Sale of Shares and Businesses:
Law, Practice and Agreements

7 Day

University of Plymouth
Charles Seale Hayne Library
Subject to status this item may be renewed
via your Voyager account

http://voyager.plymouth.ac.uk
Tel: (01752) 232323

Sale of Shares and Businesses:
Law, Practice and Agreements

SECOND EDITION

Andrew Stilton
Partner, Martineau

SWEET & MAXWELL

THOMSON REUTERS

First edition   2006
Second edition   2008

Published in 2008 by Thomson Reuters (Legal) Limited
(Registered in England & Wales,
Company No 1679046.
Registered Office and address for service:
100 Avenue Road, London, NW3 3PF)
trading as Sweet & Maxwell

For further information on our products and services, visit
www.sweetandmaxwell.co.uk

Typeset by LBJ Typesetting Ltd of Kingsclere
Printed and bound in Great Britain by
Printed in the UK by CPI William Clowes, Beccles NR34 7TL

No natural forests were destroyed to make this product;
only farmed timber was used and re-planted.

British Library Cataloguing in Publication Data

A CIP catalogue record for this book is available from the British Library

ISBN 978 1 8470 36032

Contents

Appendix 1

Typical areas that may be covered in a financial due diligence report

Appendix 2

Precedents

Preface

This second edition consolidates into the main body of the book the changes made (and to be made) by the Companies Act 2006, references to most of which were contained in the supplement which was published in Autumn 2007.

It also reflects various other changes to the law and to practice, of which the most significant are probably the changes to the financial assistance regime (taking effect on October 1, 2008) and their practical implications (discussed in Chapter 17) and the significant changes to the tax regime applicable to sales of shares by individuals and trustees as a result of the abolition of taper relief (discussed in Chapter 13).

Unless otherwise indicated, the book reflects the law as at 31 August 2008

Other changes/additions that have been made include:

- revisions to Chapter 5 in order to reflect the new anti-money laundering legislation;
- the inclusion of some additional wording in Chapter 7 to deal with information technology (IT) aspects of transactions;
- changes to Chapter 16 (accounting for acquisitions) in order to reflect changes in accounting standards;
- changes to Chapter 18 to reflect changes in competition law and practice;
- expanded wording in Chapter 19 (property issues) in order (in particular) to give more coverage to planning issues;
- changes to Chapter 20 to reflect changes to environmental law and practice; and
- amending Chapter 21 in order to reflect case law and other TUPE-related changes.

I have also added a number of additional precedents:

- auditor's resignation letter;
- deed of novation;
- patent assignment;
- trade mark assignment;
- short-form warranties (both for share deals and assets deals); and
- simple wording for an overage/anti-embarrassment provision.

I would like again to express particular thanks to David Horsburgh and Paul Johnson of Baker Tilly in Birmingham who were responsible for revising the chapters on financial due diligence and accounting for acquisitions and Peter Rayney of BDO in London, who contributed the chapters on tax issues (Chapters 13 and 14). The eagle-eyed reader will be able to see that while I, with a typical lawyer's lack of imagination, named the parties in my examples with such highly original names as "Buyer" and "Seller", Peter drew his inspiration from 1960s Tamla Motown. Perhaps in future editions we will try to reach out for a younger readership by using members of Girls Aloud.

I am very grateful, also, to the colleagues at Martineau who have contributed to this edition, including James Dilley (Competition Law), Iain Johnston (Environmental Issues), Ian Marshall and David Faulkner (Employment Aspects), Mario Conti and Louise Pope (Pensions Issues), Helen Driscoll (Intellectual Property), Diane Price (Money Laundering) and a monstrous regiment of property lawyers, including John Rice, Simon Coghlan, Clive Read and Mavis Neale.

I also received enormous help from vacation students, including Tori Corser-Sproson and Natasha Price.

My special thanks to Wendy Fradley, who did the lion's share of the typing, along with Jo Denton (who also managed to keep me vaguely organised), Liz Grice, Alison Ashwell, Karen Edwards, Christine Taylor, Ruth Anani, Debbie Waters and Bali Kehla.

Thanks also to the team at Sweet & Maxwell and especially to John Pacione for his enormous help and for progress-chasing with his usual blend of charm and efficiency.

Finally, my thanks to Ruth, Lucy and Anna for keeping me sane.

Andrew Stilton
November 2008

Table of Cases

Table of Statutes

Table of Statutory Instruments

Table of European Legislation

Part 1
Pre-acquisition/Disposal

Chapter 1

Deal Structures—Shares or Assets?

There are two basic structures for buying and selling a business: a sale and purchase of some or all of the assets (subject to some or all of the liabilities) of that business or, if the business is being carried on by a company, a sale and purchase of the shares in that company.

On a sale of the assets of a business, the seller will sell and the buyer will buy all of the assets (or, possibly, certain agreed assets) of the business and the ownership of each of those assets will be transferred from the seller to the buyer. On the sale and purchase of the shares in a company, on the other hand, the assets and liabilities of the business will continue to belong to the company and its existing contractual relationships will be unaffected—the only change of ownership will be in respect of the shares in that company.

For example, Buyer PLC (Buyer) may wish to acquire the business which is being carried on by Target Limited (Target), a subsidiary of Seller Limited (Seller): on a sale and purchase of assets, Target will sell to Buyer the undertaking and assets of its business and each of those assets will be transferred from Target to Buyer while, on a sale and purchase of shares, Seller will sell the shares in Target to Buyer but the undertaking and assets of the business will continue to be owned by Target.

Whether or not a particular transaction proceeds as a sale and purchase of the assets of the business or of the shares of the company which carries on the business will be a matter for discussion and negotiation and it is quite likely that one party (more often than not, the buyer) will prefer the transaction to proceed as a sale and purchase of assets while the other (more often than not, the seller) will prefer a sale and purchase of shares. In particular, there may be tax considerations which make a sale of shares more attractive for a seller while there may be commercial considerations which make a purchase of assets more attractive to a buyer.

1.1　Tax considerations for the seller

Tax issues are discussed in more detail in Chs 13 and 14 but, in summary, individual sellers are likely to want to structure the transaction as a sale and purchase of shares as the sale proceeds will then be received by them personally and will normally be subject to more attractive capital gains tax rates. A sale of assets may well give rise to a "double charge" to tax as the selling company is likely to pay tax on the sale of its assets and, if the intention is to distribute the net sale proceeds to the shareholders of the selling company, a further tax charge is likely to arise. Similarly, a corporate seller who is entitled to the Substantial Shareholdings Exemption, which is discussed in Ch.14, is likely to want to make sure that the transaction is structured as a sale and purchase of shares.

These issues are discussed in detail in 13.1 and 14.1 below.

1.2   Tax considerations for the buyer

Although tax considerations are likely to make a purchase of assets more attractive for a buyer, a purchase of shares may also offer some advantages.

1.2.1   On a purchase of assets, the buyer may be able to obtain a deduction as a trading expense for corporation tax purposes of the cost of any trading stock which forms part of the assets acquired and is likely therefore to wish to argue for a relatively high apportionment of the purchase price to trading stock, rather than to assets (such as goodwill) which do not qualify for deduction as a trading expense.

1.2.2   The cost of acquiring industrial buildings, plant and machinery and some intellectual property rights will attract capital allowances and will therefore qualify for a deduction against income for tax purposes, which will effectively reduce the purchase price. For the seller, on the other hand, there is the risk of balancing charges if the assets in question are sold for more than their written-down value.

In recent years, increases in the rate of stamp duty and, subsequently, the introduction of stamp duty land tax have made acquisitions of assets less attractive to a buyer than was previously the case — currently, on a purchase of shares, stamp duty will be payable at 0.5 per cent of the consideration while on a purchase of assets, which include interests in freehold or leasehold property, stamp duty land tax may be payable at up to four per cent of the purchase price payable for those interests.

One result of this has been that a prospective buyer of a property which is owned by a company may well be prepared to consider acquiring the shares in the company rather than acquiring the property directly, in order to pay the reduced rate of stamp duty.

Inevitably, of course, this will be subject to other considerations which are discussed below and, in particular, the buyer will wish to be certain that the company he is acquiring is "clean" or that appropriate warranties and indemnities are in place in respect of any unexpected or contingent liabilities.

Stamp duty issues are discussed in more detail in Ch.15.

1.3 Other considerations

In addition to tax issues, there are likely to be other reasons which may make a sale and purchase of shares more—or less—attractive to one or both parties than a sale of assets:

1.3.1   The principal advantage to a seller of selling shares is likely to be the fact that the seller will, on completion, be able to walk away from the business, save to the extent of any warranties or indemnities which he may have to give to the buyer.

On a sale of assets, by contrast, the rules regarding privity of contract will mean that, as between the seller and the third parties concerned, the seller will remain liable for all creditors and other liabilities incurred by him and for all goods sold by him before the sale, despite the fact that, as between the seller and the buyer, the buyer may agree to assume those liabilities. If the buyer fails to do so, it is very likely that the third parties concerned will pursue the seller, who will have to rely on his ability to enforce any relevant covenants or indemnities given to him by the buyer, which may be of no value if the buyer is in financial difficulties.

If, therefore, Seller Limited sells the entire issued share capital of Target Limited to Buyer PLC, Buyer will acquire Target "warts and all", with all of its assets and liabilities. If, however, the transaction proceeds as a sale and purchase of assets, then all liabilities of the business will, as between Target and the third parties concerned, remain with Target and, if Buyer fails to satisfy them, the only remedy of Seller/Target will be to pursue Buyer under any covenants or indemnities which he may have given in the sale and purchase agreement.

This can be a particular concern if it is proposed that Target should sell its undertaking and assets to Buyer and should then be put into members' voluntary liquidation, with the intention of returning the sales proceeds and any other assets it may have to its shareholders, i.e. to Seller. It may be difficult for the directors of Target to make the necessary declaration of solvency if Target has residual liabilities to third parties in the event of Buyer failing to discharge the obligations that it has agreed to assume or has liabilities (for example) in respect of goods or services supplied by Target before completion. Even if the directors are able to make their declaration, the insolvency practitioner who is appointed as liquidator will be reluctant to make a distribution of Target's assets until enough time has elapsed for him to feel confident that no unexpected claims will be brought against Target. In practice, if Seller is a substantial company, the insolvency practitioner may be prepared to make a distribution on the basis of an indemnity.

1.3.2   A sale and purchase of assets involves the need to identify every single asset and liability of the business and to determine whether that asset or liability is to transfer to the buyer or is to remain with the seller. It will therefore be absolutely essential to ensure that the sale and purchase agreement identifies—by lists or by generic descriptions — exactly which assets and which liabilities are to transfer to the buyer and which are to remain with the seller.

1.3.3   It will also be necessary to comply with all necessary formalities for the transfer of title to each and every asset which is included in an assets sale and purchase: for example, moveable plant and equipment will normally be transferred by delivery, while it will be necessary to have formal transfers or assignments of certain other assets, such as contracts, debtors and land.

On a sale and purchase of shares, however, all that is needed is a formal transfer of the shares in the company in question and all underlying assets and liabilities of the company will then pass to the buyer along with the shares — to be more precise, there will be no change in their ownership at all, simply a change in the ownership of the company which owns them.

This obviously has the advantage of simplicity and (generally) speed.

1.3.4   One of the consequences of the need to transfer each and every asset from the seller to the buyer on a sale and purchase of assets is that it may well be necessary to obtain the consent of third parties to the transfer and this would not be an issue in the same way on a sale and purchase of shares.

For example, on a sale and purchase of assets, it will be necessary to have a formal assignment of any property leases and the consent of the landlord is likely to be required.

Similarly, there may well be contracts with key customers or suppliers which may contain terms which prohibit their being transferred or assigned without the consent of the other party — even if that is not the case, the law of privity of contract is likely to make it desirable (at the very least) to approach the other parties to key contracts in order to ensure that they will continue to deal with the business once its ownership has transferred to the buyer.

The buyer will want to do so, if at all, before entering into a legally binding obligation to make the acquisition, while the seller is likely to be concerned about the potential damage to the business if approaches are made to third parties before there is a legally binding commitment from the buyer.

This issue is discussed in more detail in Ch.4.

1.3.5   Apart perhaps from tax considerations, the principal attraction for a buyer of buying assets rather than shares is that, on an acquisition of shares the buyer acquires the company with all of its historic, current, prospective and contingent liabilities, whether the buyer is aware of them or not.

The buyer will seek protection against such matters by appropriate warranties and/or indemnities in the sale and purchase agreement but such contractual protections may be of limited value: they will inevitably be subject to limitations, there may be issues over quantification of the buyer's loss (particularly in the context of warranty claims), litigation is inevitably time-consuming and expensive and, ultimately, the best drafted warranty or indemnity will be of no value whatsoever if, when the buyer seeks to enforce it, the seller does not have the financial means to satisfy the claim.

On a sale and purchase of assets, by contrast, the buyer will have the opportunity of agreeing specifically which assets and liabilities are to be included in the sale and which are to be excluded. For example, the buyer may (subject to negotiation) be able to take over the burden only of those contracts of the business which he wishes to take over and may therefore (again, subject to negotiation) be able to exclude unknown or loss-making contracts.

A purchase of assets is therefore particularly attractive where the selling company is subject to a major claim in litigation or some other contingent liability or where the business being acquired is one which is likely to attract significant product liability or employers' liability claims which the buyer would not want to assume, although, even on a purchase of assets, some employers' liability claims may pass to the buyer by virtue of the operation of the Transfer of Undertakings (Protection of Employment) Regulations 2006 ("TUPE"), which are discussed in more detail in Ch.21.

The perceived ability to leave behind all contractual liabilities may, however, be illusory—if there are product warranty or similar claims from customers arising from the seller's ownership of the business, the buyer may well have to accept that he will have to deal with these problems if he wishes to retain the customers and, in these circumstances, the buyer should seek to agree with the seller a basis on which the buyer will deal with such claims but at the cost of the seller.

1.3.6   The ability to exclude unwanted or unknown liabilities will generally mean that, when buying assets, the buyer's due diligence process can be more limited, in that it need not cover matters which are to be excluded from the sale. One attraction for a seller of selling assets may therefore be that the warranties and indemnities to be given on a sale of assets are likely to be less than on a sale of shares. The downside of that, however, for the seller is that such liabilities will not be the subject of warranties and indemnities but will instead remain the direct responsibility of the seller.

1.4   Situations where circumstances dictate a sale and purchase of assets

There are some circumstances where the only realistic choice is a sale and purchase of assets rather than a sale and purchase of shares, and these include:

1.4.1   Where the business being acquired is a division of the selling company rather than a separate subsidiary, there may be no real alternative to a sale and purchase of the assets of that division.

1.4.2   In years gone by, where there were potentially valuable tax losses in the business, it was common for the assets to be hived down into a new subsidiary of the seller and for the buyer then to acquire the shares in that company, but changes to tax law have rendered that structure far less common, not least because there is likely to be a double charge to stamp duty—a charge to stamp duty land tax on the hive down of any property interests into the new subsidiary and stamp duty on the transfer of the shares to the buyer.

1.4.3   Where the seller is a company in administration, receivership, or liquidation, the transaction will almost invariably proceed by way of a sale and purchase of assets, as the buyer will not wish to assume responsibility for all of the creditors and other liabilities of an insolvent company and receivers, administrators and liquidators will refuse to give any warranties or indemnities.

1.4.4   Where the structure of the deal, if it took place as a sale and purchase of shares, would involve unlawful financial assistance by the target company for the purchase of its own shares in contravention of the prohibition which are now contained in ss.678 and 679 of the Companies Act 2006 and which are discussed in Ch.17.

1.4.5   Where the business being acquired includes a leasehold property and there are difficulties in obtaining the consent of the landlord to the assignment of the lease (see Ch.19).

1.4.6   If the buyer wants to acquire 100 per cent of the business and the company which carries on the business has minority shareholders who do not wish to sell, in the absence of "drag along" or similar rights in its articles of association, the only alternative may be for the transaction to proceed by way of a sale and purchase of assets. This may, however, be fraught with difficulties as, even if there is nothing in the articles of association of the company or in any shareholders' agreement to prevent a sale of the business without the consent of the shareholders concerned, those shareholders may try to block the sale by making an application to the court under the provisions of s.994 of the Companies Act 2006 on the grounds that the proposed sale would be unfairly prejudicial to the interests of its members generally or to some part of its members.

Whether such an application would be likely to succeed would depend upon all of the facts but the risk of such an application being made and the potential delays (as well as the potential costs) may deter the parties from proceeding with a sale and purchase of assets in such a situation.

Where the interests of the seller dictate one particular structure and the interests of the buyer another, the structure which is finally adopted will inevitably be a matter for negotiation and may ultimately depend upon the respective bargaining positions of the parties. It is important that negotiation of the structure of the deal takes place at the same time as negotiation of the price—that does mean that if, for example, the buyer insists upon buying assets but this is likely to have adverse tax consequences for the seller, the seller may be able to negotiate a higher purchase price in return for accepting the buyer's preferred deal structure and the resulting tax consequences.

FIRST STEPS—METHODS OF SALE AND MARKETING AND CONFIDENTIALITY

Chapter 2

First Steps—Methods of Sale and Marketing and Confidentiality

This chapter deals with the usual methods of selling a business and with the legal issues which arise when marketing a business to a number of possible buyers. The following matters are beyond the scope of this chapter (and indeed beyond the scope of this book):

- The likely reasons of the seller for selling the business.

- The likely objectives of the buyer in making a particular acquisition or in looking for acquisition opportunities generally.

- "Grooming" a business for sale.

- Choosing the best timing for an exit.

- Identifying potential buyers or (as the case may be) potential acquisition targets.

- Valuing the target business and agreeing the price.

- "Financial engineering", such as (on a share sale) taking out excess land or other assets, the value of which is unlikely to be reflected in a purchase price which is based on earnings.

- The basis for selection of a preferred buyer in an "auction" situation.

- Incentivising management to complete the deal.

These are matters on which the seller will normally be advised by his lead adviser who will typically be an investment bank, a firm of accountants or a mergers and acquisitions "boutique".

2.1   Methods of sale

Whether the transaction takes effect as a sale and purchase of assets or of shares, the sale of a business will normally be by negotiation with a specific buyer or by an "auction" process, which will be intended to lead to the identification of a "favoured" buyer, with whom the seller will then enter into detailed negotiations. The auction process will typically be used where the business in question is a substantial one or one which is likely to attract a fair amount of interest from potential buyers, as sellers are likely to conclude that the competitive nature of the process is more likely to enable them to maximise the price which they receive than negotiation with one particular buyer. They may also believe that a competitive auction may enable them to obtain the best possible terms generally (for example, it may be possible for a seller to take advantage of the competitive process in order to get away with giving less extensive warranties and indemnities than might otherwise have been the case).

The auction will generally be a confidential, "closed" process and the confidential nature of the process (by comparison with, for example, advertising the business for sale in the *Financial Times* or trade press) will be a further attraction to sellers. In an auction, the role of the lead adviser is key as his role will be to identify potential buyers (in consultation with the seller), identify potential "deal-breakers" at an early stage and take steps to address them, and manage the whole sale process. It is therefore essential to appoint a skilled lead adviser and to have one who has good sector knowledge which will help him to identify potential buyers and to identify the issues which are likely to arise in the course of the transaction. The need to appoint a lead adviser may mean that the auction process will be more expensive for a seller. In any event, the auction process will not, generally, be appropriate where the business is unlikely to be attractive to many potential buyers or where the costs of the exercise are likely to be out of proportion to the price that is likely to be obtained.

The auction process will normally involve providing potential buyers with identical pre-packaged due diligence information, with prospective buyers being required to make their bids on the basis of this information and on certain other specified bases, so that the seller can be satisfied that all bidders will be submitting their offers on the basis of the same information and on the basis of the same deal structure (for example, a competitive auction may be unworkable if some bidders state that they wish to buy assets, while others say that they wish to buy shares).

The auction process will generally be used where it is the seller who has taken the decision to "put the business up for sale" rather than where the seller is responding to approaches from one or more prospective buyers but there may be cases where the seller receives approaches from buyers but decides to test the market rather than simply negotiate with those parties who have expressed interest.

Apart from the following section (which deals with confidentiality and non-disclosure agreements), most of the remainder of this chapter is concerned with sales by auction or other competitive process, rather than where the seller is simply negotiating with one specific buyer.

2.2   Confidentiality and non-disclosure agreements

Whichever method of sale is adopted, the seller is likely to be required to provide a certain amount of information about the business to any prospective buyer before detailed negotiations can begin. However, unless and until a binding sale and purchase agreement has been entered into, the seller will almost certainly want to keep confidential the fact that the business is "for sale" and the fact that discussions/negotiations are taking place with one or more interested buyers. The fact that the business is for sale may well unsettle its employees (who are likely to be distracted by concerns as to who the new owner might be and how a change of ownership may impact on them) and once the news (or even rumours) that a business is up for sale reaches "the trade", relationships with customers and suppliers may suffer.

It may be particularly unfortunate if it becomes common knowledge that a particular buyer is proposing to buy a business and then, for whatever reason, the transaction does not proceed — employees, customers and suppliers may continue to feel that they face an uncertain future, while there will inevitably be speculation as to why the transaction did not go ahead, and the fact that one buyer is seen to have withdrawn from a deal may weaken the seller's negotiating position with other potential buyers.

The formal sale and purchase agreement will almost invariably contain a clause which obliges both parties to keep the terms of the transaction confidential and not to disclose them, or make any announcements about the transaction, without the consent of the other, but the seller will want to have similar protection in respect of the period prior to entering into the sale and purchase agreement.

Of even greater concern will be the consequences of making available to potential buyers (who may well already be competitors) confidential business information relating to the business — its customers, suppliers, prices and the like. It could be extremely damaging for a business if such information is provided to a competitor with a view to a sale to that competitor which never takes place and, in many cases, the seller will be concerned that a competitor who has expressed an interest in buying the business has no real intention of doing so but simply wants to find out as much information as possible about it and then use that information to compete with it more aggressively — for example, by attacking its customer base or poaching its key employees.

Although the common law does give some protections in such circumstances, it is almost universal practice for sellers to insist upon a formal confidentiality or nondisclosure agreement before entering into any negotiations with a prospective buyer and before providing any information of a confidential nature. A precedent for a confidentiality agreement is contained in App.2 (Precedent 5) and is typical of the sort of agreement which a seller will require. Key provisions of it include:

2.2.1   An agreement not to make any announcement or disclosure of the buyer's interest in the business without the prior written consent of the seller.

2.2.2   A clear definition of what constitutes "confidential information".

2.2.3   An undertaking from the buyer that he will use confidential information only for the purpose of his proposed acquisition of the business.

2.2.4   An undertaking from the buyer not to disclose any confidential information, or the fact that discussions or negotiations are taking place or any of the proposed terms of the transaction, other than to appropriate employees and to the buyer's professional advisers (in which case, the seller should consider whether to obtain similar confidentiality agreements from those advisers).

2.2.5 An obligation on the buyer to keep a record of all confidential information provided and of the persons holding it.

2.2.6 An obligation on the buyer to return all confidential information to the seller on demand or to destroy it (although the buyer may want to replace the seller's right to require the information to be returned or destroyed on demand with a right to do so if the transaction has not completed by a specified date and may also want an exception to allow the buyer and his advisers to retain copies of due diligence reports and the like prepared by him or by his advisers on his behalf in respect of the business, but on the basis that the buyer will keep confidential any information of a confidential nature which is contained within those reports).

2.2.7 An undertaking that the buyer will not attempt to solicit key employees of the business for an agreed period after the date on which negotiations come to an end.

2.2.8 An acknowledgement by the buyer that the seller will be entitled to injunctive relief if the buyer breaches the terms of the agreement or threatens to do so, on the basis that the seller will generally want to prevent the misuse of confidential information rather than sue for damages after the event (although a buyer may well try to resist this provision and whether or not it is included will ultimately depend on the respective negotiating positions of the buyer and of the seller).

2.2.9 A recognition that there will be certain information to which the confidentiality agreement will not apply—such as information which was already in the public domain or was already known to the buyer—and a provision to allow disclosure where required by law or any regulatory or government authority.

If the buyer is a public body, however, it will be necessary to take account of the provisions of the Freedom of Information Act 2000 ("FOIA") and of the Environmental Information Regulations 2004 ("EIR"). Public authorities are under a statutory duty to disclose to members of the public information held by them under these two regimes, subject to various exemptions. Under the FOIA, there is an absolute exemption from disclosing information received from the seller, provided that the information is genuinely confidential in nature. The wording should, insofar as possible, specify the information which is confidential and any time limits, if appropriate, rather than seek to impose a broad duty, which may be unenforceable in any event. Information which, if not confidential, may prejudice the commercial interests of the seller (or buyer) if disclosed, may also benefit from an exemption from disclosure. The caveat is that this exemption will only apply if the public interest in protecting the relevant commercial interests outweigh the public interest in disclosing the information. While the public authority is the ultimate arbiter with regard to disclosure decisions (subject to the statutory enforcement mechanism), the seller should insert a clause requiring the buyer to consult it, should a request for access to commercially sensitive information be made. The EIR regime affords more liberal access to environmental information, though there are some exceptions for adverse effects on intellectual property rights and, in a more limited sense, the confidentiality of commercial information. It should be noted that the FOIA and the EIR will be equally applicable where it is the seller which is the public body, although in that case, of course, its particular relevance will be in relation to any confidentiality obligations imposed on the seller under the formal sale and purchase agreement.

Apart from the legal protection which such an agreement may provide, one advantage of obliging the buyer to sign a well-drafted confidentiality agreement is that it should help to "concentrate the mind" and deter a buyer who is intending to go on a "fishing expedition" for information about the seller's business, rather than being a serious buyer.

Where the seller has particular concerns about the buyer's motives, he may wish to consider imposing on the buyer an obligation not to solicit any of the customers of the business for an agreed period after the date on which negotiations come to an end, although the enforceability of such a provision would be subject to the "reasonableness" test which applies to all restrictive covenants (this issue is discussed in more detail in Ch.8). An alternative approach might be to provide details of customers (and perhaps of employees) without specifying their names—so that, for example, the buyer may be told that "Customer No. 1" placed £100,000 of orders with the business in the last 12 months but is not told the identity of that customer unless and until the formal sale and purchase agreement has been entered into.

If the seller is a listed company, the directors of the seller may be concerned about the possibility of the buyer acquiring shares in the seller with the benefit of "inside" information supplied to it by the seller and may therefore require the buyer to undertake not to do so for an agreed period.

The seller must always bear in mind, however, that no matter how well drafted the confidentiality agreement may be, it will only confer protection if the seller is able to demonstrate that the information in question was actually disclosed and the seller should therefore maintain a written record of all information which may have been provided, when it was provided and to whom it was provided, and should require his solicitors and other professional advisers to do the same. Rather than just being handed over, information should be provided under cover of a letter, memorandum or email which clearly lists exactly what information is being provided.

The seller should also bear in mind that the agreement will only bind those who are party to it, which is why the seller should consider whether to obtain confidentiality agreements directly from the buyer's professional advisers. Where the buyer is a member of a group of companies, the seller should insist on the ultimate holding company of the group entering into the confidentiality agreement and agreeing to procure that all other companies in its group will comply with its terms.

Even if a confidentiality agreement is in place, the seller must always consider whether he is legally permitted to disclose any particular item of information—for example, he may be asked by the buyer to disclose the terms of agency or distribution agreements, joint ventures or other commercial agreements which may themselves contain confidentiality undertakings which prevent their disclosure without the consent of the other party to them. The seller should also consider the implications of the Data Protection Acts before disclosing any personal data which is covered by that legislation.

Well drafted confidentiality agreements should not in any event mean that the seller should not take every possible practical step to prevent rumours leaking out to the work force, the trade or the local (or national) press: it is amazing how much information can be discovered by eavesdropping on conversations on trains or in restaurants and confidentiality agreements will offer no protection against indiscreet discussions between the seller and his colleagues or advisers and will not prevent rumours from beginning to circulate if the seller's receptionist starts to wonder why the buyer is telephoning the seller on a daily basis or why different firms of accountants or surveyors are turning up at the company's premises. It may be possible to reduce the dangers by making sure that all telephone calls come through to a direct line and that all faxes and emails are sent to a secure address, as well as by making sure that all meetings and site visits take place outside working hours but, the longer negotiations go on, the more difficult it becomes to prevent rumours from spreading.

2.3   Preparation of the information memorandum

Where the seller is negotiating individually with a specific buyer, it is likely to be the buyer who specifies the information that he requires but, where a formal auction process is undertaken, the seller will need to make sure that the same information is given to all prospective buyers and this is normally done by preparing an information memorandum relating to the business and distributing it to prospective buyers.

2.3.1   The information memorandum will normally be prepared by the seller's lead adviser, but on the basis of information provided by the seller and, where relevant, by the seller's solicitors and other professional advisers. The information to be given can be as extensive or as limited as the seller may choose and the seller may therefore choose to have the information memorandum contain as much information as possible, or may prefer it to contain sufficient information to whet the appetites of prospective buyers but with other information (typically, information which is likely to be more commercially sensitive) being held back until a later stage.

2.3.2   The information memorandum will contain a summary of the sale process and this is likely to include the proposed timetable, the required format and contents of bids, and the procedure for submitting bids. Sellers will normally wish to be prescriptive on these points in order to be confident that the competing bids will be submitted on a consistent basis, so that the seller should be "comparing like with like" rather than "comparing apples with pears". The seller will almost certainly wish to specify the deal structure (i.e. a sale and purchase of shares or a sale and purchase of assets) which he requires and will normally wish to specify any other underlying principles on which bids must be submitted such as, for example, a requirement that they must be submitted on the basis that the buyer will be acquiring the target company "cash-free/debt-free". Where prospective buyers are private companies or buy-in teams, the seller will also require them to provide "proof of funds", i.e. confirmation from their financial backers that they are prepared, in principle, to finance the transaction.

The information memorandum will, typically, include the following information about the target company or business:

- executive summary, including key strengths and future strategy;

- its history;

- its current ownership;

- a description of the business;

- products and services;

- premises;

- patents, trademarks and other intellectual property rights;

- a summary of the market in which the business operates;

- the business's position in that market;

- customers and suppliers;

- directors and senior management;

- organisational structure;

- employees;

- management information and IT systems;

- financial record;

- current trading and future prospects.

Even if it is not formally verified to the same extent as a prospectus, the seller and his advisers should take great care to ensure the accuracy of the information contained in the information memorandum, not least because buyers will base their bids on that information and, if there are any errors or ambiguities, that is likely to encourage the buyer to try to renegotiate the price at a later stage—this may cause immense problems if all other interested parties have been "stood down", with the result that the seller may be left in a very weak negotiating position.

In addition, although the information memorandum will normally contain a wide "disclaimer" to the effect that the information in it does not constitute a representation or warranty and purporting to exclude liability for any false or misleading statements, it should not be automatically assumed that any such wording will be effective to prevent any false or misleading statements from giving rise to a claim for misrepresentation. Further, the inclusion of any false or misleading statements may constitute a criminal offence under s.397(1) of the Financial Services and Markets Act 2000 ("FSMA"). Any such statement may also give rise to liability at common law for negligent misstatement.

When the parties come to negotiate the formal sale and purchase agreement, the buyer may press for a warranty as to the accuracy of information contained in the information memorandum and perhaps even as to the accuracy or reasonableness of forecasts in it. The seller will normally argue against this, on the basis that the purpose of the information memorandum was to enable potential buyers to decide whether they wished to enter into negotiations which would, in turn, be followed by detailed due diligence work, while the buyer may argue that it was the information in the information memorandum which was fundamental to his decision to make the acquisition. A seller should be very cautious about giving any such warranty, as the sale and purchase agreement is likely to be entered into some months after the preparation of the information memorandum and it is almost certain that some of the information originally provided will have become out of date—even if the business's current trading and prospects have not changed, customers and suppliers are likely to have been won and lost, there are likely to have been changes in the workforce and there may well have been wage and salary reviews or other changes to contracts of employment. In practice, sellers will normally be successful in resisting a general warranty in respect of the information memorandum but, if there is information in there which the buyer continues to regard as absolutely fundamental, the seller may have to accept that it will be necessary to give a specific warranty regarding the accuracy of that information.

2.4 Distributing the information memorandum

Businesses will sometimes be advertised for sale in the *Financial Times* or elsewhere but that approach is normally more appropriate where it is by no means clear who the prospective buyers are likely to be. Advertising the business may result in considerable interest at a superficial level but is likely to encourage a lot of "time wasters". It is therefore preferable for the seller (with his advisers) to identify prospective buyers and then to approach them. As has already been explained, it is beyond the scope of this book to discuss how the seller and his advisers are likely to go about identifying potential buyers but the approach will normally be made by the seller or his lead adviser and may be made verbally or in writing. Where the approach is made in writing, it will normally be accompanied by a very brief note (often referred to as a "flyer") about the business, which will be used to elicit initial interest. For confidentiality reasons, this initial approach will sometimes be made on a "no names" basis.

If potential buyers do show initial interest, the seller and his advisers will normally make sure that they obtain a confidentiality undertaking from them and will then provide them with the information memorandum.

Where the seller is proposing to sell the assets of the business rather than the shares in the company which carries on the business (see Ch.1), there will be no legal restrictions on the distribution of information to potential buyers. If, however, he is proposing to sell shares, he will need to consider the implications of s.21 of the FSMA (which provides that any "financial promotion" must be issued or approved by an "authorised person" unless an appropriate exemption applies). Contravention is a criminal offence and any agreement to which the financial promotion relates may be unenforceable against the other party, who may also be entitled to reimbursement and possible compensation.

A financial promotion is defined as any communication in the course of business which is an invitation or inducement to engage in "investment activity". Investment activity, very broadly, includes an agreement relating to the purchase of securities, such as shares (an offer for business assets is not a financial promotion). The definition covers both written and oral communications, whether solicited or unsolicited.

An authorised person is one who is authorised under the FSMA to carry on certain regulated financial services activities.

Whether or not a communication amounts to a financial promotion is likely to depend on the circumstances and the precise wording of the approach. The Financial Services Authority ("FSA") has published guidance (Ch.8, Perimeter Guidance Manual) which will not be legally binding, but will nevertheless be persuasive. The following general points are worthy of note:

2.4.1   A financial promotion can include all types of communication, oral and written, real time (such as face-to-face visits and telephone conversations) and non-real time (such as letters, materials displayed on websites and emails). It also encompasses "cold calling" and solicited and unsolicited communications.

2.4.2   The financial promotion regime catches offers as well as invitations to treat.

2.4.3   There are many exemptions to the financial promotion prohibition contained in the Financial Services and Markets Act 2000 (Financial Promotion) Order 2005 (SI 2005/1529) (the "Financial Promotion Order"). Those which are most likely to be relevant are:

- Communications made to "investment professionals" (art.19).

- "One-off communications" made to one recipient or group of recipients in the expectation that they will engage in an investment activity which relates to a specific subject-matter (e.g. a specific acquisition) (art.28).

- A non-real time communication (such as an information memorandum) will be exempt provided that it is made only to one recipient or only to a group of recipients in the expectation that they would engage in any investment activities jointly and in the *Perimeter Guidance Manual* the FSA gives as examples married couples, directors of a company, partners in a firm, participants in a joint enterprise, or the managers or prospective managers of a company who are involved in a management buy-out or buy-in. The communication must be tailored to the circumstances of the recipient(s) and must not simply be sent out as part of a general mail shot. A number of communications could be made, all of which could be "one-off", and this would include subsequent communications with prospective buyers.

- Communications made to "certified high net worth individuals" (art.48), high net worth companies, unincorporated associations and trusts (art.49) and associations of high net worth or sophisticated investors (art.51)).

- Communications made to "sophisticated investors", which includes individuals who are certified (including self certification) as such (that is, persons sufficiently expert to understand the risks involved) (arts 50 and 50A).

- Communications by, or on behalf of, a body corporate, a partnership, an individual or a group of connected individuals in relation to the acquisition or disposal of shares in a body corporate (art.62).

The *Perimeter Guidance Manual* states that the FSA views this exemption as being aimed at the sale of a corporate business by a person who, either alone or with others, controls the business, to another person who, either alone or with others, proposes to control the business.

The shares in question must consist of, or include, shares carrying 50 per cent or more of the voting rights exercisable at any general meeting of the body corporate (i.e. the target company) in question or must do so when aggregated with any shares already held by the person proposing to acquire them. In any event, the prospective seller must be a body corporate, a partnership, a single individual or a group of connected individuals and the prospective buyer must also be one or other of these.

Even if these criteria are not satisfied, however, art.62 (2)(b)(ii) provides that the exemption will still apply if the communication is by or on behalf of a single individual, a company, a partnership or a group of connected individuals, and relates to the proposed acquisition or disposal of shares in a body corporate or is entered into for the purposes of such an acquisition or disposal and (in either case) the object of the transaction may reasonably be regarded as being the acquisition of day-to-day control of the company.

Article 62(4) provides that a group of connected individuals includes persons who are, or who are close relatives of, a director of manager of the target company and persons who are, or who are close relatives of, a person who is to be a director or manager of the target company and also includes trustees and nominees of any such person.

The FSA has provided guidance on this exemption in the *Perimeter Guidance Manual* but the exemption is difficult to interpret and should be considered carefully, alongside the FSA guidance, in each case in order to establish whether or not it applies.

Any approach to prospective buyers may potentially, therefore, amount to financial promotion and may need to be issued or approved by an authorised person, unless one of the exemptions applies. In practice, the distribution of an information memorandum to potential buyers is reasonably likely to fall within one or more of these exemptions but that should not automatically be assumed to be the case and the seller should take appropriate advice before taking steps to have the document distributed.

2.5   Shortlist

Where the business has been marketed to a number of prospective buyers, the seller and his advisers will ask for initial expressions of interest and indicative offers based on the information memorandum and, on the basis of those indicative offers, will normally draw up a shortlist of prospective buyers.

If only one of the indicative offers is at a price and on other terms which are acceptable in principle to the seller, the seller will normally begin detailed negotiations with that party, in the hope of reaching an agreement in principle with him. After that, the buyer in question will almost certainly want to carry out detailed due diligence on the business before being prepared to enter into a formal sale and purchase agreement (the due diligence process is discussed in detail in Chs 5, 6 and 7). This may also be the case where one party's indicative offer is sufficiently more attractive than the others that the seller does not consider it worthwhile continuing negotiations with the others.

Where, however, there are a number of prospective buyers whose indicative offers might be acceptable to the seller (or which the seller or his advisers beleve to be capable of being "negotiated up"), the seller will normally make available to all of the shortlisted parties more detailed information relating to the target company/business, together with a draft sale and purchase agreement. The seller will normally also arrange for management to do a presentation to the shortlisted buyers and will normally also arrange site visits.

Depending upon the amount of information in question, the seller may deliver to each of the shortlisted buyers a "pack" of due diligence information but where the sheer volume of information makes this impracticable, the seller will normally make the information available to prospective buyers in a "data room".

On some transactions (particularly where the information memorandum is only being supplied to a comparatively small number of prospective buyers) the seller may decide to make the data room information available at the outset of the process and to any party to whom the information memorandum had been provided, rather than to a shortlist only. If so, the seller will normally also make available to interested parties a draft sale and purchase agreement, as discussed below.

2.6   Data rooms

The data room is often established "off site" (typically, at the offices of one of the seller's advisers) both in the hope of maintaining confidentiality with the work force and with customers and suppliers and in order to minimise disruption to the day-to-day running of the business. Often, of course, pure space constraints make it more logical to locate the data room off site.

One possible alternative might be to establish a "virtual" data room with remote computer access to data available, albeit restricted by password security, but it is far more common for there to be a physical data room containing hard copies of relevant documentation.

Preparing a data room which contains all of the information which is likely to be material to a prospective buyer is likely to be time consuming and it is therefore essential to plan ahead and start preparing the data room at the same time as the information memorandum is being prepared, rather than trying to do so at a later stage, when interested parties are pressing for access to it.

It is essential that the data room is organised in a way which is "user-friendly" to the parties visiting it and it is important that different aspects of the data room are contained in separate files—for example, all financial information should be kept separate from all other information and similarly with information relating to employment, pensions, property interests and so on. Those files should be carefully and clearly indexed and labelled.

It is also essential that the information in the data room is as complete as possible: it is particularly frustrating for buyers and their advisers if they are presented with undated and/or unsigned copies of contracts (particularly when they have "draft" written all over them) or where they receive incomplete correspondence relating to a particular issue, or copies of the correspondence without copies of the documents referred to. Data room documents should be prepared clearly and unambiguously—visiting a data room should not be a modern day equivalent of consulting the oracle at Delphi.

The information which would normally be included in a data room is similar to that which a buyer would expect to obtain through his financial and legal due diligence and it is generally in the best interests of the seller to make sure that the data room contains all information which prospective buyers may reasonably expect to find there but, particularly where the prospective buyers include competitors, the seller may wish to withhold commercially sensitive information until the preferred buyer has been selected. This may be attractive to prospective buyers too, as they may be concerned about buying a business in the knowledge that competitors may have obtained commercially sensitive information about it through the data room. If the seller chooses to do so, he should make it quite clear to prospective buyers that this is the case. He should, however, be wary of withholding information which, once disclosed, may affect the preferred buyer's decision to proceed or the price which he is prepared to pay.

It may be particularly helpful, especially if the seller wants to move to an early completion once the preferred bidder has been chosen, for the data room to contain a certificate of title from the seller's solicitors in respect of each of the business's freehold properties or at least for the seller's solicitors to have carried out the normal local authority and other searches that a buyer would normally expect to carry out and for copies of those to be contained in the data room, along with copies of the leases relating to any leasehold premises which the target company or business may occupy and any other material property documents.

Once the data room has been prepared, each interested party will be allowed access to it at a specified time, along with its professional advisers. The seller or his advisers will normally produce rules governing access to the data room—opening times, the number of people who may attend and so on. One issue which can cause particular difficulties is the question of whether or not bidders should be entitled to request copies of documents in the data room for further review. The principal purpose of the data room will be defeated if the seller winds up having to provide copies of a lot of the information in there, but prospective buyers will typically argue that there are documents which they need to review in a more leisurely fashion or which they want to have reviewed by other members of the team and in practice the rules will normally permit bidders to request copies of documents to a reasonable extent. A precedent for a reasonably typical set of data room rules is contained in App.2 (Precedent 6).

Prospective buyers visiting the data room may request additional information and the data room rules should specify how such requests may be made. They will normally be made via the buyer's solicitors and the seller and his advisers will normally wish to ensure that any additional information which is provided to one prospective buyer is also provided to the others so that the seller can be confident that each interested party has the same information and is submitting his final offer on the same basis. This will also help to show that the seller has established a "level playing field" for all interested parties.

The buyer will normally wish to make sure that information in the data room is warranted to be true and accurate and this may take the form of a general warranty as to the information in the data room or (more commonly) specific warranties regarding specific categories of information contained in the data room (for example, contractual information, employment information and so on).

From the buyer's perspective, a data room has the advantage of pulling together at least the majority of core information for the exercise into one place. It is also easier to record what information has been made available to the due diligence teams. The process of compiling a data room may also require the seller to review and "cross check" information before submission, so in some cases it may improve the quality of information provided. On the downside, however, the use of a data room denies the due diligence team the chance to see the business in action (for example, does morale seem good in the business, how quickly can information be accessed in response to specific questions and so on?). There can be an even greater need than normal in a data room environment to think about what information is "missing".

Sellers will, sometimes, seek to make information available via a data room even where there is only one potential buyer and the justification for that will normally be that it should help to maintain confidentiality and minimise disruption to the business. A cynical buyer might, however, wonder whether the seller's real intention is to restrict his access to management and to make it more difficult for him to "get under the skin" of the business and find out material issues.

2.7 Best and final offers

The seller will require interested parties to submit their "best and final offers" by a specified date and time and this will normally be by way of "sealed bid". The seller will normally have supplied to all shortlisted parties an identical draft sale and purchase agreement and will require best and final offers to be accompanied by a "mark up" of the draft, showing the changes which the buyer would wish to make if he were to become the preferred bidder.

The principal advantage of this approach is that it should help to establish before a preferred bidder is finally selected whether, even if a particular party is prepared to offer a price which is acceptable to the seller, his offer is likely to be subject to other terms (for example, retentions or indemnities) which may not be acceptable. In addition, where the buyer knows that he is in competition with others, he is likely to mark up the draft with a lighter hand than might be the case if he were marking it up at a point when he had already become the preferred bidder. This is because buyers will not want to lose an attractive deal by taking a heavy-handed approach to the draft sale and purchase agreement, whereas they may be inclined to negotiate more aggressively once they have become preferred bidders. This can therefore create quite a dilemma for the buyer, who will be keen to become preferred bidder but will appreciate that, if there are material issues on the draft agreement which he fails to raise at this stage, it may be more difficult for him to do so at a later stage.

Buyers will therefore try to mark up the draft agreement with general comments such as "additional warranty protection to be discussed in the light of further due diligence" but sellers and their advisers may attempt to prevent this by making it clear that any comments on the draft agreement must be specific rather than general.

Once the preferred buyer has been selected, the next step is likely to be to agree a set of "heads of terms" which record the agreement that they have reached (see Ch.3).

In practice, most sellers will appreciate that, once a preferred buyer has been selected, there will be some further negotiation on the draft sale and purchase agreement and this is particularly likely to be the case if the preferred bidder is obtaining finance from a venture capitalist or acquisition finance from a bank, as the financiers will not be prepared to proceed unless they are happy with the form of the sale and purchase agreement and related documents.

Although the preferred buyer will have reviewed the information in the information memorandum and in any data room, the length of time that is likely to have passed since that information was prepared will almost certainly mean that the buyer will want to carry out some further financial and commercial due diligence in order to ascertain whether there have been any changes and there may well be further, more detailed, legal due diligence work which the buyer will require to be carried out. This is particularly the case where the preferred buyer is obtaining external finance.

2.8   Negotiation with a specific buyer

Preparing and distributing the information memorandum, compiling a shortlist, establishing a data room and obtaining best and final offers will not, of course, be relevant where the seller does not initiate an auction or similar competitive process but instead simply enters into negotiations with one specific buyer. In those cases, the principal steps in the transaction are likely to be:

- buyer entering into a confidentiality agreement;

- provision of information to the buyer in order to enable him to make an offer;

- agree deal in principle and sign heads of terms and perhaps grant buyer exclusivity (Ch.3);

- buyer to carry out due diligence (Chs 5, 6 and 7);

- negotiate and complete the sale and purchase agreement.

2.9   Buyers approaching potential targets

This chapter has concentrated principally on the position of the seller but many transactions do not involve the marketing of the target company or business but are instead initiated by an approach by or on behalf of the buyer to the seller or his advisers. In doing so, the buyer must take care not to contravene the provisions of the FSMA and in particular those relating to financial promotions.

These issues are discussed in more detail in Ch.23, as are the implications of the City Code on Takeovers and Mergers. The principal steps involved where the seller is responding to an approach from the buyer will typically be similar to those summarised at 2.8 above.

Chapter 3

Heads of Terms and Exclusivity

3.1   Heads of terms

When the buyer and seller have agreed a deal in principle—whether for a sale and purchase of shares or a sale and purchase of assets—they would be well advised to set out the principal terms of their agreement in writing and such a record is what is meant by "heads of terms", "heads of agreement", a "term sheet" or a "memorandum of understanding".

Heads of terms will generally be non-legally binding but the principal advantage of having them is to avoid future misunderstandings (as it is by no means unusual for parties to shake hands on a deal only to find that they have different understandings of what they have actually agreed) and identify potential "deal-breakers" at an early stage.

In both cases, the advantage of identifying misunderstandings or deal-breakers early is that it reduces the risk of wasting professional and other time and expense in working towards formalising a deal which has never actually been agreed between the parties and reduces the risk of incurring abortive time and expense if there is a fundamental issue which cannot be resolved and prevents the transaction from proceeding—if there are any such issues, the sooner they can be identified, the better. If heads of terms have been signed, the parties can proceed to instruct their professional and other advisers with some degree of confidence that there is a good prospect of bringing the deal to a satisfactory conclusion (subject, of course, to matters which may arise from the due diligence exercise).

It may be a difficult decision as to whether the heads of terms should be a very simple document, setting out only the very basic terms of the deal (parties, price and payment) or a more lengthy legal document which (at the extreme) seeks to address all of the issues which tend to become bones of contention when negotiating and agreeing the formal sale and purchase agreement—for example, the non-competition undertakings to be given, the warranties and indemnities and the limitations and qualifications that are to apply to them and issues such as whether or not the buyer should have the right to set off any warranty or indemnity claims against any deferred element of the purchase price.

On the one hand, of course, the advantage of having very detailed heads of terms is that, once they have been negotiated and agreed, the process of negotiating and agreeing the formal sale and purchase agreement should be much less difficult and time-consuming as, by definition, the likely "sticking points" will have been resolved (although, no matter how detailed the heads of terms may be, there is always the danger of an unexpected issue arising—typically, as a result of the buyer's legal, financial or tax due diligence but often simply because it was originally overlooked).

On the other hand, there is a danger that the parties will spend time and effort (and, as a result, delay the deal) in fine-tuning the heads of terms and discussing detailed legal points which would be better dealt with at a later stage.

There is a school of thought that, once heads of terms have been signed, the parties are morally (if not legally) committed to the deal and will be much more inclined to work together to overcome any issues which may subsequently arise than might be the case if those issues were being discussed at the time of the heads of terms. On the other hand, however, once a point appears in the heads of terms, it becomes very difficult for either of the parties to re-open that point in the light of changed circumstances or in the light of information which may subsequently come to light and that is perhaps a reason for having heads of terms which are not over detailed.

There are no hard and fast rules as to what is appropriate—each transaction should be considered on its merits but, as a rule of thumb, very simple heads of terms are more likely to be appropriate where there is a good relationship between the parties and each party has confidence that the other will co-operate with a view to reaching a mutually acceptable agreement but more detailed heads of terms may be appropriate where the relationship is (for whatever reason) not so good. In any event, the heads of terms should state clearly that they are not intended to constitute an exhaustive note of the terms and conditions of the transaction.

If, as is usually the case, the heads of terms are not intended to be legally binding, they should clearly be marked "subject to contract" and it is advisable that there should be a formal statement that they are not legally binding and that no legally binding obligations will arise unless and until the formal sale and purchase agreement has been signed and (if conditional) become unconditional in accordance with its terms.

If there are parts of the heads of terms which are to be legally binding (e.g. any confidentiality or exclusivity provisions, assuming that they are not contained in separate agreements), this needs to be made clear in the wording of the heads of terms and there must be consideration given in accordance with normal contractual principles.

Although, as a general rule, the heads of terms should be confined to stating points of principle rather than going into the level of detail that would normally be reserved for the formal sale and purchase agreement, it is essential that what goes into the heads of terms is not capable of more than one interpretation at a later date.

For example, if the deal is to be structured on a "cash-free/debt-free" basis, the heads of terms should spell out in words of one syllable what that expression actually means in the context of the particular transaction.

Similarly, if all or part of the price is to be determined by reference to net assets or pre-tax profits, the heads of terms should state in as much detail as possible how these are to be determined and should specify any specific adjustments or deductions which have to be made before arriving at the final figure.

Precedents 38 and 39 in App. 2 are examples of typical heads of terms for share sales and purchases and assets sales and purchases respectively.

3.2 Exclusivity

A buyer would be well-advised, at the same time as entering into heads of terms, to insist upon an exclusivity or "lock-out" agreement, under which the seller undertakes with the buyer that he will not enter into negotiations with a third party for the sale of the business in question (or of the company which owns it) and that the buyer will have the exclusive right to negotiate with him, in each case for an agreed period of time.

A seller will, by definition, be inclined to resist having to grant exclusivity but will generally have to accept some period of exclusivity if the buyer requires it, which is particularly likely to be the case where the buyer is a management buy-out team with limited resources or the preferred bidder in an auction process or is funded by venture capitalists (who will almost certainly make it a condition of their committing time and resources to the transaction that a realistic period of exclusivity is granted).

The attraction of an exclusivity arrangement from the buyer's point of view is that it allows the buyer time to carry out the required due diligence and to finalise negotiations without having to worry that the seller may just be using the buyer as a "stalking horse" to try to attract higher offers from elsewhere.

Equally importantly, the buyer will be concerned not to incur a considerable amount of professional and other costs, only to find that the seller then ends negotiations and sells to a third party—the exclusivity agreement should be helpful in this respect, particularly if it is coupled with an agreement that the seller will meet the buyer's abortive professional and other costs if the seller breaches its terms.

It should be noted that an agreement to "lock-in" a seller to negotiations is unlikely to be enforceable, as an agreement to continue to negotiate is no more than an agreement to agree. A "lock-out" agreement, however, under which the seller agrees for good consideration not to enter into discussions or negotiations with a third party for a specified period, is likely to be enforceable.

The consideration for the seller entering into an exclusivity agreement is generally stated to be the buyer's incurring professional fees and other costs, charges and expenses in connection with the proposed acquisition.

The seller should obviously be advised to accept the shortest possible exclusivity period that will be acceptable to the buyer, partly to encourage the buyer to progress the transaction as rapidly as possible but also because, once the exclusivity has expired, there is nothing to prevent the seller from entering into discussions or negotiations with other parties, even if negotiations are still continuing with the original buyer.

In any event, the seller should try to ensure that the exclusivity ceases when negotiations with the buyer come to an end: the buyer will want to limit this right to the situation where the buyer formally withdraws from negotiations, while the seller will want the right to withdraw if he believes that the buyer is not genuinely moving the transaction forward with a view to completion within the agreed timescale.

If the exclusivity agreement is coupled with an agreement on the part of the seller to reimburse the buyer's costs if the seller breaches its terms, then care needs to be taken to make certain that the agreement identifies precisely what costs are covered (for example, does the undertaking apply only to legal and accountancy fees and other third party costs or does it extend to the buyer's internal costs?) and the basis on which those costs are to be calculated.

It is worth adding that a "lock-in" agreement (that both parties will continue to negotiate in good faith for an agreed period) may be given some "teeth" by wording to the effect that, if one party ceases to carry on bona fide negotiations within the agreed period, it will meet the other's costs. Such provisions are notoriously difficult to draft— such a provision might be enforceable if one party formally withdraws from negotiations but, if there is such an agreement in place, that is most unlikely to happen and a recalcitrant party is more likely to "drag his feet" until the exclusivity period has expired. There is often then a debate as to whether the costs undertaking should be capable of being invoked if negotiations come to an end for any reason or only if they come to an end for no good reason—for example, what happens if the buyer withdraws from negotiations because of a major uninsured contingent liability which comes to light during the course of his due diligence? What happens if the seller wishes to withdraw from negotiations because the buyer's financiers have withdrawn their offer, notwithstanding that the buyer is still keen to proceed, subject to arranging alternative finance?

These are difficult and complex areas and such agreements should not be entered into without full consideration of all of the consequences. A precedent for an exclusivity agreement is contained in App.2 (Precedent 7). Whether or not all of its provisions are appropriate in any particular case will depend upon the circumstances and on whether it is being drafted on behalf of a seller or a buyer.

Chapter 4

Conditions Precedent—Consents, Approvals, Releases, etc.

It will often be advisable (and, in many cases, necessary) to obtain certain third party consents or approvals to a sale and purchase of a business.

Some of these are relevant whether the transaction takes the form of a sale and purchase of shares or of assets, whereas others will normally only be relevant to one structure or the other.

4.1 All acquisitions

4.1.1 Shareholder approvals

4.1.1.1 *The buyer*

If the seller is a director of the buyer (or of the buyer's holding company) or a person "connected" with such a director within the meaning of s.252 of the Companies Act 2006, the approval of the shareholders of the buyer will normally be required under s.190 of that Act.

Section 191 provides that members' approval is only required where the value of the asset exceeds £100,000 or 10 per cent of the company's assets but no approval is required if the value of the asset in question is less than £5,000 (an increase from £2,000 previously). Section 190(1) changes the law by allowing a company to enter into a contract which is conditional on members' approval but s.190(3) states that the company is not liable under the contract if such approval is not obtained.

Approval of the buyer's holding company will also be required if the seller is, or is connected with, a director of the buyer's holding company.

Section 321 of the 2006 Act contains various exceptions to the general requirement to obtain shareholder approval under s.320, including transactions in the course of winding-up (other than a members' voluntary winding-up) and intra-group transfers. Buyers and sellers should beware of the fact that s.190 may apply to sales by companies in receivership but there is a helpful change in the 2006 Act in that s.193(1)(b) provides that approval is not required where the company concerned is in administration.

The approval of the shareholders of the buyer may also be required if the consideration for the transaction includes the issue of shares in the buyer as, unless the buyer has sufficient authorised but unissued share capital, an ordinary resolution will be required to increase the buyer's share capital and, unless the allotment of such shares falls within an existing general authority for the allotment of shares granted pursuant to s.80 of the Companies Act 1985 (to be replaced by s.549 of the Companies Act 2006 with effect from October 1, 2009), an ordinary resolution will be required to authorise the allotment of those shares.

Where the consideration for the acquisition includes shares in the buyer, the statutory pre-emption rights conferred by s.89 of the Companies Act 1985 (to be replaced by s.561 of the Companies Act 2006 with effect from October 1, 2009), which require new issues of shares to be offered first of all to existing shareholders in proportion to their respective holdings, do not apply where the shares are, or are to be, issued wholly or partly paid-up otherwise than in cash. Nevertheless, the buyer's articles of association may contain similar pre-emption rights which may need to be disapplied (usually by special resolution) or its articles of association may contain other restrictions on the issue of share capital (for example, where the buyer's share capital is divided into shares of more than one class, the issue of further shares may require class consents).

There may also be an agreement between the shareholders of the buyer (particularly where there are venture capitalists or other third party investors) under which major transactions (such as acquisitions) require the prior consent of certain shareholders of the buyer or of a specified proportion of the shareholders of the buyer.

In addition, if the buyer (or its ultimate holding company) is a listed company or its shares are traded on any similar market, the approval of shareholders may be required by the Listing Rules of the UK Listing Authority or by the equivalent rules governing any other market. These issues are discussed in more detail in Ch.24.

If the buyer is a public company which is itself the subject of a takeover offer, r.21 of the City Code on Takeovers and Mergers may mean that the prior approval of its shareholders will be required for any acquisition.

Finally, for completeness, although this is not strictly a consent matter, s.103 of the Companies Act 1985 (to be replaced by s.593 of the

Companies Act 2006 with effect from October 1, 2009) provides that, subject to certain exceptions, a public company may not allot shares credited as paid-up (in whole or in part) for a consideration other than in cash unless that consideration has been independently valued under s.108, a report on its value has been made to the company by a person appointed by the company during the six months immediately preceding the allotment of the shares, and a copy of the report has been sent to the proposed allottee. The valuation and report must generally be made by a person qualified at the time of the report to be appointed or to continue to be the auditor of the company (and may therefore be the existing auditor, although that person may commission or accept an expert valuation from a third party (so that, for example, he may instruct a firm of surveyors to value property interests)).

There are however certain exceptions to this requirement and these are:

- The issue of shares by a buyer in consideration of the acquisition of some or all of the share capital of another company, provided that it is open to the holders of all of the shares in the other company (or all the holders of a particular class) to take part in the arrangement.

- The issue of shares as consideration for the acquisition by a buyer of all the assets and liabilities of another company, but only where those shares are issued to the shareholders of that other company. Accordingly, an issue of shares by a buyer to a seller in consideration of the sale and purchase of the assets of the seller will not fall within that exception and, before issuing the shares, the buyer is likely to have to comply with the provisions of s.103.

4.1.1.2   *The seller*

The prior approval of the shareholders of the seller may be required under s.190 of the Companies Act 2006 if the buyer is a director of the seller (or its holding company) or is connected with such a director, and the value of the shares or assets being acquired exceeds the requisite value referred to above. Particular care will therefore have to be taken on management buy-outs.

Shareholder approval may also be required under the Listing Rules (or equivalent) if the seller or its holding company is a listed company or its shares are traded on any other market or if it is a public company which is itself the subject of a take-over offer.

In the same way as for a buyer, the articles of association of a selling company may impose a requirement to obtain the prior approval of shareholders (or of the holders of a class of its shares) for any such transaction or a similar requirement may be contained in a shareholders' agreement between the shareholders of the seller.

In any event, although the articles of association of a selling company are likely to state that the management of the company will be delegated to the directors, it is debatable whether that extends to the sale of the undertaking and assets of the company and it is therefore recommended that the sale should be approved by the shareholders, particularly where the sale is likely to be followed by the winding-up of the seller.

4.1.1.3 *The target company*

On a sale and purchase of shares, there may be circumstances in which the consent of the shareholders of the target company will be required — for example, by virtue of provisions contained in its articles of association. There may also be elements of a transaction such as a purchase of own shares under ss.162–170 of the CA 1985 (to be replaced by ss.690–732 of the CA 2006 with effect from October 1, 2009) which require prior shareholders' approval.

4.1.2 **Contracts and agreements**

The seller or the buyer may have entered into contracts or agreements under which the consent or approval of a third party may be necessary or desirable and there may be contracts entered into by the target company (on a sale and purchase of shares) or by the target business (on a sale and purchase of assets) under which consents or approvals may be necessary or desirable.

4.1.2.1 *Loan or other funding agreements*

Either the seller or the buyer may have entered into loan or other funding agreements under which the consent of the lender or other funder is required for a sale or purchase of shares in a company or for the sale or purchase of all or a substantial part of the undertaking and assets of a business. Banks' term loan agreements will typically contain covenants prohibiting any such transaction without the prior consent of the bank and the same is likely to be the case with loan stock instruments. If a buyer who has issued convertible loan stock wishes to issue shares as consideration for an acquisition, the loan stock instrument may well contain provisions preventing the issue of shares without the prior consent of the stockholders (or trustees for stockholders).

4.1.2.2 *Mortgages and charges*

If the seller has created any mortgage, charge or other security over his assets, it will be necessary to see whether the shares or other assets which are to be sold to the buyer are subject to that security and, if so, it will almost certainly be necessary to obtain the consent of the holder of the security, together with a formal deed of release of assets which are subject to a fixed charge and a letter of non-crystallisation in respect of any assets which are subject to a floating charge.

It is very often the case that the holder of the security will only consent to the sale and release his security if he receives the sale proceeds in reduction or repayment of the amount owing to him and so there can be a timing problem in that the buyer will want to see the appropriate consents and releases, while the holder of the security will not be prepared to issue them until he has received the sale proceeds.

The solution to this is normally for the purchase price to be paid to the seller's solicitors and for them to undertake to the holder of the security that the appropriate amount will be paid to him and to undertake to the buyer that he will do so and for this to be coupled with an undertaking from the security holder to release his security on receipt of those funds. Where, however, the buyer is borrowing the money to fund the purchase price, his financier may well insist upon the consents and releases being handed over on completion and this is typically achieved by having the security holder attend completion or by having them issued by the security holder and held by the seller's solicitors on an undertaking to hold them to the order of the security holder until completion has taken place.

Apart from mortgages, charges and other security, on a sale and purchase of shares there may be guarantees given by the target company in respect of borrowings and other liabilities of other companies in the seller's group or letters of set-off or similar arrangements between the companies in the group. The buyer will want to make sure that those will be released on completion and, again, this is likely to involve obtaining a release which is conditional on the bank or other beneficiary under the guarantees receiving all or part of the sale proceeds. The seller will have similar concerns if other companies in the seller's group have given guarantees in respect of the target company or where the seller is an individual and has given personal guarantees in respect of the target company. These issues are discussed in more detail in Ch.8.

It may take some time to obtain formal consents and releases and so, where there are third party security holders involved or where there are guarantees to be released on completion, the third parties concerned should be approached well ahead of completion, so that these formalities will not delay completion.

4.1.2.3 *Commercial contracts and agreements*

As regards commercial contracts entered into by the business which is the subject of the transaction, the issue of consents will need to be considered differently depending upon whether the transaction is a sale and purchase of shares or of assets.

On a sale and purchase of shares in a company, the company will continue to be the contracting party but it will be necessary to consider whether any of its contracts or agreements contain provisions under which they may be terminated—or another party's rights under them may be accelerated—in the event of a change of control of the company. For example, it is common for loans or finance leases to be subject to a term that they become immediately repayable if control of the borrowing company or lessee changes and, if the buyer wishes the company to continue to enjoy the benefit of those loans or agreements, the buyer should ensure that the consent of the lender or finance company is obtained to the continuation of those arrangements before the change of control takes place. Similarly, government or other grants often contain a provision under which they may become repayable if there is a change of control of the recipient of the grant within a specified period.

Care will also have to be taken on a sale and purchase of shares where the target company is a shareholder in another company (such as a joint venture company) and the articles of association of that company or an agreement between its shareholders contain provisions requiring the consent of one or more other parties to a change of control or give one or more other parties the right (often under an option agreement) to acquire the shares held by the target company.

On a sale and purchase of shares, a buyer should always bear in mind that these issues will not only apply to the activities of the company whose shares he is buying but will apply also to the activities of any subsidiary, as a change of control of its ultimate—or intermediate—holding company is likely to be treated as a change of control of the subsidiary.

On a sale and purchase of assets, on the other hand, it will be necessary to transfer the benefit of the business's contractual arrangements to the buyer and, if the buyer wishes to obtain the benefit of any such arrangements, he will have to establish whether such contracts can be transferred to him without the consent of the third party concerned or whether the consent of the third party should be obtained, either by way of consent to the assignment of the benefit of the contract to the buyer or by way of novation (see Ch.9).

In any event, even if a contract does not contain any prohibition on assignment, only the benefit—and not the burden—of a contract will normally be assignable and so, where the continuation of trade or other contracts is important to the future of the business, a buyer may be well-advised to seek assurances (at the very least) from the third party concerned that he will agree to the buyer fulfilling the contract in place of the seller.

Where there are customers which are absolutely key to a business (whether on a sale and purchase of shares or a sale and purchase of assets), even if the customers' consent is not strictly required, the buyer may well insist upon approaching each of those customers in advance in order to obtain assurances that his custom will not be lost following the change of ownership and perhaps even to agree the terms of a new supply agreement, so that the buyer can be confident that that customer will continue to do business with the buyer, at least for an agreed minimum term. Similarly with key suppliers.

The risk of approaching a third party for consent, or indeed for any form of assurance, is that the proposed transaction will cease to be confidential and will soon become public knowledge—or, at least, well known "in the trade". A seller is therefore likely to be reluctant to allow the buyer to speak to any customers or suppliers or to any other third parties until as late a stage as possible and, ideally not until the sale and purchase agreement has been signed—which is unlikely to be attractive to the buyer, who will want to have the right to withdraw from the transaction if it becomes apparent that a key customer or key supplier will be lost.

The buyer and the seller should also bear in mind that approaching a third party for consent in advance may give that party considerable leverage in agreeing commercial terms—for example, a customer may press for lower prices or better credit terms as a condition of giving his consent, while a supplier may take the opportunity to try to negotiate higher prices or a guaranteed minimum volume of supplies.

Another point which is particularly relevant to a buyer, although not strictly a consent matter, is that, where he is buying a business out of a group of companies, there may be group arrangements in which the business will need to participate for a period after completion, failing which alternative arrangements will have to be made with effect from completion. Typically, these services may include information technology and payroll services but, in addition, there may be arrangements, such as insurances, which are provided on a group basis and which may need to be continued after completion, if possible, for an agreed period.

It is always possible, of course, that the business which is being sold provides services to other parts of the seller's group and, in those circumstances, the seller may need to make arrangements for those services to be continued or provided from elsewhere.

It is impossible to give an exhaustive list of the contractual arrangements which may be in place and which may mean that third party consents will be required, because that will depend upon the nature and terms of the contracts entered into by the seller, buyer or target and the extent to which the sale and purchase will impact on them but a buyer would be strongly advised to carry out detailed due diligence on the contractual commitments of the business in question in order to establish, as far as possible, the extent to which third party consents may be necessary or desirable. In addition to contracts with customers and suppliers, the contracts which the buyer should review in the course of his due diligence will include:

- leasing, rental, hire and hire-purchase agreements;

- agency and distribution agreements;

- agreements for the supply of computer services;

- service and maintenance agreements;

- software licence agreements.

- other intellectual property licence agreements;

- agreements for the supply of services such as telephones, electricity and gas;

- joint venture, consortium or similar agreements.

Such due diligence will normally be supported by a warranty from the seller to the effect that all contracts which may be terminated on a change of control of the company concerned or (on a sale and purchase of assets) which are stated to be non-assignable, have been disclosed to the buyer. The buyer may also request a warranty to the effect that the seller knows of no reason to believe that any material customer or supplier of the business will be lost as a result of the change of ownership of the business but a seller should be very cautious about giving any such warranty.

4.1.3   Regulatory approvals and requirements

There are various business activities which may not be carried on without a licence, permit or other regulatory approval and, if the business in question is such a business or has any such licence or approval, it is likely that the buyer will need to ensure that it continues in force or will need to obtain a new licence or approval in his own name.

On a sale and purchase of shares, the company which carries on the business after completion of the transaction will be the same as before and so the parties will have to consider whether there will have to be formal consents to the change of ownership or whether the licences or approvals may be capable of being withdrawn as a result of the change of ownership.

On a sale and purchase of assets, it will be necessary to consider whether the licences or approvals are capable of being transferred with the business (which is unlikely), whether any existing licences or approvals of the buyer will cover the business activities being acquired or (if not) whether new licences or approvals must be taken out in the name of the buyer.

It is impossible to give an exhaustive list of the business activities for which licences or approvals will be required and it is essential that the buyer makes certain that he is fully aware of the regulatory regime to which the business is subject but examples include:

4.1.3.1   Activities which are regulated by the FSA under the FSMA: on a sale and purchase of assets it will be necessary for the buyer to ensure that the activities in question fall within any permission which he currently holds and, if that is not the case, to obtain a new or extended permission while, on a sale and purchase of shares, the buyer will need to be satisfied that the continued authorisation will not be affected by a change of ownership.

4.1.3.2   When acquiring an insurance company, a buyer needs to be aware that there are regulatory issues relating to change of control under the FSMA, which governs the regulation of insurers in the UK. The acquisition of, or increase in the level of control of, a UK authorised insurer or reinsurer is subject to prior approval by the FSA. Since January 14, 2005, it is a criminal offence to help customers buy or claim on insurance products without the appropriate permission or exemption from the FSA.

4.1.3.3   Businesses which sell alcohol or provide public entertainment, such as live music, theatre or cinema, or which sell hot food or drink after 11pm, are regulated by the Licensing Act 2003.

Following the acquisition of entertainment businesses such as cinemas, pubs, bars and nightclubs, or even supermarkets, restaurants, late night takeaways, off-licences, convenience stores, hotels and guesthouses, the buyer will need to ensure that he has both a Premises Licence for the premises where alcohol is to be sold (which is likely to be transferred with the business) and a Personal Licence for the person(s) who will actually be selling alcohol. A Personal Licence is issued for ten years in the first instance and will be renewed on application for a further ten years if the licence holder has not been convicted of any relevant or foreign offence. It may therefore be essential that the individual concerned actually transfers to the buyer in addition to making sure that the buyer can comply with the other conditions of these licences.

4.1.3.4 Businesses which carry on betting and gaming activities are regulated by the provisions of the Gambling Act 2005, which implemented new gambling laws in the UK and put in place the Gambling Commission, which will took over the responsibility for regulating and enforcing gambling in the UK from the Gaming Board.

Under the Gambling Act 2005, directors and other persons holding positions of authority or influence over betting operators, such as bingo halls, casinos or games arcades, require an operating licence from the Gambling Commission and have to undergo a "fit and proper" test, assessing the suitability of the applicant to take on such a role and the knowledge and professional competence of the applicant, as well as a financial standing test.

If, therefore, the buyer does not already hold such a licence, he (and, where relevant, his co-directors and other relevant staff) will have to undergo these tests.

4.1.3.5 The buyer of a residential or nursing home has to comply with the provisions of the Care Standards Act 2000, which requires that establishments providing residential accommodation and personal care have to register with the Commission for Social Care Inspection ("CSCI"). A residential or nursing home, as a registered provider, also has to appoint an officer to be registered as a "responsible person" and, where that person is not involved in the day-to-day running of the care home, it must appoint an individual who will be registered in his own right as the registered manager of the care home.

The buyer will therefore have to make sure that he is able to comply with these requirements and it may be essential that the registered manager is transferred to the buyer.

4.1.3.6 A business involved in the treatment, keeping or disposal of controlled waste must hold a waste management licence. On a sale and purchase of its assets, such licence may be transferred to the buyer and the licence holder and the buyer must jointly make an application for the transfer to the waste regulation authority which granted the licence. If, on such an application, the authority is satisfied that the proposed transferee is a fit and proper person, the authority must effect a transfer of the licence to the proposed transferee. In case of rejection of the application by the waste regulation authority, the buyer may appeal to the Secretary of State.

4.1.3.7   A buyer acquiring a transport or haulage business will have to ensure that the licence requirements under the Goods Vehicles (Licensing of Operators) Act 1995 are complied with and that any person involved in the carriage of goods by road in the course of a trade or business has a licence which is obtainable from the Traffic Commissioner.

If the buyer is buying assets and the business operates from different centres, the buyer will have to ensure that he makes an application in each area where the business operates. The buyer may hold separate operators' licences in respect of different areas, but he must not at any time hold more than one such licence in respect of the same area.

Even where licences and approvals are not essential, the buyer will wish to ensure that all licences or approvals which are desirable for the carrying on of the business will continue in force or (on a sale and purchase of assets) will be capable of being transferred to him.

On a sale and purchase of shares, a buyer should remember that these issues will not only apply to the target company but will also apply to the activities of any subsidiary, as a change of control of its ultimate—or intermediate—holding company is likely to be treated as a change of control of the subsidiary.

4.1.4   Competition law issues

Transactions involving the change of ownership of certain industries will automatically require clearance from the competition authorities, while others may give rise to competition law considerations: this will depend upon the size of the transaction and the market shares involved. These issues are discussed in more detail in Ch.18.

4.1.5   Data protection

Most businesses are likely to store personal records (e.g. employee records) electronically and as a result they will be subject to the data protection legislation. It will be necessary for the buyer to establish whether the transaction will involve the transfer of data which is subject to a data protection registration and, if so, it will be necessary for the buyer to obtain his own registration. This subject is discussed in more detail in Ch.7.

4.2   Share sales and purchases

4.2.1   There are occasions when there are so many selling shareholders (or potential selling shareholders) that it is impractical to have all shareholders sign a single sale and purchase agreement and is more appropriate for the buyer to issue a formal offer document to all shareholders. One particular advantage of this approach is that, if the buyer is able to obtain acceptances from the holders of at least 90 per cent of the share capital (or, if the offer extends to more than one class of share, the holders of at least 90 per cent of the shares of each such class), he will be able compulsorily to acquire any shareholders who have not accepted the offer.

Any offer document which is issued to the shareholders is, however, likely to amount to a "financial promotion" and it may then need to be issued by an "authorised person" or its contents may need to be approved by an authorised person. This issue is discussed in detail in Ch.23.

4.2.2   In some transactions, it may also be necessary or desirable to obtain specific "tax clearances" and these are discussed in Chs 13 and 14.

4.3   Assets sales and purchases

Apart from the matters previously discussed in this chapter, a particular concern on the sale and purchase of assets is where there are leasehold properties involved and the lease specifies that the written consent of the landlord must be obtained to any assignment or under-letting.

If the financial position of the buyer is not as strong as that of the seller, the landlord may refuse to consent to the assignment without ensuring that the seller remains liable under the lease if the buyer defaults—this is likely to be a particular concern in management buy outs (where the buyer is likely to be a newly-incorporated and highly-geared company) and when a smaller company is buying a business from a much larger company.

Alternatively, as a condition of giving his consent, the landlord may insist upon personal guarantees from the shareholders of the buyer, advance rent deposits or other security for the rent and other obligations of the tenant under the lease.

Where the obtaining of the landlord's consent is likely to be a major difficulty, the only solution may be for the transaction to proceed as a sale and purchase of shares, in which event there will be no change of ownership of the property and therefore no need to obtain the consent of the landlord (unless, of course, the lease is expressed to be capable of termination on a change of control of the tenant company).

Leases and other property-related issues are considered in more detail in Ch.19.

4.4   Impact of changes to the law relating to directors' duties

The directors of a party which is a company will have to consider the impact of the changes to the law relating to directors' duties which were made by the Companies Act 2006. Most of these came into force on October 1, 2007 and the remainder on October 1, 2008.

Previously, most of the law relating to directors' duties derived from the common law and various equitable principles but the Companies Act 2006 introduced a statutory statement of directors' duties and codified them, while making it clear (s.170(3)) that the duties specified in the new Act are based on those common law rules and equitable principles and have effect in place of them. The Act provides (s.170(4)) that those duties are to be interpreted and applied in the same way as the common law rules or equitable principles and that regard should be had to the corresponding common law rules and equitable principles in interpreting and applying the statutory duties.

The DTI has produced guidance which states that the statutory statement of duties is "essentially the same as the existing duties established by case law" with the only exception being the new procedures for dealing with conflicts of interest (discussed below).

A detailed summary of the relevant provisions of the new Act is beyond the scope of this book but this chapter considers briefly how some of the changes may impact on corporate transactions.

4.4.1 Duty to act within powers

Section 171 provides that a director of a company must act in accordance with the company's constitution and only exercise powers for the purposes for which they are conferred.

4.4.2 Duty to promote the success of the company

Section 172 provides that a director must act in the way he considers, in good faith, would be most likely to promote "the success of the company for the benefit of its members as a whole".

What has provoked a considerable amount of discussion is that s.172(1) goes on to provide that, in fulfilling this duty, a director must have regard (amongst other matters) to:

- the likely consequences of any decision in the long term;

- the interests of the company's employees;

- the need to foster the company's business relationship with suppliers, customers and others;

- the impact of the company's operations on the community and the environment;

- the desirability of the company maintaining a reputation for high standards of business conduct; and

- the need to act fairly as between the members of the company.

The list is not exhaustive—for example, if the company looks like becoming insolvent, the directors' primary duty is to act in the interests of the creditors (s.172(3)).

What "success for the benefit of the company's members as a whole" means is unclear but the government has stated that "success" in this context will usually mean "long-term increase in value" for commercial companies.

The practical concern that has been expressed is how much weight should directors give to the different factors?

For example, the directors may receive an offer for part of their company's business which is very attractive from a financial point of view but which will result in the business being relocated and most of the existing workforce being made redundant, with a consequent impact on the local community. Is the general duty of the directors to have regard to the long-term increase in the value of their company to be outweighed by their responsibility towards the employees and the local community?

There has been a lot of concern expressed about this as the Act does not give any guidance on the point but the Government has suggested that it will simply be a judgment call for the directors as to which should prevail and that, provided that they act in good faith, their decisions are unlikely to be challenged because somebody thinks that they got it wrong.

It is not clear what the position will be if a director acts in good faith but does not actually have regard to the various factors. The Government has stated that it did not intend it to be possible for a director who is acting in good faith to be held liable for a "process failure" where that could not have affected the outcome but the Act is silent on the point.

It is important to remember too that these duties will be owed to the company (s.170(1)) and that only the company will be able to enforce them. Directors will have to take account of the interests of the various "stakeholders" but those stakeholders will not be able to enforce them in their own right (in certain circumstances, they might, if they are or become shareholders, be able to bring a "derivative claim" (as discussed below) but this would essentially be on the company's behalf).

Directors of subsidiaries may be particularly concerned if their parent company has made the decision that the subsidiary should sell all or part of its business as it would (on a sale and purchase of assets) be the directors of the subsidiary who would ultimately have to approve the sale. Should they focus on the interests of their particular company or may they take account of the interests of the wider group?

This point does is not addressed in the Act but the reality is that, while directors do owe their duties to their own company rather than to other companies in the group, the over-riding duty is to promote the success of the company "for the benefit of its members as a whole" and, as its members will be one or more other companies in the group, it is hard to see what risks there could be for directors in acting in accordance with the wishes of their parent company, save where their company is insolvent or in danger of becoming insolvent (at which point their duties would be owed primarily to its creditors).

In any event, there are court cases which suggest that it is acceptable for directors of a company which is part of a group to take into account the wider interests of the group and those principles are unlikely to be affected by the new Act. It should be borne in mind, however, that this will only be the case if it is in the best interests of the company of which the individual is a director for him to do so. The test set out in *Charterbridge Corp Ltd v Lloyds Bank Ltd* ([1970] Ch.62) is "whether an intelligent and honest man in the position of a director of the company concerned could, in the whole of the existing circumstances, have reasonably believed that the transaction was for the benefit of the company". The court made it clear that the directors of a particular company are not entitled to sacrifice the interests of that company in order to promote the interests of the group.

The position may not be as straightforward where the company is not a wholly-owned subsidiary, particularly in view of the fact that directors must have regard to the need to act fairly as between the members of the company.

As has already been mentioned, the position will change if a company (or group of companies) is in danger of becoming insolvent as, at that point, the individual directors' duties will become owed primarily to the creditors of their company and these are likely to be different from group company to group company. Directors must recognise the point when this shift takes place and they must then become much more careful in considering whether a particular decision is really in the best interests of all creditors of a particular company.

When a company is in financial difficulties, a sale of the assets of the company (or a sale of the share capital of a subsidiary) may be put forward as a potential solution. A detailed analysis of the relevant provisions of insolvency law is beyond the scope of this book but, in those circumstances, directors will need to consider the implications of the Insolvency Act 1986, including those relating to wrongful trading and voidable preferences (which may be an issue on a sale and purchase of assets which is likely to result in some creditors being paid at the expense of others).

If the company concerned is a member of a group, it is essential that its directors consider the interests of the creditors of their particular company rather than the interests of other companies in the group or of creditors of other companies in the group—this can be particularly difficult for those who are directors of more than one company within a group and, when they are concerned about the financial position of their companies, they should consider obtaining independent professional advice at an early opportunity.

There has been some discussion as to whether or not board minutes will have to be more detailed in order to record the fact that the directors have taken into account the matters specified in s.172 and the general view is that, for routine business at least, this will not be appropriate.

Where, however, decisions are being taken which may be regarded as unusual or exceptional (whether because of their size or their very nature) or which may be controversial, it is recommended that the chairman should initiate a detailed discussion which does take account of the various factors and, in those circumstances, it would be appropriate to have more detailed board minutes than might normally be the case in order to show that there was a discussion which took into account the factors required by the Act.

A sale or purchase of a company or of the assets and undertaking of a business is exactly the sort of area where this approach may be appropriate, particularly where redundancies are envisaged or where there are minority shareholders involved.

The minutes should, however, be a record of a genuine discussion which actually took place, rather than an attempt to lay a "paper trail".

Sections 171 and 172 of the Companies Act 2006 were briefly considered by the Scottish Court of Session in the case of *West Coast Capital (Lios) Ltd* [2008] ScotsCS CSOH 72. The Court expressed the view that these sections appeared to do little more than set out the pre-existing law on the subject but it does not appear that they were the subject of specific legal argument or detailed consideration by the Court.

4.4.3   Duty to exercise independent judgement

Under s.173, a director must exercise independent judgement but this duty is not infringed by a director acting in accordance with an agreement entered into by the company which restricts the future exercise of the directors' powers or acting in a way authorised by the company's constitution.

This is likely to be particularly relevant in the context of a venture capital investment where the investment agreement will normally oblige the directors (along with the other parties) to act in accordance with the terms of the agreement and to abide by any restrictions in it.

For example, venture capitalists ("VCs") will often insist upon investment agreements which oblige the directors of the investee company to take steps to seek out an "exit" (typically, either a sale or a flotation) at an agreed point and may go further and oblige the directors to take steps to implement a particular exit opportunity if that is acceptable to the VC investors.

Clearly, the duty of the directors to exercise independent judgment should not be infringed if they are acting in accordance with their obligations under the investment agreement (although the directors would be well-advised to make sure that the company itself is a party to the investment agreement as otherwise it would not be "an agreement entered into by the company").

4.4.4   Duty to exercise reasonable care, skill and diligence

Section 174 provides that a director must exercise the care, skill and diligence which would be exercised by a reasonably diligent person with both the general knowledge, skill and experience that may be reasonably expected of a person carrying out the functions of that director and the actual knowledge, skill and experience that that director has. In applying this duty, regard must be had to the functions of the particular director, including his specific responsibilities and the circumstances of the company.

It is reasonable to assume that the finance director would be expected to have a level of financial awareness which is appropriate to someone acting in that capacity and that will be the case even if (for example) a junior accountant is promoted beyond his competence to the position of finance director.

4.4.5   Duty to avoid conflicts of interest

The provisions of the Act relating to conflicts of interest are contained in s.175, which came into force on October 1, 2008, and provide that a director must avoid situations in which he has or can have a direct or indirect interest that conflicts with—or may conflict with—the company's interests. This applies in particular to the exploitation of property or information or a business opportunity (whether or not the company could take advantage of the property, information or opportunity).

An example of how this duty may be relevant in the context of mergers and acquisitions is if Tom, Dick and Harriet, the directors of a company, consider and reject a particular acquisition opportunity but Harriet decides that she would like to pursue the opportunity herself as a "buy in" candidate.

Before she can do that, she must obtain formal authorisation from the company.

Otherwise, she would be in breach of her duties to the company and may have to account to the company for any profits she makes.

Before s.175 came into force, she would have been required to obtain prior authorisation from the shareholders but, under the new law, this may not necessarily be the case. In summary:

- For private companies incorporated after the legislation came into force, the directors can authorise an arrangement which would otherwise have given rise to a conflict (assuming that the articles permit and do not require any such authorisation to be given by the shareholders).

- In the case of private companies incorporated before the legislation came into force, there are transitional arrangements requiring them to obtain the approval of their members (or to amend their articles) if they want to permit board authorisation for any particular opportunity, the intention being to preserve whatever current arrangements existing companies have with regard to this.

- In the case of public companies, the directors may give the necessary authorisation, provided that the articles allow them to do so (failing which the authorisation would have to come from the shareholders).

- It should be noted that, where board authorisation is permitted, it must be given by independent directors—any directors who have an "interest" in the arrangements will not count towards the quorum and will not be allowed to vote.

In the example, therefore, Harriet would not be allowed to vote on the proposal to authorise her to pursue the acquisition opportunity and would have to rely on authorisation from Tom and Dick.

4.4.6   Duty not to accept benefits from third parties

Section 176 of the 2006 Act provides that a director must not accept any benefit from a third party if the acceptance of the benefit can reasonably be regarded as likely to give rise to a conflict of interest.

Section 176(3) makes it clear that benefits received by a director from a person by whom his services (as a director or otherwise) are provided to the company are not regarded as benefits from a third party and so the provision does not stop a director providing services to the company through another company.

An example of how s.176 may impact on mergers and acquisitions is where Seller PLC is in the course of disposing of a subsidiary through an "auction" process and, before a preferred bidder has been chosen, a couple of its directors receive lavish entertainment from a corporate finance firm who are representing one of the interested parties.

Responsible directors should all know where the line between normal corporate hospitality and bribery falls but this duty may well result in companies developing a formal policy regarding acceptance of corporate hospitality and gifts generally and of keeping a central register of hospitality or gifts received.

In any event, if there is any doubt at all as to whether or not any particular arrangement may be caught by this section, the safest course is for the director to make a formal declaration to the board of his having received the benefit in question and for the minutes of the board meeting to record why the board considered that receipt of the benefit did not give rise to a conflict of interest.

4.4.7   Duty to declare interest in proposed transaction or arrangement with the company

These provisions require a director to declare to the other directors the nature and extent of any interest, direct or indirect, in a proposed transaction or arrangement with the company if this interest can reasonably be regarded as likely to give rise to a conflict of interest.

This may be done at a board meeting or in writing but must be done before the company enters into the transaction or arrangement.

There are similar provisions where a director has an interest in an existing transaction or arrangement entered into by his company.

The relevant provisions are s.177 (duty to declare interest in proposed transaction or arrangement) and s.182 (declaration of interest in existing transaction or arrangement), along with ss.178–181 and 183–187.

The requirement to declare both the nature and extent of the director's interest will mean that declarations of interest may have to be more detailed than had previously been the case.

To give a practical example, Tom, Dick and Harriet may be the directors of Seller Limited (Seller), which receives an approach from Buyer PLC (Buyer), which expresses an interest in buying a division of Seller. Tom is a director of Buyer and holds 10 per cent of its issued share capital.

Tom is required to declare to the board of Seller that he is interested in the proposed transaction as a director of Buyer and as a 10 per cent shareholder in Buyer.

One helpful provision, however, is that the Act states that a sole director of a private company will not have to hold a meeting alone and make the declaration to himself and then record it in the minutes.

4.4.8   Derivative claims

In the past, the ability of a shareholder to bring an action on behalf of his company for a wrong done to the company is very limited but the 2006 Act specifies a wider range of circumstances in which such a "derivative claim" may be brought by a shareholder.

For example, a derivative action will now be available for breach of duty by the directors, even if the director concerned has not benefited personally from the breach and it will not be necessary (as previously) to show that those directors who were responsible for the wrong doing control the majority of the company's shares.

The Act contemplates a two-stage procedure for obtaining permission to proceed with such a claim. First of all, the shareholder will be required to show that there is a prima facie case for bringing the action and the Court will consider this without requiring evidence from the company.

Assuming that he is able to show a prima facie case, the court may require evidence from the company prior to the start of the action.

Under s.260(4) the cause of action may arise before the shareholder became a member and there is a concern that this will lead to activists taking a stake in a company solely for the purposes of challenging some particular action that the company has taken (for example, decisions on environmental policies).

The requirement to present a prima facie case before a claim can continue and the ability of the court to make a Costs Order against an applicant are intended to prevent vexatious claims or claims made without any real grounds.

The new court procedure will be used for claims begun on or after October 1, 2007 but, where the act or omission giving rise to the claim occurred before that date, the court will determine the outcome on the basis of the common law applicable at the time of the act or omission in question.

Most of the concerns raised in the press have been about the dangers of actions being brought by special interest groups and the like but, in practice, it is hard to see how any actions could ever result in an award of damages unless the company can be shown to have suffered loss as a result of the director's actions and, in practice, more significant claims may arise out of merger and acquisition activity.

For example, the directors of a listed company may receive an approach from a potential offeror which would value the shares at 10 pounds per share and may reject that approach, only to find that the share price subsequently plummets to one pound per share.

In those circumstances, there must be a possibility that disaffected shareholders will try to mount an action against the directors for failing to accept what turned out (with the benefit of hindsight) to have been a good offer.

In practice, provided that directors were acting in good faith and in accordance with professional advice, it is hard to see how a successful action could ever be brought against the directors but the risk will be there and it is precisely to cover this sort of situation that directors should make sure that there are board minutes which record how the directors' decision was reached and show that the decision was taken on the basis of professional advice and after due consideration of the various factors specified in the Act.

These changes are of particular concern to directors when viewed in the light of the changes in the law relating to directors' duties and boards should review their directors' and officers' liability insurance policies to ensure that defence of derivative claims is covered by the policies.

4.4.9   Ratification by shareholders

As under the common law, under the 2006 Act shareholders may ratify conduct of a director which might otherwise have amounted to negligence, breach of duty or the like but there is a significant change in the law in that, under s.239 of the 2006 Act, ratification must be by the members without reliance on the votes of the director concerned or any person connected with him.

For example, the directors of a company are Tom, Dick and Harriet and they are all shareholders—Tom holding 60 per cent and Dick and Harriet 20 per cent each. The company's solicitors advise that some action on Tom's part was in breach of his duties as a director.

Before the 2006 Act, unless his breach was in bad faith, Tom could have used his majority interest in order to procure the passing of an ordinary resolution to ratify his own breach of duty but, in the future, his votes would have to be ignored. Inevitably, there is a concern that this may lead to more actions against directors.

Chapter 5

Due Diligence—General Principles

5.1 Introduction

Due diligence is the process by which the buyer and his professional and others advisers will investigate the target business and its assets and liabilities before entering into a legally-binding sale and purchase agreement. The principle of caveat emptor (let the buyer beware) will apply to most aspects of the sale and purchase of a business, whether that transaction proceeds by way of a sale and purchase of shares or a sale and purchase of assets. A seller will not generally be liable for non-disclosure of relevant information or the provision of untrue or misleading information unless this constitutes a misrepresentation or breach of a contractual term and, as a result, it has become almost universal practice for buyers to insist upon contractual warranties concerning the target business and its assets and liabilities.

Warranties will rarely be given by an administrator, receiver or liquidator and in some transactions (such as a management buy-out or a sale by a seller in a very strong negotiating position) the warranties may be very limited. Otherwise, a seller will have to accept that, if he wants to sell, he will have to give the buyer the benefit of warranties (and probably some indemnities) in respect of a whole host of matters.

Warranties and indemnities will be discussed in more detail in Ch.10 but a buyer should not regard warranties or indemnities as cast iron protection against any problems which may arise: no matter how widely drafted the warranties or indemnities may be, they may not necessarily cover every conceivable situation and, even if they do cover any particular issue, they are likely to be subject to limitations, there may be issues over quantification of loss, they will be expensive and time-consuming to enforce and they will be of no value whatsoever if the seller does not ultimately have the financial means to satisfy the claim in full.

A buyer should therefore regard warranties and indemnities as very much a fall-back position and should instead carry out as much investigation as possible into what he is buying before entering into a legally binding sale and purchase agreement: in that way, if a major issue does come to light before then, the buyer will have the opportunity to negotiate a specific indemnity or retention to cover the issue, may be able to negotiate a price reduction which takes account of it or, as a last resort, may walk away from the deal altogether.

On a sale and purchase of assets, rather than of shares, the due diligence is likely to be less extensive, as it need only cover the specific assets and liabilities which are to be transferred to the buyer, so that (for example) a buyer of assets may only need to carry out minimal due diligence into the tax affairs of the business. On a sale and purchase of shares, on the other hand, all assets and liabilities will transfer and the due diligence work needs to reflect that.

The extent of the due diligence work to be carried out on any particular transaction will also depend on other circumstances, such as the time available to the buyer for such work to be done and the importance of the transaction to the buyer.

For example, where there are pressing commercial or other reasons for a transaction to be completed rapidly, the buyer may have to accept that he will only be able to carry out a limited amount of due diligence work. Similarly, a large company acquiring a small business may be more inclined to "take a view" and limit its due diligence work than a smaller buyer, for whom the threshold of materiality is likely to be far lower.

Although the primary purpose of the due diligence exercise is to enable the buyer to find out in advance any material issues which may affect his decision to buy the business and/or the price at which he is prepared to buy it, one of the advantages of obtaining as much information as possible about the business in advance is that, once the buyer becomes the owner of the business, he should have a considerable amount of information about the business which will be helpful on a day-to-day basis—details of its relations with its customers and suppliers, with its employees and so on. This is likely to be invaluable where the buyer is going to be having a "hands on" involvement in the running of the business.

In any transaction, there may well be particular factors which prompted the buyer to offer to buy the business and/or which were taken into account in arriving at the price offered and it is obviously essential that particular attention be given to such matters in the course of the due diligence exercise.

5.2 Examples of due diligence investigation

On most (but by no means all) acquisitions, the buyer will instruct a firm of accountants or other financial advisers to carry out a financial due diligence exercise into the financial position of the business (see Ch.6) and will also instruct his solicitors to carry out legal due diligence (see Ch.7). Depending on circumstances, the buyer may instruct other advisers to carry out appropriate investigations. These may include some or all of the following:

5.2.1 "Market" or "commercial" due diligence

5.2.1.1 If deemed to be required, a due diligence review of the markets and competitive position of the target business can be undertaken, usually by specialist commercial due diligence firms (some of the larger accountancy firms have in-house commercial due diligence specialists).

For some, typically smaller, transactions, however, the accountants may be asked to undertake some limited market analysis as "non-experts" as part of their financial due diligence. Generally this utilises publicly available information and also discussions with target management.

5.2.1.2   Areas that can be covered in a commercial due diligence review include:

- size and description of the target's markets;

- technological, regulatory and economic development, competitor activity and other developments affecting these markets;

- major competitors, their market share and their strengths and weaknesses compared to the target business;

- pricing trends in the industry; and

- other key issues for the industry, such as raw material supply or product substitution.

5.2.1.3   Commercial due diligence will also often include direct interviews with customers, suppliers and competitors, typically under a "cover story" about market research or performance feedback. Some buyers (particularly where backed by venture capitalists) may request access to major customers and suppliers but, for the reasons given in Ch.4, sellers will, almost invariably, resist this very strongly.

5.2.2   Technical due diligence

This is particularly relevant where the business depends on complex technology or is undertaking important research and development projects, the viability of which may be uncertain.

5.2.3   Operational due diligence

This will, typically, cover areas such as supply chain management and production processes. The operational due diligence team will often be tasked with identifying opportunities to take cost out of the business.

5.2.4   Management due diligence

This is particularly important where a buyer plans to keep the existing management team in place post-acquisition. For financial investors, the competence and suitability of the management team can be one of the most important areas for consideration in the due diligence process. This may involve the formal assessment of the management team through interviews, psychometric testing and referencing by HR specialists.

Other due diligence providers on the transaction may be asked for their views on the effectiveness of the management team.

5.2.5   **Environmental due diligence**

Where the nature of the business activity on the site (either past or present) might cause pollution, a specialist environmental due diligence review may be advisable.

This review typically comprises two phases:

"Phase I"   initial desktop review, sometimes with a site visit to identify any potential environment hazards; and

"Phase II"   a more extensive exercise, to quantify the potential problems identified in "Phase I".

Environmental issues are discussed in detail in Ch.20.

5.2.6   **Pensions**

A specialist review of pension provision in the target business may be appropriate, particularly where there is a defined benefit final salary pension scheme.

The power of the Pensions Regulator to influence a deal where there is a defined benefit scheme in deficit can be a major factor in corporate acquisitions.

Pensions issues can be very complex and time consuming to resolve and so need to be addressed as early as possible in the process. They are discussed in more detail in Ch.22.

5.2.7   **Surveyors/valuers**

If property forms a significant part of the value of the target business, then it may be appropriate to commission an independent valuation of the property portfolio.

In addition, there are asset valuation specialists who can carry out specialist valuations of stocks and plant.

Invoice discounting/factoring providers will typically carry out their own review of the target's debtor book and cash collection/credit control procedures.

5.2.8   **Insurance due diligence**

A specialist review of current insurance provision and an estimate of likely insurance costs after completion.

5.3   Report

On the basis of the work carried out, the advisers concerned will report to the buyer on the outcome. This will normally be by way of formal due diligence reports, but experienced buyers may well instruct their legal advisers to report on an "exceptions only" basis or simply to draw their attention to anything which is reasonably likely to affect their decision to proceed with the transaction at the proposed price. One advantage of a less extensive report from the point of view of the buyer is that it should save him from having to wade through a lengthy report which, almost invariably, includes information which is of no real interest to him and which is totally immaterial in the context of the transaction in question. It should also help to reduce his professional costs.

The advisers concerned, on the other hand, may well prefer to prepare a "full" report (or something approaching it)—not because (as a cynical client may claim) they wish to increase their fees but because of a concern about potential negligence claims if their judgment as to whether or not a particular matter should be material to their client turns out to be incorrect. Nevertheless, if the buyer is experienced in acquisitions and mergers and asks for a more limited form of report, it should just be a matter of the advisers agreeing with the buyer in advance (and in writing) the basis on which they will prepare their report and what should be regarded as "material".

5.4   In-house due diligence

The buyer may also carry out some due diligence himself—larger companies may have the resources in-house to enable them to carry out all or part of the due diligence work and, particularly when buying a manufacturing business, the buyer may himself want to inspect the plant, see it working and generally "kick the tyres".

5.5   Heads of terms and exclusivity

Because of the high costs which may be involved in a due diligence exercise, a buyer will generally insist upon having signed heads of terms before instructing his advisers to begin their work and, wherever possible, the buyer should also make sure that there is a realistic exclusivity agreement in place.

5.6   Relationship between advisers

It will be appreciated from this chapter and Chs 6 and 7 that there can be significant areas of overlap/interaction between the various areas of investigation being undertaken by the buyer or his advisers. For example, the accountants may look at the terms and conditions of employment from a financial perspective (what are overtime rates and levels, what benefits are given, etc.) whilst the legal advisers may also review contractual terms from a legal perspective. It is important that the scope of the financial and legal due diligence avoids, wherever possible, duplication of the work of other due diligence providers and close liaison between advisers is therefore required to ensure that the due diligence process is undertaken efficiently. It is important that this should take place throughout the due diligence exercise as it is unhelpful to the buyer or to his other advisers if (for example) his solicitors receive, as the transaction approaches completion, a draft of an extensive financial due diligence report which highlights a concern and goes on to make the comment that the accountants recommend that appropriate warranty or indemnity protection be obtained in respect of the matter in question. There is the danger that such a comment may be "lost" in all the details of the report or that the lawyers will not be aware of the issue until the sale and purchase agreement is regarded as more or less finalised, at which point it may be difficult to introduce additional protections.

Similarly, it is unhelpful if the buyer's solicitors issue a legal due diligence report which refers (for example) to a particular tax issue and simply contains the statement that the solicitors recommend that advice be taken from the accountants who are dealing with the financial due diligence. Where one set of advisers becomes aware of an issue which may be material to another, they should not wait for this to be dealt with in a formal report but should instead take steps to draw the matter to the attention of the buyer and his other advisers as soon as possible so that they can be confident that it will not be overlooked or left until too late a stage.

5.7 The duty of professional advisers to disclose information under anti-money laundering legislation

5.7.1   Accountants, solicitors and certain other professional advisers (who fall within the regulated sector) are covered by two pieces of anti-money laundering legislation—the Proceeds of Crime Act 2002 ("POCA") (as amended) and the Money Laundering Regulations 2007 ("MLR"), along with the Terrorism Act 2000 (as amended ("TA")). The POCA and the TA require individual professional advisers to report money laundering activities to the Serious Organised Crime Agency ("SOCA"). They also create individual money laundering offences which can be committed both by the parties to a transaction and their professional advisers. The MLR imposes on the firms of such professionals a duty to undertake risk assessments and verification of identity in relation to their clients. The MLR also require them to establish internal controls, monitor compliance, provide training to all relevant staff and to keep records. They are required under the POCA to make a report as soon as practicable to the SOCA if they become aware of any circumstances which give rise to knowledge, or suspicion, or reasonable grounds for suspicion, of a money laundering offence. Accountants and solicitors as individuals must report as soon as practicable knowledge or suspicions of money laundering (whether involving a client or another party) to SOCA in accordance with their firm's anti-money laundering procedures, or otherwise face the prospect of criminal liability.

Money laundering for this purpose is very widely defined, and includes possessing, or in any way dealing with, or concealing, the proceeds of any crime. Any person involved in any known or suspected money laundering activity in the UK risks a criminal conviction carrying a jail term of up to 14 years.

5.7.2   Someone commits a money laundering offence under the legislation if they:

5.7.2.1   conceal, disguise, convert, transfer or remove (from the UK) criminal property;

5.7.2.2   enter into or become concerned in an arrangement which, they know or suspect, facilitates (by whatever means) the acquisition, retention, use or control of criminal property by or on behalf of another person; or

5.7.2.3   acquire, use or have possession of criminal property

and they know or suspect that the property in question constitutes or represents a benefit from criminal conduct.

Any person involved in any known or suspended money laundering activity in the UK risks a criminal conviction carrying a jail term of up to 14 years.

The offence set out in 5.7.2.2 means that a solicitor or other regulated professional adviser can be liable for money laundering carried out by a client event if the criminal proceeds do not pass through the client account of the firm.

5.7.3   Property is criminal property if it:

5.7.3.1   constitutes a person's benefit, in whole or in part, from criminal conduct; or

5.7.3.2   represents such a benefit, directly or indirectly, in whole or in part; and

5.7.3.3   the alleged offender knows or suspects that it constitutes such a benefit.

5.7.4   Criminal conduct is conduct which constitutes an offence in any part of the UK. An element of intent is required before a criminal offence can be committed in a country or territory outside the UK. Where there is no element of knowledge or suspicion, no money laundering can arise.

5.7.5   Regulated professional advisers are required under s.330 of the POCA to make a report as soon as practicable to SOCA if they become aware of any circumstances which give rise to knowledge, or suspicion, or reasonable grounds for suspicion of a money laundering offence. Such advisers which includes accountants and solicitors must, in their individual capacity report as soon as practicable such money laundering activity (whether involving a client or another party) to the Money Laundering Officer within their firm ("MLRO") or otherwise face the prospect of criminal liability. The maximum jail sentence for such an offence is five years.

5.7.6   The "tipping off" of a money launderer (or suspect) also constitutes an offence under the POCA. It is a further criminal offence to tell anyone that a disclosure has been made—for example, to the MLRO or SOCA—or that an investigation into allegations that a money laundering offence has been committed has been initiated or is being contemplated—provided that such an action is likely to prejudice any investigation. For this reason, accountants or solicitors finding a reportable event at a target business when carrying out a due diligence review may decide that they cannot inform their client (or the seller) that they have submitted a report to SOCA. Obviously, the submission of such a report makes an investigation by the authorities much more likely and, as a consequence, the crystallisation of any related liability in the target business more probable.

A professional adviser can inform a professional adviser of the same kind (for example, legal adviser to legal adviser) that a disclosure has been made or an investigation is taking place, provided they share the same client or are involved in the same transaction. A legal adviser can also inform his client for the purpose of dissuading the client from engaging in conduct amounting to an offence.

5.7.7   Clients who have knowledge or suspicion of money laundering activity may report it to SOCA but, unlike professional advisers, are under no duty to do so. If they themselves become involved in the money laundering activity they will be guilty of a criminal offence. However, they cannot be criminally liable if they fail to report an offence but they can commit the offence of prejudicing an investigation, which is similar to tipping off.

If, therefore, a prospective buyer becomes aware of activities of the target business which amount to criminal conduct, he will not be obliged to report it and will not be criminally liable if they point out to the seller that he is doing something which amounts to criminal conduct but, if the activities in question continue once the buyer has acquired the business, he is likely himself to be guilty of money laundering.

5.7.8   The law provides that the making of a report under the money laundering regulations takes precedence over client confidentiality considerations for the professional advisers and provides protection to them for such disclosure. Where providing directly comparable services to lawyers, accountants operate under the same rules of legal privilege as set out in s.330(6) of the POCA. The application of legal privilege to money laundering is a complex area but, in general, it is a defence for professional advisers to a money laundering offence, provided the communications was made for the purpose of giving or receiving legal advice. Most documents disclosed in due diligence are not made for such purpose.

5.7.9   Set out below are some examples of activities that could fall under the definition of money laundering, some of which may not at first sight appear obvious:

- cost savings resulting from breaches of health and safety regulations;

- late payment of tax;

- if a customer has overpaid and the business does not reflect this liability in its books without first obtaining consent from the customer or taking reasonable steps to return the money;

- if a company employing five or more employees has not facilitated access for the employees to a stakeholder pension scheme;

- cartel offences under the Enterprise Act;

- tax evasion, which includes tax offences committed abroad if the action would have been an offence were it to have taken place in the UK; and

- breaches of environmental or health and safety legislation.

5.7.10 Tax evasion includes the under-declaring of income and over-claiming of expenses. For direct tax, common criminal offences generally involve some criminal intent or dishonesty. For indirect tax, s.167(3) of the Customer and Excise Management Act 1979 provides that a wide range of "innocent/accidental errors" are criminal offences, even though in practice they are generally dealt with through the civil penalty regime.

Disclosure to SOCA is not required for innocent errors. However, where the situation is not rectified once the error is realised, a report to SOCA should be made, using the simplified Limited Intelligence Value report.

5.7.11 The disclosure letter—particularly in relation to tax and environmental warranties, where a breach results in both a crime and criminal proceeds—may also highlight matters which should be reported to SOCA.

5.7.12 Money laundering reports need to be made irrespective of the quantum of the benefits derived from, or the seriousness of, the offence—there is no de minimis level or exclusion for "immaterial" amounts.

5.7.13 One of the greatest practical concerns for professional advisers who have made a report to SOCA is what happens after that. For example, if a solicitor acting for a buyer becomes aware that the target company or business has breached environmental legislation and makes a report to SOCA, he may only take limited steps to further the transaction until he has been given (or is deemed to have been given) clearance by SOCA to proceed. He should certainly not complete the transaction without such clearance.

In circumstances where completion cannot take place without seeking consent from SOCA, particularly if the timetable is tight, the solicitor may come under considerable pressure from the seller and his solicitors to proceed more rapidly. In practice, it is normally possible to obtain a rapid clearance from SOCA but, if the matter in question comes to his attention as a result (for example) of a last-minute disclosure, he will find himself in an extremely difficult position.

This does not purport to be anything approaching an exhaustive summary of the money laundering rules and the way in which they impact on transactional work but is simply intended to remind professional advisers of the need always to be mindful of those rules when engaged on a corporate transaction. Professional advisers who have particular concerns are strongly recommended to refer to the guidance issued by their own professional body.

Chapter 6

Due Diligence—Financial

6.1 The purpose of financial due diligence

Financial due diligence investigations typically provide an appraisal of financial matters (such as accounting policies and methodologies, trading results, assets and liabilities), as well as the provision of information on other areas such as employees, management organisation, and systems. The main purposes of financial due diligence investigations can include:

6.1.1 to identify any issues or areas of risk of which the buyer and any funders may not be already be aware and which may affect the purchase arrangements;

6.1.2 to confirm the reasonableness of the key financial information presented by the seller;

6.1.3 to assist the buyer in determining the purchase consideration;

6.1.4 to identify matters in respect of which the buyer should seek warranties and indemnities from the seller;

6.1.5 to assess the level of ongoing working capital requirements for the target business;

6.1.6 to help the buyer develop plans for the post acquisition management and development of the target business; and

6.1.7 to "test" any synergy benefits assumed by the buyer to arise in respect of the acquisition.

It is important to appreciate that, typically, a financial due diligence investigation does not constitute an audit of the target business, with no detailed "audit" verification work being carried out in accordance with International Standards on Auditing (UK and Ireland) issued by the Auditing Practices Board or any other auditing standards. In many cases, the accountant will accept the explanations and assurances received from the Target's directors, officers and employees. The accountant will normally satisfy himself that information received is internally consistent.

This chapter considers financial due diligence work in connection with a trade purchase or a management buy-out or buy-in. It is not intended to cover the work of a reporting accountant on a Stock Exchange transaction, although due diligence procedures form the basis of much of the reporting accountants' work in producing their "long form report" and their "working capital report" on such assignments.

6.2 Contractual terms with accountants

6.2.1 Prior to taking on a due diligence assignment, the accountants must carry out various professional checks to confirm that they can carry out the work, including an assessment of any potential conflicts of interest (if, for example, they as a firm have a relationship with more than one party to the transactions) and of any other ethical reasons why they may not be able to act.

6.2.2 Once these checks are completed the accountants should provide a formal letter of engagement for their due diligence assignment in advance of commencement of their work. This would normally include the following matters:

6.2.2.1 scope and purpose of the due diligence;

6.2.2.2 limitations in scope, making it clear what areas the accountants will not cover in their review;

6.2.2.3 timetable and reporting requirements;

6.2.2.4 limitation of liability;

6.2.2.5 fee arrangements;

6.2.2.6 communication and complaints procedure; and

6.2.2.7 detailed contractual terms.

Where external funding is a feature of the transaction, the accountants may be engaged to provide a report addressed to both the buyer and the bank, venture capitalist or other third party investor. In such circumstances, the accountant must assess any conflict of interest before accepting the engagement; for example, the accountant could not advise the buyer on bank funding and the terms of any such funding while, at the same time, accepting a duty of care and issuing that same report to the bank.

In the case of a management buy-out or buy-in, a "Newco" is often formed as the vehicle to acquire the target business. The Newco may not be in existence at the time that the accountants are commissioned to undertake the work. In such circumstances, it is usual for the letter of engagement to provide for the Newco to subsequently sign up to the letter and thereby become an addressee of the accountants' report, upon formation of the company.

6.2.3 Accountants will usually seek to limit their financial liability on due diligence assignments against any claim arising out of the engagement. The basis of limitation and the way it is put in place will vary from firm to firm. The financial limit may be expressed by reference to a multiple of the fee or a fixed amount, sometimes set by reference to a scale based on transaction size. What is an appropriate financial limit can vary substantially between transactions.

6.2.4   Some of the larger accountancy firms have reached an agreement with the British Venture Capital Association for limitation of liability where one of their members is involved in a transaction and this has become the general market "norm" for private equity transactions. The agreement may be summarised as follows:

Value of Transaction	Liability cap
Under £10 million	Value of transaction
£10 million to £55 million	£10 million plus one third of the excess of the value of the transaction over £10 million (resulting in a cap which progressively rises to £25 million in a £55 million transaction)
Over £55 million	£25 million, together with proportionality*
Proportionality is the apportionment of liability between parties by reference to responsibility or blame for the situation giving rise to a claim. Without proportionality, the liability for all of a loss could fall on the accountants, irrespective of their culpability.	

6.2.5   Accountants may seek further to reduce their level of liability cap when they are engaged on a "limited scope" piece of work.

6.2.6   Fees for financial due diligence work can be based on stated charge out rates applied to hours worked or, more usually, to a fixed fee for the work specified in the engagement letter (albeit this can be expected to be tied to a number of assumptions, such as the reasonable availability of information within an agreed timetable or the number of revisions of forecasts to be reviewed).

6.2.7   In order to guard against any risk to the accountant's objectivity, the professional standards prohibit fees on due diligence work to be undertaken on a contingent basis (i.e. the total fee being conditional upon the transaction proceeding). It does allow a "differential" fee level, dependent upon whether the transaction is completed, provided that this reflects any additional risk and responsibility to the due diligence provider if the transaction takes place. This allows for separate "fail" and "success" fees to be quoted. While there is no set range for a success or an abort fee, anything outside a range of + or − 30% of the "base fee" could be regarded as excessive and could leave the accountant open to challenge. This could cause difficulty where the client has limited funds to pay for the due diligence if the transaction fails (as can sometimes be the case, for example, on a management buy-out). It is rare for a bank to underwrite due diligence fees on a transaction, but some venture capital houses may do so.

6.3   Setting the scope of work

6.3.1   Setting the right scope of work is a key area to address early in the process, as financial due diligence can vary widely in scope and content, depending on circumstances. It can cover aspects of the broad range of a target's business or be very focused on a few areas of specific interest to the buyer. This will typically depend on:

6.3.2.1   the existing knowledge of the buyer and/or investor and/or financier;

6.3.2.2   the perceived degree of risk involved;

6.3.2.3   the size and complexity of the target business;

6.3.2.4   whether the transaction is an asset or share purchase;

6.3.2.5   the value of the transaction; and

6.3.2.6   the time available.

6.3.3   In the case of a purchase of assets, due diligence may be focused principally on the categories of assets being acquired and liabilities being assumed. In the case of a share purchase, where the liabilities of the target company are being assumed, a more extensive investigation is typically required. However, even in the case of an assets purchase, an understanding of underlying trading history is generally advisable.

6.3.4   An experienced buyer buying in a sector in which he already operates, may choose to carry out a large part of the due diligence in-house.

6.3.5   Typically, private equity investors will require more due diligence by professional advisers than a trade buyer. Accountants experienced in due diligence work can make recommendations as to particular areas of focus for their review—for example, identifying likely areas of judgment in the preparation of the accounts.

6.3.6   If a buyer requires external acquisition finance, prospective funders will often require independent due diligence (with a principal focus on forecast performance) to be undertaken on both the target and the enlarged group.

6.3.7   Set out in App.1 as a guide, are certain typical sections and areas of focus that can be covered in a financial due diligence report. It is important to emphasise, however, that the scope of any review should be tailored for each project.

6.3.8   Sometimes the buyer's solicitors may not be fully aware of the scope given to the accountants who are carrying out the financial due diligence and vice versa. There can therefore be a danger of something "slipping through the net"—for example, the accountants may be instructed to report on the tax affairs of the target company on a sale and purchase of shares but it is always possible that their instructions will not extend to advice on the tax structure of the transaction generally. The buyer's solicitors should also therefore make sure that the scope of their work is clearly set out and agreed.

6.4   The financial due diligence process

6.4.1   As discussed earlier, accountants are not permitted to work on a "contingent" fee basis, so to appoint a financial due diligence provider represents a cost investment for the buyer. Partly as a consequence, financial due diligence is typically commissioned only after Heads of Agreements have been signed (ideally granting the prospective buyer a period of exclusivity on the deal). It is also quite common for the seller to be asked to underwrite at least part of the buyer's due diligence fees in circumstances where the seller unreasonably causes the transaction to be aborted. These issues are discussed in more detail in Ch.3.

6.4.2   To be most effective, the accountants need a full understanding of their client's objectives and strategy for the acquisition and his key commercial drivers. There may be occasions when the specialist nature of the target business requires accountants with specific industry or sector experience to carry out the due diligence.

6.4.3   Once terms of engagement and scope have been agreed, and the initial planning of the work has been completed, the typical steps in undertaking a financial due diligence exercise are as follows:

6.4.3.1   detailed search of public information sources (websites, Companies House, etc.);

6.4.3.2   issue an information request list to target (many firms have a standard checklist which they can tailor for a specific assignment. It is often most efficient to co-ordinate requests with other due diligence providers). Care is needed not to "over burden" the target management with a list which is not properly tailored to the scope of work and the target's business;

6.4.3.3   initial meeting with management of target;

6.4.3.4   obtain and analyse information and undertake detailed questioning of target management;

6.4.3.5   assess information/answers for reasonableness, testing key information as necessary;

6.4.3.6   ongoing liaison with other due diligence providers; and

6.4.3.7   drafting of the report, issue of factual sections of the draft report to the Target for confirmation of factual accuracy, issue of the report in draft to the buyer for comment and finalisation of the report.

6.4.4   For the reasons given in Ch.5, experience shows that the most effective due diligence exercises occur when the buyer, accountants and other due diligence providers work as part of an overall team, sharing key information and views as the exercise progresses, albeit with clearly defined areas of responsibility.

6.5   Access to information

6.5.1   Typically, the accountants will require access to:

6.5.1.1   the financial records of the target;

6.5.1.2   senior management of the target;

6.5.1.3   audit and tax files of the auditors; and

6.5.1.4   financial forecasts.

6.5.2   The level and extent of information available will obviously vary from business to business. A small owner-managed business may not produce regular and very detailed management reports, whilst the expectations for larger businesses will be higher.

6.5.3   It is generally preferable to undertake the fieldwork at the target's premises as this gives a sense of how the business operates in practice. Where a target business has more than one location, the specific locations to be visited need to be determined. This will take into account various factors, such as the relative size and complexity of operation, the management structure, and the commonality (or otherwise) of systems across the target business. For reviews of large, multi-location operations, sites may be categorised ("a", "b", "c" etc.) for the financial due diligence review and a particular scope of work applied for each specific category. Access to target businesses can sometimes however be restricted because of the seller's concerns over maintaining confidentiality on the transaction, a wish to minimise disruption to the day-to-day running of the business, or simply physical space constraints.

6.5.4   As discussed in Ch.2, particularly where the sale takes the form of an auction or other competitive process, the seller will generally establish a "data room", which is often housed at the offices of one of the seller's advisers.

6.5.5   The seller may insist that the accountants do not disclose commercially sensitive information (such as the identify of key customers) until the negotiations between the parties are at an advanced stage. The accountants should make their client aware of any such restrictions as soon as possible. There can be no arrangement whereby the seller acquires editorial rights to the accountants' report. Additionally, the accountant should refuse to allow his report to be "disclosed" by the seller as an attachment to the sale and purchase agreement as this creates a conflict of interest and might allow the seller to claim no responsibility for incomplete disclosure (maintaining that it should have been covered by the accountant).

6.6   Review of auditors' files and other "hold harmless" arrangements

6.6.1   Often a financial due diligence exercise will include a review of the files of the auditors and/or tax advisors of the target business. This can provide a valuable source of information to the investigating accountants.

6.6.2   In the UK, a buyer cannot generally rely only a company's audited accounts to give it any comfort as to the state of the business, unless the auditors expressly assume any responsibility to it (*Caparo Industries v Dickman* [1990] 2 W.L.R. 358).

6.6.3   The working papers of the auditor (including working papers prepared to support their client's tax computations) are the auditors' legal property and they can restrict or decline access to them. The Institute of Chartered Accountants in England and Wales has issued guidance to auditors on this topic, to the effect that, where access to the auditors' papers is granted, this will be under "hold harmless" arrangements, with the auditors. Such arrangements involve written authorisation from the target business to disclose confidential information to the buyer and the investigating accountants and agreement from the seller, the target business and its directors that the auditors will not be held responsible for the consequences of giving access to the working papers and disclosure of confidential information and written confirmation from the buyer and the investigating accountants that:

●   no duty of care is owed by the auditors as a result of permitting access and that they have no liability to the buyer and investigating accountants and accordingly that they will not bring any claims against the auditors;

●   restrict the buyer and the investigating accountants from passing information obtained from the review to other parties;

●   provide for the investigating accountants to include a brief notice in standard form in their due diligence report explaining the characteristics of the working papers and disclaiming any duty of care by the auditors as a result of providing access to the working papers;

●   provide for the buyer to agree to indemnify the auditors against any claims arising from any breach of the release letter by the buyer or the investigating accountants.

Many buyers may be reluctant to give an indemnity but access is unlikely to be granted by the auditors unless the indemnity is given. If it is given, care will be required to ensure that it is not extended to cover the liability that the auditors would otherwise have in respect of their audit responsibilities. This can be a complex area, and specialist legal advice may be appropriate. Funders are typically reluctant to sign up to any indemnity so it is often the corporate acquirer left providing the indemnity. In the case of a buy-out, where that entity may be a "Newco" which may not have been formed at the time of the due diligence, individuals within the management team may be asked to sign up to the "hold harmless" letter.

6.6.4   In some circumstances, the investigating accountants may be asked to release a copy of their due diligence report to a third party to whom it is not addressed (for example to a bank). The accountants would typically require a "hold harmless" letter from both their client (the buyer) and the proposed recipient of the report before its release. This is similar in form to the auditors letters discussed above.

6.7   Extent of verification of information

6.7.1   Financial due diligence investigation generally does not constitute an audit of the target business. In accordance with International Standards on Auditing (UK and Ireland) issued by the Auditing Practices Board or any other auditing standards. No "true and fair" opinion is given and, unless specifically requested by the client, no detailed verification work is carried out. In contrast to an audit, there is limited regulatory requirement or specific professional guidance on the conduct of financial due diligence.

6.7.2   It is obviously of limited value if the accountants simply re-present information already available to their clients and the key approach to effective due diligence is to review the information available (seeking access to key documentation as considered appropriate), highlighting gaps or inconsistencies, prepare the relevant analysis and ask the right questions. The answers obtained should be critically assessed for reasonableness and consistency.

6.7.3   The accountants are not normally required to verify formally in detail all the information they obtain. They should specify the sources of the key information that they have obtained. If, however, the accountants consider that any particular information is critical to the assessment being made by the readers of the report, they should discuss with the client the steps that should be taken to ensure that the information has been derived from a reliable source.

6.7.4   Depending upon circumstances, it is usual for the accountants to require target management to confirm that the draft report contains no material error of fact and that no material relevant information has been omitted from the report. This may be through a formal "letter of representation" mechanism. This confirmation process may not be possible if the report contains information confidential to the buyer or commercially sensitive to the deal (i.e. it may be used in purchase price negotiations). It is advisable therefore for the structure of the report to allow such confidential information to be readily extracted, allowing the rest of the report to be confirmed by target management.

6.8   Corporation tax review

6.8.1   Tax due diligence will typically encompass a review of PAYE, national insurance and VAT, as well as corporation tax, to ensure that a target company's tax affairs are up-to-date and that there are no potential undisclosed liabilities that could fall on the buyer.

6.8.2   The current UK corporation tax rules are that after 12 months have elapsed from the filing deadline of a company's tax return (itself generally 12 months after the year end), the UK tax authorities cannot retrospectively make enquiries about an issue that was disclosed by a company in its return. However, it can make enquiries where the issue was not disclosed. It can be difficult for the buyer to assess what has, and what should have been disclosed by the target company in relation to its past dealings. Typically, the accountants will be asked to review the corporation tax affairs for the last six years, being the period over which the tax authorities can seek to revise tax liabilities (assuming that the tax returns for earlier periods have been agreed — including potentially those of other group companies which could have an impact on the target's tax position).

6.8.3   It is clearly not possible to anticipate in this chapter all the potential tax issues that can be encountered as part of the due diligence process. Set out below are some of the more common areas to be considered as part of the exercise on the UK tax liabilities:

6.8.3.1   Is the target up-to-date with its tax affairs, including meeting payment deadlines and the filing of returns — does the target business fall within the quarterly payment regime for tax and if so, has this been dealt with correctly?

6.8.3.2   Are there any significant areas of judgment in the accounts impacting upon the quantum and timing of tax payable which may be challenged by the tax authorities?

6.8.3.3   Are there any open periods or areas where HMRC have not determined taxable profits or losses?

6.8.3.4   Are there any matters currently in dispute with HMRC?

6.8.3.5   Are there any liabilities arising as a result of the target business leaving the seller's group — for example in respect of assets acquired within the preceding six years from another group undertaking?

6.8.3.6   Is there a risk that transfer pricing or "thin capitalisation" rules apply — when group companies trade on a non-arm's length arrangement?

6.8.3.7   Is there a risk that trading losses may be lost where there has been, or is likely to be, a change in the nature or conduct of trade?

6.8.3.8   Are there any potential tax liabilities on employees of the target business selling their shares as part of the transaction, which could either in practice fall on the target business or disrupt employee relations?

6.9   Reporting findings

6.9.1   The timing, style and nature of the financial due diligence report will be dictated by the circumstances of the particular engagement, ranging from a short verbal presentation to a full "long form" report. Most clients value forthright views and opinions being given by the accountants in their reports. In addition to raising issues, a good due diligence advisor will also seek to provide solutions to those issues or put forward actions to mitigate their impact.

6.9.2   A principal focus of the due diligence exercise is to identify risk (some clients require reporting by exception, detailing only adverse matters or areas of risk). This can produce an unduly negative view of the target business. It is important that a level of balance is maintained as much as possible.

6.9.3   The form of the report may be particularly important to funders, with a requirement, for example, for an executive summary in a particular form to satisfy their internal approval procedures (ultimate sign off often being given by a "credit committee").

6.9.4   Some clients will ask their accountants to provide their views (verbally on an "off the record") basis on matters such as the competence of particular managers and the effectiveness of the overall management team.

6.9.5   Most firms will include certain standard caveats in their reports, including:

6.9.5.1   that, other than as required in the agreed scope of work or to the extent indicated in the report itself, the accountants have not independently verified the information contained in the report, that they have not carried out an audit, and that they express no opinion on the financial information contained in the report,

6.9.5.2   that the report is confidential, it is for the information of the addressees only and that no duty of care or liability towards any other party is accepted;

6.9.5.3   that the report should not be copied or disclosed to any party other than professional advisers assisting in the transaction, without the prior written consent of the accountants; and

6.9.5.4   that the financial due diligence should not be taken as a recommendation or otherwise to proceed with the transaction. as this will depend on other matters additional to the scope of the accountants' due diligence (for example, management's own due diligence and that of other specialist reviews commissioned in respect of the transaction).

6.9.6   In practice, there can sometimes be a significant elapse of time between the preparation of a due diligence report in draft and the formal signing of the final report in anticipation of completion. The accountants may well not update their review in finalising the report, for events since their draft report was issued, unless specifically requested to do so. Their report should make it clear if this is the case. It is important, however, that the accountants are requested to provide a finalised version of their report in advance of completion, so as to ensure that there is no question over the level of reliance that can be placed on the accountants' work if the report stays as a "draft".

6.9.7   The accountants are sometimes asked to review the sale and purchase agreement and the disclosure letter to raise any issues, particularly in relation to the warranties, based upon the knowledge they have gained through their review. The accountants will typically make it clear that, due to the limitations on the scope of their work, this review can not be expected to identify all issues which should be addressed. This will rely on input from all aspects of due diligence carried out or commissioned by the buyer.

6.10   Vendor due diligence

6.10.1   The seller may sometimes commission a due diligence report by a firm of third party accountants on its own business in anticipation of its sale. This is termed "vendor due diligence" or "sell side" due diligence. It is employed to:

6.10.1.1 assist the seller in preparing information for potential buyers in a professional manner;

6.10.1.2 identify key issues that are likely to be raised by a buyer upon carrying out his due diligence so that the seller can mitigate these as far as possible or at least anticipate them in negotiation;

6.10.1.3 highlight all the key selling points of the business being sold; and

6.10.1.4 allow the seller to better control the sale process. For instance, if there are several potential buyers, they can each be given a copy of the vendor due diligence report to facilitate their due diligence process and thereby reduce the disruption to the target business.

6.10.2   The vendor due diligence report seeks to anticipate and give answers to the same questions that a prospective buyer will raise.

6.10.3   In vendor due diligence, the accountants preparing the report will be initially engaged, and sometimes paid, by the seller. The accountants will normally release their report, once finalised, to interested parties—initially on a "hold harmless" basis but they will ultimately assume a duty of care to the party that becomes the buyer by addressing their report to the buyer. At the same time, the seller will agree that the accountants cease to owe them a duty of care, thus avoiding a conflict of interest.

6.10.4   It is likely that there will be some areas where the potential buyer will require further information or investigation over and above that provided in the vendor due diligence report and the potential buyer may also require his own advisers to provide him with an independent view of the target (including a review of the vendor due diligence report).

6.10.5   Some buyers remain wary of the vendor due diligence process, believing that the report may carry a bias in favour of the seller but, if a vendor due diligence report has been prepared, it is clearly worthwhile for a potential buyer to review it, assess the scope of work and the credibility of the report (perhaps including direct discussion with the accountants), before determining what additional procedures are necessary.

Chapter 7

Due Diligence—Legal

Legal due diligence will normally consist of a number of different elements: enquiries of the seller, searches and enquiries of public registers (such as the register of companies at Companies House and the Land Registry and other property registers) and a review of the information provided by the seller, either in response to the enquiries raised or by way of disclosure against the warranties proposed by the buyer (see Ch.10). Where the sale is taking place by way of competitive auction, rather than submitting enquiries, the buyer and his solicitors will normally review "pre-packaged" due diligence information provided by the seller (which, as discussed in Ch.2, is often provided by way of a data room and then (upon becoming preferred bidder) update that work and/or carry out any additional legal due diligence which may be regarded as appropriate).

As with financial due diligence, it is important to set the scope of the legal due diligence work, not least because it is likely that formal disclosures will be made via the buyer's solicitors (see 10.2.5 below).

Appendix 2 contains a precedent for a reasonably typical set of legal due diligence enquiries (Precedent 8).

The principal areas which would normally be covered in legal due diligence are as follows.

7.1   Share capital and shareholders

On a sale and purchase of shares, it is obviously fundamental to make sure that those who are purporting to sell the shares are indeed the owners of such shares and that they have good title to them.

7.1.1   The starting point will normally be to obtain from the seller (by way of reply to due diligence enquiries) details of the authorised and issued share capitals of the target company and a list of its shareholders and of their shareholdings but the buyer should also carry out a Companies Registry search against the company in order to ensure that the details of the shareholders and shareholdings shown on the register at Companies House accord with those in the list provided by the seller (or that any differences are explained). A Companies Registry search will only show the names of the shareholders shown in the last annual return and details of any subsequent allotments of shares and will not therefore reflect any transfers of shares which have taken place since the last annual return but is nevertheless essential.

It is important, however, to bear in mind that the accuracy of the information on file at Companies House is not guaranteed as it is information provided by the seller or by the target company and a buyer should also review the target company's register of members as, so far as the company is concerned, it is the registered shareholder who may vote, receive dividends and transfer the shares.

The buyer should nevertheless make enquiries as to whether or not the beneficial ownership is held by somebody other than the registered holder and, if the buyer is aware that that is the case, should require that person to be party to the sale and purchase agreement in order to transfer beneficial ownership.

7.1.2 In addition to making sure that the seller is the registered holder of the shares in question, the buyer should ideally investigate the seller's title to them by following the trail of entries in the registers of allotments and transfers and in the register of members in order to satisfy himself that there are entries in these registers which show how the shares devolved upon those purporting to sell them.

7.1.3 The buyer should also endeavour to obtain from the seller (by way of reply to due diligence enquiries) whether the seller has created any mortgages or charges over any of his shares or has granted any options over them in favour of a third party and, if the seller is a company, the buyer should carry out a Companies Registry search against the seller in order to establish whether the seller has created any fixed or floating charges over those shares.

If any such mortgages, charges, options or any other encumbrances have been created over the shares, it should be a term of the sale and purchase agreement that appropriate consents, releases or letters of non-crystalisation are obtained on completion.

7.1.4 The buyer should also check the articles of association of the target company in order to establish whether there are any pre-emption rights or any other restrictions on the transfer of shares. This is unlikely to be a major concern if the entire issued share capital of the target company is being sold, as all shareholders will normally be party to the sale and purchase agreement and, in that agreement, will agree to waive any such rights that they may have but, where that is not the case (for example where not all shareholders are selling their shares), then the buyer should insist upon specific written waivers of those rights.

7.1.5 The buyer should also obtain details of all redemptions by the company of redeemable shares and of any purchases of its own shares which may have taken place and should obtain copies of all relevant documentation in order to ensure (insofar as he is able to do so) that all of the formalities prescribed by the Companies Act have been complied with. This is important as, if that has not been the case, in some circumstances the former shareholders in question may claim that they have the right to have their name restored to the register as the holder of the shares—particularly if they feel, with hindsight, that they sold their shares at too low a price. At the very least, any such claim would have a nuisance value.

7.2   Capacity of the seller

It will be necessary for the buyer to establish that the seller has the necessary legal capacity to enter into the sale and purchase agreement and to sell the shares or assets in question:

7.2.1   The buyer should carry out a bankruptcy search in the Land Charges Registry against individual sellers as, if there is an outstanding bankruptcy order or a bankruptcy petition, the consent of the trustee in bankruptcy (where there is a bankruptcy order) or of the court (where a bankruptcy petition has been presented and a bankruptcy order is subsequently made) will be required. In such circumstances, the buyer should obtain certified copies of the bankruptcy order and of the trustee in bankruptcy's certificate of appointment or, where a bankruptcy petition has been presented, a certified copy of the court order approving the sale.

7.2.2   Care should be taken if the seller is a minor (i.e. is under 18 years of age) as the general common law rule was that a contract made by a minor was capable of being set aside at his option. The rules regarding contracts made by minors are however beyond the scope of this book.

7.2.3   If the seller is a company, the buyer should obtain a copy of its memorandum and articles of association in order to establish that it has the power to sell the shares or assets in question and to establish that the directors are authorised to exercise that power and whether there are any restrictions on their ability to exercise it.

After October 1, 2009, however, the position will be rather more complicated. A detailed analysis of the relevant changes made by the Companies Act 2006 is beyond the scope of this book but, in essence, the objects of a company incorporated after that date will be unrestricted, unless any restrictions on them are specifically set out in its articles of association, while an existing company may make its objects unrestricted by amending its articles to that effect.

In the case of a company incorporated after October 1, 2009, therefore, the buyer should review its articles in order to see whether there is any express limitation on the seller's objects while, in the case of a company incorporated before that date, the buyer should check whether steps have been taken to give it unlimited objects.

In any event, if the directors are able to exercise the power to sell, the buyer should obtain a certified copy of the minutes of a meeting of the directors of the seller, should ensure that such meeting is quorate in accordance with the seller's articles, that any directors who are personally interested in the transaction declare their interest and refrain from voting (unless they are permitted to do so by the seller's articles of association) and that those who actually sign the sale and purchase agreement were duly authorised to do so by the board.

7.2.4   The buyer should also carry out a Companies Registry search against a corporate seller in order to establish whether it is in receivership, administration or liquidation. A detailed analysis of these procedures and of the powers of the office holders concerned is beyond the scope of this book and, in each case, the buyer should obtain expert advice. They can, however, be summarised briefly as follows:

7.2.4.1   Administrative receivers are appointed under a security document which usually confers fixed charges over certain specified assets and floating charges over all other assets, past, present or future. The buyer should obtain a copy of the security pursuant to which the administrative receiver was appointed and a copy of the formal appointment of the receiver. An administrative receiver will normally have the power to sell the assets of the company in respect of which he is appointed, either pursuant to the security under which he was appointed or pursuant to the Insolvency Act 1986.

7.2.4.2   Where receivers are appointed under fixed charges (often known as "Law of Property Act receivers" because such charges usually grant powers under the Law of Property Act 1925), the buyer should obtain a copy of the charge in order to ensure that the receiver was appointed in accordance with it and that the charge itself is valid, as well as to make sure that the shares or assets in question are caught by the fixed charge pursuant to which the receiver is appointed.

7.2.4.3   When buying from a court-appointed receiver, the buyer should obtain a sealed or certified copy of the court order under which the receiver is appointed.

7.2.4.4   An administrator may be appointed by the court or by the holder of a floating charge.

Following the making of an administration order or (as is more common) the appointment of an administrator out of court (and with effect from the presentation of a petition for the appointment of an administrator or the filing of notice of intention to appoint) there is a moratorium to prevent creditors from taking precipitate action against the assets of the company.

Administrators have the power to sell the company's assets but the administrator's proposals must in certain circumstances be approved by creditors.

7.2.4.5   Liquidators have the power to sell the company's property but a buyer should be aware that, if a winding-up order is made, the winding-up will be deemed to have begun on the presentation of the winding-up petition and disposals of the company's property after that point will be void unless the court otherwise orders.

A search of the register of pending petitions (for liquidation and administration) which is maintained at the Royal Courts of Justice in The Strand should be made at the latest possible time before completion (the search can be made by telephone) in order to establish whether there are any pending winding-up or administration petitions. The Companies Registry search should also be renewed at the latest possible point in order to establish whether any notices of resolutions or appointments or intention to appoint have been filed.

If the search reveals that a receiver, administrator or liquidator has been appointed in respect of the seller, the buyer should not continue to progress the transaction with the directors of the seller — the powers of the directors to deal with the assets of the company will have come to an end and, from then on, the seller may only act through its receiver, administrator or liquidator. All subsequent discussions and negotiations should therefore take place with the insolvency practitioner concerned. If the search at the Royal Courts of Justice reveals that a petition has been presented for the appointment of an administrator or for a winding-up but that the administration order or winding-up order (as the case may be) has not yet been made, the buyer should exercise extreme caution as, if the order is subsequently granted, the sale to the buyer will be void, unless it is approved by an order of the court. Even if the buyer is assured that a winding-up petition is vexatious or that the debt owing to the creditor in question has been satisfied, there is the danger that other creditors will have supported the petition and that it will be too late to prevent the winding-up order being made. In any event, it is likely to take some time to have the petition formally withdrawn.

7.3   Corporate structure

The buyer should obtain (amongst other things) the following information:

7.3.1   A copy of the original certificate of incorporation and of any subsequent certificates of incorporation on change of name of the target company or (on a sale and purchase of assets) of the seller, in order to make sure that the company whose shares or assets he is buying is the correct company.

7.3.2   On a sale and purchase of shares, copies of the memorandum and articles of association of the target company, in order to ensure that the target company's current activities are permitted by its objects clause, that the objects clause is wide enough to cover everything that the target company is likely to be doing under its new ownership (including the giving of mortgages, charges and guarantees), that there are no restrictions on the ability of the directors to manage the company's business and that there are no pre-emption rights or other restrictions on the ability of the seller to sell the shares in the target company.

If any concerns arise, the buyer should make it a term of the sale and purchase agreement that all necessary amendments to the memorandum and/or articles of association take place on or before completion and that all pre-emption rights or other restrictions on the transfer of shares are formally waived. The position will be rather different after October 1, 2009 and the changes to the law which will take effect from that date are summarised in 7.2.3.

7.3.3   On a sale and purchase of shares, details of all subsidiaries and other companies in which the target company holds any shares or other interests.

Any legal due diligence enquiries should be expressed to apply not just to the target company but to any subsidiaries and (perhaps to a more limited extent), to any other company in which the target (or any subsidiary of the target) holds shares.

7.3.4   Copies of all documents relating to the sale or purchase of any other company or business—at least where it was sufficiently recent for there still to be warranties and indemnities or other rights or liabilities outstanding. If the buyer is buying assets, he can probably be less concerned about warranties and indemnities as he is unlikely to agree to assume any liability under them but, as would be the case if he were buying shares, he will want to make certain that there are no restrictions on the ability of the seller to sell to him and that there are no non-competition clauses or other provisions which purport to bind the seller's successors in title—even though the buyer would not be a direct party to any such provisions, there is always the danger that the other party to the original transaction may allege that, in some way, the buyer has induced the seller to breach his contract with that other party.

7.4   Insurance

7.4.1   Detailed consideration of the insurance cover which a buyer might reasonably expect the target company to have in place falls outside the scope of this book but, on a sale and purchase of shares, the buyer will acquire the target company with all contingent and other liabilities and will need therefore to be satisfied that all liabilities which are required by law, or which the buyer would normally expect, to be covered by insurance are indeed covered. The buyer should satisfy himself as to the adequacy of the scope and amount of the cover and also check the terms of the policies as regards exclusions, excesses and so on. The buyer should also obtain details of the recent "claims history" (which may have an impact on premiums) and details of any outstanding insurance claims.

The buyer should consider obtaining expert advice in relation to this whole area—either from his solicitors (if they have the appropriate expertise) or from a specialist firm of insurance advisers.

7.4.2   On a sale and purchase of assets, the buyer is likely to be less concerned about the business's insurance cover as any claims arising out of anything done (or not done) before completion will normally be the responsibility of the seller and will fall to be dealt with under the seller's insurances. One exception to this may, however, be employers' liability cover, as the buyer may take on liability for such claims under TUPE (see Ch.21). In any event, the buyer is likely to find it helpful to have details of the insurance cover that has been in place in the past in order to enable him to consider the extent of the cover that he should take out in the future and, in the interests of maintaining the goodwill of the business, the buyer will generally like to know that the seller has appropriate product liability and public liability insurance.

7.4.3   On a sale and purchase of assets, it is essential that the buyer makes sure that he has insurance cover in respect of the business and the assets which he is buying as from the point when insurance risk passes to him (normally, but not necessarily, completion). On a sale and purchase of shares, the target company may have its own insurance cover which will continue after completion but, if it is being bought out of a group of companies and has the benefit of group insurance cover, that cover may cease on completion, in which case it will be necessary for the buyer to put his own cover in place.

7.5   Legal compliance

7.5.1   The buyer will want to be satisfied that the seller has obtained all licences, permits and other regulatory approvals which are required in order to enable the business to be carried on or which should ideally be obtained. The buyer should, therefore, obtain details of all such licences and approvals, together with copies and details of any correspondence or other communication from any regulatory body which indicates that there may have been breaches of any such licence or approval or that any such licence or approval may be withdrawn or not renewed (or renewed subject to conditions). Examples of businesses for which licences or approvals are likely to be required are given in Ch.4 but, in addition to considering the impact of the transaction on those licences and approvals, the buyer will need to know whether there have been any breaches of them. On a sale and purchase of shares, the buyer will take on liability for any such breach and, although that will not normally be the case on a sale or purchase of assets, if any such breach results in the withdrawal or non-renewal of any licence or approval, that may prevent the business from being carried on. In addition, if any of the business practices are in breach of any licence or approval, then the buyer would have to consider the implications of its continuing to carry on the business in the same way and the costs and other implications of making sure that the business complies with all appropriate licences and approvals in the future.

7.5.2 Apart from making sure that the seller has complied with all such licences and approvals, the buyer will want to be certain that the seller has complied with all other legal and regulatory requirements, including (amongst other things):

7.5.2.1 Health and Safety at Work legislation;

7.5.2.2 the data protection legislation, including the Data Protection Acts 1984 and 1998 and the Telecommunications (Data Protection and Privacy) Direct Marketing Regulations 1998;

7.5.2.3 UK and EU competition law (which are discussed in more detail in Ch.18);

7.5.2.4 environmental laws and regulations (which are discussed in more detail in Ch.20);

7.5.2.5 planning regulations and planning permissions (which are discussed in more detail in Ch.19);

7.5.2.6 employment legislation;

7.5.2.7 all laws and regulations regarding pensions (which are discussed in more detail in Ch.22).

7.5.3 The buyer should obtain details of any prosecutions pending or threatened against the business, of any litigation or other claims pending or threatened against it and of any disputes or other circumstances which are reasonably likely to lead to litigation or prosecution. On a sale and purchase of shares, the buyer will assume liability for any such claims; that may not be the case on a sale and purchase of assets but the buyer will normally wish to obtain details of any such matters as claims from customers, suppliers or the like may lead to their custom or supply being lost or may otherwise damage the goodwill of the business.

7.6   Finance

The matters which should be covered by any financial due diligence are dealt with in Ch.6.

In addition to the "pure" financial due diligence, on a share acquisition the buyer should obtain details of the following (and copies of all relevant documentation):

7.6.1 All outstanding overdraft, loan, asset finance and other facilities available to the target company—if the intention is to leave these in place after completion, the buyer will need to review the terms in order to ensure that they are commercially acceptable and in order to make sure that there is no term allowing the facilities to be withdrawn on a change of control of the company. If it is not intended to leave such facilities in place after completion, the buyer will need to establish what needs to be done in order to bring them to an end and, in particular, needs to ensure that there are no early repayment or other penalties.

7.6.2   All mortgages, charges, debentures or other security over the assets of the business — if the facilities or other obligations which are secured by such security are to be repaid or otherwise discharged on completion, the buyer will need to establish what needs to be done in order to effect this and will need to make sure that all necessary releases and discharges will be available on completion.

7.6.3   Details of all guarantees, indemnities, bonds and suretyship arrangements given by, or for the benefit of, the target company — both between the seller (and, where the seller is a company, other companies in its group) and the target company and those given by banks, insurance companies and other third parties.

Where a target company has given guarantees in respect of a corporate seller and other companies in its group, it is essential to make sure that these are formally released on completion or (if this is not possible) that appropriate counter-indemnities are given from a person, firm or company of appropriate financial standing. In practice, however, it will be very rare for a buyer to agree to complete an acquisition where there are outstanding guarantees in respect of the seller — this normally only happens when time pressures do not permit such guarantees to be released on completion and the buyer is satisfied that the financial strength of the seller is such that they are most unlikely ever to be called.

7.6.4   The seller will wish to ensure that all such arrangements entered into by the seller or (in the case of a corporate seller) its other group companies are released on completion so that the seller will have no continuing liability in respect of the obligations and liabilities which are being guaranteed. There are, however, occasions where (for example) the landlord of a leasehold property will not agree to release a parent company from its guarantee of its subsidiary's obligations under the lease and the seller will then have to consider whether it is prepared to proceed with the sale on the basis of a counter-indemnity from the buyer.

If the timescale or the confidentiality requirements of the deal do not allow steps to be taken before completion in order to obtain the release of a parent company or other guarantee, then the sale and purchase agreement should set out specifically any obligations which are to be imposed on the buyer with a view to obtaining such release after completion — for example, whether personal guarantees or a bank guarantee should be offered, if necessary, in order to obtain the release.

7.6.5   The buyer should also obtain details of all loans made to or by the target company, including loans from the seller and the directors of the target company. Where the business is being sold out of a group of companies, it is very likely that there will be inter-company loans and also that there will be inter-company trading balances and it will be necessary to establish the amounts outstanding as accurately as possible.

Ideally, the parties should identify the amounts owing and arrange for them to be repaid on completion or (if this is not possible or if other arrangements have been agreed) should specify the repayment terms in the sale and purchase agreement.

This is particularly important from the point of view of the buyer who will want certainty as to amounts owing to the seller and will not want to receive a claim from the seller after completion in respect of undisclosed amounts owing to the seller.

In some cases, however—particularly with large groups of companies—there are transactions entered into between the various companies in the group on a daily basis in the ordinary course of business and it may not then be possible to agree a definitive figure for these balances in advance.

In that case, the parties should agree the repayment terms for any such trading balances in the sale and purchase agreement and should be quite clear as to what they may cover—for example, the buyer may be prepared to pay for goods ordered from another company in the same group in the ordinary course of business but is most unlikely to be prepared to accept management charges and the like from the seller in respect of periods down to completion.

7.6.6   There can be particularly difficult issues when buying a company out of a larger group where there are services which are provided or paid for centrally and which are then re-charged to the various group companies periodically—typically, insurance premiums, audit fees and pension contributions. As with all other inter-company balances, the amounts should be established on completion and all balances owing to and from the target company should be settled. Where, however, this is simply not practicable, the parties should specify in the sale and purchase agreement how any such re-charges are to be calculated, together with the payment terms for them.

Such issues will not generally be relevant on a sale and purchase of assets but there may be transactions on which performance or other bonds may have been given for the benefit of the business—either by the seller or, more likely, by a bank or an insurance company, on the basis of a back-to-back counter-indemnity from the seller.

These may typically be performance bonds given in connection with construction contracts or VAT or customs duty deferment bonds. Such bonds will have been given for the benefit of the seller and the benefit of them is most unlikely to be transferable to the buyer, who will therefore need to make alternative arrangements.

7.7   Title to the assets of the business

The buyer will need to make sure that the target company (on a sale and purchase of shares) or the seller (on a sale and purchase of assets) owns all of the assets which it uses or needs to use in order to enable it to carry on its business or, where that is not the case, that there is a valid lease, hire, rental or licence agreement which enables it to use the assets in question:

7.7.1   Where plant, equipment and other assets are on lease, contract hire, rental, hire-purchase or similar financing arrangements, the buyer will need to review the terms in order to ensure that they are acceptable commercially and (on a sale and purchase of shares) in order to ensure that the owner of the assets is not permitted to terminate the financing arrangements on a change of ownership of the seller. On a sale and purchase of assets, the buyer will need to check the terms regarding assignment but it is almost invariably the case that any such agreement will be stated to be personal to the seller, so that (if he wishes to continue to use the assets in question) the buyer should make sure that an approach is made to the owner as soon as possible in order to ensure that its consent is obtained before completion to the transfer of the benefit of the relevant arrangements.

   If this is not done, the seller will have breached the terms of the finance agreement in parting with possession of the assets in question to the buyer and there is the risk that the owner will exercise its rights to repossess the items in question or that it will demand a "ransom payment" in consideration for agreeing to give its consent.

   Where assets are held subject to a licence from a third party, similar considerations apply.

7.7.2   It will be essential to establish that the assets in question are owned by the target company (on a sale and purchase of shares) or by the seller (in the case of a sale and purchase of assets) rather than (for example) by a company in the same group as the seller or otherwise associated with it. For example, it is by no means unusual to find that, in a group of companies, freehold and leasehold property or intellectual property rights are owned by one company in the group and leased or licenced to others.

7.7.3   The buyer will also wish to ensure that the assets are held free from any mortgages, debentures, charges or other security and will therefore need to carry out a Companies Registry search on the target company or the seller (as the case may be) in order to establish what security there may be and in order to obtain confirmation that all necessary releases and letters of non-crystalisation are available on completion in order to enable the buyer to ensure that the target company has title to the assets in question free from such encumbrances or (on a sale and purchase of assets) in order itself to obtain good title to them. The buyer will also seek to establish (by way of enquiries of the seller) whether there are any options or liens or other similar encumbrances granted to any third party.

7.8 Intellectual property rights

7.8.1 It is rare for a business to have no intellectual property rights at all. The principal intellectual property rights could include trade marks, patents, copyright, design rights domain names, software licences and know-how. It is possible that a UK company will hold rights which may be registered in other jurisdictions. However, the buyer should start with a search of the registers and databases held by the UK Patent Office. The UK Patent Office is responsible for the updating and maintenance of the UK Trade Marks Register, the Patent Office database and the UK Registered Designs Register.

A search can reveal details of both pending and granted trade marks and patents and granted registered designs. The registers may also give details of assignments and some licences. However, the searches of these registers cannot be taken to be conclusive and should not replace detailed enquiries of the seller to ascertain the current position of each right to ensure, inter alia, that title to the right rests with the seller, whether the right has been licensed, (and, if so, to whom and on what terms), and that the right is in force and meets the buyer's requirements—for example, in the case of a registered trade mark that it is registered in respect of the goods or services for which the buyer intends to use the mark or that it is registered in the jurisdiction in which the buyer intends to use the mark.

Foreign rights can be more difficult to identify, as not all patent offices provide information either over the internet or in English. Where foreign rights are important, the buyer should insist that the seller provides written confirmation of those foreign rights, together with copies of certificates where available, and refer these to the buyer's solicitor or patent agent for verification.

The availability of domains and ownership of registered domains can be checked online using a *whois.net* search engine.

7.8.2 As intellectual property rights can be very valuable to a business, shortcuts are not advised. It is advisable to instruct a specialist intellectual property solicitor or patent agent to clarify what is being sold and identify any potential problems before the sale is completed. Issues to be considered could include the likelihood of a pending trade mark application succeeding to registration or overcoming objections or potential oppositions. Of course, where the initial right is embroiled in problems, this could be useful information for the buyer, not only in negotiating the value of the right but also in assessing future costs which may be applicable. The buyer should, at least, obtain details of any search report, official objection or opposition that has been lodged in respect of any application for registration and of any application for rectification or cancellation of a registered intellectual property right. Specialist advice should then be taken as to how likely it may be that the objection or opposition will be upheld.

If the intellectual property rights are a particularly important part of the transaction, it may be advisable to ask a specialist intellectual property solicitor or patent agent to make an evaluation of the strength of each intellectual property right by assessing it against any prior rights in the same field.

7.8.3   Unregistered rights such as copyright and know-how can be more difficult to identify and the extent of work, which can be time and cost intensive in respect of such rights, will depend on the importance of those rights to the buyer. Where such rights are likely to be important, consideration of the seller's documentation and record-keeping procedures may be vital to establishing subsistence and ownership of unregistered rights and will often be worthwhile, as they will be indicative of the likely ease or difficulty of asserting or defending them. Where software is involved, the buyer should check all software licences and ensure these may be transferred and that the terms of the licence are acceptable. If they are not acceptable, consideration should be given to the negotiation of new licences.

7.8.4   On a sale and purchase of assets, it will be particularly important to identify exactly what intellectual property rights there may be and make sure that all intellectual property rights (and the benefit of all agreements relating to intellectual property rights) are transferred to the buyer. This will involve:

- in the case of intellectual property rights which are owned by the business, the execution by the seller of appropriate assignments in favour of the buyer;

- in the case of intellectual property rights which are used in the business but which are owned by a third party and licensed for use in the business, assignments of the benefit (subject to the burden) of the licences or (in the case of trade marks) registered user agreements pursuant to which those rights are used—bearing in mind that such arrangements will almost certainly require the consent of the owner of the rights in question before they can be assigned to the buyer;

- in the case of any intellectual property rights which are owned by the business but used by a third party under licence from the seller, assignments of the benefit (subject to the burden) of such agreements to the buyer—again, subject to obtaining any necessary consents from the third parties to whom the rights are licensed.

7.8.5   On a sale and purchase of shares, the main concern will be to ensure that all intellectual property rights are owned by the company whose shares are being acquired (rather than, for example, by the seller or another company in the same group) and to make sure that, where intellectual property rights are used under licence from a third party or are licensed to a third party, the licence or registered user agreements do not contain provisions which allow the other parties to terminate them on a change of control of the target company. If such provisions are included, the buyer will want to obtain confirmation from the third party concerned that it will not invoke its right to terminate.

7.8.6　This section is intended to give no more than a general overview of the work that will generally need to be undertaken but, where the business in question is a technology business (i.e. one whose principal assets are intellectual property rights and other intangible assets) more extensive legal and commercial due diligence is likely to be appropriate and this is discussed in more detail in Ch.6. The contents of that chapter will, in practice, be equally relevant to other businesses which would not necessarily be regarded as technology businesses but which, nevertheless, have valuable patents, trade marks or other intellectual property rights.

7.9　Contracts

Almost any business will have in place various contracts and agreements, which may range from formal agency and distribution agreements, leasing, hire-purchase and similar agreements and intellectual property licences to orders placed by or with customers and suppliers, some or all of which may have been accepted or placed informally or even orally.

The buyer will therefore wish to review all contracts and agreements which are likely to be material in the context of the business and, in practice, this is likely to mean all contracts other than routine orders. The buyer is also likely to require details of all major customers and suppliers of the business.

The buyer will be particularly concerned to consider the following issues:

7.9.1　Whether there are any contracts or orders which should be regarded as particularly significant because of their size.

7.9.2　Whether there are any contracts of a long-term nature, i.e. contracts which cannot (or are unlikely to) be performed within (say) three months after completion or which the buyer will not be able to terminate on less than three months' notice without payment of compensation or damages for breach of contract.

7.9.3　Contracts which are inherently unprofitable or which are (or appear to be) likely to be loss-making.

7.9.4　Copies of all agency or distribution agreements—the buyer will need to review their commercial terms but will also need to establish whether, under the laws of the UK or elsewhere, compensation may be payable to the other party on the termination of the agreement, even if such termination takes place in accordance with its terms. Where the other party is outside the UK, the buyer should consider obtaining local legal advice in order to establish whether or not there are any provisions in the laws of the country concerned for compensation to be payable on such termination.

7.9.5   Copies of all joint venture, franchising, partnership, consortium agreements or technical assistance arrangements.

7.9.6   Any contracts or agreements which contain provisions under which the other party may terminate them on a change of ownership of the business—on a sale and purchase of shares, the buyer will need to establish whether any such contracts or agreements can be terminated upon a change of ownership of the shares while, on a sale and purchase of assets, the buyer will need to consider the extent to which such contracts may be assignable to him.

7.9.7   Details of any contracts which may be regarded as outside the ordinary course of business—whether because the subject-matter is outside the ordinary course of the business or because any of the terms are unusual (for example, where there are unusual payment terms or a particularly onerous warranty has been given) or because the contract concerned is with the seller or anybody connected with the seller and may not therefore be on arm's length terms.

7.9.8   Any contracts or agreements under which there will be a continuing liability to pay any fee, commission or royalty.

7.9.9   The contractual terms which have been agreed with any major customers and suppliers of the business and any other customers and suppliers who may be regarded as key to the business.

The buyer should also obtain copies of the business's standard terms and conditions of sale and purchase (if any) and should review these (or instruct lawyers to do so) in order to ensure that they are appropriate commercially and (in particular) that any exclusions or limitations of liability will be enforceable. The buyer should also obtain (via replies to legal due diligence enquiries) details of any contracts which have been entered into other than on those standard terms (for example, where any unusual discounts or payment terms have been agreed).

On a sale and purchase of shares, the target company will continue to be the contracting party and so, when the buyer acquires the shares, he will take on all contracts and agreements, whether he wishes to do so or not and whether they have been disclosed to him or not. In addition, therefore, to carrying out a due diligence exercise, the buyer should insist upon warranties that all such contracts as are listed above have been disclosed to him. If he is able to find out in advance about contracts which are unprofitable or which he regards as unattractive for any other reason, he will at least have the opportunity of seeking a lower purchase price to take account of them or (as a last resort) of walking away from the deal altogether.

On a sale and purchase of assets, on the other hand, the business's contractual arrangements will not automatically transfer to the buyer and it will therefore be necessary to identify all of the contracts which are to transfer and to take steps for them to be transferred, with the consent of the third party concerned, where necessary. This makes it more important for the buyer (via his due diligence) to establish exactly what contractual arrangements there may be but, on the other hand, it does afford the buyer the opportunity of refusing to take on contracts which he may not want to assume — whether because the terms are onerous or because they relate to areas of business in which the buyer has no interest. Whether or not such contracts can be left behind with the seller is a matter of negotiation in each case — the seller will not generally be in a position to perform such contracts once he has sold the business and is likely to be left with having to pay compensation to the other party to the contract. The outcome of such negotiations may well therefore be that the buyer will agree to take on the contracts concerned but with the purchase price being reduced in order to reflect the fact that the buyer is taking over contracts which he does not want.

The issue of assignment and novation of contracts and agreements is dealt with in more detail in Ch.9.

7.10   Employees

As with other contracts, on a sale and purchase of shares, the contracts of employment of the employees of the business will continue with the target company, notwithstanding the change of ownership of that company.

On a sale and purchase of assets, however, TUPE will normally apply and will operate as a statutory novation of the contracts of employment so that, on completion of the sale and purchase, they will take effect as if they had originally been entered into between the employee and the buyer. Unlike on a sale and purchase of shares, the identity of the employer will change but the buyer will take on nearly all rights, obligations and liabilities towards the employees. TUPE is discussed in more detail in Ch.21.

As a result, whether the transaction proceeds as a sale and purchase of shares or of assets, the buyer will effectively take on the employees of the business with their accrued continuity of employment and will assume liability for any unpaid wages or salaries or other breaches of the contracts of employment and for any other claims which the employees may have against their employer.

In all cases, therefore, the buyer will need via the due diligence exercise to identify the employees of the business, obtain details of their contractual terms of employment and other employment-related agreements, as well as details of any potential employment-related claims.

The buyer's due diligence should therefore include at least the following:

7.10.1   Obtaining a schedule of employees, including all relevant information such as names, start dates, dates of birth, job titles, place of work, hours of work, salary, expenses and all other benefits and emoluments. Particularly on an agreement for the sale and purchase of assets, this schedule should appear in the sale and purchase agreement but, in any event, the buyer should require the seller to warrant its completeness and accuracy. As discussed in Ch.21, there may be some assets deals where the question of exactly which employees transfer will be something of a "grey area" and it may therefore be necessary for the buyer to "dig deeper", particularly where the business in question is only one of a number of separate trading divisions of the seller or where there are "head office" staff who devote some (but not necessarily all) of their time to the business in question.

7.10.2   The buyer should obtain copies of all standard terms and conditions of employment and of all service agreements or other written contracts of employment and should review their terms, partly to enable him to assess the extent of the commitments of the business to its employees as regards salary, bonuses and so on, but also in order to ensure that all standard terms and conditions of employment and all service agreements and other contracts of employment comply with current employment legislation and contain the provisions which an employer would normally wish to see included.

7.10.3   The buyer should obtain details of any disputes with any employee or former employee and of any claims by employees or former employees, together with details of any circumstances which may be likely to give rise to any such claim. The information to be obtained should therefore include details of any grievance raised by any employee or any warning outstanding against any employee, together with details of any involvement with the Equality and Human Rights Commission, the Health and Safety Inspector and HM Revenue and Customs.

7.10.4   The buyer should also obtain details of any redundancies or other dismissals in the months leading up to completion as, on a sale and purchase of shares, the buyer will inherit liability for any claims arising out of any such situations and may in some cases do so on a purchase of assets. The buyer should also obtain details of any employees who have given notice to terminate their employment—the buyer will need to know this information from an operational point of view but may also be keen to know the circumstances in case there is any question of claims for constructive dismissal.

7.10.5   The buyer should obtain details of any redundancy schemes, policies or agreements which may have been put in place (for example, arrangements under which employees will receive enhanced payments if they are made redundant) and of any collective bargaining or similar agreements.

7.10.6   The buyer should obtain details of all claims made by employees or former employees for industrial injury, industrial illness and the like and of any circumstances which are likely to give rise to any such claims. The buyer would be well-advised to back this up by reviewing the accident book in order to see whether there are any circumstances recorded there which are likely to give rise to claims.

On a sale and purchase of shares, the buyer will inherit all such liabilities but, on a sale and purchase of assets, the buyer will only assume liability under TUPE in respect of claims by employees who pass to him under TUPE.

Such liabilities should be covered by employers' liability insurance but the buyer should consider obtaining an indemnity in respect of any such claims, to the extent to which they are not in fact covered by insurance.

7.10.7   The buyer should seek to establish which are the key employees required to run the business—for example, those who have the know-how or the relationships with customers and suppliers which are vital to the continued prosperity of the business.

If there are individuals whose continuing involvement with the business is essential, the buyer should consider meeting with those individuals in advance and making sure, as far as possible, that they will continue to remain with the business. If key employees are employed on terms which allow them to terminate their employment on reasonably short notice, the buyer should consider negotiating new contracts of employment with them in advance, which provide for a minimum period of employment and/or a longer notice period.

The buyer should also ensure that the key individuals are actually employed by the target company (on a sale and purchase of shares) or the target business (on a sale and purchase of assets). It is not unusual, where the target company forms part of a larger group or the target business is just one of several businesses carried on by the seller, to find that there are key individuals whose contracts of employment are not with the target company or (on an assets sale and purchase) will not be allocated to the target business and hence will not automatically transfer under TUPE. If that is the case, the buyer is likely to have to negotiate arrangements with the seller and with the individuals concerned in order to secure their future services (either as full-time employees or on some other basis).

7.10.8   The buyer should seek to establish whether, in addition to the express terms of the employees' contracts of employment, there are any other practices which are regarded by the seller as discretionary but which may, over time, become implied terms of the contracts of employment—for example, bonus arrangements, enhanced redundancy packages and the like.

The purpose of the due diligence work in respect of employees is two-fold: to acquire all of the information about the employees and their terms and conditions which a buyer will need as their new employer but also, if redundancies or other changes in the work force are likely, in order to enable the buyer to assess his ability to implement such changes or redundancies (and the procedures for doing so) and (ultimately) the costs that would be involved in any redundancy programme among the work force of the business and/or among his own work force.

7.11   Pensions

Pensions issues are dealt with in detail in Ch.22.

7.12   Freehold, leasehold and other property

Property matters are dealt with in detail in Ch.19.

7.13   Tax

Tax issues are dealt with in more detail in Chs 13 and 14.

7.14   Data protection

7.14.1   Introduction

The Data Protection Act 1998 ("DPA") regulates the processing of personal data and sensitive personal data. Personal data is information from which a living individual can be identified or information that expresses an opinion about a living individual, such as name, address or appraisal forms. Sensitive personal data includes information regarding the sexuality, race, religion, politics, criminal record, etc. of a living individual. It will impact on mergers and acquisitions as information must be disclosed to buyers to get a deal done, yet disclosure is often in breach of the DPA and can create expensive problems for sellers and buyers. It is therefore important to consider the DPA in connection with due diligence and also in warranty and indemnity protection.

7.14.2   Due diligence

The seller should try to ensure that disclosing information during the due diligence process is DPA-compliant through the following steps:

7.14.2.1   Identify what personal data and sensitive personal data is used by the business. This should include a review of the nature of the data and an evaluation of compliance with the DPA.

7.14.2.2   Disclosure of personal data for the purposes of a sale amounts to "processing" under the DPA and will be in breach of the DPA, unless the data subject consents or there is some other valid justification. It is unlikely that consent can be obtained, but businesses should consider amending their data protection notices, contracts and employment contracts, specifically to address the possibility of transferring personal data for the purposes of a corporate sale or restructuring.

7.14.2.3 In the more common situation where consent has not been obtained, the seller will need to justify disclosing personal data by showing that disclosure is necessary for the legitimate reasons of the seller and (in a sale and purchase of shares) of the target company and that the rights and freedoms of the data subjects are not prejudiced. On a sale and purchase of shares, the target company may be the person in breach of the DPA because of due diligence disclosures. Sellers should therefore create a package of measures to protect the personal data and the rights of the relevant data subject, which might include:

- Limiting the personal data which is disclosed—can some data be withheld (or does it actually need to be disclosed?) until a preferred bidder is identified?

- Making the personal data as anonymous as possible—is it necessary to reveal names? Receipt of personal data will make the buyer a data controller in respect of the DPA and therefore subject to the legislation.

- Imposing contractual conditions on access to, and use of, personal data. For example, if the personal data is held in a data room, it should be subject to controlled access and the seller should maintain a record of all people who had access to such data and what copies were made. Where electronic data rooms are being used, extra care will be required.

- In addition, ensuring that confidentiality agreements restrict the use of the personal data, limit onward disclosure to funders and advisers and require return or destruction of the data if the acquisition does not proceed.

- If the buyer is from North America, or otherwise outside the European Economic Area ("EEA"), additional restrictions will be required.

7.14.3 Data protection and the share deal

On a sale and purchase of shares, a buyer must consider the following through due diligence:

7.14.3.1 Has the target company been (and does it continue to be) DPA-compliant and are there any outstanding liabilities for breaches of the DPA?

7.14.3.2 Does the target company have a valid notification with the Office of the Information Commissioner and is the notification accurate?

7.14.3.3 Are there any outstanding complaints, legal actions, prosecutions, investigations or other queries from any person, including data subjects and the Office of the Information Commissioner, in respect of processing activities?

7.14.3.4 Has there been any act or omission by the target company, its employees or representatives which may constitute a breach of the DPA?

7.14.3.5 Does the target company have a data protection policy and documented procedure which reflect best practice?

7.14.3.6 Are third parties (such as another company in the same group) used to process personal data on behalf of the target company?

Warranty protection should also be sought and indemnities or a retention or price reduction may be necessary if any major issues are identified.

The outgoing directors and responsible officers of the target company will remain personally liable for any breaches of the DPA committed during their time in office.

7.14.4 Data protection and the assets deal

In addition to the points detailed above, on a sale and purchase of assets, buyers and sellers should also consider the following:

7.14.4.1 Can the data be lawfully sold and/or transferred and, if so, can the data be used in the manner intended by the buyer without the need to incur further costs? An examination of the nature of the data subjects' consent held by the seller is required. This will involve checking the seller's data protection notices.

7.14.4.2 Is there valid consent or other lawful justification to sell the personal data? This will involve asking for evidence from the seller of such consent or justification plus an explanation of how it was obtained.

7.14.4.3 How many data subjects is the seller responsible for? This should be broken down into lists of customers, employees, suppliers, etc. This will help a buyer establish how much work and expense may be involved in obtaining consent, if necessary.

7.14.5 Data protection post completion

Once the transaction is complete the buyer should formalise his position as data controller over the personal data and will need to do the following:

7.14.5.1   On a share sale and purchase, update the existing notification, giving new contact details, etc. On an assets sale and purchase, submit a new notification to the Office of the Information Commissioner.

7.14.5.2   Undertake a request for consent to process data—perhaps, in the form of a mail shot to all data subjects.

7.14.5.3   On an assets sale and purchase, even where valid consents exist for the continuing data processing activities, the data subject must be advised of the new data controller's identity. Again, the most practical solution may be a mail shot.

7.14.5.4   If required, record and manage policies and procedures centrally and train all staff in their use.

7.14.6   Conclusion

The Information Commissioner is entitled to issue enforcement or information notices (irrespective of whether there have been complaints from the data subjects concerned) for each breach of the DPA and this may result in fines which can be unlimited. Additionally, a data controller may face civil proceedings from any data subject suffering damage, or damage and distress (but not distress alone), as a result of a data controller's failure to comply with the DPA. The risk of such actions is increased where employees have union representatives.

Proper planning and considering the DPA from the outset will make it possible to complete the transaction while managing the risk of non-compliance and avoiding prejudice to data subjects.

7.15   Information technology (IT) issues

IT is of great importance to most businesses and, in some cases, it is absolutely fundamental to the continued operation of the business. The buyer will therefore need to establish the significance of IT at an early stage and then work out whether all the IT systems of the business need to be transferred to him or whether other arrangements need to be put in place, such as transitional arrangements under which the seller will provide IT services to the buyer for an agreed period after completion.

The IT system(s) of a business will generally comprise hardware, software and communication networks. Most businesses will also have a website, which may simply be their "shop window" but may also be used as a means of selling their goods and services and other means of interaction. It is likely to be necessary for the buyer to consider each of these various elements of the IT system in order to establish which elements are essential to the operation of the business in the future.

Where the software used is standard packaged software, the buyer will normally be able to ensure its continuing use (either by obtaining the consent of the licensor or by purchasing a new licence) but there may well be bespoke software which has been written or modified specifically for the business in question and specific arrangements may need to be made if the buyer is to be able to use that software after completion.

It will then be necessary for the lawyers to deal with the legal formalities for transferring the IT systems or (as the case may be) the provision of IT services to the business by the seller.

In practice, the buyer's pre-acquisition planning may well be carried on in parallel with the legal due diligence process and there are a number of IT-related questions which (although not necessarily, in every case, strictly legal matters) will be raised with the seller and his advisers through the buyer's legal due diligence enquiries.

Where, however, the IT systems are essential to the continued operation of the business or particular concerns have been identified, the buyer would be well-advised to arrange for a technical audit of the business' IT systems — whether by a firm of external consultants or by members of his own IT department.

A detailed analysis of the matters to be considered by the buyer in relation to IT is beyond the scope of this book but they will include the following (which includes the main IT-related issues in respect of which the buyer is likely to request warranty protection):

7.15.1   What IT systems are actually used in the business?

7.15.2   Which software is owned by the business and which software is used under licence? If used under licence, the buyer should consider the terms of those licences – their extent, their duration and (on a sale and purchase of shares) whether the licensor can terminate the licence on a change of control of the business or (on a sale and purchase of assets) whether they are assignable. Also, will additional licence fees be triggered following the sale? For example, this may occur if the licence is site specific, or once the business is no longer part of a "group licence".

7.15.3   Has any of the software been developed by the business for its own use? If so, it will be necessary to check whether the employees' contracts of employment provide that software will belong to the employer.

7.15.4   Has any software been developed by an external consultant or some other third party on behalf of the business? If so, copyright in that software will normally belong to the consultant or other third party unless a written contract formally assigns it to the business.

7.15.5   Has any software been created from open source software? If so, are there any implications for the exploitation of this software and has the buyer complied with the relevant terms?

7.15.6   Does the business rely on IT services provided by third parties? Typical examples of such services will include facilities management, help desk support, break-fix services, on-line network services (for example, where the website is hosted by a third party), disaster recovery services and general IT support services.

7.15.7   Do the IT systems operate on a "stand-alone" basis or do they depend on any group licences or services? It is very common, in a group of companies, for accounts and payroll systems, in particular, to be shared across a group and, if so, these arrangements may need to be split or transitional arrangements may need to be put in place to allow the business to continue to use those systems for a transitional period after completion. Similar problems are likely to arise on an assets sale and purchase, where the business in question is one of several divisions of the seller.

7.15.8   There may also be software licences which are provided on a group basis and which (in the absence of new arrangements being put in place) the business would not be able to use after completion, in the absence of some sort of transitional arrangements.

7.15.9   If software is used under licence, has anything been done (or not done) which may give the other party the right to terminate the licence? For example, have all licence fees been paid up-to-date? Also, if the licence is contingent on the business being within the group, will a new licence have to be purchased?

7.15.10 Will the business require access (or appropriate rights of access) to the source code of any software which is held under licence? This may be necessary in order to ensure adequate maintenance and updating of the software in question and, if so, the buyer's solicitors should review the terms of the agreements in question.

7.15.11 Is there any hardware which is on lease or hire-purchase? On a sale and purchase of shares, it will be necessary to check whether they are capable of being terminated by the other party on a change of control of the business while, on a sale and purchase of assets, it will be necessary to check to see whether they are capable of being assigned with or without the consent of the other party.

7.15.12 Has the hardware been satisfactorily maintained and supported and are there appropriate maintenance and support agreements in place? The buyer will want to know that that is the case and his solicitors will normally wish to review all relevant agreements in order to ensure that they do provide for an appropriate level of maintenance and support and in order to establish when they fall to be renewed. Again, on a sale and purchase of shares, it will be necessary to check whether the other party can terminate any relevant agreements on a change of control of the business while, on a sale and purchase of assets, it will be necessary to check to see whether the consent of the other party is needed to assign the agreements.

7.15.13 Has any part of the IT function being outsourced to a third party? If so, when and how will the arrangement end and has it been managed successfully? Are any service levels appropriate for business requirements and are there sufficient sanctions to encourage the supplier to meet them?

7.15.14 Does the business own the copyright in the design and contents of its website?

7.15.15 Is it essential for the buyer to acquire the IT systems in their entirety or would it be possible to make arrangements for a migration of the data and programs to the buyer's own computer system, typically with there being some transitional arrangements which allow the buyer access to the seller's systems for a limited period after completion?

It is quite possible, of course, that there may be good reasons why the buyer may not want to acquire some of the IT systems of the business — for example, if it is out-dated, unreliable or unsupported.

7.15.16 Will the employees who will transfer to the buyer with the business include sufficient technically competent and trained IT specialists to ensure that the IT systems will be able to continue to operate after completion? There may well be IT specialists whose continuing involvement will be essential in order to enable the buyer to make use of the IT systems and, when the buyer is buying a company out of a larger group or acquiring a business which is just one of several divisions of the seller, these staff may not transfer as a matter of course. If that is the case then, assuming that the seller wishes to retain the individuals concerned, there may need to be transitional arrangements under which key members of the seller's IT department are seconded to the buyer for an agreed period after completion.

7.15.17 Are the computer systems Euro compliant? If the business trades in the EU, it will be important to ensure that its IT systems will be able to convert financial amounts into and out of the Euro.

7.15.18 Are the IT systems capable of handling date information correctly? Most solicitors have now got round to removing warranties regarding Year 2000 compliance but it is still advisable to ensure that the systems are able to process dates correctly and will operate without interruption irrespective of the date or the format of any date-related information.

7.15.19 Are there adequate disaster recovery plans in effect to ensure that the hardware and software and the data stored on it can be replaced or substituted without material disruption to the business?

7.15.20 Is there adequate internal and external security in place? This should include procedures for preventing unauthorised access, anti-virus protection, and taking and storing both on-site and off-site back-up copies of software and data.

Perhaps one of the most fundamental questions of all is whether there have there been any recurring technical problems with the IT systems. The best way for the buyer to satisfy himself on this point is to arrange for a technical audit or, alternatively, for members of his IT department to see the system in operation. The seller is unlikely to give unequivocal replies to legal due diligence enquiries in this area and is unlikely to be prepared to give a warranty which goes beyond a warranty that the IT systems perform adequately and that there have not been any IT failures which have had a material impact on the operation of the business. Although unhelpful from the buyer's point of view, it is understandable why a seller should be reluctant to give any stronger warranty protection than that—few users of IT systems fail to find it a frustrating experience at times and most IT departments would say that they could improve performance of the IT systems if they were not constrained by a limited budget. The seller will also want to avoid the risk of a warranty claim as a result of minor issues inherent in any IT system, e.g. a technical "glitch" which (he would argue) could normally be addressed by the IT specialist's time-honoured solution of telling the user to turn his computer off and then turn it on again.

Part 2
The Agreement

Chapter 8

Sale and Purchase Agreements—Share Sales

8.1 General principles

The transfer of title to a share can be effected very simply by the seller executing a stock transfer form and delivering it, together with the share certificate (or an indemnity if the certificate is missing), to the buyer who will then (subject of course to the company's articles of association) lodge it with the company. Subject again to the articles of association of the company, its board will then approve the transfer and the buyer will be entered in the register of members as the holder of the shares. Unless, however, the transfer falls within one of the statutory exemptions, it is unlawful to register a transfer unless it has been stamped and duty at the rate of £5 per £1,000 or part thereof has been paid on it. Once the transfer has been registered, the buyer becomes a member of the company and is entitle to delivery of a share certificate within two months thereafter.

Although this will be sufficient to transfer title to the buyer, on a sale and purchase of the entire issued share capital of a company there will generally be a formal sale and purchase agreement and, in practice, this will also be the case where the shares being sold represent 50 per cent or more of the issued share capital of the target company, as there will almost certainly be particular terms which either or both of the parties will want to see formally documented. For example, if any part of the purchase price is being deferred rather than being paid on completion, the parties will want the payment terms to be formally documented and there are in any event particular provisions which a buyer will wish to see in a formal sale and purchase agreement, such as any warranties and indemnities (see Ch.10) and any non-competition clauses (see later in this chapter).

In some cases, however, it may be necessary or desirable for the sale and purchase to take the form of an offer from the buyer to each of the target company's shareholders, for example:

8.1.1   If the City Code on Takeovers and Mergers (the "Takeover Code") applies, i.e. if the target company is considered by the Panel on Takeovers and Mergers (the body responsible for administering the Takeover Code) (the "Panel") to be resident in the UK, the Channel Islands or the Isle of Man and is:

- a public company (listed or unlisted) or a Societas Europaea;

- a private company, the equity share capital of which has been admitted to the Official List of the FSA at any time during the period of 10 years prior to the relevant date;

- a private company, in relation to which dealings and/or prices at which persons were willing to deal in its equity share capital have been published on a regular basis for a continuous period of at least six months in the 10 years prior to the relevant date, whether via a newspaper, electronic price quotation system or otherwise;

- a private company, the equity share capital of which has been subject to a marketing arrangement as described in s.693(3) of the Companies Act 2006 (that is, traded on a recognised investment exchange, as defined in FSMA) at any time during the ten years prior to the relevant date;

- a private company, which has filed a prospectus for the issue of equity share capital with the Registrar of Companies at any time during the ten years prior to the relevant date.

In each of the above cases, the relevant date is the date on which an announcement is made of a proposed or possible offer for the target or the date on which some other event occurs in relation to the target company which has significance under the Takeover Code.

8.1.2   Where the target company has a large number of shareholders — particularly where they are unconnected — it may be impractical to enter into negotiations with them all (or with all of their various advisers) or to obtain their signatures to an agreed form of sale and purchase agreement.

8.1.3   Where (as is normally the case) the buyer wishes to acquire 100 per cent of the share capital of the target company but there is a dissentient minority of shareholders, unless the articles of association of the target company contain "drag along" rights which allow a specified majority to compel a specified minority to sell their shares to a buyer to whom the majority wishes to sell, the only way in which the dissentient minority can be compelled to sell is by the buyer taking advantage of the procedures set out in ss.974–991 of the Companies Act 2006. These provisions enable a buyer who has made an offer to acquire all the shares, or all the shares of any class or classes, in a company, compulsorily to acquire the shares of a dissenting minority holding less than 10 per cent of any class of shares in the target company to which the offer relates. These procedures can also be used to enable the buyer to acquire the shares of shareholders who cannot be traced or who simply fail to respond to the buyer's offer.

In summary, these provisions allow a buyer to acquire the minority's shares for the price paid to the accepting shareholders provided that the buyer receives acceptances in respect of 90 per cent of the shares to which the offer relates (ignoring any shares which the buyer owned at the time of making the offer). Within two months of reaching the 90 per cent threshold, the buyer must serve a statutory notice (Form 429(4)) on any shareholders who have not accepted the offer and must send a copy of the notice to the target company, together with a statutory declaration signed by a director of the buyer stating that the conditions for serving the notice have been fulfilled. Once he has done so, the buyer is entitled and bound to acquire the shares of the minority for the price paid to the accepting shareholders.

8.1.4   Where the target company's articles of association do contain a drag along right but its exercise is dependant upon an offer being made.

Chapter 23 deals with transactions for which it is necessary or desirable to proceed via an offer rather than having a sale and purchase agreement. This chapter deals with sales and purchases of shares through a sale and purchase agreement, the first draft of which is traditionally prepared by the buyer's solicitors, although where the sale is by "auction", then the seller will very often prepare a first draft and submit it to prospective buyers (see Ch.2). Precedents 1 and 2 in App.2 are typical examples of the form of agreement which is appropriate for the sale and purchase of the entire issued share capital of a private company, Precedent 1 being drafted to cover the situation where the seller is a company and Precedent 2 to cover the situation where the sellers are individuals. Both precedents have primarily been drafted from the point of view of the buyer, although some provisions have been included in order to reflect the likely requirements of the seller.

There follows a brief commentary on some of the principal provisions of these precedents. In practice, many of these are applicable also to an agreement for the sale and purchase of assets but points which are specific to assets deals are discussed in Ch.9.

References to a "clause" are (unless otherwise stated) references to the clause of that number in Precedent 1 and Precedent 2. Similarly with reference to a "Schedule".

8.2   Parties

The parties will normally be the shareholders of the target company (or, where not all of the sharcholders are selling shares, those who are selling) and the buyer. On a sale by a corporate seller out of a group, however, it may be appropriate for the seller's holding company and possibly also other companies in its group to be made party to the agreement, for example:

8.2.1   where the buyer requires the obligations of the seller (for example, under the warranties and any indemnities) to be guaranteed by a company which he regards as more substantial;

8.2.2   where the buyer wishes to seek restrictive covenants from the other members of the seller's group of companies, in which case it will be necessary to make the ultimate holding company a party to the agreement and oblige it to give the restrictive covenants on behalf of all members of its group or to make all of the members of the group as parties to the agreement.

Similarly, where the buyer is a company, the seller may require the buyer's ultimate holding company or (as appropriate) individual shareholders personally to guarantee the obligations of the buyer in respect of any deferred consideration or other sums payable by the buyer after completion.

Precedent 2 in App.2 (for use where there are individual sellers) has been drafted on the basis that all of the sellers will be parties to the warranties and the tax covenant but, as has already been seen, that may not be necessarily be the case and where only some of the sellers are giving the warranties and the tax covenant then they will have to be identified separately as "the Warrantors" and at appropriate points in the agreement it will be necessary to change references to "the Sellers" to "the Warrantors".

If the beneficial ownership of any shares is held by somebody other than the registered holder and the buyer is aware that that is the case, he should require that person to be party to the sale and purchase agreement in order to transfer beneficial ownership.

8.3   Definitions and interpretation (cl.1)

Most agreements will contain a "definitions" section which will include a number of definitions of expressions which are used regularly throughout the agreement and these will need to be considered carefully in the context of each point at which they are used. There will usually be other provisions to clarify the interpretation of the agreement, some of which may be of a clarificatory nature only but others of which may have a more substantive effect.

8.4   Conditions (cl.2 and Sch.7)

It has already been explained (Ch.4) that it will often be advisable (and in many cases necessary) to obtain certain third party consents or approvals to a sale and purchase of a company or of a business, while Ch.18 explains that in some circumstances there may be competition law requirements which have to be satisfied before the transaction can take place. Where possible, these consents or approvals should be obtained and any competition law requirements should be satisfied before entering into the sale and purchase agreement, principally to avoid the damage that could be caused by announcing a transaction which then does not take place because one of the conditions cannot be satisfied — but also because if an agreement is entered into before those conditions have been satisfied, then the parties have to consider what happens during the period between the signing of the agreement and the satisfying of the conditions, what happens if the conditions are not in fact satisfied, and the (often vexed) questions of whether the warranties "speak" at the point when the agreement is signed or whether they speak also at completion and what happens if a breach of warranty arises in the intervening period (these issues are discussed in detail in Ch.10).

Where, however, it is not possible to delay signing the sale and purchase agreement until the conditions have been satisfied (or where there are pressing commercial reasons not to delay), the sale and purchase agreement will have to set out those conditions precedent subject to which the agreement is signed.

Where that is the case, the conditions should be drafted as clearly and as unambiguously as possible and if at all possible subjective conditions should be avoided. For example, a condition to the effect that the buyer must be "satisfied" that certain key customers will continue to do business with the target company is totally subjective to the buyer and allows the buyer the opportunity to walk away from the deal if, for whatever reason, he has a change of heart. Ideally, the parties should endeavour to agree and set out in the agreement exactly what is required in order for the condition to be satisfied (for example, written confirmation from each key customer to the effect that he will continue to do business with the target company for an agreed period after completion and with no material changes to the terms on which he is prepared to do so) but, if that is unrealistic, there should be an obligation on the buyer to act reasonably in deciding whether or not what is received is acceptable to him. Where a seller is pressing to have a sale and purchase agreement signed as soon as possible, the buyer will sometimes suggest that an agreement be signed which is conditional on the buyer's funding but the seller should nearly always refuse point blank to accept this—in reality, it is no more than a one-way option in favour of the buyer.

In practice, the most common conditions precedent are obtaining the approval of the shareholders of the buyer or of the seller to the transaction and Precedents 1 and 2 include in Sch.7 wording to cover the situation where the transaction requires the prior approval of the shareholders of the buyer. The Precedents make these "conditions precedent" rather than "conditions subsequent" and state that unless and until those conditions are satisfied, only certain specified provisions of the agreement will be legally binding so that beneficial ownership in the shares will not pass to the buyer until all of the conditions have been satisfied (or waived).

The agreement should specify a date by which the conditions must be satisfied, failing which the agreement will lapse (see para.1 of Sch.7). The precedents have been drafted on the basis that if the conditions are not satisfied, then the agreement will be of no further effect, although where the conditions are included at the behest of one party only (for example, because it is only the seller who is obliged to obtain shareholder approval) the other party may press for the inclusion of a provision under which he will be reimbursed all or part of his costs if the party concerned fails to procure that the condition is satisfied.

The agreement should oblige all parties to use reasonable endeavours to procure that the conditions are satisfied (see Pt I of Sch.7) and where it is subject to the approval of the shareholders of any party the agreement will normally oblige that party to send a circular letter to its shareholders which contains a unanimous recommendation of the transaction by its directors and the other party may also press for the directors or other key shareholders of the party concerned to give irrevocable undertakings to vote in favour of the resolution to approve the transaction. Any commitments from directors to vote in favour of the resolution to approve the transaction may however be overridden by their fiduciary duties (*Fulham Football Club v Cabra Estates Plc* (1992) 65 P. & C.R. 284; [1994] 1 B.C.L.C. 363 CA).

The precedents contain a mechanism under which notice is to be given by one party to the other once a particular condition has been satisfied and the agreement may well allow a party to waive a condition which has been included for his benefit (see paras 5 and 6 of Pt I of Sch.7).

As has already been seen, where the sale and purchase agreement is subject to conditions (or where for any other reason there is an interval between the signing of the sale and purchase agreement and completion) it will be necessary to consider the question of whether the warranties should "speak" both as at the date of signing the agreement and at completion and what happens if there is a breach of warranty or a material adverse change in the business during that interval. These issues are discussed in detail in Ch.10.

Whatever is agreed as regards warranties, the buyer will almost certainly insist on the seller undertaking to procure that during that time the target company and any subsidiaries carry on business in the normal way and that during that period they will not enter into certain specified transactions, which are likely to include:

8.4.1   Creating any mortgages, charges or other encumbrances.

8.4.2   Disposing of any property or assets, or than trading stock in the ordinary course of business on arm's length terms.

8.4.3   Entering into any guarantee or indemnity.

8.4.4   Creating or issuing any share capital or granting any options over share capital.

8.4.5   Enter into any leasing or similar agreements.

8.4.6   Declaring or paying any dividend or bonus.

8.4.7   Entering into any transaction outside the ordinary course of business.

8.4.8   Doing anything which may make any circular to be sent by the buyer to its shareholders inaccurate or misleading (which could mean that it would be necessary for the buyer to send a further circular to shareholders).

Part 2 of Sch.7 contains the sort of restrictions which a buyer is likely to request: sellers will normally accept the principle of such provisions but should try to avoid very general provisions, such as an undertaking not to do anything which may render the company's financial position less favourable or which may damage its goodwill. The precise wording is likely to be a matter of negotiation in every case.

8.5   Sale and purchase (cl.2)

8.5.1   The sale and purchase agreement will specify exactly which shares are being sold; where there is only one seller, then it may simply refer to the entire issued share capital of the target company but where there is more than one seller there will normally be a schedule which lists the sellers and the shares which each is selling. Particular care will be needed where not all shareholders are selling. As there are no implied terms that the seller will sell the shares with good title, the sale and purchase agreement will normally provide for the seller to sell the shares with "full title guarantee", a term introduced by the Law of Property (Miscellaneous Provisions) Act 1994 and which implies covenants as to title where a sale is made with "full title guarantee" or with "limited title guarantee".

A seller who agrees to sell shares with "full title guarantee" impliedly covenants that:

- he has the right to dispose of them;

- he will at his own cost do all that he reasonably can to give the title he purports to give; and

- he is disposing of the shares free from all charges and encumbrances and other rights exercisable by third parties, other than any charges, encumbrances or rights which he does not know and could not reasonably be expected to know about.

8.5.2   Where the shares are transferred with "limited title guarantee", instead of the implied covenant that he is disposing of the shares free from all charges and encumbrances, the seller impliedly covenants that he has not since the last disposition for value:

- charged or encumbered the shares by means of any charge or encumbrance which subsists at the time of transfer or granted third party rights in relation to the shares which subsist at the time of transfer; or

- suffered the shares to be so charged or encumbered or subjected to any such rights;

and that he is not aware that anyone else has done any of those things since the last disposition for value.

The seller will not be liable under the implied covenants in respect of any matter to which the transfer of the shares is made subject or anything which at the time of transfer is within the actual knowledge of the buyer or which is a necessary consequence of facts then within the actual knowledge of the buyer. Buyers may therefore wish to specify in the agreement that the seller will be liable notwithstanding that the matter in question is within the actual knowledge of the buyer or is a necessary consequence of facts within his actual knowledge.

8.5.3   Even where the sale is made with full title guarantee, the buyer should check the articles of association of the target company in order to ascertain whether there are any restrictions on the transfer of shares. This is particularly important where there is more than one shareholder in the target company as its articles may well contain pre-emption rights under which, before transferring any shares, the shareholder concerned must first offer those shares to the other shareholders. If so, the sale and purchase agreement should contain a waiver from all of the sellers of any pre-emption rights to which they are entitled but, if there are any shareholders who are not selling all of their shares or if there are any sellers who are not party to the sale and purchase agreement, then separate waivers will be needed from them in order to avoid having to comply with the pre-emption provisions.

8.6   Consideration (cl.3)

The sale and purchase agreement will set out the purchase price or (as the case may be) the way in which it is to be determined, together with the time and manner in which it is to be paid or otherwise satisfied. These provisions will be most straightforward where the purchase price is to be paid in full in cash on completion of the transaction, but that is the case in only a minority of transactions: the buyer may not necessarily be in a position to pay the purchase price in full on completion or he may be unwilling to do so (for example, because he wishes part of the price to be retained as security for warranty and indemnity claims). In any event, the final amount of the purchase price may not be known at completion but it may fall to be determined after completion by reference to the net assets of the target company or business, as shown by completion accounts, or (in part, at least) by reference to future profits (an earn out) or some other formula.

It is possible also that all or part of the purchase price may be satisfied in shares or loan stock of the buyer.

Accordingly, therefore, the purchase price may be, in whole or in part:

- a fixed amount;

- dependant upon completion accounts;

- subject to an earn out or similar arrangement;

- payable on completion;

- payable by instalments;

- subject to a retention against warranty and indemnity claims (which may involve part of the price being retained by the buyer or being retained in a solicitors' escrow account);

- payable in cash;

- satisfied other than in cash—typically, by the issue of shares, loan stock or loan notes by the buyer to the seller.

These issues are discussed in more detail in Ch.12.

In practice, it is reasonably rare for completions to take place within banking hours and so it is very common for the purchase price to be:

- held by the buyer's solicitors and for completion to take place on the basis of their undertaking to transfer the funds to the seller as soon as possible after completion; or

- transferred to the seller's solicitors before completion and for completion to take place on the basis of their undertaking to hold those funds to the buyer's order until completion has taken place.

Precedents 9 and 10 in App.2 are undertakings to cover these situations: it is important to draft such undertakings correctly and to make it clear to whose order the funds are being held at any particular time as there is always the danger, however remote, of (for example) a buyer's solicitors undertaking to pay the purchase price to the seller the following day, only to find that a winding-up petition is presented in relation to the buyer or a receiver or administrator is appointed over the buyer's assets before the transfer of funds has actually taken place. If it is made clear that, with effect from completion, the funds are being held by the buyer's solicitors to the order of (i.e. on behalf of) the seller, that should make it very difficult for it to be argued that those funds still remain assets of the buyer at the point of winding-up, receivership or administration (as the case may be).

8.7   Warranties (cl.4)

The warranties to be given will normally be defined as "the Warranties" and will then be set out in a separate schedule, for convenience. It will be necessary for the sale and purchase agreement to contain a clause to the effect that the seller warrants to the buyer that each of those warranties is true and accurate and, where there is an interval between signing the sale and purchase agreement and completing it, that clause should make it clear whether the warranties are to "speak" only at the point at which the agreement is signed or also at completion. That clause will specify whether the warranties are to be given on a joint and several basis or on a several basis. Warranties are discussed in detail in Ch.10.

As explained in Ch.10, the parties will normally agree various limitations on the liability of the seller under the warranties which will normally be contained in a separate schedule to which reference should be made in the "main body" of the agreement (cl.4.3). If there is to be a tax covenant rather than a separate tax deed (see Ch.11), reference should also be made to that in the main body of the agreement.

8.8   Completion (cl.5)

The sale and purchase agreement should specify the date, time and place at which the transaction is to be completed, although in many cases the signature of the agreement will simply be followed by completion. Where, however, there is a gap between signing the agreement and completion (typically where the agreement is subject to one or more conditions precedent) then it is particularly important to ensure that there is a fixed date and time in the agreement or that the agreement provides for completion to take place within an agreed period after the conditions have all been satisfied. The agreement should also specify exactly what is to take place at completion and Precedents 1 and 2 in App.2 contain a typical clause (cl.5) to deal with this. The clause specifies exactly what each party is to deliver to the other and any other steps that each party is to take, including, of course, payment of the purchase price. It will be seen that there is a lengthy list of completion requirements and, to avoid wasting time at the completion meeting itself, the parties' solicitors should prepare and agree a completion agenda well in advance and this should specify who will be needed at completion, anything which needs to be done before completion can formally take place, all documents and other items required to be produced (with a note of who is to take responsibility for producing them) and a step-by-step summary of the completion process. A specimen completion agenda is contained in App.2 as Precedent 11. Particular points to note include the following:

8.8.1   It is essential to establish as soon as possible exactly who will need to attend completion and if there are any concerns over availability then the party concerned should be asked to sign a power of attorney which is sufficiently widely drawn to cover all that is required to be done at completion (see Precedents 12 and 13 in App.2). Where the buyer, the seller or any other party to the agreement is a company, that party should be required to produce certified copy board minutes to approve the transaction and to authorise the signature/ execution of the sale and purchase agreement and all related documents (see Precedents 14 and 15 in App.2).

8.8.2   The sellers will be required to hand over their share certificates at completion and so it is important that these are located as early as possible. If any share certificates are missing, the buyer will normally accept an appropriate indemnity (see Precedent 16 in App.2).

8.8.3   If the sale and purchase agreement does not contain a waiver from all of the sellers of any pre-emption rights to which they are entitled or if there are any shareholders who are not selling all of their shares or sellers who are not party to the agreement, the buyer should obtain separate waivers of pre-emption rights from them as discussed above.

8.8.4   The statutory books will need to be handed over at completion (cl.5.2.13) and it is important to ensure that they are written up-to-date before then.

8.8.5   The buyer may well require some or all of the directors of the target company to resign from office on completion and the buyer will typically ask them to sign an acknowledgement that they have no claims against the company (cl.5.2.14) (Precedent 17 in App.2 is a resignation letter which contains such an acknowledgement).

Where the directors are also the sellers, this should not be difficult to achieve but, where the individuals concerned are employees of the target company, the buyer may insist upon their signing formal compromise agreements under (amongst other legislation) the Employment Rights Act 1996, the Sex Discrimination Act 1985, the Race Relations Act 1976 and the Disability Discrimination Act 1995, which is the only effective way of making certain that none of the individuals concerned subsequently claims that, by asking him to resign, the company repudiated his contract of employment and "constructively" dismissed him (giving rise to a claim for breach of contract and unfair dismissal under the Employment Rights Act 1996).

For a detailed consideration of these issues and of the sums which may be involved, reference should be made to a specialist employment law text book and, where appropriate, specialist employment law advice should be obtained.

A seller who is also an executive director (i.e. an employee) of the target company may wish to consider structuring the transaction so that part of the consideration which would otherwise be paid to him takes the form of a payment by way of compensation for termination of his employment, as the first £30,000 of any such compensation payment may be free of tax, which would make such a payment attractive to the seller concerned. It should not however be assumed as a matter of course that the £30,000 exemption will be available—for example, it may not be available where there is a clause in the individual's contract of employment to the effect that the employer may terminate his contract of employment without giving the full contractual notice, provided that it does so by making a payment in lieu of notice. Before agreeing to any such compensation payment, the buyer should review the individual's contract of employment and establish whether or not there is such a clause as, if there is not, terminating the contract of employment and making a compensation payment will be a breach of the contract of employment, bringing the contract to an end so that it would no longer be possible to enforce provisions of the contract which would normally continue after its termination or expiry—such as restrictive covenants and confidentiality provisions. The sale and purchase agreement will normally, of course, contain confidentiality provisions and restrictive covenants but this is a point of which the buyer should be particularly aware if there are directors resigning on completion who are not also sellers and who are not therefore party to the sale and purchase agreement (see below).

To the extent that any compensation payment exceeds £30,000, it will be taxable and so (where the individual concerned is a seller) it is normally more attractive for him if the compensation payment is limited to £30,000.

A compensation payment should not in any event exceed the net value of the salary and other benefits to which the individual would have been entitled had he received his full contractual notice period as any payment in excess of the amount to which the individual is contractually entitled could constitute unlawful financial assistance by the target company for the acquisition of its own shares as discussed in Ch.17.

Particular care will be needed where there are directors of the target company whom the buyer wishes to resign but who are not sellers, as they are unlikely to have the same incentive to co-operate. Where the buyer requires them to resign both from office as directors and from their employment, it is essential to ensure that agreement is reached with them well in advance of completion and that that agreement is embodied in a formal compromise agreement entered into at completion.

The buyer will often wish to change the composition of the Board completely and may therefore wish directors to resign, even if he wishes to retain their services as employees after completion. In order to avoid the risk of the individual concerned claiming that his being asked to step down from the board constitutes a repudiation of his contract of employment or constructive dismissal, the buyer should obtain a formal variation to his contract of employment.

The parties should consider the implications of ss.215–222 of the Companies Act 2006, which replaced ss.312–316 of the 1985 Act, dealing with payments to directors (or those connected with them) by way of compensation for loss of office.

Section 215 provides that shareholder approval must be obtained before a company may make a payment to a director by way of compensation for loss of office as a director or loss of any other office or employment with the company or any of its subsidiaries. These provisions also cover payments made in connection with retirement and are extended to apply to payments to connected persons (s.215(3)) and payments made by another person at the direction of (or on behalf of) the company (s.215(4)). Where a company is to make a payment for loss of office to a director of its holding company, the proposal must be approved by a resolution of both the company and the holding company (s.217(2)) but no approval is required in the case of a wholly-owned subsidiary or a company which is not a UK-registered company.

Section 218 provides that shareholder approval must be obtained before any person (i.e. not just the company concerned) may make a payment for loss of office to a director of a company in connection with a transfer of the whole or any part of the undertaking or property of the company, while s.219 contains similar provisions relating to payments for loss of office to a director of a company in connection with a transfer of shares in the company (or in any of its subsidiaries) resulting from a takeover bid.

It will therefore be necessary to consider these issues both on a sale and purchase of shares and a sale and purchase of assets.

Members' approval will not however be required for a payment made in good faith in discharge of an existing legal obligation, by way of damages for breach of such an obligation, by way of settlement or compromise of any claim arising in connection with the termination of a person's office or employment or by way of pension in respect of past services (s.220(1)).

In the case of a payment by the company concerned to which s.217 applies, reference to an existing legal obligation means an obligation of the company, or any associated company, which was not entered into in connection with, or in consequence of, the event giving rise to the payment for loss of office.

In the case of payments to which ss.219 or 218 apply, an existing legal obligation means an obligation of the person making the payment which was not entered into for the purposes of, in connection with or in consequence of, the transfer in question. Sections 218 and 219 can apply to payments made under an arrangement which was entered into as part of a transfer which took place within one year before or two years after the agreement for the transfer.

In essence, therefore, approval will not be required where the payment represents no more than the contractual entitlement of the individual concerned and will not generally affect arrangements under which a director agrees to resign on the basis that he will receive a payment in lieu of his contractual notice period.

It will be necessary to bear these provisions in mind if there are proposals which may involve directors being given new service agreements (with more generous notice periods) ahead of a proposed sale.

These paragraphs are only intended to give a brief introduction to the relevant provisions of the 2006 Act and, in any circumstances to which these provisions may apply, reference should be made to the provisions of the Act itself.

8.8.6   The buyer may also wish the company secretary to resign on completion and similar issues may arise.

8.8.7   Conversely, there may be directors or other key individuals whose services the buyer considers essential to retain after completion and, unless he is satisfied with their existing terms and conditions of employment, the buyer may well make it a completion requirement that the individuals concerned enter into new contracts of employment.

8.8.8   Under the Companies Act 1985, shareholder approval was required for directors' fixed term service contracts which were not terminable by notice within five years or less and s.188(1) of the Companies Act 2006 reduces that period to two years. The 2006 Act also introduces a definition of a director's service contract and makes it clear that it will cover not just a contract of employment but a contract for the provision of services (such as a consultancy agreement) and (amongst other things) an agreement under which a company is to provide the director's services to the company concerned.

8.8.9   The buyer may well wish the existing auditors to resign on completion and for them to be replaced by a firm of his choosing: it will normally therefore be a completion requirement that the auditors deliver a written resignation on completion, along with the statement required by s.519 of the CA 2006, which provides that where an auditor of an unquoted company ceases for any reason to hold office, he shall deposit at the company's registered office a statement of any circumstances connected with his ceasing to hold office which he considers should be brought to the attention of the members or creditors of the company or, if he considers that there are no such circumstances, a statement that there are none (cl.5.2.2.4) (the position is slightly different in the case of a quoted company, where the resigning auditor is obliged to deposit a statement of the circumstances connected with his ceasing to hold office). The buyer will normally expect there to be a statement that there are no such circumstances and the buyer may also require the auditors to provide an acknowledgement that they have no outstanding fees, billed or unbilled, in order to avoid the risk of the company receiving a bill after completion for audit or other services provided before completion. The buyer may also be particularly concerned to make sure that the auditors (or other advisers of the seller) do not subsequently attempt to invoice the company for advice which the buyer considers should properly be paid by the seller.

Precedent 18 is a specimen form of resignation letter which can be adapted to meet the circumstances in question.

8.8.10   Unless the buyer is intending to leave the target company's existing banking or other facilities in place, the buyer will normally require a formal release on completion of all mortgages or other charges over the assets of the target company and of any guarantees given by the target company for the benefit of (typically) any other company in the seller's group, while the seller will normally expect there to be formal releases of any guarantees which he (or, where the seller is a corporate seller, any other company in his group) has given in respect of the target company (cl.5.2.2.5). In any event, the buyer will require a formal release of any mortgages, charges or other encumbrances over the seller's shares in the target company (Precedent 28 in App.2 can be adapted for this purpose).

8.8.11   The buyer is likely to require a formal release from all sellers of any claims which they may have against the target company or any of its subsidiaries — he sale and purchase agreement will normally contain a warranty to that effect but, rather than run the risk of receiving a claim from a seller and then having to make a claim against the sellers under the warranties (to which issues of disclosure, knowledge, mitigation and quantification of loss would apply), the buyer is likely to require a formal release so that he can be satisfied that no such claims may arise. This requirement is contained in cl.5.2.2.8 of Precedent 1 and cl.5.2.2.7 of Precedent 2 and it will be seen that, where the seller is a company, the buyer will expect the release to extend not just to claims by the seller but claims by the seller and any other company in the same group as the seller.

8.8.12   The sale and purchase agreement will normally require the seller to procure
          that a meeting of the board of directors of the target company is held in order
          to deal with everything which is necessary to transfer control of the company
          to the buyer, including approval of the share transfers, the appointment of new
          directors, the resignation of the existing directors, change of auditors, change
          of registered office, change of accounting reference date, change of bankers or
          bank mandates and so on. The form of the minutes which are to be passed will
          be agreed between the parties' solicitors in advance. A typical set of comple-
          tion board minutes is contained in the completion agenda which is Precedent
          11. It is important for the seller to make sure that a quorum of the board of
          directors of the target company will be available to enable that meeting to be
          held although modern articles of association normally permit board meetings
          to be held by way of conference telephone call or the like and in practice that
          is how such meetings often take place.

Where the signature and exchange of the sale and purchase agreement is not immediately followed by completion, the form of all documents which are required on completion (directors' resignations, compromise agreements, new contracts of employment,
completion board minutes, etc.) should be agreed on or before the point when the sale
and purchase agreement is signed and it is normal for the sale and purchase agreement
to refer to such documents as documents "in the Agreed Terms" or "in Agreed Form",
with their being initialled by the parties to show that their form has been agreed.

8.9   Failure to complete (cl.5.4)

The sale and purchase agreement will normally address the possibility of one party failing to comply with its obligations in respect of completion—for example, if a director
refuses to resign or the release of a guarantee is not forthcoming. This is not really an
issue where the intention is to sign the sale and purchase agreement and then immediately complete it as the parties will make sure that everything required for completion is
in place before they enter into the agreement and, if it is not, then they will normally
delay signing until it is. Where, however, there is an interval between the signing of the
agreement and completion, this point will need to be addressed and the sale and purchase
agreement will normally provide that in those circumstances the party who is not in
default may defer completion for a reasonable period, complete the transaction but without prejudice to his rights (for example, to sue for breach of contract or specific performance) or rescind the agreement. Both parties will therefore be particularly concerned to
make sure that they do not agree in the sale and purchase agreement to deliver or do anything on completion which for any reason they may be unable to deliver or do—partly
because neither party will want to run the risk of being in breach of contract but also
because neither party will want to give the other a "get out" if (for whatever reason) that
other party changes his mind about the deal before completion. The seller should therefore be particularly careful to avoid accepting obligations which are expressed in very
general terms, such as an obligation "to execute or procure the execution of such documents and do or procure the doing of such acts or things as the buyer may reasonably
require for the purpose of vesting the Shares in the buyer and of assuring to the buyer
the full benefit of this agreement". At the very least, such an obligation should only

extend to matters which the buyer may "reasonably require". Ideally, the sale and purchase agreement should specify exactly what will be required and, as has already been explained, those documents should be agreed in advance and initialled as being "in Agreed Terms" so that all parties are in no doubt as to exactly what is required.

8.10   Declaration of trust (cl.5.5)

The buyer will want to be able to exercise all voting and other rights attaching to the shares with effect from completion but will not legally be able to do so until he is entered in the register of members as the holder of the shares. The buyer cannot be registered as the holder of the shares until the share transfer form has been stamped with the appropriate amount of stamp duty and this will almost invariably take place a few days after completion (and longer if the transfer requires adjudication by HM Revenue and Customs). The solution to this is normally for the seller to agree that, while he remains the registered holder of the shares, he will hold them (and all dividends received in respect of them) on trust for the buyer and will exercise all voting and other rights in respect of the shares in accordance with the directions of the buyer. In this way, the buyer will be able to exercise control with effect from completion. It is not unusual for the declaration of trust to be coupled with a provision under which the seller appoints the buyer as his attorney in order to enable him to sign any written resolution of the shareholders of the target company, all proxy forms, consent to short notice and other documents which may be necessary in order to enable the buyer to exercise the rights attaching to the shares (in which event the agreement should be expressed to be a deed).

8.11   Confidential information (cl.6)

The seller will almost certainly have confidential information relating to the target company and its business and the buyer will invariably require an undertaking from the seller that he will not use any such information and will not disclose it to any third party.

As in the case of a confidentiality agreement entered into at the beginning of negotiations (as discussed in Ch.2), the agreement should contain a clear definition of what constitutes "confidential information" and, from the seller's point of view, should recognise that there will be certain information to which the confidentiality provisions will not apply and that it will be necessary to allow disclosure where required by law or any regulatory or government authority. The Freedom of Information Act 2000 and the Environmental Information Regulations 2004, which are discussed in Ch.2, will be relevant where the seller is a public body.

8.12   Restrictive covenants (cl.7)

8.12.1   The buyer will inevitably be concerned to protect the goodwill (the trade connection) of the business and will want to do whatever he can to make sure that its customers (or, at least, those customers which the buyer wishes to retain) will continue to do business with it following the change of ownership. The buyer will therefore want to do whatever he can to make sure that the seller does not simply pocket the sale proceeds and then set up a competing business (or join a competitor) and take away the company's customer base. Accordingly, the sale and purchase agreement is likely to contain restrictive covenants in order to prevent the seller from doing so. These will normally include the following elements:

- an undertaking not to solicit customers of the company (which may extend to an undertaking not even to have any dealings with any such customers;

- an undertaking not to interfere with the sources of supply to the company;

- an undertaking not to solicit away the company's key employees;

- an undertaking not to be involved in a competing business.

All these types of clauses are designed to protect the buyer's interests until he has had adequate opportunity to build or rebuild relationships with clients and customers and to fill any void left by the seller.

8.12.2 As a matter of public policy, the general rule is that restrictive covenants are unenforceable as being in restraint of trade. However, they may be enforceable if they are designed to protect the legitimate business interests of the party seeking to enforce them, such as customer or supplier relationships or confidential information.

A buyer cannot prevent a seller from competing or exploiting existing relationships forever. In the case of individual sellers, a balance has to be struck between (on the one hand) the seller's right to earn a living and use the knowledge and skills obtained from his former employment and (on the other hand) protecting the buyer's interests; in the case of corporate sellers, the balance which has to be struck is between the public interest in allowing businesses to compete and the protection of the buyer's legitimate commercial interests.

Restrictive covenants will, therefore, only be enforceable if they are reasonable and necessary to protect the buyer's interests. A seller's activities should not be restricted any further than is reasonably necessary.

What is reasonable will depend on the particular circumstances and will be assessed as at the date the restrictions were entered into.

8.12.3 Set out below are various issues affecting the reasonableness of restrictive covenants. Some of these are, by their very nature, only relevant where the seller is an individual but others will be equally relevant where the seller is a company (or indeed a partnership):

- The nature of the seller's role: this may need particular thought where there are a number of sellers and it may be necessary to consider the position of each seller separately. In the case of a seller who had close contact with clients or customers, then a restriction is more likely to be reasonable than if he had little client/customer contact.

- The activities prohibited, if, for example, there are a number of sellers of a company which operates in several different business areas, it may be appropriate for each only to be restrained in connection with the particular area in which he has worked.

- Whether the restriction is limited to the clients or customers with whom the individual concerned had personal dealings within a reasonable period immediately preceding termination.

- The geographical scope of the restriction: with non-competition restrictions, it is usually important to restrict the area to which the covenant applies, so rather than seeking to impose a restriction which covers the whole of the UK or even the whole of the world, a restriction is more likely to be regarded as reasonable if it is limited to the parts of the UK or parts of the world in which the business actually operates (or, in appropriate cases, in which the individual concerned worked).

At one extreme, in the case of a multi-national business, it may be appropriate for the restriction to cover large areas of the globe while, at the other, in the case of a business which is very localised, it may only be reasonable for the restriction to cover a few miles' radius of the place from where the business has been carried on.

- The period of time the restrictions are to last. Generally speaking any covenant which purports to last for longer than 36 months will be unreasonable, but it will depend on all the circumstances and in some cases it may be unreasonable for restrictions to last for 12 or even six months.

- Similar issues, of course, arise where a contract of employment contains restrictive covenants but, as a general rule, a buyer of a company orbusiness is likely to be able to persuade a court to accept as reasonable restrictions which may well be regarded as unreasonable in a contract of employment. The reason for this is that the buyer is (presumably) paying a price for the goodwill and trade connection which has been agreed on arm's length terms and he would normally therefore be regarded as entitled to restrict the activities of the seller to a greater extent than would be the case if the seller was simply an employee who had left his employment and was seeking alternative employment.

8.12.4   Where the seller is a company, it will also be necessary to consider the possible impact of EC competition law and UK competition law. These issues are discussed in detail in Ch.18.

8.12.5   Whether the seller is an individual or a company, restrictive covenants need
          very careful drafting and it is important to seek specialist advice when intro-
          ducing them.

          If a restrictive covenant goes beyond what is reasonable in the particular cir-
          cumstances it will be unenforceable and the courts will not enforce it to a
          lesser, more reasonable, extent. For example, a court will not look at a three
          year non-solicitation clause and say that it is unreasonable, but substitute a six
          month restriction; it will say that the whole restriction is unenforceable to any
          extent. This means that it is crucial to ensure that restrictions are reasonable.
          The buyer should not simply adopt the approach of "let's see if we can get
          away with five years" but should consider carefully with his legal advisers
          what is reasonable in the circumstances of the particular case.

          However, if only part of a restriction is unreasonable and the unenforceable part
          can be severed from the rest of the clause, leaving what is left making inde-
          pendent sense, without modifying the wording or changing the sense of the
          contract, then (if the wording of the agreement permits this (see cl.20)) a court
          may strike out individual words or phrases. This is called the "blue pencil test".

          For example, if a non-competition clause purports to cover the UK, France and
          Germany and a court found that it was unreasonable in the circumstances to
          extend protection to Germany, it could strike out the reference to this country,
          leaving the rest of the clause to be enforceable.

          If a buyer would like a restriction to last (for example) for three years but is
          concerned that a court might regard that that length of time as unreasonable, it
          might be worthwhile having a restriction which lasts for two years and
          11 months, in the hope that the court might strike out the 11 months if it
          thought that only two years was reasonable or might strike out the two years
          if it thought that only 11 months was reasonable. There is no certainty that that
          approach would work, but it may be worth considering.

8.12.6   A buyer will normally expect any restrictive covenants to be drafted widely
          enough to prevent the seller from setting up in competition or joining a com-
          petitor but also from competing indirectly—for example, by using part of the
          sale proceeds to enable a member of his family to set up a competing business
          in which the seller has (typically "behind the scenes") an involvement.

8.12.7   If there are activities in which the seller wishes to be involved during the
          relevant period and which might infringe any restriction, he would be well-
          advised to be open with the buyer and negotiate an acknowledgement from the
          buyer that those activities will not infringe the restriction (assuming, of course,
          that the buyer is prepared to agree to that).

8.12.8   There may be particular concerns where a business is being bought out of a
          group of companies, such as where Buyer PLC (Buyer) is acquiring the entire

issued share capital of Target Limited (Target), which is a wholly-owned subsidiary of Seller Limited (Seller), which is itself a wholly-owned subsidiary of Parent PLC (Parent). In that situation, Buyer will be concerned that an existing subsidiary of Parent (whether a direct subsidiary of Parent or a subsidiary of Seller) may set up in competition with Buyer. Buyer is likely therefore to argue that Parent should be made party to the sale and purchase agreement and should covenant that neither it, not Target nor any of Parent's other group companies will solicit customers of the business, be involved in a competing business, etc. Whether or not this would be enforceable would depend upon all the circumstances, but a court may well conclude that it is perfectly reasonable to structure the non-competition covenants in this way, in order to prevent their being rendered worthless simply by the competing business being carried on through a different legal entity, rather than by Seller.

If, in that example, Parent is a large and acquisitive company, it may well argue that it should not be prevented from acquiring other companies or groups of companies which may happen to include a business which competes with the business which is being sold to Buyer. For example, Parent and its subsidiaries may be involved in the construction industry and may be selling their house-building activities to Buyer, in order to enable them to concentrate on commercial developments. Buyer will argue that Parent and its subsidiaries should covenant that they will not compete with Buyer in house-building for an agreed period but Parent is likely to argue that, if it has the opportunity of acquiring another construction company which is also focused on commercial developments, it should not be prevented from doing so merely because the company in question also has a house-building operation, notwithstanding that it represents a comparatively minor part of its operations. If the point is agreed, there will be an exception from the restrictive covenants, which will normally be worded so as to apply where the competing activities do not represent more than an agreed proportion of the turnover being acquired (typically either five per cent or 10 per cent). In other words, Parent will agree that it will not deliberately go out and acquire another house-building business but Buyer will accept the possibility of Parent acquiring a house-building business as an incidental part of a larger acquisition. Depending on the relative bargaining strengths of the parties and on all other circumstances, Buyer may try to persuade Parent to agree that, if that happens, Parent will use all reasonable endeavours to dispose of the competing business within a reasonable period after completion and may go further and ask it to agree to offer to sell the competing business to Buyer at a fair market price. Such provisions may be difficult to enforce but may nevertheless be helpful in laying down some "ground rules".

It may also make restrictive covenants look more reasonable if there is an express provision to the effect that they will not apply to any activities in which the target company and the buyer have ceased to be involved (cl.72.4).

The restrictive covenants in cl.7 have been drafted as separate sub-clauses so that, if the court finds that any one or more covenants to be unreasonable, it may choose to strike out the covenant(s) in question, while allowing the others to be enforced.

Some of these issues were considered in the case of *Beckett Investment Management Group Ltd v Hall* [2007] EWCA Civ. 613 in which the Court of Appeal reversed the decision of the court at first instance that the non-dealing covenants in the contracts of employment of two relatively senior independent financial advisers ("IFAs") were unenforceable. In doing so, the court reviewed the principles applicable to covenants in restraint of trade in employment contracts.

The background is that Beckett Investment Management Group Ltd ("BIMG") was a holding company for two subsidiaries which provided the services of IFAs. BIMG did not trade but effectively provided the services of its employees to the subsidiaries for a management charge. H was a director of all three companies but was only an employee of BIMG. Y was employed as a senior IFA and both he and H worked at the same office of BIMG.

The terms of their contracts of employment contained a "non-dealing" clause as follows:

"17.3 The Employee HEREBY AGREES with the Company that for the period of his . . . employment and for the period of twelve months immediately following the termination of his . . . employment with the Company he . . . shall not, whether on his . . . own account or with, through, for or on behalf of any other person, firm, company or organisation, directly or indirectly, deal with or attempt to deal with, any Relevant Client for the purpose of supplying, or of seeking to supply, thereto any Prohibited Services."

The contracts of employment defined "Prohibited Services" as follows:

"the provision of advice in relation to pensions, life assurance, investments and other advice of a type provided by the Company in the ordinary course of its business at the date of the termination of the Employee's employment with it"

The expression "Relevant Client" was defined as follows:

"any person, firm, company or organisation who or which was at any time during the period of twelve months immediately prior to the termination of the Employee's employment a client of the Company (or Subsidiary Company) with whom or which the Employee dealt in the course of his/her employment during the twelve month period."

However, the definition contained a second limb as follows:

"if the Employee so dealt with an individual in that individual's capacity as an officer, employee or representative of any firm, company or organisation, that firm, company or organisation shall be deemed to be a Relevant Client and the individual shall also be deemed to be a Relevant Client in his or her personal capacity as well. If the Employee had, on behalf of the Company, during the twelve month period, dealt with an individual on behalf of others, that individual and those others shall be deemed to be Relevant Clients as well."

Y left and set up his own business and H left and joined him. Through their new business, they continued to deal with Beckett Group clients and argued that the non-dealing restriction was unenforceable.

The claim was dismissed at first instance but the Court of Appeal allowed the appeal on the basis that it was impossible to arrive at the conclusion that the parties intended that the term "Prohibited Services" should be defined so as to render the restriction devoid of practical utility and that "the business of the Company" should be construed as including that undertaken by the subsidiaries, as BIMG clearly had legitimate interest in the client base of its subsidiaries.

The Court of Appeal held that the 12 month restriction was reasonable, having regard to the nature of the IFA business and the seniority of the individuals concerned.

Finally, the Court of Appeal held that, while the second limb of the definition of "Relevant Client" was unreasonable in its width, it could be severed from the first limb of the definition, which the Court did regard as reasonable.

8.13   Guarantees (cl.8)

It has already been seen that, if the seller has given any personal guarantees in respect of liabilities of the target company (for example, to its bankers or its landlord), he should ideally take steps to have those guarantees released on completion. Sometimes, however, that is not possible — for example, because of the constraints of time or confidentiality. This is particularly likely to be the case with guarantees in favour of landlords, who have no particular incentive to make an early decision as to whether or not to agree to release a guarantee and, before doing so, may require a fair amount of financial and other information about the buyer and about any person or company whom the buyer is proposing to offer as a guarantor in place of the seller.

The seller may therefore in some instances have to accept that it is not going to be possible to have the guarantee released on completion and that he may have to rely on an undertaking from the buyer to attempt after completion to obtain the release of the guarantee and to indemnify the seller against any liability which arises after completion under the guarantee.

Ideally, the seller should insist on an undertaking from the buyer to use "best endeavours" to procure the release of the guarantee but the buyer is unlikely to be prepared to accept that as it is potentially an onerous obligation and could oblige the buyer (for example) to make payments to the landlord (or other beneficiary of the guarantee) if that is what is required in order to have the guarantee released.

The parties would be well-advised to specify in the agreement exactly what the buyer does or does not have to do in order to comply with his obligations under the clause — does he have to make any payment (such as a rent deposit) or give any other security? Does he have to offer himself as a substitute guarantor? There is an obvious risk for the seller in completing the transaction without obtaining the release of any guarantees and inevitably there will be some transactions where the party in whose favour a guarantee has been given may simply refuse point blank to release the guarantee — particularly where the seller is an individual or a company of substance and the buyer is of weaker financial standing. This will typically be the case in a sale out of a group of companies to a management buy-out or buy-in team, who will almost certainly make the acquisition via a newly-incorporated and highly-leveraged company, whose shareholders have few assets other than their shareholdings in the new company.

In such cases, the beneficiaries of the guarantees are unlikely to agree to release them and the seller's only remedy is likely to be to claim under an indemnity from the buyer if he suffers any liability under his guarantee and, by definition, the fact that the guarantee has been called is likely to mean that the buyer is in financial difficulty and that that indemnity is worthless.

Where therefore there are significant guarantees, one of the factors which the seller should take into account in deciding whether or not to sell to a particular buyer should be the financial strength of that buyer and the likelihood of his being acceptable as a replacement guarantor in place of the seller.

If the seller is prepared to proceed on the basis of an undertaking from the buyer to use reasonable endeavours to obtain the release of any guarantees and an indemnity from the buyer against any liability arising under any of them, then it is in the interests of both parties to make sure that the guarantees in question are carefully listed in the disclosure letter or in the agreement itself.

8.14   Indemnities (cl.9)

Matters which are typically covered by indemnity are discussed in Ch.10.

8.15   Boilerplate

Sale and purchase agreements will typically contain a number of clauses which do not have great commercial significance but which the lawyers normally like (for good reason) to see in the agreement and these include:

8.15.1   Following the Contracts (Rights of Third Parties) Act 1999, which allows someone who is not a party to a contract to enforce a term of the contract where the contract expressly so provides and where a term purports to confer a benefit on the third party (and it appears that the parties intended him to have the right to enforce it), the agreement should specify any provisions which are to be capable of enforcement by a third party and should state that otherwise no such rights are conferred on any third party (cl.10).

8.15.2   A clause which states the extent (if any) to which the parties may assign their rights under the agreement (cl.11). Clause 11 prohibits assignment by one party without the prior written consent of the other party, save that the seller may assign its rights (principally, the right to receive the purchase price) to another company in the same group. The seller may likewise be prepared to allow the buyer to assign the benefit of the agreement (principally, the benefit of the warranties and any indemnities and of any restrictive covenants) to another company in the same group as the buyer but sellers will generally be reluctant to allow the buyer to assign to a third party — the seller's principal concern is likely to be to prevent the buyer selling on the company to an unconnected third party with the benefit of the warranties and indemnities given by the seller. The buyer will, of course, be keen to be allowed to do so if he consider that there is a serious possibility of selling the company on within a comparatively short period after completion, although the extent to which warranties, in particular, may be enforced by an assignee is unlikely to be a straightforward matter.

If the seller is prepared to agree, in principle, that the benefit of the agreement should be capable of being assigned, he may wish to add a provision to ensure that any such assignment may not have the effect of increasing any liability of the seller above what it would have been were it not for such assignment. For example, the *Zim Properties* case, which is discussed in 11.1, means that there may be situations in which payments made pursuant to indemnities may be taxable and, as a result, it has become common to include a "grossing-up" clause, pursuant to which, if any such payment is taxable in the hands of the buyer, the seller will pay to the buyer such additional amount as is necessary to leave the buyer (net of tax) with the amount to which he would otherwise have been entitled (see, for example, para.5 of Pt 4 of Sch.4 to Precedents 1 and 2). It would be unreasonable for the seller to have to make such an additional payment if a payment made by him was taxable in the hands of an assignee of the sale and purchase agreement but would not have been taxable in the hands of the buyer.

If the first draft of the sale and purchase agreement contains a provision which allows the buyer to assign the benefit of the agreement to third parties, simply deleting that clause is unlikely to be sufficient to prevent the buyer from assigning it, as the benefit of an agreement will generally be assignable unless it is expressed not to be assignable.

8.15.3   A clause specifying that the formal sale and purchase agreement (and all related documents) represent the entire agreement between the parties in relation to the transaction and supersede all prior agreements, understandings and discussions (such as, for example, any heads of terms) (cl.12). This will normally be coupled with a provision excluding liability in respect of misrepresentations made before entering into the agreement and making it clear that the only representations and warranties are those contained in the agreement. As will be seen, however (see 10.1.2 below), following the decision in the

Thomas Witter case, any such clause should not purport to exclude liability for fraudulent misrepresentations.

Doubts over the effectiveness of such clauses have, however, been raised by the case of *Lloyd v Sutcliffe* [2007] EWCA Civ. 153.

In that case, L controlled N Ltd, which had been granted options to buy two sites (Site D and Site W). L verbally agreed with S that S would project manage, design and construct a residential development on each site. In return, S would become a 50 per cent shareholder in N Ltd and would share equally in the profits.

It was subsequently agreed to modify this original agreement so that, instead of being transferred to N Ltd, Site W would be transferred to a new company owned by L and his partner, W, although S would still be involved in its redevelopment.

The shares in N Ltd were duly transferred to L and S, who entered into a shareholders' agreement which dealt primarily with Site D, but contained references to N Ltd exercising the option for the purchase of Site W and transferring it to a company owned by L and W. It also contemplated that directors would charge for any work carried out at either site on a particular basis.

The agreement contained the following clause:

> "This Agreement supersedes any previous agreement between the parties in relation to the matters dealt with herein and represents the entire understanding between the parties in relation thereto."

The option over Site W was assigned to L and W's new company, MGL, which then bought the site. S indirectly helped to fund the purchase by lending money to N Ltd, which then lent money to MGL.

S carried out a certain amount of project management work in relation to Site W and, becoming concerned over the lack of any formal agreement relating to Site W, instructed his professional advisors to draw up a joint venture agreement. The relationship between L and S broke down without such an agreement being signed.

The High Court held that all the elements for a proprietary estoppel were present and that an equity had arisen in favour of S.

MGL and L appealed, on the following grounds, amongst others:

- The "entire agreement clause" precluded S from relying on extraneous material.

- The parties were astute businessmen who anticipated entering into a form of agreement relating to Site W but never did so. L and MGL never suggested to S that their promises were irrevocable or created an enforceable obligation.

The appeal was dismissed on the basis that the agreement only represented the entire agreement between the parties "in relation to the matters dealt with" in it. However, the arrangements between L and S in relation to Site W were not "dealt with" in the agreement and the clause was therefore not relevant. The agreement did not dispose of the important issues relating to its development and profits.

Also, the court held that the entire agreement clause could only preclude reliance on extraneous matters arising before the date of the agreement. L and S had clearly reiterated the terms of their understanding for the development of Site W by their words and conduct after the date of the agreement.

This case will cause some concern as such clauses are intended to prevent a party from claiming that the formal agreement did not cover all of the terms that were agreed but the case would allow a party to argue that such a clause will not be effective for the reason that it did not fully cover everything that was agreed. Parties should assume that such a clause will only apply to matters agreed before the date of the formal legal agreement and make sure that any subsequent changes are formally agreed in writing.

8.15.4   The buyer will normally require a clause to make it clear that if he fails to enforce his rights on one occasion, that will not be treated as a waiver of those rights for the future. For example, the buyer may not consider it cost-effective to pursue a potential warranty claim but may want to be free to do so if other claims subsequently arise and will want to prevent the seller from arguing that, by not pursuing the first claim, he has waived the right to pursue the subsequent claims. Similarly, where there is more than one seller, the buyer may wish to be free to release one seller (perhaps a seller who has continued to be employed by the buyer) from liability, without being treated as having released all of them (cl.13).

8.15.5   Both parties will normally require a clause to make it clear that to the extent that any provisions of the agreement have not been performed at completion, they will continue in full force and effect after completion (cl.14). This is to avoid any argument that once completion has taken place, the warranties and any other continuing obligations of the parties will come to an end.

8.15.6   It is normal to state (assuming that this is the intention) that English law will apply to the agreement (cl.15) and, in addition, there are a number of possible alternatives as regards jurisdiction—the agreement may provide that any disputes under it will be subject to the exclusive jurisdiction of the English (or any other) courts, may provide that such jurisdiction will be non-exclusive or will be exclusive for one party but not for the other (cl.16).

A detailed analysis of these alternatives is beyond the scope of this book but an exclusive submission to the English courts will normally be appropriate where the agreement is subject to English law, save where there is a distinct possibility that proceedings may have to be brought outside the UK.

8.15.7   It is normal to include a further assurance clause, under which the seller will agree to do whatever the buyer may reasonably require for the purpose of giving him the full benefit of the agreement, which is intended to give the buyer the assurance that, if he needs any further documents signing or anything further doing in order to perfect his title to the shares, the seller will oblige (cl.17). A seller will normally agree to this but there may be a debate as to who should bear any costs of any such action: the seller will argue that, once completion has taken place, any such costs should be for the account of the buyer, while the buyer will argue that, if there are any issues over the seller's title, then the seller should bear the cost of remedying them.

In practice, this is likely to be more of an issue on an assets sale and purchase where, as will be seen, rather more formalities are required.

8.15.8   It is normal to include a "counterparts" clause in order to make it clear that it is not necessary for all parties to sign the same piece of paper but that different parties may sign different (counterpart) copies of the agreement, which will then be deemed to constitute one and the same agreement (cl.18).

8.15.9   The parties will normally want the agreement to say that each party will bear its own costs, save that where there is a gap between signing the agreement and completion, one of the parties may in certain circumstances wish to oblige the other to bear his costs (for example, where the buyer has a right to rescind and exercises that right) (cl.19).

8.15.10 Both parties will normally require a provision which specifies what press and other announcements (for example, announcements to employees, customers and suppliers) may be made and preventing either party from issuing any other announcement without the consent of the other (cl.21). It is normal for all press announcements to have to be agreed between the parties but the buyer is likely to want to be free to make his own announcements to employees, customers and suppliers, while the seller may also want these to be in an agreed form. In any event, any party will need to be free to make any announcement which may be required by law or any regulatory authority such as the Stock Exchange.

8.15.11 As with any other legal agreement, there will almost invariably be a clause specifying that any formal notices to be given pursuant to the agreement (e.g. notice of any warranty claims) must be given in writing and specifying how and where any such notice must be served (cl.23). This is particularly important where there are a number of sellers and, where any of the sellers is an individual, there should be express provision governing the service of notice on a seller who has died. Where one or more of the parties is outside the UK, it would be wise to include a provision under which that party appoints somebody in the UK (typically a firm of solicitors) as his process agent in order to receive on his behalf service of process in any proceedings in this country.

8.16   Schedules

The agreement is likely to contain a number of schedules, as it is normally more convenient to deal with matters such as warranties, tax covenants and any completion accounts or any similar price-fixing mechanism in a separate schedule. In addition, there will normally be schedules containing basic details of the target company and of any subsidiaries and particulars of its or their freehold or leasehold properties, with the accuracy of such details then being formally warranted. The agreement will normally contain a provision to make it clear that the schedules arc an integral part of the agreement (cl.15).

Chapter 9

Sale and Purchase Agreements—Asset Sales

9.1   General principles

By contrast with a sale and purchase of shares, where all that is needed is a transfer of shares in the target company in order to transfer ownership of that company and its assets and liabilities to the buyer, a sale and purchase of assets is much more complex as it will be necessary to identify every single asset and liability (or category of assets and liabilities) of the business in question and to determine whether or not each particular asset or liability will transfer to the buyer or remain with the seller. Having done that, it will be necessary to comply with all necessary formalities for the transfer of title to each and every asset which is to transfer and possibly also for the novation of any liabilities which are to transfer.

Accordingly, as in the case of a sale and purchase of shares, there will almost invariably be a formal sale and purchase agreement, both to specify exactly what assets and liabilities are (and are not) to transfer to the buyer but also (as in the case of a sale and purchase of shares) to formalise other terms of the transaction, such as the payment terms, warranties and indemnities and any non-competition clauses.

In the past it was reasonably common for the seller's solicitors to prepare the first draft of an agreement for the sale and purchase of assets, on the basis that the seller was best-placed to know exactly what assets were used in the business in question and to instruct his solicitors accordingly. In recent times, however, it has become more normal for the first draft to be prepared by the buyer's solicitors, save in the case of a sale and purchase from receivers or administrators or (as in the case of a sale and purchase of shares) where the sale is by auction or similar competitive process. Precedents 3 and 4 in App.2 are typical examples of the form of agreement which is appropriate for the sale and purchase of all (or substantially all) of the undertaking, and assets of the business of a company, Precedent 3 being drafted to cover the situation where the debtors and creditors of the business are included in the sale and Precedent 4 to cover the situation where they are being retained by the seller. Both precedents have primarily been drafted from the point of view of the buyer, although some provisions have been included in order to reflect the likely requirements of the seller.

There follows a brief commentary on some of the principal provisions of these precedents but to the extent that some of these provisions are common to a share sale and purchase agreement and have been discussed in Ch.8 in relation to the precedent share sale and purchase agreements, no attempt is made in this chapter to duplicate the comments that have already been made and instead this chapter will concentrate on those provisions which are specific to a sale and purchase of assets or at least represent a change from the equivalent provision in a typical agreement for the sale and purchase of shares.

9.2   Parties

The parties will normally be just the selling company and the buyer, unless the buyer requires the obligations of the seller to be guaranteed by its holding company or (where it is owned by individuals) its shareholders or the seller requires a similar guarantee in respect of the obligations of the buyer. The buyer's concern is likely to be that the selling company may, if it has sold all of its assets, be no more than a "cash shell" and that it may then be wound up or its cash may otherwise be returned to its shareholders, with the result that it will not be worth suing if (for example) any breaches of warranty arise; the seller, on the other hand, if he has any doubts as to the financial strength of the buyer, will be concerned that any liabilities which the buyer has agreed to assume will nevertheless, as between the seller and the third party concerned remain direct liabilities of the seller and that, if the buyer fails to satisfy them, the seller will have to do so.

As part of his due diligence the buyer should take steps to make sure that all of the assets in question are vested in the seller, rather than (for example) other companies in the same group as the seller or its shareholders. It is very common for a company to trade from a property which is owned by (or leased to) its shareholders or (where it is part of a group) another company in the same group. Similarly with patents, trade marks or other intellectual property rights.

The seller may well wish to have the agreement drafted so that it is only assets which are owned by the seller or used exclusively in its business which are included in the transaction, while the buyer will wish to make certain that all assets which are used in the business are included, regardless of who owns them.

Particular care will need to be taken when buying assets from a group of companies where the business in question has been "divisionalised", i.e. transferred from the group company which originally carried it on into another group company, which then operates it as a trading division. There may be residual assets or liabilities remaining with the original company and the problems may be more acute where (as is quite common) the business continues to be carried on in the name of the original company, but as "undisclosed agent" of the company to which the business has been transferred.

For example, Seller Limited (Seller) may have a trading subsidiary, Subsidiary Limited (Subsidiary), and may decide for tax, accountancy or other reasons to transfer the undertaking and assets of the business of Subsidiary into Seller. There may, however, be considerable goodwill in the name of Subsidiary and Seller may want to retain that goodwill by making the outside world (customers, suppliers and perhaps employees) believe that they are still continuing to deal with Subsidiary, which is typically achieved by having contracts with customers and suppliers entered into in the name of Subsidiary but on the basis of an agreement entered into "behind the scenes" pursuant to which

Subsidiary agrees that it is doing so as agent for Seller, but on an undisclosed basis. In this way, it is hoped that those dealing with Subsidiary will be completely unaware of the agency agreement and believe that they are dealing with Subsidiary as principal rather than as agent. In these situations, there may be doubt as to whether the benefit of contracts and other rights which the buyer wishes to acquire are vested in Seller or in Subsidiary and there may be uncertainty as to whether the employees of the business are technically employed by Seller or Subsidiary. A detailed analysis of the law of agency is beyond the scope of this book but in such circumstances the buyer should ensure that both Seller and Subsidiary are party to the agreement and agree to sell their respective rights in the undertaking and assets of the business—this is likely to be helpful for Seller also as Seller is likely to be concerned to ensure that both Seller and Subsidiary have the benefit of any undertaking from the buyer to take over contracts, creditors and any other liabilities which are to pass to the buyer.

Where there may be issues as to whether a particular asset "belongs to" one division or another, rather than trying to rely on "clever" drafting, the parties should work together to identify any assets over which there may be any issues and have a specific agreement as to whether or not each such asset is included in the sale.

9.3   Definitions (cl.1)

The agreement for the sale and purchase of assets is likely to contain rather more definitions than an agreement for the sale and purchase of shares and these definitions should be as clear as possible in order to reduce the risk of a subsequent dispute as to whether or not a particular asset or liability transferred to the buyer or remained with the seller. As the current assets of a business may be constantly changing (for example, in the course of a day, raw materials may be purchased, raw materials may be converted into work-in-progress, work-in-progress may be converted into finished goods and stocks of finished goods may be sold and converted into debtors) it is normal to agree a particular time at which the sale and purchase is deemed to take effect (in Precedents 3 and 4 this is defined as the "Transfer Point") and draft the definitions by reference to the Transfer Point, so that the stocks of finished goods to be included in the sale will be those remaining in stock and unsold as at the Transfer Point and so on. The Transfer Point will typically (although not necessarily) be the close of business (or, if there is doubt as to when that is, then midnight) on the day before completion or the day of completion.

9.4   Conditions (cl.2 and Sch.10)

It has already been explained that, as in the case of a sale and purchase of shares, it will often be advisable (if not essential) to obtain certain third party consents or approvals to any sale and purchase of a business and, as discussed in Ch.4, these may be more extensive on a sale and purchase of assets where there will actually be a change in the legal entity which carries on the business. It may therefore be necessary to obtain the consent of the third parties concerned to the transfer of any commercial contracts or agreements, to transfer any licences, permits or other regulatory approvals which may be required and, where there are leasehold properties involved, to obtain the consent of the landlord. As in the case of a sale and purchase of shares, wherever possible these consents should be obtained before entering into the sale and purchase agreement but, where that is not possible, the sale and purchase agreement should set out clearly any conditions precedent to which the agreement is subject. Where any conditions concern third party consents or approvals (such as the transfer of licences, permits or other regulatory approvals) the seller should make sure that the agreement obliges the buyer to take appropriate steps to obtain them and this may be expressed as a "reasonable endeavours" obligation or may more specifically oblige the buyer to contact the third party concerned within an agreed period and to provide all information which the third party requires in order to decide whether or not consent is to be given. The buyer may also want to oblige the seller to provide all reasonable assistance. Detailed provisions are likely to be required where the sale and purchase agreement is conditional on the obtaining of landlord's consent to the assignment of the lease of any leasehold property used by the business and this is discussed in more detail in Ch.19.

9.5   Sale and purchase (cl.2)

The sale and purchase agreement will specify which assets are included in the sale and these will normally be defined as "the Assets" or the like. As has already been mentioned, in order to avoid subsequent disputes it is important to specify as clearly as possible exactly what is (or is not) included in the sale and the list of assets to be sold therefore needs to be read very carefully in conjunction with all relevant definitions. As in the case of a sale and purchase of shares, the buyer will expect the seller to sell with full title guarantee.

Sellers may attempt to frame the definitions of (for example) plant and machinery so as to refer to items "owned" by the seller but the buyer should not generally accept that wording as it means that items which are not owned by the seller will not be included in the sale and instead the seller should agree to sell with full title guarantee all the plant and machinery of the business, save for items which are separately identified as not being owned by it.

The assets to be sold and bought will normally include some or all of the following:

9.5.1   The goodwill of the business and the right for the buyer to carry on the business in succession to the seller (including the right to use any business names which the parties have agreed will transfer).

9.5.2   Plant, machinery, equipment, vehicles, fixtures and fittings and the like (which in Precedents 3 and 4 have been defined as "Plant"). The definition of what is to be included will need careful consideration and the buyer will normally require a general definition which extends to all such items used in the business (and/or held at the seller's premises) at the Transfer Point but would be well-advised to make sure that as far as possible the items which are to be included in the sale and purchase are listed in a schedule to the agreement, notwithstanding that it may not be possible for that schedule to be exhaustive. For reasons already given, the buyer should not generally accept a definition which is limited to items "owned" by the seller as the buyer will wish to make certain that all necessary plant, machinery, etc. is included in the sale and that, if it is not actually owned by the seller, arrangements are made for title to transfer to the buyer or at least for the buyer to be given the right to use it. As has already been explained, particular issues will arise where the items in question are used by other companies in the seller's group (which is typically the case with computer equipment but may also be the case with plant and machinery) and where the business in question is one of several divisions of the seller and these are compelling reasons for there to be a schedule of Plant which is as complete as possible.

9.5.3   Stocks of raw materials, work-in-progress, finished goods and the like which will normally be defined as the items held at the Transfer Point (with their then being verified by a physical stock-take to be carried out on or immediately after completion, particularly where there are to be completion accounts (see Ch.12)). Both parties will need to take particular care where raw materials, components or even finished goods are supplied to the seller by suppliers whose terms and conditions purport to reserve title to them unless and until the buyer has paid for them (reservation of title clauses may in fact go further and purport to reserve title unless and until all sums owing by the seller to the supplier have been paid). A detailed analysis of reservation of title clauses is beyond the scope of this book but the seller will be unable to agree to sell with full title guarantee where there are items which purport to be subject to third party reservation of title clauses.

The buyer should attempt to identify through his due diligence the extent to which this is likely to be an issue and ideally would require the seller to pay off the suppliers concerned before completion, so that the buyer can be confident of acquiring good title. That is, of course, unlikely to be realistic in the majority of cases and so, where creditors of the business remain the responsibility of the seller, the buyer will normally impose an obligation on the seller to pay off the suppliers concerned in the ordinary course of business and to indemnify the buyer against any failure to do so. Where the buyer has concerns as to the ability of the seller to do so or simply does not trust the seller to do so, he may wish to consider some sort of escrow account mechanism in order to make sure that those suppliers are paid. Where the buyer is agreeing to assume the creditors of the business, however, reservation of title should be of less concern to him as he can obtain good title by complying with his obligations under the sale and purchase agreement to pay creditors as and when they fall due.

9.5.4   Contracts with customers, suppliers and the like. The seller will normally seek to oblige the buyer to assume responsibility for all outstanding orders and all current contracts and agreements, while the buyer will normally be concerned that a very wide definition may oblige him to assume responsibility for orders, contracts and agreements, the terms of which have not been disclosed to him and which may be onerous for a variety of reasons.

Ideally, in the interests of certainty, the sale and purchase agreement will contain a definitive schedule of those which the buyer is to take over but in many cases this is simply not possible—either because there are so many contractual commitments or because orders are constantly being received and contracts are constantly being entered into, so that it is impossible at any given time to provide a definitive "snap shot" of those that are current. In those circumstances, the buyer will normally offer to take over all orders, contracts and agreements which have been entered into in the ordinary course of the business, to which the seller is likely to respond that he is selling the business in its entirety and does not want to be faced with a dispute at a later date as to whether or not a particular order or contract was in the ordinary course of business.

An alternative approach would be for the sale and purchase agreement to specify that the buyer will take over all orders, contracts and agreements and then for the seller to warrant that there are no contracts which have been entered into outside the ordinary course of business but that approach is less attractive for the buyer, as it is likely to mean that he will be obliged to assume the liability in question and then do what he can to recover from the seller under the warranties (which will be subject to his duties to mitigate his loss and subject to any limitations on the seller's liability, such as time limits, maximum and minimum liability and so on).

If the sale and purchase agreement refers to orders, contracts and agreements "outstanding" or "remaining to be completed" at the Transfer Point, the buyer should consider whether that wording may open up the possibility of his assuming responsibility for liabilities beyond those which he was expecting to assume. For example, if the business involves the supply of goods on the basis that warranties will be given to the customers in respect of any defects (for example, entitling the customer to have the goods repaired or replaced free of charge if any such defects emerge within an agreed period), it could be argued that the effect of the wording is to oblige the buyer to assume responsibility for all goods sold by the seller before completion, regardless of the fact that payment for the goods in question may already have been made to the seller. This issue is discussed in detail below but, where appropriate, the buyer should make sure that the definition of "Contracts" does not extend to obligations in respect of goods delivered or services supplied by the seller before the Transfer Point.

9.5.5   There may be other contractual commitments of the seller which should be excluded from the definition of "Contracts" such as the contracts of employment of the employees of the business, which will normally be the subject of separate provisions (see 9.14 below and Ch.21).

9.5.6   Patents, trade marks, copyrights and other intellectual property rights (which will normally be defined as widely as possible).

9.5.7   Any freehold or leasehold property of the business.

9.5.8   The book debts of the business (see 9.11 below).

9.5.9   Certain books and records of the business: the parties will normally wish to agree which books and records are to transfer to the buyer and which are to be retained by the seller but they will normally agree that for a period after completion the seller will have the right to inspect (and take copies of) books and records which have transferred to the buyer and vice versa (cl.20).

9.5.10   Rights against third parties in respect of other assets which the buyer is acquiring, such as the benefit of manufacturers' warranties in respect of plant and machinery or finished goods.

9.6   Excluded assets (cl.3)

The buyer will naturally be concerned to ensure that all assets of the business are included in the sale and may request a provision in the agreement to the effect that all assets are included, whether or not specifically mentioned. The seller on the other hand may wish to say that no assets will be included in the sale unless they are specifically mentioned and that is particularly likely to be the case where only part of a business is being sold or where the business being sold represents only one of a number of businesses being carried on by the seller. Whatever approach is adopted, there will normally be a clause in the agreement making it clear that certain assets are excluded from the sale and these will typically include cash, any VAT repayment and any assets which are on lease, hire-purchase or similar financing arrangements to which the seller will not have title and which the seller will not therefore be able to sell and in respect of which specific arrangements will need to be agreed (see below).

9.7   Consideration (cl.4)

The agreement will specify the purchase price and the comments made in respect of the consideration for share sales and purchases will for the most part apply equally to sales and purchases of assets. Where, however, the buyer is agreeing to assume the creditors of the business, then that will normally be treated as part of the consideration for the assets. For example, if a buyer agrees to pay £1,000,000 in cash for a business but as part of the transaction agrees to take over £4,000,000 of creditors, the total consideration for the transaction will, for legal purposes, normally be regarded as £5,000,000.

One major difference between a sale and purchase of assets and a sale and purchase of shares is that on a sale and purchase of shares the consideration will all be attributable to the shares in the target company whereas, on a sale and purchase of assets, the consideration is attributable to the various assets and for tax and accounting reasons it is normal to apportion the price between the assets (or categories of assets). The basis on which the purchase price is to be apportioned will normally be a matter for discussion and negotiation between the parties.

The buyer will normally wish to apportion as much as possible to those assets (primarily plant and machinery) which attract capital allowances, whereas the seller may not be in favour of this, as it may result in balancing charges. The buyer may also wish to apportion as much as possible to stocks, which may be less attractive to the seller as the amount in question may then be treated as income.

Depending on the respective bargaining positions of the buyer and a seller, they normally work together with their advisers to try to agree a basis of apportionment which is fair and reasonable to both of them and if the basis of apportionment proposed by the buyer has adverse tax consequences for the seller or vice-versa, that may be a matter to be used as a bargaining lever in the course of negotiations.

9.8   VAT (cl.5)

9.8.1   Almost invariably, the sale and purchase of a business will be a "transfer of a business as a going concern" for the purposes of art.5 of the Value Added Tax (Special Provisions) Order 1995 (SI 1995/1268) and will be regarded as neither a supply of goods nor of services for VAT purposes. The seller will wish to ensure that the price is expressed to be exclusive of VAT so that, in the event that VAT is chargeable, it is payable in addition to the price. If the agreement is silent, the price will be assumed to be inclusive of VAT (s.19 of the Value Added Tax Act 1994) and, if it is subsequently found to be the case that VAT should have been charged, the seller will be liable to account for it, with no recourse to the buyer. If VAT is chargeable, the seller must produce a VAT invoice.

9.8.2   To fall within art.5, the transferor must be a taxable person.

9.8.3   The transferee must also be a taxable person. A taxable person for this purpose means not only a person who is registered for VAT, but also one who is liable to be registered for VAT, for example by virtue of the transfer and the supplies he will be making in consequence of that transfer. It is not therefore necessary for the transferee to have registered for VAT before completion of the transfer but the seller of a business may reasonably require confirmation that the buyer is either registered or will be liable to be registered for VAT purposes following completion of the transaction. HM Revenue & Customs ("HMRC") was previously of the view that the assets transferred had to be used by the transferee in carrying on the same kind of business as the transferor but it appears that they may no longer be taking that view.

9.8.4   Where part of an existing business is transferred, the same rules apply, with an additional requirement that the part of the business transferred is capable of independent operation (art.5(1)(b)).

9.8.5   If land (freehold or leasehold) is one of the assets transferred, as is commonly the case, there are further complications. Where the sale of the land (and any buildings) would be a standard-rated supply if the exemption did not apply, the exemption will only be available if, on or before completion of the sale, the buyer makes an election in relation to the land or buildings in question and notifies HMRC of that election and does not revoke it. Where the sale includes land and buildings for which the seller has elected to tax or which is less than three years old or (in the case of a building) unfinished, the exemption will only be available if the buyer's option to tax will not be exercised and the transferee notifies the seller before completion that this will be the case.

This is a difficult and technical area, on which specialist advice should be taken.

If the seller has waived his exemption in respect of the supply of his land pursuant to Sch.10 para.2 to the Value Added Tax Act 1994, or the land to be transferred includes the freehold of a new commercial building or civil engineering work (i.e. the practical completion of which was within the three years prior to the transfer) then, notwithstanding the other provisions of art.5, VAT will still be chargeable unless the buyer has both waived his exemption in respect of those buildings and notified HMRC that he wishes to do so prior to completion of the sale (arts 5(2) and (3) of the VAT (Special Provisions) Order 1995).

9.8.6   Before September 1, 2007, the seller of a business which was transferred as a going concern was obliged to pass the business's VAT records to the buyer, unless HMRC agreed to their retention by the seller. HMRC would normally wish to be convinced that there were genuine commercial needs for the seller to hold onto the records before giving such agreement.

Section 100 of the Finance Act 2007 changes the rules in respect of transactions which involve the transfer of a business as a going concern pursuant to a contract entered into on or after September 1, 2007.

From September 1, 2007, the position will depend on whether the buyer takes over the seller's VAT registration.

If the buyer does not take over the seller's VAT registration, there will be no requirement for the seller to transfer the VAT records to the buyer. This means that the seller must retain the VAT records of the business for six years (para.6 of Sch.11 to the Value Added Tax Act 1994 ("VATA 1994") and reg.31 of the VAT Regulations 1995). New provisions have also been inserted into s.49 of the VATA 1994 by the Finance Act 2007 to ensure that the buyer can gain access to the VAT records of the business. Where there is a transfer of a business as a going concern and the seller is required to keep the records, the buyer can require the seller to do the following, so far as is necessary, to enable the buyer to comply with his own VAT obligations:

●   give the buyer, within such time and in such form as the buyer may reasonably require, such information contained in the records as the buyer may reasonably specify;

●   give the buyer, within such time and in such form as the buyer may reasonably require, such copies of documents forming part of the records as the buyer may reasonably require;

- make the records available for the buyer's inspection at such time and place as the buyer may reasonably require (and permit the buyer to take copies of or make extracts from those documents).

The parties cannot contract out of or restrict the buyer's rights and the treatment of VAT records is entirely governed by the legislation so that there is no need to make express provision in the sale and purchase agreement in relation to VAT records. From the seller's point of view it may be preferable for the agreement to remain silent on the point as an express provision which is inconsistent with the statutory requirements could lead to the seller being in breach of his statutory duty.

The position is different where the buyer takes over the seller's VAT registration. Regulations have been made which provide that where, on a transfer of a business as a going concern, the buyer takes over the seller's VAT registration, the seller must transfer the VAT records to the buyer unless the seller obtains a direction from HMRC that the seller should retain the records (VAT (Amendment) (No. 5) Regulations 2007 (SI 2007/2085)). Where the VAT records pass to the buyer, the seller should obtain an undertaking from the buyer to provide the seller with access to the records. Where the seller obtains a direction from HMRC allowing him to keep the records, the seller will, from September 1, 2007, be under the same statutory obligations to provide access to the records as where the buyer does not take over the VAT registration.

Section 100 of the Finance Act 2007 also makes it clear that the rules relating to transfer and retention of VAT records apply where part of a business is transferred as a transfer of a business as a going concern.

9.8.7 The sale and purchase agreement should also contain provisions covering any VAT deferment accounts. When goods are imported from outside the EU, VAT must be paid at the point of importation on the value of the goods imported. A VAT deferment account enables payment to be postponed. Provision of the VAT deferment account number to the supplier allows the goods to be imported and HMRC will then collect the duty via a direct debit from a bank account, which has to be supported by a bank guarantee in favour of HMRC. It is important, when acting for a seller, to ensure that employees or agents of the business realise that the old VAT deferment account number must not be used and that, where necessary, guarantees are reduced or cancelled. The buyer must make his own VAT deferment account arrangements and will need to make sure that, if necessary, these are in place on completion.

9.9   Completion (cl.6)

As with a share sale and purchase agreement, the assets sale and purchase agreement should specify exactly what is to take place at completion and Precedents 3 and 4 contain a typical clause (cl.6) to deal with this. The completion requirements will primarily be the formalities which are required in order to transfer the various assets (or categories of assets) from the seller to the buyer and these are likely to include some or all of the following:

9.9.1   An assignment of the goodwill (see Precedent 22 in App.2).

9.9.2   An assignment of all contracts and agreements with customers, suppliers and the like which the buyer is to assume (see Precedent 22 in App.2).

9.9.3   An assignment of any book debts which are included in the sale and purchase.

9.9.4   A "blanket" assignment of all intellectual property rights included in the sale (whether registered or unregistered) (see Precedent 22 in App.2).

9.9.5   Formal assignments of any registered intellectual property rights (patents, trade marks, service marks and registered designs) and applications for any such rights, which will then need to be registered with the UK patent office and other relevant patent offices Precedents 24 and 25 are simple assignments of UK patents and trade marks respectively.

9.9.6   A transfer (in the prescribed form) of any freehold or leasehold property title to which is registered at the Land Registry, which will after completion need to be stamped and then registered at the Land Registry, and a conveyance of any unregistered land.

9.9.7   A formal assignment of the lease of any leasehold property the title to which is unregistered and (where required under the terms of the lease) a licence to assign from the landlord (see Ch.19).

9.9.8   Formal releases in respect of all fixed charges and formal releases and/or letters of non-crystalisation in respect of all floating charges affecting any of the assets (see Precedents 28 and 29 in App.2).

9.9.9   The seller will give vacant possession of any freehold or leasehold property to the buyer.

9.9.10   The seller delivering to the buyer possession of the books and records which it has agreed to sell and possession of the plant and machinery, stocks and any other assets which are capable of passing by delivery. It should be noted that the seller must deliver to the buyer any VAT records of the business unless he receives permission from the local VAT office to retain them which may be granted, for example, where only part of a business is being sold, for which there are no separate VAT records (see 9.8 above).

9.9.11   If the buyer wishes to make use of the seller's corporate name after completion, a resolution changing its name.

9.9.12   If it is proposed that a director of the seller should be paid compensation for loss of office as a director or loss of any other office or employment with the seller (or any of its subsidiaries), it will be necessary to consider the implications of ss.215–222 of the Companies Act 2006 which are discussed in Ch.8.

9.10   Agency (cl.7)

If the parties wish the business to be transferred with effect from a date which is earlier than the date of completion (so that the Transfer Point will pre-date completion) the sale and purchase agreement may include a provision under which the seller will be deemed to have acted as the agent of the buyer as from that date, so that the benefit of trading during the interim period will accrue to the buyer. This is because it is not possible to back-date an agreement or to pass title with effect from an earlier date, although any such deemed agency provision is likely to have limited effect. Nevertheless, there is no reason why the parties should not contractually agree that the buyer will have the benefit of trading during the interim period, although it will generally be preferable to achieve this by adjusting the purchase price. That approach is preferable as HMRC will treat the income arising between the Transfer Point and completion as income of the seller whatever the agreement provides and it will be the responsibility of the seller to charge and pay VAT as principal during that interim period.

9.11   Debtors and creditors (cl.8)

When agreeing the terms of a sale and purchase of assets, one of the major issues to be considered is whether or not the debtors and creditors of the business should be taken over by the buyer (who will then collect the debtors and discharge the creditors) or retained by the seller (in which case, the seller will collect the debtors and pay the creditors (although sometimes the buyer will agree to do so as his agent)). Traditionally, one particular reason for excluding debtors and creditors was that stamp duty would be payable by the buyer on the proportion of the purchase price which was attributable to the debtors and, in determining the amount of stamp duty payable, the value of the creditors which the buyer was assuming would be treated as part of the purchase price. However, stamp duty is no longer payable on debtors and so is no longer an issue.

A buyer will often wish to take over debtors and creditors so that he can take over the relationship with customers and suppliers and may be concerned that otherwise the seller may damage the relationships by being too heavy handed in collecting debts from customers or may be dilatory in paying suppliers. Against that, the buyer may be reluctant to pay book value for debtors which may subsequently not be collected (or at least which it may take some time and effort to collect).

Precedent 3 covers the situation where debtors and creditors are included in the sale and Precedent 4 the situation where they are being retained by the seller and the relevant provisions of the agreements will be different in a number of respects:

9.11.1   Where debtors and creditors are included in the sale, then it will be necessary to make sure that there is clarity as to exactly which debtors and which creditors are to transfer as there may be debtors or creditors which the buyer does not wish to assume.

Where the seller is part of a group of companies, the buyer will not generally wish to acquire (and pay for) sums owing to the seller by other companies in the same group, particularly where these are loan accounts rather than normal trading accounts. As the seller will remain part of the group, it is far more logical for it to retain the benefit of those intra-group debtors and to collect them as it sees fit. In the same way, there may well be sums owing by the seller to other members of its group and the buyer will not normally wish to assume those liabilities. It is also likely that the buyer and the seller will wish to exclude any repayment of VAT or any other tax refund to which the seller may be entitled and any liabilities of the seller for VAT or any other tax and it is likely that the seller's bank overdraft and other sums owing to its bankers will remain the responsibility of the seller.

Particular care will be needed with pre-payments made by or to the seller before the Transfer Point, such as pre-payments of insurance premiums made by the seller or deposits paid to the seller by customers. It will normally be appropriate for pre-payments made by the seller (defined in Precedents 3 and 4 as "Pre-payments") to be treated as debtors and for pre-payments received by the seller (defined in Precedents 3 and 4 as "Accruals") to be treated as creditors.

If debtors are included in the sale, there should be a formal assignment of them pursuant to s.136 of the Law of Property Act 1925 and, in order to enable the buyer to pursue the debts in his own name, it will be necessary to give notice in writing to each of the debtors, as required by that section. This can be quite time-consuming and in many cases the buyer will want to adopt a more "low key" and "business as usual" approach to customers rather than give them formal notices and so in practice the buyer may decide only to do so if and when it actually becomes necessary to take formal proceedings to recover a debt.

Where the buyer is agreeing to take over creditors, the seller should insist upon an indemnity against any failure on his part to do so.

Whether or not debtors or creditors are included in the sale, the buyer would be well-advised to make sure that there is a clause stating expressly that he is not obliged to assume any liabilities of the seller other than those which he expressly agrees to assume (cl.8.2 of Precedent 3 and cl.8.7 of Precedent 4).

9.11.2   Where debtors and creditors are not included, the principal concerns of the parties will be to make sure that sums which are payable to the seller are not retained by the buyer and vice versa and, from the buyer's point of view, to try to make sure that the relationship with the customers of the business is not damaged as a result of action taken by the seller in collecting its debtors.

As the buyer will normally be continuing to operate the business from the same address and is likely to be using the same staff to collect debtors, it is quite common for the buyer to agree that he will act as the agent of the seller in collecting pre-completion book debts and will then pay over to the seller the amounts which he recovers (cl.8.1 of Precedent 4). If so, the sale and purchase agreement will normally set out the practical arrangements for this and in particular the time period within which the buyer must account to the seller for the amounts received (cl.8.2 of Precedent 4). The seller is likely to require the buyer to keep accurate records of all sums received and to provide the seller with regular statements, together with supporting documents (cl.8.3 of Precedent 4). Whether or not this approach is adopted or the seller collects the debtors himself, the parties will have to address the possibility of payments being received from debtors which cover sums owing both to the seller and to the buyer or which are not specifically stated to relate to any particular debt. Each party will be concerned that the other may pressurise the debtor into stating that the payment relates to a debt owing to him rather than to the other party and so it is common to say that if a payment is not specifically stated to relate to a particular debt, the party receiving the payment will ask the debtor to specify the debt to which the payment relates (but without putting undue pressure on the debtor), failing which the payment will generally be treated as being in payment of the debt which has been outstanding the longest, unless it is fairly obvious that that was not the debtor's intention (for example, because the debt which has been outstanding the longest is still disputed by the customer) (cl.8.6 of Precedent 4).

If the buyer does agree to collect the debtors as agent of the seller, the seller will wish the agreement to prevent him from compromising or releasing any of the debtors (which he might otherwise be tempted to do in order to ingratiate himself with customers) and if it becomes apparent that litigation is going to be necessary, this will normally be handled by the seller (although the buyer may wish the seller to consult with him before doing so) (cl.8.5 of Precedent 4). If it is the seller who is responsible for collecting the book debts then the buyer may wish to agree with the seller what action the seller may take in order to recover those debts and when he may do so. In other words, the parties may agree a credit control procedure which allows the seller to take reasonable steps to recover debtors owing to him but in a way which is not too heavy handed when looked at from the point of view of the buyer, who has every incentive to maintain a good relationship with the debtors (while the seller, of course, may have no such incentive).

Where debtors and creditors are not included in the sale and purchase, it will also be necessary to agree a basis for apportioning overheads and income which do not fall within the definitions in the Precedents of Pre-payments and Accruals. It is normal to agree that rent, rates, wages, salaries and the like will be apportioned on a time basis (by reference to meter readings where relevant) and that licence fees, royalties and similar sums payable to the seller shall be apportioned (cll.8.8 and 8.9 of Precedent 4). Where debtors and creditors are included in the sale then this should be less of an issue, particularly where there are to be completion accounts as all of these apportionments will normally be dealt with through the mechanism of the completion accounts.

9.12   Contracts (cl.9)

It is possible to assign the benefit of a contract provided that the contract does not prohibit assignment or limit the ability to assign it (typically, by providing that no assignment is permitted without the prior written consent of the other party to the contract). In any event, even if the benefit of a particular contract is capable of being assigned, the burden of the contract (i.e. the obligations of the party concerned under that contract) cannot be assigned or otherwise transferred to the buyer without the consent of the other party to it. If, for example, Buyer PLC (Buyer) is acquiring the undertaking and assets of Seller Limited (Seller) and Seller has entered into a contract with a major customer which Buyer wishes to take over, Buyer will have to establish whether or not it is possible for Seller to assign the benefit of that contract without the prior written consent of the customer; if assignment is permitted, Seller will be able to assign to Buyer the right to be paid by the Customer. However, a customer who has a contract for the supply of goods or services by Seller cannot be forced to accept that those goods or services will instead be supplied by Buyer, with whom he has no contractual relationship. Whatever the sale and purchase agreement may say, Seller will continue to remain directly liable to the customer under the contract. The ideal solution to this, from Seller's point of view, will be to have the contract novated, which involves a three-way agreement under which the customer agrees that, with effect from an agreed time, his contract with Seller will come to an end and will be replaced by a new contract with Buyer. If this approach is adopted, Buyer will normally require the novation agreement to specify that he will be liable for the obligations of Seller as from the point of novation rather than stepping into the shoes of Seller from the point when the contract was entered into, as that would make him liable for all past breaches.

Novation may be appropriate where a business has only a handful of contracts with customers which are absolutely key to the continuation of the business (for example, where the business is a construction business and its principal assets are construction contracts) but generally formal novation is seen as unduly time-consuming and unlikely to be conducive to good relations with customers and suppliers; it is therefore more common for there to be a formal assignment of the benefit of the contracts, coupled with an agreement by both parties to use all reasonable endeavours to obtain all necessary third party consents and an agreement on the part of the seller to allow the buyer to perform the contracts as the agent of the seller (cl.8.2), with the buyer undertaking to do so (cl.8.1). If that is what is agreed, the seller will continue to remain directly liable to the third parties concerned under the various contracts and so should require an indemnity from the buyer against any liabilities which the seller incurs as a result of any failure on the part of the buyer to perform those contracts. The buyer should require a similar indemnity against any losses which the buyer may suffer as a result of any breach or non-performance of any of the contracts by the seller before completion (cl.9.3). In order to avoid any argument from the third party concerned that a contract has been breached by virtue of the seller purporting to assign it without the consent of that third party, it is common for the sale and purchase agreement to provide that the seller will hold the contracts concerned on trust for the buyer and that the buyer will perform them as agent for the seller, as discussed above.

As is the case with an assignment of book debts, the buyer should consider whether to give formal notice of assignment to the third parties to the various contracts but is likely in practice to be reluctant to do so unless and until it becomes necessary to take action to enforce the contract concerned.

9.13   Defective goods (cl.10)

In most transactions, the parties will need to agree how to deal with claims received after completion as a result of goods or services supplied by the seller before completion which are alleged to be defective. Where the buyer is taking over the debtors, he will want to be certain that where warranty work has to be done or goods have to be replaced in order to enable him to obtain payment of those debtors, then that work will be done at the seller's expense. Where debtors are excluded from the sale, the seller will be concerned to make sure that all work is carried out which is necessary to enable him to obtain payment of the sums due to him and will also be conscious of the fact that, as the original contracting party, any claims in respect of goods or services supplied before completion will be his direct responsibility.

Even where debtors are not included in the sale, the buyer will wish to make certain that all product warranty claims are satisfied as he is likely to need that to be done in order to maintain relations with customers and protect the goodwill of the business.

In practice, after selling the business, the seller is most unlikely to be able to satisfy any such claims and so it will generally be accepted that any such claims will be dealt with by the buyer. The buyer will want to make sure that, if he does so, then it will be at the expense of the seller, while the seller will want to be certain that there is an agreed basis on which the buyer will charge for such work and that that basis is fair to the seller.

The seller will also be concerned that, in order to carry favour with customers, if he knows that he can do so at the expense of the seller the buyer will be tempted to accept all customer returns and agree to repair or replace defective goods, regardless of whether the customer's complaint is valid. The seller will normally therefore press to have a provision in the sale and purchase agreement under which the buyer will not do work at the expense of the seller without the prior agreement of the seller, at least where the sums involved are above a specified level. What is fair and reasonable will inevitably depend upon all the circumstances—the parties' views may be very different when the business is a supplier of relatively cheap consumer goods from when it supplies expensive plant and machinery.

9.14   Employees (cl.11)

As discussed in more detail in Ch.21, by virtue of the provisions of TUPE the employees of the business will transfer automatically to the buyer and the buyer will therefore take over the rights and powers of the seller in relation to those employees, but also all of the seller's duties and liabilities to them. To all intents and purposes, therefore, there will be a statutory novation of the contracts of employment and, subject to certain limited exceptions, the buyer will stand in the shoes of the seller as if the contracts of employment had originally been entered into with the buyer rather than the seller.

These issues and the provisions which, as a result, will normally be required in an agreement for the sale and purchase of assets are discussed in Ch.21.

9.15   Property (cll.12 and 13)

The property provisions are discussed in detail in Ch.19.

9.16   Warranties (cl.14)

As has already been seen, the warranties to be included in an agreement for the sale and purchase of assets will generally be less extensive than those which are appropriate to a sale and purchase of shares. The extent of the warranty protection which is appropriate will inevitably, however, be dependent upon the extent to which the buyer agrees to assume contractual and other obligations or liabilities of the seller as the buyer will not normally require warranties in respect of liabilities which are remaining with the seller. In any event, on a sale and purchase of assets, the tax warranties which are likely to be appropriate will be far less extensive than would be appropriate on a sale and purchase of shares and there will be no tax covenant. There are however a limited number of tax warranties which may be appropriate as an information-gathering exercise, if nothing else. Particular care will be needed where part only of a business is being sold or where the business being sold represents only one of a number of businesses being carried on by the seller—for example, in the latter case a warranty regarding the audited accounts of the seller is unlikely to be at all helpful and the buyer should instead be looking for warranties in respect of the management or divisional accounts in respect of the business in question.

9.17   Restrictive covenants (cl.16)

On a sale and purchase of assets, the buyer is likely to expect the seller to enter into similar restrictive covenants to those which would normally be given on a sale and purchase of shares and would be subject to the same "reasonableness" requirement and (where relevant) to UK and EC competition laws in exactly the same way (see Ch.18).

On a sale and purchase of shares, it will be the seller who enters into the sale and purchase agreement and agrees to be bound by any restrictive covenants but the position may be more difficult on a sale and purchase of assets. For example, Buyer PLC (Buyer) may be acquiring the undertaking and assets of a business from Seller Limited (Seller), a company owned by Tom, Dick and Harriet. It will be Seller who will be the selling the assets and it would normally therefore be Seller who entered into the restrictive covenants. Buyer may, however, be concerned that Tom, Dick and Harriet may set up a competing business using their connections with Seller's customer base and might feel particularly aggrieved if, shortly after completion of the sale, Seller were wound-up and the proceeds of sale were distributed to Tom, Dick and Harriet, who then used those proceeds to set out in competition.

Tom, Dick and Harriet may well argue that the sale proceeds would be coming into Seller and that it would therefore be unreasonable for them personally to accept any restriction, but Buyer may respond by arguing (if this is the case) that Tom, Dick and Harriet have all the trade connections and that, in order to protect the goodwill of the business, it is only reasonable that they should be bound by the restrictions, along with Seller. Whether or not this would be enforceable will depend upon all the circumstances and Buyer would be well-advised to make sure that the restrictive covenants are drafted in such a way that, if the personal restrictions were found to be unreasonable, they may be struck out, while leaving the restrictions on Seller to be enforceable.

9.18   Use of names (cl.17)

On the sale and purchase of assets, the buyer will not as a matter of course acquire the right to use the seller's corporate name or any trading name used by the business but the definition of goodwill may include the right to use all or any of such names. If the buyer wants to be able to use the seller's corporate name, the sale and purchase agreement should oblige the seller to change its name at completion and then to file the name change resolution (together with the relevant fee) with the registrar of companies. Where there are names that the buyer wishes to acquire, the sale and purchase agreement will normally contain provisions obliging the seller to cease using them — either immediately or after an agreed period.

9.19   Title (cl.18)

It may be worth including a provision to the effect that (unless any reservation of title is intended) title to the assets will pass to the buyer at completion and the seller may wish to include a provision to make it clear that risk in the assets (e.g. the risk of loss of destruction) shall pass to the buyer at that point. It is essential that the buyer takes out appropriate insurance cover in his own name with effect from the point where risk passes.

9.20   Third party assets (cl.21)

Most businesses will use plant, equipment or vehicles which are subject to lease, rental, hire or hire-purchase arrangements and to which the seller will therefore be unable to pass title to the buyer, unless either the seller or the buyer agrees to pay off the finance company. These may range from franking machines, photocopiers and other items which are easily replaced to major items of plant and machinery without which the business will be unable to function. It will be necessary for the parties to establish exactly what there is and then agree whether there are any items which are so important that the sale and purchase agreement should not be entered into until arrangements have been made with the finance company concerned for the transfer of the finance agreements to the buyer or the agreement should be conditional on such arrangements being made. In practice, where there are key items of plant and machinery, the parties may well enter into discussions with the finance company before the agreement is signed so that the buyer knows that he will be able to continue to use the plant and machinery in question after completion but in the case of items which are not regarded as essential to the operation of the business the parties will normally leave this until after completion. If they do decide to complete without having formalised the transfer of the finance agreements to the buyer, the buyer runs the risk that the finance company will repossess the assets in question once it becomes aware that the seller has delivered them into the possession of the buyer (which is likely to be a breach of the finance agreements).

Where the parties do agree to deal with such matters after completion, the sale and purchase agreement will normally oblige both the buyer and the seller to use reasonable endeavours to obtain the consent of the finance company as soon as possible after completion and will normally oblige the buyer to comply with the terms of the finance agreements (paying the rentals and so on) until that consent has been obtained. There is always the danger for the buyer that the finance company will demand a ransom payment as a condition of giving its consent and the buyer may wish to make it clear that its obligations to use reasonable endeavours do not oblige it to make any such payment.

If the seller does allow the buyer to take possessions of any such assets, he will normally expect an indemnity from the buyer against any liability which the seller may suffer as a result of any failure of the buyer to comply with the terms of the finance agreement. Where the seller is a receiver or administrator, he may want to extend that indemnity so that the buyer has to bear any claims which may be brought against the receiver or administrator as a result of his having given possession of the assets in question to the buyer.

9.21 Schedules

An agreement for the sale and purchase of assets will normally contain rather more schedules than an agreement for the sale and purchase of shares as it makes sense, in the interest of certainty, to list in schedules to the agreement assets or liabilities which are to transfer to the buyer, to the extent that this is practical. It may not be practicable to have schedules of stocks and in many businesses it will be impossible have up to date schedules of contracts and orders, but there are likely to be schedules of:

9.21.1 employees;

9.21.2 registered intellectual property rights and applications for them;

9.21.3 plant and machinery and other major items of fixed assets;

9.21.4 third party assets (in particular, assets which are subject to finance agreements).

Chapter 10

Warranties and Indemnities—General Principles

As has already been seen, the principle of caveat emptor will apply to most aspects of the sale and purchase of a business but, in agreeing to make the acquisition and in agreeing the purchase price, the buyer will inevitably have relied upon information provided to him by or on behalf of the seller and on various assumptions. A seller will not generally be liable for the provision of untrue or misleading information or the failure to disclose information which may be material to the buyer unless this constitutes a misrepresentation or breach of a contractual term and, as a consequence of this, on most transactions the buyer will insist upon the sale and purchase agreement containing warranties regarding the business and its assets and liabilities, in order to compensate him if the information or assumptions on which he is relying prove to be incorrect.

Warranties normally take the form of a series of statements of fact (but sometimes including statements of opinion as well) which the seller warrants to be true and which the buyer's solicitors may want to frame as "representations" as well as framing them as "warranties". Where however a specific risk has been identified as one in respect of which the buyer requires protection, it may be more appropriate for it to be covered by an indemnity than by a representation or a warranty—an indemnity being a promise by one party (in this case, the seller) to reimburse another (in this case, the buyer) for any loss which that party suffers as a result of the event or circumstances in question.

10.1 Warranties, representations and indemnities

Warranties, representations and indemnities all provide a way of helping the buyer to recover his loss in particular circumstances but the measure of the damages which may be awarded to the buyer may be different in each case and a claim under an indemnity is likely to be easier to establish than a claim for breach of warranty or misrepresentation.

10.1.1 Warranties

The measure of damages for a breach of warranty will be whatever is required to put the buyer in the position he would have been in had the warranty concerned been true—to compensate the buyer for his loss of bargain. The damages to which the buyer is entitled will normally be the difference between the actual market value of the business and the market value that it would have had if the warranty had been true. For example, if a buyer buys a company for £1 million and the seller warrants that all of the plant used by the company is owned by it but after completion the buyer finds out that a major item of plant was actually on lease and the effect of that is to reduce the value of the company to £950,000, the damages to which the buyer will be entitled for breach of warranty are likely to be £50,000.

This example assumes that the purchase price paid by the buyer represents what would have been the market value of the company if the warranties had been true, but that may not always be the case: the seller may be able to show that the buyer overpaid for the business or the buyer may be able to show that he underpaid and that the market value of the company was higher than the price which he paid. If, therefore, in the example, the seller is able to show that the buyer paid £1,000,000 for a company worth £950,000, the buyer may not be entitled to any damages at all. If, on the other hand, the buyer is able to show that he paid £1,000,000 for a company worth £1,050,000, he is likely to be able to recover damages of £100,000.

It may be more difficult to determine the market value with the warranty breached and this is likely to depend upon the basis on which the parties arrived at the purchase price. Using the example given above, if the purchase price were determined by reference to the net assets of the company and the value of the plant in question is £50,000, then the value of the company with the warranty breached is likely to be £950,000. If, on the other hand, the purchase price had been determined by reference to the company's profits (for example, on a multiple (a price/earnings multiple) of five times the profits for the previous financial year), then, if the plant in question were repossessed by the finance company but its absence did not affect the company's capacity to earn profits, its value may be unaffected. If, however the buyer found that the company had to pay £20,000 per year in leasing payments if it wished to continue to use the plant, the reduction in the company's value may well be five times the amount by which the company's earnings are reduced, i.e. £100,000.

Buyers should note that the case of *Senate Electrical Wholesalers Ltd v Alcatel Submarine Networks (formerly STC Submarine Systems Ltd)* [1999] 2 Lloyd's Rep. 423 suggests that buyers should not assume that the fact that a breach of warranty directly affects the earnings of the business will mean that the courts will assess damages by applying a multiple to the amount by which earnings were reduced. That case involved the sale of the assets of an electrical business by Alcatel to Senate and Senate was awarded damages for breach of a warranty regarding the management accounts of the business, which overstated its profitability. Senate argued that damages should be assessed by applying a price/earnings multiple of 13.67 to the difference between the profit shown by the management accounts and the actual profit. The trial judge rejected this and the decision was upheld by the Court of Appeal, on the basis that it would only be appropriate to apply a price/earnings multiple where the original purchase price had been arrived at in the same way or if valuation experts were to agree that this was the proper basis for assessing damages. The court concluded that, in that particular case, the purchase price was not arrived at by reference to a price/earnings multiple and that, as there was no such agreement between valuation experts, it would be inappropriate to calculate damages in that way.

Where a buyer has used a price/earnings multiple in valuing the company or business which he is buying, he may wish to consider inserting a clause in the sale and purchase agreement to the effect that the parties acknowledge that the purchase price has been calculated on this basis and that any damages for breach of warranty will therefore be calculated by reference to the same multiple. It is unlikely that a court would regard any such clause as conclusive but it is likely to be helpful to the buyer to have an express acknowledgement of the way in which the purchase price has been arrived at, although it is important that any such clause does constitute a reasonable pre-estimate of the buyer's loss so that it will not be rendered unenforceable as being a penalty. Precedents 1, 2, 3 and 4 contain sample clauses to address this point (in Precedents 1 and 2, these are para.11.2 of Sch.6, while in Precedents 3 and 4 the relevant provisions are cl.14.9).

There may be situations where the assets of the company or business are less than they were warranted to be, or its liabilities are greater than they were warranted to be, but where that fact does not materially affect its value. For example, if a company or business is bought by reference to a price/earnings multiple of five, the fact that it has a "one off" undisclosed liability of (say) £25,000 may not actually affect its value. The buyer would, however, expect to be compensated for the additional liability and would normally expect to be compensated for its full amount. As a result, he will normally seek to include in the sale and purchase agreement a clause under which he will be entitled to recover on a "pound for pound" basis the amount by which the assets of the company or business are less than would have been the case were it not for the circumstances giving rise to the breach of warranty or (as the case may be) the amount by which its liabilities are increased as a result of those circumstances. Precedents 1, 2, 3 and 4 contain sample clauses to address this point (in Precedents 1 and 2, the relevant provisions are para.11.1 of Sch.6, while in Precedents 3 and 4 the relevant provisions are cl.14.8). Most sellers will, however, resist the inclusion of such a clause on the basis that it is unreasonable for the buyer to be compensated if he has not suffered any actual loss as a result of the circumstances in question. Whether or not such a clause is ultimately included is likely to depend on the relative bargaining positions of the parties but, even if the seller accepts it in principle, he will need to consider the wording very carefully as (for example) an agreement by the seller to pay to the buyer whatever sum is necessary to put him into the position in which he would have been if the breach of warranty had not taken place may be extremely onerous.

To give a simple illustration, a buyer may have bought a company for £1 million by reference to a price-earnings multiple of five times the profits for the previous financial year and the sale and purchase agreement may have contained a warranty that all of the plant and machinery of the business was in good working order and fully complied with all health and safety and other legal requirements. There may be some plant which has been written down to nil in the books of the company and which is rarely used but which is found to be in need of a major overhaul, involving a cost of £30,000, in order to make it compliant with health and safety requirements.

The business could function perfectly well without the plant and so, if it were scrapped, there would be no impact at all on earnings; the damages to which the buyer would normally be entitled for the breach of the warranty would therefore be nil. The inclusion of such a clause may, however, mean that the seller would be liable to pay £30,000 to the buyer in order to put him into the position in which he would have been if the warranty had been true.

The inclusion of such a clause will also impact upon the buyer's common law duty to mitigate his loss: this generally means that, even if the buyer is able to demonstrate that there has been a breach of warranty and that the market value with the warranty breached is less than it would have been if it had not been breached, he should not assume that he has an automatic right to damages equal to the reduction in value of the company but must take all reasonable steps to minimise the loss that he suffers as a result of the seller's breach of warranty.

Buyers need to be aware of the implications of this common law duty and should bear in mind also that the seller will almost certainly seek to include in the sale and purchase agreement various "seller's protection" provisions to supplement this duty. These are discussed in more detail later in this chapter.

10.1.2 Misrepresentation

A misrepresentation is a false statement of fact which induces the buyer to enter into the transaction and such a statement will be a misrepresentation if it is in fact false.

The measure of damages in the event of a misrepresentation will be the amount required to put the buyer in the same financial position as he would have been in if the misrepresentation had not been made, i.e. the difference between the amount actually paid by the buyer and the actual value of the business.

If, for example, a buyer is induced by a misrepresentation to pay £1 million for a company of which the actual value is £950,000, the buyer should be able to recover £50,000.

That would be the case even if the buyer made a good deal and the value of the company would have been £1.2 million if the representation had been true whereas, if the representation in question had also been included in the sale and purchase agreement as a warranty, the buyer should be entitled to recover £250,000, being the difference between the market value that the company would have had if the warranty had been true and the value of the company with the warranty breached.

It is common to state in a sale and purchase agreement that the warranties will take effect as both representations and warranties but it is arguable that that will not be effective to give a separate claim for misrepresentation, as the misrepresentation, will not have been made before the sale and purchase agreement was entered into.

Although damages are the normal remedy for misrepresentation, rescission may also be available, but will only be ordered if the parties can be returned to the position that they were in before the representation was made. For this reason, rescission may often be impractical if the misrepresentation comes to light after completion, but it may be of greater value where there is a gap between signing the sale and purchase agreement and completing it. The remedy will in any event be unavailable if, after discovering the misrepresentation, the buyer has taken some action to affirm the sale and purchase agreement—for example, if he sells some of the assets that he has bought.

If the buyer wishes to have the right to rescind the agreement, therefore, he should make sure that there is an express right to rescind and such a provision is very often included where there is a gap between signing the agreement and completion (see 10.6 below).

Apart from that particular situation, a seller will seek a provision which excludes the buyer's right of rescission and states that his remedy for any misrepresentation must lie in damages only. Where there is a gap, the seller may have to accept that the buyer will have the right of rescission if any misrepresentations come to light during that period (see 10.6) but will want to limit that right to material misrepresentations and will want to provide expressly that once completion has taken place, the buyer's only remedy will lie in damages.

A seller would also be well-advised to seek to include in the sale and purchase agreement a provision which excludes liability for pre-contractual misrepresentations, as there will inevitably have been discussions and negotiations during the course of the transaction and it is reasonable to require that any representations on which the buyer wishes to rely should be contained in the sale and purchase agreement, with an exclusion of liability in respect of any other representations which may have been made before entering into the agreement. The wording of any such clause, however, needs to be considered carefully, in the light of the decision in *Thomas Witter ER Ltd v TBP Industries Ltd* [1996] 2 All E.R. 573 in which a clause which purported to exclude liability for any pre-contractual misrepresentations whatsoever was rendered ineffective by virtue of the provisions of the Misrepresentation Act 1967 s.3 (as amended by the Unfair Contract Terms Act 1977 s.8) which restricts the ability to contract out of the Misrepresentation Act 1967 unless the requirement of reasonableness is satisfied. In that case the judge held that the exclusion was too wide to satisfy the reasonableness test, as it purported to exclude liability for fraudulent misrepresentation as well as negligent or innocent misrepresentation. Any such clause should not therefore purport to exclude liability in respect of fraudulent misrepresentations.

The buyer's solicitors should make sure that the buyer appreciates the implications of any such clause and the buyer should be made aware of the fact that information provided to him will not be warranted unless it is the subject of a specific warranty in the sale and purchase agreement or is covered by a general warranty as to the accuracy of information provided to the buyer. The buyer should therefore be asked whether there is any particular information on which he is relying and which should be the subject of specific warranty protection.

It should be emphasised that this is only a very brief summary of the law relating to misrepresentation and that a more detailed analysis can be found in the standard contract law text books.

It should also be mentioned that a seller who makes a false representation may be guilty of an offence under s.1(2)(a) of the Fraud Act 2006, if it can be proved that the representation is false (defined as "untrue or misleading"), dishonest and intended to make a gain or cause a loss to another. A conviction for the offence of fraud can be punished by up to 10 years' imprisonment and/or an unlimited fine. In the case of a company, the officers of the company can be prosecuted personally if the representation was made with their "consent or connivance".

The Fraud Act also makes it an offence in certain circumstances to fail to disclose information (see 10.2.6 below).

An analysis of the new statutory offence of fraud is beyond the scope of this book. However, it is of note that it remains possible that advisers to a seller who makes a false representation may themselves be liable as secondary parties to the offence and advisers would be wise to "tread carefully" if they believe that their client intends to make a false representation.

10.1.3 **Indemnities**

If the seller agrees to indemnify the buyer against a particular set of circumstances and those circumstances arise, then (provided that the indemnity is sufficiently widely drawn) the buyer can require the seller to compensate him for all of the loss which he suffers as a result of the circumstances in question. An indemnity may therefore have a number of advantages over a warranty:

10.1.3.1   The general contractual principles of remoteness and foreseeability of loss will not (if it is sufficiently widely drafted) apply to an indemnity and so, under an indemnity, it may be possible to claim in respect of losses which were so difficult to foresee that a court would not allow them to form the subject of a claim for breach of contract.

10.1.3.2   A claim under an indemnity is a claim for a debt rather than for a breach of contract and so the common law rules requiring parties to take reasonable steps to mitigate their loss will not apply.

If, for example, the sale and purchase agreement contains a warranty that the business has no claims in litigation against it and the buyer subsequently discovers that there is an outstanding claim, the buyer would be expected to mitigate his loss by defending the claim (where it is reasonable to do so) or at least endeavouring to negotiate the best possible settlement.

If, on the other hand, the sale and purchase agreement contains an indemnity against any losses which may arise as a result of any claims in litigation, in the absence of wording to the contrary, the seller must bear all losses which the buyer may suffer in connection with any such claim, even if those losses could have been avoided or at least reduced. In practice, therefore, before agreeing to such an indemnity, a seller should insist on provisions which require the buyer to act reasonably and to take all reasonable steps to avoid (or mitigate) any liability before bringing a claim against the seller.

10.1.3.3   An appropriately worded indemnity may enable the buyer to recover all of his legal costs, whether or not they would be awarded by a court—a seller should, of course, seek to limit the ability of the buyer to do so.

10.1.3.4   It will be seen that the seller normally has the right to avoid liability under warranties by making a formal disclosure of circumstances which would otherwise constitute a breach of warranty and this will not normally be the case with indemnities.

Similarly, the issues discussed in 10.2.4 below regarding actual knowledge of the buyer will not be relevant in the case of an indemnity.

Indemnities will normally be included in the sale and purchase agreement in order to cover specific risks which are of particular concern to the buyer and, in particular, issues arising out of the buyer's due diligence. For example, on a sale and purchase of shares, if the buyer is aware of a potential claim in litigation against the target company and is not prepared to bear any resulting liability, he is unlikely to be content to rely upon warranty protection and, if the seller is prepared to bear any liability which might result from the circumstances in question, the appropriate way of dealing with this is through an indemnity.

Other areas where indemnities may be appropriate (depending upon all the circumstances) will include:

- potential claims by directors or secretaries who are resigning from office and/or from their employment on completion (although the better approach would be to insist upon a formal compromise agreement, as discussed in Ch.8);

- on a sale and purchase of shares, any residual liabilities under any leases of premises formerly occupied by the target company;

- on a sale and purchase of shares, any defect or alleged defect in any goods produced or sold by the company, or any services supplied by it, before completion;

- on a sale and purchase of shares, any industrial or other work-related illness or injury suffered by any employee or former employee before completion;

- on a sale and purchase of assets, various employment and related liabilities which may transfer to the buyer under TUPE (as discussed in Ch.21);

- on a sale and purchase of assets, any liabilities of the business which the buyer has not agreed to assume and which should therefore remain with the seller (a similar indemnity being given by the buyer to the seller in respect of liabilities which he (the buyer) has agreed to assume but which, under the doctrine of privity of contract, will, as between the seller and the third party concerned, remain liabilities of the seller);

- on the sale of purchase of shares, any liabilities incurred by the target company as a result of its being part of a group VAT registration which includes other companies which are not included in the transaction.

10.2 Disclosure

10.2.1 Disclosure—general principles

In most transactions, the buyer will require warranties from the seller which the seller knows to be untrue—for example, a buyer will invariably require a warranty that there is no current or threatened litigation and that there are no circumstances known to the seller which are likely to give rise to litigation but in practice there may well be claims in litigation or at least disputes which (if not resolved) are likely to lead to litigation.

Rather than amend the warranties themselves in order to make exceptions for matters known to the seller which would render them untrue, it is almost universal practice in the UK to provide in the sale and purchase agreement that warranties will apply "save as disclosed" in a formal "disclosure letter"—a letter from the seller to the buyer (or, sometimes, from the seller's solicitors to the buyer's solicitors) identifying matters which would otherwise amount to a breach of warranty. The disclosure letter is normally divided into two parts: general disclosures, which apply to all warranties, and specific disclosures, which are by reference to the particular warranties which they qualify (although the seller will normally require the disclosure letter to state that, even where specific disclosures are made by reference to specific warranties, they should nevertheless qualify all other warranties and this is not generally unreasonable as a sale and purchase agreement normally contains warranties of a very general nature as well as warranties of a specific nature). The purpose of the seller in making disclosures will be to avoid any liability under the warranties in respect of the matters which have been disclosed and so the seller will wish to make sure that the disclosure exercise is carried out as thoroughly as possible. This will also be in the interests of the buyer as one of the purposes of the warranties is to "flush out" disclosures from the seller and therefore to obtain from the seller material information which might not otherwise have come to light. The process of putting forward warranties and obtaining disclosures should therefore complement the buyer's due diligence work.

10.2.2   General disclosures

A typical (and reasonably fair) set of general disclosures is contained in the precedent disclosure letters (Precedents 31 and 32 in App.2) and these contain a number of general disclosures. A buyer should, however, approach general disclosures with caution and should not accept them without considering their full implications, particularly in the light of the extent of the due diligence work which the buyer has been, or will be, able to carry out. For example:

10.2.2.1   It is customary for there to be a general disclosure of the most recent accounts of the business but the buyer should (for example) resist general disclosures of matters "provided for" in the accounts as the provision in question may be part of a general provision for bad debts or for creditors or other liabilities or there may be insufficient information in the accounts to enable the buyer to appreciate the full significance of the matter in question.

10.2.2.2   The seller will normally include a general disclosure of information on file at Companies House: as a general principle, the buyer should be expected to make appropriate searches and the seller should therefore be entitled to exclude liability for matters which appear from those searches. The buyer should, however, require such disclosure to extend only to matters on file as at the date on which he last carried out a search (which in practice is likely to be a day or so before completion) and the buyer should also bear in mind that, if the company in question is long-established, there may be so much information on file as to make it impracticable for him to review it all, in which event the buyer should only accept disclosure of information filed within a limited period before completion.

10.2.2.3   The seller will normally seek to include a general disclosure of information apparent from the property deeds or which would be revealed by normal conveyancing searches or physical inspection of the properties and the extent to which deemed disclosure of information available from the deeds or from searches will be acceptable will depend upon the extent of the property warranties to be given. It may also depend upon the extent to which the buyer has actually carried out those searches or has had the opportunity (within the agreed timescale of the deal) to carry them out. For example, if the buyer has sufficient time to carry out the normal conveyancing searches but chooses not to do so, it may be reasonable for the buyer to accept a deemed disclosure of the normal searches (which should ideally be listed in the disclosure letter) but such a deemed disclosure may not be appropriate if the time constraints have not allowed the buyer to carry out the searches which would normally be carried out. If the buyer has carried out those searches and is prepared to accept such a general disclosure, it should be limited to matters which would be revealed by searches carried out on the date on which his searches were actually carried out. If the buyer has not carried out the searches but is nevertheless prepared to accept a general disclosure, it should extend only to matters which would have been revealed if the searches had been carried out on a specific date.

A general disclosure of matters apparent from a physical inspection should be resisted unless the buyer has agreed to obtain and rely upon a detailed survey of the properties—even then, general disclosure might be reasonable as a qualification to warranties regarding the state and condition of the properties but it could be argued that reference to a physical inspection of the properties would be wide enough to cover matters such as boundaries, the presence of asbestos or other hazardous materials, drains and the state and condition of the plant and equipment on the premises and the buyer would be well-advised to allow the general disclosure to extend only to matters which are actually revealed by the surveyor's report.

The buyer should certainly not accept a general disclosure of matters which would be revealed by an inspection of the plant of the business unless he has had the plant inspected by a plant engineer or somebody else suitably qualified (but even then there is always the danger of a fault arising after that inspection has taken place but before completion).

10.2.2.4 The seller will normally require a general disclosure of information contained in the statutory books of the company concerned and the buyer should only accept such disclosure if he has had a reasonable opportunity to review the information contained in the statutory books—not just the register of members but the minute books and the other registers which form part of the statutory books. If the company in question is long-established, the buyer should not generally be expected to review every single set of minutes since the incorporation of the company and should therefore seek to limit the disclosure to meetings taking place during a limited period of time before completion.

10.2.2.5 Where there has been detailed financial or legal due diligence, the seller will wish to exclude from the warranties matters which have been revealed in the course of that exercise or which should have been revealed if the work had been done thoroughly. A seller will often therefore seek to include a very wide general disclosure, to the effect that the buyer and its professional advisers have been given the opportunity to inspect the business of the plant and its books and records and that anything which would be apparent from such inspection is deemed to have been disclosed. On behalf of the seller, it may be argued that there is no point in allowing the buyer the opportunity to carry out detailed due diligence if the seller nevertheless has to accept responsibility under the warranties for matters of which the buyer is fully aware or of which he would have been made aware if his advisers had done their job properly. On behalf of the buyer, on the other hand, it may be argued that the purpose of the due diligence work was not to look for matters which would constitute breach of the warranties (which may not even have been drafted at the time when the due diligence work was done) but to report to the buyer on key issues which may affect his willingness to proceed with the transaction or the price which he is prepared to pay.

Depending upon the relative bargaining strengths of the parties, the buyer may in practice have to accept some general disclosure of matters revealed by due diligence but should make sure that such disclosure is as narrow as possible, perhaps by limiting the general disclosure to the contents of any due diligence reports issued to him.

10.2.2.6   Sellers may try to include a general disclosure of all information which could be obtained by searches of the registers and databases maintained by the UK Patent Office but, where there are registered intellectual property rights which are considered to be important, the buyer should be wary about accepting such a disclosure as there may be information which can be obtained by searching those registers but only after a lot of time and effort. The buyer should certainly resist attempts to extend such a general disclosure to "any information" which may be obtained by searching any similar public register, anywhere in the world.

10.2.2.7   The buyer should not accept a general disclosure of information revealed by "the books and records" of the business as that would include every single customer order, every single supplier order, every single personnel file and so on and there is always the danger that a dishonest seller may make sure that any material documents have been removed or even shredded before the buyer has had the opportunity to look at them. If the buyer has to accept some sort of general disclosure to that effect, he should insist that it refers very specifically to specific information which he has actually seen. The buyer should also bear in mind the implications of the decision in the *Infiniteland* case which is discussed later in this chapter.

10.2.2.8   The first draft of a disclosure letter may well contain a general disclosure of "all information which is in the public domain" and the principal purpose of this is to avoid general warranties (for example, a warranty that there has been no change in the financial position or prospects of the business) being breached as a result of circumstances of general application (such as a general downturn in economic conditions) rather than circumstances which relate specifically to the business in question. Nevertheless, the buyer should not generally accept such a disclosure as (for example) there may be information regarding the sector in which the business operates or about its customers which has been made public but of which the buyer may not necessarily be aware for example, there may have been speculation that a major customer of the business is in financial difficulties but that speculation may have been confined to newspapers which are local to the area where the customer is based.

10.2.2.9   Sellers' solicitors will sometimes attempt to include a general disclosure of all information provided by the seller to the buyer or by any of the sellers' professional advisers to any of the buyer's professional advisers and may not limit this to information provided in writing. If the buyer is prepared in principle to accept such a wide disclosure, he should limit it to information provided in writing and ideally should insist upon copies of the correspondence and documents in question being included in the "disclosure bundle" referred to below. If time constraints or the sheer volume of paperwork make this impractical, the buyer should insist upon the items in question being listed, with that list then being scheduled to the disclosure letter or included in the disclosure bundle. Sellers should normally be prepared to agree to this, as it is likely to be in the interests of the seller, as much as in the interests of the buyer, to have a definitive list of exactly what information is to be covered by the disclosures, in order to avoid arguments at a later date as to whether or not the buyer ever actually received a particular item of correspondence or a particular document. Sellers should also be aware that disclosures of this nature may backfire if the buyer insists upon the seller warranting the accuracy of the disclosure letter—depending upon the precise wording of the warranty, the seller may find himself warranting the accuracy of information provided by his professional advisers which he may never even have seen, let alone reviewed to ensure its accuracy.

10.2.2.10 Sellers' solicitors will often seek to include a general provision in a disclosure letter to the effect that, if a contract or other document is mentioned in the disclosure letter, its full terms are deemed to be disclosed and that, if part of a contract or other document is disclosed, then it is to be deemed to have been disclosed in its entirety. While it is understandable that a seller may not wish to provide a copy of every single order received from every single customer or placed with every single supplier, it is totally unreasonable for the seller to maintain that, by disclosing the existence of a particular document, he should be regarded as having made an effective disclosure to the buyer of terms and conditions which the buyer has not seen and which have not themselves been summarised (or which may have been inaccurately summarised) in the disclosure letter. For example, a seller may disclose that the business has a six-month supply contract with a particular customer but may not in that disclosure mention the fact that, under that contract, he has agreed to give the customer a 20 per cent discount on his usual selling prices. In those circumstances, it is reasonable for the seller to be regarded as having made an effective disclosure against a warranty that there are no long term supply contracts but it would be unreasonable for that same disclosure to qualify a warranty to the effect that no discounts or rebates have been offered to any customers. In the light of the *Infiniteland* decision which is discussed below, a provision such as discussed in this paragraph should only be accepted if it is subject to a proviso to the effect that the information which has actually been provided to the buyer must of itself constitute a fair disclosure and must give sufficient details to enable the buyer to identify the nature and scope of the matter disclosed.

10.2.3   Specific disclosures

The specific disclosures will normally include both disclosures of matters which would (if not disclosed) constitute a breach of the warranties and matters which are required by the express terms of the warranties to be included in the disclosure letter — for example, it is common for the sale and purchase agreement to include a warranty that the disclosure letter contains a list of all customers who in the last financial year accounted for more than a specified proportion of the turnover of the business and a warranty that the copies of the memorandum and articles of association which are attached to the disclosure letter are complete and up-to-date.

It has become more or less standard practice to prepare a "disclosure bundle" which contains copies of all documents which are referred to in the disclosure letter or which are required to be attached to it by the terms of the warranties — for example, copies of the memorandum and articles of association. The seller should prepare two copies of the disclosure letter and of the disclosure bundle — one to be delivered to the buyer and a duplicate to be retained by the seller. Before completion, the parties should compare the bundles in order to ensure that they are identical, and ideally, the documents in the disclosure bundles should be initialled in order to avoid any argument that a document has not been attached or as to which version of a particular document has been attached to the disclosure letter.

In order to assist with this exercise, the seller (or, ideally, his solicitors) should take or retain copies of all documents as and when they are disclosed to the buyer and should prepare an index of the information provided, which will eventually form the index to the disclosure bundle. It is preferable for the seller's solicitors to deal with this, not least in order to enable them to review the information before it is actually handed over to the buyer.

If the seller is considering making a disclosure of circumstances which may give rise to litigation or which are the subject of litigation, he should be aware of the fact that, if he discloses to the buyer a document which is the subject of legal professional privilege, that professional privilege may be lost, with the consequence that the document in question would no longer be privileged from production during legal proceedings, which could prejudice the seller or the target company in those proceedings.

A detailed discussion of the nature and extent of legal professional privilege is beyond the scope of this book.

10.2.4 Effective disclosure, buyer's knowledge and the *Infiniteland* case

In order to strike a fair balance between the respective interests of the buyer and of the seller, the sale and purchase agreement, instead of simply limiting the warranties by reference to matters "disclosed" in the disclosure letter, may provide that the warranties will only be qualified where the matters are "fairly disclosed", "fully and fairly disclosed" or "fully, fairly and accurately disclosed" in the disclosure letter and in the past the courts have taken a fairly relaxed approach to the construction of these different phrases.

For example, in the Scottish case of *Prentice v Scottish Power plc* [1997] 2 B.C.L.C. 264, warranties were given "save as disclosed in the disclosure letter" and the court held that, although the word "fair" did not appear in the relevant clause, any disclosure, to be effective, "would require to be fair" and that "there must be fair disclosure of facts and circumstances material to the bargain sufficient in detail to identify the nature and scope of the matter disclosed and to enable the buyer to form a view. Thus disclosure of a source of information may not be sufficient if this does not adequately draw attention to the matter that is being disclosed".

The question of what constitutes effective "disclosure" has recently been considered by the Court of Appeal in *Infiniteland Ltd v Artisan Contracting Ltd* [2005] EWCA Civ. 758 and that case also considered the question of whether the buyer would be entitled to claim for breach of warranty if he was aware of the breach before entering into the sale and purchase agreement.

In that case, the seller gave a set of warranties qualified "save as disclosed in the Disclosure Letter". The sale and purchase agreement also provided that the buyer's rights in respect of a breach of warranty was not to be affected by any investigation made by it or on its behalf, except to the extent of the buyer's actual knowledge (a "knowledge saving provision"). The disclosure letter made a general disclosure of all papers provided to the investigating accountants and also made a number of specific disclosures.

The warranties given included the standard accounts warranty—that the accounts showed "a true and fair view" of the profit and loss of the company concerned for the period to which they related. However, the profit and loss account did not provide a true and fair view as the cost of sales had been inappropriately recorded by including a credit from the holding company. By understating the cost of sales, profits were inflated. This defect in the accounts was not included in the specific disclosures but was apparent from the papers supplied to the buyer's investigating accountants. The investigating accountants did not report the defect to their client, the buyer. When the defect in the accounts became apparent to the buyer, it sued for breach of the accounts warranty and the seller's defence was based, first, upon the knowledge of the investigating accountants and, secondly, on a carve-out to the knowledge saving provision in the sale and purchase agreement.

The Court of Appeal found for the seller, on the basis that disclosure had been fairly made. The Court of Appeal's reasoning will impact upon transactions although, to an extent, it may have turned upon the particular circumstances and the fact that the court clearly felt sympathy for the seller.

The Court of Appeal's approach in *Infiniteland* was to pay more attention to the wording used in the sale and purchase agreement regarding what is fair disclosure. In that case, the standard of disclosure was only "save as set out in the disclosure letter" and the buyer had accepted general disclosure of all papers provided to the investigating accountants. The Court of Appeal ruled that anything contained in the papers supplied to the investigating accountants was disclosed if it could fairly be expected that the investigating accountants would become aware from the examination of the documents in the ordinary course of their due diligence exercise that the relevant breach would be identified.

As a result of this case, it will now be far more important for a buyer to pay attention to the standard to which disclosure must be made, as a court will not apply an overriding "fairness" qualification. Wording in the sale and purchase agreement along the following lines may now be appropriate:

> "The Warranties are subject to matters fairly disclosed (with sufficient details to identify the nature and scope of the matter disclosed) in the Disclosure Letter."

Ideally, the buyer should refuse to accept general disclosure of papers that may have been supplied in correspondence and/or to investigating accountants. This is particularly important if the more precise wording identified in the preceding paragraph has not been accepted.

Late disclosure or imprecise disclosure may affect a court's view as to whether disclosure is fair, but the reverse of this is that, if the buyer has had plenty of time and used a range of expert advisers, then a court may accept a lower standard of disclosure as being fair.

Sellers can now expect much more detailed provisions regarding what constitutes fair disclosure and they can expect lengthy negotiations, although in the *Infiniteland* case the Court of Appeal accepted that general disclosure could be effective, which is helpful for sellers.

Many sellers will continue to press strongly for some form of warranty or acknowledgement from the buyer that he is not actually aware of a breach of warranty. Not only is this good comfort for sellers, but it also enables sellers to be confident that the buyer is not exchanging contracts in the knowledge that he has a warranty claim.

It is very common for sale and purchase agreements to contain a knowledge saving provision: in *Infiniteland*, the judge at first instance considered the implications of the knowledge saving provision which was contained in that sale and purchase agreement and, although his comments were obiter and do not therefore set a binding precedent, the following points can probably be stated as being applicable to a buyer's knowledge of a breach of warranty prior to a transaction being exchanged:

10.2.4.1   It is implicit in the *Infiniteland* decision that a buyer is not prohibited from suing for breach of warranty, even if he was aware of the breach before entering into the transaction.

10.2.4.2   The sale and purchase agreement can exclude the right of the buyer to sue if the buyer is aware of the breach before entering into the transaction. However, in the absence of such an exclusion, the buyer's damages may be limited as the seller will argue that the buyer has not suffered any loss if he was aware of the breach but nevertheless proceeded with the transaction at the agreed price.

10.2.4.3   A knowledge saving provision is capable of being effective but the wording of the clause must be very carefully considered, as the court may well be reluctant to give it effect if the buyer is trying to sue for a breach of warranty of which he was already aware.

One consequence of this case should be that buyers will seek specific indemnities where there are particular concerns of which they are aware. Buyers' solicitors and other professional advisers should make certain that they notify the buyer of any points arising out of the disclosure exercise which are likely to be material and they would be well-advised to do so in writing—either via a formal due diligence report or at least by way of formal letter. They would also be well-advised to provide the buyer with copies of all disclosed documents which may be material. Sellers' solicitors will hopefully realise that inundating the buyer with last minute disclosures may be counter-productive and may not constitute "disclosure" at all.

Some of the issues which were considered in the *Infiniteland* case were also discussed in *MAN v Freightliner* and that case is discussed later in this chapter.

10.2.5   Buyer's approach to disclosures

The buyer will wish to receive a draft of the disclosure letter at a reasonably early stage in the transaction: clearly, the seller and his solicitors cannot prepare this until they have seen the draft sale and purchase agreement and are able to see the warranties against which they will be required to disclose but, although the precise form and extent of the warranties will inevitably be subject to a fair amount of negotiation, the buyer will want to start receiving disclosures against those warranties which are not the subject of negotiation, in order to "flush out" as soon as possible any information which may affect his decision to proceed or the price which he is prepared to pay.

All disclosures should be channelled through the buyer's solicitors and whoever is given primary responsibility for this part of the transaction should make sure that relevant material is copied to the buyer for review and, where relevant, to the buyer's other professional advisers (accountants, surveyors, pension advisers, tax advisers and so on). Where the buyer's legal team includes specialist lawyers (for example, property, employment, pensions or intellectual property specialists) relevant disclosures should also be passed for review to the lawyers concerned).

The buyer's solicitors would be well advised to have a clear understanding with their client as to who will take responsibility for reviewing disclosures in particular areas: for example, if copies of commercial agreements are received, is the buyer happy to review these himself or does he require his solicitors to review them and report on their terms? If there are any disclosures of tax issues and the buyer's solicitors pass them to the buyer's tax advisers for comment, can they assume that they are not expected to comment further. These issues reinforce the need to set the scope of each of the buyer's professional advisers' due diligence work.

It has been seen that the purpose of the seller in making disclosures will be to transfer to the buyer the commercial risk in respect of the matters disclosed. The seller will therefore be concerned to ensure that any disclosure is effective to do so, while the buyer will only want to accept disclosures which are fairly made, with sufficient detail and clarity to enable the buyer fully to appreciate their implications. A buyer will be particularly concerned not to be swamped with barely comprehensible disclosures or by substantial disclosures made at a very late stage. The seller, on the other hand, will want to make it the responsibility of the buyer to review all disclosures and understand their implications and will want to be able to carry on making disclosures until the last possible moment. To an extent, this is reasonable as the business will continue to operate and employees may join or leave, customers may be won or lost, claims may be threatened and so on.

The buyer may, therefore, have to accept that there may be late (or even last-minute) disclosures as circumstances change. The buyer is, however, entitled to object if the seller attempts to swamp him with last-minute disclosure of matters which ought reasonably to have been disclosed earlier—he may well be concerned (and quite possibly with every justification) that the seller is attempting to sneak through a disclosure of a material issue by disclosing it at such a late stage that the buyer is unlikely to be able properly to consider all of the implications of the disclosure.

Where their negotiating position allows them to do so, buyers may well refuse to accept such disclosures but this may be unwise in the light of the decision in the *Infiniteland* case and because, if there are issues, it is better to grasp them and (if appropriate) negotiate indemnity protection or a price reduction or retention, rather than press on to completion and rely upon the hoped-for ability to bring a claim under the warranties. If, therefore, the seller does attempt to make any eleventh hour disclosures which appear to be material, the buyer would be well advised to delay completion until he has had the opportunity of considering the issues disclosed and how best to address them.

10.2.6 Deliberate non-disclosure

If a seller is aware of a particular problem but chooses not to disclose it to the buyer, this would not of itself amount to a misrepresentation under general law, as there is no general duty to disclose relevant facts. A seller may well therefore be aware of a material problem which, if known to the buyer, would be likely to affect his decision to proceed with the transaction or the price which he was prepared to pay but would not be under a general duty to disclose it to the buyer. If, however, the sale and purchase agreement contains a warranty which is rendered untrue by the issue in question and which the seller is unable to persuade the buyer to delete from the agreement, the seller may be tempted to keep quiet about the problem, proceed with the transaction and take the risk of receiving a warranty claim at a later date.

The seller should, however, be aware that in those circumstances his failure to disclosure may constitute a misrepresentation, which may potentially give the buyer the right to apply to the court to have the transaction rescinded (see 10.1.2 above). In addition, on a sale and purchase of shares, s.397(1) of the FSMA makes it a criminal offence if a person, broadly, conceals information or makes misleading statements in order to induce another party to enter into an investment agreement (which would include an agreement to buy shares). The buyer would have no civil remedy under this section but an action for civil remedies could be brought by the FSA under the FSMA. The seller's professional advisers would run the risk of being ordered to pay compensation to a buyer who suffers loss as a result of a breach of s.397(1) if they were "knowingly concerned" in such breach.

As discussed in 10.1.2, it is also possible that an offence may be committed under the Finance Act 2006.

10.3 Who gives the warranties?

On a sale and purchase of assets, the warranties and any indemnities will normally be given by the selling company (to which the purchase price will be payable) but on a sale and purchase of shares they will be given by the selling shareholders and it is a matter for discussion and negotiation (depending on all the circumstances and on the respective bargaining positions of the parties) whether they are to be given by all of the sellers, those who are major shareholders, those who are active in the management of the business, or by any other combination. Where all of the sellers have material share-holdings and are actively involved in management, it is normally reasonable for them all to be party to the warranties and indemnities but that may not be the case where shares are held by "business angel" or other investors with little or no day-to-day involvement, by trustees or by the personal representatives of a shareholder who has died. A particular concern arises where shares are held by a venture capitalist or other institutional investors as any such investor will almost certainly refuse point blank to give any warranties or indemnities (indeed, most such investors make it a term of their investment that they will not accept any such liability).

The fact that one or more selling shareholders refuse to be party to the warranties or indemnities may be a major commercial issue, as the buyer will almost certainly insist upon receiving an appropriate level of cover and his starting point in negotiations is likely to be that he should have the benefit of warranty protection up to the amount of the total purchase price (see 10.7.2). If (for example) the buyer is paying £10 million to acquire the share capital of a company of which 40 per cent is held by a venture capitalist, the buyer is likely to insist upon warranty cover up to the full £10 million and will argue that it is for the sellers to make sure that it is available.

Difficult negotiations are likely to follow, as those of the sellers who are prepared to be party to the warranties and indemnities will not want to accept a liability of up to £10 million when they are only receiving £6 million between them. They may also consider that, as they are only receiving (between them) 60 per cent of the purchase price, they should only accept 60 per cent of the liability for any claim (in other words, if a claim is received for £1 million, they may argue that their liability for that claim should be limited to £600,000).

The final outcome of those negotiations will inevitably depend upon the relative bargaining positions of the parties and on how keen the sellers are to sell and the buyers are to buy but, in order to get the deal done, the buyer is likely, in the example given, to have to accept that the level of warranty protection will have to reflect the proportion of the shares held by those sellers who are prepared to give the warranties and indemnities and those sellers will have to accept that between them, they will have to bear 100 per cent of any claim, up to a limit to be agreed, albeit one which is less than the total purchase price. Alternatively, it may be possible to use warranty and indemnity insurance cover to provide an outcome which is acceptable to all parties — this is discussed in detail later in this chapter.

The position may be different if (for example) the company is owned by members of a family who have put a significant proportion of their shares into a trust — in that situation, if the trustees are not prepared to be party to the warranties and indemnities, it may well be perfectly reasonable for the remaining shareholders to accept the share of liability which would otherwise have fallen upon the trustees.

In some cases, it may be inappropriate for certain shareholders to be party to the warranties, as they are simply in no position to know whether or not the warranties are true, but they may nevertheless be prepared to share the risk of any claim which may arise. For example, a company may have three directors who hold 20 per cent of the share capital each, with the remaining 40 per cent being held between a number of passive investors. In that situation, the directors may well argue that they should not bear all the risk of any claims which may arise and may therefore be able to agree with the other shareholders that, although the directors will give the warranties, the other shareholders will enter into a separate contribution agreement under which, if any claims actually arise, they will bear their pro rata share of any liability.

As between the sellers and the buyer, those smaller shareholders would have no responsibility to the buyer under the warranties but instead there would be a "back-to-back" arrangement between the sellers under which they would agree to make such payments between them as may be necessary to ensure that the smaller shareholders did actually pick up their appropriate share of the liability.

10.4   Joint and several liability

Where the warranties (or any indemnities) are given by more than one person, the buyer will normally request that they be given on a joint and several basis, which means that the buyer would have the right to recover the full amount of the claim from any one of the sellers concerned, which gives him the maximum possible flexibility.

To give an example: four individuals, each holding 25 per cent of the share capital, may agree to sell a company and may give warranties on a joint and several basis. If a warranty claim arises for (for example) £500,000, the buyer will be able to recover the full amount of that claim (£500,000) from any one of the sellers, leaving him to seek to obtain a contribution from the other sellers. The Civil Liability (Contribution) Act 1978 gives him the right to seek such a contribution and entitles the court to determine a just and equitable basis for apportioning the liability between the sellers, having regard (amongst other things) to the extent of each seller's responsibility for the claim in question, and so the court might, at one extreme, conclude that a particular seller should have no liability at all, while, at the other extreme, it may conclude that he should be liable for the whole amount of the claim. It is more common, however, for the sellers to enter into a contribution agreement under which they agree, as between themselves, to share liability for any warranty claims in specified proportions (typically, in proportion to their respective shareholdings). Any such agreement is, however, a "domestic" matter as between the sellers and does not affect the rights of the buyer. Precedent 30 in App.2 is a reasonably typical form of contribution agreement.

The sellers may be prepared to accept joint and several liability where there is a close connection between them (typically, when they are all members of the same family) but otherwise a seller is likely to be reluctant to accept the risk that he may have to accept the entire liability for a particular claim and then do what he can to obtain contributions from the other sellers—who may by then have spent the sale proceeds or may (for example) have moved off shore where it is difficult to make any recovery from them.

In those circumstances, therefore, the sellers will press for the warranties to be given on a several basis and for each seller only to be liable for an appropriate proportion of any claim which may arise (which will normally be the same as his proportion of the purchase price).

The buyer is then likely to respond that he does not want the inconvenience of having to try to recover the appropriate proportion of any claim from each shareholder and that he should not have to bear the risk of any of the sellers being unable to satisfy his proportion of any claim. In the example given above, where a company is sold by four shareholders each holding 25 per cent of the shares, if the warranties are given on a several basis and with each seller only being responsible for an appropriate proportion of any claim, a claim may arise for £500,000 and the buyer may be able to recover £375,000 from three of the sellers but the fourth may have spent his share of the sale proceeds or taken all of his assets off shore, leaving the buyer with a shortfall of £125,000.

Whether or not liability is to be joint and several or several will be a matter for negotiation and will inevitably depend upon the circumstances of the transaction and the respective bargaining positions of the buyer and the seller. Possible compromises would be to have joint and several liability but with the liability of each seller being limited to the sale proceeds which he actually receives (so that each seller can at least feel comfortable that he will not have the risk of paying out more than he receives) or to have several liability, but with a reasonable proportion of the sale proceeds being held on an escrow account for an agreed period after completion in order to give the buyer comfort that, if a claim does arise, the funds will be available to satisfy it (see 10.9 below). Similarly, if the sellers have to accept joint and several liability, they may be well-advised to have an arrangement between them under which part of the sale proceeds will be held in an escrow account in order to make sure that, even if the buyer recovers damages from only one of them, the funds will be available for the seller concerned to recover appropriate contributions from the other sellers.

The question of who gives the warranties, and on what basis, can be a potential deal-breaker and, where there are likely to be issues, the parties should address them in the heads of terms rather than allow them to become a sticking point at a later stage. From the point of view of the buyer, this may give the opportunity of negotiating a lower purchase price in return for accepting that warranties need only be given severally.

10.5   Extent of the warranties

10.5.1   The matters to be covered by warranties will vary considerably depending on whether the buyer is buying shares or assets, the nature of the business in question, the identities of the parties and the projected timescale for completion of the transaction. As explained in Ch.1, there will normally be less extensive warranties on a sale and purchase of assets than on a sale and purchase of shares but some businesses will inevitably be regarded as more "risky" than others and so are likely to involve more extensive warranties than might otherwise have been the case. Circumstances where the identities of the parties may affect the extent of the warranties will include:

10.5.1.1   As has already been seen, venture capitalists will rarely give any warranties and, on a sale and purchase of shares of which the majority are held by a venture capitalist, the buyer may have to accept that the other shareholders (normally management) may not be prepared to give "full" warranties (although in that situation the buyer will usually expect to receive the normal warranty protection, on the basis that liability under the warranties will be limited to the proportion of the purchase price which is payable to the smaller shareholders). There are likely to be similar issues where the majority of the shares are held by a shareholder with no active part in the management of the business (such as the widow of a former director of the company or the personal representatives of a shareholder who has died). The seller and his advisers will normally maintain in those situations that the buyer should rely to a large extent on his due diligence and that the warranties will be very limited but whether or not the buyer accepts that is a matter for negotiation—ultimately, the buyer may be prepared to accept more limited warranty protection if the risks of doing so are reflected in the purchase price.

10.5.1.2 Where the buyer is a large and experienced acquirer, he may be more prepared to "take a view" on what is material and therefore on what needs to be covered by warranties than (for example) a smaller and more highly leveraged buyer.

10.5.1.3 Receivers, administrators or liquidators are most unlikely to agree to give any warranties or indemnities. As has already been seen, such transactions are almost invariably structured as sales and purchases of assets and this will, to a large extent, allow the buyer to leave behind all creditors and historic and contingent liabilities of the business but other risks (for example, the risk that the seller may not have good title to all of the assets) should be reflected in the purchase price which the buyer is prepared to pay.

10.5.1.4 The method of sale may also affect the extent of the warranties that are to be given: as discussed in Ch.1, where a business is likely to be attractive to potential buyers, the seller will often arrange for it to be sold by auction, in the hope that this will stimulate competition between potential buyers and result in a higher price than might otherwise have been achieved. The auction process will normally involve the seller providing all potential buyers with identical draft transactional documentation and requiring them to submit, with their final bids, the amendments which they would be seeking to the draft contractual documentation. This will almost certainly be drafted with the seller's interests in mind and will therefore include less warranty protection than a buyer would normally expect. Most buyers will be reluctant to risk losing a deal by being seen to be "going overboard" by requiring a significant amount of additional warranty protection and so a sale by auction may enable the seller to get away with less warranties than might otherwise have been the case.

An astute buyer will, of course, try to counter this by waiting until he has achieved preferred bidder stage and then, when the more detailed negotiation of the sale and purchase agreement begins, pressing for additional warranty protection. If the purchase price is being financed with external funding, the buyer should make it clear that his initial response to the draft sale and purchase agreement is subject to the requirements of his funders and then, in due course, try to negotiate additional warranties from the seller on the basis that he will not be able to obtain funding for the transaction otherwise.

10.5.1.5 On a management buy-out where the business is being bought by a management team which is already familiar with it, the seller's starting point will normally be that the warranty protection should be limited to matters outside the knowledge of the management team—in particular, when buying out of a group of companies, arrangements which are normally handled at group level rather than operating company level, such as tax, pensions and insurances. The management team may well regard that approach as perfectly reasonably but most management buyouts are funded with the benefit of external finance and the financiers will almost certainly require additional warranty (and possibly indemnity) protection in order to help to protect the value of their investment.

10.5.2 Once a deal has been agreed in principle, it is very tempting for the buyer and his solicitors to "press the button" and send out to the seller and his solicitors their standard form share sale and purchase agreement or (as the case may be) assets sale and purchase agreement but they should take time to consider a number of questions before doing so as the answers to some of those questions may materially impact on the form of agreement that is actually sent to the sellers:

10.5.2.1 What are the key factors which have influenced the buyer's decision to make the acquisition? For example, is it the customer base of the business? Its intellectual property rights? Its property assets? The buyer and his solicitors should not just rely on standard wording but should make sure that those matters are the subject of appropriate warranty protection.

10.5.2.2 How is the purchase price arrived at? By reference to net assets or a multiple of profits or on some other basis? If by reference to net assets, the buyer is likely to insist upon a warranty that net assets at completion will not be less than a specified amount (unless this is to be established through completion accounts, with a corresponding price adjustment) and, if the price has been arrived at by reference to profits, the buyer is likely to require warranty protection in respect of matters which are particularly likely to impact on profitability.

10.5.2.3 Does the nature of the business mean that there are particular areas which would normally be covered by warranties but, in the particular case, will be irrelevant? It is always annoying for sellers and their advisers to receive a draft agreement which (for example) contains pages of warranties in respect of patents, trade marks and other intellectual property rights where the business is a haulage operation which is most unlikely to have any. Similarly, it is frustrating to receive warranties regarding customers and their likely loyalty when the business comprises a chain of retail outlets. It is better to exclude irrelevant warranties like that before the agreement is sent to the seller rather than risk damaging relations between the parties by submitting an agreement which has clearly been drafted without any real thought for what is relevant.

10.5.2.4   How good is the relationship between the parties and their respective advisers? It is normal for buyer's solicitors to prepare a first draft which contains very extensive warranties in the full knowledge that some of those warranties will be deleted in the course of negotiations but, where the relationship is a good one, it makes sense for the parties and their solicitors to agree that the buyer's solicitors will produce a reasonably even-handed draft, in order to reduce the amount of time that is likely to be spent in negotiation.

10.5.2.5   How sophisticated are the seller and his advisers? Will they be familiar with the sort of warranties that are normally expected? Is there a danger of the seller walking away from the deal because he is unhappy with what he is being asked to sign?

10.5.3   Precedents 1 and 2 are sale and purchase agreements for use in connection with a sale and purchase of shares and Precedents 3 and 4 are agreements for use in connection with a sale and purchase of assets. These contain examples of the warranties which would normally be requested on such a transaction. Precedent 26 is a set of "short form" (non-tax) warranties which could form the basis of a set of warranties to be used in share sales and purchases where it is agreed that a reasonably basic level of warranty protection will be given.

Precedent 27 is a similar set of warranties for use in connection with assets sales and purchases.

In each case, the draft assumes that the buyer will be relying on due diligence in respect of matters such as competition law, IT and property and that the aim of the warranties will be to back up that due diligence work, rather than flush out disclosures from the seller.

The warranties that may be regarded as essential will inevitably vary from business to business and transaction to transaction and so these precedents should not be used without careful consideration with the buyer and his other professional advisers.

This book does not purport to contain a detailed analysis of them all but it should be noted that the matters which are normally covered by warranties are predominantly those which would also form the subject of due diligence, as discussed in Chs 6 and 7, including:

10.5.3.1 *Capacity and title*

Any buyer will insist on warranties that the seller has the necessary power to enter into the transaction and that he owns the shares or assets in question free from all encumbrances. These warranties are so fundamental that the buyer will not normally allow them to be qualified by any provisions regarding maximum or minimum levels of liability (see later in this chapter) and the buyer may wish to consider whether to allow the seller to disclose against these warranties—for example, on a share sale and purchase, a general disclosure of the statutory books of the target company may be an unreasonable disclosure against these warranties where the company is long-established and there have been numerous transfers and allotments of shares.

10.5.3.2 *Corporate structure*

On a sale and purchase of shares, the buyer will expect the seller to warrant a schedule of particulars about the target company (its registered number, registered office, directors, secretary, authorised and issued share capitals and so on) and will also expect the seller to provide him with copies of the memorandum and articles of association of the company and to warrant them as correct. The buyer will also require the seller to warrant (on a sale and purchase of shares) that the target company's statutory books and accounting records have been properly maintained and are up-to-date and that all documents that should have been filed with the Registrar of Companies have been filed.

10.5.3.3 *Insurances*

The buyer will normally require the seller to warrant that the business has maintained adequate insurance cover against all normal risks, that the premiums have been paid and that the policies are in force. The seller may prefer to provide the buyer with details of those insurances and warrant them to be correct but then to leave it up to the buyer to decide whether or not they are adequate. This may be less of an issue on a sale and purchase of assets than on a sale and purchase of shares as, on a sale and purchase of assets, most risks which would normally be covered by insurance (for example, product liability claims or public liability) would normally remain with the seller but that is not necessarily the case with employer's liability claims and, in any event, the buyer will be keen to have details of the insurance cover that has been thought appropriate in the past and the claims history in order to enable him to decide what cover to put in place for the future.

Whether the transaction proceeds as a sale and purchase of shares or of assets, the buyer is likely to require a warranty that there are no current or pending insurance claims and that the seller has not done anything which might invalidate any of the insurance cover.

10.5.3.4 *Legal compliance*

The buyer will require warranties that the seller has complied with all licences, permits or other regulatory approvals which are applicable to the business and with all other legal and regulatory requirements and this issue is discussed in more detail in Ch.7. The seller will normally argue that he can only warrant that this is the case to the best of his knowledge and in most transactions a debate then follows as to whether that is reasonable or whether the seller should accept responsibility for any non-compliance, even if he was unaware of it at the time, on the basis that he is in a much better position than the buyer to assess whether or not there has been any non-compliance. Whether or not the buyer accepts that the warranties may be qualified in this way will normally depend upon the respective bargaining positions of the parties and on the nature of the business in question—for example, whether or not it is one which is heavily regulated and whether failure to comply with legal or regulatory requirements may have significant consequences.

Sale and purchase agreements normally contain some general warranties regarding legal compliance and then a whole host of warranties regarding compliance with specific statutory requirements— environmental legislation, competition laws, the Data Protection Acts, health and safety legislation and so on. If the seller is able to negotiate the deletion of some of these specific warranties, he should be aware of the implications of the more general warranties—for example, there is no point in devoting a lot of time and energy to negotiating the deletion of all environmental warranties if the agreement still contains a general warranty regarding compliance with all applicable laws and regulations, as that would almost certainly cover environmental matters. In those circumstances, the seller should make sure that the agreement contains specific wording to the effect that none of the warranties extend to environmental laws or regulations.

Environmental warranties and other environmental issues are discussed in more detail in Ch.20.

10.5.3.5 *Financial position*

A buyer will almost certainly insist upon a general warranty that the most recent audited accounts have been prepared in accordance with all applicable laws and regulations and generally accepted accounting practices, on a consistent basis with previous years and so as to "show a true and fair view". The buyer may also require more detailed warranties regarding provisions in the accounts, stock valuation and so on and whether or not these are acceptable will normally depend upon the particular circumstances. The seller should not normally agree to a warranty to the effect that the accounts make full provision for all liabilities, as that would extend to contingent liabilities for which it is not necessarily appropriate to make full provision.

The buyer will almost certainly expect the seller to give warranties regarding the conduct of the business in the period between the date of the last audited accounts and completion and it is normally reasonable for a seller to warrant that he has carried on the business in the same way as previously. It may also be reasonable for the seller to warrant that in that period the target company or business has not entered into any transaction outside the ordinary course of business or any capital commitments, that there have been no unusual discounts offered to customers and that creditors have been paid in the ordinary course of business: all of these are factual warranties and the seller should be in a position to know whether or not they are true. The seller should, however, be wary of giving any forward-looking warranties regarding the business's financial position or prospects.

The buyer may require a warranty regarding the accuracy of the most recent management accounts but the seller should ensure that the wording of the warranty reflects the fact that management accounts are unlikely to have been prepared to the same standard as audited accounts.

10.5.3.6   *Finance*

On a sale and purchase of shares (but not normally on a sale and purchase of assets) the buyer will expect the seller to warrant that he has disclosed to the buyer details of all overdraft, loan and other facilities available to the target company, of all mortgages, charges, debentures or other security created by the target company over its assets and of all guarantees or similar arrangements given by or in respect of the target company. This is likely to be the case even where the target is being acquired on a "debt-free" basis as the buyer will need to be certain that all existing facilities are being repaid and that all security given by the target company is being released.

On a sale and purchase of assets, the buyer will normally only require a warranty that there are no mortgages, charges or other security over the assets which he is buying but, in some instances, it may be appropriate to obtain a warranty that there are no outstanding performance or other bonds given in respect of the business (as it will be important to the buyer to establish whether any such arrangements exist, so that he can make arrangements for them to be continued or replaced).

10.5.3.7 *The assets of the business*

On a sale and purchase of shares, the buyer will insist upon a warranty that the target company owns all of the assets which it uses in its business and that none of them are on lease, contract hire, rental, hire-purchase or similar financing arrangements.

One area which may be particularly emotive on a sale and purchase of shares or (where debtors are included in the sale) of assets is that a buyer will normally request the seller to warrant the collectability of the debtors of the business. The seller will normally be reluctant to accept a warranty which is more onerous than a warranty that he knows of no reason to believe that any of the debtors will not be recovered within a specified period, on the basis that after completion the collection of debtors will largely be in the hands of the buyer and the seller cannot guarantee that customers will not run into financial difficulties in the future. Depending, of course, on how the purchase price was arrived at, the buyer may argue in response that if a debt is bad, even if the seller had no reason for expecting that to be the case, he has overpaid for the business and should be compensated accordingly. If the seller does agree to give such a warranty, it should not apply to the extent of any provision or reserve made in the last audited accounts or in any completion accounts, the seller should require the buyer to take all reasonable commercial steps to obtain payment and should consider obliging the buyer to assign the debt to the seller at (normally) face value, so that the seller can then at least take his own steps to try to obtain payment if he has had to pay damages for breach of a warranty as a result of its not being paid.

Another difficult area can be the extent to which the seller is to warrant the state and condition of the tangible assets of the business and this again may be an issue on a sale and purchase of shares or of assets. The buyer may request a warranty to the effect that the plant, machinery and equipment of the business is in a good state of repair and condition and in good working order, while the seller may be reluctant to give such a warranty, on the basis that he will not want to be liable for breach of warranty if an item of plant breaks down unexpectedly shortly after completion. The seller will normally therefore be reluctant to warrant anything more than that the plant, machinery and equipment has been regularly maintained and is in reasonable working order, having regard to its age and normal wear and tear. Whether or not that is likely to be acceptable to the buyer will depend (amongst other things) on the extent to which the business is dependent upon its plant, machinery and equipment—this is likely to be less of an issue in the case of an information technology business, for example, than a manufacturing business. If there are major items of plant and machinery which are absolutely key to the operation of the business, the buyer would be well-advised to have them inspected by a plant engineer as part of the due diligence process. In the case of a haulage business or any other business involving a number of motor vehicles, they should be inspected as near to completion as possible by somebody who is appropriately qualified, in order to ensure their roadworthiness and to ensure that they have been properly maintained and are in an acceptable state of repair and condition.

Most businesses are dependant to a greater or lesser extent upon information technology ("IT") and the buyer is therefore likely to require warranties to the effect that all hardware has been properly maintained and supported and (amongst other things) that the business has all necessary software licences. It is reasonable for the seller to give warranties which are purely factual but sellers should be wary of giving warranties regarding the capacity or capability of the IT systems or warranties which could be breached if there was a "crash" after completion. Most buyers' solicitors have now got out of the habit of including warranties regarding millennium compliance but nevertheless buyers may press for warranties regarding the IT systems' ability to handle date information. Sellers should be wary of giving an absolute warranty to that effect.

10.5.3.8 *Intellectual property*

Where the business is one which is likely to have patents, service marks, trade marks, copyright, designs, know how or other intellectual property rights, then the buyer will require warranties regarding the ownership and use of such rights.

Areas where the buyer will normally seek warranty protection and where the seller will normally be reluctant to give it (other than in respect of matters known to him) will include whether or not the business is infringing the intellectual property rights of a third party and whether or not a third party is infringing the intellectual property rights of the business.

The issues which are likely to be of particular concern to a buyer are discussed at 7.8 in Ch.7.

10.5.4 **Contracts**

Chapter 7 summarises the issues which are likely to be of particular concern to a buyer in respect of the contractual commitments of the business (see 7.9) and the buyer will expect these issues to be covered by appropriate warranty protection, save that more limited protection may be appropriate on a sale and purchase of assets where the buyer is only taking over a limited number (or a limited type) of contracts. These are generally warranties of a factual nature which the seller ought to be able to give, provided that appropriate disclosure is made, but the seller should beware of very general or subjective warranties, such as a warranty that there are no contracts of an "unusual" or "onerous" nature.

Depending on the nature of the business, the buyer may require warranties which require the seller to disclose the major customers and suppliers of the business—typically, those who accounted for an agreed percentage of the sales by, or supplies to, the business in the last financial year. Any such warranty is of a factual nature and, provided that the information is available, should be capable of being given, but the seller should beware of any forward-looking warranties in respect of customers and suppliers, such as a warranty that no customers or suppliers have been or are likely to be lost.

10.5.5 **Employees**

Chapter 7 summarises the issues relating to the employees of the business which are likely to be of concern to a buyer (see 7.10) and these are the areas which are likely to be the subject of warranties. The implications of TUPE mean that the level of warranty protection is unlikely to be materially different whether the transaction proceeds as a sale and purchase of assets or of shares.

10.5.6 **Pensions**

The extent and wording of the pension warranties will vary according to whether the transaction is a sale and purchase of assets or of shares and according to whether the target company or business has its own self-contained money purchase scheme or a final salary scheme. These issues are discussed in Ch.22.

10.5.7 **Freehold, leasehold and other property**

The extent of the property warranties which are appropriate will depend in part upon the significance of the property interests in question and in part on whether the buyer's solicitors are investigating title or relying upon a certificate of title from the seller's solicitors. Typical property warranties include warranties as to title, disputes, compliance with planning and other regulations, compliance with obligations under all property leases, the state of repair and condition of the premises and there being no residual liabilities under leases of premises formerly occupied by the target company. Property issues are discussed in detail in Ch.19.

10.5.8 Tax

On a share sale and purchase, there will almost invariably be extensive tax warranties, even where there is a separate tax covenant or indemnity (see Ch.11). The principal purpose of including detailed tax warranties is to flush out as much disclosure as possible from the seller, so that the buyer can feel reasonably confident that he is acquiring the company with sufficient knowledge of its tax position and, in particular, so that the buyer will be aware in advance of any potential tax issues.

The tax warranties which would normally be expected are discussed in Ch.11.

On a sale and purchase of assets, the tax warranties tend to be far more limited as, if the seller is a company, the buyer will not be taking over the seller's ongoing corporation tax liabilities and the position is similar where the seller is an individual or a partnership. Buyers may nevertheless look for warranties in respect of issues such as capital allowances, PAYE, national insurance contributions and VAT, as these may affect the business going forward.

10.5.9 Material disclosure

The first draft of the sale and purchase agreement will normally include a very general warranty to the effect that the seller is not aware of anything which might reasonably affect the willingness of the buyer to buy the shares or assets (as the case may be) at the price and on the other terms specified in the sale and purchase agreement. The seller's response should be that, if the buyer is requiring a whole host of specific warranties on a whole range of subjects then, if there are any other issues about which he may be concerned, he should seek additional and specific warranty protection in respect of them, rather than try to rely on a "catch all" which is generally too widely drafted to be acceptable—not least, because it is almost impossible to disclose against any such warranty. Such a warranty may perhaps be considered where the time available does not permit the buyer to carry out the normal due diligence work or does not allow detailed warranty protection to be negotiated but otherwise a seller will normally be reluctant to accept anything more onerous than a warranty that he has not deliberately withheld any material information which is within his actual knowledge.

A more difficult question is whether or not the contents of the disclosure letter should be warranted and the seller will normally seek to resist this, on the basis that, if there is an error or inaccuracy in the disclosure letter, its effect is likely to be that the disclosure in question will be ineffective to qualify the warranty or warranties to which it relates. The buyer is likely to respond that his solicitors are issuing any legal due diligence report to him on the basis not just of the replies to their legal due diligence enquiries, but also on the basis of the information contained in the disclosure letter and that he should therefore have a right of action if that information is untrue or inaccurate, without having to be able to show that the error in the disclosure letter means that one or more warranties is or are breached.

If the seller has to accept such a warranty, he should ensure that it only extends to factual information and not statements of opinion and (in most cases) that it does not extend to reports provided by third parties, such as the seller's professional advisers. Otherwise, for example, if the disclosure letter refers to a report by environmental consultants and the seller warrants the accuracy of the disclosure letter, the seller may find himself effectively warranting the contents of that report and so giving an extensive environmental warranty "by the back door".

Similar issues arise if the seller is asked to warrant all information provided to the buyer — any such warranty should be limited to written information and, ideally, all information which is warranted should be specifically listed.

10.6   Warranties—date from which they speak

10.6.1   The signature and exchange of a formal sale and purchase agreement will often be followed immediately by completion but this is not always possible and, as a result, there may be a lapse of time between entering into the agreement and completion of the transaction. This will often be because the transaction has to be subject to one or more conditions precedent but there may be other reasons why the parties agree to give each other the certainty of a signed sale and purchase agreement but on the basis that completion will not take place until a later date. A typical example is on a sale and purchase of assets where it is necessary for the employee consultations required by TUPE (see Ch.21) to take place. The seller will not want to announce the transaction to his employees without a signed agreement, which may well be conditional only upon those consultations taking place. It will be necessary for there to be a gap between signing the agreement and completion which is long enough for those consultations to take place. In those circumstances, the business will usually continue to be run by the seller and the buyer will therefore expect provisions in the sale and purchase agreement governing the way in which the business will be carried on and (on a sale and purchase of shares) the way in which the affairs of the target company will be conducted during that gap. These provisions will normally be to the effect that nothing will be done outside the ordinary course of business and there will normally be a list of things that the seller will agree not to do (these are discussed further at 8.4 in Ch.8 and typical wording is contained in Sch.7 to Precedents 1 and 2 and in Sch.10 to Precedents 3 and 4).

In addition, however, the buyer will want the representations and warranties to apply both at the point at which the agreement is signed and also at completion and perhaps even at every moment throughout the period between the entering into of the agreement and completion, as he will want to protect himself, as far as possible, against any material issues which may arise during that period when, of course, the business will generally be run by the seller and with the buyer having little or no "say" in the way in which it is being run.

The seller will wish to resist this as far as possible as he is likely to argue that, once the sale and purchase agreement has been signed, the business should be carried on at the buyer's risk but in practice the seller is likely to have to accept that, to a greater or lesser extent, the application of the warranties will extend until completion—either by their being repeated as at completion or by the seller agreeing not to do anything or to permit anything to be done which would have constituted a breach of the warranties if they had been so repeated.

The extent to which that is the case is likely, however, to depend upon all the circumstances, including the reasons for there having to be a gap between signing the agreement and completing it.

10.6.2   If the gap is a requirement of the buyer (for example, in order to enable him to finalise his funding arrangements or because the consent of the buyer's shareholders is required) the seller is likely to argue that he (the seller) would have been ready, willing and able to complete the transaction at the point when the agreement was signed and that, as the delay in completion was a requirement of the buyer alone, the buyer should accept the risk of anything untoward which may arise during that period. For example, if Seller Limited (Seller) is selling the entire issued share capital of Target Limited (Target) to Buyer PLC (Buyer) and the sale and purchase agreement has to be conditional on the approval of Buyer's shareholders, Seller's starting point is likely to be that the warranties should only "speak" as at the date of the agreement and should not be repeated down to completion. Seller is nevertheless likely to accept the usual obligations regarding the carrying on of the business down to completion and may also have to accept a general obligation not to do anything or permit anything to be done (or, in the case of a sale and purchase of shares, to procure that the target company does not do anything or permit anything to be done) which would have constituted a breach of the warranties if they had been repeated down to completion. Buyer will doubtless press for the warranties to be repeated down to completion—particularly if Buyer is a company whose shares are publicly traded and Buyer is proposing to finance the acquisition, in whole or in part, by a rights issue, an open offer to shareholders or any other issue of new shares.

10.6.3   If the gap between signing the agreement and completion is as a result of a requirement of Seller, it may be more difficult for Seller to argue against the general principle that the warranties will have to speak from completion as well as from the point when the agreement is signed.

10.6.4   If it is agreed that the warranties will be repeated down to completion, Seller should consider each warranty carefully, in order to decide whether or not it is acceptable for it to be repeated as at completion. In practice, most of the warranties should be capable of being repeated as they are matters of fact and, as it will be Seller who will be carrying on the business, it will be in a position to ensure that there is no breach. Nevertheless Seller is likely to be concerned about being asked to repeat warranties which may be breached as a result of matters arising before completion and which are outside its control.

For example, Seller will be able to ensure that there are no amendments to the memorandum and articles of association of Target, that the existing insurance cover is maintained, that no further mortgages, charges or other security are created, that there are no acquisitions or disposals of assets outside the ordinary course of business and that no contractual commitments are entered into outside the ordinary course of business. Seller is likely to be more concerned however where there are warranties which it knows to be true as at the date when the sale and purchase agreement is signed but which may subsequently be rendered untrue by something unexpected arising before completion — for example, Seller may be able to warrant when the agreement is signed that there are no circumstances known to it which are likely to give rise to a claim in litigation but may, between then and completion, receive a threat of litigation in respect of something of which it was totally unaware (and such threat may be totally spurious). Similarly, Seller may feel able to warrant when the agreement is signed that it is not aware of any breaches of any statutory or regulatory requirements but, between then and completion, Target may receive a notice alleging (for example) a breach of health and safety or environmental regulations.

Of even more concern still will be forward-looking warranties regarding the business's financial position and prospects, warranties regarding customer loyalty and warranties regarding the collectability of book debts, all of which may be rendered untrue before completion by circumstances outside Seller's control and not of Seller's or the business's making. For example, Seller may be prepared to warrant, when the agreement is signed, that it is not aware of any reason to indicate that any major customer of the business will be lost but what if, before completion, Target is informed that a major customer has gone into receivership or administration or has simply decided to take its business elsewhere?

Seller is likely therefore to argue that those warranties should speak only from the point when the agreement is signed and should not be repeated down to completion, while Buyer will doubtless argue that, if any such matter arises while the business is under Seller's ownership and control, then it should be the responsibility of Seller and that Buyer should be compensated if as a result it winds up overpaying for the business.

10.6.5   Where there is a gap between exchange and completion and the issue of repetition of warranties arises (as it almost certainly will), various related issues are also likely to arise, including:

- Whether, during the period before completion, the seller should be entitled to make further disclosures against the warranties by reference to a supplemental disclosure letter.

- Whether any right to make further disclosures should extend to circumstances as at the date when the agreement was signed or whether the seller should only be entitled to disclose circumstances arising between the signing of the agreement and completion — for example, if the seller is prepared to warrant that he is not aware of any circumstances which are likely to give rise to a claim in litigation, it may be reasonable for him to be allowed to make an appropriate disclosure if he becomes aware of a potential claim between the signing of the agreement and completion but it may be less reasonable to allow him to disclose a potential claim of which he was aware when the agreement was signed but which (for whatever reason) he failed to disclose at that time.

- Whether the seller should be obliged to notify to the buyer any circumstances arising between the signing of the agreement and completion which would render any of the warranties untrue.

- The remedies available to the buyer if a breach of warranty comes to light before completion — the buyer's starting point is likely to be that in those circumstances he will want the right either to complete the transaction and then bring a claim for damages or to rescind the agreement and recover his abortive costs and any other damages to which he may be entitled. However, that is unlikely to be acceptable to the seller.

- The extent to which the seller's liability in respect of breaches of warranty arising during the gap between signing the agreement and completion should be subject to an agreed materiality level.

- The way in which these provisions relate to the usual provisions governing the conduct of the business during the period between signing the agreement and completion.

- Whether or not there should also be a "material adverse change" clause (see 10.6.6 below).

As ever, what is agreed in each case is likely to depend upon the particular circumstances, including the relative bargaining strengths of the parties and whether the need for the gap between exchange and completion is a requirement of the seller or of the buyer. Even the question of whether the gap is a requirement of the seller or of the buyer is not always straightforward — for example, the consultations required by TUPE are simply a consequence of structuring the transaction as a sale and purchase of assets and it is in the interests of both parties that the required consultations take place.

In appropriate cases, the following may be a reasonable compromise:

- The warranties to be given as at the point when the sale and purchase agreement is signed and to be deemed to be repeated immediately prior to completion, save to the extent that the seller is able to persuade the buyer to agree that certain warranties should not be repeated in this way.

- The seller to be entitled to make further disclosures against the warranties during the period before completion by way of a supplemental disclosure letter.

- That right, however, only to extend to circumstances arising between the signing of the sale and purchase agreement and completion and not to circumstances existing as at the date when the agreement was signed.

- The seller, in any event to be obliged to notify the buyer in writing of any circumstances coming to light before completion which would render any of the warranties untrue.

- If, before completion, the buyer becomes aware of a material breach of any of the warranties as at the date when the agreement was signed, he will be entitled either to complete the transaction and claim damages or to rescind the agreement and recover his costs and any other damages to which he may be entitled.

- If the seller discloses in a supplemental disclosure letter any circumstances which would otherwise have constituted a material breach of the warranties as repeated at completion (but which do not constitute breaches of warranty as at the date when the agreement was signed), the buyer to be entitled either to complete the transaction (in which event he would not be entitled either to bring a claim for damages in respect of the circumstances so disclosed, (assuming of course, that the disclosure complied with any requirements of the agreement as to fairness, etc.) or to rescind (but without any right to damages).

- The seller to agree that, between signing the agreement and completion, the business will be carried on in the normal way and to enter into reasonable restrictions governing the carrying on of the business (and, in the case of a sale and purchase of shares, the conduct of the affairs of the target company) between signing the agreement and completion.

- Questions of materiality to be determined by reference to any minimum threshold for claims in the sale and purchase agreement (see 10.7.3), so that if, for example, no claims can be brought unless the total amount claimed is £50,000 or more, a breach would not be regarded as material unless the amount capable of being claimed in respect of it may reasonably be regarded as likely to exceed £50,000.

- Where the gap is a requirement of the buyer and the seller is able to persuade the buyer to agree that the warranties need not be repeated at completion, the parties may agree something along the following lines:

  - The warranties to speak only as at the date on which the sale and purchase agreement is signed.

  - No right for the seller to make further disclosures if any circumstances come to light before completion which constitute a breach of warranty as at the date when the agreement was signed.

  - The seller nevertheless to be obliged to notify the buyer of any such circumstances.

- If the buyer does become aware of any such circumstances, he will be entitled either to proceed to completion and then bring a claim for damages or to rescind the agreement and recover his costs and any other damages to which he may be entitled.

- The seller to agree that, during the gap before completion, he will not (or, in the case of a sale and purchase of shares, will procure that the target company will not) actively do anything or permit anything to be done which would have constituted a breach of the warranties if they had been repeated at completion.

- The seller to agree that, between signing the agreement and completion, the business will be carried on in the normal way and to enter into reasonable restrictions governing the way in which it is carried on in that period (and, on a sale and purchase of shares, governing the conduct of the affairs of the target company during that period).

- If the seller commits a material breach (determined by reference to any minimum threshold for claims) of those restrictions, the buyer to be entitled either to complete the transaction and claim damages for breach of contract or to rescind the agreement and recover his costs and any other damages.

10.6.6 Material adverse change clauses

An issue which is closely allied to the question of whether or not the warranties should be repeated down to completion is whether or not where there is a gap between entering into the sale and purchase agreement and completion, there should be a "material adverse change" ("MAC") clause. Such a clause would give the buyer the right to walk away from the transaction if, before completion, there is a material adverse change in the business in question or its financial position, profits or prospects. In a takeover offer which is regulated by the Takeover Code (see Ch.23), there will normally be a condition to that effect, although on a recommended takeover the target company will normally seek to delete reference to "prospects". In any event the Panel on Takeovers and Mergers will apparently allow the buyer to invoke such a condition only in very exceptional circumstances.

On transactions which are not governed by the Takeover Code, the extent to which there is a MAC clause is normally a matter for negotiations and will be dependant, in part, upon the prospective negotiating strengths of the parties and in part on whether or not the buyer is relying on third party finance, which may itself be subject to a MAC condition, which needs to be mirrored in the terms of the acquisition.

The buyer will often attempt to incorporate a MAC condition by including a warranty that, since a specified date (typically the date of last audited accounts) there has not been any material adverse change in the business, or financial position, profits or prospects of the target company or business and will then press for that warranty to be repeated on completion, with the buyer having the right to walk away from the transaction if the warranty, when repeated on completion, is not true.

This is, however, one of the warranties which the seller will be reluctant to repeat, on the basis that it relates to matters outside his control. The seller is likely to argue that the buyer should instead rely on the seller's covenants regarding the conduct of the business down to completion.

Where the seller is prepared to accept the principle that the buyer should be entitled to withdraw if there is a MAC, rather than giving a warranty and agreeing to repeat it at a point (completion) when the warranty may not necessarily be true, the seller may prefer to express the MAC clause as a condition precedent.

Whether it is expressed as a warranty or as a condition, the seller will want to remove reference to "prospects", while the buyer will inevitably argue that it should be included, in order to cover the situation where something untowards happens which does not immediately damage the business but is likely to have a material adverse impact on it in the future.

Another difficult issue can be whether or not the MAC clause applies to cover changes in stock market or other general economic conditions, changes in conditions generally affecting the sector in question and legal or other regulatory changes. What happens if another "9/11" takes place? Should the buyer still be bound to go ahead in that situation?

The seller will generally argue that such risks should be the buyer's and, as has already been seen, the position that is ultimately agreed is likely to depend both on the negotiating positions of the parties and on whether the buyer has financing arrangements which themselves contain a MAC condition, with the result that he cannot accept the risk of his funding being unavailable but his nevertheless being bound to complete the purchase from the seller. One possible compromise may be for there to be a MAC clause which does not allow the buyer to withdraw from the transaction as a result of general changes in economic conditions but does allow him to withdraw if the circumstances in question have a disproportionately severe impact on the seller (for example, if the business in question is one which is highly-regulated, there may be changes in regulation which have a particularly severe impact on the business).

Another approach may be to have a MAC clause which is rather more in the nature of a "force majeure" clause, allowing the buyer to withdraw if (for example) there is a serious fire or flood which has a material adverse affect on the business and, if a significant proportion of the business's customers or suppliers are based in jurisdictions which are notoriously volatile, the wording might make specific reference to civil unrest, terrorist attacks, war and the like.

10.7   Warranties—limitations on liability

The seller will almost invariably seek to restrict his liabilities under the warranties in various ways and the sale and purchase agreement will normally contain a separate "seller's protection" schedule which will contain whatever limitations are agreed. Precedent 33 in App.2 is a reasonably typical set of limitations, which should be read in conjunction with the precedent share sale and purchase agreement for use where there are individual sellers (Precedent 2). It can be adapted (by making appropriate amendments) where the seller is a corporate seller and for the sale and purchase of assets.

The precedent has been drafted on the basis that most of the limitations which are to apply in respect of the tax warranties and tax covenants will appear in a separate tax schedule rather than with the other limitations on liability.

The precedent seeks to strike a fair balance between the buyer and the sellers and, in practice, there may be additional limitations which a seller may seek to include and some limitations contained in the precedent which a buyer would not want to accept in every case. The first draft of the sale and purchase agreement will generally be produced by the buyer who will generally only include very basic limitations on the seller's liability and so the seller is likely to seek to introduce additional limitations, with the extent to which these are included in the final version being a matter for commercial negotiations.

Limitations which will typically be agreed include (references to paragraphs are to the appropriate paragraph of the schedule which forms Precedent 33):

10.7.1   Time limits (paras 1 and 2)

A seller will not normally be prepared to accept the risk of warranty claims hanging over him for an indefinite period and, in relation to normal trading liabilities a buyer will normally start by offering to accept a limitation period of three years within which claims have to be notified, while the seller will be pressing for a shorter period of (perhaps) 12 months. Claims will very often come to light as a result of the audit of the target company or (in the case of a sale and purchase of assets) the buyer after completion and the parties will normally settle on a time limit which gives enough time for either two or three full audits to be carried out.

Any such provision is likely to state that, when notifying a potential claim, the buyer must specify in reasonable detail the matter giving rise to the claim, the nature of the claim and the amount claimed, in order to give the seller the opportunity to assess the strength (or otherwise) of the claim and to consider whether any action should be taken to mitigate it. In the case of *Laminates Acquisition Co v BTR Australia Ltd* [2003] EWCH 2540 (Comm), the court held that, where a sale and purchase agreement contains wording to that effect, the buyer must show that he has complied with its requirements and, in that particular case, it was held that the buyer had failed to do so. It is reasonable for a buyer to accept such a provision (although he may wish to include wording to the effect that he only need give details of the claim by reference to the information then available to him) but, before actually taking steps to notify a claim, the buyer should review the sale and purchase agreement and make sure that the notice which is given does comply with its strict requirements.

Tax claims may take longer to come to light and HMRC's time limit for making an assessment to tax is six years from the end of the financial year in question and 20 years where there has been fraud or negligent conduct. Accordingly, the buyer will normally insist on the limitation period for making claims under the tax warranties (or tax covenants) being between six and seven years and it will be difficult for a seller to argue against that on a share sale and purchase (less so, perhaps, on a sale and purchase of assets, where tax warranties should be less of an issue).

There may be some other warranties and some indemnities where a longer period is appropriate, depending upon the circumstances of the case — for example, environmental warranties or indemnities and indemnities in respect of residual liabilities in respect of leasehold properties where the target company was the original tenant. Buyers will in any event argue that the time limits should not apply in the event of fraud, dishonesty or wilful non-disclosure. Where the limitation period is longer than six years, the sale and purchase agreement may need to be executed as a deed because the statutory limitation period will be six years for an agreement which is not a deed but will be 12 years for a deed.

It should be noted, however, that an express or implied agreement not to plead the Limitation Act 1980 is valid if supported by consideration and that it should therefore be possible to agree a contractual limitation period which is longer than the statutory limitation period. An express provision which (for example) specifies a 20 year limitation period where there has been fraud or negligent conduct may be regarded as excluding the operation of the Limitation Act by implication but it may nevertheless be wise to include an express exclusion.

Sellers will often also seek to include a provision to the effect that any claim which has been notified will be deemed to have been waived unless the buyer issues and serves proceedings within a specified period after the date on which he originally notified the claim. The intention of this is to prevent the buyer from notifying claims and then leaving them hanging over the seller indefinitely. Buyers will often argue against such a provision, on the basis that it is likely to precipitate litigation, but that should not be the case if the period is of an appropriate length (typically, either six or twelve months).

10.7.2 Maximum liability (para.3.1)

The seller will be very reluctant to accept liability under the warranties in excess of the purchase price and the sale and purchase agreement will very often state that the maximum liability of the seller under the warranties and under the tax covenants (and also, perhaps, under any specific indemnities) will be limited to the purchase price. A buyer will normally accept this, but there may be some circumstances where a higher figure is appropriate, to reflect the fact that, in addition to the specified purchase price, the buyer is agreeing to make other payments or is agreeing to accept liabilities which may reasonably be regarded as part of the consideration for the transaction — for example, where (on a sale and purchase of shares) the buyer is agreeing to procure the repayment of intra-group or other loans or where (on an asset sale and purchase) the buyer is agreeing to take over responsibility for the creditors of the business.

By the same token, depending on the extent of the due diligence work which the buyer is able to do and on the outcome of such work and depending also upon the respective bargaining positions of the parties, the seller may in some transactions be able to persuade the buyer to accept a maximum liability which is below the purchase price. A seller may be particularly keen to fix his liability at a level which takes account of the costs and expenses of sale and of any tax liability arising out of the sale.

10.7.3 Minimum liability (para.3.2)

To avoid the possibility of claims being brought for trivial breaches and to avoid wasting time and expense in defending very small claims, the seller will wish to agree with the buyer that claims may not be brought where the amount claimed is below a specified level. This will normally be the case both with individual claims and the aggregate of all claims. A buyer will nearly always accept that there should be minimum thresholds for claims so that (for example) on a transaction where the purchase price is £1 million, the sale and purchase agreement may specify that no claims may be brought unless the aggregate of all claims amounts to (say) £10,000 or more and that in determining whether or not that figure of £10,000 has been reached, individual claims of less than (say) £1,000 will be ignored altogether. There may also be some debate as to whether, once claims exceed the minimum liability, the buyer should be able to recover the whole amount of his claim or just the excess over the minimum, but normally the buyer will insist upon the right to recover the full amount in those circumstances. The minimum liability levels which are appropriate will vary from transaction to transaction and will to a large extent depend upon the size of the deal (as what is trivial in the context of a £100 million transaction may be very material in the context of a £1 million transaction).

Sellers will naturally tend to focus rather more on the maximum liability figure than on the minimum, as the maximum may appear to be an alarmingly high figure but, provided that the seller can be satisfied that he has carried out a thorough and accurate disclosure exercise and assuming that he is not aware of any circumstances which are likely to give rise to significant claims (such as uninsured product liability claims), he may be well-advised to concentrate his energies on trying to negotiate the highest possible threshold (i.e. minimum liability) for claims, rather than being unduly concerned over the maximum liability, as it is more likely that any claims will be at the lower end of the scale.

It is normal for the parties to agree that claims under any tax covenants or tax indemnity will not be subject to any minimum level.

10.7.4 Nature of liability (para.4)

As has already been seen, sellers will normally press for their liability to be several and for liability in respect of any claim to be borne between them in the proportions in which they share the purchase price. In any event, it should always be made clear that each seller shall only be liable for any breach of any of the warranties regarding title and capacity where they relate to his own lack of title or lack of capacity.

10.7.5 Reduction of consideration (para.5)

For tax reasons, it may be helpful to specify that any payment for breach of any of the warranties or under the tax covenants will constitute a reduction in the purchase price as this may reduce any chargeable gain made by the seller.

10.7.6 Conduct of claims (para.6)

Although, if any breaches of warranty arise, the buyer will have a common law duty to mitigate his loss, a seller will normally want to reinforce that duty by making sure that the buyer takes steps to defend any third party claims which may give rise to a warranty claim. For example, particularly on a sale and purchase of shares, if the seller has warranted that the target company has not sold any defective goods and after completion a customer claims that goods have been supplied to him which were defective, the seller will be concerned to make sure that the buyer contests that claim if it is reasonable for him to do so and does not simply accept the claim and seek to recover his loss from the seller under the warranties.

10.7.7 Insurers and other third parties (paras 7 and 8)

If the customer's claim is covered by product liability insurance, then the seller will normally expect the buyer to claim on his insurance rather than make a claim against the seller. The sale and purchase agreement will normally therefore oblige the buyer to endeavour to recover under any insurance policy before bringing a claim against the seller. Similarly where there is a right of recovery against any other third party—for example, where the claim results from defective goods sold by the target company and the target company has a claim against the original manufacturers.

If the seller pays damages for breach of warranty and then the buyer does subsequently succeed in a claim against his insurers or another third party, then the sale and purchase agreement will normally provide for the seller to be reimbursed, to the extent that the buyer has been able to recover his loss.

10.7.8 Set-off (para.9)

If part of the purchase price is deferred, the seller should include a provision to the effect that it must be paid in full, without set-off or deduction, in order to prevent the buyer from withholding payment on the basis that he considers that he has a warranty or indemnity claim and proposes to set that claim off against the payment that would otherwise fall to be made. The seller's principal concern is likely to be that the buyer will make spurious claims and then use them as a device to delay payment for as long as possible and thereby perhaps obtain a reduction in the purchase price. The buyer, on the other hand, is likely to argue that, if he believes that he has a claim, he should not be obliged to pay the seller and then have the problem of trying to get back the money that he has paid. This issue is discussed in more detail at 10.9 below but, if the buyer does produce a draft sale and purchase agreement which gives him the right to set claims off against sums otherwise due to the seller, the seller should note that it is not enough simply to delete that provision, as the buyer is likely to have a right of set off at common law, and that will be the case unless it is expressly excluded by the terms of the agreement.

10.7.9 Double recovery (para.10)

Where there has been a breach of any of the tax warranties, the circumstances in question will be likely also to give the buyer a claim under the tax covenants and the seller will normally require a provision to prevent the buyer from recovering more than once in respect of the same loss.

10.7.10 Misrepresentations (para.11)

As has already been seen at 10.1.2 above, a seller will normally seek to include a provision which excludes liability for pre-contractual misrepresentations but the wording of any such clause will need to be considered carefully, in the light of the decision in the *Thomas Witter* case. In particular, any such clause should not purport to exclude liability in respect of fraudulent misrepresentations.

10.7.11 Ordinary course of business (para.12)

Sellers will normally seek to include a provision excluding liability for any loss or damage which results from anything done by the buyer or (on a sale and purchase of shares) by the target company after completion and this may be acceptable, provided that it is limited to things done in the ordinary course of business and does not extend to things done pursuant to pre-existing contractual obligations.

10.7.12 Completion accounts (para.13)

Where the purchase price is to be determined by reference to completion accounts, the seller should require a provision to make it clear that the buyer may not recover under the warranties to the extent that the circumstances giving rise to the claim have already been reflected in the completion accounts and hence in the purchase price. For example, if the seller has warranted that all book debts are recoverable and there is a book debt which turns out to be irrecoverable but in respect of which a bad debt provision was made in the completion accounts, then the purchase price will have been reduced by the amount of that provision and it would be unreasonable for the buyer also to be able to recover damages for breach of warranty in that situation.

The same principle will apply when the purchase price is to be determined by reference to future profits of the company or business (an earn out). If the seller warrants that no material customers have taken their business elsewhere during the last 12 months and this turns out to be untrue, the effect of the loss of the customer in question is likely to be to reduce the future profitability of the business, with the result that the buyer is likely to pay less for it.

10.7.13 Buyer's warranty (para.15)

Sellers will often seek to include a provision in which the buyer warrants to the seller that he is not entering into the sale and purchase agreement with knowledge of any circumstances which amount to a breach of any of the warranties, but buyers should be wary of giving such a "reverse warranty" as there may be issues of which the buyer has some knowledge but of which he does not have sufficient knowledge to appreciate all of the implications and, depending on the wording of the provision in question, he could be prevented from bringing a claim in such circumstances.

10.7.14 Knowledge qualification

A buyer will normally accept from the outset that some of the warranties in the sale and purchase agreement may be qualified so that they apply only to matters within the seller's knowledge and are therefore given "so far as the seller is aware" or "to the best of the knowledge and belief of the seller" or with similar wording (the knowledge qualification). For example, a buyer will normally expect a warranty to the effect that no third party is infringing the intellectual property rights of the business but will normally accept that the seller may simply not be in a position to know whether or not that is the case (for example, if the business is the design, manufacture and sale of carpets, the seller's designs could quite easily be copied by a competitor anywhere in the world) and the buyer will normally therefore accept that such a warranty may be subject to the knowledge qualification, with the result that the seller will have breached the warranty if he was aware of the infringement, but (subject to the precise wording of the knowledge qualification in the agreement) will have no liability if he was genuinely unaware of it.

The buyer will normally produce the first draft of the sale and purchase agreement with very few of the warranties qualified in this way but the seller and his solicitors will normally try to make sure that as many warranties as possible are qualified by the knowledge qualification. Whether or not such qualification is appropriate is ultimately a question of allocation of risk: should it be the seller or the buyer who bears the risk of a claim as a result of a contingent liability of which the seller had no knowledge? For example, the buyer will normally require a warranty that there has been no breach of any legal or regulatory requirements and the seller may genuinely believe that to be the case, only for the buyer to receive a few days after completion a visit from the Health and Safety Executive inspectors who may maintain that a particular working practice contravenes the health and safety legislation and threatening enforcement action unless the situation is remedied (which may involve the buyer in considerable expense). Should it be the seller or the buyer who bears that risk? The seller will normally argue that he has taken all reasonable steps to make sure that the business does comply with the health and safety legislation and that he can only therefore warrant that he is not aware of any breaches, while the buyer will normally respond by saying that, even if the seller is not aware of any breaches, if he (rather than the buyer) was responsible for them, then it is the seller who should bear the consequences.

Whether or not particular warranties are subject to the knowledge qualification will normally depend upon the nature of each particular warranty (as there will inevitably be some warranties where the knowledge qualification may be appropriate and others where it is not), the nature of the business in question and, of course, the respective bargaining positions of the parties.

Much may depend on whether or not the business is one which is heavily regulated and on whether failure to comply with legal or regulatory requirements may have significant consequences.

For example, where it is a financial services business which is regulated by the FSA, failure to comply with all permissions held by the seller and with the legal and regulatory framework generally may lead to substantial fines or, ultimately, to the business being unable to continue. In those circumstances, it may be more reasonable for the buyer to insist on a warranty from the seller which is not limited to matters within his knowledge and it may even be reasonable for the buyer to require an indemnity.

The time available to complete the transaction will also be relevant — if the timescale for completion is short and it is the buyer who is responsible for that timetable, then the seller is likely to be better-placed to negotiate qualifications to the warranties than where the timescale is a long one or where it is the seller who requires completion within a comparatively short time.

If the buyer does accept that certain warranties may be subject to the knowledge qualification, he will normally be concerned to make sure that the seller does not give the warranty blindly but actually takes appropriate steps to ensure that the warranty is true before giving it. Accordingly, sale and purchase agreements typically state that, where a warranty is given subject to the knowledge qualification, the seller warrants that he has made due and careful enquiry into its subject-matter.

A seller may, however, be reluctant to accept the words "due and careful enquiry" and may prefer to replace them with "reasonable enquiry" as, otherwise, the wording might mean that, for example, before warranting that there is no reason to believe that any major customers will be lost, the seller actually has to contact all of the major customers and obtain assurances from them that that is the case.

If it is agreed in principle that all that is required is "reasonable enquiry", then the buyer may well require the agreement to specify a list of individuals or entities of whom enquiry must be made, such as professional advisers and certain specified directors, officers and employees. The buyer will normally want the agreement to state that that list is not exhaustive and that "reasonable enquiry" should not be confined to those individuals or entities but should also be made of anybody else of whom it would be reasonable to make enquiry, while the seller will normally be keen to agree an exhaustive list, in the interests of certainty.

Where the seller is a corporate seller, there may be issues as to whether or not the fact that particular circumstances are known to a particular officer or employee of the seller means that those circumstances are to be regarded as known to the seller and it may well therefore be in the interests of both the seller and the buyer to include a list of the individuals of whom enquiry must be made. Similarly, on a sale of shares by individual sellers, the issue may arise as to what happens where circumstances are known to one of the sellers but not to all of them and the individual concerned chooses not to inform the others. In those circumstances, the buyer may wish to make it clear that anything known to one of the sellers is deemed to have been known to them all.

From the buyer's point of view, the inclusion of wording obliging the seller to make enquiries (whether those enquiries have to be due and careful enquiries or reasonable enquiries) rather begs the question as to what happens if enquiries are made but the information in question does not come to light as a result of those enquiries and as a result is not disclosed to the buyer: for example, the salesmen may be asked whether they know of any reason to believe that any of the major customers may be lost and a salesman who is aware of a particular difficulty with a particular customer may choose to withhold that information because he is concerned about retaining his job. In that situation, the seller would have satisfied his duty to make enquiries and would (in the absence of wording to the contrary) have no liability for breach of warranty—but is that fair? Should it not be the seller rather than the buyer who takes the risk of those enquiries not resulting in a truthful answer? From the buyer's point of view, it may therefore be appropriate to provide both that the seller will be deemed to be aware of anything of which he would have become aware if he had made all reasonable enquiries and to provide that he will be deemed to be aware of anything which was known to any individual or entity in the agreed list (professional advisers, directors and other officers, specified employees and so on).

10.8   MAN v Freightliner

10.8.1   The case of *MAN Nutzfahrzeuge AG v Freightliner Ltd* [2005] EWHC 2347 (Comm) raises a number of practical issues, both for sellers and for buyers, in connection with representations, warranties, disclosures and, indeed, due diligence. This was a claim by MAN Nutzfahrzeuge AG ("MAN") against Freightliner Ltd ("Freightliner") for losses MAN sustained after it purchased ERF Holdings Plc ("ERF") from Freightliner's predecessor company, Western Star Trucks (Holdings) Ltd ("Western Star") in March 2000.

The price was agreed on the basis of audited accounts which indicated that ERF was making a small profit and had net assets of around £25 million. The sale and purchase agreement included a representation and warranty that the relevant accounts "fairly represented" the financial position of ERF. The warranties were subject to a limitation period of 12 months, other than claims in respect of fraud or fraudulent misrepresentation.

The information deemed to be disclosed to MAN under the terms of the sale and purchase agreement included:

"all matters that would be revealed by . . . an inspection of the books and records of the ERF Companies . . . any matter which is or should be revealed by inspection of the statutory registers and books and minutes . . . or which would have been revealed by the making of such inspection as would have been made by a prudent buyer . . ."

In July 2001 MAN discovered that ERF's financial controller, E, had been fraudulently manipulating the accounts since 1996. In reality, ERF was making losses and had net liabilities of around £75 million.

MAN sought damages from Freightliner on the basis that Western Star had been involved very heavily in negotiations leading up to the sale and MAN's due diligence investigation into ERF. Western Star knew nothing of E's fraud and a claim under the representations and warranties in the sale and purchase agreement was not possible because the 12-month time limit for claims had expired. However, MAN argued that:

- E's dishonest knowledge could be attributed to Western Star and that, as a result, the contractual representations were given fraudulently, so that the 12-month time limit did not apply to the claim.

- E acted as Western Star's agent when he misrepresented ERF's financial position to MAN in the period leading up to the contract and Western Star was vicariously liable for E's pre-contractual statements, giving rise to liability in tort for fraud.

The court held that:

- Although E was involved on Western Star's behalf in the negotiations, he was not a director or an employee of Western Star and there was no evidence that he was involved in deciding the price or other terms of the deal. The contractual representations were contained only in the sale and purchase agreement itself and E was not involved in the decision as to whether or not Western Star should give them. Therefore, E's dishonest knowledge could not be attributed to Western Star for the purposes of the agreement, unless it contained a provision to that effect. There was no such provision and so no claim could be brought under the representations and warranties in the agreement, because of the 12-month time limit.

- E acted as Western Star's agent when he misrepresented ERF's financial position to MAN during negotiation meetings between Western Star and MAN. Western Star had put him forward to speak about the accounts and financial position of ERF at those meetings in such a way as to hold him out as having authority to speak about such matters on its behalf, with the result that Freightliner was vicariously liable for E's fraud.

One of E's frauds included false completion of VAT returns. Freightliner argued that the management accounts and VAT returns of ERF had been disclosed, that those accounts and returns were inconsistent, and that that inconsistency should have led MAN to conclude that the VAT returns were not honestly completed. However, the court held that the VAT returns had not been disclosed because they did not fall within the meaning of "books and records" or "statutory registers and books and minutes" in the general disclosures. The judge also commented (obiter) that the matters deemed to be disclosed did not include inferences to be drawn from the items inspected but suggested that a disclosure letter which was appropriately drafted could include such inferences.

10.8.2 Implications for buyers

10.8.2.1 The case indicates that, on a sale and purchase of shares, it may be difficult to make a seller liable for statements made by employees of the target company during due diligence but that the seller may well be liable for statements made by employees or advisers of the seller during that process. Where statements are made in the course of the due diligence exercise on which the buyer wishes to rely, he should make sure that they are incorporated into the sale and purchase agreement as formal representations and/or warranties and ensure that those representations/warranties are not watered down by widely-drawn disclosures.

10.8.2.2 *Infiniteland* illustrates the need for a buyer to pay attention to the standard to which disclosure must be made and indicates that buyers should be wary of accepting widely-worded general disclosures. This is reinforced by MAN as the case shows that, if the buyer accepts widely-drafted general disclosures, this can seriously erode his warranty protection. Buyers will need to be particularly cautious before accepting deemed disclosure of matters which would be discoverable from "a reasonable investigation", "thorough examination" or the like.

10.8.2.3 Buyers should also be very aware of the time limits for bringing warranty claims and should put in place arrangements to review matters which are covered by the warranties on a regular basis, so that potential claims are more likely to come to light within the limitation period. Solicitors acting for buyer would be well-advised to make a diary note to remind their clients of the impending expiry of the time limits and this should be done comfortably before the expiry of the time limits, in order to give the buyer sufficient time to take whatever steps are necessary to establish whether there are any potential claims.

10.8.3   Practical lessons for sellers

10.8.3.1 Sellers may be vicariously liable for statements of their employees and advisers made during negotiations or due diligence. On a sale and purchase of shares, they may also be liable for statements made by target company employees during negotiations (but this is less likely during due diligence where they are more likely to be considered to be speaking on the target company's behalf). Sellers should be particularly aware of these risks on a sale and purchase of assets, as the seller is likely to be the company which is carrying on the business in question and the employees concerned are likely to be employees of the seller, with the result that, even during the due diligence exercise, they must (by definition) be speaking on behalf of the seller.

10.8.3.2 Sellers should attempt to protect themselves against these risks through wording in the sale and purchase agreement although, as has already been seen, clauses which exclude or restrict liability for misrepresentation will only be upheld if they satisfy the requirement of reasonableness and a clause which purports to exclude liability for fraudulent misrepresentation is likely to be ineffective. A clause in which the buyer acknowledges that he is not relying on any statements made by the seller or any other information provided by the seller which are not included in the agreement as formal representations and/or warranties (non-reliance clauses) will only be effective if the person making the representation believed it to be true and, by definition, that will not be the case in a situation such as arose in the *MAN v Freightliner* case. Sellers will therefore have to accept that "entire agreement" and non-reliance clauses will be of little value where misrepresentations are made fraudulently.

10.8.3.3 Sellers should, however, take the obvious practical step of making sure that only trusted employees and advisers are involved in negotiations and that anybody who may be regarded as a "loose cannon" should be kept away from direct contact with the buyer or should be left in no doubt as to what he may or may not say. Sellers need to exercise particular caution in bringing target employees on to the negotiating team.

10.8.3.4 Sellers should not assume that they will be able to pass liability on to the company's auditors if the auditors have been negligent in auditing the target company's statutory accounts.

In *MAN*, Freightliner failed to pass on liability to the auditors despite the fact that it was admitted that their audit of ERF's 1998 and 1999 accounts had been negligent.

Auditors do not owe a duty of care to shareholders or prospective buyers in undertaking an ordinary statutory audit but only if they have taken on a "special audit duty" (that is, according to the judge in *MAN*, that they knew and intended "that their statement as to the company's accounts would be communicated to and relied on by a particular person ... for a particular purpose in connection with a particular transaction").

In *MAN* the judge thought that there was "no evidence of anything passing between Western Star and [the auditors] to indicate that Western Star was intending to rely on the accounts for any particular purpose in its negotiations with MAN or that it was seeking an assurance from [the auditors] that it could safely do so". The basis for this view appears to have been that the auditors knew that a due diligence exercise was being carried out (and indeed accelerated completion of their audit so that the accounts could be available to be provided to MAN in connection with the transaction) but were not consulted about it and played no part in it—despite the fact that the auditors knew that it was likely that MAN and Western Star would rely on the audited accounts in connection with the transaction and indeed made their audit working papers available to another firm of accountants for the purposes of the due diligence exercise.

10.9   Set-off and security for warranty and indemnity claims

A buyer may have a well-drafted set of warranties, may be able to show that they have been breached, may overcome the hurdles of remoteness and the common law duty to mitigate his loss and obtain an award of damages in his favour, but this will be to no avail if he is unable to recover those damages from the seller. The value of warranties and indemnities ultimately turns on the financial strength of the seller giving them and, if he is the proverbial "man of straw", the buyer may find it difficult, if not impossible, to recover from him.

If the seller is an individual, he may have taken himself and the sale proceeds off shore, may have given it away to his nearest and dearest, may have used it to repay his mortgage or other borrowings or may simply have frittered it away. A corporate seller may have paid the sale proceeds to its shareholders by way of dividend, may have sold its remaining assets and then returned all of its cash to shareholders in a members' voluntary winding-up, may have used the sale proceeds to repay its bank overdraft or other borrowings or may have become insolvent after the sale.

The buyer should therefore consider the financial strength of the seller and, if he has any concerns, there are various ways in which he may obtain a measure of security for any claims which may arise.

10.9.1 Guarantee from shareholders/parent company

Where the seller is a company, he may be able to obtain a guarantee from its share-holders, whether they are individuals or a holding company. Even then, of course, the buyer will have to consider the financial strength of whoever is to give the guarantee.

10.9.2 Bank guarantee

From the buyer's point of view, it would be preferable to obtain a guarantee from the seller's bank, although the seller will doubtless be very reluctant to provide such a guarantee because of the likely costs involved (particularly if the guarantee is to last for the entire life span of the warranties and any indemnities).

10.9.3 Retention

Part of the purchase price (typically around 10 per cent) may be retained by the buyer for an agreed period (typically around 12 months) in order to satisfy any warranty or indemnity claims which may arise during that period. The sale and purchase agreement will then contain a provision allowing the buyer to set off any claims against the amount which would otherwise be payable to the seller.

To give a practical example: if Buyer PLC (Buyer) is buying the entire issued share capital of Target Limited (Target) from Tom, Dick and Harriet (Sellers) for £1,000,000 and is concerned about the ability of Sellers to satisfy any claims which may arise, he may be able to persuade Sellers that only £900,000 will be paid on completion and that the balance of £100,000 will be paid on the first anniversary of completion, less any amount which Buyer claims to be due to it in respect of any warranty claims which have arisen before that first anniversary.

If Sellers accept the principle of this, they in turn may have some concern as to Buyer's ability to make the appropriate payment to Sellers when it falls due and will therefore have to consider whether they should be requesting a guarantee or some other security for that payment. The normal solution to this is for Sellers to agree to a retention of £100,000, provided that the money is not actually retained by Buyer but is placed into a designated deposit account (typically, an account in the joint names of Sellers' solicitors and Buyer's solicitors) until the first anniversary of completion, at which point any balance remaining in the account, after any payment of damages to Buyer, will be paid to Sellers, with all interest earned on the account being paid to Buyer and Sellers in proportion to the amount of principal which they each receive. That deposit account (normally referred to as an escrow account) will be opened on terms under which there may be no withdrawals from the account without the agreement of both sets of solicitors, which means that both parties should be able to feel confident that it cannot be taken by the other. There will normally be an "escrow agreement" in order to reflect these arrangements and Precedent 34 in App.2 is an example of a fairly typical escrow agreement.

Apart from concerns over Buyer's ability to pay, another reason to have the retention held on an escrow account rather than simply being retained by Buyer is that Sellers are likely to be concerned that Buyer may simply put forward some spurious warranty or indemnity claims and then claim to be entitled to set them off against the £100,000 retention. Sellers would certainly be wise to assume that, if Buyer is retaining part of the purchase price against warranty and indemnity claims, Buyer will be looking for every opportunity to make a claim, in order to enable it to delay paying the retention as long as possible, which may have cashflow advantages and may put Buyer in a position to negotiate a reduction of the purchase price.

For example, Buyer may have genuine claims totalling £25,000 but will inevitably be tempted to "throw in the kitchen sink" and allege various other breaches of warranty: as a result, his total claims may (for example) amount to £110,000. Although Buyer may only be likely to recover £25,000 and may be unlikely to be able to substantiate the balance of £85,000, nevertheless he will (depending on the wording of the sale and purchase agreement—see below), unless the retention is paid into an escrow account, be able to retain the whole retention of £100,000 for months (or even years) beyond the date on which it would otherwise have been payable. Sellers will want to receive payment as soon as possible and Buyer is therefore likely to be in a good position to open negotiations with Sellers with a view to "cutting a deal" under which (for example) Buyer will accept £60,000 in full and final settlement of the claims which he has notified and agrees to pay just £40,000 of the retention to Sellers. Effectively, therefore, he will have obtained a £60,000 price reduction, despite the fact that, if he had had to pursue Sellers for damages, he may have struggled to have recovered more than £5,000.

If Sellers have to accept that the retention will be held by Buyer rather than held on an escrow account, they are likely to argue that the £100,000 retention must be paid in full on the due date save to the extent of any warranty or indemnity claims which have been notified to them before that date and in respect of which they have either agreed that they are liable (and the amount of their liability) or in respect of which liability has been determined by a court. Buyer would, however, argue against that, on the basis that, if the retention is only to last for one year, it is almost inconceivable that a claim would have been litigated to a conclusion before the courts before the end of the retention period, while there would obviously be no incentive for Sellers to agree liability during the retention period.

Buyer may offer to address Sellers' concerns by including a provision to the effect that he may not withhold payment of the retention on account of an outstanding warranty claim unless he can produce an opinion from suitably experienced counsel to the effect that Buyer does have a good prima facie claim but that will not be of great comfort to Sellers, as counsel will inevitably give his opinion on the basis of the facts presented to him in his instructions and those instructions will have been drafted by Buyer.

If the retention is held in an escrow account for the agreed 12-month period, rather than simply being held back by Buyer, at least Buyer will derive no cashflow benefit from putting forward spurious claims in order to delay payment, which may give Buyer an incentive to resolve any claims sooner rather than later. If the retention is to be held on an escrow account, the sale and purchase agreement should make it clear that the retention should be paid on the due date, save to the extent of any warranty or indemnity claims which have been notified before that date and the seller should seek as much protection as possible against the possibility of spurious claims.

10.9.4 Set-off against deferred consideration

If only part of the purchase price is payable on completion and the balance is payable on a later date (for example, because the seller is prepared to accept payment by instalments or because part of the purchase price is dependant upon an earn out or a similar arrangement) the buyer will have the right to set-off any warranty or indemnity claims against the deferred element of the purchase price. The seller will inevitably argue against this, on the basis that such an arrangement is quite different from the situation where there is a retention as security for claims, but the buyer will respond to that by saying that it would be unreasonable to expect him to pay the seller at a time when he considers that he has a claim—an obvious concern is that, if the seller knows that there is a potential claim, he may take the money off shore or may take other steps to make it difficult for the buyer to recover any damages which he may ultimately be awarded.

The issues to be considered will be similar to those to be considered when a retention is agreed and a reasonable solution may be to agree that, if there are any outstanding claims as at the date when any balance of the purchase price falls to be paid, the buyer will pay into an escrow account an amount equal to his best (and bona fide) estimate of the amount which he would be entitled to recover if the claim were successful and for the balance to be paid over to the seller. The money on the escrow account would then be held there until the buyer's claim had been resolved, either by agreement or by a court, and any interest earned on the account would be paid to the parties in proportion to their entitlements to the principal amount.

Such an arrangement may be difficult if the buyer has provided a guarantee from his bankers for the deferred element of the purchase price but the difficulties are not insuperable—the bank may not be prepared to be embroiled in any disputes between the parties as to whether or not the buyer has the right to exercise his right of set-off and will insist on being entitled to pay upon receipt of an appropriate demand from the seller but it should be possible to make arrangements with the bank so that, in the absence of agreement between the parties to the contrary, any payment under the guarantee will be made into a solicitors' escrow account, where it will remain until the buyer's claim has been determined by agreement or by a court.

10.10 Warranty and indemnity insurance

In appropriate cases, sellers (and sometime also buyers) should consider the possibility of taking out insurance cover against liability under warranties and indemnities arising on a transaction. Warranty and indemnity insurance ("W & I insurance") is at its most useful where there is a commercial gap between the warranty cover being offered by the sellers (normally on a sale of shares) and the amount of warranty cover required by the buyer. This typically arises in the following cases:

- One or more of the sellers is a venture capitalist ("VC") who as a matter of policy refuses to give warranties.

- The seller is returning the consideration to lenders or shareholders (see 1.3.1 above).

- One or more of the sellers has solvency issues or is outside the UK, so that recovery will be difficult.

- The sellers include trustees who have no knowledge of the business and are unwilling to put the assets of the trust at risk for warranty claims.

- Some of the sellers are unwilling to give full warranty cover, whether because of a lack of knowledge or an unwillingness to take on risk.

- Due diligence throws up a problem which, though very unlikely to crystallise, is of a magnitude which neither the seller nor the buyer is prepared to accept. An example of this would be technical breaches of planning restrictions.

10.10.1 Traditional model

In a fairly typical situation where the management team (for example) owns 40 per cent of a company and a VC 60 per cent, the warranty liability risk on sale might be divided as follows:

- management—the first 40 per cent of the purchase price;

- buyer—the balance of the risk (i.e. the sellers' total liability is capped at four per cent of the purchase price);

- VC—no risk.

In this example, the buyer is getting (arguably) a reasonable level of warranty cover and has management responsible for warranties, disclosures and due diligence. The buyer might also have taken the view that the purchase price was structured in such a way as to take into account the lack of warranty cover.

10.10.2 Larger buy-outs/Institutional buy-outs ("IBOs")

Applying the traditional model to larger buy-outs' exits would give a buyer warranty cover up to management's proportion of the consideration and the buyer would be at risk for the balance of the consideration. However, this is a structure which may well be unacceptable to both management and the buyer.

Consider a substantial IBO where management have only 10 per cent of the equity: management would be taking the first 10 per cent of the risk (that portion of the consideration with the highest risk). The buyer, who is paying a significant sum, is only receiving warranty cover to the extent of 10 per cent of the purchase price and that limited cover is given by management, who may be critical to the ongoing future of the business. (It is assumed that management will receive 10 per cent of the consideration but, more often, senior debt and VC debt must be repaid first, leaving management with a much smaller share of the purchase price).

An insurance product could be written to give the buyer greater warranty protection. Here management might accept liability for more than their share of the consideration, with the first slice of that protection being covered by the consideration received by management and the second slice being covered by insurance.

Although this form of seller W & I insurance appears attractive, there are a number of issues which mean that both management and the buyer will have difficulties with the proposal:

10.10.2.1 The seller W & I insurance policy will exclude liability in the following situations:

- Fraud or material non-disclosure on the part of management. This is a key exclusion for buyers who are relying upon management being able to call upon a valid insurance policy to satisfy a warranty claim and will be equally significant to management who will want to feel confident that they will be able to do so. W & I insurance policies are covered by the same principles as normal insurance policies and the proposer (in this case management) has a duty of utmost good faith in applying for insurance. It is quite possible that the circumstances which give rise to a claim will be circumstances known to management but overlooked (whether intentionally or not) in the disclosure exercise and therefore excluded from insurance cover.

- Issues which have come to light through the due diligence or disclosure process will be excluded from the insurance cover, which means that some form of price adjustment will be necessary.

- Completion accounts/net assets adjustments are not covered.

- Forward-looking warranties, such as collectibility of debtors, are excluded — and sometimes the definition of "forward looking" can be interpreted very widely by underwriters.

- Environmental, product liability and pension liabilities are nearly always excluded, though bespoke insurance may be available from some specialists.

- Warranties regarding the insurances of the target will not be covered.

- The wording of management accounts and stock warranties will be carefully considered by the insurers.

10.10.2.2 Who bears the substantial premiums—management, VC and/or buyer?

10.10.2.3 The general issues discussed below will also apply.

10.10.3 Buyer W & I insurance

Some of the problems with seller W & I insurance can be overcome by the buyer taking out his own policy. In this case, management still gives warranties but the buyer takes out an insurance policy as a "top slice" above the extent of management's warranty cover. Buyer W & I insurance is increasingly used in secondary buy-outs.

Often there will be an element of self-insurance by the buyer between the management warranty cover and the buyer's W & I insurance cover, particularly as an element of self-insurance usually reduces the premium. Co-insurance is also an option which reduces the premium.

The issues relevant to buyer's warranty and indemnity cover are:

10.10.3.1 As it is the buyer who is the proposer, the buyer is not exposed to the risk of management fraud or material non-disclosure undermining the insurance policy. However, the buyer's knowledge is now relevant to the insurance policy and the buyer will need to be sure that the results of his due diligence, whether legal, financial or commercial, are properly disclosed to the insurer.

10.10.3.2 A buyer policy is not a reason to avoid normal due diligence. The insurer will wish to be sure that proper due diligence has been undertaken, without which the premium will be significantly higher (or the insurer may refuse cover altogether).

10.10.3.3 The standard exclusions referred to above for W & I insurance will continue to apply (completion accounts/net asset adjustments, forward-looking warranties, environmental, product liability, insurance and pension issues and management accounts and stock warranties).

10.10.4 Other issues

In addition to the structural problems discussed above, there are a number of other factors to be borne in mind where W & I insurance is being considered:

10.10.4.1 Cover can be quite expensive—typically starting at two per cent of the sum insured. There are, though, no hard and fast rules on the cost of the cover.

10.10.4.2 It is important to use an experienced broker who can structure bespoke cover to the transaction.

10.10.4.3 Obtaining cover can delay transactions, as the broker/underwriters will need to investigate the transaction thoroughly, which includes understanding the business, the warranties, reasons for insurance being sought and so on. Additionally the insurers will obtain their own legal advice on the sale and purchase agreement and disclosure letter and this will be at the proposer's cost.

10.10.4.4 W & I insurance cover can be obtained once a transaction has completed, although obviously there is a risk that cover may not be available or that it may be available at prohibitive rates. It also becomes less easy to match the sale and purchase agreement risk to the cover being written.

10.10.4.5 Where sellers are seeking insurance for all their warranty liability they will inevitably seek to match the warranties that they are giving to the insurance cover available and (as far as possible) avoid giving any warranties in respect of which insurance cover is not available. As a result, the buyer may find warranties being renegotiated, and the sale process extended, as insurers and their lawyers comment on the sale and purchase agreement. Conversely sellers should seek to match the warranties to the insurance cover available.

10.10.4.6 In any form of W & I insurance, insurers are keen for the insured to bear some of the pain, preferably by the insured taking on some of the risk between the minimum threshold for claims in the sale and purchase agreement and the level at which the insurance begins to apply. A degree of self-insurance will also reduce the premium.

Chapter 11

Tax Covenants, Tax Deeds and Tax Warranties

11.1 Tax covenants and tax deeds

On sales and purchases of shares, it has long been recognised that it is appropriate for certain tax liabilities to be the subject of indemnity (rather than warranty) protection and this gradually developed into the concept of a separate tax deed, containing a blanket indemnity against any tax liability, with a very wide definition of the kinds of tax covered by the indemnity. That indemnity would sometimes be structured as an indemnity in favour of the target company itself but then the case of *Zim Properties Ltd v Procter (Inspector of Taxes)* [1985] 58 T.C. 371 suggested that a payment to the target company could be taxable but that this was unlikely to be the case where the payment was made to the buyer, with the result that tax deeds are generally now structured so as to constitute an indemnity in favour of the buyer. It is not in fact strictly correct to refer to it as a tax indemnity as it is not an indemnity in favour of the target company and it is very often referred to today as a tax covenant, which is the expression used in this book. It is also very common nowadays for the tax covenant to be contained in a schedule to the sale and purchase agreement, along with all other tax provisions (tax warranties, limitations on liability and so on), rather than in a separate tax deed and that is the approach which has been adopted in Precedents 1 and 2 in App.2.

The principal provisions of a typical tax covenant can be summarised as follows.

11.1.1 Basic principles

The tax covenant will generally oblige the seller to compensate the buyer on a pound for pound basis for any tax liability of the target company which exceeds the tax provision in its last audited accounts and any tax liability which arises after the date to which those accounts were made up but before completion, but only to the extent that it arises other than the ordinary course of business of the target company.

Although it is almost invariable practice for the seller to be liable on a pound for pound basis, his advisers should always consider whether that is really appropriate, rather than unthinkingly accept that their client should automatically be liable for the full amount of every claim.

On some transactions, there is no real commercial logic to having a tax indemnity which applies on a strict pound for pound basis—for example, the sale and purchase agreement may provide that the purchase price will reduce if completion accounts show net assets of less than £1,000,000, with no provision for an increased price if net assets are more than that. If net assets were, in fact, £1,050,000 and a tax liability, for which provision had not been made in the completion accounts, for £60,000 subsequently arose, the buyer would almost certainly expect to be able to recover the full £60,000 but that would not be particularly logical—if the liability had come to light before completion and provision had been made for it in the completion accounts, the purchase price would only have reduced by £10,000.

Occasionally, there will be transactions where the buyer's solicitors have similar issues which they should consider. For example, the purchase price may have been agreed on the basis that completion accounts will show net assets of at least £1,000,000 but, in order to avoid arguing over comparatively small amounts, the parties may have agreed that there will be a "buffer" of £25,000 either side of that figure, so that the price will only increase if net assets are more than £1,000,025 and will only reduce if net assets are less than £975,000—but on the basis that if (for example) net assets turn out to be £1,030,000 or £970,000, the price will increase or reduce (as appropriate) by the full amount by which net assets are greater/less that £1,000,000 (i.e. by £30,000).

If the completion accounts showed net assets of £980,000 but an unexpected tax liability of £30,000 then arose, the buyer will, arguably, have overpaid by £50,000 (as the price would have reduced by that amount if provision for the liability had been made in the completion accounts).

The practice of leaving the tax covenant to be negotiated directly between the seller's solicitors' and the buyer's solicitors' tax specialists often means that the tax covenant "acquires a life of its own" and is not necessarily being considered in the context of the overall commercial transaction. It is essential to ensure that the tax specialists fully understand the structure of the transaction and (in particular) the way in which the purchase price is to be arrived at, rather than being allowed to negotiate the tax provisions in a vacuum.

11.1.2 Completion accounts

Where the purchase price is dependant upon completion accounts, it will generally be inappropriate for the tax covenant to operate by reference to tax liabilities in excess of the provision in the last audited accounts and in those circumstances the seller will normally have to compensate the buyer for any tax liability arising before completion, save to the extent of any tax provision in the completion accounts.

11.1.3 Events

The tax covenant will normally be drafted so that a claim will arise if the tax liability results from an "event" occurring on or before completion and the buyer will normally want to extend this to cover the situation where a tax liability arises after completion but which arises in part as a result of something happening before completion. The buyer may be concerned, for example, that a payment giving rise to a tax liability may be received after completion but pursuant to a contract entered into before completion and there are a number of specific situations were the combination of two acts can give rise to a tax charge. The seller, on the other hand, will be concerned about the wide-ranging effect of such a clause and is likely to want to delete it. There are various possible compromises, including a provision to the effect that the seller will only be liable if what was done before completion was outside the ordinary course of business, while what happened after completion was in the ordinary course of business.

11.1.4 Tax reliefs

Where a tax relief is taken into account in determining the tax provision to be made in the accounts, the loss or withdrawal of such a relief will give rise to a higher tax liability and, in those circumstances, the buyer will normally expect the seller to be liable under the tax covenant. The buyer is also likely, initially, to word the tax covenant so that, if there are tax losses which have not been utilised at completion, the seller will be liable under the tax covenant if they cease to be available as a result of something happening before completion. That is unlikely to be acceptable to the seller unless the value of those tax losses has been taken into account in arriving at the purchase price but the seller will normally have to accept that there may be a claim under the tax covenant if the accounts show the right to a repayment of tax as an asset and that right is lost.

The seller should not normally be liable where there are tax reliefs available to shelter the tax liability in question and these have arisen before completion, save where they have been taken into account in arriving at the tax provision in the accounts. If, for example, a tax liability arises for which no provision was made but which can be eliminated by utilising previously unutilised tax losses which arose before completion but were not treated as an asset in the accounts, the seller should not have any liability under the tax covenant. The position would normally, however, be different where the tax losses in question have arisen after completion, as those would then be losses which rightly belong to the buyer, who should not be obliged to use them to relieve a tax liability which should be the responsibility of the seller.

11.1.5 Mitigation

There are various situations in respect of which the seller will normally seek to limit or exclude his liability under the tax covenant, including:

11.1.5.1 Where the tax in question was paid before the date of the accounts and that fact was reflected in those accounts.

11.1.5.2 To the extent that specific provision or reserve has been made in the accounts (i.e. the latest audited accounts or the completion accounts, as appropriate), which accords with the general principle under which tax covenants are normally given (but note that whether or not this should include deferred tax provisions will need careful consideration).

11.1.5.3 To the extent that the tax liability arises or is increased as a result of changes in tax legislation or any increase of tax announced after completion and with retrospective effect, although it is a matter for negotiation as to whether this risk should be borne by the seller or by the buyer.

11.1.5.4 To the extent that the liability would not have arisen but for transactions after completion and other than in the ordinary course of business: in principle, this may be reasonable but the buyer may wish to limit the exclusion so that it only applies if the act in question could reasonably have been avoided and was not entered into pursuant to an obligation incurred before completion.

11.1.5.5 To the extent that there are tax reliefs available at completion to eliminate the liability in question (see 11.1.4 above).

11.1.5.6 To the extent that the buyer is able to make recovery in respect of the same liability under the tax warranties, in order to avoid double recovery (although the buyer will generally prefer to bring a claim under the tax covenant rather than under the tax warranties as the tax covenant is likely to give a more favourable basis for recovery).

11.1.5.7 If the buyer fails to give notice to the seller of the potential liability or fails to act in accordance with the reasonable instructions of the seller in connection with any dispute with tax authorities.

11.1.5.8 Sellers' solicitors will sometimes seek to amend the sale and purchase agreement so as to make the disclosure letter qualify the tax covenant, with the intention that the covenant should not apply to any circumstances which are disclosed in the disclosure letter. It would be very rare, however, for a buyer to accept this—for example, the disclosure letter may refer to a particular set of circumstances but it may be difficult (if not impossible) for the buyer to consider all of the possible tax consequences of those circumstances and few buyers would wish to become embroiled in a debate as to whether or not such a disclosure constituted a fair disclosure. The buyer should therefore refuse to accept that the tax covenant should be qualified in this way but should instead insist on the principle that, if there are any particular tax liabilities (or circumstances which may give rise to tax liabilities) which the seller wishes to exclude from the tax covenant, the seller should propose specific exclusions in the tax covenant itself, which the buyer may or may not accept (depending upon the nature and size of the liability and the respective bargaining strengths of the parties).

11.1.5.9 As discussed in 10.7.1 of Ch.10, there will normally be a limitation period of between six and seven years within which claims under a tax covenant have to be notified.

11.1.5.10 As discussed in 10.7.3 of Ch.10, it is normal for the parties to agree that claims under any tax covenant or tax indemnity will not be subject to any minimum threshold for claims.

11.1.6 Conduct of claims

The seller will normally want to oblige the buyer and the target company to take such action as the seller may reasonably require to resist, appeal or compromise any potential tax liability which may give rise to a payment under the tax covenant and the tax covenant will normally contain specific provisions to cover the extent to which they are obliged to do so.

The seller may seek to negotiate a provision under which it is the seller and his advisers who have the conduct of negotiations with and all claims by or against the tax authorities but whether or not the buyer accepts that or insists upon having conduct of claims himself is likely to depend on all the circumstances. The seller will almost certainly be keen to retain the conduct of negotiations but, if the buyer insists upon having conduct himself, then the seller may well argue that, if the buyer has conduct and fails to act in accordance with the reasonable instructions of the seller, then the seller should have no liability under the tax covenant. Most buyers will agree to act in accordance with the reasonable instructions of the seller but will be reluctant to accept that the seller should have no liability if they fail to do so as failing to do so may make no difference at all to the extent of the tax liability which is incurred.

11.2 Tax warranties

As discussed in 10.5 of Ch.10, there will almost invariably be extensive tax warranties on a sale and purchase of shares, even where there is a separate tax covenant or tax indemnity. The principal purpose of what, at first sight, appears to be "belt and braces" protection is to flush out as much disclosure as possible from the seller, so that the buyer can obtain as much information as possible about the tax position of the company and can (hopefully) become aware in advance of any tax issues which may need to be the subject of specific covenants or indemnities.

Typical tax warranties are contained in Pt 2 of Sch.4 to Precedents 1 and 2 and these include warranties as to the following:

11.2.1 Submission of returns, etc. to the tax authorities.

11.2.2 Disputes with the tax authorities.

11.2.3 Maintenance of PAYE, National Insurance, VAT and other records.

11.2.4 Payment of tax.

11.2.5 Reliance on extra-statutory or other concessions.

11.2.6   The making of all necessary deductions and withholdings in respect of tax (including PAYE and National Insurance contributions).

11.2.7   PAYE inspections, etc.

11.2.8   Close companies.

11.2.9   Potential tax liabilities in respect of capital gains.

11.2.10 Capital allowances.

11.2.11 Payment of stamp duty, stamp duty land tax and stamp duty reserve tax.

11.2.12 Anti-avoidance.

11.2.13 VAT.

11.2.14 Group tax.

11.2.15 Foreign connections.

11.3   Group VAT registrations

If a group VAT registration is in force, then additional considerations arise. The effect of a group registration is to enable all companies within the scope of that registration to make supplies from one to the other without accounting for VAT (s.43(1) of the Value Added Tax Act 1994). The representative member is liable to account to or recover from HM Revenue and Customs all VAT payable by or due to the group, but all the members of the group will be liable jointly and severally for any VAT due from the representative member.

If the target and its subsidiaries include all the companies within the group registration, then the buyer will probably wish to continue with that registration and may in due course wish to include the acquired companies within any group registration of his own. If, on the other hand, the group registration includes companies in the seller's group which the buyer is not acquiring, the terms of the group registration will need to be amended. Whether the buyer takes over the group registration will depend in part upon whether the representative member is included in the target and its subsidiaries or whether it is a company retained by the seller. Agreement will have to be reached between the parties and arrangements made either to separate out the group members and apply for a new group registration for the target and its subsidiaries or for inclusion of the target and its subsidiaries in the buyer's group registration.

Where there is a group registration which includes companies in the seller's group which the buyer is not acquiring, the sale and purchase agreement should contain an indemnity against any liability falling on the target or its subsidiaries for VAT which is attributable to any other member of the seller's group (see para.1.2 of Pt 4 of Sch.4 to Precedents 1 and 2).

11.4 Conduct of tax returns

The sale and purchase agreement may contain provisions for the preparation, submission and agreement of the corporation tax computations and returns for periods ended on or before the date of the last audited accounts.

It will typically be agreed that the seller will be responsible for these (see, for example, para.10 of Pt 4 of Sch.4 to Precedents 1 and 2).

Chapter 12

Paying the Purchase Price—Consideration Structures

Paragraph 8.6 of Ch.8 sets out various alternative arrangements for the payment of the purchase price or satisfaction of any other consideration for a sale and purchase and this chapter discusses some of the issues surrounding these various alternatives, as well as discussing a number of related issues. For convenience, they are generally discussed in the context of a sale and purchase of shares but the points discussed will generally be equally applicable to sales and purchases of assets. Tax planning (both for the buyer and for the seller) often plays a key part in determining the structure which is appropriate for the particular transaction and the tax issues which are most likely to arise in practice are discussed in detail in Chs 13 and 14.

12.1   Purchase price payable in full in cash on completion

Where the purchase price is payable in full in cash on completion, then the relevant provisions of the sale and purchase agreement will be very straightforward as it will simply be necessary to specify the amount of the purchase price, the requirement that it be paid in full on completion and the way in which it is to be paid—the seller will require payment to be made in cleared funds and this will either take the form of a banker's draft or a direct bank transfer to a specified account. In practice, the payment will normally be made via the seller's solicitors and it is customary to include a provision to the effect that a payment to them will satisfy the buyer's obligations and that the buyer need not be concerned to make sure that the money actually reaches the seller (see, for example, cl.3.6.2 of Precedent 1 in App.2).

As discussed in 9.7 of Ch.9, it should be noted that, on a sale and purchase of assets where the buyer is agreeing to assume the amounts owing to creditors of the business, that will normally be treated as part of the consideration for the assets. The consideration will therefore comprise the agreement of the buyer to assume liability for the amounts owing to creditors, plus any agreed cash payment. Clause 4 of Precedent 3 in App.2 has been drafted on that basis.

12.2   Purchase price payable by instalments

If the purchase price is to be paid by instalments, the sale and purchase agreement will specify the dates on which those instalments are to be paid and, if there is more than one instalment payable after completion, the seller will normally require a provision to the effect that, if the buyer fails to pay one instalment, it will render the remaining instalments immediately due and payable. The seller may also require a provision under which the outstanding balance of the purchase price will become immediately due and payable if certain specified "events of insolvency" take place—typically, the taking of steps for the winding-up of the buyer or for the appointment of a receiver or adminis-trator over all or part of the buyer's assets. If the seller is prepared to accept payment by instalments, he should also endeavour to include a provision in the sale and purchase agreement to the effect that the amounts in question will be paid in full on the due date and with the buyer having no right to set off any warranty, indemnity or similar claims against the amount payable (this subject is discussed in 10.9.4 of Ch.10).

As a matter of course, the seller should consider the financial strength of the buyer and, if he has any concerns, he should press for appropriate security for the outstanding amount (see 12.9 below).

12.3   Purchase price subject to retention

If it is agreed that part of the purchase price will be retained as security for warranty and indemnity claims, the first draft of the sale and purchase agreement is likely to give the buyer the right to set off any amount claimed by him against the retention. The seller, however, will be concerned that the buyer will simply put forward spurious or inflated claims in order to delay payment and should therefore press for the amount of the retention to be put into a designated bank account, which will normally be in the joint names of the buyer's solicitors and the seller's solicitors, rather than simply being retained by the buyer. Whether or not the seller is able to persuade the buyer to agree to this, he should insist upon some mechanism for establishing the genuineness of the claim and the amount of the claim, with the amount claimed being paid into a joint solicitors' account until the claim has been resolved and the balance of the retention being paid on the due date. For example, if there is a retention of £500,000 and the buyer is able to show that he has a prima facie claim for £100,000, on the date when the retention is due to be paid the buyer should be obliged to pay £400,000 to the seller and to pay £100,000 into the joint account, pending resolution of his claim. If it is sub-sequently agreed or determined by a court that the buyer is entitled to damages of £60,000 for breach of warranty, he will be entitled to £60,000 from the joint account, with the balance of £40,000 being payable to the seller and any interest earned on the account being apportioned between the buyer and the seller in the same proportions.

Where money is to be (or may be) paid into a joint solicitors' (or similar) account, the terms on which it is to be held (and, in particular, the circumstances in which payments out of the account are to be permitted) should be set out clearly in the sale and purchase agreement or in a separate escrow agreement. Precedent 34 in App.2 is an example of a fairly typical escrow agreement.

It will also be necessary to make sure that the account mandate is appropriate for the circumstances so that if, for example, the account is to be opened in the joint names of the parties' solicitors, any withdrawal from the account should require the signature of at least one representative of each firm.

These issues are discussed in more detail in 10.9.3 of Ch.10.

12.4   Purchase price subject to adjustment in accordance with completion accounts

12.4.1   Introduction

In many transactions, the precise amount of the purchase price is not fixed at the point when the sale and purchase agreement is signed but, instead the parties agree a provisional figure which is subject to adjustment by reference to a set of accounts of the target company or business prepared as at (or shortly before or shortly after) completion (completion accounts). Typically, the parties will agree that the purchase price will be subject to adjustment if the net assets being acquired vary from a specified figure or if the profits down to completion vary from an historic level.

For example, Buyer PLC may have agreed to acquire the entire issued share capital of Target Limited from Seller Limited for a purchase price of £5,000,000, that price having been arrived at on the basis that Buyer will on completion acquire a company (Target) with net assets of at least £4,000,000. As Target will continue to trade down to completion, it is most unlikely that Buyer would be able to satisfy himself through due diligence that there will be net assets of at least £4,000,000 on completion and so the sale and purchase agreement will provide (if this is what the parties agree) that the provisional purchase price of £5,000,000 will reduce on a pound for pound basis if and to the extent that the net assets of Target, as shown by completion accounts, are less than £4,000,000. For example, therefore, if the completion accounts showed net assets of £3,500,000, the purchase price would reduce to £4,500,000.

Depending on all the circumstances, Seller may argue that there should be a similar price adjustment if net assets are above £4,000,000 and so, if that is agreed and the completion accounts show net assets of £4,250,000, the purchase price will increase to £5,250,000.

Precedents 1 and 2 in App.2 contain an alternative version of cl.3 to deal with transactions where the purchase price is subject to adjustment by reference to the net assets of the target company, as shown by completion accounts.

Precedents 3 and 4 in App.2 similarly contain alternative versions of cl.4 although, on a sale and purchase of assets where debtors and creditors are not included, the exercise is likely to be more straightforward.

12.4.2   Preparation of the completion accounts

12.4.2.1   In the example given above, every £1 variation in net assets will mean that the purchase price will increase or decrease by £1 and so, inevitably, when it comes to the preparation and finalisation of the completion accounts, there is every incentive for Seller to argue for the highest possible figure and for Buyer to argue for the lowest possible figure. The rules governing the preparation and finalisation of those accounts will be set out in the sale and purchase agreement and it is essential to make the drafting as precise as possible in order to minimise subsequent uncertainty and dispute. Quite subtle use of wording in the rules can mean that they work to the advantage of one party over the other, with potentially substantial financial consequences. It is important therefore that the rules are reviewed by someone with a high degree of financial literacy.

12.4.2.2 It is important also to bear in mind that issues which might be disregarded when preparing and finalising statutory accounts, on the basis that they are not "material", may be far more material in the context of completion accounts, on which an increase or decrease in the purchase price may depend.

The due diligence work undertaken by accountants can mean that they are well placed to do this and the parties' legal advisers would be well-advised to make it clear to their clients that the parties should rely on their accountants (or other financial advisers) to ensure that the wording in the agreement is appropriately drafted.

12.4.3 **Principles to be applied**

The sale and purchase agreement will normally provide that the completion accounts must be prepared in accordance with a number of principles and these will typically be:

12.4.3.1 specific accounting policies and methodologies, to be set out as the detailed rules in the sale and purchase agreement;

12.4.3.2 policies and methodologies consistent with those adopted in the target's latest statutory and/or management accounts;

12.4.3.3 compliance with generally accepted accounting principles in the UK ("UK GAAP").

Schedule 9 to Precedents 1 and 2 in App.2 and Sch.11 to Precedents 3 and 4 have been drafted on that basis.

However, as explained in Ch.16, the accounting rules in the UK are going through some fundamental changes with the introduction of International Financial Reporting Standards ("IFRS") and, in appropriate cases, it will be necessary to consider whether references to "UK GAAP" continue to be appropriate.

12.4.4 **Conflicting principles**

One of the key tasks in drafting the rules for the preparation of the completion accounts is to establish a clear order of precedence in the event of conflict between the various principles. This is important as, for example, the parties will normally wish to make sure that the specific policies set out in the agreement apply, regardless of whether their application would be consistent with previous accounts or would comply with UK

GAAP. Similarly, if it is agreed that the completion accounts will be prepared in accordance with policies which are consistent with past accounts, one or both parties will normally wish to make sure that those policies are applied, regardless of whether or not they comply with UK GAAP—for example, the seller will want to prevent the buyer from being able to argue that the policies which have been used for valuing stock do not comply with UK GAAP and that more "conservative" policies should be used instead, thereby reducing the net assets and, as a result, the purchase price. A typical order of priority is:

- first of all, the specific policies set out in the agreement; then

- "consistency"; and then

- compliance with UK GAAP.

The order of priority between "consistency" and UK GAAP which is most beneficial for a buyer can, however, vary, depending on the particular circumstances of the target company or business. In the example given above, it would be in the best interests of the buyer to argue that stock should be valued in accordance with UK GAAP if that means that it would then be valued on a more conservative basis but the opposite may be the case where the buyer is aware that, in the past, stock has been valued very conservatively and with generous provisions for slow-moving and obsolete stock. In that situation, the buyer will not want to leave open the possibility of the seller being able to argue that such provisions are not required by UK GAAP and that stock should therefore be valued more "aggressively". Schedule 9 to Precedents 1 and 2 in App.2 and Sch.11 to Precedents 3 and 4 have been drafted on that basis.

With precision in drafting, the specific rules provide the most certainty of outcome. The "consistency" principle may not always cover the particular circumstances encountered in the completion accounts, whilst UK GAAP is not a simple set of rules and in some areas can be open to broad interpretation (Ch.16 provides further details on the meaning of the phrase "UK GAAP"). Moreover, the introduction of IFRS is resulting in major revisions to UK GAAP, which can have a major impact on completion accounts prepared under "UK GAAP" (what was UK GAAP a year ago may no longer be so).

The application of "consistency" in the completion accounts may also have to distinguish between consistency of treatment in the target's statutory accounts and in its management accounts.

For a buyer, a due diligence report which clearly sets out the key accounting policies and methodologies of the target (and any recent change thereto) and a comparison with UK GAAP can be a very helpful guide in relation to drafting the rules for the preparation of completion accounts.

Buyers should take particular care before agreeing to accept "consistency" when buying a business which is a division of a larger company rather than a separate legal entity and when buying a business from a large corporate seller which, by comparison to the rest of the seller's operations, would be regarded as very small. In the case of a division, there will not have been separate audited accounts and the basis of accounting in the past may not have been as precise as should have been the case. Similarly, where the target business is one which is so small as barely to "appear on the radar screen" of the seller's parent company, the parent company may not have taken steps to make sure that its basis of accounting accords with the group's policies.

12.4.5 "True and fair"

It is sometimes tempting (particularly for lawyers who are not as financially literate as their colleagues in the accountancy profession) to include a requirement that the completion accounts must "show a true and fair view" of the financial position of the target company or business at the date to which they are prepared and of its profits or losses for the period which they cover but this will not normally be appropriate.

Where the completion accounts are to be prepared as statutory accounts (for example, where completion coincides with the financial year end of a target company), the sale and purchase agreement should provide for statutory accounts to be prepared which do "give a true and fair view" and for a separate statement of net assets then to be prepared, in accordance with the provisions of the sale and purchase agreement, which is not required to do so and on which any adjustment to the purchase price will be based.

12.4.6 Common problems

Experience shows that some common areas that are sometimes not adequately dealt with in the provisions regarding the preparation of completion accounts include:

12.4.6.1 Provisions for doubtful debts:

- Often provisioning in this area in the accounts of the target business can be based solely on subjective assessment by management.

- To introduce a more objective measure, the specific rules for completion accounts sometimes state that provision should be made for "all debts remaining unpaid for [(say)] three months after the completion date". But, depending on the precise wording, this could exclude known doubtful debts not yet this old (a customer may be known to be in deep financial difficulty but its debts may be quite recent). Similarly under this scenario, if a debt is paid sometime after being outstanding for three months after the completion date, should the provision remain in the completion accounts?

- Should VAT recovery on the doubtful debt be assumed in setting up the provision?

- Should provision be made for all credit note requests from customers or should a provision be made only for those credit notes expected or actually raised in a defined period?

- Is it necessary to take account of insurance against bad debts?

- Care is needed in relation to certain types of business.

For example, the invoices sent by suppliers to many major retail chains are generally ignored by the retailers. The retail chains operate a "self billing" system. They count the goods received and price them at what they consider to be the agreed price and then pay the supplier what they consider to be payable. Reconciling the supplier's debtors with their customer's accounts can therefore be a key issue in this sector.

12.4.6.2 Elimination of intra group profits:

- If the completion accounts require stocks to be valued on a basis consistent with that employed in the statutory accounts of the target business, this may include an element of intra group profit in stock on product sourced from another company in the seller's group.

- The buyer may seek specifically to exclude any intra group profit in stock in the completion account rules.

12.4.6.3 Valuation of stock and work-in-progress

The valuation of stock and work-in-progress, particularly in a manufacturing business, is not straightforward. Any wording to define the method of gross valuation of stock and the provisioning for slow moving, excess or absolute stock require careful drafting. There can be many methods of determining "actual" cost.

- If stocks are a material asset, a stock take as at the date of the completion accounts is recommended for the following reasons:

  - physical existence of stock can be confirmed; and

  - damaged slow moving, excess or obsolete stock can be identified.

- It is particularly helpful to have representatives of the buyer at the stock take (particularly a member of his production team), because they will be able to use their experience to identify obsolete and slow moving stock.

- Companies normally rely on their accounting and costing systems to generate the gross value of work in progress but these systems are not infallible. For example, a manufacturer of lorries used its standard costing system to value the lorries held in stock, but a review of the breakdown of the product costing identified that the standard cost included two engines.

- Stock and work-in-progress which has no economic value because it is slow moving or obsolete should be written off. For example, the company manufacturing lorries mentioned above had decided, some years before the sale, to diversify its product range into taxis and had invested in sufficient parts to manufacture an initial 20 taxis. In fact, only one taxi had been manufactured and it had not been possible to obtain any orders for more; therefore the whole of this stock simply had scrap value.

- Stocks of high technology parts (such as electronic parts) require very careful storage or they become damaged. A company manufacturing electronic parts found itself with too much stock to store in its own warehouse and rented space off site to house the excess. At the stock take it was established that the components had become damaged and had to be written off.

12.4.6.4 Long term contracts

Long term contracts are those for delivery of a large project or provision of a service which typically but not necessarily will take in excess of a year. Often, the precise profit earned on the project is not capable of being established until the project concludes and therefore there are difficulties as to what profit (if any) should be taken in the interim.

Where the outcome of a long term contract can be assessed with reasonable certainty before its conclusion, an appropriate level of attributable profit should be recognised (as the difference between turnover and reported costs) for that contract. In some cases, separate parts of a contract may fail to be treated as, in effect, a separate contract for profit recognition purposes.

Accounting for long term contracts can be a particular issue in a company which does not undertake long term contracts as part of its core business. For example, a small division of a large company obtained a contract to develop a new engine for the Navy. Regular payments were received from the Ministry of Defence and these were credited to sales and the costs incurred written off. The management at head office paid little attention to the contract until it became clear that no further payments were due from the Ministry of Defence but the development of the engine was substantially incomplete. The costs of completing the contract then had to be provided, resulting in a large loss for the division. Had the contract been correctly identified as a long term contract then the payments received from the Ministry of Defence would only have been released to profit as appropriate stages of development had been completed.

Provision should be made for "foreseeable losses" on a contract as soon as such losses are foreseen.

In determining attributable profit (or, if applicable the foreseeable loss) adequate allowance needs to be made for any estimated remedial/snagging works, if applicable, and the costs of any "guarantee" period for maintenance, as well as future increases in costs not recoverable under the terms of the contract.

The timing and quantification of the recognition of variations (an instruction from the customer for a change in the scope of work under a contract) and claims (for the recovery of costs for matters not envisaged in the contract) can be a difficult area in preparing accounts.

Generally, revenue from variations approved by the customer can be taken into account. For claims, there can be a very high level of uncertainty and therefore it will not be prudent to anticipate claim monies until negotiations with a customer are close to finalisation, such that the customer's acceptance of the claim and the relevant minimum level of payment is clear.

12.4.6.5 Accounting for leased assets

Are lease incentives (for example, rent free or reduced-rent periods or contributions to fit out costs) properly spread over the term of the lease rather than recognised immediately?

12.4.6.6 Fixed assets:

- How are tangible fixed assets to be accounted for—at cost or valuation? Where there are freehold or leasehold properties, the parties should agree in advance the values that are to be attributed to them and these should be specified in the agreement.

- Are there any individual assets which require separate-mention?

- Is there a risk of impairment in the value of fixed assets and, if so, how is this treated?

- Should finance costs on borrowings directly attributable to a specific asset be capitalised as part of the cost (under UK GAAP such capitalisation is permitted but is not mandatory).

- Has any "own labour" been capitalised? If so, have appropriate costs been included?

- Fixed assets which have no economic value to the business should be written off.

  For example, a company invested in a new factory and specific plant and machinery in order to manufacture a new innovative product. A substantial order had been obtained from an overseas company which was currently supplied by an overseas supplier with a similar product. Before the company had supplied a single product, the overseas supplier brought a successful action for patent infringement. Because the equipment was specific to manufacture of the product, the whole of the investment had to be written off by the company.

- Difficulties can also arise in relation to fixed assets which have been manufactured by the company itself. In principle, the cost capitalised in respect of self-constructed assets should be the cost to bring the assets to their current condition and location. Part of the grooming of the business for sale is to review the valuation of such fixed assets to make sure that an appropriate amount of labour and overheads has been capitalised.

- When dealing with a private business, assets which are not used in the business (for example, holiday homes or cars for members of family) may be included in fixed assets. Provision needs to be made for these assets to be transferred to the owners and treated as part of the purchase consideration (with appropriate adjustments for taxation if necessary).

12.4.6.7 Creditors

Completeness of creditors is a most important factor in preparing completion accounts.

For example, a business sold products to a customer in the Middle East on which substantial commissions were payable to agents. The company's practice was to account for these on payment rather than accrue them on sale of the products and the completion accounts identified that creditors were significantly understated because of this.

12.4.6.8 Is account to be taken of any liability or other matter which could form the subject-matter of a claim under the warranties and/or any tax covenant or tax indemnity?

12.4.6.9 Currency conversion issues:

- How are foreign currency transactions to be dealt with?

- Which method of translation is to be used?

- Valuation of debtors, etc. where they are expressed in a foreign currency.

12.4.6.10 Where there is a defined benefit scheme the accounting can be very complex, with potentially large sums involved. As a result, typically, this would have been a major area of focus of the buyer's due diligence exercise. How the accounting for refined benefit schemes is addressed in the Completion Accounts will need to draw on this work, and may require further specialist advice to make sure that the application of the accounting rules (principally FRS 17) does not give rise to any unexpected result.

12.4.6.11 Holiday pay

Should a provision for holiday entitlement earned but not yet taken be established (some businesses accrue for such costs whilst others charge the costs as they fall)?

12.4.6.12 Taxation

As the acquisition date is not generally at a year end, a mechanism for determining the tax charge in the completion accounts may well need to be in place. Matters to consider can include:

- Should a full tax computation be prepared or is it adequate simply to apply a defined tax rate to profit before tax and (typically) goodwill amortisation?

- What effective tax rate (this can alter, inter alia, on a change of parent company) should be used?

- Should a deferred tax asset be recognised in respect of available tax losses?

- The completion accounts rules may specifically require a provision to be made which would not be generally permissible under UK GAAP—should tax relief be assumed on this?

12.4.6.13 Provisions and contingent liabilities/assets:

- Although it is often advisable to address the specific treatment of significant provisions and contingent balances in the completion accounts rules, it is not always possible to anticipate all such matters.

- The treatment of provisions, contingent liabilities and contingent assets in completion accounts, left to be determined on the basis of consistency with past practice, or UK GAAP, can often be an area of dispute.

- A provision is defined as "a liability of uncertain timing or amount" (FRS 12 para.2). For a provision to be permissible under UK GAAP, there needs to be a present obligation (either legal or constructive) as a result of a past event that probably (as opposed to possibly) requires a transfer of economic benefit (i.e. incurring expenses or losses). It is also necessary that a reliable estimate of the amount of the obligation can be made. Provisions are not allowed under UK GAAP in respect of expenses and losses that are likely to arise in the future but for which no obligation exists at the accounts date.

- "Probable" in this context means that the "probability that the event will occur is greater than that it will not". This suggests that a level of likelihood of over 50 per cent is required.

- It is clear that provisions cannot be made for future operating losses as they are not the result of a past event (although anticipated future losses may well indicate the need for an impairment review of asset values or the presence of onerous contracts).

- An onerous contract is defined as "a contract in which the unavoidable costs of meeting the obligations under it exceed the economic benefits expected to be received under it" (FRS 12 para.2). Where a contract is onerous and cannot be cancelled without penalty, then the accounting rules may require a provision for the onerous element

- A contingent liability is defined for accounting (in FRS 12 para.2) as:

"a) a possible obligation that arises from past events, and whose existence will be confirmed only by the occurrence of one or more uncertain future events not wholly within the entity's control; or

b) a present obligation that arises from past events but is not recognised because:

      i)   it is not probable that a transfer of economic benefits will be required to settle the obligation or;

    ii) the amount of the obligation cannot be measured with sufficient reliability".

- Again, the underlying principle in respect of contingent liabilities under UK GAAP is that provision should not be made unless, inter alia, the likelihood of the liability crystallising is assessed as "probable" (rather than simply "possible"). This can be a subjective area.

- Under UK GAAP, contingent assets should not be recognised in the accounts unless it is virtually certain that the asset will arise.

The above examples of points to consider are obviously not exhaustive. Given the complexity of accounting rules, it is advisable that the Completion Accounts rules are subject to scrutiny by an accounting expert.

12.4.7   Who should prepare the completion accounts?

12.4.7.1 Typically, the sale and purchase agreement will set out which party will prepare the completion accounts and provide for a mechanism for these to be reviewed and agreed by the other party. This may involve the completion accounts being audited by one party's accountants and reviewed by the other's.

12.4.7.2 The sale and purchase agreement sometimes requires the accountants to "prepare and audit" the completion accounts. In fact, accountants are not permitted to audit accounts that they have prepared and so the completion accounts should be prepared either by the seller or by the buyer. Generally, as the new owner of the target business, the buyer is best placed to prepare the completion accounts, although this is not always the case.

12.4.7.3 There can be an advantage in taking responsibility for preparing the completion accounts, as it is then left for the other party to justify amendment. Where, for example, it is debatable whether a provision should or should not be made, the preparer of the completion accounts can take the view most advantageous to his position, and then the onus is on the other party to show that the approach adopted is demonstrably wrong.

12.4.7.4 The sale and purchase agreement will set out the timetable for the preparation of the completion accounts, their delivery to the other party and their subsequent agreement or determination. The amount of time given should be realistic but should not be unduly generous and, in order to prevent the other party from dragging its feet, the agreement will normally state that the party preparing the completion accounts will deliver them to the other within an agreed period and that, if that other does not raise any queries or objections within a specified period after that, he will be deemed to have accepted the completion accounts as supplied to him.

12.4.7.5 Although it can take weeks or months for the parties to "agree" the completion accounts, there is often no explicit mechanism in place for the party preparing the completion accounts to seek to revise them for subsequent events or information after they have been passed to the other party for review. If the buyer is preparing the accounts, it may be advisable to seek to include such a mechanism to allow him to seek justifiable revisions to the draft completion accounts.

12.4.8 Tie-break mechanism

In any event, the sale and purchase agreement should include a mechanism under which any disagreements on the completion accounts which cannot be resolved by negotiation will be determined by an appropriate third party (typically, an independent accountant, acting as an expert and not as an arbitrator).

In practice, this is likely to be expensive and time-consuming and parties will normally "horse trade" and reach an agreement without actually invoking the tie-break procedure.

Parties who agree a deal which is based on completion accounts should accept that, the less precise the wording in the sale and purchase agreement, the more likely it is that disputes will arise and that they will have to come back to the negotiating table. Even where there is precise drafting, there is likely to be some haggling and some compromises are likely to be required.

In view of the time and expense that can be incurred in trying to "fine tune" the completion accounts to the nearest pound, it may be worth agreeing that there will be no price adjustment if the amount of the net assets varies within specified tolerance levels: for example, if Buyer PLC is acquiring the entire issued share capital of Target Limited from Seller Limited and it is agreed in principle that the purchase price will increase or decrease to the extent that the net assets of Target, as shown by completion accounts, are greater than or less than £4,000,000, the parties might be prepared to agree that there will be no adjustment if the net assets turn out to be within £25,000 either side of that figure, i.e. if they are between £4,975,000 and £5,025,000.

12.4.9 Adjusting payments

As it is likely to take some time to prepare and finalise the completion accounts, the parties will normally agree that, on completion of the transaction, the buyer will make a payment to the seller on account of the purchase price, such payment to be of an amount which is appropriate in all the circumstances.

The amount to be paid on completion will be a matter for negotiation and agreement, as the seller will inevitably be pressing for the highest possible amount to be paid, while the buyer will be keen to keep the payment as low as possible, not least because he may be concerned about the difficulties of trying to recover sums that he has already paid to the seller, if it turns out that he has overpaid. The buyer is likely to be particularly concerned if he is buying from a number of individual sellers or from a company whose financial position may not be particularly strong, while the seller may have similar concerns as to the ability of the buyer to pay any additional consideration which may turn out to be payable.

Typically, therefore, the parties will agree that a payment on account will be made to the seller which is reasonably close to (but not more than) the parties' best estimate of the purchase price, with a further amount then being paid into an escrow account (normally in the joint names of the buyer's and the seller's solicitors) pending final agreement or determination of the net asset value.

For example, if Buyer is acquiring the entire issued share capital of Target from Tom, Dick and Harriet (Sellers) for a purchase price of £5,000,000, subject to adjustment to the extent that the net assets of Target are more or less than £4,000,000, the parties may agree that it is almost inconceivable that net assets will be less than £3,600,000, and it may therefore be agreed that Buyer will pay £4,600,000 to Sellers on completion and that £400,000 (or perhaps more, if there seems to be a reasonable possibility of net assets being more than £4,000,000) will be paid into an escrow account and held there until the final amount of the purchase price has been agreed or determined.

The sale and purchase agreement will provide for any further payment by Buyer or any repayment by Sellers to be made within a few business days after the final purchase price has been agreed or determined and that any such payment or repayment will first of all be satisfied from the escrow account.

Schedule 9 to Precedents 1 and 2 in App.2 and Sch.11 to Precedents 3 and 4 contains typical wording regarding the preparation of the completion accounts, their subsequent agreement or determination, the making of a payment "on account" at completion and the making of any subsequent payment or repayment.

12.5   Purchase price subject to an earn-out or similar arrangement

All or (far more commonly) part of the purchase price may be dependant upon the future performance of the target company or business and this will typically (although not necessarily) mean that it will be determined by reference to a multiple of the profits for an agreed period after completion. In practice, this is likely to be the case where the parties are unable to agree on the valuation of the target company or business, with the result that the buyer is not prepared to pay the price that the seller is looking for unless he can be satisfied that the profits after completion show that that price can be justified. It may also be appropriate where some or all of the sellers are key to the success of the company or business, as an earn-out may help to retain their loyalty and incentivise them to maximise profits.

To give a typical example, Buyer may agree to acquire the entire issued share capital of Target from Tom, Dick and Harriet (Sellers) for a total consideration of £1,000,000 plus a sum equal to three times the average of the pre-tax profits of Target over the period of two years immediately following completion. As where there are completion accounts, it will be necessary for the sale and purchase agreement to set out these arrangements as clearly and as precisely as possible and particular concerns of the parties will be:

- making sure that it is clear how the parties are to arrive at the profit figure to which the multiple is to be applied—for example, if it is agreed that the multiple will be based on pre-tax (rather than post-tax) profits, then that will need to be stated;

- specifying the accounting practices and principles which are to apply in arriving at that profit figure;

- from Sellers' point of view, how to make sure that Buyer, as the new owner of Target, does not do anything to make it difficult for Sellers to maximise their entitlement under the earn-out;

- from Sellers' point of view, to make sure that Buyer does not take steps to manipulate the profits of Target downwards so as to reduce the earn-out entitlement;

- from Buyer's point of view, to make sure that Sellers do not take steps artificially to increase profits and thereby increase their entitlement under the earn-out;

- from Buyer's point of view, to make sure that the business is run properly during the earn-out period;

- to make sure that there is an agreed timetable and procedure for determination of Sellers' entitlement under the earn-out and for the payment of any additional consideration to which they may be entitled.

12.5.1 Definition of "profit"

The profits to which the agreed earn-out multiple is to be applied will be based on accounts for the relevant period and these may be statutory accounts (if the earn-out period coincides with a year-end) or accounts prepared specifically for the purpose. The sale and purchase agreement will normally provide that, on the basis of those accounts, the buyer will produce a statement of the "profit" for the relevant period and will specify how that figure should be arrived at. The starting-point for determining the profit is likely to be the accounting practices and principles which were used in the preparation of the target's last statutory accounts but, as in agreeing the rules for the preparation of completion accounts, it may well be necessary to consider the order of priority between "consistency" and UK GAAP which are discussed in 12.4.3. It is likely also that there will be other points which will need to be considered and which may result in adjustments to the figure that would otherwise have been produced and these include:

12.5.1.1 Whether the figure is to be determined before (as in the example given above) or after tax.

12.5.1.2 Whether the figure is to be determined before or after interest.

12.5.1.3 Whether the figure should be before or after exceptional items—these will very often be excluded from the calculation but the parties will need to give particular consideration to any "one-off" costs which they are anticipating—for example, any post-completion redundancy or relocation costs. Similarly with any "one-off" income.

12.5.1.4 Whether (as would normally be the case) the figure should be determined before taking account of any dividends paid or payable in respect of the period in question.

12.5.1.5 Whether or not account should be taken of profits or losses on the revaluation of fixed assets.

12.5.1.6 Whether the figure should be determined before or after depreciation and/or amortisation.

12.5.1.7 Whether management or other charges by the buyer or other companies in the buyer's group should be taken into account.

12.5.1.8 Whether adjustments should be made to take account of any additional costs or any cost-savings which may result from the target company or business becoming part of the buyer's group (for example, reductions in insurance premiums as a result of being able to benefit from group rates).

These are just some of the points which are likely to arise and there are many other points which may, in particular circumstances, fall to be considered and which, it may be agreed, will give rise to adjustments in arriving at the profit for the purposes of the earn-out.

In appropriate cases, it will also be necessary to consider whether the introduction of IFRS means that references to UK GAAP will no longer be appropriate and, in any event, it may be necessary to consider the impact of the likely convergence between UK GAAP and IFRS.

12.5.2 Protection of ability to maximise earn-out

In the example given above, Sellers will be very conscious of the fact that, after completion, Target will be controlled by Buyer and that there will be various ways in which

Buyer would be able to prevent their maximising the profits of Target and their earn-out entitlement, including:

> 12.5.2.1 Preventing Tom, Dick and Harriet from devoting their time to managing the business of Target and enhancing its profitability—for example, by diverting them to other projects within Buyer's group or, ultimately, dismissing them from their employment.
>
> 12.5.2.2 Transferring the assets and business of Target to Buyer or another company in its group (with the result that Target would no longer be trading as a separate limited company and would not be making any profits).
>
> 12.5.2.3 Diverting profitable business from Target to another company in Buyer's group.
>
> 12.5.2.4 "Starving" Target of the working capital which is necessary in order to maximise its profitability.
>
> 12.5.2.5 Arranging for Target to buy or sell goods from or to Buyer or other companies in Buyer's group other than on normal arm's length terms—for example, if there are other companies in Buyer's group which are suppliers to Target, Buyer may arrange for those goods to be supplied at a price which is sufficiently high to eliminate any profit margin in Target.
>
> 12.5.2.6 Reducing or eliminating any profit in Target by levying management or similar charges on Target.
>
> 12.5.2.7 Incurring substantial development costs which may impact on profits during the earn-out period but which may have significant financial benefits in the medium to long term.
>
> 12.5.2.8 Incurring significant capital expenditure which may have a serious impact on the profits for the earn-out period, but may result in medium to long term benefits.

Sellers will therefore expect the sale and purchase agreement to include provisions which restrict Buyer's ability to take any of these steps (and there will no doubt be other similar provisions which sellers will want to include).

The extent to which such restrictions are acceptable to Buyer will be a matter of negotiation, but most buyers will accept that sellers are entitled to this sort of protection.

Buyer may, however, insist on the ability to levy genuine management charges and Sellers may therefore have to accept that Buyer may charge for management and other services (for example, payroll, accounting and IT services) provided that it does so at a commercial rate. Buyer will expect also to be able to re-charge the costs of third party services such as audit fees and fees for tax advice and that should be reasonable, provided that the proportion to be allocated to Target is fair and reasonable.

Alternatively, Sellers may be prepared to agree to there being no restrictions on the ability of Buyer to impose management or similar charges, provided that the amount charged, to the extent that it exceeds a reasonable commercial charge for services actually provided, is added back for the purposes of determining the earn-out profits.

Issues concerning development costs or capital expenditure are more difficult to resolve as Sellers may press for a restriction on the target incurring such costs or expenditure without the prior consent of Sellers, but Buyer will want to have an unfettered right to do so if he considers that it would be in the best interests of the business.

A further concern of Buyer may also be that the inclusion of these restrictions for the benefit of Sellers will delay the integration of Target and its business into Buyer's group.

12.5.3 Buyer's concerns

In the example give above, in the same way that Sellers will be concerned that Buyer may be able to prevent their maximising the profits of Target or may be able to take artificial steps to reduce the profits on which the earn-out is based, Buyer will be concerned that Sellers will run the business with their eyes fixed firmly on the earn-out rather than what is in the best interests of the business. As discussed above, a particular concern will be that Sellers will be tempted to take a short term view and seek to defer development expenditure or capital expenditure until after the earn-out period, even if that would not be in the best interests of Target. Buyer will also be concerned that Sellers may take artificial steps to increase the earn-out profits, for example:

12.5.3.1 Sellers may sell profitable product lines and keep loss-making lines in stock.

12.5.3.2 Sellers may offer generous discounts to customers in order to boost sales—even if the profit margin is greatly reduced, the fact that the earn-out is based on a multiple of three times profits may make this attractive to Sellers.

12.5.3.3 Sellers or parties connected with them may buy goods or services from Target on uncommercial terms, with a view to increasing the profits—for example, if Target normally supplies sand and gravel at 10p per tonne, Sellers may be tempted to set up a company which buys from Target at 12p per tonne—even if that company then has to sell the goods to its customers at 10p per tonne, that loss will be outweighed by the fact that Sellers will be receiving a multiple of three times the additional profit in Target.

The sale and purchase agreement will normally contain a provision to address the possibility of transactions with "connected parties" but they would not cover the possibility where the sales are to their "mates", rather than to anybody formally connected with Sellers—assuming, of course, that Sellers can find somebody who is prepared to pay 12p per tonne, with Sellers personally then refunding to them (say) 3p per tonne as a "thank you".

12.5.3.4   Similarly, if there are debts from customers which appear to be bad and which would otherwise fall to be written off as bad debts, it may be in the best interest of Sellers to pay those debts themselves on the basis that, if they pay £10,000, they will receive £30,000 back under the earn-out.

In reality, where a deal includes an earn-out element, the parties have to accept that it will be almost impossible to prevent one or both parties from taking steps to manipulate profits.

In practice, the parties will very often agree provisions to address specific concerns and then have a general provision to the effect that, during the earn-out period, they will act towards each other in good faith and that none of them will enter into any transaction or do anything else with the intention of increasing or (as the case may be) reducing the amount of the earn-out. Such a provision would, at least, provide protection against any blatant manipulation of the earn-out profit but the precise wording will need careful consideration—for example, a buyer may be concerned that he should not be prevented from doing anything in the ordinary course of business which happens to have the effect of reducing the earn-out profit and may wish therefore to limit the application of the wording to situations where reducing the amount of the profit is the "specific" or "primary" intention.

One further point which may be a concern to a buyer is if he believes that there is a possibility of selling the target company or business (in whole or in part) during the earn-out period. Sellers may press for an absolute prohibition on any such sale but that is unlikely to be acceptable to buyers. Possible solutions include having earn-out payments which are determined in some way by reference to the consideration for the sale or providing for the earn-out to become payable early on such a sale—perhaps by reference to the profits earned down to completion of that sale but with an adjustment to reflect the fact that the sale was taking place before the end of the earn-out period.

12.5.4   **Practical steps for determining the amount of the earn out profit**

The sale and purchase agreement will specify the practical arrangements for preparing and finalising the calculation of the earn-out profit and this is likely to involve the preparation of a profit and loss account for the relevant period (which may be an audited profit and loss account if the relevant period coincides with an accounting reference period), on the basis of which (normally) the auditors of the target company (or, on a sale and purchase of assets, the auditors of the buyer) will produce a certificate or statement of the earn-out profits and submit it to the seller. The comments made in 12.4.6.4 of this chapter in connection with completion accounts will be equally relevant in the context of an earn-out. The sale and purchase agreement will require any earn-out consideration to be paid within a specified number of days after the amount of the earn-out profit has been agreed or otherwise determined.

12.6   Consideration to be satisfied other than in cash

It is reasonably common for all or part of the consideration to be satisfied other than in cash and the non-cash element will typically comprise:

- listed shares in the capital of the buyer;

- unlisted shares in the capital of the buyer (i.e. where the buyer is not a company whose shares are publicly traded); or

- loan notes or loan stock issued by the buyer.

12.6.1   Issue of listed shares

The seller may be prepared to accept that all or (more typically) part of the consideration may be satisfied by the issue to him of shares in the capital of the buyer (consideration shares) and, inevitably, that is more likely to be the case where the buyer is a company whose shares are traded on the Official List or on the Alternative Investment Market ("AIM") or a similar market.

Apart from tax considerations (which are discussed in Chs 13 and 14), it will be necessary for the parties and their advisers to consider (amongst other points) the following, some of which are discussed in more detail in 4.1.1 of Ch.4:

> 12.6.1.1 Whether or not the acquisition will require the approval of the share-holders of the buyer in accordance with the Listing Rules, the AIM Rules or equivalent rules for any other market as, if that is the case, the sale and purchase agreement will have to be conditional on obtaining the necessary approval. This is discussed in detail in Ch.23. This point is significant as, if shareholder approval is required, there will have to be a delay between signing the sale and purchase agreement and completing it, in order to obtain the necessary shareholders' meeting to be convened and held, and that then begs the question of whether the number of shares which the seller is to receive will be determined when the sale and purchase agreement is signed or whether it will be determined at or shortly before completion—this point is discussed in more detail below.
>
> Where the buyer is an AIM company, it will be necessary to consider the implications of the Prospectus Rules (which are discussed briefly in 24.13.8 of Ch.24).

12.6.1.2 Whether the buyer has a sufficient margin of authorised, but unissued, share capital or whether it will be necessary to convene a general meeting of the buyer in order to increase its authorised share capital.

12.6.1.3 Even if the buyer does have a sufficient margin of authorised, but unissued, share capital, whether the directors of the buyer have the necessary authority under s.80 of the Companies Act 1985 (to be replaced by s.549 of the Companies Act 2006, with effect from October 1, 2009) to enable them to issue the consideration shares to the buyer or whether it will be necessary to convene a general meeting to obtain the necessary authority. They will also have to consider whether the articles of association of the buyer contain other restrictions on the issue of share capital (for example, where its share capital is divided into shares of more than one class, class consents may be required).

12.6.1.4 Whether the number of consideration shares to be issued to the seller will be determined before the sale and purchase agreement is signed or between then and completion: if there is to be no gap between signing the agreement and completion, this will not be an issue but it will need to be considered if the sale and purchase agreement is conditional (for example, on the shareholders of the buyer approving the transaction or an increase in the authorised share capital of the buyer) or if completion is to be deferred for any other reason.

For example, Buyer (Buyer) may be acquiring the entire issued share capital of Target (Target) from Tom, Dick and Harriet (Sellers) for a consideration of £5,000,000, of which £1,000,000 is to be satisfied by the allotment and issue to Sellers of ordinary shares in the capital of Buyer. Under the Listing Rules, the transaction requires the prior approval of the shareholders of Buyer.

At the point when the sale and purchase agreement is about to be signed, the Buyer's ordinary shares may be trading at a price of (say) £2 per share, so that Sellers would be expecting to receive 500,000 shares.

If Buyer's share price is prone to volatility, Sellers may be concerned that, in the period between signing the sale and purchase agreement and completion, there may be a significant fall in Buyer's share price—for example, if by completion Buyer's share price had dropped to £1.80 per share, Sellers would be unhappy because they would then be receiving shares with a market vale of only £900,000, which they would regard as an effective reduction in the purchase price.

Buyer is likely to want certainty and is likely therefore to press for the number of "consideration shares" to be agreed in advance and specified in the sale and purchase agreement, while Sellers may argue that the precise number of shares should be determined by reference to Buyer's share price immediately before completion.

Where Sellers' negotiating position is strong enough to enable them to persuade Buyer to agree to this, a possible compromise may be for the sale and purchase agreement to provide for Sellers to receive 500,000 consideration shares unless, between signing the sale and purchase agreement and completion, there is a major fall in Buyer's share price, in which event the number of consideration shares will be adjusted— typically, by reference to the average of the middle market quotations for the Buyer's shares over an agreed number of days immediately before completion (typically, somewhere between three and five days).

If that was agreed and the average of the middle market quotations over the agreed period was £1.60 per share, the number of consideration shares would increase to 625,000.

12.6.1.5   If consideration shares fall to be issued after completion (for example, following a completion accounts adjustment or an earn-out), it is most unlikely that the sale and purchase agreement will specify the number of consideration shares and it would almost certainly provide instead for that number to be determined by reference to a formula as discussed above.

12.6.1.6   The rights attaching to the consideration shares: if they are ordinary shares, they are likely to rank pari passu with Buyer's existing ordinary shares but it will nevertheless be necessary to consider the dividend rights which will attach to them (typically, they will not rank for any dividend or other distribution which is declared, made or paid by reference to a record date before completion of the transaction).

If the consideration shares are preference shares, the sale and purchase agreement will normally state that they will have the rights (and be subject to the restrictions) set out in the articles of association of the company but, if (as is likely) a new class of preference share is being created specifically for the purpose, the agreement will normally state that they will have the rights (and be subject to the restrictions) set out in a pre-agreed resolution of the buyer's shareholders, with the transaction being conditional (amongst other things) on the passing of that resolution.

12.6.1.7   The extent to which Sellers will be subject to a "lock-in" after completion, i.e. the extent of any restrictions on their ability to dispose of the consideration shares.

Buyer will normally be concerned about the potential impact on its share price if Sellers decided to "unload" their consideration shares (or a substantial proportion of them) shortly after completion and will normally therefore insist on a provision in the sale and purchase agreement limiting their ability to dispose of consideration shares within a specified period after completion, save in certain limited circumstances. The precise terms of the "lock-in" will vary from transaction to transaction but may, for example, provide that there will be no disposals of consideration shares for an initial period after completion and that after that any disposals must be made through brokers nominated by Buyer. Particularly where Sellers are receiving very limited cash out of the transaction, they will want to have the right to sell consideration shares in order to satisfy any warranty or indemnity claims and Buyer is likely to be sympathetic to that concern.

12.6.1.8 A related concern may arise where there is an earn-out which is to be satisfied to a large extent by the issue of consideration shares: if any warranty claims have arisen by then, Buyer will be looking for ways in which he can have a right of set-off against the earn-out consideration shares, while Sellers may want to be in a position where they can satisfy the claim by giving up all or part of their entitlement to earn-out consideration shares rather than have to find cash to satisfy the claim.

The parties may therefore wish to explore mechanisms which would involve the earn-out consideration shares being issued and then immediately sold in order to provide Sellers with cash to enable them to satisfy the claim or under which the number of shares to be issued is reduced (for example, by a number of shares to be arrived at by dividing the amount of the claim by the buyer's share price at the relevant time (see above)). Inevitably, Sellers would only want the Buyer to have a right of set-off where a claim has been agreed or determined by a court and there may therefore have to be a mechanism under which the issue of shares would be delayed pending resolution of any outstanding claim.

12.6.1.9 The sale and purchase agreement should oblige all parties to use reasonable endeavours to procure that the conditions are satisfied and this point is discussed in more detail in 8.4 of Ch.8. In addition, Sellers should make sure that there are provisions obliging Buyer to procure the passing of all necessary board resolutions to allot the consideration shares and the registration of Sellers as the holders of such shares.

12.6.1.10 The inevitable requirement of Sellers that completion must be conditional on the admission of any consideration shares to the Official List or (as the case may be) to trading on AIM or other relevant market: as discussed in 24.12 of Ch.24, this may involve a two-stage completion.

12.6.1.11 Whether the provisions of s.103 of the Companies Act 1985 (to be replaced by s.593 of the Companies Act 2006, with effect from October 1, 2009) apply, with the result that the non-cash consideration will have to be independently valued under s.108 of that Act (to be replaced by s.593 of the Companies Act 2006, with effect from October 1, 2009) before the consideration shares are allotted: this point is discussed in 4.1.1 of Ch.4 and, as discussed in that chapter, there is an exception to this requirement where the shares are being issued as consideration for a sale and purchase of shares, provided that it is open to the holders of all of the shares in the company whose shares are being acquired (or all the holders of a particular class) to take part in the arrangement. If there are some holders who are not receiving consideration shares, it may be appropriate for the sale and purchase agreement to contain an acknowledgement that it was nevertheless open to them to take part in the arrangement.

As explained in that chapter, an issue of shares by a buyer to a seller in consideration of the sale and purchase of the assets will not fall within any exception and, before issuing the consideration shares, the buyer is likely to have to obtain an independent valuation. Partly for this reason and partly because merger relief under s.612 of the Companies Act 2006 will not be available where shares are being issued as consideration for the sale and purchase of assets, it is not particularly common to have the consideration for the sale and purchase of assets satisfied by the issue of consideration shares.

12.6.1.12   Whether Buyer should have the right to satisfy the whole of the consideration in cash (for example, if there are likely to be difficulties or delays in obtaining any necessary approvals for the issue of shares). Sellers may propose that they should have the right to take cash if there is a substantial fall in Buyer's share price between signing the sale and purchase agreement and completion but that is unlikely to be acceptable to Buyer.

Appendix A to Precedents 1 and 2 in App.2 contains typical wording to cover the situation where all or part of the consideration is to be satisfied by an issue of consideration shares.

12.6.2   Issue of unquoted shares

The consideration for an acquisition may sometimes include the issue of consideration shares by a buyer whose shares are not listed on the Official List or traded on AIM or any other market. Examples of this are where the transaction is more in the nature of a "merger" of two companies or businesses rather than an acquisition by one of the other or where (typically on a management buy-out or a buy-in) the seller is agreeing to "roll over" part of his shareholding in the target company into shares in the buyer—which may be equity shares or may be redeemable preference shares. This is discussed in more detail in Ch.25 below.

In such cases, as with any other transaction, the parties will have to consider whether the approval of the shareholders of the buyer will be required under s.190 of the Companies

Act 2006 (see 4.1.1.1 of Ch.4) or under the articles of association of the buyer or any agreement between the shareholders of the buyer and they will also have to consider the following points (which are discussed in more detail in 4.1.1 of Ch.4):

12.6.2.1 Whether it will be necessary to increase the buyer's authorised share capital.

12.6.2.2 Whether an ordinary resolution will be required under s.80 of the Companies Act 1985 (to be replaced by s.549 of the Companies Act 2006, with effect from October 1, 2009) to authorise the allotment of the consideration shares.

12.6.2.3 Whether there are any pre-emption rights in the buyer's articles of association which require new shares to be offered first of all to existing shareholders and which may therefore need to be disapplied.

12.6.2.4 Whether the buyer's articles of association contain other restrictions on the issue of share capital (for example the need to obtain class consents).

12.6.2.5 Whether there is any agreement between the shareholders of the buyer under which consents are required either for the issue of consideration shares or for the transaction itself.

12.6.2.6 Where the buyer is a public limited company, it will be necessary to consider the implications of s.103 of the Companies Act 1985 (to be replaced by s.593 of the Companies Act 2006, with effect from October 1, 2009), notwithstanding that the buyer's shares may not be publicly traded.

12.6.2.7 The rights attaching to the consideration shares (where practicable, sellers should also consider pressing for a shareholders' agreement where they are going to become minority shareholders in the buyer).

12.6.2.8 Whether there are any "financial promotion" issues (these are discussed briefly in 2.4 of Ch.2) or whether there may be any issues under the Prospectus Rules (which are discussed briefly in 24.13.8 of Ch.24—in practice, there is unlikely to be an issue).

It is possible (although unlikely) that the sale and purchase agreement may be signed conditionally upon obtaining any necessary approval or other resolution from the shareholders of the buyer—for example, if for some reason it is impractical to obtain a written resolution of the shareholders of the buyer or to hold a general meeting of the buyer on short notice. In those circumstances there would not, of course, be the same concern over movements in the buyer's share price as would be the case on an acquisition by a company whose shares are publicly traded and the number of the consideration shares will simply be written into the sale and purchase agreement when it is signed.

12.6.3 **Loan notes and loan stock**

It is reasonably common for part of the purchase price to be satisfied by the issue of loan notes or loan stock by the buyer to the seller—these are debt securities of the buyer and are provided as an alternative to cash. They are typically used where the seller has a liability to capital gains tax (or, in the case of a corporate seller, to corporation tax on chargeable gains) arising from the sale and which the seller wishes to defer. This is discussed in detail in Ch.13.

Alternatively, they may be used where the purchase price is to be paid in cash but the buyer is unable or unwilling to pay the whole of the purchase price in cash on completion. There is no particular reason, however, to have loan notes or loan stock where it is not required for tax reasons unless the seller wishes to have an instrument which he can "discount" or against which he can borrow—particularly if repayment is guaranteed by a bank or similar financial institution, it may be possible for the seller to borrow against the security of the loan notes/loan stock. The loan notes or loan stock will be of a nominal amount equal to the amount of the consideration which is to be satisfied by their issue and will be constituted by a loan note/loan stock instrument. Precedent 35 in App.2 is a reasonably typically example of a loan note instrument for use where there is more than just one seller—where there is a single seller, the provisions can normally be simplified. The detailed terms of the loan notes or loan stock will, to an extent, be driven by tax considerations but the principal terms will include:

12.6.3.1 The principal amount.

12.6.3.2 The interest rate—typically, where the buyer would be prepared to pay cash on completion but the seller wishes to take loan notes or loan stock for tax reasons, that rate will be a reasonably "neutral" rate, i.e. one which does not make the transaction more expensive for the buyer than would have been the case if he had paid cash on completion.

12.6.3.3 The repayment terms.

12.6.3.4 Any provisions for early repayment (for example, in the event of certain specified events of default).

12.6.3.5 The extent to which they may be transferred.

12.6.3.6 Any security for the buyer's obligations—where the seller is to receive loan notes or loan stock, issues such as guarantees and other security, set-off, etc. will need to be considered in the same way as when the purchase price is being deferred (in whole or in part) for any other reason (see below). Where the buyer agrees to provide a bank guarantee, he may well argue that the interest rate payable to the seller should reduce in order to take account of the cost to the buyer of providing the guarantee and whether or not the seller agrees to that will depend on all the circumstances.

12.7   Vendor placings

Where the buyer is a company whose shares are publicly traded, it may fund any cash consideration by a "vendor placing", which essentially involves the consideration being satisfied by the issue of shares in the capital of the buyer, which are immediately sold to "placees" in order to realise the cash to pay the seller. Vendor placings are discussed in detail in Ch.24.

12.8   Repayment of loans and other indebtedness

On many sales of shares, the seller will have been funding the target company by way of loan rather than just by way of subscription for share capital and so at completion there may well be loans or other amounts owing by the target company to the seller. If the buyer wishes to acquire the target company on a "debt-free" basis, this would on the face of it involve the elimination of those loans before completion.

For example, if Buyer is proposing to acquire Target from Seller for £5,000,000 on a "debt-free" basis and Target has loans of £2,000,000 owing to Seller, the starting-point would be that Seller would have to eliminate those loans. The alternatives would be for the loans to be assigned by Seller to Buyer, for them to be waived by Seller or for them to be capitalised, i.e. satisfied by the issue of shares to Seller, credited as fully paid. For tax reasons, however, the parties will often, in practice, agree to reduce the purchase price by the amount of the loans so that, in the example, Buyer would on completion pay £3,000,000 to Seller for the shares and advance £2,000,000 to Target in order to enable Target to repay Seller.

Similarly, where the loans are owing to a third party (such as Target's bank), it will often be agreed that the purchase price will be reduced by the amount of the third party loan and that, on completion, the buyer will advance funds to the target company in order to enable it to repay the third party.

There may, however, be situations in which this is impossible, for example, when the target company has been making losses and the purchase price which the buyer is prepared to pay is less than the amount of the loans in question or where the buyer is unable or unwilling to part with the required amount of cash (for example, where the purchase price (or the greater part of it) is to be satisfied other than in cash). In these situations, where the loans are owed to the seller, there is unlikely to be any alternative but to have them assigned by the seller to the buyer, waived or capitalised and the way in which they are dealt with in practice will depend upon tax considerations. Clearly, these approaches are unlikely to be appropriate where the lender is a bank or other third party.

12.9   Security for any deferred element of the purchase price

Whenever any part of the purchase price falls (or may fall) to be paid after completion—whether because the parties agree on deferred payment terms or a retention, the purchase price is subject to adjustment in accordance with completion accounts or is dependent upon an earn-out or the consideration is to be satisfied by an issue of loan notes or loan stock—the seller should carefully consider the buyer's financial strength and, if he has any concerns, should request appropriate security for the buyer's obligations.

Depending upon the circumstances, possible security may include:

12.9.1   A bank guarantee: this would obviously be ideal from a seller's point of view, although the buyer may be concerned about the cost of providing such a guarantee.

12.9.2   A guarantee from the buyer's shareholders or parent company (if there is one): the buyer would, of course, have to consider the financial strength of whoever is to give the guarantee.

12.9.3   A guarantee from the target company, supported by a debenture or other security over its assets: this may, however, be of limited value if the buyer's group (as enlarged by the acquisition of target) is highly geared and the target will be required to give guarantees to the buyer's bank in respect of the buyer and other companies in the buyer's group and to support any such guarantee by security over its assets. The buyer's bank will inevitably insist upon its security having priority over the security to be granted to the seller.

It should also be noted that any security over the target company's assets would potentially be "financial assistance" by the target company for the acquisition of its own shares (see Ch.17). This would not, of course, be an issue on a sale and purchase of assets.

12.9.4   On a sale and purchase of shares, a charge over the shares which the buyer is acquiring: this is likely to be of limited value on its own as the shares will be caught by any security which the buyer may have given (or may give) to its bankers and the bank would no doubt require priority. In any event, the shares in the target company are unlikely to have any security value if the target company has guaranteed the bank and other borrowings of the buyer and secured its obligations under that guarantee by a charge over its assets.

12.10   Default interest

As in any commercial agreement, the seller is likely to require a provision under which interest is payable at a "penal" rate if any sums are not paid on the due date. The buyer is likely to require a similar provision (for example, to cover late payment of any sums which may become payable for breach of warranty).

12.11   Overage and anti-embarrassment agreements

On a sale and purchase of shares or assets, particularly where the business has been acquired out of public ownership or from a VC, it is quite common for the sale and purchase agreement to include a provision which entitles the seller to an "overage" or "anti-embarrassment" payment if the buyer sells the business or any material part of its assets within a reasonably short period after the buyer acquired them. A typical example of this is where there is land which the seller considers to have development potential but where there is no immediate prospect of that land being developed, so that the price which the buyer is prepared to pay will not reflect the development potential of the land.

An overage or anti-embarrassment arrangement will, typically, provide that the seller will be entitled to receive, by way of deferred consideration, a sum equal to an agreed percentage of the extent to which the sale proceeds exceed an agreed base figure, provided that the subsequent sale takes place within an agreed period after completion.

Issues for the parties to consider in connection with such arrangements include:

12.11.1   The seller will wish to make sure that the payment falls to be made whether the subsequent transaction is a sale of assets or a sale of shares.

12.11.2   The seller will want to make certain (as far as he can) that the buyer cannot avoid having to make any payment to him by agreeing a sale within the agreed period but completing it outside that period—for example, if the overage/anti-embarrassment arrangements continue for a two-year period, the buyer might enter into a contract in the twentieth month after acquiring the business, with such contract providing for completion outside the two-year period. The seller will therefore need to ensure that the overage/anti-embarrassment payment falls to be paid if a subsequent sale takes place outside the relevant period, provided that it takes place pursuant to a contract entered into (or option granted) within that period.

12.11.3   The seller will want to prevent the buyer from selling the business, property or other assets to a connected party (for example, another company owned by the buyer) for a price which does not trigger an overage/anti-embarrassment payment and then having that connected party make the subsequent sale (in respect of which, in the absence of any agreement to the contrary, no overage/anti-embarrassment payment would be payable).

12.11.4   The seller will want to ensure that the buyer cannot avoid having to make an overage/anti-embarrassment payment by structuring the subsequent transaction as something other than an outright sale—for example, a long term lease of a property.

12.11.5   The buyer may wish to ensure that the payment is to be calculated by reference to the amount ultimately received by him, net of the costs of obtaining and implementing planning permissions and so on, in order to ensure that the payment only falls to be calculated by reference to his actual "profit". This is particularly relevant where the transaction giving rise to the payment is the sale of a property but it may also be relevant to the sale of a company—particularly if it is likely that the buyer will have to incur a significant amount of capital expenditure or redundancy or other costs in order to be able to make an onward sale at a profit.

Precedent 36 contains the wording for a very basic anti-embarrassment provision which has been drafted in connection with a sale and purchase of shares and which is focused on an onward sale of the shares or of the assets of the company concerned, rather than a property transaction. It is very basic and should only be used when a simple arrangement is all that is required.

This provision has been drafted from the point of view of the seller.

Part 3
Specialist Areas

Chapter 13

Sale by Individual/Trustee Sellers—Main Tax Issues and the New Post April 5, 2008 Capital Gains Tax ("CGT") Regime

This chapter discusses the main tax implications of the sale of an owner-managed company by an individual/trustee seller. It also covers a number of tax planning issues that should be considered in appropriate cases.

Most owner–managers selling under the new post April 5, 2008 regime are likely to qualify for the new-style entrepreneurs' relief ("ER"). This effectively retains the benefit of a 10 per cent CGT rate, which was previously available under the pre April 6, 2008 business taper relief rules. However, in contrast to CGT business taper, ER is restricted to the first £1 million of (eligible) share sale gains. Any gains in excess of the £1 million limit (which is a lifetime allowance) are chargeable at the new flat CGT rate of 18 per cent.

Under the new CGT rules, an important planning consideration will be to ensure that maximum possible use is made of ER and some owner managers may wish to fragment their shareholdings to other family members to achieve this. Given that the flat CGT rate of 18 per cent applies to all gains, ER achieves an effective 10 per cent rate by reducing the relevant gains (up to the £1 million limit) by 4/9ths. Thus, for example, a capital gain of (say) £450,000 arising on the sale of a 25 per cent holding in a trading company would be reduced by 4/9ths (being £200,000). This would leave a taxable gain of £250,000 taxed at 18 per cent—£45,000 (which equates to 10 per cent of £450,000).

When compared with the "old" pre April 6, 2008 taper system, owner managers should broadly pay the same CGT tax on share sale gains up to £1 million. (The treatment of owner-managed company sales under the pre April 6, 2008 regime was covered extensively in the first edition of this book.)

However, the owner-manager's CGT liability will progressively rise on larger gains, as demonstrated in the comparative table overleaf.

However, this analysis simplifies the true position, since the post April 5, 2008 CGT regime contains some other noteworthy changes for individual and trustee shareholders.

The abolition of the taper relief system is also accompanied by the complete withdrawal of indexation relief. For those shareholders who acquired their shares (well) before April 1998, the loss of indexation may prove to be costly in terms of additional CGT.

	CGT payable	
Gains on shares	Before 6 Apr 08 (with 75% business taper)	After 5 Apr 08 (with ER)
£000	£000	£000
100	10	10
200	20	20
300	30	30
400	40	40
500	50	50
750	75	75
1,000	100	100
1,500	150	190
2,000	200	280
5,000	500	820

March 1982 rebasing is now compulsory for shares held at March 31, 1982. In many cases, this should not affect the shareholder's capital gain (since the March 1982 rebasing value will be used in any case). However, it will no longer be possible to use the original cost of the shareholding if that produces a *lower* gain.

Allied to the abolition of taper relief, the special share identification rules introduced in the Finance Act 1998 become otiose. Thus, from April 6, 2008, all shares in a particular company (of the same class) are generally treated as a single "pooled" asset, regardless of when they were actually acquired.

In recent years, HMRC have begun to apply the "Transaction in Securities" anti-avoidance rules in (what is now) s.684 of the Income Tax Act 2007 ("ITA") more vigorously (see 13.6). It is therefore very important for the selling shareholders to make use of the statutory clearance procedure under the ITA s.701. Provided that the main aspects of the transaction have been fully disclosed, the seller can obtain some certainty before the sale that HMRC are satisfied that the transaction is being made for good commercial reasons and will not subsequently be challenged under this legislation.

13.1   Sale of shares v sale of assets

In the majority of cases, sellers will seek to structure the deal as a sale of their shares. This is attractive for a number of reasons. The sale proceeds are received directly in their hands and will normally be subject to the attractive CGT rates—in many cases, the owner-manager will benefit from an effective 10 per cent rate under ER, with gains in excess of the £1 million ER limit being charged at the (still relatively low) rate of 18 per cent. In addition as discussed in Ch.1, a share sale also limits the seller's commercial exposure, subject to the protection obtained by the buyer through warranties and indemnities in the sale and purchase agreement.

In contrast, an assets deal frequently gives rise to an element of double taxation. This is because capital gains and "clawbacks" of previously claimed capital allowances typically arise on the company's sale of the assets (such as goodwill and plant). A further tax charge then arises when the company's post-tax sale proceeds are extracted by the shareholders. The basic tax treatment of a sale of assets is covered in 13.7 of this chapter.

Buyers have tended to prefer to acquire the trade and assets, since this involves less commercial risk and the prospect of obtaining tax relief on the assets purchased, such as on goodwill and other intangible assets. However, in recent years, assets deals have become likely to be more expensive in terms of stamp duty land tax ("SDLT"), where the acquisition contains a substantial element of UK land and property. For example, if the amount paid for (say) some trading premises exceeds £500,000, the SDLT cost would be four per cent of the amount paid (goodwill and all transfers of intellectual property and debts no longer attract any stamp taxes). On the other hand, share purchases only attract stamp duty at 0.5 per cent but this is levied on the total value of the company (reflecting the value of non-dutiable assets, but reduced by the company's debt and liabilities).

13.2 Basic capital gains tax ("CGT") rules on share sales

13.2.1 Date of disposal

The seller will normally generate a capital gain when he sells his shares. A disposal of an asset will be recognised for CGT purposes when an unconditional contract is executed for its sale (s.28(1) of the Taxation of Chargeable Gains Act 1992 ("TCGA 1992")). In the case of a conditional contract, the date of disposal is deferred until the relevant condition precedent is satisfied (or waived) (s.28(2) of the TCGA 1992). A condition precedent refers to an event which is outside the control of the contracting parties—for example obtaining satisfactory tax clearances or relevant regulatory approval, etc. (on the other hand, a "condition subsequent" is merely a term of the contract required to be fulfilled by one of the parties and does not create a conditional contract for CGT).

Cash consideration is immediately chargeable to CGT in the tax year of disposal (s.28 of the TCGA 1992). Tax must be paid on any fixed (i.e. ascertainable) deferred consideration, even if it is conditional, although the HMRC will refund the tax when it is satisfied that the conditional amount will not be paid. Instalment relief may be available for the tax payments, given the difficulty of paying the tax before the full cash proceeds are received (ss.48 and 280 of the TCGA 1992). However, fixed deferred consideration is usually best structured through the use of loan notes, as this enables the relevant tax to be held-over.

13.2.2 Calculation of capital gain

In broad terms, an individual or trustee seller's capital gain is calculated as the amount by which the sale proceeds (net of allowable incidental costs of disposal) exceeds the amount they originally paid for the shares—often referred to as the "base cost".

For disposals made after April 5, 2008, the gain cannot be reduced by either indexation relief or taper relief (since both are now abolished—readers should refer to Ch. 13 in the first edition of this book for a detailed discussion of the pre April 6, 2008 CGT regime.

Where the seller held their shares at March 31, 1982, they must deduct the market value of their shareholding at March 31, 1982 as their base cost (instead of their pre-March 1982 acquisition cost).

Example 1—Comparative CGT computation for sale of shares (under old and new CGT regimes)

For some months, Dylan has been in serious negotiations for the sale of "his" company, Rolling Stone Limited. He expects to sell his company for a cash consideration of £4 million (net of legal and professional costs). Dylan acquired his 100 per cent shareholding in June 1993 for £100,000. Rolling Stone Limited has always been a trading company.

Indicative CGT liabilities for a sale before April 6, 2008 and afterwards are given below:

	Pre-6 April 2008	Post-5 April 2008
	£	£
Net sale proceeds	4,000,000	4,000,000
Less: Acquisition cost (June 1993)	(100,000)	(100,000)
Indexation relief		
£100,000 × 0.153 (RPI increase between	(15,300)	–
June 1993 to April 1998)		
Chargeable gain	3,884,700	3,900,000
Less: Business asset taper relief		
£3,884,700 × 75%	(2,913,525)	–
Less: ER – £1,000,000 (max) × 4/9		(444,444)
Tapered gain/Chargeable gain	971,175	3,455,556
Less: Annual exemption	(9,200)	(9,600)
Taxable gain	961,975	3,445,956
CGT @ 40%	£ 384,790	
CGT @ 18%		£ 620,272

13.3   Entrepreneurs' relief ("ER")

13.3.1   Main qualifying conditions

For normal share sales the following conditions must be satisfied throughout the one year before the disposal (TCGA 1992 s.169I(1)(2)(c)(5)(6)). The seller shareholder must:

- hold shares in a trading company or holding company of a trading group; and

- be a director or employee of that company (or fellow group company) and it must be their "personal company"—i.e. they must own at least five per cent of the ordinary share capital (carrying at least five per cent of the voting rights).

Most owner managers should have little difficulty in satisfying the relevant tests. However, the "director/employee" requirement should not be that onerous, since there is no requirement to work on a "full time" basis—part time working would therefore suffice. The five per cent "shareholding/votes" test must be satisfied by the individual seller alone (for example, there is no attribution of spouses' or relatives' shares).

ER must be claimed (broadly) 22 months after the end of the relevant tax year in which the share sale is made. Thus, for example, an ER claim on a qualifying gain in 2008/09 must be made by January 31, 2011. Once claimed, ER is applied to the complete eligible gain (up to the maximum £1 million cumulative threshold)—it cannot be restricted in any way. However, some flexibility could be provided by selling shares in separate tranches, with an ER election being made against specific disposals.

The ER conditions are more restrictive than those which applied to the (pre April 6, 2008) business taper regime. For example, a large number of minority and employee shareholders will be unable to meet the conditions necessary to secure ER. They will therefore suffer a significantly higher CGT rate of 18 per cent under the new regime (compared with their typical rate of 10 per cent under the pre April 6, 2008 taper regime).

Trustees can also claim ER in certain special cases where their trust has one or more beneficiaries holding an "interest in possession" (see 13.3.4).

13.3.2 Basic mechanics of ER

ER is modelled on the old "retirement relief" regime, although there is no minimum age requirement (and there is no need to retire). The shares only need to be held on a qualifying basis for at least one year to obtain ER.

ER provides that the first £1 million of "qualifying business gains" are effectively taxed at a lower rate of 10 per cent. This £1 million ER allowance is given to both husband and wife, separately, which may be an important consideration when structuring shareholdings.

The 10 per cent effective ER CGT rate is achieved computationally by reducing relevant gains up to the £1 million limit by 4/9ths. The following example shows the computation of ER for different levels of qualifying business gains:

Example 2—ER available on varying levels of eligible gains

	£000	£000	£000
Eligible gain	500	1,000	2,000
Less: ER – (4/9ths reduction)	(222)	(444)	(444)
Taxable gain	278	556	1,556
CGT @ 18%	50	100	280

13.3.3   Trading company/group test

The ER "trading company/group" test is virtually the same as the one that previously applied for business asset taper relief and is therefore relatively stringent (TCGA 1992 s.165A). Broadly, the relevant company/group must be wholly engaged in carrying on trading activities, subject to the de minimis rule for "substantial" non-trading activities.

HMRC practice is to interpret this rule as permitting non-trading activities, provided they do not exceed 20 per cent of the company's/group's total activities (although this is not a statutory test). Vulnerable non-trading activities would include property letting to third parties, investment in shares, etc. loans to shareholders/connected companies, and surplus cash not required for future trading activities which is actively managed as an investment activity.

HMRC generally test whether non-trading activities are within the 20 per cent benchmark by looking at a range of measures, such as:

- turnover;

- the asset-base of the company;

- expenses;

- time spent by management and employees.

Thus, for example, the turnover/sales income from a company's non-trading activities would be compared with the total turnover generated by the company and so on. It may be necessary to build-up the correct picture over time and this may involve striking a balance between all these factors (see *IR Tax Bulletin*, Issue 62).

Although many considered that substantial surplus cash could invalidate a company's trading status, HMRC now seem to have a more relaxed approach in this area. It would appear that, provided that the cash had been generated from a company's trading operations and it has not been applied for an investment purpose, then it should be treated as a trading asset.

When determining whether a company/group satisfies the "trading" status test for ER, qualifying equity investments in joint venture trading companies (which would otherwise be regarded as investment activities) are deemed to represent an appropriate part of the trading activities of a trading company/group. A shareholding in a "joint-venture" company qualifies for "trading" treatment provided the participating company (or group) holds at least 10 per cent of its ordinary shares and:

- the joint-venture company is a trading company or holding company of a trading group; and

- at least 75% of the joint-venture company's equity share capital is held by five or fewer participating shareholders (irrespective of their tax residence status).

It is possible to obtain an advance clearance from HMRC as to whether the company satisfies the relevant "trading" company/group criteria for ER.

13.3.4 Disposals by trustees

Trustees can also claim ER in certain special cases where their trust has one or more "qualifying" beneficiaries holding an "interest in possession" (over the entire trust fund or the relevant part (such as a "sub-fund") containing the shares) (TCGA 1992 s.169J).

The main trust conditions are directed at the "qualifying beneficiary" rather than the trustees. Thus, the trustees can make a claim for ER provided the *qualifying beneficiary*:

- is a director or employee of the company (or any fellow-group company), *and*

- holds at least five per cent of the ordinary shares in the company (carrying at least five per cent of the voting rights) in their own right.

There is no minimum shareholding condition for the trustees. These "trust" conditions must be satisfied throughout a period of *one year* ending within the *three years* before the sale. The company must also be a trading company or a holding company of a trading group throughout this period.

The conditions mean that, to facilitate a potential ER claim by a trust, the (qualifying) beneficiary must have a personal holding of at least five per cent of the shares (carrying at least five per cent of the votes). However, the trustees do *not* have their own separate £1 million ER allowance. The qualifying beneficiary effectively assigns to the trustees all or part of their unused ER allowance (by entering into a joint election). Therefore, if the beneficiary has used all their £1 million allowance, this will preclude any ER claim by the trustees.

13.3.5 ER on associated disposals of personally held property

Where an individual qualifies for the relief on the disposal of shares, they can also obtain relief on an associated disposal of an asset that has been used by the company

(TCGA 1992 s. 169K). This would typically be a property that is personally owned by a shareholder/director which has been used by the company for its business, but it might also cover the sale of intellectual property that is personally held (outside the company) by the seller shareholder.

The relief is only allowed for "associated" disposals, so they must therefore take place at the same time as (or shortly after) the share sale—an isolated disposal of personally-held property will not qualify for any relief (even though it generally attracted business taper on a pre April 6, 2008 sale).

Section 169K requires the following conditions to be satisfied for a qualifying "associated disposal" (in the context of an ER-related share sale):

• The seller shareholder must make the "associated disposal" as part of their "withdrawal from participation" in the business carried on by the company. (There is no statutory definition to assist with the interpretation of the "withdrawal from participation" requirement, although in practice HMRC consider that this test is met so long as the individual sells all or part of their shareholding interest).

• Throughout the one-year period (normally) prior to the sale of the shares, the relevant property is used for the purposes of the company's trade.

The conditions for associated disposal relief are therefore quite restrictive in terms of timing. For example, the sale of the property some time before the share sale would not qualify (since it would then have been used for the purposes of the company's trade up to the date of the share sale).

The ER on an associated disposal can be also scaled down on a "just and reasonable" basis (under the TCGA 1992 s.169P) to reflect cases where (amongst other things):

• the property has only been partly used for the purposes of the company's trade throughout the seller's period of ownership;

• a rent has been charged by the "seller to the company for its use of the property".

These restrictions are generally tested from when the property was originally acquired, despite the fact that strong representations were made to HMRC for a April 6, 2008 "base" date in applying this rule. However, in the case of the "rental" restriction, which reduces the available ER (on a just and reasonable basis) to the extent that a commercial rent has been charged, only rent charged *after* April 6, 2008 is taken into account. (This is sensible, since under the pre April 6, 2008 taper regime, the payment of rent did not affect the availability of business taper on personally held property let to trading companies etc. However, the retention of a rent charge after April 6, 2008 will reduce the qualifying (associated disposal ER gain) on a "just and reasonable" basis from that date (TCGA 1992 s.169P and FA 2008 Sch.3 para.6).

13.4 Treatment of sale consideration satisfied by shares/loan notes in the acquirer

13.4.1 Different types of consideration

Sellers may sell their shares for a consideration satisfied in cash, loan notes or shares issued by the acquiring company. Very often the seller is likely to be offered a combination of cash and loan notes/shares. In some cases, sellers may also be given additional deferred consideration in the form of an "earn-out".

13.4.2 Consideration shares in the acquirer

Many private company takeovers, particularly by quoted companies, will entail the buyer issuing new shares to the seller shareholders as part of the sale consideration.

Many company takeovers, particularly by listed companies, will entail the buyer issuing new shares to the seller shareholders as part of the sale consideration. This enables the seller to defer their capital gain until the shares are sold. The CGT reorganisation rule in the TCGA 1992 s. 127 is applied here so that the seller does not make any disposal of their old shares and is treated as receiving the new "consideration" shares at the same time and cost as their old shares.

The share for share exchange "reorganisation rules" are circumscribed by the "commercial purpose" test in the TCGA 1992 s.137. Consequently, the beneficial CGT treatment will only apply where the transaction is being undertaken for genuine commercial reasons and where one of the main purposes is not to obtain a tax advantage. Advance clearance should generally be applied for under the TCGA 1992 s.138 to obtain certainty that HMRC agree that these requirements are satisfied in relation to the proposed deal.

The "commercial purpose" test in the TCGA 1992 s.137 does not apply to very small minority shareholders (i.e. those holding no more than five per cent of the target company), presumably because they are not in a position to influence the structure of the transaction (TCGA 1992 s.137(2)).

13.4.3 Special election to obtain ER on share exchange

Because the "reorganisation" rule provides there is no CGT disposal, the seller would normally be unable to claim ER on the value of the acquirer's shares received as part of their sale consideration. This would be unfortunate if the seller was unable to claim ER on a later sale of their "consideration" shares—for example, because they did not possess the requisite five per cent shareholding in the acquiring company.

The ER legislation recognises this problem and provides that the seller can make a special election (under the TCGA 1992 s.169Q) to opt out of the normal share-for-share exchange treatment. By making a s.169Q election the seller is treated as having made a normal CGT disposal with the value of the acquirer's shares being reflected as all/part of their overall sale consideration. In such cases, the benefit of the ER would be reflected in the (higher) market value base cost of the shares in the acquiring company.

Example 3—Effect of special ER election on share exchanges

Peggy Sue has been a "management" shareholder since June 2000 and holds 10 per cent of the equity share capital of Holly Limited (a successful music publishing and recording company). She acquired her 10,000 £1 shares at their full market value of £20,000.

In October 2008 Holly Limited was taken over by Buddy plc. As part of this transaction, Peggy Sue received sale consideration of £600,000, which was satisfied as follows:

		£
Cash		200,000
Shares in Buddy plc, valued at		400,000

Peggy Sue's shares in Buddy plc represented a three per cent shareholding (with commensurate voting rights). She was therefore unlikely to qualify for ER on their subsequent sale. However, by making a TCGA 1992 s.169Q election, she could benefit from ER on the total consideration received on the October 2008 sale, as shown below:

		£
Sale consideration	Cash	200,000
	Buddy plc shares	400,000
		600,000
Less: Base cost		(20,000)
		580,000
Less : ER – £580,000 × 4/9		(257,777)
Gain after ER		322,223
Less : Annual exemption		(9,600)
Taxable gain		312,623
CGT @ 18%		£56,272

Peggy Sue's base cost of her Buddy plc shares would be their full market value of £400,000 (as opposed to £13,333 (4/6 × £20,000), being the pro-rata original cost of her Holly Limited shares if the reorganisation rules had applied).

13.4.4 Making a s.169Q election

The s.169Q election is made on an "all or nothing" basis. It is not therefore possible to restrict its application to gains of £1 million. Such elections must be made within 22 months after the end of the tax year in which the sale occurs.

The potential consequences of making a s.169Q election should always be considered when structuring any deal. Because the reorganisation rule is disapplied, the seller would generally incur a CGT liability on the "ER-relieved" gain. The seller would therefore need to ensure they had sufficient cash consideration to fund the tax liability. Furthermore, the timing of any future tax liability (when the higher base cost comes into play) must also be considered.

Clearly, such an election would not be appropriate where the "cash" element of a company share sale produced chargeable gains exceeding the ER limit of £1 million.

13.4.5 Consideration satisfied in loan notes

In many deals, the seller may agree to accept deferred payment for part of the sale consideration by taking loan notes in the acquiring company. As a general rule, where the buyer satisfies part of the consideration by issuing loan notes, an appropriate part of the seller's gain is deferred until the loan note is redeemed for payment. The precise mechanics of the deferral depends on the tax status of the loan note, as this varies between Qualifying Corporate Bonds ("QCBs")(see 13.4.6) and non-QCBs (see 13.4.9).

These CGT deferral rules are subject to HMRC being satisfied that the loan note has been issued for genuine commercial reasons and not mainly to avoid tax (TCGA 1992 s. 137)(see 13.4.2). The seller would normally apply for a TCGA 1992 s. 138 clearance to seek advance confirmation of this point from HMRC.

13.4.6 Dealing with QCBs

Broadly, most "non-convertible" loan notes will represent QCBs. The capital gains deferral mechanism for a QCB is governed by the rules in the TCGA 1992 s. 116(10). These provide that the chargeable gain on the loan note consideration is computed at the date of sale. This gain is then postponed and becomes taxed only when the loan note is encashed (or disposed of outside the cases specified in the TCGA 1992 s. 116(11)).

Where QCBs are received on a post April 6, 2008 share sale, any available ER is deducted in arriving at the gain held-over under the TCGA 1992 s.116(10). This means that the "carried-forward" gain reflects any ER that was available and claimed at the original sale date.

Example 4—Claiming ER on QCBs

In July 2008, John sold his 40 per cent shareholding in Imagine Limited to Instant Karma plc for £2,500,000 of which:

- £500,000 was paid in cash on completion; and

- £2,000,000 was satisfied by the issue of a QCB loan note (bearing interest at nine per cent, bank guaranteed and redeemable after 12 months).

John subscribed for his 40,000 £1 shares in Imagine Limited at par in May 2002.

John would incur a CGT liability on the cash consideration and would be able to defer the capital gain on the part satisfied in QCBs.

2008/09 – CGT on cash consideration

			£
Cash			
Sale consideration	– Cash		500,000
Less: Base cost	£40,000 ×	£500,000	
		£500,000 + £2,000,000	(8,000)
Capital gain			492,000
Less : ER – £492,000 × 4/9			(218,667)
Gain after ER			273,333
Less : Annual exemption			(9,600)
Taxable gain			263,733
CGT @ 18%			£47,472

Postponed QCB gain (with ER)

			£
QCB consideration			2,000,000
Less: Base cost	£40,000 ×	£2,000,000	
		£500,000 + £2,000,000	(32,000)
Capital gain			1,968,000
Less : ER – £508,000 (£1,000,000 less £492,000) × 4/9			(225,778)
Postponed gain			1,742,222
Postponed CGT			313,600

13.4.7 Transitional ER for pre April 6, 2008 QCBs

Special rules apply to QCB loan notes that were acquired as consideration for a pre April 6, 2008 share sale. Taper relief ceases to be relevant where QCB gains are crystallised under the new CGT regime. However, the benefit of any indexation allowance that was built into the held-over gain is retained on a post April 5, 2008 redemption.

After strong representations, HMRC considered that it would be inequitable not to grant any form of transitional relief in such cases. There are, therefore, special rules which enable ER to be claimed against the QCB gain becoming chargeable on a post April 5, 2008 redemption (FA 2008 Sch.3 para.7). Clearly, the QCB holder must have unused ER available to offset against the crystallised gain. However, relief is only given provided the seller would have been entitled to ER on the original pre April 6, 2008 share sale (on the assumption that the ER legislation had been in force at that time). ER relief will not always be available—for example, the seller may have sold a very small (less than five per cent) holding on the original sale.

For these purposes, the transitional ER claim must be made within 22 months following the tax year in which the held-over gain crystallises.

13.4.8 QCB loss problem

No capital loss relief is available as a QCB is not a chargeable asset for CGT (TCGA 1992 s. 115). Furthermore, any capital gain deferred under s.116(10) of the TCGA 1992 can also triggered if the purchasing company defaults on a QCB loan note which is cancelled or settled via a "compromise arrangement". In these dire circumstances, HMRC generally permit the worthless loan note to be "gifted" to a charity without triggering the held-over gain. Having said all that, sellers should always seek to obtain "commercial bank" guarantees for their loan notes to avoid these types of "nightmare" scenarios!

13.4.9 Non-qualifying corporate bonds (non-QCBs)

Different rules apply where the buyer issues non-QCB loan notes. The terms of such loan notes will be designed so as to fall outside the criteria for a QCB. Thus, for example, a non-QCB loan note would be one which is convertible into the acquirer's shares or contains the right to subscribe for additional shares or securities. Where such notes are issued in exchange for shares, they are deemed to be a security (and therefore do not necessarily have to be "marketable", readily transferable and so on) (TCGA 1992 s. 251(6)).

Non-QCB loan notes represent a security for CGT purposes and the CGT reorganisation rule in the TCGA 1992 s.127 is applied here (by virtue of the share exchange rules in the TCGA 1992 s.135) so that the seller does not make any disposal of their old shares and is treated as receiving the new "consideration" shares at the same time and cost as their old shares. The appropriate part of the seller's original base cost in the target company's shares is therefore treated as given for the non-QCB security at the original acquisition date(s). (Non-QCBs were often used under the taper relief regime to extend the seller's taper relief period, but these taper relief issues cease to be relevant after April 5, 2008.)

Since the CGT deferral in relation to sale consideration satisfied by non-QCBs is governed by the CGT reorganisation rules in the TCGA 1992 s.127, it is possible for ER to be claimed on the non-QCB consideration (assuming the relevant ER conditions are satisfied) by making a TCGA 1992 s.169Q election (TCGA 1992 s.169Q(1)). By making this special election, the value of the non-QCB consideration is brought into the seller's CGT computation at the date of the sale (as explained in 13.4.3). Before structuring any deal or deciding whether an election would be beneficial, the relevant factors in 13.4.4 should be considered.

Where the seller is unable to obtain a commercial bank guarantee for the loan note, many feel that a non-QCB would be a more prudent alternative—this avoids the QCB-type risk of triggering a CGT charge on the cancellation of the loan note (for example, where the acquiring company becomes insolvent)(see 13.4.8).

13.5 Earn-out deals

13.5.1 Basic tax treatment of "cash-based" earn-outs

Owner-managed companies are sometimes sold on an "earn-out" basis with deferred consideration being provided, calculated on a formula basis relating to the post-sale profits over (normally) the next two or three years. This will generally enable the seller to enjoy extra consideration, calculated by reference to a formula based on the level of profits achieved by the target company in the two or three years following the sale. An earn-out also limits the buyer's "downside" risk as the seller will receive little or nothing if the anticipated profits are not met.

Under the principles established in the case of *Marren v Ingles* [1980] S.T.C. 500, the expected net present value of the earn-out right falls to be included as part of the seller's taxable consideration for the disposal of the shares. Thus, where the seller's share sale gain qualifies for ER, the value of the earn-out right will effectively attract the relief (subject to the £1 million threshold).

As and when the earn-out payments are received, further CGT charges will arise in respect of the earn-out right itself (representing capital sums derived from the right to receive the earn-out (under TCGA 1992 s. 22) and not the disposal of shares). Thus, assuming the seller had unused ER relief, this would not be available against the disposals of the earn-out right (since these do not constitute a disposal of shares).

Capital gains on the earn-out payments (taxed under TCGA 1992 s. 22), which are based on the earn-out payment received less the appropriate deductible base value of the right, will therefore attract CGT at the flat rate of 18 per cent.

One of the main potential problems arising from the "*Marren v Ingles*" treatment is the risk of being taxed on an unrealised gain, i.e. the seller would suffer tax on the value of the right (when their shares are sold). In an extreme case, if the earn-out falls (well) below expectation, this could result in a capital loss arising on the disposal of the right in a subsequent tax year. In such cases, it is now possible to make an election under the TCGA 1992 s. 279A to carry the subsequent loss back to reduce the seller's original capital gain.

13.5.2   Earn-outs satisfied in shares/loan notes under the TCGA 1992 s.138A

An earn-out may also be structured so that it must be satisfied in the form of shares and/or loan notes in the acquiring company (when the relevant earn-out consideration is determined). This enables the "deferral" mechanism in the TCGA 1992 s. 138A to apply (automatically, without the need for an election) and thus avoids the "up-front" tax charge based on the value of the right. Broadly speaking, provided the original share sale could meet the conditions for a TCGA 1992 s.135 share exchange (but there does not necessarily have to be one), the seller is automatically treated as (partly) exchanging their original shares for the deemed s.138A security.

This treatment was particularly beneficial under the (pre April 6, 2008) taper relief regime. Since the seller was in effect "rolling-over" into a non-QCB, their taper relief would continue to accrue (normally) at the business rate. This treatment generally enabled sellers to obtain full business taper on their earn-out payments (when they redeemed their actual loan notes). Thus, even where an earn-out was originally proposed to be settled in cash, sellers were advised to amend its terms so as to require the buyer to satisfy the agreed earn-out amounts in the form of short-dated loan notes. Typically, the sale agreement would require the buyer to issue these loan notes once the earn-out profits had been computed and the seller"s entitlement had been agreed. After a minimum six-month redemption period, the seller would encash their loan notes and pay the relevant CGT on their earn-out "gains" at an effective CGT rate of around 10 per cent.

This was the standard tax advice for sellers selling "their" companies before the Pre-Budget Report 2007. By ensuring that the earn-out could only be satisfied in the form of loan notes, the seller would automatically enjoy the CGT deferral mechanism offered by the TCGA 1992 s.138A. However, with the abolition of taper relief from April 6, 2008, the seller's CGT profile is now markedly different (and this includes sellers who entered into their earn-out transaction before the Pre-Budget Report 2007).

13.5.3 Treatment of s.138A earn-outs after April 5, 2008

When the earn-out is quantified, the acquiring company will issue the relevant loan note or shares for the agreed amount.

13.5.3.1   QCB loan notes

Where the earn-out consideration is satisfied in the form of a QCB loan note, this will be dealt with under the company security conversion/exchange rules in the TCGA 1992 s.132. This treats the event as a CGT reorganisation hence brings the special QCB rules in the TCGA 1992 s.116(10) into play.

Broadly, the gain held-over against the QCB would be the amount of the relevant earn-out consideration, less the pro-rata base cost. (The pro-rata base cost is derived from the original cost of the shares that was carried into the deemed security when the seller sold their original shares—see 13.4.2 and 13.4.9). The postponed gain would generally be taxed at the 18 per cent CGT rate when the QCB is finally encashed (HMRC permit a minimum redemption period of six months from issue).

13.5.3.2   Shares/non-QCB loan notes

In some cases, the acquiring company satisfies the earn-out in the form of a fresh issue of its shares (or a non-QCB). The number of shares issued would generally depend on the earn-out consideration and the (agreed) prevailing market price/value of the acquirer's shares. In such cases, a combination of the TCGA 1992 s.132 exchange and the TCGA 1992 s.127 CGT reorganisation rules will apply to treat the new shares/security as having been acquired at the same time, and (pro-rata) base cost as the seller's original shares.

Any subsequent gain on sale/encashment would generally attract CGT at 18 per cent.

Exceptionally, there may be cases (assuming the seller has unused ER relief available) where the subsequent disposal of the shares/non-QCB securities could attract ER. However, the seller would generally need to have satisfied the relevant ER conditions from the time the shares/securities were issued as part of the earn-out. This is because (assuming they remain employed in the target company) it is only from this date that they would generally be able to satisfy the five per cent ordinary shares/voting rights test — see 13.2.2).

13.5.4 Share/loan note-based earn-outs straddling the CGT changes

Where a sale has been concluded before April 6, 2008 with an earn-out satisfied in loan notes/shares, the normal "deferral" rule in TCGA 1992 s. 138A should apply. In broad terms, the effect is twofold:

- there is no initial CGT charge on the value of the right; and

- the CGT on the gains relating to the "earn-out" loan notes is taxed when they are redeemed.

As mentioned above, following the announcement of the radical changes to the CGT regime, many sellers had to revise their anticipated CGT tax position on their earn-out payments. In many cases, they were now looking at a CGT charge of 18 per cent on their earn-out gains (rather than the hoped-for 10 per cent effective "business-tapered" CGT rate).

Where all or substantially all the "earn-out" loan repayments would fall to be taxed under the post April 5, 2008 18 per cent flat rate regime, sellers should consider whether it would be advantageous to make a s. 138A(2A) election to disapply the s. 138A deferral. The overall effect of this election would be to bring the earn-out to tax under the general principles established in *Marren v Ingles* (see 13.5.1), despite the fact the earn-out is being settled in loan notes/shares. This means that the value of the earn-out right would then be taxed at the date of the original share sale.

Assuming the original share sale qualified for maximum business taper, the value of the earn-out would then be effectively taxed at 10 per cent. The overall benefit of this treatment would depend on the seller agreeing a "high" up-front value of the earn-out right with HMRC — Shares & Asset Valuation. The election would therefore bring forward additional gains into the (pre April 6, 2008) 10 per cent CGT net and minimise the amount taxed at 18 per cent (post April 5, 2008). The election would only be beneficial where the total CGT payments are lower than those that would arise under the s.138A route (taking into account the timing of the tax cash flows).

The election for earn-out sales in 2006/07 and 2007/08 must be made by January 31, 2009 and January 31, 2010 respectively.

13.6 Application of the ITA 2007 s. 684 anti-avoidance rules

Under these provisions, an owner-managed company will invariably constitute what is known as a "s.684" (circumstance D) company and the sale of the company would constitute a "transaction in securities". HMRC are particularly likely to seek to apply this legislation where the seller:

- still retains a material equity interest in the company post-sale; or

- sells the company to a connected party (such as a trust or connected company).

If HMRC succeed in applying the ITA 2007, s. 684 (previously ICTA 1988 s. 703), all or part of the seller's sale proceeds would effectively be taxed as a distribution/dividend at a higher (25 per cent) tax rate.

This legislation does not apply where (amongst other things) the sale has been motivated by genuine commercial reasons (rather than tax avoidance motives). Sellers should always make use of the advance clearance procedure in the ITA 2007 s. 701 (previously ICTA 1988 s. 707), which enables them to obtain comfort before the deal takes place that HMRC are satisfied that transaction is being made for commercial reasons and not for tax avoidance so that the ITA 2007 s. 684 would not be applied.

HMRC's willingness to litigate in this area is demonstrated by the recent case of *Lloyd v R&C Commrs* [2008] S.T.C. 681 SCD, where the taxpayer lost on the "tax avoidance" issue even though the Special Commissioner accepted there was also a commercial rationale for the transaction.

13.7 Sale of assets

13.7.1 Dealing with a sale and purchase of assets

Although sellers will invariably prefer to structure the deal as a share sale, there will be cases where the seller will have to accept that the deal will be structured as a sale and purchase of assets and carefully manage the attendant tax costs.

13.7.2 Overview of tax consequences of a sale and purchase of assets

A sale of a company's trade and assets is likely to trigger a number of tax costs within the company and there would be a further tax liability if its seller shareholders wish to take the sale proceeds out of the company. In some cases, the seller may be able to minimise the corporation tax charges (for example, if the company is generating significant tax losses which are available to shelter the profits and gains). However, many sellers find that an assets deal is likely to be much less attractive, since their sale proceeds will suffer two "layers" of tax. Furthermore, the sellers still retain any contingent commercial, legal and tax risks relating to the company's previous dealings and transactions.

13.7.3 Summary of tax consequences of sales of assets

The main tax consequences of a sale of assets are summarised below:

- **Company's corporation tax accounting period ("CTAP")**

  The sale of the company's trade and assets will trigger the end of a CTAP (unless the company is continuing to carry on at least one other trade) (s.12(3)(c) the ICTA 1988). This is likely to accelerate the payment of the company's tax liabilities.

- **Unrelieved trading losses**

  If the company has unrelieved trading tax losses, these will be forfeited on the cessation of the trade. This is because unused trading losses can only be set-off against profits of the same trade (s.393(1) of the ICTA 1988). In such cases, the seller company's planning strategy must be to minimise the amount of losses which would otherwise be wasted — for example, by ensuring that a "realistic" amount of the total sale proceeds has been allocated to the sale of trading stock and plant etc.

- **Sale of trading stock**

  The closing trading stock will be brought into the company's corporation tax computation at the actual transfer price (provided it is sold at arm's length). Consequently, a certain amount of flexibility is available in agreeing the disposal value of trading stock (s.100(1)(a) of the ICTA 1988).

- **Capital allowance clawbacks**

  The sale of the trade will trigger a balancing adjustment on plant and machinery for capital allowance purposes. If the sale proceeds exceeds the tax written down value ("TWDV") of the plant, etc. a taxable balancing charge arises. Conversely, if the TWDV exceeds the sale proceeds, there would be a balancing allowance to deduct against the company's profits (s.61(1)(f), (2) (Table, item 6) of the Capital Allowances Act 2001 ("CAA 2001")).

  The sale of industrial buildings and hotels no longer produce any balancing charge. In preparation for the gradual phasing-out of IBAs and HBAs, any post March 20, 2007 disposal of an industrial building or qualifying hotel is no longer subject to any balancing adjustment. The post-sale residue of qualifying expenditure is deemed to be the same as the pre-sale residue. This means that the buyer takes over the seller's unrelieved qualifying expenditure and claims IBAs (on the same basis as the seller would have done) under the transitional phase-out rates until March 31, 2011, after which no IBAs/HBAs can be claimed.

- **Capital gains on sale of trading property and goodwill**

The sale of property and goodwill invariably produces taxable capital gains (after deducting indexation relief which remains available for corporate sellers).

If the company is continuing to trade or is part of a group, then it may be possible to "roll-over" (i.e. defer) the gains. Broadly, if the company or group is planning to reinvest in new qualifying assets (such as trading property, fixed plant, etc.) within the relevant one/three year period, the gains can be sheltered (s.152 and s.175 of the TCGA 1992).

The sale of "old-regime" goodwill (i.e. goodwill held on April 1, 2002) is taxed as a capital gain under the normal rules—it is not treated as an income receipt under the Finance Act 2002 ("FA 2002") Intangibles regime (para.118 Sch.29 to FA 2002). However, any gain on goodwill can now only be "rolled-over" against the purchase of goodwill and other intangible assets under the FA 2002 Intangibles regime (paras 37 to 41 of Sch.29 to FA 2002).

- **VAT treatment**

As explained in 9.8, the sale of the trade will usually qualify for VAT transfer of going concern ("TOGC") relief, which means that no VAT should be accounted for on the sale of the assets/trade (art.5 of the VAT (Special Provisions) Order 1995). Where the goodwill of the trade is being transferred, the employees are being taken on by the buyer, and the same business is being carried on post-sale, HMRC will generally accept TOGC treatment. HMRC are no longer prepared to give informal rulings on whether "straightforward" transactions qualify as a TOGC.

13.7.4 Allocation of the total sale consideration

The overall price paid for the assets which make up the business will be determined commercially. However, because a bundle of assets are being acquired, this may give rise to an opportunity for tax savings, by appropriate allocation of the global price amongst the individual assets. However, the tax objectives of the seller and buyer may conflict and, in practice, a compromise allocation is usually negotiated. The "break-down" of the sale price amongst the various assets should be included in the sale and purchase agreement. This will carry considerable weight, although it does not necessarily bind HMRC.

The tax legislation gives HMRC the power to re-apportion the consideration. However, in practice, HMRC rarely interfere with any apportionment agreed at arm's length between unconnected parties, unless it is clearly artificial. The seller and buyer should therefore try to ensure that the amounts attributed to each asset fall within the accepted parameter of values which can be substantiated.

13.7.5 Buyer's acquisition of goodwill and intangibles

Under the Sch.29 intangibles regime, the tax deductions available for the acquisition of goodwill and intangibles are generally based on the amount reflected in the acquiring company's statutory accounts. The amounts allocated to the relevant assets acquired as part of the business purchase are often subject to FRS 7. Broadly, this requires the acquiring company to reflect the acquired assets at their fair market value—which may not necessarily be the amount reflected in the sale and purchase agreement.

If there is a disparity between the contract allocation and the FRS 7 fair value for goodwill/intangibles, the buyer's tax relief will be based on the goodwill reported in the accounts after applying the FRS 7 "fair value" process. HMRC accept that this is the correct analysis for goodwill and other intangibles. From a planning perspective, any amount eligible for relief under the Sch.29 intangibles regime is circumscribed by the overriding "just and reasonable" rule in the FA 2002 Sch.29 para.105.

In such cases, HMRC may also contend that it is necessary to follow the "fair-value" apportionment for other assets using their powers in, for example, s.52(4) of the TCGA 1992 (for chargeable gains) and ss.562 and 563 of the CAA 2001 (for capital allowances). There is growing evidence that HMRC are pressing for the FRS 7 values for capital allowances and chargeable gains as well.

13.7.6 Extracting the sale proceeds from the company

Sellers will often wish to extract the post-tax sale proceeds from the company in the most tax-efficient way. If the seller shareholders are entitled to business taper relief, they will wish to take their entitlement in a "capital form". In practical terms, this will mean that the company has to be liquidated (under a members voluntary winding-up). The liquidator will then arrange to pay the net proceeds (possibly together with the company's retained trading profits and share capital) to the shareholders as a capital distribution. The receipt of a capital distribution is treated as a (part) disposal of the shares for CGT purposes (s.122 of the TCGA 1992)—see 13.2 for computation of capital gains and Example 5 below.

Capital distributions made during a winding-up (or distributions treated as capital under the concessionary ESC C16 treatment) are eligible for ER, since they are treated as a disposal of an interest in shares under the TCGA 1992 s.122 (TCGA 1992 s.169I (2)(c)).

As a general rule, ER should be available where the capital distribution is made within *three years* of the cessation of trade, in such cases, provided the conditions in the TCGA 1992 s.169I(7) are satisfied. These are:

- The company must be a trading company (or holding company of a trading group) in the one year before it ceases to trade (or ceases its "holding company of a trading group" status).

- Throughout the one year before the company ceases to trade (or be a qualifying holding company), the recipient shareholder is required to have:

  - held at least five per cent of the ordinary share capital (carrying at least five per cent of the voting rights) in the one year;

  - served as a director or employee of the company (or fellow group company).

Example 5—CGT on receipt of capital distribution

In December 2008, Jimmy Mack received a final capital distribution of £3,500,000 from his 100 per cent owned company, Supremes Limited. The capital distribution represented the net proceeds of the sale of the company's trade and assets in August 2008 (after allowing for the tax liability attributable to the sale of £375,000 and liquidation fees of £25,000).

Jimmy Mack set up the company in June 1965 and has agreed with HMRC—Share Valuation that his 100 per cent shareholding was worth £500,000 in March 1982.

On the basis that Jimmy makes a claim for ER against his "capital distribution" gain, his tax liability would be calculated as follows:

	£
Capital distribution	3,500,000
Less: March 1982 base cost	(500,000)
Capital gain	3,000,000
Less: ER – £1,000,000 (max) $\times$ 4/9	(444,444)
Gain after ER	2,555,556
Less: Annual exemption	(9,600)
Taxable gain	2,545,956
CGT @ 18%	458,272

13.8   Seller tax planning—some final thoughts

Carefully structured tax planning is an essential pre-requisite for those wishing to sell their company. Sellers will normally seek to sell their shares (to avoid the additional corporate tax costs that arise on asset sale and to reduce their commercial risk).

For many owner-managed companies, the main focus will now be securing the availability of ER, which will provide an "exit" CGT rate of 10 per cent. However, ER is limited to gains of £1 million (computed on a "lifetime" basis). Thus, where the owner manager is likely to realise gains of more than £1 million on a sale, they may wish to increase the amount of available ER by (for example) transferring an appropriate number of shares to their spouse. Provided that the spouse satisfied the relevant conditions in their own right (see 13.3.1), there would be a further ER allowance of £1 million available (attracting a 10 per cent CGT rate). However, this would need to be planned for well before a sale was planned, since the spouse would have to have held at least five per cent of the (voting) ordinary shares in their own right and be an employee/director (although not necessarily "full time") throughout the year before the sale.

To the extent that ER is not available, the seller shareholder's CGT rate will be 18 per cent. Following the abolition of the business taper regime which gave an unlimited 10 per cent CGT rate on sale, sellers will now have to be re-educated and accept that 18 per cent is still a pretty reasonable rate to pay on their "exit" gains.

Some sellers may wish to consider emigration, but this brings its own problems. Whilst this route may be initially appealing, many sellers are "put off" by the inherent restrictions (such as the upheaval of their family and the inability to regularly watch their favourite football team play on Saturday afternoons). All this requires careful consideration and specialist tax advice both in the UK and the destination country.

Obtaining carefully considered tax planning advice on the sale of an owner-managed company is essential. Such sales often represent a "once in a lifetime" opportunity to realise the benefits of many years hard work. Both the tax and commercial "grooming" must be considered many months in advance—it should not be an "eleventh hour" exercise. And, as with all tax planning exercises, the seller's commercial objectives should take precedence. Nevertheless, it should not be forgotten that a failure to address a key tax issue can often turn a good deal into a bad one.

Chapter 14

Sale by Corporate Sellers—Main Tax Issues

Following the introduction of the Substantial Shareholdings Exemption ("SSE") in April 2002, most companies should be able to sell their shareholdings in a subsidiary company (or perhaps an equity stake in a joint venture company) on a tax-exempt basis. However, the availability of the SSE cannot be assumed, since a number of detailed conditions have to be satisfied (see 14.2). The tax implications of selling shares in a company (such as a subsidiary company) which does not qualify for the SSE are dealt with at 14.3.

Sales by corporate sellers (which are part of a 75 per cent group) may also give rise to other tax charges, such as degrouping charges under s.179 of the Taxation of Chargeable Gains Act 1992 ("TCGA 1992") or "clawbacks" of stamp duty/stamp duty land tax ("SDLT") as a result of the target company leaving the seller's group (see 14.4).

14.1 Sale of shares v sale of assets

In cases where a corporate seller is entitled to SSE, it will seek to ensure that the transaction is structured as a share sale (as opposed to an assets sale). However, if a corporate seller is under some pressure (e.g. where a subsidiary or group has financial problems), then a shrewd purchaser is likely to insist that he purchases the trade and assets. In such cases, the sale of the assets is likely to trigger various tax liabilities within the subsidiary (see 13.7.3 for detailed tax consequences of a sale of assets).

In cases of a "distressed" sale, the post-tax sale proceeds will often be used to repay intra-group or bank debt. Any amounts available for the group will normally be extracted by way of dividend (tax-free in the recipient's hands). Thus, a further tax charge will only arise where the individual shareholders of the parent take some or all of the sale proceeds as a dividend (see 13.7.5).

14.2 Share sales—the substantial shareholdings exemption ("SSE")

14.2.1 Key SSE conditions

The SSE provides an extremely valuable tax relief for corporate disposals of subsidiaries and certain other equity investments. Provided that the detailed conditions in Sch.7AC to the TCGA 1992 are satisfied, any capital gain on the sale should be exempt from corporation tax. The SSE exemption is not restricted to eligible shareholdings in UK resident companies—it also applies to exempt gains arising on the sale of non-resident subsidiaries, etc.

On the other hand, if the disposal satisfies all the SSE conditions but produces a capital loss, that loss will not count as an allowable loss for reducing the company's/group's capital gains (s.16(2) of the TCGA 1992).

The key pre-conditions for the main SSE are:

14.2.1.1   The "investing company" (i.e. the seller) must be a sole trading company or a member of a trading group throughout the "qualifying period" which begins at the start of the relevant 12-month "substantial shareholding" period (see below) and ends when the substantial shareholding is sold. It must also be a sole trading company or trading group member immediately after the disposal — (see 14.2.3 and 14.2.4) (para.18 Sch.7AC to the TCGA 1992).

14.2.1.2   The relevant shareholding investment must qualify as a "substantial shareholding" held throughout a 12-month period starting not more than two years before the shares are disposed of (see 14.2.7) (para.7 Sch.7AC to the TCGA 1992).

14.2.1.3   The company in which the shares are held (i.e. the investee company) must be a qualifying trading company or qualifying holding company of a trading group throughout the "qualifying period" defined in 14.2.1.1 above and also immediately after the disposal (see 14.2.8) (para.19 Sch.7AC to the TCGA 1992).

These key conditions will now be examined in more detail.

14.2.2   Investing company conditions

In the two-year period before the sale of the substantial shareholding, the investing company must have been a "trading company" (see 14.2.3) or trading group member (see 14.2.4) for at least a 12-month period. Furthermore, the investing company must also be a sole trading company or "trading group" member immediately after the sale (para.18 Sch.7AC to the TCGA 1992).

The requirement for the investing company to be a trading company or member of a trading group (see 14.2.3.) immediately after the disposal could deny relief where, for example, a holding company sells its only (trading) subsidiary company. In this case, the holding company will normally be left with the sale proceeds and would only satisfy the post-sale "trading requirement" where the seller company planned to acquire another trade or a significant equity interest in a trading company or group within the near future.

Alternatively, in such cases, it should generally be possible to exempt the gain under the so-called "para 3" exemption. This provides a "secondary" SSE where (broadly speaking) the seller company would have qualified for the main SSE on a notional sale in the past two years (the "trading requirements" are deemed to have been satisfied for these purposes). However, SSE relief can only be enjoyed where the seller company is liquidated (as soon as is reasonably practical) with the sale proceeds being distributed to its shareholders (para.3 Sch.7AC to the TCGA 1992).

14.2.3 Trading company

The SSE "trading company" and "trading group member" definitions are virtually identical to the ones applying for CGT entrepreneurs' relief (see 13.3.4) Thus, a "trading company" is a company carrying on trading activities that does not to any substantial extent include non-trading activities. In practice, HMRC apply a 20 per cent de minimis limit for "non-trading" activities. Where a company has "non-trading" activities or investments, HMRC may look at a range of possible measures, depending on the facts of the particular case (see 13.3.4).

Activities carried out for the purposes of preparing to trade also count as trading. A very helpful extension to the meaning of "trading activities" embraces activities carried on with a view to:

- acquiring or starting to carry on a trade; or

- purchasing a significant (i.e. 51 per cent or eligible joint venture) shareholding in another trading company or "trading group".

In such cases, the acquisition must be made "as soon as reasonably practicable in the circumstances". This means that a holding company may still qualify for SSE relief if it sells its only trading subsidiary and reinvests the sale proceeds in buying a 51 per cent stake in another trading company (see 14.2.2) (para.20 Sch.7AC to the TCGA 1992).

14.2.4 "Trading group" member

A member of a trading group also qualifies and does not therefore have to carry out a trade in its own right. A "trading group" is defined in much the same way as a sole trading company. For these purposes, a group broadly consists of a principal or parent company and its 51 per cent subsidiaries on a "worldwide" basis. A trading group is one where, taking all the activities of the group together, it carries on trading activities, ignoring any non-substantial (i.e. no more than 20 per cent) non-trading activities (para.21 Sch.7AC to the TCGA 1992). The legislative requirement to take all the activities of the group together ensures that any intra-group transactions are effectively ignored—the group's activities are effectively looked at on a "consolidated" basis. Thus, for example, loans made or property leased to another 51 per cent group member is not regarded as an investment/non-trading activity.

Where the net sale proceeds generated from an SSE sale of a subsidiary are paid out to the parent company's shareholders by way of a dividend within a "reasonable" period, such amounts would not be treated as "non-trading" funds. This should usually enable the seller group to satisfy the "trading group" test immediately after the disposal as required by para.18(1)(b) Sch.7AC to the TCGA 1992.

14.2.5   Special "look-through" rule for joint venture holdings

Where the group holds non-controlling equity investments, these would normally fall to be treated as a "non-trading" activity and may therefore potentially prejudice the seller's trading status, subject to the 20 per cent de minimis test for investments, etc. (see 14.2.3 and 14.2.4 above).

However, most types of joint venture investments should benefit from the helpful "transparency" rule in para.23 Sch.7AC to the TCGA 1992. This provides that where the seller company/group holds at least 10 per cent of the (underlying) joint venture company's ("JVC's") ordinary shares, it should generally be possible to treat it as carrying on an appropriate part of the JVC's trade. Consequently, the seller company/group is deemed to carry on the appropriate part of the JVC's trading activities. However, this beneficial treatment only applies where five or fewer individual or corporate shareholders hold 75 per cent or more of the JVC's ordinary shares.

14.2.6   Risk issues and HMRC's advance "non-statutory" clearance procedure

In many cases, it will be clear as to whether the seller group and target company meet the appropriate "trading" tests for SSE. However, there will often be marginal cases, where the impact of certain "non-trading" activities/assets on the seller's SSE relief is less clear.

HMRC accept that there will be cases of genuine uncertainty in determining whether the relevant requirements are satisfied for the SSE—for example, there may be questions surrounding the group's trading status or the technical application of the legislation to an "unusual" case. In such cases, the seller company can seek advance confirmation from HMRC as to whether SSE will apply under the non-statutory advance clearance procedure. This helpful procedure enables the seller to obtain greater certainty as to whether SSE is available before implementing a sale. HMRC will only deal with applications for advance clearance where it can be demonstrated that the transaction is commercially significant to the business and is genuinely contemplated. The seller must effectively put "all its cards on the table" and highlight the areas of uncertainty and its own tax analysis and conclusions. HMRC aims to respond within 28 days, though complex cases may take longer.

Where the underlying facts clearly show that it would be difficult to sustain a claim for the SSE, alternative tax planning could be considered to mitigate the seller's taxable gain (see 14.3).

14.2.7   The "substantial shareholding" requirement

The SSE is also dependent on the investing company having a substantial shareholding in the relevant "investee" company throughout a 12-month period within the two years before the shares are sold (para.7 Sch.7AC to the TCGA 1992). It is possible to "look through" any no gain/no loss transfer (such as an intra-group transfer under s.171 of the

TCGA 1992) and include the transferor's period of ownership for the purpose of satisfying the above condition.

The investing company satisfies the substantial shareholding requirement provided that it is beneficially entitled to at least 10 per cent of the:

- investee company's ordinary share capital;

- profits available for distribution to the investee company's equity holders (see Sch.18 to the ICTA 1988);

- assets that would be distributed on a winding up of the investee company.

14.2.8 Investee company requirements

The investee company in which the shares are held must be a sole trading company, holding company of a trading group (or trading subgroup) throughout the "qualifying period" which runs from the start of the relevant 12-month "substantial shareholding" period until the disposal date, as well as immediately after the disposal (para.16 Sch.7AC to the TCGA 1992).

The investee company's "trading" status ceases to be under the seller's control post-sale and therefore actions taken by the buyer could invalidate the seller's SSE. For example, the buyer may arrange for the investeee company's trade to be hived-up. Consequently, the seller should obtain an appropriate warranty from the buyer to the effect that the investee company will continue to satisfy the "trading" requirement for SSE purposes after the sale.

It is clearly important that any "non-trading" activities carried on by the investee company or group fall within the de minimis 20 per cent threshold (see 14.2.3 and 14.2.4) as, otherwise, the disposal would not be protected by the SSE and thus potentially exposed to a tax charge.

14.2.9 Dealing with different types of disposal consideration (including earn-outs)

The SSE relief is available where the seller receives the consideration in cash or in shares in the acquiring company. Any share element in the consideration effectively overrides the normal capital gains "reorganisation" reliefs. Thus, a sale of the shares wholly or partly in exchange for the acquirer's shares is "tax-free" under the SSE. (The SSE "trumps" the general share exchange relief in s.135 of the TCGA 1992 (para.4 Sch.7AC to the TCGA 1992)). The seller company acquires the new shares at their market value. (Special rules apply where shares in a group company are transferred to a fellow group member in exchange for a fresh issue of shares.)

The SSE is beneficial since otherwise s.127 of the TCGA 1992 would have deemed there to be no disposal for tax purposes with the "new" consideration shares having been acquired at the same time and cost as the old shares (see 13.4.2). Hence, if a subsequent sale of the new shares did not attract the SSE, the gain on the old shares would be taxed as part of the overall gain.

Care should be taken on "earn-out" transactions since the capital gains arising on earn-out payments does not qualify for the SSE. This is because the actual payments derive from the earn-out right as opposed to the sale of the original shares, following the dicta in *Marren v Ingles* [1980] S.T.C. 500 (see 13.5.1). In some cases, it may be possible to alleviate this problem by making the deferred consideration ascertainable. The maximum amount payable would then be included in the consideration for the original SSE sale (under s.48 of the TCGA 1992), although this may increase the buyer's stamp duty liability on the share purchase. If the relevant post-acquisition profits fell short of the required targets, there would be a retrospective reduction in the initial consideration but the entire transaction would have been tax exempt.

Example 1 — Basic operation of the SSE

The Motown Group is a large diversified group, specialising in publishing, e-learning solutions, niche music concerts and conferences. The group makes up its accounts to December 31 each year.

The current corporate structure of The Motown Group Ltd is summarised below (indicating the relevant percentage of ordinary share capital and voting rights held for each holding) and has remained the same for many years.

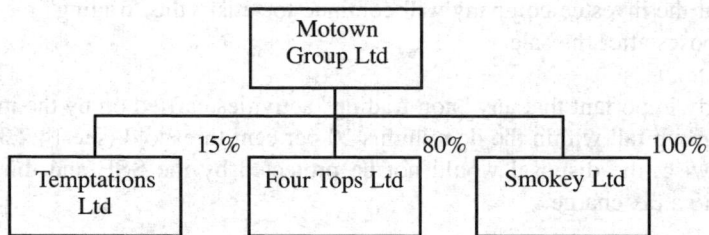

```
                        ┌──────────────┐
                        │   Motown     │
                        │  Group Ltd   │
                        └──────┬───────┘
            ┌──────────15%─────┼─────80%──────────────100%─────────┐
     ┌──────┴───────┐   ┌──────┴───────┐        ┌──────┴───────┐
     │ Temptations  │   │ Four Tops Ltd│        │  Smokey Ltd  │
     │     Ltd      │   │              │        │              │
     └──────────────┘   └──────────────┘        └──────────────┘
```

Ruffin Spa, an Italian resident company, holds the remaining 85 per cent of Temptations Ltd's ordinary share capital. 20 per cent of Four Tops Ltd is owned by Renee plc.

The group is currently considering an offer to sell the entire share capital of Smokey Ltd to Clown plc. Smokey Ltd runs a successful publishing business. The group incorporated Smokey Ltd with 100,000 £1 ordinary shares (issued at par) in 1975. It is estimated that Smokey Ltd's shares were worth about £500,000 at March 31, 1982. Smokey Ltd has never acquired capital assets from other members of the group.

The sale of Smokey Ltd is likely to take place within the next few months and legal Heads of Agreement for a share sale were finalised some weeks ago. The expected sale consideration is £4 million, of which £3 million is to be satisfied in cash and £1 million in shares in Clown plc.

The sale of the entire share capital of Smokey Ltd should qualify for the SSE. Based on the facts provided, the relevant pre-conditions for relief appear to be satisfied as follows:

- The investing company, The Motown Group Ltd, should qualify as a member of a trading group for at least a 12-month period in the two years before the impending sale. As all the group members are engaged in trading activities, the group should have little difficulty in satisfying the "trading group" definition (see 14.2.4). Although the 15 per cent shareholding in Temptations Ltd might appear to be treated as an investment activity, The Motown Group Ltd is favourably deemed to carry on 15 per cent of Temptations Ltd's trading activities under the special rules for joint venture companies (see 14.2.5).

- The entire share capital of Smokey Ltd clearly represents a "substantial shareholding" held throughout the same relevant period.

- Smokey Ltd has been a trading company during the relevant period.

Clearly the SSE provides a valuable relief in this case as it avoids an immediate tax liability of around £556,500 on the sale, which would have been calculated as follows:

Sale proceeds—cash element 3,000,000

Less: Deemed base value at March 31, 1982

Less: £500,000 × £3m/(£3m + £1m) (375,000)

Less: Indexation (March 1982 to date) £375,000 × (say) 170% (637,500)

Capital gain 1,987,500

Corporation tax thereon at (say) 28% £556,500

As the SSE applies to the entire £4 million sale consideration, including the part satisfied by the shares issued by Clown plc, The Motown Group Ltd will acquire its "consideration" shares in Clown plc at a capital gains base cost of £1 million (rather than at a pro-rata proportion of original base cost in Smokey Ltd's shares).

There are no other tax charges to consider as Smokey Ltd has not received any chargeable assets by way of intra-group transfer within the previous six years.

14.3   Tax treatment of sales that do not qualify for the SSE

14.3.1   Minimising seller's capital gain

There will be cases which do not qualify for the SSE—for example, where the seller group company does not satisfy the stringent "trading" requirement. The seller group would then be faced with a taxable capital gain on the sale of the target company's shares. The seller's main objective will then be to minimise the tax liability on the sale of the subsidiary's shares as well as reducing any other hidden tax costs of disposal.

Example 1 above illustrates how the company's capital gain might be calculated in the absence of the SSE. Thus, the corporate seller's gain is broadly calculated as the amount by which the sale proceeds (net of allowable incidental costs of disposal) exceeds the amount it originally paid for the shares. Special rebasing rules apply where the seller company (or a fellow group company) held the shares in the target subsidiary, etc. at March 31, 1982. In such cases, the seller can deduct the market value of the target's shares at March 31, 1982 as the base cost (where this is higher than the pre-March 31, 1982 acquisition cost). In such cases, sellers can normally deduct the market value of the shareholding at March 31, 1982 as their base cost.

If the sale proceeds are less than the seller's base cost, a capital loss arises (which can be offset against other capital gains made by the seller).

Corporate sellers are entitled to deduct an indexation allowance against their gain (although this was abolished completely for individuals/ trustees from April 6, 2008). Broadly, the indexation allowance gives a measure of relief for inflation — by taking the increase in the Retail Prices Index ("RPI") between the disposal date and the date the shares were acquired (or March 1982, where rebasing is used). (The relevant RPI increase is represented as an "indexation" factor (expressed as a decimal, calculated to three places), which is then applied to the shareholder's base cost, as shown in example 1 above.) Indexation cannot give rise to or create a capital loss.

Detailed attention must also be paid to the impact of the vast amount of anti-avoidance legislation which impinges on the disposal of the subsidiary company's shares.

14.3.2   **Pre-sale dividends**

Where a proposed sale of a subsidiary is likely to give rise to a taxable gain (for example, because the sale does not qualify for the SSE), it is normally possible to reduce that gain through the use of a pre-sale dividend.

In simple terms, the holding company/seller would procure the payment of an appropriate dividend from the subsidiary company. The dividend payment would have various legal and tax consequences:

- it would generally reduce the value of the subsidiary (so that the buyer would generally be willing to reduce the sale consideration (on a "£ for £" basis);

- the dividend would be tax-free in the holding company's hands (s.208 of the ICTA 1988);

- the lower sale consideration would lead to a pro-rata reduction in the holding company's taxable gain on the sale of the subsidiary.

In practice, the amount of dividend that could be "stripped-out" legitimately would be limited by the amount of the subsidiary's distributable reserves but not necessarily its available cash. Typically, the subsidiary company would pay the relevant dividend to its holding company, with the amount being immediately lent back to the subsidiary. The purchasing company would then repay the consequent holding company debt (by injecting suitable funds into the "target" subsidiary on a loan account). As a result of these arrangements, the buyer would pay a commensurately lower amount for the subsidiary's shares (thus saving stamp duty).

It is important to ensure that the "consideration" clause of the sale and purchase agreement is correctly drafted to ensure that HMRC is not able to tax the amount of the agreed sale consideration before the reduction for the pre-sale dividend, as occurred in *Spectros International plc (in voluntary liquidation) v Madden* [1997] S.T.C. 114. The *Spectros* case is an instructive lesson in the importance of correct legal drafting — the judge confirming that the seller is taxed by reference to the strict construction of the contract.

The payment of pre-sale dividends is circumscribed by various anti-avoidance rules. Thus, for example, if the payment of a pre-sale dividend creates a capital loss on the sale of the shares, the amount of the seller's allowable loss would be restricted on a "just and reasonable" basis under the depreciatory transaction rules (ss.176–177 of the TCGA 1992). Similarly, the seller's capital gain could be increased to the extent that dividends have been paid from "artificially generated" profits that have not been subjected to corporation tax (ss.30–31 of the TCGA 1992). Dividends paid out of normal taxed profits are not affected by these rules and can therefore be used to mitigate capital gains (as described above).

Example 2—Use of pre-sale dividends to mitigate tax payable on sale of subsidiary

Jackson Holdings Ltd is planning to sell one of its wholly owned subsidiaries, Ben Ltd. Ben Ltd was incorporated in April 1992 with issued share capital of 100,000 £1 ordinary shares and currently has distributable reserves of around £2,000,000 (which have all arisen from trading profits).

The buyer, ABC Ltd, is seeking to acquire all the shares in Ben Ltd for £3,000,000.

If no planning is done, Jackson Holdings Ltd will be liable to pay corporation tax of around £795,200 on the gain from the sale of Ben Ltd. However, with a pre-sale dividend of around £2,000,000 (equivalent to the current distributable profits), the tax liability reduces to £235,200. The relevant indicative calculations are summarised below.

	Initial proposal £	Pre-sale dividend £	With pre-sale dividend £
Sale proceeds	3,000,000	(2,000,000)	1,000,000
Less: Base cost	(100,000)		(100,000)
Less: Indexation Less: £100,000 × (say) 60%	(60,000)		(60,000)
Chargeable gain	2,840,000		840,000
Corporation tax @ 28%	795,200		235,200

The payment of a pre-sale dividend would therefore save the seller about £560,000 in tax (i.e. £2,000,000 × 28 per cent).

14.3.3   Pre-sale extraction of assets from the target company

If the subsidiary holds assets which are not required by the buyer or which the seller wishes to retain, they can be extracted prior to the sale via an intra-group transfer. It may therefore be possible to reduce the value of the subsidiary's shares (and hence the capital gain) by arranging for the relevant asset(s) to be transferred out at an under-value, which will be effective provided the asset is transferred for an amount at least equal to its cost (in the accounts) (see ss.30–32 of the TCGA 1992).

Where such transactions lead to the creation of a capital loss, the depreciatory transaction rules in s.176 of the TCGA 1992 will generally nullify that loss.

14.3.4   Use of group capital losses

If the group has legitimate unused capital losses, these could also be used fully or partly to shelter the seller's capital gain on the sale. Since FA 2000, it is no longer necessary first to route the "third-party" disposal through the group company with the capital losses. Under s.171A of the TCGA 1992, the holding company/seller can treat the disposal of the shares in the subsidiary, etc. as though it had been made by another group member (provided a competent "no gain/no loss" transfer could have been made between the group companies under s.171, of the TCGA 1992).

Both group members must jointly elect to deem that the shares in the subsidiary, etc. are first transferred to the other group member (with capital losses) on a no gain/no loss basis. The deemed recipient member is then treated as selling the subsidiary etc. to the third party buyer for tax purposes and will therefore recognise the capital gain or loss in its own tax computation.

14.4   Degrouping charges

14.4.1   Capital gains degrouping charge under s.179 of the TCGA 1992

The sale of the target subsidiary may trigger a s.179 of the TCGA 1992 degrouping tax charge (as a result of it leaving the group). A degrouping charge will arise where the target subsidiary has received chargeable assets from other group companies within the previous six years which it still holds when it leaves the group.

The tax charge (which crystallises in the subsidiary) is based on a deemed disposal (and reacquisition) of the relevant asset at its market value at the date of the original intra-group transfer (s.179(1)(3) of the TCGA 1992). However, the deemed capital gain will arise immediately after the beginning of the corporation tax accounting period in which the subsidiary leaves the group (or, if later, at the date of the original intra-group transfer) (s.179(4) of the TCGA 1992).

In the context of a sale, the buyer effectively "picks" up the degrouping tax charge since it is triggered in the subsidiary. However, a well-advised buyer will normally obtain an indemnity for the s.179 of the TCGA 1992 tax from the seller. The seller will therefore have a strong incentive to mitigate any degrouping tax charge.

Given that the degrouping gain is normally treated as arising at the start of the accounting period in which the subsidiary leaves the group, it may often be possible to shelter it using group relief losses (the "arrangements" rule would usually only break the group relief relationship at a later time in that accounting period—see 14.6).

Further ways in which degrouping gains can be eliminated/reduced include:

- Exempting the gain under the SSE—this would apply in relation to a deemed s.179 of the TCGA 1992 disposal of a subsidiary or other substantial shareholding that satisfied the SSE rules (see 14.2).

- Electing to allocate all/part of the gain to other members of the seller group— such re-allocations may enable the gain to be sheltered by capital losses, etc. within those companies (s.179A of the TCGA 1992).

- Rolling-over the gain against qualifying reinvestment within the seller group under the normal roll-over relief provisions (s.175 of the TCGA 1992). The degrouping gain would then be rolled-over/held-over against group acquisitions of (for example) property or fixed plant and machinery within the three years after the gain arises (or within the previous 12 months). Since April 2002, goodwill is no longer an eligible "reinvestment" asset for this purpose. Similarly, any degrouping charge arising on goodwill (for example, as a result of a hive-down of the trade to the degrouped subsidiary) must be rolled-over against group reinvestment in goodwill and other intangible assets under the Sch.29 to the FA 2002 regime. (This form of roll-over is less beneficial since the rolled-over gain effectively reduces the tax allowable depreciation charge on the new goodwill/intangible assets).

- Making use of the associated companies' exemption in s.179(4) of the TCGA 1992. Where two or more companies are leaving the group together (in a "sub-group" relationship), there is no degrouping charge in relation to assets that have previously been transferred between those companies. In appropriate cases, it may therefore be thought that the associated companies exemption could be obtained by transferring the original transferor company to the degrouped subsidiary. However, this is unlikely to be effective following the recent Court Of Appeal ruling in *Johnston Publishing (North) Ltd v HMRC* [2008] EWCA Civ. 858. The Court of Appeal judges (on a two to one verdict) confirmed HMRC's view that the associated companies exemption is only available if the relevant companies are in a "sub-group" relationship at the time of the original transfer as well as when they leave the group.

The important ruling in *Johnston Publishing* contradicts the long held view amongst many advisers that the relevant "sub-group" relationship does not necessarily have to subsist at the time of the original intra-group transfer. The legislation does not clearly state this as a pre-condition. Had the draftsman intended it to do so, surely they would have specifically stated this in the legislation (in line with typical legislative practice). Nevertheless, following the decision in *Johnston Publishing*, the associated companies' exemption is now more restrictive. It can only be relied on to prevent a degrouping charge on assets that were transferred between members of the same sub-group which leave the group together (provided they were still in that same sub-group relationship at the time of the original intra-group transfer). (The decision in *Johnston Publishing* is final since leave to appeal to the House of Lords was refused.)

14.4.2   Degrouping charge on held-over gains

An unexpected form of degrouping charge arises where the subsidiary leaving the group has gains held-over under the depreciating asset provisions.

Under s.175(3) of the TCGA 1992, all members of the group are treated as carrying on the same trade. When the subsidiary leaves the group, it ceases to carry on the "single group" trade. HMRC argue that where a subsidiary leaves the group, it ceases to carry on the "deemed" group trade and this therefore crystallises a charge on gains held-over against depreciating assets held by the degrouped subsidiary (s.154(2) and s.175(3) of the TCGA 1992).

14.4.3   Clawback of stamp duty land tax/stamp duty group relief

Where the target subsidiary has acquired property or shares from a fellow-group company it may be vulnerable to a clawback of the relevant stamp duty land tax ("SDLT") or stamp duty.

An SDLT degrouping charge will arise (clawing back the SDLT relief on the original intra-group transfer) where the subsidiary leaves the group:

-     within three years of the intra-group transfer; and

-     continues to hold the land or property that was transferred from a fellow group member (para.4 Sch.7 to the FA 2003).

In such cases, the subsidiary will incur an SDLT charge (based on the SDLT that would have been payable at the time of the original transfer if SDLT group relief did not apply). Thus, the SDLT is based on the market value of the property at the time of the original transfer using the SDLT rates at that time. If the SDLT remains unpaid after six months, HMRC can recover tax from other "related" parties, including the seller and certain companies in the purchaser's group (para.5 Sch.7 to the FA 2003). A buyer would invariably seek an appropriate indemnity for any SDLT degrouping charges from the seller (as part of the sale and purchase agreement).

Similar rules apply for stamp duty purposes in relation to shares previously transferred to the target company within the previous three years.

Stamp duty and SDLT are discussed in detail in Ch.15.

14.5   Denial of group relief

Companies which are part of a 75 per cent group relationship often participate in group relief, which enables the current tax losses of one group member to be surrendered to another group company for offset against its taxable profits. However, special care is required where negotiations are taking place for a company to leave a group. In such cases, a company will not be able to participate in group relief where there are arrangements in existence for it to be sold. "Arrangements" are given a very wide meaning for these purposes and cover any form of agreement for the disposal of the subsidiary, even if it is not enforceable (SP3/93 and s.410(1) of the ICTA 1988)

Following *Shepherd v Law Land plc* [1990] S.T.C. 795, the degrouped subsidiary would not be able to benefit from any group relief losses for the period in which arrangements were in existence for it to leave the group. This will normally mean that the "current" accounting period is split at the point where the relevant arrangement starts and only the period up to that date can be accessed by group relief claims.

14.6   Section 684 of the ITA 2007—transactions in securities anti-avoidance rules

A straightforward sale of shares in a subsidiary company at arm's-length to an unconnected purchaser is unlikely to give rise to a problem under s.684 of the ITA 2007. These are the corporation tax provisions which are designed to counteract any tax advantage arising from certain transactions in securities or shares. However, if there are unusual features, such as abnormal dividends, it is normally sensible to apply for advance clearance under s.701 of the ITA 2007.

Chapter 15

Stamp Duties

Since 2003, the scope of stamp duty has been significantly reduced so that transfers of assets such as book debts and other receivables are no longer subject to stamp duty. Accordingly, stamp duty is only now chargeable on:

- instruments (for example, forms of transfer) relating to stock (for example, shares) or marketable securities;

- land, where the conveyance or transfer is pursuant to a contract for sale entered into on or before July 10, 2003;

- transfers of partnership interests.

Stamp duty land tax ("SDLT") is charged in accordance with Pt 4 of the Finance Act 2003 on "land transactions". A "land transaction" is any acquisition of a "chargeable interest" and SDLT applies however the acquisition of the chargeable interest is effected (ss.43(1) and (2) of the Finance Act 2003). A "chargeable interest" is defined as an estate, interest, right or power in or over land in the UK or the benefit of an obligation, restriction or condition affecting the value of any such estate, interest, right or power (but subject to certain exemptions which are discussed below). The general principle is therefore that SDLT is charged on the acquisition of an interest in land in the UK.

In practice, therefore, stamp duty will be payable on a sale and purchase of shares and SDLT will be payable on sales and purchases of assets, to the extent that the transaction includes a chargeable interest in land.

A sale and purchase of shares may, however, involve an ancillary land transaction on which SDLT will be payable (for example, the transfer of a property from the target company to the seller or the grant of a new lease of the target company's premises) and similarly, a sale and purchase of assets may involve an ancillary transfer of shares on which stamp duty will be payable.

This chapter is intended to be a brief summary of the practical impact of stamp duty and SDLT in the context of such transactions and does not purport to be anything more than a brief summary of the way in which these duties will impact on a typical transaction.

15.1 Sales and purchases of shares

15.1.1 Stamp duty is chargeable on transfers of registered shares from a seller to a buyer. Unless stock transfer forms are presented for stamping within 30 days a penalty is payable and the company secretary will be liable to a £10 fine under s.17 of the Stamp Act 1891, if he registers a transfer which is not duly stamped. Duty is payable by the buyer and is chargeable at the rate of £5 per £1,000 (or part) of the consideration. If, therefore, Buyer PLC is acquiring the entire issued share capital of Target Limited for £4,444,444, stamp duty amounting to £22,225 will be payable by Buyer.

15.1.2   A transfer of loan capital will generally be exempt from stamp duty but, if the buyer agrees to pay to the seller the amount of any indebtedness which is due from the target company to the seller, that amount may, under s.57 of the Stamp Act 1891, be treated as consideration for the shares and may be subject to stamp duty. This will not, however, be the case if the buyer undertakes to procure that the target company itself will repay the loan, unless it is clear that the target company does not have sufficient resources to make the repayment. In the example given above, therefore, if, in addition to paying £4,444,444 for the share capital of Target, it is agreed that a loan of £2,000,000 from Seller to Target should be repaid on completion, Buyer should not itself assume responsibility for the repayment but should instead undertake to put Target in funds (normally by way of loan) in order to enable it to repay the loan.

15.1.3   Duty is charged on so much of the consideration as is ascertainable at the date on which the transfer is stamped and the consideration is ascertainable if the information exists from which it may be calculated. If, therefore, the amount of the purchase price is to be determined following the preparation of completion accounts, the buyer should present the transfer for stamping within the 30 day period and the duty should then be paid once the completion accounts have been finalised and the amount of the purchase price has been determined.

The position will, however, be different if the consideration is unascertainable at the date that the transfer is stamped—for example, where all or part of the purchase price is dependent upon an earn-out. In those situations, by virtue of the "contingency principle", all contingencies (e.g. achieving the profit targets to which the earn-out is linked) will generally be ignored. Accordingly, on an earn-out deal, the element of the consideration which is linked to the earn-out will not be subject to stamp duty, unless there is a specified maximum or a minimum amount which will be payable in any event.

On an earn-out deal, therefore, the buyer should ensure that the whole of that element of the purchase price is contingent and that there will be no minimum earn-out payment and no maximum earn-out payment. If he does so, stamp duty will only be payable on that part of the purchase price which is ascertainable at the date the transfer is stamped—any part of the purchase price which is fixed at completion or is to be determined by reference to completion accounts. Buyers will sometimes seek to impose a cap on the amount which will be payable under an earn-out but should be aware that, if they do so, stamp duty will be payable by reference to that maximum.

The contingency principle will apply whether the additional consideration is to be satisfied by way of cash or shares or other securities (such as loan notes or loan stock).

15.1.4 Stamp duty reserve tax ("SDRT") is chargeable where there is an agreement to transfer "chargeable securities". The charge to tax arises on the date the agreement is made (or, if the agreement is conditional, on the date the condition is satisfied) and is chargeable at the rate of 0.5 per cent of the consideration. The tax is due and payable on the last day of the month following that in which the agreement was made. Where the agreement is completed later, but within six years, repayment of the SDRT may be obtained if the duty stamped instrument of transfer is presented to the Stamp Office.

Under s.99(3) of the Finance Act 1986, "chargeable securities" include stocks and shares but do not include shares in companies incorporated outside the UK (unless recorded in a register kept in the UK) or most forms of loan capital. Renounceable letters of allotment are, however, subject to the tax.

SDRT will not usually be of concern to a buyer who is buying shares in a private company as he will wish to complete the purchase and have the shares registered in his name, unless (for example) he intends that on completion the shares should be transferred into the beneficial ownership of another company within his group. If he does intend to do so, the buyer should ensure that the sale and purchase agreement allows him to substitute the other company as the transferee on completion as, otherwise, a direct transfer of the shares from the seller to that other company would give rise to SDRT. Otherwise, the buyer should take a transfer from the seller, pay stamp duty on it and register it and then enter into a separate transfer of the shares in favour of the associated company. Relief under s.42 of the Finance Act 1930 may then be claimed in respect of the latter transfer and the sale and purchase agreement will not be subject to SDRT, as it will have been duly completed by a stamped instrument.

15.1.5 Section 42 of the Finance Act 1930 gives relief from stamp duty on certain transactions between companies in the same group, provided that certain conditions are met. In summary:

15.1.5.1 The parties to the transaction must be bodies corporate that are "associated", which means that one company must be the parent of another or both must have the same parent. The test of whether one company is the parent of another will be satisfied if one company beneficially owns, either directly or indirectly, at least 75 per cent of the issued ordinary share capital (essentially, share capital other than fixed rate preference shares of the other), is beneficially entitled to not less than 75 per cent of any profits available for distribution to equity holders of the other or would be beneficially entitled to not less than 75 per cent of any assets of the other available for distribution to its equity holders on a winding-up.

15.1.5.2 The transfer in question must pass beneficial ownership of the asset in question from one company to the other.

15.1.5.3 By virtue of s.27(3) of the Finance Act 1967, it must be shown to the satisfaction of HMRC that the instrument in question was not executed "in pursuance of or in connection with an arrangement" in which:

- the consideration is provided or received directly or indirectly by a non-associated person;

- a non-associated person previously conveyed the interest or;

- the transferee company was to cease to be the subsidiary of the transferor or another group company.

A detailed discussion of these anti-avoidance provisions is beyond the scope of this chapter but they should be considered when there have been transfers from one group company to another, particularly if they have taken place at a time when a sale of the transferee is in the offing.

There are additional anti-avoidance provisions where land is concerned—in the past, land would often have been transferred to a "shell" subsidiary prior to any arrangements to sell it and s.42 relief would be obtained, with the company owning the land being sold at a later date and the buyer paying stamp duty at the rate of 0.5 per cent on the sale of the shares, rather than the duty which would otherwise have been payable on a sale of land. Such arrangements have now been curtailed and, under s.111 Finance Act 2002, there is a claw back of group relief where land has been transferred between two companies and then within three years of that transfer the transferee company ceases to be a member of the same group as the transferor. It will therefore be necessary for the buyer to establish through due diligence whether there have been any transactions to which these anti-avoidance rules may apply and to obtain warranty or indemnity protection where appropriate.

This is no more than a brief introduction to the issues and, whenever these rules appear to be relevant, professional advice should be taken. In practice, the equivalent anti-avoidance provisions relating to SDLT are more likely to be relevant where land is concerned.

15.1.6 The relief from stamp duty on transactions between companies in the same group and the related anti-avoidance provisions are largely replicated in the

SDLT regime (para.1 of Sch.7 to the Finance Act 2003). In addition, however, there are more extensive anti-avoidance provisions relating to the availability of the relief and its subsequent claw back.

Group relief will not be available if the relevant transaction is not effected for bona fide commercial reasons or the transaction forms part of arrangements of which the main purpose, or one of the main purposes, is the avoidance of tax (para.2(4)a of Sch.7 to the Finance (No. 2) Act 2003)—this provision can be difficult to apply in practice.

The relief can be clawed back if, within three years of the effective date of the intra-group land transaction, the "buyer" of the land leaves the group of which it and the seller of the land were members and the buyer, or a company associated with it, holds the land in question. The relief will also be subject to claw back where the buyer of the land leaves the group after three years but pursuant to arrangements in place within three years.

Further anti-avoidance provisions were introduced by the Finance (No. 2) Act 2005, which inserted a new para.4A into Sch.7 to the Finance Act 2003 which applies where:

- a company is subject to a change of control;

- that company has claimed group relief within the last three years (or longer pursuant to arrangements made before that date);

- it does not suffer a claw back of the group relief under the original claw back rules referred to above.

In those circumstances and where there was an earlier transaction under which the relief was claimed and which took place within three years of the change of control of the buyer of the land and which related to a chargeable interest which was the same as, or was derived from, the chargeable interest in respect of which the relief was claimed, then claw back rules mentioned above are re-applied as if the seller under the later transaction were the seller under the earlier transaction.

15.2   Sales and purchases of assets

15.2.1   It will be necessary to consider whether or not SDLT is payable whenever there is a sale and purchase of assets which involve a "land transaction", i.e. the acquisition of a "chargeable interest" over land, other than an "exempt interest".

15.2.2   As already discussed, "chargeable interest" is defined as an estate, interest, right or power in or over land in the UK or the benefit of an obligation, restriction or condition affecting the value of any such estate, interest, right or power, while "exempt interest" includes a licence to use or occupy land, a tenancy at will and a "security interest" (such as a mortgage). Chargeable interests therefore, include freehold and leasehold interests and the equivalent rights under the laws of Scotland and Northern Ireland. The definition covers both legal and equitable interests. SDLT will therefore be payable, for example, whenever the sale and purchase involves the transfer of freehold or leasehold land or (amongst other things):

- the grant of a new lease (which will be treated as an acquisition by the lessee and a disposal by the lessor);

- the surrender of a lease (which will be treated as a disposal by the lessee and an acquisition by the lessor);

- the variation of a lease (which may be a disposal or acquisition by either party).

15.2.3   The "buyer" in a land transaction must deliver a land transaction return to HMRC within 30 days after the "effective date" of the transaction and it is the effective date which is the key date for triggering an SDLT liability. The effective date of a land transaction will generally be the date on which it is completed (for example, the date of completion of a transfer of a freehold interest or the grant of a lease) but s.44(4) of the Finance Act 2003 provides that where a contract relating to land is "substantially performed" before being completed, the contract will be treated as a separate land transaction and the effective date will be the date on which the contract is substantially performed.

A discussion of the concept of "substantial performance" is beyond the scope of this book but its purpose was to prevent arrangements under which a buyer would enter into a contract to buy land and would go into occupation without taking a formal transfer on which stamp duty would be payable.

15.2.4   SDLT is charged as a percentage of the "chargeable consideration" for the land transaction and the current rates of SDLT are set out below.

Residential Consideration	Rate	Non-residential/mixed consideration	Rate
Not more than £125,000	0%	Not more than £150,000	0%
More than £125,000 but not more than £250,000	1%	More than £150,000 but not more than £250,000	1%
More than £250,000 but not more than £500,000	3%	More than £250,000 but not more than £500,000	3%
More than £500,000	4%	More than £500,000	4%

SDLT is payable at the relevant percentage on the whole of the chargeable consideration—not just the amount above the various thresholds.

If VAT is chargeable on a commercial property, then SDLT is chargeable at the relevant rate on both the purchase price and the VAT element as well.

There are however provisions under which, where a land transaction is one of a number of "linked transactions", the land subject to SDLT will be all of the land comprised in all of the linked transactions and the consideration on which SDLT will be payable will be the aggregate chargeable consideration for all of the transactions in question.

15.2.5   SDLT is charged in respect of leases or any premiums paid for the grant of the lease and also on any rent. A summary of the relevant statutory provisions is beyond the scope of this book. It should be noted also that there are specific provisions dealing with the grant of an agreement for a lease which is substantially performed prior to the grant of the actual lease.

15.2.6   Where a company acquires the whole or part of the undertaking of another company and certain conditions are met, the rate of SDLT on any land transaction entered into for the purposes of or in connection with that acquisition is limited to 0.5 per cent. The relevant conditions are that:

●   the consideration for the acquisition must be satisfied in its entirety by the issue of non-redeemable shares to the seller or (where that is not the case) such part of the consideration as does not consist of the issue of non-redeemable shares must comprise either or both of cash not exceeding 10 per cent of the nominal value of the shares and/or the assumption and discharge of liabilities of the seller;

●   the buyer must not be associated with another company that is party to arrangements with the seller relating to shares of the buyer that have been issued.

This relief (acquisition relief) is subject to the "main purpose" anti-avoidance provisions which apply to group relief and which are discussed in 15.1.5 of this chapter.

15.2.7   It should be noted that any part of the purchase price which is attributable to fixtures and fittings (in the case of a lease, whether landlord's fixtures or tenant's fixtures), which form an integral part of the land, will be subject to SDLT. In essence, this will be the case where the item in question is sufficiently annexed to the land that it cannot be removed without causing significant damage and so it will be necessary to consider, for example, the extent to which plant and machinery has been annexed to the land on which it is situated.

15.2.8   SDLT adopts a more flexible approach to contingent consideration than stamp duty as it is not automatically payable on any maximum ascertainable sum and the legislation provides for the possibility of deferral of SDLT and the repayment of any tax paid on a greater amount of consideration than is ultimately payable.

Where the consideration is payable (in whole or in part) only if an uncertain future event occurs, the amount or value of the consideration for SDLT purposes is determined on the assumption that it is in fact payable (or, as the case may be, does not cease to be payable). Where the amount of the consideration is uncertain (because it depends on an uncertain future event, such as a subsequent sale of the land in question) or is unascertained, SDLT is payable on the basis of a reasonable estimate.

These provisions therefore cover situations where the consideration is neither contingent nor uncertain but is unascertained (for example, because it is dependant upon a set of completion accounts), situations where the consideration is contingent (in which case, it is assumed to be payable) and uncertain as to amount, when a reasonable estimate at the effective date of the transaction will be required. There is an obligation to file a further land transaction return and make a payment of any further tax due when the outcome of the contingency is known or when any uncertain or unascertained consideration becomes known.

It is possible to apply to defer payment of SDLT where the amount payable depends on the amount or value of consideration which is contingent or uncertain at the effective date and falls to be paid on one or more future dates, of which at least one falls (or may fall) more than six months after the effective date of the transaction.

Where the buyer is unable to defer payment of SDLT where the consideration is contingent or uncertain then, where it is contingent and the contingency does not happen, he can file a further return and reclaim the over-payment while, if it is uncertain or has yet to be ascertained, he must make a reasonable estimate of the final consideration as at the effective date and can file a further return and reclaim the over-payment if the initial payment was too high. If the initial payment is too low, a subsequent return must be made and the additional payment made.

15.2.9　It will be necessary for the buyer to pay the SDLT at the same time as he delivers the land transaction return to HMRC (i.e. within 30 days after the effective date of the transaction). Buyers and their advisers will need to be familiar with the compliance requirements particularly if a further return is likely to be required at a later date. Some changes have in fact been made since the introduction of SDLT in order to reduce the burden on buyers on land.

It should be emphasised that SDLT is a reasonably new tax and the SDLT regime is extremely complex in a number of respects. Professional advice on the SDLT implications should therefore be obtained before entering into any transactions involving land.

Chapter 16

Accounting for Acquisitions

Accounting for acquisitions in UK accounts is a complex and, particularly with the introduction of International Financial Reporting Standards ("IFRS"), a rapidly changing area. It is intended, therefore, that this should provide only an introduction to the principal rules and some of the potential issues that can arise in acquisition accounting under UK Generally Accepted Accounting Principles ("UK GAAP"). Readers are recommended to obtain professional advice on any specific matters with which they are concerned.

16.1 The impact of International Financial Reporting Standards

16.1.1 The accounting rules in the UK are going through a period of fundamental change with the introduction of IFRS. Since late 2000, nearly all the new accounting standards in the UK have been to a very large extent copies of IFRSs.

16.1.2 Under EU regulation, listed groups on the main market have been required to prepare their consolidated financial statements using IFRS for periods commencing on or after January 1, 2005. There is a process by which the EU reviews IFRSs and endorses individual standards. The IFRSs used by UK companies must be those endorsed by the EU.

16.1.3 Companies in the same group must all use either EU-adopted IFRS or UK GAAP, unless there are "good reasons" not to do so (there is DTI guidance on what represents "good reasons"). An exception to this rule is that, where a parent company adopts EU-adopted IFRS in both its consolidated financial statements and its individual financial statements, it is not required to ensure that all its subsidiaries use EU-adopted IFRS as well.

16.1.4 An AIM listed company incorporated in a European Economic Area ("EEA") country (comprising at the date of publication of all EU Member States together with Norway and Liechtenstein, as well as the Channel Islands and the Isle of Man) is required to prepare its consolidated accounts under IFRS for financial periods commencing on or after January 1, 2007 (with restated comparative information). AIM companies incorporated in EEA countries that do not produce consolidated accounts can continue to produce their published accounts under local GAAP (i.e. UK GAAP in the case of UK companies). AIM companies that are not incorporated in an EEA country must present their accounts in accordance with either:

16.1.4.1   International Accounting Standards;

16.1.4.2   US GAAP;

16.1.4.3   Canadian GAAP; or

16.1.4.4   Australian International Financial Reporting Standards.

16.1.5   For non-listed UK companies, EU regulation provides an option to adopt IFRS or remain on UK GAAP. To date, the number of non-listed companies that have moved from UK GAAP to IFRS has been limited.

In 2007, the International Accounting Standards Board issued an exposure draft on a version of IFRS for small and medium-sized entities, which puts forward a simplified version of IFRS. Once this is developed into a finalised standard, wider adoption of IFRS amongst unlisted companies in the UK may result.

16.1.6   In the UK, the Accounting Standards Board ("ASB") is working to harmonise its own standards with IFRSs. In due course, therefore, IFRS and UK GAAP should in principle converge. Some commentators are arguing that UK GAAP should remain different, tailored for the UK business environment. This debate is ongoing. What is clear is that the accounting framework in the UK is subject to a greater number of increasingly complicated rules. For users of accounts, the level of change can represent a major challenge in the interpretation of reported financial performance. Partly in recognition of this, to provide a period of greater stability in financial reporting under IFRS, it was announced in July 2006 that companies will not be required to apply any future new IFRSs or major amendments to existing standards before January 1, 2009.

16.1.7   The timing of revenue recognition in a company may be changed by IFRS, impacting upon the timing of tax payments. The impact of IFRS on distributable profits and therefore dividend policy can also be a major issue.

16.1.8   Banking covenants may need to be re-defined in the light of IFRS reporting (including the adoption of IFRS into UK GAAP).

16.1.9   Even where IFRS has not been adopted, the financial forecasts of a target business may need to anticipate the impact of future introduction.

16.1.10   All this can be very complex. A key challenge for the accountants in a due diligence investigation is to present the impact of any changes in accounting policies and methodologies as clearly as possible to their clients.

16.2   What is "UK GAAP"?

16.2.1   Generally Accepted Accounting Principles in the United Kingdom ("UK GAAP") is still used by most unlisted companies in the UK and by most individual entities in listed groups. UK GAAP is a very common but not very well defined term. There is no definition in the Companies Act 1985 or the Companies Act 2006 of "UK GAAP" or of "generally accepted accounting principles".

16.2.2   The core components of "UK GAAP" come from the provisions of:

    16.2.2.1   the Companies Act 1985 and Companies Act 2006 as it is implemented;

    16.2.2.2   Accounting Standards—that is Statements of Standard Accounting Practice ("SSAPs") and since 1990, Financial Reporting Standards ("FRSs");

    16.2.2.3   abstracts issued by the ASB's Urgent Issues Task Force ("UITFs");

    16.2.2.4   for listed companies, the Listing Rules; and

    16.2.2.5   statements issued by the ASB.

16.2.3   UK GAAP can also be taken to include the following components:

    16.2.3.1   statements from professional bodies, such as the ICAEW Technical Releases (previously called "FRAGs") or Statements of Recommended Practice ("SORPs") providing sector-specific guidance;

    16.2.3.2   statements issued by the ASB, including its statement of principles for financial reporting;

    16.2.3.3   findings from the Financial Reporting Review Panel ("FRRP"), which comments on accounting policies of individual companies; and

    16.2.3.4   established practice—as may be set out, for example, in guidance issued by leading accountancy firms.

16.2.4   Smaller companies can choose to adopt the Financial Reporting Standard for Smaller Entities ("FRSSE") but must disclose in the accounts that they have done so. For this purpose (for financial periods beginning on or after April 6, 2008), to qualify as "small", a company must meet two of the following size criteria for two consecutive years (these criteria are periodically updated):

    16.2.4.1   annual turnover not exceeding £6.5 million;

    16.2.4.2   balance sheet aggregate totals (net assets) not exceeding £3.26 million; and

    16.2.4.3   average number of employees not exceeding 50.

16.2.5   The FRSSE provides in a single document the "cut down" accounting standards and the accounting requirements of company law applicable to smaller companies. It therefore largely defines "UK GAAP" for those smaller companies adopting it. The FRSSE is periodically updated to reflect developments in wider UK GAAP.

16.2.6 If the FRSSE is adopted, the company is exempt from other accounting standards (apart from certain standards which apply when preparing consolidated accounts). That said, inevitably there are circumstances that may not be covered in the FRSSE, so other standards are then relevant as a guide to best practice.

16.3 Accounting for acquisitions and mergers

16.3.1 Under current UK GAAP, there are two methods of accounting for acquisitions in consolidated accounts:

16.3.1.1 acquisition accounting—this is by far the most common method and follows the rules set out in reporting standards, FRS 2, FRS 6, FRS 7, FRS 10, and the Companies Act legislation; and

16.3.1.2 merger accounting—mandatory in certain limited circumstances when strict conditions, as set out in FRS 6, are met, but otherwise not permissible.

Under IFRS, merger accounting is prohibited.

16.3.2 There are three principal differences between acquisition accounting and merger accounting:

16.3.2.1 in acquisition accounting, the consolidated financial statements reflect the acquired company's results from the date of acquisition but in merger accounting they incorporate the results of the combined company as if the companies had always been combined (i.e. the date of merger has no relevance);

16.3.2.2 in acquisition accounting, the acquiring company should record at "fair value" the identifiable assets and liabilities of the acquired company at the date of acquisition. In merger accounting, existing book values rather than fair values are used, adjusted only to bring the accounting policies into line between the two companies; and

16.3.2.3 unlike in acquisition accounting, no goodwill arises in merger accounting.

16.4 Acquisition accounting under UK GAAP

The following paragraphs summarise the principal rules, and some of the main issues, in acquisition accounting under UK GAAP.

16.4.1 When does a company become a subsidiary?

According to the relevant accounting standard (FRS 2), a company becomes the subsidiary of another when that other acquires the power to control the company. For this purpose "control" (or the power to control) is defined as:

"The ability of an undertaking to direct the financial and operating policies of another undertaking with a view to gaining economic benefits from its activities" (FRS 2 para.6).

16.4.2 How should a new subsidiary be consolidated?

16.4.2.1   The UK accounting rules for consolidating a subsidiary when it is first acquired are broadly:

16.4.2.1.1   include the identifiable assets and liabilities of the subsidiary acquired at their fair values as at the date of acquisition;

16.4.2.1.2   the income and expenditure of the subsidiary acquired should be included in the consolidated financial statements of the parent company from the date of acquisition; and

16.4.2.1.3   the difference between the acquisition cost of the group interest in the shares of the subsidiary acquired and the fair value of the identifiable assets and liabilities identified at 16.4.2.1.1 above represents goodwill if positive, and if negative, represents "negative" goodwill. Both positive and negative should be included in the consolidated balance sheet (within fixed assets).

16.4.2.2   in summary, goodwill is determined as follows:

	£m
Purchase consideration	W
Plus expenses of acquisition	X
Less: Fair value of identifiable net assets	(Y)
Goodwill (either positive or negative)	Z

16.4.2.3   The derivation of each of the balances above is considered in the following section.

16.5 Determining the fair values of identifiable net assets

The fair value of the identifiable net assets is used as the carrying value of these assets and liabilities in the buyer's consolidated accounts.

16.5.1   The accounting standard (FRS 7) which deals with fair value accounting is based on two main underlying principles:

16.5.1.1   the identifiable assets and liabilities to be recognised should be those of the acquired entity that existed at the date of the acquisition; and

16.5.1.2   such assets and liabilities should be measured at fair values that reflect the conditions at the date of acquisition.

16.5.2   Under these rules, the costs of any post-acquisition reorganisation of the target business planned by the buyer should not be included as part of the fair value exercise to determine the liabilities of the target at acquisition, but rather fall as a post acquisition charge against profits.

16.5.3   The basic definition of "fair value" in the accounting rules is:

"The amount at which an asset or liability could be exchanged in an arm's length transaction between informed and willing parties, other than in a forced or liquidation sale" (FRS 7 para.2).

16.5.4   Fair value is therefore a market value concept. The difficulty in practice is that, typically, many of a target company's assets and liabilities are not regularly "exchanged in an arm's length transaction".

16.5.5   FRS 7 provides the following valuation methodology to determine fair values:

16.5.5.1   market values—where the similar assets are traded on a readily accessible market—if there are separately identifiable values ascribed to a particular asset in a sale and purchase agreement then, provided that this is a proper arm's length value, this could represent the fair value of the asset; and

16.5.5.2   replacement cost—if market values are not available (or not appropriate to the particular circumstances of the acquired company), fair values should be valued at replacement cost. For stocks, for example, replacement cost would be the cost at which the stocks would have been replaced by the acquired entity, reflecting its normal buying process and sources of supply and prices available to it—that is, the current cost of bringing the stocks to their present location and condition.

This valuation at replacement cost is subject to an overriding requirement that the fair value of an asset should not exceed its recoverable amount.

For this purpose, the recoverable amount of an asset is the greater of the net realisable value of an asset and, where appropriate, its value in use. The "value in use" is defined as "the present value of the future cash flows obtainable as a result of the asset's continued use, including those resulting from the ultimate disposal of the asset". (FRS 7 para.2). This assessment of recoverable amount can involve quite complex calculations, and can be a highly subjective valuation methodology as it is based on future projections.

16.5.6   Behind these valuation principles, there are detailed rules about how to determine these values (for example, should market value of a property be determined on an open market value or an existing use value basis).

16.5.7   UK GAAP requires that the identifiable assets and liabilities of an acquired entity should be recognised and measured in accordance with the buyer's accounting policies.

16.5.8   It is possible that some identifiable assets and liabilities that need to be recognised by the buyer may not have been previously recognised in the accounts of the acquired entity. Examples of such items may include liabilities that specifically crystallise on a change of ownership, such as compensation clauses in directors' service contracts. It may also be that the buyer takes a different view on the likelihood of an existing liability occurring, requiring provision to be made whereas none was previously held, and vice versa.

16.5.9   Sometimes it is not possible to align the fair value of assets and liabilities of an acquired business, as held in the buyer's consolidated accounts with those in the acquired company's own financial statements. For example, where the fair value of stocks is above their cost to the acquired company, the carrying value of stocks cannot be increased in the acquired company's accounts (it must be held at the lower of its cost and net realisable value). This necessitates the maintaining of separate records to track stocks recorded at fair values in excess of cost to the acquired company, for group accounts purposes.

16.5.10 Two potentially complex areas for the fair value exercise relate to pensions and onerous contracts.

        16.5.10.1 Where the acquired business has a pension scheme or provides other post retirement benefits to employees, the UK accounting rules require the fair value of the following to be recognised as assets or liabilities in the buyer's consolidated accounts:

            • an asset a surplus in a funded scheme (i.e. a defined benefit pension scheme)—but only to the extent it can be recovered through reduced contributions or through refunds from the scheme;

            • a liability a deficiency in a funded scheme; and

            • a liability accrued obligations in respect of an unfunded scheme (e.g. a defined contribution scheme).

            • Under 16.5.10.1 and 16.5.10.2 above, an actuarial valuation will typically be required to determine the quantum of the asset/liability.

        16.5.10.2 Provision for onerous contracts (where the contractual obligation exceeds its current market value) should be included as an identifiable liability in the fair value exercise. For long term purchase contracts, both losses and gains against current market values should be recognised in the fair value exercise.

16.6   How long is permitted to complete the fair value exercise?

16.6.1   So far as possible, the fair value exercise should be completed in time for publication of the buyer's first post-acquisition financial statements. Where this is not practicable, provisional fair values should be included in these accounts (and must be disclosed as such). These provisional values are then amended if necessary in the next annual financial statements, with a resultant adjustment to the goodwill balance. The absolute time allowance to complete the fair value exercise is, therefore, dependent on the timing of the acquisition in relation to the year end of the buyer.

16.6.2   After approval of the buyer's annual financial statements in which non-provisional fair values are included, any adjustments to fair values should normally be dealt with in the profit and loss account, and not as an adjustment to goodwill. The principal exception to this is where the adjustments arise from fundamental errors in the fair value exercise, in which case a prior year adjustment would be required with the goodwill balance being revised.

16.7   Determining the fair value of purchase consideration

16.7.1   The purchase consideration can be a combination of the following components:

- cash consideration; and

- fair value of other consideration (such as shares or loan notes and can also include the assumption of liabilities including the repayment of loans in the target business).

16.7.2   The acquisition cost is the aggregate of the purchase consideration and the relevant expenses of acquisition.

16.7.3   For non-monetary consideration such as the swapping of shares in a third party or other assets for an interest in the target business, the fair values should be determined by reference to market prices, estimated realisable values or other available evidence.

16.7.4   For quoted shares given as consideration, the fair value is usually taken as the mid-market price at the date of acquisition.

16.7.5   Where no market value is available for shares, in most cases, their fair value should be determined by appropriate share valuation methods (for example based on a multiple of earnings). Similar methodologies can be applied to determine the fair value of other securities such as loan stock.

16.7.6   Sometimes the purchase and sale agreement provides for payments to the sellers for "non-compete" provisions or for future bonus payments if the sellers remain as employees/officers in the target business post acquisition. This can be a grey area for accounting. As a general rule, if such payments are not dependent upon the recipient providing future services to the target business, they are prima facie part of the purchase consideration.

16.7.7   Deferred cash consideration may need to be discounted to its present value to determine its fair value at the date of acquisition. As with other non-share deferred consideration, the difference between the fair value at which the liability is stated at the date of acquisition and the total amounts payable at future dates, represents an interest cost for accounting purposes.

16.7.8   For contingent consideration (for example dependent upon the future profit levels of the target business), the UK accounting rules require "a reasonable estimate" of the fair values of amounts expected to be payable in the future. This may involve a need to discount future amounts payable to present value.

16.7.9   Such estimates will be subject to revision until the final amount payable is actually determined. Such revisions to the purchase consideration will result in equivalent revisions to the goodwill balance in the accounts of the buyer.

16.8   Accounting for acquisition expenses

Costs incurred on an acquisition fall into three categories:

16.8.1   Costs of raising capital for the acquisition and of issuing capital instruments in consideration for the acquisition.

Generally such costs should be deducted from the proceeds of those capital instruments. For shares, the costs of issue should be deducted from reserves (a permissible use of the share premium account). For debt, these costs are off-set against the gross debt and then written off in the profit and loss account over the term of the debt (or a shorter period if there is a realistic commercial prospect that the debt will be repaid earlier).

16.8.2   Fees—excluding costs of raising capital—incurred directly in making an acquisition (excluding internal costs) should be added to the cost of acquisition.

16.8.3   Other costs, not falling under 16.8.1 or 16.8.2 above, should be written off to profit and loss account as incurred.

Generally, for UK corporation tax purposes, tax relief on expenses should be available for the costs of raising debt finance when the expenditure is charged to the profit and loss account in accordance with applicable accounting standards.

16.9   Accounting for goodwill on consolidation

16.9.1   Purchased goodwill is simply the difference between the acquisition cost of a business and the fair values of its identifiable assets and liabilities at the date of acquisition.

16.9.2 Under UK GAAP, internally generated goodwill (i.e. not associated with an acquisition) cannot be carried as an asset on the balance sheet.

16.9.3 The UK accounting rules require purchased goodwill to be held as an asset (within fixed assets) on the balance sheet. If that goodwill has a limited useful economic life (as it obviously has, except in quite rare circumstances), it should be amortised systematically (in most cases on a straight line basis) over that life.

16.9.4 The accounting rules provide that there is a rebuttable presumption that the useful economic life will not exceed 20 years.

16.9.5 A longer life than 20 years, or an indefinite life, may be adopted. However, this must be subject to a potentially onerous annual impairment test, to confirm that the present value of the future cash flows that will be generated by the acquired business are sufficient to justify the carrying value of the goodwill. If shown to be insufficient, an impairment write down of goodwill will be required. This can remove the predictability of the goodwill amortisation charge and subject the business to large one-off write downs.

16.9.6 For goodwill being amortised over 20 years or less, an impairment review is required at the end of the first full financial year following acquisition, but thereafter only if adverse events bring the carrying value of goodwill into question.

16.9.7 In practice, many companies seem to adopt a 20-year write off period almost as a default position. This may not be correct.

16.9.8 The useful economic life of goodwill may be revised, but the carrying value of goodwill cannot be increased by revaluation.

16.10 Negative goodwill

16.10.1 Where the fair value of the identifiable assets less liabilities exceed the cost of acquisition, negative goodwill arises. This is shown as a negative item within the fixed assets category on the balance sheet.

16.10.2 Negative goodwill generally arises because:

16.10.2.1 the acquirer has made a genuine bargain purchase (for example where the seller has had to sell its business quickly to raise funds); or

16.10.2.2 the purchase price has been reduced to take account of future costs or losses (such as where the acquired business requires substantial reorganisation).

16.10.3 Where negative goodwill arises in the case of 16.10.2.2 above, it is necessary to re-confirm that the adverse trading position of the acquired business has been fully and properly reflected in the fair values ascribed to the identifiable net assets acquired.

16.10.4 Negative goodwill up to the fair values of "non-monetary" assets (principally fixed assets and stocks) should be credited (i.e. shown as "income") in the profit and loss account in the periods in which these assets are recovered (whether through depreciation, in the case of fixed assets or cost of sale as in the case of stocks).

16.10.5 Any remaining negative goodwill should be credited to the profit and loss account in the period expected to benefit (for example, if unusually some negative goodwill was left to be attributed to debtors, that element of negative goodwill should be taken to profit as the debtors are collected).

16.11 Accounting for goodwill in entity accounts of the buyer

16.11.1 Where the transaction proceeds as a sale and purchase of assets, it is still necessary to determine the fair value of the identifiable assets and liabilities acquired and to account for any resulting goodwill.

16.11.2 The fair values of the identifiable net assets acquired and resultant goodwill should be introduced into the entity accounts of the buyer.

16.11.3 The amortisation of such goodwill (excluding certain goodwill in relation to a property) currently attracts tax relief in the UK, whilst the amortisation of goodwill arising on consolidation does not (this can be one of the incentives for the buyer to press for the transaction to proceed as a sale and purchase of assets rather than a sale and purchase of shares).

16.11.4 The shares acquired should be shown in the buyer's entity accounts at cost (subject to merger relief) as an "investment in group undertakings" within "fixed asset investments".

16.12 Acquisition accounting—comparison with IFRS

16.12.1 The main components of a set of IFRS financial statements are broadly similar to those required for UK financial statements. They include:

16.12.1.1 an income statement;

16.12.1.2 a balance sheet;

16.12.1.3 a statement showing changes in equity;

16.12.1.4 a cash flow statement; and

16.12.1.5 explanatory notes (including accounting policies).

16.12.2 However, IFRS does not prescribe the strict order or format in which items are to be shown in the financial statements. This can make it more difficult to achieve consistency in comparison between companies. For example, under IFRS, entities may, if they wish, strike a sub-total to disclose operating profit, however, unlike under UK GAAP, this is not mandatory.

16.12.3 IFRS requires the disclosure of material judgments made in the process of applying accounting policies, whilst the obligation here is less explicit under UK GAAP although FRS 18 does require a general description of the methods adopted.

16.12.4 IFRS 3 "Business Combinations" deals with acquisition accounting in consolidated accounts under IFRS. In overview, it provides for the following principal differences compared to current UK GAAP:

16.12.4.1 all business combinations should use acquisition accounting (i.e. merger accounting as permitted under current UK GAAP is not allowed);

16.12.4.2 goodwill is deemed to have an indefinite useful life and is therefore not amortised but is subject to an annual impairment test. In contrast, under current UK GAAP, goodwill should be amortised over its useful economic life, unless this life is regarded as being indefinite. Goodwill amortised over more than 20 years (or not amortised) should be subject to an annual impairment review under UK GAAP;

16.12.4.3 negative goodwill—described under IFRS as "the excess of acquirer's interest in the net fair value of acquiree's identifiable assets, liabilities and contingent liabilities over cost"—is recognised immediately in the profit and loss account. Under current UK GAAP, negative goodwill is recognised as income in the periods in which non-monetary assets (typically fixed assets and stocks) are recovered through depreciation or sale, with any remaining balance recognised in the periods expected to benefit;

16.12.4.4 IFRS 3 requires that all the intangible assets of the acquired business at acquisition should be recognised separately in the consolidated accounts (if they comply with the definition of an intangible asset in IFRS and their fair value can be measured reliably) and not subsumed within goodwill. Under IFRS, an intangible asset for this purpose must:

● be separable—that is capable of being sold, transferred, licensed, rented or exchanged, separately from the entity; or

● arise from contractual or other legal rights (even if not "separate").

Under current UK GAAP, many intangibles (for example customer lists and internally generated brands) are effectively subsumed into the goodwill balance.

16.12.4.5 revisions to any provisional fair values must be made within 12 months of the acquisition date (UK GAAP provides for a potentially longer period). These revisions must be effected by restating the comparative information (whereas under UK GAAP any adjustment to provisional fair values are accounted for in the period during which adjustments are made); and

16.12.4.6 where an acquisition takes place in stages, under IFRS 3, although accounting for the acquisition commences when control is obtained, each "exchange transaction" (including previous transactions) is assessed separately to determine fair values and resultant goodwill, whereas under current UK GAAP, this is undertaken at the date that the target business becomes a subsidiary.

16.13 Merger accounting under UK GAAP

16.13.1 The objective of merger accounting is to show the results and financial position of the combined companies as if they had always been combined. Therefore, under merger accounting the combined group's accounts should show the income and expenditure and cash flows for the entire period in the year of merger (i.e. including the period before the merger). Comparative results should also show the position as if the entities have always been merged.

16.13.2 As discussed earlier, under UK GAAP merger accounting can only be used in limited circumstances but, when those circumstances are met, it must be used (the only exception being for some group reconstructions meeting certain criteria, where merger accounting is not mandatory). Merger accounting is not permitted under IFRS.

16.13.3 For this purpose a merger is defined as "a business combination that results in the creation of a new reporting entity formed from the combining parties, in which the shareholders of the combining entities come together in a partnership for the mutual sharing of the risks and benefits of the combined entity, and in which no party to the combination in substance obtains control over any other, or is otherwise seen to be dominant, whether by virtue of the proportion of its shareholders' rights in the combined entity, the influence of its directors or otherwise" (FRS 6 para.2).

16.13.4 The criteria for the use of merger accounting draws on both the Companies Act and FRS 6 (which are sometimes are not wholly consistent in this area). The seven criteria are summarised below:

16.13.4.1 All but an immaterial element of the consideration to acquire the shares in the other entity must be in the form of equity shares (as defined in FRS 6).

16.13.4.2 At least 90 per cent of the nominal value of the "relevant shares" in an undertaking acquired (taking into account any existing holdings) must be held by the buyer (or its subsidiaries). For this purpose, relevant shares are those that carry unrestricted rights to participate both in distributions by the undertaking and in its assets upon a liquidation.

16.13.4.3 The fair value of any cash or non-equity consideration cannot exceed more than 10 per cent of the nominal value of the equity shares issued as part of the consideration for the arrangement. For this purpose, any acquisition by one of the combining parties of equity shares in the other within two years of the other should be taken into account. The 10 per cent limit is taken from the Companies Act, whilst FRS 6 makes reference to "immaterial" amounts but does not define this numerically.

16.13.4.4 There should be no identifiable acquirer or acquiree—that is, no party should be dominant over the other.

16.13.4.5 The boards of each combining party should participate in setting up the management structure, and selecting key management appointments, for the combined entity.

Provided structures or appointments reflect the wishes of all the combining parties, it is not relevant if most of the key management positions are filled by staff from one of the parties.

16.13.4.6 The relative sizes of the combining entities should not be so different that one party can dominate because of this. In terms of the proportion of the equity of the combined entity attributable to each of the combined parties, one party is presumed to dominate if it is more than 50 per cent larger than each of the other parties to the combination. This presumption can be rebutted based on the specific circumstances of the merger.

16.13.4.7 No equity shareholders of any of the combining entities retain any material interest in the future performance of only part of the combined entity.

16.13.5 Under merger accounting, the carrying values of assets and liabilities of the combining parties are not adjusted to fair value on consolidation. Adjustments are required to ensure uniformity of accounting policies for the combined entity.

16.13.6   Any difference between the amount recorded as share capital issued, plus any additional consideration and the amount recorded for the share capital acquired, is adjusted through reserves (typically shown as a merger reserve).

16.13.7   Any merger expenses should be charged to profit and loss account at the date of merger.

16.14   Merger accounting for group reconstructions

16.14.1   Merger accounting may (i.e. non-mandatory) be used for group reconstructions, even when this does not satisfy the definition of a merger provided that:

16.14.2   the ultimate shareholders remain the same and their rights remain unchanged;

16.14.3   no minority's interest in the net assets of the group are altered by the combination; and

16.14.4   the requirement of the Companies Act for merger accounting are met (the additional requirements of FRS 6 do not have to be met). These Companies Act requirements are:

> 16.14.4.1   at least 90 per cent of the nominal value of the relevant shares in the undertaking acquired are held by the parent company and its subsidiary and this was attained pursuant to an arrangement providing for the issue of equity shares by them;
>
> 16.14.4.2   the fair value of any cash or non-equity consideration does not exceed 10 per cent of the nominal value of the equity shares issued; and
>
> 16.14.4.3   adoption of the merger method of accounting accords with generally accepted accounting principles or practices.

16.15   Merger relief

16.15.1   Quite distinct from merger accounting, the Companies Act provides for merger relief, which gives relief from the need (under s.612 CA 2006) to transfer to a share premium account the difference between the nominal value of any shares issued by the company in order to acquire the shares in another company, and the fair value of those issued shares.

16.15.2   The advantage of merger relief is that there are tight restrictions on the uses of share premium account (for example, it can only be distributed if the legal procedure for a reduction of capital is followed).

16.15.3   To obtain merger relief the following three conditions have to be met:

16.15.3.1 the acquiring company must secure at least 90 per cent of the nominal value of each class of equity shares of another company as a result of an arrangement;

16.15.3.2 the arrangement must provide for the allotment of equity shares in the acquiring company; and

16.15.3.3 the consideration for the shares above must be either:

- the issue, or the transfer, to the acquiring company of equity shares in the acquired company; or

- the cancellation of any of the equity shares in the acquired company not already held by the acquiring company.

16.15.4 If the above conditions are met, merger relief is compulsory. It results in the cost of an investment in the acquiring company's own accounts being at the nominal value of the number of the shares in that company issued to acquire the share capital of the acquired company (along with the fair value of any other consideration).

Chapter 17

Financial Assistance

Subject to certain exceptions it is unlawful for a UK public company whose shares are being acquired (or for any of its UK subsidiaries) to give financial assistance for the purpose of that acquisition. It is also unlawful for any such company to give any financial assistance after the acquisition to reduce or discharge any liability incurred by the acquirer or any third party for the purpose of the acquisition but only if, at the time when the assistance is given, the company whose shares have been acquired is a public company.

There is a similar prohibition against a UK public company giving financial assistance for the purpose of the acquisition of shares in its private holding company and that prohibition extends to the giving of financial assistance after the acquisition in order to reduce or discharge any liability incurred for the purpose of the acquisition.

Those provisions were originally introduced to protect the creditors of the company concerned and any minority shareholders but their width and complexity means that it is essential, on a sale and purchase of shares in the capital of a public company or of shares in a company in a group which includes a public company, to consider their implications on the structure of the transaction itself, on any related transactions and on the funding of the purchase price and any related security arrangements.

This statutory prohibition originally extended to the giving of financial assistance for the acquisition of shares in a private company but this statutory prohibition was removed by the Companies Act 2006, with effect from October 1, 2008.

Although the abolition of the financial regime for private companies has generally been welcomed, the legal profession, in particular, had been pressing for many years for the financial assistance rules as a whole to be clarified and for specific exemptions to be introduced for various transactions which are generally considered to be entirely unobjectionable but which might nevertheless be caught by the financial assistance regime. There was, therefore, some disappointment that the opportunity was not taken in the Companies Act 2006 to address these issues, which will continue to be of concern when dealing with acquisitions where a public company is involved. The prohibition against public companies giving financial assistance is a requirement of the EU Second Company Law Directive and could not have been abolished but it would certainly have been helpful if the law had been clarified to make it clear that transactions such as the giving of warranties and indemnities in relation to an issue of shares will not of themselves constitute financial assistance—these examples will be particularly relevant where a listed company is proposing to issue shares in order to fund an acquisition and the bank, broker or other institution which is agreeing to place the shares or to under-write their issue requires warranties and indemnities from the company concerned.

Practitioners will also be disappointed that some of the exemptions have not been redrafted in a way which will make them more useful (see 17.3).

As discussed later in this chapter, transactions entered into in connection with a sale and purchase of shares will be subject to the provisions of the Companies Act 2006 relating to directors' duties and maintenance of capital and to the provisions of insolvency legislation in the same way as any other transaction and it will be important to ensure that these requirements are not overlooked.

Confusingly, the financial assistance rules in the Companies Act 1985 will, generally, continue in force until October 1, 2009, when they will be replaced by the relevant provisions of the Companies Act 2006, but the Companies Act 2006 (Commencement No. 5, Transitional Provisions and Savings) Order 2007 (SI 2007/3495) (the Fifth Commencement Order) provides that those provisions of the Companies Act 1985 (ss.151–153) will be repealed, with effect from October 1, 2008, to the extent that they apply to the giving of financial assistance by private companies.

Until October 1, 2009, therefore, it will be necessary to refer to ss.151–153 of the Companies Act 1985 and, from October 1, 2009, the relevant provisions will be ss.678–683 of the Companies Act 2006.

To avoid confusing readers by referring to the relevant provisions of the 1985 Act and the 2006 Act and, in view of the fact that those provisions of the 1985 Act will be repealed altogether from October 1, 2009, this chapter generally refers only to the provisions of the Companies Act 2006. In the period down to October 1, 2009, the safest approach, for section numbers and wording, would be to refer to the corresponding chapter of the First Edition of this book or to the supplement to that edition which was published in 2008.

17.1   The basic prohibition

The basic prohibitions against giving financial assistance are now contained in s.151 of the Companies Act 1985 but, from October 1, 2009, will be contained in ss.678(1), 678(3), 679(1) and 679(3) of the Companies Act 2006.

Section 678(1) (replacing s.151(1) of the Companies Act 1985) prohibits the giving of financial assistance before, or at the same time as, the acquisition of shares and provides that:

> ". . . Where a person is acquiring or proposing to acquire shares in a public company, it is not lawful for that company or a company that is a subsidiary of that company, to give financial assistance directly or indirectly for the purpose of that acquisition before or at the same time as the acquisition takes place."

Section 678(3) (replacing s.151(2) of the Companies Act 1985) prohibits the giving of financial assistance after the acquisition of shares and provides that:

> "Where:
>
> (a) person has acquired shares in a company, and
>
> (b) liability has been incurred (by that or any other person), for the purpose of that acquisition
>
> it is not lawful for that company, or a company that is a subsidiary of that Company to give financial assistance directly or indirectly for the purpose of reducing or discharging the liability if, at the time the assistance is given, the company in which the shares were acquired is a public company."

The words at the end of s.678(3) were intended to make it clear that the prohibition against post-acquisition assistance only applies if the company in which the shares were acquired is a public company at the time when it is proposed that the assistance should be given. Accordingly, on a public-to-private transaction, where the target company was a public company when it was acquired but was subsequently re-registered as a private company and remains a private company at the time when the assistance is given, this prohibition will not apply—the relevant date is the date on which the assistance is proposed to be given, rather than the date of the acquisition.

This wording does not appear in the Companies Act 1985 as the provisions of the 1985 Act applied equally to public companies and private companies.

Section 679(1) contains the prohibition against a public company giving financial assistance for the acquisition of shares in its private holding company and s.679(3) extends that prohibition to post-acquisition assistance.

There are a number of initial comments to be made on the wording of these provisions:

17.1.1   There must be an acquisition, whether actual or proposed—whether by purchase or by subscription and whether for cash or otherwise—of shares in a UK company. The financial assistance rules have no relevance on a sale and purchase of assets.

17.1.2   The company giving the financial assistance must be a UK-registered company and so the legislation should not prevent a foreign subsidiary from providing financial assistance for the acquisition of shares in its UK parent (see *Arab Bank Plc v Mercantile Holdings Ltd* [1994] 2 W.L.R. 307), although it would be necessary to consider whether the arrangements might be prohibited by the laws of the jurisdiction in which the subsidiary is incorporated.

In the *Arab Bank* case, Millett J. was considering a transaction in which the foreign subsidiary of a target company incorporated in England had allowed a property in England which belonged to it to be charged to a bank to secure an advance by the bank to its parent, which it then used to enable it to buy the share capital of the target company. The judge held that "the mere giving of financial assistance by the subsidiary" did not of itself also constitute the giving of such assistance by the parent company.

The judge did, however, go on to state that the giving of financial assistance by a foreign subsidiary may involve unlawful conduct of the UK parent in procuring the assistance in question so that (for example) the hiving down of an asset by a UK company to a foreign subsidiary, in order to enable it to be made available as security to finance an acquisition of shares in the UK company, would clearly constitute the giving of indirect financial assistance by the UK company.

This case was considered by the High Court in the 2008 case of *AMG Global Nominees (Private) Ltd v SMM Holdings Ltd* [2008] EWHC 221 (Ch), in which it was held that the participation of a UK company, by passing a resolution in general meeting of its overseas subsidiary and not taking steps to prevent the subsidiary from procuring a particular payment, could not be distinguished from the facts in the *Arab Bank* case and that, accordingly, there was no contravention of the financial assistance rules.

The reasoning in the *Arab Bank* case suggests that the financial assistance rules would not apply to prevent a UK public company from giving financial assistance for the acquisition of shares in its foreign parent, although this specific point has not come before the courts.

17.1.3   For the purposes of s.678(3), "a reference to a person incurring a liability includes his changing his financial position by making an agreement or arrangement (whether enforceable or unenforceable, and whether made on his own account or with any other person) or by any other means" (s.683(2)(a) (replacing s.152(3)(a) of the 1985 Act)).

An example of this is where the buyer obtains a loan from a third party in order to obtain funds to finance the purchase of shares. It should be noted that it should not be necessary that the person concerned worsens his financial position — all that is required is that he changes it.

17.1.4   The reduction or discharging of a liability for the purposes of s.678(3) includes a company "giving such assistance for the purpose of wholly or partly restoring [the] financial position [of the person concerned] to what it was before the acquisition took place" (s.678(2)(b) (replacing s.152(3)(b) of the 1985 Act)).

An example of this is where the buyer acquires the shares using his own cash but subsequently obtains a loan from the target company in order to replenish his cash balances.

17.1.5   The prohibitions against post-acquisition financial assistance are not limited to any particular period after the acquisition of the shares and so will continue to apply indefinitely. Buyers and their financiers will therefore have to bear in mind the implications of the financial assistance rules if the buyer ever wishes to refinance the funds that he has borrowed for the acquisition, even if that refinancing takes place years later and is partly also for working capital purposes.

17.2   What is "financial assistance"?

There is no definition of "financial assistance" in the Companies Act 2006 but its meaning has from time-to-time been considered by the courts. In *Charterhouse Investment Trust Ltd v Tempest Diesels Ltd* [1986] B.C.L.C. 1, Hoffmann J. said that the words "giving financial assistance" "have no technical meaning and their frame of reference is in my judgment the language of ordinary commerce. One must examine the commercial realities of the transaction and decide whether it can be described as the giving of financial assistance by the company, bearing in mind that the section is a penal one and should not be strained to cover transactions which are not fairly within it".

In *Robert Chaston v SWP Group Ltd* [2002] All E.R. D 345, Arden L.J. identified the general mischief against which the statutory prohibition is directed as follows:

> "Namely, that the resources of the target company and its subsidiaries should not be used directly or indirectly to assist the Purchaser financially to make the acquisition. This may prejudice the interests of the creditors of the target and the interests of any shareholders who do not accept the offer to acquire their shares or to whom the offer is not made."

Arden L.J. went on to talk of assistance which "smoothed the path" to the acquisition and also emphasised the importance of focusing on the "commercial substance of the transaction", concluding that, as a matter of the commercial substance and reality, unlawful financial assistance for the purpose of acquiring its shares may have been given by a company in a particular case notwithstanding that:

- the assistance was given in advance of the transaction, rather than in the course of it;

- it could not necessarily be shown that the target company has suffered any detriment;

- the assistance may have no impact on the purchase price;

- the assistance was given by the target company in circumstances where its directors had acted bona fide in the best interests of the company;

- only one of the purposes for which the transaction was carried out was to assist the acquisition of shares.

The identity of the recipient of the assistance is irrelevant but it must be "financial". That does not however mean that the assistance must be monetary. It may (for example) involve the transfer of a property or some other non-cash asset to the person to whom the assistance is being given.

Section 677(1)(a) of the Companies Act 2006 (replacing s.152(1)(a) of the 1985 Act) sets out the four heads of financial assistance which will generally fall within the scope of the prohibition.

17.2.1 Financial assistance given by way of gift (s.677(1)(a)).

A sale of an asset at an undervalue will not be a "gift" (although such a transaction may fall within s.677(1)(d) (see below)), but a transfer of an asset at nil value will be a gift.

17.2.2 Financial assistance given by way of guarantee, security or indemnity, other than an indemnity in respect of the indemnifier's own neglect or default, or by way of release or waiver (s.677(1)(b)).

This covers more indirect financial assistance, such as where the buyer obtains a loan from a third party in order to fund the acquisition of the shares and the company guarantees the repayment of that loan.

17.2.3 Financial assistance given by way of loan or any other agreement under which any of the obligations of the person giving the assistance are to be fulfilled at a time when, in accordance with the agreement, any obligation of another party to the agreement remains unfulfilled, or by way of the novation, or assignment of rights arising under, a loan or such other agreement (s.677(1)(c)).

Financial assistance by way of loan or by way of novation or assignment of rights under a loan is self-explanatory but the remaining wording of this subsection would cover (for example) the situation where the company agrees to transfer assets to another company in reliance upon an indemnity from that other company—the company whose shares are being acquired would be fulfilling its obligations (completing the sale) at a time when the other company would have unfulfilled obligations (the indemnity).

17.2.4 Any other financial assistance given by a company the net assets of which are reduced by it to a material extent or which has no net assets (s.677(1)(d)).

An example of this type of financial assistance is a sale of a property or any other asset at an undervalue.

"Net assets" here means the aggregate of the company's assets, less the aggregate of its liabilities, and refers to the actual values of the assets and not their book values.

The net assets must be reduced to a "material extent" and it is generally accepted that a reduction of less than one per cent would fall outside the prohibition but 1 per cent and over would amount to a material reduction. A company without net assets cannot lawfully give any form of financial assistance.

It is important to note that the other heads of financial assistance are not subject to any de minimis rule and that (for example) financial assistance by way of gift would be rendered unlawful even if the amount of the gift was minimal.

17.3   The "principal purpose" and "larger purpose" exemptions

Section 678(2) (replacing s.153(1) of the 1985 Act) identifies two instances where financial assistance may be provided without infringing s.678(1).

Section 678(2) provides that financial assistance is not in breach of s.678(1) if:

"(a) the company's principal purpose in giving the assistance is not to give it for the purpose of [the] acquisition, or

(b) the giving of the assistance for that purpose is only an incidental part of some larger purpose of the company,

and the assistance is given in good faith in the interests of the company."

Section 678(4) provides an equivalent exemption in relation to financial assistance given after the acquisition (that is, financial assistance prohibited by s.678(3)) while s.679(2) and (4) provide equivalent exemptions in relation to financial assistance given by a public company for the acquisition of shares in its private holding company (that is, financial assistance prohibited by ss.679(1) or (3)).

For the principal purpose exemption to apply, there must be a principal purpose behind the actions in question other than to give financial assistance. For the larger purpose exemption to apply, the financial assistance will be intended but it must be incidental to some larger purpose of the company.

The corresponding provisions of the Companies Act 1985 were considered by the House of Lords in *Brady v Brady* [1988] 2 All E.R. 617, where the "larger purpose" exemption was given a very narrow construction. For a detailed analysis of this case reference should be made to one of the standard company law textbooks but, in view of that decision advisers are very reluctant to rely on either of those exemptions and it is generally accepted that they have been construed so narrowly as to be of little avail.

It was hoped that the wording of these exemptions might be revisited in the Companies Act 2006 but that did not happen.

17.4   Unconditional exceptions

Section 681 of the Companies Act 2006 (replacing s.153(3) of the 1985 Act) sets out a
number of unconditional exceptions to the statutory prohibitions against giving financial assistance and these are:

17.4.1   A distribution of a company's assets by way of dividend lawfully made or a
distribution made in the course of the company's winding up (s.681(2)(a)).
This would, for example, allow the seller to take some or all of the profits of
the company by way of pre-completion dividend, which in the past was generally attractive from a tax point of view but is less attractive since the introduction of taper relief. This exemption may also be useful where there is an
asset (perhaps a property) which the seller wishes to retain and which the
buyer is happy to exclude from the sale, as (provided that there are sufficient
distributable reserves) it may be possible to transfer that asset to the seller
by way of dividend in specie. Similarly, it may be helpful for a buyer to have
the company pay a dividend after completion in order to enable the buyer
to reduce loans which he has taken out in order to fund the acquisition.
Care should however be taken if, in order to fund a cash dividend, it would
be necessary for the company to obtain a third party loan and create security
for the repayment of that loan as there are suggestions in the *Robert Chaston*
case (discussed earlier in this chapter) that that could constitute financial
assistance.

17.4.2   An allotment of bonus shares (s.681(2)(b)).

17.4.3   A reduction of capital under Ch.10 of Pt 17 of the Companies Act 2006
(s.681(2)(c)), which will include a "new style" reductions of capital made
pursuant to ss.642–644 of the Companies Act 2006, as well as a reduction
confirmed by the court pursuant to ss.645–649.

17.4.4   A redemption of shares or purchase by a company of its own shares
(s.681(2)(c)). Again, however, there are suggestions in the *Robert Chaston*
case that there might be financial assistance if the company borrows the
money to fund the purchase price and gives security to support those borrowings. The prevailing view has generally been that that should not be the case
and it had been hoped that this point would be clarified in the 2006 Act.

17.4.5   Schemes of arrangement made pursuant to a court order pursuant to the provisions of ss.895–901 of the Companies Act 2006 (s.681(2)(e)).

17.4.6   Any matter carried out under an arrangement made in accordance with s.110
of the Insolvency Act 1986 (acceptance of shares by a liquidator in a winding
up as consideration for the sale of property) (s.681(2)(f)).

17.4.7   Anything done pursuant to a voluntary arrangement (s.681(2)(g)).

17.5   Conditional exceptions

Section 682(1) (replacing s.153(4) of the 1985 Act) states that certain transactions will not fall within the financial assistance prohibitions if they are carried out by a private company or are carried out by a public company which has net assets that are not reduced by the giving of the assistance or, to the extent that its net assets are so reduced, the assistance is provided out of distributable profits.

The transactions in question include lending money in the ordinary course of business and anything done for the purpose of employee share schemes.

These exceptions may be helpful in certain circumstances but are unlikely to be helpful on a normal corporate transaction where one company is acquiring the entire issued share capital of another company (or, at least, a controlling interest in it).

17.6   Financial assistance—practical examples

On and after a share sale and purchase or subscription, all transactions proposed to be entered into by the target company and its subsidiaries will need careful consideration to see whether they may contravene the financial assistance prohibition. Some typical examples (all based on the situation where Tom, Dick and Harriet (Sellers) are selling the entire issued share capital of Target Limited (Target) to Buyer PLC (Buyer), Target having a wholly-owned subsidiary called Subsidiary Limited ("Subsidiary")) include the following.

17.6.1   Sale of property

Target may have a freehold property which Sellers wish to retain and which Buyer is happy to exclude from the sale, the property having a market value of £1,000,000 and a book value of £800,000. The parties will have to consider how the property can be excluded from the sale without contravening the financial assistance prohibition:

> 17.6.1.1   If Target were to transfer the property to Seller for nil consideration, this would be financial assistance given by way of gift within s.677(1)(a).

> 17.6.1.2   If Sellers buy the property at a price below market value, there will be financial assistance within s.677(1)(d), if this results in the net assets of Target being reduced to a material extent. It would not be enough simply to transfer the property at its book value of £800,000 as, in determining whether the assistance reduces net assets by a material extent, reference has to be made to the actual values of the assets and not their book values.

> The parties would also have to take account of the provisions of s.845 of the Companies Act 2006, which are discussed in 17.9.2 below, together with the

provisions of the Insolvency Act 1986 relating to transactions at an under-value, which are discussed in 17.9.3 below.

17.6.1.3 If Sellers buy the property for its market value of £1,000,000 but with the purchase price being payable on deferred terms, there will be financial assistance by way of loan or "any other agreement under which any of the obligations of the person giving the assistance [Target] are to be fulfilled at a time [completion of the sale of the property] when in accordance with the agreement any obligation of another party to the agreement [the obligation of Sellers to pay the purchase price] remains unfulfilled" in breach of s.677(1)(c)(i).

17.6.1.4 If Sellers buy the property at its market value of £1,000,000 and pays for it in cash on completion of the purchase, there is no financial assistance. This is unlikely however to be particularly attractive to the parties as the purchase price for Target will doubtless reflect the fact that it will be receiving £1,000,000 in cash for the property, which will mean additional stamp duty and may lead to an increased tax liability for Sellers.

17.6.1.5 Target may transfer the property to Sellers by way of distribution in specie, provided that Target has distributable profits which are at least equal to the book value of the property (i.e. at least £800,000) and this will not amount to unlawful financial assistance as it will fall within the exemption for distributions.

17.6.2 Giving of security

If, in order to fund the acquisition, Buyer obtains a loan from a third party, who requires a guarantee from Target in respect of the repayment of that loan, this will be financial assistance by way of guarantee within s.677(1)(b)(i) and, if Target gives a debenture or any other security in respect of its obligations under that guarantee, then that will be financial assistance by way of security within that section. Similarly, if Subsidiary gives a guarantee (with or without supporting security). Whether the financial assistance falls within s.678(1) or (3), will depend upon the way in which completion is structured and the stage at which the guarantee and/or security is given. If the guarantee and (where relevant) security are executed on or before the point when Buyer acquires the shares in Target, it will fall within s.678(1) but if the completion arrangements are structured so that Buyer acquires the shares before the guarantee and/or security is given, it will fall within s.678(3) (as a person (Buyer) will have acquired shares in a company (Target) and will have incurred a liability (the third party loan or the obligation to pay the price) for the purpose of the acquisition and Target will then be giving financial assistance for the purpose of enabling Buyer to discharge that liability).

Buyer may be able to fund the acquisition of Target out of its own cash resources or on the security of its own assets and those of its existing subsidiaries and that will not be financial assistance. After completion, however, Buyer may wish to refinance and may well ask how long has to elapse after completion before it is "safe" to bring Target into any cross-guarantee structure required by Buyer's financiers as part of the refinancing.

Section 683(2)(b) provides that reference to a company giving financial assistance for the purpose of reducing or discharging a liability incurred for the purpose of the acquisition includes its giving such assistance for the purpose of wholly or partly restoring the financial position of the party concerned to what it was before the acquisition took place and this may (depending upon all the circumstances) mean that Target will be giving financial assistance in contravention of s.678(3) if it gives a guarantee and/or security in respect of borrowings incurred by Buyer as part of a refinancing which takes place long after completion of the acquisition, on the basis that Target may be doing so in order to enable Buyer to replenish his financial resources.

If the acquisition of Target was funded by way of a loan taken out specifically for the purpose of the acquisition, it may be possible for Target to give a guarantee in respect of Buyer's bank borrowings once that loan has been repaid but that is not necessarily the case as any new facilities which are obtained in order to refinance a loan which was taken out for the purpose of the acquisition may themselves be a "liability" which has been incurred "for the purpose of the acquisition" within the meaning of s.677(3)(b).

If the purchase price has been funded out of a bank overdraft, the position is likely to be even more complicated and it is likely to be necessary for the overdraft to have reduced below the level at which it stood immediately prior to the acquisition before it may be permissible for Target to give any guarantees.

Financial assistance may even be relevant where the acquisition was funded out of Target's own cash resources and in those circumstances it will be necessary to establish whether the refinancing is for the purpose of enabling Buyer to replenish those cash resources or purely to provide working capital facilities for the future.

17.6.3 Release of debt

If as part of the deal Target is to release loans owing to it by Sellers this will amount to financial assistance by way of release of waiver within s.677(1)(b)(ii). If the intention is to eliminate these loans, it will be necessary to consider alternative structures, such as capitalising them or having Sellers assign them to Buyer for a nominal consideration. The appropriate route will inevitably depend upon tax advice.

These issues tend to be particularly relevant where the company in question is being brought out of a group of companies and there are various inter-company loans and other balances.

17.6.4 Repayment of existing loan

If, as part of the transaction, Target is to repay any loans owing by it, whether to Sellers or to any third party, it will be necessary to consider the repayment terms in order to establish whether this may involve financial assistance. Repayment of an overdraft or a loan which is repayable "on demand" will not constitute financial assistance but, if the loan is repayable on a particular date or dates, early repayment of the loan could amount to financial assistance. Whether or not it does will depend on whether Target has net assets and (if it does) whether there will be a material reduction in net assets within the meaning of s.677(1)(d)(i). There may be a material reduction in net assets if (for example) there is a financial penalty for early repayment.

This point was considered in the case of *Anglo Petroleum Ltd v TFB (Mortgages) Ltd* [2006] EWHC 258 which concerned the acquisition of a company (APL) by Kaluna Limited (Kaluna).

Immediately prior to the acquisition, APL owed £30 million to its parent (RUK) as an "on demand" inter-company loan. Prior to the sale of APL, RUK entered into a compromise agreement with APL, pursuant to which RUK agreed to write off half of the £30 million loan in exchange for immediate repayment of £6 million and the grant of security over the assets of APL to secure the outstanding balance of £9 million, which would bear interest. Kaluna then acquired the whole of the issued share capital of APL for £1.

Some months later APL borrowed £14 million from TFB, in part to repay the outstanding loan to RUK. The TFB loan was secured by charges over the assets of APL and a personal guarantee from the owner of Kaluna. Subsequently APL went into receivership and APL and the guarantor sought to avoid liability to TFB by claiming that the refinancing and/or the security granted to TFB were unlawful financial assistance.

The court held as follows:

17.6.4.1   The granting of security by APL to RUK and the rescheduling of the debt were not financial assistance as the commercial reality was that APL benefited substantially from the debt reduction and rescheduling and thus the granting of the security was simply part of the overall arrangement, which so benefited APL.

17.6.4.2   The repayment of a debt which is properly due from a company does not constitute the giving of financial assistance. The court did not however consider whether the outstanding debt being repaid has to be on demand or whether (as is generally thought to be the case) the early repayment of term money would constitute financial assistance.

The case subsequently went to appeal but the appeal was dismissed.

Toulson L.J. commented as follows:

"Standing back from the minutiae of the arguments, and looking at the transactions attacked by APL from a commercial perspective, I do not consider that they exemplify the mischief against which the section is aimed ... I begin with the [compromise agreement], the nature of which was that APL's liability to [RUK] was reduced. I do not consider that it should be characterised as giving financial assistance to the purchaser on account of the fact that it thereby made the company a more attractive acquisition and can thus be said to have smoothed the path to its acquisition.

> Just because it smoothed the path to the acquisition, it does not follow that it amounted to financial assistance. Nor can the [charge], by which APL gave security to [RUK] for its reduced indebtedness, properly be described as financial assistance to the purchaser."

Toulson L.J. went on to state that he agreed with the Judge's reasoning that "if it is lawful for a company to repay its own indebtedness and there is a genuine commercial justification, it must also equally be lawful [for] the company to assist that repayment by providing security".

17.6.5   Making a loan

It may be necessary for Target to lend money to Buyer at completion in order to enable Buyer to fund the purchase price or it may be necessary for Target to lend money to Buyer after completion in order to enable Buyer to service the interest and capital repayments on borrowings taken out by Buyer from a third party in order to enable it to fund the purchase price.

This will be financial assistance by way of loan (s.677(1)(c)(i)).

17.6.6   Hive-up

Buyer may wish the assets and undertaking of Target to be hived-up into Buyer after completion in order to enable Buyer to service the interest on borrowings which it has taken out in order to fund the acquisition. There may also be tax reasons why a hive-up is desirable. If the hive-up takes place at less than market value, there may be financial assistance within the meaning of s.677(1)(d) and, if it takes place at market value, but with all or part of the purchase price being deferred, there will be financial assistance by way of loan. It is therefore necessary for the hive-up to take place at market value and with the purchase price being paid in full on completion. Even then, however, there may be financial assistance if, for example, the effect of the hive-up is that Target remains liable to its creditors but has an indemnity against them from Buyer—that would be financial assistance within the meaning of s.677(1)(c)(i) as Target would be fulfilling its obligations (the transfer of its assets and undertaking) at a time when the other party to the hive-up agreement (Buyer) would have obligations (under the indemnity) remaining unfulfilled.

17.6.7   Golden handshakes etc.

It has been reasonably common for sellers to request that part of the overall "consideration" for the deal should take the form of a compensation payment on termination of their employment, as the first £30,000 will be tax-free and the purchase price (and hence the seller's taxable gain) will reduce accordingly (although as a result of the introduction of taper relief (see Ch.13) the potential tax savings are now less significant and transactions are therefore less likely to be structured in this way). A "golden handshake" to a director or other employee who is resigning from office on completion may be financial assistance by way of gift within s.677(1)(a) or (if it constitutes a material reduction in net assets) pursuant to s.677(1)(d), assuming that it is a payment to which he is not entitled under his contract of employment or that it is in excess of his contractual entitlement. It will therefore be essential to establish the individual's contractual entitlement in order to ascertain whether financial assistance may be an issue.

Similar concerns will apply where "loyalty" or similar bonuses are payable to staff on completion — for example, in recognition of their loyalty and co-operation during a time of uncertainty. There may be less of an issue if, at a time when no sale is even being considered or no specific person is proposing to acquire the shares, incentives are put in place under which key staff are to be paid bonuses, the payment of which will be triggered by the sale. Whether or not financial assistance will be an issue will, however, depend upon all the circumstances. In practice, any such payment is more likely to be financial assistance if the arrangements are put in place when discussions are taking place with a potential buyer.

17.6.8 Surrender of group relief

If Target is a member of a group, it is common to agree arrangements under which past trading losses may be surrendered to other members of the group which Sellers are retaining, to the extent that they have not already been utilised by Target. Whether or not those losses are recognised as an asset in Target's accounts, they represent an asset of Target and their surrender would constitute financial assistance (within s.677(1)(d)) if Target had no net assets or if the surrender resulted in a material reduction in its net assets (for example, because they were being surrendered for no payment or for an inadequate payment). It may therefore be a case of putting a value on the benefit of those losses and making sure that Target does receive a payment of what may reasonably be regarded as their market value.

17.6.9 Break fees

It is reasonably common to have arrangements for break fees (otherwise known as inducement fees or termination fees) in both public takeover offers (particularly public to private transactions) and private acquisitions and disposals. A break fee is an arrangement entered into between the parties under which an agreed sum is paid to one of the parties if a specified event occurs which prevents the transaction from completing.

For Target to pay the break fee (or agree to do so) could amount to unlawful financial assistance if:

17.6.9.1   The break fee operates as an indemnity — for example, an indemnity in respect of Buyer's costs, charges and expenses in negotiating the deal and carrying out due diligence work. This would be rendered unlawful by s.677(1)(b)(i) and, to avoid this, the parties should agree at the outset a pre-determined fee which is not based on actual or anticipated costs, charges or expenses.

17.6.9.2   The break fee is of an amount which reduces Target's net assets to a material extent (that is, more than one per cent), as this would be financial assistance within s.677(1)(d)(i). The parties should therefore ensure that the agreed sum is less than one per cent.

17.6.9.3   Target has no net assets (as this would be financial assistance within s.677(1)(d)(ii)).

17.6.9.4   No consideration is given for the break fee as this could amount to financial assistance by way of gift within s.677(1)(a). The parties should therefore ensure that the break fee is expressed to be payable in consideration of Buyer entering into negotiations and/or carrying out due diligence and/or making its offer.

17.6.10 Rescues and refinancings

The prohibitions against post-acquisition financial assistance in ss.678(3) and 679(3) may have a serious impact on company rescues and refinancings.

For example, Buyer has acquired the entire issued share capital of Target for a cash consideration, which it funded by way of a five-year term loan.

Three years later, Buyer is in financial difficulties and needs to obtain additional facilities from its bank.

In order to enable it to provide its bank with additional security, it is proposed that Target should guarantee repayment of the loan—but that would be financial assistance within s.677(1)(b)(i). The reason for this is that a person (Buyer) has acquired shares in a company (Target) and has incurred a liability for the purpose of the acquisition (the liability to repay the loan) and it would not therefore be lawful for Target or any of its subsidiaries to give financial assistance directly or indirectly for the purpose of reducing or discharging that loan. If it were to give a guarantee, that would be financial assistance by way of guarantee and, if its liabilities under that guarantee were to be secured, that would be financial assistance by way of security.

The position may be even more complicated where, since the date of the original acquisition of Target, there have been substantial changes in the financing of the Buyer and its group of companies—for example, where a number of other acquisitions have taken place, along with the refinancing of some loans and the repayment of other loans (for example, out of the proceeds of disposals or new share issues).

In such cases, it is extremely difficult to establish whether any part of the loan currently outstanding still represents the original loan incurred to purchase the shares in Target and, accordingly, whether any guarantee by Target of any of the debt of Buyer or other companies in its group would be "tainted" by financial assistance.

17.6.11 "Finder's fees"

An arrangement under which the advisers or brokers who find a buyer for Target would receive a fee for doing so from Target may be financial assistance by way of a gift within s.677(1)(a) or (if it constitutes a material reduction in net assets or if Target has no net assets), pursuant to s.677(1)(d) and these issues were considered in 2007 in the case of *Corporate Development Partners v E-Relationship Marketing Ltd* [2007] EWHC 436 (Ch).

In that case, ERM Limited had entered into an agreement with CDP, pursuant to which CDP had agreed to seek out potential acquisitions, joint ventures or strategic alliances for ERM. Red Eye was identified as a potential acquisition target. The original agreement was then replaced by a second agreement for commercial reasons. It was on similar terms but made express provision for a deal with Red Eye and for a reduced fee (payable to EDP). Red Eye then acquired ERM.

CDP sought payment under the second agreement for putting together the deal between Red Eye and ERM, but ERM argued that the relevant provisions of that agreement were unenforceable as such payment would constitute illegal financial assistance.

ERM's argument was that the original introduction of Red Eye to ERM facilitated, or smoothed the path towards an acquisition of ERM by Red Eye, that the payment commitment in the second agreement was by way of a reward for that introduction and that, therefore, that commitment (or payment if ultimately made) itself facilitated the acquisition and so amounted to the giving of unlawful financial assistance for the purpose of the acquisition.

The Court rejected ERM's argument and held that there was no unlawful financial assistance in this case on the basis that CDP was playing no role in the negotiation of the acquisition (and was neither intended nor required to do so) and, therefore, the commitment to pay the fee to it was not intended to and did not in fact assist or advance the acquisition at all.

The payment commitment was not a condition of the takeover, it would not serve to reduce Red Eye's acquisition obligations, and it was neither intended to, nor did, smooth the path towards any ultimate acquisition.

It is reasonable to assume that, to a considerable extent, this case turned on its own particular and rather unusual facts, in that the arrangements which did smooth the path to the relevant acquisition arose in connection with an agreement that had been replaced for good commercial reasons. If CDP and ERM had negotiated and replaced the original agreement with the second agreement for reasons other than good commercial reasons, there could arguably have been financial assistance. Certainly, the Court seems to have considered it important that the parties had not simply varied the first agreement but had terminated it and replaced it with a new one.

It is interesting to note that the Judge commented that the fact that assistance is being given to the seller rather than to the buyer would not, of itself, preclude it being unlawful financial assistance.

17.7   Penalties

The Companies Act 2006 (s.680) provides that contravention of the financial assistance prohibitions renders the company liable to a fine and every officer in default liable to a fine or up to two years' imprisonment or both.

"Officers" include directors, managers and secretaries (s.1121 of the 2006 Act). Officers who may be liable are those who authorise or permit, participate in, or fail to take all reasonable steps to prevent, the giving of financial assistance (s.1122 of the 2006 Act).

In addition to the criminal penalties, there are various civil consequences of a breach of the financial assistance prohibition:

17.7.1 The transaction itself will be void and unenforceable (*Brady v Brady* [1989] A.C. 755), as will be any security or guarantee given in contravention of the prohibition although it may be possible in certain cases to sever the illegal part of a transaction and leave the rest enforceable. If therefore the terms relating to the sale and purchase of the shares can be severed from the terms relating to the illegal financial assistance, then the terms relating to the sale and purchase can be enforced. Otherwise, the whole agreement will be void. In a case where the purchase price was to be secured by a charge which amounted to unlawful financial assistance, it was held that the charge could be severed from the sale and purchase agreement and that the sellers were entitled to recover the purchase price (*Carney v Herbert* [1985] A.C. 301).

17.7.2 A director who procures that the company enters into an unlawful transaction will be in breach of his fiduciary duties to the company and can be sued by the company for breach of trust and required to make good any loss suffered by the company. For example, in *Re In A Flap Envelope Company Ltd* [2004] 1 B.C.L.C. 64 Ch D (Companies Ct) the Court held that a director was in breach of his fiduciary duties in participating in arrangements which constituted financial assistance. Similarly, in the (so far unreported) case of *Robert Edward Caunce Cook and M&S Tarpaulins Ltd (in liquidation) v Green* May 2, 2008, the Court held that a company was entitled to damages for breach of fiduciary duty and in negligence from a director who had caused loss to the company by causing or permitting the company to provide unlawful financial assistance.

17.7.3 A person who receives a company's funds in circumstances where he knew or ought to have known that he is doing so as a result of unlawful financial assistance may be required to account to the company for such funds as constructive trustee (*Belmont Finance Corp Ltd v Williams Furniture Ltd (No. 2)* [1980] 1 All E.R. 393) and the parties to a scheme or arrangement which infringes the financial assistance prohibition may be liable in damages in tort for conspiracy.

17.7.4 If the company is subsequently liquidated, a director or officer who has participated in the breach may be subject to misfeasance proceedings under s.212 of the Insolvency Act 1986.

17.8 The whitewash procedure

It has been seen that there are various transactions which are typically entered into in connection with a sale and purchase of shares and which are likely to amount to unlawful financial assistance. There will be particular concerns in a management buy-out where the financiers will almost invariably be relying on the assets of the target company for security to support the borrowings of the buy-out vehicle, which is likely to be a newly-incorporated company, with no assets of its own other than the shares in the target company. Guarantees by the target company and its subsidiaries and the granting of security in support of those guarantees will almost certainly constitute financial assistance. Trade buyers may also need to finance the acquisition on the security of assets of the target company and many of the other arrangements which have been given as examples of financial assistance may be proposed, whether the buyer is a management team, a trade buyer or otherwise. As a result, in the past, there were many transactions which could not have taken place at all (or which might have to have been restructured as sales and purchases of assets) because of the financial assistance rules, were it not for the fact that ss.155–158 of the Companies Act 1985 provided a procedure (normally known as the "whitewash procedure" but sometimes also as the "gateway procedure") to permit private companies to give financial assistance which would otherwise have been rendered unlawful.

The whitewash procedure enabled a private company to give financial assistance for the acquisition of shares in that company or a subsidiary to give financial assistance for the acquisition of shares in its holding company, provided that the holding company was a private company and there was no intermediate public company and provided that there was strict compliance with the requirements of the procedure.

The abolition of the financial assistance regime for private companies means that the Companies Act 2006 no longer contains a whitewash procedure but, as will be seen, an understanding of the whitewash procedure may be helpful to enable directors and advisers to understand the post-2006 Act position. They may also be helpful in order to anticipate the approach that bankers and other lenders are likely to take.

An understanding of the pre-2006 Act law and of the whitewash procedure may also be helpful when doing due diligence on a company which has been acquired previously or which has itself made acquisitions.

The whitewash procedure was, basically, as follows:

17.8.1   The company giving the financial assistance was required to have the capacity to enable it to do so.

17.8.2   The directors of the company were required to sign a statutory declaration of solvency.

17.8.3   That declaration was required to be supported by a report from the auditors stating that they have enquired into the state of affairs of the company and were not aware of anything to indicate that the opinion expressed by the directors in the declaration was unreasonable in all the circumstances.

17.8.4   The shareholders of the company were required to pass a special resolution in general meeting authorising the financial assistance (unless it was a wholly-owned subsidiary).

17.8.5   The company giving the financial assistance was required to have net assets
          (as shown in its current accounting records, not its latest audited accounts)—
          that is, its assets were required to exceed its liabilities (including contingent
          and prospective liabilities) and those net assets could not be reduced by the
          financial assistance or, to the extent that they were, the assistance was required
          to be provided out of distributable profits. In other words, to the extent that the
          giving of the financial assistance reduced the net assets of the company, the
          amount of the reduction could not exceed its distributable profits. If (for exam-
          ple) the giving of the financial assistance reduced the net assets by £100,000,
          the company was required to have distributable profits of at least that amount.

          It was therefore necessary to establish the extent that the financial assistance
          would reduce the company's net assets and ensure that the company had distrib-
          utable profits of an amount equal to, or in excess of, the amount of the reduc-
          tion. For this purpose, it was necessary to look at the book (not market) value
          of net assets and at the impact of the financial assistance on that book value.

17.9   Reform of the financial assistance rules—Companies Act 2006

It came as a great relief to lawyers involved in mergers and acquisitions (and probably
even more so to the clients who have to pay their fees) when it was announced that what
is now Pt 18 of the Companies Act 2006 was to abolish the prohibition on private companies giving financial assistance and with it the whitewash procedure. The Government's
reasoning was that the interests of shareholders and of creditors should be adequately
protected by the law relating to directors' duties and by insolvency law.

There was, however, a major concern among the legal profession that, despite the
abolition of the financial assistance prohibition, there may be circumstances in which
common law rules on maintenance of capital could still operate to prevent a private
company from giving financial assistance, in the absence of any express provision to
disapply them. These common law rules stem from cases such as *Trevor v Whitworth*
[1887] 12 App. Cas. 409, in which the House of Lords decided that a company might
not (under the then law) purchase its own shares, on the ground that "neither the paid
up nor the nominal capital of the company shall be reduced otherwise than in the
manner permitted by [Act of Parliament]".

There was some discussion as to whether or not the enactment of the original predecessors to the current financial assistance prohibitions caused the earlier case law to cease
to have effect and one argument that was put forward was that practitioners have,
generally, concluded that the whitewash procedure provided a "safe harbour" and that it
was not necessary, where a transaction was being whitewashed, to be concerned about
issues such as whether or not the arrangements were in the best interests of the company
(commercial benefit) and the maintenance of capital rules. Once that "safe harbour" was
removed (it was argued), these issues fell to be addressed.

The 2006 Act does not address these concerns but, in response to pressure from the
legal profession and elsewhere, a "saving" provision was introduced via the Fifth
Commencement Order in order to make it clear that common law does not have the

effect of re-activating the statutory prohibition against the giving of financial assistance by private companies (and does not override other legal considerations relating to the giving of financial assistance) para. 52 Sch.4 to the Fifth Commencement Order).

The effect of this is to preserve the application of the common law rules on maintenance of capital, if and to the extent that they were not replaced by the statutory prohibition on financial assistance. In essence, if an arrangement is proposed which, ignoring the fact that it was being entered into for the purpose of the purchase of the acquisition of the shares of the company concerned, would be unlawful under the common law, it will continue to be unlawful under the common law and will not be made lawful because it happens to be entered into in connection with a purchase of shares.

On any acquisition, therefore, it will be necessary to take these common law rules into account and also any relevant statutory provisions, as the abolition of the financial assistance prohibition for private companies will not override any other statutory provisions which may be applicable.

It will also be necessary to consider whether the company has the necessary capacity to enter into the transaction in question and, in the case of companies whose articles incorporate the 1948 Act version of Table A before it was amended by the Companies Act 1981 (with effect from December 2, 1981), it will be necessary to remove or disapply Reg.10 of that version of Table A, which prohibits the giving of financial assistance.

The prevailing view (and one which is reflected in some very helpful notes prepared by the City of London Law Society) is that, in future, in addition to questions of corporate capacity, it will be necessary to consider the following:

- Is the transaction in the best interests of the company? In causing their company to enter into the arrangements in question, are the directors acting in the way that would be most likely to promote "the success of the company for the benefit of its members as a whole" (as required by s.172 of the Companies Act 2006)?

- Do the arrangements involve an unlawful distribution or otherwise amount to an unlawful reduction of capital?

- Are they open to challenge under the provisions of the Insolvency Act 1986— in particular, ss.238 (transactions at an undervalue) and 239 (preferences) and (in the case of Scottish companies ss.242 (gratuitous alienations) and 243 (unfair preferences).

Each of these is considered in turn below.

17.9.1 Best interests of the company

The legal position will generally be the same as for any other transaction between a company and its parent/shareholders, including "up stream" guarantees and inter-company loans. There should be board minutes which confirm that the board has considered whether or not the arrangements in question are in the best interests of the company and has resolved that that is the case and that the transaction in question should be approved.

It would be advisable for the board minutes to identify what the directors consider to be the "commercial benefit" of the transaction in question and, in order to take account of s.172 of the Companies Act 2006, it may be advisable for the minutes to be more detailed than might have been the case in the past, in order to show that the directors have considered the various factors which they are required to take into account under s.172(1) (see 4.4.2 in Ch.4).

For example, where the buyer is borrowing the purchase price on the security of the assets of the target company, there should be board minutes in which the directors of the target company consider the guarantee and security that their company is being asked to give and recite (for example) that they consider it to be in the best interests of the company to become (or remain) part of the buyer's group and to provide financial support to the buyer for that purpose. Similarly, where the target company is being asked to lend to the buyer the funds which the buyer needs to make the acquisition.

What goes into the minutes in order to demonstrate that the directors have considered the various factors specified in s.172(1) will vary from company to company and transaction to transaction but (for example) s.172(1) requires the directors to have regard to the likely long-term consequences of any decision and, where their company is being asked to give a guarantee and supporting security, they would need to demonstrate that they have considered the extent of the liabilities that their company is being asked to guarantee and the likelihood of that guarantee being called. That, in turn, is likely to mean that it will be necessary for them to consider the financial position of the buyer (and of any other group companies whose liabilities are being guaranteed).

It will also be necessary for them to consider the solvency of their own company as, if their company is insolvent or in danger of becoming insolvent, their duties will be owed to its creditors but, otherwise, their duties are owed to the shareholders (who, depending on timing, will presumably be either the seller or the buyer). For this reason, the arrangements should be approved by a special resolution of the shareholders—although, if at all possible, the directors would be well-advised to have the arrangements approved by a unanimous resolution of the shareholders, in order to eliminate the risk of shareholder challenge altogether.

It should be borne in mind, also, that s.239 of the Companies Act 2006 provides that ratification of any conduct which might otherwise have amounted to negligence, breach of duty or the like by the directors may be ratified, but such ratification must be without reliance on the votes of the director concerned or any person connected with him (see 4.4.9).

In some cases, such as a sale of an asset at an undervalue (the example given in 17.6.1), the release of a debt owing to the target company (the example given in 17.6.3), early repayment of an existing loan (the example given in 17.6.4), a hive-up (the example given in 17.6.6), a golden handshake (the example given in 17.6.7) or the surrender of valuable group relief (the example given in 17.6.8), it may be difficult to see any obvious benefit to the target company itself, save for the fact that the arrangement in question smooths the path to a change of ownership, which the directors may consider to be in the best interests of the company. In these cases, approval of the arrangements by the shareholders is even more important.

17.9.2 No reduction of capital

The impact of the rules regarding distributions and reductions of capital will depend on the nature of the arrangements in question.

17.9.2.1   If there is a gift involved—for example, the seller's group want to strip out valuable tax losses free of charge or to acquire a property without paying for it—the transaction may be treated as a dividend and it will be necessary to make sure that the company has sufficient distributable reserves.

17.9.2.2   If there is a sale of an asset at less than market value, it will be necessary to comply with the provisions of s.845 of the Companies Act 2006. This section provides that, for determining the amount of a distribution consisting of, or including, or treated as arising in consequence of, the sale, transfer or other disposition by a company of a non-cash asset at less than market value, the amount of the distribution will be determined by reference to book values provided that, at the time of the transaction in question, the company has sufficient distributable profits. Section 845(2) provides that, if the transaction takes place at book value, the amount of the distribution will be zero and that, in any other case, it will be the amount by which the consideration is less than the book value of the asset in question.

The significance of this is that, if the amount of the distribution would exceed the amount of the Company's distributable profits, the distribution would be unlawful and would amount to an impermissible return of capital to the Company's shareholders. It is worth adding, however, that this should, generally, only be the case where the transaction in question is with (or at the direction of) one or more shareholders of the Company.

To give a practical example: Buyer PLC (Buyer) is proposing to acquire the entire issued share capital of Target Limited (Target) from Seller PLC and Target has a property with a book value of £800,000 but a market value of £1 million. It has been agreed that the property will be excluded from the sale and that Seller may retain it. Seller, naturally, wants to pay as little as possible for the property and Buyer is happy to accommodate the Seller in that respect (as the purchase price for the shares in Target will reflect the facts that Seller is retaining the property).

This is very similar to the example given in 17.6.1.

The effect of s.845 is that, as long as Target has some distributable reserves, the property can be transferred to Seller at book value and there will then be deemed to have been a distribution of nil amount.

If however, Target does not have any distributable profits, there would be deemed to be a distribution of the difference between market value (£1 million) and book value (£800,000) and that would be unlawful, because Target does not have any distributable reserves. The transfer would have to take place at market value.

If Target had distributable reserves of £300,000, it would be possible (as a matter of company law, but taking account of the issues discussed in 17.9.1) for the transfer of the property to take place for a consideration of £500,000, which would result in a distribution of £800,000.

If, on the other hand, Target had distributable reserves of £800,000, it would be possible (again, as a matter of company law, but taking account of the issues discussed in 17.9.1) for the transfer of the property to take place for a nil consideration, which would result in a distribution of £800,000.

It will, therefore, be necessary to establish the extent to which the transaction in question would reduce Target's net assets and ensure that it has distributable profits of an amount equal to, or in excess of, the amount of the reduction and this will involve the same exercise as was previously required in order to consider whether any financial assistance whitewash was possible.

In the example given above, it is reasonably straightforward to establish the extent to which net assets would be reduced but, in other cases, the position is likely to be less clear. If financial assistance is given by way of a guarantee or security, this would not lead to a reduction in net assets, unless the giving of the security or guarantee requires any provision to be made in the accounts of the company giving the guarantee — this depends on the likelihood of the guarantee being called. Similarly, where the financial assistance takes the form of a loan or the sale of an asset on deferred terms, whether or not there is any reduction in net assets will depend on the likelihood of the loan being repaid or (as the case may be) the deferred consideration being paid. The directors of the company giving the financial assistance will, therefore, have to consider the financial position of the party whose obligations they are guaranteeing or (as the case may be) from whom the loan or deferred consideration is owing and then consider whether a provision should be made in the accounts in respect of the liability or (as the case may be) debt.

In the example given in 17.6.2, therefore, where Buyer PLC (Buyer) is acquiring the entire issued share capital of Target Limited (Target) and is funding the acquisition with a loan from its bank, who require repayment of the loan to be guaranteed by Target, the directors of Target will have to consider the financial position of Buyer and consider whether, in the light of that, a provision should be made in the accounts of Target in respect of the liability under the guarantee.

Similarly, in the example given in 17.6.5, where it is proposed that Target should lend money to Buyer in order to enable Buyer to fund the purchase price or to service borrowings incurred for the purpose of the acquisition, it will be necessary for the directors of Target to consider the likelihood of that loan being repaid and whether a provision should be made against it.

It should not be assumed that every single transaction entered into by a private company and which would previously have amounted to financial assistance will be caught by the capital maintenance rules—for example, the early repayment of an existing loan from a third party (the example given at 17.6.4) would not involve a distribution (actual or deemed)—but the majority of such arrangements will be entered into with the Buyer, the Seller or with group companies or others connected with the Buyer or the Seller and, in such cases, it will be necessary to consider the impact on the net assets of the Target Company and (if net assets are reduced) whether there are sufficient distributable profits to cover the amount of the reduction. The directors of the companies concerned would be well-advised to ensure that there are carefully-worded board minutes which show that they have considered these issues and the bases on which they have arrived at their conclusions. These minutes are likely to be very similar to the board minutes that have traditionally been prepared for a company in connection with a financial assistance whitewash.

If the directors are uncertain as to whether or not a provision should be made in the accounts of their company in respect of an inter-company guarantee or a loan owing to their company, they should take professional advice—typically, from the firm of accountants who have carried out any financial due diligence or who have otherwise acted as financial advisers to the deal. As discussed below, banks and other lenders may well require this—particularly on leveraged transactions.

It is worth adding that, although issues of "commercial benefit" and the implications of insolvency legislation have been considered as a matter of course in connection with inter-company guarantees, in particular, lenders have not (as a matter of course) considered the impact of the capital maintenance regime in relation to such arrangements and they may, therefore, ask their advisers why it is thought necessary to take these issues into account where there is an acquisition of shares when such issues have not, generally, been raised when inter-company guarantees are being put in place in other circumstances. It is possible that banking lawyers will start to raise these issues in all cases where guarantees are being taken but speculation on that point is beyond the scope of this book.

17.9.3 Insolvency Act issues

As discussed in 17.9.2.2, where there are guarantees or loans involved, it will be necessary for the directors of the company entering into the guarantee or giving the loan to consider the financial position of the company whose obligations have been guaranteed or (as the case may be) to whom the loan is to be made. In addition, however, before entering into many transactions of the nature discussed in 17.9.2.2, it will also be necessary for the directors to consider whether their company would be solvent when the transaction was entered into and whether it would still be solvent after entering into it.

The main concern will be to ensure that the arrangement in question will not be capable of being set aside pursuant to s.238 of the Insolvency Act 1986 (transactions at an undervalue), s.239 (preferences) or the corresponding provisions for Scottish companies (ss.242 and 243).

This book will focus on the law applicable to England and Wales but, if the company concerned is a Scottish company, it will be necessary to consider the implications of ss.242 and 243 and (if necessary) seek specialist advice from a specialist in Scots insolvency law.

Section 238 allows an administrator or liquidator to apply to the court to have a transaction set aside, if it was "at an undervalue" and was entered into at a "relevant time".

Section 238(4) provides that a company enters into a transaction at an undervalue if it is a gift or otherwise for no consideration or if the consideration provided by the other party is significantly less than that provided by the company. The court may not, however, order a transaction to be set aside if it is satisfied that it was entered into in good faith and for the purpose of carrying on the company's business and that, at the time when the transaction was entered into, there were reasonable grounds for believing that the transaction would benefit the company.

A sale or transfer of a property or other asset at less than market value (the example given in 17.6.1) is a fairly obvious example of a transaction which may be subject to being set aside under s.238 but it is generally accepted that guarantees (see 17.6.2) are capable of being set aside under that section. That is also likely to be the case with transactions such as a release of a debt (the example given in 17.6.3), a loan (particularly where there is a serious risk of the loan not being repaid) and many of the other arrangements referred to at 17.6.

Directors (and others involved in transactions) should also consider the impact of s.239, which allows the court to set aside a transaction, on the application of an administrator or liquidator, if the transaction had the effect of putting the other party to it into a better position in the event of the company going into insolvent liquidation than would otherwise have been the case—but only if the company giving the preference was influenced in deciding to give it by a desire to improve the position of the other party to it.

An example of an arrangement which may be entered into as part of a corporate transaction and which may be open to challenge as a preference is where Seller PLC is selling the entire issued share capital of Target Limited (Target) to Buyer PLC and, as part of the deal, Target gives security for pre-existing loans made to it by Seller which, up until then, had been unsecured. By giving security to Seller, Target is putting it into a better position in the event of Target going into insolvent liquidation than would have been the case if the loans had been unsecured and so the creation of the security is potentially open to challenge under s.239.

It is important to remember, however, that these provisions will only apply if the transaction in question was entered into at a "relevant time" and that the transaction may only be set aside if the company was unable to pay its debts (within the meaning of s.123 of the Insolvency Act 1986) at that time or becomes unable to pay its debts in consequence of that transaction.

Section 240 provides that "relevant time" means the period of six months prior to the onset of insolvency or (where the other party to the transaction in question is connected with the company) the period of two years ending with the onset of insolvency. The onset of insolvency is, essentially, the date on which the company goes into administration or winding-up.

In other words, a transaction may be capable of being set aside as a transaction at an undervalue or as a preference if the company in question goes into administration or liquidation within the period of six months or (where there are connected parties involved) two years after the date of the transaction in question, provided that the company was unable to pay its debts at the time when the transaction was entered into or became unable to pay its debts as a consequence of entering into it.

Where, therefore, there is a transaction at an undervalue or a potential preference, it will be necessary for all involved to consider the solvency of the company concerned.

In particular, banks and other lenders who are proposing to rely on inter-company guarantees and supporting security will want to be satisfied that the company in question will be solvent at the point when the guarantee and security are given and will continue to be so after giving the guarantee.

This will involve considering the financial position of that company in question and of any company whose obligations are being guaranteed.

In the case of the company giving the guarantee, it will be necessary to consider whether it has net assets as, if it has net liabilities (i.e. its liabilities exceed its assets), it will be deemed to be unable to pay its debts by virtue of the provisions of s.123(2) of the Insolvency Act 1986.

In the context of a corporate transaction, the financiers will have to consider the financial position of the target company (and of any subsidiaries that it may have) and of the buyer (and any other companies in its group whose obligations may be guaranteed by the target company (or its subsidiaries)). Where there are any concerns, lenders are likely to require some comfort as to solvency but it is hoped that, where there is a financial due diligence report, lenders will be content to rely on that and will not insist upon a specific "financial assistance" report.

Hopefully, this will not be too onerous in leveraged transactions as, in such transactions, there will almost invariably be a financial due diligence report. There may, however, be some debate between lenders and their customers as to the level of comfort that should be provided to the lenders in cases where the buyer was not expecting to incur the expense of a financial due diligence report.

One complication in the past has been that the whitewash procedure required a report from the auditors but, in future, any comfort as to solvency which may be required by lenders can be provided by the accountants who have undertaken the financial due diligence or who have otherwise been involved in the transaction, whether or not they are actually the auditors of the target company at the relevant time.

17.9.4   Summary

For private companies proposing to enter into transactions which would previously have amounted to financial assistance, the steps necessary to protect the directors and any providers of finance may well include some or all of the following:

- a special resolution (to address the commercial benefit issue);

- establishing whether or not the target company has net assets (as if it has not, it will be deemed to be unable to pay its debts, which is relevant to the question of whether or not the arrangements can be set aside as a transaction at an undervalue or as a preference);

- whether there is any reduction in net assets;

- whether, if there is a reduction, it is covered by distributable profits;

- consideration of the solvency of the target company (with comfort from a firm of accountants where there are concerns);

- consideration of the financial position of the Buyer and of any other companies in its group whose liabilities are being guaranteed (again, with external comfort where there are concerns).

Readers who are familiar with the requirements of the whitewash procedure will, no doubt, conclude that there is a danger of the whitewash procedure disappearing and being replaced by a Whitewash Procedure Mark 2.

This is particularly likely to be the case on leveraged deals, although it is hoped that, even then, lenders will not normally require anything over and above the normal financial due diligence report. There should, however, be other transactions (such as acquisitions by trade buyers) where there are no real concerns as to solvency and where no comfort will should be required.

The changes should also make restructurings and refinancings (see 17.6.10) easier, as there will no longer be the need to consider whether there are existing loans which mean that inter-company guarantees and security would be "tainted" by financial assistance.

One practical benefit of the new regime is that there will no longer be a statutory declaration of solvency by the directors and there will no longer be the usual concerns over directors being unavailable to sign a statutory declaration on the same day—it will be a relief to all concerned that, in future, it will not be necessary for directors to interrupt their holidays or business trips to far-flung places to find a local lawyer before whom a statutory declaration can be made.

Although the Companies Act 2006 has made minimal substantive changes to the financial assistance regime for public companies, further changes are likely to be made in the future to deal with the implementation of EU Directive 2006/68, which amends the Second Company Law Directive on Capital Maintenance and Share Capital. This Directive gives Member States the option to relax the prohibition on public companies giving financial assistance to third parties for the purchase of their shares, subject to certain conditions being satisfied.

Chapter 18
Competition Law Issues

This chapter considers two main issues, the way in which merger control laws apply to mergers and acquisitions and the way in which competition laws apply to restrictions contained in sale and purchase agreements.

On auction sales or other transactions where it is the seller who is approaching potential buyers, the seller should make sure that his advisers consider in advance whether particular parties, who might otherwise be potential buyers, might be prevented from buying the company or business in question by merger control laws.

Key points are as follows:

- Within the European Union ("EU") there are potentially up to 28 merger control jurisdictions, namely the EU itself and the 27 Member States. In broad terms, the EC Merger Regulation ("ECMR") requires the mandatory notification of mergers, acquisitions and certain joint ventures that exceed relevant (high) turnover thresholds. If the ECMR applies to a transaction, then national merger control rules in the EU will not do so. The ECMR leads to a "one-stop shop" for mergers in the EU. However, if the ECMR does not apply in a case, then national merger control rules may do so. In the UK, a merger may qualify for a detailed investigation if it creates or strengthens a share of supply in the UK or a substantial part of it of more than 25 per cent or if it involves the acquisition of a company or business which has a UK turnover of more than £70 million.

- Sale and purchase agreements often contain clauses which restrict the conduct of the parties and competitive activity. Restrictive covenants can be caught by EC competition law, UK competition law and the UK common law doctrine of restraint of trade. The criminal cartel offence contained in the UK Enterprise Act 2002 also covers market-sharing arrangements which are implemented or intended to be implemented in the UK.

18.1 When do merger control rules apply to a transaction?

Merger control rules normally apply to two types of transaction. First, the classic merger/acquisition/take-over situation where two (or more) undertakings[1] legally merge

[1] An undertaking is effectively any entity engaged in business activities—see [1971] O.J. L134/15.

into one or where one undertaking takes sole control of the whole or part of another. Secondly, where two or more undertakings acquire joint control of another undertaking, i.e. a joint venture or where there is a change in the degree of control exercised by a party. Both types of transaction may be referred to as a "concentration".

Intrinsic to identifying a merger situation is the notion of control. In brief, control of an undertaking denotes the ownership of shares or other rights which confer the possibility of exercising influence on that undertaking, in particular consisting of (a) the right to use all or part of the assets of the undertaking; and (b) rights which confer influence on the composition, voting or decisions of the organs of the undertaking.

Control of an undertaking does not necessarily require a majority shareholding in that undertaking. Shareholdings of less than 50 per cent are often enough to confer a sufficient element of control to bring merger control rules into play. Indeed, even a relatively small shareholding combined with important veto rights may lead to merger control rules becoming applicable. One of the most extreme examples occurs in the UK where the acquisition of 15 per cent of the voting rights in an undertaking can be considered to give the holder the ability to materially influence the policy of that undertaking which is considered a sufficient element of control for the UK merger control rules to apply.

Merger control rules normally therefore apply to any transaction which forms the subject matter of this book, whether it takes the form of a sale and purchase of shares or of assets.

18.2 Objectives of merger control

The main objective of most merger control systems is to maintain competition on a market (and therefore ultimately to protect consumers). In the UK, for example, the substantive test for assessing mergers is whether a merger may be expected to lead to a substantial lessening of competition on a market. Other issues to which some merger control systems pay regard to include the effect which a merger may have on unemployment and regional policy, whether a merger may lead to firms in a sector with too much size and power, whether mergers may result in the control of domestic firms passing to overseas companies and whether a merger involves a sector of the economy that is especially sensitive, such as media ownership.

When analysing concentrations, many merger control authorities (for example, in the UK and the EC) examine prospectively what effect a concentration is likely to have on competition on the relevant market(s)[2] upon which the parties to a concentration will operate. The authorities examine the structure of all the markets concerned and the actual or potential competition from other undertakings. A concentration may have a

---

[2] According to EC law the relevant product market is the market for goods or service upon which the parties operate and the relevant geographic market is the area in which the undertakings concerned are involved in the supply and demand of the goods or services under sufficiently homogenous conditions of competition. See the Commission's Notice on the definition of the relevant market [1997] O.J. C372/5.

positive (pro-competitive effects: the promotion of investment, development of a new product or geographical markets, diversification, assurance of supplies or outlets, promotion of innovation or transfers of technology, achievement of economies of scale and cost reductions, restructuring or rationalisation of businesses, establishment of countervailing market power), negative (anti-competitive effects: reinforcement of oligopolistic market structures (providing scope for collusion between remaining operators on market), raising of barriers to entry, market sharing, strengthening market power which can be exploited against competitors, suppliers or customers) or neutral effect on competition on the relevant market(s) and the merger control authorities normally weigh up the positive effects against the negative effects and take action based on what they predict the likely outcome of the concentration will be.

18.3   EU merger control jurisdictions

Within the EU there are potentially up to 28 merger control jurisdictions, namely the EU itself and the 27 Member States.

With so many jurisdictions it is important that there is no overlap in enforcement of the different provisions. This is achieved in two main ways. First, the European Commission has exclusive jurisdiction over concentrations which come within the ambit of the European Community Merger Regulation ("ECMR") (EC Council Regulation 139/2004) and such concentrations may not be examined by the national merger control authorities of the Member States (ECMR art.21(2)). Thus, the Commission operates as a "one-stop-shop" for concentrations with a Community dimension, although in rare cases a Member State may challenge a merger which has a Community dimension under national legislation to protect its legitimate national interests (ECMR art.21(4)).

Secondly, when the merger is not subject to ECMR control, the other States should apply the rule of their jurisdiction only to the extent that a concentration affects competition within their jurisdiction.

The possibility of transferring the investigation of a concentration between the Commission and national merger control authorities exists. The national authorities may refer to the Commission transactions that fall below the ECMR thresholds (ECMR art.22). The Commission may also refer transactions (and Member States may request that the Commission refers transactions) with a Community dimension to the national merger control authorities of a Member State in certain cases. The parties can request that the Commission takes a case in which they would otherwise have to file notifications in three or more EC Member States, and where three EC Member States agree, no national notifications are required (ECMR arts 4 and 9).

18.4   The EC Merger Regulation ("ECMR")

The ECMR requires the prior mandatory notification of mergers, acquisitions and certain joint ventures that exceed relevant turnover thresholds. Where transactions must be notified to the Commission under the ECMR, then national merger filings in individual EC Member States cannot be made.

An ECMR filing is triggered where a change of control is involved. Shareholdings of far less than 50 per cent can confer control. Control for the purposes of the ECMR is the possibility of exercising decisive influence. Control may arise as a result of both positive and negative rights (such as veto rights) including in relation to voting rights, the right to appoint directors to the company board and rights relating to a company's budget or business plan.

18.4.1   Turnover thresholds

The ECMR applies when relevant turnover thresholds are exceeded. There are two alternative sets of thresholds and if a transaction satisfies either set, then it is subject to the ECMR.

First, the ECMR will apply to an acquisition, merger or joint venture if:

- the combined aggregate worldwide turnover, which should be calculated according to the principles set out in the Commission's Consolidated Jurisdictional Notice, [2006] O.J. C251/02, of all the parties (in all cases the figures include turnover of the whole of their groups and also the turnover of any controlling shareholders in the parties) exceeds € 5 billion (approximately £3.4 billion); and

- at least two parties to the transaction each have an EU-wide turnover in excess of € 250 million (approximately £171 million) (ECMR art.1(2)).

Alternatively, the ECMR will apply to an acquisition, merger or joint venture where:

- the combined aggregate worldwide turnover of all the parties is more than € 2.5 billion (£1.71 billion approximately); and

- in each of at least three EC Member States, the combined aggregate turnover of all the parties is more than € 100 million (£68.4 million approximately); and

- in each of the three EC Member States in (b) the aggregate turnover of each of at least two parties is more than € 25 million (£17.1 million approximately); and

- the aggregate EU-wide turnover of each of at least two parties is more than € 100 million (£68.4 million approximately) (ECMR art.1(3)). (There are special rules applicable to the calculation of turnover for financial institutions and insurance undertakings—see Pt C VII of the Commission's Consolidated Jurisdictional Notice, [2006] O.J. C251/02).

The ECMR will not apply to a transaction, though, if all of the parties involved achieve more than two-thirds of their aggregate EU-wide turnover in one and the same EC Member State.

18.4.2 **Notification obligations**

Transactions caught by the ECMR must be notified to the Commission prior to their implementation. Preparing the notification involves very considerable work and, normally, meeting the Commission in Brussels. As a general rule and depending on the level of information required at least two months is normally required to prepare a notification under the ECMR.

The Commission has introduced a simplified procedure for concentrations that can be expected not to give rise to competition concerns (Commission Notice on a simplified procedure for treatment of certain concentrations, [2000] O.J. C217/32). In such cases the Commission will adopt a "short-form" decision. The procedure is available for joint ventures that have no, or negligible, activities in the EEA; for concentrations where the parties are not engaged in business activities in the same product and geographical markets; and for transactions where the parties' market shares are below 15 per cent in the case of a horizontal concentration and 25 per cent in a vertical one. In these circumstances, it should also be possible, at the Commission's discretion, to complete a short Form CO notification rather than the full version.

A notified transaction must not normally be implemented by the parties before it has been formally approved by the Commission (ECMR art.7. See also Commission Notice on Best Practices on the Conduct of EC Merger Control Proceedings).

A breach of these procedural rules can result in each party to a transaction being fined up to 10 per cent of its total worldwide group turnover. A transaction is invalid until it is approved by the Commission.

If the ECMR applies to a transaction, then national merger control rules in the EU will not do so. The ECMR leads to a "one-stop shop" for mergers in the EU. However, if the ECMR does not apply in a case, then national merger control rules may do so.

18.4.3 **Procedure**

The Commission normally has 25 working days (subject to extension in certain cases) in which to make its initial assessment of a transaction caught by the ECMR ("Phase I" investigations). This period can be lengthened where one or more distinct national markets are affected or where particular national interests are involved.

Where a transaction raises serious competition law concerns, the Commission will open an in-depth "Phase II" investigation. Such investigations are relatively unusual. The Commission has 90 working days (subject to extension in certain cases) to complete an in-depth investigation (ECMR art.10).

18.4.4 **Horizontal Merger Guidelines**

The Commission has published a set of guidelines on horizontal mergers (mergers between actual or potential competitors) (Commission Guidelines on the assessment of horizontal mergers under the Council Regulation on the control of concentrations between undertakings, [2004] O.J. C31/5) which set out five factors of which the Commission will take account in analysing mergers:

- the likelihood that the merger would have anti-competitive effects in the relevant market, in the absence of countervailing factors;

- the likelihood that buyer power would act as a countervailing force to an increase in economic power as a result of a merger;

- the likelihood that entry by new firms would maintain effective competition in the relevant markets;

- the likelihood that efficiencies would result from the merger;

- whether the failing firm defence is available.

The guidelines consider in some detail the issues that the Commission will take account of in considering whether a merger may lead to anti-competitive effects. The Commission breaks these down into two types of effect: non-co-ordinated and co-ordinated effects. Co-ordinated effects cover situations previously dealt with as collective dominance, where the concentration increases the likelihood that firms will co-ordinate their behaviour. Non-co-ordinated effects cover not only the situations previously dealt with as single firm dominance, but also situations falling in the "gap" under the dominance test, where there is no tacit collusion, and no single firm dominance, but nevertheless a significant impediment to effective competition.

The guidelines consider market share levels and suggests that the Commission is unlikely to consider that a merger leads to competition concerns where certain market share and concentration levels are not exceeded.

18.5   UK merger control provisions

18.5.1   Enterprise Act 2002 ("EA")

UK merger control provisions are contained in the EA.

Under UK merger control law, a merger situation occurs when an "enterprise ceases to be distinct". This happens when enterprises are brought under common ownership or control, or where there are arrangements whereby one or more enterprises ceases to be carried on.

A merger can therefore arise either where there is a change of control in a company (for example upon a sale or issue of shares), or where there is a change of control or ownership of a business.

There are three levels of influence over an enterprise which constitute a change of control:

- The acquisition of the ability to exercise material influence. A shareholding of 25 per cent (with equivalent voting rights) enabling the shareholder to block special resolutions, will usually amount to material influence, even if all other shares are held by one person. A shareholding of between 15 per cent and 25 per cent (with equivalent voting rights) may give material influence, depending on the size and strength of the other shareholders. A shareholding below 15 per cent (without any additional voting rights) is unlikely to involve material influence, unless the target is a large listed company with no other substantial shareholders.

- The acquisition of the ability to control policy. This amounts to de facto control. It arises when the acquirer has a sufficiently large shareholding and/or other rights in the target to enable it, in practice, to control the policy of the target, even though it has less than 50 per cent of the voting rights.

- The acquisition of a controlling interest. This is outright or legal control, which normally means a shareholding with more than 50 per cent of the voting rights in the target.

A merger situation arises either when control, at whatever level, is first acquired by the party concerned or when someone who already has some control (at the material influence or de facto control level) acquires a higher level of control.

A merger may be referred to the Competition Commission (within four months of completion or public announcement, whichever is the later) for a detailed investigation if it:

- creates or strengthens a share of supply of more than 25 per cent in the UK or a substantial part of it (the "share of supply test"); and/or

- involves the acquisition of a target company which has a UK turnover of more than £70 million (the "turnover test") (s.23 of the EA).

There are special provisions dealing with newspaper and media mergers and also for mergers involving water companies.

18.5.2 Merger notifications

The EA does not require mergers to be notified for prior clearance (i.e. the UK merger control system is voluntary). Even if a merger is not notified under the EA to the Office of Fair Trading ("OFT"), the latter may become aware of it via press coverage or following a complaint. Once it has become aware of a merger, the OFT is obliged to consider whether the EA applies to it and often sends a questionnaire to the parties, asking them to provide sufficient information to allow the OFT to determine this issue. The City Code on Takeovers and Mergers also sets out additional requirements in relation to public bids.

The parties to a merger may ask for confirmation from the OFT that it does not intend to make a reference to the Competition Commission for a detailed investigation.

There are now two ways of obtaining the OFT's view on a merger:

- By making an informal notification to obtain clearance. There is no binding timetable for this procedure, although the OFT's administrative guidelines state that it should be able to issue a decision within about 40 working days.

- By applying under the statutory merger notice procedure for clearance. The official merger notice form should be used. The OFT must respond within 20 working days, subject to extension by up to 10 working days. This procedure is not generally favoured as the official form is not easy to complete and the OFT does not like to be bound into the mandatory timetable specified by the EA.[3]

18.5.3 Changes to UK merger policy—interim withdrawal of confidential guidance ("CG") procedure and amendment to informal advice ("IA") procedure

Prior to November 2005, the CG and IA procedures allowed parties contemplating a merger to obtain a non-binding opinion from the OFT on a confidential basis as to the likelihood of a reference to the Competition Commission. The CG procedure was more detailed and lengthy than the IA procedure, but the opinion given was thought to carry greater weight. The IA process, meanwhile, involved the submission of a short paper followed by a meeting (a "fireside chat") at which the OFT expressed its preliminary views. The OFT withdrew both these procedures in November 2005.

In April 2006, the OFT adopted a Notice on its interim practice on the provision of confidential CG and IA in UK merger cases. The Notice re-introduces the IA procedure in a different form and in more limited circumstances. These interim arrangements will be in place until the OFT publishes new guidance.

Under the OFT's Interim Notice, companies will be able to seek IA, but not CG (the OFT presently sees CG as an unjustifiable call on its limited resources). Revival of IA is to be welcomed as it potentially allows parties to obtain some form of steer from the OFT prior to a merger being made public.

The main features of the revised IA procedure are:

- IA will be a pre-merger procedure for confidential transactions only.

- IA will only be available where the OFT is satisfied that there is a good faith intention to proceed, as evidenced by a likely ability to do so.

- IA will only be given where there is a genuine issue, i.e. the merger could be genuinely problematic and there could be a case for reference to the Competition Commission.

[3] See Office of Fair Trading's Booklet: "Mergers—Procedural Guidance".

The OFT will be flexible as to how it gives IA as well as "likely to refer" or "not likely to refer" type responses, it could instead say, for example, "the OFT advises that third party evidence is likely to be decisive as to whether or not it refers the merger".

As before, the fact of seeking IA and any IA given must remain confidential and any views expressed by the OFT will be non-binding.

The application for IA should be an executive summary of no more than five pages in length. The OFT will try to indicate within five days whether or not it will accept or reject the application. Where IA is only given at the end of a meeting, the OFT will endeavour to schedule that meeting within ten to fifteen working days of receipt of the original application.

As mentioned above, these interim arrangements will be in place until the OFT publishes new guidance on the long term provision of IA and CG.

On many transactions, the parties may decide to sign sale and purchase agreements which are conditional on the OFT clearing their merger and will publicly announce the deal at this stage. The parties would then formally notify the OFT for clearance of the proposed acquisition.

18.5.4 Investigation by the Competition Commission

The OFT can make a reference to the Competition Commission for a detailed investigation. The Court of Appeal's decision in *IBA Health*[4] of February 19, 2004 narrowed the OFT's discretion in relation to references. The Court of Appeal made it clear in this decision that, when assessing a merger and whether to refer it to the Competition Commission, the OFT needs only to consider whether it believes that the merger may be expected to result in a substantial lessening of competition. The OFT needs only to consider what is its view, and does not need to consider whether there could be a credible alternative opinion. The OFT does need to ensure that any decision it makes clearing a controversial merger without reference to the Competition Commission shows adequate evidence gathering and analysis and is fully justified.

The EA also allows the OFT to accept binding undertakings (see below) from the merging parties as an alternative to making a reference to the Competition Commission. The Competition Commission is normally asked to complete its investigation into a merger within 24 weeks, subject to extension in certain cases. The substantive test that the Competition Commission uses (as well as the OFT) is whether a merger may be expected to result in a substantial lessening of competition on a market.

The announcement of a reference automatically prohibits a buyer acquiring any further shares in the target (if it is a company). The OFT can also make an order, or require

---

[4] *OFT v IBA Health Ltd* [2004] 4 All E.R. 1103.

undertakings from the parties, preventing them from doing anything which might prejudice the Competition Commission's investigations. In particular, the buyer is likely to be prevented from taking any steps to consolidate the target or acquired business with its own business.

If the Competition Commission considers that a merger is likely to have serious anti-competitive effects and therefore submits an adverse report, it must indicate what steps must be taken to alleviate those effects. The steps normally required include divestiture (if the merger has already been completed), or a prohibition on completing a merger or the giving of undertakings (such as agreeing to a price cap or other restraints on prices). The steps are enforced by the OFT. The parties can appeal the remedies required for a clearance.

If the merger has been completed and divestment is ordered, the buyer must identify a new buyer for the relevant business or assets within a specific period of time. Importantly, the buyer would have to accept whatever price was on offer (this is known as a "fire sale") and, in addition, would normally have to obtain prior approval of the new buyer from the competition authorities.

18.5.5 Competition Commission Divestiture Remedies Guidelines

In 2004 the Competition Commission published Guidelines entitled "Application of Divestiture Remedies in UK Merger Inquiries". The Competition Commission puts forward the following views in relation to remedies required for potentially anti-competitive mergers:

- structural remedies such as divestiture (or prohibition) are likely to be preferable to behavioural remedies, which seek to regulate the behaviour of firms;

- the Competition Commission will normally prefer divestiture of an existing business, which can operate independently of the merger parties, to divestment of part of a business or a collection of assets, particularly a mix of assets from both merging parties[5];

- the Competition Commission proposes that in order to incentivise parties to complete an agreed divestiture a broader, more valuable group of assets could be defined (i.e. "crown jewels") which the Competition Commission would require the parties to sell if a proposed divestiture is not completed within a specified period;

- the maximum length of the divestiture period will normally be six months, but this will depend upon the particular circumstances of the case.[6]

---

[5] The Competition Guidelines on Application of Divestiture Remedies in Merger Inquiries, December 2004 paras 3.3–3.4.

[6] The Competition Commission Guidelines on Application of Divestiture Remedies in Merger Inquiries, December 2004 para. 5.5.

18.6   Other jurisdictions

Many other countries have systems of merger control in place. These vary considerably in form and effect and a detailed description is beyond the scope of this chapter. If an acquisition will have effects in or will involve businesses located in another country, it would be prudent to seek local legal advice.

18.7   Restrictive covenants

Sale and purchase agreements often contain clauses which restrict the conduct of the parties and competitive activity. There can be continuing supply or purchase obligations or licences of intellectual property rights. The most common restrictions, though, are covenants limiting competition (see Ch.8). In order to protect its investment, the buyer of a business normally requires a covenant from the seller against competing with the business acquired and may seek to extend this covenant to retiring directors or former individual shareholders of the seller. The seller, meanwhile, if it is continuing to operate in related businesses, may seek covenants from the buyer against competing with any business retained by the seller. Restrictive covenants can be caught by EC competition law, UK competition law and the UK common law doctrine of restraint of trade. Each of these areas is considered further below.

18.7.1   Article 81(1)

Article 81(1) of the EC Treaty prohibits agreements between businesses which, to an appreciable degree, may affect trade between EC Member States and which have as their object or effect the restriction, prevention or distortion of competition within the EU. Agreements under which parties accept restrictions as to with whom they do business or where they do business could fall under this prohibition on anti-competitive agreements. Article 81(1) will only apply, though, where the relevant agreement may have an appreciable effect on competition within the EU and is capable of affecting trade between EC Member States to an appreciable degree. The European Commission's guidance on this subject suggests that an agreement between non-competitors will not affect competition where the market share of each of the parties does not exceed 15 per cent and an agreement between competitors will not appreciably affect competition where the parties have a combined market share in the EU or a substantial part of the EU of 10 per cent or less, as long as the agreement does not involve hard-core restrictions such as price-fixing or market-sharing. If the agreement is of a type common in the market (i.e. at least 30 per cent of the EU market is covered by similar agreements), the threshold goes down to five per cent. The shares of the parties must include market shares of group companies.[7]

Restrictive covenants in agreements can clearly fall within art.81(1) of the EC Treaty. Under EC law, though, they will fall outside the prohibition if they are no more than is necessary to secure the successful transfer of the business in question, i.e. they must be limited in scope, duration and geographical extent. In the latest Commission Notice on

[7] Commission Notice on Agreements of Minor Importance [2001] O.J. C368/13.

restrictions (Commission Notice on restrictions directly related and necessary to concentrations, [2005] O.J. C56/03) it is stated that non-compete clauses are only justified by the legitimate objective of implementing the merger when their duration, their geographical field of application and their subject matter do not exceed what is reasonably necessary to achieve that end. Non-compete clauses on the seller on business transfers are considered to be justified for periods up to three years where there is a transfer of customer loyalty in the form of both goodwill and know-how (and for up to two years where only goodwill is involved). The covenant must also be limited to the economic activity of the business being sold. The geographical scope of a non-compete covenant must be limited to the area in which the seller has offered the relevant products or services before the transfer, since the acquirer does not need to be protected against competition from the seller in territories not previously penetrated by the seller.

18.7.2 Restrictive covenants from buyer

Non-compete covenants from a buyer are unlikely, save in exceptional circumstances, to be enforceable under EC competition law, as such a clause on the transfer of a business is unlikely to be protecting a legitimate business interest and is likely to be viewed as against the public interest—the seller of the business would often simply appear to be trying to protect itself from competition.

18.7.3 Article 82

If either of the parties has a dominant position on a relevant market, restrictions can in some circumstances also be judged under art.82 of the EC Treaty, which prohibits an abuse of a dominant market position within the EU.

18.7.4 Competition Act 1998

The UK Competition Act 1998 introduced a prohibition, known as the Chapter I Prohibition, which is closely modelled on art.81(1) of the EC Treaty. It applies where there is an effect on trade within a part of the UK, rather than between EC Member States. The Chapter I Prohibition is applied by the OFT rather than by the European Commission. The OFT's guidance on this subject suggests that an agreement between non-competitors will not affect competition where the market share of each of the parties does not exceed 15 per cent in the UK or a substantial part of it and an agreement between competitors will not appreciably affect competition where the parties have a combined market share in the UK or a substantial part of it of 10 per cent or less, as long as the agreement does not involve hard-core restrictions such as price-fixing or market-sharing. Again, if the agreement is of a type common in the market (i.e. at least 30 per cent of the market is covered by similar agreements), the threshold goes down to five per cent (OFT Guide to Agreements and Concerted Practices, December 2004).

In terms of the enforceability of restrictive covenants under the Chapter I Prohibition, identical considerations apply as in relation to art.81(1) (see above).

Again, if either of the parties has a dominant position on a relevant market, restrictions can in some circumstances also be judged under the Chapter II Prohibition of the Competition Act, which prohibits an abuse of a dominant market position in the UK.

18.7.5 Penalties

The penalties for breaching EC and UK competition laws can be very severe and, therefore, the utmost care should be taken when considering which restrictions should be included in sale and purchase agreements. It used to be possible to notify agreements to the European Commission and the OFT for individual exemption from the provisions of art.81(1) and the Chapter I Prohibition; however, notifications to both bodies were abolished in May 2004 and undertakings now need to self-assess their agreements and practices for compliance with relevant competition laws.

Restrictions which are in breach of art.81(1) and/or the Chapter I Prohibition and which are not otherwise exempt (for example via a block exemption) are automatically void and unenforceable. In serious cases, the European Commission and the OFT may, in theory, impose fines of up to 10 per cent of the parties' total group worldwide turnover for breaches of either art.81(1) or the Chapter I Prohibition. Further, where an infringement of art.81(1) and/or the Chapter I Prohibition causes damage to a third party or the other party to the agreement, that party may commence an action for damages and/or injunctive relief.

18.7.6 **Restraint of trade**

It has already been seen in Ch.8 that under the English common law doctrine of restraint of trade (which can apply in addition to art.81 and the Chapter I Prohibition discussed above), a covenant is only enforceable to the extent that it can be shown to protect a legitimate business interest, it is reasonable as between the parties in terms of geography, duration and scope of activity (subject-matter) and it is not against the public interest. Where the seller is a company, as where the seller is an individual, as discussed in Ch.8 the buyer should ensure that the restrictive covenant designed to achieve this is no wider—in terms of activities covered, geographical area and duration—than necessary to provide reasonable protection of its interests. The question of what is reasonable will depend largely on the facts of each case.

Non-compete obligations entered into by the buyer are often unenforceable under the restraint of trade doctrine on the grounds that they are not protecting a legitimate business interest. In fact, such restrictions are often seen as an attempt by the seller to contract out of competing with the buyer without any legitimate business interest (such as protecting goodwill or preventing employees from divulging know-how acquired in the course of employment, as is likely to be the case with a seller non-compete). According to English case law, a clause is likely to be in restraint of trade where the party seeking to introduce it is "really seeking to protect itself from competition and nothing else" (*Esso v Harper's Garage* [1968] A.C. 269), as is often the case with restrictions on the buyer of a business.

The EA makes it even more important that care is taken when drafting restrictions for inclusion in sale and purchase agreements. The criminal cartel offence contained in that

Act covers, among other things, market-sharing agreements which are implemented or intended to be implemented in the UK. The offence is committed where an individual dishonestly agrees with one or more other persons that at least two undertakings at the same level of business share or divide markets or customers (s.188 of the EA). Bid-rigging, price-fixing and agreements to limit supply or production can also constitute the cartel offence. The criminal cartel offence can only be committed by individuals, not by undertakings, and carries a maximum sentence of imprisonment of five years and/or an unlimited fine if tried on indictment. The offence is prosecuted by the Serious Fraud Office.

The EA also gives the OFT the power to disqualify directors for up to 15 years where they are found to have breached competition laws (s.204 of the EA).

The OFT can apply to the court for a Competition Disqualification Order disqualifying an individual from being a director if the company of which he or she is a director has breached the Chapter I Prohibition or art.81 or the Chapter II Prohibition or Art.82 and his or her conduct makes him or her unfit to be involved in the management of the company.

18.8 Due diligence

18.8.1 Cartels

One of the greatest competition law risks when purchasing a business is whether it is, or has been, involved in a cartel. Cartels are agreements between competitors and therefore have the potential to have serious anti-competitive effects. As noted above restrictions which are in breach of art.81(1) and/or the Chapter I Prohibition are void and unenforceable. Further, the European Commission and the OFT may impose fines of up to 10 per cent of the parties' total group worldwide turnover for breaches of these provisions. In addition, where an infringement of art.81(1) and/or the Chapter I Prohibition causes damage to a third party or the other party to the agreement, that party may commence an action for damages and/or injunctive relief. Cartels will generally attract high fines and, although damages actions are currently relatively rare, it is cartels that are most likely to be the subject of any proceedings. In the UK, in common with several other EU jurisdictions, participation in a cartel may amount to a criminal offence implicating individuals within the target.

It follows from the above that relationships with competitors should be carefully analysed and the terms of any agreements with competitors should be reviewed. It is also important to understand any other relationships between the target and its competitors, such as trade association memberships or other more informal meetings.

18.8.2 Other anti-competitive behaviour

Agreements with non-competitors may also contain anti-competitive restrictions to which art.81(1) and/or the Chapter I Prohibition apply and, if so, an assessment will need to be made as to whether they satisfy the criteria for exemption. This can be particularly important if the agreements in question are with important customers and the price is based on such agreements being enforceable or they have an important bearing on the operation of the business.

Article 82 of the EC Treaty and the Chapter II Prohibition, which prohibits abuse of a dominant position, may apply where the target has significant market power. It follows that questions need to be asked to establish whether the target does have a strong position on any of the markets on which it operates and, if so, further questions need to be asked to establish whether there is any possibility of an abuse. Examples of areas for investigation are where the target holds significant market power include pricing structures, discount schemes, exclusivity provisions and any examples of recent discontinuations of supply or refusals to supply. However, there is no exhaustive list of activities that may amount to an abuse of a dominant position and ultimately it may be necessary to form a view as to whether an activity may put the target at risk.

18.8.3 Regulatory compliance

A company's compliance with competition law should be evidenced by documentation in appropriate circumstances. Mergers and acquisitions may have been subject to filing requirements and the filings and approval decisions should be requested. Given that a failure to receive approval for a transaction may render it void in certain jurisdictions, it is important that a company possesses the relevant decisions. Although today it is generally not possible to request a formal decision from the European Commission or OFT as to whether an agreement can benefit from the exemption from art.81(1) and/or the Chapter I Prohibition, this was possible previously and the purchaser should ensure that it reviews the parameters of such decisions.

In relation to actual or alleged infringements involving the target there may be correspondence with competition authorities and this should be reviewed.

Finally, it is prudent to review a company's competition law compliance programme as this will give some indication as to how importantly the company treats compliance. Today it is relatively uncommon to find a company with no competition law compliance procedures at all.

18.8.4 Continuing liability of the target

It is important to understand that, if the target was or is involved in competition law infringements together with the current owner, then it is most likely that they will be held joint and severally liable in the event that a fine is imposed. Therefore, post-transaction, the target remains liable for the infringements in which it was involved and, further, if the original owner ceases to exist, then it is possible that the target may be obliged to pay the full amount of any fine.

Chapter 19

Property Issues

19.1   Property due diligence

In virtually every transaction, the business will have freehold, leasehold or tenanted property occupied by the business itself or occupied (under lease or licence) by a third party and the investigations into those property assets will be broadly (save in the case of shares where there may be a contingent or residual property liabilities) similar whether the transaction proceeds as a sale and purchase of shares or of assets. A sale and purchase of assets will, of course, involve the transfer of the seller's interest in the land while on a sale and purchase of shares the property will continue to be owned by the same company as before but, whatever the structure of the transaction, the buyer will want to be satisfied as to the seller's title. The buyer will also want to carry out due diligence into other matters relating to the seller's property assets, save in rare cases where the timetable dictates or other reasons mean that warranties only are relied upon.

The property interests of a business are normally among its most significant assets—either because of their value or because of their importance to the continuance of the business. For example, a business may operate from a freehold property, the value of which represents a significant part of the value of the business, or it may occupy premises subject to a lease which is entered into on normal commercial terms and which therefore has no market value but, nevertheless, the ability to continue to occupy those premises may be crucial to the business—perhaps because of their location or the facilities which they offer (cranage, etc.)—or the disruption that would be involved in trying to relocate the business (especially at short notice) may make it essential that it continues to operate from its existing premises. For example, it would almost certainly be a major undertaking to move a manufacturing business, involving heavy plant and machinery (much of which may be concreted into the ground or otherwise fixed to the fabric of the building), to new premises (assuming always that suitable alternative premises can be found in the locality).

In some cases, of course, such as care homes, pubs and restaurants, the essence of the business is the premises from which it operates.

Where the property assets are not significant—for example, when the business is one which operates from office premises which are held on a short-term lease—the buyer may be content to rely on warranties from the seller in respect of those premises but, in other cases the possibility of a claim in damages for breach of warranty will not be adequate protection for the buyer and the buyer will want his solicitors to carry out an investigation of title or, more rarely, may be able to obtain a certificate of title from the seller's solicitors.

19.2   Investigation of title or certificate of title?

Factors to be taken into account in deciding whether to instruct the buyer's solicitors to investigate title or to obtain a certificate of title from the seller's solicitors will include the following:

●   Timing: in order to prepare a certificate of title, the seller's solicitors will have to investigate title themselves and this may help the timing of the transaction in that, if no specific buyer has been identified, the seller's solicitors can submit searches and prepare a certificate of title which can then be offered to the buyer or buyers once these have been identified. In addition, where the seller has only recently purchased the property, or where the seller's solicitors are very familiar with the title to the property, a certificate of title would be likely to be capable of being produced more quickly by the seller's solicitors. Traditionally, there have been arguments over the precise form of certificate which the seller's solicitors are give, but such arguments have become less frequent as the standard City of London Law Society Certificate of Title tends to be used in most cases.

●   Costs: for the buyer, it will be more cost-effective to have the seller's solicitors prepare a certificate of title at the seller's expense and for the buyer's solicitors then to review that certificate than for the buyer's solicitors to carry out the title investigation. For the same reason, of course, the seller will generally prefer the buyer to incur this expense.

●   The number of properties involved and their importance to the buyer and to the business: if there are a large number of properties involved, certificates of title might be prepared by the seller's solicitors to speed up the transaction.

●   The identity of the seller's solicitors, their reputation and the level of its professional indemnity insurance cover.

●   The number of parties involved and the specific requirements of funders.

●   The knowledge of the buyer of the property: for example, on a management buy-out, the buyer's solicitors may often be responsible for providing a certificate of title to the buyer's funder.

In practice, it is more common for buyers to investigate title than for them to rely on certificates of title—this is partly for reasons of speed and efficiency but also because, where the buyer is obtaining finance from a bank, VC or other third party funder, the funders are likely to require that a certificate of title should be addressed to them and it is therefore logical for the buyer's solicitors to do that work. If the buyer does instruct his solicitors to investigate title, the exercise will involve a review of the title to the property, the raising of preliminary and other enquiries of the seller and of third parties and the carrying out of the searches that would normally be carried out as part of a property transaction. The process will therefore include:

19.2.1 The seller deducing title to the property as in any other property transaction— if the title is registered, official copies will be obtained from the Land Registry and the buyer should request an office copy or a certified copy of the lease, where the property is leasehold. In the case of unregistered land, the seller should provide an epitome of title, including certified copies of the title deeds.

19.2.2 The buyer should carry out the searches which would be carried out as part of any other property transaction, including local authority searches, environmental searches, central Land Charges Registry Searches, Land Registry Searches, and, depending where the property is situated, additional searches such as Commons Searches and Coal Mining Searches. Even in the case of non-residential property, the buyer may wish to consider carrying out a Chancel Repair search.

19.2.3 There the seller is a company or on a sale and purchase of shares, the buyer should carry out a search at Companies House in order to establish whether there are any mortgages or charges over the property which have been registered. The buyer should, however, bear in mind that the fact that no such charge has been registered gives no protection to a buyer of shares in a company—a registerable charge which is not registered is void only against a liquidator or creditor of the company and the effect of that is that the money secured by the charge becomes automatically repayable. The buyer should also bear in mind that there is a period of 21 days within which charges have to be registered and so it is always possible that a charge may have been created but not yet registered.

19.3 Property warranties

Although a certain amount of information is available from searches of public registers, the effectiveness of an investigation of title will depend to a large extent, on the quality of the information supplied by, or on behalf of, the seller—by way of copies of title deeds in the case of unregistered land and in replies to the buyer's enquiries and requisitions. The buyer, even if his solicitors investigate title, needs to be protected against any untrue or incomplete replies to enquiries or any other failure by the seller to disclose any relevant property issues and, even where the buyer's solicitors investigate title or the seller's solicitors give a certificate of title, should insist upon the seller giving some warranties regarding the property assets of the business, particularly where information can not be verified or revealed by the buyer's enquiries of third parties.

The extent of the property warranties may, in part, be dependent upon the opportunity that the buyer has had to carry out searches and upon the apparent quality of the replies to enquiries. In general, however, the property warranties should be similar whether the transaction is a sale and purchase of shares or of assets save that, on a sale and purchase of shares, the buyer will require warranties (and possibly indemnities) covering potential

liabilities in respect of leasehold premises previously occupied by the target company—
either as the original tenant or pursuant to subsequent assignments and licences to assign.
Whilst the Landlord and Tenant (Covenants) Act 1995 ("the 1995 Act") removes the
liability of the original tenant under new leases granted since January 1, 1996, the requirement of former tenants to enter into authorised guarantee agreements (an "AGA"),
mean that this warranty will be required even in relation to target companies incorporated
after January 1, 1996. There may also be residual environmental liabilities in respect of
properties formerly owned or occupied by the target company.

Whatever the structure of the acquisition, the buyer should insist upon the seller's replies
to the buyer's property enquiries being warranted and the buyer's solicitors should ideally
refuse to accept replies which would render such a warranty meaningless, such as "not so
far as the seller is aware but no warranty is given". If specific property problems or issues
are identified, these should be covered by specific indemnities.

If property warranties are qualified with reference to the seller's knowledge (for example by being given "so far as the seller is aware" or "to the best of the seller's knowledge
and belief"), in appropriate cases, the buyer should insist upon a provision in the sale and
purchase agreement to make it clear that any such warranty has been given after making
reasonable enquiries of the seller's property manager or any other employee or agent
with responsibility for property matters. The "knowledge qualification" is discussed in
more detail in 10.7.14.

Particular if the buyer has actually carried out the normal conveyancing searches
(or has, at least, had the opportunity to do so), the seller will normally seek to include
in the disclosure letter a general disclosure of information which would be apparent
from the property deeds, conveyancing searches or physical inspection of the properties
(see 10.2.2.3).

19.4   Other provisions in the sale and purchase agreement—sales and purchases of shares

On a sale and purchase of shares, it is likely that the only provisions in the sale and
purchase agreement relating to the target company's freehold and leasehold properties
will be a schedule which lists them and describes them by reference to Land Registry
title numbers or conveyancing-type descriptions and any warranties, as referred to
above. In addition, if the seller has given a guarantee of the target company's lease of
any premises, the sale and purchase agreement will normally contain a provision
regarding the release of that guarantee (see 8.13 of Ch.8).

The only circumstances in which more extensive provisions are likely to be needed are
when one or more of the target company's properties are owned by the seller or a connected party (typically the seller's pension fund or, when the target company is being
brought out of the group, another company in the group) in which case, arrangements
may need to be made for the target company to acquire the company or for a lease or
licence to be granted to the target company in order to enable it to continue to occupy
the property after completion.

Where the target company operates from premises which are owned by the seller or a connected party, the seller may, as part of his pre-sale planning, have put in place a very "landlord-friendly" lease before the sale process gets underway and, as part of the negotiations, the buyer may well press for the terms of that lease to be varied on completion, in order to make them rather less onerous from his and the company's point of view. The seller should certainly not assume that the buyer will be content to accept the terms of whatever lease the seller has put in place and the seller would therefore be well-advised to put in place a lease which a third party buyer would be likely to accept.

19.5   Other provisions in the sale and purchase agreement—sales and purchases of assets

On a sale and purchase of assets, on the other hand, the sale and purchase agreement will have to contain provisions for the transfer or assignment to the buyer of any freehold or leasehold property or (where the premises in question are excluded from the sale) arrangements allowing the buyer to continue to occupy the premises or, alternatively, vacate them.

Rather than set out in full all the terms and conditions which will apply to the transfer or assignment of any freehold or leasehold property, it is common to cross-refer to a standard and widely-accepted set of terms and conditions (typically, for business premises, the latest version of the Law Society's Standard Commercial Property Conditions).

Where, however, the business operates from freehold premises but those premises (or at least the freehold interest in them) are excluded from the sale it is normal for the agreement to provide for one of the following alternatives:

19.5.1   the grant of a lease of the property from the seller to the buyer on completion in an agreed form;

19.5.2   the grant of a short-term licence to allow the buyer to occupy the premises for an interim period;

19.5.3   an obligation on the buyer to remove the assets from the premises on or very shortly after completion.

If a lease is to be granted on completion, the parties will have to consider the normal issues which arise on the grant of any new lease. Where the parties agree to proceed by way of short-term licence rather than by way of lease, it will be important from the seller's point of view to make sure that the arrangements are drafted in such a way that they do not in fact constitute a tenancy. A detailed explanation of these issues is beyond the scope of this book and reference should be made to a specialist property law text book.

Where premises are leasehold and it is important to the buyer that the business should continue to trade from those premises after completion, both parties should wait until any necessary landlord's consent to assignment of the lease has been obtained or (if that is not possible) make sure that the sale and purchase agreement is conditional on the granting of such consent.

Before reaching a decision as to whether to wait for the landlord's consent or to enter into a conditional agreement, the parties should consider the precise wording of the lease, in order to ascertain whether the lease contains a qualified covenant against assignment (a covenant not to assign the lease without the landlord's consent), rather than an absolute prohibition on assignment). Section 19 of the Landlord and Tenant Act 1927 ("the 1927 Act") provides that the landlord may not withhold his consent unreasonably and that, if he does wish to withhold his consent, he must be able to show reasonable grounds for not believing that the buyer will be capable of paying the rent and performing the tenant's covenants in the lease. In addition, where there is a qualified covenant against assignment, under the Landlord and Tenant Act 1988 ("the 1988 Act") the landlord must give his decision (as to whether or not to consent to the proposed assignment) within a reasonable time and in writing and, if he is prepared to give his consent subject to conditions, to set out those conditions (which must be reasonable). If the landlord refuses to give his consent, he must set out the reasons for doing so.

The parties should, however, establish the precise date of the lease as, if it was granted on or after January 1, 1996, unless pursuant to a contract or option prior to that date, the 1995 Act will apply. Leases granted before January 1, 1996 are referred to as "old leases" and those granted on or after that date as "new leases". In the case of a new lease, s.19(1A) of the 1927 Act will apply and the landlord may, in the lease, impose strict pre-conditions to be satisfied before an assignment will be permitted and those may be conditions which the buyer is unlikely to satisfy. The reason why those conditions may be difficult for a buyer to satisfy is that, where the 1995 Act applies, the seller will cease, upon the assignment of the lease, to be liable under the lease whereas, where the Act does not apply, the original tenant will remain liable under the lease for the whole of its duration.

Where the sale and purchase agreement is conditional on the obtaining of the landlord's consent, the seller should ensure that he imposes on the buyer appropriate obligations to take the steps and produce the information which is likely to be necessary to enable the landlord to reach a positive decision. For example, the agreement should oblige the buyer to provide the seller with the references that a landlord is likely to require, together with such other information on the buyer (details of directors and shareholders, accounts, etc.) as the landlord is likely to request and the buyer should be obliged to provide this information on, or within a comparatively short period after, the entering into of the sale and purchase agreement.

Particular difficulties may arise where the buyer is a new company or one which has a very short trading history (this is particularly likely to be a problem on a management buy out, where the purchasing vehicle will almost certainly be a company formed specifically for the purpose). In those circumstances, it may be difficult to argue that consent has been unreasonably refused, in view of the limited nature of the information provided to the landlord, unless (for example) financial projections can be provided which should give the landlord sufficient comfort as to the financial strength of the buyer. That may be difficult as financial projections are, of course, no more than "crystal ball gazing", notwithstanding that, on a transaction of that nature, the buyer is likely to have had them prepared to a standard which meets the requirements of his financiers. The seller would be well-advised to require the agreement to oblige the buyer to provide any guarantee or other security which the landlord may require as a pre-condition to giving his consent—for example, a guarantee from the buyer's shareholders or a rent deposit. The buyer is, however, unlikely to accept an unqualified obligation to provide whatever guarantees or security the landlord may require, regardless of how reasonable or unreasonable it may be for the landlord to require them as (for example) there is likely to be a significant cost in providing bank guarantees, while the shareholders of the buyer may be unable or unwilling to give personal guarantees or other security. A typical (if not entirely satisfactory) fall-back is for the agreement to require the buyer to provide such guarantees or other security as the landlord may reasonably require.

As mentioned above, under an old lease, the original tenant will remain liable for the tenant's covenant in the lease throughout the term, notwithstanding subsequent assignments. Should a subsequent tenant not comply with the lease covenants, the landlord may look to the original tenant to remedy the breach and pay any arrears of rent. The 1995 Act abolished this onerous liability but, under s.16, did permit the landlord to require, as a condition of giving consent to an assignment, that the assigning tenant should enter into an authorised guarantee agreement ("AGA"). Under an AGA, the assigning tenant guarantees the performance of the lease covenants by its immediate assignee only.

The lease is likely to provide for the tenant to bear the costs of the landlord in connection with any application for consent to an assignment of the lease and these will include the landlord's legal costs. The sale and purchase agreement should specify whether any such costs are to be borne by the seller or by the buyer and should oblige the relevant party to pay them: it is normal for the seller to bear those costs and that is likely to be the position if the agreement is silent on the point. If, however, the assignment takes place without obtaining the landlord's consent, the seller will continue to be liable under the lease, even if the lease was subject to the 1995 Act, as the Act will not apply in those circumstances. The seller will also be subject to a potential claim for damages from the landlord, who may also forfeit the lease.

There may, of course, be transactions where it is simply not practicable to obtain the landlord's consent before the sale and purchase agreement is signed nor to make the sale and purchase agreement conditional on consent—for example where the purchase is from receivers or administrators and needs to be completed very rapidly in order to maintain the business as a going concern. In those circumstances, the seller may allow the buyer to occupy the premises on the basis of a simple licence to occupy and on the basis that the buyer will vacate the premises if the landlord forfeits the lease or otherwise begins action to repossess them. This may be a high risk approach for the buyer, as he runs the risk of severe disruption of the business (or worse) if he is unable to continue to occupy the premises until he has found suitable alternative premises and the landlord may well take advantage of that to negotiate a rent increase or to force the buyer to pay any arrears of rent for which the landlord may otherwise be an unsecured creditor. The buyer will have to weigh up the risks of that happening against the fact that the landlord may have difficulty in finding another tenant very quickly and may therefore be prepared to agree to an assignment, in order to maintain the rental stream from the premises. Whether or not that is the case will depend very much on market conditions in the area and at the relevant time.

In some transactions, particularly where there are a number of properties and the buyer is prepared to acquire the business without necessarily acquiring all of them, the sale and purchase agreement will provide for completion to take place, with the buyer being given a short-term right to occupy all of the properties and on the basis that, if it is not possible to obtain the landlord's consents by a specified date, any properties in respect of which consent to an assignment has not been obtained by then, will be excluded from the transaction altogether, with an appropriate adjustment to the price.

A typical example of this is where the business consists of a chain of retail outlets and the buyer is prepared to complete in the knowledge that he may not necessarily be able to have all of the property leases assigned to him. In those circumstances, the sale and purchase agreement may apportion the purchase price between the various properties and provide that, in respect of any of the outlets for which landlord's consent has not been obtained by an agreed date, the purchase price will reduce by the amount which has been apportioned to it.

A possible alternative to an assignment of the lease, where the landlord refuses to give consent, is to have the seller grant an underlease to the buyer as, in connection with new leases, the restrictions on granting underleases may be less extensive than the restrictions on assigning the lease—where the seller grants an underlease he will continue to be the tenant under the original lease and still be subject to his obligations under it, with the result that it would be the seller rather than the landlord who would be taking the risk of the buyer's failing to pay the rent and to perform his other obligations under the lease.

On the grant of a lease of freehold premises or an underlease of leasehold premises, the seller will need to consider the length of the term to be granted to the buyer and whether it is essential for the seller to regain possession at the end of the term. If it is essential, it will be necessary, to prevent the buyer from having any rights to renew the lease at the end of the term, for the lease or underlease to be excluded from the security of tenure provisions contained in ss.24–28 of the Landlord and Tenant Act 1954 ("the 1954 Act"). This will involve the seller, as prospective landlord, serving notice on the buyer prior to the grant of the lease to the effect that ss.24–28 of the 1954 Act will not apply and the buyer as prospective tenant producing a declaration that the consequences of the exclusion of those sections is understood. Many leases contain provisions requiring that any underlease must exclude those sections. Buyers and sellers should note that these are complicated issues and should be aware that this book can do no more than give a brief summary of them: for further information, reference should be made to the standard text books on landlord and tenant.

An underlease may also be attractive to a buyer who is happy to take over a particular set of leasehold premises but is not prepared to pay the same rent as that currently being paid by the seller. In those circumstances, if the seller is prepared to agree, he could grant the buyer an underlease at a lower rent than the rent that he is himself paying (but it would be necessary for the parties to check the terms of the head lease in order to make sure that such an arrangement would be permitted).

19.6 Planning issues

19.6.1 Background

The planning system controls and regulates the use and development of land and the principal legislative framework through which the control is exercised is the Town and Country Planning Act 1990 ("TCPA 1990") and subsidiary legislation.

Under the TCPA 1990 and subject to certain exceptions, all development needs to be authorised by way of a planning permission, subject to exceptions. Development is defined by the TCPA 1990 as:

> "The carrying out of building, engineering, mining or other operations in, on, over or under land, or the making of any material change in the use of any buildings or other land" (s.55(1) of the TCPA 1990).

If there has been a breach of planning control and development has been carried out without planning permission, the planning authority may take enforcement action requiring remedial steps to be taken or requiring cessation of the use. Enforcement action will be taken against the owner, for the time being, of the property. However, unauthorised operational development (such as building work) or changes of use are immune from enforcement action if specific periods of time have elapsed from the breach of planning control. These are four years in the case of operational development and ten years in the case of change of use. There are, however, certain procedural requirements which have to be complied with and these are discussed in 19.6.2.

19.6.2 Continuing to operate the business

Planning controls are concerned with the use of the land rather than the identity of the user and any new owner of the business, either by way of the sale and purchase of shares or by sale and purchase of assets, will therefore benefit from the planning permissions. However, the buyer will want to be satisfied that the appropriate planning consents are in place to allow the business to continue operating without any operational restrictions (such as restrictions on the hours of operation) and that no expenditure will be required to remedy prior breaches of planning control. The property due diligence should therefore establish the planning position. This is done principally by way of the local authority search and land charges search which will reveal the existence of any planning consents, planning agreements and breaches of planning legislation.

It is worth mentioning that where building works have been carried out within the last four years, they may have been carried out under a general development order, which can authorise certain minor works.

Where the business has operated for a considerable period of time from the premises, the search is likely to reveal a great deal of information which effectively tracks the development and growth of the business over the years—for example, permissions for extensions and additional buildings and structures within the perimeter of the site or erection of plant or machinery. The key points which the buyer should establish are whether:

- the current use is authorised by express planning consent;

- there are any conditions on the permission which might limit the operation of the business;

- all building works made within the last four years have been carried out pursuant to an express planning consent;

- there are any breaches of planning control and, if so, whether any enforcement action is current, pending or possible;

- which planning consents have actually been implemented (if a planning permission is not implemented within the relevant time periods stipulated in the planning conditions, it will expire).

If pre-contract enquiries reveal that the use or construction of any buildings is unauthorised, a lawful development certificate ("LDC") may be sought from the local planning authority if the requisite period of time has elapsed. An LDC is a statutory document certifying the lawfulness for planning purposes of existing operations on, or use of, land. The LDC application must be supported by evidence and the buyer should ensure that the seller is contractually obliged to provide any statutory declarations (based on his own knowledge) required to show that there has been uninterrupted use for at least ten years or that the building or structure has stood for at least four years, together with any supporting documents, such as building contracts.

If, as a result of the due diligence process, there are gaps identified in the planning background or, for example, it is discovered that covenants in planning agreements (which will bind the buyer as successor in title) remain unfulfilled and therefore impose an ongoing financial burden, it will be a matter for negotiation whether warranties or indemnities are given by the seller, to provide some level of comfort to a buyer. The pressure to complete a deal may, on occasions, outweigh the full regularisation of the planning position but it is an area in which to tread carefully—a buyer's funders may be reluctant to provide finance if a breach of planning control could lead to the business being shut down.

Buyers should be aware that planning permissions can occasionally be personal to a particular grantee and this can be an issue for a buyer of assets or on a sale and purchase of shares, where the property in question has been transferred around a group of companies.

19.6.3   Future business plans and asset management

The planning system is also plan-led, which means that decisions on applications for planning permission (which are usually determined by local planning authorities) must be made in accordance with a hierarchical structure of planning guidance and plans at national, regional and local level. If the buyer intends to carry out any development works, or alterations to the property, or alter the use of the property following completion, then he should assess the policies relevant to the property and to the proposal, in order to assess the likelihood of obtaining permission. This appraisal is often best done by a specialist planning consultant.

Where the buyer is considering the future sale and/or rationalisation of the property portfolio, it would again be prudent to take specialist planning and valuation advice to ascertain the uplift in land value which a planning permission might confer.

The reason for this is that there have been discussions regarding the introduction of a Planning Gain Supplement ("PGS"), which would tax a proportion of the difference in value of a site before and after the grant of planning permission.

This point may be particularly relevant if there is to be deferred consideration which is dependent upon the grant of planning permission, as the buyer would want to make certain that, if PGS were to be introduced, any PGS payable in future could be deducted as a cost in arriving at the amount of the deferred consideration payable.

If, in the case of a sale and purchase of assets, a planning application has already been submitted to facilitate future development, the buyer should ensure that an agency arrangement is put in place, which will enable the buyer, on behalf of the seller, to appeal the planning permission (if an appeal is considered necessary and has any prospect of success) because only the applicant has a right of appeal. If, however, an appeal has already been lodged and then turned down, the buyer may be able to challenge the decision in the courts by way of a statutory challenge under s.287 of the TCPA 1990 because the courts have held that a subsequent purchaser may be regarded as a "person aggrieved" for the purposes of an application to the High Court.

It is quite common (particularly where land has been acquired out of public ownership or from a VC) for the original agreement for sale to include a provision which entitles the seller to an "overage" or "anti-embarrassment" payment if the land is subsequently developed—this is typically the case where there is no immediate prospect of the land in question being developed and so the price originally paid will not have reflected the development potential of the land. In those circumstances, the sale agreement will generally provide for an overage payment, which allows the original seller to share in the profit made by the buyer as a result of developing the land. As part of the due diligence process, the buyer should obtain details of all such arrangements.

Chapter 20

Environmental Issues

There is a growing understanding of the need to consider environmental issues (which can involve both civil and criminal liabilities) in transactions (whether they are sales and purchases of shares or of assets), not least because of the implications on securing funding (whether for the acquisition itself or to meet future working capital requirements) and the future operation of the business. This need has arisen from the significant growth in environmental regulation in recent years.

Generally speaking, environmental liabilities and risks arise out of the condition of the property in question and from activities carried out at that property, an assessment of which is recommended at an early stage in the transaction. In this regard, environmental audits and investigations and controlled disclosure are important. Environmental liabilities can involve the buyer in significant cost—this may be the cost of carrying out whatever work is required in order to achieve compliance with environmental legislation (for example, the cost of cleaning-up the site) and/or fines from regulatory authorities. Any party involved in a transaction (whether as buyer, seller or lender) will be keen to limit his liabilities as much as possible.

Once identified, liabilities and risks can then be allocated between the parties by warranties and indemnities and/or dealt with by way of appropriate environmental insurance (although this will probably be expensive and is unlikely to apply to historic contamination). Alternatively, the buyer may achieve a reduction in the purchase price in order to reflect the liabilities which he is assuming (for example, he may be able to negotiate a reduction equal to the parties' best estimate of the costs of cleaning up the site) or the seller may agree to carry out remedial works on the site. Much will depend on the relative bargaining positions of the parties.

The seller will want a "clean break" on completion and may say that, because of the uncertainty of environmental laws, he has no knowledge of factors which may give rise to environmental liability in years to come and that such liability is a risk associated with the future operation of the business. On the other hand, the buyer will not want to take on environmental liabilities in respect of activities carried out before the transaction.

20.1   Authorisations, permits, licences and consents

20.1.1   In order to establish his potential environmental exposure, the buyer will require details of all permits, licences, authorisations, consents or other approvals required by environmental legislation in order to enable the business to operate. These include licenses issued under Pt I of the Environmental Protection Act 1990 ("EPA") (as replaced by the Pollution Prevention Control Act 1999) which provides that a licence is required for a "prescribed process" (Part A and Part B processes). Part A processes are regulated by the Environmental Agency under the Integrated Pollution Control ("IPC") system and Part B processes are regulated by the local authority under the system of Local Authority Air Pollution Control.

Following the passing of the Pollution Prevention and Control Act 1999, the IPC system is gradually being replaced by a new Integrated Pollution Prevention and Control ("IPPC") system which requires that more processes are the subject of regulation. There is stricter regulation under the new regime, permits will be given to installations rather than specific processes and inputs as well as outputs will be monitored.

As of the April 6, 2008, the Environmental Permitting (England and Wales) Regulations 2007 (SI 2007/3538) have introduced a system of "environmental permits" for all "regulated facilities". A regulated facility will be every installation and mobile plant.

It is also important to obtain copies of authorisation conditions so that the buyer can satisfy himself that the seller has been compliant. For example, there may be a condition requiring the seller to update his equipment. Where this has not been done, the buyer will need to assess the costs that are likely to be involved in taking the necessary steps to make sure that the business complies with that condition.

Up until April 6, 2008 Pt II of the EPA governed the system for the regulation of waste management. The introduction of the Environmental Permitting (England and Wales) Regulations 2007 (SI 2007/3538) has meant that there is no longer a separate regulatory regime for waste management and PPC. Both are now regulated by "environmental permits". However the same waste principles apply and the buyer will need to ensure that necessary licences are in place, to keep, treat or dispose of controlled waste. Although there has been much debate on what constitutes "controlled waste", it will, generally speaking, be anything that has been discarded and has ceased to have a utility. Licences tend to be required for businesses involved in the permanent "handling" of controlled waste and so will not be required for a "typical" business. There is also a statutory duty of care with which any business that produces controlled waste will need to have complied. The Department of the Environment, Food and Rural Affairs ("DEFRA") has produced a code of practice which will provide guidance on the duty of care entitled "Waste Management, The Duty of Care, A Code of Practice". Obligations include ensuring that ordinary and hazardous waste has been segregated and disposed of appropriately, that transfer notes or consignment notes (as applicable) are generated and that controlled waste is handed over to a licensed carrier. The Environment Agency, in practice, expects the ultimate destination of the waste to be known to the producer of the waste.

20.1.2   The buyer will also need to establish whether there are any obligations under the so-called Producer Responsibility Directives. These Directives have created the principle that certain producers have liabilities for their products when they have come to the end of their useful life. These liabilities have had a huge cost impact on the sectors affected and currently relate to packaging by virtue of the Producer Responsibility (Packaging Waste) Regulations 1997 (SI 1997/648) (now the Producer Responsibility Obligations (Packaging Waste) (Amendment) Regulations 2008) (SI 2008/413), with schemes for waste end-of-life vehicles and waste electrical and electronic equipment set to follow.

20.1.3   The buyer should seek evidence that a discharge consent from a sewerage undertaker has been obtained where trade effluence is discharged into the public sewer or surface waters and again, where appropriate, that an Abstraction Licence for the removal of water from surface waters or boreholes has been obtained.

20.1.4   Where the seller or his assets are subject to the emissions trading scheme, then particular issues will need to be considered by the buyer. The EU emissions trading scheme ("ETS") commenced on January 1, 2005 under the Emissions Allowance Trading Directive 2003/87. It requires EU Member States to set limits on emissions, initially carbon dioxide, from certain energy-intensive industries. At the UK level, affected installations are specified in a national allocation plan, which divides up the UK emissions limit amongst affected UK installations by allocating allowances, each allowance representing the right to emit one tonne of carbon dioxide into the atmosphere. The Greenhouse Gas Emissions Trading Scheme Regulations 2005 (SI 2005/925) require each affected installation to obtain a permit and oblige the operator of that installation to surrender each year allowances equal to, or more than, the total volume of actual emissions from that installation. The operator of an installation may trade allowances with other operators to meet shortfalls or dispose of surpluses. Should an operator present a shortfall of allowances against its verified emissions in any year, a penalty is payable on the shortfall, and in addition the operator is required to retire an equivalent number of allowances from the following year's allocation.

The ETS is split into phases, the first of which ran from 2005 to 2007 and the second of which runs from 2008 to 2012. In the first phase, the affected industries comprised certain combustion installations, oil refineries, coke ovens, iron and steel production, glass manufacturing, cement, clinker and lime production, brick and tile manufacturing, ceramic products, pulp and paper. Notably, a combustion installation is caught if it has a thermal capacity exceeding 20 MW and the applicable aggregation rules have meant that entities such as some universities have found themselves caught by virtue of operating a collection of small facilities across a campus. In Phase 1, the penalty on allowance shortfalls was € 40 per tonne of carbon dioxide.

The second phase of the ETS runs from 2008 to 2012, and sees an increase in the penalty on allowance shortfalls to € 100 per tonne of carbon dioxide. The scheme has also been extended to Norway, Iceland and Liechtenstein, which are in the European Economic Area but not the EU. Further, from 2012 the aviation sector will be subject to the scheme.

With the advent of the Linking Directive (2004/101), operators are able to utilise project credits in meeting their ETS commitments. These credits are derived under the so-called flexibility mechanisms of the Kyoto Protocol, namely clean development mechanism ("CDM") and joint implementation ("JI"). CDM applies to projects based in non-industrialised countries, whilst JI applies to projects based in industrialised countries. In both cases, project credits represent a reduction in emissions generated by a project against a "business as usual" scenario and are issued after the project has undergone a rigorous verification and approval process. However, project credits are unlikely to play a significant part in an operator's ETS compliance strategy until such time as an international transaction log is put in place enabling credits allocated in the name of a project developer to be traded and transferred into the name of that operator.

The EU has proposed a reform of the EU ETS for the period from 2013 to 2020. The proposal enlarges the scope of the scheme to new sectors and two new gases (nitrous oxide and perfluocarbons). In addition, a much greater percentage of allowances will be auctioned rather than handed out for free as is current practice. Some sectors will continue to get allowances for free if they are at "significant risk of carbon leakage", i.e. relocation to countries with less stringent laws. This list of sectors is still to be finalised. Further, there will be an EU wide cap on the number of emission allowances rather than 27 national caps and so there will be harmonised rules for the allocation of allowances.

From a buyer's perspective, due diligence enquiries will need to include such things as:

- Does the installation have sufficient allowances to cover its projected emissions?

- What are the contractual arrangements for verification of emissions, and for trading of allowances?

- Where in the seller's group are the allowances or project credits held, and will they be transferred as part of the deal?

- Have any penalties been levied, and paid, in respect of past compliance years?

- Has the Environment Agency taken any enforcement action for contravention of monitoring or reporting conditions?

Where these issues are of concern, the buyer is likely to require appropriate warranty and/or indemnity protection.

Where the business has been the subject of serious breaches of environmental legislation such as prosecutions or the inclusion of the business on the contaminated land register, the buyer will need to consider any damage to the reputation of the business and if this has had an impact on the value of the business and/or of the site in question. Enquiries should also be made to establish if there have been any complaints relating to breaches of environmental laws as these potential liabilities will also need to be assessed. A nuisance action claim can be very costly.

20.2   Contaminated land

20.2.1   Section 57 of the Environment Act 1995 amended the EPA by the inclusion of ss.78A–78YC of a new Pt IIA. Under these new provisions, local authorities have primary responsibility to identify contaminated land and serve a remediation notice for clean-up. The contaminated land regime is complex and has the potential to impose substantial liabilities.

The detailed requirements for this new regime, which came into force on April 1, 2000, can be found in the Contaminated Land (England) Regulations 2000 (SI 2000/227) and DETR (now DEFRA) Guidance on Contaminated Land, September 01/2006 (DETR Guidance).

Contaminated land is defined in s.78A as being:

> "... land which appears to the local authority in whose area it is situated to be in such a condition, by reasons of substances in, on or under land, that:

> (a) significant harm is being caused or there is a significant possibility of such harm being caused; or

> (b) significant pollution of controlled waters is being or is likely to be caused." ("Significant" was added by the Water Act 2003).

Whether or not land is contaminated depends therefore on whether or not there is pollution present that has the potential for significant harm. The local authorities, who are under a duty to have regard to statutory guidance, will look at the DETR Guidance for assistance on the interpretation of the "significant harm".

In 2006, Government regulation and guidance specifically recognised "radioactivity" in the definition of "contaminated land".

20.2.2   The Environment Agency must be consulted where there is water pollution and will also be the enforcement authority having responsibility for the remediation of any land which it is designated as being a "special site". Special sites involve land having the potential for "serious harm". Water is contaminated if there is a risk of water pollution (this has to change under the provisions of the Water Act 2003, whereby pollution of controlled waters is required to be "significant"). There is no requirement for significant harm with regard to water pollution.

20.2.3 Once a site has been identified as being contaminated, and unless there is imminent danger of serious harm or pollution of controlled waters, the authority is under an obligation to carry out a consultation exercise and a remediation notice will not be served where the authority is satisfied that appropriate steps are being or will be taken without the need for a notice to be served.

20.2.4 Where it has been unable to get an agreement for voluntary clean up of the site through the consultation exercise, the enforcement authority will serve a remediation notice. Here, statutory liability falls on the "appropriate person". In general terms, liability will initially rest upon a "Class A person" (the original polluter or a person who continues to allow that pollution to exist—the "causer" or "knowing permitter"). If a Class A person cannot be found, responsibility for remediation shifts to the current owners or occupiers of the land—a Class B person. It is by no means true, therefore, to assume that "the polluter pays".

Having identified the "appropriate persons", i.e. Class A persons or Class B persons, the next step is to exclude from that class group anyone who satisfies the exclusionary test(s) set out in the DETR Guidance. The DETR Guidance tests are to be applied in order, with the intention that they will cease to be applied once there is only one person remaining left in the group. Two of the six Class A exclusionary tests (the second and third) are the most relevant to transactions. Under the second test, liability can be excluded on the basis that "sufficient payment" has been provided for in the sale and purchase agreement in respect of the specific remediation of land, provided that the person paying for the remediation retains no further control over the land. Also, liability can be passed on to the buyer under the third test, often referred to as the "sold with information" test, where, in connection with sale of the freehold of, or the grant of a long leasehold (being more than 21 years) interest in, the land, the seller notifies the buyer of the risk, so that the buyer is aware of it. For Class B persons, exclusion will apply to persons occupying land under licence with no value or who pay rent for land and have no beneficial interest in the ownership of it, other than the tenancy itself.

In order to rely on the exclusionary tests, any sale and purchase agreement should include clauses reflecting the intention of the parties to transfer liabilities in this manner. It is also advisable to include indemnities having the same effect, as there is always the possibility that the enforcement authority may fail to apply the tests as the parties had intended. For Class B tenants, there should be no provisions in the lease passing liability. Indemnities are discussed further in 20.4.

The implications of the contaminated land regime differ depending on whether the transaction is a sale and purchase of assets or a sale and purchase of shares. On a sale and purchase of assets, the seller may still be liable after completion of the transaction as the person who caused or knowingly permitted the contamination. The buyer, who is not the original polluter prior to the transaction, is exposed to liability as a Class A person once the transaction has completed (as a causer or knowing permitter) or as a Class B person (as the current owner or occupier of the site). Where the site in question is not essential for the continued operation of the business, one possibility for the buyer might be to insist that any contaminated land be excluded from the sale and purchase agreement. Alternatively, the buyer could consider taking a lease of the land in the hope that he can rely on the Class B exclusionary test, should it be necessary. Similarly, where the business operates from a site of which only part is contaminated and the business could be operated without that part, it may be possible for the contaminated part to be excluded from the sale or, again, alternatively, a lease could be entered into in respect of that part of the land. There may be practical difficulties with this, however, as any licenses in place will apply to processes carried out on that specific land.

Where there is a concern over contaminated land, a sale and purchase of shares may be particularly attractive for the seller as the buyer will then acquire the target company together with all of its potential liabilities in respect of the contaminated land (although the seller should not assume that he will be able to walk away from these liabilities altogether and, in any event, on a sale and purchase of shares, the buyer is likely to press for appropriate warranty and/or indemnity protection where he has concerns over contaminated land).

For the buyer, concerns over contaminated land may make a purchase of assets more attractive than a purchase of shares as the seller will retain ownership of the target company which was the original polluter, although the buyer risks incurring liability as a causer or knowing permitter of the contamination unless he takes appropriate steps to clean up the site and remedy the contamination as soon as possible after completion of the transaction (ideally, after negotiating a reduction in the purchase price in order to take account of the costs of doing so).

For both parties, however, one attraction of a sale and purchase of shares is that the buyer will then acquire the target company along with all existing environmental permits, licences, authorisations, consents or other approvals which may be required in order to enable the business to operate, whereas on a sale or purchase of assets it is likely to be necessary to make arrangements for every single one to be transferred to the buyer, which is likely to involve an application to the relevant authority and may lead to a delay in completing the transaction. There may also be the risk that, for some reason, the authorities concerned will not give their consent to the transfer.

Since the introduction of the contaminated land regime, there has been little case law and few remediation notices served on polluters or land owners around the country. This has been partly due to a lack of resources at local level and at the Environment Agency. In practice most contaminated land is being remediated by voluntary agreement or as a result of the planning development system and the imposition of planning conditions.

20.3   Environmental audits and investigations

The environmental information provided by the seller following standard information requests is likely to be limited but should give an indication as to whether an environmental audit or investigation is required. It is unlikely that the seller will have a complete picture of the site history. The earlier in the transaction an environmental audit is carried out, the better the chances are of addressing any environmental issues.

The Law Society Contaminated Land Warning Card instructs solicitors to advise clients on contaminated land liabilities. Such advice includes making the necessary enquiries of the relevant statutory and regulatory bodies, recommending independent historical investigations on the site and carrying out a Phase 1 or Phase 2 audit where there is a likelihood of contamination.

That said, because of time, costs and confidentiality, environmental audits and investigations are not always carried out. There is no certainty that the transaction will go ahead and the buyer therefore may be concerned about "wasting" money on a report—equally the seller may be reluctant to allow the buyer to "trawl through" its confidential business information, particularly if the buyer is a competitor.

In the interests of time the seller may make available to the buyer reports on environmental audits or investigations carried out in the past. Although useful, this raises a number of issues for the buyer:

20.3.1   Is the report up-to-date? It may be of limited value as environmental laws and procedures change frequently. Where there are potential environmental issues, the buyer will need an up-to-date report on the site.

20.3.2   Can the buyer rely on the report? On the basis that the report was originally prepared for the seller, the buyer will need to establish whether he would have a remedy in tort or contract against the consultant who prepared it, in the event that the buyer suffers loss in reliance upon the report. Where the report is prepared for a third party no duty of care exists in tort. This could be addressed by requesting the consultant to re-issue the report in the name of the buyer, although the consultant may be very reluctant to do so unless he receives a payment in respect of the additional liabilities he is accepting.

20.3.3   Is the consultant who prepared the report credible and does he have the financial standing (ordinarily addressed by professional indemnity cover)? Even if the consultant has the right PI cover, it is worth checking on the level of aggregate claims already made against the consultant (if any).

In any event it is preferable for the buyer to commission his own audit. Audits generally fall within the categories of a Phase 1 audit or a Phase 2 audit. Phase 1 audits are most common and typically comprise a site visit and/or a desk top study. Due to their nature, Phase 1 audits cannot be relied upon to determine environmental risks as they are confined to identifying (or not) visible issues such as the presence of asbestos and underground storage tanks. The desk top study will provide information on proximity to environmentally sensitive areas in the locality, such as controlled waters and a historical survey of site documents. It may be that the Phase 1 audit flags up the necessity for a Phase 2 audit. Alternatively, in the circumstances, it may be preferable to go straight to a Phase 2 audit (or for that matter a combination of the two). Phase 2 audits, which are less common, could include intrusive surveys, such as drilling boreholes and taking soil samples for analysis. These audits are more likely to reveal any risks on site with respect to the areas tested and will provide a clearer picture of whether the site is actually contaminated. Where a Phase 2 audit is commissioned, the parties will need to enter into contractual documentation to provide terms for site access, removal of waste and liabilities for any damage caused. As the results of testing may take weeks, it is advisable to undertake this type of survey/audit at an early stage in the transaction.

20.4   Environmental warranties and indemnities

Whether the transaction proceeds as a sale and purchase of assets or of shares, the buyer will expect some protection against environmental liabilities by way of warranties and/or indemnities. The buyer may consider that warranty protection would only have limited value as the warranties will normally be subject to disclosure (see below and see also Ch.10) and it may be difficult to show claimable loss if the value of the business has not been reduced. Warranties would also be subject to the usual issues regarding mitigation and remoteness, while an indemnity will compensate for losses on a pound-for-pound basis, provided, of course, that the indemnity is appropriately drawn to cover the losses in question. On the other hand, the inclusion of environmental warranties in the draft sale and purchase agreement may help to elicit information about potential environmental problems and about the operation of the business and may also produce information which makes the buyer realise the importance of carrying out an environmental audit or investigation before going ahead or which may suggest that an environmental indemnity should be obtained or that the purchase price should be reduced. There may, indeed, be instances where the liabilities are so significant that the information revealed causes the buyer to withdraw from the transaction altogether.

Environmental indemnities are becoming increasingly common in view of the potential size of environmental liabilities and the fact that, unlike most business issues, environmental issues may not surface for a long time after completion of the transaction. For example, the buyer may continue to operate the site as an industrial site for many years but then the opportunity may arise for him to sell it at a huge price for residential development, only for him to find that the developer carries out far more extensive environmental investigations than the buyer considered appropriate when he acquired the site and that those investigations reveal contamination which caused the developer to reduce the value of his offer or even to withdraw it altogether.

The seller will normally attempt to persuade the buyer that the environmental risks are minimal or (even if that is not the case) that they are risks which the buyer should assume. Buyers, on the other hand, are likely to press for an environmental indemnity where the risks of environmental liabilities are considered to be high (typically because of the nature of the business in question or because the history of the site shows that, for example, it has in the past been used for heavy manufacturing industry or for some other activity which is likely to cause contamination) or where the buyer's financiers make it a condition of lending to the buyer that the buyer is given an indemnity against any environmental liabilities which may exist at completion. If the seller is prepared to give an indemnity, he will normally seek to limit its application in some or all of the following ways:

20.4.1   in time and amount;

20.4.2   by giving the seller conduct of any claim which may be brought against the buyer and which may give rise to a claim under the indemnity;

20.4.3   to exclude liability for costs incurred as a result of the buyer's voluntarily choosing to clean up the site without being ordered to do so or where the buyer notifies the authorities of any environmental issues.

The example given above concerning the desire to redevelop an industrial site for residential use is one which may be of particular concern to a seller who may argue that the authorities are unlikely to be concerned about the condition of the site while it is used for industrial purposes but that higher standards would be required if the site were to be redeveloped for residential use and that any indemnity should not therefore extend to additional costs which result from a change of use. Commonly an indemnity is linked to an action on the part of the buyer such as the clean-up of contamination existing at completion using a Phase 2 environmental audit as a bench mark for the identification of contamination existing at the time of completion.

Negotiations may be particularly difficult on a management buy-out where the management team may well sympathise with any reluctance on the part of the seller to give an environmental indemnity as they may well feel that they know the site well and on that basis feel reasonably comfortable that there are unlikely to be any major environmental risks. Their financiers, on the other hand, may well take a much less relaxed view and may insist upon indemnity protection. Similar issues may arise where the buyer is a "buy-in" team who know the industry well—they may well have assessed the environmental risks and have concluded that they are reasonably low but their financiers are unlikely to have the same knowledge and may therefore be less inclined to "take a view".

When drafting the indemnity it is important to be clear what the seller's exposure is. For example, where the indemnity relates to clean-up, will recoverable losses relate to any work done to remediate the site or will it simply relate to any losses or damages suffered as a result of a notice served by a regulatory body? In the former situation there is scope for the buyer to take advantage of the indemnity by undertaking unnecessary works. A "sliding scale" of cost apportionment between the seller and the buyer during the period in which the indemnity is in force is one solution, along with wording which specifies clearly what losses will be caught by the indemnity.

The issue of time limits for claims under an environmental indemnity is a difficult one as the normal limitation period for general warranty claims of "two or three audits" (see 10.7.1) is unlikely to be acceptable to the buyer, in view of the fact that it may take years before a problem emerges. The buyer will therefore argue that any indemnity should be unlimited in time.

One possible compromise may be to agree upon a time limit which is rather longer than for general warranty claims (perhaps six years) and for the buyer to make sure, as far as possible, that during that period he takes all possible steps to establish the extent of any potential environmental liability. The practical difficulty with that approach may be that there is no way of "crystallising" that liability within the agreed limitation period unless the buyer notifies the authorities of the contamination and agrees with them what needs to be done in order to clean up the site—a situation in which the seller will argue that the indemnity should not apply.

The buyer may need to carry out work after completion to bring the site into com-pliance. Here the buyer will argue that the seller should compensate him for the costs of such work and for any pollution arising until compliance is achieved. The seller, however, will not want to be liable for any pollution occurring after completion.

There are two principal ways of dealing with this: the buyer could have a right to bring a claim during a specified period post-completion in respect of the operation of the business or, again, there could be a "sliding scale" of cost apportionment between the seller and the buyer during the period in which an indemnity is in force. In these cir-cumstances, the buyer is likely to pursue activities speedily after completion to identify and rectify any environmental problems. Although not ideal for the seller, it would have the advantage of identifying environmental issues early on and preventing the buyer from allowing matters to continue and worsen, thus prompting a more serious claim at a future date.

Even where an indemnity is given the buyer may still want warranties. The seller will argue against this in negotiations and is likely to give the buyer the opportunity to carry out full independent investigations and then argue that the buyer should rely on those investigations (this may also be the seller's starting-point when the buyer requests an indemnity).

As with all other warranties, any environmental warranties will be given subject to matters disclosed in the disclosure letter (see Ch.10). If the buyer has carried out any environmental audits or investigations, the seller will wish to include in the disclosure letter a provision to the effect that there are deemed to have been disclosed to the buyer all matters revealed by any such audits or investigations (the seller may even try to go further and argue that there should be deemed disclosure of anything discoverable as a result of the investigations that were carried out, whether or not they were actually discovered).

It might have been thought unlikely that any such general disclosure would constitute "fair" disclosure as discussed in Ch.10 but, in the light of the *Infiniteland* case, which is discussed in Ch.10, the buyer should ideally refuse to accept such a wide-ranging gen-eral disclosure. If the buyer does accept disclosure of the contents of an environmental report, it should be made clear that that general disclosure will not operate to qualify warranties which require specific disclosure, such as a warranty that the disclosure letter contains details of all environmental authorisations that are in force.

If the specific disclosures reveal anything untoward, the buyer will either have to accept the disclosures or insist on an indemnity in respect of the matter or matters in question or negotiate an appropriate reduction in the purchase price, which (provided that an acceptable reduction can be agreed) the buyer may find preferable to relying on an indemnity.

As has been discussed in Ch.10, the seller will press for as many warranties as possible to be limited to matters within his knowledge, by qualifying them with words such as "so far as the seller is aware" ("the knowledge qualification"). This will typically be the case when it is difficult for the seller to be certain that a particular warranty is true. Environmental warranties are a good example of this as, while a seller may be able to warrant with absolute certainty that he has not received any notices alleging that his site is contaminated and may accept that he has to give a warranty that he has not caused any contamination of the site. As has already been mentioned, it is common for environmental issues to come to light years after the contamination was caused and the site may already have been contaminated by previous occupiers before the seller began to occupy it. One possible compromise would be to agree that the seller will give a warranty (which is not subject to the knowledge qualification) that he has not caused any contamination but for that warranty not to extend to historical contamination caused by previous owners or occupiers. An indemnity might be constructed on a similar basis but this is only likely to be an acceptable solution where the risk of historical contamination is low. Allocating the risk between the seller and the buyer for historical contamination would be an option, but could be difficult to agree in practice.

Nevertheless, sellers should be aware that buyers will be concerned about the risks of acquiring a site which is contaminated, whether that contamination was caused by the seller or by somebody else, and the seller may have to accept some degree of risk (whether by way of warranty or indemnity) unless the point is to become a "deal breaker".

If environmental warranties are to be given, the seller will normally seek to limit their application in the same way as he would with an environmental indemnity (see 20.4.1, 20.4.2 and 20.4.3) above

In the due diligence exercise, the buyer needs to think carefully about what environmental matters he requires information about. Asking for "the kitchen sink" may not be advisable unless the buyer has the resources (both legal and technical) to consider the vast amount of documentation which may be forthcoming. The buyer should consider what environmental information he requires and who will review that information. He will need to ensure that all disclosures relate to the warranties given by the seller and that he understands the implications of the disclosure.

20.5   Changes in environmental laws and procedures

It is reasonable to assume that environmental laws and enforcement processes are unlikely to be relaxed and that any future changes in environmental laws and procedures will therefore result in a stricter regime than at present. If the seller agrees to give environmental warranties or indemnities, he is likely to argue that he should not have any liability to the extent that the loss in question results from changes taking place after completion. Naturally this will not sit well with the buyer who will argue that the seller should be liable for environmental problems he has caused irrespective of whether the laws have changed since completion. In practice, the buyer may have to accept that the seller should not be liable in this situation but he should only do so on the basis that legislation which was in force at completion is deemed to be in force in the future so that, if stricter environmental legislation is introduced after completion, the seller will at least be liable to the extent that he would have been liable under existing legislation. The buyer should also make sure that the sale and purchase agreement provides that references to any current environmental laws will extend to any re-enactments of, or modifications to, those laws—in practice, this is normally achieved by a general clause to that effect in the "Interpretation" of the agreement (see, for example, cl.1.4 of Precedent 1 in App.2).

Chapter 21

TUPE

Introduction

The employment law issues which arise on the sale of a business are dependent on whether it is a sale and purchase of assets or a sale and purchase of shares. Where it is a sale and purchase of shares, there is no change in the identity of the employer and all rights, duties and liabilities owed by or to the employees continue to be owed to or by the target company. For example, if Buyer PLC ("Buyer") is buying the entire issued share capital of Target Limited ("Target") from Seller Limited ("Seller"), the employees of Target's business will continue to be employed by Target in exactly the same way as before—all that will happen is that the ownership of Target itself will transfer from Seller to Buyer.

Where it is a sale and purchase of assets, however, the position at common law was that employment contracts terminated for reasons of redundancy. The buyer was free to offer contracts of employment to whom it wished and on terms and conditions of its choosing. This changed as a result of the Transfer of Undertakings (Protection of Employment) Regulations 1981 ("TUPE 1981") (SI 1981/1794) (implementing the Acquired Rights Directive 1977), which introduced three new concepts into UK employment law:

- the automatic transfer of employees from the seller of the business to the buyer;

- an obligation to inform and consult with representatives of affected employees regarding the transfer; and

- a right of employees not to be unfairly dismissed in connection with a transfer.

If, for example, Buyer is buying all the undertaking and assets of Seller, on completion the contracts of employment of all of the employees of Seller will automatically be novated to Buyer and there will be transferred to Buyer not just the rights and powers of Seller in connection with those employees, but all Seller's duties and liabilities to them.

21.1 TUPE Regulations—amendments in 2006

The main aim of TUPE was to safeguard the rights of employees when the "undertaking" in which they are employed transfers from one employer to another. TUPE therefore does not apply to transfers of the ownership of a business which take place by way of a sale and purchase of shares because there is no change of employer.

From April 6, 2006 further changes were introduced to TUPE by the Transfer of Undertakings (Protection of Employment) Regulations 2006 (SI 2006/246) ("TUPE 2006"):

21.1.1   its scope was widened to expressly cover service provision changes;

21.1.2   there is an obligation on the seller to give to the buyer certain information about the transferring employees prior to the transfer;

21.1.3   where there is a transfer employers and employees can agree to changes to the terms and conditions of employment in limited circumstances;

21.1.4   sellers and buyers are jointly and severally liable for failure to inform and consult with the transferring employees; and

21.1.5   provisions were introduced to make it easier to transfer insolvent businesses to new employers.

References in this chapter (and indeed throughout this book) to "TUPE" are to TUPE 2006.

21.2   When does TUPE apply?

TUPE applies to a "relevant transfer". A relevant transfer covers both a business transfer and a service provision change.

21.2.1   Business transfers

A business transfer is defined as:

> "A transfer of an undertaking, a business or part of an undertaking or business situated immediately before the transfer in the United Kingdom to another person where there is a transfer of an economic entity which retains its identity" (reg.3(1)(a) of the TUPE 2006).

An undertaking must be a stable economic entity, which means an organised grouping of resources which has the objective of pursuing an economic activity. TUPE can apply to the transfer of all or part of an undertaking or business. Case law has established that the relevant transfer of part of an undertaking must be of an economic unit that, at least at the point of transfer, is severable and self-contained.

The undertaking must transfer from one person to another person, although the precise mechanics of the transfer are not relevant. A transfer from one subsidiary to another within the same group of companies will be a relevant transfer.

Retention of identity following the transfer is an important concept in TUPE and whether the economic entity has retained its identity should be apparent from the facts. All factors need to be considered when determining whether the entity has retained its identity including the following:

- what activities are carried on before and after the transfer;

- the extent of any disruption to the activities;

- whether goodwill has transferred;

- whether employees have transferred;

- whether plant, customers, stock and other tangible assets have transferred; and

- the value of the seller's intangible assets.

The weight or significance of the factors will vary according to the nature of the transaction, although no single factor will be conclusive.

If Buyer is buying a factory from Seller, is this a TUPE transfer? If there is just a transfer of physical assets (i.e. a factory, plus fixtures and fittings), there is no relevant transfer. Whether Buyer's acquisition of the factory is a TUPE transfer would depend on all the circumstances. If (for example) Seller makes men's suits and the agreement provides that Buyer will complete the work in hand and that Seller would provide work on a sub-contract basis for six months, Buyer can do with the asset (the factory) as it wishes. The orders given to Buyer are merely to tide it over until it is established: it is not a transfer of a business to Buyer. The court will draw a distinction between the transfer of physical assets and the transfer of a business. As a broad proposition, the business transfer must be the transfer of a going concern.

Similarly where Buyer is acquiring plant and machinery from Seller: that of itself would not amount to the transfer of a business. If, however, Buyer was also acquiring stock and work-in-progress and intended, in practice, to approach Seller's customers with a view to supplying them in place of Seller, the transaction may well be regarded as the transfer of an undertaking, even if the sale and purchase agreement does not expressly provide for Buyer to acquire goodwill and the benefit of customer orders and contracts. It is what happens in practice that matters.

Sales of restaurants, farms, pubs, petrol stations and so on may look like a sale or lease of land, and thereby an asset sale which appears to avoid TUPE. However, the circumstances of the sale must be carefully reviewed to see whether it is merely a transfer of land or whether it is also the transfer of a business. If goodwill transfers, the transfer will be of an economic entity. In *Premier Motors (Medway) Ltd v Total Oil Great Britain Ltd* [1983] I.R.L.R. 471 the Employment Appeals Tribunal ("EAT") held that the price of the sale of land on which two petrol stations stood was linked to the profitability of the petrol stations and so included captive goodwill. This was enough to convert a land sale into one of an economic entity, to which TUPE applied.

In *Celtec v Astley* [2006] I.R.L.R. 635, the House of Lords held that whether a transfer occurs is determined by TUPE, whatever the parties may agree, and must be deemed to have taken place at a particular point in time whatever the parties (including the employees) may have thought was the case.

21.2.2 **Service provision change**

TUPE 2006 expressly states that a relevant transfer includes a service provision change, codifying the principles long established by case law (*Suzen v Zehnacker Gebaudereinigung GmbH* [1997] I.R.L.R. 255).

A service provision change is defined (in reg.3(1)(b) of TUPE 2006) as a situation in which:

> "(i) activities cease to be carried out by a person ('a client') in his own behalf and are carried out instead by another person on the client's behalf ('a contractor')" [traditionally referred to as a contracting-out situation—a typical example of this is when a company has traditionally employed its own cleaning staff but then decides to contract the cleaning services out to an agency]; or

> "(ii) activities cease to be carried out by a contractor on a client's behalf (whether or not those activities had previously been carried out by the client on his own behalf) and are carried out instead by another person ('a subsequent contractor') on the client's behalf" [second generation contracting out-a typical example of this is when a company's cleaning services have been provided by Agency "A" but the company decides to terminate that contract and to appoint Agency "B" instead]; or

> "(iii) activities cease to be carried out by a contractor or a subsequent contractor on a client's behalf (whether or not those activities had previously been carried out by the client on his own behalf) and are carried out instead by the client on his own behalf" [contracting in—a typical example of this is when a company's cleaning services have been provided by an agency but the company decides to terminate the contract with the agency and to take cleaning in-house.]

There must therefore be an organised grouping of employees situated in Great Britain before the change whose principal purpose is carrying on services for the client; this could be a single employee. There will not be a service provision change where the contract is wholly or mainly for the supply of goods for the client's use or the activities are carried out in connection with a single specific event or task of short term duration. It is not clear if this exemption applies if there is a single event or a task of short term duration or if it applies to events or tasks that are both "one off" and are of short term duration. The better view is that it applies to the latter.

In *Hunt v Storm Communications Ltd and Others* (ET/2006) a Tribunal ruled that a public relations professional who worked on a client's account transferred under TUPE when the client changed its provider of public relations services. A client contracted out its public relations services to Storm Communications Ltd. However, Storm lost the account to another agency ("Wild Card") when the client decided to re-tender its contract for PR services. Prior to the re-tender, Mrs Hunt was employed by Storm as an Account Manager and had spent approximately 70 per cent of her time working on the client's account. Storm argued that the transfer of the contract to Wild Card amounted to a transfer under TUPE 2006 (by way of a service provision change) and as such, contended that Mrs Hunt's employment should automatically transfer to Wild Card. Wild Card disagreed. As the parties could not agree that TUPE applied, Mrs Hunt's employment was terminated at the same time that the client terminated its contract with Storm. Mrs Hunt brought proceedings for automatic unfair dismissal under TUPE 2006.

The Tribunal decided that Mrs Hunt alone constituted an "organised grouping of employees" and that her "principal purpose" was managing Storm's account on a daily basis. As she dedicated 70 per cent of her time to that account, the Tribunal was satisfied that the re-tendering of the contract to Wild Card amounted to a service provision change under TUPE. As such, Mrs Hunt should have had her employment transferred to Wild Card and her claim for automatic unfair dismissal was allowed to proceed against Wild Card.

In *Thomas-James and ors v Cornwall County Council and ors* (ET/2008) the Tribunal said that when considering whether a service provision change ("SPC") had occurred, there was no need for the identity of the activities to be retained but that there must be a connection between the activities of the outgoing contractor and the incoming contractor. It also accepted that an SPC could take place where the activities of an outgoing contractor were split between several new contractors, but said that the transferee who carried out the new activities after the SPC must be identifiable for there to be an SPC. In this case the ET said that there had been no SPC, as it was not possible to identify who the transferee was.

It should be noted that TUPE can apply to cross-border transfers also, provided the undertaking is situated in the UK immediately beforehand.

21.3   Who and what transfers?

Following a relevant transfer, broadly speaking, all rights and liabilities under the contracts of (existing) (see further 21.8 below) employees engaged in the transferred undertaking will transfer to the buyer.

21.3.1   Employees

Those employed by the seller and assigned "to the organised grouping of resources or employees that are subject to the relevant transfer" will transfer to the buyer on their existing terms and conditions of employment with continuity of service unbroken (reg.4(1) of TUPE 2006). This includes anyone employed immediately before the transfer. Liabilities in respect of anyone who would have been employed if they had not been dismissed because of the transfer or a reason connected with it (see below) will also transfer, but not the employees themselves.

It is a question of fact to be decided by an Employment Tribunal whether an employee in question is assigned to the organised grouping. There is no specific percentage of time which an employee must devote to a part of a business before being regarded as assigned to it. Employees temporarily assigned to the organised grouping may not transfer however—whether an assignment is temporary will depend on the facts (for example, the length of the assignment and whether the date has been set for the employees' return or reassignment, etc.).

If Buyer PLC is buying the whole of the undertaking and assets of Seller Limited and everyone who works in Seller's business is either an employee of Seller, self-employed (for example a consultant to the business) or working for Seller pursuant to a contract with a third party service provider (for example cleaners whose services are provided by an agency), then it may not be difficult to conclude that those who will transfer will be those who are employed by Seller at the point when the transfer takes place. The self-employed and third party staff will not. The position may, however, be less clear cut if the business in question is only one of a number of divisions of Seller—for example Seller may be a computer business with a hardware division and a separate software division and the deal may involve Buyer buying the hardware division, but with the software division being retained by Seller or possibly even being sold to a third party. Depending on the facts, there may well be many employees who are clearly assigned to one division or the other but there are likely to be other cases where the position is by no means obvious—for example, Seller may have accounts staff and an IT department who may provide their services to both divisions and who may not therefore be clearly assigned to one or the other. The position may be even more complicated when the divisions are operating from the same premises, as it may be necessary to consider the position of receptionists, security staff, cleaners, catering staff and the like.

Similarly, there may be complications where Seller is part of a group of companies and there may be employees who are employed by one company in the group but devote a considerable proportion of their time to another company in the group or who are employed by one company but seconded to another. This may typically be a problem with "head office" staff who are employed by the parent company but provide their services to different companies in the group, or who might be seconded from head office to one of the operating companies on a basis which might be short-term, but could equally be indefinite.

In one case, a chief executive who was employed by a parent company but devoted a substantial part of his working time to four subsidiaries, did not transfer under TUPE when the subsidiaries entered into agreements to sell the businesses which they owned. According to the EAT, he was not employed by the subsidiaries—the transferors—and therefore did not transfer.

By contrast, a group accountant and company secretary transferred under TUPE when the business of a subsidiary was sold, because a substantial part of the work he did was with that subsidiary. The EAT said that the correct approach is to determine whether the employee is an employee of the undertaking which has been transferred. This implies that by whom the employee is employed is not a crucial factor. The more significant issue is for whom they do the work. This tends to be the approach Tribunals take.

In one case (*Duncan Web Offset Ltd v Cooper* [1995] I.R.L.R. 633) the EAT commented that "tribunals will be astute to ensure that the provisions of the Regulations are not evaded by devices such as service companies, or by complicated group structures which conceal the real position". So in a situation where an individual is employed by Company X to work on Company Y's business and Company Y transfers that business to Company Z:

21.3.1.1 if the person only worked on Company Y's business, he might be viewed as being employed by Company X on behalf of Company Y and this would mean that he transfers; or, alternatively

21.3.1.2 the individual may have remained employed by Company X, who had other work for him to do.

Each case would very much depend on its facts and the Tribunal will look to at a number of factors. The EAT in *Duncan Web Offset*, recently approved by the EAT in *Kimberley Group Housing Ltd v Hambley* [2008] I.R.L.R 682, provided a non-exhaustive list of relevant factors:

- the amounts of time spent respectively in the transferred undertaking and in other parts of the business;

- the amount of value given to each part by the employee;

- the terms of the employee's contract of employment, insofar as they establish what the employee could be required to do; and

- how the costs of the employee's services have been allocated between different parts of the business.

The buyer should address these issues in the legal due diligence exercise, in order to establish (as far as possible) which employees will transfer under TUPE. It is in the interests of the seller to do likewise and in practice the buyer and the seller will normally agree a list of transferring employees and that list will then be included in the sale and purchase agreement in a schedule. They should, however, bear in mind that all employees who are engaged in the business in question will transfer to the buyer, regardless of whether or not they are on that list and, if there are employees of the business whom the buyer does not wish to take, it will not be enough simply to exclude them from the list. One recent case in the EAT held that dismissed employees reinstated on appeal by the transferor post-transfer had transferred to the transferee. Often indemnities can cover these situations, so that if the buyer inherits employees of which he was not aware, the seller will indemnify him against costs and liabilities.

If the seller wants to retain the employee concerned and the employee wants to stay in the employment of the seller, he could write to the seller to say that he objects to the transfer, although the employee would need to be sure that he did not end up losing all rights against the seller in those circumstances. In practice, most employers do not declare those employees that they wish to retain as part of the undertaking being transferred and, if the employee is happy to stay, this never becomes an issue.

It may be that there are employees of the seller who are seconded from another division on a short-term basis and so would not necessarily transfer but whom the buyer does want to take. This would simply be a matter of the individual agreeing to resign from the employment of the seller, serving appropriate notice and entering into a contract of employment with the buyer on completion, although the employee would then need to consider whether his continuity of employment was preserved.

These issues can be addressed by way of appropriate indemnities.

21.3.2   Seller's rights, powers, duties and liabilities

All of the seller's rights, powers, duties and liabilities in connection with the transferring employees will transfer to the buyer. Any acts or omissions of the seller before the transfer are therefore treated as having been done by the buyer (reg.4(2) of TUPE 2006) with limited exceptions. Effectively, the buyer steps into the shoes of the seller in respect of all the transferring employees and that means that the continuity of employment of the employees will not be broken as a result of the transfer. If, for example, an employee was employed in a particular business for five years, transferred to a buyer of the business under a TUPE transfer and was made redundant three years later, for the purposes of determining his redundancy entitlement he would be regarded as having been employed by the buyer for eight years.

Terms and conditions of employment also transfer—for example pay, holidays, notice periods, sick pay provisions and the like.

Accrued liabilities which can give rise to employment claims such as discrimination claims, equal pay, debts owed to the employees and other liabilities such as personal injury (employer's liability claims) will pass to the buyer. Alarmingly, the EAT in *Sodexo Ltd v Gutridge* [2008] I.R.L.R. 752 held that a transferred employee could bring a claim against a transferee employer (or buyer) where the seller was in breach of equal pay legislation and could do so at any time up to six months after the end of employment with the transferee. This is a worrying decision, especially as back pay can be claimed for up to six years, and therefore properly drafted indemnities are vital.

Although the seller and buyer are jointly and severally liable in relation to a failure to consult and inform under TUPE (see 21.5), the position in relation to liability for failure to consult on collective redundancies is not clear cut. At present, liability for failure to inform and consult on collective redundancy under the Trade Union and Labour Relations (Consolidation) Act 1992 does transfer to the buyer (*Kerry Foods Ltd v Creber* [2000] I.R.L.R. 10) but there have been conflicting decisions on this point.

21.3.3   Collective agreements and union recognition

All collectively agreed terms relating to the transferring employees transfer to the buyer. Whether union recognition also transfers would depend on whether the organised grouping of employees retains a distinct identity after the transfer (reg.6 of TUPE 2006). This means that some rights which are awarded only to recognised trade unions, such as the right to disclosure of information for collective bargaining, the right to be consulted on certain matters and the right to paid time off for union officials to carry out duties related to collective bargaining or for union training, are treated as transferred if the distinct identity is retained.

In some cases, TUPE has meant that the public sector collective bargaining machinery has transferred across into the private sector on a privatisation covered by TUPE, because of the particular terms of employees' contracts. Although it can be difficult to get out of bargaining arrangements, even where the buyer has no influence over them, there are not the same prohibitions on changing recognition agreements post-transfer as there are on changing terms and conditions (see below). The position on collective agreements now seems to be that a transferee will only be bound by collective bargains to which the transferor was a party prior to the transfer, *not* to such bargains reached by or affecting the transferor post-transfer.

21.3.4 Pension rights

The major exception to the principle of automatic transfer are old age, invalidity and survivors benefits under occupational pension schemes—these do not transfer.

Benefits under an occupational pension scheme which are not old age, invalidity or survivors benefits, including early retirement benefits do therefore transfer.[1] Similarly, if there is a contractual obligation to pay a percentage of salary into an employee's personal pension scheme, this will not fall within the exemption and the buyer must continue to honour such an arrangement.

Under the Pensions Act 2004 buyers may be required to meet specified levels of pension provisions for certain transferring employees (see Ch.22).

21.3.5 Other benefits

Some benefits and profit share or share option schemes are by their nature non-transferable. For example, employees might cease to be entitled to participate in the seller's group employee share option scheme following the transfer. It may be necessary for the buyer to provide an equivalent share option scheme; alternatively, it may have to buy out those employees' rights.

Restrictive covenants will transfer with the rest of the employees' contracts. However, the restrictive terms may protect only the seller's business, for example, where the restrictive covenants identify a range of activities or customers to which the restrictions relate. It may be that the buyer arranges for the restrictive covenants to be amended but this will be subject to the buyer's limited rights to make changes to the employment contracts following the transfer.

The operation of TUPE may produce some anomalous situations, particularly where a business is being bought from a large and diverse group of companies. For example, many years ago, a well-known tour operator diversified into the construction industry and all employees of the group, regardless of the division in which they were engaged, were given an entitlement to a free cruise after completing 25 years' service. A buyer of one of those construction businesses had to take on its employees and found itself having to honour that commitment to long-serving employees. This has recently been

---

[1] *Beckmann v Dynamco Whicheloe Macfarlane Ltd* [2002] 2 C.M.L.R. 45. The ECJ decided that enhanced pension benefits on redundancy are not benefits for old age and the liability to provide such benefits therefore transfers to a buyer under TUPE.

qualified by the Court of Appeal in *Jackson v Computershare Investor Services Plc* [2007] EWCA Civ 1065 in which it was held that an employee who transferred to the buyer in 2004 did not gain a right only available to persons employed by the buyer before March 2002. TUPE does not, the Court said, artificially create new rights that did not exist for transferring employees immediately before transfer.

21.4 Right to object

All employees have a right to object to the transfer under TUPE. If an employee objects, his/her employment is treated as terminating by operation of law, with effect from the transfer date. As there has been no dismissal, he/she will not be entitled to any statutory or contractual compensation on termination, unless it is shown that the objection was, for example, because of proposed changes to terms and conditions of employment in which case the employee may well have a right to claim unfair dismissal (see below). Objection can be made post-transfer where the employees do not know the buyer's identity pre-transfer – this may mean, for example, the buyer losing the protection of restrictive covenants in respect of key employees (see *New ISG Ltd v Vernon* [2008] I.R.L.R. 115).

21.5 Information and consultation

Buyers and sellers are required to inform and consult with appropriate representatives of any affected employees (reg.13 of TUPE 2006), not simply the transferring employees, through recognised trade unions or elected employee representatives. There are detailed provisions concerning the election of employee representatives for these purposes.

If the seller or the buyer does not recognise a trade union or have appropriate elected employee representatives, they will need to hold elections for these prior to the consultation commencing. Sufficient time therefore needs to be factored in for this and this may mean having to announce the proposed transfer to the workforce earlier than would ideally have been the case.

Where redundancies are planned at the same time as the transfer, the obligation to consult about collective redundancies may arise, depending on the number of redundancies. In practice, consultation would be through a single group of representatives in relation to both the proposed redundancies and the proposed transfer, with the two consultation periods running concurrently.

21.5.1 When should consultation take place?

The recognised trade union or elected employee representatives must be informed about the transfer and any measures flowing from it long enough before the transfer to enable consultations to take place. There is no minimum prescribed time limit and much will depend on the extent of any likely changes.

As a rule of thumb, however, even when the proposed changes are not major, the consultation period should cover at the very least one full working week and a weekend on either side of it. For example, if completion of the transaction is scheduled for Monday February 28, the consultations should begin not later than Friday February 18.

This requirement may cause concern for a seller as, inevitably, once the workforce has been told that a sale of the business is proposed, the deal will become public knowledge and the seller will be reluctant to begin the consultation process without the certainty of a signed sale and purchase agreement. In practice, therefore, it is often the case that the consultation process will only begin once the parties have entered into a sale and purchase agreement which is conditional only on those consultations taking place and which contains appropriate provisions governing the way in which the consultations will be carried out. The agreement will specify the agreed completion date and will require the consultations to take place between the signing of the agreement and completion.

21.5.2 What information must be given?

The following information must be given (Reg.13(2) TUPE 2006):

- The fact of the transfer, when it is to take place and the reasons for it.

- The legal, economic and social implications of the transfer for the affected employees.

- The measures which the employer, carrying out the information and consultation exercise, envisages it will take in connection with the transfer in relation to any affected employees. If no "measures"' are to be taken then that fact should be stated. The term "measures" has been held to have the widest scope, covering any action step or arrangement taken in connection with the transfer.

- The seller must also state the measures that the buyer envisages it will take in relation to transferring employees in connection with the transfer. Again, if the buyer envisages taking no measures, then that fact should be stated.

21.5.3 Obligation to consult

Both the seller and the buyer are under an obligation to consult with appropriate representatives if the buyer or the seller envisage, in connection with the transfer, taking measures in relation to any affected employees. Consultation must be with a view to seeking agreement and not merely an opportunity for the representatives to air their views. Therefore, employers must consult in good faith in all areas including proposed redundancies.

There is a limited defence for failure to inform and consult if the employer can show that there were special circumstances making it not reasonably practicable for information to be given or consultation to take place. In practice, however, this is likely to be construed very narrowly and even then an employer must do what it can. Commercial confidentiality will not be a sufficient reason to make the defence available.

Very often, the measures proposed are those of the buyer in relation to the transferring employees. Strictly speaking, the buyer cannot commence consultation on these measures before the transfer, but he is required to consult after the transfer takes place. In practice, many buyers will be afforded access to transferring employees to enable consultation to begin pre-sale.

21.5.4 **Remedies for failure to inform and consult**

Failure to comply with the obligations to inform and/or consult entitles an employee representative to bring a claim in the Employment Tribunal within three months of the transfer. A successful claim could result in an award of up to 13 weeks' actual pay for each affected employee. In awarding compensation the Employment Tribunal will start from 13 weeks' pay and then consider any mitigating circumstances which should reduce the award of compensation.

Because the buyer and the seller are jointly and severally liable for failure to inform and consult, claims are likely to be brought against either or both parties. The Tribunal can apportion liability between the parties (under the Civil Liability Contributions Act 1978) and will consider arguments put forward. A seller may argue that it was not reasonably practicable for him to give the information to the employees because the necessary information was not given to it by the buyer. In such a case the seller should tell the buyer that he intends to rely on that reason for his (the seller's) failure to comply and the buyer may become a party to the proceedings.

21.6   **Employee liability information**

TUPE 2006 introduced is a new obligation on the seller to provide information to the buyer about the transferring employees at least 14 days before the transfer, although most of this information has traditionally been provided by way of due diligence. The information that must be provided includes the following:

21.6.1   the identity and age of the employees who will transfer;

21.6.2   information contained in the employee's particulars of employment under s.1 of the Employment Rights Act 1996 (i.e. terms and conditions of employment);

21.6.3   information on any collective agreement affecting those employees which will still have effect after the transfer;

21.6.4   any disciplinary proceedings taken against any employee or grievance brought by an employee in the last two years (until April 2009 this will be confined to grievances) to which the Employment Act 2002 (Dispute Resolution) Regulations 2004 (SI 2004/752) applied);

21.6.5   any legal action taken by transferring employees against the seller in the previous two years and any potential legal action where the seller has reasonable grounds to believe that such actions might occur.

Not only is the obligation to give the information at least 14 days before the transfer, but the seller must provide written notification of any changes following the disclosure. The parties cannot contract out of this obligation and as a result any indemnity in relation to any liability arising from failure to comply with it may possibly be seen as contracting out and may therefore be ineffective.

If the seller does not provide the relevant employee information, the buyer can bring a claim in the Employment Tribunal which can award any sums which it considers just and equitable having regard to the buyer's loss and any contractually agreed terms between the parties. This is subject to a minimum award of £500 for each employee in respect of whom the information was not provided or was defective.

The statutory requirement to identify transferring employees and provide information means that the common practice of anonymising such information as part of the due diligence exercise (for compliance with the Data Protection Act) will not be necessary. It may, however, be appropriate for the practice of anonymising to continue where a specific buyer has yet to be identified and information is given to a number of potential buyers, for example, in a data room.

21.7   Changing terms of employment

21.7.1   Reason for variation

Any changes in the employees' terms of employment will be void if the sole or principal reason for the variation is:

- the transfer itself; or

- a reason connected with the transfer which is not an economic, technical or organisational reason entailing changes in the workforce ("an ETO reason").

This is irrespective of whether the changes are agreed with the employees before or after the transfer. However, it is possible for the employer and employee to agree changes to employment terms where the sole or the principal reason is:

- unconnected with the transfer; or

- connected with the transfer but is an ETO reason.

The ability to make changes to terms and conditions which are connected with the transfer, pre- or post transfer is very limited in practice. It is only permissible where there is an ETO reason which entails changes in the workforce. Changes in the workforce has been held to require a change in numbers, i.e. a reduction in staff or a change in the functions of the employees. Few contractual changes will involve changes in the workforce, as defined. Most buyers would wish to vary terms and conditions in order to harmonise the terms of transferring employees with the remainder of their workforce. Changes to terms and conditions purely for reasons of harmonisation are not permitted however and, even where employees agree to the changes, these agreements would be void and ineffective if tested.

If the changes to the terms and conditions are part of a wider reorganisation and have nothing to do with the transfer, then they will be effective. There is no specific period after which it is safe to say that the connection with the transfer has been broken—each case will be assessed on its own facts. In fact, in *Regent Security Services Limited v Power* [2008] I.R.L.R. 66 it was held that transferred employees can rely on amended terms that they regard as beneficial, whilst disregarding adverse changes as void.

21.7.2 Constructive dismissal

An employee has a right to resign and claim constructive (and unfair) dismissal where the seller or buyer commits a repudiatory breach of contract. This is expressly provided for in reg.4(11). Such a dismissal may be unfair under the normal unfair dismissal principles or it may be automatically unfair under reg.7(1) (if transfer-connected) and not for an ETO reason. Regulation 4(9) introduced a new right for transferring employees to resign if the transfer involves a substantial change to their working conditions which would be to the employees' material detriment. In this situation the employees will be treated as having been dismissed with notice by the employer. They will therefore not be able to claim pay in lieu of notice, but will still have their statutory rights (i.e. unfair dismissal). It remains to be seen how many claims arise out of this.

21.8 Protection against dismissal

21.8.1   Any dismissal will be automatically unfair where the sole or principal reason for the dismissal is:

- the transfer itself; or

- a reason connected with the transfer that is not an economic, technical or organisational reason entailing changes in the workforce ("an ETO reason").

If the employer establishes an ETO reason, then there will be no automatic unfair dismissal claim. The case will go to mainstream unfair dismissal law, where the Tribunal has to be satisfied that the decision to dismiss was reasonable in all the circumstances.

Protection against dismissal is given to those employees who transfer and to any other employee who is dismissed as a result of the transfer, whether by the seller or by the buyer. For example, if the buyer dismissed one of his existing employees in order to accommodate the transferring employees, such a dismissal could be automatically unfair because it is connected with the transfer. There is no specific period after which the automatic unfairness rule will cease to apply, although the greater the time between the dismissal and the transfer, the greater the possibility of arguing that the connection between the two has been broken.

21.8.2 Pre-transfer dismissal

Where a dismissal occurs prior to the transfer, the reason for such a dismissal will be important in determining who would be liable for unfair claims.

However, the seller and the buyer may apportion liability between themselves by way of an indemnity. Employees must have at least 12 months continuous service in order to make a complaint of unfair dismissal for TUPE-related reasons. However, this qualifying period does not apply where the employee brings a claim for unfair dismissal for asserting certain rights under TUPE related to being an appropriate representative for information and consultation purposes.

Reason for Dismissal	Automatically Unfair?	Who is liable?
Transfer itself	Yes	Buyer
Reason connected with transfer but it is *not* an ETO reason	Yes	Buyer
Reason connected with transfer which is an ETO reason	No, not automatically unfair but it could be procedurally unfair	Seller
Reason *not* connected with transfer	No, not automatically unfair but could be unfair under normal rules	Seller

It will be for the employee to prove that the dismissal was connected to the transfer. Where the dismissal happens at the time of the transfer this may be relatively easy for the employee to show. The employer will have to prove that there is no connection between the dismissal and the transfer—for example, that there was some other reason for the dismissal, such as performance, misconduct or a decision to reduce the workforce for a reason unconnected with the transfer itself.

Where a dismissal is potentially automatically unfair, the employer may avoid liability if he can show that the reason for the dismissal was an ETO reason and that it was procedurally fair. Demonstrating an ETO reason will involve producing evidence relating to profitability or market performance, or management or organisational structure. A dismissal which is effected in order for the sale to go through will not fall within the scope of an ETO reason.

Entailing changes in the workforce has been held to mean a reduction in the numbers of employees or changes in the functions of employees. Dismissal related to an attempt to harmonise terms and conditions will not be for an ETO reason because it is unrelated to the numbers or functions of employees (*Delabole Slate Co Ltd v Berriman* [1985] I.R.L.R. 305).

In many transactions, the buyer will look at the workforce and conclude that he does not want to take all of them. He will therefore seek to make it a term of the deal that those employees whom he does not want to take will be dismissed by the seller before completion.

In those situations, two alternatives are possible:

21.8.2.1 The seller could dismiss the employees (ostensibly for redundancy) prior to completion and the buyer could give the seller an appropriate indemnity. The difficulty with this is that the seller will be relying on the ETO defence to avoid unfair dismissal but the reason for the dismissal is simply so that the sale can go through, which is not sufficient to fall within the ETO category. The buyer would be liable for the unfair dismissal claims because the reason for the dismissal is a reason connected with the transfer and is not an ETO reason. This has been confirmed by the Court of Session in *Hynd v Armstrong and Others* [2007] I.R.L.R. 338. The maximum to which each employee would be entitled is over £60,000 (at current rates), as well as his notice period, and the buyer could even pick up redundancy payment liabilities. This is often too risky an option to take, especially if large numbers of employees are involved.

21.8.2.2 The employees could be allowed to transfer to the buyer on completion and then notice of redundancy could be served by the buyer. It is often more likely that the buyer would be able to demonstrate a redundancy situation, i.e. reorganisation or a diminution in the requirement of the business for employees to carry out particular work and so would have a fair reason for dismissal. Provided that a fair procedure is followed, therefore, the buyer would not be liable for compensation for unfair dismissal claims. A question which often arises in practice is when the consultation about the redundancies should take place. It is believed, though yet untested, that the seller and buyer together can consult about the proposed redundancies before the transfer (concurrently with the TUPE consultation) but cannot serve notice of redundancy until the buyer becomes the employer. This will mean that the buyer has to pay for the notice period.

Alternatively, the purchase price could be reduced in order to take account of the buyer making redundancies following the transfer.

Sometimes it is agreed that the employees concerned will transfer to the buyer but that the seller will indemnify the buyer against any costs of any dismissals taking place within an agreed period after completion. In those situations, the seller should look for appropriate wording in the sale and purchase agreement to prevent the buyer from claiming under the indemnity for dismissals by reason of redundancy that have become unfair dismissals.

21.8.3 Redundancies

There are some key points to make about redundancies in connection with a transfer. It is outside the scope of this book to address these in detail but some key points are highlighted here. If the seller or the buyer proposes to dismiss as redundant 20 or more members of staff at one establishment, within a period of 90 days or less, it is required to notify the Department for Business, Enterprise and Regulatory Reform ("DBERR") in writing of the proposal at least 30 days before notice is given of the first of the dismissals (or at least 90 days if there are to be 100 or more redundancies). Failure to do so can result in a conviction and a fine of up to £5,000.

21.8.3.1 There are minimum consultation periods depending on the number of proposed redundancies—either 30 days or 90 days before termination notices are served. Consultation under TUPE and redundancy consultation is often done at the same time and run concurrently.

The redundancy consultation should cover ways of:

● avoiding the dismissals;

● reducing the number of employees to be dismissed;

● mitigating the consequences of the dismissal.

For the purposes of consultation, the employer should disclose in writing to the appropriate representatives of affected employees:

● the reasons for its proposals;

● the numbers and descriptions of staff whom it proposes to dismiss as redundant;

● the total number of staff of any such description employed by the employer at the establishment in question;

● the proposed method of selecting the staff who may be dismissed;

● the proposed method of carrying out the dismissals, with due regard to any agreed procedure, including the period over which the dismissals are to take effect; and

● the proposed method of calculating the amount of any redundancy payment (over and above statutory redundancy payments).

Failure to comply with these obligations can lead to Tribunal claims and awards of up to 90 days' pay per member of staff.

One interesting point to note, if a buyer is proposing to make redundancies following the transfer, is that its existing workforce may form part of the selection pool for redundancy if they are at the same establishment, rather than simply the transferred employees. The selection for redundancy will have to be based on a fair and transparent process and this will mean looking at the whole of the buyer's workforce at any one establishment. As noted above, it is also uncertain whether collective consultation on post-transfer dismissals can begin before the transfer and the best course of action is to confine the whole process to the post-transfer period.

21.8.3.2 Parallel with the obligations of collective consultation set out above, every member of staff with at least a year's continuous service has an individual right not to be unfairly dismissed. In relation to redundancy, this involves warning and consulting with the individual about the proposal to terminate his/her contract by reason of redundancy before notice of such termination is given. The consultation with individuals should involve an explanation of, and opportunity to challenge, how the member of staff has been selected and the consideration of possible alternative employment.

When conducting individual consultation, the seller and the buyer should follow the minimum statutory procedures for dealing with dismissals under the Employment Act 2002 (Dispute Resolution) Regulations 2004 (SI 2004/752) (expected to be repealed in April 2009 but representative of good practice. This means that the employer should put the reasons why he is considering dismissal in writing, arrange a face-to-face meeting with the member of staff and then inform the member of staff of the decision and of his/her right to appeal. An appeal meeting should be held and the member of staff should be informed of the outcome of that appeal.

21.9   Provisions in the sale and purchase agreement

Even if the sale and purchase agreement is entirely silent on the point, if there is a relevant transfer, TUPE will apply and the contracts of all employees of the business will transfer to the buyer on completion. As has already been seen, that means that the buyer will automatically assume pretty much all of the seller's duties and liabilities in relation to those employees. The seller may therefore be reasonably content for the sale and purchase agreement to say nothing about employees, although in practice most sellers will seek an indemnity against any liability which may rebound on the seller as a result of any acts or omissions of the buyer towards the employees after completion. More importantly for a seller, any threat from a buyer to change the terms and conditions of transferring employees could rebound in constructive dismissal liabilities against the seller.

The buyer will, under TUPE, stand in the shoes of the seller as from completion and will assume responsibility for any acts or omissions of the seller towards the employees as if they had been acts or omissions of the buyer himself. The buyer will therefore be concerned to establish through legal due diligence the extent of the liabilities that he may be assuming and he will almost certainly require indemnities from the seller in respect of any liabilities that he may inherit under TUPE as a result of acts or omissions on the part of the seller while the employees were in the employment of the seller. Particular concerns of the buyer which should normally be covered by indemnity will include:

21.9.1   The risk of any of the employees resigning after completion and claiming that they had been constructively dismissed as a result of the conduct of the seller before completion.

21.9.2 The risk of an employee bringing a claim against the buyer after completion for race, sex or other discrimination as a result of the conduct of the seller before completion.

21.9.3 The risk of equal pay claims, on the basis that an employee has not received equal pay to a comparator of the opposite sex who is in the same employment and carries out like work, or work of equal value, or work related as equivalent to that of the comparator.

21.9.4 There may be employees who remain employed in the business as at completion but who have been given notice by the seller which is not yet expired and which may give rise to a claim for unfair dismissal or for a redundancy payment (and possibly also for race, sex or other discrimination).

21.9.5 There may be arrears of wages or salaries for which the buyer would become liable under TUPE (this is a particular concern if the seller is in financial difficulties when any indemnity is likely to be worthless or where the buyer is buying from a receiver or administrator, who is most unlikely to be prepared to give any indemnity).

21.9.6 There may be outstanding claims at completion for industrial illness or injury and those claims may not even have been notified to the seller as at completion. A particular concern of the buyer is likely to be that, some time (perhaps many years) after completion, somebody who was employed in the business at completion will bring a claim in respect of ill health or disability which is claimed to have resulted from the individual's employment with the seller or (more likely) both from his employment with the seller before completion and with the buyer after completion. A typical example of this is deafness, which is likely to have developed over many years. Case law has established that the benefit of employers' liability insurance also transfer to the buyer, which should be of some comfort in this regard, though not if the insurers cannot be traced.

The sums involved may be significant and the buyer should be particularly concerned that he does not assume liability for any employer's liability claims which are not covered by his insurance.

In practice, buyers of businesses will often receive employer's liability claims from employees who ceased to be employed in the business before completion but who, understandably, do not appreciate that the buyer bought the assets of the business rather than the share capital of the seller (this is particularly likely to be the case where the buyer has adopted the seller's corporate name after completion). As those employees were not employed at completion, those liabilities will not have passed to the buyer under TUPE but the buyer is nevertheless likely to require an indemnity in respect of claims made by former employees in order to cover the costs of defending any claim which might be brought against the buyer in error.

As has already been seen, the parties are likely to agree a schedule of employees or transferring employees for the purposes of the sale and purchase agreement but there is always the possibility that other employees of the seller may subsequently claim that they also transferred to the buyer under TUPE—possibly because the schedule was inaccurate but possibly also because the individual concerned claims to have been assigned to the business in question, notwithstanding that the parties had concluded that that was not the case (as has already been seen, the position is often far from being clear cut). The buyer will therefore want an indemnity against any claims which may arise as a result of any such individual being found to have transferred under TUPE—the liabilities to be covered by the indemnity would include any salary or other remuneration which the individuals concerned may seek to recover from the buyer and the cost of the buyer terminating the contract of employment of any such person.

Clause 11.2 of Precedents 3 and 4 in App.2 contain examples of the indemnities which a buyer would normally expect.

21.10 Insolvency situations

Two main changes were made by TUPE 2006 in connection with insolvency and corporate recovery situations:

21.10.1 Introduction of provisions to assist the survival of failing businesses. This would include administrations. If a business is under insolvency proceedings with a view to liquidating assets, TUPE does not apply.

21.10.2 Special provisions apply where the seller is subject to insolvency proceedings which are under the supervision of an insolvency practitioner and are not "with a view to the liquidation of the assets". To make failing businesses more attractive to a prospective buyer, some of the existing debts to the employees will be met by the Secretary of State out of the National Insurance Fund rather than passing to the buyer—these include statutory redundancy pay or notice monies. Debts that fall outside the payments made or which exceed the statutory limits would pass to the buyer. There is also more scope to vary employees' contracts in a rescue situation with the agreement of employee representatives. The seller, buyer or insolvency practitioner must agree the changes with the appropriate representatives of the employees which are the recognised trade union, or elected representatives. The agreement recording the changes must be in writing and be signed by the representatives. Prior to signature, the employer must provide all the affected employees with a copy of the agreement and any guidance which they may reasonably need in order to understand it. The varied terms must not breach any other statutory entitlement. If the sole or the principal reason for the change is the transfer itself which is not an ETO reason then it must be made with the aim of safeguarding the employment opportunities by ensuring the survival of the undertaking or business (or part of the business or undertaking).

Individual employees need not agree to the changes to their contracts for it to be effective. It is sufficient that the representatives of affected employees have agreed.

21.11 Piercing the corporate veil

Although TUPE does not generally have any application on a sale and purchase of shares, it is possible that such a transaction may be followed by a restructuring of the business of the target company or its integration into one of the existing businesses of the Buyer and that this may lead to a TUPE transfer taking place.

In *Millam v The Print Factory (London) 1991 Ltd* [2007] EWCA Civ 322, the Court of Appeal held that the employees of a company whose shares had been purchased by another company had transferred to that other company under TUPE. The tribunal found (as a matter of fact) that the activities of the target company were being carried out by its new holding company (the buyer) and this did not involve any piercing of the corporate veil.

The background is that M was employed as a printer by FPL, which was acquired by MCP in 1999 by way of a sale and purchase of shares. Both FPL and MCP went into administration separately in 2005 and the defendant company acquired the assets and undertaking of MCP in 2005. M was dismissed the day before the transfer. He brought a number of claims against the defendant and argued that, immediately before the defendant's acquisition of the assets of MCP from the administrator, he had been employed by MCP and not by FPL. The Employment Tribunal found the following facts.

Following the acquisition of the share capital of FPL by MCP, M had been told (correctly) that the identity of his employer was not changing. However he was subsequently told, in August 2000, that his employment had been continued "under the TUPE regulations".

The employees had been told at the time of the sale that it was MCP's intention fully to incorporate the business of FPL into its own.

Following the acquisition of FPL, MCP paid the employees' wages and administered the pension scheme; FPL had no payroll department of its own.

FPL and MCP continued to be separate legal entities, but there were various combined board meetings (although FPL also had its own separate quarterly meetings).

Following the acquisition of FPL, MCP began to handle FPL's sales function and a single sales representative moved from FPL to MCP. All other FPL staff continued to carry out their functions at FPL's premises. When FPL went into administration, some 50 per cent of its work was being carried on for MCP. In addition, work was transferred from MCP to FPL, partly to make FPL appear more attractive to potential buyers.

The Tribunal concluded that M's real employer was MCP rather than FPL, because the business in which he worked was not actually in the hands of the legal entity in whose name it was run (FPL) but was instead in the hands of the holding company, MCP, which in practice directed its affairs.

The defendant appealed successfully to the Employment Appeal Tribunal (EAT), which held that the Tribunal had erred in law by lifting the corporate veil in the circumstances in question and that the lack of independence (typical in a parent-subsidiary relationship) did not mean that the subsidiary's business had passed to the holding company. No assets or employees had been transferred to the holding company in order to cause TUPE to apply and the transfer of one member of the sales staff did not bring about a transfer of the whole of the undertaking. Also, the EAT considered that the fact that the pay and pension arrangements were under the control of the holding company was of no real significance, as this was frequently the case in groups of companies.

M appealed to the Court of Appeal, who allowed the appeal, holding that it was MCP which was M's employer. The Court of Appeal concluded that the Tribunal had not found that the activity was being carried on by FPL and then pierced the corporate veil to attribute that activity to MCP. Rather, it had found, as a matter of fact, that the activity was being carried on by MCP.

Although the EAT had noted the absence of factors which it would have normally have expected to have seen in a TUPE transfer, none of those factors was of itself conclusive as to whether or not a TUPE transfer had in fact occurred. On the evidence, a tribunal of fact could properly have concluded that there had been a transfer of a business to which TUPE applied and so there was no legitimate ground on which the EAT could have interfered with the ET's conclusion.

The EAT also concluded the legal structure of a corporate group was important but could not be conclusive in deciding the issue of whether, within that legal structure, control of a business had (as a matter of fact) been transferred.

This case makes it clear that the courts will look at the substance of a transaction, rather than its form, in determining whether there has been a TUPE transfer and will consider whether, as a matter of fact, there has been a transfer of the business in question from one owner to another. Buyers will need to bear this in mind where they intend to integrate the business of the target company into one of the buyer's existing businesses (or into the existing businesses of one of the buyer's other subsidiaries) and buyers should also proceed with caution if they are intending to integrate key functions (such as the financial or administrative function or the sales force) or transfer them to "head office".

Chapter 22

Pensions Issues

22.1 Background: UK pension provision

Pension provision in the UK falls into two broad types: defined benefit (final salary) and defined contribution (money purchase).

Under the former, members are promised a particular level of pension related to salary at, or near, retirement, or averaged over their working lifetime. Employee contributions are usually a fixed percentage, with employers paying the balance of the cost of the scheme. Since the cost is affected by many factors, not all of them under the employer's control, it can be both volatile and escalating. Consequently, defined benefit schemes have become increasingly unfashionable in recent years. Many have been closed, either for new entrants or for new accruals, but changes in legislation have meant that it is usually not viable to wind them up altogether (this is discussed further below).

Defined contribution schemes have the advantage that the costs are a fixed percentage of salary, giving employers much greater cost control, and they have been in the ascendancy. Benefits are based on whatever the individual's "pot" will buy at retirement. They are therefore subject to the vagaries of investment return and annuity rates, with the risks effectively being borne by the employees.

Both types of arrangement are generally registered pension schemes with HMRC which means that they enjoy important tax reliefs and concessions. Schemes can be established either on an occupational pension scheme basis—generally established under trust by the employer—or as personal pension schemes—where each individual has his own pension arrangements, which may or may not be contributed to by his employer. Historically, occupational pension schemes and personal pension schemes were subject to different regimes for tax approval but this distinction has disappeared with the introduction of the new simplified tax regime from April 6, 2006. However, the distinction between occupational and personal schemes remains valid in relation to the Transfer of Undertakings (Protection of Employment) Regulations 2006 (SI 2006/246) ("TUPE") and this is discussed in more detail below.

A stakeholder pension is a personal pension with a capped charging structure. Employers of more than four qualifying employees are required to make stakeholder pensions available to their employees and to deduct any contributions the employees wish to make from their wages. However, employers are not at present required to contribute to such arrangements. For this reason, although employers are required to designate schemes, in practice many of those schemes have no take-up by employees.

It is also quite common for senior employees to have some form of pensions top-up promise in their contracts of employment, where the employer agrees to increase the pension payable to the employee if the pension provided by the main pension scheme does not provide a high enough level of benefit. Such pension promises need to be looked at carefully, as a seemingly innocuous sentence in a service agreement can lead to an expensive commitment.

Both defined benefit and defined contribution schemes can be used to contract out of the earnings-related portion of the state pension ("S2P"). For occupational schemes, this is done on a blanket scheme-wide basis. For personal pensions, it is customary for the individual to be given the choice.

22.2   Pensions issues on share sales and purchases

Where the target company has its own pension arrangements, then the documentation relating to the pension scheme in the share sale and purchase agreement will be relatively straightforward, consisting only of warranties and indemnities relating to the scheme. The buyer will, of course, have no choice as to whether to take on the scheme; careful due diligence will therefore be key, especially where there is a defined benefit scheme in place.

If the target company participates in a group scheme, then further issues fall to be considered. The first is that, in the case of a defined benefit scheme, the buyer may wish to negotiate a transfer payment from the seller's scheme to the buyer's scheme which is higher than the transfer payments that the individual members are entitled to by law. It is customary for there to be a pension schedule to the agreement which sets out the timing, etc. for the making of the transfer payment and which has appended to it the actuarial assumptions to be used in calculating the transfer payment.

The pension schedule may also make arrangements in these circumstances for the employees to remain as members of the seller's scheme for a short while after completion. This can be helpful where the buyer does not have his own pension arrangements already in place, as it gives the buyer a breathing space in which to decide what type of scheme to offer and to go through the practicalities of setting it up.

Whether or not there is a period of continued participation, if the target participates in a defined benefit scheme, then it may trigger a debt on the target under s.75 of the Pensions Act 1995. The impact of this is considered in more detail below.

22.3   Pensions issues on assets sales and purchases

If the company from which the assets are being acquired operates its own occupational pension scheme, then it may be possible for the buyer, or a new company which has been established to buy the assets, to take over as the principal employer under that scheme. However, care should be taken to ensure that this is possible under the scheme's governing documents and that a winding up of the scheme is not inadvertently triggered—especially where it is a defined benefit scheme, because of s.75 considerations (see below). In other circumstances, the employees may transfer either to a new scheme established by the buyer or to an existing pension scheme run by the buyer. In that case, the considerations regarding calculation of transfer payments and possible continued participation are as discussed above for share sales.

Going forward, the obligations of the buyer will depend upon whether the seller's pension arrangements are occupational pension schemes or personal pensions. Personal pension schemes do not fall within the occupational pension schemes exemption from the operation of TUPE. The rights of the employees to the existing level of employer contributions to their personal pensions will therefore pass under TUPE. There may be practical issues for the buyer if, for example, it operates its own group personal pension scheme, but using a different provider, and wishes to harmonise benefit provision going forward.

Under TUPE, rights to old age, invalidity and survivors' benefits under occupational pension schemes do not pass. However, in the case of *Beckmann v Dynamco Whichelo Macfarlane* [2002] All E.R. (EC) 865, it was held by the European Court of Justice that this exemption was to be construed very narrowly; enhanced early retirement terms on redundancy did not fall within the exemption and the right to those enhanced terms passed under TUPE. It is possible, therefore, for this valuable right to pass under TUPE without the equivalent right to the remaining benefits of the scheme, leaving the new employer with an unfunded obligation to provide the rights.

Since April 6, 2005, the provisions of s.257 of the Pensions Act 2004 and of the Transfer of Employment (Pension Protection) Regulations 2005 (SI 2005/649) give some limited protection to pension rights. The provisions apply only where there is a TUPE transfer. Those covered are, as one would expect, members of the seller's scheme and employees who are waiting to complete eligibility criteria for entry to the seller's scheme; however, those employees who are eligible for membership of the buyer's scheme but have not taken up the offer of membership are also covered. This needs to be borne in mind at the due diligence stage, to ensure that employee data provided clearly identifies people in this category, as well as scheme members.

There is no requirement for the scheme to be provided by the buyer to be a mirror image of the seller's scheme. The buyer has complete freedom of choice to decide whether to provide benefits on a defined benefit or a defined contribution basis and whether the scheme to be provided should be contracted in or contracted out of S2P.

If the scheme to be provided is a defined contribution scheme, then the obligation is for the employer to match the employees' contributions to the scheme up to a maximum of six per cent of salary—salary for this purpose being basic salary only. It should be noted that, if the scheme provided by the buyer is contracted out, then the contributions referred to above must be in addition to the minimum contributions required for contracting out. At the time of writing, there is no case law on the point, but it appears that the employees have some degree of choice on the contribution matching; the Regulations do not distinguish between mandatory and voluntary contributions. If the standard rate of both employee and employer contributions is, (say) four per cent, but an employee chooses to pay six per cent, then the employer will be required to match the full six per cent.

Should the buyer wish to offer a defined benefit scheme, then that scheme must provide benefits at least at the level of the "reference scheme test" for contracting out of S2P—in broad terms, a pension for the employee of one-eightieth of the average of the final three years' salaries for each year of membership, with a 50 per cent survivor's pension.

If the buyer fails to implement any new pension arrangements, then the employees have the right to bring claims for breach of contract and may have possible constructive dismissal claims. There are, however, no penalties under the Pensions Acts of 1995 and 2004. This is to be contrasted with the position where an employer fails to designate a stakeholder arrangement, where civil penalties can be imposed.

22.4   Debts on the employer under s.75 of the Pensions Act 1995

The detailed operation of debts under s.75 was revised in March 2008 by the Occupational Pension Schemes (Employer Debt and Miscellaneous Amendments) Regulations 2008 (SI 2008/1068).

A statutory debt will arise when an employer ceases to employ active members of the scheme, so long as at least one of the other sponsoring employers continues to do so. The calculation basis for the debt begins with calculating the "liability share", which (unless the scheme rules provide otherwise) is the departing employer's proportionate share of the scheme's full buy-out deficit (i.e. the cost of securing all benefits under the scheme by way of annuity purchase), based on the liabilities in relation to its own employees' period of pensionable service with it (including any transferred-in benefits).

Where the trustees cannot determine where any liabilities should be attributed, or if the cost of the determination would be disproportionate, the Regulations provide some rough and ready solutions. Liabilities can be attributed to a member's last employer, or assigned to one or more employers in a reasonable manner. If all else fails, and the trustees cannot determine whether an employer is a member's last employer and cannot attribute the liabilities to any employer, then those liabilities are to be treated as "orphan", i.e. not attributable to any specific employer and shared by all.

The approach to valuing assets and liabilities is similarly practical. Asset valuations can be updated from the most recent accounts and there will be no need for an audited asset statement. Liabilities can be updated from the most recent actuarial valuation.

The liability share represents the full amount of the debt. However, the Regulations provide for a number of ways in which lower amounts can be paid up front. The departing employer can enter into a "scheme apportionment arrangement" whereby a smaller amount is paid on exit and the shortfall is apportioned amongst the remaining employers, provided that the trustees believe that the remaining employers will be able to make the contributions needed and that they are satisfied that the security of members' benefits is not adversely affected. Pensions Regulator approval to the arrangement is not necessary, but it will be a "notifiable event" under the Pensions Act 2004. Detailed guidance on the notifiable events regime is set out at the Pensions Regulator's website: *http://wwww.thepensionsregulator.gov.uk*

A "withdrawal arrangement" can be entered into, with part of the debt being paid by the departing employer and the remainder being guaranteed by another party or parties. Again, the trustees must be satisfied that the guarantors will have sufficient financial resources to be able to meet the guaranteed amount as and when it falls due. As long as certain requirements can be satisfied, then this, too, would not need Regulator approval, although it should be noted that various events fall under the "notifiable events" regime while there is a guarantee in place.

A variant on the withdrawal arrangement is a "regulated withdrawal arrangement" which, as the name suggests, requires Regulator approval and is subject to the same considerations regarding the "notifiable events" regime. Regulator approval can be sought in advance of triggering the employer debt.

Finally, the Regulations introduce the concept of a "regulated apportionment arrangement" for use in the limited circumstances where the scheme is either already in an assessment period for possible entry to the Pension Protection Fund or the trustees believe that there is a reasonable likelihood that the scheme will enter one in the next 12 months. Such arrangements are subject to the consent of the trustees, to Regulator approval and to receiving no objection from the PPF.

Guidance on the procedures outlined above is published by the Pensions Regulator on its website, *http://www.thepensionsregulator.gov.uk*. It is recommended that the scheme trustees, the relevant parties' pensions advisers and the scheme actuary should be involved in the process as soon as possible. It is appreciated that there may be issues of confidentiality, particularly where a deal is price-sensitive. The Pensions Regulator's office is always prepared to deal with initial queries and outline proposals on a "no-names" basis (although, of course, nothing is binding on them at that stage) and it is quite routine in the present climate for trustees to sign confidentiality agreements.

22.5   The "moral hazard" provisions of the Pensions Act 2004

The sale of the shares or business may also be the subject of a clearance application to the Pensions Regulator. Under the moral hazard provisions of the Pensions Act 2004, the Pensions Regulator is given power to impose a contribution notice on parties to the transaction and those connected or associated with them if a defined benefit occupational pension scheme subsequently goes into winding-up, the Regulator believes that the transaction was undertaken with a view to reducing or avoiding a s.75 debt and that it is reasonable in the circumstances to issue the notice. The Regulator has the power to look back six years from the date of the wind-up. It will therefore be seen that the obligation could be imposed on one of the parties at a time when it has nothing further to do with the scheme.

The Regulator also has power to impose a financial support direction where a participating employer in a defined benefit scheme is a service company or "insufficiently resourced". In those circumstances, it is not necessary for the Regulator to infer any lack of good faith on the part of the employers.

The Pensions Regulator's standpoint is that a pension scheme in deficit should be treated in the same way as any other substantial unsecured creditor and that trustees should think like bankers in relation to the unsecured liabilities. The Regulator will wish to know about all events that could have a materially detrimental effect on the ability of a scheme to meet its liabilities.

In order to assess whether a particular event has a financially detrimental effect on the pension creditor, it is necessary to consider where the pension creditor sits in the allocation of proceeds in the event of the insolvency of the employer, and then consider the impact of that event on the potential allocation.

It is possible to apply to the Pensions Regulator for advance clearance that the Regulator will not seek to impose a contribution notice or financial support direction in the future as a result of a particular event known as a "Type A" event. Type A events are defined as events which are materially detrimental to the ability of a scheme to meet its pension liabilities, usually because they will prevent the whole of a debt on the employer under s.75 of the Pensions Act 1995 from becoming due or recoverable. Clearance is given only on the facts as presented to the Pensions Regulator at the time of the application for clearance and it should be noted that, if the facts presented are incomplete or misleading, then the clearance notice could be invalidated. The clearance procedure is entirely voluntary.

Most transactions in relation to the sale of shares or assets are arguably not Type A events because of the arm's length nature of the transaction. However, if they result in the change of a group structure, which could be seen as weakening the overall employer covenant to the scheme, then they are regarded as Type A events, for which it may be prudent to seek clearance.

In particular, it should be noted that the payment of consideration for these shares or assets to a company which does not participate in the buyer's scheme or which is used to pay off creditors or make dividends may in itself be an action which could lead to the imposition of a contribution notice and is therefore a relevant factor which should be mentioned in any clearance application.

Guidance on the clearance procedure is available on the Pension Regulator's website. This guidance is updated periodically in the light of experience, most recently in April 2008, and it is recommended that the website should always be consulted for the up-to-date position before embarking on a transaction that might require a clearance application. Time to complete the clearance application process should be factored in to the timetable for the deal. The comments made above regarding confidentiality and the involvement of trustees and advisers are equally applicable to clearance applications.

22.6   Due diligence—share sales and purchases

It is important for the buyer to commence his due diligence in relation to the pension arrangements of the target company as early as possible, as the funding of any defined benefit pensions may become a serious factor in the negotiation of the purchase price.

The following information is usually requested:

- copies of the governing documentation of each scheme or other arrangement;

- copies of any announcements and explanatory booklets given to employees, including pension sections in staff handbooks;

- copy of the latest actuarial valuation;

- membership data (if a bulk transfer payment is being sought, then the data should be sufficient to enable the buyer's actuary to make a good estimate of the amount that ought to be transferred);

- details of contributions;

- confirmation that each scheme is treated as a registered pension scheme with HMRC;

- confirmation as to whether each scheme is contracted out;

- details of any discretionary benefits;

- the names of the current trustees;

- details of any complaints, including complaints to the Pensions Ombudsman, against the company and/or the trustees;

- details of any designated stakeholder pension arrangement;

- details of the scheme's investments;

- copies of the trustees' report and accounts, ideally for the last three years.

It will be appreciated that sellers are often unwilling to disclose all of this information at an early stage. In particular, actuarial information may be resisted where the target company is only one of a number of participating employers.

22.7 Due diligence—assets sale and purchases

It is sometimes argued that, as full pension rights do not pass under TUPE, very little information is required in relation to the seller's pension scheme. The difficulty with this approach is that the buyer needs to be aware of benefits to which TUPE would apply, such as enhanced early retirement pensions on redundancy or benefit promises contained in service agreements. It is therefore recommended that buyers should issue initially a questionnaire along the lines laid out above for share purchases; they can then take a view later on how much detail is required, once the nature of the current pension provision is known.

If the buyer is contemplating any period of continued participation in the seller's scheme, then thorough due diligence is essential. It should be noted that if the buyer participates in a seller's defined benefit scheme, even for a short period, on leaving the scheme a s.75 debt would be triggered and the buyer should be in possession of enough information to make an informed decision as to whether the cost of doing so makes continued participation an unattractive option.

22.8   Warranties and indemnities

Paragraph 9 of Sch.5 to Precedents 1 and 2 contains specimen warranties for inclusion (as appropriate) in share sale and purchase agreements and these can be adapted (with such changes as may be necessary) for use in connection with assets sale and purchases.

22.9   Special considerations on management buy-outs

Whilst it is customary in management buy-outs for minimal warranties to be given, as the buy-out team will have been closely involved in the day-to-day running of the company or business, special consideration needs to be given to the pensions warranties. Particularly in a large group, it is customary for pensions administration to be undertaken by a third party or by a head office function and for strategic decisions on pensions to be taken at parent company level. Accordingly, the buy-out team may know very little more about the pensions arrangements than an arm's length purchaser and it may be appropriate for more extensive warranties to be given in this area than in certain others (see Ch.25).

With regard to future benefit design, most commercial funders prefer to see defined contribution arrangements, for the certainty of cost control. However, in some industries—railways and electricity being obvious examples—employees may have a statutory right to a particular level of benefit provision. Consideration of how this is to be accomplished is necessary at an early stage.

22.10   The role of the trustees

As part of the due diligence exercise, if it is intended that the buyer will take on the target's/seller's pension arrangements, it is important for the buyer to find out who the current trustees of any occupational pension scheme are, especially where that scheme is a defined benefit scheme.

22.11   Conclusion

This is a highly specialised area and it is essential that parties should take specialist advice on any transaction. This chapter should be regarded as no more than a general overview of the subject and, for further information, reference should be made to the specialist text books.

There are so many permutations that it is impractical to produce precedents for a "pensions schedule" to a sale and purchase agreement which covers all eventualities and again, therefore, reference should be made to specialist text books for these and (in any event) specialist advice should be obtained.

Part 4
Special Situations

Chapter 23

Offers for Unquoted Companies

Chapter 9 identifies a number of situations in which it may be necessary or desirable for a sale and purchase of shares to proceed by way of a formal offer from the buyer to the shareholders of the target company rather than through a sale and purchase agreement. This chapter assumes that the company concerned is either a private company or an unquoted public company. Offers for publicly quoted companies are beyond the scope of this chapter (or indeed of this book).

23.1   Informal approaches

Before a formal offer document is prepared, a prospective buyer may wish to make an informal approach to target shareholders about their likely response to an offer. This may be done orally or in writing. Care must be taken not to contravene the provisions of the Financial Services and Markets Act 2000 ("FSMA")—in particular, those relating to financial promotions.

An informal approach, whether written or oral, to target shareholders may amount to a financial promotion for the purposes of the FSMA and, as discussed in 2.4, s.21 of the FSMA provides that a financial promotion must be issued or approved by an authorised person (i.e. one who is authorised under the FSMA to carry on certain regulated financial services activities) unless an appropriate exemption applies. Whether or not an informal approach does amount to a financial promotion is likely to depend on the circumstances and the precise wording of the communication (see 2.4). Contravention is a criminal offence and any agreement to which the financial promotion relates may be unenforceable against the other party, who may also be entitled to reimbursement and possible compensation.

As seen in Ch.2, there are many exemptions to the financial promotion prohibition contained in the Financial Services and Markets Act 2000 (Financial Promotion) Order 2005 (SI 2005/1529) (the Financial Promotion Order). In addition to those discussed in 2.4, the exemption contained in art.43 may be relevant to an approach by a potential buyer to shareholders of the potential target company.

This exemption covers non-real time and solicited real time communications by a company to (amongst others) its members and may be useful where, for example, a buyer has made an informal approach to the board of a target company and the board wish to write to shareholders giving details of the approach that it has received. The board may, however, only take advantage of this exemption where the buyer is offering cash—it will not apply where the buyer is offering shares or other securities as consideration for the proposed acquisition.

Even if a buyer is proposing to offer cash for the shares in the target company, he cannot avoid the restrictions imposed by s.21 of the FSMA by having the target company make the offer to its own shareholders on behalf of the buyer, in reliance upon the exemption in art.43 of the Financial Promotions Order, as the buyer would be "causing a communication to be made" without first having it approved by an authorised person and this would contravene s.21(13) of the FSMA.

23.2   The offer

If the City Code on Takeovers and Mergers ("the Takeover Code") applies and no waiver can be obtained (see below), then an offeror will have no choice but to make an offer which is regulated under the Takeover Code.

Whether or not the Takeover Code applies, the offer must be made or approved by an authorised person, unless it falls within an exemption. The exemption which is most likely to be relevant to a non-Takeover Code offer is that contained in art.64 of the Financial Promotion Order for any communication which is communicated in connection with a takeover offer for a "relevant unlisted company". This is defined in the Financial Promotion Order as a company which is unlisted at the time the offer is made and has been unlisted throughout the period of ten years immediately preceding the offer, which means that the target must be a private company to which the Takeover Code does not apply.

The offer must be for all the shares of the target company and so the exemption cannot be used for a partial offer. The offer must also satisfy the requirements set out in Pt I of Sch.4 to the Financial Promotion Order:

23.2.1   The offer must be recommended by all directors of the target company, other than any director who is the offeror or a director of the offeror.

23.2.2   If the offeror holds 50 per cent or less of the equity shares and makes an art.64 offer for non-equity shares or debentures, he must also make an offer for the remaining equity shares which he does not already hold.

23.2.3   The offer must be open for at least 21 days.

23.2.4   The consideration must be cash, shares or debentures of the offeror or any combination of the three.

Article 64 sets out the information which must accompany the offer and other information which must be made available for inspection. These include the most recent audited accounts of the target company and advice to the directors of the target company on the financial implications of the offer, which must be given by a competent person who is independent of, and has no substantial financial interest in, the target company or the offeror.

The requirements of art.64 are very specific and reasonably onerous and, in practice, it may well be as quick and almost as cheap to have the offer document issued by, or with the approval of, an authorised person.

Article 62 contains a further exemption (discussed in 2.4) which may be relevant and which relates to the sale of a body corporate. This provides that, subject to the satisfaction of certain conditions, the financial promotion restriction does not apply to any communication by or on behalf of a company, a partnership, a single individual or a group of connected individuals which relates to the acquisition or disposal of shares in a company. As discussed in 2.4, some of these conditions are difficult to interpret and prospective buyers should take advice before attempting to rely on this exemption but, nevertheless, it may apply in some cases.

23.3 Documents

Whether an offer is made under the Takeover Code or art.64 or otherwise, the documents required will be much the same. The main documents will be an offer document (despatched to all the target company's shareholders) and irrevocable undertakings entered into by some or all of those shareholders, before despatch of the offer document, containing, among other things, an irrevocable commitment to accept the offer.

23.3.1 Offer document

The requirements of the Takeover Code as to the contents of the offer document and of art.64 as to the information which must accompany the exempt communication differ in a number of respects and, in particular, the Takeover Code requires the provision of certain financial information about both the buyer and the target company for the last three years. In relation to the buyer, this includes a description of its financial and trading prospects. Unless the consideration includes shares in the buyer, art.64 only requires information about the assets and liabilities of the buyer from its most recent audited accounts and for the offer to be accompanied by the latest audited accounts of the target company.

Conventionally, an offer for a listed company is made by the offeror's financial adviser on behalf of the offeror. This is not necessary in relation to an unlisted company and, provided that s.21 of the FSMA is complied with, or a relevant exemption (such as art.64) applies, the buyer may make the offer himself.

The offer document will specify the terms and conditions subject to which the offer is made and the most important of these is that the offer will be subject to the offeror receiving acceptances of the offer from shareholders holding a specified proportion of the share capital of the target company and (for reasons explained below) that figure will almost invariably be 90 per cent. The buyer will, however, almost certainly reserve the right to waive that and any other condition.

If the articles of association of the target company contain pre-emption rights on the transfer of shares, the offer will almost certainly have to be conditional on the passing of a special resolution of the target company to amend its articles in order to permit the transfer of shares pursuant to acceptances of the offer and, in practice, there are various other matters on which the offer is likely to be expressed to be conditional and, depending on the circumstances, these are likely to include:

23.3.1.1   No indication that the transaction will be referred to any merger control authorities (see Ch.18).

23.3.1.2   No other action being taken or threatened by a governmental or other regulatory body or the like which may impact on the transaction.

23.3.1.3   The obtaining of all necessary authorisations, permissions and approvals for the acquisition and their not being revoked.

23.3.1.4   All authorisations, permission and approvals which are necessary for the carrying on of the target business remaining in full force and effect and there being no suggestion of any intention to revoke or vary any of them or not to renew them.

23.3.1.5   (In the case of a sale and purchase of shares) the target company not recommending, declaring or paying any dividend (other than as previously agreed) or making any changes to its authorised share capital (or agreeing to do so).

23.3.1.6   No material litigation being instituted or threatened by or against the target company or business.

23.3.1.7   No material changes to any material contracts.

23.3.1.8   No changes to the contracts of employment of any of the directors or senior executives.

23.3.1.9   No lease, mortgage, charge or other security being granted over any of the assets of the business.

23.3.1.10 (Particularly in the case of a sale and purchase of shares) no indebtedness or material contingent liability, being incurred.

23.3.1.11 No new material contracts being entered into.

23.3.1.12 No steps being taken for winding-up, administration or receivership.

23.3.1.13 No breach of any warranties that have been given to the offeror.

23.3.1.14 No material adverse change in the financial position or prospects of the target company or business.

These are only examples of the conditions to which the offeror may wish to make his offer subject and what is appropriate will depend upon the circumstances of each particular case. Before entering into irrevocable acceptances of the offer and before agreeing to recommend the offer to the other shareholders, the directors of the target company will doubtless seek to qualify as many of these conditions as possible by reference to materiality. Where the target company has a number of subsidiary and associated companies, the offeror will normally want to extend those conditions to cover all such companies (so that, for example, the offeror would have the right to withdraw his offer if there was litigation against a subsidiary).

The directors may well argue that the offeror should only have the right to withdraw if the circumstances in question were material to the target "group" as a whole—i.e. which would be material looking at the target company and its subsidiary and associated companies together. This can be a difficult point as, for example, there may be a material adverse change to the financial position of one subsidiary but the rest of the group may be unaffected. Similarly, a claim for (say) £100,000 against a subsidiary may be very material to that subsidiary but might not be regarded as material in the context of the target group as a whole. Whether or not that qualification will be appropriate will, inevitably, depend on all the circumstances and on the respective bargaining positions of the parties.

23.3.2 **Irrevocable acceptances**

Before incurring the expense of making the offer, the buyer will want to be as certain as he can be that he will ultimately acquire the entire issued share capital of the target company. He will therefore, as a condition of making the offer, almost certainly require irrevocable undertakings to accept the offer (irrevocable acceptances) from shareholders holding at least 90 per cent of each class of shares. This will put the buyer in a position where he is entitled compulsorily to acquire the balance.

For example, the directors of Target Limited (Target), Tom, Dick and Harriet, together with their families, may between them own 60 per cent of the issued share capital of the company. Buyer PLC (Buyer) may put forward terms for the acquisition of Target which are acceptable to them and their families, but the remaining 40 per cent of the shares may be held between a number of distant relatives, private investors and ex-employees, who may have little or no contact with Tom, Dick and Harriet or with the company. Buyer will not want to acquire the company with potentially awkward minority shareholders but it may simply be impractical to persuade all of the shareholders to enter into a single sale and purchase agreement, with the result that the only realistic approach is for Buyer to make an offer to each of them.

Buyer is unlikely to be prepared to incur the expense of due diligence and of making the offer without being confident that, ultimately, it will be able to acquire all of the shares and so will insist on Tom, Dick and Harriet and their respective families, together with as many "friendly" shareholders as possible, giving irrevocable acceptances. If it is possible to obtain irrevocable acceptances in respect of at least 90 per cent of the shares (or, if there is more than one class, then from the holders of at least 90 per cent of each class) then Buyer will, once it has made its offer and reached the 90 per cent threshold, know that it will be able to compel any remaining shareholders to sell by using the "squeeze out" procedure set out in ss.974–991 of the Companies Act 2006. If, however, it is not possible to obtain irrevocable acceptances from the holders of 90 per cent, Buyer will have to consider whether it is prepared to go ahead on the basis of irrevocable acceptances from the holders of a smaller percentage (for example, 75 per cent, which would at least mean that any remaining minority shareholders would be unable to block a special resolution of Target).

In the case of an offer for an unquoted company, irrevocable acceptances, may contain many of the provisions which are typically included in a share sale and purchase agreement and will commonly include:

- warranties and indemnities in respect of the target company, its assets and liabilities and its business;

- covenants not to compete with the business of the target company.

If the offeror intends to rely on the "squeeze-out" procedure to acquire the shares of a dissenting minority, then it is essential to ensure that the terms of any irrevocable acceptances do not prevent him from doing so. For example:

23.3.2.1 In order to take advantage of the compulsory acquisition procedure, the offeror must obtain 90 per cent or more of the relevant class of the target's shares pursuant to the offer. Shares which at the date of the offer are already held by the offeror are to be discounted in determining whether the buyer has acquired 90 per cent (s.974(2) of the Companies Act 2006).

"Shares already held by the buyer" will include shares which the buyer has contracted to acquire, whether unconditionally or subject to conditions being met (s.975(1) of the Companies Act 2006) but not shares which are the subject of a contract intended to secure that the holder of the shares will accept the offer when it is made and entered into by deed and for no consideration, for a consideration of negligible value or for consideration consisting of a promise by the Buyer to make the offer (s.975(2) of the Companies Act 2006).

The only consideration given by an offeror in any irrevocable acceptance should therefore be a promise by the offeror to make the offer.

23.3.2.2 The offer must be on terms which are the same in relation to all the shares (or class of shares) to which the offer relates.

This can cause concerns where, for example, some shareholders only are required to give warranties and indemnities or enter into non-competition covenants or where there are shareholders who are prepared to give irrevocable acceptances but refuse to give warranties or indemnities or to enter into non-competes—this is typically the case with venture capitalists ("VCs") and with minority shareholders who have taken no active part in the running of the company.

The prevailing view among the legal profession is that the statutory requirements will be satisfied provided that the "economic" terms—the amount and form of the consideration, the payment terms and the like—are the same for all shareholders. However, there is no case law on this point and buyers should be aware of the possibility of a dissenting minority arguing that the statutory requirements have not been satisfied because (for example) not all shareholders are being asked to give warranties. Even the inclusion of a right of set-off against some shareholders, but not others—for example, in respect of warranty or indemnity claims might be enough to take the offer outside the statutory requirements, particularly if it is structured in such a way as to be, to all intents and purposes, an adjustment to the purchase price.

The "squeeze out" procedure would not be available if some shareholders (typically, management) were offered an earn-out or similar arrangement while other shareholders received a fixed amount.

Precedent 37 in App.2 is an example of a reasonably simple form of irrevocable acceptance, which does not contain any warranties, indemnities or restrictive covenants and is therefore likely to be appropriate for a shareholder holding a small number of shares or who has had little or no involvement with the business or for a VC shareholder. In any event, it would not be unduly difficult to adapt it in order to incorporate appropriate warranties, indemnities and/or restrictive covenants.

It should be noted that it allows the shareholder giving it to withdraw the acceptance if a third party offer is received which is materially higher than the offer to which the irrevocable acceptance relates but, in practice, on an offer for an unquoted company, the offeror is likely to resist that very strongly.

23.4   Takeover Code offers

A Takeover Code offer is in many ways similar to an art.64 Offer but, if the Takeover Code applies, its Principles and Rules will need to be followed and the Panel consulted, which will inevitably involve additional complexity, time and cost for the exercise.

The application of the Rules to an offer for an unquoted company is not entirely straightforward, as they are generally more appropriate to listed company bids. The Rules which commonly give rise to specific concerns in the context of an offer for an unlisted company are:

23.4.1   The board of the target company must obtain competent independent advice (Rule 3.1). Where the target is an unquoted company, its auditors often fulfil this role, but inevitably this means additional expense.

23.4.2   If the offeror proposes to contact private individuals or small corporate shareholders with a view to seeking an irrevocable undertaking from them, then the Panel must be consulted in advance (Rule 4.3) and will wish to be satisfied that the proposed arrangements will provide adequate information about the nature of the commitment sought, a realistic opportunity to consider whether or not that commitment should be given and to obtain independent advice if required (Note to Rule 4.3).

23.4.3   An offeror must appoint a receiving agent to receive acceptances of the offer (Rule 10). In a quoted company bid, the offeror's registrars normally fulfil this role, but the appointment of registrars may be regarded as involving unnecessary expense on an offer for an unquoted company. The Panel should therefore be approached to establish whether alternative arrangements would be acceptable.

23.4.4   An offer must not normally be subject to conditions which depend solely on subjective judgments by the directors of the offeror or the fulfilment of which is in their hands (Rule 13).

           If the offeror wants to make the offer conditional and no breach of the warranties in the irrevocable undertakings having occurred or come to light before completion, it is advisable to seek specific confirmation in advance from the Panel that this will be acceptable.

           In any event, the offeror should not invoke any condition so as to cause the offer to lapse, unless the circumstances which give rise to the right to invoke the condition are of material significance to the offeror in the context of the offer. The offer must be judged by reference to the facts of each case at the time the relevant circumstances arise (Note 2, Rule 13: Panel Executive Practice Statement No. 5).

23.4.5   The offeror may not agree a special deal with favourable conditions with some of the shareholders of the target company (Rule 16). This may make it difficult for a buyer to incentivise management shareholders, via an earn-out, while other shareholders simply receive their consideration on completion. Rule 16 and General Principle 1 (which requires all shareholders to be treated equally) will not permit this.

           It may be possible to deal with this by giving management an equity shareholding (or leaving them with one) but the Panel will be concerned that there should be risks as well as rewards for management associated with such an interest. In addition, where the offeror and the management of the target together hold more than five per cent of the equity share capital of the target, the Panel will normally require these arrangements to be approved at a general meeting of the target's shareholders (Note 4, Rule 16). The Panel must be consulted in these circumstances.

Alternatively, the buyer could structure the offer so that all shareholders are offered either an earn-out based deal or payment on completion and could then make sure that irrevocable undertakings to accept the appropriate options are received before the formal offer is made. The difficulty with this, however, is that it may not be possible to obtain irrevocable acceptances from all of the shareholders. In addition, the Panel will only permit such an arrangement if the right to receive the earn-out is not linked to the continued employment of management and this may defeat the whole purpose of such an arrangement.

23.4.6   When the purchase price is to be satisfied, in whole or in part, in cash, the offer document must include confirmation by an appropriate third party that sufficient resources are available to the offeror to satisfy the cash element in full on acceptance of the offer (Rule 24.7).

Rule 24.7 states that in exceptional circumstances, with the consent of the Panel, a conditional form of confirmation may be allowed and it may be necessary to seek the consent of the Panel to a conditional confirmation where part of the consideration is, for example, dependant upon an earn-out.

23.4.7   The offer document must contain a statement to the effect that, except with the consent of the Panel, the consideration will be settled in full, without any set-off (Rule 24.11). The Panel will only grant consent in exceptional circumstances and this may make it difficult for the buyer to obtain a right of set-off in respect of warranty and indemnity or similar claims.

In any event, a Takeover Code offer document generally requires more detail than is required on an art.64 offer and will be subject to a strict (and, generally, inflexible) timetable, whereas art.64 merely requires offers to be open for 21 days. The Takeover Code also requires various announcements to be made in the course of a Takeover Code offer. All of these factors and the need to appoint an authorised person to make or approve the offer are likely to make a Takeover Code offer significantly more costly than an art.64 offer and so a buyer is likely to be keen to avoid having to make a Takeover Code offer, if at all possible.

23.5   Avoiding having to make a Takeover Code offer

If the buyer wishes to avoid the expense and complications of having to make an offer to which the Takeover Code applies, it may be possible to obtain a waiver of the requirements of the Takeover Code, failing which the only alternative is likely to be to have the target company re-registered as a private company.

23.5.1   Obtaining a takeover code waiver

The Panel is generally prepared to disapply the provisions of the Takeover Code for a specific transaction where the target company has very few shareholders and the Panel considers it inappropriate or unduly onerous to apply the Takeover Code.

The Panel has stated that this procedure will normally only be available for target companies with ten or fewer shareholders. Where, however, the shareholders in question are related in some way, such as members of the same family, then the Panel will usually treat them as a single shareholder for the purposes of this test.

A Takeover Code waiver will, in any event, only be granted if all of the target shareholders agree to it. The Panel will require written confirmation from each of them that they waive their rights under the Takeover Code and will be concerned to ensure that they have had their Takeover Code rights fully explained to them, either at a meeting or in writing, and have had the opportunity to take independent professional advice before giving this confirmation.

23.5.2   Re-registering the target company as a private company

If it is not possible to obtain a Takeover Code waiver from the Panel (for example, because the target company has more than ten shareholders) then, if the target company is an unquoted public company and the only reason why the Takeover Code would otherwise apply is the fact that it is a public limited company, the buyer will be able to avoid having to make an offer which complies with the Takeover Code if the target company re-registers as a private company before the offer is made.

Re-registration will require a special resolution of the target company's shareholders and 21 days' notice of the meeting will be required, unless it is possible to hold it on short notice. Even if it is possible to hold the meeting on short notice, if holders of not less than five per cent of the company's issued share capital or any class thereof, or over 50 of the company's members, vote against the resolution, the re-registration cannot take place until the expiry of a 28-day objection period after the date of the resolution (s.90(1) of the Companies Act 2006). It will therefore be necessary to take into account in the timetable for the transaction the notice period for the meeting (where necessary) and also the possible need to wait until the end of the 28-day period before the offer can be made. It will also be necessary to consult with the Panel about the proposed re-registration, as the Panel will be concerned to ensure that the shareholders appreciate the effect of the re-registration on them. The Panel will expect the notice of general meeting to be accompanied by a circular which contains a broad summary of the proposals resulting in the need to re-register, with a clear explanation of the rights under the Takeover Code which the shareholders will give up as a result of the re-registration. The Panel has published pro forma suggested wording for this, together with its recommended procedure for consulting with the Panel about the proposed re-registration.

23.6   Drag along rights

As explained in Ch.9, it is sometimes necessary or desirable for a sale and purchase of shares to proceed by way of a formal offer from the buyer to the shareholders of the target company because the articles of association of the target company contain "drag along" rights which entitle certain shareholders or (more typically) the holders of a specified majority of the equity share capital of the target company to compel a dissentient or unresponsive minority to accept an offer which is received from a third party and this is a convenient point at which to discuss "drag along rights" in a little more detail:

23.6.1   For example, Tom and Dick each own 333 (i.e. one-third) of the 999 issued ordinary shares of £1 in Target, with the remaining 333 shares being held as to 167 by Harriet and as to 166 by Harriet's ex-husband, Harry. The directors of the company (Tom, Dick and Harriet) receive an approach from Buyer PLC, which indicates that it would like to buy Target for £1 million, i.e. a price of approximately £1,000 per share. That offer is acceptable to Tom, Dick and Harriet but is not acceptable to Harry. If (as is likely) Buyer is only interested in proceeding if it is able to acquire the entire issued share capital of Target the transaction may fall at the first hurdle as, if Buyer were to make an offer for Target, the level of acceptances would only be 83.33 per cent, well short of the 90 per cent threshold required for the purposes of the "squeeze out" procedure set out in ss.974–991 of the Companies Act 2006.

23.6.2   It is possible, however, that the articles of association of Target may contain a provision to the effect that, if an offer is received from a third party, which is acceptable to the holders of not less than (say) 75 per cent of the issued equity share capital of Target, those shareholders who accept the offer may compel the remaining shareholders to accept it and so Tom, Dick and Harriet would be able to exercise that drag along right and compel Harry to sell his shares to Buyer.

23.6.3   A drag along provision will almost certainly provide for any shareholder who is being "dragged along" to sell his shares at the same price, and on the same terms, as those shareholders who are exercising the drag along right and so, in the example, Buyer would have to buy Harry's shares at the same price per share (£1,000) as the price which it has agreed to pay for Tom, Dick and Harriet's shares.

23.6.4   It is important to consider the wording of a drag along provision very carefully before seeking to invoke it, as some articles of association contain drag along provisions which require a formal offer to be made to all shareholders, whilst others are drafted in such a way as to avoid this. They will almost invariably require the same price per share to be paid to all shareholders but, particularly where a formal offer is necessary, may require all shareholders to sell on the same terms and, as when a Buyer wishes to rely on the statutory "squeeze-out" procedure, this can cause concerns when not all shareholders are required to give warranties or indemnities or enter into restrictive covenants.

23.6.5   In the example given above, what if the articles of association of Target did not contain a drag along provision? Tom, Dick and Harriet, between them, hold more than 75 per cent of the share capital of Target and may therefore consider the possibility of convening a general meeting to pass a resolution in order to amend the articles to incorporate a drag along right.

In the case of *Constable v Executive Connections Ltd* [2005] All E.R. (D) 156, the claimant (C) held five per cent of the share capital of a company which received an offer from a prospective buyer which he did not accept. A general meeting was held at which a resolution was passed amending the articles of association of the company (amongst other things) by the adoption of a drag along provision. C sought a declaration that the resolution was invalid (as an abuse by the majority shareholder of its powers) and an injunction preventing the company from taking steps to implement or enforce the amendment to the articles and then applied for an interim injunction pending trial or a further order in similar terms.

The court rejected the submission that there was no serious issue to be tried and granted the injunction.

This was not, of course, a full hearing but the case reinforces the view that would in any event have been taken by most cautious lawyers, that amending the articles of association in order to introduce a drag along right, with the specific intention of compelling an unwilling shareholder to accept a particular offer, may be open to challenge. In any event, even if amending the articles in this way is not open to challenge, any attempt actually to invoke the new drag along right could well precipitate an application to the court under s.994 of the Companies Act 2006 (protection of company's members against unfair prejudice).

There may be another solution if the company's articles of association incorporate regs 32(b) and 33 of Table A (1985 version) or a similar provision: reg.32(b) allows a company, by ordinary resolution, to consolidate and divide its share capital into shares of larger amounts than its existing shares, while reg.33 provides that, if a consolidation of shares results in any members becoming entitled to fractions of a share, the directors may, on behalf of those members, sell the shares representing the fractions for the best price reasonably obtainable to any person and distribute the net proceeds of sale in due proportion among those members. Regulation 33 also allows the directors to authorise some person to execute a transfer of the shares to the buyer.

In the example, Tom, Dick and Harriet may wish to consider the possibility of passing a special resolution to consolidate the shares in Target into shares of (say) £200 each. That would leave Harry with a fractional entitlement (166/200) and the directors would be entitled to sell the shares representing his (and any other) fractional entitlement and then distribute the net proceeds of sale. Assuming that the directors were satisfied that the offer from Buyer was the best price reasonably obtainable, Tom, Dick and Harriet could enter into an agreement with Buyer under which they would agree to sell their shares and procure the sale of Harry's shares using the mechanism contained in reg.33. The directors would then distribute to Harry 166/999 of the net proceeds of sale.

This may be less open to challenge than an amendment to the articles to introduce a drag along right, provided that the power to consolidate shares and to sell fractional entitlements was already in the articles: the directors would simply be exercising a power which was already conferred on them by the articles.

There is no case law on this point, but this approach is worth considering where there is a recalcitrant minority shareholder holding more than 10 per cent and where there is no drag along provision in the articles.

Chapter 24

Dealing With a Listed Company

The requirements of the FSA for companies whose shares are traded on the Official List are set out in Chs 10 to 13 of the Listing Rules issued by the FSA under Pt VI of the FSMA ("the Listing Rules").

They apply to the acquisition or disposal of assets of all kinds but the comments in this chapter are limited to the acquisition and disposal of companies and businesses. It does not attempt to consider in any detail the question of whether a prospectus will be required under the Prospectus Rules. The Listing Rules contain extensive rules regarding the content of circulars issued by listed companies, which are also beyond the scope of this book.

These requirements are generally a matter for the listed company concerned and its advisers but parties who are buying from, or selling to, a listed company will need to be aware of their potential implications on the costs of the transaction and on the timetable to completion.

In particular, where the Listing Rules require prior approval of the shareholders of the company concerned, there will have to be a gap of at least 14 clear days between signing the sale and purchase agreement and completion and there will therefore be issues regarding the conduct of the business between signing the agreement and completion and the date from which the warranties "speak" (as discussed in 10.6).

24.1 Classes of acquisition

Transactions are divided into four classes for the purposes of the Listing Rules: Class 1 Transactions, Class 2 Transactions, Class 3 Transactions, and "reverse takeovers" (Listing Rule 10.2.2). In addition, there are particular requirements (set out in Ch.11 of the Listing Rules) for "related party" transactions. Save where the transaction is a related party transaction, every transaction is classified by assessing its size in relation to that of the listed company which is proposing to enter into the transaction and the comparison is made by using the percentage ratios which result from applying the class test calculations which are set out in Annex 1 to Listing Rule 10. The class tests may be varied or modified in the case of certain specialist companies.

At various points in this chapter, the class tests are discussed by reference to the example of the purchase by Buyer PLC (Buyer) of the entire issued share capital of Target Limited (Target) from Adam and Eve (Sellers). Most of the comments will, however, apply equally to a purchase of a business and to sales as well as to purchases.

24.2   The class tests

The class tests are as follows:

24.2.1   *The gross assets test:* the gross assets which are the subject of the transaction divided by the gross assets of the listed company concerned. In the example, therefore, it would be necessary to divide the gross assets of Target by the gross assets of Buyer. For this purpose, the gross assets of Buyer or (as the case may be) of Target are its total non-current assets, plus its total current assets. Where the transaction involves the acquisition of an interest in an undertaking (as defined in s.259(1) of the Companies Act 1985) which gives rise to consolidation of the target or the disposal of an interest in an undertaking which will result in its assets no longer being consolidated in the accounts of the listed company concerned, the "gross assets the subject of the transaction" means the value of 100 per cent of the target's net assets, even if a lesser interest is acquired or disposed of. If the transaction would not give rise to consolidation or (as the case may be) to assets no longer being consolidated, then, "gross assets the subject of the transaction" means, in the case of an acquisition, the consideration together with any liabilities assumed or, for a disposal, the assets attributed to the interest in question in the listed company's accounts. In the case of an acquisition of assets, the figure is taken to be equal to the consideration or, if greater, the book value of the assets to be acquired.

If, therefore, Buyer was not acquiring the entire issued share capital of Target but nevertheless was acquiring an interest which required Target to be consolidated in the accounts of Buyer, the "gross assets the subject of the transaction" would nevertheless be the value of 100 per cent of Target's assets. If, however, the interest was not of a size which required Target to be consolidated into the accounts of Buyer, then the relevant figure would be the purchase price, together with any liabilities of Target assumed by Buyer (which, on a sale and purchase of shares, would be most likely to be reflected in the purchase price).

24.2.2   *The profits test:* the profits attributable to the net assets the subject of the transaction divided by the profits of the listed company concerned. In the example, therefore, it would be necessary to divide the profits of Target by the profits of Buyer and, for this purpose, profits are calculated after deducting all charges except taxation. As under the gross assets test, where the target is an undertaking which will be consolidated or will cease to be consolidated, 100 per cent of its profits are included in the calculation, whether or not a lesser interest is to be acquired.

24.2.3   *The consideration test:* the consideration divided by the aggregate market value of all the ordinary shares (excluding treasury shares) of the listed company concerned. In the example, therefore, it would be necessary to divide the consideration payable by Buyer for Target by the aggregate market value of all of Buyer's ordinary shares. If any part of the consideration for the acquisition was to be satisfied by the issue of shares or other securities of Buyer, the value of the consideration would be calculated by reference to their aggregate market value before the announcement. The consideration will generally be the amount to be paid but the FSA may require other amounts to be treated as part of the consideration—for example, if Buyer has agreed to discharge liabilities of Sellers. If part of the consideration is to be deferred (for example as an earn-out), the maximum amount must be used in the calculation and, if there is no maximum, the transaction will normally be treated as Class 1, irrespective of the classification into which it would otherwise fall.

24.2.4 *The gross capital test:* the gross capital of the company or business which is the subject of the transaction divided by the gross capital of the listed company concerned (the test only applying in the case of an acquisition of a company or business). In the example, therefore, it would be necessary to divide the gross capital of Target by the gross capital of Buyer. For this purpose, the "gross capital" of Target is calculated by aggregating:

- the consideration for the acquisition;

- as it is a company which is being acquired, any of its shares or debt securities which are not being acquired;

- all other liabilities (other than current liabilities) of Target, including minority interests and deferred tax;

- any excess of the current liabilities of Target over its current assets.

The gross capital of Buyer will be calculated by aggregating:

- the market value of its shares (excluding treasury shares) and the issue amount of its debt security;

- all other liabilities (other than current liabilities), including minority interests and deferred tax; and

- any excess of its current liabilities over its current assets.

The listed company's advisers will normally, at a fairly early stage in the transaction, submit a formal letter to the FSA setting out the class test calculations and requesting confirmation from the FSA that they are agreed. This must be updated and resubmitted at the date of approval of any circular and the FSA will need to be informed if the percentage ratios change after initial discussions with the FSA and before announcement.

The FSA may require the transaction to be aggregated with other transactions in the previous 12 months, for the purpose of classification. This will usually occur only if it is entered into with the same or a series of connected parties, if it relates to an acquisition of securities in the same target or, together, such transactions lead to the listed company concerned having substantial involvement in a business activity which did not previously form a significant part of its principal activities. In such a case, the latest transaction may be treated as falling with Class 1 even though, alone, it may not do so (Listing Rule 12.2.10).

There are special rules for property companies, mineral companies and scientific research-based companies.

For comparison purposes, assets and profits are generally based on the latest published audited consolidated accounts, or a published preliminary statement of annual results, if the listed company concerned has published such a statement or will have done so by the time that the terms of the transaction are agreed. If, however, a balance sheet has been published in a subsequent interim statement, then gross assets are based on that balance sheet. Figures on which the auditors are unable to report without modification must, however, be disregarded. The figures of the listed company concerned must be adjusted to take account of transactions since the last accounts or half-year results for which information has already been published and the figures of the target company or business must be adjusted to take account of such transactions where the transaction concerned would have been a Class 2 transaction or greater when classified against the target as a whole. Net assets may be adjusted to take account of transactions since the latest accounts or half-year results for which information has already been published.

24.3   Classification of transactions by reference to the class tests

24.3.1   Class 3 transactions

A Class 3 transaction is one where all of the percentage ratios are less than five per cent.

The listed company concerned must notify a regulatory information service ("RIS") if it agrees the terms of a Class 3 transaction which includes an acquisition for which the consideration includes the issue of shares or other securities for which listing will be sought and the notification must be made as soon as possible after the terms of the acquisition have been agreed. The announcement must include:

- the amount of the securities being issued;

- details of the transaction, including the name of the other party to it;

- either the value of the consideration and how this is being satisfied or the value of the gross assets being bought (or sold) (whichever is the greater). If an announcement is not required under the Listing Rules but the company nevertheless wishes to make an announcement to the public, it should make a formal notification to a RIS giving the same information as being given to the public, together with details of the transaction (including the name of the other party and either the value of the consideration and how this is being satisfied or the value of the gross assets being acquired or disposed of).

24.3.2 Class 2 transactions

A Class 2 transaction is one where any of the relevant percentage ratios amounts to five per cent or more but where none of them exceeds 25 per cent.

The listed company concerned must notify an RIS of the transaction as soon as possible after its terms have been agreed and that announcement must include:

- details of the transaction, including the name of the other party;

- a description of the business in question;

- the consideration and how it is being satisfied (including the terms of any arrangements for deferred consideration);

- the value of the gross assets which are the subject of the transaction;

- the profits attributable to those assets;

- the effect of the transaction on the company concerned, including any benefits which are expected to accrue to it as a result of the transaction;

- details of any service contracts of proposed directors of the company concerned;

- in the case of a disposal, the application of the sale proceeds;

- for a disposal, if shares or other securities are to form part of the consideration received, a statement as to whether they are to be sold or retained;

- details of key individuals important to the business or company which is the subject of the transaction.

The announcement should be made without delay after terms have been agreed and this will usually be when the sale and purchase agreement is signed. The listed company has a general obligation to notify major new developments which are not public knowledge and which may lead to a substantial movement in share price, save for transactions in the course of negotiation where the information is restricted to defined classes of individuals or certain bodies who are made aware of its confidentiality. If there are leaks or there is a possibility of a false market in the company, a warning notification will be appropriate.

24.3.3 Class 1 transactions

A Class 1 transaction is one where any percentage ratio is 25 per cent or more.

In relation to a Class 1 transaction, the listed company concerned must notify a RIS of the transaction as soon as possible after its terms have been agreed and that notification must include the information which would be required if it were a Class 2 transaction. It must also send an explanatory circular to its shareholders and obtain their prior approval (which will be by ordinary resolution) for the transaction in a general meeting. The sale and purchase agreement and any other agreement effecting the transaction must be conditional on that approval being obtained.

It is therefore essential to establish as soon as possible whether a particular transaction will be a Class 1 transaction and to build into the timetable the fact that, once the sale and purchase agreement has been signed, completion cannot take place until shareholders' approval has been obtained, which will involve a notice period of at least 14 clear days.

24.3.4 Reverse takeovers

A reverse takeover will arise where a listed company is acquiring a business, an unlisted company or assets where any of the comparisons give rise to a percentage ratio of 100 per cent or more or would result in a fundamental change in the business of the listed company or a change in board or voting control of the listed company. Where a listed company is proposing to enter into a transaction which amounts to a reverse takeover, it must comply with the Class 1 requirements in respect of that transaction.

If, for example, Buyer is acquiring the entire issued share capital of Target from Sellers and the consideration is the issue to Sellers of such a number of shares in Buyer as would result in their obtaining voting control of Buyer, the transaction would amount to a reverse takeover and Buyer must comply with the Class 1 requirements in respect of the acquisition.

Where a listed company completes a reverse takeover, the FSA will generally cancel the listing of its securities and so Buyer will be required to re-apply for listing and (generally) satisfy the relevant requirements for listing. This will involve the preparation and publication of listing particulars as if Buyer (as enlarged by the acquisition of Target) was a new applicant, subject to certain modifications. If the transaction is approved and proceeds, the original listing will be cancelled and the listing will normally be restored.

The FSA will, however, allow a transaction which might otherwise have amounted to a reverse takeover to be treated as a Class 1 transaction if the target is of a similar size to the listed company concerned and in a similar line of business, the enlarged group is suitable for listing and there will be no change of board or voting control of the listed company (Listing Rule 10.2.3).

In connection with any such transaction, it will also be necessary to consider the implications of Rule 9 of the City Code on Takeovers and Mergers which provides that, except with the consent of the Panel, when any person or group of persons acting "in concert" acquire shares in a public company which carry 30 per cent or more of the voting rights of that company, they must make a mandatory offer to acquire all other equity or voting shares in the company, for a cash consideration to be determined in accordance with Rule 9.5.

In the example given above, the Panel would regard Sellers as "acting in concert" and they would therefore be obliged to make a mandatory cash offer to the existing shareholders of Buyer, unless they were able to obtain the consent of the Panel.

In practice, the Panel will normally waive the obligation to make a mandatory offer in these circumstances provided that various requirements are satisfied and these include the approval of the waiver by a vote (on a poll) of the independent shareholders of the listed company.

This is a complex and technical area on which specialist advice should be taken at an early stage.

24.4   Related party transactions

Chapter 11 of the Listing Rules sets out the requirements which apply to transactions and arrangements between a listed company and a "related party" and will therefore apply to any sale or purchase by a listed company where the other party is a related party or under which a related party may benefit. These requirements are intended to prevent any related party from taking advantage of his position and also to prevent any perception that he may have done so.

The requirements of Chapter 11 apply both to transactions by the listed company and to transactions of any of its subsidiary undertakings.

24.4.1 Who is a "related party"?

Listing Rule 11.1.4 provides that a "related party" means:

- A substantial shareholder, being any person who is, or was within the 12 months preceding the transaction, entitled to exercise or control 10 per cent or more of the voting rights at general meetings of the company concerned or any of its parent, subsidiary, or fellow subsidiary undertakings.

- A director or shadow director of the company concerned or of any of its parent, subsidiary or fellow subsidiary undertakings, or a person who was within 12 months of the date preceding the transaction such a director or shadow director.

- A 50:50 joint venture party of the company concerned.

- A "person exercising significant influence", which is defined as a person or entity which exercises significant influence over the company concerned.

- An associate of any person mentioned above. In the case of an individual, this will mean his spouse, civil partner or child, the trustees of certain family trusts, and companies in which he or they exercise control over 30 per cent or more of the votes at general meetings or have the right to appoint or remove directors who hold the majority of voting rights at board meetings. Interests of more than one director will be aggregated for the purpose of determining whether such a company is a related party. An associate of a corporate substantial shareholder, 50:50 joint venture partner or "person exercising significant influence" means its parent, subsidiary and fellow subsidiary undertakings, any company whose directors are accustomed to act in accordance with that company's directions or instructions and any company in which it or they, together, exercise control (determined in the manner described above for an individual).

24.4.2 **What is a related party transaction?**

Listing Rule 11.1.5 defines a related party transaction as:

- a transaction (other than one of a revenue nature in the ordinary course of business) between a listed company and a related party;

- an arrangement pursuant to which a listed company and a related party each invests in, or provides finance to, another undertaking or asset; or

- any other similar transaction or arrangement (other than one of a revenue nature in the ordinary course of business) between a listed company and any other person, the purpose and effect of which is to benefit a related party.

A typical example of a related party transaction is a management buy-out, where one or more members of the management team are directors of the listed company concerned or of one or more of its subsidiaries.

If, for example, there is to be a management buy-out of Target Limited (Target) from Seller PLC (Seller) and the buy-out team consists of Tom, Dick and Harriet, one of whom is a director of Target, the buy-out will be a related party transaction.

Listing Rule 11.1.6 provides for certain exceptions to which the requirements of Ch.11 do not apply and these are set out in Annex 1R to Listing Rule 11. That which is most likely to be relevant in the context of a sale and purchase of a company or of a business is the exception for "small transactions", where each of the percentage ratios is 0.25 per cent or less.

If, therefore, on the proposed management buy-out of Target, the class tests (which would be an assessment of the size of Target in relation to that of Seller) showed that none of the percentage ratios was 0.25 per cent or more, then the exception for "small transactions" should apply.

If, on each comparison, the percentage ratio is less than five per cent but, on one or more comparisons, the percentage ratio is greater than 0.25 per cent, no shareholder approval (as referred to below) will be required if Seller notifies the FSA of details of the transaction, provides written confirmation from an independent adviser that the terms of the transaction are fair and reasonable so far as the shareholders of Seller are concerned, and undertakes to the FSA to provide details of the transaction in its next published annual accounts.

Transactions with the same, or associated, related parties must, however, be aggregated (if not otherwise approved) and shareholder approval will be required in respect of the latest if it would be a Class 2 or larger transaction (Listing Rule 11.1.10).

If a listed company is proposing to enter into a transaction which could be a related party transaction, it is required under Listing Rule 8 to obtain the guidance of a sponsor in order to assess the potential application of Listing Rule 11.

24.4.3 Requirements for related party transactions

If a listed company enters into a related party transaction, it must:

- make a notification in the same way as for a Class 2 transaction but the notification must also give the name of the related party and details of the nature and extent of the related party's interest in the transaction;

- send a circular to its shareholders;

- obtain the approval of its shareholders for the transaction before it is entered into or, if the transaction is expressed to be conditional on that approval, before it is completed;

- ensure that the related party does not vote on the relevant resolution and take all reasonable steps to ensure that the related party's associates do not vote on the relevant resolution.

In the example of the buy-out of Target by Tom, Dick and Harriet, therefore, it will be necessary for Seller to announce (notify) the transaction and then send a circular to its shareholders, in order to convene a general meeting at which a resolution will be proposed to approve the transaction. If any of Tom, Dick and Harriet hold shares in Seller, Seller must ensure that they do not vote on the resolution and must also take all reasonable steps to ensure that their associates do not vote.

It should be noted that if a meeting has been called to approve a transaction and, between the date of the notice and the holding of the meeting, a party to the transaction becomes a related party, the listed company should under Listing Rule 11.1.8 ensure that the related party concerned does not vote on the resolution and that that party takes all reasonable steps to ensure that its associates do not vote on it. In addition, the listed company is required to send a further circular, for receipt by shareholders at least one clear business day before the last time for lodging proxies for the meeting, containing any information required by the Listing Rules which was not contained in the original circular.

The variation or novation of an existing agreement with a related party will require shareholders' approval under Chapter 11 of the Listing Rules even though the person concerned was not a related party at the time of the original transaction. An example of this is where Buyer has acquired the entire issued share capital of Target from Sellers and the consideration for the acquisition consisted of the allotment and issue to Sellers on completion of shares representing 10 per cent of the issued ordinary share capital of Buyer, together with an earn-out over the next three years. The original transaction may not have been a related party transaction but if, after completion, the parties agree to vary the terms of the earn-out and at that point Sellers are still holding 10 per cent of the ordinary share capital of Buyer, that variation will require shareholders' approval as a related party transaction unless the sums involved are such that it is possible to agree with the FSA that it can be regarded as a "small transaction" (as referred to above).

24.5 Content of circulars

As has already been seen, a listed company will have to send a circular to its shareholders if the transaction is a Class 1 transaction or is with a related party. Chapter 13 of the Listing Rules sets out the requirements for the contents of all circulars and these requirements will vary depending on whether the transaction is a Class 1 transaction or is a related party transaction. It is important to note that a Class 1 circular requires an indebtedness statement and a working capital statement, which must in each case cover the target company. The timetable for the transaction should take this into account.

In addition to the contents that are required to be included by virtue of the Listing Rules, Class 1 and related party circulars will contain a notice of the meeting of the shareholders to approve the transaction and this will be the case also for a reverse takeover, in respect of which it will be necessary to comply with the Class 1 requirements.

The FSA's formal approval to the final form of a Class 1 circular is required in advance, and drafts of the circular should be submitted to the FSA as soon as possible. The same applies to related party transaction circulars. Listing Rule 13.2 contains the rules relating to the approval of circulars and Listing Rule 13.3 sets out the requirements relating to the contents of all circulars. It is beyond the scope of this book to summarise these requirements but the parties will need to build into the timetable the need to obtain the FSA's approval to the form of any circular (which must be lodged with the FSA, along with various other documents, at least ten clear business days before the date on which it is intended that the circular should be issued).

24.6 Using shares to fund an acquisition

24.6.1 If, for example, Buyer PLC is acquiring the entire issued share capital of Target Limited from Adam and Eve ("Sellers"), Buyer may wish to use its own shares in order to fund the purchase price. Sellers may be willing to accept shares in Buyer in satisfaction of part of the consideration but are likely to require that part, at least, be satisfied in cash. Unless Buyer has sufficient cash resources to finance any cash requirement, it will have to issue further shares in order to enable it to raise sufficient cash and this will normally be done by way of a rights issue or a placing. The method used will depend upon a number of considerations of which market reaction may be the most important.

24.6.1.1 A "rights issue" is an offer to existing shareholders to subscribe for new shares for cash in proportion to their existing shareholdings and this normally involves a provisional allotment to each shareholder of his proportionate entitlement, with a renounceable provisional letter of allotment then being sent to each such holder. For example, a rights issue may be made on a "one for three" basis, in which case the company will provisionally allot to each shareholder one new share for every three shares which he holds at the "record date" for the rights issue. Shareholders can sell their right to subscribe for new shares (their rights) in the market, nil paid and arrangements will be made for the sale of shares not taken up by shareholders so that, if a shareholder neither takes up his rights nor sells them in the market, he may still receive a cash payment if the shares that were provisionally allotted to him are sold in the market for more than the subscription price.

A rights issue will nearly always take place at a discount to the market value of the issuer's shares.

24.6.1.2   By contrast, a "placing" is an offer of new shares to selected persons or "placees" (often institutional investors, but possibly also individuals or companies, including existing shareholders) and this does not involve renounceable letters of allotment. A placing may be a "vendor placing" in which the new shares are (traditionally) allotted to the seller as consideration for the acquisition and then sold by him to placees in order to raise the cash consideration which he requires. Alternatively, a placing may be a "cash placing" in which the new shares are placed directly for cash, which is used to pay the seller.

In the example given above, a vendor placing would traditionally involve the allotment to Sellers of shares in Buyer which would immediately be sold by Sellers (pursuant to a pre-existing agreement with Buyer's investment bank or broker) to placees (with whom the shares will have been "placed" in advance by the bank/broker) for a price which gives Sellers the cash consideration which they require. If, on the other hand, the placing took the form of a cash placing, the new shares would not be allotted to Sellers but would instead be issued for cash to the placees and that cash would be used to fund the payment of the cash consideration.

It should not make any practical difference to Sellers which type of placing is used—they will simply be concerned to make sure that they do receive the agreed amount of cash on the due date.

Particularly on a large placing (i.e. where the shares involved represent more than five per cent of its issued share capital) Buyer may offer some or all of the shares which are being placed to its existing shareholders by way of an "open offer", with the placees taking those shares which the existing shareholders do not wish to take. Since 1987, in fact, the Association of British Insurers ("ABI") has stated that its members will expect a listed company proposing to issue its shares in order to fund an acquisition to make an offer of those shares to existing shareholders where the issue amounts to more than 10 per cent of the listed company concerned's existing capital or involves a discount of more than five per cent on the market price of the consideration shares.

24.6.1.3 Like a rights issue, an open offer is an offer of new shares to existing shareholders in proportion to their existing shareholdings but, unlike a placing, this does not involve renounceable letters of allotment and, instead involves application forms, which cannot be traded nil paid (as is the case with provisional allotment letters on a rights issue). Where a placing is coupled with an open offer, the shares are provisionally placed with institutions or other placees but with a right of "claw back" to meet applications from existing shareholders.

In an open offer, the shares will normally be offered at a finer discount to market value than would be the case on a rights issue (Listing Rule 9.5.10 provides that the discount may not exceed 10 per cent without the approval of the issuer's shareholders).

24.6.2 Underwriting

A rights issue will be underwritten, which means that it will not be announced until a bank, broker or other financial institution has entered into a binding commitment to take up the shares in question. On a rights issue, the underwriter will agree to take those rights shares not taken up by existing shareholders which cannot be sold in the market at or above the rights issue price. The period commencing with the date of this commitment (normally the announcement of the issue) and ending on the date when the shares are finally taken up is the underwriting period and the underwriters will receive a fee or commission according to its length and depending on whether or not the shares have been placed "firm" with them. For example, on a rights issue, directors or other major shareholders may agree not to take up their rights, in which event the shares to which they would otherwise have been entitled will be placed "firm". Underwriters will almost invariably have entered into agreements with "sub-underwriters" under which the sub-underwriters will agree to take up any rights shares which are not taken up by existing shareholders and which cannot be sold in the market at or above the rights issue price and this will be reflected in the commission arrangements.

Typically, the underwriter will take a commission equal to 0.75 per cent of the underwriting commitment and the sub-underwriters will receive a commission of 0.5 per cent in respect of shares which are placed firm and 1.25 per cent in respect of shares which are not placed firm, in each case for the first 30 days of the underwriting period, and one-eighth of one per cent for every week or part of a week thereafter. For this reason, the buyer will wish to keep the underwriting period as short as possible. Commissions will only be payable in respect of shares which are actually underwritten and so, where directors or other major shareholders have indicated that they intend to take up their entitlements on a rights issue or open offer, the company may wish to obtain formal irrevocable undertakings to that effect, in which event the shares in question will not form part of the underwriting commitment and the fees and commissions will be reduced as a result.

Cash placings and vendor placings are much more common than rights issues: in the case of a vendor placing, the bank or broker involved will agree to find placees who will purchase the new shares from the seller and, in the case of a cash placing, they will agree to find placees who will subscribe for the new shares, which will then be allotted by the company directly to the placees. A placing agreement will be signed and, as soon as possible after that, the bank/broker will obtain signed placing letters from the placees, under which they agree to subscribe.

One particular reason why placings are much more common than rights issues is that the length of time between signing the sale and purchase agreement and receiving the proceeds of the issue is likely to be significantly less on a placing than on a rights issue (this point is discussed further in 24.9). Smaller issues are often not formally underwritten but instead the company and the bank, broker or other institution concerned will wait until the shares have been pre-placed before signing a placing agreement.

24.7   Procedure—rights issue

Where a rights issue is proposed, a general meeting of the buyer is likely to be necessary—either because the acquisition is a Class 1 transaction or because it is necessary to increase the authorised share capital of the company and to grant the directors the necessary authority to allot the rights issue shares under s.80 of the Companies Act 1985. In the absence of any particular provisions in the articles of association, these will be ordinary resolutions which will require 14 clear days' notice.

The buyer will wish to keep the underwriting period to a minimum, both in order to enable completion to take place as soon as possible and (probably more importantly to the buyer) in order to keep underwriting fees and commissions as low as possible. It will therefore be important to ensure that the rights issue will not require the passing of a special resolution in order to disapply the statutory pre-emption rights which are contained in s.89(1) of the Companies Act 1985. A disapplication will not be required if there is an offer to existing shareholders which complies with the statutory provisions but there are particular concerns to be addressed in respect of foreign shareholders and fractional entitlements.

In order to comply with the Companies Acts, the offer must remain open for 21 clear days and that period does not start until the offer is made. Where the offer is sent by post, it is deemed to be made at the time at which it would be delivered in the ordinary course of post (s.90(2)). This poses obvious difficulties in the case of foreign shareholders, compounded by the fact that certain jurisdictions, such as the US, South Africa, Japan and Canada, have securities laws which prohibit the making of offers in those jurisdictions without regulatory filings. However, s.90(5) provides that, where a holder has no registered address in the UK, the offer may be made by publishing it in the *London Gazette*. It is the practice therefore to make the offer to overseas shareholders by those means but, in addition, to send the documents by post unless prohibited from doing so by the local law.

It should be noted that, with effect from October 1, 2009, s.80 of the Companies Act 1985 will be replaced by s.549 of the Companies Act 2006 and (subject to the provisions of the company's articles of association) it will not be necessary for the directors to be given authority to allot shares by the company concerned if it is a private company with only one class of share. Also, as from October 1, 2009, authorised share capital will be abolished. It is, however, likely that transitional provisions will be introduced in order to deal with authorities subsisting at that date and with references (in a company's articles or otherwise) to authorised share capital and it will be necessary to consider the impact of those transitional provisions very carefully.

As from October 1, 2009, the statutory pre-emption rights will be contained in s.561 of the Companies Act 2006 and it will be necessary to refer to that section and to ss.562–577. Section 562(5) provides that the offer must remain open for a period of at least 21 days beginning:

- in the case of an offer made in hard copy form, with the date on which the offer is sent or supplied;

- in the case of an offer made in electronic form, with the date on which the offer is sent;

- in the case of an offer made by publication in the *London Gazette*, with the date of publication.

Section 562(3) provides that the offer may be made by publishing it in the *London Gazette* if the holder has no registered address in an EEA state and has not given the company an address in an EEA state for the services of notices on him or is the holder of a share warrant. There is a substantive change in that an offer may not be made via the *London Gazette* if the shareholder has no registered address in the UK but does have a registered address in another EEA state or has given the company an address in the UK or another EEA state for the service of notices on him.

Unless the rights issue is on a "one for one" basis, there will almost certainly be shareholders who would become entitled to a fraction of a share and fractional entitlements will not normally be allotted, but will instead be aggregated and sold in the market. The sale in the market of the shares resulting from the aggregation of fractions amounts to a cash issue but most listed companies will at their annual general meeting obtain a limited disapplication of the statutory pre-emption rights in respect of an issue of shares for cash which does not exceed five per cent of their existing issued share capital and this will normally cover the arrangements in respect of fractional entitlements. Most listed companies will also obtain a disapplication in respect of "rights issues" and this should permit the issue of ordinary shares on a basis which does not accord strictly with the statutory requirements but it is nevertheless important to check the wording of the disapplication at an early stage in order to ensure that it is appropriately worded. Any existing disapplication is in any event unlikely to apply if the rights issue comprises the issue of a new class of share, such as convertible preference shares.

The sale and purchase agreement will be conditional on any necessary shareholders' approval and on the admission of the new shares to the Official List. The basic procedure for a rights issue may therefore be:

24.7.1   sign the sale and purchase agreement;

24.7.2   announce the transaction;

24.7.3   post the circular to shareholders;

24.7.4   hold the shareholders' meeting after at least 14 clear days' notice (21 clear days where for any reason a special resolution is required);

24.7.5   complete the transaction using "bridging" bank or similar finance;

24.7.6   post the provisional allotment letters;

24.7.7   collect the proceeds at the end of the period of 21 days within which the provisional allotments must be taken up;

24.7.8   repay the bridging finance.

This assumes, however, that the buyer is both willing and able to obtain borrowings in order to bridge the gap between the posting of the provisional allotment letters and the date on which the rights issue proceeds are received and this might not necessarily be the case, particularly if the underwriters have the ability during that period to rescind the underwriting agreement. If the buyer is unwilling or unable to pay the cash until the proceeds of the rights issue are received, completion will have to be delayed until the rights issue has closed and all the proceeds have been received, which will involve a delay of three weeks or so. In that case, the sale and purchase agreement is likely to have to be conditional on the underwriting agreement remaining in full force and effect and not being rescinded prior to the closing of the rights issue.

If the buyer's bank is prepared, in principle, to provide bridging finance, it is likely to be anxious to ensure that the bridge is "closed" and that it can be certain of being repaid out of the proceeds of the rights issue. The difficulty with that, however, is that the underwriters will almost certainly insist on having a right to rescind the underwriting agreement and "pull" the underwriting in certain circumstances and are likely to insist that that right should continue to apply until the rights issue has closed and the rights issue shares have been listed (see below). Whether or not the buyer is able to bridge is likely, therefore, to depend on whether the bank is prepared to accept the risk of the underwriting being pulled and of its not being repaid in full out of the proceeds of the rights issue.

24.8   Procedure—vendor placing

In the case of a vendor placing, the underwriting period will be shorter, even where some or all of the new shares are offered to existing shareholders. Such an offer is unlikely to be made on renounceable allotment letters and can therefore take place during the notice period for the shareholders' meeting, although the FSA requires the offer to be kept open for 15 business days.

The basic procedure for a vendor placing in this situation is therefore likely to be:

24.8.1 sign the sale and purchase agreement;

24.8.2 announce the transaction;

24.8.3 post the circular to shareholders (which will be the document containing the offer to shareholders and any necessary notice of general meeting), together with the application form pursuant to the open offer, if there is to be one;

24.8.4 hold the shareholders' meeting after at least 15 business days (or, if longer, 21 clear days if for any reason a special resolution is required);

24.8.5 assuming that it is possible to obtain cleared funds in time, complete the acquisition and placing simultaneously (together with any open offer).

There may be situations where the buyer is obliged to make an open offer to shareholders under the ABI guidelines but the sale and purchase agreement is not required to be conditional upon shareholder approval or any other condition and in those circumstances the seller is likely to argue that completion should not be delayed until receipt of funds from the placing and should not be made conditional upon receipt of those funds. Whether it is possible to complete the transaction before those funds have been received depends on whether the underwriter is prepared to part with the money (to the seller) before that has happened.

One particular risk for the underwriter would be the possibility of a placee defaulting and this will be addressed by there being a direct agreement (placing letter) between the placee and the underwriter to the effect that the placee will pay the subscription price on the due date, while the placing agreement will enable the underwriter to sell the shares in the market and keep the proceeds, while bringing a claim against the defaulting placee under the direct agreement between them. Another concern may be if the placees claim to be entitled to rescind their obligations because of a misrepresentation in the buyer's circular or listing particulars at a time when the underwriter has already paid the seller. In that situation, the only remedy of the underwriter is likely to be against the buyer (and possibly also against its directors) under the warranties and indemnities in the placing agreement.

24.9 Procedure—cash placing

In the case of a cash placing, the basic procedure is likely to be:

24.9.1 sign the sale and purchase agreement;

24.9.2 announce the transaction;

24.9.3 post the circular to shareholders (which will include any necessary notice of general meeting), together with the application form pursuant to the open offer, if there is to be one;

24.9.4   hold the shareholders' meeting, which is likely to require at least 21 clear days' notice as it is likely to be necessary to pass a special resolution to disapply the pre-emption rights contained in s.561 of the Companies Act 2006, with effect from October 1, 2008 (save in the unlikely event that the limited disapplication in respect of issues which do not exceed five per cent of the existing issued share capital will be enough to cover the issue in question);

24.9.5   complete the acquisition and placing (together with any other offer) simultaneously (if timing permits).

Where there is an open offer, the offer period must be at least 15 business days from the date of posting of the application forms (or (if earlier) from the date on which the existing shares were made "ex" the open offer entitlement) but this period will run concurrently with the notice period for the extraordinary general meeting. On a rights issue, provisional allotment letters can only be posted after the extraordinary general meeting, because the UK Listing Authority does not allow shares to be allotted provisionally on a conditional basis (i.e. conditionally on the passing of the resolutions at the general meeting) and so, where there is a rights issue, the length of time between signing the sale and purchase agreement and receipt of the proceeds of the issue is likely to be significantly greater. As a result, the underwriting period will be longer and the underwriting commissions will be greater.

24.10 Stamp duty

As has already been seen, if Buyer PLC is acquiring the entire issued share capital of Target Limited from Adam and Eve (Sellers) and the cash element of the consideration is to be financed via a vendor placing, this would traditionally involve the allotment of Buyer's shares to Sellers (which would normally be on renounceable documents) and the sale of those shares by Sellers to the placees. The transaction will, however, be subject to stamp duty reserve tax ("SDRT") and it is normal to avoid this by restructuring the vendor placing so that the cash is provided by the Buyer allotting the consideration shares direct to the placees. The consideration shares are not registered in the name of Sellers but first registration of the shares is in the name of the placees. Sellers agree in the sale and purchase agreement that the consideration for the shares in Target is the allotment and issue of the consideration shares to persons nominated by the bank or broker arranging the placing and Buyer undertakes to procure payment of the cash consideration by the bank or broker to Sellers (this being a sum equal to the cash raised by the placing of the shares). As Sellers have no entitlement to the consideration shares, there is no SDRT (and no stamp duty).

24.11 Force majeure

A bank, broker or other financial institution entering into an underwriting agreement or placing agreement will wish to rescind the agreement and walk away from its obligations if there is a breach of any of the warranties contained in the agreement, if an event occurs which renders the circular to shareholders materially accurate or misleading or if there are any material adverse changes in financial, economic or stock market conditions (any such material adverse change normally been referred to in this context as an event of "force majeure"). The extent to which there should be a force majeure clause may be an emotive one as underwriters will inevitably press very hard for one to be included, while listed companies will argue that underwriters are receiving a commission to reflect the fact that they are accepting this risk.

On a rights issue, the right to withdraw because of force majeure will not continue beyond the posting of the provisional allotment letters but, on a vendor placing or cash placing, the bank, broker or institution concerned will press for the right to continue until the new shares have been admitted (see below), although, depending on the circumstances, they will sometimes accept that the right to withdraw for force majeure will only continue until the end of the day on which the placing is announced, on the basis that by then the placees should have signed their placing letters and will therefore be bound to pay for the shares which have been placed with them. Placing letters may in fact be sent out on the day before the announcement of the placing, on the basis of a placing proof, with the result that signed placing letters should be obtained earlier.

24.12   The listing condition

Even after the FSA has approved the application for listing of the new shares, their admission to the Official List and their admission to trading on the London Stock Exchange's market for listed securities will not become effective until the decision of the FSA to admit them to listing has been announced by being disseminated by a RIS or, should the electronic systems be unavailable, posted on a noticeboard designated by the FSA (Listing Rule 3.2.7). This will not take place until after the shares have been allotted and this can cause practical problems as, on a rights issue or cash placing, the underwriters will inevitably insist that their commitment is conditional upon admission becoming effective, with the result that completion will normally have to be delayed until that happens (except on a rights issue where the buyer has already completed using bridging finance).

The problems will be even more significant on a vendor placing: using the previous example, the allotment of the new shares would normally take place on completion but listing cannot become effective until after the shares have been allotted, while Sellers will not be prepared to complete and part with their shares without receiving their cash. To complicate things further, the placees will not be prepared to pay for the shares until the listing has become effective. The risks of the application for admission being approved but admission then not taking effect, are very remote but neither Sellers nor the placees will be willing to take the risk.

The normal solution to this classic "Catch 22" problem is to go through all the completion procedures but for the parties' solicitors to hold the completion documents in escrow, subject only to listing becoming effective. If all or part of the consideration is to be satisfied by the issue of shares in the buyer and there is no vendor placing involved, there will be the usual "completion" meeting when the consideration shares will be allotted subject to formal completion taking place, the FSA will be informed of the allotment, application will be made for the shares to be admitted and then the required announcement will be made, at which point the sale and purchase agreement will complete. If there is an underwriting agreement or a placing agreement (whether the placing is a vendor placing or a cash placing), that agreement will also become unconditional when listing takes effect. Where the buyer is dependant upon a rights issue or a placing in order to enable him to fund the acquisition, the sale and purchase agreement may also have to be conditional upon the underwriting agreement/placing agreement becoming unconditional in all respects and not being rescinded (for example, by reason of force majeure) before the point when listing takes effect. This will certainly have to be the case where there is a vendor placing as the seller will not want to complete unless he is certain that there are legally-binding arrangements in place for the purchase of the new shares and the payment of cash to him.

Paragraph 2 of Pt 1 of Sch.7 to the agreements which form Precedents 1 and 2 in App.2 covers this point.

24.13 AIM

A company whose shares are admitted to trading on the Alternative Investment Market ("AIM") is subject to the AIM Rules for Companies, which are different to the Listing Rules. These rules are in many ways less prescriptive than the Listing Rules as (for example) no information is required to be published on admission of new shares by a company whose shares are already admitted to trading on AIM unless a prospectus is required under the Prospectus Rules.

24.13.1   Under the AIM Rules, a "substantial transaction" is one which exceeds 10 per cent in any of the class tests set out in Sch.3 to the AIM Rules and (as with a listed company) this includes any transaction by a subsidiary of the AIM company but excludes any transactions of a revenue nature in the ordinary course of business. It also excludes any transaction to raise finance which does not involve a change in the fixed assets of the AIM company or its subsidiaries. An AIM company must make notification to an approved Regulatory Information Service ("RIS") for distribution to the public as soon as the terms of any such transaction are agreed and that notification must contain the information which is contained in Sch.4 to the AIM Rules.

24.13.2   The class tests for AIM companies are set out in Sch.3 to the AIM Rules and may be summarised as follows:

24.13.2.1   The gross assets test involves dividing the gross assets which are the subject of the transaction by the gross assets of the AIM company — the total of its fixed assets plus total current assets, as shown by the most recent of the latest published balance sheet, an admission document produced in a reverse takeover or (where transactions are aggregated as referred to below) the latest published balance sheet prior to the earliest transaction which is aggregated.

24.13.2.2   The profits test involves dividing the profits attributable to the assets which are the subject of the transaction by the profits before tax and extraordinary items of the AIM company, as shown by the last published annual accounts, the last published preliminary statement of annual results or, where transactions are aggregated, the last such accounts or statement prior to the earliest transaction which is being aggregated.

24.13.2.3 The turnover test involves dividing the turnover attributable to the assets which are the subject of the transaction by the turnover of the AIM company, as shown by the last published annual accounts, the last published preliminary statement or, where transactions are aggregated, the last accounts or preliminary statement prior to the earliest such transaction.

24.13.2.4 The consideration test involves dividing the consideration payable by the aggregated market value of all of the ordinary shares of the AIM company on the day prior to announcement of the transaction (and if any part of the consideration is deferred or contingent, the maximum total consideration has to be treated as being payable).

24.13.2.5 The gross capital test involves dividing the gross capital of the company or business being acquired by the gross capital of the AIM company, in each case on the day prior to announcement of the transaction in question.

24.13.3 Where any of these tests produce anomalous results or where they are inappropriate to the sphere of activity of the AIM company, the Stock Exchange may (save in the case of a transaction with a related party) disregard the calculation and substitute other relevant indicators of size.

24.13.4 AIM Rule 13 applies to any transaction with a related party which exceeds five per cent under any of the class tests and the definition of "related party" includes directors of the AIM company or any of its subsidiary or parent companies and a substantial shareholder (basically, the holder of 10 per cent or more of any class of shares). The company must announce such a transaction as soon as its terms are agreed and that announcement must contain the information contained in Sch.4 to the AIM Rules, the name of the related party concerned and the nature and extent of his/her interests in the transaction and a statement that, with the exception of any director who is involved in the transaction as a related party, the directors consider, after consulting with the nominated adviser, that the terms of the transaction are fair and reasonable insofar as shareholders are concerned.

If, for example, it is proposed that Target Limited—a wholly-owned subsidiary of Seller PLC, an AIM company—should be sold to its management team of Tom, Dick and Harriet and one of them is a director of Target, AIM Rule 13 will apply to the transaction if (for example) the turnover tests shows that the turnover of Target represents more than five per cent of the turnover of Seller and its group. Seller must therefore announce the transaction and that announcement must contain the information mentioned in the previous paragraph and a statement that, with the exception of the individual concerned, the directors of Seller consider that the terms of the transactions are fair and reasonable.

24.13.5 A reverse takeover is an acquisition or series of acquisitions in a 12-month period which, for the AIM company, would exceed 100 per cent under any of the class tests, result in a fundamental change in the company's business, board or voting control or, in the case of an "investing company", depart substantially from its investing strategy.

Any agreement which would result in a reverse takeover must be conditional on shareholder approval, must be announced and must be accompanied by the publication of an admission document for the company as enlarged by the reverse transaction, which will contain notice to convene the general meeting. Where shareholder approval is given, trading on AIM will be cancelled and the enlarged company must apply for admission to AIM as if it were a new applicant.

For example, therefore, if Buyer PLC (an AIM company) is acquiring the entire issued share capital of Target Limited and the profits of Target are greater than the profits of Buyer (as shown by its last published annual accounts or any more recent preliminary statement), the sale and purchase agreement must be conditional on the prior approval of the shareholders of Buyer and the document containing notice convening the necessary general meeting of Buyer must be accompanied by an admission document for Buyer, as enlarged by the acquisition of Target. If the shareholders of Buyer vote in favour of the transaction, trading on AIM will be cancelled and Buyer (as enlarged by the acquisition) must apply for admission as if it were a new applicant.

24.13.6 AIM Rule 15 deals with disposals resulting in a fundamental change of business, which means any disposal by an AIM company which, when aggregated with any other disposal or disposals over the previous 12 months, exceeds 75 per cent by reference to any of the class tests. Any such disposal must be conditional on shareholder approval, must be the subject of an appropriate announcement and must be accompanied by the publication of a circular containing the information required by the AIM Rules and convening the necessary general meeting.

Where the effect of the proposed disposal is to divest the company of all, or substantially all, of its trading business activities, it will be treated as an "investing company" and the formal announcement and circular to shareholders must state its investing strategy. The company will then have to make an acquisition or acquisitions which constitute a reverse takeover under Rule 14 within 12 months of having obtained shareholder approval.

24.13.7 AIM Rule 16 provides for the aggregation of transactions in certain circumstances for the purposes of determining whether any particular transaction is a substantial transaction, a related party transaction, a reverse takeover or a disposal resulting in a fundamental change of business.

24.13.8 An AIM company may use its shares to fund an acquisition and may do so by way of a rights issue or placing (whether a vendor placing or a placing for cash) in the same way as a listed company and the comments made in connection with listed companies will generally apply equally to AIM companies. Issues regarding the listing condition (as referred to in 24.12 above) will similarly apply to an AIM company, as admission to AIM becomes effective only when the Stock Exchange issues a "dealing notice" to that effect.

One major difference, however, is that, where an AIM company is issuing shares as consideration for an acquisition or in order to fund the acquisition, it may be obliged to issue a prospectus under the Prospectus Rules which provide that a prospectus approved by the FSA will be required if "transferable securities" are to be offered to the public in the UK and (broadly) this will be the case where the securities being issued are shares which are not admitted to the Official List and are not subject of an application to the Official List or where they are to be admitted to trading on AIM.

A detailed analysis of these provisions is beyond the scope of this book but the allotment of shares in an AIM company or any other unlisted company in connection with an acquisition might involve an offer to the public, whether it is a simple share-for-share transaction or (where a market such as AIM exists for the shares) where there is cash consideration which is to be funded by a vendor placing, cash placing or rights issue.

In practice, a straight share-for-share exchange will almost always fall within the exemption contained in s.86(1)(b) of FSMA which applies where the shares in question are offered to no more than 100 persons. Otherwise, there is an exemption under Prospectus Rule 1.2.2 which will apply if a document is available containing information which is regarded by the FSA as being equivalent to that which is required to be contained in a prospectus (any such equivalent document must be submitted to the FSA for approval).

Where there is a vendor placing, the arrangements may be exempt because the shares are being offered to fewer than 100 persons or because the placees will constitute "qualified investors" within the meaning of s.86(7) of the FSMA. Where, however, they are to be offered to existing shareholders pursuant to an open offer or where there is a cash placing or a rights issue, a prospectus will be required, unless the arrangements fall within any of the other exemptions contained in the Prospectus Rules (for example, the exemption in Rule 1.2.3(1) for shares representing, over a period of 12 months, less than 10 per cent of the number of shares of the same class already issued to trading on the same market (i.e. AIM)).

Chapter 25

Buy-outs

This chapter considers some of the issues which are likely to need particular consideration in the context of a management buy-out, buy-in or similar transaction. In practice, the issues which arise on such transactions are likely to be very similar to those which arise on a trade sale but there are certain issues which are specific to such transactions and others which are likely to assume greater importance on such transactions than on a trade sale. This chapter does not, however, purport to consider all of the issues which will arise.

It may be helpful to begin by explaining some of the terminology that is often used and this will be done by reference to the example of the acquisition of the share capital, or undertaking and assets, of a company (Target), which is a wholly-owned subsidiary of Seller PLC (Seller):

- A management buy-out ("MBO") is where a company or business is acquired by its existing management: a simple example of this is where Target is being run by a senior management team of Tom, Dick and Harriet and they form a new company (Newco) to acquire the share capital, or (as the case may be) the undertaking and assets, of Target (typically, with the benefit of acquisition finance from a bank and/or equity finance from a venture capitalist ("VC")).

- A management buy-in ("MBI") is where the acquisition is made by a new management team: an example of this is where the shares or assets in question are acquired by a Newco formed by a new management team of Adam and Eve (with the benefit of acquisition finance from a lender and/or equity finance from a VC, unless Adam and Eve have the resources to enable them to fund the acquisition themselves).

- A buy-in/management buy-out ("BIMBO") is where one or more new managers join with existing management to make the acquisition: an example of this is where a Newco is formed by Adam and Eve and Tom, Dick and Harriet in order to make the acquisition (again, normally with the benefit of acquisition finance and/or VC funding).

- An institutional buy-out ("IBO") is where a VC or other financial institution is itself the buyer but with a management team (either the existing team or a new team) to run the business on a day-to-day basis: an example of this is where Goliath Capital PLC (VC) negotiates the acquisition from Seller and then makes the acquisition via a Newco in which Tom, Dick and Harriet hold modest shareholdings. The transaction will be funded by the VC together (almost certainly) with acquisition finance from a lender.

The issues to be considered will differ according to whether the transaction is in the nature of an MBO, MBI, BIMBO or IBO.

25.1 Conflicts of interest

If existing management (Tom, Dick and Harriet in the above example) are considering a buy-out, there is obviously potential for conflict between their interests and those of their employer and these conflicts are brought into sharper focus in the case of a member of the team who is a director of the employing company. In the above example, if Harriet is a director of Seller, she will naturally want her team to pay the lowest possible price but will have a duty to Seller to obtain the best possible price. This will be a concern both for her and for Seller.

The potential for conflict will be even greater where the management team are bidding alongside trade buyers and other interested parties in an auction or other competitive process: interested parties will inevitably want to talk to the existing management team and Seller will be concerned that Tom, Dick and Harriet, particularly if any discussions with competing bidders are unsupervised, may say things to dissuade them from proceeding or to "talk down" the price which they would be prepared to offer. Where the existing management team is seen as key to the success of the business, one obvious concern is that they will make it clear to other bidders that they will "walk" if their own offer is not accepted. The position may be rather different where management are invited to mount an MBO but if a director decides to initiate an MBO he should declare this to the board as soon as possible and obtain consent to proceed. Otherwise, he runs the risk of breaching his duties as a director and/or the terms of his contract of employment—not least because the process would inevitably involve disclosing confidential information about the business to prospective advisers and financial backers.

Prospective financial backers should be concerned to make sure that such consent is obtained as they otherwise run the risk of legal action on the basis of their having induced management to breach their contracts of employment (a concern which will apply to all employees and not just directors).

Similar concerns may well arise on an MBI, if the new management team are currently employed by a competitor and the MBI would be in breach of any restrictive covenants in their contracts of employment. Similarly if they had themselves sold a similar business in the not too distant past and were still subject to restrictive covenants given to the buyer of that business.

25.2 Conditions precedent

The comments made in Ch.4 regarding the conditions that may have to be satisfied before any sale and purchase will apply equally to an MBO, MBI, BIMBO or IBO but points which are likely to be of particular concern on an MBO (and possibly also on a BIMBO or IBO, depending on all the circumstances) include:

25.2.1   If a director of the selling company or of its holding company is involved in
         the buy-out, it may be necessary to obtain the prior approval of shareholders
         under s.190 of the Companies Act 2006 (see 4.1.1.1).

25.2.2   Where the seller or its ultimate holding company is a listed company, it will
         be necessary to consider whether it needs to be approved by shareholders as a
         "related party transaction" (see 24.4).

25.3   Due diligence

The extent of the due diligence to be carried out may depend on the nature of the
transaction and whether it is an MBO, an MBI, a BIMBO or an IBO.

The extent of the due diligence to be carried out on an MBI or an IBO is likely to be
the same as on a purchase by a trade buyer—indeed, more extensive due diligence may
in fact be required in some areas, as a trade buyer may well have more knowledge about
the business's products and customers and the markets in which it operates.

On an MBO, the management team may, depending on the circumstances, consider that
much more limited due diligence is required as they are likely to have considerable
knowledge about the business themselves. Depending, again, on the circumstances, that
may also be the case on a BIMBO.

Where, however, there is external funding involved, the financiers will almost certainly
insist on "full" due diligence in the same way as a trade buyer (and, as mentioned
above, they may in fact require due diligence on matters on which a trade buyer might
be prepared to "take a view"). Due diligence is discussed in detail in Chs 5, 6 and 7.

25.4   Warranties and indemnities

As with due diligence, the extent of the warranties and indemnities which will be
required will almost certainly depend on the nature of the transaction and on the way in
which it is being funded.

25.4.1   MBOs

As discussed in 10.5, on an MBO, the seller will almost certainly be reluctant to give
anything more than very limited warranties and indemnities and, as discussed, the general principle has traditionally been that the seller will only give warranties and indemnities in respect of matters in respect of which the management team are likely to have
only a limited knowledge.

In the example of Seller PLC selling a company (Target) or the assets of a business to
a management team of Tom, Dick and Harriet, Seller's starting point is likely to be that
it will only give warranties in respect of matters dealt with at "group" level rather than
at operating company level.

For example, matters such as insurances, pensions and tax are normally handled at group level and management may therefore only have limited knowledge of those areas.

The position may be more complicated where there are senior management who are not part of the MBO and who may be remaining with Seller—this is particularly likely where the business in question is carried on by a separate company (Target), rather than as a division of Seller, as the board of Target may well include representatives of Seller (for example, the group finance director may also act as finance director of Target).

In that situation, it is reasonable for the MBO team to expect warranties in respect of matters known to any such person but which may not be known to them.

If the target is not part of a group but is owned by one or more individual shareholders, it is quite likely that one or more of them will be involved in its management or at least a director of (or otherwise represented on the board of) the company. In those circumstances, management will expect to receive warranties in respect of matters known to the individuals concerned.

A seller may well attempt to have a "blanket" exclusion from the warranties of any matter known to the management team: this is understandable, but it will be necessary to look at the precise wording of any such limitation very carefully and, if the general principle is accepted, it may be appropriate to limit it to certain warranties only. For example, members of the management team may be aware of a particular set of circumstances but their knowledge may be incomplete or they may simply not be in a position to appreciate their full implications—this is particularly so in the case of tax matters.

In practice, however, as discussed in Ch.10, where there is acquisition finance, VC finance or other third party funding, the extent of the warranty protection from the seller will not just be a matter for management but will, to a large extent, be driven by the requirements of the funders.

Particularly in the case of VCs, the starting-point is likely to be that they will expect there to be reasonably "full" warranty and indemnity protection—either given to Newco by the seller in the sale and purchase agreement or given to them (the VCs) in their investment agreement. They will naturally prefer the warranties and indemnities to be given by the seller as far as possible as the seller is likely to be in a stronger financial position than the management team and, in any event, there must be few more certain ways of demotivating a management team than to sue them for breach of warranty, so that financiers may be unlikely to take action against management in the absence of fraud or recklessness. The argument of the VCs in negotiations with the seller is likely to be that the purpose of warranties is not just to identify the extent of the seller's knowledge but also to allocate risk between the seller and the buyer in respect of the matters in question; accordingly, the fact that the seller may not be aware of something and the fact that the management team may be aware of it should not necessarily mean that the seller should have no liability in respect of the matter in question. For this reason, financial backers are likely to be even more reluctant than management teams to accept a general exclusion of liability for matters within the knowledge of management.

Although management might otherwise be prepared to accept more limited warranties and indemnities from the seller, they are likely to find that it is in their best interest to press for more extensive protection, on the basis that that is likely then to reduce the extent of the warranties which they have to give to their financial backers.

When negotiating heads of terms, therefore, management should make it quite clear that the extent of the warranty and indemnity protection will be subject to the requirements of their funders and sellers should appreciate that, even if they persuade management to accept, when the heads of terms are signed, that only very limited warranties and indemnities will be given, the whole issue is likely to be revisited once funders become involved.

25.4.2 MBIs

An MBI team is likely to regard itself as in a similar position to a trade buyer and is likely therefore to expect the same level of warranty protection as a trade buyer.

25.4.3 BIMBOs

The level of warranty and indemnity protection which is appropriate on a BIMBO is likely to depend on all the circumstances.

In the example of a buy-in team of Adam and Eve making the acquisition alongside the existing management team of Tom, Dick and Harriet, Seller will almost certainly want to approach the transaction as if it were an MBO and only give warranties and indemnities which would be appropriate on an MBO, while Adam and Eve would argue that the transaction should be approached as if Newco were a trade buyer.

Seller will argue that Adam and Eve should rely on the knowledge of the existing management team but they are likely to be reluctant to do so as Tom, Dick and Harriet may not be worth suing and they are unlikely to want to sue their fellow shareholders in Newco, in the absence of fraud or recklessness.

What is ultimately agreed is a matter for negotiation but, as with an MBO, where there is external finance involved, the extent of the warranty and indemnity protection that is ultimately given is likely to be driven by the requirements of Newco's financial backers.

25.4.4 IBOs

On an IBO, the VCs or other institutions funding the deal will expect Newco to receive the same level of warranty protection as a trade buyer would expect. They would be most unlikely to accept an exclusion of liability in respect of matters known to management.

25.5 Financial assistance

Where transactions of the various kinds discussed in this chapter take effect as a sale and purchase of shares, it is very likely that the funding arrangements will include debt finance which is secured on the assets of the target company. As discussed in Ch.17, this will almost certainly be financial assistance by the target company for the purpose of the acquisition of its own shares.

25.5.1 Sellers "rolling over" into shares in Newco

A discussion of the documentation that will normally be involved where a transaction is being funded by acquisition finance and/or VC finance is beyond the scope of this book but, as discussed in Ch.12, if the seller is taking security for any deferred consideration he will almost certainly have to accept that such security will rank behind any security to be given to third party lenders. There will therefore have to be an agreement between the seller, Newco and Newco's financial backers which regulates the respective priorities of any security.

In practice, there will almost certainly be a detailed inter-creditor agreement which restricts the ability of Newco to make any payments to the seller without the prior approval of whoever is providing the acquisition finance.

For example, Newco may be acquiring the entire issued share capital of Target Limited from Seller PLC (Seller) for a total purchase price of £5 million, of which £4 million is payable on completion and the balance by four equal six-monthly instalments of £250,000, with the acquisition finance being provided by Loadsamoney Bank PLC (Bank) and equity finance being provided by Goliath Capital PLC (VC).

The Bank will not want Newco to pay any of the instalments to Seller if its doing so would prejudice its ability to service the interest on the Bank's loan or to meet any capital repayments to the Bank and the Bank may therefore make it a term of its lending that no such repayment may be made without its consent or, at least, that no such payment may be made if Newco's financial forecasts indicate that doing so would put it in breach of any of the financial covenants which it would be giving to the Bank under the terms of the Bank's facility documents. The Bank is likely to require similar restrictions on the payment of any interest which may be due to Seller—for example, if any part of the purchase price is to be satisfied by the issue of interest-bearing loan stock or loan notes.

On a sale and purchase of shares, sellers will sometimes agree to "roll over" part of their shareholding in the target company into shares in the buyer—typically, but not necessarily, redeemable preference shares. The issues discussed in the preceding paragraphs will almost certainly apply in such cases and there will almost certainly, therefore, be restrictions on the payment of dividends to the seller (and, indeed, to any other shareholder in Newco, including the VC) and on Newco's ability to redeem any such shares. Sellers should therefore be made aware of these issues before agreeing to accept any form of deferred payment for their shares.

The precise terms of the inter-creditor agreement are like to be subject to fierce negotiation between the bank providing the acquisition finance, any VC and the sellers and there is no hard and fast rule as to what is appropriate—it will depend upon all the circumstances and, inevitably, on the respective bargaining positions of the parties.

25.5.2 **Group services**

Particularly when a target company or business is being bought out of a group of companies, there may well be services provided "centrally" by the seller or elsewhere in its group and Newco may need to make arrangements with the seller for those services to continue to be provided for a period after completion which is long enough to allow Newco to make its own arrangements. Typical examples are payroll and IT services, but there may well be others.

It will be necessary to identify any such services before completion and make sure that whatever is agreed is reflected in the sale and purchase agreement or in a separate "services" agreement.

It will be necessary to take particular care not to breach the terms of any software licences—buyers will often want to be allowed to continue to use the business's existing accounting or payroll systems but, particularly on a sale and purchase of assets, this may infringe the terms of any third party licences.

Chapter 26

Buying from Receivers and Administrators

This chapter discusses some of the issues which are particularly likely to arise when buying from an administrator, receiver or liquidator. No precedents are given for such transactions as, in practice, the sale and purchase agreement will almost certainly be drafted on behalf of the office-holder in question, who will refuse to countenance any substantive changes to its terms other than to the extent necessary to reflect the commercial deal that has been agreed between the parties.

This chapter does not deal with purchases from liquidators where the company in question is subject to a solvent (members' voluntary) winding-up and does not in any event purport to summarise the methods of appointing administrators, receivers, or liquidators or their respective powers.

The fundamental point which prospective buyers should bear in mind when considering making acquisitions from administrators, receivers and liquidators is that they will refuse point blank to incur any personal liability and, in particular, that they will refuse to give any personal warranties, indemnities or other undertakings. Similarly, they will not commit the selling company (i.e. the company in respect of which they have been appointed) to give any warranties or indemnities. Buyers therefore have to accept that in such transactions they will be buying "as seen" and will have no come-back if (for example) any of the assets of the business are subject to an encumbrance in favour of a third party or are in a poor state of repair and condition or even if there are assets which the buyer thinks that he is buying but which he never actually manages to get his hands on—for example, there may be plant which appears in a plant register but which has in fact been scrapped or there may be stock or other assets which have "walked" in the lead-up to the appointment of the administrator, receiver or liquidator.

Prospective buyers should accept from the outset that this will be the case and should not waste time and expense by asking their legal advisers to press for warranties or indemnities. Similarly, when there are a number of prospective buyers, it is inadvisable for any prospective buyer to state in his expression of interest or offer letter that he is expecting any form of warranty or indemnity as that may suggest to the office-holder in question that he is a buyer who does not understand the rules of the game and that the office-holder would be better to negotiate with somebody who does.

It may, however, be possible to persuade the office-holder concerned to agree to a mechanism under which the price may reduce in certain circumstances such as (for example) if a particular item of plant turns out to belong to a third party and is repossessed. For example, if there are potentially valuable moulds which are believed to be with customers, the buyer may be able to negotiate a deal under which he only pays for such items as and when he manages to get his hands on them—in such cases, it would be normal to have the appropriate part of the purchase price held on an escrow account in the meantime.

Matters which a buyer will particularly need to consider on such transactions are set out below. These are generally discussed on the basis that the buyer will be buying from an administrator, rather than a receiver or liquidator, but most of them will apply equally to purchases out of receivership or liquidation. They are generally discussed also on the basis that the buyer will be buying assets, as that is how most acquisitions out of insolvency are structured (see 26.1 below).

26.1 Shares or assets?

Although the Enterprise Act 2002 made the primary duty of administrators (after September 2003) to "rescue the Company as a going concern", it is almost inconceivable that a buyer would contemplate buying the share capital of a company which is in administration, receivership or liquidation—why should a buyer acquire the share capital of an insolvent company, with all its creditors and other liabilities and, of course, subject to the burden of debt which was the cause of the insolvency? As has already been seen, the buyer would acquire the company "warts and all", with no warranties, indemnities or other recourse against the seller as a result of anything which might have happened before completion.

It is possible, however, that a buyer might be prepared to acquire the share capital of a subsidiary which is not itself in administration, receivership or liquidation. For example, Buyer PLC (Buyer) may wish to acquire the business of Target Limited, a wholly-owned subsidiary of Seller Limited, Seller (but not Target) being in administration: Buyer might in those circumstances be prepared to consider acquiring the shares in Target, which would probably be more attractive to the administrators of Seller since, if Target is not in administration, they would only be able to sell the shares in Target and would not be able to sell its assets. The alternative would be for Buyer to insist (assuming that this is possible) that Target should itself go into administration and that Buyer would then acquire the undertaking and assets of Target. That would almost certainly be more attractive to Buyer—Buyer would receive no warranties or indemnities however the transaction was structured but buying assets should at least enable him to leave behind liabilities which he did not want to take over (but subject to the comments made below).

The other situation in which a buyer will sometimes buy shares from a company in administration, receivership or liquidation is when the assets and undertaking of the company concerned are "hived down" to a new company, with Buyer then acquiring those shares.

In the above example, therefore, the undertaking and assets of Target, together with such liabilities as Buyer is prepared to assume, would be transferred to a new, clean, wholly-owned subsidiary of Target and Buyer would then acquire the share capital of that new company.

In the past, the attraction of a hive down, rather than a direct purchase of the assets, was the ability to transfer to the new company past trading losses of the insolvent company but the ability to transfer the trading losses of an insolvent company has been significantly restricted since 1986, with the result that such structures are far less common.

26.2   Appointment

A buyer should take reasonable steps to satisfy himself as to the validity of the appointment of the office-holder concerned and should also check the powers conferred on him. Section 232 of the Insolvency Act 1986 provides that the acts of an administrative receiver, liquidator or provisional liquidator of a company are valid, notwithstanding any defect in his appointment, nomination or qualifications but, although this provision may prevent his acts from being invalidated as a result of defects in formalities relating to his appointment, in the case of an administrative receiver, it may not validate his acts if the debenture under which he was appointed is invalid. In any event, s.232 does not apply to a receiver appointed under a fixed charge given by the company over some or all of its assets ("LPA Receivers"). Paragraph 104 of Sch.B1 to the Insolvency Act 1986 provides that an act of the administrator of a company is valid in spite of a defect in his appointment or qualification.

The enquiries that a buyer should make will depend on the nature of the appointment.

26.2.1   Administrators

The buyer should request copies of the following:

> 26.2.1.1 if the administrators have been appointed by the court, a copy of the court order;

> 26.2.1.2 if they have been appointed out of court:

>> • a copy of the notice of intention to appoint (if there is one);

>> • notice of appointment—the notice should have the consent of any floating charge holder endorsed on it if the administrators appointed by the company or its directors.

26.2.2   Receivers

The buyer should request copies of the following:

> 26.2.2.1 a copy of the debenture or other security under which the receiver was appointed, in order to establish the extent of his powers and any limitations on them;

> 26.2.2.2 a copy of the company's memorandum and articles;

26.2.2.3   a copy of the letter of demand on the company by the party appointing the receiver, in order to ensure that the demand has been correctly made in accordance with its provisions (assuming that the debenture provides for the sums secured by it to be repayable "on demand");

26.2.2.4   the instrument of appointment;

26.2.2.5   the receiver's acceptance of the appointment (in order to ensure that it was received within the required timescale).

26.2.3   Liquidation

The buyer should request copies of the following:

26.2.3.1   on a creditors' voluntary liquidation:

- the resolution of the members to wind the seller up and appoint the liquidator;

- the resolution of the creditors confirming this appointment.

26.2.3.2   on a compulsory liquidation:

- the court order for the winding-up of the company;

- where relevant, a copy of the Secretary of State's appointment of the liquidator (usually, after the original winding-up, a substitute liquidator is put in place).

26.3   Conditions precedent

Many of the issues discussed in Ch.4 (conditions precedent—consents, approvals, releases, etc.) will potentially be equally relevant when buying from administrators, but there is normally considerable pressure to complete the transaction very rapidly and this may mean that, in some instances, the buyer will have to "take a view" on various matters.

The following points should, however, be borne in mind:

26.3.1   When the shares or assets to be sold are subject to a mortgage, debenture or other charge in favour of a third party, it will normally be necessary to obtain formal releases from the security holder(s)—an exception to this is that an administrator may sell property which is subject to a floating charge as if it were not subject to the charge (para.70(1) of Sch.B1 to the Insolvency Act 1986).

26.3.2   If an administrator wishes to sell property which is subject to a security other than a floating charge, it will be necessary for him to obtain a court order pursuant to para.71(1) of Sch.B1 to the Insolvency Act 1986 and that is also the case with assets which are held under a hire-purchase agreement. A detailed discussion of these provisions is, however, beyond the scope of this book.

26.3.3 The provisions of s.190 of the Companies Act 2006 (formerly s.320 of the Companies Act 1985), pursuant to which substantial property contracts between a company and a director of the company require approval by a resolution of the members of the company, will apply where the company concerned is in receivership but not when it is in administration or when it is being wound-up (other than by way of members' voluntary winding up) (s.193 of the Companies Act 2006).

26.4 Reservation of title claims

It is very likely that the selling company will have acquired stock (including raw materials, parts, etc.) from suppliers whose terms and conditions of sale include a "reservation of title" clause and the administrator will almost certainly expect the buyer to take the risk of any such claims. It is likely, therefore, that the sale and purchase agreement will contain a provision under which, if any items sold to the buyer are found to be subject to such claims, the buyer will either return them or will pay off the supplier.

Unless the buyer is able to negotiate a deal under which the purchase price reduces in that situation he should take steps to establish in advance the potential risk of reservation of title claims and reflect that in the price which he is prepared to pay.

The buyer may seek to restrict the ability of the administrators to settle or compromise any reservation of title or similar claims but such restrictions are unlikely to be accepted.

26.5 Assets on lease, hire-purchase, etc.

The buyer should take steps to establish, as far as he can, the extent to which any plant, machinery or equipment is subject to leasing, hire-purchase or similar arrangements and, where there are key items and time permits him to do so, the buyer would be well-advised to approach the finance company in advance in order to establish whether it will agree to the transfer of the assets and of the financing agreements to the buyer. The buyer should also establish whether or not any of the payments due to the finance companies are in arrears as, if there are amounts unpaid, the finance company concerned may refuse to give its consent unless those arrears are discharged.

If it is not possible to make appropriate arrangements with the finance companies before completion, the buyer may be permitted to retain and use the items in question but on the basis that he will return them on demand and will indemnify the seller and the administrators against any claims resulting from his being given possession of them.

26.6 Assets held subject to licences from third parties

The buyer should take steps to establish whether any of the intellectual property rights or computer software used in the business are licensed to the seller by a third party and, if that is the case, the buyer must understand that the use of the rights in question will almost certainly contravene the terms of the licences (assuming that the administrators are prepared to authorise the buyer to use them at all). Particular care should be taken with software which is essential for the business and the buyer may well have to incur the expense of acquiring new licences if he wishes to continue to use it.

26.7   Liens

If there are any goods which the buyer is expecting to buy and which are in the possession of a third party (for example, items which are with a haulier for delivery to a customer) the buyer should try to establish whether there are sums owing to the party concerned as otherwise the third party may be able to claim a lien on them and retain them until he has been paid.

26.8   Verification of assets

If time permits, the Sale and Purchase Agreement is likely to contain a schedule which lists the principal items of plant, machinery and equipment, and, ideally, this will have been prepared shortly after the appointment of the administrators. That may not necessarily be the case, however, and time or other practicalities may mean that there is a schedule which cannot be assumed to be up to date or even that there is no such schedule at all.

In any event, there will be no warranties regarding the accuracy of the schedule and no undertaking to deliver to the buyer everything which is in the schedule and so the buyer should, to the extent that time permits, take steps to ensure that everything mentioned in the schedule is on site and is in working order. If there are items which he is expecting to buy but which are not included in the schedule, he should make sure that they are added. As discussed at 26.5 above, he should also take steps to establish the extent to which any of the items that he is expecting to buy are subject to lease, hire-purchase or similar arrangements as the administrators will only sell "such right, title and interest (if any)" as they have and, unless there is a specific price-adjustment mechanism, there will be no come-back against the administrators or the seller if (for example) a key item of plant turns out to be leased, rather than owned outright.

Particular problems can arise where there are items with third parties such as (for example) tooling which is held by out-workers, moulds or tools in the possession of customers and stock which is held by customers on consignment.

26.9   Employment issues

The implications of TUPE (see Ch.21) mean that the buyer should obtain as much information as possible about the employees of the business, including:

26.9.1   Details of all redundancies effected since the date of appointment of the administrators (as, if the redundancies could be said to be connected to the transfer of the business the dismissals of the employees would be unfair dismissals, for which the buyer would be liable (see 21.8.2)).

26.9.2   Details of any arrears of wages or salaries (liabilities for which would pass under TUPE).

26.9.3   Whether there are accrued holiday pay entitlements (responsibility for these will pass to the buyer and would therefore need to be reflected in the purchase price).

26.10   Use of seller's name

Where it is intended that a director or shadow director of the seller should become a director of the buyer or otherwise be involved in the management of the business following its acquisition by the buyer, it will be necessary to consider the implications of s.216 of the Insolvency Act 1986 which applies to anyone who was a director or shadow director of a company at any time in the period of 12 months ending with the day before it went into insolvent liquidation.

Such individuals may not, without leave of the court, be directors of, or involved in, the promotion, formation or management of a company known by a name by which the company in liquidation was known in the 12 months prior to its liquidation, or a name so similar to such a name as to suggest an association with that company and it will apply when the selling company goes into liquidation after the purchase from the administrators.

The buyer will need to consider these provisions if the intention is to use the name of the seller, or anything similar to it, in the future.

There is a specific exception under Rule 4.228 of the Insolvency Rules 1986 which applies where a company (the successor company) acquires the whole, or substantially the whole, of the business of an insolvent company, under arrangements made by an insolvency practitioner acting as its liquidator, administrator or administrative receiver or as supervisor of a voluntary arrangement and the successor company gives notice under Rule 4.228 to the insolvent company's creditors within 28 days from the completion of the acquisition. Rule 4.228 specifies the information which must be contained in such notice and if the successor company gives notice under that Rule, a person who is named in the notice in accordance with its provisions may be involved in the promotion, formation or management of the successor company without having to apply to the court. If, therefore, there are directors or shadow directors of the seller who are to be involved in the management of the business following its acquisition by the buyer, the buyer should make sure that the appropriate notices are given under Rule 4.228.

26.11   Customers and suppliers

The insolvency of the seller may have particular implications for the buyer's relationship with the customers and suppliers of the business and in particular:

26.11.1   If the seller supplied goods to customers which are alleged to be defective, the customers may well insist that the buyer repairs them or replaces them, at its own expense, before they (the customers) will continue to do business with the buyer. In this situation, it is inconceivable that the buyer would have any recourse against the seller for the costs of doing so and, indeed, the agreement may well make the buyer liable to perform such repairs or warranty work to protect the debts of the insolvent company which the administrator is seeking to collect.

26.11.2   If the buyer is acquiring the book debts of the seller, he should be aware that there may well be counter-claims from debtors and this should be taken into account in the price which the buyer is prepared to pay.

26.11.3   If there are key suppliers of the business who are owed money by the seller it is quite possible that they will insist on their debts being settled by the buyer before they will supply him.

26.12   Agency of receiver

Before completion, the buyer should take steps to establish whether or not there is a winding-up order in respect of the seller as the making of such an order will terminate a receiver's power to act as agent of the company in respect of which he is appointed. In those circumstances, the buyer should ensure that the receiver executes the sale and purchase agreement pursuant to the power of attorney which will almost certainly be granted to him in the debenture or other security document under which he was appointed, rather than as agent of the company.

There may well be good opportunities to acquire fundamentally good businesses from administrators and receivers, in particular, but buyers in such situations have to accept that there will be no warranties or indemnities and that they have to satisfy themselves, as far as possible, that they will be buying what they are expecting to buy, that it is in a decent state of repair and condition and that they will be able to acquire title to it, free from any liens or other encumbrances in favour of third parties.

Chapter 27

Sales and Purchases of Technology Businesses

This chapter deals with issues which are likely to be of particular relevance in connection with a sale or purchase of a "technology business"—in this context, a business whose principal assets are intellectual property rights and other intangible assets.

For the most part, buying and selling such businesses is similar to buying and selling any other business but what distinguishes a technology business from almost any other business is that its main assets are intangible assets (so that there are no tyres to kick), and its people who, unlike bricks and mortar and plant and equipment, can walk out of the door to join a competitor or to set up a competing business themselves.

The assets of a typical manufacturing business will, almost certainly, consist primarily of premises (which may be freehold, leasehold or tenanted), plant and equipment and other tangible assets. Similarly, the main assets of a retail business are likely to consist of premises, fixtures and fittings and stock—again, predominantly tangible assets. A manufacturing business may also have valuable patents, trade marks, copyrights and other intellectual property rights and a retailer may have valuable registered and unregistered trade marks but, generally, the bulk of their value is in their tangible assets.

In the case of a technology business, however, most of the value is likely to be in its intellectual property and other intangible rights and the buyer's legal and commercial due diligence is likely to be focused on these areas.

27.1 Due diligence

7.8 in Ch.7 summarises the due diligence that a buyer will typically want to carry out in relation to the intellectual property rights of a typical business but, when buying a technology business, the buyer would be well-advised to carry out more extensive due diligence in this area.

The first step will be to establish what intellectual property rights are key to the business and then establish the basis on which each item of those intellectual property rights is used within the business. The intellectual property rights of a technology business will normally include one or more of the following categories of intellectual property rights:

- intellectual property rights which are owned by the business outright—these may be intellectual property rights which have been developed by the company or individual carrying on the business or intellectual property rights which have been developed by a third party but the rights of which have been assigned or otherwise transferred to the business;

- intellectual property rights which the business owns, but not outright—such intellectual property rights may have been jointly developed with a third party through a joint venture or collaboration agreement or pursuant to some other commercial arrangement;

- intellectual property rights which the business does not own but which are owned by a third party and used by the business under a licence—for example, patents or trade marks which are used under a licence or registered user agreement or (as is the case with most businesses, to a greater or lesser extent) software which has been developed by a third party and which the business is using pursuant to a licence.

From a legal due diligence point of view, the work to be carried out will depend upon which of the above categories the intellectual property rights in question fall into.

27.1.1   It will often become apparent from due diligence that the position is far from clear cut, particularly in the case of intellectual property rights which were originally assumed to have been owned by the business outright.

In many technology businesses, particularly when they are in their infancy, it is very common to find that a significant amount of the development work has been carried out by third party consultants or other non-employees and it is also possible that original founders of the business may themselves have carried out all or part of the development work before establishing a company to carry on the business and without putting in place any formal assignment or other documentation to transfer the relevant intellectual property rights to the company. It is, however, essential from the point of view of a prospective seller to make sure that there is an adequate "audit trail" to satisfy the buyer that he will be acquiring the intellectual property rights which he is expecting to acquire and it is important for the buyer to follow that trail in order to verify the ownership of the rights in question.

One step which needs to be carried out at an early stage is to establish exactly who has been responsible for a particular invention or other development and then find out whether that person was, at the material time, an employee of the business or a third party consultant. The position may well be different in other jurisdictions but, in the UK, the general principle is that, if an employee develops or invents something within the course of his employment, then the resulting intellectual property rights will belong to the employer (unless the contract of employment provides to the contrary) but, where the invention or development is made by a third party consultant, the resulting intellectual property rights will belong to the consultant, unless the contract under which the consultant was engaged provides to the contrary or steps have subsequently been taken to transfer the intellectual property rights across.

The risks can be very real: when the sale of a business becomes public knowledge, it is quite common for a former employee or consultant to claim that he is the owner of some of the key intellectual property rights and it may be very difficult to refute any such claim if there is not an adequate audit trail to show that the rights do in fact belong to the business. In any event, any such claim may well have a significant nuisance value for both parties—the buyer will be concerned by the possibility of not in fact acquiring the intellectual property rights that he was expecting to acquire, while the seller will be concerned that this may result in warranty or indemnity claims from the buyer.

One situation in which particular care should be take is where the business was originally a "spin out" from a university: such businesses by their very nature, are likely to depend to a large extent on intellectual property rights and these may well have been developed, to a greater or lesser extent, by employees or researchers at the university: in such circumstances, it may well be necessary to establish that all resulting intellectual property rights vested at that point in the university and were then validly transferred by the university to the "spin out" business.

Care also needs to be taken where there have been transfers of assets and rights within a group, in order to make sure that the intellectual property rights in question have been validly transferred to the relevant group company. Even greater care needs to be taken if the transfers have taken place between companies which are not under common ownership—particularly where there are potentially hostile minority shareholders. Where appropriate, retrospective assignments should be put in place before the sale and purchase agreement is entered into but this may not be straightforward: the person or company in whom the rights are still vested may refuse to co-operate without being given some sort of incentive (almost invariably financial) to do so and there is also the risk that an individual may have died or that a company involved in the trail of ownership will have been wound up.

27.1.2 Where the intellectual property rights in question are not owned outright, it will be necessary for the buyer to check the terms of any agreement or other arrangement pursuant to which the development took place and ensure that it will be possible for the business to continue to use the rights in the event of a change in its ownership. This is likely to be of particular concern on a sale and purchase of assets but may also be relevant on a sale and purchase of shares— for example, if there is a provision under which, on a change of control of one party, the rights in question vest entirely in the other.

27.1.3. It is important for the buyer to establish exactly what intellectual property rights are licensed to the business, bearing in mind that there may be commercial agreements which do not at first sight appear to be license agreements but which do, in fact, contain a licence of intellectual property rights—examples of such agreements include collaboration agreements and sometimes even supply agreements. The buyer should review (amongst other things) the following provisions of any such licence:

- the rights which are the subject-matter of the licence;

- the duration of the licence—for example, a buyer may be particularly concerned if a vital licence was due to expire fairly shortly or was capable of being terminated on unacceptably short notice;

- provisions for "early" termination—a particular concern on a sale and purchase of shares will be to establish whether the other party can terminate the licence on a change of control of the licensee;

- on a sale and purchase of assets, whether or not the licence is capable of being assigned to the buyer;

- the nature of the licence itself—is it exclusive (which would normally prevent the licensor from using the rights himself or licensing others to use them), non-exclusive (which would limit the licensor to use the rights himself and to grant other licences to third parties), or a sole licence (which would allow the licensor to continue to use the rights but would not allow him to grant licences to others);

- the geographical extent of the licence; and

- the rate at which royalties are payable and the basis on which they are to be calculated.

27.2   Commercial evaluation

Having established what intellectual property rights there are, the buyer will want to carry out a commercial evaluation of those rights and will want to ensure that all key intellectual property rights are adequately protected by registrations in the relevant geographical areas and will also want to establish, in the case of patents, the length of time that is left before they expire. Where patents are approaching the end of their life it will be necessary for the buyer to consider whether the subject-matter of those patents can be protected in other ways. The buyer would also need to consider how easy it would be for others to compete once the patent protection has expired — what barriers to entry would there be?

The buyer may conclude that one of the most effective ways of making it difficult for others to compete would be to retain key staff of the business and this area is discussed below.

27.3   Group issues

Particular concerns may arise when a business is being bought and sold out of a group where there are intellectual property rights which are used by the business being sold but which may also be required to be used on a continuing basis by other parts of the retained group: these may be rights which are owned by the group company being sold but used by other companies in the group or they may be rights which are owned by other group companies but used by the company being sold. When buying out of a group, therefore, it will be necessary to establish what intellectual property rights are being used by the business in question but will also need to be used in the future by other group companies and then make sure that there are arrangements going forward which allow the various businesses which need to continue to be able to use the rights in question to do so and on terms acceptable to all concerned.

In such cases the starting point of the buyer is likely to be that he should acquire the rights in question and then licence the appropriate parts of the seller's group to use those rights, while (inevitably) the seller will argue that he should retain those rights and licence the buyer to use them. The obvious advantage of being the owner of the rights, rather than a licensee, is that the party concerned will not then need to be concerned about the scope of the licence, any restrictions on the use of the rights in question or the risks of losing the ability to use those rights as a result of the licence being terminated.

As is so often the case, who prevails on this point will depend on the bargaining positions of the parties, but a reasonable starting point would be to conclude that the business which has the predominant use of the rights in question should acquire them, with all other users using them under licence.

27.4   Employment issues

As has already been seen, a key asset of a technology business may well be "know-how" which may, largely, be in the heads of key people and which would therefore be lost to the business if they were to leave.

In such circumstances, the retention of those key members of staff is likely to be essential and, as discussed in 7.10.7, the buyer may wish to meet with those individuals in advance in order to make sure, as far as possible, that they will continue to remain with the business. A starting-point would be to make sure that there are appropriate service agreements or other contracts of employment or (if there are not) to have new ones put in place but that will only give the buyer limited comfort as, in practice, if an individual walks out in breach of his contract of employment, there is little that an employer can do about it and, even if the employee is made to work his full notice period, it is not ideal to have an employee in the business who is known to be leaving to join a competitor—particularly if that individual has access to key customers or suppliers of the business or access to lists of customers or other key commercial information.

The buyer will, therefore, wish to make sure that the contracts of employment contain appropriate restrictive covenants—as discussed in 8.12, these will normally include an undertaking not to solicit customers of the business, an undertaking not to solicit away other employees and an undertaking not to be involved in a competing business, in each case for an agreed period and in an agreed geographical area.

As explained in 8.12, however, the buyer should always bear in mind that such restrictions will only be enforceable if they go no further (in time and geographic area) than is reasonably necessary to protect the buyer's legitimate commercial interests.

In practice, therefore, the most effective way of retaining key employees is likely to be to make sure that there are appropriate incentives in place to persuade them to remain with the business—partly by means of attractive remuneration packages but perhaps also by giving them share options or setting up a profit-sharing or similar incentive scheme.

APPENDIX 1

APPENDIX 1

Typical areas that may be covered in a financial due diligence report

1   **Key findings and executive summary**
- This will contain a brief summary of the contents of the report and details of principal matters arising.

2   **History and description of business**
- Key events in the recent history of the target.
- Brief description of business activities and milestones in the development of the target business.
- Company structure, including capital structure, details of ownership and recent changes therein, any minority interests in subsidiaries, investments and joint ventures.
- Review of the strategy and objectives of the target business.
- Contracts and transactions involving directors.
- Details of the key legal agreements influencing the nature of the business or structure of the target business.

3   **Markets and sales**
- Markets, and competition (particularly in the light of recent and planned changes), including market growth and changes in market share (this can be on the borderline with the work of commercial due diligence specialists—see later comments).
- Sales (including strategy, sales organisation and control, dependence on individual customers, contracts, pricing, terms of trade, dependency on agency agreements, etc). Assessment of seasonality.
- Services provided (including range, description, development, revenue and contribution).
- Exposure to foreign exchange fluctuations (including extent of any hedging).
- Details of post-sales obligations, including product guarantees and servicing arrangements.
- Customer service and quality policy.

4   **Purchasing**
- Purchasing and supplies (including strategy, purchasing organisation, relationships and principal suppliers and associated purchases and relevant agreements. Exposure to raw material price movements. Details of alternative supply sources).
- Exposure to foreign exchange fluctuations (including extent of any hedging).
- Use of sub-contractors.
- Information on distribution systems.
- Review of stock control disciplines.
- Overview of research and development programmes.

5   **Premises**

- Description of premises, including location, locality, site area, current usage, date of acquisition, subsequent expenditure, analysis between freehold and leasehold. In the case of leased properties, details of terms of lease, any onerous covenants, any planning restrictions or planned development (comment on space constraints or the availability of spare space). Details of any impending or deferred repairs if significant, and any ongoing programme of maintenance.

- Any recent independent or internal valuations or insurance reports.

- The suitability and adequacy of plant and premises (based on discussion with management as non-experts). Present and future production capacity/requirements.

6   **Organisational structure, management and personnel**

- Management structure, reporting lines and division of responsibility.

- Outline of directors' and senior executives' biographies (including their age, qualifications, experience, length of service, responsibilities during the period under review, service contracts, benefits and remuneration and the role of non executives).

- Details of former directors and senior executives who have left the business over a specified period.

- Details of any relatives/friends of directors/sellers on the payroll or otherwise engaged by the target business.

- Management style, succession planning and current gaps or weaknesses in the management team (particularly in relation to the finance team).

- Analysis of employees (including total number of staff at the date of the report, analysis between full-time and part-time employment and by function, movement in numbers over the recent past, length of service and age profile).

- Basis of remuneration of employees (including salary/wages structure, comparison with industry average rates, and dates of salary reviews). Overtime and sickness levels. Holiday pay arrangements.

- Current state of labour relations and any past disputes together with details of any trade union membership.

- The use of agency or temporary staff (has PAYE/NI been correctly dealt with?).

- Pensions (including current status of the fund, existence of unfunded liabilities, level of contributions and security of assets, details of any Pensions Regulator's clearance letters) and other employment and post-employment benefits. If applicable, the financial impact of withdrawing from current seller group arrangements (this will almost certainly require specialist advice).

- Details of share incentive, share option and profit sharing schemes.

- Recruitment policy and training.

- Ability of staff to meet development plans.

7   **Financial control environment**

- Description and assessment of the key financial systems and internal controls, including estimating and forecasting, credit control and cash management procedures.

- Details of key financial (and other) information used to manage the business, including accuracy, timeliness and sufficiency (including the level of adjustment required to management accounts to produce the annual statutory accounts).

- Summaries of past budgets compared with actual results for a specified period, together with comments on the main reasons for deviations from budgets to assess past budgeting accuracy.
- Details of key computer systems (including IT strategy, systems development to date and proposed enhancements, security and disaster recovery plans, extent and effectiveness of use).
- Organisation and effectiveness of the finance function (including credit control).
- Weaknesses identified by the auditors and significant matters arising from the audit work in respect of past periods.

8   **Accounting policies**

- Details of historic accounting policies (including detailed practices and procedures adopted). Income and cost recognition policies in some businesses can be highly subjective. Imprudent revenue recognition or the excessive deferral of costs in fixed assets or stocks can be important areas for review. The mechanism for elimination of unrealised inter company profits can also be an area requiring detailed assessment.
- Impact of any changes (or of any proposed changes) in policies, methodologies and practices over a defined period (typically three years).
- Comparison with industry and "best practice", and potentially with International Financial Reporting Standards.
- When an acquisition involves a significant overseas business, a restatement of the target's accounts to UK GAAP (or the buyer's GAAP as relevant) is often required.
- A comparison of the target company's accounting policies with those of the buyer.

9   **Historic trading results**

- Summary of the profit and loss accounts over a specified period (typically three years) and the principal reasons for significant fluctuations.
- Analysis of revenues, direct costs and gross margins by relevant business segment or product category (including key operational statistics, comparison with competitors, impact of seasonality etc). Identify any low margin or loss making product groups.
- Assessment of the target's dependence upon any individual customers by reviewing an analysis of historic revenue by customer.
- Review of historic order book levels identifying key trends.
- Details of overheads together with commentary on significant fluctuations.
- Analysis of and commentary on "exceptional" and "extraordinary" items, and any significant transactions not on an "arm's length" basis.
- Analysis of interest and taxation charges.
- Details of any prior period adjustments considered by the investigating accountant to be necessary.
- Assessment of the "underlying" profitability of the target business. This can involve determining the necessary adjustments for any significant "one off" costs or revenue, or "non-arm's length" transactions. Where relevant, it may also require making allowance for the costs of operating the target business on a "stand alone" basis separate from the rest of the seller operations. This can include the loss of lower prices (for both direct costs and overheads) secured on a group wide basis by the seller's group, and the need to replace services provided by the seller group (for example, for group treasury and HR services).

10   Historic net assets

- Summary of historic balance sheets and an explanation of significant trends (typically up to the last three year ends and the latest available balance sheet per the management accounts are reviewed).

- Detailed analysis of each significant balance sheet heading including:
  - Comment on details of fixed assets and depreciation rates/asset lives (is there an asset register which adequately allows individual assets to be identified? When was the asset register last checked by physical verification of assets?). Provide details of leased assets. Identify any significant element of own labour capitalised. Review proposed capital expenditure programme and current commitments as well as past grants (and potential obligations to repay).
  - Stock verification (any stocks at third party locations or held on consignment; is all stock regularly verified; is there a history of large differences between book records and physical quantities?).
  - Stock valuation/provisioning methodologies.
  - Analysis of debtors, including sales ledger ageing, bad debt history and provisions.
  - Analysis of creditors including ageing of purchase ledger balances, accruals and basis of provisioning (provision accounting particularly for long-term liabilities can be often highly judgmental and therefore require detailed assessment as part of the due diligence review).
  - Details of banking arrangements and loan facilities (including terms, covenants and details of security granted to third parties).
  - Details of contingent liabilities.
  - Summary and implication of any off balance sheet financing arrangements.
  - Details of any material long term and/or onerous contracts.

11   Historic cash flows

- Summary of historic cash flows (again typically for up to three years and current year to date).

- Details of seasonality in working capital requirements, and also intra month patterns.

- Details of evidence of current or historic cash pressures in the target business.

12   Taxation

- Summary of the current corporation tax position of the target business with regard to the agreement of taxation computations, highlighting any important outstanding issues.

- Summary of the taxation charge within the accounts and the basis of provisioning (including an assessment of the deferred tax position).

- Summary of any available corporation tax losses.

- Impact of the acquisition on the taxation position of the target business.

- Compliance with PAYE/NI regulations and VAT regulations. In respect of these matters, work is often restricted to enquiry as to compliance with submission of returns and normal procedures and the status of any outstanding queries or issues. Has income tax/national insurance been properly accounted for on payments to employees—in instances where employees have been wrongly paid without deduction of tax, it can be very difficult for the buyer to recover the tax due from the employee. If deemed a particular risk area, a detailed review by VAT and PAYE specialists can be commissioned.

13   **Financial forecasts**

●   Review and commentary on the profit and loss, balance sheet and cash flow forecasts, a comparison with historic trading and recent experience and budget, and commentary on the assumptions underlying the forecasts. Specific consideration is typically be given to:
–   sales volume and pricing assumptions, often taking into account inter alia order book levels/level of contracted income and reliance on key customers as well as any capacity or supply issues;
–   forecast margins;
–   adequacy of forecast overhead expenditure (particularly taking into account the buyer's post acquisition planning for the target business and any anticipated step change in activity levels);
–   interest charges—the accounting for debt raising costs on acquisitions can be complex;
–   forecast tax charges—dependent on the profile of the target business and the buyer, simply applying the standard tax rate to forecast profits may not be sufficiently accurate;
–   capital expenditure forecasts;
–   forecast working capital levels (stocks, debtors and creditors); and
–   the potential impact of seasonality on the business.

●   Assess forecast compliance with debt covenant requirements.

●   Identify the key sensitivities and areas of vulnerability in the trading forecasts and cash flows.

●   Model the impact of appropriate sensitivities on the forecast model.

14   **Other matters**

●   Provide a summary of insurances (particularly where not currently on a "stand alone" basis, existing insurance cover and premiums may not remain post acquisition).

●   Summarise any current, pending or threatened significant litigation by or against any member of the target business or its directors and the adequacy of provisions associated therewith.

APPENDIX 2

APPENDIX 2

PRECEDENTS

PRECEDENT 1

Share Sale and
Purchase Agreement
Version A—Corporate Sellers

<u>DATED</u>   <u>200</u>

(1) [   ] LIMITED/PLC]
                  -and-
(2) [   ] LIMITED/PLC]

SHARE SALE AND PURCHASE AGREEMENT
-relating to-
[   ] LIMITED/PLC]
VERSION A: CORPORATE SELLER

This Agreement is made on   200 between:

(1)   [**LIMITED/PLC**], a company registered in
         England under number [   ], whose registered office is at [
                              ] ("the Seller"); and

(2)   [**LIMITED/PLC**], a company registered in
         England under number [   ], whose registered office is at
         [   ] ("the
         Buyer").

It is agreed as follows:

1.   **INTERPRETATION**

In this Agreement:

1.1   The following words and expressions shall have the following meanings:

"the Accounts"   (a) the audited accounts of the Company
                                 [and of each of the Subsidiaries] com-
                                 prising (in each case) an audited balance
                                 sheet as at the Accounts Date and audited
                                 profit and loss account for the financial
                                 period ended on the Accounts Date; [and]

                            (b) [the audited consolidated accounts of the
                                 Group comprising an audited consolidated
                                 balance sheet as at the Accounts Date and
                                 an audited consolidated profit and loss
                                 account for the financial period ended on
                                 the Accounts Date;]

                                 together (in each case) with the reports of the
                                 directors and auditors, any cash flow statements
                                 and all notes thereto;

"the Accounts Date"   [200];

"the Act"   the Companies Act 2006.

"the 1985 Act"   the Companies Act 1985;

"the Applicable Data   the Data Protection Acts 1986 and 1998 and
Protection Laws"   the Telecommunications (Data Protection and
                            Privacy) (Direct Marketing) Regulations 1998;

["the Bank"   [   ]   Bank   PLC   (
                            branch)];

"Business Day"   any day (other than Saturday) on which clearing
                            banks are open for normal banking business in
                            sterling in the City of London;

"the Buyer's Solicitors"   [   ] of   [   ]   or
                            any successor firm;

"the Company"   [Limited/PLC](of which particulars
                            are given in Part 1 of schedule 2);

"the Companies Acts"   as defined in section 2 of the Act;

"Completion"   completion of the acquisition and disposal of the
                            Shares in accordance with clause 5;

"Completion Date"	**ALTERNATIVES**
	EITHER
	the date of this Agreement;
	OR
	[200];
	OR
	[the [third] Business Day after] the date upon which the last of the Conditions to be satisfied or waived is satisfied or waived;
["the Completion NAV"	as defined in part 1 of schedule 9];
["the Conditions"	the conditions set out in part 1 of schedule 7 (each a "Condition")];
"Confidential Information"	all secret or confidential commercial, financial and technical information, know-how, trade secrets, inventions, computer software and other information whatsoever and in whatever form or medium and whether disclosed orally or in writing, together with all reproductions in whatsoever form or medium and any part or parts of it;
["Consideration Share"	an ordinary share of [ ] in the capital of the Buyer credited as fully paid;]
"the Disclosure Letter"	the letter having the same date as this Agreement from the Seller's Solicitors to the Buyer['s Solicitors];
"the Disclosed Schemes"	the GPP, the Life Assurance Scheme, the Pension Scheme(s), the Personal Pension Scheme(s) and the Stakeholder Scheme;
"Encumbrance"	any equity, right to acquire, option, right of pre-emption, mortgage, charge, pledge, lien, assignment, title retention or any other security interest, agreement or arrangement, whether monetary or not;
"Escrow Account"	a joint deposit account with the Bank in the joint names of the Buyer's Solicitors and the Seller's Solicitors;
"Escrow Agreement"	the agreement in the Agreed Terms to be entered into by the Seller's Solicitors and the Buyer's Solicitors regarding the operation of the Escrow Account;
"FRS"	a financial reporting standard in force at any material time as issued by the Accounting Standards Board;
"FSA"	the Financial Services Authority;
"GPP"	means the group personal pension plan under-written by [**name of provider**];
["the Group"	together the Company and the Subsidiaries;]

"Intellectual Property" (a)	patents, trade marks, service marks, registered designs, applications and rights to apply for any of those rights, trade, business and company names, internet domain names and e-mail addresses, unregistered trade marks and service marks, copyrights, database rights, know-how, rights in designs and inventions;
(b)	rights under licences, consents, orders, statutes or otherwise in relation to a right in paragraph (a);
(c)	rights of the same or similar effect or nature as or to those in paragraphs (a) and (b) which now or in the future may subsist; and
(d)	the right to sue for past infringements of any of the foregoing rights;
"Intellectual Property Rights"	all Intellectual Property owned, used or required to be used by the Company;
"Intellectual Property Agreements"	means agreements or arrangements relating (wholly or partly) to Intellectual Property or to the disclosure, use, assignment or patenting of any invention, discovery, improvement, process, formulae or other know-how;
"Life Assurance Scheme"	means the **[insert name of group life assurance scheme]** underwritten by **[name of provider]**;
["the Management Accounts"	the management accounts of the Company [, of each of the Subsidiaries and of the Group, in each case] for the period from the Accounts Date to [200] copies of which are attached to the Disclosure Letter;]
"Member of the "Seller's Group"	any company within the Seller's Group from time to time;
"Pension Scheme(s)"	means **[insert name of scheme(s)—to be used for occupational pension schemes]**;
"Personal Pension Scheme(s)"	means **[insert description of each scheme—to be used for personal pension schemes excluding group personal pensions]**;
"Proceedings"	any legal action or proceedings arising out of or in connection with this Agreement;
"the Property"	the property or properties briefly described in schedule 3;
"Release"	any release, waiver or compromise or any other arrangement of any kind having similar or analogous effect;
["the Seller's Group"	together the Seller and any company (including any undertaking within the meaning of section 1161 of the Act), within its group (within the meaning of section 474(1) of the Act) other than the Company [and the Subsidiaries];]
"the Seller's Solicitors	[ ], of [ ] or any [ ] successor firm;

"the Shares"	all the issued shares in the capital of the Company;
"SSAP"	a statement of standard accounting practice in force at any material time as issued by the Accounting Standards Committee and adopted by the Accounting Standards Board;;
"Stakeholder Scheme"	means the stakeholder pension scheme designated by [the Company] and underwritten by **[name of provider]**;
["the Stock Exchange"	the London Stock Exchange plc;]
["the Subsidiaries"	the companies listed in schedule 2 (each a "Subsidiary");]
"the Tax Covenants"	the obligations on the part of the Seller set out in part 3 of schedule 4;
"Tax"	as defined in part 1 of schedule 4;
"the Tax Warranties"	the warranties and representations set out in part 2 of schedule 4;
"UKLA"	the United Kingdom Listing Authority;
"the Warranties"	the warranties and representations set out in schedule 5 and the Tax Warranties;
"Warranty"	one of the Warranties (and the word "Warranty" followed by a number shall be deemed to be a reference to the paragraph of schedule 5 with that number).

1.2   References to the Property shall, where the context so admits or requires, be construed as references to all properties briefly described in schedule 3 and each of them and each and every part of each of them.

1.3   Unless the context otherwise expressly requires, words and expressions which are otherwise defined in the Companies Acts shall have the same meaning when used in this Agreement, but "company" shall mean and include both "company" and "body corporate", as in each case defined in the Act.

1.4   A reference to any statutory or other legislative provision shall be interpreted as a reference to that provision as in force at the date of this Agreement and, additionally, where the context so permits:—

1.4.1   in respect of any earlier date, as a reference to any and all provisions in force at that earlier date of which it is a re-enactment; and

1.4.2   in respect of any later date, as a reference to any and all provisions in force at that later date which are a re-enactment thereof;

in each case whether with or without modification.

1.5   The schedules form an integral part of this Agreement.

1.6   A reference to any gender shall include the other and neuter gender and a reference to a "person" includes a reference to any individual, firm, company, corporation or other body corporate, government, state or agency of a state or any joint venture, association or partnership, works council or employee representative body (whether or not having separate legal personality).

1.7 The singular shall include the plural and vice versa.

1.8 A document referred to as being in "the Agreed Terms" shall be in the form of that document signed or initialled for identification by or on behalf of the parties.

1.9 All warranties, representations, undertakings, guarantees, indemnities, covenants, agreements and obligations given or entered into by or on behalf of more than one person in this Agreement are, unless otherwise expressly stated, given or entered into jointly and severally.

1.10 Any Warranty qualified by the expression "to the best of the Seller's knowledge and belief" or "so far as the Seller is aware" or any similar expression shall [, unless otherwise expressly stated,] be deemed to include knowledge, information and belief which the Seller has or which the Seller would have had if it had made all reasonable enquiries and includes the knowledge, information and belief of each of:

1.10.1 the professional advisers who act, or at the relevant time acted, for the Company [and the Subsidiaries]; and

1.10.2 the directors, company secretary, financial controller and general managers of the Seller, and] of the Company [and of the Subsidiaries] [and of each Member of the Seller's Group.

and of any other person of whom it would be reasonable to make such enquiry or of whom it is stated that enquiry has been made.

1.11 A person shall be deemed to be connected with another if that person is connected with such other within the meaning of section 839 of Income & Corporation Taxes Act 1988.

1.12 "Associate" has the meaning given by section 435 of the Insolvency Act 1986.

1.13 References to "indemnify" and "indemnifying" any person against any circumstance include indemnifying and keeping him indemnified from and against all liabilities, losses, claims, demands, damages, costs, expenses and interest which he may suffer or incur in connection with or arising out of that circumstance.

1.14 Words shall not be given a restrictive meaning:—

1.14.1 if they are introduced by the word "other", by reason of the fact that they are preceded by words indicating a particular class of act, matter or thing; or

1.14.2 by reason of the fact that they are followed by particular examples intended to be embraced by those general words.

1.15 The word "Notice" includes any notice, demand, consent or other communication.

1.16 The headings are inserted for convenience only and shall not affect the construction of this Agreement.

1.17 The Buyer enters into this Agreement, so far as may be necessary for the enforcement of any provision for the benefit of the Company [or any of the Subsidiaries], as trustee for and on behalf of the [Company/company concerned].

1.18 References to times shall mean London time unless otherwise stated.

1.19   A reference to any English legal term for any action, remedy, method of judicial proceeding, legal document, legal status, court, official or any legal concept or thing shall in respect of any jurisdiction other than England be deemed to include what most nearly approximates in that jurisdiction to the English legal term and a reference to any English statute shall be construed so as to include equivalent or analogous laws of any other jurisdiction.

2.   [CONDITIONAL] AGREEMENT FOR SALE AND PURCHASE

2.1   Sale and purchase

On Completion the Seller shall sell the Shares with full title guarantee and the Buyer shall buy them free from any Encumbrance and together with all rights now or hereafter attaching to them, on and subject to [the Conditions and] the [other] terms of this Agreement.

2.2   The Law of Property (Miscellaneous Provisions) Act 1994

The operation of the covenants implied by sections 2 and 3 of the above Act shall be deemed to be extended so as not to exclude the liability of the Seller in respect of matters:—

2.2.1   of which the Seller does not know or could not reasonably be expected to know; or

2.2.2   which at the time of transfer are within the actual knowledge of, or the existence of which is a necessary consequence of facts then within the actual knowledge of the Buyer.

2.3   Simultaneous Completion

The Buyer shall not be obliged to complete the purchase of any of the Shares unless the purchase of all the Shares is completed simultaneously.

2.4   [Obligations and events pending Completion

Schedule 7 shall apply in respect of the period between the entering into of this Agreement and Completion.]

3.   CONSIDERATION

ALTERNATIVE A—FIXED CASH SUM WITHOUT RETENTION

3.1   The purchase price payable to the Seller for the Shares shall be the sum of £[   ] ([   ] pounds), which shall be paid in cash on Completion.

3.2   The Seller's Solicitors' receipt for the purchase price for the Shares shall be a good and sufficient discharge to the Buyer and the Buyer shall not be further concerned as to the application of the monies so paid.

ALTERNATIVE B—COMPLETION ACCOUNTS WITH JOINT ACCOUNT

3.1   Amount

The purchase price payable to the Seller for the Shares shall be a sum equal to the Completion NAV.

3.2   First Payments—on Completion

On Completion and pending the later agreement or determination of the Completion NAV, the Buyer shall pay:—

3.2.1   The sum of £[   ] (pounds) to the Seller's Solicitors (on behalf of the Seller) on account of the purchase price for the Shares; and

3.2.2   The sum of [£   ] [(pounds)] ("the Principal Sum") to the Buyer's Solicitors and the Seller's Solicitors jointly for placing into the Escrow Account, to be held under a mandate in the Agreed Terms and to be held and dealt with as set out in this clause 3.

3.3   **Second payment—following calculation of Completion NAV**

On the third Business Day after the date on which the Completion NAV is agreed or determined in accordance with schedule 9:—

3.3.1   the Buyer shall pay to the Seller's Solicitors a sum equal to the balance (if any) of the purchase price for the Shares after deducting the amount paid pursuant to clause 3.2.1, such payment to be satisfied by the payment of an equivalent sum from the Escrow Account;

3.3.2   If the purchase price for the Shares exceeds the amount paid to the Seller pursuant to clauses 3.2.1 and 3.3.1, the Buyer shall pay the amount of the excess to the Seller's Solicitors; and.

3.3.3   The balance of the Principal Sum following any payment from the Escrow Account pursuant to clause 3.3.1 (or, if no such payment falls to be made, the whole of the Principal Sum) shall be paid to the Buyer from the Escrow Account.

3.4   **The Escrow Account**

3.4.1   All interest earned on the Escrow Account shall accrue and be paid to the Seller and/or the Buyer in the proportions in which they respectively become entitled to the Principal Sum and shall be paid at the same time as any payment of all or any part of the Principal Sum is made from the Escrow Account.

3.4.2   The Seller and the Buyer shall procure that their respective solicitors shall make any payment which is required to be made from the Escrow Account pursuant to the provisions of clause 3.3.

3.5   **Clawback from first payment**

3.5.1   If the amount paid pursuant to clause 3.2.1 exceeds the purchase price for the Shares then on the third Business Day referred to in clause 3.3 the Seller shall repay to the Buyer a sum equal to the excess plus interest on an amount equal to the excess at the rate on which interest has been earned on the Escrow Account, such interest to accrue from the Completion Date until that third Business Day.

3.5.2   If the Seller defaults in making payment of any sum due under clause 3.5.1, it shall pay interest on the amount in question calculated on a daily basis from the due date until the date of actual payment (as well after any judgment as before) at the rate of 4% per year above the base rate from time to time in force of the Bank.

3.6   **Method of Payment**

3.6.1   Unless otherwise specified, any payment required to be made by the Buyer to the Seller pursuant to this clause 3 shall be made by way of a [banker's draft drawn on a UK clearing bank in favour of the Seller/Seller's Solicitors/telegraphic transfer to the following account:

Bank:

Branch:

Sort Code:

Account Name:

Account Number:

3.6.2   The Seller's Solicitors' receipt for any sums payable by the Buyer pursuant to this clause 3.6 shall be a good and sufficient discharge of the Buyer's obligation to make the payment in question and the Buyer shall not be further concerned as to the application of any sums so paid.

3.6.3   Any sum payable to the Buyer pursuant to this clause 3.6 shall, unless otherwise specified, be paid by way of a [banker's draft drawn on a UK clearing bank in favour of the [Buyer/Buyer'[s] Solicitors]/telegraphic transfer] to the following account:

Bank:

Branch:

Sort Code:

Account Name:

Account Number:]

ALTERNATIVE C—CONSIDERATION SHARES—SEE APPENDIX A

4.   **WARRANTIES AND TAXATION**

4.1   **Representations and Warranties**

With the intention of inducing the Buyer to enter into this Agreement (and acknowledging that the Buyer does so in reliance on the Warranties) the Seller represents to the Buyer in the terms of the Warranties and warrant to the Buyer that each of the Warranties is true and accurate in all respects and not misleading at the date of this Agreement [and will continue up to and including Completion to be true and accurate in all respects and not misleading.]

4.2   **Tax Covenants**

The Seller undertakes with the Buyer in the terms of the Tax Covenants.

4.3   **Claims procedure and determination and Seller's safeguards**

Schedule 6 shall apply in relation to the determination of the rights and remedies of the Buyer in respect of the Warranties and the Tax Covenants.

4.4   **[Application to Subsidiaries**

Each of the Warranties and of the Tax Covenants shall apply equally to each of the Subsidiaries and shall take effect as if the name of each Subsidiary were in turn substituted for "the Company" throughout schedule 4 and schedule 5.]

5.   COMPLETION

5.1   **Date of Completion**

Completion shall [,subject to schedule 7,] take place on the Completion Date at [   ].

5.2   **Seller's obligations**

On Completion the Seller shall:

5.2.1   deliver to the Buyer:

5.2.1.1   transfers of the Shares by the registered holders thereof in favour of the Buyer together with the relative share certificates and certified copies of any power of attorney under which any of such transfers may have been executed;

5.2.1.2   [certificates in respect of all issued shares in the capital of each of the Subsidiaries and duly executed transfers of all such shares held by any nominee in favour of such persons as the Buyer shall direct;]

5.2.1.3   all the statutory and other books (duly written up to date) of the Company [and each of the Subsidiaries] and [its/their] certificate[s] of incorporation or registration and certificate[s] of incorporation on change of name and common seal[s] (if any);

5.2.1.4   letters of resignation in the Agreed Terms executed by the persons resigning as directors [and secretary] of the Company [and each of the Subsidiaries] pursuant to clause 5.2.2.3;

5.2.1.5   [a certificate in the Agreed Terms from the Seller's Solicitors as to the title of the Company [and the Subsidiaries] to the Property;]

5.2.1.6   [the title deeds to the Property;]

5.2.1.7   [the resignation of the trustees of the [Pension Scheme] and the appointment in their place of such persons as the Buyer shall nominate [and the appointment of [the Buyer] as principal employer in respect of [the Pension Scheme];

5.2.1.8   all credit and charge cards held to the account of the Company and all other papers and documents relating to the Company which are in the possession of or under the control of the Seller or any director of the Company; and

5.2.1.9   the Disclosure Letter, duly executed;

5.2.2   procure:

5.2.2.1   the transaction of the other business referred to in the completion board minutes in the Agreed Terms;

5.2.2.2   such persons as the Buyer may nominate to be validly appointed as additional directors of the Company [and the Subsidiaries];

5.2.2.3   upon such appointment, the resignation of the directors [other than [   ]] [and the secretary] of the Company [and each of the Subsidiaries] both from their respective offices and as employees;

5.2.2.4 the written resignation [in the Agreed Terms] of the auditors of the Company [and each of the Subsidiaries] incorporating an acknowledgment that they have no claim against the Company [or any of the Subsidiaries] for any fees or disbursements, whether billed or unbilled, in respect of the period up to Completion and the statement referred to in section 519 of the Act;

5.2.2.5 [the release in the Agreed Terms of the Company [and the Subsidiaries] from all banking arrangements of the Seller's Group, including all guarantees, sureties and indemnities given by [any one or more of] the Company [and the Subsidiaries] in respect of the obligations of Members of the Seller's Group and all securities and authorities given by [any one or more of] the Company [and the Subsidiaries] in respect thereof];

5.2.2.6 the release [in the Agreed Terms] of all 'Encumbrances given by the Company [and each of the Subsidiaries] (whether to its bankers or otherwise) and of all guarantees given by the Company [and each of the Subsidiaries] in respect of the obligations of Members of the Seller's Group or of any third party;

5.2.2.7 the repayment (by such method as the Buyer directs) without deduction or set-off of any and all sums owed to the Company [and to each of the Subsidiaries] by the Seller, any Member of the Seller's Group, the directors of the Company [and of the Subsidiaries] and any person who is an associate of or connected with any of them;

5.2.2.8 the release [in the Agreed Terms] of any and all claims against the Company [and the Subsidiaries] by the Seller, each Member of the Seller's Group and any person who is an associate of or connected with any of them, incorporating an acknowledgment by each that there is no agreement or arrangement under which any such claim might arise in the future;

5.2.2.9 [that the Company and [   ] and [   ] enter into [service] [consultancy] agreements in the Agreed Terms; and]

5.2.2.10 that [each of] the Company [and the Subsidiaries] convenes an extraordinary meeting on short notice and, at such meeting[s], adopt[s] new articles of association in the Agreed Terms.

5.3 **Buyer's obligations**

On Completion, and against compliance by the Seller with its obligations under clause 5.2, the Buyer shall:

5.3.1 make the payments required to be made on Completion in accordance with clause 3;

5.3.2 acknowledge receipt of the Disclosure Letter; [and]

5.3.3 [deliver to the Seller's Solicitors share certificates in respect of the Consideration Shares.]

OR

5.3.3 [if it has not already done so, submit an application [to the UKLA for the Consideration Shares to be admitted to the Official List of the Stock Exchange and to the Stock Exchange [for the Consideration Shares to be admitted to trading on the Stock Exchange's main market for listed securities] [for the Consideration Shares to be admitted to trading on the Alternative Investment Market of the Stock Exchange] and instruct its registrars to prepare and deliver to the Seller share certificates in respect of the Consideration Shares].

5.4 **Failure to complete**

If in any respect the preceding provisions of this clause 5 are not complied with on the Completion Date, then (without prejudice to any and all rights of action it may have pursuant to the terms of this Agreement or otherwise) the party not in default may:

5.4.1 defer Completion to a date not more than 28 days after the Completion Date (and so that the provisions of this clause 5, apart from this clause 5.4.1, shall apply to Completion as so deferred); or

5.4.2 proceed to Completion so far as practicable (without prejudice to its rights hereunder or otherwise); or

5.4.3 rescind this Agreement by notice in writing to the Seller.

5.5 **Declaration of trust in relation to the Shares**

The Seller declares that, for so long as it remains the registered holder of any of the Shares after Completion, it will:

5.5.1 stand and be possessed of them and of all dividends and other rights arising out of or in connection with them in trust for the Buyer and its successors in title;

5.5.2 at all times thereafter deal with and dispose of them and all such dividends and rights as the Buyer or any such successor may direct; and

5.5.3 at the request of the Buyer or any such successor vote at all meetings which he or she shall be entitled to attend as the holder of them in such manner as the Buyer or any such successor may direct.

[The Seller hereby irrevocably appoints the Buyer or any such successor to be its attorney and in its name and on its behalf to sign any written resolution of the members of the Company and to execute all instruments of proxy or other documents which the Buyer or any such successor may reasonably require and which may be necessary or expedient to enable the Buyer or any such successor to attend and vote at any such meeting[1].]

6. CONFIDENTIAL INFORMATION AND USE OF NAMES

6.1 The Seller shall, and shall procure that each Member of the Seller's Group shall, after Completion, keep and procure to be kept secret and confidential all Confidential Information which relates to the Company or its business or

---

[1] If this wording is used, the agreement must be executed as a deed and it will be necessary to check the articles of association of the Sellers in order to ensure that they permit the appointment of an attorney.

is used in its business and shall not use or disclose to any person any such Confidential Information.

6.2 The obligations of confidentiality in this clause shall not extend to any matter which is in or becomes part of the public domain otherwise than by reason of a breach of the obligations of confidentiality in this Agreement or which the Seller receives from a third party independently entitled to disclose it or which the Seller is required by law or regulatory authority to disclose.[2]

6.3 The Seller shall not, and shall procure that no Member of the Seller's Group shall, at any time after Completion, use in connection with any trade or business any corporate name, trade name, or logo, domain name or e-mail address which is confusingly similar to the name of the Company [or of any of the Subsidiaries] or to any corporate name, trade name, logo, domain name or e-mail address used by the Company [or any of the Subsidiaries] [at any time during the period of 5 years before Completion].

7. **RESTRICTIVE UNDERTAKINGS**

7.1 **Customers, suppliers and employees**

The Seller undertakes with the Buyer that it will not, and will procure that no Member of the Seller's Group from time to time will,] at any time during the period of [   ] year[s] and [   ] months after Completion, directly or indirectly and whether alone or in conjunction with, or on behalf of or by way of assistance to, any other person:

7.1.1 canvass or solicit the custom of any person who was at any time during the period of [   ] months before Completion a customer of the Company [or any of the Subsidiaries] for the supply of goods and/or services which are competitive with any of those supplied to such person at any time during the period of [   ] months before the Completion Date by the Company [or any of the Subsidiaries]; or

7.1.2 do anything which it knows or ought reasonably to know would cause or be reasonably likely to cause any person who was at any time during the period of [   ] months before the Completion Date a supplier to the Company of goods and/or services to cease or materially reduce its supply of those goods and/or services to the Company [or any of the Subsidiaries]; or

7.1.3 solicit or entice away from the Company or employ or (directly or indirectly) offer employment or a consultancy to any person who is then an employee of the Company and who at Completion was an employee of the Company and likely (in the reasonable opinion of the Buyer) to be in possession of Confidential Information relating to, or able to influence the customer relationships or connections of, the Company or **[specify job titles]**; or

7.1.4 solicit or entice away from the Company [or any of the Subsidiaries] or employ or offer employment to any person who at, or at any time during the period of 6 months prior to, Completion was an employee of the Company [or any of the Subsidiaries] and likely (in the reasonable opinion of the Buyer) to be in possession

---

[2] If a public body is a party, it will be necessary to add additional wording to take account of the Freedom of Information Act 2000 and the Environmental Information Regulations 2004.

of Confidential Information relating to, or able to influence the customer relationships or connections of, the Company [or any of the Subsidiaries]; or

7.1.5   except as the holder for investment of less than 5% in nominal value of the issued share capital of a company whose shares are listed on a recognised investment exchange (within the meaning of the Financial Services and Markets Act 2000) [or as the holder of Consideration Shares] be engaged, concerned or interested within the Restricted Area in any Relevant Business.

7.2   **Definitions**

For the purposes of clause 7.1, "Relevant Business" means any business which consists of or includes to a material extent [**Description of business activities**] and "Restricted Area" means [**Specify geographical area to be covered**].

7.3   **Reasonableness of undertakings**

Each of the undertakings in clause 7.1 is:

7.3.1   considered by the parties to be reasonable;

7.3.2   a separate undertaking by the Seller and is enforceable by the Buyer (on behalf of itself and [any one or more of] the Company [and the Subsidiaries]) separately and independently of its right to enforce any one or more of the other undertakings in clause 7.1; and

7.3.3   given for the purpose of assuring to the Buyer the full benefit of the business and goodwill of the Company [and the Subsidiaries] and in consideration of the agreement of the Buyer to acquire the Shares on the terms of this Agreement.

Accordingly, if one or more of such undertakings is held to be against the public interest or unlawful or in any way an unreasonable restraint of trade, the remaining undertakings shall continue to bind the Seller.

7.4   **Cessation of business**

Nothing in the undertakings set out in clause 7.1 shall be deemed to prohibit any action in respect of any business or part of any business in which (otherwise than as a result of any breach of any of those undertakings by the Seller) the Company[, the Subsidiaries] and the Buyer and every other subsidiary of the Buyer have ceased to be involved prior to any event giving rise to a claim, or which would but for this clause 7.4 give rise to a claim, under this clause 7.

8.   **GUARANTEES**

The Buyer undertakes with the Seller after Completion to use all reasonable endeavours (short of actual payment of any money and the substitution of the guarantee of any person other than the Buyer or any company within the Group) to procure the release of the Seller [and any Member of the Seller's Group at the date of this Agreement] from liability under any and all outstanding guarantees given by the Seller or any Member of the Seller's Group at the date of this Agreement and listed below in respect of monies borrowed and obligations undertaken by the Company [and/or any of the Subsidiaries] and to indemnify the Seller and any such Member of the Seller's Group against any such liability arising after Completion. The guarantees in question are:
[**Details**]

Thank you for purchasing the second edition of **Sale of Shares and Businesses.**

☑ Don't miss important updates

So that you have all the latest information, **Sale of Shares and Businesses** is supplemented regularly. Sign up today for a Standing Order to ensure you receive the updating supplements as soon as they publish. Setting up your Standing Order with Sweet & Maxwell is hassle-free. Simply tick, complete and return this FREEPOST card and we'll do the rest.

You may cancel your Standing Order at any time by writing to us at Sweet & Maxwell, PO Box 2000, Andover, SP10 9AH stating the Standing Order you wish to cancel.

Alternatively, if you have purchased your copy of **Sale of Shares and Businesses** from a bookshop or other trade supplier, please ask your supplier to ensure that you are registered to receive the new editions.

All goods are subject to our 30 day Satisfaction Guarantee (applicable to EU customers only)

Yes, please send me new supplements to **Sale of Shares and Businesses** to be invoiced on publication, until I cancel the standing order in writing.

Name

Organisation

Job title

Address

Postcode

Telephone

Email

S&M account number (if known)

PO number

All orders are accepted subject to the terms of this order form and our Terms of Trading. (see www.sweetandmaxwell.co.uk). By submitting this order form I confirm that I accept these terms and I am authorised to sign on behalf of the customer.

Signed

Print Name   Date

(LBU007) V7

Goods will normally be dispatched within 3-5 working days of availability. The price charged to customers, irrespective of any prices quoted, will be the price specified in our price list current at the time of dispatch of the goods, as published on our website, unless the order is subject to a specific offer or discount in which case special terms may apply. Delivery Charges are not made for titles supplied in the UK. For deliveries in Europe the following charges apply: £7/€10 for first item, £2.50/€4 for each additional item. For deliveries outside Europe please add £30/€42 for first item, £15/€21 for each additional item.

UK VAT is charged on all applicable sales at the prevailing rate except in the case of sales to Ireland where Irish VAT will be charged at the prevailing rate. Customers outside the EU will not be charged UK VAT. UK VAT Number: GB 900 5487 43. Irish VAT Number: IE 9513874E. For customers in an EU member state (except UK & Ireland) please supply your VAT Number. VAT No

Thomson Reuters (Legal) Limited (Company No. 1679046. Registered in England & Wales. Registered Office and address for service: 100 Avenue Road, London NW3 3PF) trades using various trading names, of which a list is posted on its website at www.sweetandmaxwell.co.uk, and is part of Thomson Reuters.

"Thomson Reuters" and the Thomson Reuters logo are trademarks of Thomson Reuters and its affiliated companies.

SWEET & MAXWELL   **THOMSON REUTERS**

SWEET & MAXWELL

FREEPOST

PO BOX 2000

ANDOVER

SP10 9AH

UNITED KINGDOM

9.   INDEMNITIES

The Seller shall indemnify the Buyer [and/or the Company] [and each of the Subsidiaries] against and shall pay to the Buyer a sum equal to all liabilities suffered or incurred by the Company as a result of or in connection with: —

9.1   any breach, whether before or after Completion, of any covenant or any other term contained or implied in any lease of property assigned by the Company [or by any of the Subsidiaries] before Completion to any third party;

9.2   any defect or alleged defect in any goods produced or sold by the Company [or by any of the Subsidiaries] prior to Completion;

9.3   any industrial or other work-related illness or injury suffered by any employee or former employee of the Company [or any of the Subsidiaries] in respect of or in relation to any period ending on or before Completion; [or]

9.4   any VAT chargeable against any Member of the Seller's Group[; or]

9.5   **[other issues arising out of due diligence]**

save, (in the circumstances specified in clauses 7.2 and 9.3) to the extent that recovery is made by the Company [or by the Subsidiary concerned] under any policy of insurance.

10.   THIRD PARTY RIGHTS

10.1   For the avoidance of doubt [and save as expressly provided in clause [ ]],nothing in this Agreement shall confer on any third party the right to enforce any provisions of this Agreement.

10.2   Notwithstanding that any provision of this Agreement may be enforceable by any third party this Agreement and its provisions may be amended, waived, modified, rescinded or terminated by the parties to this Agreement without the consent or approval of any third party.

11.   ASSIGNMENT

11.1   This Agreement shall be binding upon and enure for the benefit of the successors and assignees of the parties and in the case of individuals their respective estates and, subject to any succession or assignment being permitted by this Agreement, any such successor or assignee of the parties shall in its own right be able to enforce any term of this Agreement.

11.2   Save as permitted under this Agreement, none of the parties nor their respective successors and assignees shall be entitled to assign its rights or obligations under this Agreement without the prior written consent of the others save that the Seller may assign its rights under this Agreement to a member of the Seller's Group ("Permitted Assignee") subject always to the following: :

11.2.1   where such assignee ceases to be a member of the Seller's Group such assignee shall be obliged as soon as reasonably practicable after such cessation to assign the rights under this Agreement back to a member of the Seller's Group; and

11.2.2   the assignor shall remain liable in respect of its obligations under this Agreement notwithstanding any such assignment, including for the avoidance of doubt the provisions of this clause 11.

11.2.3   The Buyer may at any time charge, grant security over or assign by way of security all or any of its rights under this Agreement.

12.   WHOLE AGREEMENT

12.1   This Agreement together with all documents entered into or to be entered into pursuant to its provisions constitutes the entire agreement between the parties in relation to its subject matter and supersedes all prior agreements, understandings and discussions between the parties, other than representations made fraudulently.

12.2   Each of the parties acknowledges that it is not relying on any statements, warranties or representations given or made by the others in relation to the subject matter of this Agreement, save those expressly set out in this Agreement and other documents referred to above and that it shall have no rights or remedies with respect to such subject matter otherwise than under this Agreement (and the documents executed at the same time as it or entered into pursuant to it) save to the extent that they arise out of the fraud or fraudulent misrepresentation of any party.

13.   WAIVER

The rights and remedies of a party in respect of this Agreement shall not be diminished, waived or extinguished by the granting of any indulgence, forbearance or extension of time by a party to another nor by any failure of or delay by a party in ascertaining or exercising any such rights or remedies. Any Release by a party shall not affect its rights and remedies as regards any other party nor its rights and remedies against the party in whose favour it is granted or made except to the extent of the express terms of the Release and no such Release shall have effect unless granted or made in writing. The rights and remedies in this Agreement are cumulative and not exclusive of any rights and/or remedies provided by law.

14.   PROVISIONS SURVIVING COMPLETION

Insofar as the provisions of this Agreement shall not have been performed at Completion, they shall remain in full force and effect notwithstanding Completion.

15.   PROPER LAW AND JURISDICTION

This Agreement shall be governed by the laws of England and Wales.

16.   JURISDICTION

Any dispute arising under this Agreement shall be subject to the [exclusive/non-exclusive] jurisdiction of the English courts and the parties waive any objection to Proceedings in such courts on the grounds of venue or on the grounds that Proceedings have been brought in an inappropriate forum.

17.   FURTHER ASSURANCE

The Seller shall at its own expense do such acts and things and execute such documents as the Buyer may at any time reasonably require for the purpose of assuring to the Buyer the full benefit of this Agreement and of any document to which it refers.

18.   COUNTERPARTS

This Agreement may be executed in any number of counterparts and by the parties on separate counterparts, each of which, when so executed and delivered, shall be an original, but all the counterparts shall together be deemed to constitute one and the same agreement.

19. **COSTS**

Each party shall, except where otherwise stated, pay its own costs of and incidental to this Agreement and its subject matter [except that, if the Buyer shall lawfully exercise any right hereby conferred to rescind this Agreement, the Seller shall indemnify the Buyer against all expenses and costs incurred by it in connection with this Agreement and its subject matter.]

20. **SEVERABILITY**

The provisions of this Agreement are severable and distinct from one another, and, if at any time any of such provisions is or becomes invalid, illegal or unenforceable, the validity, legality or enforceability of the others shall not in any way be affected or impaired thereby.

21. **PUBLICITY**

21.1   The parties shall forthwith upon [the signing of this Agreement/Completion] make or procure to be made a press announcement and announcements to the employees of the Company and to the customers and suppliers of the Company in the Agreed Terms.

21.2   [The Buyer shall be entitled to send a circular to its shareholders convening a general meeting for the purposes set out in schedule 7 and shall give the Seller a reasonable opportunity to comment on the contents of such circular in so far as it relates to it and to the Company.]

21.3   Each of the parties shall both before and after Completion, but subject to clauses 21.1 and 21.2, keep the contents of this Agreement strictly private and confidential and shall not without the prior written consent of the other disclose any or all of them to any person or make any other announcement relating to the transactions hereby agreed upon except to the extent required by law, [the FSA, UKLA, the Stock Exchange or the Panel on Take-overs and Mergers] and except that the Buyer and the Seller shall be entitled to make references to the transactions hereby agreed upon in their respective future annual reports and financial statements.

22. **PENSION SCHEME**

Schedule 8 shall apply in relation to the Pension Scheme.

23. **NOTICES**

23.1   Any Notice relating to this Agreement shall be in writing delivered personally or sent by pre-paid first class post or facsimile transmission to the address of the party to be served given herein or such other address as may be notified for this purpose.

23.2   Any such Notice shall, if sent by post, be deemed to have been served 24 hours after despatch and, if delivered by hand or sent by facsimile transmission, be deemed to have been served at the time of such delivery or transmission.

If, however, in the case of delivery by post a period of 24 hours after despatch would expire on, or if, in the case of delivery by hand or facsimile transmission, such delivery or transmission occurs on, a day which is not a Business Day or after 4.00 p.m. on a Business Day, then service shall be deemed to occur on the next following Business Day.

23.3   In proving service it shall be sufficient to prove, in the case of a letter, that such letter was properly stamped, addressed and placed in the post and, in the case of a facsimile transmission, it shall be sufficient to produce a transmission report showing that transmission was duly and fully made to the correct number.

[**SIGNED** by or on behalf of the parties the day and year first before written]

OR

[**IN WITNESS** of which this deed has been executed and unconditionally delivered the day and year first above written.]

SCHEDULE 1

The Company

Name:

Registered in England no:

Date of incorporation:

Authorised share capital: £[   ] divided into [
    ] ordinary shares of [   ] each [and [   ] [
    ] shares of [   ] each]

Issued share capital: £[   ] divided into [
                    ] ordinary shares of [   ] each [and [
            ]   [   ] shares of [   ] each]

Directors:

Secretary:

Auditors:

Registered office:

SCHEDULE 2

The Subsidiaries

Name:

Registered in England no:

Date of incorporation:

Authorised share capital: £[   ] divided into [   ] ordinary
                    shares of [   ] each [and [
                    ] [   ] shares of [   ] each]

Issued share capital: £[   ] divided into [   ] ordinary shares
                    of [   ] each [and [   ] [
                    ] shares of [   ] each]

Directors:

Secretary:

Auditors:

Registered office:

Shareholders:

       Name   Number and class of shares

SCHEDULE 3

The Property

SCHEDULE 4

TAX

Part 1 Definitions

1.   INTERPRETATION

1.1   In this schedule, unless the context otherwise requires, the following words and expressions shall have the following meanings:

"Accounts Relief"	(a) any Relief which was treated as an asset of the Company in the Accounts; or
	(b) any Relief which was taken into account in computing (and so reducing or eliminating) any provision for Tax which appears in the Accounts or which would have appeared in the Accounts but for the presumed availability of such Relief;
"Event"	any act, omission, event, fact or circumstance whatsoever (whether actual or deemed or treated as occurring for any purpose);
"ICTA"	Income and Corporation Taxes Act 1988;
"ITEPA"	Income Tax (Earnings and Pensions) Act 2003;
"loss"	includes the loss, denial, clawback or cancellation in whole or in part of any Relief and derivative word (such as "lost") shall be construed accordingly;
"Post Completion Relief"	includes any Relief which arises as a result of any Event which has occurred or occurs after the Accounts Date or in respect of any period commencing on or after the Accounts Date;
"Relevant Person"	the Seller and any person (except the Buyer or the Company);
	(a) who before Completion was a Member of the same group of companies for any Tax purpose ("Group Person"); or
	(b) with whom, before Completion the Company or, at any time, the Seller or any Group Person is connected; or
	(c) any person who stands or has stood in a direct or indirect relationship with the Company at any time before Completion such that failure by such person at any time to pay any Tax could result in an assessment on the Company under section 767A or section 767AA ICTA;
"Relief"	(a) any relief, allowance, exemption, set-off, deduction or credit available from, against, or in relation to, Tax or in the computation for any Tax purpose of income, profits or gains; and

	(b)	any right to repayment of Tax;
"Tax"	(a)	any tax, duty, impost, levy, deduction or withholding, past or present, of the United Kingdom or elsewhere; and
	(b)	any interest, charge, surcharge, penalty, fine or other imposition relating to or arising in connection with any tax, duty, impost, levy, deduction or withholding mentioned in paragraph (a) of this definition or to any account, record, form, return or computation required to be kept, preserved, maintained or submitted to any person for the purpose of any such tax, duty, impost, levy, deduction or withholding;

"Tax Authority" any authority, whether of the United Kingdom or elsewhere, competent to impose, assess or collect Tax, including HM Revenue & Customs;

"Tax Claim" any notice, demand, assessment, letter or other document issued, or action taken, by or on behalf of any Tax Authority and the submission of any Tax form, return or computation from which, in either case, it appears to the Buyer that the Company is or may be subject to a Tax Liability or other liability in respect of which the Seller is or may be liable under this schedule 4;

"Tax Legislation" any statute, statutory instrument, regulation or legislative provision providing for, imposing, or relating to, Tax;

"Tax Liability"	(a)	any liability (including a liability which is a primary liability of some other person and whether or not there is a right of recovery against another person) to make an actual payment of an amount in respect of Tax;
	(b)	any liability (including a liability which is a primary liability of some other person and whether or not there is a right of recovery against another person) to make a payment or increased payment of Tax which would have arisen but for being satisfied, avoided or reduced by any Accounts Relief or Post Completion Relief; and
	(c)	the disallowance, loss, clawback, reduction, restriction or modification of any Accounts Relief;

"Tax Warranties" the warranties contained in part 2 of this schedule 4;

"TCGA"	Taxation of Chargeable Gains Act 1992;
"VAT"	value added tax;
"VATA"	Value Added Tax Act 1994;
"VAT Group"	any group of companies for the purpose of section 43 VATA of which the Company is or has been a member on or before Completion.

1.2   In this schedule, "Company" shall in addition to the Company include every subsidiary of the Company to the intent and effect that the provisions of this schedule shall apply to and be given in respect of each subsidiary as well as the Company.

1.3   Any reference to an Event or the consequences of an Event occurring on or before Completion shall include the combined effect of:

    1.3.1   any two or more Events, all of which shall have taken place or be deemed (for the purposes of any Tax Legislation) to have taken place on or before Completion; or

    1.3.2   any two or more Events, at least one of which shall have taken place or be deemed (for the purposes of any Tax Legislation) to have occurred on or before Completion.

1.4   Any reference to a Tax Liability in respect of income profits or gains earned, accrued or received on or before Completion shall include a Tax Liability in respect of income profits or gains deemed to have been or treated or regarded as earned, accrued or received for the purposes of any Tax Legislation on or before Completion and any reference to Tax Liability on the happening of any Event shall include a Tax Liability where such Event (for the purposes of the Tax Legislation in question) is deemed to have occurred or treated or regarded as having occurred.

1.5   Any stamp duty which would be payable on any document in order for it to be produced as evidence in Court (whether or not such document is presently within the United Kingdom), provided that such document is either necessary to establish the title of the Company to any asset or is a document in the enforcement or production of which the Company is interested, and any interest, fine or penalty relating to any such stamp duty will be deemed to be a liability of the Company to make an actual payment of Tax on the date on which the document was executed and "Tax Liability" shall be construed accordingly.

1.6   In determining for the purposes of this schedule 4 whether a charge on, or power to sell, mortgage or charge, any of the shares or assets of the Company exists at any time, the fact that any Tax is not yet payable or may be paid by instalments shall be disregarded and such Tax shall be treated as becoming due and the charge or power to sell, mortgage or charge shall be treated as arising on the date on which HM Revenue & Customs gave notice of the liability to the Company or the Buyer.

Part 2 Tax Warranties

1.   **RETURNS, NOTICES AND RECORDS**

    1.1   All accounts, computations, notices and returns required to be made or submitted by the Company to any Tax Authority and all notices and information required to be given by the Company to any Tax Authority (including all returns and other documents or information in respect of

PAYE and National Insurance) have been properly and duly prepared and punctually made, submitted or given by the Company and are up-to-date and correct.

1.2   The Company is not and, in the period of three years ended on the date of this document, has not been, in dispute with or subject to enquiry or investigation by any Tax Authority (other than routine enquiries concerning the corporation tax computations of the Company, all of which have been resolved) and, so far as the Seller is aware there are no facts or circumstances likely to give rise to or be the subject of any such dispute, enquiry or investigation.

1.3   The Company has (to the extent required by law) preserved and retained in its possession complete and accurate records relating to its Tax affairs (including PAYE and National Insurance records, VAT records and records relating to transfer pricing) and the Company has sufficient records relating to past events to calculate the profit, gain, loss, balancing charge or balancing allowance (all for Tax purposes) which would arise on any disposal or on the realisation of any assets owned at the Accounts Date or acquired since that date but before Completion.

2. PAYMENT OF TAX

The Company has duly and punctually paid all Tax (including Tax required to be deducted or withheld from payments) to the extent that the same ought to 'have been paid and has not in the last three years paid or become liable to pay any penalty or interest charged by virtue of the provisions of any Tax Legislation.

3. CONCESSION

The Company has not during the period of three years ending on the date of this document relied on any formal or informal unpublished concession, dispensation or practice (whether general or specific to the Company) which affects the amount of Tax chargeable on the Company or which purports to modify or provide exemption from any obligation to make or submit any computation notice or return to any Tax Authority.

4. DEDUCTIONS AND WITHHOLDINGS

The Company has made all deductions and withholdings in respect of, or on account of, any Tax (including amounts required to be deducted under the PAYE and National Insurance contributions) from any payments made by it which it is obliged or entitled to make and (to the extent required to do so) has accounted in full to the relevant Tax Authority for all amounts so deducted or withheld.

5. PAYE

The Company has not been notified that any PAYE audit or visit by HM Revenue & Customs will be or is expected to be made. The Disclosure Letter gives full details of all dispensations or notices received by the Company under Section 65 of ITEPA (dispensations) and of all PAYE settlement agreements entered into under Chapter 5 of Part 11 of ITEPA by the Company.

6. CLOSE COMPANIES

6.1   The Company is not and never has been a close investment holding company within the meaning of section 13A ICTA.

6.2 The Company has not at any time:

6.2.1 made any loan, advance or payment or given any consideration falling within sections 419 to 422 ICTA (charges to tax in connection with loans) or released or written off or agreed to release or write off the whole or any part of such loans or advances; or

6.2.2 made a transfer of value which is or may be liable to Taxation under the provisions of sections 94, 99 or 199 of the Inheritance Act 1984.

6.3 The Company has never made any distribution within section 418 ICTA.

7. CAPITAL GAINS

7.1 The sum which would be allowed as a deduction from the consideration under section 38 TCGA (acquisition and disposal costs etc) of each asset of the Company (other than trading stock) if disposed of on the date of this document:

7.1.1 would not be less than (in the case of an asset held on the Accounts Date) the book value of that asset shown or included in the Accounts or (in the case of an asset acquired since the Accounts Date) an amount equal to the consideration given for its acquisition; and in particular

7.1.2 would not be treated or deemed for the purposes of Tax to have been reduced by reason of any claim made under sections 152 (roll-over relief), 153 (assets only partly replaced), 165 (relief for gifts of business assets) or 175 (group rollover) TCGA or by reason of the operation of section 17 (disposals and acquisitions treated as made at market value) or sections 126 to 140 TCGA (reorganisation of share capital, conversion of securities etc).

7.2 No transaction has been entered into by the Company to which the provisions of section 18 (transactions between connected persons) TCGA have been or could be applied.

8. CAPITAL ALLOWANCES

No balancing charge in respect of any capital allowances claimed or given would arise if any asset of the Company (or, where computations are made for capital allowances purposes for pools of assets, all the assets in that pool) were to be realised for a consideration equal to the amount of the book value thereof as shown or included in the Accounts (or, in the case of any asset acquired since the Accounts Date, for a consideration equal to the consideration given for the acquisition).

9. SECONDARY LIABILITY

So far as the [Seller] is aware, no Event has occurred in consequence of which the Company is made or held liable to pay or bear any Tax which is primarily chargeable against or attributable to some person, firm or company other than the Company.

10. STAMP DUTIES

10.1 Each document in the possession or under the control of the Company or to the production of which the Company is entitled and on which the Company relies or may rely on for any purpose whatsoever and which in the United Kingdom requires any stamp has been properly stamped or marked as appropriate and no such document which is outside the United Kingdom would attract stamp duty if it were to be brought into the United Kingdom.

10.2 The Company does not hold any interest in real property situated in the United Kingdom which was granted or transferred to it in the three years prior to the date of this agreement where such grant or transfer was the subject of an application for relief from stamp duty under section 42 of the Finance Act 1930, section 151 of the Finance Act 1995 or section 76 of the Finance Act 1986 or for relief from stamp duty land tax under any of the provisions of schedule 7 to the Finance Act 2003.

10.3 The Company has not entered into any agreement for the sale of an estate or interest in real property situated in the United Kingdom in the 90 days prior to Completion.

10.4 The Company has complied in all respects with the provisions of Part IV of the Finance Act 1986 (Stamp Duty Reserve Tax) and any regulations made under such legislation.

10.5 The Company is not and has never been party to a "land transaction" for the purposes of section 43 Finance Act 2003.

11. ANTI-AVOIDANCE

The Company has never been party to any non-arm's length transaction or been party to or otherwise involved in any scheme or arrangement the main purpose, or one of the main purposes, of which was to avoid Tax.

12. VALUE ADDED TAX

12.1 The Company is registered as a taxable person for VAT purposes in the United Kingdom under schedule 1 VATA and has never been treated as (nor applied to be) a member of a group of companies for VAT purposes.

12.2 The Company is not registered (nor required to be registered) for local VAT or its equivalent in any state other than the United Kingdom.

12.3 The Company has complied in all material respects with all the requirements of VATA and all application regulations and orders, and has fully maintained complete, correct and up-to-date records, invoices and other necessary documents.

12.4 The Company is not in arrears with any payment and has not failed to submit any return (fully and properly completed) or information required in respect of VAT and is not liable or likely to become liable to any abnormal or non-routine payment or default surcharge or any forfeiture or penalty or subject to the operation of any penal provision.

12.5 No circumstances exist whereby the Company would or might become liable for VAT pursuant to the provisions of sections 47 (agents etc) or 48 (tax representatives) VATA.

12.6 The Company has not made and is not otherwise bound by any election made pursuant to paragraph 2 of schedule 10 VATA.

12.7 The Company has not been party to a transaction to which Article 5 of the Value Added Tax (Special Provisions) Order 1995 (transfer of business as a going concern) has (or has purported to have been) applied.

12.8 No asset of the Company is a capital item, the input tax on which could be subject to adjustment in accordance with the provisions of Part XV of the Value Added Tax Regulations 1995.

13. GROUPS

13.1 No Tax is or may become payable by the Company pursuant to section 190 TCGA (tax on one member or group recoverable from another member) in respect of any chargeable gain accruing prior to Completion.

13.2 The Company has not at any time within the period of six years ending with the date of this document acquired any asset (other than as trading stock) from any other company which at the time of the acquisition was a member of the same group of companies as the Company (as defined in section 170 TCGA (groups of companies: definitions)) and no member of any group of companies of which the Company is, or has at any material time been, the principal company (as defined in section 170 TCGA (groups of companies: definitions)) has so acquired any asset.

13.3 The Company has not in the last seven years ceased to be a member of a group of companies for the purposes of section 178 or 179 TCGA (company ceasing to be member of a group).

13.4 There are no assets currently owned by the Company in respect of which a charge may arise on the sale of the Company pursuant to this Agreement under Section 179 TCGA (company ceasing to be a member of a group).

14. LOAN RELATIONSHIPS

14.1 Each amount in relation to which the Company is a debtor or creditor and reflected in the Accounts or existing on the date of this agreement constitutes a loan relationship of the Company.

14.2 No Tax Liability or non-trading deficit would arise from any loan relationship of the Company as a result of any debt under such loan relationship being settled in full or in part at Completion.

14.3 In relation to each of its loan relationships, the Company operates and has, in each accounting period of the Company ending after 31 March 1996, operated an accruals basis of accounting authorised under section 85 of the Finance Act 1996.

15. INHERITANCE TAX

There is no unsatisfied liability to inheritance tax attached or attributable to the assets of the Company or the shares of the Company and neither such assets nor such shares are subject to an HM Revenue & Customs charge.

16. FOREIGN CONNECTIONS

16.1 The Company has never been resident outside the United Kingdom for the purposes of any tax legislation.

16.2 The Company does not have (and in the period of three years ending on the date of this document has not had) any branch agent, or permanent establishment (within the meaning of the OECD Model Double Taxation Agreement) outside the United Kingdom.

16.3 The Company does not have (and has not in the last seven years had) any interest in a controlled foreign company within the meaning of sections 747 and 752 ICTA.

Part 3 Tax Covenants

1. SELLER'S COVENANT

Subject to part 4 of this schedule, the Seller covenants with the Buyer to pay to the Buyer an amount equal to:

1.1 any Tax Liability of the Company:

1.1.1 arising in respect of, by reference to or in consequence of, any Event which occurred on or before Completion; or

1.1.2 arising in respect of, by reference to, or in consequence of, any income profits or gains earned, accrued or received on or before or in respect of a period ended on or before Completion; or

1.1.3 arising or assessed as a consequence of the failure of a Relevant Person at any time to pay Tax;

1.2 any Tax Liability which arises as a result of any supply, acquisition or importation made or deemed to be made for the purposes of VAT by any member of any VAT Group other than the Company;

1.3 any liability of the Company to make a payment in respect of, or in consequence of, any indemnity, covenant or guarantee relating to Tax given by the Company on or before Completion;

1.4 any liability in respect of inheritance tax which:

1.4.1 is at or becomes after Completion, as a result of the death of any person within seven years after a transfer of value (or a deemed transfer of value) on or before Completion, a charge on any of the shares or the assets of the Company or gives rise to a power to sell, mortgage or charge any of the shares or the assets of the Company; or

1.4.2 arises as a result of a transfer of value occurring or being deemed to occur on or before Completion whether or not in conjunction with the death of any person (whenever occurring) which increased or decreased the value of the estate of the Company;

1.5 any Tax Liability in respect of the emoluments or benefits in kind of employees or directors of the Company arising in respect of periods ended on or before Completion and arising from their employment or directorships with the Company or in respect of services rendered by an individual to the Company where Tax has not been properly accounted for or proper returns have not been made in respect of emoluments and which the Company decides to pay, whether or not the liability for such Tax may be the liability of the employees or directors; and

1.6 any reasonable costs, fees or expenses incurred by the Company or the Buyer in connection with:

1.6.1 any Tax Liability or other liability in respect of which the [Seller] is liable under any of paragraphs 1.1 to 1.5 above; or

1.6.2 taking or defending any action (including legal proceedings) under this schedule at the request or direction of the [Seller].

Part 4 Limitations and procedure

2.   RESTRICTION ON SELLER'S LIABILITY

2.1   The provisions of paragraphs 2.1 (maximum liability) and 1.2 (time limits) of schedule 6 shall apply to this schedule as if the same were set out herein in full and the liability of the Seller under this schedule shall be limited or excluded accordingly.

2.2   The covenants contained in part 3 of this schedule shall not extend to any Tax Liability to the extent that:

2.2.1   such Tax Liability was paid or discharged on or before the Accounts Date [and such payment or discharge was reflected in the Accounts];

2.2.2   specific provision or reserve (other than a deferred tax provision or reserve) in respect of that Tax Liability was made in the Accounts;

2.2.3   such Tax Liability arises or is increased as a result of any change in Tax Legislation or any increase in rates of Tax (in each case) announced after Completion which has retrospective effect;

2.2.4   such Tax Liability would not have arisen but for any voluntary act or transaction carried out after Completion by the Buyer or Company, provided that this paragraph 2.2.4 shall not apply to any act or transaction:

2.2.4.1   required by law or carried out or effected by the Company pursuant to a legally binding commitment created or entered into before Completion; or

2.2.4.2   which consists of communicating information to any Tax Authority; or

2.2.4.3   carried out or effected by the Company in the ordinary course of its business.

2.3   The Seller shall not be liable in respect of a breach of any of the Warranties if and to the extent that the loss occasioned thereby has been recovered under the Tax Covenants and vice versa in respect of the same subject matter.

3.   RECOVERY FROM THIRD PARTIES

3.1   If, before the sixth anniversary of the date of this document, the Company recovers from any other person any amount which is referable to a Tax Liability of the Company in respect of which the Seller has made a payment under this schedule, the Buyer will repay to the Seller the lesser of:

3.1.1   the amount so recovered (less any losses, costs, damages and expenses properly and reasonably incurred by the Company, or the Buyer or any other member of the same group of companies as the Buyer as a result of effecting recovery of that amount); and

3.1.2   the amount paid by the Seller under this schedule in respect of the Tax Liability in question, less any part of such amount previously repaid to the Seller under any provision of this agreement or otherwise.

4. NO DEDUCTIONS OR WITHHOLDINGS

4.1 Save only as may be required by law, all sums payable by the Seller under this schedule shall be paid free and clear of all deductions or withholdings whatsoever.

4.2 If any deductions or withholdings are required by law to be made from any payment under this schedule, the Seller shall pay such sum as will, after the deduction or withholding has been made, leave the Buyer with the same amount as it would have been entitled to receive in the absence of any such requirement to make a deduction or withholding.

5. TAX ON PAYMENTS

If any sum payable by the Seller to the Buyer under this schedule is (or but for the availability of any Accounts Relief or Post Completion Relief would be) subject to a Tax Liability in the hands of the Buyer, the Seller shall pay to the Buyer such sum as is necessary to ensure that the amount received by the Buyer is not less than the amount it would have received had the payment not been subject to Tax.

6. DATE FOR PAYMENT

6.1 Where the Seller becomes liable to make a payment pursuant to the provisions of this schedule, the due date for the making of that payment in cleared funds shall be:

6.1.1 the date falling 5 Business Days after the date on which the Company or (as the case may be) the Buyer has notified the Seller of the amount of the payment required to be made; or

6.1.2 in any case involving a liability of the Company or the Buyer to make an actual payment (whether or not a payment of Tax), the later of the date falling 5 Business Days after the date on which the Company or (as the case may be) the Buyer has notified the Seller of the amount of the payment required to be made and the date falling 5 Business Days before the last date on which the payment in question is required to be made to the person entitled to the payment (after taking into account any postponement of the due date for payment of any Tax which is obtained).

7. INTEREST ON LATE PAYMENTS

If any payment required to be made by the Seller under this schedule is not made by the due date for payment thereof, then that payment shall carry interest from that due date until the date when the payment is actually made at the rate of 4 per cent above the base rate from time to time of [   ] Bank PLC compounded quarterly.

8. PRICE REDUCTION

Any payment by the Seller under this schedule shall (so far as possible) be treated as a reduction in the consideration paid for the Shares, provided that nothing in this paragraph 7 shall limit or exclude the liability of the Seller under this Agreement.

9. TAX CLAIMS

9.1 If the Buyer or the Company shall become aware of any Tax Claim which is likely to give rise to a liability of the Seller under this schedule the Buyer shall (or shall procure that the Company shall) as soon as reasonably practicable give notice thereof to the Seller but so that such notice shall not be a condition precedent to the liability of the Seller hereunder.

9.2　　If the Seller shall indemnify the Company and the Buyer to the reasonable satisfaction of the Buyer against all losses, costs, damages and expenses (including interest on overdue Tax) which may be incurred thereby, the Buyer shall (and shall procure that the Company shall), in accordance with any reasonable instructions of the Seller promptly given by notice to the Buyer (but subject to paragraphs 9.2.1 to 9.2.3 inclusive), seek to avoid, dispute, resist, appeal, compromise or defend such Tax Claim provided always that:

9.2.1　　the Company shall not be obliged to appeal against any assessment for Tax raised on it if, having given the Seller notice of the receipt of that assessment, it has not within 15 days thereafter received instructions from the Seller, in accordance with the provisions of this paragraph 9.2.1, to make that appeal;

9.2.2　　the Buyer and the Company shall not be obliged to comply with any instruction of the Seller which involves contesting any assessment for Tax before any court or other appellate body (excluding the Tax Authority in question) unless the Seller furnishes the Buyer with the written opinion of Tax Counsel of at least 5 years' call to the effect that an appeal against the assessment for Tax in question will, on the basis of probabilities, be won;

9.2.3　　the Buyer and the Company shall not in any event be obliged to comply with any instruction of the Seller to make a settlement or compromise of a Tax Claim which is the subject of a dispute or agree any matter in the conduct of such dispute which it reasonably considers to be materially prejudicial to the business of the Company or the Buyer or likely increase the future liability of the Company or the Buyer in respect of Tax.

10.　　[TAX AFFAIRS

10.1　　The Seller or its duly authorised agents or advisers shall, at the expense of the Company to the extent provided for in the Accounts and thereafter at the expense of the Seller, prepare, submit and agree the corporation tax computations and returns of the Company ("Tax Computations") for its accounting period(s) (within the meaning of section 12 of the Taxes Act) ended on or before the Accounts Date ("Relevant Accounting Period(s)").

10.2　　The Seller shall deliver to the Buyer for comments any Tax Computation return document or correspondence and details of any information or proposal ("Relevant Information") which it intends to submit to HM Revenue & Customs before submission to HM Revenue & Customs and shall take account of the reasonable comments of the Buyer and make such amendments to the Relevant Information as the Buyer may reasonably require in writing within 30 days of the date of delivery of the Relevant Information prior to its submission to HM Revenue & Customs.

10.3　　The Seller shall deliver to the Buyer copies of any correspondence sent to, or received from, HM Revenue & Customs relating to the Tax Computations and returns and shall keep the Buyer fully informed of its actions under this paragraph.

10.4　　Subject to paragraphs 10.2 and 10.3, the Buyer shall procure that:

10.4.1　　the Company properly authorises and signs the Tax Computations and makes and signs or otherwise enters into all such elections, surrenders and claims and withdraws or disclaims such elections, surrenders and claims and gives such notices and signs such other documents as the Seller shall require in relation to the Relevant Accounting Period(s);

10.4.2 the Company provides to the Seller such information and assistance, including such access to its books, accounts and records which may reasonably be required to prepare, submit, negotiate and agree the Tax Computations;

10.4.3 any correspondence which relates to the Tax Computations shall, if received by the Buyer or any Company or its agents or advisers, be properly copied to the Seller.

10.5 In respect of any matter which gives or may give the Buyer a right to make a Tax Claim, the provisions of paragraph 8 with respect to appeals and the conduct of disputes shall apply instead of the provisions of this paragraph 9.

10.6 The Seller shall use all reasonable endeavours to agree the Tax Computations as soon as reasonably practicable and shall deal with all such matters promptly and diligently and within applicable time limits.]

SCHEDULE 5

The Warranties

1.   THE COMPANY AND THE SELLER

1.1   **Capacity**

The Seller has full power to enter into and perform the provisions of this Agreement, which constitutes a binding agreement on the Seller in accordance with its terms.

1.2   **Ownership of the Shares**

The Seller is the beneficial owner of the Shares and has the right to dispose of them to the Buyer or as it directs free from any Encumbrance and together with all rights now or hereafter attaching to them.

1.3   **Transfers at an undervalue**

Neither the Shares nor any asset owned or used by the Company has been the subject of a transfer at an undervalue (within the meaning of section 238 or section 239 of the Insolvency Act 1986) within the period of five years prior to the date of this Agreement.

1.4   **Liabilities owing to or by the Seller**

There is not outstanding any indebtedness and there are no contracts, arrangements or liabilities (actual or contingent) remaining in whole or in part to be performed between the Company and any Member of the Seller's Group or any director of the Company or any director of any Member of the Seller's Group or any person who is an associate of or connected with any of them.

2.   THE COMPANY'S SCHEDULED PARTICULARS AND CONSTITUTIONAL AND ADMINISTRATIVE AFFAIRS

2.1   **Schedule 1**

2.2   The particulars of the Company set out in schedule 1 are true, complete and accurate; no person is a shadow director of the Company and its issued share capital is fully paid.

2.2.1   The Company:

2.2.1.1   has not since its incorporation had any group undertaking [other than the Subsidiaries]; [and]

2.2.1.2   [is the beneficial owner (directly or indirectly) free from any Encumbrance of the whole of the issued share capital of each of the Subsidiaries; and]

2.2.1.3   has not since its incorporation been a subsidiary of any other company.

2.3   **Memorandum and Articles**

The copy of the memorandum and articles of association of the Company attached to the Disclosure Letter is true and complete.

2.4   **Options**

No person has the right (whether exercisable now or in the future and whether or not contingent) to call for the allotment, issue or transfer of any share or loan capital of the Company under any option or other agreement (including without limitation conversion rights and rights of pre-emption).

2.5 **Purchase of own shares**

The Company has not at any time purchased any of its own shares or redeemed or forfeited any shares in its capital.

2.6 **Statutory and other books and records**

2.6.1 All registers, accounts, books, ledgers, financial and other records of the Company have been fully, properly and accurately kept and maintained, are in the possession of the Company and contain true and accurate records of all matters required by law to be entered therein and no notice or allegation that any of them is incorrect or should be rectified has been received by the Company or the Seller.

2.6.2 The Company's accounting records:

2.6.2.1 comply with the requirements of sections 386 of the Act;

2.6.2.2 are sufficient to show and explain the Company's transactions;

2.6.2.3 disclose with reasonable accuracy, at any time, the financial position of the Company at that time; and

2.6.2.4 do not contain or reflect any material inaccuracy or discrepancy.

2.7 **Filing of documents**

All returns and other documents required to be filed with the Registrar of Companies, or with any other authority, in respect of the Company have been duly filed and were when filed correct.

2.8 **Insurances**

2.8.1 The Company maintains, and at all material times has maintained, adequate insurance cover against all risks normally insured against by companies carrying on a similar business, for the full replacement or reinstatement value of its business and assets, and in particular has maintained all insurance required by statute, product liability and professional indemnity insurance, and insured against loss of profits for a period of not less than six (6) months and for loss of rent for a period of not less than three (3) years.

2.8.2 The Disclosure Letter sets out full details of all policies of insurance maintained by or on behalf of the Company, all of which are in full force and effect.

2.8.3 All premiums in respect of policies of insurance maintained by or on behalf of the Company have been paid as and when due, and there are no circumstances which might lead to any liability under such insurance being avoided by the insurers or (being circumstances not affecting businesses generally) the premiums being increased, and there is no claim outstanding under any such policy, nor is the Seller aware of any circumstances likely to give rise to a claim thereunder.

2.8.4 The Disclosure Letter sets out full details of all insurance claims made by or on behalf of the Company within the period of three years immediately prior to the date of this Agreement.

2.8.5   There are no claims outstanding or threatened or, so far as the Seller is aware, pending against the Company which are not fully covered by insurance.

2.9   Agency

No person, as agent or otherwise, is entitled or authorised to bind or commit the Company to any obligation outside the ordinary course of business.

3.   THE COMPANY AND THE LAW

3.1   Compliance with laws

3.1.1   The Company has conducted and is conducting its business in accordance with all applicable laws and regulations of any relevant jurisdiction and neither the Company nor any of its officers, agents or employees have committed, or omitted to do, any act or thing capable of giving rise to any fine, penalty, default proceedings or other liability on the part of the Company.

3.1.2   There is no order, decree or judgment of any court or any governmental agency of any jurisdiction outstanding against the Company or which may have any adverse effect upon the assets or business of the Company; no such order, decree or judgment is pending, and there are no circumstances likely to give rise to any such order, decree or judgment.

3.1.3   There is not pending or in existence any investigation or enquiry by or on behalf of any governmental or other body in respect of the affairs of the Company.

3.2   Licences

3.2.1   The Company has obtained all licences, consents, permits and authorities of a statutory or regulatory nature necessary or expedient to enable it to carry on its business effectively in the places and in the manner in which it is now carried on.

3.2.2   All such licences, consents, permits and authorities are valid and subsisting, and the Seller knows of no reason why any of them should be suspended, cancelled or revoked or renewed or continued subject to any term or condition which does not currently apply thereto.

3.3   Litigation

3.3.1   The Company is not engaged in any dispute with any customer or supplier or in any litigation or other proceedings.

3.3.2   So far as the Seller is aware:

3.3.2.1   no litigation or other proceedings are pending or threatened by or against the Company;

3.3.2.2   there are no circumstances likely to give rise to any litigation or other proceedings; and

3.3.2.3   the Company has not been a party to any undertaking or assurance given to any court or governmental agency which is still in force.

3.4 **Insolvency**

3.4.1 The Company has not become unable to pay its debts as they fall due within the meaning of section 123 of the Insolvency Act 1986 or received any written demand pursuant to section 123(1)(a) of the Insolvency Act 1986.

3.4.2 No order has been made or petition presented or resolution passed for the winding up of the Company; no proposal has been made under part I of the Insolvency Act 1986 for a voluntary arrangement; no person has appointed or applied to any court of competent jurisdiction to appoint a receiver or an administrative receiver or an administrator; and no distress, execution or other process has been levied against the Company.

3.5 **Fair trading**

3.5.1 No agreement, practice or arrangement currently or previously carried on by the Company or to which the Company is or has been a party infringes any competition, anti-restrictive trade practice, anti-trust or consumer protection law or legislation applicable in any relevant jurisdiction ("Competition Laws").

3.5.2 The Company has not given any undertaking to any court, person or body and is not subject to any act, decision, regulation, order or other instrument under any Competition Laws.

3.6 **Products**

The Company has not manufactured, sold or supplied any product or provided any service which does not or did not at any material time comply with the terms of any contract entered into by the Company or with any applicable regulation, standard or statutory requirement, or which was in any other way defective.

3.7 **Pollution of the environment**

3.7.1 [No hazardous substances have been used or stored or otherwise handled by the Company on the Property or elsewhere.] [The Company has at all times held all licences, consents, permits and authorities necessary to enable it to use, store or otherwise handle or dispose of any hazardous substances used, stored, otherwise handled or disposed of by it, whether on the Property or elsewhere.]

3.7.2 There has been no pollution of the environment by the Company, the Company has no responsibility or liability for any pollution of the environment by any third party and there has been no act or omission by the Company which could give rise to any pollution of the environment.

3.7.3 The Company has complied and has adequate systems and facilities to continue to comply with:

3.7.3.1 all laws and regulations relating to pollution of the environment;

3.7.3.2 all laws and regulations relating to pollution of the environment which apply to any person carrying on any process carried on by the Company;

3.7.3.3 all EC Directives relating to pollution of the environment (whether or not they have been implemented in any relevant jurisdiction).

For the purposes of this paragraph 3.7 the expressions "pollution of the environment" and "process" shall have the same meanings as in section 1 of the Environmental Protection Act 1990.

3.8 **Data Protection**

3.8.1 The Company has at all times complied with the Applicable Data Protection Laws, and there exist no circumstances likely to give rise to any allegation of non-compliance.

3.8.2 The Company has made all necessary notifications or registrations under the Applicable Data Protection Laws, and such registrations or notifications are appropriate given the Company's actual data processing activities.

3.8.3 The Company has not received any enforcement, information or other official notice or request under the Applicable Data Protection Laws.

3.8.4 The Company has not received any communication from any data subject or official alleging a breach of the Applicable Data Protection Laws.

3.8.5 The Company has not been required to pay compensation in respect of any breach of the Applicable Data Protection Laws, no claims for compensation are outstanding and there are no circumstances likely to give rise to such a claim.

3.8.6 The Company has complied with all data subject requests including requests for access to personal data or cessation of specified processing activities.

3.9 **Health and Safety**

3.9.1 The Company has complied with all its obligations under the Health & Safety at Work etc Act 1974 ("the Health & Safety Act") and all regulations passed thereunder ("the Regulations").

3.9.2 The Company has not been served with any Improvement Notices.

3.9.3 The Company has not been served with any Prohibition Notices.

3.9.4 The Company has not been cautioned for any breach of the Health & Safety Act or the Regulations.

3.9.5 The Company has not been prosecuted for any breach of the Health & Safety Act or the Regulations.

3.9.6 There are no circumstances likely to give rise to the service of an Improvement Notice or Prohibition Notice, or to a prosecution for a breach of the Health & Safety Act or the Regulations.

3.9.7 The Company has not been the subject of a prosecution (whether by the Crown Prosecution Service, the Health and Safety Executive, or any other responsible body) as a result of or in connection with any work-related death and there are no circumstances likely to give rise to such a prosecution.

3.9.8 For the purposes of this paragraph 0, the expression "Improvement Notice" and "Prohibition Notice" shall have the same meanings as in sections 21 and 22 of the Health & Safety Act.

4.   THE COMPANY'S FINANCIAL POSITION

   4.1   **The Accounts**

            The Accounts:

            4.1.1   have been prepared in accordance with the requirements of the Act
                     and all other applicable statutes and regulations and in accordance
                     with generally accepted accounting practices, including all appli-
                     cable SSAPs and FRSs and statements from the Urgent Issues Task
                     Force;

            4.1.2   have been prepared on bases and principles and using methods
                     which are consistent with those used in the preparation of the
                     audited accounts of the Company [and the audited consolidated
                     accounts for the Group in each case] for any accounting period
                     falling wholly or partly within the period of six years ended on the
                     Accounts Date; and

            4.1.3   show a true and fair view of the state of affairs of the Company
                     [and of the Group] as at the Accounts Date and of the profit or loss
                     of the Company [and of the Group] for the accounting period
                     ended on that date.

   4.2   **Provisions in the Accounts**

            The Accounts:

            4.2.1   fully provide for all liabilities (other than contingent liabilities
                     which are not expected to crystallise) and fully disclose all contin-
                     gent liabilities which are not expected to crystallise and all capital
                     and revenue commitments of the Company in each case as at the
                     Accounts Date;

            4.2.2   fully provide for all bad and doubtful debts as at the Accounts
                     Date;

            4.2.3   attribute a value to stock which does not exceed the lower of direct
                     cost and net realisable value as at the Accounts Date after wholly
                     writing off all redundant, obsolete, old, unusable, unsaleable, slow-
                     moving, deteriorated and excessive stock; and

            4.2.4   are not affected (except as disclosed in the Accounts) by any
                     extraordinary or exceptional event, circumstance or item.

   4.3   **Events since the Accounts Date**

            Since the Accounts Date:

            4.3.1   the Company has carried on its business in the ordinary and usual
                     course and without any interruption or alteration in the nature,
                     scope or manner thereof;

            4.3.2   the Company has not acquired or disposed of any asset, assumed
                     any liability, made any payment or entered into any other transac-
                     tion which was not in the ordinary course of its business and for
                     full value;

            4.3.3   the Company's turnover and margins of profitability have not been
                     less than its turnover and margins of profitability for the correspon-
                     ding period in the accounting period which ended on the Accounts
                     Date, and there has been no deterioration in its financial position or
                     prospects. In particular, there has been no reduction in the value of

the net tangible assets of the Company on the basis of the valuations used in the Accounts;

4.3.4   the Company has paid its creditors within the times agreed with such creditors, and there are no debts now outstanding by the Company which have been outstanding for more than [   ] days or which are now overdue for payment (whether in whole or in part);

4.3.5   the Company has not entered into, or agreed to enter into, any capital commitment;

4.3.6   the Company has not repaid or become liable to repay any loan or indebtedness in advance of its stated maturity;

4.3.7   the Company has not received notice (whether formal or informal) from any lender of money to the Company requiring repayment or intimating the enforcement by it of any security which it may hold over any assets of the Company, and there are no circumstances likely to give rise to such notice;

4.3.8   no part of the amounts included in the Accounts, or subsequently recorded in the books of the Company as owing by any debtors, has been outstanding for more than [   ] days or has been released on terms that any debtor pays less than the full book value of his or its debt or has been written off or has proved to any extent to be irrecoverable;

4.3.9   the Company has not factored or discounted any of its debts or agreed to do so;

4.3.10 the Company has not offered any price reduction or discount or allowance on sales of stock below a selling price which achieves a gross margin of [   ]% or sold any stock at less than its book value;

4.3.11 the Company has not sought to accelerate payment by its trade debtors other than in the ordinary and normal course of business.

4.4   **Working capital**

[Having regard to existing bank and other facilities, the Company has sufficient working capital for the purpose of continuing to carry on its business in its present form and at its present level of turnover for the period to [200]] [The financial forecasts of the Company for the [three] year period ending on [   ] 200 (a copy of which is attached to the Disclosure Letter) have been prepared by or on behalf of the Seller in good faith and on the basis of assumptions which are reasonable.

4.5   **Grants**

The Company has not made any application for or received any financial assistance from any supranational, national or local authority or governmental agency.

4.6   **Debts**

There are no debts owing by or to the Company other than debts which have arisen in the ordinary course of its business, nor has the Company lent any money which has not been repaid.

4.7 Management Accounts

The Management Accounts have been prepared using the same accounting principles, policies and bases as used in the Accounts (consistently applied), fairly reflect the trading position of the Company as at the date and for the period to which they relate and are not affected by any extraordinary, exceptional, unusual or non-recurring income, capital gain or expenditure or by any other factor known to the Seller rendering profits or losses for the period covered exceptionally high or low.

5. THE COMPANY AND ITS FINANCIERS

5.1 Borrowings

The total amount borrowed by the Company from its financiers does not exceed its facilities and the total amount borrowed by the Company from whatsoever source does not exceed any limitation on borrowing imposed upon it in its articles of association or otherwise.

5.2 Continuance of facilities

Full and accurate details of all overdrafts, loans or other financial facilities outstanding or available to the Company are contained in the Disclosure Letter (and true and complete copies of all documents relating thereto are attached to the Disclosure Letter), and neither the Seller nor the Company has done anything whereby the continuance of any such facilities in full force and effect might be affected or prejudiced.

5.3 Bank accounts

A statement of all the bank accounts of the Company and of the credit or debit balances on such accounts as at a date not more than two days before the date of this Agreement and a reconciliation of such credit or debit balances to the books and records of the Company as at the date of this Agreement are attached to the Disclosure Letter and are true, complete and accurate. The Company does not have any other bank or deposit account. Since the date to which such statement is drawn up there have been no payments out of, and no instructions given for any payments out of, and no cheques drawn against, any such accounts except for routine payments out of current account in the ordinary course of business.

5.4 Guarantees

No person has given any guarantee of or security for any overdraft, loan or loan facility granted to or obligations undertaken by the Company. The Company is not a party to any guarantee, suretyship, indemnity or similar commitment.

6. THE ASSETS OF THE COMPANY

6.1 Assets and charges

6.1.1 The Company owns free from any Encumbrance all assets included in the Accounts or acquired by the Company since the Accounts Date except for current assets subsequently disposed of by the Company in the ordinary course of its business [, the Properties] and stock which is the subject of retention of title terms contained in standard terms of trading imposed by suppliers in the ordinary course of their business and owns free from any Encumbrance any other asset used by it.

6.1.2   The Company has possession of all such assets and none of such assets, nor any of the undertaking, goodwill or uncalled capital of the Company, is subject to any Encumbrance or any agreement or commitment to give or create any Encumbrance.

6.1.3   The assets owned by the Company, together with assets held under hire-purchase, leasing and rental agreements (copies of which are attached to the Disclosure Letter), comprise all assets necessary for the continuation of its business as now carried on.

6.1.4   No asset is shared by the Company with any Member of the Seller's Group at the date of this Agreement, and the Company does not depend for its business upon or make use of any assets, facilities or services owned or supplied by any Member of the Seller's Group at the date of this Agreement

6.2   **Stocks**

The stock of raw materials, packaging materials and finished goods now held by the Company is not excessive and is adequate in relation to the current trading requirements of the business of the Company; none of it is obsolete, slow-moving or unusable and it is capable of being sold by the Company in the ordinary course of its business in accordance with current price lists without rebate or allowance to a Buyer.

6.3   **Debts**

The amounts due from debtors are recoverable in full in the ordinary course of business and in any event not later than [ninety] days following the date of this Agreement, and none of these debts is subject to any counterclaim or set-off.

6.4   **Intellectual Property**

6.4.1   The Company:

6.4.1.1   is the sole and beneficial owner and (where it is capable of registration) the registered proprietor of the Intellectual Property used by it, all of which are valid and in full force and effect;

6.4.1.2   does not own or use any Intellectual Property other than that listed in the Disclosure Letter and other than copyrights, design rights, technical know-how and confidential information and does not require any other Intellectual Property to carry on its business;

6.4.1.3   has not entered into any Intellectual Property Agreements other than any listed in the Disclosure Letter or authorised any person to make any use of or to do anything which would or might otherwise infringe any Intellectual Property Rights; and

6.4.1.4   has not disclosed (except in the ordinary course of its business) any of its know-how, trade secrets or customer details to any other person.

6.4.2   The Company owns the copyright or design right (whether registered or unregistered) in the designs of all its products and is the proprietor of any registrations or applications to register any such designs.

6.4.3   None of the processes or products of the Company [(so far as the Seller is aware)]:

6.4.3.1   infringes any Intellectual Property of any other person; or

6.4.3.2   involves the unlicensed use of confidential information or know-how disclosed to the Company by any person.

6.4.4   None of the Intellectual Property Rights are being used by, or are being or have been claimed, disputed, opposed or attacked by any other person.

6.4.5   All Intellectual Property Agreements to which the Company is a party are valid and binding on the parties thereto; the Company has at all times observed and performed all of the provisions of each of them and nothing has been done or omitted to be done by the Company which would enable any of them to be terminated.

6.4.6   None of the records, systems, data or information of the Company is recorded, stored, maintained, operated or otherwise wholly or partly dependent on or held or accessible by any means (including any electronic, mechanical or photographic process, whether computerised or not) which are not under the exclusive ownership and direct control of the Company.

6.4.7   No person has the right to require the Company to change its corporate name or to cease using any trade name, logo, trading style, domain name or e-mail address currently used by the Company.

6.5   Plant

Each item of the plant and machinery and all vehicles and office and other equipment used in connection with the business of the Company:

6.5.1   is in good repair and condition (subject to fair wear and tear) and in satisfactory working order;

6.5.2   is capable, over the period of time during which it is to be written down to a nil value in the accounts of the Company, of doing the work for which it was designed or purchased; and

6.5.3   is not surplus to the requirements of the Company.

6.6   [Net asset value

The value of the net tangible assets of the Company, determined in accordance with the same accounting policies as those applied in the preparation of the Accounts (and on the basis that each of the fixed assets of the Company is valued at a figure no greater than the value attributed to it in the Accounts or, in the case of any fixed assets acquired by the Company after the Accounts Date, at a figure no greater than cost), is not less than the value of the net tangible assets of the Company at the Accounts Date as shown in the Accounts.]

6.7   Computer Systems

6.7.1   The Computer Systems are capable of the following functions:

6.7.1.1   handling date information involving all and any dates including, accepting date input, providing date output and performing date calculations in whole or part;

6.7.1.2   operating accurately without interruption on and in respect of any and all dates and without any change in performance;

6.7.1.3   responding to and processing two digit year input without creating any ambiguity as to the century; and

6.7.1.4   storing and providing date output information without creating any ambiguity as to the century.

6.7.2   The Computer Systems and each element of them passes and will continue to pass date information between each other (and any third parties' computer systems with which they habitually communicate) in a way which does not, and will not, create inaccuracies.

6.7.3   The Hardware has been satisfactorily maintained and supported and has the benefit of an appropriate maintenance and support agreement which is not capable of being terminated by the contractor by less than 24 months' notice.

6.7.4   The Hardware and the Software have adequate capability and capacity for the projected requirements of the Company for not less than 4 years following Completion.

6.7.5   Disaster recovery plans are in effect and are adequate to ensure that the Hardware, Software and Data can be replaced or substituted without material disruption to the business of the Company.

6.7.6   In the event that any person providing maintenance or support services for the Computer Systems ceases or is unable to do so, the Company has all necessary rights and information to procure the carrying out of such services by employees of by a third party without undue expense or delay.

6.7.7   The Company has sufficient technically competent and trained employees to ensure proper handling, operation, monitoring and use of the Computer Systems.

6.7.8   The Company has adequate procedures to ensure internal and external security of the Computer Systems and of the Data, including procedures for preventing unauthorised access, preventing the introduction of a virus, taking and storing on-site and off-site back-up copies of Software and Data.

6.7.9   Where any of the records of the Company are stored electronically, the Company is the owner of all hardware and software licences necessary to enable it to keep, copy, maintain and use such records in the course of its business and does not share any hardware or software relating to the records with any person.

6.7.10   The Company has all the rights necessary (including rights over the source code) to obtain, without undue expense or delay, modified versions of the Software which are required at any time to improve in any regard the operation and/or efficiency of the Software.

6.7.11   The Company owns, and is in possession and control of, original copies of all of the manuals, guides, instruction books and technical documents (including any corrections and updates) required to operate the Computer Systems effectively.

6.7.12   The Computer Systems have never unduly interrupted or hindered the running or operation of the Company's business and have no defects in operation which so affect the Company's business.

6.7.13   In this paragraph 6.7:-

6.7.13.1 "Data" means any data or information used by or for the benefit of the Company at any time and stored electronically at any time;

6.7.13.2 "Hardware" means any computer equipment used by or for the benefit of the Company at any time including, without limitation, PCs, mainframes, screens, terminals, keyboards, discs, printers, cabling and associated and peripheral electronic equipment but excluding all Software;

6.7.13.3 "Software" means any set of instructions for execution by microprocessor used by or for the benefit of the Company at any time, irrespective of application, language or medium;

6.7.13.4 "Computer Systems" means all Hardware, Software and any other items that connect with any or all of them which in each case are used by or for the benefit of the Company.

7. THE CONTRACTS OF THE COMPANY

7.1 Documents

All title deeds and all agreements to which the Company is a party are in the possession of the Company and are properly stamped and free from Encumbrance.

7.2 Material contracts

The Company is not a party to or subject to any agreement, transaction, obligation, commitment, understanding, arrangement or liability which:

7.2.1 is incapable of complete performance in accordance with its terms within three months after the date on which it was entered into or undertaken or cannot be terminated, without giving rise to any liabilities on the Company, by the Company giving three months' notice or less;

7.2.2 is known by the Seller or by the Company to be likely to result in a loss to the Company on completion or performance;

7.2.3 cannot readily be fulfilled or performed by the Company on time;

7.2.4 involves or is likely to involve obligations, restrictions, expenditure or revenue of an unusual, onerous or exceptional nature; or

7.2.5 requires an aggregate consideration payable by the Company in excess of £[ ] ([ ] pounds);

7.2.6 is in any way otherwise than in the ordinary and proper course of the business of the Company and on arm's length terms.

7.3 Defaults

Neither the Company nor any other party to any agreement with the Company is in default thereunder, being a default which would be material in the context of the financial or trading position of the Company nor (so far as the Seller is aware) are there any circumstances likely to give rise to any such default.

7.4   **Insider contracts**

There is not outstanding, and there has not at any time during the last three years been outstanding, any agreement or arrangement between the Company and any Member of the Seller's Group at any material time and the Company is not a party to, nor has its profit or loss or financial position during such period been affected by, any such agreement or arrangement or any other agreement or arrangement which is not entirely of an arm's length nature.

7.5   **Customers/suppliers**

7.5.1   In the accounting period ended on the Accounts Date, no customer or supplier of the Company represented [%] or more of the Company's sales or purchases in that period (any such customer or supplier being a "Major Customer" or "Major Supplier") save for those specifically identified in the Disclosure Letter as Major Customers or Major Suppliers.

7.5.2   No Major Customer or Major Supplier has since the Accounts Date ceased to do business with the Company or has since such date substantially reduced its purchases from or supplies to the Company and since the Accounts Date no indication has been received by the Company of any material change in the prices or other terms upon which any customer or supplier is prepared to contract or do business with the Company.

7.5.3   The Seller is not aware of any reason to indicate that any of the existing customers of or suppliers to the Company are likely materially to reduce the volume of their purchases from or supplies to the Company in the future by comparison with the value of their purchases from or supplies to the Company during the period of [   ] months prior to the date of this Agreement.

8.   **THE COMPANY AND ITS EMPLOYEES**

8.1   **General**

8.1.1   There is no employment or other contract or engagement between the Company and any of its directors or other officers. The Company is not a party to a consultancy contract.

8.1.2   There is no employment contract between the Company and any of its employees which cannot be terminated by the Company by three months' notice or less without giving rise to a claim for damages or compensation (other than a statutory redundancy payment or statutory compensation for unfair dismissal). The Company has not received notice of resignation from [*key personnel*].

8.1.3   There is no employment or consultancy contract or other contract of engagement between the Company and any person which is in suspension or has been terminated but is capable of being revived or enforced or in respect of which the Company has a continuing obligation.

8.1.4   The Disclosure Letter contains details of:

8.1.4.1   the total number of the Company's employees including those who are on maternity leave or absent because of disability or other long-term leave of absence and who have or may have a right to return to work with the Company;

8.1.4.2   the name, date of start of employment, period of continuous employment, salary and other benefits, grade and age of each employee of the Company and, where an employee has been continuously absent from work for more than one month, the reason for the absence; and

8.1.4.3   the terms of the contract of each director, other officer and employee of the Company entitled to remuneration at an annual rate, or an average annual rate over the last three financial years, of more than £[ ].

8.1.5   The basis of the remuneration payable to the Company's directors, other officers and employees is the same as that in force at the Accounts Date. The Company is not obliged to increase, nor has it made provision to increase, the total annual remuneration payable to its directors, other officers and employees by more than [three] per cent. or to increase the rate of remuneration of a director, other officer or employee entitled to annual remuneration of more than £[ ].

8.1.6   The Company owes no amount to a present or former director, other officer or employee of the Company (or his dependant) other than for accrued remuneration or reimbursement of business expenses.

8.1.7   There is no agreement or arrangement between the Company and an employee or former employee with respect to his employment, his ceasing to be employed or his retirement which is not included in the written terms of his employment or previous employment. The Company has not provided, or agreed to provide, a gratuitous payment or benefit to a director, officer or employee or to any of their dependants.

8.1.8   The Company has maintained up-to-date, full and accurate records regarding the employment of each of its employees (including details of terms of employment, payments of statutory sick pay and statutory maternity pay, income tax and social security contributions, working time, disciplinary and health and safety matters) and termination of employment.

8.2   **Payments on termination**

Except as disclosed in the Accounts, the Company has not:

8.2.1   incurred a liability for breach or termination of an employment contract including, without limitation, a redundancy payment, protective award and compensation for wrongful dismissal, unfair dismissal and failure to comply with an order for the reinstatement or re-engagement of an employee;

8.2.2   incurred a liability for breach or termination of a consultancy agreement;

8.2.3   made or agreed to make a payment or provided or agreed to provide a benefit to a present or former director, other officer or employee of the Company or to any of their dependants in connection with the actual or proposed termination or suspension of employment or variation of an employment contract.

8.3   Compliance with law

The Company has complied with:

8.3.1   each obligation imposed on it by, and each order and award made under, statute, regulation, code of conduct and practice, collective agreement, (including any agreement or arrangement under the ICE Regulations 2004), custom and practice relevant to the relations between it and its employees or a trade union or the terms of employment of its employees; and

8.3.2   each recommendation or code of practice made by the Advisory, Conciliation and Arbitration Service and each award and declaration made by the Central Arbitration Committee.

8.4   Redundancies and transfer of business

Within the year ending on the date of this Agreement the Company has not:

8.4.1   given notice of redundancies to the relevant Secretary of State or started consultations with appropriate representatives under Chapter II of Part IV of the Trade Union and Labour Relations (Consolidation) Act 1992 or failed to comply with its obligations under Chapter II of Part IV of that Act; or

8.4.2   been a party to a relevant transfer (as defined in the Transfer of Undertakings (Protection of Employment) Regulations 2006) or failed to comply with a duty to inform and consult appropriate representatives under those Regulations.

8.5   Trade Unions

8.5.1   The Company has no agreement or arrangement (whether under the Information and Consultation of Employees Regulations 2004 or otherwise) with and does not recognise a trade union, works council, staff association or other body representing any of its employees and the Company has not received any notice or request nor are there any negotiations which may lead to any such agreement or arrangement).

8.5.2   The Company is not involved in, and no fact or circumstance exists which might give rise to: —

8.5.2.1   a dispute with a trade union, works council, staff association or other body representing any of its employees; or

8.5.2.2   any proceedings before the Central Arbitration Committee or an Employment Tribunal in relation to any collective bargaining agreement or any arrangement under the ICE Regulations 2004.

8.6   Incentive schemes

The Company does not have and is not proposing to introduce a share incentive, share option, profit sharing, bonus or other incentive scheme for any of its directors, other officers or employees.

9.   PENSIONS

9.1   Disclosed Schemes

The Disclosed Schemes are the only arrangements under which the Company has or could have any liability to provide or contribute towards relevant benefits as defined in Chapter 2 of Part 6 of the Income Tax (Earnings & Pensions) Act 2003.

9.2   **Details Supplied**

The Seller has supplied to the Buyer documents containing full, accurate and up to date details of each of the Disclosed Schemes and of the Company's obligations and liabilities under it.

9.3   **Eligibility Requirements**

No amendments have been proposed or announced in relation to the eligibility requirements for entry to the Disclosed Schemes, contribution rates or benefits.

9.4   **Legal Compliance**

Each of the Disclosed Schemes complies and has at all times complied with all legal and regulatory requirements (including equal treatment and data protection requirements) applicable to it.

9.5   **Stakeholder Pension Scheme**

The Company complies and has at all times complied with any duty to facilitate access to a stakeholder pension scheme under section 3 of the Welfare Reform and Pensions Act 1999.

9.6   **Deduction of Contributions**

All contributions deducted from the salaries of employees of the Company who are members of the Disclosed Schemes and all contributions payable by the Company to and in respect of the Disclosed Schemes have been paid and passed to the trustees of the Pension Scheme or the provider[s] of the Personal Pension Schemes, GPP, Life Assurance Scheme and the Stakeholder Scheme, as appropriate, in full and within the prescribed time limits applicable in each case.

9.7   **Payments**

All levies payable in respect of the Pension Scheme have been paid in full and on or by the due date in each case.

9.8   **Claims and Disputes**

No claim, dispute, complaint or investigation (including, but not limited to, complaints to the Pensions Ombudsman and investigations by the Pensions Regulator) has arisen which relates to the Disclosed Schemes or to the provision of retirement or death benefits in respect of each member of the Group's current and former employees and there is no reason why any such claim, dispute, complaint or investigation could arise.

9.9   **Registered Pension Scheme**

Each of the Disclosed Schemes is a registered pension scheme (within the meaning of Chapter 2 of Part 4 of the Finance Act 2004) and there is no reason why HM Revenue & Customs could withdraw that registration.

9.10   **Contracting Out**

The Pension Scheme is [not] a contracted out scheme within the meaning of section 8 of the Pension Schemes Act 1993.

9.11   **Death in Service Benefits**

All death in service benefits under the [Pension Scheme/Life Assurance Scheme] are fully insured on normal terms for persons in good health.

9.12   **Equalising Benefits**

The Pension Scheme has complied fully with its obligations to equalise benefits for men and women.

9.13   **Eligibility Criteria**

The eligibility criteria for access to the Disclosed Schemes have not been operated so as to discriminate on the grounds of sex, race, disability, religion or belief, sexual orientation or [on and after 1 October 2006] age.

9.14   **Money Purchase Basis [Only relevant to defined contribution schemes]**

All benefits under the Pension Scheme (other than those which are fully insured) are calculated on a money purchase basis only and the Company has given no assurance or contractual promise to any employee of the Company that his benefits at retirement will be based on his salary at or near to retirement.

9.15   **Funding [Only relevant to defined benefit schemes]**

As at [date of last actuarial valuation] the Pension Scheme was fully funded on a [scheme specific funding/ FRS 17] basis, contributions since that date have been paid in accordance with the current schedule of contributions in accordance with section 58 of the Pensions Act 1995, and nothing has occurred since that date which would have an adverse effect on the funding position.

9.16   **Discretions and Powers [Only relevant to defined benefit schemes]**

No discretion or power has been exercised under the Pension Scheme in respect of any employee or director, or former employee or director of the Company to

9.16.1   augment benefits

9.16.2   admit to membership an employee or director who would not otherwise have been eligible for membership

9.16.3   provide in respect of a member a benefit which would not otherwise be provided in respect of that member

9.16.4   provide or pay a benefit on more favourable terms.

9.17   **Transfer Payments [Only relevant to defined benefit schemes]**

No transfer payment has been made from the Pension Scheme whose amount exceeds the lower of 5% of the assets of the Pension Scheme and £1.5m.

9.18   **Benefits [Only relevant to defined benefit schemes]**

No member is in receipt of or entitled to receive benefits from the Pension Scheme whose value exceeds the lower of 5% of the assets and £1.5m.

9.19   **Notifiable Events [Only relevant to defined benefit schemes]**

No notifiable event within the meaning of section 67 of the Pensions Act 2004 has occurred in relation to the Pension Scheme or the Company.

9.20   Effect of sale [Only relevant to defined benefit schemes—where target company participates in group scheme]

The sale and purchase of the [Shares/Company] in accordance with this agreement will not cause the Company to cease to be an employer of persons in the category or categories of employment to which the Pension Scheme relates

10. MATERIAL DISCLOSURE

10.1 Disclosure letter

All information contained in or referred to in the Disclosure letter is true and accurate, and the Disclosure Letter does not omit anything which renders any such information misleading or which might reasonably affect the willingness of an acquirer to acquire the Shares on the terms (including without limitation as to price) of this Agreement.

10.2 Commission

No person is entitled whether, actually or contingently, to receive from the Company any finder's fee, brokerage, or other commission in connection with the acquisition or disposal of shares in the Company.

10.3 Consequence of share acquisition by the Buyer

The sale of the Shares to the Buyer will not by virtue of the terms of any agreement or arrangement to which the Company is a party:

10.3.1 cause the Company to lose the benefit of any right or privilege it presently enjoys, entitle any person to terminate any contract with, or obligation to, the Company or, so far as the Seller is aware, cause any person who normally does business with the Company not to continue to do so on the same basis as previously; or

10.3.2 result in any present or future indebtedness of the Company becoming due or capable of being declared due and payable prior to its stated maturity.

10.4 [Circular letter

The information (including without limitation any negative statement) contained in the extracts from the circular letter to the shareholders of the Buyer (which are signed or initialled by or on behalf of the parties for the purposes of identification) is, so far as the Company and the Seller is concerned, in accordance with the facts and does not omit anything which renders any such information misleading.]

10.5 Legal Due Diligence Enquiries

The replies to the Legal Due Diligence Enquiries dated [ ] 200 raised on behalf of the Buyer were when given and remain true complete and accurate.

11. PROPERTY

11.1 Particulars

The Particulars of the Property shown in schedule 4 are true and correct and the Company has good and marketable title to and the exclusive occupation and possession of the Property free from any mortgage, debenture or charge (whether specific or floating, legal or equitable) rent charge, lien or other encumbrance, lease, sub-lease, tenancy or right of occupation, reservation, covenant, stipulation, profit a prendre, wayleave, grant, restriction, easement, quasi-easement or any agreement for any of the same or any privilege in favour of any third party.

11.2   **Rights and easements**

There are appurtenant to the Property all rights and easements necessary for its use and enjoyment.

11.3   **Title deeds and documents**

The Company has in its possession or under its control all duly stamped deeds and documents which are necessary to prove title to the Property.

11.4   **Disputes etc**

The Property is not affected by any of the following matters nor is it likely to become so affected:-

11.4.1   any dispute, notice or complaint or any exception, reservation, right, covenant, restriction, overriding interest or condition and in particular (but without limitation) any of those matters which is of an unusual nature or which affects or might in the future affect the use of any of the Property for the purpose for which it is now used or which affects or might in the future affect the value of the Property; or

11.4.2   any notice, order, demand, requirement or proposal made or issued by or on behalf of any government or statutory authority, department or body for the acquisition, clearance, demolition or closing or the carrying out of any work upon any building, the modification of any planning permission, the discontinuance of any use or the imposition of any building or improvement line; or

11.4.3   any compensation received as a result of any refusal of any application for planning consent or the imposition of any restrictions in relation to any planning consent; or

11.4.4   any commutation or agreement for the commutation of rent or payment of rent in advance of the due dates for payment thereof.

11.5   **State of repair and condition**

The Property is in a good and substantial state of repair and condition and is fit for the purpose for which it is presently used and no high alumina cement, woodwool, calcium chloride, sea dredged aggregates, asbestos or other deleterious material (not in accordance with good building practice) was used in the construction thereof and there are no development works, redevelopment works or fitting out works outstanding in respect of the Property.

11.6   **Restrictions, conditions and covenants**

All restrictions conditions and covenants (including any imposed by or pursuant to any lease) affecting the Property have been duly and punctually observed and performed and no notice of any breach of any of the same has been received or is likely to be received.

11.7   **Compliance with legislation**

The use of the Property and all machinery and equipment thereon and the conduct of any business thereon complies and has at all times complied in all respects with all relevant statutes and regulations, including the Factories Act 1961, the Offices, Shops and Railway Premises Act 1963, the Fire Precautions Act 1971, the Health and Safety at Work etc., Act 1990 and with all rules, regulations and delegated legislation thereunder and all necessary licences and consents required thereunder have been obtained.

11.8   **Use of property**

There are no restrictive covenants or provisions, legislation, or orders, charges, restrictions, agreements, conditions or other matters which preclude the use of the Property for the purpose or purposes for which the Property is now used and each such use is the permitted use under the provisions of the Town and Country Planning Acts 1971 to 1990 and any statutory re-enactment thereof and all statutory instruments and regulations made thereunder and is in accordance with the requirements of any Local Authority and all restrictions, conditions and covenants imposed by or pursuant to the said Town and Country Planning Acts have been observed and performed and no agreements have been entered into under section 52 of the Town and Country Planning Act 1971, section 106 of the Town and Country Planning Act 1990 or section 33 of the Local Government (Miscellaneous Provisions) Act 1982 in respect of the Property.

11.9   **Replies to enquiries**

All replies by or on behalf of the Seller to enquiries relating to the Property made by or on behalf of the Purchaser were when given and are now true complete accurate and correct.

11.10   **Encumbrances**

There are no options agreements for sale, mortgages, charges (whether specific or floating) rights of pre-emption or of first refusal affecting the Property.

11.11   **Outgoings**

The Property is not subject to the payment of any outgoings (except national non domestic rates and water rates and sewerage service charges). The Property abuts onto an adopted public highway maintainable at public expense to which it has access without crossing land not in the ownership of the Company.

11.12   **Compulsory purchase orders**

There are no compulsory purchase notices, orders or resolutions affecting the Property.

11.13   **Properties previously occupied**

The Company has no existing or contingent liabilities in respect of any properties previously occupied by it or in which it owned or held any interest (or as a surety for the obligations of any other person in relation to such property) including leasehold premises assigned surrendered or otherwise disposed of and the Company has not at any time received any indication whatsoever from any party that any claim has been made or will be made in respect of any such existing or contingent liabilities.

11.14   **No further land and buildings**

The Property comprises all the land and buildings owned, leased or occupied by the Company.

SCHEDULE 6

Claims procedure and determination and Seller's safeguards

1.   NOTICE OF CLAIMS AND TIME LIMITS

No claim in respect of any breach of any of the Warranties (other than the Warranty in paragraph 1 of schedule 5) or pursuant to the Tax Covenants shall be made (except in any case of fraud, dishonesty or wilful non-disclosure) unless notice thereof has been given by or on behalf of the Buyer before:

1.1   in respect of any breach of any of the Warranties other than the Tax Warranties, the expiry of the period of [   ] years following Completion; or

1.2   pursuant to the Tax Covenants or in respect of any breach of any of the Tax Warranties, the expiry of the period of six months following the end of the accounting reference period of the Company in which the sixth anniversary of Completion falls.

2.   LIMITATION OF LIABILITY—MAXIMUM AND MINIMUM AMOUNTS

Except in any case of fraud, dishonesty or wilful non-disclosure:

2.1   the Seller shall have no liability in damages in respect of any claim by the Buyer under any of the Warranties (except for claims in respect of any breaches of the Warranties in paragraph 1 of schedule 5) or the Tax Covenants if and to the extent that such liability would, when aggregated with the amount of any damages paid to the Buyer by the Seller in respect of all and any such claims, exceed, the consideration received by the Seller/[A] ([A] pounds) [the amount set against their names respectively in column [   ] of Schedule 1];

2.2   the Seller shall have no liability in damages in respect of any claim by the Buyer under the Warranties unless such claim:

2.2.1   equals or exceeds, [B] ([B] pounds); and

2.2.2   would, when aggregated with all other such claims against the Seller of, [B] ([B] pounds) or more equal or exceed, [C] ([C] pounds);

but any such claim shall not be limited to the excess over the amounts specified in this paragraph 2.2 and for the purposes of this paragraph 2.2 all claims arising out of the same subject-matter shall be treated as one single claim rather than as individual claims.

3.   NO PREJUDICE FROM PRIOR INVESTIGATION

The rights and remedies of the Buyer in respect of the Warranties and the Tax Covenants shall not be affected by Completion, by any investigation made by or on behalf of the Buyer into the affairs of the Company [or any of the Subsidiaries], by any actual, constructive or imputed knowledge of the Buyer (save as provided in the next following paragraph), by any rescission of (or failure to rescind) this Agreement or by any other event or matter except a specific waiver or release by the Buyer in accordance with the terms of this Agreement.

4.   DISCLOSURE LETTER

The Buyer shall not be entitled to bring any claim in respect of any breach of any of the Warranties if and to the extent that such inconsistency has been fairly disclosed in the Disclosure Letter with sufficient details to identify the nature and scope of the matters disclosed.

5.   SEPARATE WARRANTIES

Each Warranty is a separate warranty and shall not be limited or restricted by reference to or inference from any other Warranty.

6.   RIGHTS OF CONTRIBUTION

The Seller shall not if any claim is made against it by the Buyer under the terms of this Agreement, make any claim against the Company [or any of the Subsidiaries] or any director or any employee of the Company [or of any of the Subsidiaries] on which or on whom it may have relied before agreeing to any term of this Agreement or authorising any statement in the Disclosure Letter.

7.   COSTS

The Seller shall indemnify the Buyer against any costs (including without limitation legal costs on a full indemnity basis) and expenses which it may incur, either before or after the instigation of any legal proceedings, in connection with any legal proceedings for breach of any of the Warranties or pursuant to the Tax Covenants in which judgment is given to the Buyer and the enforcement of any such judgment.

8.   REDUCTION OF CONSIDERATION

Any payment by the Seller for breach of any of the Warranties or under the Tax Covenants shall constitute pound for pound a repayment of and reduction in the consideration for the Shares.

9.   NOTIFICATION

The Buyer shall as soon as reasonably practicable notify the Seller (but any failure to give such notice shall not affect the rights of the Buyer) in writing of any claim made against it by a third party which may give rise to a claim for breach of Warranty (other than a claim relating to a Taxation) (in this paragraph 9 "a Claim").

10.   SET-OFF

Without prejudice to any other right or remedy which it may have, the Buyer shall have the right to set off any sum claimed by it under this Agreement or otherwise against any of its obligations hereunder not then fulfilled in which event any sum otherwise payable by it under this Agreement shall be reduced by the amount of such set-off.

11.   DAMAGES

In the event of a breach of the Warranties, the Seller shall at the election of the Buyer pay to the Buyer on demand an amount equal to either:

11.1   the reduction caused in the value of the Shares; or

11.2   if the value of an asset of the Company is or becomes less than the value would have been had the breach not occurred, the reduction in the value of the asset; or

11.3   if the Company is subject to, or incurs, a liability or an increase in a liability, which it would not have been subject to, or would not have incurred, had the breach not occurred, then the amount of the liability or increased liability.

12.   DAMAGES FOR BREACH OF PENSION WARRANTIES

In determining the damages flowing from any breach of any Warranty in paragraph 9 of schedule 5, it shall be assumed that:

12.1   the Company [is/,and each of the Subsidiaries is,] under a liability to make whatever payments provide the benefits under the [Disclosed Schemes] (as defined in that paragraph) on the basis that any power to amend or discontinue any of the [Disclosed Schemes] is disregarded; and

12.2   the Company [is/,and each of the Subsidiaries is,] under a liability to provide and to continue to provide any benefit (including without limitation gratuities) which it now provides or is now proposing to provide and at the rate at which each respectively is now provided or proposed to be provided and to maintain without amendment any schemes or funds of a kind referred to in that paragraph which are now in existence.

13.   DOUBLE RECOVERY

The Seller shall not be liable in respect of any breach of the Warranties if and to the extent that the losses occasioned thereby have been recovered under the Tax Covenants (and vice versa).

14.   NOTIFICATION

The Seller shall notify the Buyer immediately it becomes aware of any fact or circumstance which constitutes or which may constitute a breach of the Warranties.

SCHEDULE 7

Conditional agreement

Part 1

Conditions

1. **PRINCIPAL CONDITIONS**

The provisions of clauses 2, 3, 6, 7, 8 and 9 are conditional upon the fulfilment of all the following conditions not later than, and the continuance in full force and effect of their fulfilment at, [   ] or such later date as may be agreed in writing between the Seller and the Buyer:

1.1 the passing of a[n ordinary] resolution in general meeting of the Buyer approving the transaction hereby agreed upon [or the Stock Exchange indicating to the Buyer in writing that it does not require the Buyer to submit such transaction to its members for approval;

1.2 the passing of a[n ordinary] resolution in general meeting of the Seller approving the transaction hereby agreed upon [or the Stock Exchange indicating to the Seller in writing that it does not require the Seller to submit such transaction to its members for approval;

1.3 no action having been taken or intimated by HM Government (or any department or agency thereof) or any third party to restrain the transaction hereby agreed upon;

1.4 no receiver and/or manager or administrator or administrative receiver having been appointed of the whole or any part of the assets and undertaking of the Company [or of any of the Subsidiaries] [or of any Member of the Seller's Group from time to time];

1.5 no order having been made and no resolution having been passed for the winding- up of the Company [or of any of the Subsidiaries] [or of any Member of the Seller's Group from time to time];

1.6 no application having been made for an administration order in respect of the Company [or of any of the Subsidiaries] [or of any Member of the Seller's Group from time to time] and no petition having been presented and no notice having been given (whether or not by the Company [or of any of the Subsidiaries] and whether or not by any members) relating to the winding-up of the Company [or of any of the Subsidiaries] [or of any Member of the Seller's Group from time to time];

1.7 [the [underwriting/placing] agreement dated the date of this Agreement between (1) [   ], (2) [   ] and (3) [   ] becoming or being declared unconditional and being completed in accordance with its terms except as to completion of the transaction hereby agreed upon and [   ] not having exercised any right to rescind the agreement thereby constituted; and]

1.8 the Buyer not having exercised any right to rescind this Agreement.

2. **ESCROW COMPLETION**

2.1 The provisions of this Agreement are further conditional upon UKLA admitting the Consideration Shares to the Official List of the Stock Exchange and the Stock Exchange admitting the Consideration Shares to trading on the Stock Exchange's main market for listed securities, in each case, on, or within a period of three working days after, the Completion Date by the posting of the appropriate notices under] [Rule 3.2.7 of the Listing Rules published by the FSA] [the Consideration Shares being admitted to trading on the Alternative Investment Market of the Stock Exchange ("AIM") and such admission being announced in accordance with paragraph 16.6 of the AIM Admission Rules on, or within a period of 3 working days after, the Completion Date.]

2.2   The documents and things required to be delivered by the Buyer to the Seller and vice versa at Completion shall be held in escrow pending the satisfaction of the condition contained in paragraph 2.1 and shall be irrevocably released from escrow forthwith upon the satisfaction of such condition.

3.   THE PARTIES' ENDEAVOURS

Each of the parties shall use all reasonable endeavours to procure that all the provisions of this Agreement become unconditional in accordance with their terms[, and [the Seller] [and] the Buyer shall in particular, but without limitation, procure that the circular letter[s] to be sent to [its/their respective shareholders relating to the resolution[s] referred to in paragraph[s] 1.1 [and 1.2] contains[s] [a] unanimous recommendation[s] by the directors of the Seller] [and] the Buyer [respectively] and a confirmation that each intends to vote in favour of such resolution[s] in respect of his own holding and that the general meeting[s] referred to in paragraph[s] 1.1 [and 1.2] [is/are] held no later than [200]].

4.   NON-FULFILMENT

If any one or more of the Conditions are not fulfilled on or before [LONG STOP DATE], the agreement constituted by this Agreement shall thereupon become void and of no effect except as regards and without prejudice to any and all rights of action of the parties for any prior breach of any of the provisions of this Agreement. In that event the parties shall promptly return to one another all documents and other things already delivered in connection with the transaction hereby agreed upon.

5.   WAIVER

The Buyer shall be entitled at its option to waive any one or more of the Conditions [other than that set out in paragraph 1.2], and, if it does so, the Seller shall be deemed to have done so also. [The Seller shall be entitled at its option to waive the Condition set out in paragraph 1.2, and, if it does so, the Buyer shall be deemed to have done so also.]

6.   NOTICE OF FULFILMENT OF CONDITIONS

6.1   When the Conditions other than that set out in paragraph 1.2 have been fulfilled, the Buyer shall forthwith give written notice to that effect to the Seller, and such notice shall be conclusive and binding on the parties as to the fulfilment thereof.

6.2   When the Condition set out in paragraph 1.2 has been fulfilled, the Seller shall forthwith give notice to that effect to the Buyer, and such notice shall be conclusive and binding on the parties as to the fulfilment thereof.

Part 2

Obligations and events pending Completion

1.   RESTRICTIONS

The Seller shall procure that prior to Completion the Company [and the Subsidiaries] carry on business in the normal way so as to maintain the same as a going concern and that, except with the prior written consent of the Buyer, [neither] the Company [nor any of the Subsidiaries] will [not]:

1.1   grant any Encumbrance over any property or assets or dispose of any property or assets other than trading stock in the ordinary course of business on arm's length terms;

1.2   enter into or agree to enter into any Intellectual Property Agreement or enter into any assignment of any Intellectual Property;

1.3   grant or issue, or agree to grant or issue, any guarantee or indemnity;

1.4   create or issue, or agree to create or issue, any share or loan capital or any security convertible into share or loan capital or give or agree to give any option or other right in respect thereof;

1.5   acquire any asset on lease, lease-purchase, hire-purchase or deferred terms;

1.6   declare and/or pay any dividend or bonus or make any distribution of profits or assets;

1.7   pass any resolution of its members in general meeting;

1.8   do or allow to be done or omitted any act or thing which may render its financial position less favourable than at the date hereof;

1.9   do or allow to be done or omitted any act or thing which may reduce or vitiate the cover afforded by any current insurance policy;

1.10   enter into any transaction outside the ordinary course of its business;

1.11   make any payment pursuant to any guarantee or indemnity paid in respect of any obligation or liability of any member of the Seller's Group; [nor]

1.12   do anything which would or might render in any way untrue or inaccurate or misleading the circular to the shareholders of the Buyer [and/or the prospectus in respect of the Buyer as contemplated by paragraph 7 of part 1 of this schedule].

2.   ACCESS TO RECORDS

The Seller shall at all times prior to Completion give to the Buyer and its professional advisers, in all cases with reasonable despatch upon request, all such information and make available for inspection all such documents and records as it or they may reasonably require and as may be under the control of the Seller and so far as possible take and procure to be taken all such steps as may be required to implement the terms of this Agreement.

Part 3

Warranties

1.   MAINTENANCE OF WARRANTIES

The Seller shall procure that (save only as may be necessary to give effect to the terms of this Agreement) neither it nor the Company [nor any of the Subsidiaries] shall allow to occur, at any time at or before Completion, any change of circumstances:

1.1   such that, if the Warranties were repeated at that time, any of them would not then be true and accurate; and/or

1.2   which would entitle the Buyer, assuming this Agreement were unconditional and that Completion had taken place, to make a claim under the Tax Covenants.

2.   SELLER'S DUTY TO DISCLOSE BREACHES

The Seller shall immediately disclose to the Buyer anything which comes to its notice before Completion which is or may be inconsistent with any of the Warranties.

3.   RESCISSION

The Buyer shall not be bound to complete the acquisition of the Shares, and may by notice in writing to the Seller's Solicitors rescind this Agreement without liability on its part, if:

3.1   on the date of this Agreement:

   3.1.1   any of the Warranties are not true and accurate; and/or

   3.1.2   the Buyer would be entitled, assuming this Agreement were unconditional and that Completion had taken place, to make a claim under the Tax Covenants; and/or

3.2   at any time at or before Completion or the fulfilment of the Conditions there is a change of circumstances:

   3.2.1   such that, if the Warranties were repeated at that time any of them would not then be true and accurate; and/or

   3.2.2   which would entitle the Buyer, assuming this Agreement were unconditional and that Completion had taken place, to make a claim under the Tax Covenants; and/or

3.3   the Seller is in breach of part 2 of this schedule

[and (in any such case) the amount which the Buyer is entitled to claim or would be entitled to claim if the Warranties were repeated or if Completion had taken place amounts to at least £[   ] ([   ] pounds).

4.   [Rescission shall be without prejudice to the rights of the [parties/Buyer] in respect of any prior breach of any of the provisions of this Agreement.]

SCHEDULE 8

[This schedule to contain any operative provisions regarding pension arrangements]

SCHEDULE 9

Calculation of Completion NAV

Part 1

Interpretation

In this Agreement the following words and expressions shall have the meanings set out opposite each respectively:

"the Completion NAV"	the net asset value of the [Company/Group] being the aggregate of:

    (a)   the amounts paid up or credited as paid up on the issued share capital of the [Company/Group], and

    (b)   any balance standing to the credit of the profit and loss account of the [Company/ Group][3]

less:

    (c)   any debit balance on the profit and loss account of the [Company/Group][4]

as stated by the Buyer's Accountants and agreed (or deemed to be agreed) by the Seller's Accountants or, as the case may be, as determined by the Independent Accountant, in accordance with this schedule;

"the Completion Statement"	as defined in paragraph 3.1 of part 2 of this schedule;
"Independent Accountant"	a chartered accountant agreed upon by or on behalf of the Seller and the Buyer or, if they fail to agree, nominated on the application at any time of the Seller or of the Buyer by the President for the time being of the Institute of Chartered Accountants in England and Wales (the costs of such accountant, and, if applicable, of such President, in nominating such accountant to be borne as he may direct);
"the Buyer's Accountants"	[ ] of [ ];
"the Seller's Accountants"	[ ] of [ ].

Part 2
Calculation

1.   [The Company [and each of the Subsidiaries] shall carry out a physical stock-take within days after the Completion Date at which a representative of each of the Buyer, the Buyer's Accountants, the Seller and the Seller's Accountants shall be entitled to be present and] the Buyer shall procure the [Company/Group] to prepare within [   ] days after the Completion Date accounts comprising a [consolidated] balance sheet dealing with the state of affairs of the [Company/Group] to the close of business on the

---

[3] Consider whether it will be necessary to refer to other reserves, such as a revaluation reserve.

[4] Consider whether it will be necessary to refer to other reserves.

Completion Date and a [consolidated] profit and loss account for the [Company/Group] for the period from the Accounts Date to the close of business on the Completion Date in accordance with part 3 of this schedule. ("the Completion Accounts").

2. The Seller shall provide such information and assistance as the Buyer and the [Company/Group] may reasonably require for the preparation of the Completion Accounts.

3. The Buyer shall instruct the Buyer's Accountants to:

3.1 report on the Completion Accounts and on the basis of the Completion Accounts produce a dated statement of the Completion NAV ("the Completion Statement"); and

3.2 deliver the Completion Statement and provide access to all working papers to the Seller's Accountants;

within [   ] days following delivery to the Buyer's Accountants of the Completion Accounts.

4. If such queries and observations as the Seller's Accountants raise within [twenty-one] days following delivery to them of the Completion Statement have not been dealt with to their satisfaction and reflected in any amendments within [twenty-one] days following delivery to the Buyer's Accountants of such queries and observations, it shall be open to the Seller or the Buyer to request an Independent Accountant to determine the Completion NAV, and his determination shall, in the absence of manifest error, be final and binding on the parties.

5. If the Seller's Accountants do not raise any queries or observations in respect of the Completion Statement within [twenty-one] days following delivery thereof to them or if they agree the Completion Statement, then the Completion Statement shall be final and binding on the parties, and the Completion NAV shall be as set out in the Completion Statement.

6. In stating, agreeing or determining (as the case may be) the Completion NAV, the Buyer's Accountants, the Seller's Accountants and, if applicable, the Independent Accountant shall act as experts and not as arbitrators.

7. The Buyer and the Seller shall promptly provide and render or cause to be provided and rendered to the Buyer's Accountants, the Seller's Accountants and the Independent Accountant such information and assistance as they or any of them may reasonably require to enable the Buyer's Accountants and the Seller's Accountants to agree the Completion Statement (and to make the report referred to in paragraph 3) or to enable the Independent Accountant to determine the Completion NAV.

8. The Seller shall bear and pay all of the costs of the Seller's Accountants, and the Buyer shall bear and pay all the costs of the Buyer's Accountants, incurred in each case in connection with the matters referred to in this schedule.

Part 3
Accounting principles, methods and bases

1. Subject to paragraph 2, the Completion Accounts shall be prepared in accordance with:

1.1 generally accepted United Kingdom accounting principles, methods and bases; and

1.2   subject thereto (and to the extent they are disclosed in the Disclosure Letter or in the notes to the Accounts), the accounting principles, methods and bases applied and used in the preparation of the Accounts, consistently applied.

2.   The following specific provisions shall apply to the preparation of the Completion Accounts:

[Any detailed provisions to be inserted here]

Signed by [   ] for and
on behalf of [   ]
LIMITED/PLC in the presence of:

OR

Signed as a deed by [   ]
LIMITED/PLC acting by [   ],
a director,
in the presence of:

OR

Signed as a deed by [   ]
LIMITED/PLC acting by two
directors or a director and its secretary:

          director
          [director/secretary]

OR

Signed as a deed by [   ]
LIMITED/PLC acting by [   ],
a director,
in the presence of:

OR

Signed as a deed by [

LIMITED/PLC] acting by two

directors or a director and its secretary:

director

[director/secretary]

APPENDIX A

ALTERNATIVE C—CONSIDERATION SHARES

3. **CONSIDERATION**

3.1 The consideration for the Shares shall be the allotment at Completion (credited as fully paid,) to the Seller of [ ] Consideration Shares.

OR

3.1 The consideration for the Shares shall be the allotment at Completion (credited as fully paid) to the Seller of the number of Consideration Shares (excluding fractions) nearest to but not less than A in the formula:

$$A = \frac{B}{C}$$

Where:

B = £[NOTIONAL CONSIDERATION]

C = whichever is the greater of:

(a) the average of the middle market quotations for an ordinary share of [ ] in the capital of the Buyer [as shown by the daily Official List of the Stock Exchange/on the Alternative Investment Market] for each of the last [ ] days on which the Stock Exchange is open for business ending with the last such day but one before Completion; and

(b) the nominal value of such an ordinary share.

3.2 **Dividends**

The Consideration Shares shall rank pari passu in all respects with the existing ordinary shares of [ ] each in the capital of the Buyer and shall carry the right to receive in full all dividends and other distributions declared, made or paid after the date of this Agreement [except that they shall not carry the right to participate in the [interim/final] dividend of the Buyer for the accounting reference period ending on [200] [declared/to be declared] on [or about] [200]].

3.3 **Retention of Consideration Shares**

The Seller undertakes that it will not:-

3.3.1 except with the prior written consent of the Buyer, dispose of any interest in any of the Consideration Shares for a period of [ ] months following Completion; or

3.3.2 for a period of [ ] months thereafter, dispose of any interest in any such shares, except with the prior written consent of the Buyer, such consent not to be unreasonably withheld or delayed provided that any such disposal is (in the reasonable opinion of the Buyer) on an orderly market basis and made through the Buyer's [stockbroker for the time being] [Nominated Broker for the time being].

3.4 **Cash Alternative**

    3.4.1   If the Buyer so elects, the consideration for the Shares may be either:

        3.4.1.1   wholly satisfied by a cash payment to the Seller, in which event:

            (a)   on Completion the Buyer shall pay the amount described as B in clause 3.1; and

            (b)   clauses 3.1 to 3.3 inclusive shall not apply; or

        3.4.1.2   partly satisfied by a cash payment to the Seller of an amount which is less than the amount described as B in clause 3.1, in which event on Completion the Buyer shall pay that lesser amount and clauses 3.1 to 3.3 inclusive shall apply to the extent, and on the basis only, that the amount described as B in clause 3.1 is reduced by the amount of the cash payment made on Completion pursuant to this clause. **[This wording will require amendment if the first version of clause 3.1 applies.]**

3.5 **Cash payment**

    3.5.1   If a cash payment is made on Completion pursuant to clause 3.4:

        3.5.1.1   it shall be made [by way of a banker's draft drawn on a UK clearing bank in favour of the [Seller/Seller's Solicitors]] by telegraphic transfer to the following account:-

            Bank:

            Branch:

            Sort Code:

            Account Name:

            Account Number:]; and

        3.5.1.2   the Seller's Solicitors' receipt for such payment shall be a good and sufficient discharge to the Buyer, and the Buyer shall not be further concerned as to the application of any monies so paid

PRECEDENT 2

**Share Sale and
Purchase Agreement
Version B—Individual Sellers**

DATED   200

(1) [   ] AND OTHERS]

-and-

(2) [   ] LIMITED/PLC]

SHARE SALE AND PURCHASE AGREEMENT

-relating to-

[   ] LIMITED/PLC]

**VERSION B: INDIVIDUAL SELLERS:
LONG FORM AGREEMENT**

This Agreement is made on　　　　　　　200 between:

(1)　　　**THE INDIVIDUALS** whose names and addresses are set out in column 1 of Schedule 1 (each a "Seller" and together "the Sellers"); and

(2)　　　[　　　　　　　　　　　　　　　　　　**LIMITED/PLC**], a company registered in England under number [　　　　　　　　　　], whose registered office is at [　　　　　　　　　　　　　　　　　　　　　　　　　　] ("the Buyer").

It is agreed as follows:

1.　　　INTERPRETATION

In this Agreement:

　　1.1　　The following words and expressions shall have the following meanings:

"the Accounts"	(a) the audited accounts of the Company [and of each of the Subsidiaries] comprising (in each case) an audited balance sheet as at the Accounts Date and audited profit and loss account for the financial period ended on the Accounts Date; [and]
	(b) [the audited consolidated accounts of the Group comprising an audited consolidated balance sheet as at the Accounts Date and an audited consolidated profit and loss account for the financial period ended on the Accounts Date;]
	together (in each case) with the reports of the directors and auditors, any cash flow statements and all notes thereto;
"the Accounts Date"	[　　　　　　　　　200];
"the Act"	the Companies Act 2006;
"the 1985 Act"	the Companies Act 1985
"the Applicable Data Protection Laws"	the Data Protection Acts 1986 and 1998 and the Telecommunications (Data Protection and Privacy) (Direct Marketing) Regulations 1998;
["the Bank"	[　　　]　　　Bank　　PLC　　(branch)];
"Business Day"	any day (other than Saturday) on which clearing banks are open for normal banking business in sterling in the City of London;
"the Buyer's Solicitors"	[　　　] of [　　　] or any successor firm;
"the Companies Act"	as defined in section 2 of the Act;
"the Company"	[　　　　　　Limited/PLC](of which particulars are given in Part 1 of schedule 2);
"Completion"	completion of the acquisition and disposal of the Shares in accordance with clause 5;

"Completion Date"	**ALTERNATIVES**
	EITHER
	the date of this Agreement;
	OR
	[200];
	OR
	[the [third] Business Day after] the date upon which the last of the Conditions to be satisfied or waived is satisfied or waived;
["the Completion NAV"	as defined in part 1 of schedule 9];
["the Conditions"	the conditions set out in part 1 of schedule 7 (each a "Condition")];
"Confidential Information"	all secret or confidential commercial, financial and technical information, know-how, trade secrets, inventions, computer software and other information whatsoever and in whatever form or medium and whether disclosed orally or in writing, together with all reproductions in whatsoever form or medium and any part or parts of it;
["Consideration Share"	an ordinary share of [ ] in the capital of the Buyer credited as fully paid;]
"the Disclosure Letter"	the letter having the same date as this Agreement from the Sellers' Solicitors to the Buyer['s Solicitors];
"the Disclosed Schemes"	the Life Assurance Scheme, the Pension Scheme(s), the Personal Pension Scheme(s) and the Stakeholder Scheme;
"Encumbrance"	any equity, right to acquire, option, right of pre-emption, mortgage, charge, pledge, lien, assignment, title retention or any other security interest, agreement or arrangement, whether monetary or not;
"Escrow Account"	a joint deposit account with the Bank in the joint names of the Buyer's Solicitors and the Sellers' Solicitors;
"Escrow Agreement"	the agreement in the Agreed Terms to be entered into by the Sellers' Solicitors and the Buyer's Solicitors regarding the operation of the Escrow Account;
"FRS"	a financial reporting standard in force at any material time as issued by the Accounting Standards Board;
"FSA"	the Financial Services Authority;
"GPP"	means the group personal pension plan underwritten by **[name of provider]**;

["the Group"		together the Company and the Subsidiaries;]
"Intellectual Property"	(a)	patents, trade marks, service marks, registered designs, applications and rights to apply for any of those rights, trade, business and company names, internet domain names and e-mail addresses, unregistered trade marks and service marks, copyrights, database rights, know-how, rights in designs and inventions;
	(b)	rights under licences, consents, orders, statutes or otherwise in relation to a right in paragraph (a);
	(c)	rights of the same or similar effect or nature as or to those in paragraphs (a) and (b) which now or in the future may subsist; and
	(d)	the right to sue for past infringements of any of the foregoing rights;
"Intellectual Property Rights"		all Intellectual Property owned, used or required to be used by the Company;
"Intellectual Property Agreements"		means agreements or arrangements relating (wholly or partly) to Intellectual Property or to the disclosure, use, assignment or patenting of any invention, discovery, improvement, process, formulae or other know-how;
"Life Assurance Scheme"		means the **[insert name of group life assurance scheme]** underwritten by **[name of provider]**;
["the Management Accounts"		the management accounts of the Company [, of each of the Subsidiaries and of the Group, in each case] for the period from the Accounts Date to [200] copies of which are attached to the Disclosure Letter;]
"Pension Scheme(s)"		means **[insert name of scheme(s)—to be used for occupational pension schemes]**;
"the Personal Pension Scheme(s)"		means **[insert description of each scheme—to be used for personal pension schemes excluding group personal pensions]**;
"Proceedings"		any legal action or proceedings arising out of or in connection with this Agreement;
"the Property"		the property or properties briefly described in schedule 3;
"Release"		any release, waiver or compromise or any other arrangement of any kind having similar or analogous effect;
"the Shares"		all the issued shares in the capital of the Company;
"SSAP"		a statement of standard accounting practice in force at any material time as issued by the Accounting Standards Committee and adopted by the Accounting Standards Board;;

"the Sellers' Solicitors"	[ ], of [ ] or any [ ] successor firm;
"Stakeholder Scheme"	means the stakeholder pension scheme designated by [the Company] and underwritten by **[name of provider]**;
["the Stock Exchange"	the London Stock Exchange plc;]
["the Subsidiaries"	the companies listed in Part II of schedule 2 (each a "Subsidiary");]
"the Tax Covenants"	the obligations on the part of the Sellers set out in part 3 of schedule 4;
"Tax"	as defined in part 1 of schedule 4;
"the Tax Warranties"	the warranties and representations set out in part 2 of schedule 4;
"UKLA"	the United Kingdom Listing Authority;
"the Warranties"	the warranties and representations set out in schedule 5 and the Tax Warranties;
"Warranty"	one of the Warranties (and the word "Warranty" followed by a number shall be deemed to be a reference to the paragraph of schedule 5 with that number).

1.2   References to the Property shall, where the context so admits or requires, be construed as references to all properties briefly described in schedule 3 and each of them and each and every part of each of them.

1.3   Unless the context otherwise expressly requires, words and expressions which are otherwise defined in the Companies Acts shall have the same meaning when used in this Agreement, but "company" shall mean and include both "company" and "body corporate", as in each case defined in the Act.

1.4   A reference to any statutory or other legislative provision shall be interpreted as a reference to that provision as in force at the date of this Agreement and, additionally, where the context so permits:-

1.4.1   in respect of any earlier date, as a reference to any and all provisions in force at that earlier date of which it is a re-enactment; and

1.4.2   in respect of any later date, as a reference to any and all provisions in force at that later date which are a re-enactment thereof;

in each case whether with or without modification.

1.5   The schedules form an integral part of this Agreement.

1.6   A reference to any gender shall include the other and neuter gender and a reference to a "person" includes a reference to any individual, firm, company, corporation or other body corporate, government, state or agency of a state or any joint venture, association or partnership, works council or employee representative body (whether or not having separate legal personality).

1.7   The singular shall include the plural and vice versa.

1.8   A document referred to as being in "the Agreed Terms" shall be in the form of that document signed or initialled for identification by or on behalf of the parties.

1.9   All warranties, representations, undertakings, guarantees, indemnities, covenants, agreements and obligations given or entered into by or on behalf of more than one person in this Agreement are, unless otherwise expressly stated, given or entered into jointly and severally.

1.10   Any Warranty qualified by the expression "to the best of the Sellers' knowledge and belief" or "so far as the Sellers are aware" or any similar expression shall [, unless otherwise expressly stated,] be deemed to include knowledge, information and belief which any of the Sellers has or which the any of the Sellers would have had if it had made all reasonable enquiries and includes the knowledge, information and belief of each of:

     1.10.1   the Sellers;

     1.10.2   the professional advisers who act, or at the relevant time acted, for the Company [and the Subsidiaries]; and

     1.10.3   the directors, company secretary, financial controller and general managers of the Company [and of the Subsidiaries].
     and of any other person of whom it would be reasonable to make such enquiry or of whom it is stated that enquiry has been made.

A person shall be deemed to be connected with another if that person is connected with such other within the meaning of section 839 of Income & Corporation Taxes Act 1988.

1.11   References to "indemnify" and "indemnifying" any person against any circumstance include indemnifying and keeping him indemnified from and against all liabilities, losses, claims, demands, damages, costs, expenses and interest which he may suffer or incur in connection with or arising out of that circumstance.

1.12   "Associate" has the meaning given by section 435 of the Insolvency Act 1986.

1.13   General

Words shall not be given a restrictive meaning:—

     1.13.1   if they are introduced by the word "other", by reason of the fact that they are preceded by words indicating a particular class of act, matter or thing; or

     1.13.2   by reason of the fact that they are followed by particular examples intended to be embraced by those general words.

1.14   The word "Notice" includes any notice, demand, consent or other communication.

1.15   The headings are inserted for convenience only and shall not affect the construction of this Agreement.

1.16   The Buyer enters into this Agreement, so far as may be necessary for the enforcement of any provision for the benefit of the Company [or any of the Subsidiaries], as trustee for and on behalf of the [Company/company concerned].

1.17   References to times shall mean London time unless otherwise stated.

1.18   A reference to "the Sellers" shall include a reference to each of them and, unless the context otherwise expressly requires, to each of their respective personal representatives.

1.19   A reference to any English legal term for any action, remedy, method of judicial proceeding, legal document, legal status, court, official or any legal concept or thing shall in respect of any jurisdiction other than England be deemed to include what most nearly approximates in that jurisdiction to the English legal term and a reference to any English statute shall be construed so as to include equivalent or analogous laws of any other jurisdiction.

2.   [CONDITIONAL] AGREEMENT FOR SALE AND PURCHASE

2.1   Sale and purchase

On Completion each of the Sellers shall sell the Shares with full title guarantee and the Buyer shall buy them free from any Encumbrance and together with all rights now or hereafter attaching to them, on and subject to [the Conditions and] the [other] terms of this Agreement.

2.2   The Law of Property (Miscellaneous Provisions) Act 1994

The operation of the covenants implied by sections 2 and 3 of the above Act shall be deemed to be extended so as not to exclude the liability of the Sellers in respect of matters: —

2.2.1   of which the Sellers do not know or could not reasonably be expected to know; or

2.2.2   which at the time of transfer are within the actual knowledge of, or the existence of which is a necessary consequence of facts then within the actual knowledge of the Buyer.

2.3   Waiver

Each of the Sellers waives all rights of pre-emption and other restrictions on transfers conferred on or enjoyed by him in respect of the Shares, whether under the articles of association of the Company or otherwise.

2.4   Simultaneous Completion

The Buyer shall not be obliged to complete the purchase of any of the Shares unless the purchase of all the Shares is completed simultaneously.

2.5   [Obligations and events pending Completion

Schedule 7 shall apply in respect of the period between the entering into of this Agreement and Completion.]

3.   CONSIDERATION

ALTERNATIVE A—FIXED CASH SUM WITHOUT RETENTION

3.1   The purchase price payable to the Sellers for the Shares shall be the sum of £[ ] ([ ] pounds), which shall be paid in cash on Completion in the Due Proportions.

3.2   The Sellers' Solicitors' receipt for the purchase price for the Shares shall be a good and sufficient discharge to the Buyer and the Buyer shall not be further concerned as to the application of the monies so paid.

ALTERNATIVE B—COMPLETION ACCOUNTS WITH JOINT ACCOUNT

3.1   Amount

The purchase price payable to the Sellers for the Shares shall be a sum equal to the Completion NAV [up to a maximum purchase price of [(pounds)], which sum shall be payable in the Due Proportions.

3.2   **First Payments—on Completion**

On Completion and pending the later agreement or determination of the Completion NAV, the Buyer shall pay:—

3.2.1   The sum of £[   ] (pounds) to the Sellers' Solicitors (on behalf of the Sellers) on account of the purchase price for the Shares; and

3.2.2   The sum of [£   ] [(pounds)] ("the Principal Sum") to the Buyer's Solicitors and the Sellers' Solicitors jointly for placing into the Escrow Account, to be held under a mandate in the Agreed Terms and to be held and dealt with as set out in this clause 3.

3.3   **Second payment—following calculation of Completion NAV**

On the third Business Day after the date on which the Completion NAV is agreed or determined in accordance with schedule 9:—

3.3.1   the Buyer shall pay to the Sellers' Solicitors a sum equal to the balance (if any) of the purchase price for the Shares after deducting the amount paid pursuant to clause 3.2.1, such payment to be satisfied by the payment of an equivalent sum from the Escrow Account;

3.3.2   If the purchase price for the Shares exceeds the amount paid to the Sellers pursuant to clauses 3.2.1 and 3.3.1, the Buyer shall pay the amount of the excess to the Sellers' Solicitors; and.

3.3.3   The balance of the Principal Sum following any payment from the Escrow Account pursuant to clause 3.3.1 (or, if no such payment falls to be made, the whole of the Principal Sum) shall be paid to the Buyer from the Escrow Account.

3.4   **The Escrow Account**

3.4.1   All interest earned on the Escrow Account shall accrue and be paid to the Sellers and/or the Buyer in the proportions in which they respectively become entitled to the Principal Sum and shall be paid at the same time as any payment of all or any part of the Principal Sum is made from the Escrow Account.

3.4.2   The Sellers and the Buyer shall procure that their respective solicitors shall make any payment which is required to be made from the Escrow Account pursuant to the provisions of clause 3.3.

3.5   **Clawback from first payment**

3.5.1   If the amount paid pursuant to clause 3.2.1 exceeds the purchase price for the Shares then on the third Business Day referred to in clause 3.3 the Sellers (in the Due Proportions) shall repay to the Buyer a sum equal to the excess plus interest on an amount equal to the excess at the rate on which interest has been earned on the Escrow Account, such interest to accrue from the Completion Date until that third Business Day.

3.5.2   If any of the Sellers defaults in making payment of any sum due under clause 3.5.1, he shall pay interest on the amount in question calculated on a daily basis from the due date until the date of actual payment (as well after any judgment as before) at the rate of 4% per year above the base rate from time to time in force of the Bank.

3.6 **Method of Payment**

3.6.1 Unless otherwise specified, any payment required to be made by the Buyer to the Sellers pursuant to this clause 3 shall be made by way of a [banker's draft drawn on a UK clearing bank in favour of the Sellers/Sellers' Solicitors/telegraphic transfer to the following account:

Bank:

Branch:

Sort Code:

Account Name:

Account Number:

3.6.2 The Seller's Solicitors' receipt for any sums payable by the Buyer pursuant to this clause 3.6 shall be a good and sufficient discharge of the Buyer's obligation to make the payment in question and the Buyer shall not be further concerned as to the application of any sums so paid.

3.6.3 Any sum payable to the Buyer pursuant to this clause 3.6 shall, unless otherwise specified, be paid by way of a [banker's draft drawn on a UK clearing bank in favour of the [Buyer/Buyer'[s] Solicitors]/telegraphic transfer] to the following account:

Bank:

Branch:

Sort Code:

Account Name:

Account Number:]

ALTERNATIVE C—CONSIDERATION SHARES—SEE APPENDIX A

4. **WARRANTIES AND TAXATION**

4.1 **Representations and Warranties**

With the intention of inducing the Buyer to enter into this Agreement (and acknowledging that the Buyer does so in reliance on the Warranties) the Sellers jointly and severally represent to the Buyer in the terms of the Warranties and warrant to the Buyer that each of the Warranties is true and accurate in all respects and not misleading at the date of this Agreement [and will continue up to and including Completion to be true and accurate in all respects and not misleading.]

4.2 **Tax Covenants**

The Sellers jointly and severally undertake with the Buyer in the terms of the Tax Covenants.

4.3 **Claims procedure and determination and Sellers' safeguards**

Schedule 6 shall apply in relation to the determination of the rights and remedies of the Buyer in respect of the Warranties and the Tax Covenants.

4.4 **[Application to Subsidiaries**

Each of the Warranties and of the Tax Covenants shall apply equally to each of the Subsidiaries and shall take effect as if the name of each

Subsidiary were in turn substituted for "the Company" throughout schedule 4 and schedule 5.]

5.   **COMPLETION**

5.1   **Date of Completion**

Completion shall [,subject to schedule 7,] take place on the Completion Date at [   ].

5.2   **Sellers' obligations**

On Completion the Sellers shall:

5.2.1   deliver to the Buyer:

5.2.1.1   transfers of the Shares by the registered holders thereof in favour of the Buyer together with the relative share certificates and certified copies of any power of attorney under which any of such transfers may have been executed;

5.2.1.2   [certificates in respect of all issued shares in the capital of each of the Subsidiaries and duly executed transfers of all such shares held by any nominee in favour of such persons as the Buyer shall direct;]

5.2.1.3   all the statutory and other books (duly written up to date) of the Company [and each of the Subsidiaries] and [its/their] certificate[s] of incorporation or registration and certificate[s] of incorporation on change of name and common seal[s] (if any);

5.2.1.4   letters of resignation in the Agreed Terms executed by the persons resigning as directors [and secretary] of the Company [and each of the Subsidiaries] pursuant to clause 5.2.2.3;

5.2.1.5   [a certificate in the Agreed Terms from the Sellers' Solicitors as to the title of the Company [and the Subsidiaries] to the Property;]

5.2.1.6   [the title deeds to the Property;]

5.2.1.7   [the resignation of the trustees of the [Pension Scheme] and the appointment in their place of such persons as the Buyer shall nominate [and the appointment of [the Buyer] as principal employer in respect of [the Pension Scheme];

5.2.1.8   all credit and charge cards held to the account of the Company and all other papers and documents relating to the Company which are in the possession of or under the control of the Sellers or any director of the Company; and

5.2.1.9   the Disclosure Letter, duly executed;

5.2.2   procure:

5.2.2.1   the transaction of the other business referred to in the completion board minutes in the Agreed Terms;

5.2.2.2   such persons as the Buyer may nominate to be validly appointed as additional directors of the Company [and the Subsidiaries];

5.2.2.3 upon such appointment, the resignation of the directors [other than [   ]] [and the secretary] of the Company [and each of the Subsidiaries] both from their respective offices and as employees;

5.2.2.4 the written resignation [in the Agreed Terms] of the auditors of the Company [and each of the Subsidiaries] incorporating an acknowledgment that they have no claim against the Company [or any of the Subsidiaries] for any fees or disbursements, whether billed or unbilled, in respect of the period up to Completion and the statement referred to in section 519 of the Act;

5.2.2.5 the release [in the Agreed Terms] of all Encumbrances given by the Company [and each of the Subsidiaries] (whether to its bankers or otherwise) and of all guarantees given by the Company [and each of the Subsidiaries];

5.2.2.6 the repayment (by such method as the Buyer directs) without deduction or set-off of any and all sums owed to the Company [and to each of the Subsidiaries] by the Sellers, the directors of the Company [and of the Subsidiaries] and any person who is an associate of or connected with any of them;

5.2.2.7 the release [in the Agreed Terms] of any and all claims against the Company [and the Subsidiaries] by the Sellers, and any person who is an associate of or connected with any of them, incorporating an acknowledgment by each that there is no agreement or arrangement under which any such claim might arise in the future;

5.2.2.8 [that the Company and [   ] and [   ] enter into [service] [consultancy] agreements in the Agreed Terms; and]

5.2.2.9 that [each of] the Company [and the Subsidiaries] convenes an extraordinary meeting on short notice and, at such meeting[s], adopt[s] new articles of association in the Agreed Terms.

5.3 **Buyer's obligations**

On Completion, and against compliance by the Sellers with its obligations under clause 5.2, the Buyer shall:

5.3.1 make the payments required to be made on Completion in accordance with clause 3;

5.3.2 acknowledge receipt of the Disclosure Letter; and

5.3.3 [deliver to the Sellers' Solicitors share certificates in respect of the Consideration Shares.]

OR

5.3.3 [if it has not already done so, submit an application to the UKLA for the Consideration Shares to be admitted to the Official List of the Stock Exchange and to the Stock Exchange for the Consideration Shares to be admitted to trading on the Stock Exchange's main market for listed securities] [for the Consideration Shares to be admitted to trading on the Alternative

Investment Market of the Stock Exchange] and instruct its registrars to prepare and deliver to the Sellers share certificates in respect of the Consideration Shares].

5.4   **Failure to complete**

If in any respect the preceding provisions of this clause 5 are not complied with on the Completion Date, then (without prejudice to any and all rights of action it may have pursuant to the terms of this Agreement or otherwise) the party not in default may:

5.4.1   defer Completion to a date not more than 28 days after the Completion Date (and so that the provisions of this clause 5, apart from this clause 5.4.1, shall apply to Completion as so deferred); or

5.4.2   proceed to Completion so far as practicable (without prejudice to its rights hereunder or otherwise); or

5.4.3   rescind this Agreement by notice in writing to the Sellers.

5.5   **Declaration of trust in relation to the Shares**

Each of the Sellers declares that, for so long as he remains the registered holder of any of the Shares after Completion, he will:

5.5.1   stand and be possessed of them and of all dividends and other rights arising out of or in connection with them in trust for the Buyer and its successors in title;

5.5.2   at all times thereafter deal with and dispose of them and all such dividends and rights as the Buyer or any such successor may direct; and

5.5.3   at the request of the Buyer or any such successor vote at all meetings which he or she shall be entitled to attend as the holder of them in such manner as the Buyer or any such successor may direct.

[Each of the Sellers hereby irrevocably appoints the Buyer or any such successor to be his attorney and in his name and on his behalf to sign any written resolution of the members of the Company and to execute all instruments of proxy or other documents which the Buyer or any such successor may reasonably require and which may be necessary or expedient to enable the Buyer or any such successor to attend and vote at any such meeting.][1]

6.   **CONFIDENTIAL INFORMATION AND USE OF NAMES**

6.1   Each of the Sellers shall, after Completion, keep and procure to be kept secret and confidential all Confidential Information which relates to the Company or its business or is used in its business and shall not use or disclose to any person any such Confidential Information.

6.2   The obligations of confidentiality in this clause shall not extend to any matter which is in or becomes part of the public domain otherwise than by reason of a breach of the obligations of confidentiality in this Agreement or

---

[1] If this wording is used, the agreement must be executed as a deed and it will be necessary to check the articles of association of the Seller in order to ensure that they permit the appointment of an attorney.

which any of the Sellers receives from a third party independently entitled to disclose it or which any of the Sellers is required by law or regulatory authority to disclose.[2]

6.3 None of the Sellers shall, at any time after Completion, use in connection with any trade or business any corporate name, trade name, or logo, domain name or e-mail address which is confusingly similar to the name of the Company [or of any of the Subsidiaries] or to any corporate name, trade name, logo, domain name or e-mail address used by the Company [or any of the Subsidiaries] [at any time during the period of 5 years before Completion].

7. RESTRICTIVE UNDERTAKINGS

7.1 Customers, suppliers and employees

Each of the Sellers undertakes with the Buyer that he will not, at any time during the period of [   ] year[s] and [cb months after Completion, directly or indirectly and whether alone or in conjunction with, or on behalf of or by way of assistance to, any other person:

7.1.1 canvass or solicit the custom of any person who was at any time during the period of [   ] months before Completion a customer of the Company [or any of the Subsidiaries] for the supply of goods and/or services which are competitive with any of those supplied to such person at any time during the period of [   ] months before the Completion Date by the Company [or any of the Subsidiaries]; or

7.1.2 do anything which he knows or ought reasonably to know would cause or be reasonably likely to cause any person who was at any time during the period of [   ] months before the Completion Date a supplier to the Company of goods and/or services to cease or materially reduce its supply of those goods and/or services to the Company [or any of the Subsidiaries]; or

7.1.3 solicit or entice away from the Company or employ or (directly or indirectly) offer employment or a consultancy to any person who is then an employee of the Company and who at Completion was an employee of the Company and likely (in the reasonable opinion of the Buyer) to be in possession of Confidential Information relating to, or able to influence the customer relationships or connections of, the Company or **[specify job titles]**; or

7.1.4 solicit or entice away from the Company [or any of the Subsidiaries] or employ or offer employment to any person who at, or at any time during the period of 6 months prior to, Completion was an employee of the Company [or any of the Subsidiaries] and likely (in the reasonable opinion of the Buyer) to be in possession of Confidential Information relating to, or able to influence the customer relationships or connections of, the Company [or any of the Subsidiaries]; or

7.1.5 except as the holder for investment of less than 5% in nominal value of the issued share capital of a company whose shares are

---

[2] If a public body is a party, it will be necessary to add additional wording to take account of the Freedom of Information Act 2000 and the Environmental Information Regulations 2004.

listed on a recognised investment exchange (within the meaning of the Financial Services and Markets Act 2000) [or as the holder of Consideration Shares] be engaged, concerned or interested within the Restricted Area in any Relevant Business.

7.2 **Definitions**

For the purposes of clause 7.1, "Relevant Business" means any business which consists of or includes to a material extent [**Description of business activities**].

7.3 **Reasonableness of undertakings**

Each of the undertakings in clause 7.1 is:

7.3.1 considered by the parties to be reasonable;

7.3.2 a separate undertaking by the Sellers and is enforceable by the Buyer (on behalf of itself and [any one or more of] the Company [and the Subsidiaries]) separately and independently of its right to enforce any one or more of the other undertakings in clause 7.1; and

7.3.3 given for the purpose of assuring to the Buyer the full benefit of the business and goodwill of the Company [and the Subsidiaries] and in consideration of the agreement of the Buyer to acquire the Shares on the terms of this Agreement.

Accordingly, if one or more of such undertakings is held to be against the public interest or unlawful or in any way an unreasonable restraint of trade, the remaining undertakings shall continue to bind the Sellers.

7.4 **Cessation of business**

Nothing in the undertakings set out in clause 7.1 shall be deemed to prohibit any action in respect of any business or part of any business in which (otherwise than as a result of any breach of any of those undertakings by the Sellers) the Company [, the Subsidiaries] and the Buyer and every other subsidiary of the Buyer have ceased to be involved prior to any event giving rise to a claim, or which would but for this clause 7.4 give rise to a claim, under this clause 7.

8. **GUARANTEES**

The Buyer undertakes with the Sellers after Completion to use all reasonable endeavours (short of actual payment of any money and the substitution of the guarantee of any person other than the Buyer or any company within the Group) to procure the release of the Sellers from liability under any and all outstanding guarantees given by him and listed below in respect of monies borrowed and obligations undertaken by the Company [and/or any of the Subsidiaries] and to indemnify each of the Sellers against any such liability arising after Completion. The guarantees in question are:

[**Details**]

9. **INDEMNITIES**

The Sellers shall indemnify the Buyer [and/or the Company] [and each of the Subsidiaries] against and shall pay to the Buyer a sum equal to all liabilities suffered or incurred by the Company as a result of or in connection with: —

9.1   any breach, whether before or after Completion, of any covenant or any other term contained or implied in any lease of property assigned by the Company [or by any of the Subsidiaries] before Completion to any third party;

9.2   any defect or alleged defect in any goods produced or sold by the Company [or by any of the Subsidiaries] prior to Completion;

9.3   any industrial or other work-related illness or injury suffered by any employee or former employee of the Company [or any of the Subsidiaries] in respect of or in relation to any period ending on or before Completion; [or]

9.4   **[other commercial issues arising out of due diligence]**

save, (in the circumstances specified in clauses 9.1 and 9.3) to the extent that recovery is made by the Company [or by the Subsidiary concerned] under any policy of insurance.

10. THIRD PARTY RIGHTS

10.1   For the avoidance of doubt [and save as expressly provided in clause [ ]],nothing in this Agreement shall confer on any third party the right to enforce any provisions of this Agreement.

10.2   Notwithstanding that any provision of this Agreement may be enforceable by any third party this Agreement and its provisions may be amended, waived, modified, rescinded or terminated by the parties to this Agreement without the consent or approval of any third party.

11. ASSIGNMENT

11.1   This Agreement shall be binding upon and enure for the benefit of the successors and assignees of the parties and in the case of individuals their respective estates and, subject to any succession or assignment being permitted by this Agreement, any such successor or assignee of the parties shall in its own right be able to enforce any term of this Agreement.

11.2   Save as permitted under this Agreement, none of the parties nor their respective successors and assignees shall be entitled to assign its rights or obligations under this Agreement without the prior written consent of the others save that the Sellers may assign its rights under this Agreement to a member of the Sellers' Group ("Permitted Assignee") subject always to the following:

11.2.1   where such assignee ceases to be a member of the Sellers' Group such assignee shall be obliged as soon as reasonably practicable after such cessation to assign the rights under this Agreement back to a member of the Sellers' Group; and

11.2.2   the assignor shall remain liable in respect of its obligations under this Agreement notwithstanding any such assignment, including for the avoidance of doubt the provisions of this clause 11.

11.2.3   The Buyer may at any time charge, grant security over or assign by way of security all or any of its rights under this Agreement.

12. WHOLE AGREEMENT

12.1   This Agreement together with all documents entered into or to be entered into pursuant to its provisions constitutes the entire agreement between the parties in relation to its subject matter and supersedes all prior agreements, understandings and discussions between the parties, other than representations made fraudulently.

12.2   Each of the parties acknowledges that it is not relying on any statements, warranties or representations given or made by the others in relation to the subject matter of this Agreement, save those expressly set out in this Agreement and other documents referred to above and that it shall have no rights or remedies with respect to such subject matter otherwise than under this Agreement (and the documents executed at the same time as it or entered into pursuant to it) save to the extent that they arise out of the fraud or fraudulent misrepresentation of any party.

13.   WAIVER

The rights and remedies of a party in respect of this Agreement shall not be diminished, waived or extinguished by the granting of any indulgence, forbearance or extension of time by a party to another nor by any failure of or delay by a party in ascertaining or exercising any such rights or remedies. Any Release by a party shall not affect its rights and remedies as regards any other party nor its rights and remedies against the party in whose favour it is granted or made except to the extent of the express terms of the Release and no such Release shall have effect unless granted or made in writing. The rights and remedies in this Agreement are cumulative and not exclusive of any rights and/or remedies provided by law.

14.   PROVISIONS SURVIVING COMPLETION

Insofar as the provisions of this Agreement shall not have been performed at Completion, they shall remain in full force and effect notwithstanding Completion.

15.   PROPER LAW AND JURISDICTION

This Agreement shall be governed by the laws of England and Wales.

16.   JURISDICTION

Any dispute arising under this Agreement shall be subject to the [exclusive/non-exclusive] jurisdiction of the English courts and the parties waive any objection to Proceedings in such courts on the grounds of venue or on the grounds that Proceedings have been brought in an inappropriate forum.

17.   FURTHER ASSURANCE

The Sellers shall at their own expense do such acts and things and execute such documents as the Buyer may at any time reasonably require for the purpose of assuring to the Buyer the full benefit of this Agreement and of any document to which it refers.

18.   COUNTERPARTS

This Agreement may be executed in any number of counterparts and by the parties on separate counterparts, each of which, when so executed and delivered, shall be an original, but all the counterparts shall together be deemed to constitute one and the same agreement.

19.   COSTS

Each party shall, except where otherwise stated, pay its own costs of and incidental to this Agreement and its subject matter [except that, if the Buyer shall lawfully exercise any right hereby conferred to rescind this Agreement, the Sellers shall indemnify the Buyer against all expenses and costs incurred by it in connection with this Agreement and its subject matter.]

20. **SEVERABILITY**

The provisions of this Agreement are severable and distinct from one another, and, if at any time any of such provisions is or becomes invalid, illegal or unenforceable, the validity, legality or enforceability of the others shall not in any way be affected or impaired thereby.

21. **PUBLICITY**

21.1 The parties shall forthwith upon [the signing of this Agreement/Completion] make or procure to be made a press announcement and announcements to the employees of the Company and to the customers and suppliers of the Company in the Agreed Terms.

21.2 [The Buyer shall be entitled to send a circular to its shareholders convening a general meeting for the purposes set out in schedule 7 and shall give the Sellers a reasonable opportunity to comment on the contents of such circular in so far as it relates to it and to the Company.]

21.3 Each of the parties shall both before and after Completion, but subject to clauses 21.1 and 21.2, keep the contents of this Agreement strictly private and confidential and shall not without the prior written consent of the other disclose any or all of them to any person or makes any other announcement relating to the transactions hereby agreed upon except to the extent required by law, [the FSA, UKLA, the Stock Exchange or the Panel on Take-overs and Mergers] and except that the Buyer and the Sellers shall be entitled to make references to the transactions hereby agreed upon in their respective future annual reports and financial statements.

22. **PENSION SCHEME**

Schedule 8 shall apply in relation to the Pension Scheme.

23. **NOTICES**

23.1 Any Notice relating to this Agreement shall be in writing delivered personally or sent by pre-paid first class post or facsimile transmission to the address of the party to be served given herein or such other address as may be notified for this purpose (or, by way of service upon all of the Sellers, to the Sellers' Solicitors, quoting their reference [ ]).

23.2 Any such Notice shall, if sent by post, be deemed to have been served 24 hours after despatch and, if delivered by hand or sent by facsimile transmission, be deemed to have been served at the time of such delivery or transmission.

If, however, in the case of delivery by post a period of 24 hours after despatch would expire on, or if, in the case of delivery by hand or facsimile transmission, such delivery or transmission occurs on, a day which is not a Business Day or after 4.00 p.m. on a Business Day, then service shall be deemed to occur on the next following Business Day.

23.3 In proving service it shall be sufficient to prove, in the case of a letter, that such letter was properly stamped, addressed and placed in the post and, in the case of a facsimile transmission, it shall be sufficient to produce a transmission report showing that transmission was duly and fully made to the correct number.

23.4   Any notice relating to this Agreement and served as provided in this clause 23 on any of the Sellers shall be deemed to have been given to each of the Sellers.

23.5   Any such notice shall be deemed to have been given to the personal representatives of a deceased Seller, notwithstanding that no grant of representation has been made in respect of his or her estate, if the Notice is given to the Sellers' Solicitors in accordance with clause 23.1, to the deceased Seller by name or to his or her personal representatives by title at the relevant Seller's address given herein or at such other address as may have been notified by them in writing to the sender as being their address for service.

23.6   Each of the Sellers irrevocably and unconditionally appoints the Sellers' Solicitors as his agent for the service of any Notice or proceedings arising out of or in connection with this Agreement and the transactions hereby agreed upon.

[**SIGNED** by or on behalf of the parties the day and year first before written]

OR

[**IN WITNESS** of which this deed has been executed and unconditionally delivered the day and year first above written.]

SCHEDULE 1

The Sellers

Name and Address of Sellers	Shares	Due Proportion of Payment/ Consideration Shares

SCHEDULE 2

Part 1

The Company

Name:

Registered in England no:

Date of incorporation:

Authorised share capital: £[   ] divided into [
    ] ordinary shares of [   ] each [and [   ] [
    ] shares of [   ] each]

Issued share capital: £[   ] divided into [
                    ] ordinary shares of [   ] each [and [
            ] [   ] shares of [   ] each]

Directors:

Secretary:

Auditors:

Registered office:

Part 2

The Subsidiaries

Name:

Registered in England no:

Date of incorporation:

Authorised share capital: £[   ] divided into [   ] ordinary
                    shares of [   ] each [and [
                        ] [   ] shares of [   ] each]

Issued share capital: £[   ] divided into [   ] ordinary shares
                    of [   ] each [and [   ] [
            ] shares of [   ] each]

Directors:

Secretary:

Auditors:

Registered office:

Shareholders:

              Name   Number and class of shares

SCHEDULE 3

The Property

SCHEDULE 4

TAX

Part 1 Definitions

1.   INTERPRETATION

1.1   In this schedule, unless the context otherwise requires, the following words and expressions shall have the following meanings:

"Accounts Relief"	(a) any Relief which was treated as an asset of the Company in the Accounts; or
	(b) any Relief which was taken into account in computing (and so reducing or eliminating) any provision for Tax which appears in the Accounts or which would have appeared in the Accounts but for the presumed availability of such Relief;
"Event"	any act, omission, event, fact or circumstance whatsoever (whether actual or deemed or treated as occurring for any purpose);
"ICTA"	Income and Corporation Taxes Act 1988;
"ITEPA"	Income Tax (Earnings and Pensions) Act 2003;
"loss"	includes the loss, denial, clawback or cancellation in whole or in part of any Relief and derivative words (such as "lost") shall be construed accordingly;
"Post Completion Relief"	includes any Relief which arises as a result of any Event which has occurred or occurs after the Accounts Date or in respect of any period commencing on or after the Accounts Date;
"Relevant Person"	the Sellers and any person (except the Buyer or the Company) who stands or has stood in a direct or indirect relationship with the Company at any time before Completion such that failure by such person at any time to pay any Tax could result in an assessment on the Company under section 767A or section 767AA ICTA;
"Relief"	(a) any relief, allowance, exemption, set-off, deduction or credit available from, against, or in relation to, Tax or in the computation for any Tax purpose of income, profits or gains; and
	(b) any right to repayment of Tax;
"Tax"	(a) any tax, duty, impost, levy, deduction or withholding, past or present, of the United Kingdom or elsewhere; and
	(b) any interest, charge, surcharge, penalty, fine or other imposition relating to or aris-

	ing in connection with any tax, duty, impost, levy, deduction or withholding mentioned in paragraph (a) of this definition or to any account, record, form, return or computation required to be kept, preserved, maintained or submitted to any person for the purpose of any such tax, duty, impost, levy, deduction or withholding;
"Tax Authority"	any authority, whether of the United Kingdom or elsewhere, competent to impose, assess or collect Tax, including HM Revenue & Customs;
"Tax Claim"	any notice, demand, assessment, letter or other document issued, or action taken, by or on behalf of any Tax Authority and the submission of any Tax form, return or computation from which, in either case, it appears to the Buyer that the Company is or may be subject to a Tax Liability or other liability in respect of which the [Sellers] are or may be liable under this schedule 4;
"Tax Legislation"	any statute, statutory instrument, regulation or legislative provision providing for, imposing, or relating to, Tax;
"Tax Liability"	(a) any liability (including a liability which is a primary liability of some other person and whether or not there is a right of recovery against another person) to make an actual payment of an amount in respect of Tax;
	(b) any liability (including a liability which is a primary liability of some other person and whether or not there is a right of recovery against another person) to make a payment or increased payment of Tax which would have arisen but for being satisfied, avoided or reduced by any Accounts Relief or Post Completion Relief; and
	(c) the disallowance, loss, clawback, reduction, restriction or modification of any Accounts Relief;
"Tax Warranties"	the warranties contained in part 2 of this schedule 4;
"TCGA"	Taxation of Chargeable Gains Act 1992;
"VAT"	value added tax;
"VATA"	Value Added Tax Act 1994;
"VAT Group"	any group of companies for the purpose of section 43 VATA of which the Company is or has been a member on or before Completion.

1.2   In this schedule, "Company" shall in addition to the Company include every subsidiary of the Company to the intent and effect that the provisions of this schedule shall apply to and be given in respect of each subsidiary as well as the Company.

1.3   Any reference to an Event or the consequences of an Event occurring on or before Completion shall include the combined effect of:

1.3.1   any two or more Events, all of which shall have taken place or be deemed (for the purposes of any Tax Legislation) to have taken place on or before Completion; or

1.3.2   any two or more Events, at least one of which shall have taken place or be deemed (for the purposes of any Tax Legislation) to have occurred on or before Completion.

1.4   Any reference to a Tax Liability in respect of income profits or gains earned, accrued or received on or before Completion shall include a Tax Liability in respect of income profits or gains deemed to have been or treated or regarded as earned, accrued or received for the purposes of any Tax Legislation on or before Completion and any reference to Tax Liability on the happening of any Event shall include a Tax Liability where such Event (for the purposes of the Tax Legislation in question) is deemed to have occurred or treated or regarded as having occurred.

1.5   Any stamp duty which would be payable on any document in order for it to be produced as evidence in Court (whether or not such document is presently within the United Kingdom), provided that such document is either necessary to establish the title of the Company to any asset or is a document in the enforcement or production of which the Company is interested, and any interest, fine or penalty relating to any such stamp duty will be deemed to be a liability of the Company to make an actual payment of Tax on the date on which the document was executed and "Tax Liability" shall be construed accordingly.

1.6   In determining for the purposes of this schedule 4 whether a charge on, or power to sell, mortgage or charge, any of the shares or assets of the Company exists at any time, the fact that any Tax is not yet payable or may be paid by instalments shall be disregarded and such Tax shall be treated as becoming due and the charge or power to sell, mortgage or charge shall be treated as arising on the date on which HM Revenue & Customs gave notice of the liability to the Company or the Buyer.

Part 2 Tax Warranties

1.   RETURNS, NOTICES AND RECORDS

1.1   All accounts, computations, notices and returns required to be made or submitted by the Company to any Tax Authority and all notices and information required to be given by the Company to any Tax Authority (including all returns and other documents or information in respect of PAYE and National Insurance) have been properly and duly prepared and punctually made, submitted or given by the Company and are up-to-date and correct.

1.2   The Company is not and, in the period of three years ended on the date of this document, has not been, in dispute with or subject to enquiry or investigation by any Tax Authority (other than routine enquiries concerning the corporation tax computations of the Company, all of which have been resolved) and, so far as the Sellers are aware there are no facts or circumstances likely to give rise to or be the subject of any such dispute, enquiry or investigation.

1.3   The Company has (to the extent required by law) preserved and retained in its possession complete and accurate records relating to its Tax affairs (including PAYE and National Insurance records, VAT records and records relating to transfer pricing) and the Company has sufficient records relating to past events to calculate the profit, gain, loss, balancing charge or balancing allowance (all for Tax purposes) which would arise on any disposal or on the realisation of any assets owned at the Accounts Date or acquired since that date but before Completion.

2.   PAYMENT OF TAX

The Company has duly and punctually paid all Tax (including Tax required to be deducted or withheld from payments) to the extent that the same ought to have been paid and has not in the last three years paid or become liable to pay any penalty or interest charged by virtue of the provisions of any Tax Legislation.

3.   CONCESSION

The Company has not during the period of three years ending on the date of this document relied on any formal or informal unpublished concession, dispensation or practice (whether general or specific to the Company) which affects the amount of Tax chargeable on the Company or which purports to modify or provide exemption from any obligation to make or submit any computation notice or return to any Tax Authority.

4.   DEDUCTIONS AND WITHHOLDINGS

The Company has made all deductions and withholdings in respect of, or on account of, any Tax (including amounts required to be deducted under the PAYE and National Insurance systems) from any payments made by it which it is obliged or entitled to make and (to the extent required to do so) has accounted in full to the relevant Tax Authority for all amounts so deducted or withheld.

5.   PAYE

The Company has not been notified that any PAYE audit or visit by HM Revenue & Customs will be or is expected to be made. The Disclosure Letter gives full details of all dispensations or notices received by the Company under Section 65 of ITEPA (dispensations) and of all PAYE settlement agreements entered into under Chapter 5 of Part 11 of ITEPA by the Company.

6.   CLOSE COMPANIES

6.1   The Company is not and never has been a close investment holding company within the meaning of section 13A ICTA.

6.2   The Company has not at any time:

6.2.1   made any loan, advance or payment or given any consideration falling within sections 419 to 422 ICTA (charges to tax in connection with loans) or released or written off or agreed to release or write off the whole or any part of such loans or advances; or

6.2.2   made a transfer of value which is or may be liable to Taxation under the provisions of sections 94, 99 or 199 of the Inheritance Act 1984.

6.3   The Company has never made any distribution within section 418 ICTA.

7.   **CAPITAL GAINS**

    7.1   The sum which would be allowed as a deduction from the consideration under section 38 TCGA (acquisition and disposal costs etc) of each asset of the Company (other than trading stock) if disposed of on the date of this document:

        7.1.1   would not be less than (in the case of an asset held on the Accounts Date) the book value of that asset shown or included in the Accounts or (in the case of an asset acquired since the Accounts Date) an amount equal to the consideration given for its acquisition; and in particular

        7.1.2   would not be treated or deemed for the purposes of Tax to have been reduced by reason of any claim made under sections 152 (roll-over relief), 153 (assets only partly replaced), 165 (relief for gifts of business assets) or 175 (group rollover) TCGA or by reason of the operation of section 17 (disposals and acquisitions treated as made at market value) or sections 126 to 140 TCGA (reorganisation of share capital, conversion of securities etc).

    7.2   No transaction has been entered into by the Company to which the provisions of section 18 (transactions between connected persons) TCGA have been or could be applied.

8.   **CAPITAL ALLOWANCES**

No balancing charge in respect of any capital allowances claimed or given would arise if any asset of the Company (or, where computations are made for capital allowances purposes for pools of assets, all the assets in that pool) were to be realised for a consideration equal to the amount of the book value thereof as shown or included in the Accounts (or, in the case of any asset acquired since the Accounts Date, for a consideration equal to the consideration given for the acquisition).

9.   **SECONDARY LIABILITY**

So far as the [Sellers] are aware, no Event has occurred in consequence of which the Company is made or held liable to pay or bear any Tax which is primarily chargeable against or attributable to some person, firm or company other than the Company.

10.   **STAMP DUTIES**

    10.1   Each document in the possession or under the control of the Company or to the production of which the Company is entitled and on which the Company relies or may rely on for any purpose whatsoever and which in the United Kingdom requires any stamp has been properly stamped or marked as appropriate and no such document which is outside the United Kingdom would attract stamp duty if it were to be brought into the United Kingdom.

    10.2   The Company does not hold any interest in real property situated in the United Kingdom which was granted or transferred to it in the three years prior to the date of this agreement where such grant or transfer was the subject of an application for relief from stamp duty under section 42 of the Finance Act 1930, section 151 of the Finance Act 1995 or section 76 of the Finance Act 1986 or for relief from stamp duty land tax under any of the provisions of schedule 7 to the Finance Act 2003.

    10.3   The Company has not entered into any agreement for the sale of an estate or interest in real property situated in the United Kingdom in the 90 days prior to Completion.

10.4   The Company has complied in all respects with the provisions of Part IV of the Finance Act 1986 (Stamp Duty Reserve Tax) and any regulations made under such legislation.

10.5   The Company is not and has never been party to a "land transaction" for the purposes of section 43 Finance Act 2003.

11.   ANTI-AVOIDANCE

The Company has never been party to any non-arm's length transaction or been party to or otherwise involved in any scheme or arrangement the main purpose, or one of the main purposes, of which was to avoid Tax.

12.   VALUE ADDED TAX

12.1   The Company is registered as a taxable person for VAT purposes in the United Kingdom under schedule 1 VATA and has never been treated as (nor applied to be) a member of a group of companies for VAT purposes.

12.2   The Company is not registered (nor required to be registered) for local VAT or its equivalent in any state other than the United Kingdom.

12.3   The Company has complied in all material respects with all the requirements of VATA and all application regulations and orders, and has fully maintained complete, correct and up-to-date records, invoices and other necessary documents.

12.4   The Company is not in arrears with any payment and has not failed to submit any return (fully and properly completed) or information required in respect of VAT and is not liable or likely to become liable to any abnormal or non-routine payment or default surcharge or any forfeiture or penalty or subject to the operation of any penal provision.

12.5   No circumstances exist whereby the Company would or might become liable for VAT pursuant to the provisions of sections 47 (agents etc) or 48 (tax representatives) VATA.

12.6   The Company has not made and is not otherwise bound by any election made pursuant to paragraph 2 of schedule 10 VATA.

12.7   The Company has not been party to a transaction to which Article 5 of the Value Added Tax (Special Provisions) Order 1995 (transfer of business as a going concern) has (or has purported to have been) applied.

12.8   No asset of the Company is a capital item, the input tax on which could be subject to adjustment in accordance with the provisions of Part XV of the Value Added Tax Regulations 1995.

13.   GROUPS

13.1   No Tax is or may become payable by the Company pursuant to section 190 TCGA (tax on one member or group recoverable from another member) in respect of any chargeable gain accruing prior to Completion.

13.2   The Company has not at any time within the period of six years ending with the date of this document acquired any asset (other than as trading stock) from any other company which at the time of the acquisition was a member of the same group of companies as the Company (as defined in section 170 TCGA (groups of companies: definitions)) and no member of any group of companies of which the Company is, or has at any material time been, the principal company (as defined in section 170 TCGA (groups of companies: definitions)) has so acquired any asset.

13.3   The Company has not in the last seven years ceased to be a member of a group of companies for the purposes of section 178 or 179 TCGA (company ceasing to be member of a group).

13.4   There are no assets currently owned by the Company in respect of which a charge may arise on the sale of the Company pursuant to this Agreement under Section 179 TCGA (company ceasing to be a member of a group).

14.   LOAN RELATIONSHIPS

14.1   Each amount in relation to which the Company is a debtor or creditor and reflected in the Accounts or existing on the date of this agreement constitutes a loan relationship of the Company.

14.2   No Tax Liability or non-trading deficit would arise from any loan relationship of the Company as a result of any debt under such loan relationship being settled in full or in part at Completion.

14.3   In relation to each of its loan relationships, the Company operates and has, in each accounting period of the Company ending after 31 March 1996, operated an accruals basis of accounting authorised under section 85 of the Finance Act 1996.

15.   INHERITANCE TAX

There is no unsatisfied liability to inheritance tax attached or attributable to the assets of the Company or the shares of the Company and neither such assets nor such shares are subject to an HM Revenue & Customs charge.

16.   FOREIGN CONNECTIONS

16.1   The Company has never been resident outside the United Kingdom for the purposes of any tax legislation.

16.2   The Company does not have (and in the period of three years ending on the date of this document has not had) any branch agent, or permanent establishment (within the meaning of the OECD Model Double Taxation Agreement) outside the United Kingdom.

16.3   The Company does not have (and has not in the last seven years had) any interest in a controlled foreign company within the meaning of sections 747 and 752 ICTA.

Part 3 Tax Covenant

1.   SELLERS' COVENANT

Subject to part 4 of this schedule, the Sellers covenant with the Buyer to pay to the Buyer an amount equal to:

1.1   any Tax Liability of the Company:

1.1.1   arising in respect of, by reference to or in consequence of, any Event which occurred on or before Completion; or

1.1.2   arising in respect of, by reference to, or in consequence of, any income profits or gains earned, accrued or received on or before or in respect of a period ended on or before Completion; or

1.1.3   arising or assessed as a consequence of the failure of a Relevant Person at any time to pay Tax;

1.2   any Tax Liability which arises as a result of any supply, acquisition or importation made or deemed to be made for the purposes of VAT by any member of any VAT Group other than the Company;

1.3   any liability of the Company to make a payment in respect of, or in consequence of, any indemnity, covenant or guarantee relating to Tax given by the Company on or before Completion;

1.4   any liability in respect of inheritance tax which:

      1.4.1   is at or becomes after Completion, as a result of the death of any person within seven years after a transfer of value (or a deemed transfer of value) on or before Completion, a charge on any of the shares or the assets of the Company or gives rise to a power to sell, mortgage or charge any of the shares or the assets of the Company; or

      1.4.2   arises as a result of a transfer of value occurring or being deemed to occur on or before Completion whether or not in conjunction with the death of any person (whenever occurring) which increased or decreased the value of the estate of the Company;

1.5   any Tax Liability in respect of the emoluments or benefits in kind of employees or directors of the Company arising in respect of periods ended on or before Completion and arising from their employment or directorships with the Company or in respect of services rendered by an individual to the Company where Tax has not been properly accounted for or proper returns have not been made in respect of emoluments and which the Company decides to pay, whether or not the liability for such Tax may be the liability of the employees or directors; and

1.6   any reasonable costs, fees or expenses incurred by the Company or the Buyer in connection with:

      1.6.1   any Tax Liability or other liability in respect of which the [Sellers] are liable under any of paragraphs 1.1 to 1.5 above; or

      1.6.2   taking or defending any action (including legal proceedings) under this schedule at the request or direction of the [Sellers].

Part 4 Limitations and procedure

2.   **RESTRICTION ON SELLERS' LIABILITY**

2.1   The provisions of paragraphs 2.1 (maximum liability) and 1.2 (time limits) of schedule 6 shall apply to this schedule as if the same were set out herein in full and the liability of the Sellers under this schedule shall be limited or excluded accordingly.

2.2   The covenants contained in part 3 of this schedule shall not extend to any Tax Liability to the extent that:

      2.2.1   such Tax Liability was paid or discharged on or before the Accounts Date [and such payment or discharge was reflected in the Accounts];

      2.2.2   specific provision or reserve (other than a deferred tax provision or reserve) in respect of that Tax Liability was made in the Accounts;

      2.2.3   such Tax Liability arises or is increased as a result of any change in Tax Legislation or any increase in rates of Tax (in each case) announced after Completion which has retrospective effect;

2.2.4   such Tax Liability would not have arisen but for any voluntary act or transaction carried out after Completion by the Buyer or Company, provided that this paragraph 2.2.4 shall not apply to any act or transaction:

2.2.4.1   required by law or carried out or effected by the Company pursuant to a legally binding commitment created or entered into before Completion; or

2.2.4.2   which consists of communicating information to any Tax Authority; or

2.2.4.3   carried out or effected by the Company in the ordinary course of its business.

2.3   The Sellers shall not be liable in respect of a breach of any of the Warranties if and to the extent that the loss occasioned thereby has been recovered under the Tax Covenants and vice versa in respect of the same subject matter.

3.   RECOVERY FROM THIRD PARTIES

3.1   If, before the sixth anniversary of the date of this document, the Company recovers from any other person any amount which is referable to a Tax Liability of the Company in respect of which the Sellers has made a payment under this schedule, the Buyer will repay to the Sellers the lesser of:

3.1.1   the amount so recovered (less any losses, costs, damages and expenses properly and reasonably incurred by the Company, or the Buyer or any other member of the same group of companies as the Buyer as a result of effecting recovery of that amount); and

3.1.2   the amount paid by the Sellers under this schedule in respect of the Tax Liability in question, less any part of such amount previously repaid to the Seller under any provision of this agreement or otherwise.

4.   NO DEDUCTIONS OR WITHHOLDINGS

4.1   Save only as may be required by law, all sums payable by the Seller under this schedule shall be paid free and clear of all deductions or withholdings whatsoever.

4.2   If any deductions or withholdings are required by law to be made from any payment under this schedule, the Sellers shall pay such sum as will, after the deduction or withholding has been made, leave the Buyer with the same amount as it would have been entitled to receive in the absence of any such requirement to make a deduction or withholding.

5.   TAX ON PAYMENTS

If any sum payable by the Sellers to the Buyer under this schedule is (or but for the availability of any Accounts Relief or Post Completion Relief would be) subject to a Tax Liability in the hands of the Buyer, the Sellers shall pay to the Buyer such sum as is necessary to ensure that the amount received by the Buyer is not less than the amount it would have received had the payment not been subject to Tax.

6.   DATE FOR PAYMENT

6.1   Where the Sellers become liable to make a payment pursuant to the provisions of this schedule, the due date for the making of that payment in cleared funds shall be:

6.1.1   the date falling 5 Business Days after the date on which the Company or (as the case may be) the Buyer has notified the Sellers of the amount of the payment required to be made; or

6.1.2   in any case involving a liability of the Company or the Buyer to make an actual payment (whether or not a payment of Tax), the later of the date falling 5 Business Days after the date on which the Company or (as the case may be) the Buyer has notified the Sellers of the amount of the payment required to be made and the date falling 5 Business Days before the last date on which the payment in question is required to be made to the person entitled to the payment (after taking into account any postponement of the due date for payment of any Tax which is obtained).

7.   INTEREST ON LATE PAYMENTS

If any payment required to be made by the Sellers under this schedule is not made by the due date for payment thereof, then that payment shall carry interest from that due date until the date when the payment is actually made at the rate of 4 per cent above the base rate from time to time of [   ] Bank PLC compounded quarterly.

8.   PRICE REDUCTION

Any payment by the Sellers under this schedule shall (so far as possible) be treated as a reduction in the consideration paid for the Shares, provided that nothing in this paragraph 7 shall limit or exclude the liability of the Sellers under this Agreement.

9.   TAX CLAIMS

9.1   If the Buyer or the Company shall become aware of any Tax Claim which is likely to give rise to a liability of the Sellers under this schedule the Buyer shall (or shall procure that the Company shall) as soon as reasonably practicable give notice thereof to the Sellers but so that such notice shall not be a condition precedent to the liability of the Sellers hereunder.

9.2   If the Sellers shall indemnify the Company and the Buyer to the reasonable satisfaction of the Buyer against all losses, costs, damages and expenses (including interest on overdue Tax) which may be incurred thereby, the Buyer shall (and shall procure that the Company shall), in accordance with any reasonable instructions of the Sellers promptly given by notice to the Buyer (but subject to paragraphs 9.2.1 to 9.2.3 inclusive), seek to avoid, dispute, resist, appeal, compromise or defend such Tax Claim provided always that:

9.2.1   the Company shall not be obliged to appeal against any assessment for Tax raised on it if, having given the Sellers notice of the receipt of that assessment, it has not within 15 days thereafter received instructions from the Sellers, in accordance with the provisions of this paragraph 9.2.1, to make that appeal;

9.2.2   the Buyer and the Company shall not be obliged to comply with any instruction of the Sellers which involves contesting any assessment for Tax before any court or other appellate body (excluding the Tax Authority in question) unless the Sellers furnish the Buyer with the written opinion of Tax Counsel of at least 5 years' call to the effect that an appeal against the assessment for Tax in question will, on the basis of probabilities, be won;

9.2.3   the Buyer and the Company shall not in any event be obliged to comply with any instruction of the Sellers to make a settlement or compromise of a Tax Claim which is the subject of a dispute or agree any matter in the conduct of such dispute which it reasonably considers to be materially prejudicial to the business of the Company or the Buyer or likely increase the future liability of the Company or the Buyer in respect of Tax.

10.   [TAX AFFAIRS

10.1   The Sellers or their duly authorised agents or advisers shall, at the expense of the Company to the extent provided for in the Accounts and thereafter at the expense of the Sellers, prepare, submit and agree the corporation tax computations and returns of the Company ("Tax Computations") for its accounting period(s) (within the meaning of section 12 of the Taxes Act) ended on or before the Accounts Date ("Relevant Accounting Period(s)").

10.2   The Sellers shall deliver to the Buyer for comments any Tax Computation return document or correspondence and details of any information or proposal ("Relevant Information") which they intend to submit to HM Revenue & Customs before submission to HM Revenue & Customs and shall take account of the reasonable comments of the Buyer and make such amendments to the Relevant Information as the Buyer may reasonably require in writing within 30 days of the date of delivery of the Relevant Information prior to its submission to HM Revenue & Customs.

10.3   The Sellers shall deliver to the Buyer copies of any correspondence sent to, or received from, HM Revenue & Customs relating to the Tax Computations and returns and shall keep the Buyer fully informed of its actions under this paragraph.

10.4   Subject to paragraphs 10.2 and 10.3, the Buyer shall procure that:

10.4.1   the Company properly authorises and signs the Tax Computations and makes and signs or otherwise enters into all such elections, surrenders and claims and withdraws or disclaims such elections, surrenders and claims and gives such notices and signs such other documents as the Sellers shall require in relation to the Relevant Accounting Period(s);

10.4.2   the Company provides to the Sellers such information and assistance, including such access to its books, accounts and records which may reasonably be required to prepare, submit, negotiate and agree the Tax Computations;

10.4.3   any correspondence which relates to the Tax Computations shall, if received by the Buyer or any Company or its agents or advisers, be properly copied to the Sellers.

10.5   In respect of any matter which gives or may give the Buyer a right to make a Tax Claim, the provisions of paragraph 8 with respect to appeals and the conduct of disputes shall apply instead of the provisions of this paragraph 9.

10.6   The Sellers shall use all reasonable endeavours to agree the Tax Computations as soon as reasonably practicable and shall deal with all such matters promptly and diligently and within applicable time limits.

SCHEDULE 5

The Warranties

1. THE COMPANY AND THE SELLERS

1.1 **Capacity**

Each of the Sellers has full power to enter into and perform the provisions of this Agreement, which constitutes a binding agreement on the Seller in accordance with its terms.

1.2 **Ownership of the Shares**

Each of the Sellers is the beneficial owner of the number of Shares set opposite his name in [part 1 of] Schedule 1 and has the right to dispose of them to the Buyer or as it directs free from any Encumbrance and together with all rights now or hereafter attaching to them.

1.3 **Transfers at an undervalue**

Neither the Shares nor any asset owned or used by the Company has been the subject of a transfer at an undervalue (within the meaning of section 238 or section 239 of the Insolvency Act 1986) within the period of five years prior to the date of this Agreement.

1.4 **Liabilities owing to or by the Sellers**

There is not outstanding any indebtedness and there are no contracts, arrangements or liabilities (actual or contingent) remaining in whole or in part to be performed between the Company and any of the Sellers or any director of the Company or any of the Sellers or any person who is an associate of or connected with any of them.

2. THE COMPANY'S SCHEDULED PARTICULARS AND CONSTITUTIONAL AND ADMINISTRATIVE AFFAIRS

2.1 **Schedule 1**

2.2 The particulars of the Company set out in schedule 1 are true, complete and accurate; no person is a shadow director of the Company and its issued share capital is fully paid.

2.2.1 The Company:

2.2.1.1 has not since its incorporation had any group undertaking [other than the Subsidiaries]; [and]

2.2.1.2 [is the beneficial owner (directly or indirectly) free from any Encumbrance of the whole of the issued share capital of each of the Subsidiaries; and]

2.2.1.3 has not since its incorporation been a subsidiary of any other company.

2.3 **Memorandum and Articles**

The copy of the memorandum and articles of association of the Company attached to the Disclosure Letter is true and complete.

2.4 **Options**

No person has the right (whether exercisable now or in the future and whether or not contingent) to call for the allotment, issue or transfer of any share or loan capital of the Company under any option or other agreement (including without limitation conversion rights and rights of pre-emption).

2.5	**Purchase of own shares**

The Company has not at any time purchased any of its own shares or redeemed or forfeited any shares in its capital.

2.6	**Statutory and other books and records**

2.6.1   All registers, accounts, books, ledgers, financial and other records of the Company have been fully, properly and accurately kept and maintained, are in the possession of the Company and contain true and accurate records of all matters required by law to be entered therein and no notice or allegation that any of them is incorrect or should be rectified has been received by the Company or the Sellers.

2.6.2   The Company's accounting records:

2.6.2.1   comply with the requirements of sections 221 and 222 of the Act;

2.6.2.2   are sufficient to show and explain the Company's transactions;

2.6.2.3   disclose with reasonable accuracy, at any time, the financial position of the Company at that time; and

2.6.2.4   do not contain or reflect any material inaccuracy or discrepancy.

2.7	**Filing of documents**

All returns and other documents required to be filed with the Registrar of Companies, or with any other authority, in respect of the Company have been duly filed and were when filed correct.

2.8	**Insurances**

2.8.1   The Company maintains, and at all material times has maintained, adequate insurance cover against all risks normally insured against by companies carrying on a similar business, for the full replacement or reinstatement value of its business and assets, and in particular has maintained all insurance required by statute, product liability and professional indemnity insurance, and insured against loss of profits for a period of not less than six (6) months and for loss of rent for a period of not less than three (3) years.

2.8.2   The Disclosure Letter sets out full details of all policies of insurance maintained by or on behalf of the Company, all of which are in full force and effect.

2.8.3   All premiums in respect of policies of insurance maintained by or on behalf of the Company have been paid as and when due, and there are no circumstances which might lead to any liability under such insurance being avoided by the insurers or (being circumstances not affecting businesses generally) the premiums being increased, and there is no claim outstanding under any such policy, nor are any of the Sellers aware of any circumstances likely to give rise to a claim thereunder.

2.8.4   The Disclosure Letter sets out full details of all insurance claims made by or on behalf of the Company within the period of three years immediately prior to the date of this Agreement.

2.8.5   There are no claims outstanding or threatened or, so far as the Sellers are aware, pending against the Company which are not fully covered by insurance.

2.9   **Agency**

No person, as agent or otherwise, is entitled or authorised to bind or commit the Company to any obligation outside the ordinary course of business.

3.   THE COMPANY AND THE LAW

3.1   **Compliance with laws**

3.1.1   The Company has conducted and is conducting its business in accordance with all applicable laws and regulations of any relevant jurisdiction and neither the Company nor any of its officers, agents or employees have committed, or omitted to do, any act or thing capable of giving rise to any fine, penalty, default proceedings or other liability on the part of the Company.

3.1.2   There is no order, decree or judgment of any court or any governmental agency of any jurisdiction outstanding against the Company or which may have any adverse effect upon the assets or business of the Company; no such order, decree or judgment is pending, and there are no circumstances likely to give rise to any such order, decree or judgment.

3.1.3   There is not pending or in existence any investigation or enquiry by or on behalf of any governmental or other body in respect of the affairs of the Company.

3.2   **Licences**

3.2.1   The Company has obtained all licences, consents, permits and authorities of a statutory or regulatory nature necessary or expedient to enable it to carry on its business effectively in the places and in the manner in which it is now carried on.

3.2.2   All such licences, consents, permits and authorities are valid and subsisting, and none of the Sellers know of no reason why any of them should be suspended, cancelled or revoked or renewed or continued subject to any term or condition which does not currently apply thereto.

3.3   **Litigation**

3.3.1   The Company is not engaged in any dispute with any customer or supplier or in any litigation or other proceedings.

3.3.2   So far as the Sellers are aware:

3.3.2.1   no litigation or other proceedings are pending or threatened by or against the Company;

3.3.2.2   there are no circumstances likely to give rise to any litigation or other proceedings; and

3.3.2.3   the Company has not been a party to any undertaking or assurance given to any court or governmental agency which is still in force.

3.4   **Insolvency**

3.4.1   The Company has not become unable to pay its debts as they fall due within the meaning of section 123 of the Insolvency Act 1986 or received any written demand pursuant to section 123(1)(a) of the Insolvency Act 1986.

3.4.2   No order has been made or petition presented or resolution passed for the winding up of the Company; no proposal has been made under part I of the Insolvency Act 1986 for a voluntary arrangement; no person has appointed or applied to any court of competent jurisdiction to appoint a receiver or an administrative receiver or an administrator; and no distress, execution or other process has been levied against the Company.

3.5   **Fair trading**

3.5.1   No agreement, practice or arrangement currently or previously carried on by the Company or to which the Company is or has been a party infringes any competition, anti-restrictive trade practice, anti-trust or consumer protection law or legislation applicable in any relevant jurisdiction ("Competition Laws").

3.5.2   The Company has not given any undertaking to any court, person or body and is not subject to any act, decision, regulation, order or other instrument under any Competition Laws.

3.6   **Products**

The Company has not manufactured, sold or supplied any product or provided any service which does not or did not at any material time comply with the terms of any contract entered into by the Company or with any applicable regulation, standard or statutory requirement, or which was in any other way defective.

3.7   **Pollution of the environment**

3.7.1   [No hazardous substances have been used or stored or otherwise handled by the Company on the Property or elsewhere.] [The Company has at all times held all licences, consents, permits and authorities necessary to enable it to use, store or otherwise handle or dispose of any hazardous substances used, stored, otherwise handled or disposed of by it, whether on the Property or elsewhere.]

3.7.2   There has been no pollution of the environment by the Company, the Company has no responsibility or liability for any pollution of the environment by any third party and there has been no act or omission by the Company which could give rise to any pollution of the environment.

3.7.3   The Company has complied and has adequate systems and facilities to continue to comply with:

3.7.3.1   all laws and regulations relating to pollution of the environment;

3.7.3.2   all laws and regulations relating to pollution of the environment which apply to any person carrying on any process carried on by the Company;

3.7.3.3   all EC Directives relating to pollution of the environment (whether or not they have been implemented in any relevant jurisdiction).

For the purposes of this paragraph 3.7 the expressions "pollution of the environment" and "process" shall have the same meanings as in section 1 of the Environmental Protection Act 1990.

3.8 **Data Protection**

3.8.1 The Company has at all times complied with the Applicable Data Protection Laws, and there exist no circumstances likely to give rise to any allegation of non-compliance.

3.8.2 The Company has made all necessary notifications or registrations under the Applicable Data Protection Laws, and such registrations or notifications are appropriate given the Company's actual data processing activities.

3.8.3 The Company has not received any enforcement, information or other official notice or request under the Applicable Data Protection Laws.

3.8.4 The Company has not received any communication from any data subject or official alleging a breach of the Applicable Data Protection Laws.

3.8.5 The Company has not been required to pay compensation in respect of any breach of the Applicable Data Protection Laws, no claims for compensation are outstanding and there are no circumstances likely to give rise to such a claim.

3.8.6 The Company has complied with all data subject requests including requests for access to personal data or cessation of specified processing activities.

3.9 **Health and Safety**

3.9.1 The Company has complied with all its obligations under the Health & Safety at Work etc Act 1974 ("the Health & Safety Act") and all regulations passed thereunder ("the Regulations").

3.9.2 The Company has not been served with any Improvement Notices.

3.9.3 The Company has not been served with any Prohibition Notices.

3.9.4 The Company has not been cautioned for any breach of the Health & Safety Act or the Regulations.

3.9.5 The Company has not been prosecuted for any breach of the Health & Safety Act or the Regulations.

3.9.6 There are no circumstances likely to give rise to the service of an Improvement Notice or Prohibition Notice, or to a prosecution for a breach of the Health & Safety Act or the Regulations.

3.9.7 The Company has not been the subject of a prosecution (whether by the Crown Prosecution Service, the Health and Safety Executive, or any other responsible body) as a result of or in connection with any work-related death and there are no circumstances likely to give rise to such a prosecution.

3.9.8 For the purposes of this paragraph 0, the expression "Improvement Notice" and "Prohibition Notice" shall have the same meanings as in sections 21 and 22 of the Health & Safety Act.

4. **THE COMPANY'S FINANCIAL POSITION**

4.1 **The Accounts**

The Accounts:

4.1.1   have been prepared in accordance with the requirements of the Act and all other applicable statutes and regulations and in accordance with generally accepted accounting practices, including all applicable SSAPs and FRSs and statements from the Urgent Issues Task Force;

4.1.2   have been prepared on bases and principles and using methods which are consistent with those used in the preparation of the audited accounts of the Company [and the audited consolidated accounts for the Group in each case] for any accounting period falling wholly or partly within the period of six years ended on the Accounts Date; and

4.1.3   show a true and fair view of the state of affairs of the Company [and of the Group] as at the Accounts Date and of the profit or loss of the Company [and of the Group] for the accounting period ended on that date.

4.2   **Provisions in the Accounts**

The Accounts:

4.2.1   fully provide for all liabilities (other than contingent liabilities which are not expected to crystallise) and fully disclose all contingent liabilities which are not expected to crystallise and all capital and revenue commitments of the Company in each case as at the Accounts Date;

4.2.2   fully provide for all bad and doubtful debts as at the Accounts Date;

4.2.3   attribute a value to stock which does not exceed the lower of direct cost and net realisable value as at the Accounts Date after wholly writing off all redundant, obsolete, old, unusable, unsaleable, slow-moving, deteriorated and excessive stock; and

4.2.4   are not affected (except as disclosed in the Accounts) by any extraordinary or exceptional event, circumstance or item.

4.3   **Events since the Accounts Date**

Since the Accounts Date:

4.3.1   the Company has carried on its business in the ordinary and usual course and without any interruption or alteration in the nature, scope or manner thereof;

4.3.2   the Company has not acquired or disposed of any asset, assumed any liability, made any payment or entered into any other transaction which was not in the ordinary course of its business and for full value;

4.3.3   the Company's turnover and margins of profitability have not been less than its turnover and margins of profitability for the corresponding period in the accounting period which ended on the Accounts Date, and there has been no deterioration in its financial position or prospects. In particular, there has been no reduction in the value of the net tangible assets of the Company on the basis of the valuations used in the Accounts;

4.3.4   the Company has paid its creditors within the times agreed with such creditors, and there are no debts now outstanding by the Company which have been outstanding for more than [   ] days or which are now overdue for payment (whether in whole or in part);

4.3.5   the Company has not entered into, or agreed to enter into, any capital commitment;

4.3.6   the Company has not repaid or become liable to repay any loan or indebtedness in advance of its stated maturity;

4.3.7   the Company has not received notice (whether formal or informal) from any lender of money to the Company requiring repayment or intimating the enforcement by it of any security which it may hold over any assets of the Company, and there are no circumstances likely to give rise to such notice;

4.3.8   no part of the amounts included in the Accounts, or subsequently recorded in the books of the Company as owing by any debtors, has been outstanding for more than [   ] days or has been released on terms that any debtor pays less than the full book value of his or its debt or has been written off or has proved to any extent to be irrecoverable;

4.3.9   the Company has not factored or discounted any of its debts or agreed to do so;

4.3.10   the Company has not offered any price reduction or discount or allowance on sales of stock below a selling price which achieves a gross margin of [   ]% or sold any stock at less than its book value;

4.3.11   the Company has not sought to accelerate payment by its trade debtors other than in the ordinary and normal course of business.

4.4   **Working capital**

[Having regard to existing bank and other facilities, the Company has sufficient working capital for the purpose of continuing to carry on its business in its present form and at its present level of turnover for the period to [200   ]] [The financial forecasts of the Company for the [three] year period ending on [ ] 200 (a copy of which is attached to the Disclosure Letter) have been prepared by or on behalf of the Sellers in good faith and on the basis of assumptions which are reasonable.

4.5   **Grants**

The Company has not made any application for or received any financial assistance from any supranational, national or local authority or governmental agency.

4.6   **Debts**

There are no debts owing by or to the Company other than debts which have arisen in the ordinary course of its business, nor has the Company lent any money which has not been repaid.

4.7   **Management Accounts**

The Management Accounts have been prepared using the same accounting principles, policies and bases as used in the Accounts (consistently applied), fairly reflect the trading position of the Company as at the date and for the period to which they relate and are not affected by any extraordinary, exceptional, unusual or non-recurring income, capital gain or expenditure or by any other factor known to the Sellers rendering profits or losses for the period covered exceptionally high or low.

5. THE COMPANY AND ITS FINANCIERS

5.1 Borrowings

The total amount borrowed by the Company from its financiers does not exceed its facilities and the total amount borrowed by the Company from whatsoever source does not exceed any limitation on borrowing imposed upon it in its articles of association or otherwise.

5.2 Continuance of facilities

Full and accurate details of all overdrafts, loans or other financial facilities outstanding or available to the Company are contained in the Disclosure Letter (and true and complete copies of all documents relating thereto are attached to the Disclosure Letter), and neither any of the Sellers nor the Company has done anything whereby the continuance of any such facilities in full force and effect might be affected or prejudiced.

5.3 Bank accounts

A statement of all the bank accounts of the Company and of the credit or debit balances on such accounts as at a date not more than two days before the date of this Agreement and a reconciliation of such credit or debit balances to the books and records of the Company as at the date of this Agreement are attached to the Disclosure Letter and are true, complete and accurate. The Company does not have any other bank or deposit account. Since the date to which such statement is drawn up there have been no payments out of, and no instructions given for any payments out of, and no cheques drawn against, any such accounts except for routine payments out of current account in the ordinary course of business.

5.4 Guarantees

No person has given any guarantee of or security for any overdraft, loan or loan facility granted to or obligations undertaken by the Company. The Company is not a party to any guarantee, suretyship, indemnity or similar commitment.

6. THE ASSETS OF THE COMPANY

6.1 Assets and charges

6.1.1 The Company owns free from any Encumbrance all assets included in the Accounts or acquired by the Company since the Accounts Date except for current assets subsequently disposed of by the Company in the ordinary course of its business [, the Properties] and stock which is the subject of retention of title terms contained in standard terms of trading imposed by suppliers in the ordinary course of their business and owns free from any Encumbrance any other asset used by it.

6.1.2 The Company has possession of all such assets and none of such assets, nor any of the undertaking, goodwill or uncalled capital of the Company, is subject to any Encumbrance or any agreement or commitment to give or create any Encumbrance.

6.1.3 The assets owned by the Company, together with assets held under hire-purchase, leasing and rental agreements (copies of which are attached to the Disclosure Letter), comprise all assets necessary for the continuation of its business as now carried on.

6.2 Stocks

The stock of raw materials, packaging materials and finished goods now held by the Company is not excessive and is adequate in relation to the current trading requirements of the business of the Company; none of it is obsolete, slow-moving or unusable and it is capable of being sold by the Company in the ordinary course of its business in accordance with current price lists without rebate or allowance to a Buyer.

6.3 **Debts**

The amounts due from debtors are recoverable in full in the ordinary course of business and in any event not later than [ninety] days following the date of this Agreement, and none of these debts is subject to any counterclaim or set-off.

6.4 **Intellectual Property**

6.4.1 The Company:

6.4.1.1 is the sole and beneficial owner and (where it is capable of registration) the registered proprietor of the Intellectual Property used by it, all of which are valid and in full force and effect;

6.4.1.2 does not own or use any Intellectual Property other than that listed in the Disclosure Letter and other than copyrights, design rights, technical know-how and confidential information and does not require any other Intellectual Property to carry on its business;

6.4.1.3 has not entered into any Intellectual Property Agreements other than any listed in the Disclosure Letter or authorised any person to make any use of or to do anything which would or might otherwise infringe any Intellectual Property Rights; and

6.4.1.4 has not disclosed (except in the ordinary course of its business) any of its know-how, trade secrets or customer details to any other person.

6.4.2 The Company owns the copyright or design right (whether registered or unregistered) in the designs of all its products and is the proprietor of any registrations or applications to register any such designs.

6.4.3 None of the processes or products of the Company [(so far as the Sellers are aware)]:

6.4.3.1 infringes any Intellectual Property of any other person; or

6.4.3.2 involves the unlicensed use of confidential information or know-how disclosed to the Company by any person.

6.4.4 None of the Intellectual Property Rights are being used by, or are being or have been claimed, disputed, opposed or attacked by any other person.

6.4.5 All Intellectual Property Agreements to which the Company is a party are valid and binding on the parties thereto; the Company has at all times observed and performed all of the provisions of each of them and nothing has been done or omitted to be done by the Company which would enable any of them to be terminated.

6.4.6 None of the records, systems, data or information of the Company is recorded, stored, maintained, operated or otherwise wholly or partly dependent on or held or accessible by any means (including any electronic, mechanical or photographic process, whether computerised or not) which are not under the exclusive ownership and direct control of the Company.

6.4.7 No person has the right to require the Company to change its corporate name or to cease using any trade name, logo, trading style, domain name or e-mail address currently used by the Company.

6.5 Plant

Each item of the plant and machinery and all vehicles and office and other equipment used in connection with the business of the Company:

6.5.1 is in good repair and condition (subject to fair wear and tear) and in satisfactory working order;

6.5.2 is capable, over the period of time during which it is to be written down to a nil value in the accounts of the Company, of doing the work for which it was designed or purchased; and

6.5.3 is not surplus to the requirements of the Company.

6.6 [Net asset value

The value of the net tangible assets of the Company, determined in accordance with the same accounting policies as those applied in the preparation of the Accounts (and on the basis that each of the fixed assets of the Company is valued at a figure no greater than the value attributed to it in the Accounts or, in the case of any fixed assets acquired by the Company after the Accounts Date, at a figure no greater than cost), is not less than the value of the net tangible assets of the Company at the Accounts Date as shown in the Accounts.]

6.7 Computer Systems

6.7.1 The Computer Systems are capable of the following functions:

6.7.1.1 handling date information involving all and any dates including, accepting date input, providing date output and performing date calculations in whole or part;

6.7.1.2 operating accurately without interruption on and in respect of any and all dates and without any change in performance;

6.7.1.3 responding to and processing two digit year input without creating any ambiguity as to the century; and

6.7.1.4 storing and providing date output information without creating any ambiguity as to the century.

6.7.2 The Computer Systems and each element of them passes and will continue to pass date information between each other (and any third parties' computer systems with which they habitually communicate) in a way which does not, and will not, create inaccuracies.

6.7.3 The Hardware has been satisfactorily maintained and supported and has the benefit of an appropriate maintenance and support agreement which is not capable of being terminated by the contractor by less than 24 months' notice.

6.7.4 The Hardware and the Software have adequate capability and capacity for the projected requirements of the Company for not less than 4 years following Completion.

6.7.5   Disaster recovery plans are in effect and are adequate to ensure that the Hardware, Software and Data can be replaced or substituted without material disruption to the business of the Company.

6.7.6   In the event that any person providing maintenance or support services for the Computer Systems ceases or is unable to do so, the Company has all necessary rights and information to procure the carrying out of such services by employees of by a third party without undue expense or delay.

6.7.7   The Company has sufficient technically competent and trained employees to ensure proper handling, operation, monitoring and use of the Computer Systems.

6.7.8   The Company has adequate procedures to ensure internal and external security of the Computer Systems and of the Data, including procedures for preventing unauthorised access, preventing the introduction of a virus, taking and storing on-site and off-site back-up copies of Software and Data.

6.7.9   Where any of the records of the Company are stored electronically, the Company is the owner of all hardware and software licences necessary to enable it to keep, copy, maintain and use such records in the course of its business and does not share any hardware or software relating to the records with any person.

6.7.10   The Company has all the rights necessary (including rights over the source code) to obtain, without undue expense or delay, modified versions of the Software which are required at any time to improve in any regard the operation and/or efficiency of the Software.

6.7.11   The Company owns, and is in possession and control of, original copies of all of the manuals, guides, instruction books and technical documents (including any corrections and updates) required to operate the Computer Systems effectively.

6.7.12   The Computer Systems have never unduly interrupted or hindered the running or operation of the Company's business and have no defects in operation which so affect the Company's business.

6.7.13   In this paragraph 6.7:—

6.7.13.1   "Data" means any data or information used by or for the benefit of the Company at any time and stored electronically at any time;

6.7.13.2   "Hardware" means any computer equipment used by or for the benefit of the Company at any time including, without limitation, PCs, mainframes, screens, terminals, keyboards, discs, printers, cabling and associated and peripheral electronic equipment but excluding all Software;

6.7.13.3   "Software" means any set of instructions for execution by microprocessor used by or for the benefit of the Company at any time, irrespective of application, language or medium;

6.7.13.4   "Computer Systems" means all Hardware, Software and any other items that connect with any or all of them which in each case are used by or for the benefit of the Company.

7.   THE CONTRACTS OF THE COMPANY

7.1   **Documents**

All title deeds and all agreements to which the Company is a party are in the possession of the Company and are properly stamped and free from Encumbrance.

7.2   **Material contracts**

The Company is not a party to or subject to any agreement, transaction, obligation, commitment, understanding, arrangement or liability which:

7.2.1   is incapable of complete performance in accordance with its terms within three months after the date on which it was entered into or undertaken or cannot be terminated, without giving rise to any liabilities on the Company, by the Company giving three months' notice or less;

7.2.2   is known by the Sellers or by the Company to be likely to result in a loss to the Company on completion or performance;

7.2.3   cannot readily be fulfilled or performed by the Company on time;

7.2.4   involves or is likely to involve obligations, restrictions, expenditure or revenue of an unusual, onerous or exceptional nature; or

7.2.5   requires an aggregate consideration payable by the Company in excess of £[   ] ([   ] pounds);

7.2.6   is in any way otherwise than in the ordinary and proper course of the business of the Company and on arm's length terms.

7.3   **Defaults**

Neither the Company nor any other party to any agreement with the Company is in default thereunder, being a default which would be material in the context of the financial or trading position of the Company nor (so far as the Sellers are aware) are there any circumstances likely to give rise to any such default.

7.4   **Insider contracts**

There is not outstanding, and there has not at any time during the last three years been outstanding, any agreement or arrangement between the Company and the Sellers, nor has its profit or loss or financial position during such period been affected by, any such agreement or arrangement or any other agreement or arrangement which is not entirely of an arm's length nature.

7.5   **Customers/suppliers**

7.5.1   In the accounting period ended on the Accounts Date, no customer or supplier of the Company represented [%] or more of the Company's sales or purchases in that period (any such customer or supplier being a "Major Customer" or "Major Supplier") save for those specifically identified in the Disclosure Letter as Major Customers or Major Suppliers.

7.5.2   No Major Customer or Major Supplier has since the Accounts Date ceased to do business with the Company or has since such date substantially reduced its purchases from or supplies to the Company and since the Accounts Date no indication has been received by the Company of any material change in the prices or other terms upon which any customer or supplier is prepared to contract or do business with the Company.

7.5.3   The Sellers are not aware of any reason to indicate that any of the existing customers of or suppliers to the Company are likely materially to reduce the volume of their purchases from or supplies to the Company in the future by comparison with the value of their purchases from or supplies to the Company during the period of [ ] months prior to the date of this Agreement.

8.   THE COMPANY AND ITS EMPLOYEES

8.1   General

8.1.1   There is no employment or other contract or engagement between the Company and any of its directors or other officers. The Company is not a party to a consultancy contract.

8.1.2   There is no employment contract between the Company and any of its employees which cannot be terminated by the Company by three months' notice or less without giving rise to a claim for damages or compensation (other than a statutory redundancy payment or statutory compensation for unfair dismissal). The Company has not received notice of resignation from [*key personnel*].

8.1.3   There is no employment or consultancy contract or other contract of engagement between the Company and any person which is in suspension or has been terminated but is capable of being revived or enforced or in respect of which the Company has a continuing obligation.

8.1.4   The Disclosure Letter contains details of:

8.1.4.1   the total number of the Company's employees including those who are on maternity leave or absent because of disability or other long-term leave of absence and who have or may have a right to return to work with the Company;

8.1.4.2   the name, date of start of employment, period of continuous employment, salary and other benefits, grade and age of each employee of the Company and, where an employee has been continuously absent from work for more than one month, the reason for the absence; and

8.1.4.3   the terms of the contract of each director, other officer and employee of the Company entitled to remuneration at an annual rate, or an average annual rate over the last three financial years, of more than £[ ].

8.1.5   The basis of the remuneration payable to the Company's directors, other officers and employees is the same as that in force at the Accounts Date. The Company is not obliged to increase, nor has it made provision to increase, the total annual remuneration payable to its directors, other officers and employees by more than [three] per cent. or to increase the rate of remuneration of a director, other officer or employee entitled to annual remuneration of more than £[ ].

8.1.6   The Company owes no amount to a present or former director, other officer or employee of the Company (or his dependant) other than for accrued remuneration or reimbursement of business expenses.

8.1.7   There is no agreement or arrangement between the Company and an employee or former employee with respect to his employment, his ceasing to be employed or his retirement which is not included in the written terms of his employment or previous employment. The Company has not provided, or agreed to provide, a gratuitous payment or benefit to a director, officer or employee or to any of their dependants.

8.1.8   The Company has maintained up-to-date, full and accurate records regarding the employment of each of its employees (including details of terms of employment, payments of statutory sick pay and statutory maternity pay, income tax and social security contributions, working time, disciplinary and health and safety matters) and termination of employment.

8.2   **Payments on termination**

Except as disclosed in the Accounts, the Company has not:

8.2.1   incurred a liability for breach or termination of an employment contract including, without limitation, a redundancy payment, protective award and compensation for wrongful dismissal, unfair dismissal and failure to comply with an order for the reinstatement or re-engagement of an employee;

8.2.2   incurred a liability for breach or termination of a consultancy agreement;

8.2.3   made or agreed to make a payment or provided or agreed to provide a benefit to a present or former director, other officer or employee of the Company or to any of their dependants in connection with the actual or proposed termination or suspension of employment or variation of an employment contract.

8.3   **Compliance with law**

The Company has complied with:

8.3.1   each obligation imposed on it by, and each order and award made under, statute, regulation, code of conduct and practice, collective agreement, (including any agreement or arrangement under the ICE Regulations 2004), custom and practice relevant to the relations between it and its employees or a trade union or the terms of employment of its employees; and

8.3.2   each recommendation or code of practice made by the Advisory, Conciliation and Arbitration Service and each award and declaration made by the Central Arbitration Committee.

8.4   **Redundancies and transfer of business**

Within the year ending on the date of this Agreement the Company has not:

8.4.1   given notice of redundancies to the relevant Secretary of State or started consultations with appropriate representatives under Chapter II of Part IV of the Trade Union and Labour Relations (Consolidation) Act 1992 or failed to comply with its obligations under Chapter II of Part IV of that Act; or

8.4.2   been a party to a relevant transfer (as defined in the Transfer of Undertakings (Protection of Employment) Regulations 2006) or failed to comply with a duty to inform and consult appropriate representatives under those Regulations.

8.5   **Trade Unions**

8.5.1   The Company has no agreement or arrangement (whether under the Information and Consultation of Employees Regulations 2004 or otherwise) with and does not recognise a trade union, works council, staff association or other body representing any of its employees and the Company has not received any notice or request nor are there any negotiations which may lead to any such agreement or arrangement).

8.5.2   The Company is not involved in, and no fact or circumstance exists which might give rise to:-

8.5.2.1   a dispute with a trade union, works council, staff association or other body representing any of its employees; or

8.5.2.2   any proceedings before the Central Arbitration Committee or an Employment Tribunal in relation to any collective bargaining agreement or any arrangement under the ICE Regulations 2004.

8.6   **Incentive schemes**

The Company does not have and is not proposing to introduce a share incentive, share option, profit sharing, bonus or other incentive scheme for any of its directors, other officers or employees.

9.   PENSIONS

9.1   **Disclosed Schemes**

The Disclosed Schemes are the only arrangements under which the Company has or could have any liability to provide or contribute towards relevant benefits as defined in Chapter 2 of Part 6 of the Income Tax (Earnings & Pensions) Act 2003.

9.2   **Details Supplied**

The Sellers have supplied to the Buyer documents containing full, accurate and up to date details of each of the Disclosed Schemes and of the Company's obligations and liabilities under it.

9.3   **Eligibility Requirements**

No amendments have been proposed or announced in relation to the eligibility requirements for entry to the Disclosed Schemes, contribution rates or benefits.

9.4   **Legal Compliance**

Each of the Disclosed Schemes complies and has at all times complied with all legal and regulatory requirements (including equal treatment and data protection requirements) applicable to it.

9.5   **Stakeholder Pension Scheme**

The Company complies and has at all times complied with any duty to facilitate access to a stakeholder pension scheme under section 3 of the Welfare Reform and Pensions Act 1999.

9.6   **Deduction of Contributions**

All contributions deducted from the salaries of employees of the Company who are members of the Disclosed Schemes and all contributions payable by the Company to and in respect of the Disclosed Schemes have been paid and passed to the trustees of the Pension Scheme or the provider[s] of the Personal Pension Schemes, GPP, Life Assurance Scheme and the Stakeholder Scheme, as appropriate, in full and within the prescribed time limits applicable in each case.

9.7   Payments

All levies payable in respect of the Pension Scheme have been paid in full and on or by the due date in each case.

9.8   Claims and Disputes

No claim, dispute, complaint or investigation (including, but not limited to, complaints to the Pensions Ombudsman and investigations by the Pensions Regulator) has arisen which relates to the Disclosed Schemes or to the provision of retirement or death benefits in respect of each member of the Group's current and former employees and there is no reason why any such claim, dispute, complaint or investigation could arise.

9.9   Registered Pension Scheme

Each of the Disclosed Schemes is a registered pension scheme (within the meaning of Chapter 2 of Part 4 of the Finance Act 2004) and there is no reason why HM Revenue & Customs could withdraw that registration.

9.10   Contracting Out

The Pension Scheme is [not] a contracted out scheme within the meaning of section 8 of the Pension Schemes Act 1993.

9.11   Death in Service Benefits

All death in service benefits under the [Pension Scheme/Life Assurance Scheme] are fully insured on normal terms for persons in good health.

9.12   Equalising Benefits

The Pension Scheme has complied fully with its obligations to equalise benefits for men and women.

9.13   Eligibility Criteria

The eligibility criteria for access to the Disclosed Schemes have not been operated so as to discriminate on the grounds of sex, race, disability, religion or belief, sexual orientation or [on and after 1 October 2006] age.

9.14   Money Purchase Basis [Only relevant to defined contribution schemes]

All benefits under the Pension Scheme (other than those which are fully insured) are calculated on a money purchase basis only and the Company has given no assurance or contractual promise to any employee of the Company that his benefits at retirement will be based on his salary at or near to retirement.

9.15   Funding [Only relevant to defined benefit schemes]

As at [date of last actuarial valuation] the Pension Scheme was fully funded on a [scheme specific funding/FRS 17] basis, contributions since that date have been paid in accordance with the current schedule of contributions in accordance with section 58 of the Pensions Act 1995, and nothing has occurred since that date which would have an adverse effect on the funding position.

9.16   Discretions and Powers [Only relevant to defined benefit schemes]

No discretion or power has been exercised under the Pension Scheme in respect of any employee or director, or former employee or director of the Company to

9.16.1   augment benefits

9.16.2   admit to membership an employee or director who would not otherwise have been eligible for membership

9.16.3 provide in respect of a member a benefit which would not otherwise be provided in respect of that member

9.16.4 provide or pay a benefit on more favourable terms.

9.17 **Transfer Payments [Only relevant to defined benefit schemes]**

No transfer payment has been made from the Pension Scheme whose amount exceeds the lower of 5% of the assets of the Pension Scheme and £1.5m.

9.18 **Benefits [Only relevant to defined benefit schemes]**

No member is in receipt of or entitled to receive benefits from the Pension Scheme whose value exceeds the lower of 5% of the assets and £1.5m.

9.19 **Notifiable Events [Only relevant to defined benefit schemes]**

No notifiable event within the meaning of section 67 of the Pensions Act 2004 has occurred in relation to the Pension Scheme or the Company.

10. **MATERIAL DISCLOSURE**

10.1 **Disclosure letter**

All information contained in or referred to in the Disclosure letter is true and accurate, and the Disclosure Letter does not omit anything which renders any such information misleading or which might reasonably affect the willingness of an acquirer to acquire the Shares on the terms (including without limitation as to price) of this Agreement.

10.2 **Commission**

No person is entitled whether, actually or contingently, to receive from the Company any finder's fee, brokerage, or other commission in connection with the acquisition or disposal of shares in the Company.

10.3 **Consequence of share acquisition by the Buyer**

The sale of the Shares to the Buyer will not by virtue of the terms of any agreement or arrangement to which the Company is a party:

10.3.1 cause the Company to lose the benefit of any right or privilege it presently enjoys, entitle any person to terminate any contract with, or obligation to, the Company or, so far as the Sellers are aware, cause any person who normally does business with the Company not to continue to do so on the same basis as previously; or

10.3.2 result in any present or future indebtedness of the Company becoming due or capable of being declared due and payable prior to its stated maturity.

10.4 **[Circular letter**

The information (including without limitation any negative statement) contained in the extracts from the circular letter to the shareholders of the Buyer (which are signed or initialled by or on behalf of the parties for the purposes of identification) is, so far as the Company is concerned, in accordance with the facts and does not omit anything which renders any such information misleading.]

10.5 **Legal Due Diligence Enquiries**

The replies to the Legal Due Diligence Enquiries dated [ ] 200 raised on behalf of the Buyer were when given and remain true complete and accurate.

11.   PROPERTY

11.1   **Particulars**

The Particulars of the Property shown in schedule 4 are true and correct and the Company has good and marketable title to and the exclusive occupation and possession of the Property free from any mortgage, debenture or charge (whether specific or floating, legal or equitable) rent charge, lien or other encumbrance, lease, sub-lease, tenancy or right of occupation, reservation, covenant, stipulation, profit a prendre, wayleave, grant, restriction, easement, quasi-easement or any agreement for any of the same or any privilege in favour of any third party.

11.2   **Rights and easements**

There are appurtenant to the Property all rights and easements necessary for its use and enjoyment.

11.3   **Title deeds and documents**

The Company has in its possession or under its control all duly stamped deeds and documents which are necessary to prove title to the Property.

11.4   **Disputes etc**

The Property is not affected by any of the following matters nor is it likely to become so affected:-

11.4.1   any dispute, notice or complaint or any exception, reservation, right, covenant, restriction, overriding interest or condition and in particular (but without limitation) any of those matters which is of an unusual nature or which affects or might in the future affect the use of any of the Property for the purpose for which it is now used or which affects or might in the future affect the value of the Property; or

11.4.2   any notice, order, demand, requirement or proposal made or issued by or on behalf of any government or statutory authority, department or body for the acquisition, clearance, demolition or closing or the carrying out of any work upon any building, the modification of any planning permission, the discontinuance of any use or the imposition of any building or improvement line; or

11.4.3   any compensation received as a result of any refusal of any application for planning consent or the imposition of any restrictions in relation to any planning consent; or

11.4.4   any commutation or agreement for the commutation of rent or payment of rent in advance of the due dates for payment thereof.

11.5   **State of repair and condition**

The Property is in a good and substantial state of repair and condition and is fit for the purpose for which it is presently used and no high alumina cement, woodwool, calcium chloride, sea dredged aggregates, asbestos or other deleterious material (not in accordance with good building practice) was used in the construction thereof and there are no development works, redevelopment works or fitting out works outstanding in respect of the Property.

11.6   **Restrictions, conditions and covenants**

All restrictions conditions and covenants (including any imposed by or pursuant to any lease) affecting the Property have been duly and punctually observed and performed and no notice of any breach of any of the same has been received or is likely to be received.

11.7 Compliance with legislation

The use of the Property and all machinery and equipment thereon and the conduct of any business thereon complies and has at all times complied in all respects with all relevant statutes and regulations, including the Factories Act 1961, the Offices, Shops and Railway Premises Act 1963, the Fire Precautions Act 1971, the Health and Safety at Work etc., Act 1990 and with all rules, regulations and delegated legislation thereunder and all necessary licences and consents required thereunder have been obtained.

11.8 Use of property

There are no restrictive covenants or provisions, legislation, or orders, charges, restrictions, agreements, conditions or other matters which preclude the use of the Property for the purpose or purposes for which the Property is now used and each such use is the permitted use under the provisions of the Town and Country Planning Acts 1971 to 1990 and any statutory re-enactment thereof and all statutory instruments and regulations made thereunder and is in accordance with the requirements of any Local Authority and all restrictions, conditions and covenants imposed by or pursuant to the said Town and Country Planning Acts have been observed and performed and no agreements have been entered into under section 52 of the Town and Country Planning Act 1971, section 106 of the Town and Country Planning Act 1990 or section 33 of the Local Government (Miscellaneous Provisions) Act 1982 in respect of the Property.

11.9 Replies to enquiries

All replies by or on behalf of the Sellers to enquiries relating to the Property made by or on behalf of the Purchaser were when given and are now true complete accurate and correct.

11.10 Encumbrances

There are no options agreements for sale, mortgages, charges (whether specific or floating) rights of pre-emption or of first refusal affecting the Property.

11.11 Outgoings

The Property is not subject to the payment of any outgoings (except national non domestic rates and water rates and sewerage service charges). The Property abuts onto an adopted public highway maintainable at public expense to which it has access without crossing land not in the ownership of the Company.

11.12 Compulsory purchase orders

There are no compulsory purchase notices, orders or resolutions affecting the Property.

11.13 Properties previously occupied

The Company has no existing or contingent liabilities in respect of any properties previously occupied by it or in which it owned or held any interest (or as a surety for the obligations of any other person in relation to such property) including leasehold premises assigned surrendered or otherwise disposed of and the Company has not at any time received any indication whatsoever from any party that any claim has been made or will be made in respect of any such existing or contingent liabilities.

11.14 No further land and buildings

The Property comprises all the land and buildings owned, leased or occupied by the Company.

SCHEDULE 6

Claims procedure and determination and Sellers' safeguards

1.   NOTICE OF CLAIMS AND TIME LIMITS

No claim in respect of any breach of any of the Warranties (other than the Warranty in paragraph 1 of schedule 5) or pursuant to the Tax Covenants shall be made (except in any case of fraud, dishonesty or wilful non-disclosure) unless notice thereof has been given by or on behalf of the Buyer before:

1.1   in respect of any breach of any of the Warranties other than the Tax Warranties, the expiry of the period of [   ] years following Completion; or

1.2   pursuant to the Tax Covenants or in respect of any breach of any of the Tax Warranties, the expiry of the period of six months following the end of the accounting reference period of the Company in which the sixth anniversary of Completion falls.

2.   LIMITATION OF LIABILITY — MAXIMUM AND MINIMUM AMOUNTS

Except in any case of fraud, dishonesty or wilful non-disclosure:

2.1   the Sellers shall have no liability in damages in respect of any claim by the Buyer under any of the Warranties (except for claims in respect of any breaches of the Warranties in paragraph 1 of schedule 5) or the Tax Covenants if and to the extent that such liability would, when aggregated with the amount of any damages paid to the Buyer by [the Sellers] [that Seller] in respect of all and any such claims, exceed, the consideration received by the Sellers/[A] ([A] pounds) [the amount set against their names respectively in column [   ] of Schedule 1];

2.2   the Sellers shall have no liability in damages in respect of any claim by the Buyer under the Warranties unless such claim:

2.2.1   equals or exceeds, [B] ([B   ] pounds); and

2.2.2   would, when aggregated with all other such claims against the Sellers of, [B] ([B] pounds) or more equal or exceed, [C] ([C] pounds);

but any such claim shall not be limited to the excess over the amounts specified in this paragraph 2.2 and for the purposes of this paragraph 2.2 all claims arising out of the same subject-matter shall be treated as one single claim rather than as individual claims.

3.   NO PREJUDICE FROM PRIOR INVESTIGATION

The rights and remedies of the Buyer in respect of the Warranties and the Tax Covenants shall not be affected by Completion, by any investigation made by or on behalf of the Buyer into the affairs of the Company [or any of the Subsidiaries], by any actual, constructive or imputed knowledge of the Buyer (save as provided in the next following paragraph), by any rescission of (or failure to rescind) this Agreement or by any other event or matter except a specific waiver or release by the Buyer in accordance with the terms of this Agreement.

4.   DISCLOSURE LETTER

The Buyer shall not be entitled to bring any claim in respect of any breach of any of the Warranties if and to the extent that such inconsistency has been fairly disclosed in the Disclosure Letter with sufficient details to identify the nature and scope of the matters disclosed.

5.   SEPARATE WARRANTIES

Each Warranty is a separate warranty and shall not be limited or restricted by reference to or inference from any other Warranty.

6.   RIGHTS OF CONTRIBUTION

None of the Sellers shall if any claim is made against him by the Buyer under the terms of this Agreement, make any claim against the Company [or any of the Subsidiaries] or any director or any employee of the Company [or of any of the Subsidiaries] on which or on whom he may have relied before agreeing to any term of this Agreement or authorising any statement in the Disclosure Letter.

7.   COSTS

The Sellers shall indemnify the Buyer against any costs (including without limitation legal costs on a full indemnity basis) and expenses which it may incur, either before or after the instigation of any legal proceedings, in connection with any legal proceedings for breach of any of the Warranties or pursuant to the Tax Covenants in which judgment is given to the Buyer and the enforcement of any such judgment.

8.   REDUCTION OF CONSIDERATION

Any payment by any of the Sellers for breach of any of the Warranties or under the Tax Covenants shall constitute pound for pound a repayment of and reduction in the consideration for the Shares.

9.   NOTIFICATION

The Buyer shall as soon as reasonably practicable notify the Sellers (but any failure to give such notice shall not affect the rights of the Buyer) in writing of any claim made against it by a third party which may give rise to a claim for breach of Warranty (other than a claim relating to a Taxation).

10.   SET-OFF

Without prejudice to any other right or remedy which it may have, the Buyer shall have the right to set off any sum claimed by it under this Agreement or otherwise against any of its obligations hereunder not then fulfilled in which event any sum otherwise payable by it under this Agreement shall be reduced by the amount of such set-off.

11.   DAMAGES

In the event of a breach of the Warranties, the Sellers shall at the election of the Buyer pay to the Buyer on demand an amount equal to either:

11.1   the reduction caused in the value of the Shares; or

11.2   if the value of an asset of the Company is or becomes less than the value would have been had the breach not occurred, the reduction in the value of the asset; or

11.3   if the Company is subject to, or incurs, a liability or an increase in a liability, which it would not have been subject to, or would not have incurred, had the breach not occurred, then the amount of the liability or increased liability.

12.   DAMAGES FOR BREACH OF PENSION WARRANTIES

In determining the damages flowing from any breach of any Warranty in paragraph 9 of schedule 5, it shall be assumed that:

12.1   the Company [is/,and each of the Subsidiaries is,] under a liability to make whatever payments provide the benefits under the [Disclosed Schemes] (as defined in that paragraph) on the basis that any power to amend or discontinue any of the [Disclosed Schemes] is disregarded; and

12.2   the Company [is/,and each of the Subsidiaries is,] under a liability to provide and to continue to provide any benefit (including without limitation gratuities) which it now provides or is now proposing to provide and at the rate at which each respectively is now provided or proposed to be provided and to maintain without amendment any schemes or funds of a kind referred to in that paragraph which are now in existence.

13.   DOUBLE RECOVERY

The Sellers shall not be liable in respect of any breach of the Warranties if and to the extent that the losses occasioned thereby have been recovered under the Tax Covenants (and vice versa).

14.   NOTIFICATION

The Sellers shall notify the Buyer immediately they become aware of any fact or circumstance which constitutes or which may constitute a breach of the Warranties.

SCHEDULE 7

Conditional agreement

Part 1

Conditions

1.   **PRINCIPAL CONDITIONS**

The provisions of clauses 2, 3, 6, 7, 8 and 9 are conditional upon the fulfilment of all the following conditions not later than, and the continuance in full force and effect of their fulfilment at, [   ] or such later date as may be agreed in writing between the Sellers and the Buyer:

1.1   the passing of a[n ordinary] resolution in general meeting of the Buyer approving the transaction hereby agreed upon [or the Stock Exchange indicating to the Buyer in writing that it does not require the Buyer to submit such transaction to its members for approval;

1.2   no action having been taken or intimated by HM Government (or any department or agency thereof) or any third party to restrain the transaction hereby agreed upon;

1.3   no receiver and/or manager or administrator or administrative receiver having been appointed of the whole or any part of the assets and undertaking of the Company [or of any of the Subsidiaries];

1.4   no order having been made and no resolution having been passed for the winding- up of the Company [or of any of the Subsidiaries];

1.5   no application having been made for an administration order in respect of the Company [or of any of the Subsidiaries] and no petition having been presented and no notice having been given (whether or not by the Company [or of any of the Subsidiaries] and whether or not by any members) relating to the winding-up of the Company [or of any of the Subsidiaries];

1.6   [the [underwriting/placing] agreement dated the date of this Agreement between (1) [   ], (2) [   ] and (3) [   ] becoming or being declared unconditional and being completed in accordance with its terms except as to completion of the transaction hereby agreed upon and [   ] not having exercised any right to rescind the agreement thereby constituted; and]

1.7   the Buyer not having exercised any right to rescind this Agreement.

2.   **ESCROW COMPLETION**

2.1   The provisions of this Agreement are further conditional upon UKLA admitting the Consideration Shares to the Official List of the Stock Exchange and the Stock Exchange admitting the Consideration Shares to trading on the Stock Exchange's main market for listed securities, in each case, on, or within a period of three working days after, the Completion Date by the posting of the appropriate notices under] [Rule 3.2.7 of the Listing Rules published by the FSA] [the Consideration Shares being admitted to trading on the Alternative Investment Market of the Stock Exchange ("AIM") and such admission being announced in accordance with paragraph 16.6 of the AIM Admission Rules on, or within a period of 3 working days after, the Completion Date.]

2.2   The documents and things required to be delivered by the Buyer to the Sellers and vice versa at Completion shall be held in escrow pending the satisfaction of the condition contained in paragraph 2.1 and shall be irrevocably released from escrow forthwith upon the satisfaction of such condition.

3. THE PARTIES' ENDEAVOURS

Each of the parties shall use all reasonable endeavours to procure that all the provisions of this Agreement become unconditional in accordance with their terms, and the Buyer shall in particular, but without limitation, procure that the circular letter[s] to be sent to its respective shareholders relating to the resolution[s] referred to in paragraph[s] 1.1 [and 1.2] contains[s] [a] unanimous recommendation[s] by the directors of the Buyer and a confirmation that each intends to vote in favour of such resolution[s] in respect of his own holding and that the general meeting[s] referred to in paragraph 1.1 is held no later than [200].

4. NON-FULFILMENT

If any one or more of the Conditions are not fulfilled on or before [LONG STOP DATE], the agreement constituted by this Agreement shall thereupon become void and of no effect except as regards and without prejudice to any and all rights of action of the parties for any prior breach of any of the provisions of this Agreement. In that event the parties shall promptly return to one another all documents and other things already delivered in connection with the transaction hereby agreed upon.

5. WAIVER

The Buyer shall be entitled at its option to waive any one or more of the Conditions, and, if it does so, the Sellers shall be deemed to have done so also.

6. NOTICE OF FULFILMENT OF CONDITIONS

When the Conditions have been fulfilled, the Buyer shall forthwith give written notice to that effect to the Sellers, and such notice shall be conclusive and binding on the parties as to the fulfilment thereof.

Part 2

Obligations and events pending Completion

1. RESTRICTIONS

The Sellers shall procure that prior to Completion the Company [and the Subsidiaries] carry on business in the normal way so as to maintain the same as a going concern and that, except with the prior written consent of the Buyer, [neither] the Company [nor any of the Subsidiaries] will [not]:

1.1   grant any Encumbrance over any property or assets or dispose of any property or assets other than trading stock in the ordinary course of business on arm's length terms;

1.2   enter into or agree to enter into any Intellectual Property Agreement or enter into any assignment of any Intellectual Property;

1.3   grant or issue, or agree to grant or issue, any guarantee or indemnity;

1.4   create or issue, or agree to create or issue, any share or loan capital or any security convertible into share or loan capital or give or agree to give any option or other right in respect thereof;

1.5   acquire any asset on lease, lease-purchase, hire-purchase or deferred terms;

1.6   declare and/or pay any dividend or bonus or make any distribution of profits or assets;

1.7   pass any resolution of its members in general meeting;

1.8   do or allow to be done or omitted any act or thing which may render its financial position less favourable than at the date hereof;

1.9   do or allow to be done or omitted any act or thing which may reduce or vitiate the cover afforded by any current insurance policy;

1.10   enter into any transaction outside the ordinary course of its business; [nor]

1.11   do anything which would or might render in any way untrue or inaccurate or misleading the circular to the shareholders of the Buyer [and/or the prospectus in respect of the Buyer as contemplated by paragraph 7 of part 1 of this schedule].

2. ACCESS TO RECORDS

The Sellers shall at all times prior to Completion give to the Buyer and its professional advisers, in all cases with reasonable despatch upon request, all such information and make available for inspection all such documents and records as it or they may reasonably require and as may be under the control of the Sellers and so far as possible take and procure to be taken all such steps as may be required to implement the terms of this Agreement.

Part 3

Warranties

1. MAINTENANCE OF WARRANTIES

The Sellers shall procure that (save only as may be necessary to give effect to the terms of this Agreement) neither they nor the Company [nor any of the Subsidiaries] shall allow to occur, at any time at or before Completion, any change of circumstances:

1.1   such that, if the Warranties were repeated at that time, any of them would not then be true and accurate; and/or

1.2   which would entitle the Buyer, assuming this Agreement were unconditional and that Completion had taken place, to make a claim under the Tax Covenants.

2. SELLERS' DUTY TO DISCLOSE BREACHES

Each of the Sellers shall immediately disclose to the Buyer anything which comes to his notice before Completion which is or may be inconsistent with any of the Warranties.

3. RESCISSION

The Buyer shall not be bound to complete the acquisition of the Shares, and may by notice in writing to the Sellers' Solicitors rescind this Agreement without liability on its part, if:

3.1   on the date of this Agreement:

3.1.1   any of the Warranties are not true and accurate; and/or

3.1.2   the Buyer would be entitled, assuming this Agreement were unconditional and that Completion had taken place, to make a claim
under the Tax Covenants; and/or

3.2   at any time at or before Completion or the fulfilment of the Conditions there
is a change of circumstances:

3.2.1   such that, if the Warranties were repeated at that time any of them
would not then be true and accurate; and/or

3.2.2   which would entitle the Buyer, assuming this Agreement were
unconditional and that Completion had taken place, to make a
claim under the Tax Covenants; and/or

3.3   the Sellers are in breach of part 2 of this schedule

[and (in any such case) the amount which the Buyer is entitled to claim or
would be entitled to claim if the Warranties were repeated or if Completion
had taken place amounts to at least £[   ] ([   ] pounds).

4.   [Rescission shall be without prejudice to the rights of the [parties/Buyer] in respect of
any prior breach of any of the provisions of this Agreement.]

SCHEDULE 8

Pension Scheme

SCHEDULE 9

Calculation of Completion NAV

Part 1

Interpretation

In this Agreement the following words and expressions shall have the meanings set out opposite each respectively:

"the Completion NAV"	the net asset value of the [Company/Group] being the aggregate of :
	(a) the amounts paid up or credited as paid up on the issued share capital of the [Company/Group], and
	(b) any balance standing to the credit of the profit and loss account of the [Company/Group][3],
	less:
	(c) any debit balance on the profit and loss account of the [Company/Group][4]
	as stated by the Buyer's Accountants and agreed (or deemed to be agreed) by the Sellers' Accountants or, as the case may be, as determined by the Independent Accountant, in accordance with this schedule;
"the Completion Statement"	as defined in paragraph 3.1 of part 2 of this schedule;
"Independent Accountant"	a chartered accountant agreed upon by or on behalf of the Sellers and the Buyer or, if they fail to agree, nominated on the application at any time of the Sellers or of the Buyer by the President for the time being of the Institute of Chartered Accountants in England and Wales (the costs of such accountant, and, if applicable, of such President, in nominating such accountant to be borne as he may direct);
"the Buyer's Accountants"	[ ] of [ ];
"the Sellers' Accountants"	[ ] of [ ].

Part 2

Calculation

1.   [The Company [and each of the Subsidiaries] shall carry out a physical stock-take within days after the Completion Date at which a representative of each of the Buyer, the Buyer's Accountants, the Sellers and the Sellers' Accountants shall be entitled to be

---

[3] Consider whether it will be necessary to refer to other reserves, such as a revaluation reserve.

[4] Consider whether it will be necessary to refer to other reserves.

present and] the Buyer shall procure the [Company/Group] to prepare within [   ] days after the Completion Date accounts comprising a [consolidated] balance sheet dealing with the state of affairs of the [Company/Group] to the close of business on the Completion Date and a [consolidated] profit and loss account for the [Company/Group] for the period from the Accounts Date to the close of business on the Completion Date in accordance with part 3 of this schedule. ("the Completion Accounts").

2.   The Sellers shall provide such information and assistance as the Buyer and the [Company/Group] may reasonably require for the preparation of the Completion Accounts.

3.   The Buyer shall instruct the Buyer's Accountants to:

3.1   report on the Completion Accounts and on the basis of the Completion Accounts produce a dated statement of the Completion NAV ("the Completion Statement"); and

3.2   deliver the Completion Statement and provide access to all working papers to the Sellers' Accountants;

within [   ] days following delivery to the Buyer's Accountants of the Completion Accounts.

4.   If such queries and observations as the Sellers' Accountants raise within [twenty-one] days following delivery to them of the Completion Statement have not been dealt with to their satisfaction and reflected in any amendments within [twenty-one] days follow-ing delivery to the Buyer's Accountants of such queries and observations, it shall be open to the Sellers or the Buyer to request an Independent Accountant to determine the Completion NAV, and his determination shall, in the absence of manifest error, be final and binding on the parties.

5.   If the Sellers' Accountants do not raise any queries or observations in respect of the Completion Statement within [twenty-one] days following delivery thereof to them or if they agree the Completion Statement, then the Completion Statement shall be final and binding on the parties, and the Completion NAV shall be as set out in the Completion Statement.

6.   In stating, agreeing or determining (as the case may be) the Completion NAV, the Buyer's Accountants, the Sellers' Accountants and, if applicable, the Independent Accountant shall act as experts and not as arbitrators.

7.   The Buyer and the Sellers shall promptly provide and render or cause to be provided and rendered to the Buyer's Accountants, the Sellers' Accountants and the Independent Accountant such information and assistance as they or any of them may reasonably require to enable the Buyer's Accountants and the Sellers' Accountants to agree the Completion Statement (and to make the report referred to in paragraph 3) or to enable the Independent Accountant to determine the Completion NAV.

8.   The Sellers shall bear and pay all of the costs of the Sellers' Accountants, and the Buyer shall bear and pay all the costs of the Buyer's Accountants, incurred in each case in connection with the matters referred to in this schedule.

Part 3

Accounting principles, methods and bases

1.   Subject to paragraph 2, the Completion Accounts shall be prepared in accordance with:

1.1   generally accepted United Kingdom accounting principles, methods and bases; and

1.2   subject thereto (and to the extent they are disclosed in the Disclosure Letter or in the notes to the Accounts), the accounting principles, methods and bases applied and used in the preparation of the Accounts, consistently applied.

2.   The following specific provisions shall apply to the preparation of the Completion Accounts:

[Any detailed provisions to be inserted here]

Signed [as a deed] by

in the presence of:-

Signed [as a deed] by

in the presence of:-

Signed [as a deed] by

in the presence of:-

Signed [as a deed] by

in the presence of:-

Signed by [   ]

for and on behalf of

[   ]

LIMITED/PLC

in the presence of:

OR

Signed as a deed by [   ]

LIMITED/PLC] acting by two

directors or a director and its secretary:

director

[director/secretary]

OR

Signed as a deed by

[**]LIMITED/PLC**

acting by

[   ],

a Director, in the presence of:

APPENDIX A

ALTERNATIVE C—CONSIDERATION SHARES

3. **CONSIDERATION**

3.1 The consideration for the Shares shall be the allotment at Completion (credited as fully paid,) to the Sellers of [ ] Consideration Shares.

OR

3.1 The consideration for the Shares shall be the allotment at Completion (credited as fully paid) to the Sellers of the number of Consideration Shares (excluding fractions) nearest to but not less than A in the formula:

$$A = \frac{B}{C}$$

Where:

B = £[NOTIONAL CONSIDERATION]

C = whichever is the greater of:

    (a) the average of the middle market quotations for an ordinary share of [ ] in the capital of the Buyer [as shown by the daily Official List of the Stock Exchange/on the Alternative Investment Market] for each of the last [ ] days on which the Stock Exchange is open for business ending with the last such day but one before Completion; and

    (b) the nominal value of such an ordinary share.

3.2 **Dividends**

The Consideration Shares shall rank pari passu in all respects with the existing ordinary shares of [ ] each in the capital of the Buyer and shall carry the right to receive in full all dividends and other distributions declared, made or paid after the date of this Agreement [except that they shall not carry the right to participate in the [interim/final] dividend of the Buyer for the accounting reference period ending on [200] [declared/to be declared] on [or about] [200]].

3.3 **Retention of Consideration Shares**

Each of the Sellers undertake that he will not:-

3.3.1 except with the prior written consent of the Buyer, dispose of any interest in any of the Consideration Shares for a period of [ ] months following Completion; or

3.3.2 for a period of [ ] months thereafter, dispose of any interest in any such shares, except with the prior written consent of the Buyer, such consent not to be unreasonably withheld or delayed provided that any such disposal is (in the reasonable opinion of the Buyer) on an orderly market basis and made through the Buyer's [stockbroker for the time being] [Nominated Broker for the time being].

3.4 **Cash Alternative**

3.4.1 If the Buyer so elects, the consideration for the Shares may be either:

    3.4.1.1 wholly satisfied by a cash payment to the Sellers, in which event:

(a) on Completion the Buyer shall pay the amount described as B in clause 3.1; and

(b) clauses 3.1 to 3.3 inclusive shall not apply; or

3.4.1.2 partly satisfied by a cash payment to the Sellers of an amount which is less than the amount described as B in clause 3.1, in which event on Completion the Buyer shall pay that lesser amount and clauses 3.1 to 3.3 inclusive shall apply to the extent, and on the basis only, that the amount described as B in clause 3.1 is reduced by the amount of the cash payment made on Completion pursuant to this clause. **[This wording will require amendment if the first version of clause 3.1 applies.]**

3.5   **Cash payment**

3.5.1   If a cash payment is made on Completion pursuant to clause 3.4:

3.5.1.1 it shall be made [by way of a banker's draft drawn on a UK clearing bank in favour of the [Sellers/Sellers' Solicitors]] by telegraphic transfer to the following account:-

Bank:

Branch:

Sort Code:

Account Name:

Account Number:]; and

3.5.1.2 the Sellers' Solicitors' receipt for such payment shall be a good and sufficient discharge to the Buyer, and the Buyer shall not be further concerned as to the application of any monies so paid

PRECEDENT 3

**Assets Sale and
Purchase Agreement
Version A — For use when
debtors and creditors are
being transferred to the Buyer**

DATED _____ 200

(1) [**LIMITED/PLC]**

(2) [**LIMITED/PLC]**

(3) [**LIMITED/PLC]**

ASSETS SALE AND PURCHASE AGREEMENT

-relating to-

[DESCRIPTION OF BUSINESS]

VERSION A—FOR USE WHEN DEBTORS AND CREDITORS ARE BEING TRANSFERRED TO THE BUYER

This Agreement is made on   200

between:

(1)   [**[LIMITED/PLC]]**, a company registered in England
           under number [   ], whose registered office is at [
           ] ("the Seller"); [and]

(2)   [**[LIMITED/PLC]]**, a company registered in England
           under number [   ], whose registered office is at [
           ] ("the Buyer")[; and

(3)   [**[LIMITED/PLC]]**, a company registered in England
           under number [   ], whose registered office is at [
           ] ("the Guarantor")].

It is agreed as follows:

1.   **INTERPRETATION**

           In this Agreement:

           1.1   The following words and expressions shall have the meanings set out or
                      referred to opposite each respectively:

                      "the Accounts"   the audited accounts of the Seller, comprising an
                                                  audited balance sheet as at the Accounts Date
                                                  and an audited profit and loss account for the
                                                  financial period ended on the Accounts Date,
                                                  together with the reports of the directors and
                                                  auditors, any cash flow statements of source and
                                                  application of funds and all notes thereto;

                      "the Accounts Date"   [200];

                      "Accruals"   the Seller's obligations in respect of all prepay-
                                                  ments made to the Seller in connection with the
                                                  Business [or the Property/(but not the Property)]
                                                  before the Transfer Point [and, to the extent not
                                                  included among "Creditors", all liabilities in
                                                  respect of expenses incurred by the Seller in
                                                  connection with the Business before the Transfer
                                                  Point and remaining unpaid as at the Transfer
                                                  Point] [, all as shown in the Completion
                                                  Statement][1];

                      "the Act"   the Companies Act 2006;

                      "the 1985 Act"   the Companies Act 1985

                      "the Applicable Data   the Data Protection Acts 1986 and 1998 and the
                      Protection Laws"   Telecommunications (Data Protection and
                                                  Privacy) (Direct Marketing) Regulations 1998;

                      "the Assets"   the assets listed in clause 2;

                      "the Bank"   Bank PLC (branch);

---

[1] This definition will have to be carefully considered alongside the provisions regarding the preparation of
any Completion Statement/Completion Accounts. Accruals and pre-payments may in practice be dealt with
in the accounting policies used in the preparation of those accounts but it is important to make sure that all
such liabilities are picked up either as Accruals or as Creditors.

"Book Debts"   together all amounts owing to the Seller in connection with the Business at the Transfer Point (whether or not invoiced before the Transfer Point and whether or not due and payable at the Transfer Point) and all Prepayments, but excluding any such amounts as are referred to in clause 3;

"the Books and Records"   the books and records maintained by the Seller relating to the Business, the Assets and the Employees other than the Retained Books and Records;

"the Business"   the business of [
                       ] carried on by the Seller at the Transfer Point at and from the Property [and elsewhere];

"Business Day"   any day (other than Saturday) on which clearing banks are open for normal banking business in sterling in the City of London;

"the Buyer's Solicitors"   [   ] of [   ] or any successor firm;

"Completion"   completion of the sale and purchase of the Business and the Assets in accordance with clause 6;

"the Companies Acts"   as defined in section 2 of the Act;

"Completion NAV"   as defined in schedule 11;

"Completion Statement"   as defined in schedule 11;

["the Conditions"   the conditions set out in part 1 of schedule 10 (each a "Condition");]

"Confidential Information"   all secret or confidential commercial, financial and technical information, know-how, trade secrets, inventions, computer software and other information whatsoever and in whatever form or medium and whether disclosed orally or in writing, together with all reproductions in whatsoever form or medium and any part or parts of it;

"Contracts" (each a "Contract")

ALTERNATIVES

EITHER

all the contracts and agreements listed in schedule 1 to the extent that they remain to be completed at the Transfer Point;

OR

all the contracts and agreements [, whether written or oral,] remaining to be completed at the Transfer Point and entered into by the Seller in the ordinary course of the Business, including

	the Listed Intellectual Property Agreements, but excluding all obligations under any such contracts and agreements in respect of goods delivered or services supplied prior to the Transfer Point, the agreements under which the Third Party Assets are held as listed in schedule 6, (to which the provisions of clause 21 shall apply), the Employees' contracts of employment (to which the provisions of clause 11 shall apply) and Creditors;
"Creditors"	all amounts owing by the Seller to creditors in connection with the Business [or the Property / (but not the Property)] at the Transfer Point (whether or not invoiced before the Transfer Point and whether or not due and payable at the Transfer Point), including wages and salaries down to the Transfer Point and Accruals [, all as shown in the Completion Statement]);
	but excluding in each case:
	all amounts owing to the Seller's bankers at the Transfer Point;
	any liabilities for Taxation;
	any VAT payable to H M Revenue & Customs in respect of taxable supplies made by or to the Seller in connection with the Business before the Transfer Point; and
	all sums owed at the Transfer Point by the Seller to other Members of the Seller's Group at the date of this Agreement [otherwise than in the normal course of trading];[2]
"the Disclosure Letter"	the letter having the same date as this Agreement from the Seller['s Solicitors] to the Buyer['s Solicitors];
"the Disclosed Schemes"	the GPP, the Life Assurance Scheme, the Pension Scheme(s), the Personal Pension Scheme(s) and the Stakeholder Scheme;
"Employee"	each person employed by the Seller and engaged in the Business at the Transfer Point and who is listed in schedule 2;
"Encumbrance"	any equity, right to acquire, option or right of pre-emption, mortgage, charge, pledge, lien, assignment, title retention or any other security interest, agreement or arrangement, whether monetary or not;

[2] This definition needs very close attention to avoid the Buyer taking on unintended liabilities and the Seller retaining liabilities which it intended to pass to the Buyer. It needs to be considered too alongside the definitions of Plant and Stocks and any provisions for the apportionment of outgoings. From the Buyer's point of view, it is helpful to say that liabilities will only be assumed to the extent that provision is made for them in the Completion Statement/Completion Accounts.

"Escrow Account"	a joint deposit account with the Bank in the joint names of the Buyer's Solicitors and the Seller's Solicitors;
"Escrow Agreement"	the agreement in the Agreed Terms to be entered into by the Seller, the Buyer, the Seller's Solicitors and the Buyer's Solicitors relating to the operation of the Escrow Account;
"FRS"	a financial reporting standard in force at any material time as issued by the Accounting Standards Board;
"Goodwill"	the goodwill relating to the Business and the exclusive right for the Buyer to represent itself as carrying on the Business in succession to the Seller [and to use the name "[ ]"];
"GPP"	means the group personal pension plan under-written by **[name of provider]**;
"ICTA"	the Income & Corporation Taxes Act 1988;
"Intellectual Property"	(a) patents, trade marks, service marks, registered designs, applications and rights to apply for any of those rights, trade, business and company names, internet domain names and e-mail addresses, unregistered trade marks and service marks, copyrights, database rights, know-how, rights in designs and inventions;
	(b) rights under licences, consents, orders, statutes or otherwise in relation to a right in paragraph (a);
	(c) rights of the same or similar effect or nature as or to those in paragraphs (a) and (b) which now or in the future may subsist; and
	(d) the right to sue for past infringements of any of the foregoing rights;
"Intellectual Property Agreements"	the agreements or arrangements relating (wholly or partly) to Intellectual Property or to the dis-closure, use, assignment or patenting of any invention, discovery, improvement, process, for-mulae or other know-how;
"Intellectual Property Rights"	all Intellectual Property owned, used or required to be used by the Seller in connection I with the Business;
"Lease"	any lease under which any of the Leasehold Property is held by the Seller;
"Leasehold Property"	any leasehold property comprised within the Property;
"Life Assurance Scheme"	means the **[insert name of group life assurance scheme]** underwritten by **[name of provider]**;
"Listed Intellectual Property"	the Intellectual Property Rights listed in schedule 3;

"Listed Intellectual Property Agreements"	the Intellectual Property Agreements listed in schedule 3;
["the Management Accounts"	the unaudited management accounts of the Seller for the period from the Accounts Date to [200], a copy of which is attached to the Disclosure Letter;]
["Member of the Seller's Group"	any company within the Seller's Group from time to time;]
"Pension Scheme(s)"	means **[insert name of scheme(s)—to be used for occupational pension schemes]**;
"Personal Pension Scheme(s)"	means **[insert description of each scheme—to be used for personal pension schemes excluding group personal pensions]**;
"Plant"	all the plant, machinery, equipment, furniture, fixtures and fittings, tools, vehicles and spare parts and other tangible assets held [on the Property] at the Transfer Point by [or on behalf of] the Seller for use in connection with the Business including, but without limitation, all the items listed in schedule 4 but excluding the Third Party Assets;[3]
"Prepayments"	all prepayments made by the Seller in connection with the Business [or the Property/(but not the Property)] before the Transfer Point;[4]
"Proceedings"	any legal action or proceedings arising out of or in connection with this Agreement;
"Property"	[the property/each of the properties] briefly described in schedule 5;
"the Property Conditions"	[the Law Society's Standard Commercial Property Conditions (Revision)];
"the Regulations"	the Transfer of Undertakings (Protection of Employment) Regulations 2006;
"Release"	any release, waiver or compromise or any other arrangement of any kind having similar or analogous effect;
"the Retained Books and Records"	the accounting records relating to the Business required to be kept by the Seller under section 386 of the Act [,the VAT Records and books and records relating to assets or liabilities of the Seller not agreed to be acquired or assumed by the Buyer under this Agreement and the statutory books of the Seller;

[3] It will be necessary to consider whether the words in square brackets are appropriate—for example, there may be Plant which is being serviced or repaired or there may be moulds or tools held by customers.

[4] This definition will have to be considered in the context of the provisions regarding the preparation of the Completion Statement/Completion Accounts. Accruals and Prepayments may in practice be dealt with via the accounting policies to be used but it is important to ensure that all such liabilities are picked up either as Accruals or as Creditors.

"the Seller's Group"	together the Seller and any company including for this purpose any undertaking (within the meaning of section 1161(1) of the Act) within its group (within the meaning of section 474(1) of the Act);
"the Seller's Solicitors"	[ ] of [ ] or any successor firm;
"SSAP"	a statement of standard accounting practice in force at any material time as issued by the Accounting Standards Committee and adopted by the Accounting Standards Board
"Stakeholder Scheme"	means the stakeholder pension scheme designated by [the Seller] and underwritten by **[name of provider]**;
["the Stock Exchange"	the London Stock Exchange plc;]
"Stocks"	all the stocks of raw materials, components, work-in-progress, finished and unfinished goods, bought-in goods, consumables and packaging materials held by [or on behalf of] the Seller [on the Property] at the Transfer Point for use in the Business which have not been invoiced by the Seller before the Transfer Point;
"Taxation"	corporation tax, advance corporation tax, income tax, capital gains tax, value added tax, stamp duty, stamp duty reserve tax, customs and other import duties, vehicle duty, general or business rates, water rates, national insurance, social security or similar contributions, and any sum payable to any person as a result of the operation of any enactment anywhere in the world relating to taxation and all penalties, charges and interest relating to any claim for taxation or resulting from any failure to comply with any enactment relating to taxation;
"Taxation Authority"	any authority, whether of the United Kingdom or elsewhere, competent to impose, assess or collect Taxation, including HM Revenue & Customs;
"Tax Warranties"	the Warranties contained in paragraph 11 of schedule 7;
"the Third Party Assets"	those assets which are used in the Business, are in the possession of the Seller subject to leasing, rental, hire or hire-purchase agreements and are listed in schedule 6;
"the Transfer Point"	**ALTERNATIVES**
	EITHER
	the close of business (which for this purpose shall be deemed to be 5.00 pm) on the date of this Agreement;

OR

	the close of business (which for this purpose shall be deemed to be 5.00 pm) on [the [third] Business Day after] the date upon which the last of the Conditions to be satisfied or waived is satisfied or waived;
"UKLA"	the United Kingdom Listing Authority;
"VAT"	value added tax;
"the VAT Act"	the Value Added Tax Act 1994;
"VAT Records"	all of the books and records referred to in section 49 of the VAT Act which relate to the Business
"the Warranties"	the warranties and representations set out in schedule 7;
"Warranty"	one of the Warranties (and the word "Warranty" followed by a number shall be deemed to be a reference to the paragraph of schedule 7 with that number).

1.2   References to the Property shall, where the context so admits or requires, be construed as references to all properties briefly described in schedule 5 and each of them and each and every part of each of them, and references to Leasehold Property shall, where the context so admits or requires, be construed as references to all Property which is leasehold.

1.3   Unless the context otherwise expressly requires, words and expressions which are otherwise defined in the Companies Acts shall have the same meaning when used in this Agreement, but "company" shall mean and include both "company" and "body corporate" as in each case defined in the Act.

1.4   A reference to any statutory or other legislative provision shall be interpreted as a reference to that provision as in force at the date of this Agreement and, additionally, where the context so permits: —

1.4.1   in respect of any earlier date, as a reference to any and all provisions in force at that earlier date of which it is a re-enactment; and

1.4.2   in respect of any later date, as a reference to any and all provisions in force at that later date which are a re-enactment of it;

in each case, whether with or without modification.

1.5   The schedules form an integral part of this Agreement.

1.6   A reference to any gender shall include the other and neuter gender and a reference to a "person" includes a reference to any individual, firm, company, corporation or other body corporate, government, state or agency of a state or any joint venture, association or partnership, works council or employee representative body (whether or not having separate legal personality).

1.7   A document referred to as being in "the Agreed Terms" shall be in the form of that document signed or initialled for identification by or on behalf of the parties.

1.8   The headings are inserted for convenience only and shall not affect the construction of this Agreement.

1.9   Any Warranty qualified by the expression "to the best of the Seller's knowledge and belief" or "so far as the Seller is aware" or any similar expression shall, be deemed to include knowledge, information and belief which the Seller has or which the Seller would have had if it had made all reasonable enquiries, and includes, the knowledge, information and belief of each of:

1.9.1   the professional advisers who act, or at the relevant time acted, for the Seller; and

1.9.2   the directors, company secretary, financial controller and general managers of the Seller [, and] [of the Guarantor] [and of each Member of the Seller's Group]

and of any other person of whom it would be reasonable to make such enquiry or of whom it is stated that enquiry has been made.

1.10   A person shall be deemed to be connected with another if that person is connected with such other within the meaning of section 839 of ICTA.

1.11   "Associate" has the meaning given by section 435 of the Insolvency Act 1986.

1.12   References to "indemnify" and "indemnifying" any person against any circumstance include indemnifying and keeping him indemnified from and against all liabilities, losses, claims, demands, damages, costs, expenses and interest which he may suffer or incur in connection with or arising out of that circumstance.

1.13   Words shall not be given a restrictive meaning: —

1.13.1   if they are introduced by the word "other", by reason of the fact that they are preceded by words indicating a particular class of act, matter or thing; or

1.13.2   by reason of the fact that they are followed by particular examples intended to be embraced by those general words.

1.14   The word "Notice" includes any notice, demand, consent or other communication.

1.15   References to time shall mean London time unless otherwise stated.

1.16   A reference to any English legal term for any action, remedy, method of judicial proceeding, legal document, legal status, court, official or any legal concept or thing shall in respect of any jurisdiction other than England be deemed to include what most nearly approximates in that jurisdiction to the English legal term and a reference to any English statute shall be construed so as to include equivalent or analogous laws of any other jurisdiction.

2.   [CONDITIONAL] AGREEMENT FOR SALE AND PURCHASE

On and subject to [the Conditions and] the [other] terms of this Agreement, the Seller shall sell with full title guarantee and the Buyer shall buy, with effect from the Transfer Point and free of any Encumbrance, the Business as a going concern and the Assets, being:

2.1   the Goodwill;

2.2   the Stocks;

2.3   the Plant;

2.4   the benefit (subject to the burden) of the Contracts;

2.5   the Intellectual Property Rights;

2.6   the Property;

2.7   the Book Debts;

2.8   the Books and Records; and

2.9   all rights of the Seller against third parties (including without limitation under warranties, representations and indemnities and under any policies of insurance) in respect of any of the assets specified in clauses 2.1 to 2.8 inclusive and in respect of any goods incorporated therein or used thereon or any services performed in relation thereto.

3.   EXCLUDED ASSETS

The following are excluded from the transaction hereby agreed upon:

3.1   all and any shares or other securities in any companies held by the Seller;

3.2   all cash in hand or at bank and all cheques and other securities representing them, in each case as at the Transfer Point, other than those, if any, representing the Book Debts;

3.3   any credit or refund of any Taxation in respect of supplies made to or by the Seller or profits or gains made or deemed to have been made by the Seller, in each case before the Transfer Point;

3.4   all sums owed at the Transfer Point to the Seller by other Members of the Seller's Group at the date of this Agreement [otherwise than in the normal course of trading];

3.5   the Retained Books and Records; and

3.6   the Third Party Assets.

For the avoidance of doubt, the amounts referred to in clauses 3.3 and 3.4 shall not be regarded as Book Debts for the purposes of this Agreement.[5]

4.   CONSIDERATION

ALTERNATIVE A—FIXED CASH SUM WITHOUT RETENTION

4.1   The consideration for the Business and the Assets shall be the Buyer's undertakings contained in this Agreement in relation to Creditors and the payment by the Buyer to the Seller of the sum of £[   ] ([pounds], which shall be paid in cash on Completion.

4.2   The Seller's Solicitors' receipt for the cash payment referred to in clause 4.1 shall be a good and sufficient discharge to the Buyer and the Buyer shall not be further concerned as to the application of the monies so paid.

4.3   The Assets shall for the purposes of the transaction hereby agreed upon have the values set opposite them respectively:—

Goodwill	£[ ]
Stocks	£[ ]
Plant	£[ ]
Contracts	£[ ]

---

[5] It is normal for the sale and purchase only to include normal trade debtors and it may well therefore be appropriate to exclude refunds of VAT or other Taxation and sums owing by other group companies, but there may be normal trading debts from other group companies which in some cases will be included.

Intellectual Property Rights	£[	]
Property*	£[	]
Book Debts	£[	]
Books and Records	£1	
The rights referred to in Clause 2.9	£1	

* apportioned as indicated in Schedule 5.

ALTERNATIVE B—COMPLETION ACCOUNTS WITH JOINT ACCOUNT

4.1 Amount

The Consideration for the Business and the Assets shall be the Buyer's undertakings contained in this Agreement in relation to Creditors and the payment by the Buyer to the Seller of a sum equal to the Completion NAV [up to a maximum of £   (pounds)] ("the Cash Consideration")].

4.2 First Payments—on Completion

On Completion and pending the later agreement or determination of the Completion NAV, the Buyer shall pay:—

4.2.1   the sum of £[   ] (pounds) to the Seller's Solicitors (on behalf of the Seller) on account of the Cash Consideration; and

4.2.2   the sum of [£   ] [(pounds)] ("the Principal Sum") to the Buyer's Solicitors and the Seller's Solicitors jointly for placing into the Escrow Account to be held under a mandate in the Agreed Terms and to be held and dealt with as set out in this clause 4.

4.3 Second payment—following calculation of Completion NAV

On the third Business Day after the date on which the Completion NAV is agreed or determined in accordance with schedule 11:—

4.3.1   the Buyer shall pay to the Seller's Solicitors a sum equal to the balance (if any) of the Cash Consideration, after deducting the amount paid pursuant to clause 4.2.1, such payment to be satisfied by the payment of an equivalent sum from the Escrow Account;

4.3.2   if the Cash Consideration exceeds the amount paid to the Seller pursuant to clauses 4.2.1 and 4.3.1, the Buyer shall pay the amount of the excess to the Seller's Solicitors;

4.3.3   the balance of the Principal Sum following any payment from the Escrow Account pursuant to clause 4.3.1 (or, if no such payment falls to be made, the whole of the Principal Sum) shall be paid to the Buyer from the Escrow Account.

4.4 The Account

4.4.1   All interest earned on the Escrow Account shall accrue and be paid to the Seller and/or the Buyer in the proportions in which they respectively become entitled to the Principal Sum and shall be paid at the same time as any payment of all or any part of the Principal Sum is made from the Escrow Account.

4.4.2   The Seller and the Buyer shall procure that their respective solicitors shall make any payment which is required to be made from the Escrow Account pursuant to the provisions of clause 4.3.

4.5   **Clawback from first payment**

4.5.1   If the amount paid pursuant to clause 4.2.1 exceeds the Cash Consideration then, on the third Business Day referred to in clause 4.3, the Seller shall repay to the Buyer a sum equal to the excess plus interest on an amount equal to the excess at the rate on which interest has been earned on the Escrow Account, such interest to accrue from the Completion Date until that third Business Day.

4.5.2   If the Seller defaults in making payment of any sum due under clause 4.5.1, it shall pay interest on the amount in question calculated on a daily basis from the due date until the date of actual payment (as well after any judgment as before) at the rate of 4% per year above the base rate from time to time in force of the Bank.

4.6   **Method of Payment**

4.6.1   Unless otherwise specified, any payment required to be made by the Buyer to the Seller pursuant to this clause 4 shall be made by way of a [banker's draft drawn on a UK clearing bank in favour of the Seller/Seller's Solicitors/telegraphic transfer to the following account:

Bank:

Branch:

Sort Code:

Account Name:

Account Number:]

4.6.2   The Seller's Solicitors' receipt for any sums payable by the Buyer pursuant to this clause 4 shall be a good and sufficient discharge of the Buyer's obligation to make the payment in question and the Buyer shall not be further concerned as to the application of any sums so paid.

4.6.3   Any sum payable to the Buyer pursuant to this clause 4 shall, unless otherwise specified, be paid by way of a banker's draft drawn on a UK clearing bank in favour of the [Buyer/Buyer's'[s] Solicitors]/telegraphic transfer to the following account:

Bank:

Branch:

Sort Code:

Account Name:

Account Number:]

5.   **VALUE ADDED TAX**

5.1   The Purchase Price payable hereunder is stated exclusive of VAT.

5.2   The Seller warrants to the Buyer that it is [and undertakes with the Buyer that it will at Completion be] duly registered for VAT purposes.

5.3   The Seller warrants to and undertakes with the Buyer that:

5.3.1   it has not made, and will not before Completion make, for VAT purposes any election to tax in respect of the Property; and

5.3.2   there are no, and will not at Completion be any, new (as defined in note 4 of item 1 of group 1 in schedule 9 to the VAT Act) or uncompleted freehold commercial buildings or civil engineering works included in the sale and purchase hereby agreed upon.[6]

5.4   The Buyer warrants to the Seller that [it is [and undertakes with the Seller that it will at Completion be] duly registered/it is by virtue of the transaction hereby agreed upon liable to be duly registered] for VAT purposes.

5.5   The parties shall use all reasonable endeavours to procure that the transaction hereby agreed upon is deemed to be a transfer of a business as a going concern for the purposes of section 49 and paragraphs 8(1)(a) and 8(2)(b) of schedule 4 to the VAT Act and article 5(1) of the Value Added Tax (Special Provisions) Order 1995 and is treated neither as a supply of goods nor as a supply of services.

5.6   **ALTERNATIVES**

EITHER

The Seller and the Buyer intend that section 49 of the VAT Act shall apply to the transaction hereby agreed upon but they do not intend to make a joint application to HM Revenue and Customs for the Buyer to be registered for VAT under the VAT registration number of the Seller, pursuant to Regulation 6 (1) (d) of the VAT Regulations 1995.

OR

5.6.1   The Seller and the Buyer intend that section 49 of the VAT Act shall apply to the transaction hereby agreed upon and they intend to make a joint application to HM Revenue and Customs for the Buyer to be registered for VAT under the VAT registration number of the Seller, pursuant to Regulation 6 (1) (d) of the VAT Regulations 1995. If HM Revenue and Customs register the Buyer under the Seller's VAT registration number.

IF BUYER TO KEEP VAT RECORDS

5.6.1   The Seller shall, on Completion, deliver to the Buyer all VAT Records;

5.6.2   The Seller shall not make any request to HM Revenue & Customs for the VAT Records to be preserved by the Seller rather than the Buyer;

5.6.3   The Buyer shall preserve the VAT Records for such period as may be required by law and, during that period, permit the Seller reasonable access to them to inspect or make copies of them; and

5.6.4   The Buyer may fulfil its obligations under clause 5.6.3 by procuring that any future transferee of the Business or any other person preserves the VAT Records and permits reasonable access as mentioned in that clause, in which case the Buyer shall notify the Seller of the name of that person.

OR [IF THE SELLER TO KEEP VAT RECORDS—these are alternative versions of 5.6.1–5.6.4]

5.6.1   The Seller shall immediately make a request to HM Revenue & Customs for a direction that the VAT Records be preserved by the Seller;

---

[6] The "going concern" exemption may not be available if this warranty cannot be given.

5.6.2   The Seller shall promptly notify the Buyer of the result of that request;

5.6.3   If HM Revenue & Customs do not grant the request referred to in clause 5.9.1, the Seller shall deliver the VAT Records to the Buyer as soon as reasonably practicable; and

5.6.4   If clause 5.9.3 applies, the Buyer shall:

5.6.4.1   preserve the VAT Records in the United Kingdom for such period as may be required by law;

5.6.4.2   so long as it preserves the VAT Records, permit the Seller reasonable access to them to inspect or make copies of them; and

5.6.4.3   not at any time cease to preserve the VAT Records without giving the Seller a reasonable opportunity to inspect and remove such of them as the Seller wishes.]

5.7   If H M Revenue & Customs shall determine in writing that VAT is payable on the whole or any part of the consideration payable hereunder, the Buyer shall, within [fourteen] days following delivery to it by the Seller of an invoice in respect thereof valid for VAT purposes and a copy of H M Revenue & Customs' written determination to that effect, pay to the Seller the amount of VAT as so assessed by H M Revenue & Customs.

5.8   [The Seller and the Buyer acknowledge that the provisions of Section 47(2)(a) of the VAT Act will apply in respect of transactions made by the Seller as agent for the Buyer in the period between the Transfer Point and Completion and will issue VAT invoices accordingly].[7]

6.   COMPLETION

6.1   [Schedule 10 shall apply between the entering into of this Agreement and Completion].

6.2   Completion shall[, subject to schedule 10,] take place on the day of the Transfer Point at [the offices of the Buyer's Solicitors].

6.3   On Completion the Seller shall:

6.3.1   execute, or procure execution (as the case may be) of, and deliver to the Buyer:

6.3.1.1   assignments in the Agreed Terms in respect of the Goodwill, the Intellectual Property, the Book Debts and the rights specified in clause 2.9;

6.3.1.2   a [transfer] [conveyance] in the Agreed Terms in respect of the Property;

6.3.1.3   [a transfer] [an assignment] in the Agreed Terms in respect of the Leasehold Property;

6.3.1.4   a licence to assign the Lease in the Agreed Terms, duly executed by the landlord of the Leasehold Property;

6.3.2   deliver duly executed releases and letters of non-crystallisation in the Agreed Terms in respect of all fixed and floating charges affecting any of the Assets;

6.3.3   deliver the Disclosure Letter duly signed;

[7] This is only relevant where there is a gap between the Transfer Point and Completion.

6.3.4   give vacant possession of the Property to the Buyer; and

6.3.5   deliver to the Buyer:

6.3.5.1   the Books and Records; and

6.3.5.2   possession of such of the Assets as are capable of passing by delivery and of the Third Party Assets

6.4   On Completion, the Seller and the Buyer shall enter into an election under section 198 of the Capital Allowances Act 2001 in the Agreed Terms.

6.5   On Completion the Buyer shall make the payment[s] referred to in clause [4.1/4.2 as provided in clause 4].

6.6   The Buyer shall not be obliged to complete the purchase of any of the Assets unless the purchase of all of the Assets is completed simultaneously.

6.7   If in any respect the preceding provisions of this clause 6 are not complied with on the Completion Date, then (without prejudice to any and all rights of action it may have pursuant to the terms of this Agreement or otherwise the party not in default may:

6.7.1   defer Completion to a date not more than 28 days after the Completion Date (and so that the provisions of this clause 6.7, apart from this clause 6.7.1, shall apply to Completion as so deferred); or

6.7.2   proceed to Completion so far as practicable (without prejudice to its rights hereunder or otherwise); or

6.7.3   rescind this Agreement by notice in writing to the Seller.

7.   AGENCY

As from the Transfer Point, the Seller shall be deemed to have acted as agent for the Buyer, it being the intention of the parties that the benefit of the trading activities of the Business shall accrue to the Buyer from the Transfer Point. Accordingly, the Buyer shall be entitled to the right to receive payment for goods or services supplied by the Seller in connection with the Business after the Transfer Point and the Seller shall account to the Buyer on Completion for any payments received by the Seller in respect of goods or services so supplied. In respect of the period between the Transfer Point and Completion, the Seller shall arrange for the interest of the Buyer to be noted on the policies relating to its public liability, product liability, employers' liability, motor and business interruption insurances and any other insurances where this is possible.[8]

8.   CREDITORS

8.1   The Buyer shall discharge the Creditors on their due dates for payment and shall assume responsibility for all Accruals.

8.2   The Buyer shall not be required to take on or discharge any obligation or liability of the Seller except for any which it expressly agrees in this Agreement to take on or discharge.

9.   CONTRACTS

9.1   The Buyer shall, subject to clause 9.3, perform and fulfil the Contracts on its own account with effect from the Transfer Point in the place of the Seller.

9.2   If the benefit of any of the Contracts cannot be assigned without the consent of a third party:

---

[8] This is only relevant where there is a gap between the Transfer Point and Completion.

9.2.1   nothing in this Agreement shall operate as an assignment or purported assignment of the benefit of such Contracts;

9.2.2   the parties shall each use all reasonable endeavours to obtain all necessary consents to assignment as soon as possible after the Transfer Point; and

9.2.3   from the Transfer Point and until such consents are obtained the Seller shall hold the benefit of the Contracts concerned in trust for the Buyer, the Buyer shall at its own cost and for its own benefit perform and fulfil the Contracts concerned as the Seller's agent and the Seller shall promptly account to the Buyer without deduction or set-off for any sums it may receive from any third party in respect thereof.

9.3   Subject to the provisions of clause 9.1, the Seller shall remain liable under the Contracts in respect of all goods and services supplied by or to it pursuant thereto before the Transfer Point and generally under the Contracts to the extent that they have then been performed or should then have been performed, and shall indemnify the Buyer against any act or omission of the Seller before the Transfer Point in relation to any of the Contracts.

9.4   The Seller shall at the request of the Buyer give to the Buyer all reasonable assistance to enable the Buyer to enforce each of the Contracts against the other contracting party or parties.

10.   DEFECTIVE GOODS

The Buyer shall satisfy all legally valid claims which may be made against the Seller (and which are notified in writing to the Buyer together with appropriate evidence as to their validity) or against the Buyer for the repair or replacement of, or for reimbursement of the price of, defective goods sold by the Seller, and the Seller shall in any such case reimburse to the Buyer (at cost) the cost to the Buyer of performing its obligations under this clause 10.

11.   EMPLOYEES

11.1   The parties acknowledge that the sale of the Business and the Assets pursuant to this Agreement is a relevant transfer under the Regulations and accordingly the employment of each Employee shall at the Transfer Point be transferred to and taken over by the Buyer under the Regulations.

11.2   The Seller shall indemnify the Buyer against all liabilities arising out of:

11.2.1   the employment of any Employee during the period ending at the Transfer Point or the employment at any time (whether or not by the Seller) of any employee of the Seller who is not an Employee or of any former employee of the Seller;

11.2.2   the termination before or at the Transfer Point of the employment of any Employee;

11.2.3   the termination at any time (and whether or not by the Seller) of the employment of any employee of the Seller who is not an Employee or of any former employee of the Seller;

11.2.4   any act or omission of the Seller which is deemed by virtue of the Regulations to be an act or omission of the Buyer;

11.2.5   any industrial or other work-related illness or injury suffered or allegedly suffered by any Employee in respect of or relating to any period ending on or before the Transfer Point;

11.2.6 any bonus payable to any Employee in respect of the financial year ended [200] (which shall, as between the Seller and the Buyer, remain the responsibility of the Seller);

11.2.7 any failure by the Seller to comply with its obligations under regulation 11 or regulation 13 of the Regulations or under Part IV of the Trade Union & Labour Relations (Consolidation) Act 1992;

and/or otherwise arising by virtue of the Regulations.

11.3 The Buyer will indemnify the Seller against all liabilities arising out of the employment or termination of employment of any Employee after the Transfer Point.

11.4 [Without prejudice to the provisions of part 3 of schedule 11, the Seller shall remain liable for all wages, salaries and other emoluments payable to the Employees in respect of all periods down to the Transfer Point and appropriate Accruals will be made (or, where relevant, such items will be treated as Prepayments) in the Completion Statement in respect of salaries payable in respect of the period from [ ] to [ ] and in respect of holiday entitlements as at the Transfer Point.][9]

11.5 The Seller represents and warrants to the Buyer that it has provided, and undertakes that it shall provide, to the Buyer such information as the Buyer may from time to time request in writing in order to enable it to verify compliance with the laws and regulations referred to in clause 11.2.7.

11.6 Schedule 8 shall apply in relation to pension arrangements in respect of the Employees.

12. PROPERTY

12.1 The Property Conditions shall be deemed to be incorporated herein insofar as they are not varied by or inconsistent with the terms of this Agreement except that conditions [ ] thereof shall not apply.

12.2 Title shall be deduced by the Seller's Solicitors supplying to the Buyer certified copies of the deeds and documents of title listed in column 2 of schedule 6.

12.3 For the purposes of condition [ ] of the Property Conditions, the contract rate shall be [2]% above the base rate of the Bank from time to time in force.

12.4 The assurance of the Property to the Buyer shall be executed by the Buyer as well as by the Seller and shall be in the Agreed Terms.

12.5 [That part of the Transfer Point Value attributable to the Property shall be deemed to be exclusive of VAT, and, whenever pursuant to this Agreement any charge for VAT purposes shall be made in respect of the Property, the Buyer shall within [fourteen] days following delivery to it by the Seller of the appropriate invoice valid for VAT purposes pay to the Seller, in addition to the amount charged, the amount of VAT in respect thereof.]

OR (WHERE THE PROPERTY IS EXCLUDED FROM THE SALE)

12. The Buyer shall [as soon as reasonably practicable/no later than [200]] remove or procure the removal from the Property of all the Assets and shall use all reasonable endeavours to:

[9] This provision will not be necessary provided that the provisions dealing with the preparation of the Completion Statement/Completion Accounts properly address the apportionment of wages and salaries but, in the absence of any such provision, these would become the responsibility of the Buyer under TUPE.

12.1   procure that such removal is carried out in such a way as not to cause any injury, annoyance or damage to any third party upon or near the Property or to the Property or to any other property of the Seller or of any third party; and

12.2   make good any injury, annoyance or damage which it may cause but without any obligation on the Buyer to fill in or repair any holes left following such removal.

13.   LEASEHOLD PROPERTY

The following additional provisions shall apply in relation to the Leasehold Property:

13.1   the Leasehold Property shall be sold and assigned subject to the rents reserved by and the covenants on the part of the tenant and all the other provisions contained in the relevant lease;

13.2   [Any further provisions relating to the Leasehold Property to be inserted here]

14.   WARRANTIES

14.1   With the intention of inducing the Buyer to enter into this Agreement (and acknowledging that the Buyer does so in reliance on the Warranties) the Seller represents to the Buyer in the terms of the Warranties and warrants to the Buyer that each of the Warranties is at the date of this Agreement [, and will continue up to and including Completion to be] true and accurate in all respects and not misleading.

14.2   The Seller shall indemnify the Buyer against any costs (including without limitation legal costs on a full indemnity basis) and expenses which it may incur, either before or after the instigation of any legal proceedings, in connection with any legal proceedings for breach of any of the Warranties in which judgment is given to the Buyer and the enforcement of any such judgment.

14.3   The rights and remedies of the Buyer in respect of the Warranties shall not be affected by Completion, by any investigation made by or on behalf of the Buyer into the Business, by any rescission of (or failure to rescind) this Agreement or by any other event or matter except a specific waiver or release by the Buyer in accordance with the terms of this Agreement.

14.4   Each Warranty is a separate warranty and shall not be limited or restricted by reference to or inference from any other Warranty.

14.5   The Seller shall not, if any claim is made against it by the Buyer under the terms of this Agreement, make any claim against the Buyer or any Employee on which or on whom it may have relied before agreeing to any term of this Agreement or authorising any statement in the Disclosure Letter.

14.6   Any payment by the Seller for breach of any of the Warranties shall constitute pound for pound a repayment of and reduction in the consideration for the Business and the Assets.

14.7   Without prejudice to any other right or remedy which it may have, the Buyer shall have the right to set off any sum claimed by it under this Agreement or otherwise against any of its obligations hereunder not then fulfilled.

14.8   In the event of a breach of any of the Warranties, the Seller shall, without restricting the rights of the Buyer or the ability of the Buyer to claim damages on any other basis available to it, pay to the Buyer on demand a sum equal to the amount necessary to put the Buyer into the position which would have existed if each of the Warranties had been true and accurate.

14.9   The provisions of schedule 9 shall apply in respect of the liabilities of the Seller under the Warranties.

15.   CONFIDENTIAL INFORMATION AND USE OF NAMES

15.1   The Seller shall, and shall procure that each Member of the Seller's Group shall, after Completion keep and procure to be kept secret and confidential all Confidential Information which relates to, or is used in, the Business and shall not use nor disclose to any person any such Confidential Information.

15.2   The obligations of confidentiality in this clause shall not extend to any matter which is in or becomes part of the public domain otherwise than by reason of a breach of the obligations of confidentiality in this Agreement or which the Seller receives from a third party independently entitled to disclose it or which the Seller is required by law or regulatory authority to disclose.[10]

15.3   The Seller shall not [,and shall procure that no Member of the Seller's Group shall,] at any time after Completion use in connection with any trade or business any corporate name, trade name, logo, domain name or e-mail address which is confusingly similar to "[   ]" [or "[   ]" or to any corporate name, trade name, logo, domain name or e-mail address which is confusingly similar to any corporate name, trade name, logo, domain name or e-mail address used by the Seller in connection with the Business, at any time during the period of 5 years before Completion.

16.   RESTRICTIVE UNDERTAKINGS

16.1   **Customers, suppliers and employees**

The Seller undertakes with the Buyer that it will not[, and will procure that no Member of the Seller's Group from time to time will,] at any time during the period of [   ] years and [   ] months after Completion directly or indirectly and whether alone or in conjunction with, or on behalf of or by way of assistance to, any other person:

16.1.1   canvass or solicit the custom of any person who was at any time during the period of [   ] months before Completion a customer of the Business for the supply of goods and/or services which are competitive with any of those supplied by the Business at any time during the period of [   ] months before the Completion Date; or

16.1.2   do anything which it knows or ought reasonably to know would cause or be reasonably likely to cause any person who was at any time during the period of [   ] months before Completion a supplier to the Business of goods and/or services to cease or materially reduce its supply of those goods and/or services to the Business;

16.1.3   solicit or entice away from the Buyer or employ or (directly or indirectly) offer employment or a consultancy to any person who is then an employee of the Buyer and who at Completion was:-

16.1.3.1   an employee of the Buyer and likely (in the reasonable opinion of the Buyer) to be in possession of Confidential Information relating to, or able to influence the customer relationships or connections of, the Buyer or [*specify job titles*]; or

---

[10] If a public body is a party, it will be necessary to add additional wording to take account of the Freedom of Information Act 2000 and the Environmental Information Regulations 2004.

16.1.3.2   a senior employee, earning a salary of more than £[x pa];

16.1.4   solicit or entice away from the Business or employ or offer employment to any person who at, or at any time during the period of 6 months prior to, Completion was an employee of the Business and likely (in the reasonable opinion of the Buyer) to be in possession of Confidential Information relating to, or able to influence the customer relationships or connections of, the Business; or

16.1.5   except as the holder for investment of less than 5% in nominal value of the issued share capital of a company whose shares are listed on a recognised investment exchange (within the meaning of the Financial Services and Markets Act 2000) be engaged, concerned or interested, whether directly or indirectly, within the Restricted Area in any Relevant Business.

16.2   **Definitions**

For the purposes of clause 16.1, "Relevant Business" means any business which consists of or includes to a material extent [**Description of business activities**] and "Restricted Area" means [**Specify geographical area to be covered**].[11]

16.3   **Reasonableness of undertakings**

Each of the undertakings in clause 16.1 is:

16.3.1   considered by the parties to be reasonable;

16.3.2   a separate undertaking by the Seller and is enforceable by the Buyer separately and independently of its right to enforce any one or more of the other undertakings in clause 16.1; and

16.3.3   given for the purpose of assuring to the Buyer the full benefit of the Business and of the Goodwill and in consideration of the agreement of the Buyer to acquire the Business and the Assets on the terms of this Agreement.

Accordingly, if one or more of such undertakings is held to be against the public interest or unlawful or in any way an unreasonable restraint of trade, the remaining undertakings shall continue to bind the Seller.

16.4   **Cessation of business**

Nothing in the undertakings set out in clause 16.1 shall be deemed to prohibit any action in respect of any business or part of any business or any area in which (otherwise than as a result of any breach of those undertakings by the Seller) the Buyer has ceased to be involved prior to any event giving rise to a claim, or which would but for this clause 16.4 give rise to a claim, under this clause 16.

17.   **NAME**

ALTERNATIVES

EITHER

The Buyer:

17.1   shall not following Completion use the Seller's corporate name or any colourable imitation thereof; and

---

[11] This will not necessarily be the same as the definition of the Business as it may be appropriate for the restrictions to apply to a narrower or a wider range of activities.

17.2   shall remove the Seller's corporate name from each of the Assets as soon as reasonably possible and in any event within a period of [three] months following Completion.[12]

OR

17.1   [the Seller The Guarantor] shall at Completion procure the passing of a special resolution by the Seller to change its name to a name which does not include the word[s] "[   ]" [or "[   ]"];

17.2   the Seller shall lodge such resolution, together with the relevant change of name fee, with the Registrar of Companies promptly after it is passed.

18.   TITLE

Property and title in and to the Assets shall [, subject in the case of the Property to clauses 12 and 13 and,] pass to the Buyer at the Transfer Point [; provided that all items of Plant, whether or not severed from the Property at Completion, shall be subject to the provisions of this clause 18 and not those of clauses 12 and 13].

19.   THE LAW OF PROPERTY (MISCELLANEOUS PROVISIONS) ACT 1994

The operation of the covenants implied by Sections 2 and 3 of the above Act shall be deemed to be extended so as not to exclude the liability of the Seller in respect of matters:-

19.1   of which the Seller does not know or could not reasonably be expected to know; or

19.2   which at the time of transfer are within the actual knowledge of, or the existence of which is a necessary consequence of facts then within the actual knowledge of, the Buyer.

20.   BOOKS AND RECORDS

20.1   The Buyer shall keep the Books and Records for a period of [three/six] years after the Transfer Point exercising the same degree of care for the safekeeping thereof as a bailee for value.

20.2   During the period referred to in clause 20.1 the Buyer shall:

20.2.1   give the Seller and its authorised representatives at the cost of the Seller such facilities to inspect the Books and Records and to take copies thereof as the Seller may reasonably require; and

20.2.2   give such additional information or explanation of the Books and Records as the Seller may reasonably require.

20.3   The Seller shall keep the Retained Books and Records for the period of [three/six] years after the Transfer Point, exercising the same degree of care for the safekeeping thereof as a bailee for value.

20.4   During the period referred to in clause 20.1 the Seller shall:

20.4.1   give the Buyer and its authorised representatives at the cost of the Buyer such facilities to inspect the Retained Books and Records and to take copies thereof as the Buyer may reasonably require; and

20.4.2   give such additional information or explanation of the Retained Books and Records as the Buyer may reasonably require.

---

[12] Consider also practical arrangements, domain names and website addresses.

20.5   The provisions of clause 5.6 rather than the provisions of this clause 20, shall apply to the VAT Records.

21.   THIRD PARTY ASSETS

21.1   The parties shall each use all reasonable endeavours to procure that the benefit of the leasing, rental, hire and hire-purchase agreements relating to the Third Party Assets is assigned, with the written consent in each case of the relevant other party thereto, as soon as reasonably practicable after the Transfer Point; provided that the Buyer shall have no obligation to make any payment demanded by any person as a condition of giving its written consent to any assignment concerned.

21.2   The Buyer shall, pending assignment of the benefit of each of the agreements referred to in clause 21.1, comply with the terms thereof (insofar as disclosed in the Disclosure Letter) as if it were the Seller [but shall make payment of any sum from time to time payable thereunder (and disclosed in the Disclosure Letter) not to the other party thereto but to the Seller within [fourteen] days following receipt of the Seller's invoice in respect thereof and its written confirmation that it has paid the sum shown on the invoice to the other party to the agreement concerned].

21.3   The Buyer shall be entitled, as regards any of the Third Party Assets in respect of which no written consent to assignment has been obtained within a period of three months following the day of the Transfer Point, at its option either:-to retain possession of the item concerned, in which case it shall continue to comply with clause 21.1 in respect of it, or return it to the Seller, in which case it shall have no further obligation in relation thereto in respect of the period from its return.

21.4   The Buyer shall indemnify the Seller against any failure by the Buyer to comply with any of its obligations under this clause 21.

21.5   The Seller shall indemnify the Buyer against any failure by the Seller to perform its obligations under any agreement relating to any of the Third Party Assets in respect of the period ended at the Transfer Point.

22.   GUARANTEES

The Buyer undertakes with the Seller after Completion to use all reasonable endeavours (short of actual payment of any money and the substitution of the guarantee of any person other than the Buyer) to procure the release of the Seller [and any Member of the Seller's Group at the date of this Agreement] from the guarantees and/or indemnities listed below and to indemnify the Seller [and any such Member of the Seller's Group] against any such liability arising after Completion. The guarantees in question are:-

[Details to be inserted—there may, for example, be counter-indemnities given in respect of bonds]

23.   GUARANTEE

In consideration of the Buyer's obligations hereunder, and in consideration of the sum of £1 paid to the Guarantor by the Buyer (the receipt and sufficiency of which the Guarantor acknowledges), the Guarantor irrevocably and unconditionally guarantees to the Buyer the due and punctual performance by the Seller of the Seller's obligations hereunder and the following provisions shall apply to this guarantee:-

23.1   The Guarantor shall not in any way or to any extent be released from its obligations under this Agreement by reason of any time or other indulgence or waiver granted by the Buyer to the Seller or to any other person, firm or company and this guarantee shall continue in force until the Seller, or the Guarantor on its behalf, shall have fully performed and discharged all of its obligations and liabilities to the Buyer under this Agreement; and

23.2   The Guarantor shall, in respect of any sum paid by it under this Agreement and in respect of any other rights which may accrue howsoever to it in respect of any sum so paid, rank and be entitled to recover or enforce the same against the Seller only after the Seller, or the Guarantor on its behalf, shall have fully performed and discharged all of its obligations and liabilities to the Buyer under this Agreement; and

23.3   Any security for the time being and from time to time held by the Guarantor from the Seller in respect of the obligations and liabilities of the Seller under this Agreement shall be held by it upon trust for the Buyer as security for such obligations and liabilities; and

23.4   This guarantee shall extend to any costs and expenses (including legal expenses), together with VAT thereon, incurred by the Buyer in taking any proceedings or steps of any kind with a view to enforcing this guarantee and in suing for and/or recovering any or all of the amount or amounts payable by the Guarantor under this Agreement; and

23.5   Without prejudice to the rights of the Buyer against the Seller as principal debtor, the Guarantor shall, as between the Buyer and the Seller, be deemed principal debtor in respect of its obligations under this Agreement and not merely a surety, and accordingly it shall not be necessary for the Buyer, before seeking to enforce this guarantee, to seek to enforce any security it may hold from the Seller or otherwise to take any steps or proceedings against the Seller; and

23.6   This guarantee shall extend to the obligations of the Seller under any documents referred to in this Agreement as if the same formed part of this Agreement.

24.   THIRD PARTY RIGHTS

24.1   For the avoidance of doubt and save as expressly provided in clause [   ],nothing in this Agreement shall confer on any third party the right to enforce any provisions of this Agreement.

24.2   Notwithstanding that any provision of this Agreement may be enforceable by any third party this Agreement and its provisions may be amended, waived, modified, rescinded or terminated by the parties to this Agreement without the consent or approval of any third party.

25.   SUCCESSORS

The provisions of this Agreement shall be enforceable and enure for the benefit of any successor in title to the Business or any of the Assets.

26.   WHOLE AGREEMENT

26.1   This Agreement together with all documents entered into or to be entered into pursuant to its provisions constitutes the entire agreement between the parties in relation to its subject matter and supersedes all prior agreements, understandings and discussions between the parties, other than representations made fraudulently

26.2   Each of the parties acknowledges that it is not relying on any statements, warranties or representations given or made by the others in relation to the subject-matter of this Agreement, save those expressly set out in this

Agreement and other documents referred to above and that it shall have no rights or remedies with respect to such subject-matter otherwise than under this Agreement [and the documents executed at the same time as it or entered into pursuant to it] save to the extent that they arise out of the fraud or fraudulent misrepresentation of any party.

27. WAIVER

The rights and remedies of a party in respect of this Agreement shall not be diminished, waived or extinguished by the granting of any indulgence, forbearance or extension of time by a party to another nor by any failure of or delay by a party in ascertaining or exercising any such rights or remedies. Any Release by a party shall not affect its rights and remedies as regards any other party nor its rights and remedies against the party in whose favour it is granted or made except to the extent of the express terms of the Release and no such Release shall have effect unless granted or made in writing. The rights and remedies in this Agreement are cumulative and not exclusive of any rights and/or remedies provided by law.

28. PROVISIONS SURVIVING COMPLETION

In so far as the provisions of this Agreement shall not have been performed at Completion, they shall remain in full force and effect notwithstanding Completion.

29. PROPER LAW AND JURISDICTION

This Agreement shall be governed by the laws of England and Wales.

30. JURISDICTION

Any dispute arising under this Agreement shall be subject to the [exclusive/non-exclusive] jurisdiction of the English courts and the parties waive any objection to Proceedings in such courts on the grounds of venue or on the grounds that Proceedings have been brought in an inappropriate forum.

31. FURTHER ASSURANCE

The Seller shall at its expense do such acts and things and execute such documents as the Buyer may at any time reasonably require for the purpose of assuring to the Buyer the full benefit of this Agreement and any document to which it refers and, in particular, shall at the request of the Buyer execute specific assignments in favour of the Buyer of specific Book Debts as the Buyer may from time to time reasonably require and in such form as the Buyer may reasonably require.

32. COUNTERPARTS

This Agreement may be executed in any number of counterparts and by the parties on separate counterparts, each of which, when so executed and delivered, shall be an original, but all the counterparts shall together be deemed to constitute one and the same agreement.

33. COSTS

Each party shall, except where otherwise stated, pay its own costs of and incidental to this Agreement and its subject-matter [except that, if the Buyer shall lawfully exercise any right hereby conferred to rescind this Agreement, the Seller shall indemnify the Buyer against all expenses and costs incurred by it in connection with this Agreement and its subject-matter].

34. SEVERABILITY

The provisions of this Agreement are severable and distinct from one another, and, if at any time any of such provisions is or becomes invalid, illegal or unenforceable, the validity, legality or enforceability of the others shall not in any way be affected or impaired thereby.

35. PUBLICITY

35.1 The parties shall forthwith upon [the signing of this Agreement/Completion] make or procure to be made a press announcement and announcements to the employees of the Business and to the customers and suppliers of the Business in the Agreed Terms.

35.2 [The Buyer shall be entitled to send a circular to its shareholders convening a general meeting for the purposes set out in schedule 10 and shall give the Seller a reasonable opportunity to comment on the contents of such circular in so far as it relates to it.]

35.3 Each of the parties shall both before and after Completion, but subject to clauses 35.1 and 35.2, keep the contents of this Agreement strictly private and confidential and shall not without the prior written consent of the Buyer (in the case of the Seller) or of the Seller (in the case of the Buyer) disclose any of the terms of this Agreement to any person or make any other announcement relating to the transactions hereby agreed upon except to the extent required by law, [UKLA, the Stock Exchange or the Panel on Take-overs and Mergers] and except that the parties shall be entitled to make references to the transactions hereby agreed upon in their respective future annual reports and financial statements.

36. NOTICES

36.1 Any Notice relating to this Agreement shall be in writing delivered personally or sent by pre-paid first class post or facsimile transmission to the address of the party to be served given herein or such other address as may be notified for this purpose.

36.2 Any such Notice shall, if sent by post, be deemed to have been served 24 hours after despatch and, if delivered by hand or sent by facsimile transmission, be deemed to have been served at the time of such delivery or transmission.
If, however, in the case of delivery by post a period of 24 hours after despatch would expire on, or, in the case of delivery by hand or facsimile transmission, such delivery or transmission occurs on, a day which is not a Business Day or after 4.00 p.m. on a Business Day, then service shall be deemed to occur on the next following Business Day.

36.3 In proving service it shall be sufficient to prove, in the case of a letter, that such letter was properly stamped, addressed and placed in the post and, in the case of a facsimile transmission, it shall be sufficient to produce a transmission report showing that transmission was duly and fully made to the correct number.

37. CERTIFICATE OF VALUE

It is certified that the transaction effected by this Agreement does not form part of a larger transaction or of a series of transactions in respect of which the amount or value or the aggregate amount or value exceeds the sum of [£60,000/£250,000/£500,000] *[amount set out in words also]*.

SIGNED by or on behalf of the parties the day and year first before written.

OR

IN WITNESS of which this deed has been executed and unconditionally delivered the day and year first above written.

SCHEDULE 1

Contracts

SCHEDULE 2

Employees

SCHEDULE 3

Part I

Registered intellectual property and applications

Part II

Listed Intellectual Property Agreements

SCHEDULE 4

Plant

SCHEDULE 5

Property

1.	2.	3.
Property	Title	Apportionment of price

SCHEDULE 6

Third Party Assets

Agreement

Asset	Owner	Description	Date

SCHEDULE 7

Warranties

1.   **THE BUSINESS AND THE SELLER['S GROUP]**

1.1   **Capacity**

[The Seller has/The Seller and the Guarantor each have] full power to enter into and perform the provisions of this Agreement, which constitutes a binding agreement on [the Seller/each of them] in accordance with its terms.

1.2   **Ownership of the Assets**

The Seller is the beneficial owner of the Assets and has the right to dispose of them to the Buyer or as it directs free from any Encumbrance and together with all rights now or hereafter attaching to them.

1.3   **Transfers at an undervalue**

None of the Assets have been the subject of a transfer at an undervalue (within the meaning of section 238 or section 239 of the Insolvency Act 1986) within the period of five years prior to the date of this Agreement.

1.4   **Liabilities owing to or by the Seller**

There is not outstanding any indebtedness and there are no contracts, arrangements or liabilities (actual or contingent) remaining in whole or in part to be performed between the Business and any Member of the Seller's Group or any director of the Seller or any director of any Member of the Seller's Group or any person who is an associate of or connected with any of them.

2.   **CONSTITUTIONAL AND ADMINISTRATIVE AFFAIRS**

2.1   **Books and records**

All accounts, books, ledgers, financial and other records of the Seller relating to the Business have been fully, properly and accurately kept and maintained, are in the possession of the Seller and contain true and accurate records of all matters required by law to be entered therein and no notice or allegation that any of them is incorrect or should be rectified has been received by the Seller [or the Guarantor].

2.1.1   The Seller's accounting records, insofar as they relate to the Business:

2.1.1.1   comply with the requirements of the Acts;

2.1.1.2   are sufficient to show and explain the Seller's transactions;

2.1.1.3   disclose with reasonable accuracy, at any time, the financial position of the Seller at that time; and

2.1.1.4   do not contain or reflect any material inaccuracy or discrepancy.

2.2   **Insurances**

2.2.1   The Disclosure Letter sets out full details of all policies of insurance maintained by or on behalf of the Seller in relation to the Business, all of which are in full force and effect.

2.2.2   All premiums in respect of policies of insurance maintained by or on behalf of the Seller have been paid as and when due, and there are no circumstances which might lead to any liability under such insurance being avoided by the insurers or (being circumstances not affecting businesses generally) the premiums being increased, and there is no claim outstanding under any such policy, nor is the Seller [or the Guarantor] aware of any circumstances likely to give rise to a claim thereunder.

2.2.3 The Disclosure Letter sets out full details of all insurance claims made by or on behalf of the Seller in relation to the Business within the period of three years immediately prior to the date of this Agreement.

2.2.4 There are no claims outstanding or threatened or, so far as the Seller is aware, pending against the Seller in relation to the Business which are not fully covered by insurance.

3. THE SELLER AND THE LAW

3.1 Compliance with Laws

3.1.1 The Seller has conducted and is conducting the Business in accordance with all applicable laws and regulations of any relevant jurisdiction.

3.1.2 There is no order, decree or judgment of any court or any governmental agency of any jurisdiction outstanding against the Seller or which may have any adverse effect upon any of the Assets or the Business; no such order, decree or judgment is pending, and there are no circumstances likely to give rise to any such order, decree or judgment.

3.2 Licences

3.2.1 The Seller has obtained all licences, consents, permits and authorities of a statutory or regulatory nature necessary or expedient to enable it to carry on the Business effectively in the places and in the manner in which it is now carried on.

3.2.2 All such licences, consents, permits and authorities are valid and subsisting, and [neither] the Seller [nor the Guarantor] knows of any reason why any of them should be suspended, cancelled or revoked or renewed or continued subject to any term or condition which does not currently apply thereto.

3.3 Investigations

There is not pending or in existence any investigation or enquiry by or on behalf of any governmental or other body in respect of the Business.

3.4 Litigation

3.4.1 The Seller is not engaged in any dispute with any customer or supplier or in any litigation or other proceedings in respect of the Business or any of the Assets or any of the Third Party Assets.

3.4.2 So far as the Seller [and the Guarantor] [is/are] aware:

3.4.2.1 no litigation or other proceedings are pending or threatened by or against the Seller in relation to the Business or any of the Assets or any of the Third Party Assets;

3.4.2.2 there are no circumstances likely to give rise to any litigation or other proceedings in relation to the Business or any of the Assets or any of the Third Party Assets; and

3.4.2.3   the Seller has not been a party to any undertaking or assurance in relation to the Business or any of the Assets or any of the Third Party Assets given to any court or governmental agency which is still in force.

References in sub-paragraphs 3.4.1 and 3.4.2 to the Seller shall be deemed to include also any person for whom or which the Seller may be or become vicariously liable.

3.5   **Fair trading**

3.5.1   No agreement, practice or arrangement in respect of the Business or to which the Seller is or has been a party infringes any competition, anti-restrictive trade practice, anti-trust or consumer protection law or legislation applicable in any relevant jurisdiction ("Competition Laws").

3.5.2   The Seller has not given any undertaking to any court, person or body and is not subject to any act, decision, regulation, order or other instrument under any Competition Laws and which (in each such case) may affect the Business or any of the Assets.

3.6   **Products**

The Seller has not in the course of the Business manufactured, sold or supplied any product or provided any service which does not or did not at any material time comply with the terms of any contract entered into by the Seller or with any applicable regulation, standard or statutory requirement or which was in any other way defective or dangerous or not in accordance with any representation or warranty, express or implied, given in respect of it.

3.7   **Pollution of the environment**

For the purposes of this paragraph 3.7 the expressions "pollution of the environment" and "process" shall have the same meanings as in section 1 of the Environmental Protection Act 1990.

3.7.1   [No hazardous substances have been used or stored or otherwise handled by the Seller on the Property or elsewhere.] [The Seller has at all times held all licences, consents, permits and authorities necessary to enable it to use, store or otherwise handle or dispose of any hazardous substances used, stored, otherwise handled or disposed of by it, whether on the Property or elsewhere.]

3.7.2   There has been no pollution of the environment nor contamination of land by the Seller in the course of the Business and the Seller has no responsibility or liability for any pollution of the environment or for any contaminated land by any third party, and there has been no act or omission by the Seller in the course of the Business which could give rise to any pollution of the environment or contaminated land.

3.7.3   The Seller has complied and has adequate systems and facilities to continue to comply in relation to the Business, with:

3.7.3.1   all laws and regulations relating to pollution of the environment;

3.7.3.2   all laws and regulations relating to pollution of the environment which apply to any person carrying on any process carried on by the Seller;

3.7.3.3   all EC Directives relating to pollution of the environment (whether or not they have been implemented in any relevant jurisdiction).

3.8   **Data Protection**

The Seller has:

3.8.1   at all times complied with the Applicable Data Protection Laws, and there exist no circumstances likely to give rise to any allegation of non-compliance;

3.8.2   made all necessary notifications or registrations under the Applicable Data Protection Laws, and such registrations or notifications are appropriate given the Seller's actual data processing activities;

3.8.3   not received any enforcement, information or other official notice or request under the Applicable Data Protection Laws;

3.8.4   not received any communication from any data subject or official alleging a breach of the Applicable Data Protection Laws;

3.8.5   not been required to pay compensation in respect of any breach of the Applicable Data Protection Laws, no claims for compensation are outstanding and there are no circumstances likely to give rise to such a claim; and

3.8.6   complied with all data subject requests including requests for access to personal data or cessation of specified processing activities.

3.9   **Health and Safety**

3.9.1   The Seller has complied with all its obligations under the Health & Safety at Work etc Act 1974 ("the Health & Safety Act") and all regulations passed thereunder ("the Regulations").

3.9.2   The Seller has not been served with any Improvement Notices.

3.9.3   The Seller has not been served with any Prohibition Notices.

3.9.4   The Seller has not been cautioned for any breach of the Health & Safety Act or the Regulations.

3.9.5   The Seller has not been prosecuted for any breach of the Health & Safety Act or the Regulations.

3.9.6   There are no circumstances likely to give rise to the service of an Improvement Notice or Prohibition Notice, or to a prosecution for a breach of the Health & Safety Act or the Regulations.

3.9.7   The Seller has not been the subject of a prosecution (whether by the Crown Prosecution Service, the Health and Safety Executive, or any other responsible body) as a result of or in connection with any work-related death and there are no circumstances likely to give rise to such a prosecution.

3.9.8   For the purposes of this paragraph [   ], the expression "Improvement Notice" and "Prohibition Notice" shall have the same meanings as in sections 21 and 22 of the Health & Safety Act.

4.   **THE SELLER'S FINANCIAL POSITION**

4.1   **The Accounts**

The Accounts:

4.1.1   have been prepared in accordance with the requirements of the Companies Acts and all other applicable statutes and regulations and in accordance with generally accepted accounting principles and practices, including all applicable SSAPs and FRSs;

4.1.2   have been prepared on bases and principles and using methods which are consistent with those used in the preparation of the audited accounts of the Seller for any accounting period falling wholly or partly within the period of six years ended on the Accounts Date; and

4.1.3   show a true and fair view of the state of affairs of the Seller as at the Accounts Date and of the profit or loss of the Seller for the accounting period ended on that date.

4.2   **Provisions in the Accounts**
The Accounts:

4.2.1   fully provide for all liabilities (other than contingent liabilities which are not expected to crystallise) and fully disclose all contingent liabilities which are not expected to crystallise and all capital and revenue commitments of the Seller in each case as at the Accounts Date;

4.2.2   fully provide for all bad and doubtful debts as at the Accounts Date;

4.2.3   attribute a value to stock which does not exceed the lower of direct cost and net realisable value as at the Accounts Date after wholly writing off all redundant, obsolete, old, unusable, unsaleable, slow-moving, deteriorated and excessive stock;

4.2.4   are not affected (except as disclosed in the Accounts) by any extraordinary or exceptional event, circumstance or item.

4.3   **Events since the Accounts Date**
Since the Accounts Date:

4.3.1   the Seller has carried on the Business in the ordinary and usual course and without any interruption or alteration in the nature, scope or manner thereof;

4.3.2   the Seller has not in relation to the Business acquired or disposed of any asset entered into any transaction, assumed any liability, made any payment or entered into any other transaction which was not in the ordinary course of the Business and for full value;

4.3.3   turnover and margins of profitability of the Business, have not been less than its turnover and margins of profitability for the corresponding period in the accounting period which ended on the Accounts Date and there has been no deterioration in its financial position or prospects. In particular, there has been no reduction in the value of the net tangible assets of the Business on the basis of the valuations used in the Accounts;

4.3.4   the Seller has paid the creditors of the Business within the times agreed with such creditors, and there are no debts now outstanding by the Seller in relation to the Business which have been outstanding for more than [   ] days or which are now overdue for payment (whether in whole or in part);

4.3.5   the Seller has not entered into, or agreed to enter into, any capital commitment in relation to the Business;

4.3.6   no part of the amounts included in the Accounts, or subsequently recorded in the books of the Seller as owing by any debtors has been outstanding for more than [   ] days or has been released on terms that any debtor pays less than the full book value of his or its debt or has been written off or has proved to any extent to be irrecoverable or is now regarded by the Seller as, or as likely to become, irrecoverable in whole or in part;

4.3.7 the Seller has not factored or discounted any of the Book Debts or agreed to do so;

4.3.8 the Seller has not in the course of the Business offered any price reduction or discount or allowance on sales of stock below a selling price which achieves a gross margin of [   ]% or sold any stock at less than its book value;

4.3.9 the Seller has not sought to accelerate payment by the trade debtors of the Business other than in the ordinary and normal course of the Business.

4.4 **Options**

There is no option or pre-emption right in favour of any third party in relation to the Business or any of the Assets.

4.5 **Debts**

There are no debts owing by or to the Seller in relation to the Business other than debts which have arisen in the ordinary course of its business, nor has the Seller lent any money which has not been repaid.

4.6 **Management Accounts**

The Management Accounts have been prepared using the same accounting principles, policies and bases as used in the Accounts (consistently applied) fairly reflect the trading position of the Business as at the date and for the period to which they relate and are not affected by any extraordinary, exceptional, unusual or non-recurring income, capital gain or expenditure or by any other factor known to the [Seller] [Guarantor] rendering profits or losses for the period covered exceptionally high or low.

5. **THE ASSETS USED IN THE BUSINESS**

5.1 **Assets and charges**

5.1.1 The Seller owns all of the Assets free from any Encumbrance all assets except for current assets subsequently disposed of by the Seller in the ordinary course of its business [, the Properties] and stock which is the subject of retention of title terms contained in standard terms of trading imposed by suppliers in the ordinary course of their business and owns free from any Encumbrance any other asset used by it.

5.2 **Assets sufficient for the business**

5.2.1 The Seller owns all of the Assets free from any Encumbrance and the Assets, together with the Third Party Assets, comprise all assets necessary for the continuation of the Business as now carried on and none of the Assets is shared by the Business with any other person.

5.2.2 The Assets are the only assets used by the Seller in connection with the Business other than those specified in clause 2.

5.2.3 The Seller has possession of all those of the Assets which are tangible assets and of all of the Third Party Assets.

5.2.4 The Seller does not in relation to the Business share any asset with any member of the Seller's Group or depend upon or make use of any assets, facilities or services owned or supplied by any Member of the Seller's Group at the date of this Agreement.

5.3   **Stocks**

The Stocks are adequate and not excessive in relation to the current trading requirements of the Business; none of them is obsolete, slow-moving, unsaleable, unmarketable, unusable or inappropriate or of limited value in relation to the Business; and they are capable of being sold in the ordinary course of the Business in accordance with current price lists without rebate or allowance to a Buyer.

5.4   **Debts**

Each of the Book Debts is recoverable in full in the ordinary course of the Business and in any event not later than [ninety] days following the date of this Agreement, and none of them is subject to any counterclaim or set-off.

5.5   **Intellectual property**

5.5.1   The Seller:

5.5.1.1   is the sole and beneficial owner of the Intellectual Property Rights all of which are valid and in full force and effect);

5.5.1.2   is (where such rights are capable of registration) the registered proprietor of the Intellectual Property Rights;

5.5.1.3   does not own or use in connection with the Business any Intellectual Property other than the Intellectual Property specified in schedule 3 and other than copyrights, design rights, technical know-how and confidential information;

5.5.1.4   does not require any other Intellectual Property to carry on the Business;

5.5.1.5   has not entered into any Intellectual Property Agreements other than those specified in schedule 3 or authorised any person to make any use of or to do anything which would or might otherwise infringe any Intellectual Property owned or used by it; and

5.5.1.6   has not disclosed (except in the ordinary course of the Business) any of its know-how, trade secrets or customer details to any other person.

5.5.2   The Seller owns the copyright or design right (whether registered or unregistered) in the designs of all its products and is the proprietor of any registrations or applications to register any such designs.

5.5.3   None of the processes used in or products of the Business [(so far as the Seller is aware)]:

5.5.3.1   infringes any Intellectual Property of any other person; or

5.5.3.2   involves the unlicensed use of confidential information or know-how disclosed to the Seller by any person.

5.5.4   None of the Intellectual Property Rights are being used (other than by the Seller) or are being or have been claimed, disputed, opposed or attacked by any person.

5.5.5   The Intellectual Property Agreements are the Intellectual Property Agreements to which the Seller is a party, all of them are valid and binding on the parties thereto, and the Seller has at all times observed and performed all of the provisions of each of them. Nothing has been done or omitted by the Seller which would enable any of them to be terminated or which in any way constitutes a breach of the terms of any of them.

5.5.6   None of the records, systems, data or information relating to the Business is recorded, stored, maintained, operated or otherwise wholly or partly dependent on or held or accessible by any means (including) any electronic, mechanical or photographic process, whether computerised or not) which are not under the exclusive ownership and direct control of the Seller.

5.5.7   No person has the right to require the Seller to change its corporate name or to cease using any trade name, logo, trading style, domain name or e-mail address currently used by it in relation to the Business.

5.6   Plant

Each item of Plant:

5.6.1   is in good repair and condition (subject to fair wear and tear) and in satisfactory working order;

5.6.2   is capable, over the period of time during which it is to be written down to a nil value in the accounts of the Seller, of doing the work for which it was designed or purchased;

5.6.3   is not surplus to the requirements of the Business, and

5.6.4   is safe to operate and complies with all relevant Health and Safety at Work legislation and rules.

5.7   Third Party Assets

A true and complete copy of each of the leasing, rental, hire and hire-purchase agreements relating to any of the Third Party Assets is attached to the Disclosure Letter.

5.8   Computer Systems

5.8.1   The Computer Systems are capable of the following functions:

5.8.1.1   handling date information involving all and any dates including, accepting date input, providing date output and performing date calculations in whole or part;

5.8.1.2   operating accurately without interruption on and in respect of any and all dates and without any change in performance;

5.8.1.3   responding to and processing two digit year input without creating any ambiguity as to the century;

5.8.1.4   storing and providing date output information without creating any ambiguity as to the century; and

5.8.1.5   converting sterling into euros.

5.8.2   The Computer Systems and each element of them passes and will continue to pass date information between each other (and any third parties' computer systems with which they habitually communicate) in a way which does not, and will not, create inaccuracies.

5.8.3   The Hardware has been satisfactorily maintained and supported and has the benefit of an appropriate maintenance and support agreement which is not capable of being terminated by the contractor by less than 24 months' notice.

5.8.4   The Hardware and Software have adequate capability and capacity for the projected requirements of the Business for not less than 4 years following Completion.

5.8.5   Disaster recovery plans are in effect and are adequate to ensure that the Hardware, Software and Data can be replaced or substituted without material disruption to the Business.

5.8.6   In the event that any person providing maintenance or support services for the Computer Systems ceases or is unable to do so, the Seller has all necessary rights and information to procure the carrying out of such services by employees or by a third party without undue expense or delay.

5.8.7   The Employees include sufficient technically competent and trained employees to ensure proper handling, operation, monitoring and use of the Computer Systems.

5.8.8   The Business has adequate procedures to ensure internal and external security of the Computer Systems and of the Data, including procedures for preventing unauthorised access, preventing the introduction of a virus, taking and storing on-site and off-site back-up copies of Software and Data.

5.8.9   Where any of the records of the Business are stored electronically, the Seller is the owner of all hardware and software licences necessary to enable it to keep, copy, maintain and use such records in the course of its business and does not share any hardware or software relating to the records with any person.

5.8.10   The Seller has all the rights necessary (including rights over the source code) to obtain, without undue expense or delay, modified versions of the Software which are required at any time to improve in any regard the operation and/or efficiency of the Software.

5.8.11   The Seller owns, and is in possession and control of, original copies of all of the manuals, guides, instruction books and technical documents (including any corrections and updates) required to operate the Computer Systems effectively.

5.8.12   The Computer Systems have never unduly interrupted or hindered the running or operation of the Business and have no defects in operation which so affect the Business.

5.8.13   In this paragraph 5.8

5.8.13.1   "Data" means any data or information used by or for the benefit of the Business at any time and stored electronically at any time;

5.8.13.2   "Hardware" means any computer equipment which is comprised within the Assets or the Third Party Assets including, without limitation, PCs, mainframes, screens, terminals, keyboards, discs, printers, cabling and associated and peripheral electronic equipment but excluding all Software;

5.8.13.3   "Software" means any set of instructions for execution by microprocessor used by or for the benefit of the Seller in relation to the Business at any time, irrespective of application, language or medium;

5.8.13.4   "Computer Systems" means all Hardware, Software and any other items that connect with any or all of them which in each case are comprised within the Assets or the Third Party Assets.

6. THE CONTRACTS OF THE BUSINESS

6.1 Documents

All title deeds and agreements relating to the Business or any of the Assets to which the Seller is a party are in the possession of the Seller and are properly stamped and free from Encumbrance.

6.2 Material contracts

[The Seller is not a party to or subject to any agreement, transaction, obligation, commitment, understanding, arrangement or liability relating to the Business which:/None of the Contracts:][13]

6.2.1   is incapable of complete performance in accordance with its terms within three months after the date on which it was entered into or undertaken or cannot be terminated, without giving rise to any liabilities on the Seller, by the Seller giving three months' notice or less;

6.2.2   is known by the Seller to be likely to result in a loss on completion or performance;

6.2.3   cannot readily be fulfilled or performed on time;

6.2.4   involves or is likely to involve obligations, restrictions, expenditure or revenue of an unusual, onerous or exceptional nature;

6.2.5   requires an aggregate consideration payable by the Seller in excess of £[   ] ([   ] pounds);

6.2.6   is in any way otherwise than in the ordinary and proper course of the Business and on arm's length terms[;

and a true and complete copy of each of the Contracts is attached to the Disclosure Letter].

6.3 Defaults

Neither the Seller nor any other party to [any agreement with the Seller relating to the Business or any of the Assets/any of the Contracts] is in default thereunder, being a default which would be material in the context of the financial or trading position of the Business nor (so far as the Seller is aware) are there any circumstances likely to give rise to any such default.

6.4 Insider contracts

There is not outstanding, and there has not at any time during the last three years been outstanding, any agreement or arrangement between the Seller and Member of the Seller's Group at any material time and the Seller is not a party to, nor has its profit or loss or financial position during such period

---

[13] The wording to be used will depend on the definition of Contracts.

been affected by, any such agreement or any other agreement or arrangement in relation to the Business which is not entirely of an arm's length nature.

6.5   **Customers/suppliers**

6.5.1   In the accounting period ended on the Accounts Date, no customer or supplier of the Business represented [%] or more of the Seller's sales or purchases in that period in relation to the Business (any such customer or supplier being a "Major Customer" or "Major Supplier") save for those specifically identified in the Disclosure Letter as Major Customers or Major Suppliers;

6.5.2   No Major Customer or Major Supplier has since the Accounts Date ceased to do business with the Seller or has since such date substantially reduced its purchases from or supplies to the Seller; since the Accounts Date no indication has been received by the Seller of any material change in the prices or other terms upon which any customer or supplier is prepared to contract or do business with the Seller;

6.5.3   The Seller is not aware of any reason to indicate that any of the existing customers of or suppliers of the Business are likely materially to reduce the volume of their purchases from or supplies to the Business in the future by comparison with the value of their purchases or supplies during the period of [   ] months prior to the date of this Agreement.

7.   **EMPLOYEES**

7.1   **General**

7.1.1   No person is employed in the Business other than the Employees.

7.1.2   There is no employment contract or other contract of engagement between the Seller and any of the Employees which cannot be terminated by the Seller by three months' notice or less without giving rise to a claim for damages or compensation (other than a statutory redundancy payment or statutory compensation for unfair dismissal). The Seller has not received notice of resignation from any of the Employees.

7.1.3   There is no employment contract or consultancy contract or other contract of engagement between the Seller and any person which is in suspension or has been terminated but is capable of being revived or enforced or in respect of which the Seller has a continuing obligation.

7.1.4   The Disclosure Letter contains details of:

7.1.4.1   the total number of the employees of the Business including those who are on maternity leave or absent because of disability or other long-term leave of absence and who have or may have a right to return to work;

7.1.4.2   the name, date of start of employment, period of continuous employment, salary and other benefits, grade and age of each Employee and, where an Employee has been continuously absent from work for more than one month, the reason for the absence; and

7.1.4.3   the terms of the contract of each Employee entitled to remuneration at an annual rate, or an average annual rate over the last three financial years, of more than £[   ].

7.1.5   The basis of the remuneration payable to the Employees is the same as that in force at the Accounts Date. The Seller is not obliged to increase, nor has it made provision to increase, the rate of remuneration of any Employee.

7.1.6   There is no agreement or arrangement between the Seller and an Employee with respect to his employment, his ceasing to be employed or his retirement which is not included in the written terms of his employment or previous employment. The Seller has not provided, or agreed to provide, a gratuitous payment or benefit to any Employee or to any of their dependants.

7.1.7   The Seller has maintained up-to-date, full and accurate records regarding the employment of each of its employees (including details of terms of employment, payments of statutory sick pay and statutory maternity pay, income tax and social security contributions, working time, disciplinary and health and safety matters) and termination of employment.

7.1.8   The Seller has not made or agreed to make a payment or provided or agreed to provide a benefit to an Employee or to any dependants of any Employee in connection with the actual or proposed termination or suspension of employment or variation of an employment contract.

7.2   **Compliance with law**

The Seller has complied with:

7.2.1   each obligation imposed on it by, and each order and award made under, statute, regulation, code of conduct and practice, collective agreement (including any agreement or arrangement under the Information and Consultation of Employees Regulations 2004), custom and practice relevant to the relations between it and the Employees or a trade union or the terms of employment of the Employees; and

7.2.2   each recommendation or code of practice made by the Advisory, Conciliation and Arbitration Service and each award and declaration made by the Central Arbitration Committee.

7.3   **Redundancies and transfer of business**

Within the year ending on the date of this Agreement the Seller has not:-

7.3.1   in relation to any Employee given notice of redundancies to the relevant Secretary of State or started consultations with appropriate representatives under Chapter II of Part IV of the Trade Union and Labour Relations (Consolidation) Act 1992 or failed to comply with its obligations under Chapter II of Part IV of that Act; or

7.3.2   been a party to a relevant transfer (as defined in the Regulations) or failed to comply with a duty to inform and consult appropriate representatives under those Regulations.

7.4   **Collective Bargaining and Consultation**

7.4.1   The Seller has no agreement or arrangement (whether under the Information and Consultation of Employees Regulations 2004 or otherwise) with and does not recognise a trade union, works council, staff association or other body representing any of its Employees and the Seller has not received any notice or request nor are there any negotiations which may lead to any such agreement or arrangement).

7.4.2   The Seller is not involved in, and no fact or circumstance exists which might give rise to:-

7.4.2.1   a dispute with a trade union, works council, staff association or other body representing any of its Employees; or

7.4.2.2   any proceedings before the Central Arbitration Committee or an Employment Tribunal in relation to any collective bargaining agreement or any arrangement under the ICE Regulations 2004.

7.5   Incentive schemes

The Seller does not have and is not proposing to introduce a share incentive, share option, profit sharing, bonus or other incentive scheme for any of the directors, other officers or employees.

8.   PENSIONS

8.1   Disclosed Schemes

The Disclosed Schemes are the only arrangements under which the Seller has or could have any liability to provide or contribute towards relevant benefits, as defined in Chapter 2 of Part 6 of the Income Tax (Earnings & Pensions) Act 2003.

8.2   Details Supplied

The Seller has supplied to the Buyer documents containing full, accurate and up to date details of each of the Disclosed Schemes and of the Seller's obligations and liabilities under it.

8.3   Eligibility Requirements

No amendments have been proposed or announced in relation to the eligibility requirements for entry to the Disclosed Schemes, contribution rates or benefits.

8.4   Legal Compliance

Each of the Disclosed Schemes complies and has at all times complied with all legal and regulatory requirements (including equal treatment and data protection requirements) applicable to it.

8.5   Stakeholder Pension Scheme

The Seller complies and has at all times complied with any duty to facilitate access to a stakeholder pension scheme under section 3 of the Welfare Reform and Pensions Act 1999.

8.6   Deduction of Contributions

All contributions deducted from the salaries of Employees who are members of the Disclosed Schemes and all contributions payable by the Seller to and in respect of the Disclosed Schemes have been paid and passed to the trustees of the Pension Scheme or the provider[s] of the Personal Pension Schemes, GPP, Life Assurance Scheme and the Stakeholder Scheme, as appropriate, in full and within the prescribed time limits applicable in each case.

8.7   Payments

All levies payable in respect of the Pension Scheme have been paid in full and on or by the due date in each case.

8.8   **Claims and Disputes**

No claim, dispute, complaint or investigation (including, but not limited to, complaints to the Pensions Ombudsman and investigations by the Pensions Regulator) has arisen which relates to the Disclosed Schemes or to the provision of retirement or death benefits in respect of the Employees and there is no reason why any such claim, dispute, complaint or investigation could arise.

8.9   **Registered Pension Scheme**

Each of the Disclosed Schemes is a registered pension scheme (within the meaning of Chapter 2 of Part 4 of the Finance Act 2004) and there is no reason why HM Revenue & Customs could withdraw that registration.

8.10   **Contracting Out**

The Pension Scheme is [not] a contracted out scheme within the meaning of section 8 of the Pension Schemes Act 1993.

8.11   **Death in Service Benefits**

All death in service benefits under the [Pension Scheme/Life Assurance Scheme] are fully insured on normal terms for persons in good health.

8.12   **Equalising Benefits**

The Pension Scheme has complied fully with its obligations to equalise benefits for men and women.

8.13   **Eligibility Criteria**

The eligibility criteria for access to the Disclosed Schemes have not been operated so as to discriminate on the grounds of sex, race, disability, religion or belief, sexual orientation or [on and after 1 October 2006] age.

8.14   **Money Purchase Basis [Only relevant to defined contribution schemes]**

All benefits under the Pension Scheme (other than those which are fully insured) are calculated on a money purchase basis only and the Seller has given no assurance or contractual promise to any Employee that his benefits at retirement will be based on his salary at or near to retirement.

8.15   **Funding [Only relevant to defined benefit schemes]**

As at [date of last actuarial valuation] the Pension Scheme was fully funded on a [scheme specific funding/ FRS 17] basis, contributions since that date have been paid in accordance with the current schedule of contributions in accordance with all applicable statutory requirements and nothing has occurred since that date which would have an adverse effect on the funding position.

8.16   **Discretions and Powers [Only relevant to defined benefit schemes]**

No discretion or power has been exercised under the Pension Scheme in respect of any Employee to:

8.16.1   augment benefits

8.16.2   admit to membership an employee or director who would not otherwise have been eligible for membership

8.16.3   provide in respect of a member a benefit which would not otherwise be provided in respect of that member

8.16.4   provide or pay a benefit on more favourable terms.

8.17   **Transfer Payments [Only relevant to defined benefit schemes]**

No transfer payment has been made from the Pension Scheme whose amount exceeds the lower of 5% of the assets of the Pension Scheme and £1.5m.

8.18   **Benefits [Only relevant to defined benefit schemes]**

No member is in receipt of or entitled to receive benefits from the Pension Scheme whose value exceeds the lower of 5% of the assets and £1.5m.

8.19   **Notifiable Events [Only relevant to defined benefit schemes]**

No notifiable event within the meaning of section 67 of the Pensions Act 2004 has occurred in relation to the Pension Scheme or the Seller.

9.   PROPERTY

9.1   **Particulars**

The Particulars of the Property shown in schedule 4 are true and correct and the Seller has good and marketable title to and the exclusive occupation and possession of the Property free from any mortgage, debenture or charge (whether specific or floating, legal or equitable) rent charge, lien or other encumbrance, lease, sub-lease, tenancy or right of occupation, reservation, covenant, stipulation, profit a prendre, wayleave, grant, restriction, easement, quasi-easement or any agreement for any of the same or any privilege in favour of any third party.

9.2   **Rights and easements**

There are appurtenant to the Property all rights and easements necessary for its use and enjoyment.

9.3   **Title deeds and documents**

The Seller has in its possession or under its control all duly stamped deeds and documents which are necessary to prove title to the Property.

9.4   **Disputes etc**

The Property is not affected by any of the following matters nor is it likely to become so affected:-

9.4.1   any dispute, notice or complaint or any exception, reservation, right, covenant, restriction, overriding interest or condition and in particular (but without limitation) any of those matters which is of an unusual nature or which affects or might in the future affect the use of any of the Property for the purpose for which it is now used or which affects or might in the future affect the value of the Property; or

9.4.2   any notice, order, demand, requirement or proposal made or issued by or on behalf of any government or statutory authority, department or body for the acquisition, clearance, demolition or closing or the carrying out of any work upon any building, the modification of any planning permission, the discontinuance of any use or the imposition of any building or improvement line; or

9.4.3   any compensation received as a result of any refusal of any application for planning consent or the imposition of any restrictions in relation to any planning consent; or

9.4.4   any commutation or agreement for the commutation of rent or payment of rent in advance of the due dates for payment thereof.

9.5   **State of repair and condition**

The Property is in a good and substantial state of repair and condition and is fit for the purpose for which it is presently used and no high alumina cement, wood, wool, calcium chloride, sea dredged aggregates, asbestos or other deleterious material (not in accordance with good building practice) was used in the construction thereof and there are no development works, redevelopment works or fitting out works outstanding in respect of the Property.

9.6   **Restrictions, conditions and covenants**

All restrictions conditions and covenants (including any imposed by or pursuant to any lease) affecting the Property have been duly and punctually observed and performed and no notice of any breach of any of the same has been received or is likely to be received.

9.7   **Compliance with legislation**

The use of the Property and all machinery and equipment thereon and the conduct of any business thereon complies and has at all times complied in all respects with all relevant statutes and regulations, including the Factories Act 1961, the Offices, Shops and Railway Premises Act 1963, the Fire Precautions Act 1971, the Health and Safety at Work etc., Act 1990 and with all rules, regulations and delegated legislation thereunder and all necessary licences and consents required thereunder have been obtained.

9.8   **Use of property**

There are no restrictive covenants or provisions, legislation, or orders, charges, restrictions, agreements, conditions or other matters which preclude the use of the Property for the purpose or purposes for which the Property is now used and each such use is the permitted use under the provisions of the Town and Country Planning Acts 1971 to 1990 and any statutory re-enactment thereof and all statutory instruments and regulations made thereunder and is in accordance with the requirements of any Local Authority and all restrictions, conditions and covenants imposed by or pursuant to the said Town and Country Planning Acts have been observed and performed and no agreements have been entered into under section 52 of the Town and Country Planning Act 1971, section 106 of the Town and Country Planning Act 1990 or section 33 of the Local Government (Miscellaneous Provisions) Act 1982 in respect of the Property.

9.9   **Replies to enquiries**

All replies by or on behalf of the Seller to enquiries relating to the Property made by or on behalf of the Purchaser were when given and are now true complete accurate and correct.

9.10   **Encumbrances**

There are no options agreements for sale, mortgages, charges (whether specific or floating) rights of pre-emption or of first refusal affecting the Property.

9.11   **Outgoings**

The Property is not subject to the payment of any outgoings (except national non domestic rates and water rates and sewerage service charges). The Property abuts onto an adopted public highway maintainable at public expense to which it has access without crossing land not in the ownership of the Seller.

9.12   **Compulsory purchase orders**

There are no compulsory purchase notices, orders or resolutions affecting the Property.

9.13   **No further land and buildings**

The Property comprises all the land and buildings owned, leased or occupied by the Seller for the purposes of the Business.

10.   MATERIAL DISCLOSURE

10.1   **Disclosure Letter**

All information contained in or referred to in the Disclosure letter is true and accurate, and the Disclosure Letter does not omit anything which renders any such information misleading or which might reasonably affect the willingness of an acquirer to acquire the Business and the Assets on the terms (including without limitation as to price) of this Agreement.

10.2   **Relationships**

To the best of the knowledge and belief of the Seller [(but without having made any enquiry of any customer or supplier of the Seller)], the transaction hereby agreed upon is not of itself likely to have any adverse effect on the relationships of any customer or supplier of the Business with the Business or upon the performance of any Employee.

10.3   **Legal Due Diligence Enquiries**

The replies to the legal due diligence enquiries dated [   ] 200 raised on behalf of the Buyer were when given and remain true, complete and accurate.

11.   TAXATION

11.1   The Seller has no material agreements with any Taxation Authority relating to transactions entered into in the course of the Business pursuant to which such transactions will be subject to Taxation on a basis which is not strictly in accordance with the relevant legislation.

11.2   The Seller is not aware of any dispute or any circumstances likely to give rise to any dispute with any relevant Taxation Authority in connection with the Business.

11.3   The Seller does not conduct and has not conducted any part of the Business through a branch, agency or permanent establishment outside the United Kingdom, and the Business has not involved the Seller acting as branch or agent of any person not resident for any taxation purpose in the United Kingdom.

11.4   No material sum of an income nature paid under any existing contract or commitment relating to the Business which will continue after Completion has been disallowed wholly or in part as a deduction or charge in compiling the Seller's profits for Taxation purposes.

11.5   The [Fixtures] will not be given a disposal value in the capital allowances computation of the Seller which is less than the value set out therefor in this Agreement by virtue of the operation of section 185 of the Capital Allowances Act 2001.

11.6   The amount of the consideration allocated to the [Building] in this Agreement is not less than the eligible cost therefor for industrial buildings allowances purposes.

11.7   There is no P11D dispensation in force in relation to any of the Employees.

11.8   The Seller is not transferring any assets pursuant to this Agreement to which Part XV of the Value Added Tax Regulations 1995 (Capital Goods Scheme) applies.

SCHEDULE 8

Pension arrangements

SCHEDULE 9

Claims procedure and determination and Seller's safeguards

1.   NOTICE OF CLAIMS AND TIME LIMITS

No claim in respect of any breach of any of the Warranties (other than Warranty 1) shall be made (except in any case of fraud, dishonesty or wilful non-disclosure) unless notice thereof has been given by or on behalf of the Buyer before:

1.1   in respect of any breach of any of the Warranties other than Warranty 1 and the Tax Warranties, the expiry of the period of [ ] years following Completion; **or**

1.1   in respect of any breach of any of the Tax Warranties, the expiry of the period of six months following the end of the accounting reference period of the Buyer in which the sixth anniversary of Completion falls.

2.   THE DISCLOSURE LETTER

2.1   The Buyer shall not be entitled to bring any claim in respect of any breach of any of the Warranties if and to the extent that such inconsistency has been [fairly] disclosed in the Disclosure Letter with sufficient details to identify the nature and scope of the matter disclosed.

3.   LIMITATION OF LIABILITY – MAXIMUM AND MINIMUM AMOUNTS

The Seller shall have no liability in damages in respect of any claim by the Buyer under any of the Warranties (except for claims in respect of any breaches of the Warranties in paragraph 1 of schedule 7 and except in any case of fraud, dishonesty or wilful non-disclosure):

3.1   if and to the extent that such liability would, when aggregated with the amount of any damages paid to the Buyer by the Seller in respect of all and any other such claims, exceed £[A   ] ([A   ] pounds); and

3.2   unless such claim:

      3.2.1   equals or exceeds £[B   ] ([B   ] pounds); and

      3.2.2   would, when aggregated with all other such claims against the Seller of £[B] ([B] pounds) or more equal or exceed £[C] ([C]pounds);

but any such claim shall not be limited to the excess over the amounts specified in this sub-paragraph 3.2.

SCHEDULE 10

Conditional agreement

Part 1

Conditions

1. **CONDITIONS**

    The provisions of this Agreement (other than clauses 14, 19 and 23 to 37 and schedules 1, 2, 3, 4, 5, 6, 7, 8 and 9) are conditional upon the fulfilment of all the following conditions not later than, and the continuance in full force and effect of their fulfilment at [   ], or such later date as may be agreed in writing between the Seller and the Buyer:

    1.1   the passing of a[n ordinary] resolution in general meeting of the Buyer approving the transaction hereby agreed upon [or the Stock Exchange indicating to the Buyer in writing that it does not require the Buyer to submit such transaction to its members for approval; and

    1.2   the passing of a[n ordinary] resolution in general meeting of the Seller approving the transaction hereby agreed upon or the Stock Exchange indicating to the Seller in writing that it does not require the Seller to submit such transaction to its members for approval; and

    1.3   [no action having been taken or intimated by HM Government (or any department or agency thereof) or any third party to restrain the transaction hereby agreed upon; and]

    1.4   no receiver and/or manager or administrator or administrative receiver having been appointed of the whole or any part of the assets and undertaking of the Seller [or of the Guarantor]; and

    1.5   no order having been made and no resolution having been passed for the winding up of the Seller [or of the Guarantor]; and

    1.6   no application having been made for an administration order in respect of the Seller [or the Guarantor] and no petition having been presented and no notice having been given (whether or not by the Seller [or the Guarantor] and whether or not by any members) relating to the winding-up of the Seller [or the Guarantor]; and

    1.7   the Buyer not having exercised any right to rescind this Agreement.

2. **THE PARTIES' ENDEAVOURS**

    Each of the parties shall use all reasonable endeavours to ensure that the said provisions of this Agreement become unconditional in accordance with their terms[, and [the Seller] [and] [the Buyer] shall in particular, but without limitation, procure that the circular letter[s] to be sent to [its/their respective] shareholders relating to the resolution[s] referred to in paragraph[s] 1.1 [and 1.2] contain[s] unanimous recommendation[s] by the directors of [the Seller] [and] [the Buyer] [respectively] and a confirmation that each intends to vote in favour of such resolution in respect of his own holding and that the general meeting[s] referred to in paragraph[s] 1.1 [and 1.2] [is/are] held no later than [200]].

3. **NON-FULFILMENT**

    If any one or more of the Conditions are not fulfilled on or before [   ], the agreement constituted by this Agreement shall thereupon become void and of no effect except as regards and without prejudice to any and all rights of action of the parties for any prior breach of any of the provisions of this Agreement. In that event the parties shall promptly return to one another all documents and other things already delivered in connection with the transaction hereby agreed upon.

4.   **WAIVER**

The Buyer shall be entitled at its option to waive any one or more of the Conditions [other than that set out in paragraph 1.2 above], and, if it does so, the Seller [and the Guarantor] shall be deemed to have done so also. [The Seller shall be entitled at its option to waive the Condition set out in paragraph 1.2, and, if it does so, the Buyer shall be deemed to have done so also.]

5.   **NOTICE OF FULFILMENT OF CONDITIONS**

5.1   [When the Conditions [other than that set out in paragraph 1.2] have been fulfilled, the Buyer shall forthwith give written notice to that effect to the Seller or the Seller's Solicitors, and such notice shall be conclusive and binding on the parties as to the fulfilment thereof.]

5.2   [When the Condition set out in paragraph 1.2 has been fulfilled, the Seller shall forthwith give written notice to that effect to the Buyer, and such notice shall be conclusive and binding on the parties as to the fulfilment thereof.]

Part 2

Obligations and events pending Completion

1.   **RESTRICTIONS**

The Seller shall prior to Completion carry on the Business in the normal way so as to maintain it as a going concern and, except with the prior written consent of the Buyer, shall not:

1.1   grant any Encumbrance over any of the Assets or, except for trading stock in the ordinary course of the Business on arm's length terms, dispose of any of the Assets;

1.2   grant or agree to grant any licence or make or agree to make any assignment or enter into any agreement with any person in relation to any Intellectual Property;

1.3   acquire any asset on lease, lease-purchase, hire-purchase or deferred terms;

1.4   do or allow to be done or omitted any act or thing which may render its financial position less favourable than at the date of this Agreement;

1.5   enter into any transaction outside the ordinary course of the Business[; nor

1.6   do or allow to be done or omitted any act or thing which may reduce or vitiate the cover afforded by any current insurance policy;

1.7   [do anything which would or might render in any way untrue or inaccurate or misleading the circular to the shareholders of the Buyer as contemplated by paragraph 6 of part 1 of this schedule.

2.   **ACCESS TO RECORDS**

The Seller shall at all times prior to Completion give to the Buyer and its professional advisers, in all cases with reasonable despatch upon request, all such information and make available for inspection all such documents and records as it or they may reasonably require and as may be under the control of the Seller [or the Guarantor] and so far as possible take and procure to be taken all such steps as may be required to implement the terms of this Agreement.

Part 3

Warranties

1. **MAINTENANCE OF WARRANTIES**

The Seller shall procure that (save only as may be necessary to give effect to the terms of this Agreement) there shall not occur, at any time at or before Completion, any change of circumstances such that, if the Warranties were repeated at that time, any of them would not then be true and accurate.

1.1   **Notice of change in circumstances**

The Seller [and the Guarantor] shall [each] forthwith notify the Buyer if and as soon as it becomes aware of any such change of circumstances at any time at or before Completion.

1.2   **Rescission**

The Buyer shall not be bound to complete the acquisition of the Business and of the Assets, and may by notice in writing to the Seller of the Seller's Solicitors rescind this Agreement without liability on its part, if:

1.2.1   on the date of this Agreement any of the Warranties are not true and accurate; and/or

1.2.2   at any time at or before Completion or the fulfilment of the Conditions there is a change of circumstances such that, if the Warranties were repeated at that time, any of them would not then be true and accurate; and/or

1.2.3   the Seller is in breach of part 2 of this schedule [and (in any such case) the amount which the Buyer is entitled to claim or would be entitled to claim if the Warranties were repeated or if Completion had taken place amounts to at least £[   ] ([   ] pounds).

1.3   [Rescission shall be without prejudice to the rights of the [parties/Buyer] in respect of any prior breach of any of the provisions of this Agreement.]

SCHEDULE 11

Calculation of Completion NAV

Part 1

Interpretation

In this schedule the following words and expressions shall have the meanings set out opposite each respectively:

"the Buyer's Accountants"	[ ] of [ ];
"the Completion NAV"	the net value at the Transfer Point of the Assets sold to the Buyer pursuant to this Agreement, being the aggregate value of the Assets less the aggregate amount of the Creditors, as determined in accordance with this schedule;
"Independent Accountant"	a chartered accountant agreed upon by or on behalf of the Seller and the Buyer or, if they fail to agree, nominated on the application at any time of the Seller or of the Buyer by the President for the time being of the Institute of Chartered Accountants in England and Wales (the costs of such accountant, and, if applicable, of such President, in nominating such accountant to be borne as he may direct);
"the Seller's Accountants"	[ ] of [ ].

Part 2

Calculation

1.   [The Buyer shall carry out a physical stock-take within [   ] days after the Completion Date at which a representative of each of the Buyer's Accountants, the Seller and the Seller's Accountants shall be entitled to be present and] the Buyer shall prepare within [   ] days after the Transfer Point accounts comprising a balance sheet dealing with the state of affairs of the Business at the Transfer Point and a profit and loss account for the Business for the period from the Accounts Date to the Transfer Point in accordance with part 3 of this schedule ("the Completion Accounts").

2.   The Seller shall provide such information and assistance as the Buyer may reasonably require for the preparation of the Completion Accounts.

3.   The Buyer shall instruct the Buyer's Accountants to:

   3.1   report on the Completion Accounts and on the basis of the Completion Accounts produce a dated statement of the Completion NAV ("the Completion Statement"); and

   3.2   deliver the Completion Statement to, and provide access to all working papers to, the Seller's Accountants;

   within [   ] days following delivery to the Seller's Accountants of the Completion Accounts.

4.   If such queries and observations as the Seller's Accountants raise within [twenty-one] days following delivery to them of the Completion Statement have not been dealt with

to their satisfaction and reflected in any amendments within [twenty-one] days following delivery to the Buyer's Accountants of such queries and observations, it shall be open to the Seller or the Buyer to request an Independent Accountant to determine the Completion NAV, and his determination shall, in the absence of manifest error, be final and binding on the parties.

5. If the Seller's Accountants do not raise any queries or observations in respect of the Completion Statement within [twenty-one] days following delivery thereof to them or if they agree the Completion Statement, then the Completion Statement shall be final and binding on the parties, and the Completion NAV shall be as set out in the Completion Statement.

6. In stating, agreeing or determining (as the case may be) the Completion NAV, the Buyer's Accountants, the Seller's Accountants and, if applicable, the Independent Accountant shall act as experts and not as arbitrators.

7. The Buyer and the Seller shall promptly provide and render or cause to be provided and rendered to the Buyer's Accountants, the Seller's Accountants and the Independent Accountant such information and assistance as they or any of them may reasonably require to enable the Buyer's Accountants and the Seller's Accountants to agree the Completion Statement (and to make the report referred to in paragraph 3) or to enable the Independent Accountant to determine the Completion NAV.

8. The Seller shall bear and pay all of the costs of the Seller's Accountants, and the Buyer shall bear and pay all the costs of the Buyer's Accountants, incurred in each case in connection with the matters referred to in this schedule.

Part 3

Accounting principles, methods and bases

1. Subject to paragraph 2, the Completion Accounts shall be prepared in accordance with:

    1.1   generally accepted United Kingdom accounting principles, methods and bases; and

    1.2   subject thereto (and to the extent they are disclosed in the Disclosure Letter or in the notes to the Accounts), the accounting principles, methods and bases applied and used in the preparation of the Accounts, consistently applied.

2. The following specific provisions shall apply to the preparation of the Completion Accounts:

    [Insert here any specific provisions]

3. The Assets shall for the purposes of the transaction hereby agreed upon have the values ascribed to them in the Completion Statement, save that the following Assets shall have the values set opposite them respectively as follows:

Goodwill	£
Contracts	£1.00
Books and Records	£1.00
The rights referred to in clause 2.9	£1.00

Signed by [   ] for and
on behalf of [

LIMITED/PLC] in the presence of:

OR

Signed as a deed by [
LIMITED/PLC] acting by [   ],
a director, in the
presence of:

OR

Signed as a deed by [

LIMITED/PLC] acting by two

directors or a director and its secretary:

        director

        [director/secretary]

[Appropriate form to be repeated for each party]

PRECEDENT 4

**Assets Sale and
Purchase Agreement
Version B—For use when
debtors and creditors are not
being transferred to the Buyer
but are being retained by the Seller**

DATED   200

(1) [**LIMITED/PLC]**
(2) [**LIMITED/PLC]**
(3) [**LIMITED/PLC]**

ASSETS SALE AND PURCHASE AGREEMENT

-relating to-

[DESCRIPTION OF BUSINESS]

VERSION B—FOR USE WHEN DEBTORS AND CREDITORS ARE NOT BEING TRANSFERRED TO THE BUYER BUT ARE BEING RETAINED BY THE SELLER

This Agreement is made on 200

between:

(1)   [**[LIMITED/PLC]]**, a company registered in England
        under number [   ], whose registered office is at [
        ] ("the Seller"); [and]

(2)   [**[LIMITED/PLC]]**, a company registered in England
        under number [   ], whose registered office is at [
        ] ("the Buyer")[; and

(3)   [**[LIMITED/PLC]]**, a company registered in England
        under number [   ], whose registered office is at [
        ] ("the Guarantor")].

It is agreed as follows:

1.   **INTERPRETATION**

        In this Agreement:

        1.1   The following words and expressions shall have the meanings set out or
                referred to opposite each respectively:

                "the Accounts"   the audited accounts of the Seller, comprising an
                                                audited balance sheet as at the Accounts Date
                                                and an audited profit and loss account for the
                                                financial period ended on the Accounts Date
                                                together with the reports of the directors and
                                                auditors, any cash flow statements and all notes
                                                thereto;

                "the Accounts Date"   [200];

                "Accruals"   the Seller's obligations in respect of all prepay-
                                                ments made to the Seller in connection with the
                                                Business [or the Property/(but not the Property)]
                                                before the Transfer Point [and, to the extent not
                                                included among "Creditors" all liabilities in
                                                respect of expenses incurred by the Seller in
                                                connection with the Business before the Transfer
                                                Point and remaining unpaid as at the Transfer
                                                Point;

                "the Act"   the Companies Act 2006;

                "the 1985 Act"   the Companies Act 1985;

                "the Applicable Data   the Data Protection Acts 1986 and 1998 and the
                Protection Laws"   Telecommunications (Data Protection and
                                                Privacy) (Direct Marketing) Regulations 1998;

                "the Assets"   the assets listed in clause 42;

                "the Bank"   Bank PLC (branch);

                "Book Debts"   together all amounts owing to the Seller in con-
                                                nection with the Business at the Transfer Point
                                                (whether or not invoiced before the Transfer
                                                Point and whether or not due and payable at the
                                                Transfer Point) and all Prepayments;

"the Books and Records"	the books and records maintained by the Seller relating to the Business, the Assets and the Employees other than the Retained Books and Records;
"the Business"	the business of [ ] carried on by the Seller at the Transfer Point at and from the Property [and elsewhere];
"Business Day"	any day (other than Saturday) on which clearing banks are open for normal banking business in sterling in the City of London;
"the Buyer's Solicitors"	[ ] of [ ] or any successor firm;
"Completion"	completion of the sale and purchase of the Business and the Assets in accordance with clause 6;
"the Companies Acts"	as defined in section 2 of the Act;
"Completion Statement"	as defined in schedule 11;
"Completion Value"	as defined in schedule 11;
["the Conditions"	the conditions set out in part 1 of schedule 10; (each a "Condition");]
"Confidential Information"	all secret or confidential commercial, financial and technical information, know-how, trade secrets, inventions, computer software and other information whatsoever and in whatever form or medium and whether disclosed orally or in writing, together with all reproductions in whatsoever form or medium and any part or parts of it;
"Contracts" (each a "Contract")	**ALTERNATIVES** **EITHER** all the contracts and agreements listed in schedule 1 to the extent that they remain to be completed at the Transfer Point; **OR** all the contracts and agreements [, whether written or oral,] remaining to be completed at the Transfer Point and entered into by the Seller in the ordinary course of the Business, including the Listed Intellectual Property Agreements, but excluding all obligations under any such contracts and agreements in respect of goods delivered or services supplied prior to the Transfer Point, the agreements under which the Third Party Assets are held as listed in schedule 6, (to which the provisions of clause 4 shall apply), the Employees' contracts of employment (to which the provisions of clause 11 shall apply) and Creditors;

"Creditors"	all amounts owing by the Seller to creditors in connection with the Business [or the Property /(but not the Property)] at the Transfer Point (whether or not invoiced before the Transfer Point and whether or not due and payable at the Transfer Point), including:

(a) wages and salaries down to the Transfer Point;

(b) all Accruals;

(c) all amounts owing to the Seller's bankers at the Transfer Point;

(d) any liabilities for Taxation;

(e) any VAT payable to H M Revenue & Customs in respect of taxable supplies made by or to the Seller in connection with the Business before the Transfer Point; and

(f) all sums owed at the Transfer Point by the Seller to other Members of the Seller's Group at the date of this Agreement;

"the Disclosure Letter"	the letter having the same date as this Agreement from the Seller['s Solicitors] to the Buyer['s Solicitors];
"the Disclosed Schemes"	the GPP, the Life Assurance Scheme, the Pension Scheme(s), the Personal Pension Scheme(s) and the Stakeholder Scheme;
"Employee"	each person employed by the Seller and engaged in the Business at the Transfer Point and who is listed in schedule 2;
"Encumbrance"	any equity, right to acquire, option or right of pre-emption mortgage, charge, pledge, lien, assignment, title retention or any other security interest, agreement or arrangement, whether monetary or not;
"Escrow Account"	a joint deposit account with the Bank in the joint names of the Buyer's Solicitors and the Seller's Solicitors;
"Escrow Agreement"	the agreement in the Agreed Terms to be entered into by the Seller, the Buyer, the Seller's Solicitors and the Buyer's Solicitors relating to the operation of the Escrow Account;
"FRS"	a financial reporting standard in force at any material time as issued by the Accounting Standards Board;
"Goodwill"	the goodwill relating to the Business and the exclusive right for the Buyer to represent itself as carrying on the Business in succession to the Seller [and to use the name "[ ]"];
"GPP"	means the group personal pension plan underwritten by [name of provider];

"ICTA"	the Income & Corporation Taxes Act 1988;
"Intellectual Property"	(a) patents, trade marks, service marks, registered designs, applications and rights to apply for any of those rights, trade, business and company names, internet domain names and e-mail addresses, unregistered trade marks and service marks, copyrights, database rights, know-how, rights in designs and inventions;
	(b) the rights under licences, consents, orders, statutes or otherwise in relation to a right in paragraph (a);
	(c) rights of the same or similar effect or nature as or to those in paragraphs (a) and (b) which now or in the future may subsist; and
	(d) the right to sue for past infringements of any of the foregoing rights;
"Intellectual Property Agreements"	the agreements or arrangements relating (wholly or partly) to Intellectual Property or to the disclosure, use, assignment or patenting of any invention, discovery, improvement, process, formulae or other know-how;
"Intellectual Property Rights"	all Intellectual Property owned, used or required to be used by the Seller in connection with the Business;
"Lease"	any lease under which any of the Leasehold Property is held by the Seller;
["Leasehold Property"	any leasehold property comprised within the Property;]
"Life Assurance Scheme"	means the **[insert name of group life assurance scheme]** underwritten by **[name of provider]**;
"Listed Intellectual Property"	the Intellectual Property Rights listed in schedule 3;
"Listed Intellectual Property Agreements"	the Intellectual Property Agreements listed in schedule 3;
["the Management Accounts"	the unaudited management accounts of the Seller for the period from the Accounts Date to [200], a copy of which is attached to the Disclosure Letter;]
["Member of the Seller's Group"	any company within the Seller's Group from time to time;]
"Pension Scheme(s)"	means **[insert name of scheme(s) — to be used for occupational pensions schemes]**;
"Personal Pension Scheme(s)"	means **[insert description of each scheme—to be used for personal pension schemes excluding group personal pensions]**;
"Plant"	all the plant, machinery, equipment, furniture, fixtures and fittings, tools, vehicles and spare

parts and other tangible assets held [on the Property] at the Transfer Point by [or on behalf of] the Seller for use in connection with the Business including, but without limitation, all the items listed in schedule 4, [but excluding the Third Party Assets].[1]

"Prepayments"   all prepayments made by the Seller in connection with the Business [or the Property/(but not the Property)] before the Transfer Point;

"Proceedings"   any legal action or proceedings arising out of or in connection with this Agreement;

"Property"   [the property/each of the properties] briefly described in schedule 5;

"the Property Conditions"   [the Law Society's Standard Commercial Property Conditions (Revision)];

"the Regulations"   the Transfer of Undertakings (Protection of Employment) Regulations 2006;

"Release"   any release, waiver or compromise or any other arrangement of any kind having similar or analogous effect;

"the Retained Books and Records"   the accounting records relating to the Business required to be kept by the Seller under section 386 of the Companies Act 2006 [,the VAT Records] and books and records relating to assets or liabilities of the Seller not agreed to be acquired or assumed by the Buyer under this Agreement and the statutory books of the Seller;

"the Seller's Group"   together the Seller and any company including for this purpose any undertaking (within the meaning of section 1161(1) of the Companies Act 2006) within its group (within the meaning of section 474(i) of the Companies Act 1989);

"the Seller's Solicitors"   [   ] of [ ] or any successor firm;

"SSAP"   a statement of standard accounting practice in force at any material time as issued by the Accounting Standards Committee and adopted by the Accounting Standards Board;

"Stakeholder Scheme"   means the stakeholder pension scheme designated by **[the Seller]** and underwritten by **[name of provider]**;

["the Stock Exchange"   the London Stock Exchange plc;]

"Stocks"   all the stocks of raw materials, components, work-in-progress, finished and unfinished goods, bought-in goods, consumables and packaging materials held by [or on behalf of] the

---

[1] It will be necessary to consider whether the words in square brackets are appropriate – for example, there may be Plant which is being serviced or repaired or there may be moulds or tools held by customers.

	Seller [on the Property] at the Transfer Point for use in the Business which have not been invoiced by the Seller before the Transfer Point;
"Taxation"	corporation tax, advance corporation tax, income tax, capital gains tax, value added tax, stamp duty, stamp duty reserve tax, customs and other import duties, vehicle duty, general or business rates, water rates, national insurance, social security or similar contributions, payments due under section 559 ICTA, and any sum payable to any person as a result of the operation of any enactment anywhere in the world relating to taxation and all penalties, charges and interest relating to any claim for taxation or resulting from any failure to comply with any enactment relating to taxation;
"Taxation Authority"	any authority, whether of the United Kingdom or elsewhere, competent to impose, assess or collect Taxation, including HM Revenue & Customs;
"Tax Warranties"	the Warranties contained in paragraph 11 of schedule 7;
"the Third Party Assets"	those assets which are used in the Business, are in the possession of the Seller subject to leasing, rental, hire or hire-purchase agreements and are listed in schedule 6;
"the Transfer Point"	**ALTERNATIVES**

EITHER

the close of business (which for this purpose shall be deemed to be 5.00 pm) on the date of this Agreement;

OR

the close of business (which for this purpose shall be deemed to be 5.00 pm) on [the [third] Business Day after] the date upon which the last of the Conditions to be satisfied or waived is satisfied or waived;

"UKLA"	the United Kingdom Listing Authority;
"VAT"	value added tax;
"the VAT Act"	the Value Added Tax Act 1994;
"VAT Records"	all of the books and records referred to in section 49 of the VAT Act which relate to the Business;
"the Warranties"	the warranties and representations set out in schedule 7;
"Warranty"	one of the Warranties (and the word "Warranty" followed by a number shall be deemed to be a reference to the paragraph of schedule 7 with that number).

1.2 References to the Property shall, where the context so admits or requires, be construed as references to all properties briefly described in schedule 5 and each of them and each and every part of each of them, and references to Leasehold Property shall, where the context so admits or requires, be construed as references to all Property which is leasehold.

1.3 Unless the context otherwise expressly requires, words and expressions which are otherwise defined in the Companies Acts shall have the same meaning when used in this Agreement, but "company" shall mean and include both "company" and "body corporate" as in each case defined in the Act.

1.4 A reference to any statutory or other legislative provision shall be interpreted as a reference to that provision as in force at the date of this Agreement and, additionally, where the context so permits:-

1.4.1 in respect of any earlier date, as a reference to any and all provisions in force at that earlier date of which it is a re-enactment; and

1.4.2 in respect of any later date, as a reference to any and all provisions in force at that later date which are a re-enactment of it;

in each case, whether with or without modification.

1.5 The schedules form an integral part of this Agreement.

1.6 A reference to any gender shall include the other and neuter gender and a reference to a "person" includes a reference to any individual, firm, company, corporation or other body corporate, government, state or agency of a state or any joint venture, association or partnership, works council or employee representative body (whether or not having separate legal personality).

1.7 A document referred to as being in "the Agreed Terms" shall be in the form of that document signed or initialled for identification by or on behalf of the parties.

1.8 The headings are inserted for convenience only and shall not affect the construction of this Agreement.

1.9 Any Warranty qualified by the expression "to the best of the Seller's knowledge and belief" or "so far as the Seller is aware" or any similar expression shall, be deemed to include knowledge, information and belief which the Seller has or which the Seller would have had if it had made all reasonable enquiries, and includes, the knowledge, information and belief of each of:

1.9.1 the professional advisers who act, or at the relevant time acted, for the Seller; and

1.9.2 the directors, company secretary, financial controller and general managers of the Seller [, and] [of the Guarantor] [and of each Member of the Seller's Group]

and of any other person of whom it would be reasonable to make such enquiry or of whom it is stated that enquiry has been made.

1.10 A person shall be deemed to be connected with another if that person is connected with such other within the meaning of section 839 of ICTA.

1.11 "Associate" has the meaning given by section 435 of the Insolvency Act 1986.

1.12 References to "indemnify" and "indemnifying" any person against any circumstance include indemnifying and keeping him indemnified from and against all liabilities, losses, claims, demands, damages, costs, expenses and interest which he may suffer or incur in connection with or arising out of that circumstance.

1.13 Words shall not be given a restrictive meaning:-

1.13.1 if they are introduced by the word "other", by reason of the fact that they are preceded by words indicating a particular class of act, matter or thing; or

1.13.2 by reason of the fact that they are followed by particular examples intended to be embraced by those general words.

1.14 The word "Notice" includes any notice, demand, consent or other communication.

1.15 References to time shall mean London time unless otherwise stated.

1.16 A reference to any English legal term for any action, remedy, method of judicial proceeding, legal document, legal status, court, official or any legal concept or thing shall in respect of any jurisdiction other than England be deemed to include what most nearly approximates in that jurisdiction to the English legal term and a reference to any English statute shall be construed so as to include equivalent or analogous laws of any other jurisdiction.

2. [CONDITIONAL] AGREEMENT FOR SALE AND PURCHASE

On and subject to [the Conditions and] the other terms of this Agreement, the Seller shall sell with full title guarantee and the Buyer shall buy, with effect from the Transfer Point and free of any Encumbrance, the Business as a going concern and the Assets, being:

2.1 the Goodwill;

2.2 the Stocks;

2.3 the Plant;

2.4 the benefit (subject to the burden) of the Contracts;

2.5 the Intellectual Property Rights;

2.6 the Property;

2.7 the Books and Records; and

2.8 all rights of the Seller against third parties (including without limitation under warranties, representations and indemnities and under any policies of insurance) in respect of any of the assets specified in clauses 2.1 to 2.7 inclusive and in respect of any goods incorporated therein or used thereon or any services performed in relation thereto.

3. EXCLUDED ASSETS

The following are excluded from the transaction hereby agreed upon:

3.1 all and any shares or other securities in any companies held by the Seller;

3.2 all cash in hand or at bank and all cheques and other securities representing them, in each case as at the Transfer Point;

3.3 any credit or refund of any Taxation in respect of supplies made to or by the Seller or profits or gains made or deemed to have been made by the Seller, in each case before the Transfer Point;

3.4 the Retained Books and Records; and

3.5   the Third Party Assets.

For the avoidance of doubt, the amounts referred to in clauses 3.1, 3.2 and 3.3 shall not be regarded as Book Debts for the purposes of this Agreement.

4.   CONSIDERATION

ALTERNATIVE A—FIXED CASH SUM WITHOUT RETENTION

4.1   The purchase price for the Business and the Assets shall be the payment by the Buyer to the Seller of the sum of £[   ] ([pounds] which shall be paid in cash on Completion.

4.2   The Seller's Solicitors' receipt for the cash payment referred to in clause 4.1 shall be a good and sufficient discharge to the Buyer and the Buyer shall not be further concerned as to the application of the monies so paid.

4.3   The Assets shall for the purposes of the transaction hereby agreed upon have the values set opposite them respectively:—

Goodwill   £[   ]

Stocks   £[   ]

Plant   £[   ]

Contracts   £[   ]

Intellectual Property Rights   £[   ]

Property*   £[   ]

Books and Records   £1

The rights referred to in

clause 2.7   £1

*apportioned as indicated in schedule 5.

ALTERNATIVE B—COMPLETION ACCOUNTS WITH JOINT ACCOUNT

4.1   **Amount**

The purchase price for the Business and the Assets ("the Purchase Price") shall be the payment by the Buyer to the Seller of the sum of £[   ] ([pounds]) plus a sum equal to the Completion Value [up to a maximum of £[   ] ([pounds]).

4.2   **First Payments—on Completion**

On Completion and pending the later agreement or determination of the Completion Value, the Buyer shall pay:—

4.2.1   the sum of £[   ] (pounds) to the Seller's Solicitors (on behalf of the Seller) on account of the Purchase Price; and

4.2.2   the sum of [£   ] [(pounds)] ("the Principal Sum") to the Buyer's Solicitors and the Seller's Solicitors jointly for placing into the Escrow Account to be held under a mandate in the Agreed Terms and to be held and dealt with as set out in this clause 4.

4.3   **Second payment—following calculation of Completion NAV**

On the third Business Day after the date on which the Completion Value is agreed or determined in accordance with schedule 11:—

4.3.1   the Buyer shall pay to the Seller's Solicitors a sum equal to the balance (if any) of the Purchase Price, after deducting the amount paid pursuant to clause 4.2.1, such payment to be satisfied by the payment of an equivalent sum from the Escrow Account;

4.3.2   if the Purchase Price exceeds the amount paid to the Seller pursuant to clauses 4.2.1 and 4.3.1, the Buyer shall pay the amount of the excess to the Seller's Solicitors;

4.3.3   the balance of the Principal Sum following any payment from the Escrow Account pursuant to clause 4.3.1 (or, if no such payment falls to be made, the whole of the Principal Sum) shall be paid to the Buyer from the Escrow Account.

4.4   The Account

4.4.1   All interest earned on the Escrow Account shall accrue and be paid to the Seller and/or the Buyer in the proportions in which they respectively become entitled to the Principal Sum and shall be paid at the same time as any payment of all or any part of the Principal Sum is made from the Escrow Account.

4.4.2   The Seller and the Buyer shall procure that their respective solicitors shall make any payment which is required to be made from the Escrow Account pursuant to the provisions of clause 4.3.

4.5   Clawback from first payment

4.5.1   If the amount paid pursuant to clause 4.2.1 exceeds the Purchase Price then on the third Business Day referred to in clause 4 the Seller shall repay to the Buyer a sum equal to the excess plus interest on an amount equal to the excess at the rate on which interest has been earned on the Escrow Account, such interest to accrue from the Completion Date until that third Business Day.

4.5.2   If the Seller defaults in making payment of any sum due under subclause 4, it shall pay interest on the amount in question calculated on a daily basis from the due date until the date of actual payment (as well after any judgment as before) at the rate of 4% per year above the base rate from time to time in force of the Bank.

4.6   Method of Payment

4.6.1   Unless otherwise specified, any payment required to be made by the Buyer to the Seller pursuant to this clause 4 shall be made by way of a [banker's draft drawn on a UK clearing bank in favour of the Seller/Seller's Solicitors/telegraphic transfer to the following account:

Bank:

Branch:

Sort Code:

Account Name:

Account Number:]

4.6.2   The Seller's Solicitors' receipt for any sums payable by the Buyer pursuant to this clause 4 shall be a good and sufficient discharge of the Buyer's obligation to make the payment in question and the Buyer shall not be further concerned as to the application of any sums so paid.

4.6.3   Any sum payable to the Buyer pursuant to this clause 4 shall, unless otherwise specified, be paid by way of a banker's draft drawn on a UK clearing bank in favour of the [Buyer/Buyer's'[s] Solicitors]/telegraphic transfer to the following account:

Bank:

Branch:

Sort Code:

Account Name:

Account Number:]

5.   VALUE ADDED TAX

5.1   The Purchase Price payable hereunder is stated exclusive of VAT.

5.2   The Seller warrants to the Buyer that it is [and undertakes with the Buyer that it will at Completion be] duly registered for VAT purposes.

5.3   The Seller warrants to and undertakes with the Buyer that:

5.3.1   it has not made, and will not before Completion make, for VAT purposes any election to tax in respect of the Property; and

5.3.2   there are no, and will not at Completion be any, new (as defined in note 4 of item 1 of group 1 in schedule 9 to the VAT Act) or uncompleted freehold commercial buildings or civil engineering works included in the sale and purchase hereby agreed upon.[2]

5.4   The Buyer warrants to the Seller that [it is [and undertakes with the Seller that it will at Completion be] duly registered/it is by virtue of the transaction hereby agreed upon liable to be duly registered] for VAT purposes.

5.5   The parties shall use all reasonable endeavours to procure that the transaction hereby agreed upon is deemed to be a transfer of a business as a going concern for the purposes of section 49 and paragraphs 8(1)(a) and 8(2)(b) of schedule 4 to the VAT Act and article 5(1) of the Value Added Tax (Special Provisions) Order 1995 and is treated neither as a supply of goods nor as a supply of services.

5.6   **ALTERNATIVES**

EITHER

The Seller and the Buyer intend at section 49 of the VAT Act shall apply to the transaction hereby agreed upon that they do not intend to make a joint application to HM Revenue and Customs for the Buyer to be registered for VAT under the VAT registration number of the Seller, pursuant to Regulation 6 (1) (d) of the VAT Regulations 1995.

OR

The Seller and the Buyer intend that section 49 of the VAT Act shall apply to the transaction hereby agreed upon and they intend to make a joint application to HM Revenue and Customs for the Buyer to be registered for VAT under the VAT registration number of the Seller, pursuant to Regulation 6 (1) (d) of the VAT Regulations 1995. If HM Revenue and Customs register the Buyer under the Seller's VAT registration number

---

[2] The "going concern" exemption may not be available if this warranty cannot be given.

6.   AGENCY

As from the Transfer Point, the Seller shall be deemed to have acted as agent for the Buyer, it being the intention of the parties that the benefit of the trading activities of the Business shall accrue to the Buyer from the Transfer Point. Accordingly, the Buyer shall be entitled to the right to receive payment for goods or services supplied by the Seller in connection with the Business after the Transfer Point and the Seller shall account to the Buyer on Completion for any payments received by the Seller in respect of goods or services so supplied. In respect of the period between the Transfer Point and Completion, the Seller shall arrange for the interest of the Buyer to be noted on the policies relating to its public liability, product liability, employers' liability, motor and business interruption insurances and any other insurances where this is possible.

7.   DEBTORS AND CREDITORS

7.1   The Buyer shall as agent for the Seller receive and use reasonable endeavours to collect all Book Debts within the normal credit period allowed by the Seller to each debtor respectively.

7.2   The Buyer shall account to the Seller for all sums received by it in respect of the Book Debts either:

7.2.1   if the debtor's cheque is in respect only of Book Debts and it is possible to pay it into the Seller's Bank Account, by doing so within [five] Business Days following the day after the Buyer receives it;

7.2.2   if the debtor's cheque is in respect only of Book Debts and it is not possible to pay it into the Seller's Bank Account, by paying it into its own bank account within [five] Business Days following the day the Buyer receives it and by paying a cheque drawn on such account in the amount of the Book Debts covered by the debtor's cheque into the Seller's Bank Account not later than [five] Business Days thereafter, unless the Buyer's Bank shall have notified the Buyer that the debtor's cheque has not cleared (in which event the Buyer shall promptly notify the Seller to that effect); or

7.2.3   if the debtor's cheque is in respect of both Book Debts and any sum owed to the Buyer, by paying it into the Buyer's Bank Account within [five] Business Days following the day the Buyer receives it and by paying a cheque drawn on such account in the amount of the Book Debts covered by the debtor's cheque into the Seller's Bank Account not later than [five] Business Days thereafter, unless the Buyer's Bank shall have notified the Buyer that the debtor's cheque has not cleared (in which event the Buyer shall promptly notify the Seller to that effect).

7.3   The Buyer shall keep full and accurate records and prepare [monthly] statements of all sums received by it on behalf of the Seller in respect of Book Debts and shall send the Seller such statements promptly upon preparation with all supporting remittance advice and other documents.

7.4   The Buyer shall not compromise or release any of the Book Debts.

7.5   The Buyer shall not begin or carry on any litigation in respect of any of the Book Debts except as mentioned in this clause 8.2. If it becomes apparent that recovery of any of them is not likely to be possible within a reasonable period without beginning litigation, the Buyer shall promptly notify the Seller to that effect and give the Seller full details of all steps it has taken to effect recovery. [If the Seller begins litigation in respect of any of the Book

Debts, it shall first [notify/consult with] the Buyer, and the Buyer shall provide such information as the Seller may reasonably require].

7.6   Any payments made by a debtor which owes money in connection with the Business both to the Seller and to the Buyer shall be allocated to the debt to which the debtor expressly allocates its payment in writing. If it makes no such allocation at or before the time of payment, the Buyer shall request the debtor in question to make such an allocation, and, if none is made within [fourteen] days following payment, the payment concerned shall be allocated to the oldest unpaid debt incurred by the debtor in question, unless the payment corresponds with the exact amount of a later invoice and save to the extent that such oldest unpaid debt is disputed by the debtor.

7.7   The Buyer shall not be required to take on or discharge any obligation or liability of the Seller except for any which it expressly agrees in this Agreement to take on or discharge and in particular, but without limitation, the Creditors shall remain the sole responsibility of the Seller.

7.8   All periodical charges and outgoing attributable to the Business [and the Property/(but not the Property)] and all liabilities in relation to salaries, wages, accrued holiday pay, national insurance, pension contributions, PAYE remittance and all other payments to or in respect of the Employees shall be apportioned on a time basis (but reference to meter reading where possible). Similarly all rents, licences, fees, royalties and similar sums receivable in respect of the Business shall be apportioned on the same basis. The Seller shall within 10 Business Days after Completion prepare and deliver to the Buyer a schedule of apportionments, Pre-payments and Accruals and the Seller and the Buyer shall then endeavour to agree any net payment due from one to the other.

7.9   If such schedule is not agreed within 20 Business Days following Completion, the matter or matters in dispute may be referred by the Seller or the Buyer for determination to an independent chartered accountant to be appointed by agreement between the Seller and the Buyer or, failing agreement, upon the application either of the Buyer or of the Seller by the President for the time being of the Institute of Chartered Accountants in England and Wales. Such independent chartered accountant shall act as an expert and not as an arbitrator and his determination shall be final and binding on the parties. The costs of such independent chartered accountant shall be borne as he may decide (and otherwise by the parties in equal shares) and each party shall be responsible for its own costs of presenting its case to him.

8.   CONTRACTS

8.1   The Buyer shall, subject to clause 8.3, perform and fulfil the Contracts on its own account with effect from the Transfer Point in the place of the Seller.

8.2   If the benefit of any of the Contracts cannot be assigned without the consent of a third party:

8.2.1   nothing in this Agreement shall operate as an assignment or purported assignment of the benefit of such Contracts;

8.2.2   the parties shall each use all reasonable endeavours to obtain all necessary consents to assignment as soon as possible after the Transfer Point; and

8.2.3   from the Transfer Point and until such consents are obtained the Seller shall hold the benefit of the Contracts concerned in trust for the Buyer, the Buyer shall at its own cost and for its own benefit perform and fulfil the Contracts concerned as the Seller's agent and the Seller shall promptly account to the Buyer without deduction or set-off for any sums it may receive from any third party in respect thereof.

8.3 Subject to the provisions of clause 9.1, the Seller shall remain liable under the Contracts in respect of all goods and services supplied by or to it pursuant thereto before the Transfer Point, and generally under the Contracts to the extent that they have then been performed or should then have been performed, and shall indemnify the Buyer against any act or omission of the Seller before the Transfer Point in relation to any of the Contracts.

8.4 The Seller shall at the request of the Buyer give to the Buyer all reasonable assistance to enable the Buyer to enforce each of the Contracts against the other contracting party or parties.

9. DEFECTIVE GOODS

The Buyer shall satisfy all legally valid claims which may be made against the Seller (and which are notified in writing to the Buyer together with appropriate evidence as to their validity) or against the Buyer for the repair or replacement of, or for reimbursement of the price of, defective goods sold by the Seller, and the Seller shall in any such case reimburse to the Buyer (at cost) the cost to the Buyer of performing its obligations under this clause 9.3)

10. EMPLOYEES

10.1 The parties acknowledge that the sale of the Business and the Assets pursuant to this Agreement is a relevant transfer under the Regulations and accordingly the employment of each Employee shall at the Transfer Point be transferred to and taken over by the Buyer under the Regulations.

10.2 The Seller shall indemnify the Buyer against all liabilities arising out of:

10.2.1 the employment of any Employee during the period ending at the Transfer Point or the employment at any time (whether or not by the Seller) of any employee of the Seller who is not an Employee or of any former employee of the Seller;

10.2.3 the termination before or at the Transfer Point of the employment of any Employee;

10.2.3 the termination at any time (and whether or not by the Seller) of the employment of any employee of the Seller who is not an Employee or of any former employee of the Seller;

10.2.4 any act or omission of the Seller which is deemed by virtue of the Regulations to be an act or omission of the Buyer;

10.2.5 any industrial or other work-related illness or injury suffered or allegedly suffered by any Employee in respect of or relating to any period ending on or before the Transfer Point;

10.2.6 any bonus payable to any Employee in respect of the financial year ended [200] (which shall, as between the Seller and the Buyer, remain the responsibility of the Seller);

10.2.7 any failure by the Seller to comply with its obligations under regulation 11 or regulation 13 of the Regulations or under Part IV of the Trade Union & Labour Relations (Consolidation) Act 1992;

and/or otherwise arising by virtue of the Regulations.

10.3   The Buyer will indemnify the Seller against all liabilities arising out of the employment or termination of employment of any Employee after the Transfer Point.

10.4   Without prejudice to the provisions of clause 10.7, the Seller shall remain liable for all wages, salaries and other emoluments payable to the Employees in respect of all periods down to the Transfer Point and in respect of holiday entitlements as at the Transfer Point.

10.5   **ALTERNATIVES**

EITHER

Without prejudice to clauses 10.3 and 10.4 the Buyer shall pay to the Seller without [deduction or set-off] on [   ] 200] the sum of £[   ] ([pounds) in respect of holiday taken by Employees before the Transfer Point in advance of the entitlement thereto falling due.

OR

Without prejudice to clauses 10.3 and 10.4, the Seller shall pay to the Buyer without deduction or set-off on [200] the sum of £[   ] ([pounds]) in respect of the holiday entitlements of the Employees due or accrued due at the Transfer Point.

10.6   The Seller represents and warrants to the Buyer that it has provided, and undertakes that it shall provide, to the Buyer such information as the Buyer may from time to time request in writing in order to enable it to verify compliance with the laws and regulations referred to in clause 10.2.7.

10.7   Schedule 8 shall apply in relation to pension arrangements in respect of the Employees.

11.   PROPERTY

11.1   The Property Conditions shall be deemed to be incorporated herein insofar as they are not varied by or inconsistent with the terms of this Agreement except that conditions[   ] thereof shall not apply.

11.2   Title shall be deduced by the Seller's Solicitors supplying to the Buyer certified copies of the deeds and documents of title listed in column 2 of schedule 6.

11.3   For the purposes of condition [   ] of the Property Conditions, the contract rate shall be [2]% above the base rate of the Bank from time to time in force.

11.4   The assurance of the Property to the Buyer shall be executed by the Buyer as well as by the Seller and shall be in the Agreed Terms.

11.5   [That part of the Transfer Point Value attributable to the Property shall be deemed to be exclusive of VAT, and, whenever pursuant to this Agreement any charge for VAT purposes shall be made in respect of the Property, the Buyer shall within [fourteen] days following delivery to it by the Seller of the appropriate invoice valid for VAT purposes pay to the Seller, in addition to the amount charged, the amount of VAT in respect thereof.]

OR (WHERE THE PROPERTY IS EXCLUDED FROM THE SALE)

11.   THE BUYER SHALL [AS SOON AS REASONABLY PRACTICABLE/ NO LATER THAN [200]] REMOVE OR PROCURE THE REMOVAL FROM THE PROPERTY OF ALL THE ASSETS AND SHALL USE ALL REASONABLE ENDEAVOURS TO:

11.1   procure that such removal is carried out in such a way as not to cause any injury, annoyance or damage to any third party upon or near the Property or to the Property or to any other property of the Seller or of any third party; and

11.2   make good any injury, annoyance or damage which it may cause but without any obligation on the Buyer to fill in or repair any holes left following such removal.

12.   LEASEHOLD PROPERTY

The following additional provisions shall apply in relation to the Leasehold Property:

12.1   the Leasehold Property shall be sold and assigned subject to the rents reserved by and the covenants on the part of the tenant and all the other provisions contained in the relevant lease.

12.2   **[Any further provisions relating to the Leasehold Property to be inserted here]**

13.   WARRANTIES

13.1   With the intention of inducing the Buyer to enter into this Agreement (and acknowledging that the Buyer does so in reliance on the Warranties) the Seller represents to the Buyer in the terms of the Warranties and warrants to the Buyer that each of the Warranties is at the date of this Agreement [, and will continue up to and including Completion to be] true and accurate in all respects and not misleading.

13.2   The Seller shall indemnify the Buyer against any costs (including without limitation legal costs on a full indemnity basis) and expenses which it may incur, either before or after the instigation of any legal proceedings, in connection with any legal proceedings for breach of any of the Warranties in which judgment is given to the Buyer and the enforcement of any such judgment.

13.3   The rights and remedies of the Buyer in respect of the Warranties shall not be affected by Completion, by any investigation made by or on behalf of the Buyer into the Business, by any rescission of (or failure to rescind) this Agreement or by any other event or matter except a specific waiver or release by the Buyer in accordance with the terms of this Agreement.

13.4   Each Warranty is a separate warranty and shall not be limited or restricted by reference to or inference from any other Warranty.

13.5   The Seller shall not, if any claim is made against it by the Buyer under the terms of this Agreement, make any claim against the Buyer or any Employee on which or on whom it may have relied before agreeing to any term of this Agreement or authorising any statement in the Disclosure Letter.

13.6   Any payment by the Seller for breach of any of the Warranties shall constitute pound for pound a repayment of and reduction in the consideration for the Business and the Assets.

13.7   Without prejudice to any other right or remedy which it may have, the Buyer shall have the right to set off any sum claimed by it under this Agreement or otherwise against any of its obligations hereunder not then fulfilled.

13.8   In the event of a breach of any of the Warranties, the Seller shall, without restricting the rights of the Buyer or the ability of the Buyer to claim damages on any other basis available to it, pay to the Buyer on demand a sum equal to the amount necessary to put the Buyer into the position which would have existed if each of the Warranties had been true and accurate.

13.9   The provisions of schedule 9 shall apply in respect of the liabilities of the Seller under the Warranties.

14.   CONFIDENTIAL INFORMATION AND USE OF NAMES

14.1   The Seller shall, and shall procure that each Member of the Seller's Group shall after Completion keep and procure to be kept secret and confidential all Confidential Information which relates to, or is used in, the Business and shall not use nor disclose to any person any such Confidential Information

14.2   The obligations of confidentiality in this clause shall not extend to any matter which is in or becomes part of the public domain otherwise than by reason of a breach of the obligations of confidentiality in this Agreement or which the Seller receives from a third party independently entitled to disclose it or which the Seller is required by law or regulatory authority to disclose.[3]

14.3   The Seller shall not [,and shall procure that no Member of the Seller's Group shall,] at any time after Completion use in connection with any trade or business any corporate name, trade name, logo, domain name or e-mail address which is confusingly similar to "[   ]" [or "[   ]" or to any corporate name, trade name, logo, domain name or e-mail address which is confusingly similar to any corporate name, trade name, logo, domain name or e-mail address used by the Seller in connection with the Business, at any time during the period of 5 years before Completion.

15.   RESTRICTIVE UNDERTAKINGS

15.1   **Customers, suppliers and employees**

The Seller undertakes with the Buyer that it will not[, and will procure that no Member of the Seller's Group from time to time will,] at any time during the period of [ ] years and [   ] months after Completion directly or indirectly and whether alone or in conjunction with, or on behalf of or by way of assistance to, any other person:

15.1.1   canvass or solicit the custom of any person who was at any time during the period of [   ] months before Completion a customer of the Business for the supply of goods and/or services which are competitive with any of those supplied by the Business at any time during the period of [   ] months before the Completion Date; or

15.1.2   do anything which it knows or ought reasonably to know would cause or be reasonably likely to cause any person who was at any time during the period of [   ] months before Completion a supplier to the Business of goods and/or services to cease or materially reduce its supply of those goods and/or services to the Business;

15.1.3   solicit or entice away from the Company or employ or (directly or indirectly) offer employment or a consultancy to any person who is then an employee of the Company and who at Completion was:-

15.1.3.1   an employee of the Company and likely (in the reasonable opinion of the Buyer) to be in possession of Confidential Information relating to, or able to influence the customer relationships or connections of, the Company or *specify job titles*; or

15.1.3.2   a senior employee, earning a salary of more than £[x pa];

15.1.4   solicit or entice away from the Business or employ or offer employment to any person who at, or at any time during the period of 6 months prior to, Completion was an employee of the Business

---

[3] If a public body is a party, it will be necessary to add additional wording to take account of the Freedom of Information Act 2000 and the Environmental Information Regulations 2004

and likely (in the reasonable opinion of the Buyer) to be in possession of Confidential Information relating to, or able to influence
the customer relationships or connections of, the Business; or

15.1.5   except as the holder for investment of less than 5% in nominal
value of the issued share capital of a company whose shares are
listed on a recognised investment exchange (within the meaning of
the Financial Services and Markets Act 2000) be engaged, concerned or interested, whether directly or indirectly, within the
Restricted Area in any Relevant Business.

15.2   **Definitions**

For the purposes of clause 15.1, "Relevant Business" means any business
which consists of or includes to a material extent [   ] and "Restricted
Area" means [   ].[4]

15.3   **Reasonableness of undertakings**

Each of the undertakings in clause 15.1 is:

15.3.1   considered by the parties to be reasonable;

15.3.2   a separate undertaking by the Seller and is enforceable by the
Buyer separately and independently of its right to enforce any one
or more of the other undertakings in clause 15.1; and

15.3.3   given for the purpose of assuring to the Buyer the full benefit of the
Business and of the Goodwill and in consideration of the agreement of the Buyer to acquire the Business and the Assets on the
terms of this Agreement.

Accordingly, if one or more of such undertakings is held to be against the
public interest or unlawful or in any way an unreasonable restraint of trade,
the remaining undertakings shall continue to bind the Seller.

15.4   **Cessation of business**

Nothing in the undertakings set out in clause 15.1 shall be deemed to prohibit
any action in respect of any business or part of any business or any area in
which (otherwise than as a result of any breach of those undertakings by the
Seller) the Buyer has ceased to be involved prior to any event giving rise to
a claim, or which would but for this clause 15.1 give rise to a claim, under
this clause 15.

16.   **NAME**

ALTERNATIVES

EITHER

The Buyer:

16.1   shall not following Completion use the Seller's corporate name or any
colourable imitation thereof; and

16.2   shall remove the Seller's corporate name from each of the Assets as soon as
reasonably possible and in any event within a period of [three] months
following Completion.[5]

---

[4] This will not necessarily be the same as the definition of the Business as it may be appropriate for the
restrictions to apply to a narrower or a wider range of activities.

[5] Consider also practical arrangements, domain names and websites addresses

OR

16.1   [the Seller The Guarantor] shall at Completion procure the passing of a spe-
        cial resolution by the Seller to change its name to a name which does not
        include the word[s] "[   ]" [or "[   ]"];

16.2   the Seller shall lodge such resolution, together with the relevant change of
        name fee, with the Registrar of Companies promptly after it is passed.

17.   TITLE

Property and title in and to the Assets shall [, subject in the case of the Property to
clauses 11 and 12 and,] pass to the Buyer at the Transfer Point [; provided that all items
of Plant, whether or not severed from the Property at Completion, shall be subject
to the provisions of this clause 17 and not those of clauses 11 and 12].

18.   THE LAW OF PROPERTY (MISCELLANEOUS PROVISIONS) ACT 1994

The operation of the covenants implied by Sections 2 and 3 of the above Act shall be
deemed to be extended so as not to exclude the liability of the Seller in respect of matters:-

18.1   of which the Seller does not know or could not reasonably be expected to
        know; or

18.2   which at the time of transfer are within the actual knowledge of, or the exis-
        tence of which is a necessary consequence of facts then within the actual
        knowledge of, the Buyer.

19.   BOOKS AND RECORDS

19.1   The Buyer shall keep the Books and Records for a period of [three/six] years
        after the Transfer Point exercising the same degree of care for the safekeeping
        thereof as a bailee for value.

19.2   During the period referred to in clause 19.1 the Buyer shall:

    19.2.1   give the Seller and its authorised representatives at the cost of the
              Seller such facilities to inspect the Books and Records and to take
              copies thereof as the Seller may reasonably require; and

    19.2.2   give such additional information or explanation of the Books and
              Records as the Seller may reasonably require.

19.3   The Seller shall keep the Retained Books and Records for the period of
        [three/six] years after the Transfer Point, exercising the same degree of care
        for the safekeeping thereof as a bailee for value.

19.4   During the period referred to in clause 19.3 the Seller shall:

    19.4.1   give the Buyer and its authorised representatives at the cost of the
              Buyer such facilities to inspect the Retained Books and Records
              and to take copies thereof as the Buyer may reasonably require;
              and

    19.4.2   give such additional information or explanation of the Retained
              Books and Records as the Buyer may reasonably require.

19.5   The provisions of clause 5.6, rather than the provisions of this clause 19,
        shall apply to the VAT Records.

20.   THIRD PARTY ASSETS

20.1   The parties shall each use all reasonable endeavours to procure that the
        benefit of the leasing, rental, hire and hire-purchase agreements relating to

the Third Party Assets is assigned, with the written consent in each case of the relevant other party thereto, as soon as reasonably practicable after the Transfer Point; provided that the Buyer shall have no obligation to make any payment demanded by any person as a condition of giving its written consent to any assignment concerned.

20.2   The Buyer shall, pending assignment of the benefit of each of the agreements referred to in clause 20.1, comply with the terms thereof (insofar as disclosed in the Disclosure Letter) as if it were the Seller [but shall make payment of any sum from time to time payable thereunder (and disclosed in the Disclosure Letter) not to the other party thereto but to the Seller within [fourteen] days following receipt of the Seller's invoice in respect thereof and its written confirmation that it has paid the sum shown on the invoice to the other party to the agreement concerned].

20.3   The Buyer shall be entitled, as regards any of the Third Party Assets in respect of which no written consent to assignment has been obtained within a period of three months following the day of the Transfer Point, at its option either:- to retain possession of the item concerned, in which case it shall continue to comply with clause 20.1 in respect of it, or return it to the Seller, in which case it shall have no further obligation in relation thereto in respect of the period from its return.

20.4   The Buyer shall indemnify the Seller against any failure by the Buyer to comply with any of its obligations under this clause 20.

20.5   The Seller shall indemnify the Buyer against any failure by the Seller to perform its obligations under any agreement relating to any of the Third Party Assets in respect of the period ended at the Transfer Point.

21.   GUARANTEES

The Buyer undertakes with the Seller after Completion to use all reasonable endeavours (short of actual payment of any money and the substitution of the guarantee of any person other than the Buyer) to procure the release of the Seller [and any Member of the Seller's Group at the date of this Agreement] from the guarantees and/or indemnities listed below and to indemnify the Seller [and any such Member of the Seller's Group against any such liability arising after Completion. The guarantees in question are:-

[Details to be inserted—there may, for example, be counter-indemnities given in respect of bonds.]

22.   GUARANTEE

In consideration of the Buyer's obligations hereunder, and in consideration of the sum of £1 paid to the Guarantor by the Buyer (the receipt and sufficiency of which the Guarantor acknowledges), the Guarantor irrevocably and unconditionally guarantees to the Buyer the due and punctual performance by the Seller of the Seller's obligations hereunder and the following provisions shall apply to this guarantee:-

22.1   The Guarantor shall not in any way or to any extent be released from its obligations under this Agreement by reason of any time or other indulgence or waiver granted by the Buyer to the Seller or to any other person, firm or company and this guarantee shall continue in force until the Seller, or the Guarantor on its behalf, shall have fully performed and discharged all of its obligations and liabilities to the Buyer under this Agreement; and

22.2   The Guarantor shall, in respect of any sum paid by it under this Agreement and in respect of any other rights which may accrue howsoever to it in respect of any sum so paid, rank and be entitled to recover or enforce the same against the Seller only after the Seller, or the Guarantor on its behalf, shall have fully performed and discharged all of its obligations and liabilities to the Buyer under this Agreement; and

22.3   Any security for the time being and from time to time held by the Guarantor from the Seller in respect of the obligations and liabilities of the Seller under this Agreement shall be held by it upon trust for the Buyer as security for such obligations and liabilities; and

22.4   This guarantee shall extend to any costs and expenses (including legal expenses), together with VAT thereon, incurred by the Buyer in taking any proceedings or steps of any kind with a view to enforcing this guarantee and in suing for and/or recovering any or all of the amount or amounts payable by the Guarantor under this Agreement; and

22.5   Without prejudice to the rights of the Buyer against the Seller as principal debtor, the Guarantor shall, as between the Buyer and the Seller, be deemed principal debtor in respect of its obligations under this Agreement and not merely a surety, and accordingly it shall not be necessary for the Buyer, before seeking to enforce this guarantee, to seek to enforce any security it may hold from the Seller or otherwise to take any steps or proceedings against the Seller; and

22.6   This guarantee shall extend to the obligations of the Seller under any documents referred to in this Agreement as if the same formed part of this Agreement.

23.   THIRD PARTY RIGHTS

23.1   For the avoidance of doubt and save as expressly provided in clause [   ], nothing in this Agreement shall confer on any third party the right to enforce any provisions of this Agreement.

23.2   Notwithstanding that any provision of this Agreement may be enforceable by any third party this Agreement and its provisions may be amended, waived, modified, rescinded or terminated by the parties to this Agreement without the consent or approval of any third party.

24.   SUCCESSORS

The provisions of this Agreement shall be enforceable and enure for the benefit of any successor in title to the Business or any of the Assets.

25.   WHOLE AGREEMENT

25.1   This Agreement together with all documents entered into or to be entered into pursuant to its provisions constitutes the entire agreement between the parties in relation to its subject-matter and supersedes all prior agreements, understandings and discussions between the parties, other than representations made fraudulently.

25.2   Each of the parties acknowledges that it is not relying on any statements, warranties or representations given or made by the others in relation to the subject-matter of this Agreement, save those expressly set out in this Agreement and other documents referred to above and that it shall have no rights or remedies with respect to such subject-matter otherwise than under this Agreement [and the documents executed at the same time as it or entered into pursuant to it] save to the extent that they arise out of the fraud or fraudulent misrepresentation of any party.

26. **WAIVER**

The rights and remedies of a party in respect of this Agreement shall not be diminished, waived or extinguished by the granting of any indulgence, forbearance or extension of time by a party to another nor by any failure of or delay by a party in ascertaining or exercising any such rights or remedies. Any Release by a party shall not affect its rights and remedies as regards any other party nor its rights and remedies against the party in whose favour it is granted or made except to the extent of the express terms of the Release and no such Release shall have effect unless granted or made in writing. The rights and remedies in this Agreement are cumulative and not exclusive of any rights and/or remedies provided by law.

27. **PROVISIONS SURVIVING COMPLETION**

In so far as the provisions of this Agreement shall not have been performed at Completion, they shall remain in full force and effect notwithstanding Completion.

28. **PROPER LAW AND JURISDICTION**

This Agreement shall be governed by the laws of England and Wales.

29. **JURISDICTION**

Any dispute arising under this Agreement shall be subject to the [exclusive/non-exclusive] jurisdiction of the English courts and the parties waive any objection to Proceedings in such courts on the grounds of venue or on the grounds that Proceedings have been brought in an inappropriate forum.

30. **FURTHER ASSURANCE**

The Seller shall at its expense do such acts and things and execute such documents within its power as the Buyer may at any time reasonably require for the purpose of assuring to the Buyer the full benefit of this Agreement and any document to which it refers.

31. **COUNTERPARTS**

This Agreement may be executed in any number of counterparts and by the parties on separate counterparts, each of which, when so executed and delivered, shall be an original, but all the counterparts shall together be deemed to constitute one and the same agreement.

32. **COSTS**

Each party shall, except where otherwise stated, pay its own costs of and incidental to this Agreement and its subject-matter [except that, if the Buyer shall lawfully exercise any right hereby conferred to rescind this Agreement, the Seller shall indemnify the Buyer against all expenses and costs incurred by it in connection with this Agreement and its subject- matter].

33. **SEVERABILITY**

The provisions of this Agreement are severable and distinct from one another, and, if at any time any of such provisions is or becomes invalid, illegal or unenforceable, the validity, legality or enforceability of the others shall not in any way be affected or impaired thereby.

34. **PUBLICITY**

34.1   The parties shall forthwith upon [the signing of this Agreement/Completion] make or procure to be made a press announcement and announcements to the employees of the Business and to the customers and suppliers of the Business in the Agreed Terms.

34.2 [The Buyer shall be entitled to send a circular to its shareholders convening a general meeting for the purposes set out in schedule 10 and shall give the Seller a reasonable opportunity to comment on the contents of such circular in so far as it relates to it.]

34.3 Each of the parties shall both before and after Completion, but subject to clauses 34.1 and 34.2, keep the contents of this Agreement strictly private and confidential and shall not without the prior written consent of the Buyer (in the case of the Seller) or of the Seller (in the case of the Buyer) disclose any of the terms of this Agreement to any person or make any other announcement relating to the transactions hereby agreed upon except to the extent required by law, [UKLA, the Stock Exchange or the Panel on Take-overs and Mergers] and except that the parties shall be entitled to make references to the transactions hereby agreed upon in their respective future annual reports and financial statements.

35.   NOTICES

35.1 Any Notice relating to this Agreement shall be in writing delivered personally or sent by pre-paid first class post or facsimile transmission to the address of the party to be served given herein or such other address as may be notified for this purpose.

35.2 Any such Notice shall, if sent by post, be deemed to have been served 24 hours after despatch and, if delivered by hand or sent by facsimile transmission, be deemed to have been served at the time of such delivery or transmission.

If, however, in the case of delivery by post a period of 24 hours after despatch would expire on, or, in the case of delivery by hand or facsimile transmission, such delivery or transmission occurs on, a day which is not a Business Day or after 4.00 p.m. on a Business Day, then service shall be deemed to occur on the next following Business Day.

35.3 In proving service it shall be sufficient to prove, in the case of a letter, that such letter was properly stamped, addressed and placed in the post and, in the case of a facsimile transmission, it shall be sufficient to produce a transmission report showing that transmission was duly and fully made to the correct number.

36.   CERTIFICATE OF VALUE

It is certified that the transaction effected by this Agreement does not form part of a larger transaction or of a series of transactions in respect of which the amount or value or the aggregate amount or value exceeds the sum of [£60,000/£250,000/£500,000] *[amount set out in words also]*.

SIGNED by or on behalf of the parties the day and year first before written.

OR

IN WITNESS of which this deed has been executed and unconditionally delivered the day and year first above written.

SCHEDULE 1

Contracts

PRECEDENT 4

SCHEDULE 2

Employees

SCHEDULE 3

Part I

Registered intellectual property and applications

Part II

Listed Intellectual Property Agreements

SCHEDULE 4

Plant

SCHEDULE 5

Property

1.	2.	3.
Property	Title	Apportionment of price

SCHEDULE 6

Third Party Assets

Agreement

Asset	Owner	Description	Date

SCHEDULE 7

Warranties

1.   THE BUSINESS AND THE SELLER['S GROUP]

1.1   **Capacity**

[The Seller has/The Seller and the Guarantor each have] full power to enter into and perform the provisions of this Agreement, which constitutes a binding agreement on [the Seller/each of them] in accordance with its terms.

1.2   **Ownership of the Assets**

The Seller is the beneficial owner of the Assets and has the right to dispose of them to the Buyer or as it directs free from any Encumbrance and together with all rights now or hereafter attaching to them.

1.3   **Transfers at an undervalue**

None of the Assets have been the subject of a transfer at an undervalue (within the meaning of section 238 or section 239 of the Insolvency Act 1986) within the period of five years prior to the date of this Agreement.

1.4   **Liabilities owing to or by the Seller**

There is not outstanding any indebtedness and there are no contracts, arrangements or liabilities (actual or contingent) remaining in whole or in part to be performed between the Business and any Member of the Seller's Group or any director of the Seller or any director of any Member of the Seller's Group or any person who is an associate of or connected with any of them.

2.   CONSTITUTIONAL AND ADMINISTRATIVE AFFAIRS

2.1   **Books and records**

All accounts, books, ledgers, financial and other records of the Seller relating to the Business have been fully, properly and accurately kept and maintained, are in the possession of the Seller and contain true and accurate records of all matters required by law to be entered therein and no notice or allegation that any of them is incorrect or should be rectified has been received by the Seller [or the Guarantor].

2.1.1   The Seller's accounting records, insofar as they relate to the Business:

2.1.1.1   comply with the requirements of the Acts;

2.1.1.2   are sufficient to show and explain the Seller's transactions;

2.1.1.3   disclose with reasonable accuracy, at any time, the financial position of the Seller at that time; and

2.1.1.4   do not contain or reflect any material inaccuracy or discrepancy.

2.2   **Insurances**

2.2.1   The Disclosure Letter sets out full details of all policies of insurance maintained by or on behalf of the Seller in relation to the Business, all of which are in full force and effect.

2.2.2   All premiums in respect of policies of insurance maintained by or on behalf of the Seller have been paid as and when due, and there are no circumstances which might lead to any liability under such insurance being avoided by the insurers or (being circumstances not affecting businesses generally) the premiums being increased, and there is no claim outstanding under any such policy, nor is the Seller [or the Guarantor] aware of any circumstances likely to give rise to a claim thereunder.

2.2.3   The Disclosure Letter sets out full details of all insurance claims made by or on behalf of the Seller in relation to the Business within the period of three years immediately prior to the date of this Agreement.

2.2.4   There are no claims outstanding or threatened or, so far as the Seller is aware, pending against the Seller in relation to the Business which are not fully covered by insurance.

3.   THE SELLER AND THE LAW

3.1   Compliance with Laws

3.1.1   The Seller has conducted and is conducting the Business in accordance with all applicable laws and regulations of any relevant jurisdiction.

3.1.2   There is no order, decree or judgment of any court or any governmental agency of any jurisdiction outstanding against the Seller or which may have any adverse effect upon any of the Assets or the Business; no such order, decree or judgment is pending, and there are no circumstances likely to give rise to any such order, decree or judgment.

3.2   Licences

3.2.1   The Seller has obtained all licences, consents, permits and authorities of a statutory or regulatory nature necessary or expedient to enable it to carry on the Business effectively in the places and in the manner in which it is now carried on.

3.2.2   All such licences, consents, permits and authorities are valid and subsisting, and [neither] the Seller [nor the Guarantor] knows of any reason why any of them should be suspended, cancelled or revoked or renewed or continued subject to any term or condition which does not currently apply thereto.

3.3   Investigations

There is not pending or in existence any investigation or enquiry by or on behalf of any governmental or other body in respect of the Business.

3.4   Litigation

3.4.1   The Seller is not engaged in any dispute with any customer or supplier or in any litigation or other proceedings in respect of the Business or any of the Assets or any of the Third Party Assets.

3.4.2   So far as the Seller [and the Guarantor] [is/are] aware:

3.4.2.1   no litigation or other proceedings are pending or threatened by or against the Seller in relation to the Business or any of the Assets or any of the Third Party Assets;

3.4.2.2   there are no circumstances likely to give rise to any litigation or other proceedings in relation to the Business or any of the Assets or any of the Third Party Assets; and

3.4.2.3   the Seller has not been a party to any undertaking or assurance in relation to the Business or any of the Assets or any of the Third Party Assets given to any court or governmental agency which is still in force.

References in sub-paragraphs 3.4.1 and 3.4.2 to the Seller shall be deemed to include also any person for whom or which the Seller may be or become vicariously liable.

3.5   **Fair trading**

3.5.1   No agreement, practice or arrangement in respect of the Business or to which the Seller is or has been a party infringes any competition, anti-restrictive trade practice, anti-trust or consumer protection law or legislation applicable in any relevant jurisdiction ("Competition Laws").

3.5.2   The Seller has not given any undertaking to any court, person or body and is not subject to any act, decision, regulation, order or other instrument under any Competition Laws and which (in each such case) may affect the Business or any of the Assets.

3.6   **Products**

The Seller has not in the course of the Business manufactured, sold or supplied any product or provided any service which does not or did not at any material time comply with the terms of any contract entered into by the Seller or with any applicable regulation, standard or statutory requirement or which was in any other way defective or dangerous or not in accordance with any representation or warranty, express or implied, given in respect of it.

3.7   **Pollution of the environment**

For the purposes of this paragraph 3.7 the expressions "pollution of the environment" and "process" shall have the same meanings as in section 1 of the Environmental Protection Act 1990.

3.7.1   No hazardous substances have been used or stored or otherwise handled by the Seller on the Property or elsewhere.] [The Seller has at all times held all licences, consents, permits and authorities necessary to enable it to use, store or otherwise handle or dispose of any hazardous substances used, stored, otherwise handled or disposed of by it, whether on the Property or elsewhere.]

3.7.2   There has been no pollution of the environment nor contamination of land by the Seller in the course of the Business and the Seller has no responsibility or liability for any pollution of the environment or for any contaminated land by any third party, and there has been no act or omission by the Seller in the course of the Business which could give rise to any pollution of the environment or contaminated land.

3.7.3   The Seller has complied and has adequate systems and facilities to continue to comply in relation to the Business, with:

3.7.3.1   all laws and regulations relating to pollution of the environment;

3.7.3.2   all laws and regulations relating to pollution of the environment which apply to any person carrying on any process carried on by the Seller;

3.7.3.3   all EC Directives relating to pollution of the environment (whether or not they have been implemented in any relevant jurisdiction).

3.8   **Data Protection**

The Seller has:

3.8.1   at all times complied with the Applicable Data Protection Laws, and there exist no circumstances likely to give rise to any allegation of non-compliance;

3.8.2   made all necessary notifications or registrations under the Applicable Data Protection Laws, and such registrations or notifications are appropriate given the Seller's actual data processing activities;

3.8.3   not received any enforcement, information or other official notice or request under the Applicable Data Protection Laws;

3.8.4   not received any communication from any data subject or official alleging a breach of the Applicable Data Protection Laws;

3.8.5   not been required to pay compensation in respect of any breach of the Applicable Data Protection Laws, no claims for compensation are outstanding and there are no circumstances likely to give rise to such a claim; and

3.8.6   complied with all data subject requests including requests for access to personal data or cessation of specified processing activities.

3.9   **Health and Safety**

3.9.1   The Seller has complied with all its obligations under the Health & Safety at Work etc Act 1974 ("the Health & Safety Act") and all regulations passed thereunder ("the Regulations").

3.9.2   The Seller has not been served with any Improvement Notices.

3.9.3   The Seller has not been served with any Prohibition Notices.

3.9.4   The Seller has not been cautioned for any breach of the Health & Safety Act or the Regulations.

3.9.5   The Seller has not been prosecuted for any breach of the Health & Safety Act or the Regulations.

3.9.6   There are no circumstances likely to give rise to the service of an Improvement Notice or Prohibition Notice, or to a prosecution for a breach of the Health & Safety Act or the Regulations.

3.9.7   The Seller has not been made the subject of a prosecution (whether by the Crown Prosecution Service, the Health and Safety Executive, or any other responsible body) as a result of or in connection with any work-related death and there are no circumstances likely to give rise to such a prosecution.

3.9.8   For the purposes of this paragraph 3.9, the expression "Improvement Notice" and "Prohibition Notice" shall have the same meanings as in sections 21 and 22 of the Health & Safety Act.

4.   **THE SELLER'S FINANCIAL POSITION**

4.1   **The Accounts**

The Accounts:

4.1.1   have been prepared in accordance with the requirements of the Companies Acts and all other applicable statutes and regulations and in accordance with generally accepted accounting principles and practices, including all applicable SSAPs and FRSs;

4.1.2   have been prepared on bases and principles and using methods which are consistent with those used in the preparation of the audited accounts of the Seller for any accounting period falling wholly or partly within the period of six years ended on the Accounts Date; and

4.1.3   show a true and fair view of the state of affairs of the Seller as at the Accounts Date and of the profit or loss of the Seller for the accounting period ended on that date.

4.2.   **Provisions in the Accounts**

The Accounts:

4.2.1   fully provide for all liabilities (other than contingent liabilities which are not expected to crystallise) and fully disclose all contingent liabilities which are not expected to crystallise and all capital and revenue commitments of the Seller in each case as at the Accounts Date;

4.2.2   fully provide for all bad and doubtful debts as at the Accounts Date;

4.2.3   attribute a value to stock which does not exceed the lower of direct cost and net realisable value as at the Accounts Date after wholly writing off all redundant, obsolete, old, unusable, unsaleable, slow-moving, deteriorated and excessive stock;

4.2.4   are not affected (except as disclosed in the Accounts) by any extraordinary or exceptional event, circumstance or item.

4.3   **Events since the Accounts Date**

Since the Accounts Date:

4.3.1   the Seller has carried on the Business in the ordinary and usual course and without any interruption or alteration in the nature, scope or manner thereof;

4.3.2   the Seller has not in relation to the Business acquired or disposed of any asset entered into any transaction, assumed any liability, made any payment or entered into any other transaction which was not in the ordinary course of the Business and for full value;

4.3.3   turnover and margins of profitability of the Business, have not been less than its turnover and margins of profitability for the corresponding period in the accounting period which ended on the Accounts Date and there has been no deterioration in its financial position or prospects. In particular, there has been no reduction in the value of the net tangible assets of the Business on the basis of the valuations used in the Accounts;

4.3.4   the Seller has paid the creditors of the Business within the times agreed with such creditors, and there are no debts now outstanding by the Seller in relation to the Business which have been outstanding for more than [   ] days or which are now overdue for payment (whether in whole or in part);

4.3.5   the Seller has not entered into, or agreed to enter into, any capital commitment in relation to the Business;

4.3.6   no part of the amounts included in the Accounts, or subsequently recorded in the books of the Seller as owing by any debtors has been outstanding for more than [   ] days or has been released on terms that any debtor pays less than the full book value of his or its debt or has been written off or has proved to any extent to be irrecoverable or is now regarded by the Seller as, or as likely to become, irrecoverable in whole or in part;

4.3.7   the Seller has not factored or discounted any of the Book Debts or agreed to do so;

4.3.8   the Seller has not in the course of the Business offered any price reduction or discount or allowance on sales of stock below a selling price which achieves a gross margin of [   ] % or sold any stock at less than its book value;

4.3.9   the Seller has not sought to accelerate payment by the trade debtors of the Business other than in the ordinary and normal course of the Business.

4.4   **Options**

There is no option or pre-emption right in favour of any third party in relation to the Business or any of the Assets.

4.5   **Debts**

There are no debts owing by or to the Seller in relation to the Business other than debts which have arisen in the ordinary course of its business, nor has the Seller lent any money which has not been repaid.

4.6   **Management Accounts**

The Management Accounts have been prepared using the same accounting principles, policies and bases as used in the Accounts (consistently applied) fairly reflect the trading position of the Business as at the date and for the period to which they relate and are not affected by any extraordinary, exceptional, unusual or non-recurring income, capital gain or expenditure or by any other factor known to the [Seller] [Guarantor] rendering profits or losses for the period covered exceptionally high or low.

5.   **THE ASSETS USED IN THE BUSINESS**

5.1   **Assets and charges**

5.1.1   The Seller owns all of the Assets free from any Encumbrance all assets except for current assets subsequently disposed of by the Seller in the ordinary course of its business [,the Properties] and stock which is the subject of retention of title terms contained in standard terms of trading imposed by suppliers in the ordinary course of their business and owns free from any Encumbrance any other asset used by it.

5.2   **Assets sufficient for the business**

5.2.1   The Seller owns all of the Assets free from any Encumbrance and the Assets, together with the Third Party Assets, comprise all assets necessary for the continuation of the Business as now carried on and none of the Assets is shared by the Business with any other person.

5.2.2   The Assets are the only assets used by the Seller in connection with the Business other than those specified in clause 2.

5.2.3   The Seller has possession of all those of the Assets which are tangible assets and of all of the Third Party Assets.

5.2.4   The Seller does not in relation to the Business share any asset with any member of the Seller's Group or depend upon or make use of any assets, facilities or services owned or supplied by any Member of the Seller's Group at the date of this Agreement.

5.3   Stocks

The Stocks are adequate and not excessive in relation to the current trading requirements of the Business; none of them is obsolete, slow-moving, unsaleable, unmarketable, unusable or inappropriate or of limited value in relation to the Business; and they are capable of being sold in the ordinary course of the Business in accordance with current price lists without rebate or allowance to a Buyer.

5.4   Debts

Each of the Book Debts is recoverable in full in the ordinary course of the Business and in any event not later than [ninety] days following the date of this Agreement, and none of them is subject to any counterclaim or set-off.

5.5   Intellectual property

5.5.1   The Seller:

     5.5.1.1   is the sole and beneficial owner of the Intellectual Property Rights all of which are valid and in full force and effect);

     5.5.1.2   is (where such rights are capable of registration) the registered proprietor of the Intellectual Property Rights;

     5.5.1.3   does not own or use in connection with the Business any Intellectual Property other than the Intellectual Property specified in schedule 3 and other than copyrights, design rights, technical know-how and confidential information;

     5.5.1.4   does not require any other Intellectual Property to carry on the Business;

     5.5.1.5   has not entered into any Intellectual Property Agreements other than those specified in schedule 3 or authorised any person to make any use of or to do anything which would or might otherwise infringe any Intellectual Property owned or used by it; and

     5.5.1.6   has not disclosed (except in the ordinary course of the Business) any of its know-how, trade secrets or customer details to any other person.

5.5.2   The Seller owns the copyright or design right (whether registered or unregistered) in the designs of all its products and is the proprietor of any registrations or applications to register any such designs.

5.5.3   None of the processes used in or products of the Business [(so far as the Seller is aware)]:

     5.5.3.1   infringes any Intellectual Property of any other person; or

     5.5.3.2   involves the unlicensed use of confidential information or know-how disclosed to the Seller by any person.

5.5.4   None of the Intellectual Property Rights are being used (other than by the Seller) or are being or have been claimed, disputed, opposed or attacked by any person.

5.5.5   The Intellectual Property Agreements are the Intellectual Property Agreements to which the Seller is a party, all of them are valid and binding on the parties thereto, and the Seller has at all times observed and performed all of the provisions of each of them. Nothing has been done or omitted by the Seller which would enable any of them to be terminated or which in any way constitutes a breach of the terms of any of them.

5.5.6   None of the records, systems, data or information relating to the Business is recorded, stored, maintained, operated or otherwise wholly or partly dependent on or held or accessible by any means (including) any electronic, mechanical or photographic process, whether computerised or not) which are not under the exclusive ownership and direct control of the Seller.

5.5.7   No person has the right to require the Seller to change its corporate name or to cease using any trade name, logo, trading style, domain name or e-mail address currently used by it in relation to the Business.

5.6 Plant

Each item of Plant:

5.6.1   is in good repair and condition (subject to fair wear and tear) and in satisfactory working order;

5.6.2   is capable, over the period of time during which it is to be written down to a nil value in the accounts of the Seller, of doing the work for which it was designed or purchased;

5.6.3   is not surplus to the requirements of the Business, and

5.6.4   is safe to operate and complies with all relevant Health and Safety at Work legislation and rules.

5.7 Third Party Assets

A true and complete copy of each of the leasing, rental, hire and hire-purchase agreements relating to any of the Third Party Assets is attached to the Disclosure Letter.

5.8 Computer Systems

5.8.1   The Computer Systems are capable of the following functions:

5.8.1.1   handling date information involving all and any dates including, accepting date input, providing date output and performing date calculations in whole or part;

5.8.1.2   operating accurately without interruption on and in respect of any and all dates and without any change in performance;

5.8.1.3   responding to and processing two digit year input without creating any ambiguity as to the century;

5.8.1.4   storing and providing date output information without creating any ambiguity as to the century; and

5.8.1.5   converting sterling into euros.

5.8.2 The Computer Systems and each element of them passes and will continue to pass date information between each other (and any third parties' computer systems with which they habitually communicate) in a way which does not, and will not, create inaccuracies.

5.8.3 The Hardware has been satisfactorily maintained and supported and has the benefit of an appropriate maintenance and support agreement which is not capable of being terminated by the contractor by less than 24 months' notice.

5.8.4 The Hardware and Software have adequate capability and capacity for the projected requirements of the Business for not less than 4 years following Completion.

5.8.5 Disaster recovery plans are in effect and are adequate to ensure that the Hardware, Software and Data can be replaced or substituted without material disruption to the Business.

5.8.6 In the event that any person providing maintenance or support services for the Computer Systems ceases or is unable to do so, the Seller has all necessary rights and information to procure the carrying out of such services by employees or by a third party without undue expense or delay.

5.8.7 The Employees include sufficient technically competent and trained employees to ensure proper handling, operation, monitoring and use of the Computer Systems.

5.8.8 The Business has adequate procedures to ensure internal and external security of the Computer Systems and of the Data, including procedures for preventing unauthorised access, preventing the introduction of a virus, taking and storing on-site and off-site back-up copies of Software and Data.

5.8.9 Where any of the records of the Business are stored electronically, the Seller is the owner of all hardware and software licences necessary to enable it to keep, copy, maintain and use such records in the course of its business and does not share any hardware or software relating to the records with any person.

5.8.10 The Seller has all the rights necessary (including rights over the source code) to obtain, without undue expense or delay, modified versions of the Software which are required at any time to improve in any regard the operation and/or efficiency of the Software.

5.8.11 The Seller owns, and is in possession and control of, original copies of all of the manuals, guides, instruction books and technical documents (including any corrections and updates) required to operate the Computer Systems effectively.

5.8.12 The Computer Systems have never unduly interrupted or hindered the running or operation of the Business and have no defects in operation which so affect the Business.

5.8.13 In this paragraph 5.8.13:-

5.8.13.1 "Data" means any data or information used by or for the benefit of the Business at any time and stored electronically at any time;

5.8.13.2 "Hardware" means any computer equipment which is comprised within the Assets or the Third Party Assets including, without limitation, PCs, mainframes, screens, terminals, keyboards, discs, printers, cabling and associated and peripheral electronic equipment but excluding all Software;

5.8.13.3   "Software" means any set of instructions for execution by microprocessor used by or for the benefit of the Seller in relation to the Business at any time, irrespective of application, language or medium;

5.8.13.4   "Computer Systems" means all Hardware, Software and any other items that connect with any or all of them which in each case are comprised within the Assets or the Third Party Assets.

6.   THE CONTRACTS OF THE BUSINESS

6.1   Documents

All title deeds and agreements relating to the Business or any of the Assets to which the Seller is a party are in the possession of the Seller and are properly stamped and free from Encumbrance.

6.2   Material contracts

[The Seller is not a party to or subject to any agreement, transaction, obligation, commitment, understanding, arrangement or liability relating to the Business which:/None of the Contracts:][6]

6.2.1   is incapable of complete performance in accordance with its terms within three months after the date on which it was entered into or undertaken or cannot be terminated, without giving rise to any liabilities on the Seller, by the Seller giving three months' notice or less;

6.2.2   is known by the Seller to be likely to result in a loss on completion or performance;

6.2.3   cannot readily be fulfilled or performed on time;

6.2.4   involves or is likely to involve obligations, restrictions, expenditure or revenue of an unusual, onerous or exceptional nature;

6.2.5   requires an aggregate consideration payable by the Seller in excess of £[   ] ([   ] pounds);

6.2.6   is in any way otherwise than in the ordinary and proper course of the Business and on arm's length terms[; and

and a true and complete copy of each of the Contracts is attached to the Disclosure Letter].

6.3   Defaults

Neither the Seller nor any other party to [any agreement with the Seller relating to the Business or any of the Assets/any of the Contracts] is in default thereunder, being a default which would be material in the context of the financial or trading position of the Business nor (so far as the Seller is aware) are there any circumstances likely to give rise to any such default.

6.4   Insider contracts

There is not outstanding, and there has not at any time during the last three years been outstanding, any agreement or arrangement between the Seller and any Member of the Seller's Group at any material time and the Seller is

[6] The wording to be used will depend on the definition of Contracts.

not a party to, nor has its profit or loss or financial position during such period been affected by, any such agreement or any other agreement or arrangement in relation to the Business which is not entirely of an arm's length nature.

6.5   **Customers/suppliers**

6.5.1   In the accounting period ended on the Accounts Date, no customer or supplier of the Business represented [%] or more of the Seller's sales or purchases in that period in relation to the Business (any such customer or supplier being a "Major Customer" or "Major Supplier") save for those specifically identified in the Disclosure Letter as Major Customers or Major Suppliers;

6.5.2   No Major Customer or Major Supplier has since the Accounts Date ceased to do business with the Seller or has since such date substantially reduced its purchases from or supplies to the Seller; since the Accounts Date no indication has been received by the Seller of any material change in the prices or other terms upon which any customer or supplier is prepared to contract or do business with the Seller;

6.5.3   The Seller is not aware of any reason to indicate that any of the existing customers of or suppliers of the Business are likely materially to reduce the volume of their purchases from or supplies to the Business in the future by comparison with the value of their purchases or supplies during the period of [   ] months prior to the date of this Agreement.

7.   **EMPLOYEES**

7.1   **General**

7.1.1   No person is employed in the Business other than the Employees.

7.1.2   There is no employment contract or other contract of engagement between the Seller and any of the Employees which cannot be terminated by the Seller by three months' notice or less without giving rise to a claim for damages or compensation (other than a statutory redundancy payment or statutory compensation for unfair dismissal). The Seller has not received notice of resignation from any of the Employees.

7.1.3   There is no employment contract or consultancy contract or other contract of engagement between the Seller and any person which is in suspension or has been terminated but is capable of being revived or enforced or in respect of which the Seller has a continuing obligation.

7.1.4   The Disclosure Letter contains details of:

7.1.4.1   the total number of the employees of the Business including those who are on maternity leave or absent because of disability or other long-term leave of absence and who have or may have a right to return to work;

7.1.4.2   the name, date of start of employment, period of continuous employment, salary and other benefits, grade and age of each Employee and, where an Employee has been continuously absent from work for more than one month, the reason for the absence; and

7.1.4.3   the terms of the contract of each Employee entitled to remuneration at an annual rate, or an average annual rate over the last three financial years, of more than £[   ].

7.1.5   The basis of the remuneration payable to the Employees is the same as that in force at the Accounts Date. The Seller is not obliged to increase, nor has it made provision to increase, the rate of remuneration of any Employee.

7.1.6   There is no agreement or arrangement between the Seller and an Employee with respect to his employment, his ceasing to be employed or his retirement which is not included in the written terms of his employment or previous employment. The Seller has not provided, or agreed to provide, a gratuitous payment or benefit to any Employee or to any of their dependants.

7.1.7   The Seller has maintained up-to-date, full and accurate records regarding the employment of each of its employees (including details of terms of employment, payments of statutory sick pay and statutory maternity pay, income tax and social security contributions, working time, disciplinary and health and safety matters) and termination of employment.

7.1.8   The Seller has not made or agreed to make a payment or provided or agreed to provide a benefit to an Employee or to any dependants of any Employee in connection with the actual or proposed termination or suspension of employment or variation of an employment contract.

7.2   **Compliance with law**

The Seller has complied with:

7.2.1   each obligation imposed on it by, and each order and award made under, statute, regulation, code of conduct and practice, collective agreement (including any agreement or arrangement under the Information and Consultation of Employees Regulations 2004), custom and practice relevant to the relations between it and the Employees or a trade union or the terms of employment of the Employees; and

7.2.2   each recommendation or code of practice made by the Advisory, Conciliation and Arbitration Service and each award and declaration made by the Central Arbitration Committee.

7.3   **Redundancies and transfer of business**

Within the year ending on the date of this Agreement the Seller has not:-

7.3.1   in relation to any Employee given notice of redundancies to the relevant Secretary of State or started consultations with appropriate representatives under Chapter II of Part IV of the Trade Union and Labour Relations (Consolidation) Act 1992 or failed to comply with its obligations under Chapter II of Part IV of that Act; or.

7.3.2   been a party to a relevant transfer (as defined in the Regulations) or failed to comply with a duty to inform and consult appropriate representatives under those Regulations.

7.4   **Collective Bargaining and Consultation**

7.4.1   The Seller has no agreement or arrangement (whether under the Information and Consultation of Employees Regulations 2004 or otherwise) with and does not recognise a trade union, works council, staff association or other body representing any of its Employees and the Seller has not received any notice or request nor are there any negotiations which may lead to any such agreement or arrangement).

7.4.2 The Seller is not involved in, and no fact or circumstance exists which might give rise to:-

7.4.2.1 a dispute with a trade union, works council, staff association or other body representing any of its Employees; or

7.4.2.2 any proceedings before the Central Arbitration Committee or an Employment Tribunal in relation to any collective bargaining agreement or any arrangement under the ICE Regulations 2004.

7.5 Incentive schemes

The Seller does not have and is not proposing to introduce a share incentive, share option, profit sharing, bonus or other incentive scheme for any of the directors, other officers or employees.

8. PENSIONS

8.1 Disclosed Schemes

The Disclosed Schemes are the only arrangements under which the Seller has or could have any liability to provide or contribute towards relevant benefits, as defined in Chapter 2 of Part 6 of the Income Tax (Earnings & Pensions) Act 2003.

8.2 Details Supplied

The Seller has supplied to the Buyer documents containing full, accurate and up to date details of each of the Disclosed Schemes and of the Seller's obligations and liabilities under it.

8.3 Eligibility Requirements

No amendments have been proposed or announced in relation to the eligibility requirements for entry to the Disclosed Schemes, contribution rates or benefits.

8.4 Legal Compliance

Each of the Disclosed Schemes complies and has at all times complied with all legal and regulatory requirements (including equal treatment and data protection requirements) applicable to it.

8.5 Stakeholder Pension Scheme

The Seller complies and has at all times complied with any duty to facilitate access to a stakeholder pension scheme under section 3 of the Welfare Reform and Pensions Act 1999.

8.6 Deduction of Contributions

All contributions deducted from the salaries of Employees who are members of the Disclosed Schemes and all contributions payable by the Seller to and in respect of the Disclosed Schemes have been paid and passed to the trustees of the Pension Scheme or the provider[s] of the Personal Pension Schemes, GPP, Life Assurance Scheme and the Stakeholder Scheme, as appropriate, in full and within the prescribed time limits applicable in each case.

8.7   **Payments**

All levies payable in respect of the Pension Scheme have been paid in full and on or by the due date in each case.

8.8   **Claims and Disputes**

No claim, dispute, complaint or investigation (including, but not limited to, complaints to the Pensions Ombudsman and investigations by the Pensions Regulator) has arisen which relates to the Disclosed Schemes or to the provision of retirement or death benefits in respect of the Employees and there is no reason why any such claim, dispute, complaint or investigation could arise.

8.9   **Registered Pension Scheme**

Each of the Disclosed Schemes is a registered pension scheme (within the meaning of Chapter 2 of Part 4 of the Finance Act 2004) and there is no reason why HM Revenue & Customs could withdraw that registration.

8.10   **Contracting Out**

The Pension Scheme is [not] a contracted out scheme within the meaning of section 8 of the Pension Schemes Act 1993.

8.11   **Death in Service Benefits**

All death in service benefits under the [Pension Scheme/Life Assurance Scheme] are fully insured on normal terms for persons in good health.

8.12   **Equalising Benefits**

The Pension Scheme has complied fully with its obligations to equalise benefits for men and women.

8.13   **Eligibility Criteria**

The eligibility criteria for access to the Disclosed Schemes have not been operated so as to discriminate on the grounds of sex, race, disability, religion or belief, sexual orientation or [on and after 1 October 2006] age.

8.14   **Money Purchase Basis [Only relevant to defined contribution schemes]**

All benefits under the Pension Scheme (other than those which are fully insured) are calculated on a money purchase basis only and the Seller has given no assurance or contractual promise to any Employee that his benefits at retirement will be based on his salary at or near to retirement.

8.15   **Funding [Only relevant to defined benefit schemes]**

As at [date of last actuarial valuation] the Pension Scheme was fully funded on a [scheme specific funding/ FRS 17] basis, contributions since that date have been paid in accordance with the current schedule of contributions in accordance with section 58 of the Pensions Act 1995, and nothing has occurred since that date which would have an adverse effect on the funding position.

8.16   **Discretions and Powers [Only relevant to defined benefit schemes]**

No discretion or power has been exercised under the Pension Scheme in respect of any Employee to

8.16.1   augment benefits

8.16.2   admit to membership an employee or director who would not otherwise have been eligible for membership

8.16.3   provide in respect of a member a benefit which would not otherwise be provided in respect of that member

8.16.4   provide or pay a benefit on more favourable terms.

8.17   Transfer Payments [Only relevant to defined benefit schemes]

No transfer payment has been made from the Pension Scheme whose amount exceeds the lower of 5% of the assets of the Pension Scheme and £1.5m.

8.18   Benefits [Only relevant to defined benefit schemes]

No member is in receipt of or entitled to receive benefits from the Pension Scheme whose value exceeds the lower of 5% of the assets and £1.5m.

8.19   Notifiable Events [Only relevant to defined benefit schemes]

No notifiable event within the meaning of section 67 of the Pensions Act 2004 has occurred in relation to the Pension Scheme or the Seller.

9.   PROPERTY

9.1   Particulars

The Particulars of the Property shown in schedule 4 are true and correct and the Seller has good and marketable title to and the exclusive occupation and possession of the Property free from any mortgage, debenture or charge (whether specific or floating, legal or equitable) rent charge, lien or other encumbrance, lease, sub-lease, tenancy or right of occupation, reservation, covenant, stipulation, profit a prendre, wayleave, grant, restriction, easement, quasi-easement or any agreement for any of the same or any privilege in favour of any third party.

9.2   Rights and easements

There are appurtenant to the Property all rights and easements necessary for its use and enjoyment.

9.3   Title deeds and documents

The Seller has in its possession or under its control all duly stamped deeds and documents which are necessary to prove title to the Property.

9.4   Disputes etc

The Property is not affected by any of the following matters nor is it likely to become so affected:-

9.4.1   any dispute, notice or complaint or any exception, reservation, right, covenant, restriction, overriding interest or condition and in particular (but without limitation) any of those matters which is of an unusual nature or which affects or might in the future affect the use of any of the Property for the purpose for which it is now used or which affects or might in the future affect the value of the Property; or

9.4.2   any notice, order, demand, requirement or proposal made or issued by or on behalf of any government or statutory authority, department or body for the acquisition, clearance, demolition or closing or the carrying out of any work upon any building, the modification of any planning permission, the discontinuance of any use or the imposition of any building or improvement line; or

9.4.3   any compensation received as a result of any refusal of any application for planning consent or the imposition of any restrictions in relation to any planning consent; or

9.4.4   any commutation or agreement for the commutation of rent or payment of rent in advance of the due dates for payment thereof.

9.5   **State of repair and condition**

The Property is in a good and substantial state of repair and condition and is fit for the purpose for which it is presently used and no high alumina cement, wood, wool, calcium chloride, sea dredged aggregates, asbestos or other deleterious material (not in accordance with good building practice) was used in the construction thereof and there are no development works, redevelopment works or fitting out works outstanding in respect of the Property.

9.6   **Restrictions, conditions and covenants**

All restrictions conditions and covenants (including any imposed by or pursuant to any lease) affecting the Property have been duly and punctually observed and performed and no notice of any breach of any of the same has been received or is likely to be received.

9.7   **Compliance with legislation**

The use of the Property and all machinery and equipment thereon and the conduct of any business thereon complies and has at all times complied in all respects with all relevant statutes and regulations, including the Factories Act 1961, the Offices, Shops and Railway Premises Act 1963, the Fire Precautions Act 1971, the Health and Safety at Work etc., Act 1990 and with all rules, regulations and delegated legislation thereunder and all necessary licences and consents required thereunder have been obtained.

9.8   **Use of property**

There are no restrictive covenants or provisions, legislation, or orders, charges, restrictions, agreements, conditions or other matters which preclude the use of the Property for the purpose or purposes for which the Property is now used and each such use is the permitted use under the provisions of the Town and Country Planning Acts 1971 to 1990 and any statutory re-enactment thereof and all statutory instruments and regulations made thereunder and is in accordance with the requirements of any Local Authority and all restrictions, conditions and covenants imposed by or pursuant to the said Town and Country Planning Acts have been observed and performed and no agreements have been entered into under section 52 of the Town and Country Planning Act 1971, section 106 of the Town and Country Planning Act 1990 or section 33 of the Local Government (Miscellaneous Provisions) Act 1982 in respect of the Property.

9.9   **Replies to enquiries**

All replies by or on behalf of the Seller to enquiries relating to the Property made by or on behalf of the Purchaser were when given and are now true complete accurate and correct.

9.10   **Encumbrances**

There are no options agreements for sale, mortgages, charges (whether specific or floating) rights of pre-emption or of first refusal affecting the Property.

9.11   **Outgoings**

The Property is not subject to the payment of any outgoings (except national non domestic rates and water rates and sewerage service charges). The Property abuts onto an adopted public highway maintainable at public expense to which it has access without crossing land not in the ownership of the Seller.

9.12 Compulsory purchase orders

There are no compulsory purchase notices, orders or resolutions affecting the Property.

9.13 No further land and buildings

The Property comprises all the land and buildings owned, leased or occupied by the Seller for the purposes of the Business.

10. MATERIAL DISCLOSURE

10.1 Disclosure Letter

All information contained in or referred to in the Disclosure letter is true and accurate, and the Disclosure Letter does not omit anything which renders any such information misleading or which might reasonably affect the willingness of an acquirer to acquire the Business and the Assets on the terms (including without limitation as to price) of this Agreement.

10.2 Relationships

To the best of the knowledge and belief of the Seller [(but without having made any enquiry of any customer or supplier of the Seller)], the transaction hereby agreed upon is not of itself likely to have any adverse effect on the relationships of any customer or supplier of the Business with the Business or upon the performance of any Employee.

10.3 Legal Due Diligence Enquiries

The replies to the legal due diligence enquiries dated [   ] 200 raised on behalf of the Buyer were when given and remain true, complete and accurate.

11. TAXATION

11.1   The Seller has no material agreements with any Taxation Authority relating to transactions entered into in the course of the Business pursuant to which such transactions will be subject to Taxation on a basis which is not strictly in accordance with the relevant legislation.

11.2   The Seller is not aware of any dispute or any circumstances likely to give rise to any dispute with any relevant Taxation Authority in connection with the Business.

11.3   The Seller does not conduct and has not conducted any part of the Business through a branch, agency or permanent establishment outside the United Kingdom, and the Business has not involved the Seller acting as branch or agent of any person not resident for any taxation purpose in the United Kingdom.

11.4   No material sum of an income nature paid under any existing contract or commitment relating to the Business which will continue after Completion has been disallowed wholly or in part as a deduction or charge in compiling the Seller's profits for Taxation purposes.

11.5   The [Fixtures] will not be given a disposal value in the capital allowances computation of the Seller which is less than the value set out therefor in this

Agreement by virtue of the operation of section 185 of the Capital Allowances Act 2001.

11.6 The amount of the consideration allocated to the [Building] in this Agreement is not less than the eligible cost therefor for industrial buildings allowances purposes.

11.7 There is no P11D dispensation in force in relation to any of the Employees.

11.8 The Seller is not transferring any assets pursuant to this Agreement to which Part XV of the Value Added Tax Regulations 1995 (Capital Goods Scheme) applies.

SCHEDULE 8

Pension arrangements

SCHEDULE 9

Claims procedure and determination and Seller's safeguards

1.   NOTICE OF CLAIMS AND TIME LIMITS

No claim in respect of any breach of any of the Warranties (other than Warranty 1) shall be made (except in any case of fraud, dishonesty or wilful non-disclosure) unless notice thereof has been given by or on behalf of the Buyer before:

1.1   in respect of any breach of any of the Warranties other than Warranty 1 and the Tax Warranties, the expiry of the period of [   ] years following Completion; or

1.2   in respect of any breach of any of the Tax Warranties, the expiry of the period of six months following the end of the accounting reference period of the Buyer in which the sixth anniversary of Completion falls.

2.   THE DISCLOSURE LETTER

The Buyer shall not be entitled to bring any claim in respect of any breach of any of the Warranties if and to the extent that such inconsistency has been fairly disclosed in the Disclosure Letter with sufficient details to identify the nature and scope of the matter disclosed.

3.   LIMITATION OF LIABILITY—MAXIMUM AND MINIMUM AMOUNTS

3.1   The Seller shall have no liability in damages in respect of any claim by the Buyer under any of the Warranties (except for claims in respect of any breaches of the Warranties in paragraph 1 of schedule 7 and except in any case of fraud, dishonesty or wilful non-disclosure):

      3.1.1   if and to the extent that such liability would, when aggregated with the amount of any damages paid to the Buyer by the Seller in respect of all and any other such claims, exceed £[A] ([A] pounds); and

3.2   unless such claim:

      3.2.1   equals or exceeds £[B] ([B] pounds); and

      3.2.2   would, when aggregated with all other such claims against the Seller of £[B] ([B] pounds) or more equal or exceed £[C] ([C]pounds);

but any such claim shall not be limited to the excess over the amounts specified in this sub-paragraph 3.2.

SCHEDULE 10

Conditional agreement

Part 1

Conditions

1. **CONDITIONS**

The provisions of this Agreement (other than clauses 13, 18 and 23 to 37 and schedules 1, 2, 3, 4, 5, 6, 7, 8 and 9) are conditional upon the fulfilment of all the following conditions not later than, and the continuance in full force and effect of their fulfilment at [
], or such later date as may be agreed in writing between the Seller and the Buyer:

1.1   the passing of a[n ordinary] resolution in general meeting of the Buyer approving the transaction hereby agreed upon [or the Stock Exchange indicating to the Buyer in writing that it does not require the Buyer to submit such transaction to its members for approval; and

1.2   the passing of a[n ordinary] resolution in general meeting of the Seller approving the transaction hereby agreed upon [or the Stock Exchange indicating to the Seller in writing that it does not require the Seller to submit such transaction to its members for approval; and

1.3   [no action having been taken or intimated by HM Government (or any department or agency thereof) or any third party to restrain the transaction hereby agreed upon; and]

1.4   no receiver and/or manager or administrator or administrative receiver having been appointed of the whole or any part of the assets and undertaking of the Seller [or of the Guarantor]; and

1.5   no order having been made and no resolution having been passed for the winding up of the Seller [or of the Guarantor]; and

1.6   no application having been made for an administration order in respect of the Seller [or the Guarantor] and no petition having been presented and no notice having been given (whether or not by the Seller [or the Guarantor] and whether or not by any members) relating to the winding-up of the Seller [or the Guarantor]; and

1.7   the Buyer not having exercised any right to rescind this Agreement.

2. **THE PARTIES' ENDEAVOURS**

Each of the parties shall use all reasonable endeavours to ensure that the said provisions of this Agreement become unconditional in accordance with their terms[, and [the Seller] [and] [the Buyer] shall in particular, but without limitation, procure that the circular letter[s] to be sent to [its/their respective] shareholders relating to the resolution[s] referred to in paragraph[s] 1.1 [and 1.2] contain[s] unanimous recommendation[s] by the directors of [the Seller] [and] [the Buyer] [respectively] and a confirmation that each intends to vote in favour of such resolution in respect of his own holding and that the general meeting[s] referred to in paragraph[s] 1.1 [and 1.2] [is/are] held no later than [200   ]].

3. **NON-FULFILMENT**

If any one or more of the Conditions are not fulfilled on or before [   ], the agreement constituted by this Agreement shall thereupon become void and of no effect except as regards and without prejudice to any and all rights of action of the parties for any prior breach of any of the provisions of this Agreement. In that event the parties shall promptly return to one another all documents and other things already delivered in connection with the transaction hereby agreed upon.

4.   WAIVER

The Buyer shall be entitled at its option to waive any one or more of the Conditions [other than that set out in paragraph 1.2 above], and, if it does so, the Seller [and the Guarantor] shall be deemed to have done so also. [The Seller shall be entitled at its option to waive the Condition set out in paragraph 1.2, and, if it does so, the Buyer shall be deemed to have done so also.]

5.   NOTICE OF FULFILMENT OF CONDITIONS

5.1   [When the Conditions [other than that set out in paragraph 1] have been ful-
           filled, the Buyer shall forthwith give written notice to that effect to the Seller
           or the Seller's Solicitors, and such notice shall be conclusive and binding on
           the parties as to the fulfilment thereof.]

5.2   [When the Condition set out in paragraph 1.2 has been fulfilled, the Seller
           shall forthwith give written notice to that effect to the Buyer, and such notice
           shall be conclusive and binding on the parties as to the fulfilment thereof.]

Part 2

Obligations and events pending Completion

1.   RESTRICTIONS

The Seller shall prior to Completion carry on the Business in the normal way so as to maintain it as a going concern and, except with the prior written consent of the Buyer, shall not:

1.1   grant any Encumbrance over any of the Assets or, except for trading stock in
           the ordinary course of the Business on arm's length terms, dispose of any of
           the Assets;

1.2   grant or agree to grant any licence or make or agree to make any assignment
           or enter into any agreement with any person in relation to any Intellectual
           Property;

1.3   acquire any asset on lease, lease-purchase, hire-purchase or deferred terms;

1.4   do or allow to be done or omitted any act or thing which may render its
           financial position less favourable than at the date of this Agreement;

1.5   enter into any transaction outside the ordinary course of the Business[; nor

1.6   do or allow to be done or omitted any act or thing which may reduce or
           vitiate the cover afforded by any current insurance policy;

1.7   [do anything which would or might render in any way untrue or inaccurate
           or misleading the circular to the shareholders of the Buyer as contemplated
           by paragraph 6 of part 1 of this schedule.

2.   ACCESS TO RECORDS

           The Seller shall at all times prior to Completion give to the Buyer and its pro-
           fessional advisers, in all cases with reasonable despatch upon request, all such
           information and make available for inspection all such documents and records
           as it or they may reasonably require and as may be under the control of the
           Seller [or the Guarantor] and so far as possible take and procure to be taken
           all such steps as may be required to implement the terms of this Agreement.

Part 3

Warranties

1.   MAINTENANCE OF WARRANTIES

The Seller shall procure that (save only as may be necessary to give effect to the terms of this Agreement) there shall not occur, at any time at or before Completion, any change of circumstances such that, if the Warranties were repeated at that time, any of them would not then be true and accurate.

1.1   **Notice of change in circumstances**

The Seller [and the Guarantor] shall [each] forthwith notify the Buyer if and as soon as it becomes aware of any such change of circumstances at any time at or before Completion.

1.2   **Rescission**

The Buyer shall not be bound to complete the acquisition of the Business and of the Assets, and may by notice in writing to the Seller of the Seller's Solicitors rescind this Agreement without liability on its part, if:

1.2.1   on the date of this Agreement any of the Warranties are not true and accurate; and/or

1.2.2   at any time at or before Completion or the fulfilment of the Conditions there is a change of circumstances such that, if the Warranties were repeated at that time, any of them would not then be true and accurate; and/or

1.2.3   the Seller is in breach of part 2 of this schedule

[and (in any such case) the amount which the Buyer is entitled to claim or would be entitled to claim if the Warranties were repeated or if Completion had taken place amounts to at least £[   ] ([   ] pounds).

1.3   [Rescission shall be without prejudice to the rights of the [parties/Buyer] in respect of any prior breach of any of the provisions of this Agreement.]

SCHEDULE 11

Calculation of Completion Value

Part 1

Interpretation

In this schedule the following words and expressions shall have the meanings set out opposite each respectively:

"the Buyer's Accountants"	[ ] of [ ];
"the Completion Value"	the value at the Transfer Point of the <u>Stocks,</u> as determined in accordance with this schedule;
"Independent Accountant"	a chartered accountant agreed upon by or on behalf of the Seller and the Buyer or, if they fail to agree, nominated on the application at any time of the Seller or of the Buyer by the President for the time being of the Institute of Chartered Accountants in England and Wales (the costs of such accountant, and, if applicable, of such President, in nominating such accountant to be borne as he may direct);
"the Seller's Accountants"	[ ] of [ ].

Part 2

Calculation

1.   [The Buyer shall carry out a physical stock-take within [   ] days after the Completion Date at which a representative of each of the Buyer's Accountants, the Seller and the Seller's Accountants shall be entitled to be present and] the Buyer shall prepare within [   ] days after the Transfer Point accounts comprising a balance sheet dealing with the state of affairs of the Business at the Transfer Point and a profit and loss account for the Business for the period from the Accounts Date to the Transfer Point in accordance with part 3 of this schedule ("the Completion Accounts").

2.   The Seller shall provide such information and assistance as the Buyer may reasonably require for the preparation of the Completion Accounts.

3.   The Buyer shall instruct the Buyer's Accountants to:

   3.1   report on the Completion Accounts and on the basis of the Completion Accounts produce a dated statement of the Completion Value ("the Completion Statement")'; and

   3.2   deliver the Completion Statement to and provide access to all working papers to the Seller's Accountants

within [   ] days following delivery to the Seller's Accountants of the Completion Accounts.

4.   If such queries and observations as the Seller's Accountants raise within [twenty-one] days following delivery to them of the Completion Statement have not been dealt with to their satisfaction and reflected in any amendments within [twenty-one] days following delivery to the Buyer's Accountants of such queries and observations, it shall be open to the Seller or the Buyer to request an Independent Accountant to determine the Completion Value, and his determination shall, in the absence of manifest error, be final and binding on the parties.

5.   If the Seller's Accountants do not raise any queries or observations in respect of the Completion Statement within [twenty-one] days following delivery thereof to them or if they agree the Completion Statement, then the Completion Statement shall be final and binding on the parties, and the Completion Value shall be as set out in the Completion Statement.

6.   In stating, agreeing or determining (as the case may be) the Completion Value, the Buyer's Accountants, the Seller's Accountants and, if applicable, the Independent Accountant shall act as experts and not as arbitrators.

7.   The Buyer and the Seller shall promptly provide and render or cause to be provided and rendered to the Buyer's Accountants, the Seller's Accountants and the Independent Accountant such information and assistance as they or any of them may reasonably require to enable the Buyer's Accountants and the Seller's Accountants to agree the Completion Statement (and to make the report referred to in paragraph 3) or to enable the Independent Accountant to determine the Completion Value.

8.   The Seller shall bear and pay all of the costs of the Seller's Accountants, and the Buyer shall bear and pay all the costs of the Buyer's Accountants, incurred in each case in connection with the matters referred to in this schedule.

Part 3

Accounting principles, methods and bases

1.   Subject to paragraph 2, the Completion Accounts shall be prepared in accordance with:

1.1   generally accepted United Kingdom accounting principles, methods and bases; and

1.2   subject thereto (and to the extent they are disclosed in the Disclosure Letter or in the notes to the Accounts), the accounting principles, methods and bases applied and used in the preparation of the Accounts, consistently applied.

2.   The following specific provisions shall apply to the preparation of the Completion Accounts:

[Insert here any specific provisions]

3.   The Assets shall for the purposes of the transaction hereby agreed upon have the values ascribed to them in the Completion Statement save that the following Assets shall have the values set opposite them respectively as follows:

Goodwill	£
Contracts	£1.00
Books and Records	£1.00
The rights referred to in clause 8	£1.00

Signed by [   ] for and

on behalf of [

LIMITED/PLC] in the presence of:

OR

Signed as a deed by [

LIMITED/PLC] acting by [   ], a director,

in the presence of:

OR

Signed as a deed by [

LIMITED/PLC] acting by two

directors or a director and its secretary:

      director

        [director/secretary]

[Appropriate form to be repeated for each party]

PRECEDENT 5

Confidentiality Agreement

PRECEDENTS

Confidentiality agreement

The directors   [DATE]
[TARGET COMPANY NAME AND ADDRESS]

Dear Sirs

[**Limited/PLC] ("the Company")**

We confirm that this company is interested in obtaining further information in connection with the possible sale and purchase by us of [the entire issued share capital of] [the undertaking and assets of] the Company ("the Proposed Transaction"). In this letter, "the Permitted Purpose" means the purpose of considering or furthering the Proposed Transaction and/or advising in relation to it.

The undertakings contained in this letter are given in consideration of you supplying to us (and/or to our officers, employees and advisers) commercial, financial and technical information and other material and data of a secret, confidential or proprietary nature relating to the Company in whatever form or medium and whether disclosed orally or in writing (together "Confidential Information", which shall include all reproductions in whatsoever form or medium of all or any parts of such information). **[If the buyer is a public body, in order to take account of the Freedom of Information Act 2000 and of the environmental information regulations 2004, try as far as possible to specify the information which is genuinely confidential rather than rely on wide general wording.]**

We agree and undertake that:

1.   Prior to execution of a legally binding agreement, no announcement or disclosure of our interest in [the Company] [the undertaking and assets of the Company] will be made or solicited by us or on our behalf without your prior written consent. If we should determine that, by reason of any legal requirement or of any rule or regulation of any regulatory or governmental authority having jurisdiction over us or any of the Permitted Disclosees (as such term is defined in paragraph 4 below) or with whose directions we or any of the Permitted Disclosees are bound to comply, we or any of the Permitted Disclosees are required to make any announcement as to any such matter, we shall consult with you with a view to agreeing the timing and content of any such announcement and will not release any such announcement without your prior consent.

2.   We will at all times hereafter treat all Confidential Information as strictly private and confidential and will take all necessary steps (including, but not limited, to those required by this letter) to preserve such confidentiality. We will not use, copy or store any Confidential Information in an externally accessible computer or similar system, nor transmit it over or via any such system

3.   We will use Confidential Information for the Permitted Purpose and for no other purpose whatsoever and in particular, but without limitation, will not use any Confidential Information so as to procure any commercial advantage over the Company.

4.   We will be permitted to disclose Confidential Information to those responsible employees and [,subject to your further written consent being given] to those advisers to whom in each case disclosure is proper and necessary for the Permitted Purpose (together the "Permitted Disclosees"). We will procure that the Permitted Disclosees and each other person to whom such disclosure is made adheres to the terms of this letter as if he or she were a party.

5.   We will not disclose any Confidential Information to any person other than a Permitted Disclosee without your prior written consent nor disclose to any person other than a Permitted Disclosee either the fact that discussions or negotiations are taking place concerning the Proposed Transaction or any of the proposed terms and conditions.

6.   This undertaking does not apply to information or Confidential Information:

    6.1.1   which at the time of its disclosure is in the public domain;

    6.1.2   which after disclosure comes into the public domain for any reason except our failure, or failure on the part of any of the Permitted Disclosees, to comply with the terms of this letter;

    6.1.3   which we can show was lawfully in our possession prior to such disclosure; or

    6.1.4   which is subsequently received by us from a third party independently entitled to disclose it.

7.   Paragraph 2 of this letter shall not apply to information or Confidential Information, to the extent to which we or any of the Permitted Disclosees are required to disclose it by law or any regulatory or government authority. In the event that we or any of the Permitted Disclosees become so required to disclose any Confidential Information, we will give prompt notice of such fact to you so that you may seek any appropriate court order or other suitable remedy in respect of your rights hereunder or waive compliance with the conditions of this letter and will in particular, but without limitation, consult with you should you be required to disclose any information which we may reasonably regard as commercially sensitive.

8.   We shall keep a record of the Confidential Information provided to us and Permitted Disclosees and of the location of such information and of any persons holding such information.

9.   Upon written demand from you we will promptly return to you or (as you may specify) destroy all Confidential Information in whatever form held by us and the Permitted Disclosees and where Confidential Information is held or stored on any computer, word-processor or similar system, we shall delete such Confidential Information from such system. We shall then confirm to you in writing that all Confidential Information is so returned or destroyed.

[This paragraph 9 shall apply to all reports, notes and materials prepared by you or Permitted Disclosees or otherwise on your behalf and which contain Confidential Information]. [This paragraph 9 shall not, however, apply to reports, notes and materials prepared by us or Permitted Disclosees which contain Confidential Information ("Secondary Material") provided that the provisions of this undertaking shall continue to apply to Confidential Information contained in the Secondary Materials and/or not returned to you or destroyed.] [We may retain a copy of any reports created by us or the Permitted Disclosees which contain Confidential Information provided that the provisions of this letter shall continue to apply to such Confidential Information.]

10.   We will not for a period of two years following the date on which demand is made on us under paragraph 9 above procure or attempt to procure that any employee of the Company at the date of this letter [in a senior/managerial role] [with a salary of £[ ] pa or more] leaves his or her employment and will not within such period engage or offer to engage any such person as an employee or consultant or otherwise. **[Consider extending this to cover non-solicitation of customers and perhaps, where the seller**

is a public company, including a restriction on making an offer for the seller using information which may be price-sensitive.]

11.   We acknowledge that documents, whether containing Confidential Information or otherwise, made available to us or our advisers prior to, in the course of, or for the purposes of, negotiations will not constitute an offer by you or on your behalf and that, neither the Company nor its shareholders makes any representation or warranty, express or implied, as to the correctness, accuracy or completeness or otherwise of any Confidential Information save as may subsequently be agreed in writing, provided that this paragraph 11 shall not exclude liability or any remedy for or in respect of any fraudulent misrepresentation.

12.   Without prejudice to any other rights or remedies that you may have, we acknowledge that damages may not be an adequate remedy for any breach by us or the Permitted Disclosees of the provisions of this letter and that accordingly you shall be entitled without proof of special damage to remedies of injunction, specific performance and other equitable relief for any threatened or actual breach by us of the provisions of this letter.

13.   No failure or delay by you in exercising any right, power or privilege under this letter shall operate as a waiver thereof, nor shall any single or partial exercise thereof pre-clude any further exercise thereof or the exercise of any right, power or privilege hereunder or otherwise.

14.   We acknowledge that the Confidential Information may contain personal data or sensi-tive personal data within the meaning of the Data Protection Act 1998 and that the pro-visions of this letter are, in part, to enable you to comply with the provisions of the Data Protection Act 1998.

15.   We confirm that we are entering into the undertakings contained in this letter for our-selves and for and on behalf of our subsidiary companies for the time being and we hereby undertake to procure that each such subsidiary complied with this letter and such undertakings as if it were a party to them.

16.   Any notice given under in connection with this letter shall be in writing and may be served on us by hand, by post, by email or by fax addressed to the company secretary at [our registered office for the time being].

17.   This letter shall be governed by and construed in accordance with the laws of England. For your benefit, in relation to any legal action or proceedings arising out of or in con-nection with this letter, each of the parties irrevocably submits to the exclusive juris-diction of the English courts and waives any objection to proceedings in such courts on the grounds of venue or on the grounds that proceedings have been brought in an inappropriate forum.

18.   We shall be discharged from our obligations under this letter upon completion of the acquisition by us or any subsidiary of ours of all or substantially all of the [shares in the Company.] [undertaking and assets of the Company].

Yours faithfully

For and on behalf of

[Buyer]

PRECEDENT 6

Data Room Rules

[   ] LIMITED ("THE TARGET")

Data Room Rules

These rules set out the basis upon which potential buyers and their advisers shall be given access to the data room relating to the possible disposal of the [entire issued share capital of the Target/assets and undertaking of the Target] (**"the Proposed Transaction"**).

References in these rules to the Sellers mean:

1.   LOCATION

The data room is located at the offices of [   ] at [
                    ].

2.   APPOINTMENTS

2.1   The data room will be open Mondays to Fridays between the hours of [   ] am and [   ] pm (and outside these hours by special arrangement). Access is by appointment only.

2.2   Appointments to visit the data room can be made by contacting [   ] of [   ] on [   ] or, in his absence, [   ] on [   ] and any changes to appointments should be discussed with these individuals. Initial appointments will be for [   ] consecutive days, but further visits may be arranged if time permits.

2.3   Potential buyers should provide [   ] with a list of team members, their titles and, where appropriate, their respective firms as well as the name of the designated team leader who will represent the potential buyer's team on all matters relating to the visit to the data room. This information should be provided at least [   ] business days before any visit. Each potential buyer's team shall be limited to those persons essential to any review process and may not in any event exceed [   ] persons at any one time. Only those persons named on the list shall be permitted access. Any proposed additions to the list shall be notified to [   ] not later than [   ]pm on the business day prior to the day of the proposed visit.

3.   CONDITIONS OF ADMISSION

3.1   Access to the data room is conditional upon compliance at all times with these rules and the terms of the Confidentiality Agreement. Potential buyers are required to ensure that each member of their team is fully aware of these rules, including the obligations of confidentiality and the fact that information in the data room shall only be used for the purpose of assisting potential buyers to consider the submission of an offer to acquire [the entire issued share capital of the Target/the undertaking and assets of the Target.]

3.2   The Sellers reserve the right to refuse entry to the data room to any member of a potential buyer's team, even if an appointment to visit the data room has been made.

3.3   All persons visiting the data room shall sign a visitors' log when entering and leaving the premises. After doing so, please ask for [   ] who shall then accompany the individuals concerned to the data room. During all visits to the data room, members of a potential buyer's team shall comply with any security or safety regulations imposed by [   ].

3.4   Persons visiting the data room may leave it at any time but shall not enter any parts of the building in which it is located other than the data room and the public areas of the building.

4.   USE OF THE DATA ROOM

4.1   Access to the data room shall be supervised and the instructions of the data room supervisor shall be complied with at all times.

4.2   Members of a potential buyer's team will be allowed to take calculators, lap top computers and writing materials into the data room, but the use of cameras, camera phones, photocopiers, scanners, dictating machines and other recording devices is expressly prohibited.

4.3   The information in the data room is in various lever arch files and may be removed from the files to enable them to be read but all documents and files shall be returned to their original location before leaving the data room.

4.4   No documents may be marked, altered, modified, varied (including varying the sequence of them), damaged or destroyed in any way.

4.5   Under no circumstances shall any documents be removed from the data room or be copied.

5.   CONTENTS

5.1   The information which is currently contained in the data room is listed in the attached index. Further documents may be added to the data room at any time during the process and documents which are currently contained in the data room may at any time be removed from it. In either of these circumstances, a revised or supplementary index shall be distributed. There are a number of documents which are referred to in the index but which are not currently contained in the data room and these are documents which are considered to be commercially sensitive and are expected to be made available [in due course].

5.2   Potential buyers should note that the information in the data room does not purport to be a complete description of all matters which would be material for consideration by a prospective buyer. It has not been verified by the Sellers or any of their advisers and no representation or warranty is, or shall be, made or given and no responsibility or liability is, or shall be, accepted by the Sellers or any of their advisers as to the accuracy or completeness of the information contained in the data room.

5.3   No information made available in the data room shall constitute an offer to sell, or an invitation to purchase or tender for any shares in the capital of the Target or any of its assets and no such information shall form the basis of any contract.

5.4   It shall be a term of any sale and purchase agreement relating to the Target that the information contained in the data room including, for the avoidance of doubt, the contents of all documents contained in the data room, shall be deemed to be disclosed against any warranties contained in the sale and purchase agreement, although no warranty shall be given as to the completeness or accuracy of such information.

6.   CONFIDENTIALITY

The information contained in the data room is made available, and any copies of it are supplied, subject to and on the terms contained in the confidentiality agreement given by potential buyers in respect of information made available to them and their advisers in connection with the Proposed Transaction ("the Confidentiality Agreement"). Potential buyers and their advisers are reminded of the restrictions on disclosure and the use of such information contained in the Confidentiality Agreement. Where these data room rules conflict with the terms of the Confidentiality Agreement, the terms of the Confidentiality Agreement shall prevail.

7.   COPIES OF DOCUMENTS

At their absolute discretion, the Sellers may accede to requests for copies of documents in the data room. Such requests for copies shall be limited to documents that are significant enough to require detailed consideration away from the data room. Please complete the photocopying request form available in the data room and hand it to the supervisor in attendance at the data room or, at the end of the day, to [   ], who shall arrange for requests to be considered. If the Sellers agree to copy any documents comprised in the request, the copies shall be forwarded as soon as reasonably practicable. A record shall be kept of all copies made.

8.   ADDITIONAL INFORMATION

8.1   Questions of an administrative nature shall be addressed to [   ]. Any matters which cannot be resolved shall be noted and passed on to [   ] who shall endeavour to deal with the matter raised as soon as possible.

8.2   Questions of a substantive nature shall be submitted in writing to [   ] after the potential buyer has visited the data room and the sellers, at their absolute discretion, may answer any such questions. [Where the Sellers provide further information to a prospective buyer in response to any such question, the same information will be provided as soon as possible to all other prospective buyers.]

9.   SERVICES

9.1   Tea, coffee and soft drinks may be ordered by asking the data room supervisor or [   ].

9.2   The data room will be equipped with a telephone. International calls shall be made on a reverse charge basis. Incoming callers should ask for the [   ] Room (direct dial: [   ]).

THE SCHEDULE

FORM OF ACKNOWLEDGEMENT FROM POTENTIAL BUYER

[On headed notepaper of [POTENTIAL BUYER]]

To:

("Sellers")

In consideration of you granting us access to the data room containing information relating to [   ] and situated at the offices of [   ] ("Data Room"), we agree to, and further agree to procure that each member of our team shall agree to:

Comply fully with the attached data room rules ("Data Room Rules") and any other instructions relating to the Data Room which are notified to us by [   ] or [   ] and in particular:

- not to remove any documents from the Data Room;
- not to mark, amend, deface or otherwise damage any document in the Data Room;
- not to change the order in which the documents appear in the Data Room;
- not to copy or to transmit a fax of any document in the Data Room otherwise than in accordance with the Data Room Rules;
- to notify the supervisor of the Data Room immediately if any document is found to be missing or incomplete; and
- to submit to any reasonable security regulations and procedures in relation to the data room notified from time to time.

We acknowledge that the documents contained in the Data Room are subject to, and that we are bound by the terms of, the Confidentiality Agreement made between us and dated [   ].
[   ] 200

Signed on behalf of

[   ]

REQUEST FOR PHOTOCOPYING

From: [*intended buyer*] ....

Address for copies to be sent: ....

For the attention of: ....

We request copies of the following documents from the Data Room:

Index No	Pages required

PRECEDENT 7

Exclusivity Agreement

EXCLUSIVITY AGREEMENT

To: [Prospective Buyer]

Dear Sirs

[   ] **Limited**

1.   **DEFINITIONS**

In this letter:

"the Assets"	means all the assets of the Target used in connection with the Business;
"the Business"	means the business of the Target;
"the Exclusivity"	means the agreements on the part of the Sellers which are contained in paragraph 2;
"the Exclusivity Period"	means the period beginning on the date of this letter and ending at midnight on [ ];
"the Proposed Transaction"	means the proposed acquisition of the Shares by the Buyer;
"the Buyer"	means [ ] Limited, a company registered in England under company number [ ] whose registered office is at [ ];
"Shares"	means the entire issued share capital of the Target; and
"the Target	means [ ] Limited, a company registered in England under company number [ ] whose registered office is at [ ];
"the Sellers"	means [ ].

2.   **EXCLUSIVITY**

In consideration of the Buyer continuing negotiations relating to the Proposed Transaction and incurring expense in connection with its proposed review of the business, assets and affairs of the Target, the Sellers hereby agree (subject to paragraph 3) that during the Exclusivity Period, none of the Sellers will directly or indirectly:

2.1   solicit, initiate or encourage any inquiry, discussion or proposal;

2.2   continue, propose to negotiate with or hold discussions or negotiations or

2.3   enter into any agreement or understanding with any other person for or in connection with the sale or other disposal by the Sellers of some or all of the Shares or by the Target of the whole or any substantial part of the Assets or the Business.

The Sellers further agree that during the Exclusivity Period neither of them will provide any information to or assist any person (other than the Buyer and its representatives and advisors) for the purpose of evaluating or determining whether to make or pursue any inquiry or proposal with respect to any such sale or disposal.

3.   REVOCATION OF EXCLUSIVITY

The Sellers reserve the right to revoke the Exclusivity and to negotiate with all interested parties in the following circumstances:

3.1   If the Buyer indicates any reduction in the purchase price of £[   ] which the Buyer has indicated that it is willing to pay for the [Shares] or if any material issue is raised by the Buyer which has not been discussed with the Sellers prior to the date of this letter which may in the Sellers' reasonable opinion have a material effect on the consideration payable to, or liabilities accepted by the Sellers in respect of the sale of the [Shares] or the Buyer suggests any material change in the terms and conditions set out in the heads of terms dated [   ] ("the Heads of Terms").

3.2   If, in the reasonable opinion of the Sellers, negotiations between the Sellers and the Buyer are no longer being conducted in good faith by the Buyer;

3.3   If the Buyer breaches in a material way any of the terms of the confidentiality agreement signed by the Buyer or any of the terms contained in this letter and such breach is incapable of remedy or (if capable of remedy) is not remedied within seven days of the Sellers giving written notice to the Buyer giving details of such breach.

4.   BUYER NOT WISHING TO PROCEED

If the Buyer decides that it does not wish to proceed with the Proposed Transaction it will immediately give written notice of such fact to the Sellers and the Exclusivity shall thereupon forthwith cease.

5.   DUE DILIGENCE INFORMATION

The Buyer will use reasonable endeavours to review information made available to it as part of the due diligence process on a timely basis and with all due speed and to take all reasonable steps that a determined Buyer would take to ensure that such information is promptly and properly reviewed in order to ensure that completion of the Proposed Transaction occurs on or prior to [   ] 200. The Sellers will respond on a timely basis to the reasonable requests of the Buyer for the provision of information to it.

6.   COSTS

Each party agrees that it shall bear its own costs and expenses incurred in connection with the preparation and negotiation of this letter.

7.   INDEMNITY

The Sellers acknowledge that the Buyer will incur significant costs, fees and expenses by relying on the Exclusivity and, if any Seller is in breach of the Exclusivity, the Sellers shall (without prejudice to any other remedies which the Buyer may have) indemnify and keep indemnified the Buyer for an amount equal to all of the [reasonable] costs, fees, disbursements and expenses (plus any applicable VAT) which have been or will be incurred by the Buyer in connection with the Proposed Transaction, including, without limitation, the investigation of the Target and the negotiation of the Heads of Terms and other documents connected with the Proposed transaction.

OR

The Sellers acknowledge that the Buyer will incur significant costs, fees and expenses by relying on the Exclusivity and if any Seller is in breach of the Exclusivity, the Sellers shall pay the Buyer liquidated damages in the sum of [£[AMOUNT]] for each day from the date of the Heads of Terms up to and including the Buyer becoming aware of such breach.

8.   END OF EXCLUSIVITY

Subject to the provisions of paragraphs 3 and 4, the Exclusivity shall end on the earlier to occur of:

8.1   The execution of the definitive sale and purchase and other agreements in respect of the Proposed Transaction; and

8.2   [   ] 200,

unless it is extended by mutual agreement in writing between the Sellers and the Buyer. Paragraphs 6 and 11 of this letter shall survive the termination or expiry of the Exclusivity.

9.   LEGAL REQUIREMENTS

9.1   The Sellers and the Buyer acknowledge and confirm that:

9.1.1   the provisions of this letter are considered by them to be reasonable;

9.1.2   they intend this letter to be legally binding on them; and

9.1.3   and in the event that any provision of this letter is held to be unenforceable, then the remaining provisions shall continue in full force and effect and shall be legally binding on them.

9.2   Nothing in this letter shall prevent the Sellers or any of the directors, employees, agents or advisers of the Target from discussing as required by law the Proposed Transaction with all appropriate regulatory authorities whether in the United Kingdom or overseas.

10.   ACKNOWLEDGEMENT

This agreement shall be governed by and interpreted in accordance with English law.

11.   JURISDICTION

This letter shall be governed by the laws of England and Wales and any dispute arising under it shall be subject to the [exclusive/non-exclusive] jurisdiction of the English courts. The parties waive any objection to proceedings in such courts on the grounds of venue or on the grounds that proceedings have been brought in an inappropriate forum.

12.   NOTICES

[Appropriate provision to be included for the service of notices similar to those contained in Precedents 1 and 2]

Kindly confirm your agreement to the terms of this letter by signing the acknowledgement on the enclosed duplicate and returning the duplicate to us.

Yours faithfully

....

....

[on duplicate]

We agree to the terms set out in the letter of which this is a duplicate.

Dated............................200

For and on behalf of

[   ] Limited

....

Director

PRECEDENT 8

**Legal Due Diligence
Enquiries**

DATED _____ 200[   ]

LEGAL DUE DILIGENCE ENQUIRIES

relating to

[   ] Limited/Plc

LEGAL DUE DILIGENCE

ON

[   ] [LIMITED/PLC] ("the Company")

Please supply copies of the following documents and other requested information in relation to the Company and each of its subsidiaries. Where reference is made to "the Company", this includes each subsidiary.

1. **SHARE CAPITAL & SHAREHOLDERS**

1.1   The authorised and issued share capital of the Company, including classes of shares.

1.2   Names and addresses of all registered shareholders, including number and class of shares held.

1.3   If different from the registered shareholders, names and addresses of all beneficial shareholders, showing the number and class of shares held.

1.4   All agreements granting options over, or the right to call for, the issue of any share or loan capital of the Company.

1.5   Any rights of pre-emption on the transfer of any share capital which are not contained in the Company's articles of association.

1.6   Details of any impediments to the transfer of the full legal and beneficial ownership in any shares in the Company to the Purchaser.

1.7   Documents effecting all redemptions and repurchases of shares or other reductions of capital since incorporation.

1.8   Details of any direct or indirect interest of any of the shareholders or directors in any customer, supplier or competitor of the Company.

2. **CORPORATE STRUCTURE**

2.1   The current memorandum and articles of association, including certificate of incorporation and all certificates on change of name.

2.2   The registered office.

2.3   A list of all subsidiaries, including number of shares held and percentage of share capital owned.

2.4   Whether subsidiaries are trading or dormant and if dormant please specify the date on which such subsidiary became dormant.

2.5   Names and addresses of all directors and the secretary of the Company.

2.6   All documents relating to the acquisition of any company or business since [incorporation].

2.7   A list of the Company's holdings and interests in other companies and businesses.

3. **INSURANCE**

3.1   Details of all claims made under insurance policies which are outstanding.

3.2   A schedule of all current insurances.

4. LEGAL COMPLIANCE

4.1 Details and copies of all licences, authorisations, approvals and consents obtained by the Company in relation to its business, including any consumer credit or data protection licences.

4.2 Details of all licences, authorisations, approvals and consents necessary or desirable in relation to the Company's business which have not been obtained.

4.3 Details of any prosecutions, litigation or other disputes in which the Company is currently engaged, any litigation or other disputes known to be pending or threatened and any circumstances likely to lead to any litigation or prosecutions.

4.4 Copies of any outstanding judgments or orders affecting the Company.

4.5 Details of any material breach or default by the Company under the terms of any agreement, arrangement or licence.

5. FINANCE

5.1 Last audited accounts of the Company.

5.2 Details of any outstanding loan notes or loan stock, including copies of the constituting instrument.

5.3 Details of all bank, invoice discounting, factoring and other financing facilities, including currency hedging arrangements.

5.4 Details of any grant or other financial assistance received by the Company since incorporation.

5.5 Details of all guarantees, indemnities, bonds and suretyship arrangements given by or for the Company, including intra-group arrangements.

5.6 Details of all loans made to or by the Company, including all intra-group and directors' loans and indebtedness.

5.7 Copies of all outstanding mortgages, charges, or debentures or other security over any of the assets of the Company.

5.8 Details of any security held by the Company over the assets of any third party.

5.9 Details of any material off-balance sheet finance commitments.

6. ASSETS

6.1 Any independent valuations of fixed assets (excluding land) obtained in the last three years.

6.2 Details of any hire, hire purchase, leasing, credit sale or similar agreements to which the Company is a party and copies of such agreements or where the gross payments under such contracts exceed £[   ].

7. INTELLECTUAL PROPERTY

7.1 Details of all the Company's registered intellectual property including copies of registrations and pending applications.

7.2 Any official objection or opposition in respect of any application for, or an application for rectification or cancellation of, a registered intellectual property right.

7.3   Details of all registrable intellectual property owned by the Company which has not been registered.

7.4   Details of any trade or business names or styles used by the Company.

7.5   In the case of intellectual property that is used but not owned by the Company, copies of the Company's licence or other right to use (excluding off the shelf software packages).

7.6   Details of any licences or other rights to use granted by the Company in respect of intellectual property owned or used by the Company.

7.7   Details of any disclosure to any third party of any intellectual property, trade secrets or confidential information of the Company.

7.8   Details of any actual or suspected infringements of the Company's intellectual property, including business or trading names.

8.   MATERIAL CONTRACTS

8.1   Details of all contracts involving an outstanding obligation to pay in excess of [£   ].

8.2   Details of all contracts with a performance period of more than three months, or which cannot be terminated on three months' or less notice without payment of compensation.

8.3   Details of all contracts which are or may be loss-making.

8.4   Copies of all agency or distributorship or similar agreements.

8.5   Copies of all joint venture, franchising, partnership or consortium agreements or technical assistance arrangements to which the Company is a party.

8.6   Copies of the Company's standard terms and conditions of purchase and/or sale.

8.7   Copies of all agreements or arrangements which will be (or are capable of being) terminated or varied upon a change of control of the Company.

8.8   Details of any agreement or arrangement entered into otherwise than by way of a bargain at arms length or otherwise than in the ordinary course of business.

8.9   Details of any agreement or arrangement which is outstanding [or was outstanding since incorporation] in which any shareholder or director was directly or indirectly interested.

8.10   Details of any restrictions entered into by the Company restricting or limiting the Company's ability to carry on business in any part of the world.

8.11   A list of major customers/suppliers (i.e. those accounting for more than [10]% of turnover) in the current and last financial years.

8.12   Details of any long term, unusual, onerous or other material contracts or commitments.

8.13   Details of any agreements/licences and consents in respect of which a fee, commission or royalty is paid.

9.   EMPLOYEES

9.1   Details of all the terms and conditions of employment of any director or shareholder (or their family members) employed by the Company.

9.2 A schedule comprising in respect of each employee, (and person due to begin employment) start date, date of birth, age, job title, location, hours per week worked, salary (including date of the most recent increase and details of any proposed increases, reviews or current negotiations), overtime pay, notice periods, entitlement to bonuses (whether contractual or discretionary), commission, other benefits and emoluments (including accommodation), car and expenses and amount of parental leave (if any) taken.

9.3 Copies of the Company's standard terms and conditions of employment and copies of all service agreements.

9.4 Details of any outstanding dispute with any employee or former employee and any matters which might give rise to such, including details of any grievance raised by any employee or warning outstanding against any employee.

9.5 Copies of any written enquiry, correspondence or contact between the Company and the Commission for Racial Equality, the Equal Opportunities Commission, the Health and Safety Inspector and the Inland Revenue concerning employees.

9.6 Details of any consultancy arrangement or agreement and labour—only sub-contractors including name, purpose, terms and duration of engagement.

9.7 Details of any current employee who has given or who has been given notice of termination of employment (including the reasons for termination).

9.8 Details of all employees currently on maternity, paternity or parental leave or absent from work on the grounds of ill health, disability or any other reason or arrangement pursuant to which they have a right to return to work.

9.9 Details and copies of any redundancy schemes or policies or agreements (if any), whether or not contractual.

9.10 Details of any collective bargaining agreements, including details of any arrangements adopted by agreement or default under the ICE Regulations 2004, and any requests, ballots negotiations or notices which may lead to an arrangement under those regulations, and any complaints to the Central Arbitration Committee or to an Employment Tribunal threatened or made under those regulations.

9.11 Details of any life assurance, permanent medical health and accident insurance schemes in respect of employees and a list of all participating members.

10. PENSIONS

10.1 Details of any existing or former occupational pension scheme(s).

10.2 Copies of scheme documentation including (but not limited to) deeds of amendment, member announcements, scheme booklets and circulars and details of any enhancement in benefit which may have been promised to employees but which are not yet reflected in the pension scheme documents.

10.3 Copies of any announcements and explanatory booklets given to employees, including pension sections in staff handbooks.

10.4 Copy of the latest actuarial valuation.

10.5 Membership data (if a bulk transfer payment is being sought, then the data should be sufficient to enable the buyer's actuary to make a good estimate of the amount that ought to be transferred).

10.6 Details of contributions.

10.7   Confirmation that each scheme is treated as a registered pension scheme with HMRC.

10.8   Confirmation as to whether each scheme is contracted out.

10.9   Details of any discretionary benefits.

10.10   The names of the current trustees.

10.11   Details of any complaints, including complaints to the Pensions Ombudsman against the company and/or the trustees.

10.12   Details of any investigation into the scheme by the Pensions Regulator.

10.13   Details of any designated stakeholder pension arrangement.

10.14   Details of the scheme's investments.

10.15   Copies of the trustees' report and accounts, ideally for the last three years.

10.16   Details of any discretionary practices relating to pension schemes.

11.   TAXATION

11.1   Details of all periods for which tax computations are outstanding.

11.2   Details of all disputes with any taxation authority.

11.3   Details of any VAT group of which the Company is a member.

12.   PROPERTY

12.1   Details (including a plan) of any property owned or occupied by the Company, and a copy of the existing lease in the case of leasehold property.

12.2   Details of any contingent liability which the Company may have in relation to any leasehold property formerly occupied by it.

[More detailed property enquiries will follow depending on the nature of the Company's property interests]

13.   DATA PROTECTION

13.1   Copies of documents evidencing the information provided by the data controller to the data subjects (for example, privacy statement or policies).

13.2   Evidence of consent obtained from all Data Subjects in relation to all the Personal Data held by and processed by the Company.

13.3   Copies of all notifications registered with the Office of the Information Controller and a copy of the certificate of registration.

13.4   Copies of all data processor contracts.

13.5   Copies of all data subject requests (eg. to gain access to personal data) together with documents evidencing the data controller's response (including any correspondence with the Office of the Information Commissioner).

13.6   If personal data is transferred outside the European Economic Area, details of the countries concerned and details of consents given to cross-border data transfers.

13.7   Copies of any enforcement notices or information notices from the Information Commissioner and of any responses.

13.8   Details of any compensation paid or claimed by a data subject or any circumstances likely to give rise to a claim for unlawful processing.

13.9   Details of any failure (or alleged failure) to comply with the requirements of the Data Protection Act 1998.

[More detailed enquiries may be appropriate if there are particular concerns regarding data protection issues.]

14.   COMPETITION

14.1   Provide details of the Company's market share by service or product produced or supplied within each member state of the European Union where such market share is in excess of 5%.

14.2   Provide details of the Company's market share by service or product produced, supplied or acquired by the Company within the UK where such market share is in excess of 10%.

14.3   If there is a regional market for the services or products in the UK please provide details of the market share for each such product or service of the Company by regions.

[This may be deleted if irrelevant but, if there are likely to be serious competition law issues, more detailed enquiries will be required.]

[   ] 200[   ]

Ref: [   ]

PRECEDENT 9

Undertaking—For use when acting for Buyer

Undertaking by solicitors to send completion monies when acting for Buyer

[On Letterhead]

To: [Sellers/Sellers' Solicitors]

[Address   ]

FAO [   ]

[Date]

Dear Sirs

Proposed Acquisition by [   ] PLC/Limited ("the Buyer") of the entire issued share capital of [   ] Limited from [   ] ("the Seller(s)" ("the Acquisition")

We confirm that we hold the sum of £[   ] in cleared funds in our client account which we have received from the Buyer ("the Completion Sum").

We undertake that, subject to and with effect from completion of the Acquisition, we will hold the Completion Sum to your order and will instruct our bankers to telegraphically transfer the Completion Sum (together with all interest earned on the Completion Sum in our client account from today's date) to the account set out below. We will give such instruction to our bankers as soon as reasonably practicable on [   ] 200[   ].

Bank:
Account Name:
Account No:
Sort Code:

This undertaking supersedes and replaces any prior discussion between us relating to the giving of an undertaking by us.

Yours faithfully

[Buyer's Solicitors]

On Duplicate of Undertaking

We hereby confirm that completion of the Acquisition has taken place

[To be signed by all parties to the Share Sale and Purchase Agreement]

PRECEDENT 10

Undertaking—For use when acting for Seller

Undertaking by Solicitors to hold completion monies to order pre-completion when acting for Seller

[On Letterhead]

To: [Buyer/Buyer's Solicitors]

    [Address]

FAO: [   ]

[Date]

Dear Sirs

Proposed Acquisition by [   ] PLC/Limited ("the Buyer") of the entire issued share capital of [   ] Limited from [   ] ("the Seller(s)") ("the Acquisition")

We understand that the sum of £[   ] will be transferred by [you] [the Buyer] to our sterling client account for value today. The undertaking in this letter is effective from the time at which we receive the Funds referred to below.

We undertake to hold the sums that we receive from [you/the Buyer] ("the Funds") to the order of the Buyer until the time of completion of the Proposed Acquisition.

This undertaking will automatically terminate and be released in all respects upon completion of the Proposed Acquisition. We will then hold the Funds to the order of the Seller(s) and will distribute the Funds as they direct.

We will account to the Buyer for all interest earned by us on the Funds in our client account for the days we hold the Funds to the Buyer's order (and we may, in our discretion, make transfers of the Funds to deposit accounts for the purpose of holding the Funds while this undertaking remains in force).

This letter supersedes and replaces any prior discussion between us relating to the giving of an undertaking by us.

Yours faithfully

[Buyer/Buyer's Solicitors]

On Duplicate of Undertaking

We hereby confirm that completion of the Proposed Acquisition has taken place and that you are therefore released from the undertaking of which this letter is a copy.

....

[Addressee of Undertaking]

PRECEDENT 11

Completion Agenda

DATED

COMPLETION AGENDA

RELATING TO THE ACQUISITION BY
[LIMITED/PLC]
OF THE [WHOLE OF THE] ISSUED SHARE CAPITAL OF
[LIMITED]

[Note: This precedent presumes that the acquisition will be effected by way of a share sale and purchase agreement rather than by way of an offer to the shareholders of the target company and that there will be a simultaneous "exchange" and completion of the agreement.]

COMPLETION AGENDA

RELATING TO THE ACQUISITION BY
[LIMITED/PLC]
OF THE [WHOLE OF THE] ISSUED SHARE CAPITAL OF
[LIMITED/PLC]

Time and date: [am/pm] on [200]

Place: [

                                                                    ]

<u>To be present:</u>   <u>Represented by:</u>

(1)   [   ] Limited   [
       ("Company")   ]

(2)   [   ]   [
       ("Seller[s]")   ]

(3)   [   ]   [   ]
       acting for Seller[s] ("SSols")

(4)   [[   ]
       Limited/PLC] ("Buyer")

(5)   [   ] acting for Buyer   [   ]
       ("BSols")

Words and expressions defined in or for the purposes of the share sale and purchase agreement bear the same meanings when used in this completion agenda.

A.   **BEFORE COMPLETION**

The following items will be needed at completion with responsibility for their production as follows:

No.	Item	Responsibility
1.	Share sale and purchase agreement (2 engrossments)	BSols
2.	Disclosure Lette	SSols
3.	Executed transfers of all shares in the Company in favour of the Buyer or its nominees	[Seller[s]/SSols]
4.	Share certificates for all issued shares in the Company	[Seller[s]/SSols]
5.	Executed indemnities in respect of lost or defaced share certificates	[Seller[s]/SSols]
6.	Certified copies of any relevant power of attorney	SSols
7.	Certified copy board minutes of the Seller approving the transaction	[Seller[s]/SSols]
8.	Certified copy board minutes of the Buyer approving the transaction	[Buyer/BSols]
9.	Executed transfers of shares (not registered in the name of the Company) in the [Subsidiary/Subsidiaries] in favour of the Buyer or its nominees	[Seller[s]/SSols]
10.	Share certificates for all issued shares in the Subsidiary/Subsidiaries]	[Seller[s]/SSols]
11.	Executed indemnities in respect of lost or defaced certificates in respect of shares in the [Subsidiary/Subsidiaries]	[Seller[s]]Ssols]
12.	Statutory and other books (duly written up to date) of the Company [and the Subsidiary/Subsidiaries]	[Seller[s]/SSols]
13.	Certificates of incorporation on registration and on change of name of the Company [and the [Subsidiary/Subsidiaries]]	[Seller[s]/SSols]
14.	Common seals] of the Company [and the [Subsidiary/Subsidiaries]]	[Seller[s]/SSols]
15.	Letters of resignation [in the Agreed Terms] executed by the persons resigning as directors [and secretary] of the Company [and the [Subsidiary/Subsidiaries]]	[Seller[s]/SSols]
16.	Certificate [in the Agreed Terms] from SSols as to the title of the Company [and the [Subsidiary/Subsidiaries]] to the Property	Ssols
17.	Title deeds to the Property	[Seller[s]/SSols]

18.	[Resignation of existing trustees and appointment of new trustees of the Pension Scheme]	[Seller[s]/SSols]
19.	Appointment of the buyer as principal employer in respect of the Pension Scheme	[Seller[s]/SSols]
20.	All credit and charge cards held to the account of the Company by the Seller[s] or any director of the Company	Seller[s]
21.	Cheque books and unused cheques for the Company [and the [Subsidiary/Subsidiaries]]	Seller[s]
22.	All papers and documents relating to the Company which are in the possession of or under the control of the Seller[s] or any director of the Company	Seller[s]
23.	Board minutes [in the Agreed Terms] for the Company [and the [Subsidiary/Subsidiaries]]	BSols
24.	Notice of change of directors/secretary (form 288) for the Company [and the [Subsidiary/Subsidiaries]] [with consents to act pre-signed]	BSols
25.	Auditors' resignations [in the Agreed Terms] in respect the Company [and the [Subsidiary/Subsidiaries]]	[Seller[s]/ SSols]
26.	Revocation [in the Agreed Terms] of authorities to the bankers of the Company [and the [Subsidiary/Subsidiaries]]	Seller[s]/SSols
27.	Release [in the Agreed Terms] from all banking arrangements of the Vendor's Group in respect of the Company [and the [Subsidiary/Subsidiaries]]	[Seller[s]/SSols]
28.	Release of Shares from security in favour of third parties as follows: 28.1 [Letter of non-crystallisation from [ ]] 28.2 [Consent to disposal from [ ]] 28.3 [Release from fixed charge from [ ]] [(all dated the day of Completion)]	SSols
29.	Release [in the Agreed Terms] of all Encumbrances and all guarantees in respect of third party obligations given by the Company [and the [Subsidiary/Subsidiaries]]	[Seller[s]/SSols]
30.	Release [in the Agreed Terms] of all claims against the Company [and the Subsidiary/ Subsidiaries] by Seller[s]	Seller[s]/SSols

31.	Repayment (by [telegraphic transfer/bankers' draft[s] drawn on a UK clearing bank]) of the sum of £[ ] in satisfaction of sums owed by Seller[s] to the Company [and the [Subsidiary/Subsidiaries]]	Seller[s]
32.	Service agreements [in the Agreed Terms] between the Company and:	BSols
	32.1 [ ]	
	32.2 [ ]	
33.	EGM documentation for the Company [and the [Subsidiary/Subsidiaries]]	
34.	Banker's draft drawn on a UK clearing bank/ Telegraphic transfer] in favour of SSols in [part] satisfaction of the consideration for the Shares	Buyer
35.	Banker's draft drawn on a UK clearing bank/ Telegraphic transfer] in the sum of £[ ] for crediting to the Account	Buyer
36.	Mandate [in the Agreed Terms] for the Account	[ ]
37.	Receipt of SSols for payment	SSols
38.	Share certificates for the Consideration Shares	Buyer
39.	Notice of change of accounting reference date (form 225 [(1)/(2)] for the Company [and the [Subsidiary/Subsidiaries]]	BSols
40.	Notice of change of registered office (form 287) for the Company [and the [Subsidiary/Subsidiaries]]	BSols
41.	New forms of bank mandate for the Company [and the [Subsidiary/Subsidiaries]]	[Buyer]
42.	Cheque for £[ ] in favour of Bsols for stamp duty	Buyer

A.   AT COMPLETION

1.   Check that all items under A above are present and correct and executed as appropriate

2.   Check that any necessary conditions precedent have been fulfilled

3.   Exchange share sale and purchase agreement and Disclosure Letter

4.   Hold a board meeting of the Company to convene an EGM and hold a general meeting (GM) of the Company on short notice

OR

1.   Pass written resolution[s] of the Company in place of a GM

2.   Hold a completion board meeting of the Company to deal with the matters specified in clause 5 of the share sale and purchase agreement

ALTERNATIVES

EITHER

1.   Hold a board meeting of [the/each] Subsidiary to hold a GM of the company concerned on short notice

OR

1.   Pass written resolution[s] of [the/each] Subsidiary in place of a GM

2.   Hold a completion board meeting of [the/each] Subsidiary to deal with the matters specified in clause 5 of the share transfer agreement

3.   Collect and deliver as appropriate items under A above

[**LIMITED/PLC**]

Minutes of a meeting of the board of directors of the company held at [

], on [200] at [am/pm].

Present:

In attendance:

ALTERNATIVES EITHER—EGM ON SHORT NOTICE

1.   CHAIRMAN

Mr. [   ] took the chair and declared that a quorum was present.

2.   DISCLOSURE OF DIRECTOR'S INTERESTS

Messrs [   ] and [   ] declared the nature and extent of their interests in the business of the meeting in accordance with the requirements of Section 177 of the Companies Act 2006 and of the Company's Articles of Association as follows:

[Specify]

It was noted that, notwithstanding their interests, the directors concerned were entitled to be counted towards a quorum and to vote on the matters before the meeting pursuant to the Articles of Association of the Company.

3.   EXTRAORDINARY GENERAL MEETING

There were produced to the meeting:

3.1   A notice of a general meeting to be convened to consider resolutions for the following purposes:

3.1.1   To adopt new articles of association;

3.1.2   To [   ]; and

3.1.3   To [   ]; and

3.2   A form of consent to short notice of the general meeting.

It was resolved that the notice of general meeting be and hereby is approved and the general meeting be convened and held forthwith on short notice for the purpose of considering and, if thought fit, passing the resolution[s] set out in the said notice.

The meeting was then adjourned for the holding of the general meeting.

It was reported when the meeting reconvened that the resolution[s] set out in the notice of general meeting held immediately before the meeting had been duly passed.

OR—WRITTEN RESOLUTION[S]

3.   WRITTEN RESOLUTION[S]

There was presented to the meeting a print of [a] written resolution[s] duly signed by all the members entitled to attend and vote at general meetings of the Company.

4.   CHANGE OF SECRETARY AND DIRECTORS

There was produced to the meeting a letter from Mr [   ] notifying his resignation as secretary.

It was resolved that such resignation be and hereby is accepted and Mr [   ] be and hereby is appointed secretary.

It was noted in connection with the said resignation that Mr [   ] had no claim against the company.

It was resolved that:

4.1   Messrs [   ] and [   ] be and hereby are appointed additional directors;

4.2   Mr [   ] be and hereby is appointed chairman.

The directors so appointed thereupon took their seats upon the board.

There were produced to the meeting letters from Messrs [   ] and [   ] notifying their resignations as directors.

It was resolved that such resignations be and hereby are accepted.

It was noted in connection with the said resignations that [neither/none] of the directors resigning had any claim against the company.

5.   DIRECTORS' INTERESTS

There were produced to the meeting general notices of declaration of interest by the directors specified below, dated [   ] and given under Section 185 of the Companies Act 2006 to the effect set out below and it was noted that each was accordingly to be regarded as interested in any contract or arrangement which might be made by the company with him or for his benefit.

Name	Company/Firm	Details of Interest

[ANY OTHER INTERESTS IN THE BUSINESS BEING TRANSACTED?]

Messrs [   ] and [   ] produced to the meeting written notification of their respective interests in securities of the companies therein specified, as follows:

Company	Security	Number/Amount
Mr [ ]		
Mr [ ]		

6.   TRANSFER OF SHARES

There were produced to the meeting the following forms of transfer of [ordinary] shares of [   ] each:

Name of transferor	Name of transferee	No. of [ordinary] shares

together with the relative share certificates in the names of the transferors.

It was resolved that:

6.1 Such transfers be and hereby are approved, subject to stamping, and, subject to that, the secretary be and hereby is authorised to register them in the register of members; and

6.2 Subject to that, share certificates be issued to the transferees.

7. CHANGE OF AUDITORS

There was produced to the meeting a letter of resignation from Messrs [ ] as auditors with a statement under section 519 of the Companies Act 2006.

It was resolved that such resignation be and hereby is accepted and Messrs [ ] be and hereby are appointed as auditors.

8. CHANGE OF ACCOUNTING REFERENCE DATE

It was resolved that the accounting reference date of the Company be and hereby is changed to [ ] with effect from [ ].

9. CHANGE OF REGISTERED OFFICE

It was resolved that the registered office of the company be and hereby is changed to [ ].

10. BANK MANDATES

It was resolved that all existing bank instructions be cancelled forthwith and [ ] Bank PLC ([ ] branch) be and hereby are appointed bankers and the new bank mandate in the bank's standard form be signed and sent to the bank. A copy of the new bank mandate is attached to these minutes.

11. NOTICES AND RETURNS TO REGISTRAR OF COMPANIES

It was resolved that, consequent upon the business transacted [at the general meeting/by written resolution of the members] and at the meetings of the board of directors of the company held this day, Messrs [ ] be instructed to deliver the following to the Registrar of Companies:

11.1 print of resolution[s] passed;

11.2 print of altered articles of association of the Company;

11.3 notice of change of secretary (form 288a/288b);

11.4 notice of change of directors (form 288a/288b);

11.5 letter from Messrs [ ] notifying their resignation as auditors;

11.6 notice of change of accounting reference date (form 225[(1)/(2)]; and

11.7 notice of change of registered office (form 287).

There being no further business, the meeting then ended.

....

Chairman

C.   **AFTER COMPLETION**

The following action will be needed following completion with responsibility as follows:

No.	Item	Responsibility
1.	Make any agreed Stock Exchange announcement	Buyer
2.	Make any agreed employee announcement	Buyer
3.	Make any agreed press announcement	Buyer
4.	Notify customers and suppliers	Buyer/Company
5.	Endeavour to procure release of Seller[s] from any guarantees disclosed	Buyer
6.	Change letterhead to remove names of former directors and show new registered office	Buyer/Company
7.	Stamp share transfers	Bsols
8.	Cancel old share certificates and issue new share certificates	[Buyer/Bsols]
9.	Implement new banking arrangements	Buyer
10.	Make returns as necessary to Registrar of Companies	Bsols
11.	Consider adoption of new conditions of sale and order	Buyer/Bsols
12.	Consider adoption of new objects clause and articles of association	Buyer/Bsols
13.	Implement pensions arrangements [as follows:]	Buyer
14.	Implement new insurance arrangements	Buyer
15.	Integrate into any employees' share schemes	Buyer
16.	Make group tax elections	Buyer/Company

PRECEDENT 12

Power of Attorney—Individual Sellers

THIS POWER OF ATTORNEY is made by [   ] of [
            ] on 200

I APPOINT [   ] of [   ] ("my Attorney") to be my true and lawful attorney and, as my attorney, for me and in my name and on my behalf, to perform any or all acts and to approve, execute, sign and deliver all or any deeds, documents, acts or things in relation to those shares or securities in [   ] Limited ("the Company") for the time being registered in my name or in my beneficial ownership ("the Shares") which are desirable or necessary to effect the following:

1.   The sale, exchange or other disposal of all or any of the Shares and the entire issued share capital of the Company to [   ] Limited ("the Purchaser") ("the Disposal") and for this purpose the negotiation and execution of any agreement ("Agreement") for the Disposal on such terms and subject to such conditions (including the giving of restrictive covenants, warranties and indemnities) as my Attorney shall in his absolute discretion think fit.

2.   The receipt or authorisation of a receipt of the consideration for the Disposal and the execution of such transfer or transfers or other documents as may be necessary or desirable to transfer the Shares or any interest therein to the Purchaser and as are otherwise necessary or desirable to perform and give effect to the provisions of any Agreement.

3.   The consent to the holding on less than the statutory notice of, and the appointment of a proxy to attend and vote at, any meetings of the holders of shares or securities in the Company and the signing of any written resolutions of the shareholders of the Company or of the holders of any class of shares in the capital of the Company;

4.   [Any counter-indemnity or contribution agreement between the holders of shares in the Company.]

5.   [A deed of release, in such form as my Attorney may approve, to be executed by me in favour of the Company in terms of which any and all claims which I have against the Company will be waived and released.]

6.   Any other act or thing in relation to the Shares which would be in my power to do personally in connection with, and to effect, the Disposal.

I UNDERTAKE to ratify whatever my Attorney shall do or cause to be done hereunder and to indemnify and keep indemnified my Attorney from and against all demands, claims, costs and expenses.

I DECLARE this Power of Attorney to be irrevocable for [   ] months from the date hereof.

This Power of Attorney shall be governed by and construed in accordance with English law.

IN WITNESS whereof I have duly executed this Deed the day and year first before written.

SIGNED AND DELIVERED

as a Deed by

in the presence of:

Name

Address

Occupation

PRECEDENT 13

Power of Attorney—Corporate Sellers

THIS POWER OF ATTORNEY is made by [   ] **LIMITED**, a company registered in England under number [   ], whose registered office is at [   ], on 200 .

WE APPOINT [   ] of [   ] ("our Attorney") to be our true and lawful attorney and, as our attorney, for us and in our name and on our behalf, to perform any or all acts and to approve, execute, sign and deliver all or any deeds, documents, acts or things in relation to those shares or securities in [   ] Limited ("the Company") for the time being registered in our name or in our beneficial ownership ("the Shares") which are desirable or necessary to effect the following:

1. The sale, exchange or other disposal of all or any of the Shares and the entire issued share capital of the Company to [   ] Limited ("the Purchaser") ("the Disposal") and for this purpose the negotiation and execution of any agreement ("Agreement") for the Disposal on such terms and subject to such conditions (including the giving of restrictive covenants, warranties and indemnities) as our Attorney shall in his absolute discretion think fit.

2. The receipt or authorisation of a receipt of the consideration for the Disposal and the execution of such transfer or transfers or other documents as may be necessary or desirable to transfer the Shares or any interest therein to the Purchaser and as are otherwise necessary or desirable to perform and give effect to the provisions of any Agreement.

3. The consent to the holding on less than the statutory notice of, and the appointment of a proxy to attend and vote at, any meetings of the holders of shares or securities in the Company and the signing of any written resolutions of the shareholders of the Company or of the holders of any class of shares in the capital of the Company;

4. [Any counter-indemnity or contribution agreement between the holders of shares in the Company.]

5. [A deed of release, in such form as our Attorney may approve, to be executed by us in favour of the Company in terms of which any and all claims which we have against the Company will be waived and released.]

6. Any other act or thing in relation to the Shares which would be in our power to do personally in connection with, and to effect, the Disposal.

WE UNDERTAKE to ratify whatever our Attorney shall do or cause to be done hereunder and to indemnify and keep indemnified our Attorney from and against all demands, claims, costs and expenses.

WE DECLARE this Power of Attorney to be irrevocable for [   ] months from the date hereof.

This Power of Attorney shall be governed by and construed in accordance with English law.

IN WITNESS whereof we have duly executed this Power of Attorney as a deed the day and year first before written.

SIGNED as a Deed by

[   ] LIMITED

acting by two directors or a director and its secretary

Director

[Director/Secretary]

PRECEDENT 14

Board Minutes of Buyer—
Share Sales and Purchases

[   ] LIMITED

MINUTES of a Meeting of the Board of Directors of the Company held at

on the   day of   200   at   am/pm.

PRESENT:

IN ATTENDANCE:

1.   CHAIRMAN

Mr. [   ] took the chair at the meeting and declared that a quorum was present.

2.   DISCLOSURE OF DIRECTOR'S INTERESTS

Messrs [   ] and [   ] declared the nature and extent of their interests in the business of the meeting in accordance with the requirements of Section 177 of the Companies Act 2006 and of the Company's Articles of Association as follows:

[Specify]

It was noted that, notwithstanding their interests, the directors concerned were entitled to be counted towards a quorum and to vote on the matters before the meeting pursuant to the Articles of Association of the Company.

3.   BACKGROUND

The chairman reported that negotiations had been taking place for the acquisition by the Company ("the Acquisition") of the whole of the issued share capital of [ ] Limited from [ ] ("the Seller") for a purchase price of £[   ],   [subject to adjustment by reference to completion accounts]. The purchase price would be payable as follows:-

[Specify payment terms]

4.   DOCUMENTATION

There were produced to the meeting final drafts of:

4.1   a share sale and purchase agreement relating to the Acquisition ("the Agreement"); and

4.2   a disclosure letter to be issued by the [Seller] to the Company ("the Disclosure Letter")

together with the other documents referred to in the Agreement (together the "Acquisition Documents").

5.   APPROVALS[1]

IT WAS UNANIMOUSLY RESOLVED THAT:

5.1   the Acquisition was in the best commercial interests of the Company and likely to promote the success of the Company for the benefit of its members as a whole;

---

[1] In appropriate cases, it may be appropriate to expand the wording of the minutes in order to demonstrate that the directors have taken account of the various factors specified in Section 172 (1) of the Companies Act 2006 but the directors should ensure that the minutes are an accurate reflection of discussions that have actually taken place rather than a mere "paper trail".

5.2   the terms and performance of, and the execution and delivery by the Company of, the Agreement be and hereby are approved;

5.3   the Disclosure Letter be and hereby is approved and that any director be and hereby is authorised to counter-sign it on behalf of the Company;

5.4   the terms and performance of, and the execution and delivery by the Company of each of the other Acquisition Documents be and are hereby approved;

5.5   any director or the company secretary of the Company (each of them an "Authorised Signatory") be and hereby is authorised to execute and deliver such of the Acquisition Documents as require execution under hand;

5.6   each Authorised Signatory be and hereby is authorised to execute and deliver such of the Acquisition Documents as require execution as a deed;

5.7   each Authorised Signatory be and is hereby authorised to agree such amendments, variations or modifications to any or all of the Acquisition Documents as he may in his absolute discretion think fit and to do all acts and things so as to carry into effect the Acquisition and the Acquisition Documents.

6.   NO FURTHER BUSINESS

There being no further business the meeting then ended.

....

Chairman

PRECEDENT 15

**Board Minutes of Seller—
Share Sales and Purchases**

MINUTES of a Meeting of the Board of Directors of the Company held at

on the   day of   200   at   am/pm.

PRESENT:

IN ATTENDANCE:

1.   **CHAIRMAN**

Mr. [   ] took the chair at the meeting and declared that a quorum was present.

2.   **DISCLOSURE OF DIRECTOR'S INTERESTS**

Messrs [   ] and [   ] declared the nature and extent of their interests in the business of the meeting in accordance with the requirements of Section 177 of the Companies Act 2006 and of the Company's Articles of Association as follows:

[Specify]

It was noted that, notwithstanding their interests, the directors concerned were entitled to be counted towards a quorum and to vote on the matters before the meeting pursuant to the Articles of Association of the Company.

3.   **BACKGROUND**

The chairman reported that negotiations had been taking place for the sale by the Company ("the Sale") of the undertaking and assets of [   ] Limited ("the Seller") to [   ] ("the Buyer") for a purchase price of £[   ], [subject to adjustment by reference to completion accounts]. [The purchase price would be payable as follows:-

[Specify payment terms]

4.   **DOCUMENTATION**

There were produced to the meeting final drafts of:

4.1   an assets sale and purchase agreement relating to the Sale ("the Agreement"); and

4.2   a disclosure letter to be issued by the [Company] to the Buyer ("the Disclosure Letter")

together with the other documents referred to in the Agreement (together the "Sale Documents").

5.   **APPROVALS**[1]

IT WAS UNANIMOUSLY RESOLVED THAT:

5.1   the Sale was in the best commercial interests of the Company and likely to promote the success of the Company for the benefit of its members as a whole;

5.2   the terms and performance of, and the execution and delivery by the Company of, the Agreement be and hereby are approved;

---

[1] In appropriate cases, it may be appropriate to expand the wording of the minutes in order to demonstrate that the directors have taken account of the various factors specified in Section 172 (1) of the Companies Act 2006 but the directors should ensure that the minutes are an accurate reflection of discussions that have actually taken place rather than a mere "paper trail".

5.3   the Disclosure Letter be and hereby is approved and that any director be and hereby is authorised to sign it on behalf of the Company;

5.4   the terms and performance of, and the execution and delivery by the Company of each of the other Sale Documents be and are hereby approved;

5.5   any director or the company secretary of the Company (each of them an "Authorised Signatory") be and hereby is authorised to execute and deliver such of the Sale Documents as require execution under hand;

5.6   each Authorised Signatory be and hereby is authorised to execute and deliver such of the Sale Documents as require execution as a deed;

5.7   each Authorised Signatory be and is hereby authorised to agree such amendments, variations or modifications to any or all of the Sale Documents as he may in his absolute discretion think fit and to do all acts and things so as to carry into effect the Sale and the Sale Documents.

6.   NO FURTHER BUSINESS

There being no further business the meeting then ended.

....

Chairman

PRECEDENT 16

Indemnity in Respect of Missing/Lost Share Certificate

To: The Directors

[   ] Limited ("the Company")

Dear Sirs

Indemnity for Missing, Destroyed, or Lost Share Certificate

The share certificate issued in the name of [ ] for [ ] [ordinary] shares in the capital of the Company may have been mislaid, destroyed or lost or may never have been issued.

I hereby undertake to indemnify the Company against all claims, costs and expenses which may be brought against or made against, or incurred by, the Company as a consequence of such certificate being mislaid, destroyed or lost or not issued or a replacement certificate being issued. I further undertake to return the original share certificate and any duplicates (if any) to the Company, or its successors or assigns, for cancellation if they should come to hand.

Signed as a Deed by

in the presence of:-

PRECEDENT 17

Director's Resignation Letter

RESIGNATION OF DIRECTOR/SECRETARY

To: [Limited/PLC] ("the Company") [and its subsidiary companies]

[200]

Dear Sirs,

I, [   ] of [   ], resign my office as [director/secretary] of the Company [and of those of its subsidiary companies of which I am a [director/secretary]] and resign also from any other office or employment which I may have with the Company [or any of its subsidiaries] with effect from [200 /today's date].

I confirm that I have no claim against the Company [or any of its subsidiary companies], nor against any other person, firm or company, for compensation for loss of office or at common law or under any statute or (without limitation) on any other account and that [, except for [   ],] there is no agreement or arrangement, whether performed or executory, under which the Company [or any of its subsidiary companies] might be or become liable to me on any account.

Signed as a deed by

[   ]

in the presence of:

PRECEDENT 18

Auditor's Resignation Letter

To: [   ] Limited/plc

Dear Sirs

[   ] Limited/PLC ("the Company")

We hereby resign our office as auditors of the Company with immediate effect.

(FOR UNQUOTED COMPANIES WHERE THERE ARE NO CIRCUMSTANCES TO BE STATED)

In accordance with section 519 of the Companies Act 2006, we confirm that there are no circumstances connected with our resignation which we consider should be brought to the attention of the members or creditors of the Company.

OR (FOR QUOTED COMPANIES OR FOR UNQUOTED COMPANIES WHERE THERE ARE CIRCUMSTANCES TO BE STATED)

In accordance with section 519 of the Companies Act 2006, the circumstances to be connected with our ceasing to hold office as auditor of the Company and which we consider should be brought to the attention of the members or creditors of the Company are as follows: **[STATE CIRCUMSTANCES]:**

We confirm that there are no amounts owing to us by the Company in respect of unpaid fees or on any other account.

We hereby authorise and request you to deliver a copy of this notice of resignation to the Registrar of Companies.

Yours faithfully

For and on behalf of **[NAME OF FIRM]**

PRECEDENT 19

Completion Agenda—Assets Sales and Purchases

DATED

COMPLETION AGENDA
RELATING TO THE ACQUISITION BY
[LIMITED/PLC]
OF THE UNDERTAKING AND ASSETS OF
[LIMITED/PLC]

COMPLETION AGENDA

RELATING TO THE ACQUISITION BY

[LIMITED/PLC]

OF THE UNDERTAKING AND ASSETS OF

[LIMITED/PLC]

Time and date: [am/pm] on [200]

Place: [   ]

<u>To be present:</u>   <u>Represented by:</u>

(1)   Limited/PLC   [   ]
        ("Seller")

(2)   [   ] acting for Seller[s]
        ("SSols")   [   ]

(3)   [Limited/PLC] ("Buyer")   [   ]

(4)   [   ] acting for Buyer
        ("BSols")   [   ]

Words and expressions defined in or for the purposes of the assets sale and purchase agreement bear the same meanings when used in this completion agenda.

A.   BEFORE COMPLETION

The following items will be needed at completion with responsibility for their production as follows:

No.	Item	Responsibility
1.	Assets sale and purchase agreement (2 engrossments)	BSols
2.	Disclosure Letter	SSols
3.	Certified copy board minutes of the Seller approving the transaction	Seller/SSols
4.	Certified copy board minutes of the Buyer approving the transaction	[Buyer/BSols]
5.	Assignments [in the Agreed Terms] in respect of:	
	5.1 Goodwill	
	5.2 Intellectual Property	
	5.3 [Book Debts]	
	5.4 Rights against third parties	BSols
6.	Title deeds to the Property	SSols
7.	Transfer/conveyance [in the Agreed Terms] in respect of the Property.	BSols
8.	[Transfer] [Assignment] [In the Agreed Terms] in respect of the Leasehold Property.	BSols
9.	Licence to assign the Lease [in the Agreed Terms]	SSols
10.	Books and Records	[Seller]
11.	Release of Assets from security in favour of third parties as follows:	
	11.1 [Letter of non-crystallisation from [ ]]	
	11.2 [Consent to disposal from [ ]]	
	11.3 [Release from fixed charge from [ ]] [(all dated the day of Completion)]	[Seller]
12.	A special resolution of the Seller changing its name	Seller
13.	Election under S.198 of the Capital Allowances Act 2001	[Buyer]
14.	[Banker's draft drawn on a UK clearing bank/ Telegraphic transfer] in favour of SSols in [part] satisfaction of the consideration for the Assets	Buyer
15.	[Banker's draft drawn on a UK clearing bank/ Telegraphic transfer] in the sum of £[ ] for crediting to the Escrow Account	Buyer

16.   Mandate [in the Agreed Terms] for the Account   [   ]

17.   Receipt of SSols for payment   SSols

B.   AT COMPLETION

1.   Check that all items under A above are present and correct and executed
           as appropriate

2.   Check that any necessary conditions precedent have been fulfilled

3.   Exchange assets sale and purchase agreement and Disclosure Letter

4.   Collect and deliver as appropriate items under A above

C.   AFTER COMPLETION

The following action will be needed following completion with responsibility as follows:

No.	Item	Responsibility
1.	Make any agreed Stock Exchange announcement	Buyer
2.	Make any agreed employee announcement	Buyer
3.	Make any agreed press announcement	Buyer
4.	Notify customers and suppliers	Buyer
5.	Make SDLT returns and stamp property documents	Buyer
6.	HM Land Registry registrations	BSols
7.	Consider adoption of new conditions of sale and order	Buyer/BSols
8.	Implement pensions arrangements [as follows:]	Buyer
9.	Implement new insurance arrangements	Buyer
10.	Notify employees of change of employer	Buyer

PRECEDENT 20

**Board Minutes of Buyer—
Assets Sales and Purchases**

[   ] LIMITED

MINUTES of a Meeting of the Board of Directors of the Company held at
on   the day of   200   at   am/pm.

PRESENT:

IN ATTENDANCE:

1.   **CHAIRMAN**

Mr. [   ] took the chair at the meeting and declared that a quorum was present.

2.   **DISCLOSURE OF DIRECTOR'S INTERESTS**

Messrs [   ] and [   ] declared the nature and extent of their interests in the
business of the meeting in accordance with the requirements of Section 177 of the
Companies Act 2006 and of the Company's Articles of Association as follows:

[Specify]

It was noted that, notwithstanding their interests, the directors concerned were entitled
to be counted towards a quorum and to vote on the matters before the meeting pursuant
to the Articles of Association of the Company.

3.   **BACKGROUND**

The chairman reported that negotiations had been taking place for the acquisition by
the Company ("the Acquisition") of the undertaking and assets of [   ] Limited ("the
Seller") for a purchase price of £[   ], [subject to adjustment by reference to completion accounts]. The purchase price would be payable as follows:-

[Specify payment terms]

4.   **DOCUMENTATION**

There were produced to the meeting final drafts of:

4.1   an assets sale and purchase agreement relating to the Acquisition ("the
         Agreement"); and

4.2   a disclosure letter to be issued by the Seller to the Company ("the Disclosure
         Letter")

together with the other documents referred to in the Agreement (together the
"Acquisition Documents").

5.   **APPROVALS**[1]

IT WAS UNANIMOUSLY RESOLVED THAT:

5.1   the Acquisition was in the best commercial interests of the Company;

5.2   the terms and performance of, and the execution and delivery by the
         Company of, the Agreement be and hereby are approved;

---

[1] In appropriate cases, it may be appropriate to expand the wording of the minutes in order to demonstrate
that the directors have taken account of the various factors specified in Section 172 (1) of the Companies
Act 2006 but the directors should ensure that the minutes are an accurate reflection of discussions that have
actually taken place rather than a mere "paper trail".

5.3   the Disclosure Letter be and hereby is approved and that any director be and hereby is authorised to counter-sign it on behalf of the Company;

5.4   the terms and performance of, and the execution and delivery by the Company of each of the other Acquisition Documents be and are hereby approved;

5.5   any director or the company secretary of the Company (each of them an "Authorised Signatory") be and hereby is authorised to execute and deliver such of the Acquisition Documents as require execution under hand;

5.6   each Authorised Signatory be and hereby is authorised to execute and deliver such of the Acquisition Documents as require execution as a deed;

5.7   each Authorised Signatory be and is hereby authorised to agree such amendments, variations or modifications to any or all of the Acquisition Documents as he may in his absolute discretion think fit and to do all acts and things so as to carry into effect the Acquisition and the Acquisition Documents.

6.   NO FURTHER BUSINESS

There being no further business the meeting then ended.

....

Chairman

PRECEDENT 21

**Board Minutes of Seller—
Assets Sales and Purchases**

[   ] LIMITED

MINUTES of a Meeting of the Board of Directors of the Company held at
on   the day of   200   at   am/pm.

PRESENT:

IN ATTENDANCE:

1. **CHAIRMAN**

    Mr. [   ] took the chair at the meeting and declared that a quorum was present.

2. **DISCLOSURE OF DIRECTOR'S INTERESTS**

    Messrs [   ] and [   ] declared the nature and extent of their interests in the business of the meeting in accordance with the requirements of Section 177 of the Companies Act 2006 and of the Company's Articles of Association as follows:

    [Specify]

    It was noted that, notwithstanding their interests, the directors concerned were entitled to be counted towards a quorum and to vote on the matters before the meeting pursuant to the Articles of Association of the Company.

3. **BACKGROUND**

    The chairman reported that negotiations had been taking place for the sale by the Company ("the Sale") of its undertaking and assets of [   ] Limited ("the Seller") to [   ] ("the Buyer") for a purchase price of £[   ], [subject to adjustment by reference to completion accounts]. [The purchase price would be payable as follows:-

    [Specify payment terms]

4. **DOCUMENTATION**

    There were produced to the meeting final drafts of:

    4.1   a share sale and purchase agreement relating to the Sale ("the Agreement"); and

    4.2   a disclosure letter to be issued by the Company to the Buyer ("the Disclosure Letter")

    together with the other documents referred to in the Agreement (together the "Sale Documents").

5. **APPROVALS[1]**

    IT WAS UNANIMOUSLY RESOLVED THAT:

    5.1   the Sale was in the best commercial interests of the Company and likely to promote the success of the Company for the benefit of its members as a whole;

---

[1] In appropriate cases, it may be appropriate to expand the wording of the minutes in order to demonstrate that the directors have taken account of the various factors specified in Section 172 (1) of the Companies Act 2006 but the directors should ensure that the minutes are an accurate reflection of discussions that have actually taken place rather than a mere "paper trail".

5.2   the terms and performance of, and the execution and delivery by the Company of, the Agreement be and hereby are approved;

5.3   the Disclosure Letter be and hereby is approved and that any director be and hereby is authorised to sign it on behalf of the Company;

5.4   the terms and performance of, and the execution and delivery by the Company of each of the other Sale Documents be and are hereby approved;

5.5   any director or the company secretary of the Company (each of them an "Authorised Signatory") be and hereby is authorised to execute and deliver such of the Sale Documents as require execution under hand;

5.6   each Authorised Signatory be and hereby is authorised to execute and deliver such of the Sale Documents as require execution as a deed;

5.7   each Authorised Signatory be and is hereby authorised to agree such amendments, variations or modifications to any or all of the Sale Documents as he may in his absolute discretion think fit and to do all acts and things so as to carry into effect the Sale and the Sale Documents.

6.   NO FURTHER BUSINESS

There being no further business the meeting then ended.

....,
Chairman

PRECEDENT 22

Deed of Assignment

[**LIMITED/PLC]**

-and-

[**LIMITED/PLC]**

DEED OF ASSIGNMENT

-pursuant to-

ASSETS SALE AND PURCHASE AGREEMENT

This deed of assignment is made on   200

between:

(1)   [**[LIMITED/PLC]]**, a company registered in England under number [   ], whose registered office is at [   ] ("the Seller"); and

(2)   [**[LIMITED/PLC]]**, a company registered in England under number [   ], whose registered office is at [   ] ("the Buyer");

pursuant to an agreement dated [the date of this deed/   200] and entitled "[assets sale and purchase agreement]" between (1) the Seller and] (2) the Buyer ("the Agreement").

It is agreed as follows:

1.   INTERPRETATION

In this document:

1.1   The following words and expressions shall have the meanings set out or referred to opposite each respectively:

"Book Debts"   as defined in the Agreement;

"Contracts"   as defined in the Agreement;

"Goodwill"   as defined in the Agreement;

"Intellectual Property"   as defined in the Agreement;

"Proceedings"   as defined in the Agreement.

1.2   The headings are inserted for convenience only and shall not affect the construction of this deed.

1.3   This deed is without prejudice to the terms of the Agreement, and the assignment hereby made is made with the benefit for the Buyer of all relevant provisions of the Agreement.

2.   ASSIGNMENT

The Seller with full title guarantee assigns to the Buyer:

2.1   The benefit of each of the Book Debts in consideration of [the aggregate sum of £[   ] ([   ] pound[s]);

2.2   The benefit of each of the Contracts in consideration of the aggregate sum of £[   ] ([   ] pound[s]);

2.3   The Goodwill in consideration of the sum of £[   ] ([   ] pound[s]);

2.4   In consideration of the aggregate sum of £[   ] ([   ] pound[s]), the Intellectual Property, together with all rights and powers arising or accrued therefrom, including, without limitation, the right to sue for damages and all other remedies in respect of any past infringement; and

2.5   The rights of the Seller against third parties specified in clause 2.9 of the Agreement in consideration of the sum of £[   ] ([   ] pound[s]);

to hold them to the Buyer absolutely and the Seller confirms that the assignment hereby made is made with the goodwill attaching to the Intellectual Property and all the business in respect of which the Intellectual Property has in the past been used.

3. RECEIPT

The Seller acknowledges the receipt and sufficiency of the consideration specified in clause 2.

4. GENERAL

4.1 Proper law

This deed shall be governed by the laws of England and Wales

4.2 Jurisdiction

Any dispute arising under this deed shall be subject to the [exclusive/non-exclusive] jurisdiction of the English courts and the parties waive any objection to Proceedings in such courts on the grounds of venue or on the grounds that Proceedings have been brought in an inappropriate forum.

4.3 Further assurance

The Seller shall [(at its own expense)/] do such acts and execute such documents as the Buyer may at any time reasonably require for the purpose of assuring to the Seller the full benefit of this deed.

IN WITNESS of which this deed has been executed and unconditionally delivered the day and year first above written.

Signed as a deed

on behalf of [

LIMITED/PLC]

acting by [   ],

a director, in the presence of:

Signed as a deed by [

LIMITED/PLC acting by two directors

or a director and its secretary]:

director

[director/secretary]

PRECEDENT 23

Novation Deed

DATED   20

(1) [   ]

-and-

(2) [   ]

-and-

(3) [   ]

**NOVATION DEED
SUBJECT TO CONTRACT**

SUBJECT TO CONTRACT

Reference:

Draft Date:

THIS DEED is dated 2008

PARTIES

1.   [   ] **LIMITED** incorporated and registered in England and Wales with company number [   ]whose registered office is at [   ] **(Seller)**.

2.   [   ] **LIMITED** incorporated and registered in England and Wales with company number [   ] whose registered office is at [   ] **(Buyer)**.

3.   [   ] **LIMITED** incorporated and registered in England and Wales with the company number [   ] whose registered office is at [   ]) **Continuing Party)**.

BACKGROUND

(A)   This Deed is supplemental to [details] dated [   ].

(B)   The Seller wishes to be released and discharged from the Contract as from the date of this Deed ("the Effective Date") and the Continuing Party has agreed to so release and discharge the Seller, from the Effective Date upon the terms of this Deed.

AGREED TERMS

1.   BUYER'S OBLIGATIONS

1.1   As from the Effective Date, the Continuing Party accepts the Buyer as a party to the Contract in place of the Seller and, from the Effective Date, the Buyer undertakes to each of the Seller and the Continuing Party to perform the Contract and be bound by its terms and conditions in every way as a party thereto.

1.2   Subject to clause 4, the Buyer and the Continuing Party shall do all such acts and things and execute all such deeds and documents as may be necessary to perfect the release referred to in clause 2.2.

2.   RELEASE

2.1   The Seller and the Continuing Party hereby mutually release each other from their obligations under the Contract as from the Effective Date, save as provided in clause 3.

2.2   The Continuing Party releases and discharges the Seller from all future claims and demands whatsoever in respect of the Contract and accepts that, from the Effective Date, the Buyer shall be responsible for the performance of the Contract.

3.   PRE-EXISTING CLAIMS

3.1   Nothing in this Deed shall affect or prejudice any claim or demand whatsoever which either the Seller or the Continuing Party may have against the other relating to matters arising under or in connection with the Contract prior to the Effective Date ("Pre-Existing Matters").

3.2   Nothing in this Deed shall cause or require the Buyer to be, become or assume any liability or responsibility whatsoever for, or in connection with, any Pre-Existing Matters and neither the Seller nor the Continuing Party shall make, or attempt to make, any claim against the Buyer in respect of any Pre-Existing Matters.

3.3   The Continuing Party and the Seller represent and warrant to the Buyer that:

      3.3.1   there are no claims, one against the other, either made or in contemplation in respect of any Pre-Existing Matters; and,

      3.3.2   to the best of their respective knowledge and belief, there are no grounds upon which either of them could raise a claim against the other in respect of any Pre-Existing Matters; and

      3.3.3   each has performed the Contract according to its terms in all respects.

4.   VARIATION

4.1   The Buyer shall make all consequential amendments to the Contract as are required to give full effect to the Contract, after the date of this Deed in accordance with the provisions of this Deed.

4.2   The Buyer shall notify the Continuing Party of all amendments required in relation to clause 4.1 above within 3 months after the date of this Deed.

4.3   The Continuing Party confirms and agrees that there are no further, or other, conditions or formalities to be completed to effect novation pursuant to the Contract, otherwise.

5.   GOVERNING LAW, JURISDICTION AND COUNTERPARTS

5.1   This Deed and any disputes or claims arising out of or in connection with its subject matter are governed by and construed in accordance with the law of England.

5.2   The parties irrevocably agree that the courts of England have exclusive jurisdiction to settle any dispute or claim that arises out of or in connection with this Deed.

5.3   The parties intend this document to be a deed and agree to deliver and executive it as a deed.

5.4   This Deed may be executed in any number of counterparts, each of which, when executed and delivered, shall be an original and all the counterparts together shall constitute one and the same Deed.

IN WITNESS WHEREOF the parties have executed this Deed the day and year first above written.

Signed as a Deed by

[   ] **LIMITED**

acting by:

        Director:

        Director/Secretary:

Signed as a Deed by

[   ] **LIMITED**

acting by:

        Director:

        Director/Secretary:

Signed as a Deed by

[   ] **LIMITED**

acting by:

        Director:

        Director/Secretary:

PRECEDENT 24

UK Patent Assignment

DATED   **200**

(1) [LIMITED/PLC]

-and-

(2) [LIMITED/PLC]

UK PATENT ASSIGNMENT

THIS ASSIGNMENT is made on

BETWEEN:

(1)   [**LIMITED/PLC],** a company registered in England under number [   ]
whose registered office is at [   ] ("the Assignor"); and

(2)   [**LIMITED/PLC]** a company registered in England under number [   ]
whose registered office is at [   ] ("the Assignee").

RECITALS

A.   The Assignor is the owner of [a] certain patent[s]; and

B.   The Assignee wishes to purchase and the Assignor is willing to sell to the Assignee
the said patent[s] upon the terms and conditions of this Assignment.

IT IS HEREBY AGREED as follows:

DEFINITIONS

In this Assignment Deed the following terms shall have the following meanings:

"Patents"	means the patent[s] listed in the Schedule [and any of them];
"Rights"	means all right title and interest in and to the Patents together with all rights powers privileges and immunities thereby conferred on the proprietor thereof in every jurisdiction including without limitation all accrued rights of action and remedies in respect of any infringement of such rights.

2.   ASSIGNMENT

In consideration of the payment of [   ] now paid by the Assignee to the Assignor
(receipt whereof the Assignor hereby acknowledges) the Assignor **ASSIGNS** the
Rights to the Assignee with full title guarantee.

3.   WARRANTY

The Assignor hereby warrants that:

3.1   The Assignor is the true inventor of the inventions comprised in the Patent[s];

3.2   There are no persons entitled to claim any rights in the Patent[s] nor to claim
compensation from the Assignor pursuant to Section 40 of the Patents Act
1977 nor under equivalent laws of any other country in respect of the Patents;

3.3   To the best of its knowledge and belief the Patents do not and exploitation of
the same by the Assignee will not infringe any valid and subsisting patent or
any intellectual property rights of any other third party.

4.   LAW

This Assignment shall be governed by the laws of England and Wales

5.   **JURISDICTION**

Any dispute arising under this Assignment shall be subject to the [exclusive/non-exclusive] jurisdiction of the English courts and the parties waive any objection to proceedings in such courts on the grounds of venue or on the grounds that proceedings have been brought in an inappropriate forum.

SIGNED by or on behalf of the parties the day and year first before written

SCHEDULE 1

The Patents

Number	Date of Grant	Title

SIGNED by   [   ]   )

for and on behalf of   [   )

LIMITED/PLC] I   )

in the presence of   )

SIGNED by [   ]   )

for and on behalf of   [   )

LIMITED/PLC]] I   )

in the presence of   )

PRECEDENT 25

Trade Mark Assignment

DATED   **200**

(1)[**LIMITED/PLC]**

-and-

(2)[**LIMITED/PLC]**

TRADE MARK ASSIGNMENT

THIS ASSIGNMENT is made the

BETWEEN:

(1)   [**LIMITED/PLC**], a company registered in England under number [   ] and having its registered office at [   ] (the "Assignee"); and

(2)   [**LIMITED/PLC**], a company registered in England under number [ ] and having its registered office at [ ] (the "Assignee").

RECITAL

(1)   The Assignor is the registered proprietor of (a) certain trade mark(s).

(2)   The Assignee wishes to acquire and the Assignor is prepared to assign the said trade mark(s) to the Assignee subject to the provisions of this Assignment.

IT IS NOW HEREBY AGREED as follows:—

1.   **DEFINITIONS**

          In this Assignment the following expression shall have the following meaning:

          "Mark(s)"   means the trade mark(s) set out in the Schedule;

          "Rights"   means all property right title and interest in the Mark(s) together with all and any related common law rights including all accrued rights to sue in respect of infringements [and related goodwill].

2.   **ASSIGNMENT**

          In consideration of the payment of the sum of [   ] by the Assignee to the Assignor (receipt whereof is hereby acknowledged) the Assignor **HEREBY ASSIGNS** the Rights to the Assignee with full title guarantee.

3.   **LAW**

          This Assignment shall be governed by the laws of England and Wales.

4.   **JURISDICTION**

          Any dispute arising under this Assignment shall be subject to the [exclusive/non-exclusive] jurisdiction of the English courts and the parties waive any objection to proceedings in such courts on the grounds of venue or on the grounds that proceedings have been brought in an inappropriate forum.

          SIGNED by or on behalf of the parties the day and year first before written

SCHEDULE 1

Mark	Country	Class	Description of Goods	Date of Next Renewal
SIGNED by	[	]		
for and on behalf of	[	)		
LIMITED/PLC I		)		
in the presence of:		)		
SIGNED by	[ ]	)		
for and on behalf of [		)		
LIMITED/PLC I		)		
in the presence of:		)		

PRECEDENT 26

Short Form Warranties (Non-Tax)—Share Sales and Purchases

1. THE COMPANY AND THE SELLER

1.1 Capacity

The Seller has full power to enter into and perform the provisions of this Agreement, which constitutes a binding agreement on the Seller in accordance with its terms.

1.2 Ownership of the Shares

The Seller is the beneficial owner of the Shares and has the right to dispose of them to the Buyer or as it directs free from any Encumbrance and together with all rights now or hereafter attaching to them.

1.3 Liabilities owing to or by the Seller

There is not outstanding any indebtedness and there are no contracts, arrangements or liabilities (actual or contingent) remaining in whole or in part to be performed between the Company and any Member of the Seller's Group or any director of the Company or any director of any Member of the Seller's Group or any person who is an associate of or connected with any of them.

2. THE COMPANY'S SCHEDULED PARTICULARS AND CONSTITUTIONAL AND ADMINISTRATIVE AFFAIRS

2.1 Schedule 1

The particulars of the Company set out in schedule 1 are true, complete and accurate and its issued share capital is fully paid.

2.2 Subsidiaries

The Company is the beneficial owner (directly or indirectly) free from any Encumbrance of the whole of the issued share capital of each of the Subsidiaries.

2.3 Memorandum and Articles

The copy of the memorandum and articles of association of the Company attached to the Disclosure Letter is true and complete.

2.4 Options

No person has the right (whether exercisable now or in the future and whether or not contingent) to call for the allotment, issue or transfer of any share or loan capital of the Company under any option or other agreement (including without limitation conversion rights and rights of pre-emption).

2.5 Statutory and other books and records

2.5.1 All registers, accounts, books, ledgers, financial and other records of the Company have been fully, properly and accurately kept and maintained, are in the possession of the Company and contain true and accurate records of all matters required by law to be entered therein and no notice or allegation that any of them is incorrect or should be rectified has been received by the Company or the Seller.

2.5.2 The Company's accounting records comply with the requirements of the Companies Acts.

2.6 Filing of documents

All returns and other documents required to be filed with the Registrar of Companies, or with any other authority, in respect of the Company have been duly filed and were when filed correct.

2.7   **Insurances**

2.7.1   The Company maintains, and at all material times has maintained, adequate insurance cover against all risks normally insured against by companies carrying on a similar business, for the full replacement or reinstatement value of its business and assets and in particular has maintained all insurance required by statute, product liability and professional indemnity insurance.

2.7.2   The Disclosure Letter sets out full details of all policies of insurance maintained by or on behalf of the Company, all of which are in full force and effect.

3.   **THE COMPANY AND THE LAW**

3.1   **Compliance with laws**

3.1.1   The Company has conducted and is conducting its business in accordance with all applicable laws and regulations of any relevant jurisdiction and neither the Company nor any of its officers, agents or employees have committed, or omitted to do, any act or thing capable of giving rise to any fine, penalty, default proceedings or other liability on the part of the Company.

3.1.2   There is no order, decree or judgment of any court or any governmental agency of any jurisdiction outstanding against the Company or which may have any adverse effect upon the assets or business of the Company; no such order, decree or judgment is pending, and there are no circumstances likely to give rise to any such order, decree or judgment.

3.1.3   The Company has not been party to any undertaking or assurance given to any court or governmental agency which is still in force.

3.2   **Licences**

3.2.1   The Company has obtained all licences, consents, permits and authorities of a statutory or regulatory nature necessary or expedient to enable it to carry on its business effectively in the places and in the manner in which it is now carried on.

3.2.2   All such licences, consents, permits and authorities are valid and subsisting, and the Seller knows of no reason why any of them should be suspended, cancelled or revoked or renewed or continued subject to any term or condition which does not currently apply thereto.

3.3   **Litigation**

3.3.1   The Company is not engaged in any dispute with any customer or supplier or in any litigation or other proceedings.

3.3.2   So far as the Seller is aware:

3.3.2.1   no litigation or other proceedings are pending or threatened by or against the Company; and

3.3.2.2   there are no circumstances likely to give rise to any litigation or other proceedings.

3.4   **Insolvency**

3.4.1   The Company has not become unable to pay its debts as they fall due within the meaning of section 123 of the Insolvency Act 1986 or received any written demand pursuant to section 123(1)(a) of the Insolvency Act 1986.

3.4.2 No order has been made or petition presented or resolution passed for the winding up of the Company; no proposal has been made under part I of the Insolvency Act 1986 for a voluntary arrangement; no person has appointed or applied to any court of competent jurisdiction to appoint a receiver or an administrative receiver or an administrator; and no distress, execution or other process has been levied against the Company.

3.5 **Pollution of the environment**

3.5.1 [No hazardous substances have been used or stored or otherwise handled by the Company on the Property or elsewhere.] [The Company has at all times held all licences, consents, permits and authorities necessary to enable it to use, store or otherwise handle or dispose of any hazardous substances used, stored, otherwise handled or disposed of by it, whether on the Property or elsewhere.]

3.5.2 There has been no pollution of the environment by the Company, the Company has no responsibility or liability for any pollution of the environment by any third party and there has been no act or omission by the Company which could give rise to any pollution of the environment.

For the purpose of this paragraph 3.5, the expressions "pollution of the environment" and "process" shall have the same meanings as in section 1 of the Environmental Protection Act 1990.

4. **THE COMPANY'S FINANCIAL POSITION**

4.1 **The Accounts**

The Accounts:

4.1.1 have been prepared in accordance with the requirements of the Act and all other applicable statutes and regulations and in accordance with generally accepted accounting practices;

4.1.2 have been prepared on bases and principles and using methods which are consistent with those used in the preparation of the audited accounts of the Company [and the audited consolidated accounts for the Group in each case] for any accounting period falling wholly or partly within the period of six years ended on the Accounts Date; and

4.1.3 show a true and fair view of the state of affairs of the Company [and of the Group] as at the Accounts Date and of the profit or loss of the Company [and of the Group] for the accounting period ended on that date.

4.2 **Provisions in the Accounts**

The Accounts:

4.2.1 fully provide for all liabilities (other than contingent liabilities which are not expected to crystallise) and fully disclose all contingent liabilities which are not expected to crystallise and all capital and revenue commitments of the Company, in each case as at the Accounts Date;

4.2.2   fully provide for all bad and doubtful debts as at the Accounts Date.

4.3   **Events since the Accounts Date**

Since the Accounts Date:

4.3.1   the Company has carried on its business in the ordinary and usual course and without any interruption or alteration in the nature, scope or manner thereof;

4.3.2   the Company has not acquired or disposed of any asset, assumed any liability, made any payment or entered into any other transaction which was not in the ordinary course of its business and for full value; and

4.3.3   there has been no deterioration in the financial position or prospects of the Company.

4.4   **Management Accounts**

The Management Accounts have been prepared using the same accounting principles, policies and bases as used in the Accounts (consistently applied) and fairly reflect the trading position of the Company as at the date and for the period to which they relate.

5.   **THE COMPANY AND ITS FINANCIERS**

5.1   **Continuance of facilities**

Full and accurate details of all overdrafts, loans or other financial facilities outstanding or available to the Company are contained in the Disclosure Letter (and true and complete copies of all documents relating thereto are attached to the Disclosure Letter), and neither the Seller nor the Company has done anything whereby the continuance of any such facilities in full force and effect might be affected or prejudiced.

5.2   **Bank accounts**

A statement of all the bank accounts of the Company and of the credit or debit balances on such accounts as at a date not more than two days before the date of this Agreement and a reconciliation of such credit or debit balances to the books and records of the Company as at the date of this Agreement are attached to the Disclosure Letter and are true, complete and accurate. Since the date to which such statement is drawn up there have been no payments out of, and no instructions given for any payments out of, and no cheques drawn against, any such accounts, except for routine payments out of current account in the ordinary course of business.

6.   **THE ASSETS OF THE COMPANY**

6.1   **Assets and charges**

6.1.1   The Company owns free from any Encumbrance all assets used by it.

6.1.2   The Company has possession of all such assets.

6.2   **Debts**

The amounts due from debtors are recoverable in full in the ordinary course of business and in any event not later than [ninety] days following the date of this Agreement, and none of these debts is subject to any counterclaim or set-off.

6.3   **Intellectual Property**

6.3.1   The Company:

6.3.1.1   is the sole and beneficial owner and (where it is capable of registration) the registered proprietor of the Intellectual Property used by it, all of which is valid and in full force and effect;

6.3.1.2   has not entered into any Intellectual Property Agreements other than any listed in the Disclosure Letter or authorised any person to make any use of or to do anything which would or might otherwise infringe any Intellectual Property Rights.

6.3.2   The Company owns the copyright or design right (whether registered or unregistered) in the designs of all its products and is the proprietor of any registrations or applications to register any such designs.

6.3.3   None of the processes or products of the Company [(so far as the Seller is aware)] infringes any Intellectual Property of any other person.

6.3.4   None of the Intellectual Property Rights are being used by, or are being or have been claimed, disputed, opposed or attacked by any other person.

6.4   **Plant**

Each item of the plant and machinery and all vehicles and office and other equipment used in connection with the business of the Company is in good repair and condition (subject to fair wear and tear) and in satisfactory working order;

6.5   **[Net asset value**

The value of the net tangible assets of the Company, determined in accordance with the same accounting policies as those applied in the preparation of the Accounts (and on the basis that each of the fixed assets of the Company is valued at a figure no greater than the value attributed to it in the Accounts or, in the case of any fixed assets acquired by the Company after the Accounts Date, at a figure no greater than cost), is not less than the value of the net tangible assets of the Company at the Accounts Date as shown in the Accounts.]

6.6   **Computer Systems**

6.6.1   The Hardware has been satisfactorily maintained and supported and has the benefit of an appropriate maintenance and support agreement which is not capable of being terminated by the contractor by less than 24 months' notice.

6.6.2   Where any of the records of the Company are stored electronically, the Company is the owner of all hardware and software licences necessary to enable it to keep, copy, maintain and use such records in the course of its business and does not share any hardware or software relating to the records with any person.

6.6.3   In this paragraph 6.6:-

6.6.3.1   "Hardware" means any computer equipment used by or for the benefit of the Company at any time but excluding all Software;

6.6.3.2 "Software" means any set of instructions for execution by microprocessor used by or for the benefit of the Company at any time, irrespective of application, language or medium.

7. THE CONTRACTS OF THE COMPANY

7.1 Material contracts

The Company is not a party to or subject to any agreement, transaction, obligation, commitment, understanding, arrangement or liability which:

7.1.1 involves or is likely to involve obligations, restrictions, expenditure or revenue of a long term, unusual, onerous or exceptional nature; or

7.1.2 is in any way otherwise than in the ordinary and proper course of the business of the Company and on arm's length terms.

7.2 Insider contracts

There is not outstanding, and there has not at any time during the last three years been outstanding, any agreement or arrangement between the Company and any Member of the Seller's Group at any material time and the Company is not a party to, nor has its profit or loss or financial position during such period been affected by, any such agreement or arrangement or any other agreement or arrangement which is not entirely of an arm's length nature.

7.3 Customers suppliers

The Seller is not aware of any reason to indicate that any of the existing customers of or suppliers to the Company are likely materially to reduce the volume of their purchases from, or supplies to, the Company in the future by comparison with the value of their purchases from, or supplies to, the Company during the period of [ ] months prior to the date of this Agreement.

8. THE COMPANY AND ITS EMPLOYEES

8.1 General

8.1.1 There is no employment or other contract or engagement between the Company and any of its directors or other officers, other than those, copies of which are annexed to the Company Disclosure Letter.

8.1.2 There is no employment contract between the Company and any of its employees which cannot be terminated by the Company by three months' notice or less without giving rise to a claim for damages or compensation (other than a statutory redundancy payment or statutory compensation for unfair dismissal).

8.1.3 The Disclosure Letter contains details of:

8.1.3.1 the name, date of start of employment, period of continuous employment, salary and other benefits, grade and age of each employee of the Company and the terms of the contract of employment of each such employee.

8.1.4 The Company is not obliged to increase, nor has it made provision to increase the rate of remuneration of a director, other officer or employee.

8.2 Payments on termination

Except as disclosed in the Accounts, the Company has not:

8.2.1 incurred a liability for breach or termination of an employment contract including, without limitation, a redundancy payment, protective award and compensation for wrongful dismissal, unfair dismissal and failure to comply with an order for the reinstatement or re-engagement of an employee;

8.2.2 incurred a liability for breach or termination of a consultancy agreement;

8.3 Compliance with law

The Company has complied with each obligation imposed on it by, and each order and award made under, statute, regulation, code of conduct and practice, collective agreement, custom and practice relevant to the relations between it and its employees or a trade union or the terms of employment of its employees.

8.4 Redundancies and transfer of business

Within the year ending on the date of this Agreement the Company has not given notice of redundancies to the relevant Secretary of State or started consultations with appropriate representatives under Chapter II of Part IV of the Trade Union and Labour Relations (Consolidation) Act 1992 or failed to comply with its obligations under Chapter II of Part IV of that Act.

8.5 Trade Unions

The Company has no agreement or arrangement (whether under the Information and Consultation of Employees Regulations 2004 or otherwise) with and does not recognise a trade union, works council, staff association or other body representing any of its employees and the Company has not received any notice or request nor are there any negotiations which may lead to any such agreement or arrangement).

8.6 Incentive schemes

The Company does not have and is not proposing to introduce a share incentive, share option, profit sharing, bonus or other incentive scheme for any of its directors, other officers or employees.

9. PENSIONS

9.1 Disclosed Schemes

The Disclosed Schemes are the only arrangements under which the Company has or could have any liability to provide or contribute towards relevant benefits as defined in Chapter 2 of Part 6 of the Income Tax (Earnings & Pensions) Act 2003.

9.2 Details Supplied

The Seller has supplied to the Buyer documents containing full, accurate and up to date details of each of the Disclosed Schemes and of the Company's obligations and liabilities under it.

[ADDITIONAL PENSIONS WARRANTIES TO BE INSERTED, AS NECESSARY, TO REFLECT THE FACTUAL POSITION]

10. MATERIAL DISCLOSURE

10.1 Disclosure letter

All information contained in or referred to in the Disclosure letter is true and accurate, and the Disclosure Letter does not omit anything which renders any such information misleading or which might reasonably affect the willingness of an acquirer to acquire the Shares on the terms (including without limitation as to price) of this Agreement.

10.2 Commission

No person is entitled whether, actually or contingently, to receive from the Company any finder's fee, brokerage, or other commission in connection with the acquisition or disposal of shares in the Company.

10.3 Consequence of share acquisition by the Buyer

The sale of the Shares to the Buyer will not by virtue of the terms of any agreement or arrangement to which the Company is a party cause the Company to lose the benefit of any right or privilege it presently enjoys or entitle any person to terminate any contract with, or obligation to, the Company.

10.4 Legal Due Diligence Enquiries

The replies to the Legal Due Diligence Enquiries dated [   ] 200 raised on behalf of the Buyer were when given and remain true complete and accurate.

11. PROPERTY

11.1 Particulars

The Particulars of the Property shown in schedule 4 are true and correct and the Company has good and marketable title to and the exclusive occupation and possession of the Property free from any mortgage, debenture or charge (whether specific or floating, legal or equitable) rent charge, lien or other encumbrance, lease, sub-lease, tenancy or right of occupation, reservation, covenant, stipulation, profit a prendre, wayleave, grant, restriction, easement, quasi-easement or any agreement for any of the same or any privilege in favour of any third party.

11.2 Rights and easements

There are appurtenant to the Property all rights and easements necessary for its use and enjoyment.

11.3 Title deeds and documents

The Company has in its possession or under its control all duly stamped deeds and documents which are necessary to prove title to the Property.

11.4 Use of property

There are no restrictive covenants or provisions, legislation, or orders, charges, restrictions, agreements, conditions or other matters which preclude the use of the Property for the purpose or purposes for which the Property is now used and each such use is the permitted use under the provisions of the Town and Country Planning Acts 1971 to 1990 and any statutory re-enactment thereof and all statutory instruments and regulations made thereunder and is in accordance with the requirements of any Local Authority and all restrictions, conditions and covenants imposed by or pursuant to the said Town and Country Planning Acts have been observed and performed and no agreements have been entered into under section 52 of the Town and Country Planning Act 1971, section 106 of the Town and Country Planning Act 1990 or section 33 of the Local Government (Miscellaneous Provisions) Act 1982 in respect of the Property.

11.5   **Replies to enquiries**

All replies by or on behalf of the Seller to enquiries relating to the Property made by or on behalf of the Purchaser were when given and are now true complete accurate and correct.

11.6   **Properties previously occupied**

The Company has no existing or contingent liabilities in respect of any properties previously occupied by it or in which it owned or held any interest (or as a surety for the obligations of any other person in relation to such property) including leasehold premises assigned surrendered or otherwise disposed of and the Company has not at any time received any indication whatsoever from any party that any claim has been made or will be made in respect of any such existing or contingent liabilities.

PRECEDENT 27

Short Form Warranties—Assets Sale and Purchases

Warranties

1. ## THE BUSINESS AND THE SELLER['S GROUP]

   1.1 **Capacity**

   [The Seller has/The Seller and the Guarantor each have] full power to enter into and perform the provisions of this Agreement, which constitutes a binding agreement on [the Seller/each of them] in accordance with its terms.

   1.2 **Ownership of the Assets**

   The Seller is the beneficial owner of the Assets and has the right to dispose of them to the Buyer or as it directs free from any Encumbrance and together with all rights now or hereafter attaching to them.

   1.3 **Transfers at an undervalue**

   None of the Assets have been the subject of a transfer at an undervalue (within the meaning of section 238 or section 239 of the Insolvency Act 1986) within the period of five years prior to the date of this Agreement.

   1.4 **Liabilities owing to or by the Seller**

   There is not outstanding any indebtedness and there are no contracts, arrangements or liabilities (actual or contingent) remaining in whole or in part to be performed between the Business and any Member of the Seller's Group or any director of the Seller or any director of any Member of the Seller's Group or any person who is an associate of or connected with any of them.

2. ## CONSTITUTIONAL AND ADMINISTRATIVE AFFAIRS

   2.1 **Books and records**

   All accounts, books, ledgers, financial and other records of the Seller relating to the Business have been fully, properly and accurately kept and maintained, are in the possession of the Seller and contain true and accurate records of all matters required by law to be entered therein and no notice or allegation that any of them is incorrect or should be rectified has been received by the Seller [or the Guarantor].

   2.1.1 The Seller's accounting records, insofar as they relate to the Business, comply with the requirements of the Companies Acts.

   2.2 **Insurances**

   The Disclosure Letter sets out full details of all policies of insurance maintained by or on behalf of the Seller in relation to the Business, all of which are in full force and effect.

3. ## THE SELLER AND THE LAW

   3.1 **Compliance with Laws**

   3.1.1 The Seller has conducted and is conducting the Business in accordance with all applicable laws and regulations of any relevant jurisdiction.

   3.1.2 There is no order, decree or judgment of any court or any governmental agency of any jurisdiction outstanding against the Seller or which may have any adverse effect upon any of the Assets or the Business; no such order, decree or judgment is pending, and there are no circumstances likely to give rise to any such order, decree or judgment.

3.1.3   The Seller has not been a party to any undertaking or assurance in relation to the Business or any of the Assets or any of the Third Party Assets given to any court or governmental agency which is still in force.

3.2   **Licences**

3.2.1   The Seller has obtained all licences, consents, permits and authorities of a statutory or regulatory nature necessary or expedient to enable it to carry on the Business effectively in the places and in the manner in which it is now carried on.

3.2.2   All such licences, consents, permits and authorities are valid and subsisting, and [neither] the Seller [nor the Guarantor] knows of any reason why any of them should be suspended, cancelled or revoked or renewed or continued subject to any term or condition which does not currently apply thereto.

3.3   **Litigation**

3.3.1   The Seller is not engaged in any dispute with any customer or supplier or in any litigation or other proceedings in respect of the Business or any of the Assets or any of the Third Party Assets.

3.3.2   So far as the Seller [and the Guarantor] [is/are] aware:

3.3.2.1   no litigation or other proceedings are pending or threatened by or against the Seller in relation to the Business or any of the Assets or any of the Third Party Assets;

3.3.2.2   there are no circumstances likely to give rise to any litigation or other proceedings in relation to the Business or any of the Assets or any of the Third Party Assets.

3.4   **Pollution of the environment**

For the purposes of this paragraph 3.7 the expressions "pollution of the environment" and "process" shall have the same meanings as in section 1 of the Environmental Protection Act 1990.

3.4.1   [No hazardous substances have been used or stored or otherwise handled by the Seller on the Property or elsewhere.] [The Seller has at all times held all licences, consents, permits and authorities necessary to enable it to use, store or otherwise handle or dispose of any hazardous substances used, stored, otherwise handled or disposed of by it, whether on the Property or elsewhere.]

3.4.2   There has been no pollution of the environment nor contamination of land by the Seller in the course of the Business and the Seller has no responsibility or liability for any pollution of the environment or for any contaminated land by any third party, and there has been no act or omission by the Seller in the course of the Business which could give rise to any pollution of the environment or contaminated land.

3.4.3   For the purpose of this paragraph 3.5, the expressions "pollution of the environment" and "process" shall have the same meanings as in section 1 of the Environmental Protection Act 1990.

4.   THE SELLER'S FINANCIAL POSITION

4.1   The Accounts

The Accounts:

4.1.1   have been prepared in accordance with the requirements of the Companies Acts and all other applicable statutes and regulations and in accordance with generally accepted accounting principles and practices, including all applicable SSAPs and FRSs;

4.1.2   have been prepared on bases and principles and using methods which are consistent with those used in the preparation of the audited accounts of the Seller for any accounting period falling wholly or partly within the period of six years ended on the Accounts Date; and

4.1.3   show a true and fair view of the state of affairs of the Seller as at the Accounts Date and of the profit or loss of the Seller for the accounting period ended on that date.

4.2   Provisions in the Accounts

The Accounts:

4.2.1   fully provide for all liabilities (other than contingent liabilities which are not expected to crystallise) and fully disclose all contingent liabilities which are not expected to crystallise and all capital and revenue commitments of the Seller in each case as at the Accounts Date;

4.2.2   fully provide for all bad and doubtful debts as at the Accounts Date.

4.3   Events since the Accounts Date

Since the Accounts Date:

4.3.1   the Seller has carried on the Business in the ordinary and usual course and without any interruption or alteration in the nature, scope or manner thereof;

4.3.2   the Seller has not, in relation to the Business, acquired or disposed of any asset entered into any transaction, assumed any liability, made any payment or entered into any other transaction which was not in the ordinary course of the Business and for full value; and

4.3.3   there has been no deterioration in its financial position or prospects.

4.4   Management Accounts

The Management Accounts have been prepared using the same accounting principles, policies and bases as used in the Accounts (consistently applied) and fairly reflect the trading position of the Business as at the date and for the period to which they relate. 5.

5.   THE ASSETS USED IN THE BUSINESS

5.1   Assets and charges

5.1.1   The Seller owns all of the Assets free from any Encumbrance and the Assets, together with the Third Party Assets, comprise all assets necessary for the continuation of the Business as now carried on and none of the Assets is shared by the Business with any other person.

5.1.2   The Seller has possession of all of the Assets which are tangible assets and of all of the Third Party Assets.

5.2   **Debts**

Each of the Book Debts is recoverable in full in the ordinary course of the Business and in any event not later than [ninety] days following the date of this Agreement, and none of them is subject to any counterclaim or set-off.

5.3   **Intellectual property**

5.3.1   The Seller:

5.3.1.1   is the sole and beneficial owner of the Intellectual Property Rights all of which are valid and in full force and effect);

5.3.1.2   is (where such rights are capable of registration) the registered proprietor of the Intellectual Property Rights;

5.3.1.3   has not entered into any Intellectual Property Agreements other than those specified in schedule 3 or authorised any person to make any use of or to do anything which would or might otherwise infringe any Intellectual Property owned or used by it.

5.3.2   The Seller owns the copyright or design right (whether registered or unregistered) in the designs of all its products and is the proprietor of any registrations or applications to register any such designs.

5.3.3   None of the processes used in or products of the Business [(so far as the Seller is aware)]infringes any Intellectual Property of any other person.

5.3.4   None of the Intellectual Property Rights are being used (other than by the Seller) or are being or have been claimed, disputed, opposed or attacked by any person.

5.4   **Plant**

Each item of Plant is in good repair and condition (subject to fair wear and tear) and in satisfactory working order.

5.5   **Third Party Assets**

A true and complete copy of each of the leasing, rental, hire and hire-purchase agreements relating to any of the Third Party Assets is attached to the Disclosure Letter.

5.6   **Computer Systems**

5.6.1   The Hardware has been satisfactorily maintained and supported and has the benefit of an appropriate maintenance and support agreement which is not capable of being terminated by the contractor by less than 24 months' notice.

5.6.2   Where any of the records of the Business are stored electronically, the Seller is the owner of all hardware and software licences necessary to enable it to keep, copy, maintain and use such records in the course of its business and does not share any hardware or software relating to the records with any person.

5.6.3   In this paragraph:-

5.6.3.1   "Hardware" means any computer equipment which is comprised within the Assets or the Third Party Assets but excluding all Software;

5.6.3.2 "Software" means any set of instructions for execution by microprocessor used by or for the benefit of the Seller in relation to the Business at any time, irrespective of application, language or medium;

6. THE CONTRACTS OF THE BUSINESS

6.1 Material contracts

[The Seller is not a party to or subject to any agreement, transaction, obligation, commitment, understanding, arrangement or liability relating to the Business which:/None of the Contracts:][1]

6.1.1 involves or is likely to involve obligations, restrictions, expenditure or revenue of a long term, unusual, onerous or exceptional nature;

6.1.2 is in any way otherwise than in the ordinary and proper course of the Business and on arm's length terms[; and

[and a true and complete copy of each of the Contracts is attached to the Disclosure Letter].

6.2 Insider contracts

There is not outstanding, and there has not at any time during the last three years been outstanding, any agreement or arrangement between the Seller and Member of the Seller's Group at any material time and the Seller is not a party to, nor has its profit or loss or financial position during such period been affected by, any such agreement or any other agreement or arrangement in relation to the Business which is not entirely of an arm's length nature.

6.3 Customers/suppliers

The Seller is not aware of any reason to indicate that any of the existing customers of or suppliers of the Business are likely materially to reduce the volume of their purchases from or supplies to the Business in the future by comparison with the value of their purchases or supplies during the period of [   ] months prior to the date of this Agreement.

7. EMPLOYEES

7.1 General

7.1.1 No person is employed in the Business other than the Employees.

7.1.2 There is no employment contract or other contract of engagement between the Seller and any of the Employees which cannot be terminated by the Seller by three months' notice or less without giving rise to a claim for damages or compensation (other than a statutory redundancy payment or statutory compensation for unfair dismissal).

7.1.3 The Disclosure Letter contains details of the name, date of start of employment, period of continuous employment, salary and other benefits, grade and age of each Employee and the terms of the contract of each Employee.

7.1.4 The Seller is not obliged to increase, nor has it made provision to increase, the rate of remuneration of any Employee.

---

[1] The wording to be used will depend on the definition of Contracts.

7.2   **Compliance with law**

The Seller has complied with:

7.2.1   each obligation imposed on it by, and each order and award made under, statute, regulation, code of conduct and practice, collective agreement, custom and practice relevant to the relations between it and the Employees or a trade union or the terms of employment of the Employees; and

7.2.2   each recommendation or code of practice made by the Advisory, Conciliation and Arbitration Service and each award and declaration made by the Central Arbitration Committee.

7.3   **Redundancies and transfer of business**

Within the year ending on the date of this Agreement the Seller has not:-

7.3.1   in relation to any Employee given notice of redundancies to the relevant Secretary of State or started consultations with appropriate representatives under Chapter II of Part IV of the Trade Union and Labour Relations (Consolidation) Act 1992 or failed to comply with its obligations under Chapter II of Part IV of that Act; or

7.3.2   been a party to a relevant transfer (as defined in the Regulations) or failed to comply with a duty to inform and consult appropriate representatives under those Regulations.

7.4   **Collective Bargaining and Consultation**

The Seller has no agreement or arrangement (whether under the Information and Consultation of Employees Regulations 2004 or otherwise) with and does not recognise a trade union, works council, staff association or other body representing any of its Employees and the Seller has not received any notice or request nor are there any negotiations which may lead to any such agreement or arrangement).

7.5   **Incentive schemes**

The Seller does not have and is not proposing to introduce a share incentive, share option, profit sharing, bonus or other incentive scheme for any of the directors, other officers or employees.

8.   **PENSIONS**

8.1   **Disclosed Schemes**

The Disclosed Schemes are the only arrangements under which the Seller has or could have any liability to provide or contribute towards relevant benefits, as defined in Chapter 2 of Part 6 of the Income Tax (Earnings & Pensions) Act 2003.

8.2   **Details Supplied**

The Seller has supplied to the Buyer documents containing full, accurate and up to date details of each of the Disclosed Schemes and of the Seller's obligations and liabilities under it.

8.3   **[ADDITIONAL PENSIONS WARRANTIES TO BE INSERTED, AS NECESSARY, TO REFLECT THE FACTUAL POSITION]**

9.   **PROPERTY**

9.1   **Particulars**

The Particulars of the Property shown in schedule 4 are true and correct and the Seller has good and marketable title to and the exclusive occupation and possession of the Property free from any mortgage, debenture or charge (whether specific or floating, legal or equitable) rent charge, lien or other encumbrance, lease, sub-lease, tenancy or right of occupation, reservation, covenant, stipulation, profit a prendre, wayleave, grant, restriction, easement, quasi-easement or any agreement for any of the same or any privilege in favour of any third party.

9.2 Rights and easements

There are appurtenant to the Property all rights and easements necessary for its use and enjoyment.

9.3 Title deeds and documents

The Seller has in its possession or under its control all duly stamped deeds and documents which are necessary to prove title to the Property.

9.4 Use of property

There are no restrictive covenants or provisions, legislation, or orders, charges, restrictions, agreements, conditions or other matters which preclude the use of the Property for the purpose or purposes for which the Property is now used and each such use is the permitted use under the provisions of the Town and Country Planning Acts 1971 to 1990 and any statutory re-enactment thereof and all statutory instruments and regulations made thereunder and is in accordance with the requirements of any Local Authority and all restrictions, conditions and covenants imposed by or pursuant to the said Town and Country Planning Acts have been observed and performed and no agreements have been entered into under section 52 of the Town and Country Planning Act 1971, section 106 of the Town and Country Planning Act 1990 or section 33 of the Local Government (Miscellaneous Provisions) Act 1982 in respect of the Property.

9.5 Replies to enquiries

All replies by or on behalf of the Seller to enquiries relating to the Property made by or on behalf of the Buyer were when given and are now true complete accurate and correct.

9.6 No further land and buildings

The Property comprises all the land and buildings owned, leased or occupied by the Seller for the purposes of the Business.

10. MATERIAL DISCLOSURE

10.1 Disclosure Letter

All information contained in or referred to in the Disclosure letter is true and accurate, and the Disclosure Letter does not omit anything which renders any such information misleading or which might reasonably affect the willingness of an acquirer to acquire the Business and the Assets on the terms (including without limitation as to price) of this Agreement.

10.2 Relationships

To the best of the knowledge and belief of the Seller [(but without having made any enquiry of any customer or supplier of the Seller)], the transaction hereby agreed upon is not of itself likely to have any adverse effect on the relationships of any customer or supplier of the Business with the Business or upon the performance of any Employee.

10.3 Legal Due Diligence Enquiries

The replies to the legal due diligence enquiries dated [   ] 200 raised on behalf of the Buyer were when given and remain true, complete and accurate.

11. TAXATION

11.1 The Seller has no material agreements with any Taxation Authority relating to transactions entered into in the course of the Business pursuant to which such transactions will be subject to Taxation on a basis which is not strictly in accordance with the relevant legislation.

11.2 The Seller is not aware of any dispute or any circumstances likely to give rise to any dispute with any relevant Taxation Authority in connection with the Business.

11.3 The Seller does not conduct and has not conducted any part of the Business through a branch, agency or permanent establishment outside the United Kingdom, and the Business has not involved the Seller acting as branch or agent of any person not resident for any taxation purpose in the United Kingdom.

11.4 No material sum of an income nature paid under any existing contract or commitment relating to the Business which will continue after Completion has been disallowed wholly or in part as a deduction or charge in compiling the Seller's profits for Taxation purposes.

11.5 None of the Assets are subject to the provisions on long-life assets contained in sections 90 to 104 (inclusive) of the Capital Allowances Act 2001.

11.6 The [Fixtures] will not be given a disposal value in the capital allowances computation of the Seller which is less than the value set out therefor in this Agreement by virtue of the operation of section 185 of the Capital Allowances Act 2001.

11.7 The amount of the consideration allocated to the [Building] in this Agreement is not less than the eligible cost therefor for industrial buildings allowances purposes.

11.8 There is no P11D dispensation in force in relation to any of the Employees.

11.9 The Seller is not transferring any assets pursuant to this Agreement to which Part XV of the Value Added Tax Regulations 1995 (Capital Goods Scheme) applies.

PRECEDENT 28

Deed of Release

(1) [**LIMITED/PLC]**

-and-

(2) [**LIMITED/PLC]**

DEED OF RELEASE

This deed of release is made on   200

between:

(1) [**LIMITED/PLC]**, a company registered in England under number [   ], whose registered office is at [   ] ("the Chargee"); and

(2) [**LIMITED/PLC]**, a company registered in England under number [   ], whose registered office is at [   ]("the Seller");

Pursuant to an agreement dated [the date of this deed/ [200] and entitled "assets sale and purchase agreement]" between (1) the Seller and (2) [Limited/ PLC] ("the Agreement").

It is hereby agreed as follows:-

1. **INTERPRETATION**

   In this deed:

   1.1   The following words and expressions shall have the meanings set out or referred to opposite each respectively:-

   "the Assets"   as defined in the Agreement;

   "Proceedings"   as defined in the Agreement.

   1.2   The headings and sub-headings are inserted for convenience only and shall not affect the construction of this document.

2. **RELEASE**

   2.1   The Chargee releases each of the Assets from all and any mortgages, charges and other security interests and from all claims in its favour to hold to the Seller absolutely.

   2.2   The release effected in clause 2.1 is without prejudice to the security interests and other rights of the Chargee in respect of assets of the Seller other than the Assets.

3. **GENERAL**

   3.1   **Proper law and jurisdiction**

   This document shall be governed by and construed in accordance with English law, and the parties irrevocably submit to the exclusive jurisdiction of the English courts and waive any object to Proceedings in such courts on the grounds of venue or on the grounds that Proceedings have been brought in an inappropriate forum.

   3.2   **Further assurance**

   The Chargor shall do such acts and execute such documents as the Seller may at any time reasonably require for the purpose of assuring to the Seller the full benefit of this document.

Executed as a deed by or on behalf of the Chargor on the date first set out in this document.

Signed as a deed by

[LIMITED/PLC] acting by:

director

[director/secretary]

PRECEDENT 29

Letter of Non-crystallisation

Date _____

Dear Sirs

[DEBENTURE] [FLOATING CHARGE] DATED [   ]

BETWEEN [   ] (THE "COMPANY") AND OURSELVES (THE "CHARGE")

We certify that no event has occurred, on or before the date hereof, which would cause the crystallisation of the floating charge over the assets of the Company created by the Charge and we have taken no steps ourselves to crystallise the charge.

Yours faithfully

PRECEDENT 30

Contribution Agreement

[Note: this agreement has been drafted on the basis that there will be certain of the sellers who will not be party to the warranties but will nevertheless agree "behind the scenes" to accept their proportionate share of liability. It can be adapted for use where all sellers have given warranties jointly and severally but have agreed to share liability on an agreed basis]

DATED   **200**

(1) [**]**

(2) [**]**

(3) [**]**

CONTRIBUTION AGREEMENT
-relating to-

[**] LIMITED**

THIS DEED is made on 200

BETWEEN:

(1) [   ] of [   ];

(2) [   ] of [   ]; and

(3) [   ] of [   ]

(together "the Contributors" and each a "Contributor")

RECITALS

(A)   Under the terms of the Sale Agreement the Contributors have agreed to sell the whole of the issued share capital of the Company to [ ] Limited/PLC ("the Buyer").

(B)   Certain of the Contributors ("the Warrantors") have given certain warranties, representations, indemnities and undertakings under the terms of the Sale Agreement.

(C)   The Contributors are entering into this Deed to agree to take on and share the liabilities of the Warrantors in respect of such warranties, representations, indemnities and certain of such undertakings.

IT IS AGREED as follows:-

1.   **DEFINITIONS AND INTERPRETATION**[1]

In this Deed, unless the context otherwise requires:-

    1.1   The following words have the following meanings:

"Business Day"	any day (other than Saturday) on which clearing banks are open for normal banking business in sterling in the City of London;
"Claim"	a claim made against the Warrantors under or in respect of the representations, warranties and indemnities given by the Warrantors pursuant to the Acquisition Agreement, including the Tax Covenants but excluding Excluded Claims;
"the Company"	[ ] Limited, a company registered in England number [ ];
"Excluded Claims"	Claims arising under [ ] and [ ] of Schedule [ ] to the Sale Agreement;
"Payment"	all sums paid or payable by the Contributors (or any of them) in connection with a Claim, whether by way of settlement or pursuant to the order of a court of competent jurisdiction [or by way of payment from the Retention Account (as that phrase is defined in the Sale Agreement)] and all legal and other costs and expenses incurred by the Warrantors in connection with such Claim;

[1] NOTE: Assumes that the Agreement will contain definitions of:
"the Escrow Account"
"the Buyer"
"the Seller"
"the Escrow Letter"

"Proceedings"	any legal action or proceedings arising out of or in connection with this Deed;
"Release"	any release, waiver or compromise or any other arrangement of any kind having similar or analogous effect;
"the Sale Agreement"	a sale and purchase agreement of the same date as this deed and made between the Contributors (1) and the Buyer (2) relating to the sale by the Contributors of the entire issued share capital of the Company;
"the Tax Covenants"	[Description].

1.2   A reference to any gender shall include the other and neuter gender and a reference to a "person" includes a reference to any individual, firm, company, corporation or other body corporate, government, state or agency of a state or any joint venture, association or partnership, works council or employee representative body (whether or not having separate legal personality).

1.3   The word "Notice" includes any notice, demand, consent or other communication.

1.4   The headings are inserted for convenience only and shall not affect the construction of this Deed;

1.5   A reference to "the Warrantors" or to "the Contributors" shall include a reference to each of them and to each of their respective personal representatives.

2.   CONTRIBUTION TO CLAIM

In relation to any Claim the Contributors undertake to pay to the Buyer on demand in the proportions set against their respective names in column 2 of the schedule, a sum or sums equal to all Payments in relation to such Claim.

3.   INTEREST

If any party defaults in paying within 14 days of demand any sum due under this Deed, he shall pay interest on the amount in question at the rate of 3% per year, above the base rate of [   ] Bank PLC from time to time, from the date of demand until the date of actual payment (as well after any judgment as before).

4.   SET-OFF

No party shall be entitled to withhold or delay payment of any sum due under this Deed or, in relation to any such sum, exercise any right of set-off or counter-claim.

5.   MAXIMUM LIABILITY

The maximum aggregate liability of each of the Contributors under this Deed shall not exceed the amount [of the consideration paid to that Contributor pursuant to the Sale Agreement] [set against their respective names in column 3 of the schedule].

6.   LEGAL ADVICE AND COSTS

6.1   The Contributors acknowledge that they have been recommended to take independent legal advice in connection with this Deed and that, in relation to this Deed, [   ] are not acting for them individually.

6.2   The Contributors shall bear their own costs, expenses and other charges incurred by them in connection with this Deed or (or in their capacity as Contributors) a Claim.

7. INABILITY TO CONTRIBUTE

7.1 If any Contributor ("the Defaultor") fails to satisfy in full any liability under clause 2 in relation to a claim due to bankruptcy or liquidation (or analogous process in any jurisdiction) or within six months of demand, then his unsatisfied liability shall be borne by the other Contributors on demand in the same proportions that the proportions set against their names in column 2 of the schedule respectively bear to each other (excluding for this purpose the Defaultor's proportion).

7.2 In relation to any payment made by Contributors pursuant to clause 7.1, the Defaultor undertakes to pay on demand to such Contributors an amount equal to all sums paid by such Contributors respectively pursuant to clause 7.1.

7.3 The Contributors agree to make such payments between themselves as may from time to time be necessary in order to give effect to the provisions of clause 2 and clause 7.1.

8. GENERAL

8.1 This Deed constitutes the entire agreement between the parties in relation to its subject-matter and supersedes all prior agreements, understandings or discussions between the parties, other than representations made fraudulently.

8.2 Each of the parties acknowledges that he is not relying on any statements, warranties or representations given or made by any of the others in relation to the subject-matter of this Deed, and that he shall have no rights or remedies with respect to such subject-matter other than under this Deed, save to the extent that they arise out of the fraud or fraudulent misrepresentation of any party.

9. WAIVER

9.1 The rights and remedies of a party in respect of this Deed shall not be diminished, waived or extinguished by the granting of any indulgence, forbearance or extension of time by a party to another nor by any failure of or delay by a party in ascertaining or exercising any such rights or remedies. Any Release by a party shall not affect its rights and remedies as regards any other party nor its rights and remedies against the party in whose favour it is granted or made except to the extent of the express terms of the Release and no such Release shall have effect unless granted or made in writing. The rights and remedies in this agreement are cumulative and not exclusive of any rights and/or remedies provided by law.

10. NOTICES

10.1 Any Notice relating to this Deed shall be in writing delivered personally or sent by pre-paid first class post or facsimile transmission to the address of the party to be served given in this Deed or such other address as may be notified for this purpose.

10.2 Any such Notice shall, if sent by post, be deemed to have been served 24 hours after despatch and, if delivered by hand or sent by facsimile transmission, shall be deemed to have been served at the time of such delivery or transmission.

10.3 If however, in the case of delivery by hand or facsimile transmission, such delivery or transmission occurs on, or if, in the case of delivery by post, a period of 24 hours after despatch would expire on, a day which is not a Business Day or after 4.00 p.m. on a Business Day, then service shall be deemed to occur on the next following Business Day.

10.4   In proving service it shall be sufficient to prove, in the case of a letter, that such letter was properly stamped, addressed and placed in the post and, in the case of a facsimile transmission, it shall be sufficient to produce a transmission report showing that transmission was duly and fully made to the correct number.

10.5   Any such Notice or communication shall be deemed to have been given to the personal representatives of a deceased individual, notwithstanding that no grant of representation has been made in respect of his or her estate, if the notice is given [to the [   ]'s Solicitors [Define] in accordance with clause 10.1], to the deceased individual by name or to his or her personal representatives by title at the relevant individual's address given herein or at such other address as may have been notified in writing to the sender as being his or her address for service.

11.   ASSIGNMENT

No party to this Deed shall assign, transfer or charge his rights or responsibilities under this Deed without the prior written consent of the other parties to this Deed.

12.   PROPER LAW

This Deed shall be governed by the laws of England and Wales.

13.   JURISDICTION

Any dispute arising under this Deed shall be subject to the [exclusive] jurisdiction of the English courts and the parties waive any objection to Proceedings in such courts on the grounds of venue or on the grounds that Proceedings have been brought in an inappropriate forum.

IN WITNESS of which this Deed has been executed and unconditionally delivered the day and year first above written.

SCHEDULE

The Contributors

Name	Proportion of Claims (%)	[Aggregate Liability Cap]

Signed as a deed
by [   ]
in the presence of:-
Name:
Address:

Signed as a deed
by [   ]
in the presence of:-
Name:
Address:

Signed as a deed
by [   ]
in the presence of:-
Name:
Address:

Signed as a deed
by [   ]
in the presence of:-
Name:
Address:

SIGNED as a deed
by [   ]

LIMITED acting by two directors or
a director and its secretary
Director
Director/Secretary

SIGNED as a deed
by [   ]

LIMITED acting by two directors or
a director and its secretary
Director
Director/Secretary

PRECEDENT 31

Disclosure Letter—Share Sales and Purchases

DISCLOSURE LETTER

ON SELLER'S NOTEPAPER IF A COMPANY

[TO THE BUYER]

[Registered Office]

[DATE]

Dear Sirs,

Sale and purchase of [the entire issued share capital [the undertaking and assets] of [   ] [Limited/PLC] ("the Company")

We refer to the sale and purchase agreement proposed to be dated with today's date and to be entered into between [ ] (1) ("the Seller[s]") and [ ] Limited/PLC (2) ("the Buyer"), relating to the sale of [the entire issued share capital] of the Company to the Buyer ("the Agreement").

This letter, together with the documents listed in the index and attached to it ("the Disclosure Bundle") is the disclosure letter referred to in the Agreement and words and expressions defined in the Agreement shall, where the context permits, bear the like meaning when used herein.

References herein to the accounts of a company shall mean its audited balance sheet as at the relevant accounting date and its audited profit and loss account for the accounting period ended on such date [and, in the case of a holding company, shall include also its audited consolidated balance sheet as at the relevant accounting date and its audited consolidated profit and loss account for the accounting period ended on such date] including [in each case] the directors' report and notes in relation thereto.

[References herein to "the Company" shall mean and include, as the context may require, each and all of the Company and its subsidiaries [and subsidiary undertakings].].

The matters referred to in this letter and/or in contained in the Disclosure Bundle shall constitute disclosures for the purposes of the Warranties and shall be deemed to be fairly disclosed thereunder [and for this purpose "fairly disclosed" means disclosed in such manner and in such detail as to enable a reasonable buyer to make an informed assessment of the matter concerned.]

No attempt has been made, in the event of a matter requiring disclosure under more than one of the specified circumstances set out in the Warranties, to duplicate information which might otherwise fall under several different headings and for the avoidance of doubt the contents of each statement below and of the Disclosure Bundle shall be deemed to be disclosed in relation to all the Warranties to which they may relate.

The disclosures contained in this letter are not to be taken as any admission by or on behalf of the Seller[s] that all or any of the matters call for disclosure strictly within the terms of the Agreement.

GENERAL DISCLOSURE

Against the above background, general disclosure is made as follows:

1.   all matters and information disclosed, or noted, or provided for in the audited annual accounts of the Company in respect of [the last three] accounting reference periods up to and including that ended on the Accounts Date are disclosed;

2.   all matters and information is disclosed which is disclosed, or noted, or referred to, or provided for in the Management Accounts [for the period ending [   ]], a copy of which is attached at enclosure [   ] of the Disclosure Bundle;

3.   all information is disclosed which is contained in any of the documents filed at the Companies Registry in respect of the Company as at the date two days prior to Completion;

4.   all matters and information contained in [or which may be fairly deduced from] the Agreement is disclosed;

5.   [all information is disclosed which is contained in [or which may be fairly deduced from] [a certificate of title given by [   ] on [200], addressed to the Buyer], [the deeds and/or physical inspection of] the freehold and leasehold premises of the Company ("the Property")];

        5.1   all matters contained in referred to or which would be apparent from inspection of the title deeds and the documents relating to the Property;

        5.2   all matters acts or things which are or would be revealed by a search in the Register of Commons and Town and Village Greens, an index map search, a coal mining search, a search in the Land Charges Department of HM Land Registry, a search in HM Land Registry, a search in any relevant local authority or any other statutory body, replies to preliminary enquiries and such other searches and enquiries as a prudent buyer would undertake, whether or not such searches and enquiries have been carried out, in each case as at [   ] 200;

        5.3   all matters which are or would be revealed by a physical inspection and survey of the Property by a prudent buyer and his professional advisers, whether or not such inspection and survey have been carried out;

        5.4   all matters which are or would be discoverable on an investigation properly carried out of the Company's title to or the basis of its occupation of the Property, whether or not such investigation has been carried out;

6.   all information contained in the statutory books of the Company is disclosed;

7.   all matters and information is disclosed which is contained in any of the files in relation to the Company which are open to public inspection at the Patent Office and the Trade Marks Registry as at the date two day prior to Completion;

8.   all documentation maintained by the Director General of Fair Trading and available for public inspection in respect of the Company at the date two days prior to Completion is disclosed; and

9.   all information maintained at the Central index of the Royal Courts of Justice and available for public inspection in respect of the Company at the date two days prior to Completion is disclosed.

SPECIFIC DISCLOSURES

There are further disclosed (without prejudice to the generality of the foregoing) the matters set out below. The individual Warranty numbers refer to the individual paragraphs or sub-paragraphs of schedule [   ] of the Agreement and are for ease of reference only:

Warranty
number: Disclosure

Yours faithfully

....

[each of the Seller(s)]

....

For and on behalf of

[Seller   ] Limited

We hereby acknowledge receipt of the Disclosure Letter and the Disclosure Bundle of which this is a duplicate.

For and behalf of [Buyer] Limited

PRECEDENT 31

DISCLOSURE BUNDLE

Index of Documents

PRECEDENT 32

Disclosure Letter—Assets Sales and Purchases

DISCLOSURE LETTER

ON SELLER'S NOTEPAPER IF A COMPANY

[TO THE BUYER]

[Registered Office]

                                         [DATE]

Dear Sirs,

Sale and purchase of [the undertaking and assets] of [   ][Limited/PLC] ("the Seller")

We refer to the sale and purchase agreement proposed to be dated with today's date and to be entered into between("the Seller") and [ ] Limited/PLC (2) ("the Buyer"), relating to the sale of the undertaking and assets of the Seller to the Buyer ("the Agreement").

This letter, together with the documents listed in the index and attached to it ("the Disclosure Bundle") is the disclosure letter referred to in the Agreement, and words and expressions defined in the Agreement shall, where the context permits, bear the like meaning when used herein.

References herein to the accounts of a company shall mean its audited balance sheet as at the relevant accounting date and its audited profit and loss account for the accounting period ended on such date [and, in the case of a holding company, shall include also its audited consolidated balance sheet as at the relevant accounting date and its audited consolidated profit and loss account for the accounting period ended on such date] including [in each case] the directors' report and notes in relation thereto.

The matters referred to in this letter and/or in contained in the Disclosure Bundle shall constitute disclosures for the purposes of the Warranties and shall be deemed to be fairly disclosed thereunder [and for this purpose "fairly disclosed" means disclosed in such manner and in such detail as to enable a reasonable buyer to make an informed assessment of the matter concerned.]

No attempt has been made, in the event of a matter requiring disclosure under more than one of the specified circumstances set out in the Warranties, to duplicate information which might otherwise fall under several different headings and for the avoidance of doubt the contents of each statement below and of the Disclosure Bundle shall be deemed to be disclosed in relation to all the Warranties to which they may relate.

The disclosures contained in this letter are not to be taken as any admission by or on behalf of the Seller that all or any of the matters call for disclosure strictly within the terms of the Agreement.

GENERAL DISCLOSURE

Against the above background, general disclosure is made as follows:

1.   all matters and information disclosed, or noted, or provided for in the audited annual accounts of the Seller in respect of [the last three] accounting reference periods up to and including that ended on the Accounts Date are disclosed;

2.   all matters and information is disclosed which is disclosed, or noted, or referred to, or provided for in the Management Accounts [for the period ending [   ]], a copy of which is attached at enclosure [   ] of the Disclosure Bundle;

3.   all information is disclosed which is contained in any of the documents filed at the Companies Registry in respect of the Seller as at the date two days prior to Completion;

4.   all matters and information contained in [or which may be fairly deduced from] the Agreement is disclosed;

5.   [all information is disclosed which is contained in [or which may be fairly deduced from] [a certificate of title given by [   ] on [200], addressed to the Buyer], [the deeds and/or physical inspection of] the Property];

    5.1   all matters contained in referred to or which would be apparent from inspection of the title deeds and the documents relating to the Property;

    5.2   all matters acts or things which are or would be revealed by a search in the Register of Commons and Town and Village Greens, an index map search, a coal mining search, a search in the Land Charges Department of HM Land Registry, a search in HM Land Registry, a search in any relevant local authority or any other statutory body, replies to preliminary enquiries and such other searches and enquiries as a prudent buyer would undertake, whether or not such searches and enquiries have been carried out, in each case as at [   ] 200 ;

    5.3   all matters which are or would be revealed by a physical inspection and survey of the Property by a prudent buyer and his professional advisers, whether or not such inspection and survey have been carried out;

    5.4   all matters which are or would be discoverable on an investigation properly carried out of the Seller's title to or the basis of its occupation of the Property, whether or not such investigation has been carried out;

6.   all matters and information is disclosed which is contained in any of the files in relation to the Seller which are open to public inspection at the Patent Office and the Trade Marks Registry as at the date two day prior to Completion;

7.   all documentation maintained by the Director General of Fair Trading and available for public inspection in respect of the Seller at the date two days prior to Completion is disclosed; and

8.   all information maintained at the Central index of the Royal Courts of Justice and available for public inspection in respect of the Seller at the date two days prior to Completion is disclosed.

SPECIFIC DISCLOSURES

There are further disclosed (without prejudice to the generality of the foregoing) the matters set out below. The individual Warranty numbers refer to the individual paragraphs or sub-paragraphs of schedule [   ] of the Agreement and are for ease of reference only:

Warranty
number: Disclosure

Yours faithfully

....
For and on behalf of

[Seller   ] Limited

We hereby acknowledge receipt of the Disclosure Letter and the Disclosure Bundle of which this
is a duplicate.

....
For and behalf of
[Buyer] Limited

PRECEDENT 33

Sellers' Safeguards

SCHEDULE [   ]

Claims procedure and determination and Sellers' safeguards

1. **NOTICE OF CLAIMS AND TIME LIMITS**

   No claim in respect of any breach of any of the Warranties (other than the [Title Warranties] in paragraph [   ] of schedule [   ]) or pursuant to the Tax Covenants shall be made (except in any case of fraud, dishonesty or wilful non-disclosure) unless notice thereof has been given by or on behalf of the Buyer before:

   1.1   in respect of any breach of any of the [Non-Taxwarranties], the expiry of the period of [   ] months following Completion; or

   1.2   pursuant to the Tax Covenants or in respect of any breach of any of the Tax Warranties, the expiry of the period of six years after the end of the period of six months following the end of the accounting reference period of the Company in which the sixth anniversary of Completion falls.

   Any such notice, to be valid, must give all available details of the circumstances giving rise or capable of giving rise to the claim in question.

2. **DEEMED WITHDRAWAL OF CLAIMS PREVIOUSLY NOTIFIED**

   Any claim in respect of any breach of any of the Warranties or pursuant to the Tax Covenants shall (if not previously satisfied or settled or withdrawn) be deemed to have been withdrawn at the expiry of the period of [six/twelve] months following the giving of notice of such claim pursuant to paragraph 1 of this schedule unless, before the expiry of such period, the Buyer has issued proceedings in respect of such claim and has served them on the Sellers.

3. **LIMITATION OF LIABILITY – MAXIMUM AND MINIMUM AMOUNTS**

   Except in any case of fraud, dishonesty or wilful non-disclosure and any claim in respect of any breach of the [Title warranties] in paragraph [ ] of Schedule [ ]:

   3.1   the Sellers shall have no liability in respect of any claim by the Buyer under any of the Warranties or the Tax Covenants if and to the extent that such liability would, when aggregated with the amount of any liability of the Seller in respect of all and any other such claims, exceed the sum of £[x];

   3.2   the Sellers shall have no liability in respect of any claim by the Buyer under the [Non-Tax Warranties] [or the Tax Warranties] unless such claim:

        3.2.1   equals or exceeds £[y] ([   ] thousand pounds); and

        3.2.2   would, when aggregated with all other such claims against the Sellers of £[y] or more, equal or exceed £[z] ([   ] thousand pounds);

   but any such claim shall not be limited to the excess over the amounts specified in this paragraph 3.2 and, for the purposes of this paragraph 3.2, all claims arising out of the same subject-matter shall be treated as one single claim rather than as individual claims.

4. **NATURE OF LIABILITY**

   4.1   The liability of the Sellers under the Warranties (other than the [Title Warranties] in paragraph [ ] of schedule [ ]) and under the Tax Covenants shall be several and shall be borne by the Sellers in the Due Proportions.

   4.2   Each Seller shall bear the full extent of his own liability under the [Title Warranties] in paragraph [ ] of Schedule [ ].

5.   REDUCTION OF CONSIDERATION

Any payment by any of the Sellers for breach of any of the Warranties or under the Tax Covenants shall constitute pound for pound a repayment of, and reduction in, the consideration for the Shares.

6.   CONDUCT OF CLAIMS

The Buyer shall as soon as reasonably practicable notify the Sellers in writing of any claim made against it by a third party which may give rise to a claim for breach of a [Non-Tax Warranty] (in this paragraph 6, "a Claim") and the following provisions of this paragraph 6 shall apply:

6.1   The Buyer shall procure that the conduct, negotiation, settlement or litigation of the Claim is, so far as is reasonably practicable and provided that such action in its reasonable opinion would not have a materially adverse effect on the business of the Company as carried on in the ordinary and usual course, or the goodwill of the Company or of the Buyer, or require the disclosure of any information or document in breach of any applicable data protection principles or which is covered by legal privilege, carried out in accordance with the wishes of the Sellers and at their cost, subject to (and as a precondition) their giving timely instructions to the Buyer and the Sellers reimbursing, and providing reasonable security for, any costs and expenses which might be incurred by the Buyer and the Company in taking such action.

6.2   The Buyer shall provide and shall procure that the Company provides to each of the Sellers reasonable access to its premises and personnel and to any relevant assets, documents and records within their respective powers, possession or control for the purpose of investigating any such Claim and enabling the Sellers and their advisers to take copies of any relevant documents or records at their expense (subject to such confidentiality requirements as the Buyer shall reasonable require).

6.3   The Buyer shall not (and shall procure that the Company shall not) make any admission of liability, agreement or compromise to or with any person in relation thereto without the prior written consent of the Sellers, not to be unreasonably withheld or delayed.

6.4   This paragraph 6 shall not apply if the Sellers do not notify the Buyer in writing that they wish to elect to take up their rights under this paragraph 6 as soon as reasonably practicable and in any event within [ ] Business Days of receipt of a notice from the Buyer requiring the Sellers concerned so to elect or decline.

7.   INSURERS

In the event of any claim for breach of any of the Warranties the Buyer shall (or, as the case may be, shall procure that the Company shall) first attempt to make recovery in respect of the matter giving rise to the claim in question to the fullest extent possible under any policy of insurance (whether or not such policy or any equivalent policy may have been in force at Completion) and shall abate such claim by the amount (if any) recovered from such insurance policy (less any costs, charges and expenses properly incurred by the Buyer in such recovery).

8.   THIRD PARTIES

If the Sellers have paid to the Buyer any amount in respect of a claim under any of the Warranties and the Company or the Buyer subsequently receives or recovers from a third party (including an insurer) a sum which is referable to such claim, the Buyer shall forthwith repay to the Sellers concerned the amount so received or recovered, up to the amount which has been paid by the Sellers, less any costs, charges and expenses properly incurred by the Buyer in recovering from the third party in respect of such claim.

9. SET-OFF

No party hereto shall have the right to set off any sum claimed by it under this Agreement or otherwise against any of its obligations hereunder not then fulfilled and any sum payable by it under this Agreement shall be paid in full and without set-off or deduction on any account whatsoever.

10. DOUBLE RECOVERY

The Sellers shall not be liable in respect of any breach of the Warranties if and to the extent that the losses occasioned thereby have been recovered under the Tax Covenants (and vice versa).

11. MISREPRESENTATIONS

The Buyer irrevocably and unconditionally waives any right it may have to claim damages for any misrepresentation, whether or not contained in this Agreement, or for breach of any warranty not contained in this Agreement, except where such misrepresentation was made or warranty breached fraudulently and notwithstanding that it may have been made or breached negligently, and/or to rescind this Agreement.

12. ORDINARY COURSE OF BUSINESS

None of the Sellers shall have any liability in respect of any breach of any of the Warranties, if and to the extent that such breach or claim arises or occurs out of, or as a result of, any act, omission or transaction of, or event or circumstance directly caused by, the Company (following Completion) and/or the Buyer (following the entering into of this Agreement), other than in the ordinary course of business or pursuant to a legally binding obligation of the Company entered into prior to [Completion] [the date of this Agreement].

13. COMPLETION ACCOUNTS

None of the Sellers shall have any liability in respect of any breach of any of the Warranties, nor in respect of any claim under any of the Tax Covenants, if and to the extent that the matter giving rise to the claim in question was, provided for (or otherwise taken into account in the preparation of) the Completion Accounts.

14. BUYER'S WARRANTY

The Buyer warrants to each of the Sellers that there are no circumstances within its actual knowledge [(including, for this purpose, that of its officers or professional advisors)] entitling the Buyer to make any claim against any of the Sellers for breach of the Warranties and/or under any of the Tax Covenants and acknowledges in favour of each of the Sellers that, insofar as there may be any such circumstances, any claim in respect thereof is irrevocably and unconditionally waived.

15. DUTY TO MITIGATE

The provisions of this schedule shall be in addition and without prejudice to the common law duty of the Buyer to use all reasonable endeavours to mitigate any loss and without prejudice to any rule or provision of law which may operate to the benefit of any of the Sellers.

PRECEDENT 34

Escrow Agreement

ESCROW AGREEMENT

To: [   ]

and [   ]

200

Dear Sirs,

Agreement for the sale of the [whole/part] of the Issued Share Capital of

[   ] Limited ("the Agreement")

Escrow Account Number [   ] with [   ] Bank Plc ("the Bank")

This letter, as accepted by you, constitutes the Escrow Agreement referred to in the Agreement. Words defined in the Agreement shall have the same meaning in this letter unless the context otherwise requires.

1. The Seller and the Buyer have agreed pursuant to the Agreement that the Buyer will pay the sum of [   ] (the "Retention") into a joint account with the Bank, subject to the terms of this letter. This letter sets out the instructions to you as joint holders of the Escrow Account ("Escrow Agents").

2. The Seller and the Buyer hereby instruct you:

   2.1 to open the Escrow Account as an interest bearing deposit account at the Bank on terms which include those set out in Appendix 1, such account to be designated "[   ] Escrow Account"; and

   2.2 upon receipt in the Escrow Account of the Retention, to act as Escrow Agents upon the terms as set out in the letter.

3. The funds held in the Escrow Account (including any interest accrued thereon) shall not be released except pursuant to the Escrow Agreement or as ordered by a court of competent jurisdiction or any legal or regulatory authority.

4. You shall instruct the Bank to credit to the Escrow Account all interest earned from time to time on the funds held in the Escrow Account and to aggregate it monthly (less accrued banking charges) with the principal sum held in the Escrow Account. Net interest accrued from time to time should, as nearly as possible, reflect entitlement to the Escrow Funds (as such expression is defined in paragraph 7 below).

5. All payments to be made out of the Escrow Account to the Buyer or to the Seller shall be made in the manner indicated in the payment letter, the form of which is contained in Appendix 2.

6. You shall be entitled to deduct from any interest, income or other sum earned on any funds held in the Escrow Account any withholdings, taxes or other deductions required by law to be made and to deliver such funds to the party entitled thereto in accordance with the instructions in this letter, net of any such withholdings, taxes or deductions.

7. The funds credited to the Escrow Account from time to time are referred to in this letter as the "Escrow Funds".

8.   You shall not be bound in any way by any agreement between the Seller and the Buyer to which you are not a party (whether or not you have knowledge of it) nor shall you be bound to enquire into or examine the merit of, any claim or statement by the Buyer or the Seller and your only duties and responsibilities shall be to hold the Escrow Funds and to invest and dispose of them in accordance with the terms of this letter and any instructions given in accordance with this letter or as may be ordered by a court of competent jurisdiction or any legal or regulatory authority.

9.   You may (without checking the authority of such signature) rely on, and shall be protected in acting or refraining from acting in accordance with, any written notice, instruction or request furnished to you by the Buyer and the Seller if signed on behalf of the Buyer by any of the officers whose names and specimen signatures are set out in Appendix 1 under the heading "Buyer's Signatories" and on behalf of the Seller by any of the officers whose names and specimen signatures are set out in Appendix 1 under the heading "Seller's Signatories" and it shall not be necessary for you to enquire as to the authority of any such signatory. You shall only make payments to either the Buyer or the Seller upon receipt of a payment letter signed on behalf of each of them.

10.   The Escrow Agreement may be modified or amended only with the prior written consent of the Buyer and of the Seller and any such modification or amendment shall take effect unless the effect of it is to impose upon you any duty, obligation or liability (whether actual or prospective) to which you would not otherwise be subject, in which case such modification or amendment shall also require your consent. If the Buyer and the Seller attempt to change this Escrow Letter in a manner which either of you, in your sole discretion, deem undesirable, either of you may resign as Escrow Agent by notifying the Buyer and the Seller in writing; otherwise either of you may resign as Escrow Agent at any time upon 30 days' prior written notice to the Buyer and the Seller. The Buyer and the Seller may remove either of you as Escrow Agent at any time upon 30 days' prior written notice signed by them jointly. If either of you resign or are removed, your only duty, until a successor Escrow Agent shall have been appointed and shall have accepted such appointment, shall be to hold, invest and dispose of the Escrow Funds in accordance with the provisions of the Escrow Agreement (but without regard to any notice, request, instruction or demand received by you from either or both of the Buyer and the Seller after your notice of resignation shall have been given, other than a direction by both the Buyer and the Seller that all of the Escrow Funds be paid or delivered out of the Escrow Account).

11.   The provisions of the Agreement regarding the giving of notices shall apply mutatis mutandis to any notice to be given by you pursuant to the Escrow Agreement. Any notice to you shall be effective when received at your address as set out above addressed to you, in the case of [   ], for the attention of [   ] and, in the case of [   ], for the attention of [   ], making reference in each case to [Escrow Account (Account Number)].

12.   Your fees as Escrow Agents shall be your respective standard hourly rates of charge for the time being for the persons having conduct of the subject matter of the Escrow Agreement within your organisation, plus disbursements, including (without limitation) all bank charges and VAT (if applicable). You shall also be reimbursed by the Seller and the Buyer in equal proportions for any expenses properly incurred by you in connection with the Escrow Agreement, including, without limitation, the actual cost of legal services should you reasonably deem it necessary to retain Counsel. Your ongoing fees and expenses for running the Escrow Account shall be paid by the Seller and Buyer in equal proportions. You shall bill the Seller and the Buyer directly for the fees and expenses chargeable to them. You shall have the first lien on the Escrow Funds

for payment of such fees and expenses and may make deductions therefrom in respect thereof to the extent that such fees and expenses have not been satisfied within 30 days of the relevant invoice date, provided always that you shall notify the Buyer and the Seller in writing at least 24 hours prior to your making any such deduction. No fees shall be payable merely for acting as the Escrow Agent.

13.   You shall not be liable for any action taken or omitted to be taken by you in good faith and the Seller and the Buyer jointly and severally undertake to indemnify you and keep you fully and effectively indemnified on demand against any loss, damage, cost, expense or liability whatsoever suffered or incurred by you as a result of your carrying out your functions under the terms of the Escrow Agreement, save in so far as it results from your own negligence or wilful misconduct. You shall not be responsible for any loss to the Escrow Funds resulting from the investment, delivery or payment thereof in accordance with the terms of the Escrow Agreement.

14.   You shall in no event be obliged to enquire as to the facts or circumstances set out in any notice sent to you pursuant to or in connection with the Escrow Agreement or the Agreement and shall be entitled to rely on such facts or circumstances as set out therein as if they were for all purposes true and accurate.

15.   The Seller and the Buyer each agree with you that, unless otherwise expressly set out forth in the Escrow Agreement, you shall have no responsibility at any time to ascertain whether any security interest exists in the Escrow Funds or any of them or to produce or file any statement with respect to the Escrow Funds or any part of them and if at any time any third party purports to assert an interest in the Escrow Funds or any part of them you shall be entitled to retain the Escrow Funds in the Escrow Account (notwithstanding any other terms of the Escrow Agreement) pending final resolution of the validity of such third party claim.

16.   The Buyer and the Seller will provide to you from time to time such information as you or either of you may require in connection with the arrangements the subject of the Escrow Agreement.

17.   If any instructions from the Seller and the Buyer are, in your reasonable opinion, manifestly wrong or unclear, then you may withhold making any payment (but you will immediately notify the relevant person in writing that you have done so and the reason for doing so) and, in such circumstances, you shall have no liability to the Seller or the Buyer by virtue of so doing.

18.   The Escrow Agreement shall be binding upon you and the Buyer and Seller and your and their respective legal representatives, successors and permitted assigns; provided that any assignment or transfer by either the Buyer or the Seller of its rights under this Escrow Letter or with respect to the Escrow Funds shall be void as against you unless (a) written notice of it, and appropriate documentation indicating the identity of the assignee or transferee, has been given to you, and (b) the assignee or transferee shall agree in writing, in form and substance satisfactory to each of you, to be bound by the provisions of the Escrow Agreement, and (c) each of you and the other party shall have consented to such assignment or transfer.

19.   The Escrow Agreement shall be governed by the laws of England and Wales.

20.   Any dispute arising under the Escrow Agreement shall be subject to the [exclusive/non-exclusive] jurisdiction of the English courts and the parties waive any objection to proceedings in such courts on the grounds of venue or on the grounds that proceedings have been brought in an inappropriate forum.

Please sign and return the attached copy of this letter in acknowledgement and acceptance of its terms.

Yours faithfully,

....
for and on behalf of
                    Limited

....
for and on behalf of
                    Limited

We accept appointment under the terms of the Escrow Letter, dated [200]

....
For and on behalf of   For and on behalf of
Martineau Johnson   [   ]

Appendix I

Instruction letter to Bank

1.   Interest is to be credited to the account in the normal way.

2.   Any withdrawals from the deposit account are to be made, and any other instructions relating to such account are to be given, in accordance with the written instructions addressed to the Bank provided that such instructions are signed on behalf of each of us by one of the authorised signatories listed hereunder.

3.   The Bank will be entitled to deduct its expenses and charges from the amount for the time being standing to the credit of the deposit account in accordance with normal banking practice.

List of Authorised Signatories

Name   Office Held   Signature

Dated the   day of   200

For [   ]

For [   ]

Annexure

Buyer's Authorised Signatories

....

[   ]

....

[   ]

....

[   ]

Sellers' Authorised Signatories

....

[   ]

....

[   ]

....

[   ]

Appendix 2

Payment Letter

[   ] and [   ]

[   ]

[   ]

[   ]

Reference: [   ]

Attention: [   ]

200

Dear Sirs,

We refer to our joint letter to you dated [   ] 200 (a copy of which is attached) in which we refer to the [   ] Escrow Account (the "Account").

We hereby irrevocably instruct you in accordance with clause [   ] of the Agreement to:

1.   send a banker's draft in the following amount in respect of the payment to be made pursuant to clause [   ] of the Agreement to the Seller at its address herein, for the attention of [   ]

2.   send a banker's draft in the sum of £[   ] in respect of the payment to be made pursuant to clause [   ] of the Agreement to the Buyer at its address herein, for the attention of [   ].

Please confirm safe receipt of these instructions and your confirmation that you will act in accordance with them.

. . . .

for and on behalf of   for and on behalf of
[   ]   [   ]

PRECEDENT 35

Loan Note Instrument

DATED **200**

[ ] LIMITED/PLC

INSTRUMENT CREATING
£[ ] [ ] PER CENT UNSECURED LOAN NOTES

THIS INSTRUMENT   **is dated [_____] 200**

and made by [   ] **LIMITED/PLC,** a company (registered in England under number) whose registered office is at [   ] (the "Company").

NOW THIS INSTRUMENT witnesses and it is hereby declared as follows:

1.   INTERPRETATION

In this Instrument:

1.1   The following words and expressions shall the following meanings:

"Business Day"   means a day (other than a Saturday or Sunday) on which banks are generally open for business in the sterling in the City of London;

"Certificate"   means a certificate for Notes issued in accordance with Clause 5 and in the form or substantially in the form set out in the Schedule;

"Directors"   means the Board of Directors of the Company for the time being;

"Intercreditor   the Agreement dated with the same date as this Instrument and Agreement" made between [parties];

"Interest Rate"   means in relation to any period the rate (expressed as a percentage per annum) equal to the base rate of [   ] Bank PLC for the time being in relation to such period, [plus   %] [less   %];

"Notes"   means the unsecured loan notes of the Company constituted by this Instrument or, as the case may be, the amount thereof for the time being issued and outstanding;

"Noteholders"   means the several persons for the time being entered in the Register as holders of the Notes (each a "Noteholder");

"redemption"   means repayment and "redeem" and "redeemed" shall be construed accordingly;

"Register"   means the register of the Notesholders kept by the Company pursuant to Clause 9.

1.2   In this Instrument, unless otherwise expressly provided, any reference to:

1.2.1   any statutory provision shall include a reference to such provision as from time to time re-enacted amended extended or replaced;

1.2.2   a clause or a schedule is a reference to a clause of or a schedule to this Instrument.

1.3   Save where the context otherwise requires, in this Instrument words importing the singular number shall include the plural and vice versa and words importing one gender shall include each other gender.

1.4   Headings in this Instrument are for ease of reference only and shall not affect its interpretation.

1.5   Save as expressly provided in this Instrument, words and expressions defined in the Companies Act 1985 shall bear the same respective meanings in this Instrument.

2.   TERMS OF ISSUE

2.1   The principal amount of the Notes shall be £[   ]. The Notes shall be issued in denominations and integral multiples of £1 in nominal amount, subject to and with the benefit of the provisions of this Instrument. All the obligations and covenants contained in this Instrument shall be binding on the Company and the Noteholders and all persons claiming through them.

2.2   The Notes shall rank pari passu as unsecured obligations of the Company.

2.3   No application has been or will be made to any stock exchange for the listing of, or for permission to deal in, the Notes.

3.   INTEREST

The Notes shall bear interest at the Interest Rate accruing on a daily basis from the date of issue of the Notes and payable in full on redemption of the Notes in respect of which the interest has accrued.

4.   REDEMPTION OF NOTES

4.1   Subject to the provisions of the Intercreditor Agreement, the Notes shall be redeemed at par, together with accrued interest, on [   ], save that, subject to the provisions of the Intercreditor Agreement, each Noteholder may by not more than one month's notice in writing to the Company require that the Company redeem the Notes held by him in full (but not in part) at any time after the expiry of six months from the date of issue of the Notes.

4.2   Every Noteholder whose Notes (or any part thereof) are due to be redeemed shall, not later than the due date for such redemption, deliver up to the Company at its registered office for the time being the certificate(s) for his Notes which are due to be redeemed in order that the same may be cancelled and, upon such delivery and against a receipt for the amount payable in respect of the Notes to be redeemed, the Company shall pay to the Noteholder the amount payable to him in respect of such repayment and such payment may be made through a bank on behalf of the Company if the Company shall think fit.

4.3   As and when the Notes are redeemed under the provisions of this Instrument, the Company shall pay to the Noteholders the full principal amount of the Notes to be redeemed, together with any accrued interest on such Notes.

4.4   If any deduction or withholding is required by law in respect of any payment due to the Noteholders pursuant to or in connection with the Notes, the Company shall:

4.4.1   make such deduction or withholding to the extent required by law;

4.4.2   to the extent required pay, or procure the payment of, the full amount deducted or withheld to the relevant taxation or other authority in accordance with the applicable law; and

4.4.3   promptly deliver or procure the delivery to the Noteholders of relative certificates or receipts evidencing each of the deductions or withholdings which has been made.

5.   PAYMENT PROVISIONS

5.1   If, but for this clause, any sum would become due for payment on a day which is not a Business Day, such payment shall be made on the next succeeding Business Day.

5.2   The principal amount of the Notes will be payable at the registered office of the Company or at such other place as the Company may from time to time appoint and [,subject to the provisions of clause 5.3,] shall be paid in sterling.

5.3   [

5.3.1   Subject to clauses 5.3.2 and 5.3.3, a Noteholder may elect that the principal amount of the Notes held by him shall be redeemed in US dollars. In each case the Company shall (subject to the terms of this Instrument and of the Intercreditor Agreement), on each day that principal or interest is payable, pay to the Noteholder an amount in US dollars obtained by converting the principal amount outstanding of such Notes into US dollars (at the spot rate for the purchase of US dollars with sterling prevailing at the date 30 days before the redemption date).

5.3.2   If the amount payable in US dollars under clause 5.3.1 would otherwise exceed an amount in US dollars obtained by converting 100.5% of the sterling principal amount outstanding of such Notes into US dollars at the spot rate for the purchase of US dollars with sterling at 12.00 am on the redemption date, the latter amount shall be substituted therefor.

5.3.3   If the amount payable in US dollars under Clause 5.3.1 would otherwise be less than the amount in US dollars obtained by converting 99.5% of the sterling principal amount outstanding of such Notes into US dollars at the spot rate for the purchase of US dollars with sterling prevailing at 12.00 am on the redemption date, the latter amount shall be substituted therefor.]

6.   **CERTIFICATES**

6.1   The Company shall issue duly executed Certificates for each of the Notes. The Certificates shall be in the form, or substantially in the form, set out in the Schedule.

6.2   Each Noteholder shall be entitled without charge to one Certificate for the total amount of Notes registered in his name.

6.3   If any Certificate is defaced, worn out, lost or destroyed, the Company shall issue a new Certificate on payment of such fee, not exceeding £1, and on such terms (if any) as the Directors may require as to indemnity and evidence of defacement, wearing out, loss, or destruction. In the case of defacement or wearing out, the defaced or worn out Certificate shall be surrendered and cancelled before the new Certificate is issued. In the case of loss or destruction, the person availing himself of the provisions of this Clause shall also pay to the Company (if demanded) all expenses incidental to the investigation of evidence of loss or destruction and the preparation of any form of indemnity. There shall be entered in the Register particulars of the issue of any new Certificate and any indemnity.

7.   **SURRENDER AND CANCELLATION**

7.1   Notes shall only be redeemed against surrender of the relevant Certificate(s) for cancellation in the case of full redemption.

7.2   All Notes redeemed by the Company under the provisions of this Instrument shall be cancelled and shall not be re-issued.

8. EVENTS OF DEFAULT

A Noteholder may demand immediate redemption of all or any part of the Notes held by him upon the occurrence of any of the following events:

8.1 if the Company makes default in the payment within [ ] Business Days of the due date of any [interest] which ought to be paid to him in accordance with this Instrument;

8.2 if an order shall be made or an effective resolution passed for the winding up of the Company, other than for the purpose of a reconstruction or amalgamation, the terms of which have previously been approved by the Noteholders;

8.3 if an encumbrancer shall take possession or a receiver (including an administrative receiver) shall be appointed over the whole or any substantial part of the undertaking, property or assets of the Company;

8.4 if an administrator of the Company is appointed.

9. LOAN NOTES REGISTER

9.1 The Company shall duly keep and maintain a register of the Notes and there shall be entered in the Register:

9.1.1 The names and addresses of the holders for the time being of the Notes;

9.1.2 The amount of the Notes held by every registered holder;

9.1.3 The date at which the name of every such registered holder is entered in respect of the Notes standing in his name; and

9.1.4 The serial number of each Certificate.

Any change of name or address on the part of any Noteholder shall forthwith be notified to the Company and thereupon the Register shall be altered accordingly.

9.2 Except as required by law, the Company will recognise the registered holder of any of the Notes as the absolute owner thereof and shall not be bound to take notice or see to the execution of any trust, whether express, implied or constructive, to which any Notes may be subject and the receipt of such person for the interest from time to time accruing due in respect thereof and for any moneys payable upon the redemption of the same shall be a good discharge to the Company. [??]notwithstanding any notice it may have (whether express or otherwise) of the right, title, interest or claim of any person to or in such Notes or money. No notice of any trust, express, implied or constructive, shall be entered on the Register in respect of any Notes.

10. TRANSFER OF NOTES

[Holders of the Notes are not entitled to transfer Notes without the prior written consent of the Company but, subject to that]:

10.1 The Notes are transferable in nominal amounts and integral multiples of £1.

10.2 A transfer of a Note must be by an instrument in writing which is signed by or on behalf of the transferor. The transferor shall be deemed to remain the owner of the Notes to be transferred until the name of the transferee is entered in the Register in respect thereof.

10.3 Every instrument of transfer must be delivered to the registered office of the Company or to such other place as the Company may appoint for registration accompanied by the Certificate in respect of the Notes to be transferred, together with such other evidence as the Directors, or other officers of the Company authorised to deal with the transfer, may reasonably require to prove the title of the transferor or his right to transfer the Notes.

10.4   The Company shall retain all instruments of transfer which are registered.

10.5   The Company shall not register the transfer of Notes in respect of which a notice of redemption or repayment has been given.

11.   ALTERATION OF THIS INSTRUMENT

The provisions of this Instrument and the conditions on which the Notes are held may be altered, revoked or added to with the consent in writing of the Company and of the Noteholders. The Company will endorse on this Instrument a memorandum of the execution of any deed supplemental to this Instrument.

12.   CONSENT OF NOTEHOLDERS

12.1   Any consent of, or notice from, the Noteholders pursuant to this Instrument may be given by sending it through the post in a prepaid letter addressed to the Company at its registered office for the time being.

12.2   If at any time there are two or more Noteholders, all notices, powers, rights, discretions and consents to be done, given or exercised by the Noteholders under this Instrument will be done, given or exercised by Noteholders holding not less than [75%] in nominal value of the Notes for the time being in issue.

13.   NOTICES TO NOTEHOLDERS

Any notice to the Noteholders required for any purpose pursuant to this Instrument may be given by sending it through the post in a prepaid letter addressed to each Noteholder at his registered address in the Register.

14.   THIRD PARTY RIGHTS

For the avoidance of doubt, nothing in this Instrument shall confer on any third party any benefit or the right to enforce any provisions of this Instrument.

15.   JURISDICTION

This Instrument shall be governed by and construed in accordance with the Laws of England and Wales. Any dispute arising under this Instrument shall be subject to the [(exclusive/non-exclusive)] jurisdiction of the English courts and the parties waive any objection to proceedings in such courts on the grounds of venue or on the grounds that proceedings have been brought in an inappropriate forum.

IN WITNESS whereof this Instrument had been executed and delivered as a deed on the date first above written.

SCHEDULE

Form of Loan Note Certificate

[   ] Limited/PLC

(incorporated under [the Companies Act 1985])

Certificate Number: Amount of Notes: £

ISSUE of [   ] Per Cent Unsecured Loan Notes [   ] ("Notes")

Created and issued pursuant to the Company's Memorandum and Articles of Association and a Resolution of its Board of Directors passed on [   ] 20 [   ] ("the Note").

THIS IS TO CERTIFYm that [name of Noteholder] of [address] is/are the registered holder(s) of [   ] pounds of the [   ] Per Cent Unsecured Loan Notes [   ] which are constituted by an Instrument entered into by the Company on and dated [   ] and are issued subject to the provisions contained in that Instrument.

The Notes are transferable only in nominal amounts and integral multiples of £1. No transfer of any part of the Notes represented by this Certificate will be registered unless accompanied by this Certificate [and, in any event, the Notes are not transferable without the prior written consent of the Company]. The Notes are redeemable in accordance with the terms and conditions contained in the Instrument a copy of which is available from the Company.

SIGNED AS A DEED by

[   ] **LIMITED/PLC**

acting by two directors or a director and its secretary:

       Director

       Director/Secretary

PRECEDENT 36

Overage/Anti-Embarrassment Provision

SCHEDULE

1. INTERPRETATION

In this Schedule, the following words and expressions shall have the following meanings:—

"Assets Sale"
means the sale or agreement for sale or other disposal of the whole or a substantial part of the undertaking and assets of the Company or any Group Company, by one transaction or a series of transactions;

"Completion Price"
means £[   ];

"Connected" and "Connected Persons"
shall have the meanings given to those terms by section 839 of the Income and Corporation Taxes Act 1988;

"Controlling Interest"
means an interest (of whatever nature) in shares in a company conferring rights in respect of, or an entitlement to exercise or control the exercise of, more than a majority of the voting rights in a company or a right to appoint or remove a majority of its board of directors, or a right to exercise dominant influence over a company;

"Event"
means either:

(i)   an Assets Sale; or

(ii)   a Sale; or

(iii)   a Group Company Sale; or

(iiii) the grant during the Relevant Period to any person of an option or similar right exercisable after the Relevant Period to effect one or more Events; or

(iv)   any legally binding agreement or arrangement made during the Relevant Period to effect one or more Events after the Relevant Period;

"Event Price"
means either (a) the aggregate price at which a Sale, an Assets Sale or a Group Company Sale takes place or would take place on completion of any such agreement as is referred to in paragraph (iii) or (iv) or (v) of the definition of "Event";

For this purpose, reference to price or consideration shall include any consideration (in cash or otherwise) received or receivable and which, having regard to the substance of the transaction as a whole, may reasonably be regarded as an addition to the price or other consideration paid or payable (including, for the avoidance of doubt, any additional consideration which is linked to future profits, turnover or some other measure of future performance).

"Group Company"
means the Buyer and any other company which is for the time being the holding company of the Company, any Company which is for the time being a subsidiary of the Company and any Company which is a fellow subsidiary of the same holding company as the Company and to which the assets and undertaking of the Company (or any part of either) has been transferred;

"Group Company Sale"	means the Transfer of a Controlling interest in any Group Company;
"Independent Expert"	means an independent accountant (acting as an expert and not as an arbitrator) nominated by the parties concerned or, if they cannot agree as to his identity within 14 days, appointed by the President or other senior officer for the time being of the Institute of Chartered Accountants of England and Wales upon the application of either party;
"Relevant Amount"	means:

(i) in the first [   ] months after Completion, a sum equal to [   ]% of an amount equal to the difference (if any) between the Completion Price and the Event Price;

(ii) in the period between the [   ] and [   ] months following Completion, a sum equal to [   ]% of an amount equal to the difference (if any) between the Completion Price and the Event Price;

"Relevant Period"	means the period of [ ] months from the Completion Date;
"Sale"	means the Transfer of a Controlling Interest in the Company;
"Transfer"	means the sale of (or the grant of a right to acquire or to dispose of) any legal or beneficial interest in shares in the capital of the Company or the Group Company (in one transaction or a series of transactions).

2.   ANTI-EMBARRASSMENT

2.1   If during the Relevant Period, an Event occurs, the Buyer shall, within 5 Business Days of the date on which the Event takes place, pay the Relevant Amount to the Seller in cash (by banker's draft or by transfer to such account as Seller may specify in writing), **PROVIDED THAT**, if the Relevant Amount has not been agreed by the Buyer and the Seller, the Buyer shall be obliged to pay such amount of the Relevant Amount as is not in dispute, the balance being payable within 5 Business Days of the Relevant Amount being agreed by the parties or the decision of an Independent Expert being notified to the Buyer.

2.2   The Buyer covenants with the Seller that it shall, immediately upon an Event occurring, notify the Seller of the details of the relevant Event and pay the Relevant Amount within 5 business days in accordance with paragraph 2.1 above.

2.3   The Buyer undertakes to notify Seller as soon as reasonably practicable of any actual or proposed Event and shall, so far as it is legally able, procure the provision of such information to Seller as Seller may reasonably request in relation thereto.

2.4   The Buyer hereby covenants that it will procure that neither the Company nor any Group Company shall, during the Relevant Period, transfer any legal or beneficial interest in any of its assets and/or undertaking which might (alone or with other such transfers) constitute an Event, or grant any option (or similar right) exercisable after the Relevant Period, or enter into any agreements or arrangements to effect one or more Events after the Relevant Period, other than for full value to a third party who is not a Connected Person acting in good faith and that it will not during the Relevant Period transfer or sell shares held by it in the Company or any Group Company or grant an option (or similar right) over shares exercisable after the Relevant Period or enter into any legally binding agreement or arrangement to effect one or more Events after the Relevant Period, other than for full value to a third party who is not a Connected Person acting in good faith.

2.5   Time shall be of the essence of this Schedule as regards any time, date or period, whether as originally fixed or as altered in any manner provided herein.

2.6   The Buyer shall not engage in any course of action with a view to avoiding its obligations under this Schedule or the spirit thereof (whether by devising a route which will not trigger an Event but which will deprive the Seller during the Relevant Period of a Relevant Amount to which it could reasonably claim to be entitled under the spirit of this Schedule or otherwise).

2.7   For the avoidance of doubt, the Relevant Amount shall be payable on each occasion that an Event occurs during the Relevant Period.

PRECEDENT 37

Irrevocable Undertaking to accept offer for Shares

IRREVOCABLE UNDERTAKING

To: The Directors
[Buyer Limited/PLC]

Dated: 200

Dear Sirs

[Target Limited/PLC]

This letter is written in connection with a proposal that you (or one of your subsidiaries) ("the Offeror") will make a cash offer ("the Offer") to acquire the whole of the issued share capital of the Company (other than those shares owned by you or the Offeror) at a price of not less than 200 pence per ordinary share, which (save to the extent permitted by the Panel on Takeovers and Mergers ("the Panel")) complies with requirements of the City Code on Takeovers and Mergers ("the Code").

I hereby undertake to you as follows:-

1.   IRREVOCABLE UNDERTAKINGS

1.1   Acceptance of Offer

I hereby irrevocably and unconditionally undertake to accept the Offer in respect of:

1.1.1   the shares in the Company listed in the schedule to this letter and any shares which I own or to which I am beneficially entitled not appearing in the schedule;

1.1.2   any other shares in the Company of which I may after the date of this letter become the beneficial owner or in which I may otherwise acquire any interest (as defined in Part 22 of the Companies Act 2006); and

1.1.3   any other shares in the Company deriving from shares falling within either of paragraphs 1.1.1 and 1.1.2 above (such shares together with shares falling within this paragraph 1 being referred to below as the "Shares").

I agree to fulfil this undertaking by returning to you, or as you may direct, not later than 3.00 pm on the tenth business day after despatch to the other shareholders of the Company of the formal document containing the Offer (the "Offer Document") (or, in relation to Shares falling within either of paragraphs 1.1.2 and 1.1.3 above, as soon as practicable after I become the beneficial owner of or I otherwise acquire an interest in such Shares), duly and fully completed and signed form(s) of acceptance relative to the Offer, together with such form(s) of acceptance, the share certificate(s) or other document(s) of title or an indemnity in respect of the relevant shares.

1.2   Dealings with Shares

I hereby irrevocably and unconditionally undertake :

1.2.1   notwithstanding the provisions of the Code or any terms of the Offer regarding withdrawal, not to withdraw my acceptance of the Offer in respect of the Shares;

1.2.2   except pursuant to my acceptance of the Offer, not to dispose of, charge, pledge or otherwise encumber or grant any option or other right over or otherwise deal with any of the Shares or any interest in them (whether conditionally or unconditionally);

1.2.3   in my capacity as a shareholder only, not to convene any meeting of the members of the Company nor to exercise the voting rights attaching to the shares in a manner which might frustrate the Offer or prevent the Offer becoming or being declared unconditional in all respects;

1.2.4   not to acquire any interest (as defined in Part 22 of the Companies Act 2006) in any shares in the Company other than an interest in shares deriving from shares failing within either of paragraphs 1.1.1 and 1.1.2 above; and

1.2.5   not to enter into any agreement or arrangement with any person, whether conditionally or unconditionally, to do any of the acts prohibited or required by this paragraph 1.2.

1.3   **Action to facilitate the Offer**

Unless and until the Offer lapses or is withdrawn, I hereby irrevocably agree and undertake

1.3.1   not to solicit or enter into discussions with a view to soliciting any general offer for any of the Company's shares or any other class of shares, if any, from any third party or any proposal for a merger of the Company with any other entity; and

1.3.2   to notify you forthwith in writing of the details of any approach by any third party made with a view to the making of such an offer or such a merger immediately I become aware of the relevant matter.

1.4   **Announcements**

I agree not to make any announcement in connection with the Offer or the possibility that the Offer may be made without prior consultation with you unless :

1.4.1   you shall have previously consented in writing to the making of the relevant announcement; or

1.4.2   the relevant announcement (and, where relevant, the reference to you) is required by the Code, the Panel, any applicable law or any regulatory authority ("**Applicable Requirements**"). For this purpose an announcement shall be deemed to be made by me if it is made on my behalf.

1.5   **Information**

I agree promptly on demand to supply, or procure the supply to you, of all information relative to me, and any related companies and trusts (including dealings in securities in the Company) which you may reasonably consider to be required to be contained in any document relating to the Offer by any applicable law, or the requirements of any regulatory authority.

2.   **WARRANTIES AND UNDERTAKINGS**

I represent, warrant and undertake to you:

2.1   that the Shares listed in the schedule include all the shares in the Company beneficially owned by me or in which I am interested (as defined in Part 22 of the Companies Act 2006);

2.2   that the Shares will be transferred pursuant to my acceptance of the Offer free from all claims, options, charges, liens and encumbrances and with all rights now or after the date of this letter attaching to them, including the right to all dividends declared, made or paid after the date of this letter (other than as provided by the terms of the Offer);

2.3   that I have and will continue to have full power and authority to accept the Offer and execute any document recording acceptance of it, or to undertake that the Offer will be accepted, in respect of all the Shares.

Such warranties and undertakings shall not be extinguished or affected by completion of the sale of the Shares.

3.   PUBLICITY

I consent to the announcement of the Offer containing references to me and to this letter to particulars of this letter being set out in the formal document containing the Offer and to this letter being available for inspection during all or part of the period for which the Offer remains open for acceptance.

4.   INTERPRETATION

4.1   Revised Offers

In this letter, references to the Offer shall include any revised offer made by or on behalf of the Offeror, which, in the reasonable opinion of the Offeror, is at least as favourable to shareholders of the Company as the Offer.

4.2   Obligation to procure

Each undertaking and agreement set out in this letter to do or not to do certain things shall be construed as including an undertaking or agreement to procure in so far as practicable without unreasonable expense or liability that those things are done or, as the case may be, not done.

4.3   Time

Any time date or period mentioned in this undertaking may be extended by mutual agreement between me and the Offeror but as regards any time date or period originally fixed or so extended time shall be of the essence in respect of the time for performance of the obligations set out in this letter.

5.   CONDITIONS AND TERMINATION

5.1   Conditional obligations

The undertakings, agreements, warranties, appointments, consents and waivers set out in this letter (collectively "**Obligations**") are unconditional and irrevocable, [save that the undertakings and agreements set out in this letter will cease to be binding if, before the Offer becomes or is declared unconditional in all respects, another person, firm or company (or persons acting in concert) makes an offer to acquire the whole of the issued share capital of the Company which values the entire issued share capital of the Company at a figure equal to more than 110% of the value of the Offer.]

5.2   Making of the Offer

Neither you nor any of your subsidiaries are under any obligation to make, or procure the making, of the Offer.

5.3   Lapse

My Obligations shall lapse if:

5.3.1   The Offer is not made (in accordance with the provisions of the Code) by [   ]pm on [   ] 200 .

5.3.2   the Offer lapses or is withdrawn;

provided that the lapsing of my Obligations shall not affect any rights or liabilities in respect of breaches of contract or undertaking committed prior to such lapsing.

6.   ENFORCEMENT

6.1   **Governing law**

This letter shall be governed by and construed in accordance with English law and I irrevocably submit to the exclusive jurisdiction of the English courts to settle any disputes which may arise out of or in connection with this letter and I waive any objection to any suit, action or proceedings ("**Proceedings**") in such courts on the ground of venue or on the ground that such Proceedings are brought in an inconvenient forum.

6.2   **Specific performance**

I acknowledge that if I should fail to accept or procure the acceptance of the Offer or should otherwise be in breach of any of my Obligations, that damages may not be an adequate remedy an order of specific performance would be the only adequate remedy.

6.3   **Power of attorney**

In order to secure the performance of the undertakings contained in paragraph 1 above, I appoint each director of the Offeror severally to be my attorney in my name or otherwise and on my behalf to accept the Offer, to sign a form or forms of acceptance, and generally to comply with the terms of the formal document containing the Offer and fulfil my obligations in relation to them and pursuant to this letter so far as it relates to the Shares.

Yours faithfully

SIGNED (and **DELIVERED on the date**   )
of this document) AS A DEED   )
by

Signature of witness:

Name:

Address:

Occupation:

SCHEDULE

Shares to which this letter relates

(1) Registered Holder	(2) Beneficial Owner	(3) Number of Ordinary Shares

PRECEDENT 38

Heads of Terms—Share Sales and Purchases

HEADS OF TERMS

RELATING TO THE POSSIBLE ACQUISITION BY

[LIMITED/PLC] ("THE BUYER")

OF THE WHOLE OF THE ISSUED SHARE CAPITAL OF

[LIMITED/PLC] ("THE COMPANY")

FROM

[   ] (THE SELLER[S]")

1. SALE AND PURCHASE

The Seller[s (whose obligations in relation to the transaction, except in relation to the restrictive undertakings reference in paragraph 5 below, are to be joint and several)] shall sell with full title guarantee, and the Buyer shall buy, the entire issued share capital of the Company free of all liens, charges and encumbrances.

2. PRICE AND PAYMENT

ALTERNATIVE A—FIXED CASH SUM WITHOUT RETENTION

The purchase price shall be the payment by the Buyer to the Seller[s] of the sum of £[   ] payable in full on completion by way of banker's draft drawn on a UK clearing bank or by way of telegraphic transfer in favour of the [Seller/Seller's solicitors/Sellers/Sellers' solicitors][, which shall be payable to the Sellers in proportion to their respective holdings of shares in the capital of the Company]

ALTERNATIVE B—COMPLETION ACCOUNTS WITH JOINT ACCOUNT

2.1   The purchase price shall be the payment by the Buyer to the Seller[s] of a sum equal to the Completion NAV (as hereinafter defined) [, which shall be payable to the Sellers in proportion to their respective holdings of shares in the capital of the Target].

2.2   On Completion, the Buyer shall pay:

2.2.1   the sum of £[   ] to the Seller[, which shall be payable to the Sellers in proportion to their respective holdings of shares in the capital of the Company]; and

2.2.2   the sum of £[   ] to the Buyer's solicitors and the [Seller's/Sellers'] solicitors, who will credit it to a bank account to be opened in their joint names ("the Account"), to be held on terms that interest shall follow principal and that any payments out of the Account shall require the prior approval of both the Buyer's solicitors and the [Seller's/Sellers'] solicitors.

2.3   On the third business day after the date on which the Completion NAV is determined:

2.3.1   the Buyer shall pay to the [Seller/Sellers] a sum equal to the balance (if any) of the purchase price, such payment to be satisfied by a payment from the Account; and

2.3.2   if the purchase price exceeds the amounts paid pursuant to para-
         graphs 2.2.1 and 2.3.1, the Buyer shall pay the amount of the
         excess to the [Seller/Sellers]; and

2.3.3   any balance of the principal amount standing to the credit of the
         Account after making such payments shall be paid to the Buyer; but

2.3.4   if the purchase price is less than the amount paid to the
         [Seller/Sellers] pursuant to paragraph 2.2.1, the [Seller/Sellers]
         shall repay to the Buyer a sum equal to the excess, plus interest on
         the amount in question at the rate at which interest has been earned
         on the Account.

2.4   Any payment to the [Seller/Sellers] shall in each case be by way of banker's
       draft drawn on a UK clearing bank or by way of telegraphic transfer in favour
       of the [Seller/Seller's solicitors/Sellers/Sellers' solicitors] [and subject to a
       right of set-off in favour of the Buyer in relation to any sum claimed by it
       under the sale and purchase agreement or otherwise.]

2.5   The Completion NAV shall be the net asset value of the Company [and its
       subsidiaries] being the aggregate of:

       (a)   the amounts paid up or credited as paid up on [its/their] issued
              share capital; and

       (b)   any balance standing to the credit of [its/their] profit and loss
              account[1]; less:

       (c)   any debit balance on [its/their] profit and loss account[2];
              and shall be determined as follows:

[Summary of what is agreed regarding the basis of and mechanics for calculation
and determination of the Completion NAV]

3.   WARRANTIES AND TAX COVENANTS

3.1   The Seller[s] shall give to the Buyer a "normal" full set of warranties cover-
       ing commercial, accounting, tax and legal matters relating to or affecting the
       Company and its business.

3.2   All warranties are to be given subject to matters fairly disclosed in a disclo-
       sure letter.

3.3   The Seller[s] shall give to the Buyer a tax covenant, which shall extend to
       losses and reliefs agreed with the tax authorities, amounting to an indemnity
       as to the completeness and adequacy of all tax provisions and the payment of
       all tax which has become due.

4.   QUALIFICATIONS TO WARRANTIES AND TAX COVENANTS

The liability of the Seller[s] under the warranties and tax covenant[s] shall be subject
to [various qualifications to be agreed between the Seller[s] and the Buyer including]
the following qualifications:

4.1   Liability is to cease after the expiry of the period of six years from the end of
       the accounting reference period next following completion, in respect of tax
       matters, and after the expiry of the period of [   ] following

---

[1] In some cases, it may be appropriate to refer to other reserves.
[2] In some cases, it may be appropriate to refer to other reserves.

completion, in respect of other matters, except (in each case) for claims previously notified to the Seller[s].

4.2   [A de/De] minimis limit[s] of £[A   ] for each individual claim [and £[B   ] for all claims of £[A   ] or more] [is/are] to apply, with claims not being limited to the excess.

4.3   The aggregate liability of the Seller[s] shall be limited to £[C   ].

4.4   The Buyer shall not be entitled to make recovery under the warranties or the tax covenant to the extent that recovery is made under the other [or to the extent that the matter in question has been taken into account in the determination of the Completion NAV].

5. RESTRICTIVE UNDERTAKINGS

The [Seller on behalf of itself and all its subsidiaries from time to time/Sellers] shall enter into restrictive undertakings in favour of the Buyer which will last for the period of [   ] months following completion, including undertakings that [it will not/none of them will/they will not] either [itself/themselves] or with or for any other person:

5.1   Solicit orders from any customer of the Company for the supply of [   ];

5.2   Do anything which [it/they] know[s] or ought reasonably to know would cause or be reasonably likely to cause any supplier of the Company to cease or materially reduce its supplies to the Company.

5.3   Solicit or employ or offer employment to any employee of the Company engaged in skilled or managerial work or otherwise in possession of confidential information relating to the Company or able to influence its customer relationships or connections;

5.4   Except as the holder for investment purposes only of less than 5% of the shares of a company whose shares are listed on any recognised investment exchange, be interested, directly or indirectly, within **[specify geographical area]** in any business which consists of, or includes to a material extent **[Specify]**.

6. GUARANTEES

The Buyer shall following completion use all reasonable endeavours to procure the release of the [Seller and any other company in its group/Sellers] from any guarantees or indemnities specified in the sale and purchase agreement and given in respect of the liabilities of any Company and shall indemnify the [Seller and each other company in its group/Sellers] against any liability which it may suffer under or by virtue of any such guarantee or indemnity.

7. CONFIDENTIALITY

7.1   [Neither/No] party shall make any public announcement concerning the transaction, or the negotiations relating thereto, prior to signing the formal legal agreement [unless otherwise required by law or by the rules of the London Stock Exchange]. Following completion announcements will be made to employees, and to customers and suppliers, in a form to be agreed. No other announcement concerning the transaction shall be made by [either/any] party without prior clearance with the other[s] except as required by law [or by the rules of the London Stock Exchange].

7.2   [Nothing in these heads of terms is to affect the operation of the existing confidentiality agreements, which shall continue in full force and effect, pending completion.]

8.   **COSTS**

Each party shall be responsible for its own costs whether or not the transaction proceeds to completion.

9.   **DUE DILIGENCE**

9.1   Following the signing of these heads of terms [X   ] will be permitted to carry out due diligence on behalf of the Buyer [and shall for this purpose be allowed access to the factory site for up to [   ] working days and by no more than [   ] individuals at any one time].

9.2   [All requests for information by [X   ] (or any other agents or professional advisers or agents of the Buyer)] will be made via the designated representative of the Seller[s] on the site, and access to the various parts of the site will be agreed by that representative and (if the Seller[s] require[s]) must be accompanied by the Seller[s]'[s] personnel.

9.3   Neither [X   ] nor any of the agents or other professional advisers or agents of the Buyer shall be permitted access to any of the staff of the Company without the prior written approval of the designated representative of the Seller[s], who shall be entitled to specify when and to whom such access will be permitted, as to both the timing and the extent of access. The Buyer shall ensure that neither [X   ] nor its other professional advisers or agents disclose to any of the staff of the Company the reasons for the due diligence work being carried out.]

10.   **TIMESCALE**

The parties will do all in their power to progress the transaction as rapidly as possible with the aim of completing the transaction purchase on or before [200   ].

Except for paragraphs 7 to 9 (inclusive), which are legally binding, these heads of terms and all communications, both written and oral and whether or not individually described as "subject to contract", between the parties and their respective advisers are at all times subject to contract, and no legal commitments shall arise, unless and until formal contracts are exchanged.

Signed for and on behalf of
the Buyer in the
presence of:

ALTERNATIVES
EITHER
Signed for and on behalf of
The Seller in the
presence of:

OR
Signed by [   ]
(one of the Sellers)
in the presence of:

Signed by [   ]
(one of the Sellers)
in the presence of:

Signed by [   ]
(one of the Sellers)
in the presence of:

Signed by [   ]
(one of the Sellers)
in the presence of:

PRECEDENT 39

Heads of Terms—Assets Sales and Purchases

HEADS OF TERMS

RELATING TO THE POSSIBLE ACQUISITION BY

[LIMITED/PLC] ("THE BUYER")

OF THE UNDERTAKING AND ASSETS OF THE [DESCRIPTION] BUSINESS ("THE BUSINESS") OF

1.   SALE AND PURCHASE

With effect from a date and time to be agreed ("the Transfer Point") the Seller shall sell with full title guarantee, and the Buyer shall buy, the Business as a going concern and the following assets ("the Assets") free of all liens, charges and encumbrances:

1.1   the good will of the Business and the exclusive right for the Buyer to use the name "[   ];

1.2   work-in progress and all stocks of raw materials, components, finished and unfinished goods, consumables and the like;

1.3   all the plant, machinery, equipment, furniture, fixtures and fittings, tools, vehicles and spare parts and other tangible assets of the Business;

1.4   the benefit (subject to the burden) of all contracts and agreements remaining to be completed at the Transfer Point and entered into by the Seller in the [ordinary] course of the Business ("the Contracts");

1.5   all intellectual property owned, used or required to be used by the Seller in relation to the Business;

1.6   the [freehold] property of the Seller at [description];

1.7   all book and other debts of the Business at the Transfer Point and the benefit of all pre-payments at that point;

1.8   all books and records of the Business;

1.9   all rights of the Seller against third parties in respect of any of the assets specified in paragraphs 1.1 to 1.8.

2.   EXCLUDED ASSETS

The following assets of the Seller shall be excluded from the transaction:

2.1   Shares or other securities in any other companies;

2.2   cash in hand or at bank;

2.3   any right to any credit or refund of tax;

2.4   all intra-group debts;

2.5   [specify any books and records to be excluded]; and

2.6   all assets which are subject to leasing, rental, hire or hire-purchase agreements ("the Third Party Assets") as to which the provisions of paragraph shall apply;

3.   CREDITORS

3.1   The Buyer shall not be required to take on or discharge any obligation or lia-
       bility of the Seller other than any which it expressly agrees in the formal sale
       and purchase agreement to take on or discharge.

3.2   As part of the consideration for the Business and the Assets, the Buyer shall
       assume responsibility for all creditors of the Business at the Transfer Point [if
       and to the extent that provision is made for them in the calculation of the
       Completion NAV (as herein after defined)]. The Buyer shall not however be
       required to assume the following creditors:

       3.2.1   amounts owing to the Seller's bankers;

       3.2.2   any liabilities for VAT or other taxation; and

       3.2.3   sums owing to other members of the Seller's group.

4.   PRICE AND PAYMENT

ALTERNATIVE A—FIXED CASH SUM WITHOUT RETENTION

The balance of the consideration for the Business and the Assets shall be the payment
by the Buyer to the Seller of the sum of £[   ] payable in full on completion by way
of banker's draft drawn on a UK clearing bank or by way of telegraphic transfer in
favour of the Seller/Seller's solicitors.

ALTERNATIVE B—COMPLETION ACCOUNTS WITH JOINT ACCOUNT

4.1   The balance of the consideration for the Business and the Assets shall be the
       payment by the Buyer to the Seller of a sum equal to the Completion NAV
       (as hereinafter defined).

4.2   On Completion, the Buyer shall pay:

       4.2.1   The sum of £[   ] to the Seller; and

       4.2.2   The sum of £[   ] to the Buyer's solicitors and the Seller's solic-
                itors, who will credit it to a bank account to be opened in their joint
                names ("the Account"), to be held on terms that interest shall fol-
                low principal and that any payments out of the Account shall
                require the prior approval of both the Buyer's solicitors and the
                Seller's solicitors.

4.3   On the third business day after the date on which the Completion NAV is
       determined:

       4.3.1   the Buyer shall pay to the Seller a sum equal to the balance (if any)
                of the consideration, such payment to be satisfied by a payment
                from the Account; and

       4.3.2   if the consideration exceeds the amounts paid pursuant to para-
                graphs 4.2.1 and 4.3.1, the Buyer shall pay the amount of the
                excess to the Seller; and

       4.3.3   any balance of the principal amount standing to the credit of the
                Account after making such payments shall be paid to the Buyer; but

       4.3.4   if the consideration is less than the amount paid to the Seller pur-
                suant to paragraph 4.2.1, the Seller shall repay to the Buyer a sum
                equal to the excess, plus interest on the amount in question at the
                rate at which interest has been earned on the Account.

4.4 Any payment to the Seller shall in each case be by way of banker's draft drawn on a UK clearing bank or by way of telegraphic transfer in favour of the [Seller/Seller's solicitors] [and subject to a right of set-off in favour of the Buyer in relation to any sum claimed by it under the sale and purchase agreement or otherwise.]

4.5 The Completion NAV shall be the net value at the county transfer point of the Assets (i.e. the aggregate value of the Assets less the aggregate amount of the creditors to be assumed by the Buyer and shall be determined as follows:

[Summary of what is agreed regarding the basis of and mechanics for calculation and determination of the Completion NAV] [Completion Statement]

5. VAT

5.1 The consideration is stated exclusive of VAT and the Buyer and the Seller shall use all reasonable endeavours to procure that the sale and purchase of the Business and of the Assets is deemed to be a transfer of a business as a going concern for the purposes of the VAT legislation.

5.2 If VAT is subsequently found to be payable, the Buyer will pay the amount of VAT in question within 14 days following delivery to it by the Seller of a VAT invoice and a copy of the determination of HM Revenue & Customs that VAT is payable.

5.3 **[Specify that the property is intended as regards VAT books and records.]**

6. CONTRACTS

6.1 In the formal sale and purchase agreement, the Buyer and the Seller shall agree a mechanism to enable the Buyer to obtain the benefit (subject to the burden) of any of the contracts which cannot be assigned without the consent of a third party.

6.2 The Seller shall remain liable under the Contracts in respect of all goods and services supplied before the Transfer Point and shall indemnify the Buyer against any act or omission of the Seller before the Transfer Point in relation to any of the Contracts.

6.3 If any valid claims are made against the Seller or against the Buyer for the repair or replacement of any defective goods sold by the Seller or for the reimbursement of the price of such goods, the Buyer shall satisfy such claims the Seller shall reimburse to the Buyer (at cost), the cost to the Buyer of doing so.

7. EMPLOYEES

7.1 All employees of the Business shall transfer to the Buyer and the Transfer of Undertakings (Protection of Employment) Regulations 2006 ("the Regulations").

7.2 The Buyer and the Seller shall agree appropriate indemnities in favour of each other in respect of liabilities which the one may incur as a result of acts or omissions on the part of the other, whether pursuant to the Regulations or otherwise.

7.3 The Seller will remain liable for all wages, salaries, etc, in respect of all periods down to the Transfer Point and in respect of holiday entitlements as at the Transfer Point. Appropriate provision shall be made for them in determining the Completion NAV.

7.4 **[Specify what is agreed regarding TUPE consultations with employees.]**

8.   PROPERTY

[**Specify here any necessary provisions regarding freehold or leasehold properties.**]

9.   WARRANTIES AND TAX COVENANTS

9.1   The Seller shall give to the Buyer a "normal" set of warranties which are appropriate to a sale and purchase of assets covering commercial, accounting, tax and legal matters relating to or affecting the Assets and the Business.

9.2   All warranties are to be given subject to matters fairly disclosed in a disclosure letter.

10.   QUALIFICATIONS TO WARRANTIES AND TAX COVENANTS

The liability of the Seller under the warranties and tax covenant[s] shall be subject to [various qualifications to be agreed between the Seller and the Buyer, including] the following qualifications:

10.1   Liability is to cease after the expiry of the period of six years from the end of the accounting reference period next following completion, in respect of tax matters, and after the expiry of the period of [   ] following completion, in respect of other matters, except (in each case) for claims previously notified to the Seller.

10.2   [A de/De] minimis limit[s] of £[A   ] for each individual claim [and £[B   ] for all claims of £[A   ] or more] [is/are] to apply, with claims not being limited to the excess.

10.3   The aggregate liability of the Seller shall be limited to £[C   ].

11.   RESTRICTIVE UNDERTAKINGS

11.1   The Seller on behalf of itself and all its subsidiaries from time to time shall enter into restrictive undertakings in favour of the Buyer which will last for the period of [   ] months following completion, including undertakings that it will not/none of them will/they will not] either [itself/themselves] or with or for any other person:

11.2   Solicit orders from any customer of the Business for the supply of [   ];

11.3   Do anything which [it/they] know[s] or ought reasonably to know would cause or be reasonably likely to cause any supplier of the Business to cease or materially reduce its supplies to the Business.

11.4   Solicit or employ or offer employment to any employee of the Business engaged in skilled or managerial work or otherwise in possession of confidential information relating to the Business or able to influence its customer relationships or connections.

11.5   Except as the holder for investment purposes only of less than 5% of the shares of a company whose shares are listed on any recognised investment exchange, be interested, directly or indirectly, within [**specify geographical area**] in any business which consists of, or includes to a material extent, [**specify**].

12.   THIRD PARTY ASSETS

The Buyer and Seller shall use all reasonable endeavours to obtain the assignment to the Buyer of the benefit of the agreements relating to the Third Party Assets and the formal sale and purchase agreement shall contain provisions to enable the Buyer to obtain the benefit (subject to the burden) of such agreements ending the obtaining of any necessary third party consents.

13. **CONFIDENTIALITY**

13.1 Save as provided in paragraph 7.4, neither party shall make any public announcement concerning the transaction, or the negotiations relating thereto, prior to signing the formal legal agreement [unless otherwise required by law or by the rules of the London Stock Exchange]. Following completion announcements will be made to employees, and to customers and suppliers, in a form to be agreed. No other announcement concerning the transaction shall be made by either party without prior clearance with the other except as required by law [or by the rules of the London Stock Exchange].

13.2 [Nothing in these heads of terms is to affect the operation of the existing confidentiality agreements, which shall continue in full force and effect, pending completion.]

14. **COSTS**

Each party shall be responsible for its own costs whether or not the transaction proceeds to completion.

15. **DUE DILIGENCE**

15.1 Following the signing of these heads of terms [X   ] will be permitted to carry out due diligence on behalf of the Buyer [and shall for this purpose be allowed access to the factory site for up to [   ] working days and by no more than [   ] individuals at any one time].

15.2 All requests for information by [X   ] (or any other agents or professional advisers or agents of the Buyer)] will be made via the designated representative of the Seller on the site, and access to the various parts of the site will be agreed by that representative and (if the Seller requires) must be accompanied by the Seller[s personnel.

15.3 Neither [X   ] nor any of the agents or other professional advisers or agents of the Buyer shall be permitted access to any of the staff of the Company without the prior written approval of the designated representative of the Seller[s], who shall be entitled to specify when and to whom such access will be permitted, as to both the timing and the extent of access. The Buyer shall ensure that neither [X   ] nor its other professional advisers or agents disclose to any of the staff of the Company the reasons for the due diligence work being carried out.

16. **TIMESCALE**

The parties will do all in their power to progress the transaction as rapidly as possible with the aim of completing the transaction purchase on or before [200   ].

Except for paragraphs 14 to 16 (inclusive), which are legally binding, these heads of terms and all communications, both written and oral and whether or not individually described as "subject to contract", between the parties and their respective advisers are at all times subject to contract, and no legal commitments shall arise, unless and until formal contracts are exchanged.

Signed for and on behalf of
the Buyer in the
presence of:

Signed for and on behalf of
The Seller in the
presence of:

Index

Instruction for use of the companion disc

Introduction

These notes are provided for guidance only. They should be read and interpreted in the context of your own computer system and operational procedures. It is assumed that you have a basic knowledge of WINDOWS. However, if there is any problem please contact our help line on 0845 850 9355 who will be happy to help you.

CD Format and Contents

To run this CD you need at least:

IBM compatible PC
CD-ROM drive
Microsoft Word 6.0/95

The CD contains data files of the clauses in this book. It does not contain software or commentary.

Installation

The following instructions make the assumption that you will copy the data files to a single directory on your hard disk (e.g. C:\SJoint Ventures).

Open your CD Rom drive, select and double click on setup.exe and follow the instructions. The files will be unzipped to your C drive and you will be able to open them from the new C:\SJoint Ventures folder there.

LICENCE AGREEMENT

Definitions

l. The following terms will have the following meanings: "The PUBLISHERS" means Sweet & Maxwell of 100 Avenue Road, London NW3 3PF (which expression shall, where the context admits, include the PUBLISHERS' assigns or successors in business as the case may be) of the other part on behalf of Thomson Books Limited of Cheriton House, North Way, Andover SPI0 5BE.

"The LICENSEE" means the purchaser of the title containing the Licensed Material.

"Licensed Material" means the data included on the disk; "Licence" means a single user licence;

"Computer" means an IBM-PC compatible computer.

Grant of Licence; Back up copies

2. (1) The PUBLISHERS hereby grant to the LICENSEE. a non-exclusive, non-transferable licence to use the Licensed Material in accordance with these terms and conditions.

(2) The LICENSEE may install the Licensed Material for use on one computer only at any one time.

(3) The LICENSEE may make one back-up copy of the Licensed Material only, to be kept in the LICENSEE's control and possession.

Proprietary Rights

3. (1) All rights not expressly granted herein are reserved.

(2) The Licensed Material is not sold to the LICENSEE who shall not acquire any right, title or interest in the Licensed Material or in the media upon which the Licensed Material is supplied.

(3) The LICENSEE shall not erase, remove, deface or cover any trademark, copyright notice, guarantee or other statement on any media containing the Licensed Material.

(4) The LICENSEE shall only use the Licensed Material in the normal course of its business and shall not use the Licensed Material for the purpose of operating a bureau or similar service or any online service whatsoever.

(5) Permission is hereby granted to LICENSEES who are members of the legal profession (which expression does not include individuals or organisations engaged in the supply of services to the legal profession) to reproduce, transmit and store small quantities of text for the purpose of enabling them to provide legal advice to or to draft documents or conduct proceedings on behalf of their clients.

(6) The LICENSEE shall not sublicense the Licensed Material to others and this Licence Agreement may not be transferred, sublicensed, assigned or otherwise disposed of in whole or in part.

(7) The LICENSEE shall inform the PUBLISHERS on becoming aware of any unauthorised use of the Licensed Material.

Warranties

4. (1) The PUBLISHERS warrant that they have obtained all necessary rights to grant this licence.

(2) Whilst reasonable care is taken to ensure the accuracy and completeness of the Licensed Material supplied, the PUBLISHERS make no representations or warranties, express or implied, that the Licensed Material is free from errors or omissions.

(3) The Licensed Material is supplied to the LICENSEE on an "as is" basis and has not been supplied to meet the LICENSEE'S individual requirements. It is the sole respon-sibility of the LICENSEE to satisfy itself prior to entering this Licence Agreement that the Licensed Material will meet the LICENSEE's requirements and be compatible with the LICENSEE's hardware/software configuration. No failure of any part of the Licensed Material to be suitable for the LICENSEE's requirements will give rise to any claim against the PUBLISHERS.

(4) In the event of any material inherent defects in the physical media on which the licensed material may be supplied. other than caused by accident abuse or misuse by the LICENSEE, the PUBLISHERS will replace the defective original media free of charge provided it is returned to the place of purchase within 90 days of the purchase date.

The PUBLISHERS' enure liability and the LICENSEE's exclusive remedy shall be the replacement of such detective media.

(5) Whilst all reasonable care has been taken to exclude computer viruses, no warranty is made that the Licensed Material is virus free. The LICENSEE shall be responsible to ensure that no virus is introduced to any computer or network and shall not hold the PUBLISHERS responsible.

(6) The warranties set out herein are exclusive of and in lieu of all other conditions and warranties, either express or implied, statutory or otherwise.

(7) All other conditions and warranties, either express or implied, statutory or otherwise, which relate in the condition and fitness for any purpose of the Licensed Material are hereby excluded and the PUBLISHERS shall not be liable in contract or in tort for any loss of any kind suffered by reason of any defect in the Licensed Material (whether or not caused by the negligence of the PUBLISHERS).

Limitation of Liability and Indemnity

5. (1) The LICENSEE shall accept sole responsibility for and the PUBLISHERS shall not be liable for the use of the Licensed Material by the LICENSEE, its agents and employees and the LICENSEE shall hold the PUBLISHERS harmless and fully indemnified against any claims, costs, damages, loss and liabilities arising out of any such use.

(2) The PUBLISHERS shall not be liable for any indirect or consequential loss suffered by the LICENSEE (including without limitation loss of profits, goodwill or data) in connection with the Licensed Material howsoever arising.

(3) The PUBLISHERS will have no liability whatsoever for any liability of the LICENSEE or any third party which might arise.

(4) The LICENSEE hereby agrees that

(a) the LICENSEE is best placed to foresee and evaluate any loss that might be suffered in connection with this Licence Agreement;

(b) that the cost of supply of the Licensed Material has been calculated on the basis of the limitations and exclusions contained herein; and

(c) the LICENSEE will effect such insurance as is suitable having regard to the LICENSEE's circumstances.

(5) The aggregate maximum liability of the PUBLISHERS in respect of any direct loss or any other loss (to the extent that such loss is not excluded by this Licence Agreement or otherwise) whether such a claim arises in contract or tort shall not exceed a sum equal to that paid as the price for the title containing the Licensed Material.

Termination

6. (1) In the event of any breach of this Agreement including any violation of any copyright in the Licensed Material, whether held by the PUBLISHERS or others in the Licensed Material, the Licence Agreement shall automatically terminate immediately, without notice and without prejudice to any claim which the PUBLISHERS may have either for moneys due and/or damages and/or otherwise.

(2) Clauses 3 to 5 shall survive the termination for whatsoever reason of this Licence Agreement.

(3) In the event of termination of this Licence Agreement the LICENSEE will remove the Licensed Material.

Miscellaneous

7. (1) Any delay or forbearance by the PUBLISHERS in enforcing any provisions of this Licence Agicenient shall not be construed as a waiver of such provision or an agreement thereafter not to enforce the said provision.

(2) This Licence Agreement shall be governed by the laws of England and Wales, If any difference shall arise between the Parties touching the meaning of this Licence Agreement or the rights and liabilities of the parties thereto, the same shall be referred to arbitration in accordance with the provisions of the Arbitration Act 1996, or any amending or substituting statute for the time being in force.

Disclaimer

LORD BEAVERBROOK

02365   942
"191"

MEN

and

POWER

1917   1918

HUTCHINSON
LONDON
1956

The heights by great men reached and kept
Were not attained by sudden flight,
But they, while their companions slept,
Were toiling upward in the night.

MEN AND POWER
1917–1918

LLOYD GEORGE

Pictured here with Haig and Joffre.

"Were these glittering commands to be entrusted to mediocrities, bred with obsolete tactics, and mouldering in military routine?"

CONTENTS

CONTENTS

ILLUSTRATIONS

ILLUSTRATIONS

BIOGRAPHIES

I remember—

ADDISON, Rt. Hon. Christopher

M.P. for Hoxton Division, Shoreditch, since 1910, in 1917 Addison was forty-eight years of age. He was married and had two young sons and two daughters.

Educated at Trinity College, Harrogate, and St. Bartholomew's Hospital, he was a doctor of medicine.

He was attractive in conversation, but not generally popular, though he grew in public favour through the years. His achievements in politics far outstripped his performance in medicine. Several doctors have received peerages, but only Addison could claim the Garter, an honour usually reserved for Members of the Royal Family, acquiescent aristocrats, and retiring Prime Ministers.

In 1917 he was one of Lloyd George's principal supporters. He fell out with Lloyd George soon after the war, and resigned from his Ministry. He joined the Socialist Party, becoming in time Leader of the House of Lords.

AMERY, Leopold Stennett

M.P. for South Birmingham and forty-four years of age in 1917, Amery was married to a sister of Sir Hamar Greenwood, M.P., and had one young son.

He had been educated at Harrow and Balliol College, Oxford, where he obtained a first-class degree. He was a Fellow of All Souls. He did not get a place in the Government until after the war.

A member of Lloyd George's Secretariat, although a militant Conservative, he was a warm supporter of the Prime Minister during the war. He held strong views, especially on Empire affairs. He was a good writer, though dull. Earnest in conversation, he was active in expressing his opinions and always sincere and sure of himself. Short in stature and pugnacious by temperament, he was given to making long speeches. He was generally trusted, but never reached public popularity.

In 1917 he was Assistant Secretary to the War Cabinet.

ASQUITH, Rt. Hon. Herbert Henry

M.P. for East Fife, Asquith was sixty-five years of age in 1917. He had been married twice. His first marriage was at the age of twenty-four to Helen Melland of Manchester, a match within his own social class; then he married into the fashionable world. His second wife was Margaret (Margot), the youngest daughter of Sir Charles Tennant. In 1917 he had six children, his eldest having been killed in action. Three other sons also served in the war.

Educated at the City of London School, he won a scholarship at the age of seventeen to Balliol College, Oxford. There he had a distinguished record; he obtained first classes in classical moderations and in literae humaniores, and was awarded the Craven scholarship. And in 1874 he was elected a Fellow of Balliol.

Aloof in the House, yet recognised as its greatest Member, he venerated the Sovereign and received Royal attentions with gratitude.

His friends were devoted to him. In his leisure hours he was at his best in mixed company. He gave much time to conversation, companionship and social pursuits. For recreation he played bridge, chess and golf. He wrote letters in his own hand, with vivid accounts of his colleagues.

He repeated at intervals certain cycles of stories. If his attention was directed to a portrait of Charles James Fox he made the same remarks.

Asquith resigned as Prime Minister and First Lord of the Treasury in 1916, when the second Coalition Government was formed under Lloyd George. He never held office again.

BALDWIN, Stanley

M.P. for the Bewdley Division of Worcestershire since 1908 and fifty years of age in 1917, Stanley Baldwin was married, with two sons and four daughters. He had been educated at Harrow and Trinity College, Cambridge. His eldest son was serving in the war; his second son was too young.

He was stout and sturdy, pipe-smoking frequently, and then rubbing the bowl of his pipe on his nose, possibly to polish it (the pipe).

His home life was happy, and he had a passion for a mechanical piano-player. A contented middle-class millionaire, he was not widely read, but he had literary associations and would stroll round his library, picking up a volume at random and reading out those passages which caught his eye. His simple jokes endeared him to his friends, and he was much liked and greatly respected.

Up to the outbreak of war he showed not the slightest trace of political push or ambition. He had given no sign of his great oratorical talents and immense political prescience. He was busy with the directorships of various important companies. His contemporaries regarded him as a man of affairs who had all the characteristics of a country squire. His conversation turned on the beauty of the mountain rose, and the splendour of hawthorn buds in spring.

In 1917 he began to ascend the political ladder; he had placed a foot on the first rung when he became Bonar Law's Joint Financial Secretary to the Treasury. His appointment was due to no past performance, but to the fact that he was rich enough to entertain among Members of Parliament, and popular enough to win friends for himself and for his chief.

On attaining to Junior office his character changed. Ambition marked him. Thereafter came a steady development of growing powers.

BALFOUR, Rt. Hon. Arthur James

M.P. for the City of London in 1917, Balfour was a bachelor of sixty-nine years of age. He had been educated at Eton and Trinity College, Cambridge.

Tall, slim and good-looking, like Asquith he was much admired. His intimate friends were few in number, and it is just possible that he didn't believe in anything or anybody. Asquith described him as a man of "superficial charm". Others considered that his outstanding quality was his political cunning. He was, in fact, a crafty man. During the peace conference in Paris in 1919 Clemenceau used to speak of him as 'cette vieille fille'.

Dominating the House of Commons, although an indifferent speaker, he would often hesitate as though searching for a word or phrase—but he was not really doing so. He addressed his colleagues in familiar terms, but in correspondence and conversation they frequently addressed him as Mr. Balfour.

Deposed from the leadership of the Conservative Party in November 1911, he retained membership of the Committee of Imperial Defence. He worked with Asquith's Government from the outbreak of the war, although never separating himself from his Conservative colleagues. In Asquith's First Coalition Government of May, 1915, Balfour became First Lord of the Admiralty. He was Secretary of State for Foreign Affairs in Lloyd George's Ministry in 1916, until after the war ended.

BEAVERBROOK, 1st Baron (William Maxwell Aitken)

M.P. for Ashton-under-Lyne until his *relegation* to the peerage in 1916, Lord Beaverbrook was thirty-eight years of age in 1917. He was married, with two young sons and one daughter, and was living at the Hyde Park Hotel.

He had been educated at the Government School, Newcastle, New Brunswick.

In 1915 he was a Lieutenant-Colonel in the Canadian Army and in charge of Canadian War Records. Next year he was Canadian Government Representative to the Army Overseas.

In 1918 he became Chancellor of the Duchy of Lancaster and Minister of Information in Lloyd George's Government. He was the youngest and most inexperienced member of the Administration.

BRADE, Sir Reginald Herbert

Fifty-three years of age in 1917, Sir Reginald Brade was married with no children.

Educated at St. Andrews College, Bradfield, he was Permanent Under-Secretary at the War Office.

See page 44.

CARSON, Rt. Hon. Sir Edward Henry

M.P. for Dublin University since 1892 and sixty-three years of age in 1917, Carson had been married twice. He had by his first marriage two sons serving in the war, and two daughters.

A graduate of Trinity College, Dublin, he was a loyal Ulster leader. He was a clever lawyer and a rebellious politician. His admirers believed to be clever is good, but to be rebellious is splendid.

He had an intensely emotional nature, which was nurtured by the vast crowds attending on his public appearances.

Carson spoke slowly and he had a melodious voice. His speeches were easy to hear, but difficult to read.

For nearly four years he held the issues of civil peace or civil war in his hands. He was First Lord of the Admiralty until July, 1917, when he became a member of the War Cabinet.

CECIL, Rt. Hon. Lord (Edgar Algernon) Robert (Gascoyne-)

M.P. for Hitchin, Lord Robert Cecil was fifty-three years of age in 1917. The third son of the third Marquis of Salisbury, he was married, but had no children.

Educated at Eton and University College, Oxford, he had studied law.

Highly respected and greatly admired for sturdy qualities of character, his habits were all good. He was a Free Trade member of a Tariff Party. His chief political interest was the Church.

Minister of Blockade and Under Secretary of State for Foreign Affairs in 1917, he was appointed Assistant Secretary of State for Foreign Affairs in July, 1918.

CHAMBERLAIN, Sir (Joseph) Austen

M.P. for Birmingham since 1914 and fifty-four years of age in 1917, Austen Chamberlain was married, with two young sons and one daughter. He had been educated at Rugby and Trinity College, Cambridge.

About him gathered glowing affections; there were no hatreds. He was trusted and respected and he always told the truth, rare gifts for a man born to public affairs. Lord Birkenhead said of him: "Austen always played the game, and he always lost it."

Since 1915 Chamberlain had held the appointment of Secretary of State for India. He resigned in July, 1917, returning again to the War Cabinet in 1918.

CHURCHILL, Rt. Hon. Winston (Leonard Spencer)

M.P. for Dundee and forty-three years of age in 1917, Winston Churchill was married, with three young children, and living at 41 Cromwell Road, S.W.

He had been educated at Harrow and Sandhurst. By 1917 he had won for himself a considerable reputation as a writer. His biography of Lord Randolph Churchill was acclaimed as a masterpiece. Although he had begun to paint, he had not yet received recognition as an artist. He was in this year of decision the most astonishing and the most remarkable of all the Ministers.

His conversation was pleasing, his companionship was exciting. He had no rancour and few hatreds.

He was in every sense a professional politician, having trained himself for his vocation. Impetuous in action, he was determined when resisting opposition.

He sang the popular music-hall melodies in a raucous voice, and without any instinct for tune. His bridge, which he played occasionally, was exceedingly careless, and his card sense almost non-existent.

He lived well, and ate everything. He exaggerated his drinking habits by his own remarks in praise of wine and brandy. He appeared to smoke cigars incessantly. Not at all. He smoked very little, although relighting a cigar frequently. His use of matches outstripped his consumption of cigars.

Throughout the war of 1914–18 he was involved in political storms and tempests. He tried only to do the right thing, but occasionally in the wrong way. Critics frequently found fault with him through prejudice and without reason. He had no friends in the Tory Party. Many Liberals believed that he had betrayed Asquith, and therefore they were displeased with him. The Lloyd George Liberals were none too friendly. Churchill at that time had no intimate contacts with the Labour Party.

Driven out of the Admiralty in May, 1915, he held for a short time the Chancellorship of the Duchy of Lancaster. On the issue of the evacuation of Gallipoli he resigned in November, 1915, and in the following year commanded a battalion in France. In 1916 he returned to his Parliamentary duties, and joined Lloyd George's Government as Minister of Munitions in July, 1917.

In 1917 and 1918 Churchill was a Liberal. Nobody believed that he would be a Conservative Prime Minister in years to come. If such a prediction had been made, it would have been ridiculed, although he was regarded by many as a possible future Liberal Prime Minister.

CUNLIFFE, 1st Baron of Headley (Walter Cunliffe)

Lord Cunliffe was sixty-two years of age in 1917. He had been married twice, and had two sons and three daughters. One of his sons served in the war.

He had been educated at Harrow and Trinity College, Cambridge.

Governor of the Bank of England, in 1917 he was created a G.B.E.

CURZON, 1st Earl (George Nathaniel Curzon)

Fifty-eight years of age in 1917, Curzon was married for the second time during that year. He had three daughters by his first marriage, but no sons.

Educated at Eton and Balliol College, Oxford, he was elected a Fellow of All Souls. He was a polished orator.

In 1898 he was created Viceroy of India, an office filled with pomp and ceremony, at the youthful age of thirty-nine. In his train followed long strings of elephants and retinues of gaily colourful servants. But his years of semi-kingship came to an end in 1905, when at forty-six years of age he left India an angry and embittered man.

For all the rest of his life Curzon was influenced by his sudden journey to heaven at the age of thirty-nine, and then by his return seven years later to earth, for the remainder of his mortal existence.

Lloyd George treated him roughly but gave him compensation in the form of a Marquisate, in which he took pride.

Curzon changed sides on almost every issue during his long career. Often undecided whether to desert a sinking ship for one that might not float, he would make up his mind to sit on the wharf for a day.

He had many intimates, but none of them deplored his reverses in public life.

From 1915 to 1916 Curzon held office as Lord Privy Seal, and in 1916 became Lord President and Leader of the House of Lords.

DERBY, 17th Earl of (Edward George Villiers Stanley)

In 1917 Lord Derby reached the age of fifty-two. He was married, with two sons and one daughter. One of his sons was wounded in the war, and his son-in-law was killed in action.

Derby was a tiresome speaker but a good letter-writer, often in his own hand. He ate heartily and was over-stout. But he lived to the age of eighty-three, disproving the adage that the fat die early, the thin die late.

Educated at Wellington College, Derby had been Secretary of State for War since 1916.

Popular and holding the affectionate respect of the public, he was never a heavyweight contender in Cabinet Councils. Supported by his Town Properties and his Broad Acres and the Hereditary Virtue of his House, he was the Champion in Lancashire Party organisations. He took infinite trouble to please the Press, and reaped his reward in high praise from Government and Opposition newspapers.

He was an incessant smoker of cigarettes. He pretended to confine himself to nineteen a day. In fact he deceived himself.

Always threatening resignation, he never signed off. Derby was the godfather of Haig's child, yet of him Haig wrote "like the feather pillow [he] bears the mark of the last person who sat on him."

GEDDES, Rt. Hon. Sir Eric (Campbell)

Sir Eric Geddes was forty-two years of age in 1917. He was married and had three sons, who were too young for service.

The ten years of his schooldays were spent at seven schools; six of these claim him as a distinguished old boy. At the age of seventeen he went to the U.S.A., where he worked in the Carnegie Steel Works and on the Baltimore and Ohio Railways.

He was General Manager designate of the North Eastern Railway.

In July, 1917, he took office as First Lord of the Admiralty, and in the following year became a member of the War Cabinet.

Punctuality was his passion, and routine his practice. He lived at Hassocks, near Brighton. Leaving by motor at exactly 8 a.m., returning again at 7 p.m., he spent three hours daily in these journeys. At 7.30 p.m. he sat down to dinner. At 8.15 he rose up again.

His way of life conformed to the teachings of the Shorter Catechism. He was looked on as the strong silent man of real power and influence.

In his home a telephone was on a pay-box system.

Created a Privy Councillor in 1917, he was also awarded the K.C.B. and G.B.E. in that year.

GEORGE, Rt. Hon. David Lloyd

M.P. for Carnavon since 1890 and fifty-four years of age in 1917, Lloyd George was married, with two sons and two daughters. His sons both served in the war.

He had been educated at Llanystumdwy Church of England School but never attended University.

In politics he attempted to straddle all parties. The inevitable consequence was to confuse the issues, and this led him to adopt a series of inconsistent policies.

To Lloyd George no policy was permanent, no pledge final. He became like a trick rider at the circus, as he was compelled to leap from one back to another in his party-coloured team. Thus in the middle of a great and glorious career he was faced with failure and disaster.

In 1916 with the formation of the second Coalition Government Lloyd George became Prime Minister and First Lord of the Treasury. In 1922 he was driven out of Downing Street and never held office again.

He was the only Minister who served from the outbreak of war on 4th August, 1914, to the end of it in 1918.

GUEST, Capt. Hon. Frederick Edward

M.P. for East Dorset since 1910, Guest was forty-two years of age in 1917. The third son of the 1st Baron Wimborne, he was married, with two sons and one daughter. His sons were too young for service.

Educated at Winchester, he became an officer in the East Surrey Regiment. He had served in the South African War.

He was Winston Churchill's first cousin and intimate friend and political disciple.

He served in East Africa. In 1917 he was awarded a D.S.O. He also became chief Liberal whip of the Coalition Government in the same year.

HAIG, Field-Marshal Sir Douglas

Fifty-six years of age in 1917, Haig was married, with one son and two daughters. He had been educated at Clifton and Brasenose College, Oxford, from which he went on to Sandhurst.

His war diary is a self-revealing document: frank, truthful, egotistical, self-confident and malicious. His spear knew no brother.

Careful of his health, he ate sparingly and drank with moderation, yet he died in 1928 at the age of sixty-six. With the publication of his Private Papers in 1952, he committed suicide 25 years after his death.

Throughout the war Haig held high command in France. He was Commander-in-Chief of the Expeditionary Forces in France and Flanders. In 1917 he was raised to the rank of Field-Marshal.

In 1918 he received the American Cross of Honour and the American Distinguished Service Medal. In 1918 he was offered and refused a Viscountcy. In 1919 he was offered and accepted an Earldom. The same year brought him £100,000 from Parliament and the Order of Merit. In 1920 public subscriptions provided a fund for the purchase of Bermersyde Mansion and estate.

Thereafter Lloyd George's "War Memoirs" and Haig's own Private Papers redressed the balance of public favour.

HANKEY, Lieut.-Col. Sir Maurice Pascal Alers

Forty years of age in 1917, Sir Maurice Hankey was married and had three sons too young for war service, and one daughter. Educated at Rugby, he joined the Royal Marine Artillery.

He was Secretary to the War Cabinet, to the Imperial War Cabinet and to the Committee of Imperial Defence.

He received from Parliament a gift of £25,000, his name,

BONAR LAW

"Unselfish in public affairs, he always took the best chair in the room"

BALDWIN

Mrs. Baldwin called him "Tiger"

Lieut.-Col. Sir Maurice Hankey, being included in a list of fighting Naval, Army and Air Force officers.

Protest was raised at the inclusion of officials among the fighting men. The Prime Minister explained that while he took no part in battle he was as essential to our success as any name in the list.

HOUSE, Colonel Edward Mandell

Fifty-nine years of age in 1917, Colonel House was married but had no family.

He had been educated at Cornell University, which he left without taking a degree.

Formerly a planter and farmer in Texas, he had acted as Personal Representative of President Wilson to European Governments. In 1917, he was appointed by the President to gather together material for the Peace Conference. He attended the Inter-Allied Conference at Paris as Special Representative of the U.S.A., and was designated by the President to represent the U.S.A. at Versailles in the Supreme War Council.

House walked delicately. Everything was done softly. He had a rare capacity for gaining confidences, which he always passed on to the President.

LAW, Rt. Hon. Andrew Bonar

An M.P. since 1900, Bonar Law was fifty-nine years of age in 1917. A widower, with a family of four sons and two daughters, 1917 was a tragic year for him. His two elder sons were both killed on active service, one in Palestine and the other in the air.

Educated at Glasgow High School, he left school at the age of sixteen, and did not go on to University.

Lonely and austere by nature, spare of stature but of sound constitution and good health, he smoked incessantly but never drank. Almost every idle moment he passed in playing bridge and chess. His meals—which consisted generally of vegetables, rice pudding and a glass of milk—were swallowed swiftly. Possessing a prodigious memory, he read the newspapers regularly and also light romantic novels. Upright and straightforward in conduct, he was well liked by opponents and beloved by friends. He rejected all offers of honours and decorations.

In the second Coalition Government he was Chancellor of the Exchequer and Leader of the House of Commons.

LONG, Rt. Hon. Walter Hume

M.P. for the Strand Division of Middlesex and aged sixty-three in 1917, Walter Long was married, with three children, his eldest son having been killed in January, 1917.

In his youth he attended Harrow and Christ Church, Oxford, which he left without obtaining a degree.

Generally popular, he was modest by temperament. Although of strong character, his objectives were often confused. Under medium height, but of pleasing countenance, his bald head would grow red with anger or excitement. Certainly seeking popularity, he was quick to take offence. He carried on a feud against Austen Chamberlain.

Leader of the Agricultural Section of the Conservative Party, he was not too closely tied to the Home Rule or Welsh Church Groups. Since 1916 he had held the post of Secretary of State for the Colonies.

MACLAY, Rt. Hon. Sir Joseph Paton

In 1917 Sir Joseph Maclay was sixty years of age. He was married, with four sons and two daughters. One son had been killed in action at Gallipoli. Two other sons fought in the war.

Educated in Glasgow, he had gone into business at an early age, and made a vast fortune in shipping.

While holding his ministerial office as Shipping Controller he refused to appear in the House of Commons.

MILNER, 1st Viscount (Alfred Milner)

Sixty-three years of age in 1917, Lord Milner was still a bachelor. He was born in Germany, and his father, although descended from an English family, was a German by nationality. Milner's claim to British nationality was derived from his grandfather, a native of Manchester, who settled in Germany in 1805.

He was educated in Germany and at King's College, London, and Balliol College, Oxford. His academic record was distinguished and he obtained a first-class degree, later becoming a Fellow of New College, Oxford.

Milner was a Freemason. He was a member of Brooks, and liked his club. He took little interest in food or drink. He was impressive but not attractive. Efficiency was his aim, and the unity of the Empire, political and economic, was his goal. That Britain was no part of Europe was his conviction.

He admired Bismarck's Zollverein of Central Europe, a land empire. He strove for a union of Britain and British territory, extending over lands and seas.

He was a Tory Radical, calling himself a Liberal Unionist, frowning on reductions of taxation, and favouring extensions of social welfare.

He was a Member of the War Cabinet without portfolio, and Secretary of State for War in April, 1918.

NORTHCLIFFE, 1st Viscount (Alfred Charles William Harmsworth)

Fifty-two years of age in 1917, Northcliffe was the son of a barrister practising in Ireland. Born at Chapelizod in 1865, his father moved to London two years later to take up practice there. He was married, with no children.

Self-educated, he was confused and sometimes incoherent in conversation, and had no patience with argument. His occasional speeches were badly delivered. During sixteen years of membership of the Lords he only spoke 968 words in the House.

He influenced politics, but always from the outside, priding himself on having no social relations with Ministers.

A man of brilliant creative talents, touched by the hand of genius, he was on the whole democratic in opinion, and was never carried away by royalty or aristocracy, yet he liked his titles. In the presence of men of high educational attainment he was not at ease. His intimate circle was small. He believed a newspaper proprietor should have no friends; yet he was a Freemason, although not an energetic member of that order.

He made violent attacks on public men; yet he was hurt by criticism, and would refuse to print unfavourable comments on himself.

His power was so considerable that it was of the utmost importance in all matters of public interest to secure his assistance or at any rate his neutrality.

In 1917 Northcliffe was Chairman of the British War Mission to the U.S.A. In 1918 he was Director of Propaganda in Enemy Countries.

READING, 1st Earl (Rufus Daniel Isaacs)

Fifty-seven years of age in 1917, Lord Reading was the second son of a Jewish fruit merchant. He was married and had one son serving in the war. He was created a Baron in 1914, a Viscount in 1916, and an Earl in 1917.

He had been educated in London, Brussels and Hanover. His regular schooling came to an end when he was under fourteen years of age.

Reading had a pleasing countenance. In conversation he had little to say, but when he spoke it was with authority. He did most of his talking and much of his public speaking with his hands on the lapels of his coat. He smoked cigarettes frequently and used a cigarette holder. He could sleep anywhere at any time.

Lord Chief Justice of England since 1913, he was appointed President of the Anglo-French Loan Mission to the U.S.A. in 1917.

RIDDELL, Sir George Allardice

Fifty-two years of age in 1917, Riddell had been married twice, but had no family. He began his career as a boy clerk in a solicitor's office.

On acquiring an interest in the *News of the World*, he devoted himself entirely to newspaper work. He wrote a column called "Gossip of the Day", which carried much exclusive news.

A good conversationalist, he was presentable in appearance and pleasing in manner.

His diaries, which were published in 1933, are important.

For many years he was Lloyd George's familiar companion. After Lloyd George's defeat Riddell deserted him. In the election of 1922 he turned swiftly to the support of Lloyd

George's opponents. This was described by George's friends as an act of treachery. Although the separation is shrouded in mystery, the view widely held is that Lloyd George was responsible for the parting of their ways.

ROBERTSON, General Sir William Robert

Fifty-seven years of age in 1917, Robertson was married, with two sons and two daughters. One of his sons was serving in the war.

His father was a tailor and he had been educated at the village school. After leaving school he became a domestic servant. Then in 1877, at the age of seventeen, he enlisted in the 16th Lancers as a trooper.

He dined well and drank moderately. He was fond of shooting over the fields. A frequent visitor with the Duke of Portland, his great friend, he often stayed at Langwell, the Duke's country house in Caithness-shire.

When the king dined with Lord Derby, the Chiefs of Staff and others, the drink was limited to cider because of the King's pledge that had been given when Lloyd George at the outset of the war asked for total abstinence. Derby passed the word that after the king left the party drinks would be served upstairs. The king stayed late. General Robertson asked impatiently, "When do we get our pop?"

Since 1915 Robertson had been Chief of the Imperial General Staff. He was known to the French Generals by the nickname 'General Non'.

In 1919 he got a Baronetcy from the Sovereign and £10,000 from Parliament. The money reward was inadequate considering the payments to other soldiers. Jellicoe, his opposite number at the Admiralty, dismissed in 1917, was given a Viscountcy and £50,000. But after all Robertson had taken a pot-shot at Santa Claus, and missed.

ROTHERMERE, 1st Baron of Hemsted (Harold Sidney Harmsworth)

In 1917 Rothermere was forty-nine years of age. The younger brother of Northcliffe, he had married in 1893 and had three sons. One son was killed in action in November, 1916, and another, Harold, died of wounds in February, 1918. Although

Rothermere lived entirely in hotel rooms, moving occasionally from one leading establishment to another, his sons lived with him on intimate terms, and their family relationships were close and attractive.

Rothermere had been educated at St. Marylebone Grammar School.

In 1914 he received a peerage on the nomination of Asquith, as a reward for press support, both in his own newspapers and also in the Northcliffe journals, for the Liberal measure limiting the powers of the House of Lords.

Before the outbreak of the war in the same year he had switched his newspaper support to Bonar Law and the Conservative Party, on account of the Home Rule for Ireland Bill, which he bitterly opposed.

Generous, kindly and companionable by nature, his conversation was vivacious. He had a highly developed sense of humour, which at times might be described as a sense of fun.

From 1916 to 1917 Rothermere was Director-General of the Royal Army Clothing Department. In 1917 he was appointed Air Minister.

SMITH, Rt. Hon. Sir Frederick Edwin

M.P. for the Walton Division of Liverpool and forty-five years of age in 1917, F. E. Smith was married, with one son and two daughters.

He had been educated at Birkenhead School and Wadham College, Oxford, and had obtained a first-class Final Honours in the School of Jurisprudence in 1894.

For further and fuller particulars see Chapter I.

Since 1915 he had been Attorney General.

SMUTS, Lieut.-Gen. Rt. Hon. Jan Christian

Forty-seven years of age in 1917, Smuts was married, with two sons and four daughters. He was living at the Savoy Hotel.

He had been educated at Riebeeck West School and at Victoria College, Stellenbosch. He won a scholarship to Christ's College, Cambridge, where he had a distinguished record, and was awarded a Double First in Law.

He fought against Britain in the Boer War. In 1916 he commanded the forces in British East Africa. In 1917 he held the offices of Minister of Defence and Minister of Finance in the South African Government. He was known by his opponents in South Africa as "Slim Jannie".

He joined Lloyd George in 1917, sitting with the War Cabinet although not a member until June. He was appointed to the Privy Council and to the role of Member of the Order of Companions of Honour all in the same year. In 1917 and 1918 he sat as the South African Representative on the Imperial War Cabinet.

SPRING-RICE, Sir Cecil Arthur

Fifty-eight years of age in 1917, Sir Cecil Spring-Rice was married, with one son and one daughter. His son was too young to serve in the war.

Educated at Eton and Balliol College, Oxford, where he attained first-class rank in both moderations and finals in the classical school, in 1917 he was Ambassador to the U.S.A.

He died in Canada on 14th February, 1918.

TRENCHARD, Major-Gen. Hugh Montague

Forty-four years of age in 1917, Trenchard was as yet unmarried. He failed to pass examinations for Dartmouth and Woolwich. It was through the Militia that he began his career in the Army, joining the Royal Scots Fusiliers in 1893. He served in the South African War.

A tall spare man, his loud penetrating voice won him the nickname "Boom". Endowed with a strong sense of duty and a singleness of purpose, he kept his mind firmly fixed upon his goal. A visionary by nature, he was self-centred and inarticulate. He read out his speeches from a vast bundle of manuscript written in a large sprawling hand, and very badly. He had common sense, but limited ability. In political circles he had no friends, but elsewhere he had many strong friendships and he enjoyed bitter hatreds.

Trenchard, who was Chief of the Air Staff for three months, received a Baronetcy from the monarch and £10,000 from Parliament. Sir Frederick Sykes, who was Chief of the Air Staff for over a year, got a G.B.E. "He sendeth the rain on the just and on the unjust!"

When he retired from service he acquired a number of directorships (Goodyear Tyre and Rubber Co. and United Africa Co.) which he held to the day of his death in February, 1956, at the age of eighty-three.

WILSON, Lieut.-Gen. Sir Henry Hughes

Fifty-three years of age in 1917, Sir Henry Wilson was married, with no children.

He had entered Marlborough College in 1877. Having failed to gain admission into Woolwich twice, and into Sandhurst three times, he finally obtained a commission in the Longford Militia, without examination.

He served in the South African War, and in 1914 was appointed sub-chief of the general staff of the British Expeditionary Force in France.

In March, 1917, he returned from a supply mission to Russia. In September he was appointed to the Eastern Command. In February, 1918, Wilson replaced Sir William Robertson as Chief of the Imperial General Staff.

Wilson had bitter enemies and devoted friends. Most of his colleagues in the army were opposed to him. His intellectual gifts outshone those of every other soldier. Asquith hated him; Bonar Law was his friend.

At the end of the war Wilson was given a Baronetcy and a grant of £10,000. He was a member of the House of Commons when an assassin's bullet ended his career.

WISEMAN, Sir William George Eden

Thirty-two years of age in 1917, Sir William Wiseman was married, with two daughters.

He had been educated at Winchester and Jesus College, Cambridge.

He served in the European War in 1914 and was gassed at Ypres. In 1917 he was Chief of the British Intelligence Service in the U.S.A.

Colonel House fell under his spell, declaring him to be "one of the most efficient men of his age I (had) ever met."

In 1918 he was appointed Chief Adviser on American Affairs to the British Delegation in Paris.

THE PRIVATE PAPERS OF MANY PUBLIC MEN

THIS narrative has been fortified by an immense accumulation of private and personal correspondence and various documents which are accessible to me.

Possibly my resources are more extensive than any other private collection of political papers and records of the years of the First World War.

The Lloyd George Papers comprise more than one thousand boxes and most of this material is as yet untapped. These were available for Frank Owen's brilliant book *Tempestuous Journey*.*

The Bonar Law Papers, which are in excellent order, will shortly be shipped to the University of New Brunswick. These papers were left to me by Bonar Law in his will. And I hope I have made good use of them.

The diaries and letters of Lady Lloyd George extending over twenty-five years are now in New Brunswick.

The records of Lord Bennett, who was Prime Minister of Canada for many years, are in my keeping. They are deposited in the Bennett room

* Hutchinson. 25*s.*

at the Bonar Law-Bennett Library in the University of New Brunswick.

And my own private papers have been drawn on for my narrative in no small measure.

Other manuscript collections, in Britain and in Canada and America, have been made available to me.

Lord Wargrave took a prominent and important part in the affairs of the Conservative Party over the critical years culminating in the war of 1914–1918. His papers were placed at my disposal by his great-nephew, Sir Basil Goulding.

Sir Reginald Brade, Under-Secretary at the War Office, gave me several extracts from his diaries relating to the war.

Sir John Elliot has allowed me to take a letter from the papers of his father, Mr. R. D. Blumenfeld, one-time distinguished and beloved editor of the *Daily Express*.

The papers of Sir Robert Borden, Canada's Prime Minister during the First World War, are of course in the National Archives of Canada, but I was permitted to examine the complete photographic copy at the Library of the University of Toronto. Mr. Henry Borden, Q.C., most generously made them available to me.

Extensive research has been carried out on the papers of Colonel E. M. House and of Sir William Wiseman which are held by Yale University. The library gave facilities to my colleagues and I am grateful.

Detailed research has also been performed on my

behalf covering the papers of Walter Hines Page, American Ambassador to Britain during the First War. These papers and correspondence are deposited at the Houghton Library, Harvard University and I am obliged for permission to examine them.

Fredericton,
New Brunswick,
Canada.

ACKNOWLEDGMENTS

I HAVE to acknowledge the gracious permission of Her Majesty the Queen to make use of material from the Royal Archives, Windsor Castle. Sir Owen Morshead has given me guidance in the use of this material.

I wish also to thank the Earl of Balfour; Margaret, Countess of Birkenhead; Collin Brooks, literary executor for Lord Rothermere; Lady Carson; the Public Trustee on behalf of the Northcliffe Estate; the Chamberlain Trustees; the Rt. Hon. Sir Winston Churchill, K.G.; the Marchioness of Crewe; Grace, Lady Curzon; the Earl of Derby; Henrietta, Lady Henderson; Viscount Long of Wraxall; Lord Maclay, K.B.E.; Lady Milner; the Rt. Hon. the Marquess of Reading; General Sir Brian Robertson, Bt., K.C.V.O.; Captain J. C. Smuts; Viscount Stonehaven; and Viscount Younger of Leckie for permission to publish correspondence of importance and in many instances essential to the form of my narrative.

To Sir William Wiseman I am grateful, not only for permission to publish correspondence but also for advice and material of value to my story.

ACKNOWLEDGMENTS

I acknowledge with thanks permission for the use of copyright material from:

Sir Harold Nicolson for consent to publish material from *King George V, His Life and Times*.

Dr. Charles Seymour for extracts from *The Intimate Papers of Colonel House*.

Eyre and Spottiswoode Ltd. for extracts from *The Private Papers of Douglas Haig, 1914–1919*, edited by Robert Blake; *The Unknown Prime Minister* by Robert Blake; *Reginald McKenna* by Stephen McKenna; *The World Crisis, 1916–1918* by Winston Churchill.

Ernest Benn and A. P. Watt & Son for extracts from *The Intimate Papers of Colonel House*, arranged by Charles Seymour, and from *The Life of Lord Curzon* by Lord Ronaldshay.

Constable & Co. Ltd. for extracts from *The First World War, 1914–1918* by Colonel Repington.

John Murray Ltd. for extracts from *George V. A Personal Memoir* by John Gore.

The Times Publishing Company for extracts from *The History of The Times*.

William Heinemann Ltd. for extracts from *Woodrow Wilson's Life and Letters* by R. S. Baker.

Hutchinson and Co. Ltd. for extracts from *Tempestuous Journey* by Frank Owen; *Four and a Half Years* by Christopher Addison; *The Life of Lord Oxford and Asquith* by Stephen Spender and Cyril Asquith; *My War Memories, 1914–1918* by Ludendorff; and *My Political Life* by L. S. Amery.

ACKNOWLEDGMENTS

The following literary agents have also given their consent, and I am grateful:

Messrs. Curtis Brown for extracts from *The Life of Lord Oxford and Asquith*, and *My War Memories, 1914–1918* by Ludendorff; Messrs. Albert Bonnier Forlag, Stockholm, also for extracts from *My War Memories, 1914–1918* by Ludendorff; Messrs. Pearn, Pollinger and Higham for extracts from *My Political Life* by L. S. Amery; and A. D. Peters for extracts from the *Life of Lord Carson* by Ian Colvin.

I am indebted to Mrs. Ann Cousins for research at Harvard, Yale, Toronto and New Brunswick Universities and for extensive assistance and much hard labour.

Mr. George Malcolm Thomson has been reading my proofs and at the same time making corrections.

I have relied too upon invaluable help from Mrs. Elton, the custodian of the Lloyd George and the Bonar Law records.

I owe them all my grateful thanks.

INTRODUCTION

THE year 1917 opened up in disaster for Britain. Germany was the military master of Europe. The French nation was exhausted. Russia was staggering to her doom. The British people were dispirited and a food shortage threatened the very existence of the nation.

The Army was stalemated in France, and the Navy was unable any longer to provide protection for the Mercantile Marine. The sea communications to east and west had been interrupted. Even the freedom of the Channel was challenged.

The public at large were certainly not aware of the dreadful danger, and even important Ministers were incapable of grasping the terrible truth. A few of the leading politicians spoke to each other in alarming terms and some newspapers gave repeated warnings which were almost disregarded.

Thus it was when the reins of office fell from the nerveless grasp of Asquith. Britain was in the shadows.

Lloyd George occupied the seat of power, the chair at No. 10 Downing Street where Asquith had sat for seven years, and where eminent predecessors in peace and war had dispensed patronage and exercised authority.

He was flattered and praised by his intimate circle, adored by his secretaries and courted by society—courted all the more because he rejected the overtures of the social leaders and the social climbers in the West End of London.

Bonar Law was his colleague in a coalition Government, the leader of the Tory Party which gave the Government its majority in Parliament. The Tories were at that time a cohesive party, save only for their Right Wing which accepted their leader for the time being but could not be counted on to give him unswerving allegiance in the years that lay ahead.

There were also more than a hundred Liberals willing to lend support to the Coalition. But of these many were associated personally with Lloyd George, while others had their eyes on office and employment. A few of his followers sought only recommendations for honours.

When the year 1917 opened there were forces pleading for peace in the allied countries.

In France there was a great deal of conversation and some intrigue aimed at making peace before an outright military decision had been reached on the battlefield. The lobbies of the French Chamber echoed with discussions which had peace and the advocacy of peace as their theme. Defeatism was rampant.

In London, powerful elements argued that a negotiated peace was inevitable. Lord Lansdowne, an immensely respected and influential Tory magnate, member of Asquith's Coalition Cabinet and Tory leader in the House of Lords until Lloyd George became Prime Minister, had already submitted a Peace Plan as a Cabinet paper to the Asquith Government in 1916. This document had been roughly and effectively dealt with by Lord Robert Cecil who rejected the Lansdowne plan insisting that any such peace would bring final disaster to Britain.

The Lansdowne Peace Plan was widely circulated in the early days of 1917 and fully discussed in political circles throughout the year. Finally publication in the newspapers was launched in November, 1917.

Many voices were raised in support of Lord Lansdowne. Even Colonel House, envoy extraordinary and travelling representative of the President of the United States, saw Lansdowne and discussed the terms of the "Peace Letter". He wrote to the President: "We scarcely disagreed at all."[a]

More important, however, at the outset of Lloyd George's administration, was the attitude of McKenna, who had been First Lord of the Admiralty in Asquith's government and who was the most formidable and important Liberal spokesman of the peace programme. He got support from Runciman, another influential Liberal.

Where did Asquith stand? He had been the all-powerful First Minister. He had the confidence of the King. His immediate followers were loyal to him. His political character was good; there was no blemish on his party consistency. He was trusted by the Liberal leaders, agents, managers, and in a lesser measure, by their Press.

Would he join the Lansdowne peace movement? Many predicted that he would become the leader of such a party on a convenient occasion.

Walter Page was the American Ambassador in London. He was fanatically attached to the British cause and favourable to Lloyd George's administration. He had entry to every section of political opinion in the community. When the Lansdowne letter was the subject of discussion and dispute in the private parlours and the dining-rooms of London, he reported to the President:

> Lord Lansdowne and his friends (how numerous they are nobody knows) are the loudest spokesmen of such a peace as might be made now, especially if Belgium can be restored and an agreement reached about Alsace-Lorraine. But it is talked much of in Asquith's circle that the time may come when this policy (its baldness somewhat modified) may be led by Mr. Asquith. He has up to this time patriotically supported the Government. But he is very generally suspected of intrigue, and his friends openly predict that at what they regard as a favourable moment he will take this cue.[b]

Fortunately for Britain, at the beginning of the fateful year of 1917 the men of little faith had been expelled. The men of war were in complete control of the administration. Lloyd George and Bonar Law were supported by colleagues who thought as they did and who believed in a fight until victory came. There was no room for doubters in the Ministry.

There had been in the past a great controversy between Eastern and Western schools of military strategy—a dispute whether troops should be sent to the Middle East to attempt the conquest of the Balkans, or whether all military resources should be concentrated on the battle of the Western Front.

Nearly all of the generals were the exponents of the Western strategy. Lloyd George and a few politicians expounded the plan for "victory in the East". Even after he became Prime Minister, he continued to dwell upon the benefits of an Eastern venture, but he could not carry with him the majority of his own Cabinet colleagues.

Indeed the expedition to Gallipoli, and the disaster that overtook it, had given the opponents of war in the East an argument so powerful that the issue, though frequently raised, never assumed any reality.

It had become obvious that the West was the principal theatre of war and it was impossible to contemplate any substantial diversion of the troops from that theatre.

Thus although the controversy was carried on with every appearance of a genuine struggle, the movement had really lost its force and strength. The opponents of any more Eastern escapades had little difficulty in vanquishing the arguments of the Eastern schools.

The victory of the generals over Lloyd George's Eastern yearnings gave them courage and confidence to persist in another and much more dangerous division of opinion.

The generals claimed the right to deal with the various campaigns free from political interference.

The politicians declared that, with the whole male population engaged in the war, political direction and civilian control was essential.

The generals maintained that the politicians, by their muddling, were responsible for the various defeats in the field. The politicians, for their part, blamed the generals for the military misfortunes and for the large and horrifying casualty lists.

Such was the domestic atmosphere at the beginning of the third year of war when I take up my story. This conflict between soldiers and politicians was the dominating element in the political crises which followed one after the other, almost to the day of victory.

The underlying issues of all these events may be summarised as follows:

The politicians gave little credit to the generals.

The generals denounced the politicians.

The soldiers and sailors serving in the forces had little confidence in either.

The public had no heroes.

Now it has been my intention in this work to describe these disputes and the personalities involved. I have attempted to give an account of the conduct and dispositions of many public men responsible for the higher direction of the war.

It is not my purpose to write a chronological record of the political events.

Two volumes of *Politicians and the War*, written and published by me many years ago, were an earnest attempt to provide an impartial political history from the outbreak of war to the end of the Asquith administration.*

The present work is not a continuation or a sequel to that historical record. In this book I make no attempt to deal with the general course of political events; I tell only of the crises which emerged from the general trend. They are the highlights of political history, the moments when the politicians take the centre of the stage. Certainly these politicians live and thrive in crises and on them. And it is then that public men can be studied to the best advantage.

A chance remark, a single story, a characteristic gesture may give us the man himself, as a sudden flickering flame lights up the twilight room and shows the cold or coloured face and figure set in some imperishable pose against the sombre background of history.

My labours must not be judged by literary merit. But I am in a position to give an account

* It is my intention some day to bring out a political history already in form which will be entitled *The Age of Baldwin*. And my hopes are centred on another work on the Second World War. For this task I have gathered an immense mass of material.

of vital moments in the course of great events from personal knowledge and experience.

It may be asked: "Were you there?" I was there!

I have known and worked with all the principal characters in this narrative.

My intimate knowledge of events and persons may justify me in the belief that this record might prove to be of real value to the historians of another generation.

With this brief introduction, I launch my chapters with the confidence that I have written with complete impartiality and entirely independent of party or personal affiliations.

CHAPTER I

THE CLEVEREST MAN IN
THE KINGDOM

IN 1917 my position in public life was that of a
frustrated and disappointed seeker after employment. I had hoped to get office in the Lloyd
George administration; I had failed. The best I
was offered was a tiny office of no importance.
This I had refused. I had stumbled into the House
of Lords. But I had no intention whatever of
being relegated to a dying House and I could not
take very seriously a hereditary chamber in which
I had no faith.

No sooner had I fallen into a place in the hereditary system than the absurdity and futility of the
political structure of the House of Lords became
clear to me. Certainly I had no respect for the
aristocracy as such, and no lingering admiration
for the doings of the squire and his family.

I was, of course, happy in the honour that
had been conferred on me, and the title gave
me real pleasure. Since then I have come to
take a different view, believing myself to have
lacked sound judgement when I accepted the
peerage.

I still kept a room at the War Office.* And for three of the leaders there I had great respect. Sir William Robertson was Chief of the Imperial General Staff. His deputy was Sir Robert Whigham. Sir Reginald Brade was Permanent Under-Secretary.

I was on good terms with Robertson, friendly with Whigham and intimate with Brade.

Robertson appealed to me because of his sturdy independence. He was a man whose origin was humble and who had forged steadily ahead in the army, from Private to General and at last Chief of the Imperial General Staff.† His advancement was the outcome of character, ability and determination. They are rare qualities.

Whigham, too, was a man with whom I found it easy to deal on agreeable terms. He came from the same stock as I did—a stout, sturdy Scottish family. We often talked and there were many occasions when he gave me sound advice and good direction. I was to see much of him in the future.

Brade was my friend. He was well educated, a good conversationalist, a real wit, loyal to his friends, and devoted to his task. He was a good companion and much sought after in political circles. He was short of stature, and had a pleasing countenance with a big head which gave him an appearance of importance. I was devoted to him.

* I was Canadian Government Representative for affairs concerning the Canadian Army and dealing with personnel and supply problems.

† The Chief of the Imperial General Staff was responsible for overall strategy and policy and was the Military Adviser to the Secretary of State for War and to the War Cabinet.

These three were destined to play dominating and important parts in the events of this era.

With the appearance of Lloyd George as Secretary of State for War in the summer of 1916, friction prevailed between these Army Chiefs and their civilian Minister. The reasons are easily explained. When Lord Kitchener, the former Secretary of State, was to be removed, Asquith wanted to take over the War Office while retaining the Premiership. He was willing to leave the War Administration entirely in the keeping of Robertson.

Lloyd George also wanted the War Office. He was determined to have it. He intended to deprive Robertson of some of the power already possessed by him as C.I.G.S. I quote an extract from Sir Reginald Brade's Diary, dated 13th June, 1916.

> I told him (Lloyd George) of the suggestion that I had made to the Prime Minister [Asquith], viz: that the Prime Minister should retain the seals and Lord Derby* should be President of the Army Council. He said he thought this was impracticable. It would never do.

The last two sentences are written in block capitals and underlined. There is a marginal note in Brade's handwriting, as follows:

> I did not mention Lord D. by name. I said some Provincial man not a member of the Cabinet.

In the struggle that followed, Robertson and his colleagues at the War Office stoutly opposed the appointment of Lloyd George. None the less, Lloyd George became Secretary of State for War

* Lord Derby was Under-Secretary at the War Office.

on 6th July, 1916. Bitter hostilities flared up at once, and the quarrels between Lloyd George and Robertson increased in violence up to the very day that Asquith fell from power.

But now that Lloyd George was Prime Minister it seemed likely the strife would die down. Lloyd George with his increased authority, immense public popularity and freedom from intrigue and frustration from above would be strong and sure in action, thus establishing complete leadership of politicians and generals, too.

These hopes were disappointed. The generals were to claim a freedom from restraint. They demanded the sole right to determine all military issues even though their decisions would have repercussions for the whole population of Britain, soldier and civilian, man and woman, shopkeeper and banker, financial and commercial, every section of the community.

Lloyd George found himself exposed, too, at the very outset of his Ministry to pressure from newspapers. Word had been passed to Lord Northcliffe* and others that the new administration sought to send troops to the East in defiance of military advice. The Generals claimed that all available resources should be directed to the Western Front.

A threat was spoken to the new Prime Minister by Lord Northcliffe in the early days of January, 1917. Sir Reginald Brade wrote to me on the 6th, one month after the new government was formed:

* Proprietor of The Times, the Daily Mail, the Evening News and the Weekly Dispatch.

46

6/1/17

Punch

My dear May:

You ought to know, but not from me, that L.G. & Northcliffe quarrelled in Paris when they met during this week & the latter threatened to break the former ..!

Thought for the Day

Odi profanum vulgus et arceo

[signature]

A QUARREL IN PARIS

You ought to know, but not from me, that L.G. and Northcliffe quarrelled in Paris when they met during this week and the latter threatened to break the former. Salonika was the matter in dispute. L.G. and Derby* are quite friendly.

Northcliffe was the most powerful and vigorous of the newspaper proprietors. In the rivalry between politicians and generals his attitude was not in doubt. He had "favoured the removal of Asquith because he considered that greater power should be given to Haig† and Robertson. . . . At times he used language suggesting that he almost favoured a military dictatorship."[a] In the opinion of Mr. Stanley Morison, the historian of *The Times*, "To the right soldiers he would have given almost unlimited power."[b]

But it was one thing for vague aspirations towards military rule to exist in Northcliffe's mind and among members of the public in general. It was quite another when a clash was threatened between soldiers and politicians which promised to become a struggle for power. Then the support of Northcliffe's newspapers, and most of the Conservative journals (*Morning Post, Globe*) on the side of the generals would be critical indeed.

An entry in Brade's diary gives a clear indication of the intense hostility directed against Lloyd George and the civilian Administration by the Military High Command.

---

* Lord Derby was by this time Secretary of State for War and Lloyd George was Prime Minister.

† Sir Douglas Haig's official title was Commander-in-Chief of the British Forces in France. He made immediate decisions there, though responsible for his conduct to the Chief of the Imperial General Staff.

I suggested to Lord Derby that I should try to see Rufus Isaacs (Lord Reading) and impress upon him the difficulties, and especially the certainty that L.G. would find himself up against the soldiers and *might not* get the best of it. Derby agreed and I accordingly wrote the letter.

It was my habit at that time to talk over my political problems with F. E. Smith, the Attorney-General. Early in January, 1917, I went to ask the advice of this wise counsellor. What would be the outcome of frictions between Lloyd George and the Military? What would be the immediate effect of traffic between the War Office and Fleet Street attributed to emissaries believed to be close to Sir William Robertson?

F. E. Smith was a man of supreme intellectual ability with an amazing power of making mistakes in the minor affairs of life. He was always the worst judge of his own affairs and the best judge of other people's affairs. His story was a tale of unbroken success in his public career. There was at that time no height to which his talent might not carry him.

He held a far bigger position than that of the usual political lawyer who becomes Attorney-General. In the Conservative Party, which was weak in public appeal and platform ability, he almost alone had only to put up a notice that he would speak in order to fill any meeting place in Britain. But the war had deprived him of his foremost weapon, since the guns abolished the mass meeting as the last word in politics.

He had been a member of the Privy Council for five years, a distinction that had come to him in the Coronation Honours when George V ascended the throne. The story of how it came to him illustrates F. E. Smith's strength and also demonstrates a certain weakness in the man.

Two Privy Councillorships in the Coronation Honours were designated for the Conservative Party. One honour was certainly destined for Bonar Law. F. E. Smith deserved the other but was not likely to get it. Balfour, who was then leader of the Conservatives, intended that it should be given to Hayes Fisher, a regular party hack.

Smith was indignant and Balfour endeavoured to assuage his wrath with a letter of explanation expressing strong personal appreciation. F. E. Smith regarded it as a bear might look on a bun at feeding time.

"Ah!" said Bonar Law, in an honest attempt to pour oil on the troubled waters, "but what a letter, F.E., to be able to show your son in future years!"

"Well," Smith retorted, "I do not know if my son has any brains, but if he has and thought I was put off with this letter he would say—'My father was a mug!' "*

F.E.'s friend, Winston Churchill, then took a hand. He persuaded the Prime Minister (Asquith) to declare that, in offering two Privy Councillorships to the Opposition, he was not giving Balfour a blank cheque, but one

* See *Appendix* IV, No. 1.

specifically made out in favour of Bonar Law
and F. E. Smith. This, however, did not settle
the issue. Balfour insisted on his own candidate,
Hayes Fisher, so Asquith, who had now committed himself to Smith, was compelled to hand
over to the Opposition three Privy Councillorships instead of two. Both F. E. Smith and Hayes
Fisher came under the wire.

When F. E. Smith heard the good news of the
impending honour he was jubilant. He said to
me, "The Conservative Party is the one for us.
What have the Liberals got to offer us? We are
sought out by Dukes; we are flattered by Mar-
chionesses; Countesses give us dinner parties.
What have the Liberals to offer us? Nothing but
the society of Knight's ladies!"

Alas, I had in my pocket a letter informing me
that I was to be in the Conservative list of Coronation knights. I had intended to tell him of my
good fortune. I was silent.

Yet only a few days after the announcement of
the new list of honours, F. E. Smith met Bonar
Law at a social party of a political character.
"Ah! Bonar," he exclaimed, "they don't want us
there for ourselves but simply for our brains."

This attitude in F. E. Smith was quite inconsistent with his social conduct. He really held to
the belief that he was sought after for himself, for
his own qualities of personality. And he had good
reason to think so. For he was brilliant and
witty. His conversation was like a flashing display
of fork lightning.

F. E. SMITH

A biting and witty tongue which spared no man and every woman. He had a soft heart

MILNER

He led the "Don't Hang the Kaiser" Party

RIDDELL

He controlled the *News of the World* and the *Church Family Newspaper*. He scattered his mercies

READING

The go-between

He was a man without nerves, physically brave to a point of recklessness; willing at any time to put his limbs on the board as cheerfully as a smaller stake.

Before the year was over, the Government sent him out upon an oratorical tour throughout the United States. His labours there have been recorded by him in a small book[c] which is a living embodiment of his Tory democratic principles, for after telling in the opening passage of his hurried departure from a Christmas party at Blenheim Palace it goes on to say that when he reached New York he dined with Miss Maxine Elliott (a popular Shakespearean actress) and sealed his departure by a tennis party with Miss Elsie Janis (a well-known entertainer of the Danny Kaye type).

Throughout the war he adhered always in the end to Bonar Law. Yet he never swerved in devoted and sacrificing friendship for Winston Churchill. In many ways he was in accord with Lloyd George, although he never put too much trust in the new Prime Minister.

He was throughout his career a consistent Tory, faithful to a version of the party philosophy that was not harsh or unfeeling but was full of light and sentiment and sympathy for the problems of his fellow-countrymen. In council he was sensible and prescient; in argument he was persuasive, while his methods in debate gave additional proof of his superior ability.

He was a good friend. I always thought of him as the cleverest man in the kingdom. He did not dissemble. He did not suffer fools. And of him Bonar Law said, "It would be easier for him to keep a live coal in his mouth than a witty saying."

F. E. Smith was not the man to conjure up out of nothing a menace to Lloyd George's government from generals or any other quarter. I was impressed, therefore, when he advised me to talk with Bonar Law. He believed there was a real threat to the Government. He put forward a plan for dealing with it. He recommended an immediate reorganisation of the high offices in the military command at the War Office. Why not act now? Get rid of Robertson and Haig,* too, for that matter. Both were survivors from the Asquith regime, standing in the way of the new direction. Robertson had always sought and found in Asquith protection from the fury of Lloyd George, who tried at one time to send him to Russia for the purpose of getting him out of the way.

I told F. E. Smith that Curzon, Chamberlain, Cecil and Long † had exacted a pledge from Lloyd George that he would not dismiss Haig. But there was no promise to retain Robertson. Then, "Sack him now," said F.E. in effect.

I then went off to see Bonar Law, to whom I gave my information about the developing struggle between the generals and the Prime Minister. But Bonar Law was not disposed to attach serious importance to this picture of events. He was

* Robertson was Chief of the Imperial General Staff, and Haig Commander-in-Chief in France.
† Curzon, Chamberlain, Cecil and Long were all Conservative members of Asquith's Coalition Government, holding high office.

decidedly favourable to Sir William Robertson*
and supported him in his post, expressing confidence that there would be good relations in
future between Lloyd George, now that he was
Prime Minister, and the Chief of the Imperial
General Staff. The prescience and political judgement of F. E. Smith did not move him. He spoke
of F. E. Smith as a man with the vision of an eagle
but with a blind spot in his eye.

Lloyd George shared F. E. Smith's apprehension. He was at this time nervous, perhaps unduly
nervous, about the possibility of attempts to overthrow the Government with the help of the
military and set up a new government which
would be the tool of the generals. The German
Government in 1916 had been overthrown and
replaced by Hindenburg and Ludendorff. Could
not a similar change be brought about in Britain
with Robertson playing the part of Hindenberg?

In his *War Memoirs*[e] Lloyd George wrote, at a
later date: "We were about to witness a very
determined effort—not the first nor the last—
made by this party to form a cabal which would
overthrow the existing War Cabinet and especially
its Chief, and enthrone a Government which
would be practically the nominee and menial of
this military party."

Lloyd George believed that Robertson was the
leader of the cabal. Asquith and others would
give support. Therefore the activities of the
Chief of the Imperial General Staff must be

* Bonar Law in 1916 had written to Sir Robert Borden, the Prime Minister
of Canada, saying: "in Robertson we have I believe as good a man as we could
get for the purpose."[d]

watched with anxiety. What began with obstruction would swiftly develop into a challenge to the Government which must result in the fall of the Administration or the dismissal of Robertson.

The conflict was confined at the moment to claims of prescience in military matters. Soon there would be attacks on civilian administration. Swiftly, Lloyd George believed, the military leaders might attain to a power and authority with the public excelling that of Cabinet Ministers. Then, and then only, the country would be willing to substitute what would be in effect a military dictatorship for democratic forms of government.

Lloyd George knew himself to be surrounded by political enemies, Liberals he had worsted and driven from office, Conservatives whom he could never hope to placate. A combination of ambitious generals willing to take over control of the Administration in association with political figures who were in opposition to Lloyd George's Ministry would certainly be able to turn him out in a crisis of the war.

Asquith might be a party to such a coalition, although Lloyd George did not believe that the House of Commons would turn him out of office in order to put Asquith back in power. Asquith had been given a chance and had muffed it. But Churchill was a formidable figure and Sir Edward Carson* was most dangerous.

* Carson was, of course, a member of Lloyd George's Administration. But he could not be described as a colleague. He was disgruntled and dissatisfied. The day before Lloyd George became Prime Minister, Carson was consulted about everything. The day after, nothing. Lloyd George made use of the Ulster leader when necessary and tried to push him as far out of sight as possible when no longer required.

Although there was always a great deal of newspaper support for the conception of military control of war-time policy, Lloyd George firmly believed that the Press campaign flowed from War Office sources.

Here again is an illuminative extract selected by me from an earlier entry in the diary of Sir Reginald Brade:

> Met L.G. at the office door. He suggested that I should tell W.R. [Sir William Robertson] to stop the press campaign—See D.C.* Two could play at that game and he, L.G., could do it better than most. So far he had not started.

There were many indications in the Press of the gathering storm which developed over the next year.

It is expedient to quote now from newspapers even though criticism developed slowly. It is often a practice in newspaper offices to give a new Administration a spell of repose from opposition.

The loudest and most consistent voice in the future "press campaign" was not the *Daily Chronicle* but the *Globe* newspaper. It spoke wistfully of the advantages which Germany enjoyed through the military dictatorship of Hindenburg and Ludendorff. At first the *Globe* said that only the direst necessity should induce Britain to follow the German example. The newspaper in course of time overcame its own reluctance and asked the rhetorical question, "Is there any other means of bringing this war to a swift and successful end

* The *Daily Chronicle*.

than by committing the conduct of it, and all that implies, without reserve to the greatest soldier we can find?"[f] It was not long before the *Globe* declared flatly, "Democracy has proved a failure under the stress of war.... In fact to be successful we must have a clean cut from democracy to autocracy 'for the period.'"[g]

The case that the *Globe* put bluntly the *Morning Post* argued with greater subtlety. It suggested that there should be two Cabinets, one for War and one for Civil Affairs, each under the leadership of whatever Prime Minister might be chosen, but the War Cabinet to consist of the Service Chiefs with the Secretary of State for War and the First Lord of the Admiralty.[h] The proposal fell short of military dictatorship but it would have increased enormously the power and authority of the generals. A government shared between generals and civilians would, in due course, have become a generals' government.

Such were the views of two important Conservative newspapers though the timing of their hostile outburst was delayed. There could be no doubt where the Northcliffe Press would stand if the movement for military control over policy gathered force.

As for the generals themselves, the men on whom the burden of power would fall should civilian administration be discredited, there was talk and there were expectations. General Sir Frederick Maurice, writing before the debate to which he has given his name, found it necessary to make a disavowal: "I am by descent and conviction as sincere a democrat as the Prime Minister, and the last thing I desire is to see the government of our country in the hands of the soldiers."[i] The declaration in support of democracy did credit to General Maurice, even though he failed to name the colleagues at the War Office who sought to place the government of the country in the hands of soldiers.

Ministers and others were well aware of the propaganda which threatened to undermine the Government. The effects of the Press campaign have been sardonically summed up by a great historian, Winston Churchill:

> The foolish doctrine was preached to the public through innumerable agencies that Generals and Admirals must be right on war matters, and civilians of all kinds must be wrong. These erroneous conceptions were inculcated billion-fold by the newspapers under the crudest forms. The feeble or presumptuous politician is portrayed cowering in his office, intent in the crash of the world on Party intrigues or personal glorification, fearful of responsibility, incapable of aught save shallow phrase-making. To him enters the calm, noble, resolute figure of the great Commander by land or sea, resplendent in uniform, glittering with decorations, irradiated with the lustre of the hero, shod with the science and armed with the panoply of war. This stately figure, devoid of the slightest thought of self, offers his clear far-sighted guidance and counsel for vehement action or artifice or wise delay. But his advice is rejected; his sound plans put aside; his courageous initiative baffled by political chatterboxes and incompetents. As well, it was suggested, might a great surgeon, about to operate with sure science and the study of a lifetime upon a desperate case, have his

arm jogged or his hand impeded, or even his lancet snatched from him, by some agitated relation of the patient. Such was the picture presented to the public, and such was the mood which ruled.[j]

Given a sufficiently grave turn in Britain's military fortunes, the "bumbling politicians" might be set aside and the god-like generals elevated to the summit of power. The process would probably be accomplished in two stages. First a new government would be set up dependent on military support but with civilian ministers in the home departments. And in due course this would be followed by military rule, pure and simple.

Against the background of fluctuating war, of newspaper agitation, of a precarious government and nervous ministers, the quarrel between soldiers and politicians raged, a furious struggle marked by many complex manœuvres and claiming distinguished victims.

Where would the dissensions end? Could the Prime Minister stand before the storm? Would his government go the way of the Asquith Administration?

Many political prophets predicted ruin. Few were the stalwarts who gave complete faith and undeviating confidence to the new administration.

CHAPTER II

THE FALL OF A GIANT

WHEN Churchill denounced in resounding terms "the foolish doctrine" of military control as opposed to civilian domination he was, of course, delivering an attack on Lord Northcliffe and his newspaper publications, *The Times* and the *Daily Mail*, the *Evening News* and the *Weekly Dispatch*.

And, indeed, Lord Northcliffe's position in British public life, in December 1916, when Lloyd George became Prime Minister, was a formidable one. He was fifty-one years of age and had built up a newspaper empire of enormous power and influence over which he was the undisputed ruler. Not only did he own *The Times*, politically of high importance, but he also controlled half the daily newspapers sold in London.*

To-day no parallel exists to Northcliffe's domination of newspaper sales in the metropolis. The circulation of my newspapers is the nearest approach to it. Beaverbrook Newspapers hold one-fifth of the London newspaper market. But Northcliffe held one-half.†

* Writing to H. W. Wilson, Lord Northcliffe declared that his Press was the sole source of his power. He boasted that his position was new to the world of affairs, but that he preferred it to any other as a means of getting things done.

† Beaverbrook overall circulation is now three times as great as that of Lord Northcliffe in 1917.

It conferred on him a power over the public mind and over war-time Government which he had already exerted with effect. At the outbreak of hostilities, he had defeated an attempt by Asquith to place Lord Haldane at the War Office. He had forced the Government to take in Lord Kitchener. Then, within eighteen months, he had carried out a press campaign against Kitchener which led to his being sent on a mission to Russia in 1916 on which he was drowned. Again, it was Lord Northcliffe's agitation over the Shell Shortage that had ensured the creation of a Ministry of Munitions with Lloyd George at its head.

In effecting these major changes in the administration, Northcliffe made use of a style of journalism which was highly distinctive and belonged to his character. In private conversation he never conducted an argument; in journalism, he used the same method. I once entertained him to lunch with Bonar Law and the talk turned to a discussion of the "Stomach Tax" and the election prospects. "You will lose the Election," Northcliffe said to Bonar Law. On being asked his reasons for holding this opinion, he simply repeated, "You will lose the Election."

He hammered and reiterated his themes until the point was firmly driven home.

Northcliffe may have been wrong. No one can tell. War put an end to the impending election.

For all that Lord Northcliffe's was an attractive personality; and he was capable of sudden flashes of humour that relieved the strain of his dictatorial manner. On one occasion, he instructed his newspapers to offer a substantial money reward for the discovery of a motorist who had killed a pedestrian and driven on. By an unlucky chance it turned out that the car belonged to one of his brothers, though at the time of the accident it was being driven by a chauffeur. Northcliffe never failed to remind his brother about this incident. Years later, when it was suggested that a reward should be offered for the apprehension of a train murderer, Northcliffe replied, "Better see where my brother was that day."

Northcliffe was an immensely likeable and generous man with spectacular achievements to his credit. He raised the standard of living in Fleet Street. He set up a new system of journalism. *The Times* was dying when he took charge of it and living when Northcliffe died. The man was great.

Lord Northcliffe's home was at Sutton Place, a historic and magnificent Elizabethan residence near Guildford. He spent much of his time at Broadstairs. More and more, he chose to supervise his papers from this retreat, enjoying the delights of a country villa, and retiring to bed, as was his custom, at 9.30 every evening. He avoided the social intercourse customary to a man of his position; little was known of his private life. His immediate associates may have known of his mysterious social relations. But political circles were uninformed.

In politics, Northcliffe's position was a nebulous one; he had once stood as a Tory candidate but he never had more than a very loose foothold in the Conservative camp.

His influence, however, particularly when he was assaulting the public reputations of ministers, was something which had constantly to be reckoned with. Politicians, therefore, feared and hated him. Northcliffe, for his part, never attempted to understand them or to cultivate relations of amity with them.

In the political crisis of December 1916, Northcliffe came down strongly on the side of the anti-Asquith faction. He did this because he sincerely believed that the Asquith government was a government of weak men and, as such, a peril to the country. He used his papers to urge that they should be replaced and to prepare public opinion for the reception of a new and determined administration.

His attitude was thus of the greatest value to Lloyd George; but it was given independently of that statesman and not by pre-arrangement with him.[a]

In fact, Lloyd George's relationship with Northcliffe was not a close one and there was little confidence between them. Northcliffe's sympathies lay not with the politicians but with the generals. Shortly before the fall of the Asquith Government he had declared in favour of something approaching a military dictatorship under Haig and Robertson.[b] Lloyd George later disparagingly declared that, ever since 1916, Northcliffe had become "the mere kettledrum of Sir Douglas Haig, and the mouth-organ of Sir William Robertson"[c]—the one Commander-in-Chief, the other Chief of the General Staff.

Lloyd George's distrust of Northcliffe was shared by his supporters in the Government. Four important Conservative ministers, in fact, so strongly resented the activities of the powerful Press Lord that they made it a condition of their acceptance of office under Lloyd George that Northcliffe should be given no part in the new administration.[d]

Thus, at the beginning of 1917, despite the power and influence he had built up in Fleet Street, Lord Northcliffe was hated and rejected by the political leaders. The Government had been manned at the price of his exclusion from it, and the Prime Minister had made plain his unwillingness to work with him. An attempt which I had made to secure a reconciliation between them, soon after Lloyd George moved to Downing Street, had come to nothing.[e]

In the middle of 1917, however, Lord Northcliffe's political fortunes entered a new phase. At the end of May, he was invited by the British War Cabinet to head a British Mission to the United States of America.

It was a surprising development and behind it there were complex motives.

At this time, Lloyd George was contemplating bringing Churchill into the Government, appointing the most unpopular political figure in England to be his colleague. It was a step fraught with difficulties, one of which was the fact that Lord Northcliffe's criticism of Churchill had been most bitter. Hence it was of definite concern to Lloyd George that the powerful force of Northcliffe's opposition should, on this occasion, be out of the way.

Now the idea was a splendid one. But how might it be received in the inner government circles? It was certain to provoke a considerable resistance, as events were to show.

The difficulty of bringing Churchill into the Government was serious indeed, but the difficulty of winning approval for the appointment of Northcliffe to an important American Mission was also immense. Trouble would be the portion of the Prime Minister; and well he knew it. Thus it was that Lloyd George decided to go about his business with considerable caution.

First he persuaded Bonar Law to endorse the Northcliffe appointment. He said nothing to the Conservative leader about Churchill.

Then he called together the Heads of Departments concerned with American purchases including the Admiralty, War Office, Munitions, Food, etc. Putting the question by the system adopted by the Scottish Divines who prepared the Shorter Catechism, the Prime Minister asked: Should Northcliffe represent us in America? Answer: Yes, Northcliffe.

Thereafter the Cabinet colleagues were consulted and on 25th May, 1917, approval was given to the choice of his Lordship, subject to the views

ASQUITH

Uniformed indolence, gentle indifference

NORTHCLIFFE

"I would as soon go for a sunny evening stroll round Walton Heath with a grasshopper as try and work with Northcliffe." (Lloyd George)

and opinions of Balfour, the Foreign Secretary—then completing a wartime mission in America—and also of the British Ambassador in Washington, Sir Cecil Spring-Rice.

Balfour had already requested that the question of representation on a permanent mission should be postponed until his return. He wished to present his considered view to the Government. A worthy representative must be chosen to take up a task of such importance. He did not look on Northcliffe as that "worthy representative". He cabled his earnest opposition from Ottawa. Spring-Rice, the Ambassador, was frankly and outspokenly hostile to the Northcliffe appointment.

Lloyd George, faced with this response, which in effect amounted to the rejection of his candidate, determined to find another way round the problem.

The American Ambassador in London, Mr. Walter Page, was consulted. He gave enthusiastic approval of Lord Northcliffe, transmitting his glowing message of support through the British Foreign Office.

The Cabinet met on Wednesday, 30th May. After hearing the message of Mr. Page, the Prime Minister was given the necessary authority to invite Lord Northcliffe to head a British Mission to the United States for the purpose of co-ordinating the machinery of the various branches of the administration there. Evidently the Ministers who had been consulted forgot all about the decision to seek the opinion of Balfour and Spring-Rice whose hostile views were not reported. The Cabinet agreed without further debate to the appointment of Lord Northcliffe and the offer was made to him that same day.

Northcliffe responded with enthusiasm. Indeed the invitation to represent his country in this important capacity was most attractive to him. For here was an opportunity he had long awaited. It was the first public task he had been asked to undertake and it marked a starting-point in his political office-holding career. Northcliffe accepted with joy; his role as critic and spokesman discarded in a moment. He was off without a backward glance. Within thirty-six hours he had boarded a liner for America.

From the ship he addressed a pencilled note to his brother:

Adieu, my dear Cecil. I was unable to find you ere I made my sudden and very unwilling exit.[g]

Northcliffe was on the high seas before the political pundits had observed his departure.

There was about his flight that characteristic of the flamboyant and the dramatic that always marked the major gestures in Northcliffe's life. He set off alone, without waiting for his staff, and he took elaborate precautions to veil his departure in secrecy. Before sailing, he arranged with the newspapers that his appointment should be released to the British and American Press just before his arrival in New York. Thus he made certain of balking opposition that was sure to come. He showed prescience.

There was indeed a big resistance movement. The tempest raged for many days, developing into a whirlwind of trouble. There were three separate storm centres: Northcliffe's unpopularity in political circles which stood high; the large group of enemies he had smitten who had been for long patiently lying low; and also the opposition to the Northcliffe appointment by Balfour, Secretary of State for Foreign Affairs.

In his *War Memoirs*, the Prime Minister gives the following account of the selection of Lord Northcliffe. The War Cabinet, writes Lloyd George, met on 25th May to discuss the appointment.

"Those Heads of Departments concerned who were present were of opinion that Lord Northcliffe might be a very suitable person for this appointment, and the War Cabinet decided that a telegram should be transmitted to the British Ambassador at Washington as well as to Mr. Balfour, asking them for an early expression of their views on the proposed appointment. A satisfactory response was cabled by Mr. Balfour on 28th May."[*]

But other evidence refutes this story of the satisfactory response of Balfour. Lloyd George had forgotten that the very contrary was the case.

R. S. Baker, in his book *Woodrow Wilson Life and Letters*, quotes a letter written to Wilson, dated 31st May, from his political adviser Colonel House reporting that the British Ambassador had been to see him very much perturbed over a message Balfour had received from his Government about the Northcliffe appointment and had shown House Balfour's reply, which "was a very earnest argument against sending any such representative here at this time."[i]

An examination of the diaries of Colonel House confirms this statement. It gives conclusive testimony to Balfour's very great hostility to Northcliffe's appointment to America.

Lloyd George's own papers disclose another facet of this extraordinary story.

Asquith had come into possession of a detailed account of Balfour's unfavourable reply to the telegram of 25th May. The Prime Minister at once assumed that the Foreign Office had circulated the Balfour reply to Asquith. An enquiry drew from Lord Robert Cecil, the Minister in charge during Balfour's absence, a curt and formal denial. I quote it here in full:

Prime Minister,
I find that Balfour's telegrams about Northcliffe did *not* go to Mr. Asquith. So the leakage must be elsewhere.

R.C.

Lloyd George was in fact furious about this leakage of information which could have been used most dangerously against him by his political opponents. Suspicion fell heavily on various members of the Government.

Edwin Montagu, who was serving at that time on the Committee of Reconstruction, was sus-

Robert Cecil

Prime Minister

I find that Balfour's telegrams about Northcliffe did not go to ~~Mr Secretary~~ Mr Asquith. So the leakage must be elsewhere.

R. C.

LORD CECIL TO LLOYD GEORGE

pected of making disclosures to Asquith. But Montagu had no access to Cabinet Minutes and he was therefore exonerated from the charge.

Sir Maurice Hankey was Secretary of the War Cabinet. There was no reason for his intervention except that he had been a close friend of the Asquiths and was still on good terms with them. Certainly he was aware of everything that was going on.

He wrote Lloyd George a full disclaimer of any indiscretion.[k] He denied that there was any possibility of his having let slip a hint of Balfour's telegram to anyone in the Asquith entourage. Indeed, he was at such pains to dispel any possibility of doubt in Lloyd George that he accounted for his social activities since the telegram had been received.

There was no reason for anxiety about the "leakage" so far as Asquith was concerned. He made no public reference to the Balfour message. But others were to exploit the opportunity, and with good results for themselves.

Now while Lord Northcliffe was crossing the Atlantic in one direction, Balfour was crossing it in the other. When he arrived in England on 9th June, Lord Northcliffe's appointment had already been announced.

For it was on 7th June, 1917, that news of the Northcliffe Mission was released in the British and American papers. A Press Bureau statement published by the majority of London newspapers declared:

The War Cabinet have invited Lord Northcliffe to go to America to co-ordinate the work of the several British Missions that are already established there and to continue the task so successfully initiated in that respect by Mr. Balfour. Lord Northcliffe has accepted this invitation and has already sailed for the United States.

The Times carried arresting and exciting headlines. "Lord Northcliffe's Task. Successor to Mr. Balfour." Fury was let loose. Successor to Mr. Balfour indeed! Balfour's bitter enemy appointed to a diplomatic post in Washington. Indignation and denunciation in and out of Parliament flowed from Opposition, Government supporters, Press and public, and particularly from the personal friends of Balfour.

Bonar Law, Leader in the House of Commons, was deluged with hostile questions. Had Mr. Balfour been consulted and was it upon his advice that Northcliffe went to America? Bonar Law replied that Northcliffe's appointment had been confirmed before Balfour's return and that there had been no opportunity for consultation.[']

In the House of Lords, Curzon's answers increased the state of confusion and added to the growing crisis. The *Daily News* reported that, asked whether Balfour had been consulted, Lord Curzon, "displaying considerable uneasiness, remained silent but was pressed for a reply. Rising, with marked reluctance, he said: 'I cannot possibly give an answer to that question without consulting Mr. Balfour.'"[''] The critics, comparing Bonar Law and Curzon, swiftly seized upon the confusion. There was a field day in Parliament. The

war was forgotten while the critics of the Administration tried to trip up the Government.

Lord Curzon, indeed, found himself in a position of some difficulty in the House of Lords
where attacks came from several noblemen who
were familiar with the substance of Balfour's
disapproval to the appointment. Curzon disclaimed all Government responsibility for the
announcement in *The Times*, assuring the House
that there was no analogy whatsoever between
the appointment of Lord Northcliffe and that of
Mr. Balfour.

Criticism broke loose in the Press. The *Daily
Chronicle* seized upon the inconsistencies in the
Ministers' explanations." The *Daily News* considered the choice of representative a "humiliation" to the country.° The voice of the *Morning
Post* too was raised in loud astonishment and
alarm.ᵖ

Growing public opinion hostile to Northcliffe,
with censure upon the Prime Minister, was widespread. David Davies, M.P., faithful and devoted
follower and unpaid secretary, wrote to Lloyd
George:

> If Northcliffe is to go to U.S.A. as head of the
> British Mission you will be making a damn bad
> appointment and you will raise a devil of a storm in
> the liberal party, which is just what you want to avoid
> just now. Northcliffe is one of the biggest intriguers
> and most unscrupulous people in this country. It is a
> gratuitous insult to the Americans to send him there
> —he will do more harm in a week than Balfour has
> done good in a month. He is not a business man—in

the sense that you want for this job. If you are sending him there to be rid of him, you are making a huge mistake. The restless devil will be back here in less than two months, having in the meantime played hell all round and injured your reputation. Here it will be said that you are afraid of the Harmsworth Press. Rothermere at the War Office; Cecil (Harmsworth) in the Garden City;* Northcliffe in New York. . . . We shall soon have a Government of the Harmsworths, thro' the Harmsworths, and for the Harmsworth Press.[9]

So much had been said and such furious attacks were being made, that Lloyd George gave a sharp and devastating answer to his old friend and supporter. Davies was dismissed from the Secretariat, and with contempt and derision.

While Northcliffe's appointment upset both Parliament and the Press in England, the intimation was to prove distressing to the administration on the other side of the Atlantic.

Although warm approval for the Northcliffe Mission had been secured from the American Ambassador in London, no attempt had been made to seek the President's consent, and no overtures were made to the State Department in Washington. Instead, on 31st May, Sir William Wiseman, chief of the British Intelligence Service in Washington, submitted a memorandum on the War Mission to Colonel House. Wiseman, a young man of thirty-two, had served in France before taking up his post. He had got on to good terms with Colonel House, and through

* Garden City was the name given to the yard of 10 Downing Street, where huts were set up for the overflow of secretaries.

him had influenced the President. Their relations developed into intimacy, and House in his memoirs speaks of Wiseman with admiration and affection. Wiseman's memorandum outlined the nature of the work to be undertaken and announced that the British War Cabinet proposed to appoint Lord Northcliffe.[r]

The proposal was received with genuine dismay in America. Frederick Dixon, the editor of the *Christian Science Monitor*, wrote to Balfour:

> ... Whatever induced the Government to send Lord Northcliffe here? May I explain hastily that this is not a question to which I expect an answer. It is merely a horrified note of exclamation. I thought everybody knew that the gentleman was regarded here as the British Mr. Hearst. ... The fact is, if I may so say, that I should think a man less a persona grata it would have been difficult to find, nor is it very wise surely to have as a government representative, in any way, a man with a journalistic claque always rubbing the skin off its hands, in its exertions.[s]

In official circles there was stout resistance. The appointment was particularly unacceptable to the President.

Northcliffe, self-educated and unruly, was the man least calculated to appeal to President Wilson. Hence, when the news came to him from Colonel House, the President sent an immediate rejoinder:

> Action mentioned in your letter of yesterday would be most unwise and still more unwise the choice of the person named.[t]

The appointment was equally unwelcome to Colonel House. He wrote to Wilson:

> I am sorry Northcliffe is coming, I thought Balfour's cable had headed him off . . . I am afraid his visit may stir up the anti-British feeling that at present is lying dormant."

The opinion of the State Department was so strong that the Secretary of State, Robert Lansing, sought to prevent the dispatch of the Mission.

In the event, Lansing's intervention was answered by the arrival of Northcliffe in New York.

President Wilson was thus confronted with a *fait accompli*. His hand was forced. And he was obliged to accept the appointment. Northcliffe's swift departure from Great Britain had clinched the job.

But recognition was most grudgingly given. As Northcliffe came ashore Colonel House advised the President that, as the British Government had given Northcliffe the widest possible powers, "it would therefore seem necessary to give him proper consideration".

But he added that, at his suggestion, Wiseman was advising Northcliffe not to talk through the Press and not to attempt to force his opinion upon the American people."

In fact, Northcliffe took the initiative. On the morning of his arrival in New York he telephoned to Wiseman, who was at that moment in the office of an American official.

"Is that you, Sir William Wiseman? The Prime Minister told me to get in touch with you as soon as I landed. I have been disgracefully treated. There was no one from the Embassy to meet me and no arrangements have been made for my staff, not even a secretary. I am cabling the Prime Minister to say that after this disgraceful treatment I am returning at once."

Wiseman, thinking the conversation unsuited to a public telephone, proposed to go and see Northcliffe.

"By all means," Northcliffe replied, "come and lunch with me at the St. Regis Hotel."

Arriving there, Wiseman found himself one of about ten guests, among whom were T. P. O'Connor, William Randolph Hearst and Paderewski, the Polish pianist and patriot. Paderewski was seated on Northcliffe's right and Hearst on his left. The atmosphere was strained, although Northcliffe seemed to be quite unconscious of this. For Hearst's newspapers were violently anti-British and Paderewski's sympathies were, of course, passionately on the side of Britain. He would not speak a word to Hearst, and Wiseman almost imagined that he was fingering his knife.

Northcliffe—now completely restored in temper —turned to the guest on his left, and said: "Hearst, I have known you for a long time, you are a poor journalist, you know."

In British official circles the chatter was not directed to Hearst. Everybody concentrated on criticism of Northcliffe. His appointment was particularly disagreeable to Sir Cecil Spring-Rice, the British Ambassador, who imagined he had suffered during the war from direct attacks in the Northcliffe Press.

Lord Northcliffe's reception at the Embassy was therefore a dramatic one. Later he wrote a lively description of it to Lloyd George's secretary, J. T. Davies.

My reception at the hands of the British Ambassador could not have been worse [he recorded].

I was not received on my arrival here even by the British Consul, who excused himself by telling me that, although he knew I was coming, he had not been formally notified by the Embassy. The Embassy excused themselves by saying that they were told from London to keep the matter entirely secret.

It was not secret because I was met by the usual gang of reporters, photographers, and cinematographers. That didn't matter, but it necessitated my reading to the members of the Commission my agreement with the Government, to prove my authority.

Sir Cecil Spring-Rice is an odd person. He is under the obsession that anybody who comes here is a reflection on himself. He was rude to Sir Hardman Lever and ruder to me.

Here is an account of an amazing scene which took place in his room at the Embassy, which I dictated immediately after my return . . .

"In the evening—after introducing me all day to a number of the Ministers—Sir Cecil gave a dinner to me at the Embassy. He asked me in the afternoon to come a little beforehand as he wished to go into a few private matters. I went.

"He was sitting at a table before his red boxes, and, suddenly looking up, produced a cutting from the pro-German *Evening Post* which had appeared prior to my arrival and which said, as far as I can remember, that it was odd that a man who had criticised the Ambassador in scareheads and articles (a concoction) should be coming to this appointment.

"He then suddenly rose, looked at me in a very queer way, and pointing his finger at me, said: 'You are my enemy. Apart from these criticisms, you inserted four years ago an anonymous attack in *The Times* which nearly killed me; *and Lady Spring-Rice declines to receive you on that account.*'—(There are, fortunately, other charming ladies in Washington!)

"I replied that I had never criticised him. He rejoined that he was criticised in a letter to *The Times* for his prolonged absence from the Embassy and for travelling on German ships; that his absence was due to his health, and to diplomatic circumstances which he could not publicly explain.

"I observed that, as this was his view of my visit, I proposed to leave the house, and I walked towards the door with the intention of so doing, when he rushed after me, put out his hand, and said: 'We have to work together whatever we may feel about each other.'

"I accepted his hand, and the incident was fortunately closed at that moment by the announcement of the French Ambassador.'"*

Spring-Rice gave an account of the Northcliffe incident to his chief, the Foreign Secretary, Balfour, on 13th July. It does not convey an identical record of the interview. It may be described in the words of the Scottish Psalter as "Another version of the same".

When Lord Northcliffe arrived, he sent for Gaunt*
and Wiseman and complained very bitterly that the
Embassy had not sent to meet him at the Dock. He
said it was an intentional insult and that he felt inclined
to go home again. They explained to him that strict
orders had been given to keep his movements secret. . .

On the day of his arrival, Tom Spring-Rice† and
Gaunt met him at the station with a message from me
that I was attending an entertainment in honour of the
French Scientific mission but would go at once to his
lodging if he wished to see me that night. He
preferred according to his habit to go early to bed.
The next morning he called at the Embassy and I
arranged to take him to the State Department. . . . In
the evening, he dined with me to meet the Italian
and French ambassadors. . . .

. . . He asked me how it was that the opinion
seemed to prevail that there was hostility between
himself and the Embassy. I told him that, as far as I
knew, no one in the Embassy was responsible for this
impression which certainly prevailed in the press.

The cause of it was no doubt the attacks made in
his papers on several occasions against the Embassy.
Before the war he had made in *The Times* an anonymous
and libellous attack on myself which, being an official,
I was unable to resent in the manner which my
solicitors had informed me was open to me if I
desired. During the War, his paper, in conjunction
with the *Tribune*, had attacked the Embassy for not
having imitated Count Bernstorff's policy as regards
the press. This also we had not resented and had made
no reply, but of course the impression prevailed that
his attitude towards the Embassy was as hostile now
as it had been before. I said that under present
circumstances it would be childish and wicked to allow

* Captain Guy Reginald Gaunt (later Admiral Gaunt), Naval Attaché for the
United States.
† Hon. Thomas Spring-Rice, Second Secretary at the British Embassy in
Washington.

personal antagonisms to prevail over the public advantage. He entirely agreed and our relations have been very pleasant and friendly.*

After this opening storm, Lord Northcliffe settled down to his tasks. His responsibilities raised him up. He showed traits and qualities which surprised his critics and comforted his friends. Certainly at this time his mentality was not fashioned out of marble. His character was not graven in stone. He listened to advice but not always with understanding. He was a charming and interesting companion with a gay humour. Occasionally he had entirely different manners and attitudes. Sometimes he would scold the journalists and the politicians and almost everybody about him.

He always saw a situation with truth but he invariably painted it in bright colours. Reiteration and over-emphasis, a part of his newspaper technique, still broke out in crisis. Yet he was adaptable to his surroundings and he possessed brilliant talents for improvisation. His immense prestige served him well. With swift and certain touch, he gained influence and authority in both British and Allied circles. Steadily his power developed and his prestige extended until in the early autumn of that fateful year of 1917 his administration had won the approval and praise of the staffs of British missions and even of American Government officials of high rank.

True there were occasional outbursts and now and then examples of vain and self-centred diversions. Such an incident is recorded in the Page Papers.

It was on 13th August, 1917, that Northcliffe informed the United States Ambassador in London that the British Fleet had been in danger of being put out of action for the want of fuel oil. Balfour, he declared, had put on him the "enormous responsibility" of remedying this "shortage of oil".

So, Northcliffe told Page, he got up bright and early thus protecting his countrymen from "a jump in the oil market." That day he devoted to "cautious pussyfooting". Then he got on the telephone to the Standard Oil Company and all was well. The British Navy was in action again with oil and at a "less price than we would have averaged over here."

There is no record in the Page Papers of any reply to this account of Northcliffe's pussyfooting activities. But Page might have asked: "Since the British Fleet is conveying American soldiers to the battlefront why not ask the President or the Procurement Agency for fuel oil?"

Northcliffe's enthusiasm and his powers of improvisation swiftly won for him the admiration and even the approval of his enemies. Sir Cecil Spring-Rice, writing to the Foreign Secretary not long after Northcliffe's arrival, declared:

Lord Northcliffe is making an excellent impression and is seeing a great number of prominent persons here. He must be collecting a great deal of valuable information. There is no objection to him on the part of any official and the President has given him a very favourable reception. . . . He is on very good terms with M. Tardieu [head of French Mission], who is an old friend, and this is a very important matter at the present moment.[z]

Colonel House, with whom Northcliffe worked in close co-operation, was glowing in his praise, and references in his private papers reflect an increasing admiration and even affection for Northcliffe. In August, House cabled to England that Lord Northcliffe was accomplishing wonderful work and was getting on well with everyone. Later he recorded: "He was tireless in his endeavours to stimulate the courage and energy of the Allies, and he succeeded in bringing them to a realisation of the mighty task they had on their hands."[aa]

Was there any discordant note? Yes, the voice of Lord Reading who was in America on a special mission. It is written in House's Diary. Said Reading when leaving House one day to make room for Northcliffe: "I will now turn you over to Northcliffe in order that he may tell you the things he told you the last time you met."[ab]

Northcliffe's long association with Americans stood him in good stead. He wisely acknowledged that "nothing can be gained here by threats, much by flattery and self-abnegation."[ac] He worked incessantly to bring home to the American people the measure of Britain's war effort.

He never once put a foot wrong. He moved from triumph to triumph. And he wrung a tribute from the President.

F

Northcliffe had climbed out of the Valley. Now he stood upon the Summit of the Mountain.

At the end of September, Northcliffe decided to return to England and Lloyd George was not unwilling to welcome him home again. "I have never worked so hard before"[ad] wrote the founder of the greatest newspaper power of his time. Northcliffe invited his brother, Lord Rothermere, to take on the American job and received an acceptance of the offer. He then recommended the appointment to Lloyd George. There is no trace of any answer. Certainly Lord Rothermere did not go to New York.

In November, Northcliffe's mission came to an end. By that time he had reached the ranks of successful political administrators. He returned to England to receive from the War Cabinet its thanks and congratulations, and from the Monarch a viscountcy in recognition of his work. * He stood in such favour with the public and had made such a good impression on the politicians that high office stood open to him. It was almost like Napoleon returning from Elba.

And it was in just such terms that the gossips chattered in the clubs and luncheon rooms and at dinner tables. "Northcliffe is coming! What will he say? How will he be received by Lloyd George? Will he be in the Government?" Both political parties talked of this man. His name was echoing through the corridors and the meeting places of Whitehall.

* See Chapter VII, The Birth of the Royal Air Force, p. 217.

Three days after his arrival, the answer to all these puzzles that excited the pundits was given by Northcliffe himself.

On 15th November he lunched with Lloyd George at Downing Street. In the course of their conversation Lloyd George sounded him on the subject of the Air Ministry, a new department of State.

Lord Northcliffe left the Prime Minister under the impression that, if an offer of this post was made to him, it would be accepted.

Bonar Law had been persuaded to approve of Lord Northcliffe's appointment to the Ministry. His presence in office would obviously be of considerable advantage, and his support for the Government in the gathering struggle between Soldiers and Civilians could not be under-estimated.

But before nightfall all the plans and projects crashed and perished. Lord Northcliffe released that evening through the Press Association a public rejection of the Air Ministry, condemning in outrageous terms the very ministers he had been asked to serve with as colleague and co-worker. He attacked the delays of Balfour's Foreign Office and the misuse of Censorship. Praise was given to Haig and his generals, although Northcliffe knew well that the Prime Minister was moving into a crisis on account of the conflict with the Army Chiefs, and the Military threat to the very existence of his Government.

Lord Northcliffe's open letter appeared in the Press the following morning. It opened thus:

Dear Prime Minister,

I have given anxious consideration to your repeated invitation that I should take charge of the new Air Ministry. The reasons that have impelled me to decline that great honour and responsibility are in no way concerned with the office which is rightly to be set up.

From this Northcliffe went on to contrast the "virile atmosphere" on the other side of the Atlantic with the dallying and weakness which he alleged prevailed in Britain. He spoke of obstruction in Government departments, and of men in authority "who should have been punished" but had been elevated.

We have, in my belief, the most efficient army in the world, led by one of the greatest generals, and I am well aware of the fine achievements of many others of our soldiers, sailors and statesmen; but I feel that in present circumstances I can do better work if I maintain my independence and am not gagged by a loyalty that I do not feel towards the whole of your Administration.

Northcliffe's action in publishing this letter was the grossest breach of political etiquette. *

On the day of its publication Colonel House lunched at Buckingham Palace. While he ate, he sat between the Queen and the Prime Minister. He talked mostly with Her Majesty. His diary

---

* Lloyd George described the action as "one of those lapses into blundering brutality to which his passion for the startling gesture sometimes led him".*ae*

records: "She recalled with some amusement my prediction that Northcliffe would begin an attack upon the Ministry, and cited his letter in the morning press declining to accept a Cabinet position as evidence. She seemed to talk without hesitation about matters of state or of personages, which would be embarrassing if repeated."

After eating, House "stood apart" with Lloyd George, he wrote in his diary, "telling jokes and laughing at his (Lloyd George's) predicament with Northcliffe. I told him of Northcliffe's visit and of how perturbed we were when we heard he was coming. He said, 'Of course you know why I sent him'. I gave him an account of the way we took him in hand and of how we had tried to steer him straight. George thought it was a remarkable achievement, but he said towards the end, 'I notice before he left, Northcliffe was doing much more talking, and I expected every day to have to recall him.' I asked if Northcliffe was to return to the United States. He (Lloyd George) replied: 'I hope you will ask for him because I would like to send him. I would even be willing to take Roosevelt* for a while in exchange, although,' he added quickly, 'not permanently.' . . .

"We had a good time and I am afraid the King and Queen, who I know dislike George, wondered how I could be on such friendly terms with him."*af*

Four days after this conversation the King asked House to come to Buckingham Palace.

---

* Former President Theodore Roosevelt—bitter enemy and critic of President Wilson.

House writes in his diary: "The King was full of Northcliffe and his dictatorial assumptions. He asked me to find out quietly, without using his name, if the Prime Minister intended to let Northcliffe go back to the United States. He also wanted to know whether the Prime Minister would take General Sir William Robertson, Chief of Staff, to Paris for the Inter-Allied Conference. I told him I was sure he would, and I was also certain Northcliffe would return to America whether the Prime Minister desired it or not."[ag]

Colonel House saw Lloyd George at dinner that same evening. "We talked of Northcliffe," he reported in his diary. "He (Lloyd George) evidently is afraid of him, and, unfortunately, Northcliffe knows it."[ah]

Five days after Northcliffe's offensive letter appeared in the Press, Sir Edward Carson, who by this time had become a member of the War Cabinet, said in a speech at the Constitutional Club:

> I do not understand this kind of criticism. After all, if a man has a seat in Parliament, and he thinks things are going wrong, why does he not go to his seat in Parliament and tell us what we ought to do to set them right? There he could be answered. I have had a search through the volumes of *Hansard*, and this great man, so far as I can see, has never made one single suggestion since the war from his seat in Parliament, where it can be criticised.[ai]

Austen Chamberlain, speaking later in the House of Commons, said of it:

[Lord Northcliffe] addresses to the Prime Minister a public letter which I should have thought was contrary certainly to practice and perhaps to the honourable traditions of confidence which prevail in public life to have published at all, in which, with an insolent and offensive patronage of my right hon. Friend, he combines an equally insolent and offensive criticism of my right hon. Friend's colleagues.[aj]

Not only was the letter a direct affront to the Prime Minister, but it also aimed a humiliating blow at the President of the Air Board, Lord Cowdray. Lord Northcliffe's opening reference to a "repeated" invitation was both at variance with the facts and deliberately misleading. And it was deeply wounding. Lord Cowdray never recovered from this public humiliation; and he never forgave Lloyd George. He submitted his resignation at once. In this way, thanks to Northcliffe's untimely and discourteous act, the ranks of the anti-Lloyd George Liberals received a bitter and influential recruit.

But Northcliffe himself was the real victim of his own rash act. The great newspaper Viscount, by his diplomacy and by unremitting work, had earned at last an elevated place among the politicians. Once he had been wholly rejected by them; now he had returned from a triumphant mission. He could surely take his place as a gladiator in the political arena. There seemed to be no limit to the political power that stood open to him. The Premiership itself was not beyond his grasp. Yet within days of his arrival in the country he chose deliberately to flout the prized conventions of public life and set himself at odds with the politicians. From that moment he never again set a foot right in politics.

The rise and fall of Lord Northcliffe was accomplished in the short space of six months. And it was a rise and fall unprecedented in political history. The tragedy of Lord Northcliffe was that, in his hour of political pre-eminence, he cast himself down. Never again was he invited to take high office.

Later, in the middle of 1918, he made another bid for political power. The war was going badly and Northcliffe was increasingly obsessed with the belief that he was the Man of Destiny whom public opinion would call upon to take over the Government. He would become Lord President of the Council in a Lloyd George-Northcliffe administration. He would, in effect, divide Downing Street with Lloyd George, and he would keep Fleet Street for himself. His demand amounted to that.

In making this overture for place and authority Lord Northcliffe employed two intermediaries, Lord Reading and myself. Accompanied by Sir Campbell Stuart, he then left for Scotland by motor-car. On the journey Sir Campbell Stuart telephoned frequently on Northcliffe's instruction to ask for the Prime Minister's answer. When he reached Glasgow he was told it was a downright refusal. The Coalition leader had rejected him. The Conservative colleagues of Lloyd George would not receive him.

Northcliffe was to experience a final and a

grievous disappointment. When the composition of the Peace delegation was under discussion in the Press and the lobbies, Lloyd George suggested to Lord Northcliffe that he should take a house in Paris close to the Prime Minister so that consultation between the two men might be facilitated.

Northcliffe regarded this proposal as an invitation to join the Peace delegation and informed his newspaper colleagues accordingly. When, however, Northcliffe asked Lloyd George for his warrant or commission as a Peace delegate, the Prime Minister informed him that he had no intention of including him in the British delegation.

He had now three grievances rankling in his mind continuously and exciting him to bouts of extreme and vitriolic criticism of the Prime Minister: (1) The refusal to give him a place in the Government which Northcliffe foolishly thought could be had for the asking. (2) The conviction that he was entitled to a place on the British Peace delegation. (3) The confused belief that a place had been offered and then withdrawn from him.

His fury consumed him and he made use of his newspapers to pour contempt and ridicule on the author of all his discontents.

When the General Election of December, 1918, returned Lloyd George triumphantly to power, in spite of the vituperative opposition of the Northcliffe Press, he suffered a humiliating defeat.

Night of gloom closed in upon Northcliffe. His gaiety and high spirits were memories of the past. Although he gave much attention to his newspapers, his shadow was no longer lengthening across the land.

In 1922 Lord Northcliffe's life came to a close. Yet even in his dying hours, hatred for Lloyd George dominated him. Sir Thomas Horder (later Lord Horder), that most famous of physicians, was attending him.

Horder had been recently knighted, on the recommendation of Lloyd George. He was called to Northcliffe's bedside as he lay desperately ill. As he entered the room, Lord Northcliffe brandished a revolver which had been hidden under his pillow. Pointing it at Horder he cried, "One of Lloyd George's bloody knights."* The male nurse struck at Northcliffe's hand. Lord Horder lived.

Northcliffe died.

* See *Appendix IV*, No. 2.

CHAPTER III

NABOBS AND TYRANTS

DURING the summer of 1917 one episode occurred which was destined to have a far-reaching importance. It concerned the relationship between the Chancellor of the Exchequer and the Governor of the Bank of England. It began with the firmness of Bonar Law, who, slow to anger, was finally roused to assert his principles and thus establish the authority of the Treasury over the Bank of England. And it ended, some thirty years later, with nationalization, when the strong hand of the Government was laid upon the nation's banking operations.

The Bank was the property of private investors. The Board of Directors was elected at annual meetings of shareholders. The Governor in turn was chosen by the Board. In selecting him, the Treasury was not consulted. In all financial concerns the Bank exercised coequal authority with the Government. Currency notes of five pounds and over were issued under the authority of a parliamentary charter. No other Banking house shared the Government accounts and none dared give advice or comment on financial issues at variance with Bank of England decisions.

The Governor of the Bank of England in 1917 was Lord Cunliffe. He had been elected to the post in 1913, and he had the distinction of becoming the first war-time peer created by Asquith, who announced the honour with dramatic incidence at the Guildhall, at the Lord Mayor's Banquet, on 10th November, 1914. Asquith's statement was received by the large City audience of bankers and bill-brokers and barristers with splendid enthusiasm. If the war conferred this titular honour upon him, it also brought to his office a great accession of influence and power. In fact, Lord Cunliffe soon became practically a dictator of finance.

Lloyd George's period at the Treasury * undoubtedly contributed to this result. The two men, though sharing no similarities of disposition or temperament, got on remarkably well. Lloyd George managed to penetrate the gruff, almost surly exterior of the banker and to establish a basis of understanding and respect. More important, he was ready to concede the last word to the Governor in matters of financial policy.

Nor was the financial policy at the outbreak of war at all obscure; it was in fact a stand-still order and a very necessary protection against the wave of mistrust and fear that swept through the Bank Parlours of the City. Exchanges were demoralized. Gold was in demand. Then the ameliorating measures were applied.

No maturing obligation was immediately payable except at the option of the debtor. Bills of

* Lloyd George was Chancellor of the Exchequer 1908 to 1915.

exchange were indefinitely renewed. Banks were given a holiday; thereafter restrictions were placed upon withdrawals of deposits. Cunliffe had the power; Lloyd George got the credit. The politician had saved the City. He had sustained the financial structure, giving peace and tranquillity to all those financial gentlemen who were temporarily seized with panic. Lloyd George was ever grateful to the Governor of the Bank for the credit. The Governor was always pleased and satisfied with the power.

When McKenna came to the office in the Coalition Government of 1915, he found the Exchequer already under the dominance of the Governor of the Bank of England.

But the new Chancellor had views of his own on many matters previously left to Lord Cunliffe, and he was not prepared to follow Lloyd George's methods in dealing with him. Lord Cunliffe clung tenaciously to the belief that all matters of foreign exchange were his exclusive province; McKenna thought otherwise. It was only a matter of time before there was a trial of strength between them.

At the very first encounter, McKenna yielded unwisely to the demand of Lord Cunliffe, who insisted that all meetings between the Chancellor and the Governor should be held in the presence of the Prime Minister. This arrangement considerably undermined McKenna's position. Asquith, striving to achieve a compromise where no compromise was possible, failed to give the Chancellor a proper reinforcement.

His role as negotiator between the two men left him a prey to Cunliffe's determination to assert his authority, as the following correspondence will show.

On 25th July, 1915, two months after McKenna had come to the Exchequer, the Prime Minister wrote to him:

The Governor of the Bank came to see me again yesterday morning, and I have had the opportunity of talking over the situation with the Chief Justice and Montagu.

The result is that I feel a good deal of disquietude. Without going into details, there are two or three points which seem to me to be clear:

(1) that it is of primary importance to our credit that none of the American contracts should be dropped through inability to provide exchange for the moment. I understand that provision has now been made for the immediate case;

(2) that the process of acquiring and collecting American securities here for export should be conducted as quietly and unostentatiously as possible;

(3) that every possible effort should be made to withdraw gold from circulation and accumulate it: so that a substantial reserve will always be available for export;

(4) that both Russia and France should have it made clear to them that they must be ready to part with substantial contributions of gold, if they expect us to continue to render them effective financial help.

All these are matters which cannot be put through without delicate handling, and the closest and most cordial co-operation between ourselves and the Bank of England. The Governor has rendered us invaluable service during the past year. He has (like most people) limitations of outlook and faults of temper. But I am

94

satisfied that, though not nimble either in thought or expression, his deliberate judgment is always well worth taking into account, and that he is perfectly straight.

In regard to Morgans, while I do not doubt that they have made & will continue to make all they can out of us, I see no reason to think that they have been acting unfairly, still less treacherously. The original contract with them may or may not have been wise, but it wd. be bad policy to swop horses now, or to make them suspect that we distrust them.

I have spoken with the frankness which I always use to you, and wh. you never resent.[a]

Now this was by any measure a tough letter. The use of the word "disquietude" gave the message the appearance of a severe reprimand from an angry Prime Minister to an erring subordinate. The letter carried the inference that the Lord Chief Justice and Montagu approved of these strictures on the Chancellor.

But Montagu was Financial Secretary to the Treasury. He was in effect McKenna's Under-Secretary. It was his duty to support and sustain his own chief. Only in serious circumstances could he justify hostile criticism of his Chancellor. Montagu's support for the Prime Minister's letter gave added weight to the reprimand.

Lord Reading, the Lord Chief Justice, was a formidable critic and an important influence in war-time finance. He had financial understanding, a legal training, a career in government and experience in Cabinet. He was well equipped to give good counsel and wise guidance. Holding a non-political post, he had immense advantage in relations with ministers irrespective of Party allegiance.

Reading's outstanding quality was his tact. This gift enabled him to be on intimate terms with Lloyd George, McKenna and Bonar Law, three successive Chancellors of the Exchequer, all of varying natures and diverging temperaments, yet all willing and anxious to avail themselves of Reading's fundamental qualities. Reading kept in with all three, just as he managed to keep on terms with Asquith and Lloyd George throughout the strife between these two Liberal leaders.

As a public speaker and as a parliamentary performer he was a failure. I have heard him in both the Commons and the Lords. His speeches were always dignified and dull. It is acknowledged that at the Bar he was magnificent, yet in private conversation his vocabulary was limited. He never resorted to picturesque phrases. Yet his success as an advocate was immense.

He was cautious, so cautious that he never gave an opinion until he was forced to do so. He was just and a most likeable fellow. Indeed he was a lovable man with an abundance of personal charm.

In the Walter Hines Page Papers at Harvard, there is an account of the character and conduct of Reading. It is not a penetrating analysis though an interesting human document.

London, 16th Jan., 1918.

Dear Mr. President,

You know Lord Reading and have taken measure of him, but the following facts and gossip may interest you. He is one of the ablest Englishmen living—everybody concedes that. But, with that, agreement about him here ends. The very general Conservative view of him is that he cannot be trusted. See and compare the view taken of Disraeli, the other Hebrew Earl, by his political enemies. As between the two, my judgment would be in favor of Reading. He is not so spectacular as old Dizzy was, but he is far sounder. I doubt if Dizzy was honest and I think that Reading is. As Rufus Isaacs he began life as a stockbroker. A high-sporting Jew named Joel caused Isaacs's bankruptcy by some stockbroker's trick. A bankrupt in England is likely to remain a down-and-out for the rest of his life. He suffers a far severer penalty than an American bankrupt. Joel was and is rich and he had much to do with the turf—a common highway whereon brilliant nobodies travel to association with the nobility and sometimes even with royalty. Isaacs forsook the stock exchange and took up the law. Soon after his admission to the bar, Joel became involved in a lawsuit—about something, I don't know what. When the case came to trial, lo! Isaacs appeared in court as the lawyer of the other party to the quarrel; and Joel recalled Isaacs's threat to "get even with him". When that lawsuit ended, Joel had to give up all his social ambitions, and he has lived in retirement ever since. And the event was the making of Rufus Isaacs. It soon became apparent that he was one of the most brilliant and able members of the bar. He has himself told me that for years he worked from early hours to early hours again, day in and day out, for years—a prodigy of industry. When he left the bar gossip has it that his income was not less than $200,000 a year, and his fees were prodigious.

He is, of course, a Liberal, and, under the Asquith Ministry his advancement was most rapid. He was made Solicitor-General 1910, Attorney-General 1910–1913, a Knight in 1910, Privy Councillor 1911,

Baron 1914, Viscount 1916,* Lord Chief Justice in 1913. He is the son of a London merchant and he married a daughter of a merchant named Cohen. The Isaacs and the Cohen are now swallowed up in the Earl and Viscountess, and "Reading" gives no hint of Jewry.[b]

It is necessary to point out that there are several inaccuracies in the letter, not however relevant to the very favourable estimates of Reading's character.

Page did not know that within ten years Lord Reading had paid in full all the debts he contracted when he defaulted on the Stock Exchange. He never was a bankrupt.

With the Prime Minister and McKenna's formidable Under-Secretary Montagu, and also the Chief Justice, banded together in support of the claims of the Governor of the Bank of England, the Chancellor had no choice. He was compelled to resign or give way. His letter to the Prime Minister dated the next day was by no means a fighting reply.

Your letter has caused me not less surprise than pain. I am at a loss to understand what can have been said to you by the Governor of the Bank, the Chief Justice and Montagu to lead you to write it. Nothing that I am conscious of having said or done could make you think it necessary to recommend the course of action suggested in the four propositions in your letter, in the correctness of which I concur so fully as to think that the neglect to adopt them would be most

* Lord Reading was created a Marquis in 1926. The Marchioness, his first wife, died in 1930. In August, 1931, he married Stella, the present Dowager Marchioness.

culpable. I should be glad of an opportunity of meeting the Govr.,* the C.J. and Montagu in your presence in order that I may know the precise terms of their complaints.[c]

Co-operation between Chancellor and Governor practically ceased. At best it could be said that an armed truce existed between the Treasury and the Bank. McKenna at this stage consented to the most amazing encroachment upon his authority. He agreed to a London exchange committee for the regulation of exchange. This committee was given full rights of access to all the gold, assets and securities of the Government. And Lord Cunliffe was appointed chairman. Thus power over Government assets passed from the Treasury to a privately owned banking company in the City—the Bank of England.

Lord Cunliffe was henceforth the financial dictator of Great Britain. Power had passed to him without the knowledge or consent of the House of Commons. Naturally his untrammelled authority went to his head. Like all dictators he acted as a tyrant.

And like many a tyrant his fame did not long outstrip the brief space of time when he strutted through the City like a great Gargantua. A search of the files of the British Museum fails to disclose the name of Lord Cunliffe in the catalogue of the records of the important men of Britain, although he was Governor of the Bank of England for five

---

* The Governor did not act on the Chancellor's invitation to a meeting.

years—a record term of office at that time. Nor
is his career recorded in the Dictionary of National
Biography.

Cunliffe was a second-generation hereditary
financier—a rare type among successful men of
affairs. He inherited from his father a large portion
of a fortune of over one million pounds. It was
not the fashion of those days for men of wealth
to part with their money to escape the death levy.
It is interesting to note that his Lordship at his
own departure left behind him only £650,000.

And it is indeed a deeper mystery that his name,
which was so familiar in political, financial and
Fleet Street circles has now been forgotten. It
would seem to be lost and gone forever.

But in the days of his glory, and until the fall
of the Asquith administration, Cunliffe, the Governor of the Bank of England, dominated and ruled
the greatest banking centre in the world—the City
of London.

Bonar Law, the new Chancellor of the Exchequer, was no sooner installed at the Treasury
than he experienced the full weight of the Governor's opposition. This arose over a £600,000,000
War Loan.

Bonar Law believed that a loan of this scale
could be raised in the country at an interest lower
than the current rate, which had reached the high
level of 6 per cent. He was guided by what he
considered the people would do in a spirit of
patriotism rather than as a matter of finance. He
argued that the country could be made to see the

need for money as well as munitions, and would not question the rate of interest.

This was not the opinion of Lord Cunliffe. He firmly maintained that the loan could not succeed at less than a 6 per cent interest rate; the country would not support it. As for the size of the loan, it was impossible to estimate it. The Governor of the Bank of England was convinced that the general public would take little part in the subscriptions, and he declared that the Bank could not co-operate with the Government in launching it. Bonar Law replied that, in that event, he would deal with the Joint Stock banks. This was a warning but Cunliffe was too vain to see it. Bonar Law maintained that there was a limit to the price the Government was justified in paying in loan interest and that it would therefore be better to risk a comparative failure of the loan than to commit the Government to the figure of 6 per cent. From this conviction he refused to budge.*

As I had been advocating a thousand million loan and at the rate of only 5 per cent, with the beating of drums and the blowing of bugles when the subscription lists were opened, I was called on by Bonar Law to attend at his home at Pembroke Lodge in Edwardes Square in order to give testimony to Lord Cunliffe, and possibly make an impression on him. Bonar Law thought I could

---

* Bonar Law described his attitude in an interview with an American correspondent, Mr. Lowell Mellet, reported in *Daily Express*, 5th April, 1917. "The bankers, as was natural, looked at it as a financial problem. I didn't. I considered what the people might do as a matter of patriotism, not as a matter of finance. . . . It was because of this high level of money that many men most competent to judge warned me that the loan could not succeed at less than 6 per cent."

convince most persons, particularly on financial issues. He was wrong about Lord Cunliffe.

It would be unnecessary to say that my representation to his Lordship did not improve his temper or contribute to the general amenities of the discussion. Although I lived next door to him, there was not any evidence of neighbourly sympathy or understanding.

Even though Cunliffe dismissed my arguments with some measure of impatience and displeasure, Bonar Law persisted in his plan.

Events proved him right. The War Loan, announced with a 5 per cent interest rate in January, 1917, was received with great enthusiasm. When the loan closed in February, a total of £700,000,000 had been subscribed.

In this encounter with Lord Cunliffe, Bonar Law had won a resounding success. The real test of authority was yet to come. In one matter, however, Bonar Law took a firm stand from the outset. He would have nothing to do with the condition previously imposed by Cunliffe that the Governor and the Chancellor should meet only in the presence of the Prime Minister. This stand at once consolidated his position.

Matters came to a head in the summer. Lord Cunliffe had lately come home after a three-months' visit to America with the Balfour Mission and it is fair to say that he found things, on his return, far from his liking. He believed that the position of the Exchange Committee had been usurped by the permanent officials at the Treasury and he lost no time in writing in vigorous terms of complaint to the Prime Minister.

Cunliffe contended that all the means of controlling the exchanges had been taken out of the Committee's hands and that the information guaranteed by McKenna, and subsequently by Bonar Law, was being withheld from them. The London Exchange Committee, he said, had therefore become "a mere cypher entirely superseded by Sir Robert Chalmers * and Mr. Keynes". †*d* The Governor asserted that the former Chancellor had given him a verbal promise that Keynes "should not meddle again in City matters", a promise that had been kept until McKenna went out of office.

At the same time Cunliffe made representations both in person and in writing to Bonar Law.*e* In fact, he approached the Chancellor with what amounted to a demand for the dismissal of Sir Robert Chalmers.‡

Bonar Law replied to these criticisms in a friendly manner, though he considered that Cunliffe had taken an unwarrantable liberty in suggesting the dismissal of Chalmers. He proposed that the Exchange Committee should meet at the Treasury to ensure a closer co-operation and that Stanley Baldwin, the joint Financial Secretary, should become a member of it.

* Permanent Secretary to the Treasury.
† Later Lord Keynes.
‡ In describing this occasion in his letter to Lloyd George on 9th July, 1917, Bonar Law writes: "He did not, of course, put the demand in this form but he told me that it was impossible for him to continue on the Exchange Committee under these conditions. I asked him whether that meant that he was not prepared to go on if Sir Robert Chalmers remained and he replied in the affirmative."*f*

If Cunliffe had confined his disapprobation to
a mere verbal expression, it is possible that some
workable adjustment could have been achieved.
Bonar Law was the most amenable of colleagues,
and the least sensitive about his own dignity and
status, as his fellow politicians were often to dis-
cover to their advantage. But Cunliffe had gone
beyond words and Bonar Law rightly resented
the Governor's attitude. He said to Lloyd George
that Cunliffe's demand for the replacement of
Chalmers was a proof "that he entirely mis-
understands the relations between the Government and the Bank when he ventures to dictate
to me as to the men whom I am to have as my
assistants at the Treasury."[8] Bonar Law was still
anxious to establish a practical co-operation with
the Bank.

At this time, a large quantity of gold was
held for the account of the Bank of England in
Ottawa in the care of the Canadian Government.
The precious metal had been shipped to the
Dominion so that in the event of invasion the
enemy would find at the Bank an empty cupboard.
Now it so happened that on the morning after
Bonar Law had proposed to the Governor that
Stanley Baldwin should deal with Exchange, he
received a letter from Cunliffe informing him
that, without any consultation with the Treasury,
he had instructed the Canadian Government not
to deliver any further amounts of gold when
asked by Sir Hardman Lever, Financial Secretary to the Treasury, and to place the whole
of the gold in Canada at the disposal of the

BALFOUR

Charming and ruthless

CUNLIFFE

The City tyrant

Banking House of J. P. Morgan and Co. in New York.[h]

Cunliffe, of course, contended that the gold must be held by the Bank of England as security for the note issue. This plea was looked on as so much nonsense by Bonar Law, who demanded from all sources and from every citizen the surrender of assets essential or even desirable for the fulfilment of the needs of an all-out war. All other Banks had been required to surrender their gold; insurance companies, trust companies and private citizens had been directed to give up their various American securities. Some men, Bonar Law would have said, were giving up their lives; why should others be permitted to hold their gold? The Government itself was the real backing for the note issue. There was no possible argument on which Cunliffe could resist the surrender of the gold of the Bank of England.

The instruction, therefore, of the Governor to the Dominion Government not to honour demands for gold made on behalf of the Treasury was fantastic. It was a direct contradiction of the spirit of the nation at war. It could have no precedent in banking history. In effect, Lord Cunliffe had dared to stop the Government's cheque.

I have seldom seen Bonar Law so incensed. His anger was not appeased by a letter from Cunliffe which the Prime Minister passed on to him next day.

Lord Cunliffe was then taking up the attitude, both with Lloyd George and Bonar Law, that he had made an unpardonable mistake in ever allowing anyone outside the Bank to control the Bank's gold. *

Indeed, he went so far as to assert to Bonar Law that he was sure the Court of Directors of the Bank of England would not only never permit it again, but would censure him for having betrayed his trust in ever permitting it at all. At the same time, he disclaimed any idea that the Bank's faith in the Chancellor or Sir Hardman Lever had been impaired.

This moved Bonar Law to action. He communicated his views at length to the Prime Minister. The following letter gives a clear indication of the strength of his feelings in the matter:

9th July, 1917.

My dear Prime Minister,

The letter which you handed to me from Lord Cunliffe is itself an additional proof, though that was not needed, that the present position is impossible and must be brought to an end. In that letter he says — "I will do anything you can suggest to remove the idea that the Bank's faith in you and Sir Hardman Lever is impaired as such is not the case and never has been."

It is no doubt very kind of him to make this handsome declaration, but I should be sorry to ask for a vote of confidence by the Bank of England in the Chancellor of the Exchequer.

He says also in his letter that I consider the Bank has damaged our credit in Canada. . . . This is not merely a question of damaging credit: it is an act of extraordinary disrespect towards the British Govern-

* Cunliffe wrote to Lloyd George on 7th July, 1917, enclosing this letter to Bonar Law and saying to Lloyd George on this point: "I feel you will agree that I did very wrong in ever allowing it."[i]

ment and as I think a direct insult to me who, as Chancellor of the Exchequer, had authorised Sir Hardman Lever to act for the Government. . . .

Bonar Law went on to recount his own interview with the Governor following the news of his action.

I sent for the Governor and pointed out to him that this was a step which ought not to have been taken without consultation with me. He admitted it but said that that was not the principle on which we were now working. In other words, as "reprisals" for what he considered to be a failure on the part of the Treasury to supply the Exchange Committee with the necessary information he took a step of vital importance without consultation with me although he himself admitted that this consultation ought to have taken place. . . .

For these reasons I have, as already discussed with you in conversation, come definitely to the conclusion that the present position cannot continue. There were three possible methods of dealing with it.

One was that I should cease to be Chancellor of the Exchequer and leave the Government, but this you have ruled out: the second is that Lord Cunliffe should cease to be Governor of the Bank of England. There is, however, a third possible alternative, which is that Lord Cunliffe should agree to work with me in a reasonable spirit and with a full knowledge that the Chancellorship of the Exchequer is not in commission and that the views of the British Government, as represented by me, must be carried out.

If you are willing to see him and find out from him whether or not he is ready to continue on these conditions, I should be glad, but I cannot run the risk of a repetition of the friction of the last weeks. . . .

Yours sincerely,

A. BONAR LAW.[j]

Bonar Law was quite unyielding in his determination. He was not fighting to uphold the dignity of his own place in office, but to establish the true relationship between the Government and the Bank of England. The action of the Governor, taken in a spirit of "reprisal", had entirely confounded him. He regarded the Bank of England as the wartime servant of the Government, and the policy it pursued in financial affairs must conform to the Treasury. The Governor's claim that the gold then in Ottawa was to be dealt with entirely by him was contrary to the whole principle of Government.

Bonar Law, moved to a pitch of righteous indignation, was determined to secure a true apportionment of authority once and for all. He now advised Lloyd George that he was willing to allow the present arrangement to continue only on the condition that Lord Cunliffe should send him a written declaration that he would at once resign the Governorship of the Bank on a request from the Chancellor to that effect. Should he decline to do so, Bonar Law would take steps to ensure his immediate replacement at the Bank.

Events now moved with swiftness. Lord Cunliffe soon comprehended the fatal consequences of his action. On 13th July, Bonar Law and Sir John Bradbury, the Joint Permanent Secretary to the Treasury, met the Prime Minister at No. 10 Downing Street. Their meeting produced a statement for Lord Cunliffe's signature clearly defining the Bank's relationship with the Chancellor of the Exchequer. The gist of it was the Bank must act in all things on the direction of the Chancellor for the duration of the war and must consult him in all matters affecting credit. At the same time a draft declaration was prepared to the effect that Lord Cunliffe would be prepared to retire from his position if the public interest required it.*

The documents were forwarded by the Prime Minister to the Governor that evening.

In requiring such an agreement with the Governor of the Bank, Bonar Law was not prompted by any spirit of malice. He had no desire to humiliate Lord Cunliffe. But he believed that without such a commitment the situation would remain open to all the former friction and rivalry which would seriously prejudice the country's war effort.

But Cunliffe was not ready to renounce his authority so easily. He was not prepared to put his signature to such a declaration. His reply to Bonar Law,[1] while expressing his apologies for the action he had taken, contained no acceptance of Bonar Law's demand.†

He asked for support from Lloyd George and Lord Reading. They tried and their intervention was rejected.

Mr. Brien Cokayne,‡ the Deputy-Governor of the Bank of England, now called upon Bonar

---

* The terms of the draft letter said: "the relationship between the Treasury and the Bank must, during the war, be so intimate that if you felt that there could not be complete and harmonious co-operation between yourself and me, I should not think it compatible with the public interest that I should continue to occupy my position as Governor of the Bank of England."[k]

† Cunliffe, in his reply, covers most of the same points outlined in Bonar Law's draft, but in place of the important phrase (see previous footnote) it says: ". . . the relationships with the Treasury must during the war be so intimate that complete and harmonious co-operation is of paramount importance."

‡ Later Lord Cullen of Ashbourne.

109

Law. His mission was to intercede on behalf of Lord Cunliffe. He pointed out that the Bank insisted on reserving the right to select its own Governor. This was not, he maintained, a matter for the Treasury. But to this request for consideration Bonar Law returned a firm refusal.

In the City, the repercussions of the quarrel were vast. Lord Revelstoke, a Director of the Bank of England, became identified with those favouring Cunliffe's resistance. He repeated the claim that the selection of Governor was the concern of the Bank alone and not the Treasury.

The Joint Stock banks, under the direction of Sir Edward Holden, were then called together and asked to pass resolutions supporting Lord Cunliffe.

The Times reported that all the great Clearing Banks had joined in the plea for Cunliffe. But *The Times* was in error.

Sir Edward Holden's manœuvre broke down. With Bonar Law's permission I called upon Sir William Goodenough, then chairman of Barclays Bank, and Sir Herbert Hambling, head of the London and South Western Bank, and put the case to each of them in turn. As a result, they both declared that they would not accept the proposal that the Joint Stock banks should resolve to support Cunliffe.

Bonar Law declined to give in. Thus, in August, Cunliffe fled to the north of Scotland, whence he made a final effort at appeasement. In a letter to Bonar Law on 12th August, 1917, Cunliffe stated that he was sincerely sorry to learn that both he and the Prime Minister were dissatisfied and that they looked for a personal apology. He offered it unreservedly, and he assured Bonar Law that as long as he was Governor of the Bank he would work with him loyally and harmoniously, tendering such advice as he thought necessary to offer. "I fully realize," concluded the Governor, "that I must not attempt to impose my views upon you."[m]

Protestations of loyalty so long as Cunliffe remained Governor of the Bank did not interest Bonar Law because the Chancellor was determined that there must be a change. He would have no more of Cunliffe. He replied that he would be glad to see the Governor when he returned to town. But it made no difference to Bonar Law's determination; never again did he deal with Lord Cunliffe.

When the Court of Directors of the Bank of England met early in November, the decision that Sir Brien Cokayne,* who had been carrying out the duties of Governor since early in August, should succeed Lord Cunliffe as Governor was formally announced.[n]

Even after the decision had been taken, *The Times* and the *Daily Telegraph* carried on an organized campaign to save the Governor from the consequences of his own folly. The *Telegraph* actually described him as "the kindliest and most accessible Governor".[o]

* Cokayne had been made a K.B.E. on 24th August, 1917.

There were deep rumblings in the City. Many Bank Directors and others who hoped to attain to high place in financial circles made complaints, but the trumpet gave an uncertain sound.

Such was the termination of the dispute between the Chancellor of the Exchequer and the Governor. But, of course, the significance of the quarrel went deeper. The authority of the Treasury had been explicitly exerted over the Bank of England. That authority was never relinquished. Bonar Law had established a principle on which the final seal was fixed when in 1946 the Socialist Government nationalized the Bank of England.

CHAPTER IV

"IF YOU CAN TRUST YOURSELF WHEN ALL MEN DOUBT YOU"

WINSTON CHURCHILL was the most miserable man in Britain when 1917 ushered in the fourth year of battle.

A great and critical war was unfolding its drama, yet he was playing no part in guiding the struggle—he who felt himself, who knew himself to be equipped by instinct and training for a directing role in war. Quitting Asquith's government after Gallipoli, he had gone to command a battalion in France. On 10th April, 1916, he wrote from Plugstreet (front-line trench) to Sir Edward Carson who had advised him to come home and resume his part in politics. This seemed to hold the prospect of a place in government. He returned to London and, on 20th April, 1916, Lady Carson wrote in her diary:

E. [Sir Edward Carson] and I dined with the Winston Churchills. Who would have thought that could ever have happened? He talks an awful lot and gave me the impression his tongue works faster than his brain, though it goes pretty fast.[a]

But when Lloyd George's government was formed at the close of the year 1916, Churchill was excluded from it. The Conservative Ministers refused to serve with him. Bonar Law opposed office for him. And even Carson, now First Lord of the Admiralty, wrote to the Conservative leader rejecting a proposal to appoint Churchill to a subordinate task as a Member of the Air Board, operating under the authority of the Admiralty and War Office.

Secret   20th December, 1916.

My dear Bonar Law,

I fear this matter creates much difficulty. I do not yet know what the relations between the Admiralty and the Air Board are to be, but certainly it will require great tact and forbearance all round to get any new system into working order. I should greatly fear friction if the appointment is made. I much dislike having to seem opposed to the suggestion as my personal inclination is towards utilizing Churchill's undoubted ability—especially so as he is so down in his luck at present but I hope some other, more suitable opportunity may be found.

Yours sincerely,

E. CARSON.[b]

But exclusion from office would not be regarded by Churchill as either natural or likely to last. And soon events so shaped themselves that opportunity came his way once more.

The over-riding factor in the political situation was the progress of the war. There was every appearance of defeat.

Russia was to all intents and purposes out of

the struggle. Rumania could no longer be counted on as an effective ally. News from the Italian front brought little relief from tension. More disastrous still, the offensive in France, commanded by General Nivelle, was smashed in the Battle of the Aisne in April. On this attack immense hopes were pinned. Its defeat was a correspondingly bitter blow.

If the sky of war was overcast, the scene of domestic politics was troubled and stormy. A gathering combination of forces threatened the administration of Lloyd George.

There was above all the struggle, steadily growing in its intensity, between the Prime Minister and the High Command.

Many civilians and some politicians who had been excluded from office were now talking and writing in support of placing the civil Government in the hands of the generals for the duration of the war.

In this contest, the generals drew more and more comfort and support from influence and affiliations in high places.

Lord Northcliffe persisted in his advocacy of the cause of the generals. He was their valiant champion. He supported them against every challenge from the politicians. So pronounced, indeed, were his sympathies by this time that in May 1917 he made a speech to a newspaper press luncheon at the Mansion House where he declared in favour of something approaching a dictatorship for the High Command.

Lord Northcliffe began with a tribute to the guest of honour, Sir William Robertson, the Chief of the Imperial General Staff, who had spoken in praise of the newspapers. Northcliffe continued: "Our journals felt at liberty, and they thought it their duty, to criticise politicians, because, being very close to the politicians, perhaps not greatly enamoured of them, they knew something of their wiles. [Laughter.] They thought it necessary on occasion to stimulate them to further effort and to ask them, for example, not to interfere with the Army. But there was one thing newspapers did not do. They did not criticise our generals. [Cheers.] They had no need to do so. Each one of them had proved in the last three years that he was a match for the German commander in front of him."[c]

Then there was the King, whose hostility to Lloyd George in this dispute was marked. Frequently he delivered sharp attacks on the Prime Minister urging the soldiers and sailors to defy him while counselling them never to run the risk of a General Election.

In the circumstances, it was natural that Sir Douglas Haig, Commander-in-Chief in France, should be in direct and effective contact with Buckingham Palace. This was no secret. In March, 1917, Haig paid a personal visit to the Palace. He gives this account of the interview in his private papers:

The King . . . stated that he would "support me through thick and thin", but I must be careful not to resign, because Lloyd George would then appeal to the country for support and would probably come back with a great majority. . . . The King's position would then be very difficult. . . . We went over the whole Calais Conference. . . . The King said my account agreed entirely with Robertson's. He was furious with Lloyd George, and said he was to see him tomorrow.[d]

In Parliament the generals found allies against Lloyd George among the ranks of the old administration. "The Asquith-Brass-Hat Alliance" was the name given to a group forming in opposition, slowly—but certainly in considerable strength.

In the month of May 1917 it was plain to the administration that the strength of the Brass Hats and their allies must be tested. Could the generals be detached from their alliance with Asquith? Very soon it was clear that Lloyd George could hope for nothing in that direction. Lloyd George was persisting in his demand for civilian control of strategy. The generals, for their part, were unswerving in their demand for freedom from civilian interference and looked on him as an enemy with whom there could be no truce. And Lloyd George dared not yield to the generals. Their victory would be his defeat in Parliament.

What of Asquith himself? The Prime Minister would gladly have taken him into the Government if Asquith had been willing to serve. But some gulfs are too deep and too wide ever to be bridged. The gulf between Asquith and Lloyd George was one of them. And besides, Asquith's friends were confident that his return to office and power could not be delayed for long.

The front made up of Asquith and the Generals could not therefore be broken. It represented a danger to Lloyd George's government which was formidable enough and might at any moment become fatal.

A more immediate danger than any of these elements confronted the administration in critical and even hostile guise. Winston Churchill. Here was a man of extraordinary abilities, of adroit debating strength, of originality and resourcefulness. At the height of a major war he was out of employment. Yet the greater part of his career had been occupied with problems of a military kind. He had made a thorough study of the arts of war; he had published no fewer than five books on military subjects; he had served actively in Malakand, the Sudan, South Africa and in the trenches in France. And he had held command at the Admiralty at the outbreak of the present disaster. He rightly felt that he had special talents to offer in the crisis of world war.

Instead he was extruded from the centre of action by men of lesser ability and initiative, and his knowledge and his inventiveness of mind— all were wasted. It was a time of grievous frustration for Churchill. Indeed, there were days when he feared that all might be lost if his services were denied to his country.

But for Churchill it was not a time of idleness. He wrote a series of articles for the *Sunday Pictorial*, Lord Rothermere's newspaper, for which, to the envy and admiration of all contributing journal-

CHURCHILL

He smoked matches and ate cigars

ists, he was paid £250 an article. He talked incessantly about the war and made contacts with journalists and others who helped to form public opinion.

A letter from Churchill to R. D. Blumenfeld of the *Daily Express* shows him at his best.

My dear Mr. Blumenfeld,

I was very glad to get your letter, the more so because I heard from F. E. [Smith] that you felt some compunction about the attacks which the *Daily Express* has made on me during the last year. But really there is no need for this. I am a regular reader of yr. paper and have never seen any criticism wh. I did not think perfectly fair politics. Above all, there has never been anything so far as I am concerned reflecting on private or personal conduct. That after all is the line wh. politicians and political journalists ought to draw. Also I have been greatly amused by many of your cartoons. Therefore pray banish from yr. mind any idea that there has been a breach between us.

Yours vy truly,

WINSTON S. CHURCHILL.[e]

Churchill was always free from rancour and never treacherous. Unlike the elm tree which gives no warning of falling branches, Churchill gave plenty of notice of changing dispositions; then as now, he was reliable and dependable.

He gave attention to members of Parliament, particularly important back-bench Tories. He took account of the serving soldiers' grievances and spoke in the House in support of their claims. And there were frequent meetings of a dinner club which brought him together with Ministers and other important figures. When Churchill was present at that table, war and war administration were the sole topics of discussion.

In this mood, Churchill became an outspoken critic of the Government. He was constantly formulating criticisms against the offensives in France. Even in the House of Commons he attacked the Government for their conduct in war. Strangely enough, he seldom voted—perhaps in one division out of three—and never against the Government. He sat on the Opposition Front Bench with his old Ministerial colleagues about him. Yet between Churchill and his neighbours there was a failure of sympathy. They saw him as a useful but incalculable ally. They were aware that he was seeking office under Lloyd George. In the meantime his brilliant gifts of oratory were an ever-present menace to the administration. And now that the old dividing lines of party loyalties had melted in the confusion caused by the Lloyd George Coalition, Churchill could sway the House of Commons and win it over with his eloquence.

Lloyd George's position while the war continued to go badly was therefore immensely precarious.

A great speech by Churchill, a cunning move by the generals, a direct thrust by the Asquith group—each of these or all together—might carry the day against the Government.

And there was also Carson, disgruntled and disillusioned, endowed with a mind and a temperament that could prove destructive to the Government. He had helped to put Lloyd George in. Would he decide perhaps to help to put him out again? For it could not be disputed that the whole force of the man lay in attack. He shone in opposition, and realized instinctively that his strength lay there. He had therefore always to be taken into account in estimating any political combination against the Government.

But Churchill, although hated by the Tories, and mistrusted by half the Liberals and all of the Socialists, would be the linchpin in a coalition that might and could drive Lloyd George from the seat of power.

Seeing the whole picture with the eye of a master of political tactics, Lloyd George was frightened. Very soon he had still more cogent reason for alarm.

One day, he passed a message to Bonar Law as they sat together at a meeting of the War Cabinet. It read:

My dear Bonar,
I think you ought to know that Asquith told Winston that, if he came in, he would put him in the Admiralty.

D.L.G.ʲ

The implication was clear. Churchill would be tempted to join the Asquith Alliance. Up to this point his relations with Asquith had been no more than friendly, neither strained nor intimate. He had been a powerful independent critic of the

Government. In future, he might be a captain in the hostile forces. The danger was grave indeed. At any risk, the possibility of Churchill joining the Asquith-Brass Hat Alliance must be shattered.

On 10th May, 1917, in a Secret Session, Churchill opened the debate for the Opposition. He reviewed the military position in France and Europe and spoke with intense conviction against a policy that would lead the French and British High Commands to drag each other into fresh and disastrous adventures. It was a speech of considerable power and authority, and Churchill resumed his seat amid the enthusiastic acclaim of the House.

Lloyd George, confronted with a Parliament critical of his administration, knew at once that the crisis could not be far off. He had no doubt of the urgent need for action, and little doubt what form that action should take. Churchill could not be left out of the Government. He must be fenced in, and that forthwith. What could not be squashed must be squared and what could not be squared must be squashed.

Faced with the danger of Parliamentary defeat, Lloyd George displayed his usual intrepid coolness. Indeed, his courage was always more of the moral than of the physical order.

Rising to Churchill's challenge, he delivered a speech which commanded the attention and respect of the House. Frederick Guest, the Chief Liberal Whip, wrote him a letter of congratulation that same evening:

10th May, 1917.

Dear Prime Minister,

The impression in the house, lobby, and smoking room is that you have made a great speech. It has been a good days work in more ways than one.

Winston's speech is also considered to be a fine statesmanlike effort.

Yours sincerely,
FREDDIE GUEST.[g]

This was not, however, the end of the business. After the debate, Lloyd George met Churchill behind the Speaker's Chair. What happened then is recorded by Churchill.

"In his satisfaction at the course the Debate had taken," he writes, "[the Prime Minister] . . . assured me of his determination to have me at his side. From that day, although holding no office, I became to a large extent his colleague. He repeatedly discussed with me every aspect of the war and many of his secret hopes and fears."[h]

Churchill's return to the inner circle is clearly established by two letters which he wrote to Lloyd George later that May. They are now in the Lloyd George collection.

The first is dated 17th May, 1917. It reads thus:

My dear David,

The French Government invited me to go to look at the Front Verdun etc. a fortnight ago, but I had to put this off on account of the secret session. I now think of going next Thursday for a week or so. I should be glad if you would send a personal telegram to M. Painlevé (who I only know very slightly) commending me to him and the French Military authorities. This will ensure their making my visit pleasant and interesting.

Yours sincerely,
WINSTON CHURCHILL.[i]

The second, written two days later, is brief and jubilant:

My dear David,

A line to remind you to write a letter to Painlevé and one to Haig about my visit to France.

Do not I beg you however, in writing to the latter touch on the political matters which we talked of yesterday.

We had a jolly afternoon and I hope I was not the only one who liked it.

Yours,
W.[j]

The "jolly afternoon" had cemented the new alliance. Lloyd George had set his sail to catch the wind. But he could hardly have reckoned with the buffeting he was to encounter.

The actual task of finding Churchill a place in the administration was a serious political problem confronting the Prime Minister. It could only be achieved with infinite care and preparation. At best, it must involve him in an open breach with his Conservative supporters in the Government.

The attitude of the Conservative Ministers to Churchill had been plainly defined in December, 1916; they were still rigidly opposed to his inclusion in the administration. Bonar Law was no more disposed to look with favour upon Churchill. There was, in truth, never any real sympathy between the two men. I can recall many occasions when their mutual lack of understanding came to the surface.

Bonar Law had given his opinion of Churchill to Lloyd George when the Prime Minister was pointing out the danger of Churchill as a critic of the Government. "Is he more dangerous," Lloyd George had put it, "when he is FOR you than when he is AGAINST you?" Bonar Law had replied: "I would rather have him against us every time."[k]

Bonar Law's antipathy to Churchill was of long standing, as an extract from his correspondence reveals:

> I agree with the estimate you have formed of Churchill. I think he has very unusual intellectual ability, but at the same time he seems to have an entirely unbalanced mind which is a real danger at a time like this.[l]

In a letter to Bonar Law, Sir Henry Wilson once wrote:

> A man who can plot the Ulster Pogrom,* plan Antwerp and carry out the Dardanelles fiasco is worth watching.[m]

Sir Henry Wilson's criticism would probably have Bonar Law's approval and, in substance, it summed up the whole case for Tory hatred of

* The "Ulster Pogrom" described events when troops and Navy movements took place in 1914 which threatened Ulster. Although the Rt. Hon. J. E. B. Seely, Secretary of State for War, was dismissed over the incident, the Tories believed that Churchill was the moving spirit.

Churchill. Protestant Ulster was the real obstacle to trust and confidence.

Bonar Law always accepted the "Pogrom" theory of the Ulster crisis, blaming Churchill as the real leader. Thus when Bonar Law and Churchill served in the same administration, hostility often broke out in violent controversy even in the presence of many colleagues.

On one occasion, after Churchill joined the Government and in the Prime Minister's absence, when Bonar Law was holding a meeting of Ministers, Churchill uttered prolonged denunciations of the system under which he and also the Service Ministers were excluded from the War Cabinet. These important Chiefs were precluded from exercising any influence on the general policy of the War Cabinet and therefore the Government as a whole. It was wrong, he said, in principle.

Bonar Law listened in silence, and after Churchill had concluded his remarks, said to him: "Mr. Churchill, if the Government is doing something wrong in principle, you have your remedy —why don't you resign?"

Churchill was silenced for a moment. Then he replied: "That is a question you have no right to ask. Only the Prime Minister is entitled to question his subordinate in such terms."

Even when Churchill spoke in jest Bonar Law occasionally gave him a harsh answer. When the War Office was under discussion and Churchill was asked to make up his mind to take the

War Office or the Admiralty, he said jokingly: "What is the use of being War Secretary if there is no war?" Bonar Law made the comment: "If we thought there was going to be a war we wouldn't appoint you War Secretary."

Churchill's opinion of Bonar Law was no less harsh. He attached little weight to Bonar Law's intellectual ability. Writing of him to the Prime Minister, Churchill said: "Most men sink into insignificance when they quit office. Very insignificant men acquire weight when they obtain it."[n]

But while Lloyd George had yielded to Tory antipathy to Churchill as the price of the accession of four Conservative Ministers when he formed his administration,* the situation had now fundamentally altered. The Prime Minister was faced with a mortal threat to his leadership and power. He had to choose between the danger of Conservative resistance over Churchill and the greater hazard of the rising forces of a powerful opposition. He had to choose quickly, and there was no doubt what his choice must be.

So Lloyd George began to test the political atmosphere and to prepare the ground for the return of this contentious figure to Whitehall. At the beginning of June, five weeks before Churchill re-entered the Government, a kite was flown to test the weather. He could be re-admitted to the Government either by way of the Air Board, which was to be reconstituted as a ministry with independent status, or

---

* Curzon, Chamberlain, Cecil and Long had required and received a pledge from Lloyd George that Churchill would be excluded from office.

by the Ministry of Munitions. These were the alternative suggestions Lloyd George put forward.

They won warm support from General Smuts and from Lloyd George's Liberal colleague, Dr. Addison, the Minister of Munitions. General Smuts was anxious that Churchill's initiative and great constructive ability should be used in the Air Department, and he sought to put pressure on Churchill himself to this end. He wrote enthusiastically of the idea to Lloyd George.

Savoy Hotel
London.

Personal   6th June, 1917.

Dear Mr. Lloyd George,

At the request of Capt. Guest I saw Churchill last night and expressed to him my view that if Air was offered to him instead of Munitions (which you had previously mentioned to him) he should accept it. I pointed out that Munitions had become somewhat of a routine department while Air offered great scope to his constructive ability and initiative, and that with effective help from America our aerial effort might yet become of decisive importance not only in the anti-submarine campaign but also on the Western Front in the next twelve months.

The result is that, although he prefers Munitions, he will accept an offer of Air on the assumption that real scope is given him and that he must control the higher patronage in the Air Service.

In spite of the strong party opposition to his appointment, I think you will do the country a real service by appointing a man of his calibre to this department, the vital importance of which will more and more appear.

Yours sincerely,
J. C. SMUTS.[o]

Addison, whose own promotion was under review, was ready to support Churchill's claim either to Air or Munitions, but he counselled Lloyd George to act quickly, since discussion would give opposition time to gather.[p]

Sir Edward Carson's attitude to Churchill's appointment was equivocal. Although he had receded from his opposition as stated in his letter to Bonar Law of 20th December, 1916, he made no effort to help Churchill into the Government. It is true that Churchill had confidence in Carson and believed that the First Lord of the Admiralty would support his return to office. However, there is no evidence of any such activity on Carson's part in the papers of either Lloyd George or Bonar Law. The truth is that Churchill thought more of Carson than Carson thought of Churchill. And Churchill was more friendly to Carson than Carson to Churchill.

Frederick Guest, first cousin of Mr. Churchill and his long-time personal and political friend and follower, entirely under his influence, gave Lloyd George a valuable reinforcement. He wrote encouraging him to press on with his plan to bring Churchill into the administration.

> Your will and influence with your Tory Colleagues [Guest assured Lloyd George] is greater than you have credited yourself with and . . . sooner or later you will have to test it—why not now?
> I have the strongest reasons to believe that the Tories mean to support your leadership even at the expense of their personal feelings.[q]*

* The full text of the letter appears in *Appendix IV*, No. 3.

But the news * of the proposed appointment of Churchill fell like a Big Bertha into the Conservative camp, and such an explosion resounded that the edifice of the Coalition Government trembled, and hovered precariously around Lloyd George's head.

Furious letters poured in upon the Prime Minister.

Lord Curzon expressed the most bitter indignation. He had been the target of Churchill's criticism in a speech in the House of Commons in April. Now he wrote in the most vigorous terms of protest to Lloyd George.

Confidential.

1 Carlton House Terrace,
S.W.
June 8, 1917.

My dear Prime Minister,

May I again and for the last time urge you to think well before you make the appointment (W. Ch.) which we have more than once discussed? It will be an appointment intensely unpopular with many of your chief colleagues—in the opinion of some of whom it will lead to the disruption of the Government at an early date—even if it does not lead as it may well do, to resignations now. Derby, who opened the subject to me of his own accord this evening and who has spoken to you, tells me that it will be intensely unpopular in the army. I have reason to believe the same of the Navy.

Is it worthwhile to incur all these risks and to over-ride some of those who are your most faithful colleagues and allies, merely in order to silence a

* The Press Association announced on 8th June, 1917, that Churchill would be appointed to the Air Board. This was a balloon or a kite issued by Downing Street for the purpose of sounding public opinion.

possible tribune of the people whom in my judgement the people will absolutely decline to follow?

He is a potential danger in opposition. In the opinion of all of us he will as a member of the Government be an active danger in our midst.

Yours sincerely,
CURZON.[r]

At the same time, Bonar Law received a telling reminder from Lord Curzon of the Tories' December pledge. Curzon wrote:

Confidential.

1 Carlton House Terrace,
S.W.
4th June, 1917.

My dear Bonar,

Possibly there may be no truth in what we read in the papers as to Govt. reconstruction, e.g. Addison in War Cabinet! Churchill at Air Board and so on. I just write a line to say that I hope none of these steps if contemplated will be done behind our backs.

As you know some of us myself included only joined Ll.G. on the distinct understanding that W. Ch. was not to be a member of the Govt.—It is on record and to the pledge I and I think all my colleagues adhere.

Again if it is necessary to remove Addison from Munitions, as to which I know nothing, I can see no reason why he should be lifted up to War Cabinet to which he could add neither [efficiency*] nor strength.

Yours ever,
CURZON.[s]

* The letter is written in Curzon's hand and this word is indecipherable.

An urgent warning reached the Prime Minister from the Chairman of the Unionist Party, Sir George Younger, who feared the force of the charge Lloyd George was about to explode. He used the strongest language to dissuade Lloyd George from the course of action he proposed:

8th June, 1917.

Dear Lloyd George,

I do trust there is no foundation for the persistent rumour that Winston is to join the Government. I am seriously afraid that such an appointment would strain to breaking point the Unionist [Conservative] Party's loyalty to you. His unfortunate record, the utter futility of his criticisms of your War Policy at the last Secret Session, and his grave responsibility for two of the greatest disasters in the War have accentuated the distrust of him which has prevailed both in the House and outside it for a long time past, and I feel certain that his inclusion in the Government would prove disastrous to its fortunes. I believe the Unionist Party in the House would unanimously back this opinion and I am certain that our great organisations in the country, of which, as you know, I am Chairman, would strongly assert it.

I have never in my life passed through a time of greater anxiety politically than during the last two or three months. I have been sitting on the safety valve all the time and up to now have succeeded in securing at least an official acceptance of the Government's policy.

The last difficulty was created by the Franchise Bill and Bonar Law will be able to tell you by what a narrow squeak I managed to secure acceptance of the general principles of that measure, with the result that no amendment of any kind against its main principles is being moved by the Unionist organisation.

To test their loyalty so soon again would certainly invite serious trouble, and I cannot be responsible for the result.

It would be an impertinence on my part to interfere in any way with your choice of Ministers, but it is my bounden duty to tell you, as I told Bonar Law last week, that I am satisfied from the present temper of the Unionists in the country that the greatest care is necessary not to put any further strain on their loyalty.

I write you direct as I do not care to trouble Bonar with letters just now.*

Yours sincerely,
GEORGE YOUNGER.[1]

The anxiety of Lord Derby, Secretary of State for War, was no less acute. Indeed, the prospect of serving at that post with Churchill as head of the Air Board led him to make out a list of stringent conditions which he believed should define Churchill's future relations with the War Office."† By this formula Derby sought to hold down Churchill's appointment to a minor level, to limit his influence. Thus we have the unusual spectacle of a powerful Conservative seeking to prescribe to the Prime Minister the status and authority of a colleague.

Lord Milner also was on the side of the

---

* Bonar Law had at this time received news that his second son Charlie was missing. He was full of anxiety and pinning his faith to a report that Charlie was a prisoner in Turkey. His hopes were soon to be shattered. There was no truth in the rumour.

† Derby's programme proposed that it should be clearly understood that (1) Churchill should not be a member of the War Cabinet or attend any meetings unless specially summoned for business connected with the Air Board; (2) that his duties as Chairman of the Board should be the same as were Lord Cowdray's and that he would have nothing to do with personnel and tactics, and (3) that he should receive no War Office telegrams other than those which were connected with his department. See *Appendix IV*, No. 4, for full text of letter.

discontented politicians who opposed Churchill's introduction into the Government.[v]

Criticism in the Press sounded a violent note. In almost every direction comment was unfavourable. There were, however, important and significant exceptions—the newspapers controlled by Lord Northcliffe.

Lord Northcliffe's hostility to Churchill was well known. It had been violently expressed in December when even the fact that Churchill shared with Northcliffe the disappointment of exclusion from the new Government failed to blunt the sharp edge of the newspaper magnate's criticism. Nor had the two men enjoyed at this time any amity in their personal relations to soften the asperities of public antagonism. But, the situation was altered, and in a vital respect. Northcliffe had been "squared" by his appointment in Washington and New York.

"Lord Northcliffe was on a mission to the United States," observed Mr. Churchill, "and appeased."[w] And indeed, amiable and even friendly cables to and from America passed between them, concluding before long with a message from Northcliffe to Churchill, asking for help and expressing gratitude for what he was about to receive.[x]

The reaction of the inner council of the Conservatives, expressed as it was in violent terms, came, however, as a serious setback to the Prime Minister. Indeed, the force of their outcry astonished and overwhelmed him and he lacked the faith in his own influence with the administration to drive the issue through to a conclusion. He sought to alter course and to engage Churchill in another capacity. He sent Frederick Guest to propose to Churchill that he should accept his former office of the Duchy of Lancaster, with "elaborated uses and functions". Churchill, burningly eager to serve the country in a truly national capacity, either in the War Cabinet or in charge of a war department, rejected the offer in a perfectly friendly manner. He was well aware of the potential strength of his political position.

Thus Lloyd George wavered in the uncertain political balance. His fear of Churchill impelled him onwards, but his concern for the consequences of Conservative antipathy paralysed his final action.

It was on 17th July in the afternoon that I was summoned to No. 10 Downing Street. As I walked through Whitehall my unfailing measure of optimism prompted me to believe that I would be offered at last a place in the Government dealing with war issues. My confidence was strengthened by the veiled sunshine and the warmth, with dry exhilarating air.

When I was shown into the Cabinet room, Lloyd George was genial and talkative. But he did not say the words I expected him to speak.

He reminded me that I had for long urged him to bring Churchill into the administration. Very well, the time was at hand. What, he asked, would Bonar Law say when the Conservative back-benchers howled in angry unison?

The question could not confidently be answered. Lloyd George would announce to the newspapers the changes in Government bringing into the Ministry of Munitions the much-praised and greatly abused Member for Dundee (Winston Churchill).

It would be my task to go at once to Bonar Law and tell him of this exciting news. A strange method indeed of informing the Leader of the House of Commons; but it was a line of communication which Lloyd George adopted in difficult conditions, and not for the first time.

As I was a warm supporter of Churchill the mission, although difficult and tiresome, was by no means unacceptable to me.

I found Bonar Law in his sitting-room with papers spread about him on the floor. Not newspapers but his departmental and official papers. It was not his habit to stir from his chair if he could avoid it, although he was a polite man. His pipe was lighted. It flashed through my mind, "This will put his pipe out." And it did.

Bonar Law was indignant that the Prime Minister had taken his decision without consulting him. Rufus Isaacs (Lord Reading) wrote a few days later to Lloyd George, to advise him of Bonar Law's feelings in the matter, of which I had already acquainted the Prime Minister.

July 22, 1917.

My dear L.G.,

On quite *reliable* authority I hear that B.L. is sore about the Winston appointment—his point being that

Confidential

My dear LG.

On quite reliable authority I hear that B.L. is sore about the Winston appointment - his point being that he was not told it was to be made before it was actually given to the Press. - He is not complaining of it but nevertheless is aggrieved. I thought it right to let you know.

Yours very
Rufus

LORD READING TO LLOYD GEORGE

he wasn't told it was to be made before it was actually
given to the Press. He is not complaining of it but
nevertheless is aggrieved.

I thought it right to let you know.

Yours always,
RUFUS.*y*

But Bonar Law, in spite of his distrust of
Churchill and his indignation with Lloyd George,
could not allow himself to be guided by these
two considerations alone. Opposed as he was to
Churchill's inclusion in the Government, he had
either to support Lloyd George and his administration or to retire from it. Viewed in this light,
his course of action was straightforward. He
must continue to uphold the Government. He
must give the Prime Minister the support which
was essential over the Churchill case. But he
said, "Lloyd George's throne will shake." And
it did.

The announcement of Mr. Churchill's appointment as Minister of Munitions, together with
other changes in the administration, was published in the Press on 18th July.

At this, the tempest broke with perilous force
over the Prime Minister.

The effect upon the Tory Ministers exceeded
all expectations. Lloyd George, in his *War
Memoirs*, has said: "the insensate fury they displayed . . . surpassed all my apprehensions, and
for some days it swelled to the dimensions of a
grave ministerial crisis which threatened the life of
the Government."*z*

Walter Long sent a letter immediately to the Prime Minister, advising him that the situation made it "extremely difficult for many of my friends to continue their support."[aa] This was tantamount to a threat of resignation; it therefore held the most serious implications for the Coalition. Bonar Law persuaded Long to take no further action.

In the House of Commons, the Unionist [Conservative] Business Committee * was hastily summoned by telegram. At the meeting which followed, members registered their strong dissent from the appointment. That evening a deputation waited on Bonar Law.

A resolution was passed by the 1900 Club (another Tory Committee), profoundly regretting that such "scant regard" had been paid, in appointing Churchill to the Government, to the previously expressed apprehensions and opinions of the Unionist Party, upon whose loyal aid Lloyd George's Ministry so largely depended.[ab]

Churchill's appointment was also assailed in the Conservative Press. The *Morning Post* became the spokesman of the most hostile elements. The newspaper's censure of Churchill knew no bounds: "That dangerous and uncertain quantity, Mr. Winston Churchill—a floating kidney in the body politic—is back again in Westminster."[ac] "By his appointment Mr. Lloyd George loses enormously in prestige, for it proves him to be a

---

* An important and influential group of members of both Houses of Parliament resembling in structure the American Party caucus but exercising no real power or authority.

man who allows private partiality to overcome public duty."[ad]

"The one thing certain," declared the *Morning Post*, "is that the Lloyd George Ministry has been dangerously weakened by what has happened."[ae]

Never before in history had the selection of a Minister of the Crown given rise to such a vehement opposition. A stick had been thrust into the political beehive and the rage of the drones and the workers was terrible to behold.

Lloyd George's throne tottered. But it did not fall.

Bonar Law met the deputation from the Unionist Business Committee with a stiff resistance. He had made up his mind to support the Government and he did so now with all his might.

He assured the deputation that Churchill's appointment had been accepted by the King and would stand.[af]

Nevertheless, Lloyd George was seriously damaged and he sustained prolonged and bitter hostility for his action in forcing the appointment. Walter Long represented the feeling of the Conservative Ministers to Bonar Law. "The real effect," he asserted, "has been to destroy all confidence in Ll.G. It is widely held that for purposes of his own, quite apart from the war, he has deceived and 'jockeyed' us."[ag]

In this atmosphere, Churchill returned to the administration. He was to prove a powerful reinforcement, but it was many years before the ill-feeling and the recriminations died away.

Churchill, rejoicing in the opportunity to serve the nation in an important office directly bearing upon the war, had no illusion about the feelings stirred up by his appointment. He looked round at his new Conservative colleagues with an understanding and humorous eye. As the Prime Minister set off for France a few days after the appointment, the new Minister made an amusing appeal to him.

"Don't get torpedoed;" he enjoined him, "for if I am left alone your colleagues will eat me."[ah] But he knew that he had reason to be grateful to Lloyd George.

The Prime Minister, too, had sound reasons for solid satisfaction. He had removed danger from his seat. He had regained the companionship and association of a man he liked and admired. He had shown gratitude for unflinching support at that black moment some few years before when Marconi was the principal subject of discussion in and out of Parliament. He had cancelled out his later actions.

For in 1915, Lloyd George, partly out of shrewd judgement of what was and what was not possible, partly out of pure self-interest, would not lift a finger to help Churchill when misfortune overwhelmed him over Gallipoli. Lloyd George let him fall without making any effort to save him. Asked to support him for a command in East Africa, which Bonar Law as Colonial Secretary was willing to concede, Lloyd George shook his head and murmured something of the feelings of the widows and orphans of Gallipoli.

He accepted Churchill's help in the crisis which made him Prime Minister, but denied him any reward. He pleaded Tory hostility to making Churchill a Minister, with justice and fair cause. But he added charges on his own which, if true, ought to have meant the permanent exclusion of Churchill from power. "Why," he said, "he brought Turkey into the war. Such men are too dangerous for high office."

Now these events and this indictment had been forgotten and these criticisms did not prevent Lloyd George from making Winston Churchill his Minister of Munitions on 18th July, 1917.

By January, 1919, Lloyd George's confidence in Churchill had risen to higher altitudes. Then the feeling of the widows and orphans of Gallipoli had been forgotten, and the man who was too dangerous for high office was told to choose the War Office or the Admiralty and, said Lloyd George, "whichever you take, you may carry the Air with you."

Churchill replied to Lloyd George accepting the Admiralty:

> My heart is in the Admiralty. There I have long experience, & any claim I may be granted in public goodwill rests on the fact that "the Fleet was ready". In all the circumstances of the present situation I believe I shd. add more weight to yr. Administration at the Admiralty than at the War Office.[ai] *

By the time this communication reached the Prime Minister, the option had expired. Lloyd

* See *Appendix IV*, No. 5, for full text.

George put him at the War Office. It often happened that way.

Churchill was well pleased with his new place in 1919. Colonel Seely at the Air Ministry was peeping out from behind his coat tails.

I have a picture of Churchill in my mind striding up and down in his room at the War Office, tingling with vitality. Bold and imaginative in the sweep of his conceptions, prolific of new ideas, like a machine gun of bullets and expelling his notions in much the same manner. Fertile, resourceful, courageous, he was always tolerant, though in this age occasionally wanting in prudence.

The political front was of course in confusion. These were days of broken lights of political faith. Was he nearer to Asquith's brand of Liberalism or did he freely accept Lloyd George and the Coalition? Was he a Liberal or a Tory?

He did not know himself.

Surely he had a foot in both camps. Not intentionally, but none the less, what he did abroad pleased the Tories and infuriated the Radicals. When he spoke at home, he was cheered by Radicals, and how he annoyed the Tories!

It was not inconvenient to be in a position which permitted him to step off with either foot.

He talked brilliantly and with all the ardour of middle age. Some persons said he talked too much. He never surrounded himself with those who were only good listeners. His conversation was best when he spoke with a trusted companion.

Although he had not attained to his great prestige, he was apt even then to hold sway in a large gathering, acting all the time. He was a fine actor. And occasionally he indulged in mimicry of the speech of certain of his colleagues.

He drew from his well of experience. He differed from many of his political contemporaries who had a stock of stories frequently repeated. He was always truthful. He could keep a secret.

Here I leave him. All the years of the First War may be regarded as a schooling in strategy and in politics equipping Winston Spencer Churchill as the Master Mind of the world war as yet far, far distant.

CHAPTER V

THE ULSTER PIRATE

CARSON never put his trust in Lloyd George. And Lloyd George never could rely upon uncritical support from Carson.

They had worked together in presenting an ultimatum to Asquith demanding that the direction of the war should be handed to the triumvirate of Lloyd George, Bonar Law and Carson. And when it was rejected, the Triumvirate brought Asquith down and destroyed his Government.

Now Lloyd George had climbed to power on the steps of the ladder held in position by Bonar Law and Carson. When he reached the seat of authority he forgot about the ladder. Instead of a war committee of himself, Bonar Law and Carson, the new Prime Minister called into an enlarged and somewhat decorative body, named the War Cabinet, the old cart-horse Curzon who could be relied upon to support his master providing the fodder held out and Lord Milner, a very different type.* He had been a Civil Servant. But he never was a candidate for elected office; he

* Milner's name was pressed upon Lloyd George and others by Geoffrey Dawson, Editor of *The Times*, at that moment a supporter of Lloyd George and also a powerful influence in Cabinet-making circles.

never had taken part in the hurly-burly of political meetings; he never had to defend himself in debate, even in the calm seclusion of the House of Lords, where he sat for many years. Carson was sent to the Admiralty, a post that was not suited to his abilities.

In his *War Memoirs*, Lloyd George has given two reasons for Carson's exclusion from the inner Cabinet circle and the central direction of the war. He was overridden, he says, "by the personal prejudices of the majority of the Conservative leaders against Carson. They all admired but disapproved of him".[a] His inclusion, moreover, would have tipped the balance of membership of a small war council too heavily in favour of the Conservatives.

These explanations are unsound. Lloyd George could have overridden Tory opposition without difficulty. For Carson was quite a different proposition from Churchill or Lord Northcliffe. The Tory Party chiefs had refused to serve with either of them. But no Cabinet denying ordinance fenced Carson in.

What then was the real reason for Carson's exclusion from the Triumvirate which was to have governed Britain for the duration of the war?

The explanation is a simple one. Lloyd George was suspicious and distrustful of Carson. There was no real basis of understanding and confidence between these two Celtic characters.

It is right to record that Lloyd George looked upon Carson as a potential enemy, and with some justification. He was in direct conflict with the

Irish leader over many political issues. And he often spoke of Carson's conduct in derogatory terms. Moreover he was convinced that collaboration with Carson alienated support from Liberals in Parliament and from Liberal newspapers in the country. He would use Carson when necessary. He would avoid close association when convenient. Nor were they suited to each other in social contacts.

When Carson became First Lord of the Admiralty he was in a despondent and indifferent mood. He was discontented and disaffected. "The moment that Asquith's fall was accomplished," I wrote of him in my previous volume, "a kind of incuriousness seemed to descend upon him. He was like a man whose task is accomplished."[b]

That office of state, moreover, had proved no safe harbour for the politicians appointed to it. Two eminent leaders had already held the post of war-time First Lord and both had walked the plank, Churchill and A. J. Balfour.

Churchill was the first to go overboard. Following upon his dramatic mobilisation of the Fleet on that dark night at the outbreak of war, he did not remain long in the position of responsibility where he believed his talents were used to best advantage. Within eight months he was driven from office by the forceful action of the First Sea Lord, Admiral Fisher, who pulled down the blinds and took the train to Scotland.

It is a matter for regret that Churchill was ever sacrificed. He had the spirit, the drive and the energy. He had the redoubtable Jackie Fisher to help him. But he failed to manage Fisher. This was strange because in the Second War Churchill proved to be a manager of men and a master of his colleagues.

Balfour filled the vacant place. His appointment was unsuitable. His erudition and his powers of reasoning did not equip him for the post of political head of the Admiralty at the height of a Naval war. His career there was not free from storms.

There was, in fact, one important occasion when Balfour wholly forfeited the sympathy of the public. At the end of May, 1916, the Germans engaged the British Fleet at the Battle of Jutland. News of the encounter was depressing in the extreme; Balfour believed that the nation must be given the full facts of the battle and he himself prepared a statement.

It was a catalogue of appalling disaster. Three battle cruisers and three cruisers had been sunk, five destroyers had been lost in action, six others were unaccounted for. "The enemy's losses," said the communiqué, "were serious." *ᶜ

The despatch flashed like a message of despair throughout the country.

Balfour had acted in the conviction that the people must be told the unvarnished facts. Later news was to bring brighter tidings of the battle, but in the meantime consternation and alarm had

---

* In the final score, Britain lost 3 battle cruisers, 3 cruisers and 8 destroyers at the Battle of Jutland. German losses were 1 battleship, 1 battle cruiser, 4 light cruisers and 5 destroyers.ᶜ

spread throughout the nation and to the allied countries.

So great, indeed, were their feelings first of anxiety, and then of righteous anger when comforting reports were circulated that Churchill was called in, at Balfour's own request, to write an official appreciation of the Battle of Jutland and to allay anxiety among the friendly neutrals. Balfour's prestige suffered heavily over this unhappy lapse of judgement.

In the last months of the Asquith Administration, Balfour became the subject of a vigorous campaign conducted by Lord Northcliffe to remove him from the Government. "BMG" became the popular catch-cry for the second time in one decade. "BMG"—"Balfour Must Go"—was the invention of my political friends when Balfour was pushed out of the leadership of the Tory Party in 1911. His successor was Bonar Law. Now in 1916 it was reiterated by the powerful giant of Fleet Street.

In this campaign Northcliffe was openly encouraged by the critical attitude of Lloyd George, at that time Secretary of State for War, whose views were widely disseminated by the Liberal Press. Balfour, however, was retained by the same Lloyd George when he became Prime Minister and actually promoted to the Foreign Office. Indeed his retention as a prominent member of the Administration was the hinge of the Conservatives' accession to Lloyd George's Coalition.

Now Carson's appointment to the Admiralty

gave satisfaction to the public. It was believed that he would be a stern man of action, silent in a silent service.

He was one of the most interesting personalities of the war. His position in British public life was unique. As the "uncrowned king of Ulster", the unchallenged chieftain of the stern Orangemen of Northern Ireland, and hope of the Protestant diehards of the South, he was more than a political leader. He was almost a feudal lord, commanding allegiance from devoted and ardent followers and treating with the Conservative Party as if he were an independent and equal ally.

He was a man of very high intellectual attainment, his mind possessing a startling clarity, sharpened by many encounters at the Bar; his gifts of advocacy were immense. He had the talent of lighting at once upon the defects and weaknesses in a situation. This made him formidable in counsel, powerful in opposition, but a source of danger and weakness in harness. He saw the flaws in every Administration. He was, by temperament, opposed to every Government. He was admirably adjusted to taking high place in any Administration and at the same time acting as leader of the Opposition.

Yet he took up his work at the Admiralty with a full sense of responsibility. He was eager to make a success of his task. He wrote to a friend, Gibson Bowles, "I feel full of responsibility, but you may be quite sure I will try to get the fullest play for the Navy; and I don't intend to become an amateur in naval strategy or tactics. The submarine peril is a deadly one, and I am turning all attention to it." [d]

The submarine peril was indeed deadly. The year of 1917 opened on a scene of desolation and anxiety. The survival of Britain hung in the balance. On the land, the great forces of German military power massed themselves for an offensive on the Western Front. At sea, the striking power of the U-boat accumulated a terrible intensity. The toll of shipping, with the Channel routes open to constant attack from bases at Zeebrugge, mounted with every month.

It was becoming increasingly apparent that the fate of Great Britain would be settled on the sea. Everything, indeed, turned on our ability to combat the menace of the submarines. The danger that, should we fail to do so, the country would be starved into submission had constantly to be taken into account.

It was a vital and tremendous challenge for the new First Lord.

From the very first days, however, Carson defined his position. He placed himself at once at the disposal of his expert advisers. He became to a marked degree dependent on the advice and guidance of his department. And he resisted staunchly any inclination to develop his own ideas of Naval strategy.

Indeed, he went further. In public pronouncements the First Lord proclaimed his intention to support and to protect the policy of his admirals.

In March, 1917, he made a public declaration of striking frankness which disclosed his attitude to the Administration. He would be the refuge and strength of the admirals and the protector of the generals; he would espouse their cause against the politicians.

At a luncheon gathering at the Aldwych Club, when Lord Northcliffe—that great champion of the generals—was in the chair, Carson closed his speech with these words:

"I advise the country to pay no attention to amateur strategists, who are always impatient and always ready for a gamble. We cannot afford to gamble with our Fleet.

"As long as I am at the Admiralty the sailors will have full scope. They will not be interfered with by me, and I will not let anyone interfere with them."[e]

Carson thus stood in defiant hostility to any pressure from the politicians upon the admirals. When analysed, his attitude was strange and even self-contradictory. He would see that the admirals were allowed to go their own way and pursue their own strategy. And if things went wrong—who were to be criticised? Not, it seemed, the admirals. Criticism could fall only on the politicians.

Lloyd George was, of course, the "amateur strategist". It was an open avowal of Carson's prejudice against the Administration. For the contest between Service or Civilian control of the wartime direction was in full swing. It was the topic of the political clubs, in the lobby, and in the daily newspapers. Carson had come out frankly on behalf of the generals.

It was not long before an open clash flared up between the Prime Minister and his First Lord of the Admiralty.

The question of convoys was the preoccupying problem of those grave days in the late winter of 1917.

Lloyd George at once became the ardent exponent of the convoy principle.

The Admiralty, however, did not support the proposal. Several strong arguments against the system were adduced by the Naval authorities. It was contended that the convoy offered too large a target. "The system of several ships sailing together in a convoy is not recommended in any area where submarine attack is a possibility," stated an official Admiralty publication in January, 1917. "It is evident that the larger the number of ships forming the convoy, the greater is the chance of a submarine being enabled to attack successfully, the greater is the difficulty of the escort in preventing such an attack."

It was also argued that the merchantman, sailing alone, and able to load and turn round swiftly, was a more efficient vessel than it would be as a member of a Fleet compelled to wait for the assembly of its consorts and to sail at the pace of the slowest vessel.

The experts, wrote Lloyd George, were "unanimously and stubbornly opposed" to the adoption of convoys.*f*

Carson's position in the continuing dispute was unequivocal. He firmly supported the admirals. He had been ready to concede a trial of the convoy plan, but he had no intention of pushing the project against the opinion of his Naval advisers.[*]

By April, the figures for losses of British merchant tonnage were four times as great as those of January, 1917.[†] News of sinkings became from day to day an increasing worry to the War Cabinet. Indeed, at one time, only one week's stock of wheat remained in the country.

It was in this critical emergency that Sir John Jellicoe (the First Sea Lord) submitted a memorandum entitled "The Submarine Menace and the Food Supply". It was a document of ominous character. It could not be disguised that the shipping losses would produce the most serious results for the country.

What then was the solution the First Sea Lord had to offer? Jellicoe's recommendations contained no recognition of the convoy system. Conservation of the existing food supplies and an intensification of the present methods of antisubmarine action were the measure of his remedies.

His report left the Prime Minister profoundly disquieted. Lloyd George was now convinced of the need for decisive action.

Here was his position. At the height of crisis in the war the Prime Minister found himself in

---

[*] Lloyd George writes of Carson: "Personally, he favoured a trial being made, but told me he had no official support from any quarter in his department." [g]

[†] In January, 153,512 tons of British merchant tonnage was lost by enemy action; in April the figure had reached 545,282 tons. [h]

direct opposition to his Naval advisers. And the First Lord of the Admiralty (Carson) gave his support and allegiance, not to the Prime Minister, but to the Naval staff. Yet the policy pursued by the admirals was condemned on the evidence of the shipping losses.

The Prime Minister decided the convoy plan must be adopted. This was the programme Lloyd George proposed now to force upon the Naval Board.

On 26th April, 1917, he determined to take action of a most aggressive nature. He informed the Press that fifty-five merchant ships had been sunk in seven days. Then he sent the following letter to Sir Edward Carson.

> My Dear First Lord,
> Since we met this morning I have received enclosed. There seems to me to be no doubt that it is vital to this country that we should settle this infernal question. Otherwise we might sink.
>   Ever yours,
>   D. LLOYD GEORGE.[1]

At the same time he told his colleagues of his intention to go down himself to the Admiralty and make peremptory decisions; thus establishing the convoy system of transportation by sea.

Lloyd George wanted a Conservative reinforcement. Bonar Law declined the duty, pleading his difficulties with Carson over the Irish situation. With good reason. Several sections of the Press were saying that criticisms of the Admiralty from some quarters were really attacks on Carson "for quite different reasons". One newspaper gave outspoken expression to the view that the attacks were inspired "not by any knowledge of naval affairs, but by the hope that if he can be driven from the Government Irish Home Rule will be brought appreciably nearer".[j]

Lord Curzon was chosen as the Prime Minister's bodyguard. On the day of the impending visit to Admiralty House, he wrote to the Prime Minister.

My dear Prime Minister,

Coming up in the train, I have been thinking of the subjects which I understand that you and I are to raise at the Admiralty in the investigation that is to begin at noon today.

On the accompanying sheet, I have jotted down some of these in some sort of order. Probably you have thought of many more but perhaps this list may be useful.

Yours sincerely,
CURZON.

On 30th April, with the submarine peril at its height, the Prime Minister descended upon the Admiralty and seated himself in the First Lord's chair.

This was possibly an unprecedented action. It was well within the powers and competence of the Prime Minister; yet there may be no parallels in our history. For one afternoon the Prime Minister took over the full reins of Government from the head of a major department of state. It was inevitable that, as a result, Carson's prestige suffered a serious blow.

The meeting was a minor triumph for the Prime Minister. A re-examination of the figures of shipping losses prepared by the Minister of Shipping had brought a frame of mind in which the admirals were at least willing to experiment with a convoy.

"The High Admirals," wrote Lloyd George, "had at last been persuaded by the 'Convoyers' not perhaps to take action, but to try action."[1]

Lloyd George had staged a deliberate encounter with the Naval High Command, and had emerged triumphant. But he had lost faith in Carson, Jellicoe and even his Board of Admiralty.

The main struggle had yet to be faced. There could be but one sequel: the dismissal of Jellicoe and the replacement of Carson.

"So I made up my mind," writes Lloyd George in his *Memoirs*, "to effect a change at the top in the Admiralty ... I therefore contemplated a change in the First Lord, Lord Carson, and the First Sea Lord, Admiral Jellicoe. They were both men of great influence and authority, and both possessed a formidable following, one political, the other naval."[m]

It was a brave decision. The consequences might be severe and even fatal to Lloyd George himself. Would Carson resist? Would he get extensive support? Would the Board of Admiralty resign in a body? The House of Commons might become a tribunal deciding the issue, where Carson's strength was certainly extensive, though undefined.

Yet there was the terrible toll of losses, mounting every day. The correspondence of Walter Page, U.S. Ambassador to Great Britain, gives a startling account of the Naval balance sheet. I reproduce an extract from an illuminating letter of 4th May, 1917.

London, May 4, 1917.

Dear Mr. President,

The submarines have become a very grave danger. The loss of British and Allied tonnage increases with the longer and brighter days—as I telegraphed you, 237,000 tons last week; and the worst of it is, the British are not destroying them. The Admiralty publishes a weekly report which, though true, is not the whole truth. It is known in official circles here that the Germans are turning out at least two a week—some say three; and the British are not destroying them as fast as new ones are turned out. If merely the present situation continue, the war will pretty soon become a contest of endurance under hunger with an increasing proportion of starvation. Germany is yet much the worse off, but it will be easily possible for Great Britain to suffer to the danger point next winter or earlier unless some decided change be wrought in this situation.

One help—how great it is yet somewhat too soon to know—will come when all merchantmen are armed and properly manned. Arming here is going on, and, of course, all our trans-Atlantic ships are armed.

But the greatest help, I hope, can come from us— our destroyers and similar armed craft,—provided we can send enough of them quickly. The area to be watched is so big that many submarine-hunters are needed. Early in the war the submarines worked near shore. There are very many more of them now and their range is one hundred miles, or even two hundred, at sea.

The public is becoming very restive with its half-information, and it is more and more loudly demanding all the facts. There are already angry threats to change the personnel of the Admiralty: there is even talk of turning out the Government. "We must have results, we must have results." I hear confidentially that Jellicoe has threatened to resign unless the Salonika expedition is brought back: to feed and equip that force requires too many ships.

And there are other troubles impending. Norway has lost so many of her ships that she dare not send what are left to sea. Unarmed they'll all perish. If she arm them, Germany will declare war against her. There is a plan on foot for the British to charter these Norwegian ships and to arm them, taking the risk of German war against Norway. If war come (as it is expected), England must then defend Norway the best she can. She will close the German access to Norway with mines and with such of the Grand Fleet as can be spared. And *then England may ask for our big ships to help in these waters.* All this is yet in the future, but possibly not far in the future.

For the present the only anti-submarine help is the help we may be able to give to patrol the wide area off Ireland. If we had one hundred destroyers to send the job there could, I am told, be quickly done. A third of that number will help mightily. At the present rate of destruction more than four million tons will be sunk before the summer is gone.

Such is this dire submarine danger. The English thought that they controlled the sea; the Germans, that they were invincible on land. Each side is losing where it thought itself strongest."

Carson and his friends now began to show fight. They felt that they were being knocked about. They believed that Carson was to play the role of

CARSON

No one knows to this day whether it was bluff or not

a scapegoat. They wouldn't have it. Sir Hedworth Meux, Admiral of the Fleet, spoke out strongly. At Liverpool on 2nd May he asserted:

> In Sir Edward Carson we have got what the Navy considers the right man. I hope you will not allow these attacks . . . to drive him out of office.[o]

Conservative newspapers gave their confidence and support to their old hero. They had faith in him. Then Carson's loyal friends in the House of Commons made up a mighty band of stalwart and vehement champions.

For Lloyd George the predicament was acute. He was playing two hands. He was preparing to bring into the Ministry of Munitions the weak man Churchill and he was preparing to drive out of the Admiralty the strong man Carson. Carson was a formidable and respected figure whose removal must excite the hostility, not only of the admirals and the generals and the military faction but also of a considerable section of Lloyd George's own following in the country.

Yet the shield that sheltered Jellicoe must be thrust aside. It was a political tactic requiring skill and daring, and much preliminary labour.

Another extract from the correspondence of Walter Page written to President Wilson gives a vivid picture of the tension between Lloyd George and Carson.

> A little while ago [writes Page] he [Lloyd George] dined with me, and, after dinner, I took him to a corner

of the drawing-room and delivered your message to him about Ireland. "God knows, I'm trying," he replied. "Tell the President that. And tell him to talk to Balfour." Presently he broke out—"Madmen, madmen—I never saw any such task," and he pointed across the room to Sir Edward Carson, his First Lord of the Admiralty—"Madmen." "But the President's right. We've got to settle it and we've got to settle it now." Carson and Jellicoe came across the room and sat down with us. "I've been telling the Ambassador, Carson, that we've got to settle the Irish question now—in spite of you."

"I'll tell you something else we've got to settle now," said Carson. "Else it'll settle us. That's the submarines. The press and public are working up a calculated and concerted attack on Jellicoe and me, and, if they get us, they'll get you. It's an attack on the Government made on the Admiralty, Prime Minister," said this Ulster pirate whose civil war didn't come off only because the big war was begun—"Prime Minister, it may be a fierce attack. Get ready for it."ᴾ

Now Carson had on this occasion used offensive and even insolent language to his Prime Minister and in the presence of a Foreign Ambassador. It was a measure of their relationship.

There was little or no sympathy between "the little man" (as Carson called Lloyd George) and "the Ulster Pirate" (as Page called Carson).

No doubt Lloyd George feared Carson. Yet it was imperative that he now grapple with the problem. There were dangers too great to be shirked. Should the losses of merchant ships continue at the prevailing rate, then disaster must fall upon Britain within a few weeks.

160

Carson's administration must be terminated and the Lords of the Admiralty must be brought under control. There was no escape. Lloyd George must act, and act at once.

There were other warnings that could not be neglected with safety—written warnings that might be published. Lloyd George was being bombarded with letters of complaint from the Shipping Controller, Sir Joseph Maclay, himself a wealthy shipping magnate who commanded immense respect on account of his complete integrity and who enjoyed, in addition, the esteem due to one who was the undisputed leader of Britain's shipping industry. Maclay was a deeply religious man who for many years carried on a Christian mission at Marrakesh. He compiled a volume of family prayers, "The Starting Place Of The Day".

At any moment the Shipping Controller's resignation might be tossed on Lloyd George's table. Bad enough. But made worse because Maclay had the reputation of being a "man of God", thus commanding strength and support in Lloyd George's own nonconformist circles.

All these circumstances helped Lloyd George to make up his mind; he was determined that the admirals must be subjected to civilian discipline. Someone of resource and vitality who could, if necessary, carry out a naval strategy independent of the Board, must be made First Lord. And another First Lord must be fortified by a change in his Chief Naval Adviser.

Carson, well aware of the gathering storm, took a strong line of defence. He made public declaration of his confidence in Jellicoe with a subtle suggestion that he despised his own Prime Minister.

At a luncheon gathering on 17th May in honour of the American Navy, he denounced his critics with the burning fervour that distinguished him in attack.

"I am so constituted," he said, "that I cannot get cold feet. I can divide my critics into various categories. There are my political critics. I despise them in the middle of war. Then there are the critics who have been disappointed in the past. Whenever you read criticisms of my colleague Sir John Jellicoe, try to find out what is the origin of them. But after all it does not really matter. . . . Let them grumble and growl and let us get on with our work."[9]

Lloyd George now decided to adopt an audacious method. It was full of skill and daring, and of that talent for the ingenious that put him in the front rank of political tacticians. For in preparing to instal a strong man at the Admiralty and thus reduce the influence of the admirals, Lloyd George enlisted the aid and support of the generals—Carson's natural allies in the struggle.

In the early months of 1917 there was no unified front of Army and Navy against the civilians. Had there been, events would have taken a very different turn. Instead we find the Prime Minister taking the generals into his confidence over the situation at the Admiralty, and receiving their enthusiastic backing for his plan.

At the beginning of the summer, Lloyd George spoke with Sir Douglas Haig, who was himself in danger of being handed the black spot.

In his *War Memoirs*, he records: "A conversation I had with Sir Douglas Haig in the early summer of 1917 finally decided me. The Commander-in-Chief was also alarmed at the dismaying ravages of the submarine. He was apprehensive that the War might be lost at sea before he had an opportunity of winning it on land. He had great admiration for Jellicoe's knowledge as a technical sailor, but he thought him much too rigid, narrow and conservative in his ideas. . . . Sir Douglas Haig had no opinion of his [Carson's] qualities as an administrator. . . . He strongly urged upon me the appointment of Sir Eric Geddes to that post."[r]

There has since been a great outcry by the defenders of both Carson and Jellicoe against this claim made by Lloyd George.

Ian Colvin, Lord Carson's biographer,* has rejected Lloyd George's record of his conversation with Haig and Lloyd George's assertion that Haig was responsible for convincing him that he must dismiss both Jellicoe and Carson. "Sir Douglas Haig, had he been alive," declares Colvin, "would no doubt have been flattered to know that a Minister who misprized him on land should have so deferred to him at sea."[s]

* Colvin wrote a lively biography of Lord Carson. He was, of course, the most powerful leader-writer of his time. His writings had a wide circulation in political circles and much influence.

Sir Reginald Bacon in his biography of Admiral Jellicoe * has also denied Lloyd George's story, and with asperity. Indeed he goes to the extent of declaring that there is nothing in Haig's diary or papers that gives the slightest colour to such a statement. He acquits Haig of being a collaborator.

But the publication of Haig's private papers † destroys completely the position taken up by Colvin and Bacon. Sir Douglas Haig himself discloses that he took a dominating part in driving both Carson and Jellicoe out of Admiralty House.'

Encouraged by Lloyd George, Haig became at once the Prime Minister's battering ram against the gates of Carson's stronghold at the Admiralty.

For ten days in June, 1917, he apparently spent his time in London, carrying out a well-organised, thoroughly considered and widespread campaign to drive the First Lord and also Jellicoe from their posts.

On 20th June, 1917, he visited Temporary Admiral Sir Eric Geddes (a political appointment), at this time Carson's subordinate, but by no means loyal to his chief. He agreed with Geddes that the Admiralty was in the hands of a number of incompetent sailors, Jellicoe feeble to a degree and vacillating in conduct.

Of Carson himself Haig declared: "The First Lord has recently married, he is very tired and

---

* Sir R. H. Bacon: *Life of John Rushworth, Earl Jellicoe* (London, Cassell, 1936), p. 378.
† *The Private Papers of Douglas Haig, 1914–1919,* edited by Robert Blake who deserves praise for the wisdom and discretion he has shown in his editorship. His book on Bonar Law, *The Unknown Prime Minister,* is one of the best biographies of recent times.

leaves everything to a number of incompetent sailors."

Haig promised Geddes that he would arrange for an interview with Lloyd George, so that the desperate situation at the Admiralty could be put before him. He agreed with Geddes that an audience should be sought from the King, for the same purpose.

Now Haig had immense influence at the Palace. The King relied upon him. Without doubt, he was the Keeper of the Palace gates. This close and trusting relationship is an interesting and absorbing subject, peeping out from time to time in the diaries and letters of His Majesty and his Commander-in-Chief.

Within five days (25th June, 1917) Haig had spoken to Lord Curzon, complaining about the seriously inefficient state of the Admiralty. He then saw Lloyd George and repeated his arguments, which might be summed up as "action this day".

He lunched with Balfour. Then he called on Asquith, Leader of the Opposition in Parliament. He had a talk with the "old man" (Haig's phrase) about the unsatisfactory state in the Admiralty and the ignorance of the high Naval officers.

The next day the promised interview between Geddes and the Prime Minister took place at 10 Downing Street with Haig present. It was at breakfast. When Geddes had made his complaint Lloyd George declared he was much impressed and sent for Milner who was a critic of Carson's administration.

At the breakfast party a proposal was put forward to promote Robertson to Carson's place; a proposal which suited Lloyd George admirably. For Robertson had by this time become the Prime Minister's "turbulent priest", and Lloyd George would pay any price to get rid of his tormentor.

Breakfast over, away went Haig to the War Office, but Robertson refused to become First Lord of the Admiralty, because he said it would mean he would have to become a politician.

On June 28th, 1917, after all these labours, Haig returned to his Headquarters, from which he had taken leave while promoting his intrigues in London.

It is interesting to speculate on Haig's real motives. It may have been that he was moved by genuine anxiety. He had informed Lady Haig as early as May that he looked on Jellicoe as an "old woman". Or again, it is possible that he may have been interested mainly in diverting the lightning from striking at himself, for the dismissal of Haig had been a principal objective of Lloyd George for many months.*

Haig, in fact, had managed to hold his job in defiance of Lloyd George's hostility, only through the intervention of four Tory Ministers and, more important at this time, the interest and support of the King himself.

---

* Indeed as early as February, 1917, two months after Lloyd George's pledge to his Conservative colleagues to keep Haig in command in France, a letter from Lord Derby discloses an ominous attack on Haig by the Prime Minister. See *Appendix IV*, Nos. 6 and 7. Letters of Lord Derby, 19th and 20th February, 1917.

He needed all the help he could get. For Lloyd George never did give his trust to Haig and never did cease to threaten the Commander-in-Chief with dismissal.

There is, in conclusion, a sad commentary upon the strange character and conduct of the Commander-in-Chief. Within three months Haig and Carson had a happy meeting at Army Headquarters in France. They criticised the Prime Minister, denouncing his meddling practices. "Carson," wrote Haig, "is so straightforward and single-minded.""

Even though the proposal at the breakfast party to get rid of Robertson by sending him to the Admiralty had come to nothing, Lloyd George had no hesitation in trying to mobilize Robertson's strength in the attack on Carson and Jellicoe.

But the old General was cautious. He replied in terms that might be described after the words of the Emigrant's Lament, "I am sitting on the stile".

I quote the letter in full.

26.5.17.

Dear Prime Minister,

I hear good accounts of the naval officer—Richmond. He is evidently a keen student of naval history and warfare, and is described to me as "the first naval officer met who seems to have a General Staff mind". I gather that he would be a great asset at the Admiralty—on the War Staff—and probably of far more use there than in a ship.* I am sorry I can hear nothing of the two other naval officers you mentioned. I may warn

---

* Robertson proved an accurate judge of this man. Richmond became Commandant of the Imperial Defence College. In 1929 he was appointed Professor of Imperial and Naval History at Cambridge where he published valuable works on Naval strategy.

you that it will take a *long* time to get going what you want, there is bound to be much obstruction by the old gang. It was so here, and took us years. We are progressing now because the younger generation have in recent years got into the top places. "General Staff" was anathema to our top generals even as recently as 8 years ago.

Yours sincerely,

W. R. ROBERTSON.'

At the same time the Prime Minister was mobilising the support of his Cabinet colleagues. Here the voice of Lord Milner carried a considerable authority. Milner had been originally considered for the post of First Lord when Lloyd George formed his Administration. The Prime Minister's distrust of Carson, however, had elevated Milner to the War Cabinet.

In counsel Milner's advice was moderate. He desired to carry the soldiers as far as possible with the administration.* But now, after the breakfast party at 10 Downing Street, he devised a plan and at once he wrote to Lloyd George:

26.6.17.

My dear Prime Minister,

It may seem a rather startling proposition, but I think it would be the best plan to bring Carson into the War Cabinet, where he would be excellent, and to make Geddes First Lord. In that case, with a really first-rate administrator at the Head of the Board, the great requisite in the First Sea Lord would be courage and knowledge of men, an intimate acquaintance with

---

* There was as yet no evidence of the preoccupation that caused Milner to use all his efforts at the beginning of 1918 in order to drive General Robertson from office.

the best men in the service and a determination to bring them on and put them into their right places regardless of seniority and red tape. Such a First Sea Lord can be found more easily than a naval man, who is a great administrator. That quality must be imported from outside.

Yours very sincerely,
MILNER.

I think it should be part of the bargain, that Carson helped B.L. in the House of Commons, where I think the Govt. lacks fighting power."

The Prime Minister seized on the Milner Plan. It brought wonderful relief and a magnificent escape from the perils of political strife with Carson.

Bonar Law was in agreement but he was anxious that the change should be carried out with the least possible offence to Sir Edward Carson. He recognised that Lloyd George's plan was beset with danger.

Curzon, too, was firmly behind the Prime Minister. His support had been strengthened by conversation with Haig.

But the most powerful reinforcement came from Sir Joseph Maclay, Shipping Controller, who wrote two letters on 28th June, one to Lloyd George and one to Bonar Law. I give them both here in full.

28th June 1917.

Dear Prime Minister,

I had not intended in view of your leaving for the North to trouble you today further about the shipping

169

position, but it has come to my knowledge this morning that private meetings are being held of shipmasters and others, to consider the position and there is a danger that unless something is done in connection with the Admiralty, we shall have these men refusing to go to sea.

Statistics prove that what are called the areas of concentration as now managed, have become veritable death traps for our Mercantile Marine and our men are realising this.

I am led to believe that confidence in the Admiralty has pretty well gone but the coming of a few American destroyers has given them a little heart, which is a melancholy reflection on the position. The confidence of our Mercantile Marine in the Admiralty has been flittered [sic] away and does not now exist.

I am only sending you this letter after full consultation with Sir Kenneth Anderson and Sir Norman Hill, who are of opinion it should go.

Yours very truly,

J. P. MACLAY.[x]

Private & Urgent   28th June 1917.

Dear Bonar Law,

I think it right to send you copy of letter which I have sent to the Prime Minister this morning. I will try to see you today but I am convinced that unless something is done promptly relative to the Admiralty, we shall have an exhibition somewhat along the lines of the Mesopotamia report of this morning.—The position is just as bad as it can be and my conviction is that no man or shadow of a man should be allowed to stand in the way of the country at the present juncture while the country is in such dire peril. Changes are wanted right from the top downwards, and the position should be faced.

Yours truly,

J. P. MACLAY.

Now Lloyd George turned to the King—the master move in his devious strategy. At the beginning of July he had an interview with Lord Stamfordham. Their conversation was reported in a Minute to His Majesty.

Humbly submitted.   July 5, 1917.

 I have seen the Prime Minister this afternoon. He seriously contemplates making changes at the Admiralty. When he visited the Grand Fleet last week he gathered that there was dissatisfaction with the Admiralty: the Government are of the same opinion. Sir John Jellicoe is too pessimistic: if things do not go quite right he "is apt to get 'cold feet': grouses: says the War can't go on many months more &c &c". Both Sir W. Robertson and Sir Douglas Haig think that things are not right at the Admiralty, and the Prime Minister suggested Your Majesty might perhaps speak to the latter on the subject. He is inclined to put Sir E. Carson into the War Cabinet where he would be very useful and especially in making speeches in the country which the P.M. says ought to be more done just now but unfortunately there are very few in the Government who attract public audiences! I remarked it would be difficult to find the man with "driving power" "resourcefulness" and "of an inspiriting nature" such as he said was necessary as 1st Lord "who would hearten up everyone on the Board". He replied that the man he had in his mind was Sir Eric Geddes. He had got on very well with the soldiers when once they overcame their first antagonism to the introduction of a civilian "outsider"— and he would soon have the Army working amicably with him. . . .[z]

But then it was that Lloyd George hesitated. Would Carson go quietly? Would he be willing to separate himself from Sir John Jellicoe? There was no certainty when Carson was concerned. He conjured up Carson's face on the Opposition Bench. So far, he had only been able to see the profile as they sat side by side on the Treasury Bench. What of that frown? What of those phrases tumbling out in disorder, but influencing many members? Could he really afford to take a chance? Would Carson accept a transfer to the War Cabinet, with all that it implied for the fate of Jellicoe?

He was fearful of the support Carson could command, he was nervous and distrustful of the weight of his own following should an open challenge take place. What about the Press? A sure source of trouble! One good thing, North-cliffe was three thousand miles away and he could rely on Milner to look after Geoffrey Dawson, the Editor of *The Times*. If *The Times* walked in the straight path the *Daily Mail* might come along too.

Thus the Prime Minister walked delicately.

On 6th July, 1917, he addressed the following letter to the First Lord.

My dear Carson,
　　This morning I told my colleagues the purport of my conversation with you yesterday as to the desirability of strengthening the War Cabinet with your presence. They all agreed that an additional member was needed in view of the overwhelming character of the work both in mass and in responsibility, and they were also unanimous that you would be the most helpful choice.

　　You know my opinion on the subject. I wanted you in the Cabinet from the start. My plans were then thwarted for reasons you know. The time is now ripe for reverting to my original idea. I hope therefore you will join us as a full member of the War Cabinet. We need your insight, courage and judgment. We have momentous decisions to take in the course of the next few days. I should therefore like to announce the appointment at once. Bonar foreshadowed it today.*

I tried to see you today to get your views about your successor at the Admiralty. I can see you Monday.

Ever sincerely,

D. LLOYD GEORGE.

Please let me know your desires by messenger.[aa]

At his home at Birchington, Carson was roused in the middle of the night by the message. The circumstances were not calculated to produce the most favourable reception. On the following morning, Carson despatched the messenger with a reply that left Lloyd George with no doubt of the formidable character of the man he was seeking to displace. Carson would not be hustled unceremoniously from office in order to placate the Prime Minister. He returned an austere answer:

July 7, 1917.

My dear Prime Minister,

Have received your letter by special messenger. Of course I am ready to fall in with your views that a change should be made at the Admiralty if you consider it in the public interest. It is vital that you should have confidence in the administration of so important a department. As regards my entering the Cabinet, I

---

* In the House of Commons, 6th July, 1917, Bonar Law, speaking in the debate on National Expenditure, said that he had not been able to give the time that he should have liked to have given to his duties in the War Cabinet. He said: "I think the result will be that the Prime Minister, with whom I have discussed it within the last few days, will find it necessary to make other arrangements and probably have an addition to the Cabinet to do the work that if I were free I should be able to do."

am very grateful for all you say but I should prefer not to have to give an answer today. I am suffering from a bad attack of neuralgia but hope to be all right by Monday.

Yours ever sincerely,
EDWARD CARSON.^{ab}

Surprised by the sharpness of Carson's reply, Lloyd George wrote a new letter in conciliatory tones:

July 7, 1917.

My dear Carson,

I am afraid from your letter that you have misunderstood mine. We sincerely want you in the War Cabinet, but if you cannot see your way to join the Cabinet and prefer to remain at the Admiralty then the suggestion falls to the ground. We must have your help in this terrible war. I have all along—and so has Bonar—wanted you here. But it is for you to decide.

The changes I wanted at the Admiralty could be effected under your leadership. You know my views about that. The present Board is unsatisfactory.

I am so sorry you are suffering from neuralgia. It is a plague.

We have just had a Cabinet over the air raid.

Ever sincerely,
D. LLOYD GEORGE.

P.S. We can have a talk on Monday.^{ac}

Here was the most astonishing retreat. Carson could remain at the Admiralty. The Prime Minister was showing incredible vacillation and amazing indecision. For the second time Lloyd George drew back. He hesitated and debated with friends and colleagues. Many were consulted and

174

there was much conversation. The theme varied from Carson to Churchill and back again to Carson.

At last, after ten days of vacillation, Lloyd George was driven into action by an urgent warning from Lord Milner.

Very Confidential   16.7.17.
My dear Prime Minister,

Forgive my worrying. I am very anxious about the Admiralty. It is more than a fortnight now since I think you recognised there must be a change and every week is precious. Besides, the longer we wait, the more likely it is that something will get out, and then the papers will begin gossiping and criticising and the whole thing will be blown upon. [*sic*]

It would be best to make all Ministerial changes at once, but if this is not practicable, cannot the Carson-Geddes business in any case be settled right away? It is very urgent.

Yours very sincerely,
MILNER.*ad*

On the following evening the Ministerial changes were announced in the Press.* Milner's sensible letter had precipitated the decision.

Dr. Addison, whose place at the Ministry of Munitions was taken by Churchill, gives the following description of Carson abruptly disinherited of his role as First Lord. Addison recorded in his Diary [Tuesday, 17th July, 1917]:

Carson told me that L.G. had insisted on making the announcements tonight and that he did not intend

* Carson to War Cabinet, Geddes to Admiralty, Churchill to Munitions, and other changes.

to consult his colleagues, except Milner and Bonar, himself and myself. . . .

Carson was rather sick about it. I gathered that he had not discussed it beforehand with L.G. to the same extent as I had and that this apparently needless abruptness was rather a blow to him.[ae]

Carson had been dismissed. He was despatched to the War Cabinet* while Sir Eric Geddes† took his place as First Lord of the Admiralty.

But what of Jellicoe? Geddes asked to be relieved of the First Sea Lord before taking up his duties at the Admiralty. Carson refused with indignation. He went to the War Cabinet in relentless adherence to his belief in Jellicoe.

When Geddes saw that he could not persuade Carson to dismiss Jellicoe, he did not dare to implement the transfer himself. He knew there would be an outburst of opposition if Jellicoe should be dismissed just at the time when Carson was being removed. He could not face the odium of making a change in his professional subordinates before he had the opportunity to dig in at the

---

* Thus another Conservative was in the War Cabinet. Yet Lloyd George claimed that Carson had been rejected in December, 1916, because there were three Conservatives in the War Cabinet. Now there were four.

† Geddes had been in charge of Army Transportation in France. He was an interesting character; the son of a Presbyterian family, with the influence of his upbringing upon him. He could not be called a dutiful son of the Church, but he was quite unable to throw off the effects of his early instruction. He was a man of remarkable ability, though too forceful and determined to make a real success of public life.

He had sustained a tragedy in his domestic affairs which saddened his life. He had a large family of excellent sons who gave him much satisfaction though on account of his own upbringing Geddes was a stern and unbending parent.

Geddes was fond of medals and titles. He aspired to and attained the rank of General while in France in charge of Army transport. When he joined the Admiralty he insisted on being given the rank of Admiral. Sir Philip Sassoon, Geddes's Secretary, was a shrewd and competent adviser who afterwards served Sir Douglas Haig and Lloyd George. Sir Philip's collection of Secretaryships was somewhat akin to Geddes's assumption of military and naval titles.

Admiralty. Besides Lloyd George advised his new First Lord to walk with short and cautious steps.

But Jellicoe was not backward in carrying the struggle into Geddes's domain. He claimed that he was the First Lord's colleague and not his subordinate.[af] Geddes was shocked and somewhat alarmed, possibly because he was inexperienced in public affairs.

He consulted with Bonar Law who took him to the Prime Minister. Forthwith an Order in Council dated 23rd October was handed down as from Sinai, defining the subordination of the First Sea Lord (Jellicoe) to the First Lord (Geddes).

Under Geddes's resourceful administration, however, there was a conspicuous improvement in Admiralty results. He was to prove a competent and proficient administrator. Indeed, Geddes's ability to shine in every field to which he was called won him an astonishing and, possibly, an exaggerated reputation.

By November, 1917, figures for Allied shipping losses gave testimony to his success in action. Losses of total Allied shipping had been reduced from the 900,000 tons claimed by the enemy in April, to 200,000. New ships being produced now exceeded the numbers destroyed. Here was reward and recompense. From the disastrous days when Britain's survival hung in the balance on the seas, the position had been wholly retrieved.

But for Carson there was disaffection and discontent. In the War Cabinet, he took little part in the conduct of the war, but continued to nurse his grievance. He remained faithful in his defence of Sir John Jellicoe. There was never any doubt of his allegiance. He was on the side not only of the admirals, but of the professional military advisers of the Government as a whole. As a member of the War Cabinet he extended his front while maintaining his allegiance.*

In September, 1917, Carson paid his visit to G.H.Q. in France. There he talked with Sir Douglas Haig, who three months before had helped to drive him from the Admiralty. Haig gives this account in his papers:

Sir Edward Carson arrived today and stays two nights. It is quite a rest to deal with him after Winston! He is so straightforward and single minded. He is convinced that the military experts must be given full power, not only to advise, but to carry out their plans. He is all opposed to the meddling now practised by the Prime Minister and other politicians . . .

He considers that Lloyd George has considerable value as P.M. on account of his driving powers, but he recognises his danger. He has no knowledge of strategy or military operations, yet he thinks he is well qualified to direct his Military Advisers! Carson wished me to talk freely with Mr. Asquith because the latter, though in opposition, has very great power.

Sir E. Carson left at 9.30. He said he was delighted with his visit, and he assured me that the War Cabinet would not be allowed to interfere with me or my arrangements. . . . Mr. Asquith and Bonham Carter

* Carson's willingness to help Robertson is indicated in an extract from his biography. Robertson, says Colvin, with Carson's support usually got more or less what he wanted. There was thus good reason for Carson to suppose that he could best help Robertson by remaining in the Cabinet.ag

arrived in time for dinner. Afterwards I had a long talk with Mr. A. He said that the present Government is very shaky.[ah]

Here was a truly extraordinary situation, but it was a sure indication of Carson's hostility to Lloyd George and of his bitter prejudice against the Government. In a word, he was urging the Commander-in-Chief to consult with the Leader of the Opposition at a moment when the Government, as Asquith rightly said, was "very shaky".* It was typical of the man, of his intense respect as a professional lawyer for the generals—and of the confusions of purpose that beset Carson at that time.

He returned to London and a few weeks later made what, in effect, was a public declaration of opposition to the Government of which he was a member.

> I have met in the course of my work as a member of His Majesty's government three great men—I say that advisedly—Field-Marshal Haig, Sir William Robertson and Sir John Jellicoe, with whom, while I was in the Navy, I was brought into the most intimate relations. They have my absolute confidence.[aj]

It was open defiance of the Prime Minister at a time when Lloyd George had intimated to Carson his determination to dismiss Jellicoe and had shown clearly that he intended to come to grips with the generals.

---

* It was about this time that Sir William Robertson wrote to Haig: "He [Lloyd George] is a real bad 'un. The other members of the War Cabinet seem afraid of him. Milner is a tired, dyspeptic old man. Curzon a gas-bag. Bonar Law equals Bonar Law. Smuts has good instinct but lacks knowledge."[ai]

The *Morning Post*, ever faithful to Carson, gave frantic support to the generals. "If anything could ensure the collapse and disappearance from public life of Mr. Lloyd George, it would be an attempt on his part to upset the Chief of the Imperial General Staff and the Commander-in-Chief of the British Armies in France. If he tried to replace Robertson and Haig with more amenable generals, he could not hold his office for a week."[ak]

Christmas Day dawned before the struggle with the First Sea Lord (Jellicoe) was rounded to its conclusion. On the last day of the year, a year fraught with the gravest consequences for the Navy, Carson wrote in vigorous protest to the Prime Minister.

Confidential.   31.12.17.

My dear Prime Minister,

Can I have a private interview with you today if possible.

I am very much concerned about the dismissal of Sir John Jellicoe and even more so at the appointment of Admiral Wemyss as First Sea Lord and I greatly resent the manner in which my name has been brought into the matter. I am sorry to trouble you but I cannot allow the matter to pass in silence.

Yours sincerely,
EDWARD CARSON.[al]

It was, of course, a letter from a Minister to his Chief giving notice of an intention to resign. The request for an interview carried its own implication.

The meeting followed at once. Carson made his protest, and Lloyd George made an excellent argument in favour of finding other reasons for resignation thus avoiding any possibility of stirring up anxiety and want of confidence in the Higher Command among serving sailors. It is, of course, the stock argument in such circumstances.

In January, 1918, Carson's resignation was announced. He said it was over the condition of Irish affairs. It seemed he was disturbed by the remote possibility that the Government might produce a remedy, but one of which he did not approve. He required a free hand in dealing with the Irish problem.

In any event the pretext for departure was Ireland, as on the last occasion it had been Serbia. Small nationalites could be relied upon to justify Sir Edward Carson's resignations.

But the real reason for his departure must be sought elsewhere. It would seem that Carson, having stayed in the Government to protect Jellicoe, resigned now he could no longer save him.

In March, after he had left the Government, Carson explained in Parliament what had guided his attitude during his period of office. It was a startling pronouncement. "The whole time that I was First Lord of the Admiralty," he declared, "one of the greatest difficulties I had was the constant persecution—for I can call it nothing else—of certain high officials in the Admiralty, who could not speak for themselves—constant persecution which, I have no doubt, I could have traced to reasons and motives of the most malignant character. Over and over again while I was at the Admiralty, . . . I had the most constant pressure put upon me—which I need hardly say I absolutely resisted—to remove officials, and among them Sir John Jellicoe."[am]

Carson in due course became the leader of an Opposition. He gathered round him the dissident elements in Parliament.

Not long after his resignation, he had a skirmish with Bonar Law over Ireland in which for the first time the Conservative leader defied the "King of Ulster". Bonar Law wrote:

> 11 Downing Street,
> 28th April, 1918.
>
> My dear Carson,
> Your letter, if it is to be published, must be the beginning of conflict between us and my reply, if for publication, must be of the same kind. . . .
> That may be inevitable. But I should like to delay it as much as possible.[an]

The tone of this letter showed that already the powers of Carson had waned. He had paid in loss of prestige for his excessive reliance on the judgement of the Naval technicians. He had failed to disclose the strength of mind and independence of judgement that an administrator of the first rank must possess. In fact his political career was really over when he left the Government. What came after was nothing more than the shadow of greatness—the image without the substance.

And Carson's career as a leader of an Opposition was doomed to disappointment. When his chance came at the crisis of the Maurice issue * later in May, he lacked the support to push home his assault upon the Prime Minister, and in the division that followed in the House of Commons on that dramatic day, Carson ended up voting for the Government.

Four months after the Maurice debate, Carson had ceased to be a menace to the Government. He talked with Bonar Law about the position and prospects of his old enemy Lloyd George. The war was drawing swiftly to a conclusion and war-time controversy was dying down. It was then, according to a letter written by Bonar Law to Lloyd George himself, that Carson spoke of his antagonist "very nicely" and "very kindly", telling Bonar Law among other things that "we must not kill the little man".[ao]

At the General Election of December, 1918, Carson was returned to Parliament as a Coalition member from Ulster.

His term of office in the Lloyd George Government had lasted thirteen months; seven at the Admiralty and six in the War Cabinet. It was an inglorious era in a life filled with action and studded with courage—political, moral and physical courage.

Much has been said in criticism of Carson's administration. But the Prime Minister must be given the blame for hesitation and delay in

* Lloyd George was charged by General Maurice with telling lies.

reorganizing the Admiralty. It has been shown
that he lost faith in Carson and confidence in
Jellicoe, yet he had taken three months to dismiss the politician, and another five to rid the
Admiralty of the First Sea Lord.

The charge can be answered. There was much
hostility to the Prime Minister. His parliamentary
position was weak and dangerous. To take action
without a long period of preparation and a wide
mobilisation of support might have resulted in the
destruction of Lloyd George himself. Believing
as he did that he alone could win the war, an
argument can be stated in defence of his conduct.
In any case, events were fully to justify his course
of action in sacking Carson to make Geddes
First Lord.

Nor was Sir Edward Carson in any state of
rancour against his old enemy when war was over
and peace reigned. Speaking in the House of
Commons on 3rd July, 1919, he said: "I had the
honour of serving in the Cabinet with him [Lloyd
George] in the very darkest days of our country's
history in this War. His patriotism, his courage,
and his genius . . . were the greatest contribution
that any man in the whole country has given to
the War . . . [and history will say of him] that
he did more than any other man to preserve the
liberties of the world."[ap]

Lloyd George responded generously. In the
summer of 1921, he nominated Carson for the
House of Lords, the mausoleum of weary titans.
There he carried on sham battles with his former
friend Lord Birkenhead over "Home Rule for

Ireland". Plenty of fireworks. That was all. Nothing happened.

On a dark morning in October, 1935, Lord Carson died of old age. Then it was that all men spoke well of him. But throughout his life his intimate colleagues had frequently prefaced their remarks by saying: "If I understand Carson aright."

No man possessed a greater or more overwhelming charm of manner. He appeared to be dour and grim in the eyes of his devoted followers in Ulster and Britain. His "ignorant and hostile" enemies fell into the same error. Yet such a description could only be justified by the expression of gloom which frequently marked his features. He was a rare combination of hypochondriac and man of action. His pleas of ill-health and his oft-repeated claim for sympathy over the pain and misery that oppressed him and the impending abdominal operation were, with Carson, an interesting opening gambit in many a conversation of first-class political importance. His second marriage, late in life and on the eve of war, to a beautiful and clever young woman who had the advantage of many years in age brought him much happiness.

So I leave this figure who bestrides a decade, standing in characteristic attitude of dark yet clear-cut outline against the sky of storm and strife, a hero in the eyes of his devoted young wife and of his faithful followers.

CHAPTER VI

ALL THE KING'S MEN

NOW came the decision in the long-drawn-out conflict for power between Lloyd George and Robertson.

Lloyd George, convinced that Robertson and his military colleagues now aimed at overthrowing the Government and setting up a new administration under Army control, determined that he must get rid of both Robertson, the Chief of the Imperial General Staff, and Haig, the Commander-in-Chief.

Robertson and Haig too were well aware of the Prime Minister's intention to remove them from their posts. They were bent upon holding fast.

Thus it was apparent that compromise or reconciliation became impossible. The political chief and the Army commanders looked out upon one another just as two boxers in training approach the day of trial when one or other must have the decision, even to the extent of a knock-out.

Lloyd George had real reason at this time to complain of Haig's conduct. He had muddled the battle of Cambrai.

For the first time the wonderful war-winning weapon, the tank, was launched en masse against the enemy on 20th November, 1917. The offensive was an immediate and immense triumph. Much territory was taken from the enemy and the newspapers announced the victory in terms of a military decision.

The Infantry, however, was not prepared to consolidate the gains. And when the Germans counter-attacked, within a week their lost ground was regained. After many days, slowly and reluctantly the Press was informed of the failure of Cambrai. The public had been swindled by means of suppression and deception.

The Lloyd George case against Robertson arose out of victory and not as a result of defeat. Allenby, in command of the army in Palestine, had been directed to take Jerusalem. He gave an exaggerated and extravagant estimate of the strength of the Turkish forces opposing him and asked for an extensive reinforcement of his own army. Lloyd George believed that these false claims of Turkish strength and British weakness were promoted by Robertson for the purpose of destroying the plan for the attack on Jerusalem lest the operations should interfere with the flow of manpower to the Western Front. The Lloyd George Papers and documents do not establish the charge against Robertson. Nor does Lloyd George allude to it in writing of the event in his *War Memoirs*. However, Jerusalem fell to Allenby two weeks before Christmas 1917 without the aid of reinforcements.*

* Balfour, the Foreign Secretary, sent Allenby a vast quantity of pamphlets publicising the Balfour Declaration, with its promise of a National Home for the

It was on the basis of these complaints that the Prime Minister called upon the Secretary of State for War, Lord Derby, on 11th December, 1917, asking him, in effect, to dismiss his Chief of the Imperial General Staff and also his Commander-in-Chief. He invited Derby to appoint both Sir Douglas Haig and General Robertson to sinecure posts which would remove them from Lloyd George's path. The sinecures would take the form of consolation prizes.

Lord Derby refused. He replied with a carefully reasoned and cogent statement of his own position, which is indeed a brilliant document.

It was a determined and well-argued case in support of both Haig and Robertson. Indeed it carried with it a clear indication that if Lloyd George's programme was to be carried out, Lord Derby would not remain in the Administration.

Derby's letter* was in fact the first information that he was prepared to support Haig and Robertson, even to the extent of resigning if they were dismissed.

Derby was emphatic that the Cambrai affair (the Lloyd George case against Haig) was not a just cause for hanging Haig, and he reiterated his faith in the Commander-in-Chief.

Derby then dealt with the charge made by Lloyd George that Robertson had been deliberately trying to deceive the Government. "I

Jews. These were to be distributed in Jerusalem in advance of the entry of Allenby and his triumphant army. But at this time the population of Jerusalem was made up mostly of Arabs. Allenby took the decision to reject the order from the Foreign Office and Balfour's pamphlets were consigned to other uses.

* The full text of the letter is printed in *Appendix* IV, No. 8.

ROBERTSON

Frequently answering the arguments of his opponents by
saying, "I've heard different"

confess that what you told me with regard to your suspicions today," he wrote, "has shaken my confidence but I cannot believe that he [Robertson] would deliberately ask Allenby to send in a false telegram in order to deceive the Government. I agree with you that read in the light of subsequent events Allenby's telegram asking for the enormous increase of force in order to do what he has done with the existing forces seems very ridiculous but that his former proposal should be put forward with a deliberate attempt to deceive the Government and that at the instance of Robertson, is almost beyond belief." If Robertson had deliberately deceived the Government, and it could be proved, said Derby, "I could have no further faith in him but I cannot believe it and assuming therefore that is not the case I take Robertson as I have found him and that is a very honest man endeavouring to give the Government the best advice that it is in his power to give."

As to the position of the War Cabinet, they had, said Derby, every right to change a Commander or policy at will. Some people would say that that meant the politicians interfering with the soldiers "and they may be right but I for one should never hold that opinion though naturally in one's present position one would insist on the right of resigning if one thought that the advice given was the correct one and the persons in power were most fitted to carry it out."[a]

Lord Derby's letter shattered Lloyd George's plan. His resignation over Haig and Robertson would bring strong, and indeed decisive, support from many Conservative members of the House, and all of the Liberals. Derby's voice could not be silenced or ignored. Lloyd George might indeed insist, with the support of his Cabinet, on removing Haig and Robertson. But the order of dismissal would at that time bring down in ruins the Prime Minister's own Government. Lloyd George and his two Generals would all three fall together.

Thus Lloyd George was saddled with a Secretary of State for War who professed his first allegiance to the High Command and not to the Prime Minister. While Derby remained at the War Office, Lloyd George could not rid himself of his Military Chiefs.

The very next day Derby made an amazing concession evidently intended to placate the irritated and angry Prime Minister. While continuing to defend Robertson and Haig he wrote a long letter to the Commander-in-Chief in France demanding the dismissal of many principal members of his staff at the Front. Brigadier-General Charteris, Haig's Chief Intelligence Officer, whose dismissal had been demanded by Lloyd George; Major-General Maxwell, the Quartermaster General; Lieutenant-General Sir George Fowke, Adjutant General to the Armies in France; and General Gough, Commander of the Fifth Army, were all to come under the axe.

Lord Derby gave detailed reasons for his insistence, including an account of Canadian

Decr 13th 1917

My dear S. & S.

Just read your letter. A fine straight letter that does you credit. It will do an enormous lot of good. The morale of the army must be restored at all costs.

Ever sincerely

D Lloyd George

THE LLOYD GEORGE LETTER OF
DEC. 13, 1917

opposition to Gough. "Canadians are especially bitter."[b] *

The Prime Minister, on receiving a copy of this extraordinary document, wrote a warm and even enthusiastic letter of approval. I reproduce it here.

Dec. 13th, 1917.

My dear S. of S.

Just read your letter. A fine straight letter that does you credit. It will do no end of good. The morale of the Army must be restored at all costs.

Ever sincerely,
D. LLOYD GEORGE.[c]

But the slaughter† of the innocent or guilty Generals of lesser degree did not deflect Lloyd George from his purpose. A second movement, really directed against Robertson and Haig, was launched in mid January. Lloyd George decided that the prop supporting the Generals must be removed. Another and more amenable Secretary of State must be substituted for Lord Derby.

Accordingly the Prime Minister offered to Lord Derby the post of Ambassador in Paris.

But Derby was too clever to fall into that ditch. He asked for terms sweeping in character and certainly extraordinary in practice. "Would the Ambassador in Paris be more or less of a colleague of members of the War Cabinet or would he be simply the mouthpiece of that

* The text of the letter is reproduced in *Appendix IV*, No. 9.
† Derby proposed to send four men to the guillotine; he succeeded only in beheading two, Charteris and Maxwell. Sir George Fowke escaped and remained Adjutant General till the war was over. Gough lived on as Commander of the Fifth Army until the German offensive of March, 1918.

body?"[d] he demanded in a letter to Lloyd George.*
It was apparent that the factor that would influence
his decision in accepting the Ambassadorship
would be the question of his own authority in
public concerns. Derby declared that if disagreement arose between the Military Chiefs and the
War Cabinet, he must be assured of the right to
take an independent line. He reserved, in particular, the right to resign if Robertson and Haig
should be dismissed. And Derby with such
powers could be just as dangerous to Lloyd
George in Paris as in London.

It was a skilful and cunning letter though
written in obscure terms with the evident intention
of maintaining secrecy even against his own staff.

Again Lloyd George had been frustrated in
his second plan—a plan to rid himself of the
impediment standing in the way of the dismissal
of the generals.

He tried once more, and for the third time.
He attempted the knock-out, with no question of
consolation prizes.

He made a frontal attack on Robertson and his
General Staff, charging them with communicating
to the Press, and particularly to the *Morning Post*
through Colonel Repington, a series of official
secrets.

He wrote to Derby complaining of a "grave
breach of discipline", and a "gross breach of Army
regulations". He proposed, he said, to appeal to
the House of Commons, and to take stern action.

Four days later, Lloyd George wrote again

* The letter is reproduced in full in *Appendix IV*, No. 10.

claiming that the Turks, who had been about to sue for peace,* had been bolstered up by the publication of the Repington dispatch.

Lord Derby answered. His reply was a strong defence of the Chief of the Imperial General Staff and his colleagues. The statements Repington had made, said Derby, were in the main inaccurate or were such as his long experience and profound study throughout the war, would supply. And Repington had himself affirmed that no Cabinet paper had been given to him by any soldier. He had seen the Man Power Report. But "it would lead us nowhere to threaten all recipients of the latter with dire pains and penalties." "I can see no ground", concluded Derby, "for singling out the officers of the General Staff for exclusive treatment on these lines."*†

The knock-out blow failed. The Prime Minister was checked by the overwhelming devotion of the Secretary for War to the cause of his military advisers. Besides, it was well known in Lloyd George's circles that Derby was consulting with willing helpers of high estate who honestly feared that the dismissal of Robertson would be a real national calamity. Draft copies of his letters were submitted to revision by able hands.

What now? There could be no question of Lloyd George and Robertson working together any more. Lloyd George had launched charges against Robertson that made any accommodation impossible. Indeed it is amazing that the Prime

---

* Negotiations for the surrender of Turkey were being conducted by Sir Basil Zaharoff.

† The full letter appears in *Appendix IV*, No. 11.

Minister, if he really believed these accusations, delayed so long in dismissing his Chief of the Imperial General Staff.

He was, of course, most unwilling to face a House of Commons uncertain in its loyalties. Just as Lord Derby had given his faith to the generals, so would many of the Back Bench members. Then what? Another Prime Minister and another set of Ministers! But Lloyd George believed he was the only man who could win the war. Therefore he must temporize.

Other methods must be adopted. Other plans must be matured. He would rely upon the wisdom and common sense of the old legend "If at first you don't succeed, try, try, try again".

His strength rested on the knowledge that he was sustained by Bonar Law, Leader of the Conservative Party, whose high character and good name carried conviction in the House of Commons and also in the country: and over everything on the sure and certain response which he could depend upon if a General Election could be snatched from the crisis.

He was now compelled to find some other way of dislodging his opponent at the War Office.

A programme had been prepared the previous November when the Allied Conference met at Rapallo. There, Lloyd George, pursuing a course he had long entertained, won approval for a scheme setting up a supreme directorate of the war. It was decided that a Supreme War Council should meet at Versailles with a permanent military representative from each of the participating powers.

Sir Henry Wilson was nominated to serve Great Britain in this capacity.

Loud were the outcries that this decision wrung from the generals and their political supporters. General Robertson signified his most bitter opposition. The hostile Press sprang to his defence. Lloyd George, stopping over in Paris to address a meeting and to describe the purpose of the new Supreme Council, returned to London to meet a determined outburst against him.* Even then his critics believed that this was a plan to equip himself with machinery which would enable him to receive and act on advice independent of General Robertson and the General Staff.

There were to be two sets of military advisers, said the Prime Minister's critics in his own Government.

Lord Robert Cecil, foremost amongst the opponents of the Prime Minister on this issue, expressed his grave dissatisfaction in a letter to Balfour, the Foreign Secretary.

> 100 Grosvenor Road,
> Pimlico.
> 18 November 1917

My dear Arthur,

Further reflection (in bed) has made me more distrustful than ever of the Supreme War Council. Taken with the Paris speech there can be very little

---

* Speaking in Paris on 12th November, 1917, Lloyd George, Tom Jones records, "cast such aspersions on British generals that when it was published, the immediate fall of the Government was not only desired but expected in some quarters."*f*

doubt that one of the purposes which the P.M. had in view was to enable him to over-rule the C.I.G.S. and other advocates of the Western Front.

Churchill's presence at the luncheon confirms this and so does the article in this morning's "Observer". In other words, he wants to create machinery which will enable him to receive and act on military advice independent of the General Staff. That is to say there are to be two supreme advisers to the Government on the general conduct of the war. That cannot work. It must mean division and confusion. Until therefore it can be made absolutely clear that Wilson is really and not nominally subordinate to Robertson I do not see how I can make myself responsible for the plan. I shall await the Debate on Monday without great anxiety.

Yours ever,
ROBERT CECIL

If you think right, please show this letter to the P.M. or tell him of it.[8]

Lloyd George triumphed in the parliamentary encounter. The Debate in the House of Commons on 19th November, 1917, he turned to his advantage. The Council, he repeatedly assured his anxious audience, would have no executive authority. He had also committed himself to his critics. It would be impossible, in the face of his pledge, to make use of the Supreme War Council as an alternative to the General Staff. "No executive authority" was the charter of the soldiers.

But in February, 1918, there was something more for the generals to complain of. Lloyd George saw his advantage, and took it. In the mounting conflict, he devised a scheme for achieving his desire to put an end to the Military Junta at the War Office that he feared and detested.

At the Supreme War Council meeting on the first day of the month of February, with Lloyd George present, it was determined that a General Reserve should be set up. The control would be entrusted to an Executive Committee of the permanent military representatives at Versailles.

That was that. Thus real power would now pass to the Supreme War Council.

General Robertson made another effort to hold on to his authority over the Army Reserves in France. He demanded that the British Military Representative at Versailles should come under himself as Chief of the Imperial General Staff.

Not at all. At last Lloyd George had tracked down and cornered his enemy. He refused any accommodation. In reply, he offered General Robertson the alternative of remaining on as Chief of the Imperial General Staff under the reduced dispensation, or of taking up the post of Military Representative at Versailles.

What a dilemma for Robertson! What a desperate confusion of all his hopes and aspirations. Either way he was done.

For it was apparent that if he stayed on at the War Office, military power would be vested with Sir Henry Wilson at Versailles by reason of his authority over the Reserve. If he accepted the Versailles appointment, London would become the centre of military authority where Sir Henry Wilson would fill the role of Military Adviser to the Cabinet. The Prime Minister would, of course, throw his support behind whichever post Robertson rejected.

It was an ironic and a dismal end for the old soldier. Even though he had hurled defiance at his Prime Minister denying civilian control, demanding autocratic and unquestioning authority, his enemies may well have pitied him. He could not escape extinction.

Since Robertson absolutely declined to budge from the War Office and refused to relinquish his powers, Lloyd George decided to dismiss him.

He had made up his mind. He would face the resignations and he would meet the House of Commons. He understood that Derby would resign in support of Robertson. He fully expected Haig to take the same course. And he knew that some of his colleagues would support Robertson and the Military Junta.

Would he put these grave issues to the test? Would he stand or fall by the decision of the Members of Parliament?

It would be a brave decision, for the atmosphere of the House of Commons was already prepared for an insurrection with the rumoured news of Robertson's impending dismissal.

The Debate took place on 12th February. Asquith, who was of course fully informed of Lloyd George's plan, took the opportunity to make a considered and effective attack on the Prime

HIS MAJESTY AND EARL HAIG

Lloyd George wanted to put him out: the King wanted to keep him in

Minister. He demanded on behalf of the House an assurance that no change was contemplated in the authority and power of either Haig or Robertson. "There have been many criticisms," he said, "some of them just, some of them unjust—upon the conduct of our naval and military operations during the past year, but there is nothing that has been done—I am speaking now more particularly of the military field—or left undone which has in the least shaken the confidence of the nation and of the Empire in the two great soldiers, Sir Douglas Haig, our Commander-in-Chief, and Sir William Robertson, the head of our General Staff at home."[b]

Lloyd George answered. He did not meet Asquith's challenge. Instead he intimidated the Members with an implicit threat of a dissolution and a general election. "If the House of Commons and the country," he said, "are not satisfied with the conduct of the War, and if they think there is any Government which can conduct it better, then it is their business, in God's name, to put that other Government in!"[i]

The following day, 13th February 1918, the Prime Minister sent for Sir Reginald Brade, the Permanent Under-Secretary at the War Office. Brade wrote "A Few Notes on the Recent Controversy between Sir W. R. (Robertson) and the Government." I quote an extract:

> During most of this crisis I was laid up with a poisoned foot, but Bonar and the P.M. [Prime Minister] sent for me about an hour before the latter was to see the King. . . .

P.M. told me that he was going to tell the King and his colleagues firmly that he refused to go on as he had done during the last year. He or W.R. [Sir William Robertson] was to be P.M., he did not care which.

Again I quote from Sir Reginald Brade's Notes:

On the Friday [15th February, 1918] I went with Max* to the P.M. [Prime Minister] to help in the discussion as to the P.M.'s statement to the House and as to Derby's resignation.† Hankey wrote out a long statement which Bonar was to give on the Monday, reserving for Tuesday the full statement to be made by P.M. (on Army Estimates) when his cold would probably be better. Max and I agreed it was rotten and I tried to get a shorter and more precise statement, omitting all reference to the A.C. [Army Council].

The Prime Minister had come to a solid resolution. He must announce forthwith the retirement of Robertson and the appointment of another C.I.G.S. True, the approval of the King was essential, but Lloyd George was the constitutional adviser of His Majesty and the advice would have to be accepted. The only alternative was dismissal of the Prime Minister and a change of government. Such a bold course would be dangerous indeed to the Royal master if another Government were set up and failed to find public approval.

Thus it was that Lloyd George on Friday night made a balance sheet of assets and liabilities, taking stock at the same time. None could deny that the surplus of goodwill was small. There were dissatisfied and discontented directors of the

---

* Lord Beaverbrook, then Minister of Information.
† Derby had intimated his intention to resign.

company, in the form of colleagues in the Government. Great were the forces drawn up on either side.

On the debit side of Lloyd George's balance-sheet the picture was far from encouraging, for against him there was a formidable array.

A spearhead of opposition was to be found among his colleagues and members of his Government. Lord Derby, the Secretary of State for War, was the civilian captive of the military faction, committed to supporting to the utmost his service advisers at the War Office. There was no escape for him. He was often called "Genial Judas". He would not be guilty now of betraying his two friends. He was frequently accused of changing his mind, and rightly. But in his support of Haig and Robertson he was unswerving in his devotion to his beliefs. Many efforts were made to disengage him from the generals' party. He maintained a firm front. Some observers declared that his hands were being held on high by Buckingham Palace. Certainly Derby's intimacy with the King was remarkable. They were in frequent correspondence. No doubt His Majesty influenced Derby greatly. In any event, Derby was in a position to inform His Majesty and offer advice.

Walter Long, Secretary of State for the Colonies and leader in Parliament of the country gentlemen, survival of the Tory aristocrats, was another adherent of the military caste. He wrote to Bonar Law that he was horrified over the proposal to abandon Robertson.[j]* He was convinced that it

* See *Addendum*.

would give the Government a very severe shake. It was a tremendous step, to be taken only after great consideration. It was evident that Long felt he should have been directly consulted.

Lord Robert Cecil, too, belonged to the camp of the military section. Cecil was Under-Secretary at the Foreign Office and Minister of Blockade; but in this line-up of the civilian against the military authorities, he gave his allegiance and sympathy wholly to Sir William Robertson. So strongly did he support the cause of Robertson that he wrote to Bonar Law disclaiming all share in the Cabinet's responsibility, and making a spirited justification of the generals. "I confess it seems to me more just," his letter concluded, "to say that their [the soldiers'] civilian chief ought not to have tried to force such a scheme upon them."[k]

Derby, Cecil and Long were important members of the Government, but more to be taken into account because of the positions of influence and authority they held in the Conservative Party. They could dislodge a considerable following from the Tory Benches. There was also a powerful and numerous section of members who accepted absolutely the simple formula "The Army, right or wrong."

Then there was Carson, willing at any moment to lead an attack upon the Government in the House of Commons.

Austen Chamberlain, who was at this time a private Conservative member waiting the call to office, was another whose loyalty lay outside the

administration on this grave issue. In an interview with Lord Curzon, Chamberlain had given
the impression that Lloyd George would lose his
political friendship if there was criticism of the
generals.[1]

There was, of course, a large assembly of
Liberals who were arrayed in close formation
behind the leading generals of the day. Asquith
and his Liberal ex-Ministers and all the following
of Liberal Members who looked for the return of
an Asquith Government were now aligned in
readiness for the final clash. Here was the famous
"Brass Hat Alliance", expectant of a victory in
arms.

And in advance, and behind, and in all conceivable directions, the persistent and hostile voices
of the newspapers joined the attack upon Lloyd
George. The *Globe*, the *Morning Post*, the *Westminster Gazette*, the *Daily News*, the *Daily Chronicle*,
all were the vehicles of an opinion damaging to
the Government and directly supporting military
control of the War machine.

But more important than any of these individual
influences, the positive support of the King for
the Military Advisers was a factor of the utmost
weight in this critical division and distribution of
loyalties.*

The generals were esteemed by His Majesty.
He gave them confidence and trust. Sir Douglas
Haig enjoyed his unswerving support and always

* The Memoranda of Lord Stamfordham are set out in full in *Stamfordham
Memoranda*, page 408. Readers are recommended to pay close attention to
these documents revealing at once the King's attitude to the dispute, and also
indicating Royal proceedings in public concerns.

sheltered under Royal protection."'' Robertson too had the tremendous reinforcement of the backing and endorsement of his titular Commander-in-Chief, the monarch himself.

Lloyd George, from the outset of his Premiership and for the duration of the war, never won the confidence of His Majesty. When Asquith fell the King noted in his diary: "I fear that it will cause a panic in the City & in America & do harm to the Allies. It is a great blow to me & will I fear buck up the Germans.'''

Bonar Law told His Majesty that both he and Lloyd George had for long been convinced that the war was being mismanaged.

"To this," writes Lord Stamfordham, "the King demurred and said that the politicians should leave the conduct of the war to experts. Mr. Bonar Law said that Robertson and the soldiers were all wrong, with the result that we have lost Serbia, Rumania and very likely Greece. The King expressed his entire disagreement with these views.'''

Nor did the King reserve these sentiments reflecting a distrust of his Prime Minister for his intimate advisers. He confided them to Colonel House. In turn they reached the ears of the American President. Thus we find House recording in his diary following an interview with the King at Buckingham Palace in October 1917: "He (the King) touched, with a tinge of bitterness, upon the assumption of autocratic powers by some of his Prime Ministers. He plainly referred to Lloyd George, and I could see there was considerable feeling lurking under the surface. He spoke of Grey and Asquith in the highest terms, but was guarded in what he said of his present Prime Minister."[p]

It was said of the King that "politics and the politicians of the time worried him to distraction". He was aware of "quarrels and intrigue within the Cabinet and in the Army which outraged his loyal spirit."[q]

Yet, even as the King withheld his faith in Lloyd George's judgement, he gave his trust and confidence in abounding measure to the generals.

On the side of Lloyd George a tally of good sound assets could be made. Possibly they seemed less weighty and substantial than those of his opponents on that dark winter's evening. Their true worth, however, had yet to be measured.

The Prime Minister had the solid backing of his War Cabinet. He had the allegiance of Bonar Law, the Leader of the Conservative Party, as already stated. Bonar Law's sympathies were wholly on the side of asserting civilian responsibility for the direction of the war. Smuts was squarely behind the Prime Minister. Curzon had given his encouragement to Lloyd George over the High Command ever since his excursion with the Prime Minister to the Admiralty the previous April, when they had met and beaten the resistance of the admirals.*

---

* It is necessary to record, however, that Curzon was in secret communication with Derby and was leading the War Minister to believe that if Derby's decision was in favour of resignation, then Curzon would go with him. Curzon really meant that he would go with the winning side.

Lord Milner was most active on the Prime Minister's behalf. His attitude, indeed, had undergone a striking metamorphosis for, in the previous autumn, Milner's efforts had been turned largely towards carrying the generals with the Government. Where Lloyd George had preached drastic action Milner had striven for co-operation between the rival factions. This mood had now passed. In February, 1918, Lord Milner was the outspoken advocate of a Supreme War Council, and the principal critic of Sir William Robertson.

His counsel was of the most specific kind; he advised Lloyd George that it would be better to lose Haig and Robertson than to continue at the mercy of either of them. The one vital thing, he told the Prime Minister, was "that we should be able once for all to get free to do what we know to be right".

To Bonar Law he wrote in these terms:

Confidential   18.2.18*
                              17 Great College Street, S.W.

My dear Bonar,

  . . . I have often been told, though I don't know of my own knowledge, that Percy is the man who has been working the Press & Army opinion for Robertson.

  . . . .

If R. is going to fight us, it is surely madness to let him do so from inside. As long as he retains his position, he will look the stronger party, & the large

---

* As Milner must have known of Robertson's dismissal before 18th February, it is evident that the date of writing was wrongly recorded.

number of people, who do not like the change, but would accept a *fait accompli* will rally to him. This is especially true of the Army.

The course we are pursuing, thanks to Derby, is the very course most likely to produce a considerable military combination against us.

Yours ever,
M.*

Balfour, the Foreign Secretary, had also given his loyalty. Lloyd George had sought a way of capturing Balfour's full support for his cause by using him as an emissary in the negotiations with Robertson. This was a favourite plan with Lloyd George. Often he would select an intermediary with the real intention of persuading him to swallow the case he was to present. If doubt had once clouded Balfour's mind in this issue with the soldiers, it was dispelled by his contact with Robertson. He failed to persuade the soldier, but he convinced himself.

Such then was the standing of the parties on that critical Friday evening. But there were more pressing speculations. Would the triumvirate—the two generals, Haig and Robertson, with Derby as their civilian delegate—act together? Would Sir Douglas Haig resign? If he took with him, not only Derby, but Cecil and Walter Long also, and if they were followed by eminent Conservatives outside the Government, with Austen Chamberlain and Carson at their head, would the House of Commons desert the Prime Minister? Lloyd George had good reason to worry.

What would the King do and say? There was

no certainty. His attitude was in doubt. Lloyd George had seen Lord Stamfordham, the King's Private Secretary, on Wednesday, 13th February. The Prime Minister had been told that "the King strongly deprecated the idea of Robertson being removed from the office of C.I.G.S."' The King considered that Robertson was the indispensable general and also the country had confidence in him, and so had the Army.

Lloyd George was aware that if the crisis resulted in the resignation of Derby, the withdrawal of Haig and the departure from his administration of Lord Robert Cecil and Walter Long, His Majesty might not wait upon a vote in the House of Commons. He might decide to refuse a dissolution, and dismiss his Prime Minister, setting up a new administration. Thus Lloyd George would be deprived of the opportunity of presenting his statement from the Government Bench. Instead he would have to make his case from the front Opposition Bench.

But all these speculations and questions were soon to be answered. On Saturday morning, 16th February, Lloyd George motored to Buckingham Palace from the country. It was a cold grey day. Lloyd George was resolute and forceful. In an interview with Lord Stamfordham he pointed out that if His Majesty insisted on retaining Sir William Robertson in his power and place, he would lay down his task. The King must choose other Ministers. Lloyd George declared that the Government must govern. He would not submit to military dictation on any account or in any direction. Lord Stamfordham hastened to assure Lloyd George that His Majesty had no idea of making such insistence (see *Stamfordham Memoranda*, page 408).

The King then saw his Prime Minister. His confidence in his Chief of the Imperial General Staff was absolute. There is nothing in Lloyd George's records to show that the King assented to Robertson's removal.

The news, nonetheless, of Sir William Robertson's retirement from his post at the War Office was announced by the Prime Minister late on Saturday afternoon.

Lord Derby also called upon His Majesty. Derby said that there was nothing left to him but to resign, though he appealed to the King to advise him of the proper course to follow. The King assured him there was no alternative but his resignation.

Derby then went off to consult and seek advice on resignation from several politicians and some soldiers in and about the War Office.

Lloyd George returned to his little Walton Heath home. He told his circle there: "I had one of the most anxious days I have ever had. I was with the King for an hour." In the evening he sang his favourite songs, with particular emphasis on that Calvinistic hymn, dear to orthodox Presbyterians, "And the changes that are sure to come I do not fear to see".

Haig had been summoned to London, and on

Sunday at noon, accompanied by Lord Derby, he called on Lloyd George. Now was the hour. This vital meeting might lead to anything; to a new Government, to a General Election with political strife in the constituencies, or, alternatively, to peaceful occupation of Downing Street.

The outcome was unexpected and surprising in an astonishing measure. Haig gave his allegiance to Lloyd George; Lord Derby gave his resignation. The triumvirate of Robertson, Haig and Derby was shattered in a moment. Haig's defection took Derby completely by surprise. Both he and Robertson had thought that the triumvirate was firm and strong.

What a relief for the Prime Minister! And yet what bitter disappointment! Relief because by retaining Haig, the measure of his peril in the House of Commons was lessened; disappointment because, in his heart, Lloyd George had hoped to make a clean sweep of his military advisers. To him, therefore, the outcome was a mixed blessing.

What was the reason for Haig's unexpected submission?

He must have known of Lloyd George's visit to Buckingham Palace on Saturday. Surely he had been instructed in the political realities of the situation. Possibly Lord Stamfordham may have spoken with him. He may have been told of Lloyd George's warning to the King that if Robertson's services were to be retained then His Majesty must find other Ministers.

It may have been explained that the King must

give way to his Prime Minister, for where could he turn to find another Prime Minister capable of commanding the support of the House of Commons? Bonar Law, the Conservative Leader, was fixed in his loyalty to Lloyd George. Who else could win the support of Parliament? Some advisers would say "not Asquith", because it was widely stated that he had no House of Commons following outside of the Liberal Rump. Austen Chamberlain could not secure Conservative support. He was severely damaged by a war muddle in Mesopotamia, though he had no responsibility for the tragedy. Carson was an impossibility. His Premiership would result in uniting the severed wings of the Liberal Party. He would be confronted by Lloyd George and Asquith joined together in opposition. The Irish members of Redmond's group, the O'Brien lot and the two Healys (factions among the Irish Nationalists), would all unite in assailing their old enemy. There was no possibility of a majority in the House of Commons for Carson. And if there was an election, Lloyd George would win it.*

But whatever may have been the influences prompting Haig, it is sufficient to record that he bowed at once to the civilian authority. He deserted his friends without an excuse or apology. He refused Lloyd George's suggestion that Robertson should be given command of an army in France. Lord Derby he left stranded like a whale on a sandbank.

* The Liberal leaders believed in their own fortunes and freely predicted the defeat of Lloyd George in a General Election.

Poor Derby! He had been destroyed by his zeal
and fidelity. Derided by Haig, and accused of
crooked dealing by Robertson," he was indeed a
whale on a sandbank. His threats of resignation
henceforth would no longer be political dynamite,
just Chinese firecrackers. The supreme importance he enjoyed had rested in his membership of
that dangerous triumvirate which had imperilled
the Government. Derby had been faithful to his
friends.

My home in the country was quite near to
Lloyd George's house at Walton Heath, and
Lloyd George would frequently call me to him,
especially when he was in gloom or high spirits.
On this day I was summoned and arrived at
Walton Heath shortly after Haig and Derby had
departed. I expected to see Lloyd George in low
health and possibly in a depressed mood. Instead
I found him in a state of jubilation. He was
relieved of anxiety and reaction had set in after
many days of doubt and uncertainty.

He telephoned Bonar Law to tell him of the
outcome of the visit and to instruct him to offer
the vacant Secretaryship of State for War to
Austen Chamberlain.

But in the course of the afternoon Bonar Law
rang up Lloyd George with the information that
Derby wished to withdraw his resignation. I
answered the telephone and carried the message
to the Prime Minister. Lloyd George agreed that
Derby could stay on provided he promised not
to resign again.

It was really of no interest to Lloyd George whether Derby went or stayed; his staying would make it somewhat easier for the Prime Minister in Parliament. But Lloyd George intended to dismiss him shortly anyway. Indeed, within a month he had left the Government, with the consolation prize of the British Embassy in Paris.

Sir Reginald Brade gives an account of events in his paper "A Few Notes on the Controversy between Sir. W. R. and the Government".

> Prime Minister and Bonar Law thought Derby had resigned and had wired for Austin, (I had urged P.M. previously not to appoint Milner) but at 5 [p.m.] a telephone message came from Bonar Law to say that the active MacPherson* had intimated that Derby had not resigned, so Bonar Law was told to tell Austin if he turned up that there was nothing doing for the moment but that perhaps in a month's time! [Lloyd George made no concealment of his intention to send Derby to Paris.]

The next day, Lord Derby took the precaution of nailing down his dis-resignation in a letter to Bonar Law.

18.2.18.

My dear Bonar,

I thought very carefully over what you said to me, & discussed the question of my resignation with Weir and MacPherson—and then went to see Haig. As the result of these conversations I did not put the notice in the papers, and am prepared, if you and my colleagues wish, to withdraw my resignation. You may rest assured I should loyally work and defend the scheme, but I shall quite understand it, if you think that it had better be run by somebody else.

* Under-Secretary of State for War.

I shall await your answer here and shall carry on till I do so.

I know you told MacPherson last night that you could speak in the name of the cabinet in asking me to remain—or rather in allowing me to withdraw my resignation, but I think I had better have that from you in writing after consultation with the P.M. as he may not agree.

Yours sincerely,

DERBY."*

To return to Mr. Chamberlain. He motored up to town from his country place. He had been out of the Government for eight months when this high offer of the War Office was dangled before him. He had been critical of the civilian direction of the war. Now he would return to the inner councils of wartime administration. He believed firmly that he could make a considerable contribution to the successful conduct of the war.

But when Chamberlain arrived at Downing Street, the door of office had after all been closed to him.

Chamberlain's re-entry into the Government was postponed. But he held what the Canadians call a "rain check". In April he was to become a member of the War Cabinet.

True, the developments of the Sabbath day of excitement had not finally settled the conflict. But Lloyd George was in a far, far stronger and sounder position than he had imagined likely on the Friday evening. Yet he was not too con-

---

* Derby spoke in the House of Lords on 19th February, 1918. He had the benefit of Curzon's help in preparing his statement. He said he had been asked to continue in office. He did not mention that he had himself asked permission to withdraw his resignation.

fident. He said at his house on Sunday night
after Haig had made his submission: "We have
to face a very serious crisis, and the Government
may fall." He was not, even then, sure of the
House of Commons. The issue had still to be put
to the test in Parliament. And on Tuesday, 19th
February, 1918, the House assembled to pronounce its verdict.

But the fire had been taken from the attack.
Mr. Asquith was mild and ineffective; he found
nothing to dispute in the Prime Minister's statement. Lord Robert Cecil had been won over to
acquiescence. Walter Long had been persuaded
to withdraw from opposition by Bonar Law.
He wrote:

19.ii.18.

My dear Bonar,
    Thank you for your frank and most helpful talk:
I also had some talk with Derby and Hankey. My
difficulties on the question are removed.
    From all I hear from our most reliable men the
P.M. will be well advised if he makes a very short
simple statement, avoiding detail.

Yours Ev.

WALTER H. LONG.*

Chamberlain had been fully informed of the
details of the conflict between Lloyd George and
Robertson on Sunday evening. He decided to
sustain the Prime Minister. Thus he remained
silent on the military issue but addressed himself
to civilian disputes, with considerable impact upon
his colleagues and others. He attacked the associ-

ation of the Government with the Press Lords (Northcliffe, Rothermere and me).

Lloyd George had escaped once again.

Haig, writing in his diary on Tuesday, 19th February—the day of the debate in Parliament—declared:

> I think I can fairly claim, as the result of my visit to London, that generally a saner view is now taken of the so-called military crisis, and the risk of a quarrel between "civilian and soldier" (which last Saturday seemed imminent) has been avoided.[x]

And at considerable pain to his two associates Robertson and Derby who had been faithful to Haig. Robertson, who had believed all along that Asquith would save him, was given the Eastern Command, a post of little importance. Derby was destined for dismissal before the spring tide of April.

But the quarrel between "civilian and soldier" had not been avoided. It had only been postponed.

Lloyd George had triumphed in this encounter. Walter Page, American Ambassador, who was a spectator with a seat in the front row, told the President of the United States: "His [Lloyd George's] dismissal of Robertson has been accepted in the interest of greater unity of military control, but that was a dangerous rapid he shot . . ."[y]

Indeed, his enemies were gathering for another assault. A pause that followed gave time for a remobilization of forces, before the final bid for domination was launched with all its fury.

CHAPTER VII

THE BIRTH OF THE ROYAL AIR FORCE

LORD JELLICOE had been dismissed. Sir William Robertson had been driven from the War Office. But their supporters were neither stifled nor acquiescent. Indeed, the adherents of the military clique were girding themselves for new and maybe decisive action. Their organs in the Press were sounding the challenge in words which were easily understood. Events presaged a showdown with the Prime Minister. They were a prelude to the final struggle which was fought out in the House of Commons in the Maurice Debate.

It was at this stage in the closely contested political struggle that a skirmish took place which centred upon the Air Force and involved Lord Rothermere, the Secretary of State for Air, and General Trenchard,* the Chief of the Air Staff. It was a clash of outposts yet it had some importance in relation to the main battle.

Lord Rothermere was a newcomer to the Government. His appointment to the Secretary-ship of State for Air as recently as November

* Later Lord Trenchard.

1917 had followed the astounding public rejection of that office by his elder brother, Lord Northcliffe.

Rothermere was summoned to the Ministry from his post in charge of clothing supplies for the Army, a task which he carried out with brilliant results.

In the general estimation, Lord Rothermere was a lesser figure than his illustrious brother. He was certainly a less dramatic and a less contentious one. His relations with Northcliffe were not intimate, although in private he admired his brother's courage and industry. Yet he declined to follow all of the political campaigns of that brilliant and exciting leader of Fleet Street.

I always had a very high regard for Lord Rothermere. He was a generous and devoted friend, a man of warm affections. In journalism he had achieved considerable distinction. He was the proprietor of five important newspapers, the *Daily Mirror*, the *Sunday Pictorial*, the *Leeds Mercury*, the *Glasgow Daily Record* and the *Glasgow Evening News*.

In politics, he had no party affiliations. He was on friendly terms with Bonar Law and Lloyd George. He was a good friend of Winston Churchill, whose war articles were printed in his papers. But he never gained a following in Parliament. Thus, when his own administration at the Air Ministry was breaking down under criticism, there were no friends or associates in the Houses of Parliament who could be relied upon to give him substantial aid.

General Trenchard had joined the Air Council as Chief of Air Staff at the beginning of January, 1918. The office of Chief of Air Staff was an appointment of the King* made on the advice of the Prime Minister. It was thus constitutionally the responsibility of the Prime Minister rather than, as might be supposed, the prerogative of the Secretary of State for Air. This fact was later to have considerable bearing in the conflict that involved the Government over the Ministry.

In fact, however, Rothermere had asked for Trenchard, and Lloyd George had concurred in the appointment.

Now the task of the Secretary of State was to merge the two separate services, the Royal Flying Corps which was part of the Army, and the Royal Naval Air Service which was a Naval unit.

But Trenchard, the new Chief of Staff, was strongly and even violently opposed to this reorganization, according to the records of Sir Douglas Haig.

Haig's entry in his Diary for 28th August, 1917, reads:

> The War Cabinet has evidently decided on creating a new Department to deal with Air operations, on the lines of the War Office and Admiralty. Trenchard is much perturbed as to the result of this new departure just at a time when the Flying Corps was beginning to feel that it had become an important part of the Army.[a]

* The Order in Council defining the composition of the Air Council says that, of the Members of the Air Council, the Chief of the Air Staff shall be appointed by the King (*Daily Express*, 22nd December, 1917).

Trenchard was, of course, an Army man. He did not want the divorce of the Royal Flying Corps from the Army organization. Nor, it appears, did he want the job of Chief of Air Staff under the new dispensation. On 16th December, 1917, Haig was writing in his Diary:

> General Trenchard also came to see me on his way to his H.Q. from London. Lord Rothermere (head of the Air Board) insists on him (T) going as Chief of Staff. T. stated that the Air Board are quite off their heads as to the future possibility of Aeronautics for ending the war. I told T. that it was evidently necessary that he should become C. of S. of Air, much as I regretted parting with him.[b]

Thus it was that when Trenchard came to the Air Council, he had no sympathy at all with the plans for setting up an Air Ministry. He was opposed to the policy of his own civilian chief and also the War Cabinet. He was in fact hostile to his Minister's programme, and not in accord with the task he had been called on to implement.

Trenchard had already won a high reputation when he joined the Air Ministry in January, 1918. He had served for two years in the Army as commander of the Royal Flying Corps in France and was considered, as he is to this day, the Father of the Air Arm. But he can hardly be regarded as the founder of the Royal Air Force, for, of course, he opposed the merger of the Flying Services. He was a father who tried to strangle the infant at birth though he got credit for the grown man.

From the day he took office, he was a disaffected and critical member of the newly formed Air Council. Within a few weeks of his appointment he was communicating his disloyal complaints to the Commander-in-Chief in France.

General Trenchard (now C. of Staff to Air Minister) who is on a visit to France came to report how things are developing at home [Haig recorded in his Diary on 26 January, 1918]. Lord Rothermere . . . who is Air Minister is quite ignorant of the needs or working of the Air Service, and is in great terror of newspaper criticism. Money is being squandered and officers and men wasted by being employed in creating units for performing work hitherto done by the Army (or Navy) for the Air Service. For example, Hospitals, Detention Barracks etc. All this is very sad at a time when officers and men are so badly needed. Trenchard thinks that the Air Service cannot last as an independent Ministry, and that Air Units must again return to Army and Navy. . . .

He [Trenchard] could think and talk nothing else but the rascally ways of politicians and the newspaper men.[c]

Rothermere borrowed trouble when he asked for Trenchard who disbelieved in the programme and the man. He was also lending trouble to Lloyd George.

From the outset, Trenchard exercised a strong influence upon the Air Council. This developed rapidly into a demand for a consolidation of authority in the hands of the Chief of the Air Staff at the expense of the civil head of the Department. Since Trenchard did not believe in detaching the Air Arm from the Army and did not have confidence in his own Minister, Rothermere was annoyed and frustrated by his Chief of Staff. He could not carry out his own projects.

To bring a new Ministry into working order is a difficult and trying task for men acting in harmony. But discord and dispute within swiftly bring antagonisms and hostility.

The position, as it developed, is best summed up in the words of the Parliamentary Under-Secretary to the Air Ministry, Major Baird.* "General Trenchard," he stated, "took a view as to the powers and duties of the Chief of the Air Staff which the Secretary of State for the Royal Air Force could not accept."*d*

In this conflict of authority between the civilian and the military elements, Trenchard handed in his resignation on 19th March, 1918. It may be surmised that he intended to coerce Lord Rothermere. Rothermere at once applied to the Prime Minister, who gladly came to the support of his Minister.

Lloyd George had been hearing rumours of conspiracies directed by Asquith, leader of the Liberal Opposition, and supported by Trenchard, Robertson, Jellicoe and possibly Haig. It was said that these soldiers were meeting with Asquith and considering plans for driving Lloyd George out of office. Lloyd George believed these stories.† Certainly his position was being challenged by the military faction with growing force and strength. He had no doubt on that score.

* Later Lord Stonehaven.
† Lord Milner was aware of the conspiracy and held that the Squiffites (followers of Asquith) were making use of Robertson.

The removal, therefore, of Trenchard must have been regarded favourably for no other reason than for the benefits and advantages he would gain in his struggle to hold his own place against the assaults of the political and military alliance against him.

Here was a bird Lloyd George could kill with a stone, the stone being Lord Rothermere. He threw it gladly.

Lloyd George was reinforced in his determination by the War Cabinet which met in the middle of April to discuss the question of General Trenchard. General Smuts gave the Prime Minister every encouragement; he had been commissioned by the Cabinet to investigate the situation at the Air Ministry and to advise on a successor to Lord Trenchard. He wrote to Lloyd George:

13th April, 1918.

My dear Prime Minister,

Macready has been consulted about Sykes. His position as A.G. to French at the time when the Sykes-Henderson trouble occurred gives him authority in the matter. He has no doubt whatever that Sykes is the best man to appoint, and I have accordingly told Rothermere to have him appointed without further delay.

My deepest sympathy is with you in these days of supreme peril.* If your strength continues under the load you are carrying I have no doubt you will succeed.

---

* The great Smuts was not quite right about the "supreme peril" that confronted the country in April, 1918. True the threat to the Channel ports was so serious as to involve us in decisions of momentous portent as to whether, in the event of success attending the German breach in the Allied front at Amiens, our Army would retreat to the north or follow the French forces to the south.

But such a calamity, though menacing our safety, did not mean defeat and destruction, whereas the submarine menace of 1917 threatened us with absolute and irremediable disaster.

Now is the time for quietness and strength when everybody is becoming nervous. I have no doubt whatever we shall pull through this crisis both in a military and political sense. Whatever strength or resource I have is entirely at your command.

Ever yours,

J. C. SMUTS.[e]

Lord Rothermere was given permission to accept the resignation of General Trenchard, and the announcement of the Air Ministry changes, with General Sykes as the new Chief of Air Staff, was made in the Press on 15th April.*

By an unlucky circumstance, the first intimation of the reconstruction reached Buckingham Palace through the columns of the newspapers. Very soon afterwards Lloyd George received a letter of criticism from the King's Secretary, Lord Stamfordham:

Windsor Castle.
16th April, 1918.

Dear Prime Minister,

It was only last night that the King received the Secret War Cabinet Minute of Friday, 12th instant, approving the changes on the Staff of the Air Ministry and the scheme of development of the Royal Air Force formulated by Lord Rothermere in his Memorandum of the 9th instant.

Had His Majesty seen this document or been aware of the changes advocated in it by Lord Rothermere, he would not have been surprised when, on Saturday afternoon, Lord Rothermere announced General

---

* The public turmoil over the Air Ministry was intensified by the publication on the same day of Haig's famous message: "With our backs to the wall . . . each one of us must fight to the end."

Trenchard's resignation and the appointment of General Sykes as his successor; also the King's apprehension at the consequences which he subsequently learnt might ensue by these changes, would have been considerably relieved.

His Majesty entirely appreciates how necessary and, indeed, right it is for a Secretary of State, after due consideration, to make whatever changes in both personnel and organisation he may think are required for the efficiency of his Department; it is only necessary that confident relations should exist between the Ministers and the King to avert misunderstandings such as those which occurred in this instance.

As I endeavoured to explain to you, His Majesty's one desire is that the new Air Force should be as perfect as can be, and he regrets that it should lose any of those Officers who have, since the beginning of the War, helped to build up the Royal Flying Corps and the Royal Naval Air Service respectively.

The King fully recognises and agrees with what you say as to the selection of appointments being vested in the civilian head of the Department, and that any dictation on the part of subordinates is unjustifiable. At the same time His Majesty feels sure you would be the first to realise the importance of the personal factor in dealing with the administration of Departments under the Crown, and especially those of a new creation.

Believe me,

Yours very truly,

STAMFORDHAM.[f]

No sooner had Trenchard's resignation been accepted, than conflict broke out in public. The *Daily News*[g] opened the attack on the Government. "The list is steadily growing," it declared, "of acknowledged masters of their craft for whose services in the crisis of our fate the Government has no serious use. It is the same story on every element. Thus:

The Sea, Lord Jellicoe,
The Land, Sir W. Robertson,
The Air, Sir Hugh Trenchard."

The impact of the resignation upon the Air Ministry itself was devastating. Lieutenant-General Sir David Henderson, Vice-President of the Air Council, sent in his resignation within a matter of days. In a letter to Bonar Law on 26th April, he set out the reasons for his actions. He was anxious, he said, to escape from the atmosphere of "intrigue and falsehood which has enveloped the Air Ministry for the last few months". He was unwilling, moreover, to become "a focus of discontent and opposition".[b]* Although, in fact, Henderson's task was largely completed with the fusion of the Royal Flying Corps and the Royal Naval Air Service, his decision to retire was evidently directly prompted by the appointment of General Sykes.

The departure of the Vice-President of the Air Council gave strength to the widely held belief that Trenchard's resignation must entail the dislocation of the whole Air Service.

A more serious matter was an intimation from the Parliamentary Under-Secretary to the Air Ministry, Major Baird, that he felt unable to represent Rothermere's views in the House of Commons. His letter to the Prime Minister dated

---

* Sir David Henderson's letter, with its enclosure, is given in full in *Appendix IV*, No. 12.

22nd April requested that his own opinions should be heard before the War Cabinet.

> I regret that I am unable to agree with some of the views expressed by Lord Rothermere and, consequently, could not support them in the House of Commons. In view of the Debates which are certain to take place in Parliament on this subject in the near future I thought it advisable to write to you in this sense at the earliest moment, and I most respectfully beg that I may be given an opportunity of laying my views before the War Cabinet. This course is all the more necessary because the opinions which I have formed are largely based on figures and facts which it would be impossible to make public.[i]*

His demand was tantamount to a threat of resignation and a matter of obvious concern to the Administration. By his letter Baird, in effect, declared himself a supporter of General Trenchard.

But there were other and more formidable allies of the General in the House of Commons—Sir John Simon and Lord Hugh Cecil.

Both were Flying Corps subalterns on Trenchard's staff, but they evidently had a humorous conception of the discipline demanded of non-combatant and combatant officers. For both were combining their positions on the Air Staff with violent attacks, as members of the House of Commons, on the political head of their own Service.

Both men were able Parliamentarians, exceptionally well-informed when it came to making

---

* The full text of the letter appears in *Appendix IV*, No. 13.

out a case against the Government. Sir John Simon was a leading member of the Bar, experienced in court, a redoubtable and practised advocate. There was no doubt that he and Cecil would force the issue of Trenchard's resignation to a debate in Parliament.

In the midst of this outbreak, and faced by a mounting opposition from Parliament and the Press, Lord Rothermere decided that he could not sustain the demands which the developing crisis was likely to exact from him. He went off to the country, sending in his resignation to the Prime Minister.

On the 24th April therefore I received a telephone call informing me that Rothermere had resigned, and summoning me to the Cabinet room. There I found the Prime Minister, Bonar Law and General Smuts with Lord Rothermere's resignation in front of them. The document was handed to me for my opinion. I was required to give my views without being told what was the reaction of the other three.

I had no difficulty in forming an opinion. The resignation was a devastating criticism of both Cecil and Simon, condemning them in outspoken terms for flouting disciplinary codes and for abusing their dual roles as Staff Officers and Members of Parliament.

Of his own position Rothermere declared that his work of blending the Royal Naval Service and the Royal Flying Corps was accomplished. There was hence no question of swapping horses. "The stream has been crossed."ʲ* The letter ended in eulogistic praise of Trenchard's successor in office, Major-General Sykes.

Lord Rothermere's letter of resignation at once struck me as being unsuitable, unsatisfactory and damaging to the Government.

From Lord Rothermere's point of view, it was sure to involve him in a difficult debate which he was in no condition to undertake. Rothermere had been in failing health, and he was weighed down by the heavy blows that fate had dealt him in his family. His two elder sons had been killed in action, one at Ancre at the close of 1916, and the eldest at Cambrai in February, 1918, less than two months before his letter was written. It was a burden almost greater than man could bear. He was suffering too from prolonged overwork.

Although the letter would relieve him of a task which was clearly beyond his power at that time, it would leave him to continue the controversy over the dismissal of General Trenchard even after he had left office. Indeed, it would lay him open to fierce attacks which would be based on his own communications.

Both Lord Hugh Cecil and Sir John Simon were capable of looking after themselves in the hurly-burly of Parliamentary debate. Moreover they longed to attack the Government on any and every count. The demand by Rothermere for "an enquiry by superior officers" into the conduct of these two serving soldiers in the Ministry might well become the overriding issue, thus

* The full text of the letter is reproduced in *Appendix IV*, No. 14.

raising constitutional discussion about the liberties and privileges of members of the House of Commons serving in the Armed Forces. There was no doubt also that the Prime Minister would be drawn into a heated defence of his approval of and responsibility for Trenchard's dismissal, in which the full battery of the militarists would be brought to bear against him.

Accordingly, I was opposed to accepting Lord Rothermere's letter without making energetic efforts to amend it. Bonar Law observed that if only I could be as wise in deciding my own issues as I proved myself in discussing the affairs of others, I would make a brilliant Minister.

Eventually, it was decided that a new letter of resignation should be secured from Lord Rothermere, and I was chosen as the Government's emissary charged with this task. I telephoned to Rothermere in the country, asking him to come to London to discuss the resignation with me. I met him on arrival at the Savoy Hotel. Almost immediately we were joined by Churchill, whom Rothermere had invited to take part in the discussion.

My dominating object was to help Rothermere to produce an entirely non-controversial letter which would leave him free from damaging attack and, at the same time, relieve the Government of the necessity of entering into a debate on the liberties of members of the House of Commons and also into a public defence of the dismissal of General Trenchard. My case was that unless he withdrew his present letter the whole conflict would go on more furiously than ever.

Churchill, however, gave quite different advice. He took his stand on the constitutional position that the appointment of the Chief of Air Staff rested with the Prime Minister and that it was his task to defend the removal of Trenchard and the appointment of Sykes. He said, in effect, to Rothermere, "Let the Government clear themselves." Lloyd George, he argued, had himself decided on the dismissal of Trenchard. It would not be right to throw the whole responsibility for it on Rothermere. There was something to be said for this position.

But there was another constitutional aspect which I pointed out. Lloyd George had acted on the advice and guidance of his Secretary of State and could therefore not be charged with responsibility by Lord Rothermere himself.

Churchill drafted a letter for Rothermere to sign. I advised a different approach and an entirely non-controversial letter.

Our discussion continued into the early hours of the morning. Rothermere was unable to come to any decision and we parted finally with no course of action settled. Very early next day, Lord Rothermere appeared at my rooms at the Hyde Park Hotel. He wakened me up, saying that he had decided to take my advice. He was a man worn down by anxiety and distress; the strain of the last days had greatly affected him. He was in fact quite ill. I got out of bed at once and after much discussion a letter was drafted with the promise that I should deliver it myself to the Prime Minister and bring back his reply.

Thereafter I set out for Downing Street. A meeting of the War Cabinet was in progress but I insisted on sending in a message to Lloyd George. This the secretary agreed to, provided I took full responsibility for interrupting the Cabinet. If my news pleased the Prime Minister and he wished to hear it—all would be well; if not, I was risking a snub by presenting myself in this way.

As I fully expected, however, the Prime Minister came out at once. He was delighted to see me. Together we drafted a reply to Lord Rothermere's letter.* Both Rothermere's resignation and Lloyd George's answer bear interpolations in Lloyd George's hand and mine.† Lloyd George's sole alteration in Rothermere's letter was to strike out a reference it bore to "April 1st" which he considered a necessary precaution.

I asked the Prime Minister for a recommendation of a Viscountcy for Lord Rothermere. To this Lloyd George agreed.

I reproduce both Rothermere's letter of resignation dated 25th April, 1918, and the Prime Minister's reply.

Hemsted,
Benenden, Kent.
25th April, 1918.

My dear Prime Minister,
　　I desire to relinquish my office as Secretary of State of the Air Force at the earliest possible date.

---

* Lloyd George's *War Memoirs*, Vol. IV, p. 1877, says the reply was sent "after it had been shown to and approved by my colleagues in the War Cabinet".

† The original letter and the original draft of Lloyd George's reply are preserved in the *Lloyd George Papers*.

Stansted

Benender

Kent
25 April 1918

My dear Prime Minister

I desire to relinquish my office
as Secretary of State of the Air Force at
the earliest possible date.

The Royal Air Force is now one of
the three established fighting services of the
Crown. The fusion of the Royal Naval Air
Service and the Royal Flying Corps has been
successfully accomplished

LORD ROTHERMERE'S LETTER OF
RESIGNATION

At times I have thought I would not be able to accompany the new Force so far. My second tragic loss in the war ten weeks since caused and causes me great distress of mind and body. Every day the burden of work and responsibility seemed crushing and I was suffering much from ill health and insomnia.

I felt (as I told you) my urgent primary duty to the Government and the nation required me to remain if at all physically possible until ~~1st April~~ the date of the fusion and such time (after as would suffice to establish the success of the amalgamation. My departure before might have gravely deranged what is

LORD ROTHERMERE'S LETTER OF
RESIGNATION (page 2)

The date "1st April" in the above letter was struck out by Lloyd George

now one of the nations arms of war and has
jeopardised the success of the whole scheme.

Lately I thought I might be able
to remain but a recurrence of bronchial trouble with insomnia
effectually prevents this.

I have entered into these particulars
I wish you to know
because ~~of my~~ the difficulties under which
I have been working

I cannot close this letter without
an expression of my great regard and respect.

Yours very faithfully

The Right Hon
The Prime Minister   Rothermere

The Royal Air Force is now one of the three established fighting services of the Crown. The fusion of the Royal Naval Air Service and the Royal Flying Corps has been successfully accomplished.

At times I have thought I would not be able to accompany the new Force so far. My second tragic loss in the war ten weeks since caused and causes me great distress of mind and body. Every day the burden of work and responsibility seemed crushing and I was suffering much from ill health and insomnia.

I felt as I told you my urgent primary duty to the Government and the nation required me to remain if at all physically possible until the date of the fusion and such time after as would suffice to establish the success of the amalgamation. My departure before might have gravely deranged what is now one of the nation's arms of war and have jeopardised the success of the whole scheme.

Lately I thought I might be able to remain but a recurrence of bronchial trouble with insomnia effectually prevents this.

I have entered into these particulars because I wish you to know the difficulties under which I have been working.

I cannot close this letter without an expression of my great regard and respect.

Yours very faithfully,
ROTHERMERE.[k]

The Prime Minister replied:

My dear Rothermere,

I have received your letter tendering your resignation as Secretary of State for the Air Force with the deepest regret. Your work there has been of inestimable service to the nation, and time will bring with it a full recognition of your achievement. It is no small thing to have taken over the conduct of an entirely new arm of the service in the middle of a great war, to have extricated it from the difficulties which surrounded it, co-ordinated the two services which made it up, and bestowed on its administration an initiative which has given the new force a real supremacy at the front. And all this has been done in such a brief period of time.

It is the more to be lamented that, having set the Ministry on its legs, you cannot remain to enjoy the fruition of your own brilliant work. But I feel on reading your letter that I cannot press you to stay, much as the Government must suffer from your retirement.

Your sacrifices to the National cause have been so heavy, and the strain imposed on you so cruel that it would be impossible to deny you the right to some repose. Sympathy in these matters is generally best given by silence, but I am sure that you know without my telling you how much I sympathise with you in your losses and in the way in which you have continued your public duties in spite of everything.

No Minister ever had greater difficulties to contend with than you had in effecting the fusion of the two services, and the Air Force has every right to be proud of its First Secretary of State.

I am authorised by my colleagues to state that they share fully the views I have expressed in this letter.

Yours very faithfully,

D. LLOYD GEORGE.[l]

A curious anomaly attaches to the resignation letters. When Lloyd George came to tell the story of Rothermere's resignation in his *War Memoirs* some years later, and before the death of Lord Rothermere, it was not Lord Rothermere's letter of 25th April, 1918, which he published but the earlier letter with all its implications.[m]

MINISTRY OF INFORMATION,

NORFOLK STREET,

STRAND,

LONDON, W.C. 2.

10 Downing St

P R I V A T E   April 25. 1918.

My dear Rothermere,

I have received your letter
tendering your resignation as Secretary of
State for the Air Force with the deepest regret.
Your work there has been of inestimable service
to the nation, and time will bring with it a
full recognition of your achievement. It is
no small thing to have taken over the conduct
of an entirely new arm of the service in the
middle of a great war, to have extricated it
from the difficulties which surrounded it,
co-ordinated the two services which made it up,
and bestowed on its administration an initiative
which has given the new force a real supremacy
at the front. And all this has been done in
such a brief period of time.

It is the more to be lamented
that having set the Ministry on its legs you
cannot remain to enjoy the fruition of your own
brilliant work. But I feel on reading your letter
that I cannot press you to stay, much as the
Government must suffer from your retirement. *cruel*

Your sacrifices to the National
cause have been so heavy, and the strain imposed
on your ~~mind and body~~ so ~~great~~, that it would be
impossible to deny you the right to some repose.
Sympathy in these matters is generally best given
by silence, but I am sure that you know without my
telling you how much I sympathise with you in your
losses and in the way in which you have continued your
public duties in spite of everything.

No Minister ever had greater difficulties to contend with than you had in effecting
the fusion of the two services, and the Air Force has
every right to be proud of its First Secretary of

LLOYD GEORGE'S REPLY TO LORD
ROTHERMERE

The word "cruel" was inserted by Lloyd George

States. And this I know is not only my own
opinion but that of all your colleagues.

Yours Faithfully,

D Lloyd George

I am authorized by my
colleagues to state
that they share fully
the views I have
expressed in the
letter

LLOYD GEORGE'S REPLY TO LORD
ROTHERMERE (continued)

The last sentence was added by Beaverbrook

The explanation may be a simple one. Lloyd George was dealing with a tremendous range of documents.

To continue with my narrative. Having secured the Prime Minister's reply, I returned to Lord Rothermere. I left my office and my duties and took him to my house at Leatherhead.

Rothermere, despite his judgement and ability, was not the man to grapple with a political crisis. Instead, he invariably wished to pull down the blinds. He would never take part in any debate. He would never defend himself in the House of Lords. Yet he would have made a brilliant controversialist, and a good speaker.

I had made a practice of calling to see him in his rooms regularly. He was worrying acutely over his work. His nervous concentration was too tremendous to last. He was seeking forgetfulness from his personal grief, in labour—and not succeeding in finding it. His mind was invariably running either on his task or his tragedy. He seemed quite unable to distract himself with any other set of ideas and it became obvious that such a state of affairs could not continue indefinitely. Something was bound to give way.

Lord Rothermere's letter, and the Prime Minister's reply, were published in the afternoon newspapers of 25th April.

Following the announcement, *The Times*, Lord Northcliffe's newspaper, observed Lord Rothermere's retirement "follows so close on a much-debated change in the *personnel* of the Air Staff—

a change which has been joyfully hailed by the politicians as a counter in their game—that it would have been a real advantage from every point of view to have *Lord Rothermere's* own account of his action in Debate".[n]

Lord Rothermere's own account, though brief, is set out in a letter to Bonar Law, written to the Conservative leader after the storm had blown over. Here is the letter:

> Hemsted,
> Benenden, Kent.
> 3rd May, 1918.

My dear Bonar,

I am writing to thank you for your kindness last week. The H. of C. does not like newspapers much less newspaper Ministers. Their time is not yet.

In getting rid of Trenchard I flatter myself I did a great thing for the Air Force. With his dull unimaginative mind and his attitude of "Je sais tout" he would within twelve months have brought death and damnation to the Air Force. As it was he was insisting on the ordering of large numbers of machines for out-of-date purposes.

I am very grateful to you for the message from the P.M. brought me by Max that I am, on relinquishing office, to become a Viscount.

> Yours always sincerely,
> ROTHERMERE.[o]

With the publication of the letter of resignation, the lobbies buzzed with interest and speculation. In the House of Commons on the same afternoon, that formidable critic of the Government, Sir Edward Carson, questioned the Leader of the

House. Bonar Law replied: "It is true, I regret to say, that Lord Rothermere has resigned. His successor has not yet been appointed."[p]

Four days later the changes at the Air Ministry became the subject of acrimonious parliamentary debate. The language of the opposing elements was violent and excited. Lord Hugh Cecil launched a vituperative attack. "I cannot . . . speak very respectfully," he announced, "of the Prime Minister's letter accepting that [Rothermere's] resignation, and perhaps the kindest thing to say of it is that it is the effort of a strong Celtic imagination."[q]

The accusation that service members were using information gained in the course of their official tasks did not daunt or deflect him. "If you have a man like Sir Hugh Trenchard at the head of your Air Force," he persisted, "perhaps you may find he will not always listen to the ideas of every amateur strategist in the Cabinet quite as sympathetically as that strategist might desire."[r]

This brought the Prime Minister to his feet.

"I do not think he need show himself so very sensitive" Cecil retorted. "The right hon. Gentleman really seems to care about nothing except his own retention in office—himself, personally."[s]

Sir Edward Carson made a hostile attack on the Government. He gave outspoken support to General Trenchard. Indeed he went further. He contested in the House of Commons the principle of civil authority. "When a dispute arises," Carson declared, "between the Civil head of a

great Department of the State and its great expert,
in that dispute the Civil head is the judge. If a
man goes to the Admiralty as First Lord, and
has been there only a week or a fortnight, he can
dismiss at his own will his expert advisers, and
let the public know that when it comes to be a
question whether an indispensable expert adviser,
or an ignorant civilian who has only been there a
fortnight, is to go, the decision rests with the
civilian. That is the constitutional position. It is
a very serious one, and I think that when these
things happen it is at least the duty of the Government thoroughly to investigate on a case of this
kind what has been the real cause of the State
in its throes, as it is at the present moment, losing
a great and an efficient soldier."[t] (Carson was
returning to the contemplation of his King
Charles's head, which was the dismissal of Lord
Jellicoe.)

Carson had then been out of the administration
for three months; his attack was of a most
serious and damaging character. It was an outright advocacy of military domination.

At the same time, there was a concerted demand
from the Opposition bench for the return of
General Trenchard to his post. The attempt
failed.*

For Lloyd George the storm of the morning
became the sunshine of the afternoon. He avoided
acrimonious exchanges.

Basing his defence on the letters which were

* The House of Commons was informed on 13th May, 1918, that Trenchard
had accepted the command of "a very important part of the British Air Force
in France."

composed in the Hyde Park Hotel and in the outer Cabinet office on that April morning, "General Trenchard," he said, "put in his resignation for reasons into which I do not wish to enter, because it involves a dispute which the Noble Lord himself has not thought fit to enter into, as I think wisely."[u]

He rode off, with consummate skill and ease, on Rothermere's resignation. It was a triumph of evasive action in debate.

In the House of Lords, Lord Curzon, the President of the Council, showed himself no less adroit in avoiding difficulty for the Government. Indeed, he managed to escape a debate on the question altogether. A motion tabled by Lord Sydenham, asking the Air Minister to state the reasons for the dismissal of General Trenchard, was abruptly abandoned.

Lord Curzon told the House, "an announcement has been made in the Press this afternoon as to the resignation of the Secretary of State for the Royal Air Force which puts a somewhat different complexion upon affairs. In these circumstances I feel that I have no right myself to ask the House to meet on Monday next for this debate. . . ."[v] Again Lord Rothermere's letter had served its purpose.

In carrying to the Prime Minister the request for a Viscountcy for Lord Rothermere, I was conscious that his work at the Air Ministry had produced outstanding results and the honour would please and hearten him.

But there was an immediate reaction in Royal circles against any further preferment for Lord Rothermere. On the day of his resignation Lord Stamfordham wrote to the Prime Minister.

Windsor Castle,
25th April, 1918.

Dear Prime Minister,

I have reported to the King the substance of what you told me this afternoon.

His Majesty will be prepared to approve the possible appointments you mentioned, if you finally decide to make them, but the King hopes you will not raise the question of Lord Rothermere's promotion in the Peerage. The newly constituted Air Force, of which he was Minister, has only been in existence twenty-four days when he resigns. Rightly or wrongly, his administration has been sharply criticised and is to be discussed in both Houses of Parliament. He has only just been made a Privy Councillor which, in itself, is high distinction. . . .

STAMFORDHAM.[w]

A year passed by. The Palace still maintained its resistance to the Rothermere peerage. On 11th April, 1919, Lord Stamfordham wrote to Frederick Guest, the Coalition Chief Whip, objecting once more to Lord Rothermere's name in the list of honours.

Buckingham Palace.
11th April, 1919.

Confidential

My dear Guest,

I have submitted to the King the list of honours which we discussed this morning.

As I anticipated, His Majesty takes exception to the proposed promotion of Lord Rothermere to be

STAMFORDHAM

ROTHERMERE

A firm friend and a good companion

a Viscount, and the King would like to remind the
Prime Minister that in less than nine years, Mr.
Harold Harmsworth has became a Baronet—1910,
a Peer—1914, and a Privy Counsellor, which latter
His Majesty regards as a very high honour, in 1917,
only two years ago.

. . . . . .

I pointed out to His Majesty that I gathered from
you that the Viscountcy had been promised to Lord
Rothermere, but the King says he certainly has no
recollection of this suggested promotion having
been submitted to him . . .

Yours very truly
STAMFORDHAM.[x]

On 12th April, Lord Stamfordham wrote again[y]
to inform Guest that he now recollected that the
King had raised objections the previous year,
and Stamfordham quoted his letter to the Prime
Minister of 25th April, 1918.

Bonar Law then took part in the fray. He
wrote pressing for the fulfilment of the pledge
to Lord Rothermere, given to him just a year
before.

17th April 1919

Dear Lord Stamfordham,

In the absence of the Prime Minister, I am writing
to you with reference to some remarks in your letter
to Guest about the promotion of Lord Rothermere.

I earnestly hope that this recommendation may be
allowed to go through. I must point out to you that,
while I fully realise the difficulties raised in your letter,
the Prime Minister undertook, at the time of Lord
Rothermere's resignation, that he would support this
recommendation to the King, and the Prime Minister,

I think, would personally be placed in a very unpleasant position if His Majesty could not see his way to accept the recommendation.

Although some criticisms may be passed upon the success, or otherwise, of his short administration at the Air Ministry, his intense loyalty and assistance to the Government during the later and critical days of the war, and also at the General Election, have considerably increased the obligations due to him.

Yours sincerely,

A. BONAR LAW.[z]

Lord Stamfordham replied:

Windsor Castle.

17th April, 1919.

Dear Bonar Law,

The King has read your letter of the 17th instant, urging the promotion of Lord Rothermere to a Viscountcy.

His Majesty gives his approval, but with much reluctance. He cannot help thinking that it would have been better if the Prime Minister had not given an undertaking to Lord Rothermere at the time of his resignation that he would be recommended to the King for promotion. This is another case of a quasi promise, and what is worse, a quasi committal of His Majesty!

Yours very truly,

STAMFORDHAM.[aa]

There had always been trouble over the recommendation of honours for the Press lords. Beginning with Lord Northcliffe in 1905, there was difficulty, although on that occasion the situation was in reverse.

Then two peerages were being contested, Sir

Herbert Stern's (later Baron Michelham) and Northcliffe's. The Conservatives had put forward Stern, the Palace was responsible for Northcliffe's nomination. But the Conservative Whip, Sir Alexander Acland Hood, objected to Northcliffe because he was not a reliable supporter of the Conservatives, and the Palace was not enthusiastic about an honour for Stern. In the end there was what is known in Canadian politics as a "saw-off", and King Edward VII agreed to approve a barony for Sir Herbert Stern while Hood acquiesced in the recommendation, in the name of Balfour, of the Northcliffe honour.

Then there was my own peerage. This provoked a tremendous storm. Indeed, my only regret is that the storm was not strong enough to carry me away!

On the fall of the Asquith Government, Lloyd George wanted the seat I held at Ashton-under-Lyne for Sir Albert Stanley, the new President of the Board of Trade. It is true that he also wanted a Government spokesman in the House of Lords. So he sought to promote me to the Peerage. But King George V did not see his way to approve the honour. This placed Lloyd George in a position of some delicacy as arrangements for a by-election at Ashton had already been set in motion. The King was obliged to give way; but not without a severe reproof addressed to Lloyd George.

I cannot conceal from you [wrote Lord Stamford-ham to Mr. Lloyd George] that His Majesty was surprised and hurt that this honour should have been offered without first obtaining his consent. . . . The King recognises (in view of the promises made and information given) that it is impossible for him now to withhold his approval. But, in thus signifying his acquiescence, His Majesty commands me to say that he feels that the Sovereign's Prerogative should not be disregarded; and he trusts that in future no honours whatever will be offered by any Minister until his approval has been informally obtained. His Majesty further asks that this be made clear to your Colleagues.[ab] *

There was more trouble over Lord Northcliffe in 1917. Lloyd George recommended him for a step in the varying and confusing hierarchy of nobility. He would be a Viscount. Colonel House wrote in his diary: "Wiseman tells me that the King talked to him of Northcliffe in a denunciatory way. However, he was compelled to make Northcliffe a Viscount the next day. He must have done it with a wry face."[ac]

The proposal that Sir Edward Russell, editor of the *Liverpool Daily Post*, should be given a peerage was opposed by the Palace in 1919:

I must tell you frankly [wrote Lord Stamford-ham from Windsor Castle to Frederick Guest] that His Majesty is sorry that this proposal has been revived, as you will see from my letter of the 25th February last to Davies, that the King then questioned the advisability of granting a Peerage to a person who was only a Knight Bachelor at the age of eighty-five.

* Sir Harold Nicolson referred to His Majesty's objections without mentioning me. When Robert Blake wrote his life of Bonar Law (*The Unknown Prime Minister*) I informed him of this incident and authorized him to use my name. It has always been my habit to print everything about my own career, good and bad, pleasing and disagreeable.

Still more does His Majesty now deprecate bestowing a further honour on the Press when the list already contains—Lord Burnham, Lord Rothermere, Mr. Hulton, Mr. David Duncan, Mr. Madge and Coode-Adams.*

The King would not even consent to the case being brought up again for the Birthday Gazette.[ad]

A month later, on Lloyd George's insistence, the King reluctantly consented.

The peerage of Sir Henry Dalziel, proprietor of *Reynold's News*, was delayed.

> Forgive me putting it strongly, [wrote Guest to Lloyd George on 17th May, 1920] but I feel sure that you will be sorry if you further postpone the fulfilment of this definite promise. The old warrior has faithfully and patiently played the game and has helped me in very many ways since our connection. The moment is ripe. The Court will approve.[ae]

On Sir Edward Hulton, though promised a Peerage, the Palace would not go beyond accepting a recommendation for a baronetcy.

But the greatest row of all attended Lord Riddell's elevation to the House of Lords. When his name was submitted in 1920, the King had a further ground for complaint. Riddell had been the guilty party in a divorce action. He was then the chief proprietor of the *News of the World*. King George rejected the nomination on the grounds of Riddell's divorce. But Lloyd George

---

* Lord Burnham, *Daily Telegraph*; Lord Rothermere, *Daily Mirror*; Mr. Hulton, *Manchester Daily Despatch*, and others; Mr. David Duncan, *South Wales Daily News*; Mr. Madge, *The People*, and Sir John Coode-Adams, the *Pall Mall Gazette*. It was strange that my name should have been omitted. I hope it was in compliment.

was anxious to reward this friend of long standing and of great loyalty to himself, and so he undertook the task of collecting a number of letters from the Press lords of Fleet Street testifying in praise of Riddell's admirable work on behalf of the Newspaper Proprietors' Association.*af*

Thus Riddell had the distinction of becoming the first divorced Peer to enter the House of Lords.

Lloyd George put an end to the barrier against divorced men in the House of Lords. And the Constituencies would shortly make matchwood of the barriers against divorced men in the House of Commons. The honour of destroying the ban on divorced Ministers belongs to Ramsay MacDonald, leader of the Socialist Party. The practice now extends to all parties—the Judiciary, Parliament and Governments too. The Royal Household is the last stronghold.

No divorced persons had become Peers, or Ministers either, in May, 1918. Not even a divorced member of Parliament.

And it was on May Day of the last year of war that a hurricane was blowing up about the Prime Minister. The Government had steered safely through to harbour during the Rothermere tempest. Yet the serious nature of the situation was not for a moment in doubt. It had been demonstrated in the violence of the gale in the House of Commons and in the dangerous assaults of the Opposition members against the Administration.

Within ten days, the last and worst weather would come upon Lloyd George without any warning. The Daring Pilot who had survived so many perils in a journey that had lasted for nearly a year and a half, would be tried and tested. He would need all of his courage and plenty of luck.

CHAPTER VIII

THE LOST BOX

THE whole nation was in a stormy and troubled condition. For now the crisis of the battle of the Western Front rushed across the horizon. The military reverses in France gave anxious cause for alarm; there were disputes about manpower and the responsibilities for the disasters at the Front.

At this time Lloyd George was actually contemplating a General Election. He wrote to Bonar Law:

> It looks as if the Asquithians meant to challenge an issue on Irish conscription. If they succeed in defeating that part of the Bill, we ought to consider very carefully our next step. It should be resignation or dissolution. They are relying on the 40-50 call up.[a]

But a General Election did not appeal to Bonar Law. And indeed the Asquith party had no intention of dividing the House on any question likely to precipitate a General Election without first discrediting and even destroying Lloyd George.

Thus it was that the Opposition forces came to regard the quarrel between Lloyd George and the

Generals as a vital issue. Here they might find the weapon that could sufficiently damage the Prime Minister in the judgment of the electors.

Military leaders at the War Office and in France gave out statements to their newspaper friends and others to the effect that Lloyd George had deliberately withheld troops in Great Britain instead of reinforcing the Army in France. According to his critics, his conduct was entirely responsible for the disasters of March when the Germans crashed through the British lines.

The newspapers made insistent demands that the question of war direction must come under review.

Lloyd George recorded of the time: "The militarist Press took up the cue. There was a propagandist campaign organised in the Press, in social circles, in the clubs and in the Lobbies of the House, and it ultimately culminated in the cabal which, after working assiduously but in vain to overthrow the Government for attempting to organise a General Reserve behind our threatened Army, thought that, after repeated failures, their opportunity had at last arrived."[b]

In the final clash, Sir Frederick Maurice, a devoted admirer and confidant of Sir William Robertson, and just at that time transferred from Director of Military Operations to other employment, became the standard-bearer of the soldiers and their political allies against the Government.

On 7th May, 1918, a letter from Maurice was published in several morning newspapers accusing the Government of a series of misstatements on

the military situation. It was his intention to reinforce the claims of the Government critics that the
Army in France had been starved of manpower.

Maurice arraigned the Government on three
separate counts. In the first place he challenged
the statement made by the Prime Minister in the
House of Commons on 9th April, 1918, in which
Lloyd George had declared that the Army in
France was considerably stronger in January 1918
than in January of the year before. Such a statement, Maurice claimed, was entirely erroneous.
It implied that Sir Douglas Haig's fighting strength
on the eve of the German attack in March had
not been reduced. This, he said, was not correct.

He further denied an assertion made by the
Prime Minister regarding the number of white
troops in Palestine and Egypt.

His last allegation concerned Bonar Law. The
question of the extension of the British line in
France had been recently taken up in the House.
It was a matter in which there was much interest.
Bonar Law had stated in Parliament that the
extension had not been decided by the hated
Versailles War Council. Maurice gave him the
lie direct—a bold decision considering Bonar
Law's reputation for truth and honesty.

Such was the stern nature of Maurice's charges.
Each bore on a vital matter in the disputes that
raged with increasing public attention between
the civilian and the military factions.

Yet Maurice was at pains to make clear his
motives for his attack. The letter, he affirmed,

formed no part of a military conspiracy; he was, he professed, as sincere a democrat as the Prime Minister and had no wish to see the Government of the country in the hands of the soldiers. He had written because of the widespread distrust of the Government which was impairing the morale of the troops.

Lloyd George did not credit General Maurice's protestations of devotion to democracy. He naturally supposed, in the highly charged atmosphere of the moment, that the letter was the outcome of a deliberate and organised attack upon the Government.

Indeed, a few days after the letter's publication, Sir William Robertson himself felt bound to write to Lord Milner in the following terms:

> During the past week a story has been persistently circulated in a certain section of the London Press*— the same section which suddenly and simultaneously attacked me early in the year—insinuating that Mr. Asquith, Lord Jellicoe, General Trenchard and myself met recently at a special dinner or in conference— before the Maurice letter—and conspired together to upset or cause trouble to the Government. I wish to say that so far as I am personally concerned this story is an absolute fabrication.ᶜ

In sending Robertson's letter on to the Prime Minister, Lord Milner commented:

> There is no doubt in my mind that he himself was not the principal intriguer, but that he got into bad company, Repington and the "Morning Post" crowd

* Lord Northcliffe's *Daily Mail*.

being really the devils of the piece, while no doubt the "Squiffites"* saw their chance of making use of him.[d]

This denial of Robertson's did not influence events. In fact it was received by Lloyd George after the struggle was all over. But in any case Lloyd George would not accept any denial of a conspiracy. He was convinced that the charges and counter-charges must be fought out in debate in Parliament.

For the real meaning of the Maurice charges was well known and fully understood. The intention was to reinforce the argument to which I have already referred that Lloyd George was deliberately starving the army in France of necessary reinforcements. Several reasons were offered for such conduct, most of them discreditable to Lloyd George and his Government.

Thus Maurice's imputations questioned more than ministerial veracity. They also condemned the Government on their military direction of the war. If the case were proved, the Government must inevitably fall.

The hostile Press, which had been making charges against Lloyd George holding him responsible for the weakness of the British Forces in France and for the reduction in the number of battalions, was now quick to point out that the Maurice letter put an official seal upon all the newspaper denunciations.

Here then was the crucial test.

On the day the letter appeared, Asquith gave

* Followers of Asquith.

further strength to the Opposition by putting down a private notice of his intention to ask for a Select Committee of the House of Commons.

At the same time, at a meeting of Ministers on 7th May, the whole content of Maurice's allegations was reviewed.

Bonar Law was greatly perturbed by the charges. He was directly involved; the veracity of the Prime Minister and himself had been held up to public attack. He believed that the Maurice letter reflected on his personal honour, and he was convinced that a judicial enquiry should be instituted at once to examine the accusation.

The Cabinet was moved by wider considerations. There was evident difficulty about submitting documents of a highly secret nature to a Court of Enquiry. In the same way the proposal to set up a Committee of the House of Commons had to be rejected. It was decided that the Government should invite two judges to act as a Court of Honour to enquire into the charge that misstatements had been made.

Later that day Bonar Law communicated the Government's intention to the House of Commons. The decision failed to satisfy Asquith. He intended to have the matter opened to discussion on the floor of the House; he invited the Government to name a day for a debate.

Churchill was sitting beside Bonar Law on the Front Bench. He heard the proposal for a Judicial Committee for the first time. He urged Bonar

Law to withdraw the offer. Bonar Law made no answer. Later Churchill joined Lloyd George and Bonar Law in conference. He convinced them that a Minister should never ask a Judicial Committee to enquire into his own integrity.*

Churchill's intervention was decisive. The offer of a Judicial Committee was never renewed. Asquith had blundered by failing to accept it. He had saved the Government from an embarrassing error. Churchill's wise advice had strengthened the Government's hand.

The situation, however, was now plainly exposed. It was apparent that the Maurice letter was to be treated as a vote of censure on the Administration. The *Westminster Gazette*, the mouthpiece of the Asquith Alliance, loudly proclaimed that there was an alternative government and it was time it took the reins.[e] The *Manchester Guardian*, usually friendly to the Government, assured its readers that General Maurice's statements "went to the heart of the responsibility for our recent reverses".[f] The *Morning Post* took up the cry with bitter criticism of the Prime Minister.

"It is only the seriousness of the war position, the presumed difficulty of finding a successor, and, perhaps, a shrewd suspicion of the sort of 'support' any successor would be likely to have at his hands," it proclaimed, "which has kept him at the head of the Government ever since the demission of Sir William Robertson."[g] The

* See *Appendix IV*, No. 15.

Government must come out and face the challenge.

On the evening of 7th May, therefore, the lobbies were plunged into a crisis of immense proportions. The country was even more excited than the Members of Parliament. The political sensation was the subject of discussion in every meeting place; in pubs and bank parlours, in bars and board rooms.

There were three important considerations that had to be taken into account in estimating the danger to the Government. (1) The charge of deliberately deceiving the House, if sustained, is never forgiven, and must wreck a Ministry. (2) Some of Lloyd George's colleagues believed that there was a great deal of substance in the charges. (3) The Ministry was at that period suffering from the consequences of reverses in the field, and under those conditions a serious political assault might bring the Government down.

Ministerial Whips despatched telegrams demanding the attendance of their supporters on the day of the debate. There was just as much activity in opposition circles. Sir Edward Carson entertained the hope of playing an important role. Without doubt he expected that a new government would be formed and that greater power would be accorded to the military leaders. Possibly Jellicoe would be brought back again.

Lady Carson notes in her diary for 8th May, 1918: "Heard from Edward that General Maurice's letter had made a great stir. Edward always knew that Ll.G.'s and B.L.'s statements were lies, but only knowing so from being in the Cabinet he could not say so."[h]

The Unionist War Committee was called together. L. S. Amery gives this account of the meeting: "Went to the Unionist War Committee, a very large gathering, which was discussing today's vote in the House. Salisbury opened, very hostile to the Government, and then Carson suggested that the Unionist War Committee should as a body take an independent attitude by moving the previous question, thus neither endorsing Asquith nor approving of Lloyd George."[i]

Such a decision would, as Carson well knew, be a death-blow to the Administration. If he had succeeded the Government would have fallen there and then. The War Committee rejected the proposal.

After the meeting, Carson met Colonel Repington at Lady Londonderry's luncheon table and told him that "he had been for three hours with the Unionists today, that their hate of Asquith overrides all other considerations, and that they will not back him tomorrow in the Maurice debate."[j] Carson added that it would be no use for him to speak as he would have no following.

Yet even though the Unionist War Committee refused to accept Carson's wrecking proposal, there was grave doubt of the outcome of the crisis. On the eve of the debate, the verdict could not be predicted.

The Liberal War Committee had also assembled

to discuss its course of action. There were un-known areas of weakness in the House from which a formidable opposition could be gathered. It was not possible to assess the strength of the Asquith Alliance.

As the storm grew in violence, Lloyd George displayed considerable force and determination. He had gone over the matter thoroughly with his colleagues in the Cabinet; he believed that the Government had a complete answer to its critics. He was eager to make a case in Parliament. He felt confident he could convince the House.

On 9th May, therefore, a resolute Prime Minister entered a tense and crowded House of Commons to present the case for the Government.

Asquith opened the Debate on the Motion for a Select Committee. His speech was suave and highly polished. It cannot be held to have been free from guile. Asquith concluded: ". . . I hold no brief of any sort or kind for military as distinguished from civilian and, what is called, politicians' opinion."[k]

In reply, Lloyd George dealt with the charges one by one. He referred to his own speech on 9th April, which General Maurice had challenged. He told the House that General Maurice had been at his post in the War Office some weeks after that speech had been delivered. Maurice had attended a meeting of the Cabinet, in the absence of the Chief of Staff, the very day after Lloyd George had made the speech. But, until the charges appeared in the Press, he did not say a word about the allegation that the Prime Minister's statements were inaccurate.

The most telling section of Lloyd George's defence depended on General Maurice's own figures.

"The figures that I gave," Lloyd George stated, "were taken from the official records of the War Office, for which I sent before I made the statement. If they were incorrect, General Maurice was as responsible as anyone else. But they were not inaccurate. . . . There is absolutely no doubt that there was a very considerable addition to the man-power of the Army in France at the beginning of 1918 as compared with the man-power at the beginning of 1917."[1]

Lloyd George went on to say he was not including in his estimate of the fighting strength in France the labour battalions and other non-combatant units. The combatant strength of the British Army was greater at the beginning of 1918 than at the beginning of the previous year. This information also came from General Maurice's Department at the War Office.

On a less important point, Lloyd George assured the House that his statement about the strength of British troops in the Middle East was based on official War Office information presented to the Cabinet when Sir Frederick Maurice was present, and later sent to the General for checking. Maurice had telephoned his answer, "No remarks."

It now remained for the Prime Minister to dispose of the charge concerning the veracity of

Bonar Law's statement on the extension of the British Line. He dealt with it swiftly. Not a yard, he pronounced, had been taken over by the British Army as a result of the Versailles Council. In fact, the extension agreed to between Haig and Pétain was an accomplished fact before the Council met, and Haig had reported it himself to the Versailles meeting.*

It was a triumphant reply. It was a complete vindication of Lloyd George and Bonar Law. No further attack was launched from the Opposition Front Bench.

Sir Edward Carson spoke only briefly and in a sense very different from his earlier intentions. He poured scorn on the idea that judges should be asked to decide whether the Prime Minister was, or was not, an honourable man. And he said that Asquith, his old enemy (whom he had once called a traitor), had always acted as a patriot.

He secured no backing to push home an assault. The dismal outcome of Carson's attempt to mobilize the Unionist [Conservative] War Committee was his last bid for power and his final defeat.

The House, dividing on the Motion for a Select Committee, returned an astonishing total of 293 votes for the Government. One hundred and six members registered their votes with the Opposition.

Thus Lloyd George's position was endorsed by

---

* Haig in his diary, published years after, denied that he agreed to take over any part of the French Front. He declared that this speech of Lloyd George's was "clap-trap", that the House of Commons was losing its reputation and that Maurice was not yet done with Lloyd George.[m]

an overwhelming majority. He was confirmed in the Premiership by a decisive backing in the House of Commons.

For the opposing one hundred it was a costly defeat. Indeed, for many of them it was to foreshadow their political extinction.

The importance of the Maurice Debate as an incident in political history cannot be forgotten. In the first place, it marked a turning point in Lloyd George's career. It left him in a position of considerable authority and it proved to be his conclusive victory in the struggle with the military alliance. For the first time since he had assumed the Premiership eighteen months before, it became possible to assess the strength of his support in Parliament.

But its implications went much deeper than this. For Lloyd George, the debate marked the final cleavage between his Liberal followers and those of Asquith. At the General Election that followed some months later, few of those who had voted against the Prime Minister on the Maurice question escaped exclusion from Parliament.

In the Maurice Debate were thus the seeds of the disintegration that soon overtook the Liberal Party. The party was really broken on 9th May when the division bells were ringing through the Palace of Westminster for the fateful vote. It has never since regained its political eminence. "The reverberations of the quarrel," Mr. Churchill has written of the Maurice issue, "continue to this day."[n]

General Maurice was scarcely more fortunate than the Liberal Party. He was retired from the Army on half-pay. Robert Donald offered him the position of military correspondent of the *Daily Chronicle* and from this fortress he was able to deliver an occasional glancing blow at the Administration.

But for all practical purposes, the heat of the controversy had been exhausted.

And now we come to the particular irony that surrounds an issue holding such vital consequences for English Liberalism.

In 1922, four years after the famous Maurice Debate, Sir Frederick wrote a letter to the Prime Minister.⁰ He was eager to bring forward complete evidence of what he claimed to be the facts. He said that the document from the War Office relating to the available troops in France on which Mr. Lloyd George had based his answer was prepared in a hurry. He declared that a mistake had been made and the whole strength of the Army in Italy was included in the strength of the Armies in France. With the addition of all these troops, a slight increase of the fighting strength in January, 1918, as compared with January, 1917, was shown.

Maurice affirmed that this mistake was discovered shortly afterwards, and reported to Philip Kerr, one of Lloyd George's Private Secretaries.

Therefore he declared that Lloyd George, on May 9th, 1918, had used an accidentally incorrect return to endorse his case, though he had in his possession another return showing the corrected figures.*

Where then was this document that corroborated General Maurice's claim? It would have given substance to his accusations against Lloyd George though not to the charge against Bonar Law. It was the hinge upon which the whole question hung. It invalidated the detailed defence Lloyd George had built up. But what became of it?

I now quote in full an extract taken from the Diary of Countess Lloyd George, which is included in the Lloyd George collection. It is dated 5th October, 1934.

Have been reading up the events connected with the Maurice Debate in order to help Ll.G. with this Chapter in Vol. V,† and am uneasy in my mind about an incident which occurred at the time and which is known only to J. T. Davies‡ and myself. Ll.G. obtained from the W.O. the figures which he used in his statement on April 9th in the House of Commons on the subject of man-power. These figures were afterwards stated by Gen. Maurice to be inaccurate.

I was in J. T. Davies' room a few days after the statement, and J. T. was sorting out red dispatch boxes to be returned to the Departments. As was his wont, he looked in them before locking them up and sending them out to the Messengers. Pulling out a W.O. box, he found in it, to his great astonishment, a paper from

* Lloyd George in his speech in Parliament on May 9th, 1918, declared that Sir Frederick Maurice had never made any correction of the statement of Army strength in France.

† Of the *War Memoirs*.

‡ Sir J. T. Davies, throughout the Premiership of Lloyd George, and after, his secretary and confidant; a treasurer of the Lloyd George Fund; a director of the Suez Canal.

the D.M.O.* containing modifications and corrections of the first figures they had sent, and by some mischance this box had remained unopened. J.T. and I examined it in dismay, and then J.T. put it in the fire, remarking, "Only you and I, Frances, know of the existence of this paper".

There is no doubt that this is what Maurice had in mind when he accused L.G. of mis-statement. But the amazing thing was that *the document was never fixed upon*. How was it that the matter was never clinched, and Maurice or someone never actually said: "The figures supplied by us were so and so"? They argued round and over the point, but never did one of them put any finger on it. I was waiting for the matter to be raised, and for the question to be asked: Why did L.G. not receive these supplementary figures? Or did he? But the questions never came and I could not voluntarily break faith with J.T., perhaps put L.G. in a fix, and who knows, have brought down the Government!

The only explanation is that Maurice and Co. were relying on getting their Judicial Committee, where every point would have been thrashed out in detail. When the judicial committee was turned down, it was by that time too late to bring up details again, and by that time also Maurice was beaten.

I suppose it is too late now for the matter to be cleared up and I had better keep silent. But I will talk it over with J.T. In any event, no good could come of any revelation made now, but the amazing thing to me still, is that in all these years no one has fastened on this particular point. There is a slight allusion in Colonel Repington's book about a discrepancy in figures, but this also seems to have escaped attention. And as the Official Statistics since compiled seem to justify L.G.'s statement at the time, it were better perhaps to let sleeping dogs lie.

* Director of Military Operations.

So it seems that the upward spiral of cause and effect, moving from one event to another and greater one, found its origin in a trivial event in a secretary's room at 10 Downing Street. If the amending figures sent by Maurice's department in the War Office had not been overlooked by the Prime Minister's secretary, Lloyd George would not have given misleading information to Parliament. Maurice would not have been able to make the charge which the newspapers published. There would have been no Maurice Debate. And maybe there would have been no exclusion of Asquithian Liberals at the General Election. The disruption of the Liberal Party might have been postponed or even averted.

The student of history may ponder these thoughts with humility, mingled with a sense of human comedy. Through the oversight of a secretary, Lloyd George's Government—for months the target of a military junta and the butt of powerful and contentious forces determined to drag down and utterly destroy the Prime Minister—was saved and indeed strengthened immeasurably. Never again, for the duration of the war, was Lloyd George in danger from the assaults of enemies of the right and left. The direction of the war remained unaltered. The Liberal Party was destroyed, while enemies were scattered far and wide.

Behold, how great a fire
a little matter kindleth!

Oct. 5th ..

Have been reading up the events connected with the Maurice Debate in order to help H.S. with this chapter in Vol. V., and am uneasy in my mind about an incident which occurred at the time & which is known only to J.T. Davies & myself. H.S. obtained from the W.O. the figures which he used in his statement on April 9th. in the House of Commons on the subject of man-power. These figures were afterwards stated by Gen. Maurice to be inaccurate. I was in J.T. Davies' room a few days after the statement, & J.T. was sorting out red dispatch boxes to be returned to the Departments. As was his wont, he looked in them before locking them up & sending them out by the Messengers. Pulling out a W.O. box, he found in it, to his great astonishment, a paper from the D.M.O containing modifications & corrections of the first figures they had sent, & by some mischance this box had remained unopened. J.T. & I. examined it in dismay, & then J.T. put it in the fire, remarking, "Only you & I, Frances, know of the existence of this paper."

"Only you and I, Frances, know of the existence of this paper"

CHAPTER IX

"DON'T RESIGN:
WAIT UNTIL YOU'RE SACKED"

ANOTHER crisis! February, 1918. And I was the crisis. The reason was simple. I had tumbled into office, and into trouble. Sailors had no part in the tempest that tossed my frail bark. Soldiers were not concerned with wrecking me in my stormy campaign. Politicians were my enemies, strengthened by high-born voices.

For long, public opinion in Britain had been pressing for an improvement in British war propaganda. It was felt that in this field the enemy was beating us. The demand grew and spread to the Ministers and to the brass-hats, as a consequence of the military and diplomatic reverses. There had been a mutiny in the French Army and a rebellion in Ireland. In the United States the British war effort was criticised; while in South America the conviction prevailed that the German military domination over Europe was complete and permanent. In the Far East, Japan, willing at the outbreak of war to join the allied armies in France, had come to the conclusion that Germany was the military master of the West. And in

Britain, in the factories and the shipyards discontent prevailed. Each of these conditions was in turn attributed to a well-organised system of German propaganda.

So far as Britain was concerned, this branch of the nation's effort was still in a rudimentary state. Each of the service Ministries had its propaganda section. So had the Foreign Office. A war-aims committee, set up under John Buchan* and others, was possessed of uncertain authority. While Sir Edward Carson remained a member of the War Cabinet he was charged with the duty of co-ordinating and directing these various projects. But he was hostile to the Prime Minister, critical of the Government, and nursing a grievance. His enthusiasm for the cause of propaganda was not apparent. And soon he resigned and went into opposition.

The public clamoured for a British Ministry devoted to the development of propaganda instruments able to raise morale at home, convince the Allies and the Dominions of the vast strength of the British effort, and persuade the neutrals to believe that the victorious armies of the Empire would bring peace to a war-weary world.

On 23rd January, 1918, Frederick Guest, Lloyd George's Chief Whip, wrote as follows:

12 Downing Street, S.W.

Dear Prime Minister,

I do hope you will consider *Max*† for Controller of Propaganda.

* Later Lord Tweedsmuir.
† William Maxwell Aitken, now known as Lord Beaverbrook.

He is bitten with it, knows it, and I want him anchored.

Yours sincerely,

FREDERICK GUEST.[a]

On 10th February, 1918, Lloyd George appointed me Minister of Information and Chancellor of the Duchy of Lancaster. I should be founding the first Ministry of Propaganda set up by a British government.

There was no blueprint to work on. No experience to guide the new department. There was no office, no staff. There was nothing but a decision of the War Cabinet decreeing that such a Ministry should be created and that I should be the Minister. Yet, although I had many misgivings about the appointment, these did not spring from any lack of confidence in what I was to do.

In explaining his choice of a Minister to the House of Commons the Prime Minister said:

> Lord Beaverbrook had, at the request . . . of the Canadian Government, organised a Canadian propaganda, which is acknowledged to be amongst the most successful, perhaps the most successful, piece of work of its kind on the Allied side.[b]

I had been for some time the Canadian Government representative to the Army overseas. I was the channel of communication between Sir Robert Borden, the Canadian Prime Minister, Sir Sam Hughes, the Canadian Minister of Militia and Defence at Ottawa, and the British Ministers engaged in war activities as well as the military commanders in Britain and at the front.

In addition, propaganda relating to the Canadian war effort was in my charge and—according to my critics—had given the impression in the United States that Canada was bearing the brunt of the fighting in France.

This misunderstanding was fostered by Lord Northcliffe, who telegraphed from New York[c] that the Canadian Army was given undue prominence in the American Press and that in consequence it was asked, "When are the British going to begin to fight?" English regiments, said Northcliffe, were never mentioned, yet the papers were full of the brave deeds of the Manitobas. Northcliffe was convinced, so he said, that the Canadian propaganda damaged the prestige of Britain and interfered with British applications to Washington for financial assistance. He had supreme confidence in The Power of the Press.

Northcliffe's criticism was, of course, unjustified, but I had no doubt at all that the methods I had applied to Canadian propaganda could be used with equal success for Britain's propaganda generally.

My task would be to satisfy the body of Britons living in the United Kingdom, while convincing those who lived overseas that Britain was playing her full and effective part. How could it be done? By bringing to Britain groups of newspaper proprietors from abroad—the working owners of newspapers—who would do the work of propaganda for me when they returned home again. By pictorial publications of one kind and another. And especially by the cinema, which, by this time, was just emerging from the Nickelodeon Age. By exhibitions of paintings of war scenes by the artists of quality. By assuming control of Reuters, and other news agencies, so that good news was disseminated abroad instead of gloom and apprehension. By making the acquaintance of foreign news agencies with offices in London.

Then it was necessary that the troops should be convinced that the propaganda department was working effectively. Artists and cameramen must be seen at the front and a newspaper for the soldiers must be launched.

Munition workers in Britain must be persuaded to take an interest in the soldiers on the various fighting fronts. Production in the factories could be stimulated by exciting records in the form of pictures, and particularly cinema pictures showing action in battle. And, more particularly, deeds of bravery and sacrifice.

There would be an intense enemy propaganda. Lord Northcliffe might be given charge. He would provide the necessary drive and energy.

At that time the neutral countries were giving little or no attention to Britain's immense war effort. It would be difficult to make any strong or lasting impression on these non-belligerents. The best propaganda for their edification would depend upon British victories in arms.

The programme was simple. It was easy to set in motion. Its success was assured. But if I thought on that account that my path would be smooth I was swiftly disillusioned.

A powerful complaint came from Buckingham Palace. This concerned my position as Chancellor of the Duchy. It was reported that the King was disturbed by the idea of a Presbyterian administering the ecclesiastic preferments of the Crown. I did not believe it. But of a certainty he was animated by no great personal liking for me.

I was told that he was really hostile and that his dislike flowed in part from the old story when Balfour lost the leadership of the Tory Party that behind the scenes was the "little Canadian adventurer".* Then again when Asquith tumbled down there was the charge of "intrigue" which the fallen Liberal Ministers had spread.

There were, too, real reasons for complaint. These sprang from the early days of war when I was acting as Canadian Government Representative.

I had to deal with questions relating to the Canadian forces—often difficult and tiresome issues, which exposed me to the displeasure of official circles.

For instance, there was the issue between Lord Kitchener and General Hughes over Canadian casualties. Hughes objected to the system whereby the news of casualties was transmitted to London, and thence to next-of-kin in Canada, in the name of Lord Kitchener and often days after the information had reached Canada unofficially. He asked me to demand on his behalf

---

* On 10th November, 1911, J. C. Sandars, writing to Balfour, attacked Bonar Law's methods in seizing the leadership of the Tory Party, declaring that he was run by Max Aitken, the little Canadian adventurer who sits for Ashton-under-Lyne, introduced into that seat by him.

the right to direct notification from the Battle
Front and through the Canadian Minister of
Militia. It was an obvious necessity but it proved
to be a tough assignment.

My application to Kitchener met with refusal.
Prime Minister Asquith was my next approach,
but he could not help me. He advised me to go to
Army Headquarters in France and see if matters
could be arranged there. I set out for St. Omer
and called on General Macready.*

"It's a damn cheek," said Macready when I
explained Sam Hughes's request to him.[d] Then
I approached General Maxwell.† The entry in
my diary for that day reads: "Maxwell said, 'Sam
Hughes is never satisfied with anybody or anything.' "[e]

In such circumstances I had to work and work
hard to get consent. Perhaps I worked too hard.
My insistence did not endear me to anyone.
The whole military hierarchy took a most un-
friendly view of my activities. They did not understand that Canada had grown up. I tried to explain
with patience that all Canadians would support
the Minister. Still they abused me, as though I
had personal responsibility. Thus on occasions
when I expected words of praise and commenda-
tion, I got vigorous and outspoken condemnation.

Hughes had no friends in British military
circles. He was altogether too critical not only of
equipment but also of strategy. In Royal circles

*General Sir Nevil Macready, G.C.M.G., K.C.B., was Adjutant-General to the
British Expeditionary Forces, 1914–1916.
† Major-General Sir Ronald Maxwell, K.C.B., K.C.M.G., was Quarter-
master-General to the Armies in France, 1915–1917.

he was regarded with anxiety. The Duke of Connaught, the Governor-General of Canada and uncle of the King, was his bitter enemy. The measure of his bitterness was deep indeed. A letter from the Duke to Bennett, now in the Archives of Lord Bennett at the University of New Brunswick, condemned Hughes in the most outspoken terms.*

A Minute on the reasons for the anger of the Duke will be found in an Appendix† from Mr. John Bassett, the distinguished proprietor of the *Montreal Gazette*. This gives an explanation of the origins of the quarrel.

There was an occasion when His Royal Highness, the Duke of Connaught, threatened to resign. He wrote to the Prime Minister of Canada saying:

> I must however make it quite clear to you that I must have a written apology from Sir Sam Hughes or otherwise I shall be compelled to place my resignation in the hands of the King with a full statement of my reasons for doing so.*g*

Hughes, of course, dodged the issue. He sent a memorandum to the Prime Minister. It did not serve to appease the hostility of the Governor-General.

A full account of the conflict appears in the papers of Sir Robert Borden in the Archives of

---

* The Duke of Connaught returned to England. His Governorship had been brought to an end. But his hostility to Hughes lived on. Writing to Bennett in Canada he declared that chaos reigned in all Canadian military matters and that there was ill-feeling between Imperial and Canadian military authorities. "However, it was only due to one person and now that that person is gone, let us hope forever, all will I know be right again."*f*

† *Appendix II.*

Standing, Prime Minister, Borden
Seated, Canadian Government Representative, Beaverbrook
Canadian Minister of Trade, Foster
Canadian Minister of Defence, Kemp

Ottawa, with a microfilm copy at the Library of the University of Toronto.

It was in such an atmosphere of friction and hostility towards the Canadian Minister that Sir Robert Borden authorized me during 1915 to ask for a Knighthood for General Hughes. The honour might bring Hughes into harmony with the British Service leaders. It might make rough places smooth. The Colonial Office agreed to put forward a recommendation to the King.

The Duke of Connaught made vigorous objection to the Knighthood. He joined the military hierarchy in determined opposition.

But the King rejected the protest of the Duke of Connaught and reluctantly consented to accept the recommendation of the Colonial Secretary. He expressed annoyance with me.

Now Hughes was entitled to the rank of Major-General in the British Army. In the autumn, I received the necessary authority to telegraph him as follows:

General Sir Sam Hughes, Ottawa.

16th October, 1915.

Do you wish to be gazetted Major General here stop If so Brade* will support

AITKEN[h]

Hughes asked for higher rank. I replied:

General Sir Sam Hughes, Ottawa.

Have dropped Major General and asked for Lieut. General and have assurance from very strong member

* Sir Reginald Brade, Permanent Under-Secretary at the War Office.

of Government* that he will secure consent in due course.

AITKEN[i]

Thus it was that the Secretary of State for War (Lloyd George) and the Secretary of State for the Colonies (Bonar Law) joined in recommending Hughes for the rank of Lieutenant-General.

Then the storm broke. Field-Marshal, His Royal Highness, the Duke of Connaught joined the fray. After a year of struggle the Royal Gazette heralded the Hon. Sir Sam Hughes, K.C.B., M.P., in the list of Lieutenant-Generals and quietness prevailed for a time.

But His Majesty's Secretary wrote to Sir Maurice Bonham-Carter† that the promotion had been planted on the King by Lloyd George and Bonar Law.[j]

These unfortunate but unavoidable incidents did not commend me to His Majesty and perhaps explain resistance to my being given Cabinet rank in the form of the sinecure appointment of the Duchy of Lancaster.

The objections to my appointment were set out in a letter from Lord Stamfordham to Frederick Guest, the Chief Whip, dated 8th February, 1918, saying that His Majesty

expressed much surprise that, considering past circumstances, he should now be asked to agree to Lord Beaverbrook's presiding over the Duchy, which, as it were, is the personal property of the Sovereign and

* Lloyd George.   † Secretary to the Prime Minister.

entailing closer relations between the King and its Chancellor than with many of his Ministers. . . .

I must again assure you that the Prime Minister in saying to me that he was thinking of employing Lord Beaverbrook in the Propaganda Department, never referred in merely any way to the Duchy of Lancaster. . . .[k]

Lloyd George sent a firm answer back:

I am confident [he wrote to Stamfordham] that . . . I shall receive a great accession of strength in Lord Beaverbrook's appointment. His organisation of the Canadian Propaganda Department entrusted to him by Sir Robert Borden has been a conspicuous success. On the other hand, our propaganda has been a conspicuous failure. I have sought in vain for months for a man to put it right. So far I have not succeeded. Propaganda at home and abroad is becoming increasingly important. I consulted the members of the Propaganda Committee and they thought Beaverbrook would be the best available man. I cannot get him without offering him Ministerial rank. He is a first-rate business man and will administer the Duchy well.

In these circumstances I trust the King will be graciously pleased to approve the recommendation which I have thought fit to make to him. I wish you to assure His Majesty that I attach great importance to the appointment of Lord Beaverbrook to this post.[l]

That insistence by the Prime Minister confirmed me in my dual appointment. But I had not reached the end of my troubles. Far from it!

At this time Lloyd George's government was not looked on as a stable structure. The office-seekers and those who dwell in the favour of the powerful could not determine their future allegiance. Where did the best advantage lie? Unable to make up their minds on this important issue, these unreliable followers of Lloyd George resembled a boatload of pleasure-seekers who rush from port to starboard endangering the safety of their own craft.

I became a victim of this lack of fixed and dependable allegiance to Lloyd George and his government. For in many quarters enemies of the Administration were waiting to spring out on me in the belief that I was the weakest link in the chain.

There was, of course, the group who accepted the leadership of Asquith. Their bitterness over the so-called "intrigue against Asquith", which had destroyed his Government, was directed against me.

In the Conservative Party, too, many looked on me with coldness. They were enthusiasts for the maintenance of the Parliamentary Union with Ireland, they knew that I had Irish sympathies.

The powerful Cecil family, wielding immense influence on Church and State, were angry with me for my persistent pursuit of food taxes. They held firmly to the belief that food taxes would shatter the Tory Party, thus destroying their hope of defending the establishment of the Church in Wales.

Balfour was my enemy. No doubt he too recalled the story of the little Canadian adventurer who had "intrigued" him out of the Tory leadership. Lord Milner attacked me. I don't know why he disapproved, perhaps on account of

LORD ROBERT CECIL

A sombre figure and a stalwart
supporter of the Church

DERBY

Excessive amiability

my self-confidence. Possibly he disagreed with my public performance. Certainly he did not think well of me.

There were Army chiefs who feared that the real purpose was to set up a propaganda machine, not for Britain but for Lloyd George. This thought disturbed many honest and over-anxious Members of Parliament.

Then, again, the service ministries wished to be left unmolested in possession of their own propaganda departments; they resented being deprived of officials who were in effect their P.R.O.s. And outside Whitehall some newspapers, disliking the competition of the *Daily Express*, took an unfavourable view of my appointment. So when the *Globe* spoke of "a sense of profound misgiving which we have no hesitation in believing will be shared by the nation at large",*m* the newspaper was certainly speaking for many interests and personalities.

Then, immediately after my appointment was announced, I took the step which was certain to add to my difficulties in Parliament. I told Lloyd George of my desire to appoint Northcliffe in charge of propaganda in enemy territories. Lloyd George received the recommendation with enthusiasm. He said it was an excellent appointment, and would carry public approval.

He declared that no man had qualifications surpassing Northcliffe for this post. He also mentioned that Lord Northcliffe would be likely to show a restraint in the criticism of ministerial departments if he got to know something of the trials and difficulties of conducting them. Thus possibly Lord Northcliffe's circulation of newspapers, representing one-half of all newspaper sales in London, was being loosely hitched to the Government chariot.*

Northcliffe gladly accepted the offer I made him. He showed real enthusiasm. When Bonar Law heard of my great catch he said to me: "One of you newspaper barons was too much. Now there are two. Well, you'll hear of this. I hope you have not misunderstood the Prime Minister's approval."

Bonar Law's prophecy proved to be only too accurate. By appointing Northcliffe I had made a serious blunder in political tactics; Northcliffe was feared and detested in many quarters, and particularly in the House of Commons.

Trouble came upon me swiftly. It came from a quarter damaging indeed. It was Austen Chamberlain, the most important leader in the Conservative Party outside of the Government, who opened an attack from the Government benches against Lord Northcliffe and me. His language was strong, his attitude unbending and his support on the benches very considerable indeed. He said:

> Three great newspaper owners are members of, or are intimately associated with, the Administration. . . . My right hon. Friend and his Government have

* Lloyd George displayed his usual political prescience. Northcliffe's appointment as Director of Enemy Propaganda was published on the same day as the announcement of Robertson's dismissal. His newspapers did not criticise the Government.

surrounded themselves quite unnecessarily with an atmosphere of suspicion and distrust because they have allowed themselves to become so intimately associated with these great newspaper proprietors. I tell my right hon. Friend what everyone is saying in the Lobbies, outside the House, where men meet, but what I think it is now time for someone to say publicly and as a responsible man in this House. . . . As long as you have the owner of a newspaper as a member of your Administration you will be held responsible for what he writes in the newspaper. . . . My right hon. Friend and his Government will never stand clear in the estimation of the public, and will never have the authority which they ought to have, . . . until they make things quite clear, open, and plain to all the world and sever this connection with the newspapers.[n]

On the same day the Unionist [Conservative] War Committee passed a strongly worded resolution, reading:

That in the opinion of the Unionist War Committee no member of the Government or officer holding a post under the Government should be allowed to act as the correspondent of a newspaper in respect of the conduct of the war or the fitness of any naval or military officer for the post he holds and that no one who controls a newspaper should be allowed to be a member of the Government or to hold a responsible post under it so long as he retains control of that newspaper.[o]

In forwarding the Resolution to Bonar Law, Lord Salisbury, Chairman of the Committee, put himself in a somewhat complex position. He apologised for a disagreeable letter but said that, as he had been requested by the Committee to send the Resolution, he had no choice. "I write of course as Chairman without reference to my own opinion," Lord Salisbury assured him, "though on the subject of this connection with the Press I entirely agree with the Committee."[p]

The resolution of the Unionist War Committee was in fact a long step further than Austen Chamberlain was prepared to go. Some days later, I received a letter from him dissociating himself from any connection with it.

2.3.18.

Dear Beaverbrook,

I am not in any way responsible for the terms of the resolution passed by the Unionist War Committee, nor had I seen their resolution or any part of it till I received this morning the memo enclosed in your letter.

The Committee have evidently gone far beyond my position and I am not concerned to defend theirs which is obviously open to criticism.

My publicly stated objection was to such a connection between the Government and the Press as destroys the independence of the Press and involves the Government, in responsibility for all the opinions expressed by the Press . . .

The organisation of the Bureau or Ministry of Information and its propaganda raise distinct questions into which I will not now enter. I only regret that they have been confused and prejudiced by the character of the general connection established between the Government and the Press.

You are good enough to recognise my sincerity. I spoke as a public duty—not a pleasant one—and as a well-wisher on public grounds to the present administration. Their friends may under existing conditions endure, but they will not forgive, persistence in a course of action which independent public opinion so unanimously condemns. I hope that in my speech and by my silence and inaction since, I have avoided anything in word or deed which would make it more difficult for the Prime Minister or his friends to meet public opinion and satisfy the public conscience.

Yours sincerely,

AUSTEN CHAMBERLAIN.[9]

This was a tough letter. The implication was clear. The Prime Minister would be given an opportunity to rid himself of his Minister of Information! Otherwise Chamberlain would return to the subject. He would be a formidable opponent.

The War Committee's Resolution, however, was too preposterous to be dangerous. It was directed against the Ministry of Information as a body. If acted upon, it would have made impossible any propaganda organisation whatsoever.

But the speech of Chamberlain and the action of the War Committee certainly put the Government in a position of much difficulty. Who could assess the voting strength the Committee might muster in the lobbies of the House of Commons should they decide to put the issue to the test?

Some of the Ministers thought that immediate concession should be made. But by most of his colleagues Lloyd George was stoutly urged to stand by his Press appointments. Not to do so, they argued, would only involve him in deeper difficulties; thus F. E. Smith and Winston Churchill both thought Lloyd George should not budge. As for Frederick Guest, the Chief Liberal Whip, his opinions were put before the Prime Minister in a closely argued memorandum.*

The gist of Guest's Memorandum was that if Lloyd George followed the resolution of the War Committee, then he must dismiss Northcliffe, Rothermere and me as none of us would resign. Guest declared his belief that I would continue to support Lloyd George and his Government up to and through the next General Election. Rothermere would feel inclined to do the same. "Northcliffe may do anything."

Guest's advice was that Lloyd George should stand by his friends and his appointments. He had sounded the following Ministers on the general situation and reported as follows.

"*Talbot*† is anxious to find a way out. He thinks the movement serious, but does not think it will be forced to extreme.

"*Hewart*‡ *and Illingworth*§ entirely agree with the advice which I submit.

"*F. E. Smith and W. S. C.* think that you should stand by your guns."

Guest added a note embodying his suggestions for dealing with the Unionists' objections. It is an interesting document. I reproduce it here in full.

---

* The full text of the memorandum, entitled "Notes on the Resolution Forwarded by the Unionist War Committee to the Prime Minister", is reproduced in *Appendix IV*, No. 16.
† Lord Edmund Talbot was Chief Conservative Whip and Senior Coalition Whip.
‡ Sir Gordon Hewart was the Solicitor-General.
§ A. H. Illingworth was Postmaster-General.

SUGGESTION RE UNIONIST WAR COMMITTEE'S RESOLUTION ON NEWSPAPER PROPRIETORS HOLDING OFFICE

Could it not be stated that it would be clearly prejudicial to the National interests to disturb Ministers concerned?

The Air Force is now in its most critical period of reconstruction and co-ordination.

The Department of Information, which has been so long needed, is now in process of being established.

In view however of the strong Parliamentary feeling expressed the Government think it advisable that some form of Commission should be set up to consider this and many other similar cases which have arised [*sic*] in connection with Ministerial appointments during the war, e.g.

1. Newspaper Proprietors holding office. Directorships, etc.*
2. Shipowner acting as Shipping Controller or President of the Board of Trade.†
3. Men with wide commercial interests placed in important positions in relation to contracts, etc.

This Commission might be judicial and non-party and its recommendations might prove of great constitutional value.

FREDERICK GUEST.'

There was without doubt a strong feeling, not confined to the detractors of the Government or to those supporting a military regime, against the participation of Press Lords in the war-time administration.

Austen Chamberlain, who was canvassing for

* The paper is typewritten and signed by Guest. The words "Directorships, etc." are added in Guest's handwriting.

† The words "or President of the Board of Trade" are added in Lloyd George's handwriting.

support, appears to have made a convert of Walter Long, the Colonial Secretary, even to the point of Long's offering to resign if urged to do so.'

Lord Milner wrote to the Prime Minister a long letter of advice, in which I was singled out for special attack:

> There really is more stir about this than I have yet known in any of these purely domestic rows. The important point is, that so many of our real friends are disgruntled. Of course the "Squiffites"* make the most of it. I don't mind that. But the number of people, who are your friends, and hate the notion of a return of Squiff† and Co., but are nevertheless seriously upset about the relations of Government and Press, is not negligible.
>
> I have no doubt, as I have pointed out to lots of them, that there is no motion, which can be brought forward on the subject, which cannot be riddled with criticism. The fact remains that a strong feeling exists, with which we have got to reckon.
>
> At bottom it is much more connected with the newspaper campaign than it is with the ownership of certain newspapers by members of the Government. Obviously the attacks which appeared in the Press on Jellicoe, Robertson, Derby and others, were by no means confined to papers owned by members of the Government, and Government inspiration of the Press is as easy or indeed easier, if newspaper proprietors are not Ministers. It is the *inspiration itself* or rather the clumsy and extreme nature of some of it which is objected to.
>
> Sutherland‡ is the man whom everybody has got his

---

* Asquithites.
† Asquith.
‡ William Sutherland, originally a civil servant, was Lloyd George's private secretary and dealt with the newspapers on behalf of the Prime Minister. He wielded immense power and authority, especially over patronage. He was exceedingly talkative, often revealing secrets, cunning and never disloyal to his master. Like every court favourite he suffered derision, scorn and hatred.

knife into just now, rightly or wrongly. About this
there is, I think, nothing to be done except to lie low
till the storm blows over, and *to keep the friendly Press
off the war path* as far as possible. The less people hear or
see of Northcliffe, Beaverbrook (certainly the most unpopular name of all) etc. for the next few weeks the
better.

Please don't think I exaggerate. I have been fighting
this case with all sorts of people and argumentatively
we have quite a good case. But it is no use arguing
with a really strong tide of feeling especially when it
has some justification. And there is no doubt that the
feeling is strong just now *in* quarters essentially
friendly.[t]

Yet while hostility to the newspapermen in the
Government, and possibly particularly to me,
moved men in many groups, there was no liaison
between them. Chamberlain did not seek support
from the Liberals or the Labour members. When
he renewed his enquiry into the Government's
relations with the newspapermen in the Commons on 11th March, he got plenty of support
from the Opposition Liberal benches. Their encouragement did not please him.

"They and I," he stated, "do not act from the
same motives or pursue the same objects. I have
tried from the first since this War broke out,
whether under the Premiership of my right hon.
Friend opposite (Mr. Asquith) or under the
present Prime Minister, to support the Government of the day in carrying the War to a successful
conclusion. When these hon. Gentlemen can say
the same, and not before, shall I desire their cheers
or their approval."[u]

Thus there was hope that I might escape the fury of my enemies so long as they pursued me in opposite directions.

Lord Hugh Cecil took the opportunity to criticize me. He said:

"I listened with great attention to the Prime Minister. I think he has a very strong case in respect of propaganda. The case he makes, that these gentlemen whom he has appointed to be Ministers of Propaganda are indeed experts in that function, is a case that strongly appeals to the whole House.

"The only criticism that occurred to me about that matter is that the appointment of Lord Beaverbrook as Minister of Propaganda is only one of the honours which the Government has bestowed upon him.

"It sounds to me quite reasonable to say that Lord Beaverbrook is a great expert in propaganda, and should be entrusted, therefore, with the work he so well understands. But is he also so ideally well fitted to be a Peer of the Realm? Is he also so ideally well fitted to be Chancellor of the Duchy of Lancaster? The Chancellorship of the Duchy of Lancaster is an office of very considerable distinction. I believe it brings the Minister in close contact with the Sovereign, and it has a certain amount of ecclesiastical patronage.

"It is, of course, possible that Lord Beaverbrook is equally well fitted for that function as for propaganda, but I am a little suspicious, when I find that these various distinctions have been bestowed upon him, that there is probably some other motive at work leading the Government to honour him besides his fitness for the work of propaganda."[v]

My old friend and former Parliamentary colleague, the Irish Nationalist M.P., Tim Healy, came to my defence. He was one of the ablest parliamentarians; his sling was full of sharp and witty verbal stones. He now cast one at Lord Hugh.

"I do not know what religious duties there are attaching to the post of the Duchy of Lancaster," he observed, "and no doubt the Noble Lord (Lord Hugh Cecil), whose High Churchism is one of his most distinguished attributes, has some suspicion of Lord Beaverbrook in that respect.* But I can only say for myself that an abler man or a man of clearer mind and better judgement I have never met."[w]

After this second debate, Bonar Law came to see me at my office. He told me that the temper of the House was entirely hostile to my appointment. He said it was doubtful if I could survive, and he advised me in the interests of the Administration to hand in my resignation.

I asked him to frame such a document in writing. After several attempts he handed me a draft which he thought might meet the situation.

I produce it here in facsimile.

Now, I was never given to retreat in the face of attack. And when Bonar Law informed me that the House of Lords was shortly to take up

---

* The Chancellor of the Duchy has much Church patronage. Tim Healy therefore referred to my Presbyterian allegiance.

the issue I knew that I could go there and make a very considerable defence, not only for myself but for my newspaper colleagues too. The prospect opened up possibilities.

Tim Healy responded at once to my call for advice. When he had examined the whole position and considered the proposed resignation as prepared by Bonar Law, he said to me:

"Don't resign; wait until you're sacked."

That was counsel which was congenial to me. If I was to be wrecked along with the office which I had only that moment taken on, then I would sink to the bottom with my flag at the top of the mast.

It was said that Lord Salisbury and Lord Beresford would raise the issue in the House of Lords. I attended quite often while expecting a motion on the Order Paper.

I was determined to show myself to my foes, and to give them a chance to join battle at the earliest moment. But the hullabaloo died down. Members of the House of Commons became involved in other issues. Chamberlain by this time was carrying on conversations which resulted in his rejoining the Government. He had no difficulty at an early date in entering the War Cabinet and accepting these objectionable newspaper men as his colleagues.

Apart from the troubles that I ran into on political grounds, I had also difficulties springing from the jealousies of other departments. I was no sooner established as Minister of Information

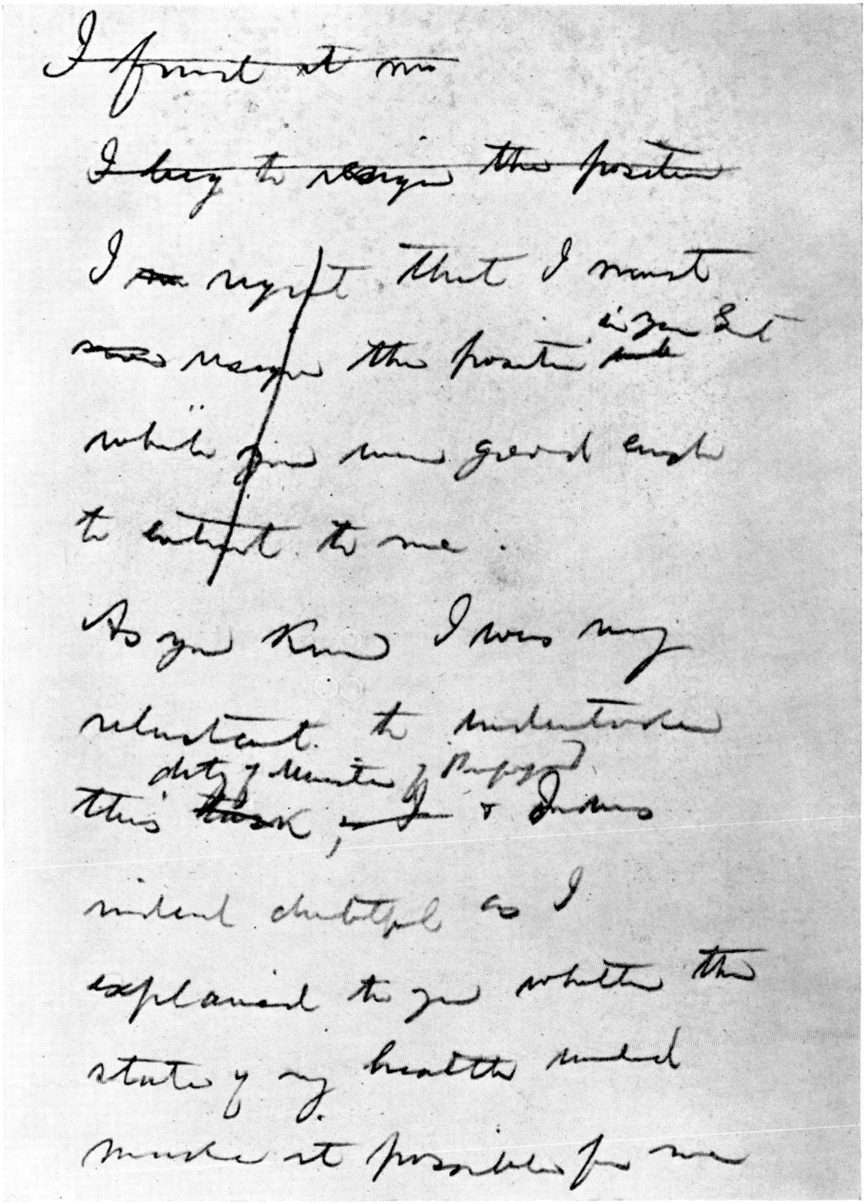

~~I must at on~~

~~I beg to resign the position~~

I ~~am~~ regret that I must

~~~~ resign the position in your Govt ~~which~~

which you were good enough

to ~~entrust~~ to me.

As you know I was very

reluctant to undertake

this ~~task~~ duty of Minister of Propaganda ~~of~~ & Information

indeed doubtful as I

explained to you whether the

state of my health would

make it possible for me

THE LETTER BONAR LAW
DRAFTED FOR ME
~~~~

Dear

give continuous attention to
faithful to perform the duties
of the office.

In view known of the belief
expressed by you that I was
specially qualified to for all
do the... I thought it my
... great... ...
duty to undertake it.

I did so in the hope that
in this way
I might be able in this
to render some small
public service but I can

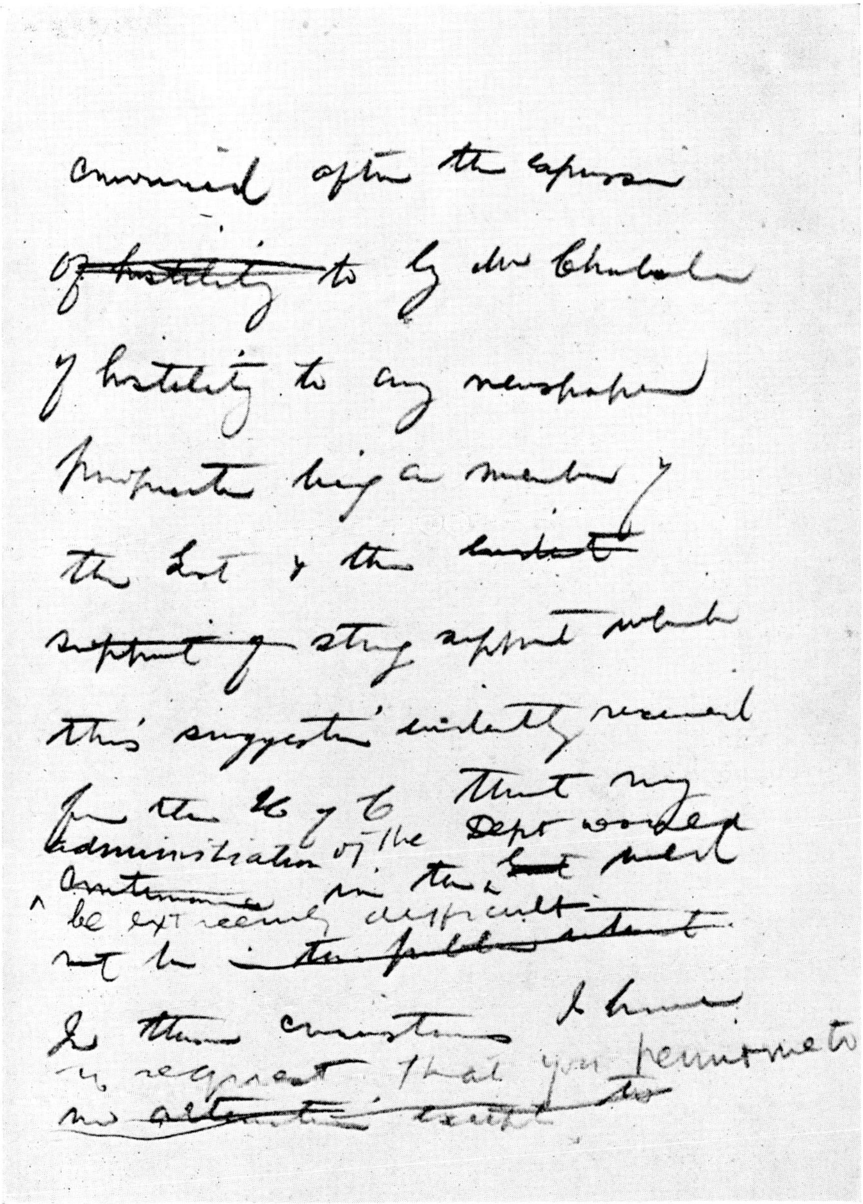

THE LETTER BONAR LAW
DRAFTED FOR ME (page 3)

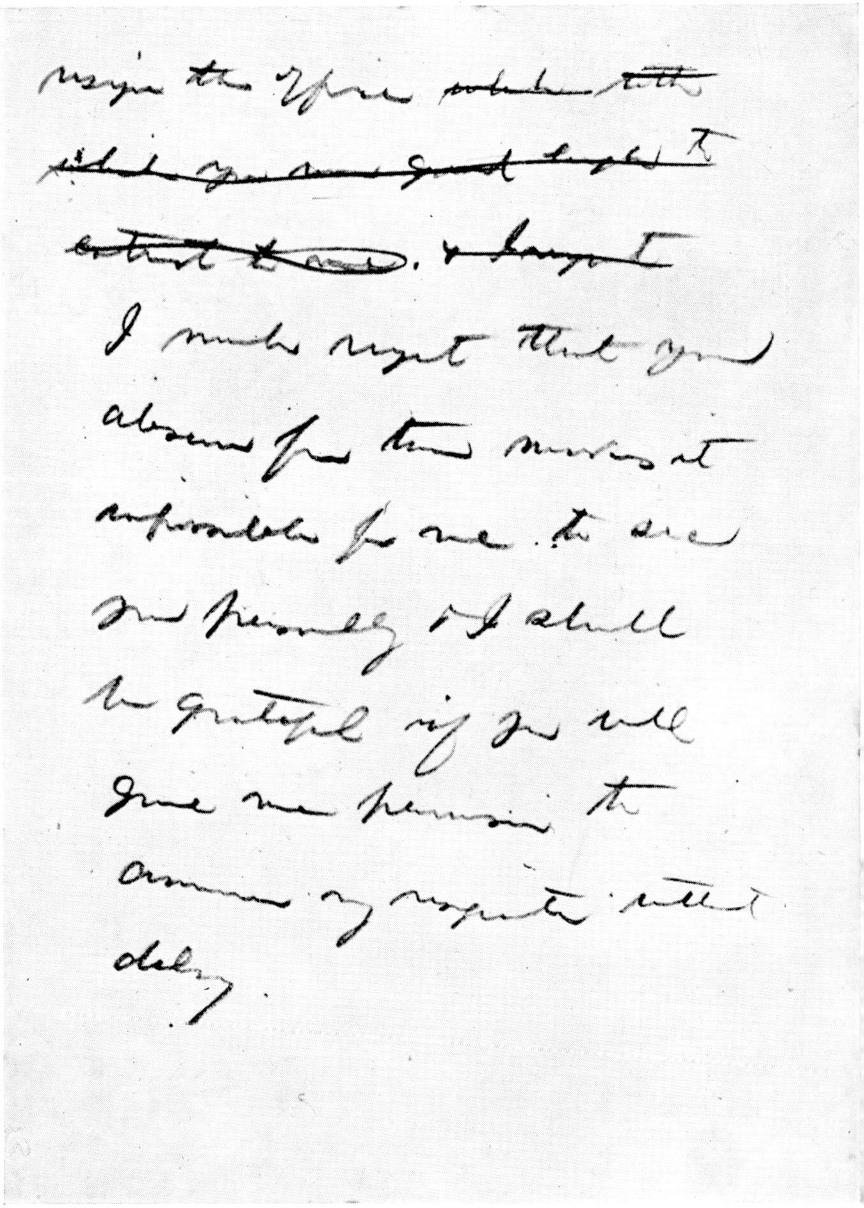
resign the Office ~~[illegible]~~

~~[illegible]~~

~~[illegible]~~

I much regret that your absence from these meetings ~~[illegible]~~ unfavourable for me to see you personally & I shall be grateful if you will give me permission to announce my resignation without delay.

THE LETTER BONAR LAW
DRAFTED FOR ME (conclusion)

than I encountered organised, vigorous and determined opposition from within the Ministries. The War Office, Admiralty and the Foreign Office all joined together in determined resistance. There is always resistance when a new Ministry is created. There is always an outcry when the ribs are removed from the old Adam and set up in the new Eve. Here, however, three Ministries were involved. And three surgical operations were necessary to set up the new organisation. All these old-established Ministries must be persuaded or compelled to hand over their propaganda functions to the new Ministry.

What a hubbub! What a hullabaloo!

These service departments and the Foreign Office sought to hold on to their authority. With what skill and letter-writing activities they tried to defeat the prospects of the little Ministry struggling to draw a breath of life! These Ministries would not yield any measure of their powers or of their work to a new department. They resolutely held on to their own propaganda machines. The Foreign Office went so far as to make a successful raid upon the staff being built up by the new Ministry of Information.

Balfour, the Foreign Secretary, was convinced that the work contemplated by my propaganda department would dislocate entirely the intelligence branch, not only of the Foreign Office, but of the Admiralty and the War Office also.

Lord Robert Cecil, the Foreign Under Secretary, shared his opinion.

At the Admiralty the disposition of the First Lord (Sir Eric Geddes) was no more favourable to me.

Thus, at a time when I was seeking by new techniques to present Britain at war to her allies and neutrals, I found myself engaged in a remorseless battle with the departments. It was a battle without compensations.

It now appeared that I must abandon the contest, accept the rebuffs of the departments, and, in a word, allow my office to suffer the same fate as befell Neville Chamberlain at the Ministry of National Service or I must carry on the fight for independent authority. I was resolved that something must be achieved.

My efforts to interest Lloyd George in my Ministry's struggle had up till then met with no positive success. Now I determined to write a letter to the Prime Minister, offering my resignation and explaining my difficulties. I set out my case in some detail.

I explained that, since the appeal of the new Ministry must be to public opinion abroad and not to diplomatic representatives, its methods must be different. But the Foreign Office, refusing to recognise this, had obstructed almost every mission which the Ministry of Information proposed to despatch abroad. And from the War Cabinet no support was forthcoming. In these circumstances, I argued, either the Ministry of Information should be abolished or given an equal status with the Foreign Office in its propaganda operations abroad.

The outcome of this offer of resignation was that Lloyd George promised to intervene to establish a working arrangement between the Ministry of Information and other departments. But his efforts were of little avail. The obstinate resistance of the Foreign Office exceeded all expectations. Yet, at this time an incident occurred which illustrated the need for a clear and official delineation of authority.

It was in relation to the Jewish National Home in Palestine.

Lloyd George directed me to make much of the fall of Palestine and the Capture of Jerusalem. The event had little or no influence on the course of war on the Western Front. But "victory" was a blessed word and the deed gave the right to widespread use of the word.

In preparing propaganda material, particularly for distribution in America, I made full use of Balfour's declaration in support of a Jewish National Home, which he had issued in November 1917.

There arose at once a fierce outcry from one section of Jewry, objecting to this conception of a National Home for the Jewish people.

Edwin Montagu, Secretary of State for India, became the passionate exponent of this viewpoint in the Government. He regarded the Jews as a religious community and himself as a Jewish Englishman. To commit the Jews to the expression of a National Home was, he argued, to prejudice their civil rights in the country of their birth. How could he, Montagu asked, as Secretary of State for India, negotiate with the peoples of India on behalf of His Majesty's Government if the world understood that His Majesty's Government regarded his National Home as being in Turkish territory?

Montagu was one of my personal friends and I had respect for his judgement. He was settled in his political philosophy and tenacious in his advocacy of his faith.

Shortly I was called upon by Sir Charles Henry, an intimate friend of Lloyd George of long standing, and Mr. Lionel de Rothschild, both Members of Parliament and prominent figures in British Jewry, both anti-Zionist. They urged me to do nothing to encourage the idea of a Jewish National Home. Sir Charles Henry reported that in an interview the Prime Minister had given his assent to the anti-Zionist view. This was an important statement, since, if it were well founded, it would have involved me in a reorientation of official propaganda on Palestine.

I asked the Prime Minister for a clear ruling. He would not answer Yes or No.

A curt letter from the Foreign Secretary dismissed the claims of the anti-Zionists and disposed of their conversations with the Prime Minister.

Dear Beaverbrook,

  The policy of His Majesty's Government in Palestine is that laid down by the Foreign Secretary in his last speech. Until it is altered officially, it is in no way affected by conversations between Sir Charles Henry and the Prime Minister.

Yours sincerely,
ARTHUR JAMES BALFOUR.[x]

Another curt letter addressed to the Prime Minister himself made complaint of my conduct in severe terms.

August 22nd, 1918.

My dear Prime Minister,

I am sorry to have to bother you when you are on holiday, but the question of the relationship between the Foreign Office and the Ministry of Information is becoming too difficult to allow the present position to continue.

As you know on November 2nd last year after prolonged discussion at Cabinet I wrote a letter setting out the policy of His Majesty's Government in regard to Zionism. The formula contained in the letter had been approved by the Cabinet.

I now find that Beaverbrook has written to you on the subject asking for a clear direction on Jewish policy. He states that he has done so because Sir Charles Henry told him that he had laid certain arguments before you which had impressed you and which you were taking into consideration; and meanwhile Zionist propaganda is being suspended. I need not go into the Zionist and anti-Zionist arguments. They were discussed at considerable length in Cabinet last year; but I think you will agree that an incident of this kind necessitates an immediate decision as to the distribution of functions of the Foreign Office and the Ministry of Information.

Yours sincerely,
ARTHUR JAMES BALFOUR.[y]

Lloyd George wrote a soft answer which gives the impression Sir Charles Henry was not entirely wrong in his interpretation of the conversation with the Prime Minister.

Brynawelon, Criccieth.
27th August, 1918.

My dear Foreign Secretary,

Your letter on Propaganda followed me down here. I quite agree that the position must be regularised, otherwise friction and misunderstanding are inevitable. I hope to be back on Friday. We can discuss the question either that day or some early day next week.

As to the Jewish policy, Henry has, I am afraid, misinterpreted the statement I made to him and his fellow anti-Zionists. I am not quite sure what he said, but I gather from your letter that he must have given a false impression of my conversation with him and Lord Swaythling when I met them some weeks ago, at their request, to hear their views.

I have always been a strong supporter of your policy on the question of Zionism and nothing that was said by Henry, Swaythling, or Philip Magnus in the least affected my opinions.

Ever sincerely,
D.Ll.G.³

At the beginning of August my Ministry again encountered stormy weather. I was told that a violent attack was going to be launched against me in the House of Commons, on the motion of Leif Jones. Many others were to join in the assault on 5th August, and I was to be "wrecked".

Having been attacked twice before in a brief period of office, I resented the injustice. The post was difficult enough in any case.

The assault was apparently to be based on some charges made in the *Westminster Gazette* that I was "a capitalist", and that my heads of departments were "capitalists".

Bonar Law would not take up the task of replying for me on the ground that our friendship was so close that his remarks might not seem impartial. He deputed the business to Stanley Baldwin, in whose parliamentary experience I had no confidence. As it turned out, I was wrong there, for Baldwin made a very good speech in my defence.

Feeling, therefore, thoroughly worried about the whole business, I wired to Tim Healy in Dublin to come over and help me. He reached my country house on Sunday, 4th August, having kept me in suspense by wiring that he would arrive "shortly after Mass"—a phrase which left me in doubt as to the time of his appearance.

When at last he came, he gave me small comfort. I wanted to show him all the documents I had accumulated for my defence. Healy put me off, talking about everything else as we wandered about the garden.

I pressed him hard to discuss the matter seriously, and asked what line he intended to take. He put me off until after lunch, when he had taken some claret. I reopened my case. He brushed my defence aside.

"Whatever line I take tomorrow," he said, "will have nothing to do with a prepared case. I shall watch the House and decide."

I tried again after dinner and champagne. He would not listen.

He laughed at my anxiety. He refused to look at the documents which I had gathered together for the purpose of supporting my defence.

"Leif Jones," he said, "is a teetotaller and can't hurt a fly. He's one of those who tried to stop the tot of rum to the soldiers in the trenches. I killed that move, and I'll checkmate him to-morrow."

"But how?" I enquired.

"Well," he said, "Neil Primrose once was angry with Lord Loreburn, the Lord Chancellor, and felt sure he would force him to resign over the non-appointment of Liberal magistrates, as Lloyd George was behind Neil. Loreburn telegraphed for me as you have done, and laid all his cards on the table at breakfast before the debate came on, and though Neil had a good case, and many Liberals were strongly with him, I beat them, for Loreburn had stood by Ireland in the old days."

I got little satisfaction out of this, and early in the morning of the next day I called on Bonar Law and told him that Tim Healy would fail me. He would not listen to my case. Bonar Law said he would stand by. This promise comforted me.

Leif Jones made his attack on the expected lines, describing me as a "menace to national freedom and Free Trade"; he spoke of a film for which my Ministry had some responsibility, *The Man Who Saved the Empire*. "Who is he?" asked Leif Jones. "It is in Lord Beaverbrook's power to decide that.

TIM HEALY AND BEAVERBROOK

Arnold Bennett is at the extreme left

He can put the Prime Minister . . . or Admiral Beatty . . . or Lord Beaverbrook.

"Is it true," he asked, "that Lord Beaverbrook wishes to take over the control of the war correspondents at the front? . . . He wants to control . . . the news to be flashed all over the world. . . . A power like that . . . is most dangerous to this country. There is talk of a daily newspaper being provided [by the Government] for soldiers. If that is to be like the films . . . it will be used for propaganda purposes. . . . A General Election is coming along. Is this newspaper to contain propaganda for the electors at the front?"[aa]

After Leif Jones came some pretty wild accusations from Mr. Pringle, the Scottish Radical.

As a matter of fact, most of what they tried to lay at my door had happened when Lord Carson from the War Cabinet had general control of propaganda.

Tim Healy would occasionally interject, "That was done in Carson's time."

Mr. Baldwin rose in my defence. "We have proof," he said, "that the work being done by the Ministry of Information is being well appreciated now, because, during the summer, there have been articles in some of the German papers to the effect that admirable work is being done now by English propaganda and suggesting that the Germans should organise themselves as efficiently."[ab]

He displayed a keen appreciation of the mood of the House in making his defence of me personally. I quote his summing up: "The Minister of

Information is a man of very strong personality. Men with strong personalities have this in common, that the magnetism which comes with that personality either attracts or repels. . . . I want to say this in all seriousness. Lord Beaverbrook has taken on a most difficult, delicate and thankless task. Do not let his pitch be queered. Give him a fair chance and judge him by results."[ac]

But as the debate was going, it was likely that I would be judged on the trend of the discussion rather than on results, and this was not likely to be satisfactory. For if a whole discussion turns on one man, more charges are made than can possibly be answered—and a bad atmosphere is created.

Then Healy spoke.

He wanted to know what all this nonsense was about. It was a waste of time in war. Anyhow, what had Carson done when he was in charge of Propaganda? And if that was all Carson had done it would not have mattered much.

But Carson had made his department an organ for anti-Irish propaganda and filled it with his nominees from Trinity College, Dublin. The result had been the absolute ruin of Irish recruiting. He spoke passionately in exposition of the whole Irish case.

On this, the vials of inter-Irish wrath were poured forth. Mr. Ronald McNeill intervened to defend Carson. Mr. Shortt, Chief Secretary for Ireland, was brought up to make a lengthy statement on behalf of the Government.

The debate was abruptly switched off from the discussion of my supposed iniquities, and a regular Irish squabble ensued. By the time Mr. Devlin had summed up for the Nationalists, the speeches of Leif Jones and Pringle had been completely forgotten, and the question of the Ministry of Information and its chief had faded out of the picture.

Healy's performance was a perfect exhibition of Parliamentary tactics.

Later Healy joined me at the Hyde Park Hotel. He said, "Get me some pea-soup and a steak and a bottle of beer, and I will tell you the fun."

After this debate my life as Minister ran a more even course. One of my most dangerous critics in Parliament, Austen Chamberlain, now a member of the administration, made no more trouble for me. Northcliffe gave me his newspaper support when criticism broke out in public.

There was an interlude when I got into difficulties over the publication in the *Daily Express* of the dismissal of Lord Derby, who, as I have told, was banished to the Embassy in Paris.

It was easy to understand the complaint of Lord Stamfordham on behalf of the King. But I was in a position to answer that I had nothing to do with the disclosure.

At the end of August the *Daily Express* printed a leading article about a proposal for a General Election in terms which irritated the Prime Minister.

"We do not want a new Khaki Election. We

cannot vote in the dark. If the Prime Minister seeks re-election as head of a Coalition Government which is to endure, he must satisfy those who are to vote for him that his views and theirs are the same. . . .

"What, for instance, is the Prime Minister's programme on Tariff Reform and Imperial Preference? . . . What would be the Irish policy of the Government which hopes to be returned? Is the Welsh Church to be sacrificed simply because the Party of Spoilers just tottering to its fall over the Irish Crisis of 1914 was saved for a moment by the outbreak of the Great War?"[ad]

From Lloyd George's point of view, the offence of the article was that it referred to his political dilemma: he had to cling to his Free Trade principles on account of his Liberal following, but the Conservative element in his Coalition wished to have tariffs included in the election platform. Lloyd George wrote indignantly to Bonar Law:

Have you seen the leader in to-day's *Daily Express*? That is Max. Having regard to the risks I ran for him and the way I stood up for him when he was attacked by his own Party, I regard this as a mean piece of treachery. It explains why no man in any Party trusts Max.

The reference to the Welsh Church is deliberately introduced to make it impossible for me to arrange matters with the Unionist [Conservative] leaders.

I am sorry, for I have sincerely tried to work with him.[ae]

Winston Churchill came to see me. He asked if I took responsibility for the substance of the

8 . 9 . 18

My dear Bonar,

Please see enclosed.

A Nitrate negotiator is not without honour save in his own country & from his own Treasury.

Look after Max or he will make a gt mistake wh all of us & he most of all will have cause to regret.

Yours sincerely

Winston S. Churchill

THE CHURCHILL LETTER TO BONAR LAW

"Look after Max"

leader. I judged his enquiry came from the Prime Minister. And I felt compelled to reply in defence of the editor, who had been encouraged by me on all occasions to promote and expound the doctrine of tariff reform and imperial preference.

On 8th September Churchill wrote to Bonar Law:

> Look after Max, or he will make a great mistake which all of us and he most of all will have cause to regret.[af]

Churchill was, of course, the real leader of the Liberal free-trade element in the Government. They all feared greatly that the policy of imperial preference would be promoted by me into an election issue, thus cutting across the Coalition structure. Hence his letter to Bonar Law.

I surely needed looking after. But not by Bonar Law. At the end of October I was stricken by an unusual and serious infection known as actinomycosis. I resigned. And I felt like the prisoner of old who was freed from the chains and the ball of servitude, even though I was compelled for more than six months to devote every hour and all of my physical resources to conquering an affliction which seldom spares its victims.

Twenty-two years after and in the Second War I had another term of duty. But that calls for another volume, on another day.

The final debate on the Ministry of Information occupied the time and attention of the House of Commons on 7th November, 1918.

The occasion was of little importance. Criticism or praise counted for nothing. The labour was over. The work was done. The blinds were pulled down; the doors were closed. Sir Edward Carson, however, took the opportunity to intervene in the debate. He had nothing to say about the Ministry.

Just as Healy had made an attack on Carson on my appearance in Parliament at the last debate, so now Carson made a bitter and vituperative assault on Northcliffe.

Baldwin answered for the Government. He made no defence of Northcliffe. For me he had words of warm praise.

"I should like to say, what I am sure the Committee will endorse, that the combination of rare vision he has shown, with ability to master details, has enabled that Department, in spite of much criticism it has received, to form itself in the short time it has had, and to become an engine this year that has really done most valuable work for the Allied cause and done it at a reasonable expense."[ag]

Sir Hamar Greenwood, a Liberal Member, who had been a critic of my appointment, told the House:

"When Lord Beaverbrook was appointed Minister of Information many people expected that things would not go right. I am, myself, only an acquaintance of Lord Beaverbrook, but I am bound to confess this, that his career at the Ministry of Information has been one of the most successful careers of any Minister in this

Coalition Government. He actually rescued from the Germans the neutral countries and America by launching out on a system of propaganda the success of which can be vouched for by everybody who has been in those countries both before the Ministry was established and since its work has commenced."[ab]

A final tribute came from a strange source. In *My War Memories* General Erich von Ludendorff said:

"We were hypnotised by the enemy propaganda as a rabbit is by a snake. It was exceptionally clever, and conceived on a great scale. It worked by strong mass-suggestion, kept in the closest touch with the military situation, and was unscrupulous as to the means it used.

". . . While Entente propaganda was doing ever more harm to the German people and the army and navy, it succeeded in maintaining the determination to fight in its own countries and armies, and in working against us in neutral countries. . . . In the neutral countries we were subject to a sort of moral blockade. . . .

"In England the whole propaganda service was placed under Lord Beaverbrook, with three directors, of whom Lord Northcliffe attended to the enemy countries, Kipling to home and colonial propaganda, and Lord Rothermere* to the work in neutral countries. . . ."[at]

---

* Rothermere joined the Ministry of Information after his retirement from the office of Secretary of State for Air. His support was of immense value.

CHAPTER X

HIS ROYAL POMP*

THE last political crisis of the war, and this time a crisis of which no whisper reached the outer world. The crisis which may be called: Lord Curzon and "Hang the Kaiser!"

The public outcry for Hanging the Kaiser resounded throughout the land. It was a favourite subject for speeches and much attention was given to the Emperor and the Rope in the political meetings up and down the country.

Now that all the dust of those ancient struggles has settled, it is difficult to realize how important the issue of "Hang the Kaiser" became. But the truth is that Lloyd George's Government won the 1918 general election on two slogans—one, "Hang the Kaiser"; the other "Make Germany Pay". Both had a powerful appeal to a public which was sick of the war and unable to tolerate the notion that the victory would yield no material spoil.†

It is easy now to see that "Hang the Kaiser" was an emotional outcry. At the end of 1918 and in the

* His Royal Pomp was the title given to His Excellency the Marquess Curzon of Kedleston, K.G., G.C.S.I., M.A., P.C., F.R.S., D.C.L., LL.D., J.P., D.L., by the American Ambassador in writing to President Wilson.

† An official statement from Downing Street set forth five election pledges. The first was Punish the Kaiser and the second, Make Germany Pay.

months immediately following, it was a serious factor in British politics. Business men might be impressed by the notion of an indemnity. The vast public were more concerned with putting the Kaiser's neck in a noose.

At the December election, candidates made ample use of this vote-catching issue. Lloyd George's huge majority was to a large extent founded on the popularity of the Hanging Craze. On that account any suspicion that Lloyd George's Government was weakening on the issue roused the whole House and threatened the Prime Minister's position. The issue became, in time, a real crisis—a crisis flowing from the war although breaking out after it was ended.

Lloyd George himself gave encouragement to the slogan. He was strengthened in his enthusiasm for this sound election plank by the vigorous denunciations of the German Emperor which flowed from the Curzon chamber.

Two days after the Armistice, Curzon wrote of it to the Prime Minister.

> Public opinion will not willingly consent to let this arch-criminal escape by a final act of cowardice. The supreme and colossal nature of the crime seems to call for some supreme and unprecedented condemnation. Execution, imprisonment, these are not, or may not be, necessary. But continued life, an inglorious and ignoble exile under the weight of such a sentence as has never before been given in the history of mankind, would be a penance worse than death.[a] *

* For the full text of the letter, see *Appendix IV*, No. 17.

On 20th November, 1918, Curzon, after consulting Clemenceau, demanded that the Kaiser and the German Crown Prince should both be brought to trial. The proposal fell in admirably with the Prime Minister's own inclinations. He agreed with Curzon, while Churchill, supported by Milner, was against it. Churchill would never give his support to anything that savoured of regicide. So far as he was concerned, monarchs were safe from the gallows.

The decision to try the Emperor was accepted by the Allies and embodied in the Peace Treaty. As the Kaiser had taken refuge in the Netherlands, that country was now invited to extradite him.

Thus Lloyd George was supported by the terms of the Peace Treaty. He would not deviate from his harsh and stern purpose. Churchill and Milner might absent themselves on the Day of Judgment. But, after all, there was Curzon. But not for long.

For Curzon listened to the King, and the King had received a memorial from three German princes, the King of Saxony, the Duke of Württemberg and the Grand-Duke of Baden, calling upon him in the name of "all unanimously thinking German Princes" with an urgent appeal, and more serious, with a warning, that should His Majesty, by tolerating the Kaiser's trial, lay hands "on the Royal Dignity of a great and at one time friendly and related Ruler, then every official authority, every throne (including the English throne) will be threatened".[b]

The King referred the memorial to the Foreign

Secretary and the Prime Minister. Lord Curzon considered it "impertinent" in tone and substance and held that no reply should be returned. The King did not share this firm view. He felt himself bound to send an answer back to his fellow monarchs. And, in due course, a change came over Curzon's attitude. A remarkable change!

For when Lloyd George announced in the House of Commons in July 1919[c] that the trial of the Kaiser would take place in London, Curzon at once began to raise every conceivable objection to the plan.

He wrote to Lloyd George an elaborate and what can only be described as hysterical composition, conjuring up the embarrassment of the Royal Family at finding their cousin up for trial within their precincts, where he had often stayed; depicting with vivid strokes the English crowd, either incommoded by the Kaiser's occupation of Hampton Court Palace or, alternatively, depressed by the shadow of despondency and gloom that would be caused by his presence in Westminster; and picturing finally the permanent and far-reaching resentment of Germany against Great Britain for this act of vengeance.

> Never mind that the Court is International [he warned], the verdict will be regarded as having been inspired, just as in all probability it will have to be executed, by ourselves. Would it be possible ever again to make friends with Germany after that? Would not it be a root of bitterness which would last till the end of time?[d] *

*The full text is reproduced in *Appendix IV*, No. 18.

Finally Curzon turned his indignation upon Holland. With the Kaiser already within her boundaries, was she not shelving her responsibilities in refusing to hold the trial there?

This passionate document failed to inspire Lloyd George. Indeed it moved him to very considerable anger, and he replied to Curzon, rebuking him in the strongest terms for his reversal of opinion.

July 8, 1919.

My dear Lord President,

The arguments you advance in your letter against trying the Kaiser in England I had already heard from the King—every one of them. I therefore assume it was the result of a conversation which you had with H.M. I can hardly, however, believe that it was his suggestion that the Cabinet should be invited to throw over its principal delegate at the Peace Conference in an important decision which he had taken on their behalf and which he had already announced to the House of Commons. If it is raised in the Cabinet I hope, at any rate, it will be after my return . . .

All the reasons which you assign are really arguments against trying the Kaiser at all. You tell me that Churchill and Milner agreed with you. Of course they did; they were firmly opposed to a trial. They are, therefore, quite consistent in their attitude. You, on the other hand, took the initiative in proposing his trial. The proposal you made was ultimately adopted by the Cabinet, pressed on their behalf on our Allies, and ultimately adopted by them after a full investigation by a very able Commission* representing the leading Allies, including Belgium. To go back on it now would indeed be not only to make the representatives of this country at the Paris Conference look

* Commission on the Responsibility of the Authors of the War.

silly, but to make Britain, France, Belgium and all the other Allies look extremely foolish. . . .

.   .   .   .   .

I took the action which was the natural sequence of decisions arrived at deliberately after long reflection and discussion by the Cabinet, and I do not like the idea of running away from them at the first difficulties that present themselves. . . .

Ever sincerely,
D. LLOYD GEORGE.[e]

It was a stinging rebuke, an insulting reply which would have driven most Ministers to hand in their resignation forthwith. Not so Lord Curzon. He remained in office unabashed. And his will, in due course, prevailed. For the Kaiser was never brought to trial. The Dutch refused to give him up. And the Allies, with varying degrees of relief and annoyance, accepted this refusal and dropped the matter.

The incident is of interest now mainly because of the light it throws on the character of Lord Curzon. What a strange man he was! And how much the reality of the man was at variance with his public reputation. For he gave the impression that his views were rigid and inflexible. Yet he had a talent for being on both sides of every controversy.

Before the outcry over "Hang the Kaiser", there had been many striking examples of Lord Curzon's capacity to carry out an agile if undignified and belated *volte face*.

The worst of all Curzon's contradictions in public life relates to the fall of Asquith.

From the outset of the first Coalition Curzon became Asquith's most active supporter in the Tory ranks. He was out-and-out an Asquith man. This was the impression in political circles and was held by Asquith himself. In the political crisis of December, 1916, it was assumed by Conservatives and Liberals alike that Lord Curzon gave his support to the Prime Minister, Asquith.

There is, however, evidence produced after the event, and now at our disposal, which reveals how Curzon, in the critical days before the fall of Asquith's Government, played an increasingly ambiguous part.

On the one hand we find him writing to his Tory colleague Lord Lansdowne on Sunday, 3rd December, describing the happenings of the Unionist meeting that afternoon.

It had been decided, he said, that Bonar Law should tell the Prime Minister that internal reconstruction of the Government was no longer possible and that Asquith should hand his resignation to the King. Should he not be willing to take that step, the Unionists would place the whole of their resignations in his hands.

"Had one felt," Curzon confided, "that reconstitution by and under the present Prime Minister was possible, we should all have preferred to try it. But we know that with him as Chairman, either of the Cabinet or the War Committee, it is absolutely impossible to win the War, and it will be for himself and Lloyd George to determine whether he goes out altogether or becomes Lord Chancellor or Chancellor of the Exchequer in a new Government, a nominal Premiership being a protean compromise which, in our view, could have no endurance."*

Yet at the same time he appeared to be working openly and actively for Asquith. Indeed, only a few hours later, on the Monday morning, Curzon despatched a friendly note of reassurance to the Prime Minister. I reproduce it here.

> 1 Carlton House Terrace,
> December 4th, 1916.

My dear Henry,

Lansdowne has, I think, explained to you that my resignation yesterday was far from having the sinister purport which I believe you were inclined to attribute to it. However, I have not written to emphasize that but to strike a note of gaiety in a world of gloom. Just now I recalled these lines of Matthew Arnold—I cannot remember in what poem:

> *We in some unknown Power's employ*
> *Move in a rigorous line;*
> *Can neither when we will enjoy*
> *Nor when we will resign.*

We are hourly expecting you to facilitate the process by asking for our seals.

> Yours ever,
> CURZON.*g*

In other words, Curzon was inviting Asquith to ask for the Seals of his Ministers just as he

* The full text of the letter is reproduced in *Appendix IV*, No. 19.

had required their Seals in 1915. Thus Asquith was to remain Prime Minister, selecting a new slate of Ministers.

Was not this, Curzon's critics ask, the limit of political cynicism? Asquith's biographers judge it so. "If the two letters were not in evidence," they write, "it would scarcely seem possible that they were written by the same hand."[b]

Asquith therefore continued to be lulled into a false sense of security. Not surprisingly. For on that critical Monday the Three C's—Cecil, Chamberlain * and Curzon—making Lord Curzon their spokesman, called on the Prime Minister at Downing Street. Lord Crewe, in his Memorandum on the crisis, has confirmed that these powerful Conservatives came, not to disclaim their fealty to Asquith but rather to explain that their consent to the Unionist resolution calling on him to resign "in no way indicated a wish that he should retire. On the contrary, they did not believe that anybody else could form a Government, certainly not Mr. Lloyd George; so that the result would be the return of the Prime Minister with a stronger Government and a greatly enhanced position."[i]

It was this apparent reinforcement that led Asquith to count noses among his supporters and to believe that his position was impregnable. Curzon's firm assurance that neither he nor the Tory Ministers for whom he was acting would take office under Lloyd George or Bonar Law[j] confirmed him in his confidence.

* Austen Chamberlain denies that he saw Asquith on the Monday.

Yet so swift and dramatic were the events of those few days, that when the Lloyd George Government was successfully formed on 7th December, Lord Curzon's participation in that administration had already been secured. He had accepted office as Lord President of the Council and as a member of the small War Cabinet.

His pledge to Asquith was ignored; nor did he delay to consult with his faithful Tory colleagues. An appeal to his patriotism from Lloyd George's envoy had clinched the matter.*

It is clearly difficult to understand a move of such startling swiftness. What is certain is that Curzon emerged elevated by the crisis, and that few men could have executed a feat of such political duality and daring.

Although Lord Curzon proved a valuable addition to the War Cabinet, from time to time he reverted to his habit of steering two opposing courses. Therefore, at the height of the military controversy, we find him at one moment defending the soldiers' cause, advising Lloyd George to seek co-operation with General Robertson and urging moderation on military issues in the House;[1] yet three months later, Curzon was supporting the Prime Minister in his dismissal of the same General Robertson, though at that moment encouraging Lord Derby in resistance.

---

* Lord Crewe, Asquith's foremost colleague and supporter, whose account of the December crisis has been accepted by Asquith and published in his *Memories and Reflections*,[k] wrote to me in October, 1928: "The prompt agreement of Curzon and one or two others to take part in the Government at the end of 1916 has always stood in need of some explanation after what they had previously said to Asquith. And it is quite true that Curzon gave the reason which you mention, that he was told it would be unpatriotic to decline at that moment of crisis."

Such was the extraordinary nature of this man that no decision of his on a point of policy could be regarded as irrevocable. Again and again he would throw over a cause with which he had been long and publicly identified without sign or warning—leaving his supporters stunned and dishevelled in the sudden gust of his departure.

Curzon's acts of desertion plainly expose him to the charge of political expediency. But there were also times when in his reversal of thought he himself exhibited no outward recognition of the change. His feelings on the question of the Coalition fell into this category.

In February, 1918, Lord Curzon addressed a letter to Bonar Law on the problem of continuing the Lloyd George Coalition Government after the end of hostilities. He flatly rejected the suggestion.

> I should like to say at once that the movement is one which not only can I not support, but which I think to be entirely mistaken. As matters stand, I agree that if there were to be a General Election in the near future, it would be the duty of our party to give the fullest support to the Prime Minister for the prosecution of the war to the end—the object, indeed the sole object, for which the Coalition was formed and still exists. But, from the idea that our party should merge its identity in some new party, or should pledge its allegiance after peace has returned, I entirely dissent and I hope that you as our Leader will give no encouragement to it.[m]

But in November, a different view had replaced his earlier misgivings. He wrote to Bonar Law:

AUSTEN CHAMBERLAIN AND CURZON

Both stumbled on the threshold of 10 Downing Street.
Disappointment was their portion

One thing is certain, viz., That the old party programmes are obsolete. Asquith's attempt to serve up
the stale dishes of his—and the reception it has met
with—are sufficient proof of this.[n]

Curzon had changed his mind again. If not
his mind, then his allegiance. He changed it
because Lloyd George asked. A letter of 12th
November, 1918, written to the Prime Minister
from Paris, where Curzon was staying at the
British Embassy, closes with this message:

I wrote to Bonar [Law] as you suggested about
General Election.[o]

Lloyd George often dragged the portly Curzon,
the President of the Council, round and round the
political arena at the tail of his chariot.

Perhaps the most amazing decision was taken
by Curzon during the dispute over Turkey.
Throughout the discussion in Office and among
his colleagues, the Foreign Secretary (Curzon)
opposed with powerful and consistent argument
the pro-Greek, anti-Turkish policy of His Majesty's
Ministers.

The moment he was overborne, he changed his
attitude and took part to the fullest extent in the
very course which he had rejected and denounced.

Could a man of such political contradictions be
taken seriously? The answer is that he could be,
and was.

The Unionist Peers may have resented Curzon's abandonment of them over the Parliament
Bill in 1911; the Carlton Club may have been

disconcerted and estranged by his sudden surrender over the suffrage cause, but in the event
both proved to be matters where Curzon's decision
put him on the right side of majority opinion of
the day. He was a political jumping-jack, but a
weary acrobat who was still called upon to
take part in the circus performance.

There was also about Lord Curzon a suspicion of
humbug, which sometimes amused but more often
annoyed his colleagues. This showed itself in
several ways.

In March, 1917, Bonar Law was asked in the
House how many state-owned cars were at the
disposal of Lord Curzon; he replied that a certain
number of cars were at the disposal of Government officials engaged in the discharge of their
duties: "Any member of the War Cabinet is at
liberty to indent upon this reserve for the use of
a car when required for official purposes only."[p]

Thus Lord Curzon was cleared of the implicit
charge that he was using official cars for private
purposes. But not all of his colleagues were
persuaded of the righteousness of his conduct.
On the very day that Bonar Law gave his answer
in the House, Lord Derby, Secretary of State for
War, political head of the department controlling
the pool of motor-cars, wrote to Bonar Law:

War Office,
Whitehall, S.W.

Personal & Confidential.   5th March, 1917.

Dear Bonar Law,

I am sorry for going away, but I really could not
stand hearing George Curzon talk, and I did not want

to enter into incriminations. As a matter of fact he has behaved disgracefully about the car, and it is undoubtedly his own fault that there is any trouble. There was a car placed at the disposal of the Air Board, but when I was Chairman I never once used it. When Curzon came to the Air Board he calmly took it for himself. He talks about it being for general use, but I should doubt a single soul having been in it except himself and his guests. He motors them down to Hackwood and uses the car for sending to the Station for his Saturday-to-Monday parties, and I should like to have asked him whether it is not true on the occasion of his Dance the other night the car came backwards and forwards to London three times. I am sure he would never deny that Lady Curzon invariably uses it, and he himself admitted to me that although he was ill in bed he had sent for the car in order to send a note down to Mrs. Harry Cust. Now this is a scandalous abuse of a Government car and needless to say makes everybody talk. He was to say the least of it incorrect as to what happened about the car in the beginning. I am going to try and find his letter, but he wrote to me, if I remember rightly, to say that the Prime Minister had authorised him to have a car. It now turns out that he telephoned to the Prime Minister to know whether he could have one and got no answer. He then told me that he meant to keep the Air Board car. I told him that was entirely a matter of agreement between him and the Air Board, but a second car would have to be supplied and it did not make the least difference which it went to, upon which he telephoned to Cowdray* (Cowdray told me this himself) to say that I had agreed, with the Prime Minister's consent, to his keeping his present car. It is very amusing his saying that his health can only be kept going by being able to go to Trent every Satur-

---

* Lord Cowdray was President of the Air Board from January to November, 1917.

day or Monday. He has only had Trent since he married.

I am going to try and get out for you the amount of petrol that he has consumed in that car since he has had it, and I think it will be surprising. Of course he kept on quoting me, and it is quite true that both in peace time as well as in war, there is a car which is supposed to be the Secretary of State's, and I do have the same car, but if that is wanted for any other military duty I should go without, and it probably will be wanted as we have to supply cars for all our Colonial Conference visitors. The real truth is he is just what he *says* he is not. He is one of the meanest men that I know. He was a tenant of mine at one time and I have good reason for knowing it.

Yours v. sincerely,

DERBY.[q]

These were bitter words, with personal resentment behind them. They were tough. Yet they illustrate how Curzon was disliked by his colleagues.

Allowance must be made for Derby's hostility to Lord Curzon. Indeed, more than a year after the motor-car dispute there was discord between them. The Lord President of the Council (Curzon) wrote to the Prime Minister while staying at the British Embassy in Paris in November 1918:

I received your orders on Sunday to stay on here in case any War Cabinet questions required to be decided. Derby was very much irritated at this. He is a sensitive person and has not shown much pleasure at my presence even though I am a guest in his house.[o]

The next day, however, Curzon's feudal spirit was uppermost. The Prime Minister was informed that Curzon's presence was required by the Belgian King when he re-entered his kingdom. On 13th November, 1918, Curzon wrote to Lloyd George:

> I have just heard from the King of the Belgians that the Queen and he re-enter Brussels on Saturday. Lady Curzon and I have always promised to be with them on that day and accordingly we are returning to Belgium by motor tomorrow for this ceremony and shall be back in England on Monday.'

The journey to the Belgians was interrupted. Lloyd George summoned the traveller to return to his own native land.

Now Curzon was to win laurels for himself. Wilson, the American President, who was journeying to Paris, refused to come to England. It was intimated to him that the King and Queen would invite him and his wife to Buckingham Palace. Wilson, however, would not have any political entanglements with Britain. Then it was that Lord Curzon concocted a plan which he rightly thought was certain to bring the American President to "this sceptred isle, set in a silver sea". And what a plan. He wrote to Lloyd George on 12th November, 1918:

> I think I helped to solve the problem of getting Wilson to come to England on his way to Paris. For, a little before leaving London I had got my University of Oxford to vote him an honorary degree and to ask him to deliver the Romanes Lecture. As soon as I told

House this he said it was the one thing the President would love and that it would bring him to England without fail—giving him an academic rather than a political excuse for his visit. He accordingly wired at once to Wilson and has no doubt of his acceptance.

Curzon captured his man, and "my" University gave Wilson his degree.

Unjust claims have been put forward on behalf of Lord Northcliffe. An American life of Wilson[r] recounts that Northcliffe was entitled to a share of the glory. But Curzon cannot be deprived of his credit. He worked the racket all by himself.

Curzon's patronage indeed extended far behind "his Oxford". He embraced in his arms Eton and the Order of the Garter. A letter written to Lloyd George in 1918 gave a clear indication of the extent of his protectorate.

> P.M.
>
> I see in the papers that Dr. Warre is about to resign the Provostship of Eton. As an old Etonian I hope I may be consulted before you fill it. On the hypothesis that the vacancy would occur in his time Asquith often spoke to me about it.
>
> It is an important appt. & difficult to fill & will require a good deal of consideration.
>
> Perhaps also later on when the time comes you will speak to me about the Garter vacant by the death of the Duke of Northumberland.
>
> The Leader of the House of Lords is rather closely interested in these matters.
>
> C.[t]

Curzon was capable of malice, though often dressed up in satire or ridicule. His characteristic disposition is revealed in a letter to Lady Curzon written on 5th November, 1923, the day of the funeral of his friend and colleague Andrew Bonar Law.

My darling girl,

I have just come back from the Abbey funeral of Bonar. It was rather a sombre performance; and one could not help thinking that many of the congregation were wondering how poor old Bonar ever got there. I met Burnham afterwards and asked him what the general sentiment on the subject was. He said that everyone knew it to be absurd; but that the Press had been stampeded by Beaverbrook who as soon as the breath was out of poor Bonar's body, turned on the full blast of the Rothermere cum Beaverbrook furnace and practically forced the entire Press into line. He concurred in thinking that in a month or two Bonar would be completely forgotten, and that in days to come people would ask who he was and how he ever got there. When we marched down from the Choir to the Nave—where a little casket containing his ashes (for he had been cremated) was let down into a small hole in the pavement, shaped like this— I found myself near the Prince of Wales. He fidgeted and looked about; never once turned a glance to the grave or the coffin, and showed himself profoundly bored with the whole perform-ance. Of course cremation has the advantage of saving a great deal of space and thereby admitting of many future interments. But it has its ridiculous side. For a sham coffin was carried under a great white pall and deposited on a catafalque before the Sanctuary in the earlier part of the service and subse-quently borne to the grave, where it was put on one side and disappeared, everyone knowing that there was no body in it at all."

This was one side of Curzon's nature. There was another. Lord Curzon was a hard-working and devoted public servant providing his own interests did not clash with the public concern. He was equipped with good understanding, a certain measure of native cunning, and an immense capacity for believing what suited his own interests.

His years in India as Viceroy had increased his endowment of pomposity, and also his measure of knowledge of conditions in the Far East. He was a real authority on native politics there.

In foreign affairs Curzon's standing was held on high by his sure grasp of the subject. Unfortunately, in his contacts with foreign potentates his manner did not correspond with his matter. In Cabinet councils he was a powerful and vigorous force.

Lord Curzon was endowed with immense social gifts. He was an entrancing conversationalist, bringing to the dinner table humour, wit, satire and plenty of malice. As an orator he was a good performer, and the painted chamber was just about the size to retain his pompous diction and his rolling periods. But to find yourself in a room with Lord Curzon was to suffer the feeling that you were being jostled mentally or physically or both. The outward sweep of the hands reminded the onlooker, like other aspects of his life, that his crest was "a popinjay rising with wings extended".

He was disliked by his colleagues, yet admired by them. He was a ceaseless intriguer. His ambition was to be leader of the Tory Party. He wished to share the crown of joint party leadership with Bonar Law, as Lord Lansdowne had done. He was always furious because he could not succeed. Only one position would have satisfied Curzon's sense of what was due to his talents and industry —the Premiership. And for four and a half hours in 1923, during the journey from Yeovil to London, Lord Curzon believed himself Prime Minister of Britain. But after he arrived at Paddington he discovered that the King had chosen as successor to Bonar Law—Stanley Baldwin.

CHAPTER XI

THE HERO

THE war was over. Lloyd George was now the most powerful man in Europe. His fame would endure for ever. He was admired and praised in all countries. His prestige in the United States was so high that men said he would be elected as their President if he could run for office there.

He had beaten his German enemies in the war. He had scattered and destroyed his British enemies at the polls in the course of a General Election which disclosed an overwhelming popular judgement in his favour. Hardly any political opponent escaped. They had fallen like autumn leaves.

It is not now possible to realise the immense position of this man Lloyd George. He had risen to such heights that only his contemporaries can understand the pre-eminence he enjoyed. Winston Churchill, whose fame has endured, never reached such a position. And the electors in 1945 showed it clearly.

When Lloyd George arrived in Paris for the Peace Conference he at once took control. He really dominated the French Prime Minister

11th NOVEMBER, 1918

"They may ring their bells now; before long they will be wringing their hands"

Clemenceau. He had immense authority with President Wilson. He was giving the law to Europe, fixing the boundaries of all the nations, giving out encouragement to some countries and severely reprimanding others. He was the arbiter of all Europe.

Bonar Law said of him, "He can be Prime Minister for life if he likes." And Bonar Law's judgement was firmly and rightly based on the facts of the situation.

In June, 1919, after the signing of the Peace Treaty, on Lloyd George's return to London he was received by the King, who drove with him through the streets to Buckingham Palace. The public reception was a delirious event.

Churchill, Secretary of State for War, recommended that the Prime Minister should be awarded the Distinguished Service Order. The recommendation was rejected. Churchill was never easily put off. In October he wrote to the King that the Army Council wished Lloyd George to have the war medals.

The Palace resisted. The King thought that Asquith should be on the same footing as Lloyd George. He objected that it would be difficult to give the medals to Lloyd George and ignore the other ministers.[a] Nor, it appeared, was he entirely persuaded that the inspiration had come from the Army Council. But he was awkwardly placed for it was probable that Lloyd George had already been told.

And, in fact, Churchill wrote again[b] on 7th

December, 1919, acknowledging that Lloyd George had been consulted and had expressed great pleasure, saying "I would rather have them than an Earldom".* On 8th January, 1920, the newspapers announced:

> At 10 Downing Street, last night, Mr. Winston Churchill and the members of the Army Council waited upon the Prime Minister to present him with the special award of the 1914–15 Star, the British War Medal, and the Victory Medal, approved by the King.
>
> The proceedings, which were private, lasted only a few minutes. The speeches of Mr. Churchill, who presented the medals, and of the Prime Minister were quite informal.
>
> We understand that the King has also approved the special award of the three war medals to Mr. Asquith.ᶜ

But in politics nothing is permanent, and often what seems to be made of marble and bronze turns out, after a little, to be composed of lath and plaster. So was it with the reputation of Lloyd George.

By the end of the first year of peace, the prestige and authority of His Majesty's Chief Minister had softened. There were signs and portents.

It was always thus. In the moment of supreme triumph decline begins to do its work, undermining, weakening and finally destroying not only the reputation but also the power and the authority of our heroes.

* After many years the Earldom came to both in time, the Earl of Oxford and Asquith in 1925 and Earl Lloyd George in 1945. Recommendations for honours flow from the Prime Ministers. Baldwin was responsible for recommending the Earl of Oxford and Asquith. Winston Churchill put forward the name of Lloyd George. But some Prime Ministers are not backward in recommending themselves. Almost every Prime Minister from Asquith to Eden has been honoured with one or other Order, excepting only Chamberlain and Bonar Law. Law disapproved of the system.

It is hard to explain to a new generation the full measure of dislike, distrust, even loathing, with which the public came to regard his government. It is easy, on the other hand, to enumerate the causes which, insufficient as they may now appear, brought about the extraordinary turn from public favour to popular animosity. Here are some of them:

(1) Lloyd George's series of foreign conferences which produced nothing and ended in futility and ridicule.

(2) His hostility to France and his preoccupation with Germany.

(3) The failure of his German policy, which finally resulted in driving Germany into the arms of Russia.

(4) The grave risk he ran when he threatened war in the Near East. At that time war was sure to involve other nations and likely to end up in another European conflict.

All the while, unemployment was widespread through the land.

Agriculture declined. The Government had given a subsidy for the production of wheat and then repealed the Act. The farmers believed themselves to have been betrayed. These domestic miseries sharpened the impatience with which the public regarded Lloyd George's busy and impulsive foreign policy.

Certain personal factors played their part. Scandal after scandal broke out over the collection of a Lloyd George Party Fund. The Prime Minister agreed to sell his memoirs to the *Daily Telegraph* for £90,000. When the public took offence over this transaction, Lloyd George was compelled to declare that the proceeds of the book would go to war charities.*

But the immediate cause of his fall may have been his arrogance coupled with the decline of the trust and confidence which he had inspired during the war. A Prime Minister without a party cannot dispense with the trust and confidence of his supporters in the House of Commons. At the very height of his popularity he became impatient, critical and dictatorial in manner.

He quarrelled with Lord Milner, who had joined his Government in 1916 as a member of the War Cabinet without departmental duties. Milner was much discussed and widely praised. He was sought after in political circles. Lord Esher, who was constantly urging a change at the Paris Embassy, frequently nominated Milner for the post.†

In 1918, when Lord Derby was moved from the War Office to the Paris Embassy, Milner succeeded him. He had discussed with Lloyd George whether Sir Maurice Hankey or himself should have the post. Milner in a letter thought he "would be more generally acceptable to the Army", but had "absolutely no feeling one way or the other. I only want the best thing done".[d]

---

* In fact, ten years passed before he returned to the book. Its earnings did not go to charity.

† In January, 1917, leading a British mission to Russia, Milner formed the impression that a revolution was not immediately likely. In January, 1919, when Germany was in revolution, he advised an easy peace for the Hohenzollerns.

Milner's friendly relations with the Prime Minister did not long survive his appointment to the War Office.

At the time of the 1918 General Election he was responsible for a scheme for newspaper propaganda among the troops in France which was a fiasco. Soon he was complaining that Lloyd George rebuked him publicly before outsiders and subordinates. On 7th December, 1918, he wrote to the Prime Minister asking for his discharge.

7.12.18
17, Great College Street, S.W.

My Dear Prime Minister,

. . . .

To be quite frank, and I know how you love frankness, my desire to withdraw from the arena has been quickened by the impatience, which you have of late frequently manifested, of my conduct of affairs at the War Office. Whether or not you are justified in that impatience, the fact remains that I am unable to do any better. I work myself as hard as I can. I press those working under me as much as I think right or wise. If the result is not satisfactory, the obvious remedy is to put some one else in my place, and I am most willing that that course should be adopted.

What I am not willing to accept is a position, in which I am exposed to such vehement charges of dilatoriness and neglect as you made yesterday in the presence of a large number of people, many of them not Ministers, in connection with the discharge of miners from the Army.

To submit to that sort of public rebuke without a protest, or to expose myself to a chance of its repetition, is, I feel, not consistent with self-respect.

The last thing I wish to do is to add to your burdens and embarrassments at the present time, and I am quite ready to carry on at the War Office till the Election is over, when there will no doubt in any case be a reconstruction of the Ministry, and my retirement can be effected with the minimum of fuss.

At the same time I should like you to feel that, if you found it convenient to make a change even before then, I am prepared at any moment to fall in with your wishes.

Believe me, my dear Prime Minister,

Yours very sincerely,

MILNER.[e]

Milner's resignation was accepted on an understanding that it should be held over until the Cabinet was reconstructed. Meanwhile rumours about Milner's position appeared in the newspapers which, he alleged, were inspired by Lloyd George's office.[f] In the end, the differences were patched up and Milner went to the Colonial Office. In this post he was concerned with the peace negotiations, especially those which related to the disposal of the German Colonies. This brought down on him a new outburst from Lloyd George.

British Delegation,

Paris.

14.5.1919.

My dear Colonial Secretary,

I earnestly hope that you will not find it necessary a second time to leave Paris without achieving a decision on the important questions entrusted to your charge. There are at least five matters essential to the peace settlement which you alone can pilot to a conclusion—Togoland, Kameroons, German East Africa, Nauru & Somaliland.

You will forgive me for saying quite emphatically that there can be no colonial business which more urgently presses for treatment than these affairs.

I could see you today at any time between 2 and 4 if that suits your convenience. Later on I am leaving to say farewell to a division with which I have been closely associated. I return Friday evening.

Ever sincerely,

D. LLOYD GEORGE.[g]

On 27th November, 1920, Milner informed the Prime Minister that he wished to resign, for private reasons, but would be willing to assist the Government in a private capacity.

At the New Year Milner refused to preside over a committee to work out the details of the proposed transfer of Palestine and Mesopotamia to the Colonial Office. He said he did not agree with the scheme and that he would not take any hand in the work. At the same time he pressed for the acceptance of his resignation.[h]

In the following month he resigned. Lloyd George's quarrel with him was indeed a stupid one. It is extraordinary that Milner was so patient and accepted so many rebukes with such good temper.

If Milner was reprimanded for leaving Paris, Lord Birkenhead (as F. E. Smith had by then become) was rebuked for the opposite reason.

Birkenhead, after being appointed Lord Chancellor, went to Paris when Lloyd George was attending the Peace Conference. Birkenhead's purpose was to interest his Prime Minister in questions concerning his office.

Lloyd George refused to see him, wrote him an angry letter telling him he had no right to leave the Kingdom, and ordered him to go back at once.

On 15th March, 1919, Lloyd George wrote a sharp letter to Birkenhead rejecting a report of the Lord Chancellor's Committee on the Land Acquisition Bill. "It has been transformed," said the Prime Minister, "into a Bill which will be represented as making sure that the landlord gets a good price, that the lawyers * get their pickings, and that there should be no undue hurry in the completion of the transaction."[i] †

Birkenhead, as Lloyd George should have remembered, was a formidable figure. He had a considerable capacity for friendship but was also capable of resenting and avenging any insult.

Lord Curzon was the real butt of Lloyd George's criticisms which were delivered on occasion in hectoring and bullying terms. It was, of course, the language his Lordship understood, though he did not like it when he was on the receiving end.

Even in the dark days of war Lloyd George was impatient and even intolerant of Lord Curzon's long and tedious harangues on public issues. There was at one time a proposal to take over the British Museum for the use of the Air Ministry. The plan found favour. Curzon then demanded a reconsideration and led off the discussion by reading a long statement setting forth his objections.

The Prime Minister checked him. Unhappily for his Lordship's pride, the Archbishop of Canterbury and Sir Frederic Kenyon, the Director of the Museum, were present to give evidence.

* Lord Birkenhead was a former Leader of the Bar.
† For full text of letter see *Appendix IV*, No. 20.

When asked if he had any alternative suggestion, Kenyon replied, "The Bethlehem Hospital—more commonly known as the Bedlam Lunatic Asylum." The Ministers felt that this would hardly be suitable accommodation.

No doubt Kenyon's good-humoured comment helped the Ministers to the revocation of the decision, thus saving the Museum for the public. But even though Curzon won the struggle his vanity was not appeased. In a weighty and dig-nified letter he protested that the Prime Minister had treated him roughly.

I reproduce a shortened version of his letter.*

Dear Prime Minister,

Although I hope I am not quick or resentful of temper, I do not like to let the incident of this morning pass without a word from me.

.   .   .   .   .

Before you came into the room Bonar Law in the Chair had asked me to open the discussion and in order to shorten the proceedings I had commenced to read my brief memo instead of recapitulating its substance. It was there that you cut me short in a manner which I venture to say left a painful impres-sion on all who heard it.

I certainly felt it acutely myself and that others felt it too was shown by the Archbishop of Canterbury, who came up to me in the H. of Lords this after-noon and said he had been astonished at the manner in which a member of the Cabinet could be treated by his Chief and at the good temper with which the latter had borne it.*j*

* The full text appears in *Appendix IV*, No. 21

Long after the war was over, Curzon still suffered from the barbs of Lloyd George's criticism. He appealed to nearly every member of the Cabinet and at last drew a response from Austen Chamberlain, a good-natured and sympathetic listener. Chamberlain wrote to Bonar Law on 6th January, 1921, inviting him to intercede, "because I know that you have an influence with him (Lloyd George) to which the rest of us cannot pretend. You will therefore be our best interpreter & you are the man most likely to put things right."*k* *

His letter was a most detailed defence of Lord Curzon, whose resignation, said Chamberlain, would be fatal to the Government and the Coalition. Churchill, he declared, had suffered a similar treatment at the hands of the Prime Minister.

But in spite of Chamberlain's appeal, there was no improvement in the relations of Lloyd George and Curzon.

The Chamberlain protest against the Prime Minister's treatment of Churchill, who was at that time Secretary of State for War,† was certainly justified. Correspondence in the Lloyd George Archives extending over these years reflects the impatience of the Prime Minister.

On unemployment Lloyd George wrote to Churchill a most intemperate letter,*l* actually charging him with attempting "to lay the blame on your colleagues for present unemployment conditions".

---

* The full text of the letter is reproduced in *Appendix IV*, No. 22.
† Churchill was transferred to the Colonial Office on February 12, 1921.

Then Lloyd George attacked Churchill on his support of "this fatuous policy" of giving out contracts for new houses in advance of the capacity of the Building Industry.

He was charged with waste in Mesopotamia where "forces far beyond the need were being kept". Churchill, as Colonial Secretary, had been given special responsibility for Mesopotamia and the Near East.

On the question of unemployment, Lloyd George concluded, "I entreat you to judge more charitably the efforts put forth by your colleagues during the last two years."

Even when Lloyd George agreed with Churchill's Irish negotiations, there were complaints that the Colonial Secretary was giving battle "on the very worst grounds" which could possibly be chosen.

In this day it is strange to read of Churchill having been bullied by Lloyd George.

But the Lloyd George letters certainly confirm the charge.

Churchill's letters preserved in the Lloyd George Archives, on the other hand, are nearly always of a conciliatory nature. When he was assailed over his views on unemployment, he replied:

> The first & greatest mistake in my opinion was leaving the profiteers in possession of their ill-gotten war wealth. Had prompt action been taken at the beginning of 1919, several thousand millions of paper wealth cd have been transferred to the State, & the internal debt reduced accordingly. The question was however deliberately held over & delayed until the moment was lost.*m*

* See *Appendix IV*, Nos. 23 and 24, for the text of correspondence between Lloyd George and Churchill, October, 1921.

The Prime Minister even quarrelled with Lord Riddell, his most intimate friend, a man who had supported and sustained him in his darkest hours. At the Paris Peace Conference the French made a great fuss of Riddell, persuading him to support their claims in opposition to Lloyd George. Then at Lucerne in 1920, when there was a dispute with the French over Turkey, Riddell warmly espoused the French cause at dinner. Lloyd George suggested that he was a traitor to his country. Riddell left for London next morning. From that moment their friendship dwindled and fell into decay. It was, in effect, the end.

When, in 1921, the partnership between Lloyd George and Bonar Law came to an end, after many strains and stresses, the Prime Minister was dealt a mortal blow.

Lloyd George, on the retirement of Bonar Law, appeared to me to be relieved. I was under the impression that he was weary of hearing that Bonar Law kept him straight. He seemed to welcome the opportunity of ruling his Government and ruling it alone. He would show that his power was supreme and his will absolute.

I was wrong.

Correspondence in the Lloyd George files shows that the Prime Minister recognised the difficulties confronting him. I quote a letter from Lord Stamfordham written to the Prime Minister on 19th March, 1921.

My dear Prime Minister,

The following are extracts from a letter just received from the King at Knowsley in reply to what I wrote after seeing you yesterday morning.

"I am sorry the Prime Minister is low on account of B.L.'s resignation: but he must not be despondent as I firmly believe *he* is now more necessary to this country than he ever was & that the vast majority of the people are behind him. He wants my views on the points he put to you this morning. They are not very easy to give from a distance. If I were talking to him it would help me to do so. I should agree to anything that would help him most. If the Cabinet resigned & there was a 'general post' & he dropped out Illingworth, Addison or any others: or if he formed (as has been advocated) a National Party: but the latter I agree would take time, as it is a big change. His difficulty will be finding a successor to B.L. Could he get the same advice and support from Chamberlain? or Horne. But the Unionists [Conservatives] will of course elect the former as their leader. You can tell the P.M. that I have complete confidence in him & will do everything in my power to help him. I will be in London on Monday & could see him that evening at any time that suits him. What a pity Balfour is away as he could give most useful advice!

I am very strong in maintaining a Coalition Govt. I am sure it is the best plan at the present moment & until these many very difficult questions have been settled. Anyhow I am against a general election which would upset everything. There really ought to be two P.M.'s! No man can do the work he L.G. has to do now. I quite understand his feeling lonely & almost lost without B.L. who did so much for him.

I fear these views will not be of much use to the P.M. What a pity I am out of London. I fear it would be almost impossible to return before Monday at 3 p.m. unless I travelled Sunday which I dislike doing—

but I am ready to do so if he wishes. I was talking to 2 Labour M.P.'s here today & they were loud in singing the P.M.'s praises & both said he is the strongest man we have had since Pitt."

Yours very truly,

STAMFORDHAM."

Now this letter is the first occasion on record when the King shows sympathetic consideration for his Prime Minister, Lloyd George. The King not only tells him of his complete confidence in him, but that he will do everything in his power to help him. He assures him that the Coalition Government must be sustained.

And all this just at the moment when Lloyd George's Ministry was showing signs of change and decay and the shadows were gathering over the Prime Minister himself.

But it could not be expected that the King would know of the many reasons why the power and glory of his great and splendid Prime Minister, triumphant in the day of battle, was now passing away.

Lloyd George had become something of a dictator without having a dictator's apparatus of power and terror. Instead his strength depended on his personal ascendancy with the public which a shift in the wind of popularity could dissolve, and upon the Conservative political machine which was only used effectively for Lloyd George's benefit so long as Bonar Law was its custodian.

After Bonar Law left the Government, Lloyd George interfered increasingly with Departmental Chiefs. He sometimes appealed to subordinates to act against and independently of the Ministers.

He often gave directions to Under-Secretaries without regard to the Ministers concerned.

A letter to Hilton-Young, who was Financial Secretary to Sir Robert Horne, Chancellor of the Exchequer, directed him to provide a plan for £250,000,000 of inflationary expenditure. Lloyd George wrote:

> Pray do not be too easily frightened by city pundits who are as stuffed with stale orthodoxies as old McKinnon, the Wee Free Minister who afflicted me yesterday with theological banking principles.[o]

To Sir Philip Lloyd Graeme, Under-Secretary to Stanley Baldwin, President of the Board of Trade, a letter from Gairloch, where the Prime Minister was holidaying, informed him:

> I am relying upon you to go into this matter very thoroughly . . . and see what can be done, and if you can wake up the Board of Trade you will, incidentally, render a great service to the community.[p]

Again, on 30th April, 1922, he wrote from Genoa a letter of remonstrance rejecting recommendations from his Cabinet.

> The strain of the Conference is great enough without further complications of that sort, and you will recognise that I cannot be expected to accept any variation of my instructions, however desirable they may seem to some of my colleagues in London, while I am doing my utmost to give effect to the agreed policy of the Cabinet under circumstances of exceptional difficulty out here in Genoa.[q]

With the exception of Lord Riddell, Press Peers, * however, did not suffer from Lloyd George's dictatorial habits. He always envied newspaper proprietors and sincerely tried to keep on good terms with them. After I retired from his Government my social relations with him were either pleasant or in abeyance. My political position might be described as much the same as the entrance to a well-known club which gives rise to the title "The In and Out Club".

We had several disputes but always I was called back to collaboration when Lloyd George would discuss with me the prospects of a General Election on the Empire issue. Nothing ever came of these discussions, but each time my hopes were again aroused.

The last occasion on which I had formed great expectation was at the Villa Valetta in Cannes.

That great event was in January, 1922. Lloyd George was of course Prime Minister. He was contemplating a General Election. And he might have been persuaded to go to the country on an Empire Commercial Union platform.

On the sunny shores of the Mediterranean he held court. Several Cabinet Ministers were in attendance, Churchill among them. Of course I was present. I always managed to be present when Empire was at issue. So was a parrot in a cage. An English parrot. A parrot endowed with a gift of prophecy.

* Lord Northcliffe had been excommunicated in 1918. He died in August, 1922.

Should Lloyd George, the Prime Minister, call for an immediate General Election? And on what issue would he seek the support of the public?

Sir Laming Worthington-Evans, the Secretary for War, spoke brilliantly in favour of an election. He had a splendid voice.

It seemed that he was carrying everything before him. When he concluded his argument, a hush fell on the company. The opponents of the election were silenced. Then suddenly, from that cage, the shriek of the English-speaking parrot cried: "You bloody fool. You bloody fool."

Evans' argument was lost in laughter. The parrot had decided the issue. There was no election.

Churchill gave me a lift back to my hotel ten miles away. As we drove through the night what do you think we talked about? The parrot.

The parrot had stood in the way of Empire policy. The parrot had put an end to the prospect of an election. The parrot had put an end to Lloyd George! Within a year he was driven from office, never to enjoy power again.

After Cannes, one more Foreign Conference and another disaster for the Prime Minister.

It was the Genoa Conference from mid April to May, 1922.

Lloyd George returned to the House of Commons high in spirits, but low in political prospects. His official life was surely ebbing to its close. For some of the representatives of Foreign Powers who sat with him at Genoa, more than power and office was ebbing to its close.

Dr. Rathenau, the German Foreign Minister, was dead within a month. Driving from his villa in the suburbs of Berlin on 24th June, to attend a Cabinet meeting in the Wilhelmstrasse, he was shot by two former Army officers.

Six months later, the Greek Prime Minister at the Conference, M. Gounaris, was put to death in circumstances of brutality and horror. Deposed by the Revolutionary Government, he was dying in hospital from typhus when his executioners seized him. He was given a heart stimulant and with four members of his Cabinet and the Commander-in-Chief of Asia Minor, he was executed before a firing squad.

M. Stambolisky, the Bulgarian Premier, too, was murdered in the following year. He had been driven out of his office by revolutionary forces. He fled to a wood, concealing himself beneath a covering of leaves. He was discovered and executed by troops who pursued him.

In the same year, violent death had claimed M. Vorovsky, a Soviet representative at Genoa. He was assassinated while dining at the Hotel Cecil in Lausanne. The accused was acquitted.

The last Foreign Conference and Failure! The last of many Foreign Conferences! And where were the triumphs? All turned to dust.

The glory departed from Lloyd George after sixteen years of power. His defeat at the General Election of 1922 was humiliating to him, and devastating to his followers. Few of his friends were returned to Parliament. In the shadows of Opposition, many of his old colleagues fell away and new political friends were hard to find. His imperious temper did not improve and his criticisms of his former Ministers increased in force and frequency.

What manner of a man was this mighty champion in the critical period of British History? How did I measure him in the last two years of the Great War?

As a witty and genial companion the Prime Minister had few equals. He was gay and generous in sharing conversation. He did not monopolize the company with monologues. He was neither egotistical nor vain, save only of some physical characteristics—his big head, long hair and small feet.

No man rallied more generously to meet any chaff which might be on the wind. "You know, George" (as Bonar Law always addressed him), "Winston * means to seize your Liberal leadership." "Maybe," said Lloyd George, "but he will get your leadership of the Conservative Party first." Lloyd George showed foresight.

His colleagues, in his glorious hours, looked upon him as a dazzling and triumphant figure. Is it possible to pierce to the heart of his real character?

Easy to detect and explain individual actions, failures and successes, his motives high and low, the caution of the man with his ear to the ground, the quality of physical weakness, joined to stark moral courage, the cool cynicism of the man of affairs, the magic of the orator, the glowing range of Celtic imagination so profound as to pass here

* At this time a Liberal Minister.

and there into the far country of idealism, the kingdom of romance.

But even so, the question reverberates, what manner of man was this wizard of Wales, as he was dubbed by some of his colleagues; "the Goat" by others?

What thread of consistency bound those dull or glistening beads together? What was the secret spring of character from which all these diverse qualities flowed?

Perhaps we are too near the masterpiece to see the real worth of the picture. We can say, however, that in the day of our dire need, when the blast of the terrible one was against the wall, a strange figure sprang into the arena to do battle.

It was clad in a jewelled breastplate set in a vesture of rags and tatters. It faltered in its walk, and yet leapt with a wonderful swiftness. The sword looked as fragile as a rapier and yet smote with the impact of a battle-axe. As it was held on high, so was the hope of Britain. And when the swordsman stumbled, anxiety filled the breasts of the multitude.

The last stumble was the worst. When the Allied line was pierced by the enemy in early 1918, hope stood still. Then the final stroke, and Britain was ablaze with glory. An Empire as broad as the earth was bathed everywhere in the sunlight of victory. Liberty was secured. The dream of a living Empire appeared to be a reality.

And in the midst of that brilliant sunlight stood

the central figure, young as Prime Ministers go, sharing the glory of Chatham and Pitt.

Then the mists gathered, other banners were unfurled, night fell.

It was my duty to deliver the speech on behalf of the Government in the House of Lords on 28th March, 1945, mourning the death of the great War Leader. I reminded the House that there were several members who served under Lloyd George, but of those of his colleagues who knew and felt the full force of his genius, those who served with him in his War Cabinet, nearly all have gone out in front of him. Many will say that Lloyd George's greatest days, his most splendid efforts were in times of peace when he put upon the Statute Book more social legislation than any single statesman in our history; but I do not hold that view. To me his greatest hour came as late as the spring of 1918, when our line of defence had been broken, our troops were in retreat, the Russian Armies were out of the war, and the American Armies had not yet come into it.

The Cabinet at that moment was concerned above all else with the dominant question, "Shall we retreat north and west to protect the Channel ports, or shall we retire south to Paris to sustain contact with the French Armies?" The history books will tell the truth. A Cabinet of strong men had been diverted for the time by the sheer gravity of the situation from the bigger issue—the issue of defeat or victory. It was at that moment that Lloyd George penetrated the gloom of doubt and indecision. It was in the hour of our peril that he refused to contemplate any plan for retreat. He would talk only of counter-attacks. It was then his leadership showed itself supreme, his courage undiminished.*

What new assessments will tomorrow bring forth, and what judgement will posterity accord to David Lloyd George, born in a cottage, brought up in a shoemaker's shop, strayed from the fields of Llanystumdwy to that narrow street so many desire to tread, yet so few deserve to enter, the path that leads to No. 10?

* For the speech in full, *see* APPENDIX VII.

MEMBERS OF THE GOVERNMENT
1917–1918

The War Cabinet

Prime Minister and First Lord of the Treasury. David Lloyd George.

Lord President of the Council. Lord Curzon.

Chancellor of the Exchequer. Andrew Bonar Law.

Lord Milner (December, 1916 to April, 1918).

General Smuts (June, 1917 to December, 1918).

Sir Edward Carson (July, 1917 to January, 1918).

Austen Chamberlain (April, 1918 to December, 1918).

Arthur Henderson (December, 1916 to August, 1917).

George Barnes (August, 1917 to January, 1918).

Ministers of Cabinet Rank.

Lord Chancellor. Lord Finlay.

Secretary of State for Foreign Affairs. A. J. Balfour.

Secretary of State for War. Lord Derby (December, 1916 to April, 1918). Succeeded by Lord Milner.

Secretary of State for the Colonies. Walter Long.

Secretary of State for India. Austen Chamberlain (December, 1916 to July, 1917). Succeeded by Edwin Montagu.

First Lord of the Admiralty. Sir Edward Carson (December, 1916 to July, 1917). Succeeded by Sir Eric Geddes.

President of the Air Board and Secretary of State for Air. Lord Cowdray (December, 1916 to November, 1917). Lord Rothermere (November, 1917 to April, 1918). Succeeded by Sir William Weir.

Secretary of State for Home Affairs. Sir George Cave.

President of the Board of Trade. Sir Albert Stanley.

President of the Board of Agriculture and Fisheries. Rowland Prothero.

President of the Board of Education. H. A. L. Fisher.

Minister of Munitions. Dr. C. Addison (December, 1916 to July, 1917). Succeeded by Winston Churchill.

Minister of Labour. John Hodge (December, 1916 to August, 1917). Succeeded by George Roberts.

Chancellor of the Duchy of Lancaster. Sir Frederick Cawley (December, 1916 to February, 1918). Succeeded by Lord Beaverbrook, who held also the office of Minister of Information.

Other Ministers Mentioned in this Narrative.

Attorney-General. Sir F. E. Smith.

Solicitor-General. Sir Gordon Hewart.

Postmaster-General. A. H. Illingworth.

Minister of Blockade and Assistant Foreign Secretary. Lord Robert Cecil.

Shipping Controller. Sir Joseph Maclay.

Minister of Reconstruction. Dr. C. Addison (July, 1917).

Joint Financial Secretaries to the Treasury. Sir Hardman Lever, Stanley Baldwin.

Parliamentary Secretaries to the Treasury. Lord Edmund Talbot, Hon. Neil Primrose (December, 1916 to May, 1917). Succeeded by Capt. Frederick Guest.

APPENDIX II

MEMORANDUM
By John Bassett

John Bassett, President and Chairman of the *Montreal Gazette*, the oldest and one of the best edited of all the morning newspapers in Canada, and President of the *Sherbrooke Daily Record*, was for long a Press Gallery Correspondent in the House of Commons at Ottawa.

When war broke out in 1914 he became Staff Officer and served throughout the war years. He was attached to General Sir Sam Hughes, accompanying him to France on all the journeys to the Front made by the Minister of Militia and Defence, which was the title in those days of the War Minister.

Mr. Bassett is Chancellor of Bishop's University and his association with that University has done much to develop and extend its influence.

THE friction between the Duke of Connaught as Governor-General of Canada and Colonel the Hon. Sir Sam Hughes, Minister of Militia and Defence, began prior to 1914. Hughes was wrongly obsessed with the idea, indeed the conviction, that there was a pro-German atmosphere at Government House, because the Governor-General was the son of Prince Albert, a German Prince, and Queen Victoria's consort, and his wife was the daughter of another German prince, and spoke English with an accent.

As everybody knows, Hughes prophesied a war with Germany from the time he became Minister of Militia in

1911 and before, until the war broke out. He expanded the Canadian forces; he built drill halls all over Canada to encourage the training of troops. So firm was his conviction that he bought surreptitiously, months before the war broke out, a huge tract of land at Valcartier. It was close to Quebec, so that the troops could embark at Gaspe. Then when the war broke out, troops assembled at Valcartier for training and mobilisation before setting sail for England.

As the troops became welded into some sort of organisation, the Duke of Connaught with his staff proceeded to interfere, and he took advantage of his position as Governor-General and Commander-in-Chief to do so.

The Minister of Militia and Defence resented his interference, and it came to a boiling point when the Duke of Connaught wished to review the troops at Valcartier on several occasions. Hughes refused, stating that he, the Duke of Connaught, was simply the titular head of the Canadian Army and that he, Hughes, was the civilian head, and therefore entitled to review, as he called them, "his boys".

The Duke of Connaught in his attitude towards Hughes was aided and abetted by one called Colonel Stanton, who was his military secretary. He had been a Governor in the Near East, and upon one occasion Hughes told him in a letter in reply to one from Stanton to mind his manners, and remember he was in Canada, and not driving a lot of "buck niggers up the Nile".

The Duke of Connaught was badly served by Stanton.

The relationship between Prime Minister Borden and Connaught was strained, due mainly to the attitude taken by the Duke of Connaught and his staff towards the Canadian military machine. Borden usually supported Hughes, although he differed with him on other matters.

It must be remembered that in the First World War one saw the deep stirrings of Canadian nationhood, and that Borden himself was responsible for insisting that Canadian Ministers should sign the Treaty of Versailles.

APPENDIX II

When the Duke of Connaught left Canada as Governor-General, a dinner was given to him by the members of the Rideau Club. Sir Robert Borden was present as a matter of courtesy as Prime Minister. Sir Wilfrid Laurier, the Leader of the Opposition, was also there.

In the speeches made Sir Robert was very non-committal about the Duke. Sir Wilfrid made one of his charming and eloquent utterances, which touched the Duke very deeply. On his return to England he sent Sir Wilfrid and Lady Laurier a loving-cup of remembrance, but gave no recognition whatever to Borden or his wife.

A study of the communications in those days between the Colonial Office and Sir Robert Borden would be interesting and illuminating. But much is to be found in the Memoirs of Sir Robert. The papers tell more than Sir Robert disclosed in his Memoirs, because Borden was very cautious in all his actions and writings.

CATALOGUE OF LETTERS PUBLISHED
FOR THE FIRST TIME

The Royal Archives, Windsor.

Stamfordham Memoranda, February, 1918.

W. S. Churchill to Lord Stamfordham, 7th December, 1919.

Bonar Law to Lord Stamfordham, 17th April, 1919.

Lord Stamfordham to Frederick Guest, 11th April, 1919.

Lord Stamfordham to His Majesty, King George V. Memorandum, 5th July, 1917.

Lloyd George Papers.

John Baird to Lloyd George, 22nd April, 1918.

A. J. Balfour to Lloyd George, 22nd August, 1918.

Sir Edward Carson to Lloyd George, 31st December, 1917.

Lord Robert Cecil to Lloyd George, June 1917.

W. S. Churchill to Lloyd George, 17th May, 1917.

W. S. Churchill to Lloyd George, 19th May, 1917.

W. S. Churchill to Lloyd George, 29th December, 1918.

W. S. Churchill to Lloyd George, 8th October, 1921.

Lord Curzon to Lloyd George, 30th April, 1917.

Lord Curzon to Lloyd George, 8th January, 1918.

Lord Curzon to Lloyd George, 12th November, 1918.

Lord Curzon to Lloyd George, 13th November, 1918.

Lord Curzon to Lloyd George, Undated (1918).

Lord Derby to Lloyd George, 19th February, 1917.

Lord Derby to Lloyd George, 20th February, 1917.

Lord Derby to Lloyd George, 8th June, 1917.

Lord Derby to Lloyd George, 11th December, 1917.

Lord Derby to Lloyd George, 18th January, 1918.

Lord Derby to Lloyd George, 29th January, 1918.

Frederick Guest to Lloyd George, 10th May, 1917.

Frederick Guest to Lloyd George, 18th June, 1917.

Frederick Guest to Lloyd George, 23rd January, 1918.

Frederick Guest to Lloyd George, 17th May, 1920.

Lloyd George to A. J. Balfour, 27th August, 1918.

Lloyd George to Lord Birkenhead, 15th March, 1919.

Lloyd George to W. S. Churchill, 1st October, 1921.

Lloyd George to Lord Curzon, 8th July, 1919.

Lloyd George to Lord Curzon, 30th April, 1922.

Lloyd George to Lord Derby, 13th December, 1917.

Lloyd George to E. Hilton Young, 26th September, 1921.

Lloyd George to Sir P. Lloyd Graeme, 26th September, 1921.

Lloyd George to Lord Milner, 14th May, 1919.

Lord Milner to Lloyd George, 26th June, 1917.

Lord Milner to Lloyd George, 16th July, 1917.

Lord Milner to Lloyd George, 27th February, 1918.

Lord Milner to Lloyd George, 19th May, 1918.

Lord Milner to Lloyd George, 7th December, 1918.

Lord Reading to Lloyd George, 22nd July, 1917.

Sir William Robertson to Lloyd George, 26th May, 1917.

Sir William Robertson to Lord Milner, 17th May, 1918.

General Smuts to Lloyd George, 13th April, 1918.

Lord Stamfordham to Lloyd George, 16th April, 1918.

Lord Stamfordham to Lloyd George, 25th April, 1918.

Lord Stamfordham to Lloyd George, 19th March, 1921.

Lord Stamfordham to Frederick Guest, 25th April, 1919.

Sir George Younger to Lloyd George, 8th June, 1917.

Countess Lloyd George, Diary Extract, 5th October, 1934.

Bonar Law Papers.

Sir Edward Carson to Bonar Law, 20th December, 1916.

Austen Chamberlain to Bonar Law, 6th January, 1921.

W. S. Churchill to Bonar Law, 8th September, 1918.

Lord Curzon to Bonar Law, 4th June, 1917.

Lord Derby to Bonar Law, 5th March, 1917.

Lord Derby to Bonar Law, 18th February, 1918.

Sir David Henderson to Bonar Law, and enclosure, 26th April, 1918.

Bonar Law to Lloyd George, 19th September, 1918.

Lloyd George to Bonar Law, 10th April, 1918.

Lloyd George to Bonar Law, 29th August, 1918.

Walter Long to Bonar Law, 19th February, 1918.

Sir Joseph Maclay to Bonar Law, 28th June, 1917.

Lord Milner to Bonar Law, 28th June, 1917.

Lord Milner to Bonar Law, 18th February, 1918.

Lord Rothermere to Bonar Law, 3rd May, 1918.

Lord Salisbury to Bonar Law, 22nd February, 1918.

Lord Stamfordham to Bonar Law, 17th April, 1919.

Sir Henry Wilson to Bonar Law, 16th May, 1915.

Beaverbrook Papers.

Lord Beaverbrook to Sir Sam Hughes, Cable, 16th October, 1915.

Lord Beaverbrook to Sir Sam Hughes, Cable, October, 1915.

Lord Beaverbrook Diary Extract, 9th March, 1915.

Sir Reginald Brade to Lord Beaverbrook, 6th January, 1917.

Sir Reginald Brade Diary, Extracts of 13th, 10th and 21st June, 1916.

Sir Reginald Brade, "A few Notes on the Recent Controversy between Sir W. R. (Robertson) and the Government."

Austen Chamberlain to Lord Beaverbrook, 2nd March, 1918.

Lord Crewe to Lord Beaverbrook, October, 1918.

E. M. House Collection, Yale University Library.

The Diary of E. M. House. Extracts of 18th and 29th October, 1917.

Walter Hines Page Papers, Houghton Library, Harvard University.

Walter Page to President Wilson, 16th January, 1918.

Walter Page to President Wilson, 7th March, 1918.

Papers of Sir Robert Borden, Toronto University.

Bonar Law to Sir Robert Borden, 1st May, 1916.

H.R.H. the Duke of Connaught to Sir Robert Borden, 18th April, 1916.

Archives of Lord Bennett, University of New Brunswick.

H.R.H. the Duke of Connaught to R. B. Bennett, 14th December, 1916.

Other Manuscript Collections.

Lord Robert Cecil to A. J. Balfour, 18th November, 1917. *Balfour Papers,* British Museum.

W. S. Churchill to R. D. Blumenfeld, 6th September, 1914. *Blumenfeld Papers.*

F. E. Smith to J. C. Sandars. *Margaret, Countess of Birkenhead.*

LETTERS PREVIOUSLY PUBLISHED IN PART; PUBLISHED IN FULL FOR THE FIRST TIME

Lloyd George Papers.

Lord Curzon to Lloyd George, 8th June, 1917.

Frederick Guest to Lloyd George, 26th February, 1917.

Lloyd George to Sir Edward Carson, 6th July, 1917.

Lloyd George to Sir Edward Carson, 7th July, 1917.

Lord Milner to Lloyd George, 7th December, 1917.

Sir Joseph Maclay to Lloyd George, 28th June, 1917.

General Smuts to Lloyd George, 6th June, 1917.

FULL TEXT OF LETTERS
AND DOCUMENTS

1

Record of Correspondence that passed between Mr. Balfour's Secretary, Mr. J. S. Sandars, and Mr. F. E. Smith (Lord Birkenhead).

Rt. Hon. J. S. Sandars, P.C., Private Secretary to Mr. Balfour, wrote:

"Your little boy will be proud of his father in the years to come for such a great act of self-sacrifice."

To which Mr. F. E. Smith replied:

"My little boy is only four, but if I thought he was such a bloody little fool as to be proud of his father for committing such an assinine act, I should indeed despair of him."

2

Correspondence between Lord Beaverbrook and Lord Horder.

21st April, 1952.

My dear Tommy,

On the 14th May, on Television, I propose to say of Northcliffe, if you have no objection, "he died with a pistol concealed under his pillow. He had just used it to threaten Lord Horder, his physician, who was struggling to save him from death that was inevitable."

Yours ever,

MAX.

LORD HORDER,
32 Devonshire Place,
London, W.1.

25.4.52.

Dear Max,

Not quite correct. When I entered the bedroom N. put his hand under the pillow and brought out a revolver. "One of G's bl—— knights," he said, & was about to fire when the male nurse struck his hand up. . . .

. . . .

Yours ever,

Tommy.

3

HOUSE OF COMMONS

Monday night
June 18, 1917.

Dear Prime Minister,

I made a tentative proposal to Winston on the grounds of the Chancellorship of the Duchy with elaborated uses and functions but without success.

He wished me to say that he regarded the offer as completely friendly.

He feels however that he could neither serve a *national purpose* nor *your purpose* by being included in this manner.

He is prepared to forego & forget all political considerations in order to help to beat the "Hun" in either of the following capacities.

1. To assist you in council in the War Cabinet, if necessary without salary.

2. To accept charge & responsibility for any War Department, as long as he has powers to actively assist in the defeat of the enemy.

I have used my utmost powers of persuasion but can do no more in this direction.

My only comment on the situation is that your will & influence with your Tory Colleagues is greater than you have credited yourself with and that sooner or later you will have to test it—why not now?

I have the strongest reasons to believe that the Tories mean to support your leadership even at the expense of their personal feelings.

Yours sincerely,
FREDERICK GUEST.

4

Derby House,
Stratford Place, W.

Confidential   8 June 1917.

Dear Prime Minister,

I much appreciated my talk with you this afternoon and I know you do not resent one saying exactly what one thinks. As to whether Winston Churchill will strengthen your Government or the reverse we must agree to differ as I do not think either could convince the other. I am really anxious to serve you and your Government and therefore feel that you will forgive me if I put before you somewhat bluntly the position as it concerns me as head of the War Office.

If Winston Churchill is only to be a second Lord Cowdray I do not mind if he will only do his work half as well. Lord Cowdray has done a real amount of good for the Air Service and has worked most cordially with the War Office without in any way attempting to interfere with the administration of that office.

While I regret Winston Churchill's inclusion in the Government—if he be included—as being a source of weakness I feel that it would not affect the War Office if it was clearly understood:—

(1) that he was not a member of the War Cabinet and did not attend any meetings unless specially summoned for business connected with the Board;

(2) that his duties as Chairman of the Board were the same as those of Lord Cowdray and that he had nothing to do with either personnel, tactics, or the nomination of the War Office representatives on the Board; and

(3) that he received no War Office telegrams other than those which were in any way connected with his particular department.

I gathered from you this afternoon that the conditions I have named were certainly those on which you would understand that he should enter the Government and that being so as far as my own office is concerned I personally can offer no objection, though I am bound to say I think there is a big 'if' in the question and that is *if* Winston Churchill will ever consent to occupy a comparatively minor position and do his own work without interfering with other people's. Perhaps you would let me know on Monday when I see you if I am right in my statement as to what your views on the position are.

I had an interesting talk with Henry Wilson this afternoon and I have a suggestion to make to you with regard to him which if you will give me 5 minutes on Monday afternoon I could easily explain. He is a great friend of mine and has in my opinion very great ability which I think might be made use of. As a Corps Commander not only is he not very good but his particular abilities would be lost to the Country.

I sent you over Ramsay Macdonald's views as to terms of peace and I am bound to say if he would stick to them I do not think his visit could do the slightest harm. I think however we are going to have great trouble with the seamen about conveying him there.

You might let me know if you could give me a few minutes on Monday afternoon any time most convenient to yourself.

Yours sincerely,

DERBY.

The Rt. Hon. D. Lloyd George, M.P.

5

My dear Prime Minister,   29. xii. 18.

I realise that you ought to have a speedy answer to the question you put to me this morning about going to the War Office or the Admiralty.

My heart is in the Admiralty. There I have long experience, & any claim I may be granted in public goodwill rests on the fact that 'the Fleet was ready'. In all the circumstances of the present situation I believe I shd add more weight to yr Administration at the Admiralty than at the War Office.

There wd be good reasons for connecting the air with the Admiralty; for aeroplanes will never be a substitute for armies & can only be a valuable accessory whereas they will almost certainly be an economical substitute for many classes of warships. The technical development of the air falls naturally into the same sphere as the mechanical developments of the Navy— & this becomes increasingly true the larger the aeroplanes grow.

Therefore I have no doubt what my choice shd be.
                                    Yours always,
                                                W.*

* Winston Churchill.

6

                                    19th February 1917.

Dear Prime Minister,

I am sorry to say Lytton has so far not arrived, and therefore I am as completely in the dark as to the circumstances under which Haig's interview was given as I was at Luncheon time. Any suggestions therefore for an answer that I could put forward to you now would be of little use. Robertson is coming back tonight and I am arranging to meet him, and we will try and draft something that will be satisfactory to you before the meeting of the War Cabinet tomorrow morning.

May I impress one thing upon you, and that is, that while definite statements appear in all the accounts of the interview, there are widely divergent accounts as to the operations proposed; in fact I do not think any two accounts agree. Nor, I suggest, should the statement that we are short of big guns be read from the light of the intimate knowledge that the War Cabinet possesses on this point. It was only an expression of opinion that has found vent in many other ways, viz., that nobody can have too many big guns. The ideal of enough big guns can probably never be reached.

Candidly also, I do not see what military information is given to the Germans by saying we have 225 miles of new railways behind the line. In the first place they know pretty well through their aeroplanes what we are doing and can estimate accordingly, and, secondly, the fact that we have got these increased railway facilities will put them more than ever in doubt as where attacks are likely to be made.

I do hope that you will check Curzon's desire to send a telegram to Haig forbidding him to have any further interviews. I am trying to find out the truth of the origin of this interview, but if, as I believe it was, at the instance of the propaganda department of the Foreign Office, his answer to the telegram will be obvious. Of course, if you like to say in a telegram that you think it would be advisable in any future interviews not to give any forecast of future operations and to confine himself entirely to past matters, I do not think the same objection would arise. I do think that to reprimand him—as this practically is—for having an interview which one of your own Departments has asked him to have, and

No. I now hear it was not.

362

at the same time to accept as gospel the account of that interview (an account which he denies) can only have one effect and that is to drive him into resignation: a state of affairs which I know you would deplore, and which I do not think the country would consider justified by this indiscretion.

Yours sincerely,

DERBY.

7

20th February 1917

Dear Prime Minister,

I was very glad to get the solution which you arrived at with regard to Haig today. It is perfectly obvious that he has been badly let down by Charteris, and I am sending an official Army Council letter to him on the subject, saying that we deplore the position which has arisen, and that we think it is indefensible that a subordinate should behave as Charteris has done, and to ask him whether he considers it is not advisable to remove the latter. I deplore the whole thing. As you know, I am a strong adherent of Haig, but I cannot help feeling that his action has undoubtedly lowered him in the eyes of others, entirely owing to the fact that words were put into his mouth which he never used, & which we could not repudiate because it would give away the French & show the incapacity of our Censors office.

Yours sincerely,

DERBY.

The Right Hon. D. Lloyd George, M.P.

8

Derby House,
Stratford Place,
W.

Strictly Confidential.　　　　　11 December, 1917.

My dear Prime Minister,

Our talk this afternoon has considerably disturbed me and while I would not ask you to look upon this as a very carefully thought out letter I want to put down what on the spur of the moment occurs to me with regard to what you said.

In the first place if you are really thinking of making a complete change in the Supreme Command both at home and abroad, it is not the least use my going out and having a very unpleasant interview with Sir Douglas Haig with regard to the dismissal of what is after all only a subordinate officer.* As it at present stands I must go out on Thursday but if you are really determined to make the big change I would not go if you would invent the excuse for me that you particularly wanted me at meetings on Thursday and Friday mornings. I leave this entirely to you but unless I hear from you to the contrary I shall go.

This requires an immediate answer

Now as regards the change of Haig and Robertson. I will deal with the former first. I do not think that the Cambrai affair is one on which you ought to hang so momentous a decision as the removal of a Commander in Chief. You may remember that the day before you went to Paris you told me that you had more confidence in Haig than you ever had before and if you had that confidence, and I believe you had, it would not be fair to remove him simply because a part of his line broke when the main attack for which he was chiefly prepared was successfully repulsed.

* It was the intention to dismiss Brigadier-General John Charteris, C.M.G., D.S.O., Haig's Chief Intelligence Officer.

I agree with you that it somewhat shakes ones confidence in anybody when you see the complete change of view that takes place between his letter of October 29th and those which he wrote subsequently but I ascribe, as I know you do, the first letter to the influence of Charteris whom it would be my mission to dismiss if I went out on Thursday. Therefore to dismiss Haig simply because of the Cambrai affair would to my mind be extremely unjust and I feel that I could not be a party to it.

Let us take however the other suggestion that it should not be a case of dismissal but rather a promotion and that he should be made Generalissimo of all the British Forces. There are certain difficulties in doing that which would have to be overcome, the principal one being the finding of a suitable Commander in Chief for the Western Front. Plumer is sound but certainly I think does not have that imagination for which you are looking. Birdwood to my mind would be absolutely out of the question. Munro would be the best man you could get and personally I look upon Rawlinson as a first class soldier. I think Haig's successor, if the change is made, should lie between Munro and Rawlinson.

Now as to Haig's position if he is made Generalissimo. I am going into the question as to what the duties and powers of the Commander in Chief of old days was but things have changed very much and I doubt whether the rules applicable then would apply now. The first question I would ask is what would be his relationship to the War Cabinet? Would he be the Chief Military Advisor to the War Cabinet? If so it is a most important post and one which anybody should hesitate before refusing. If on the other hand the advice to the War Cabinet is to be given by some other individual than the Generalissimo he is nothing more than an Inspector General, an inferior post which I do not think you could possibly ask Haig to accept.

It would be much better to dismiss him altogether rather than to ask him to take a sinecure post.

With regard to Robertson the position is equally difficult and I do not see what post you could put him in and again it would be much better to dismiss him rather than degrade him.

To return to Haig. If his position is Generalissimo and Chief Advisor to the War Cabinet it is as I have said a most important post, but supposing you do not agree to that who is to be the Chief Military Advisor of the Government? You mention Maurice as the Chief of the Staff who would come daily to the Cabinet to give the usual War information, but I did not gather from you that he would be anything more than an exponent of what had happened and you did not contemplate him as an advisor. I hope you are not thinking of making Henry Wilson in Paris the Chief Advisor. That I could not possibly support. I hope and believe he will do well in his present position but I am sure that if you put him in London as your Chief Military Advisor you would defeat the very object you have in view, namely the promotion of confidence in our Military Chiefs.

Now as to my own position. I am deeply grateful to you for what you were good enough to say with regard to your confidence in me. You know that I am not a seeker after office and that I supported you, not in any way to get official position, but I thought, as I still think, that you are the only possible Prime Minister for the country during the present crisis, and whether I remain in office or went out would make no difference in the support that I gave you. If Haig was promoted in the way that I have suggested and Robertson given suitable employment, and that they both accepted the positions voluntarily and not under compulsion, I should feel that I had nothing to reproach myself with but if on the other hand they are practically compelled to resign then I have to consider my own position and I hope not from an egotistical point of view. In the first place I do not think that my going would have the least effect on the stability of your Government. If you are right in thinking that the confidence of the Army in Haig and Robertson has gone then in going with them I should simply be looked upon as a person who supported a policy in which the Country had no confidence and you know perfectly well that no word or deed of mine would ever be used against you or your Government. Where I differ from you, and perhaps from the public, is that I have confidence in Haig and Robertson. I think Haig is very misguided in the Staff he keeps about him. He is one of those men who is so thoroughly loyal to his subordinates that he will not recognise that his own position is threatened by that loyalty but that he is the best man we have got for Command in the Field, I have no doubt whatsoever. I see nobody who can compare with him and to see him ousted from his present position, unless it is to promote him would to my mind be most prejudicial to our Military position.

With regard to Robertson. I confess that what you told me with regard to your suspicions today has shaken my confidence but I cannot believe that he would deliberately ask Allenby to send in a false telegram in order to deceive the Government. I agree with you that read in the light of subsequent events Allenby's telegram asking for the enormous increase of force in order to do what he has done with the existing forces seems very ridiculous but that his former proposal should be put forward with a deliberate attempt to deceive the Government and that at the instance of Robertson, is almost beyond belief. I want to be perfectly frank with you and confess that I was not very desirous of seeing the Jerusalem attack. I was afraid of being committed in a way which would require either a retirement or a reinforcement which we could not give. I was entirely wrong but I think

you know me well enough to realise nothing would
have induced me to be a Party to a deliberate attempt
to deceive the Government and that is what you think
Robertson did. If he did it and it can be proved, I
could have no further faith in him but I cannot believe
it and assuming therefore it is not the case I take
Robertson as I have found him and that is a very honest
man endeavouring to give the Government the best
advice that it is in his power to give. I know that he
is what you call sticky and at times a very difficult
man to deal with. I feel sometimes, and I think you do,
that there is more at the back of his mind than he will
tell one, but still I think you might go much further
and fare much worse than to accept his advice.

I am putting down my thoughts just as they occur
to me and therefore they are rather disconnected which
please forgive.

To turn to the position of the War Cabinet. I hold
that the War Cabinet has got an absolute right to
change any Commander that they may think fit and
to change any policy if they think it is right to do so.
They naturally have to take the responsibility if they
go against their military advisors but on the other
hand as they have finally to bear all responsibility
they must be allowed to insist on their policy being
carried out and get people they think best fitted to
carry it out. Some people would say that that meant
the politicians interfering with the soldiers and they
may be right but I for one should never hold that
opinion though naturally in one's present position
one would insist on the right of resigning if one
thought that the advice given was the correct one
and the persons in power were the most fitted to carry
it out. I mention this and it brings me to the end of
what I am afraid is rather a long letter. Put yourself
into my position. I have had confidence, and still
have it, in Haig and Robertson. I have told them that
I have this confidence in them time after time and if

they were suddenly superseded altogether what confidence would the new Commander in Chief have in me? He would say and with perfect justice—"You told my predecessor up to the very last moment that you had confidence in him and yet when it came to the point of showing that confidence in a practical way you deserted him". That is the position that I am sure you yourself would never take up and I know you would never ask me to.

I shall come and see you tomorrow so of course there is no need to answer this letter except on the two points (1) as to whether I should go to France on Thursday, and that requires an immediate reply; and (2) as to what position Haig as Generalissimo would occupy as regards the War Cabinet. The latter question I only want answered in view of your desire that I should discuss with a certain person the powers and position of a Commander in Chief and Generalissimo.

Yours sincerely,
DERBY

The Prime Minister.

9

Lord Derby to Sir Douglas Haig.
Strictly Personal and Confidential

12th December, 1917.

I had hoped to come over and see you tomorrow, though it was only for a flying visit, but the Prime Minister has insisted on my remaining for the discussion on Man-Power, and I agree with him it is important that I should do so as on this, in my opinion, must stand our possible success in the war. I am, therefore, obliged to deal by letter with matters which I would infinitely have preferred discussing with you.

I want to preface my remarks with a repetition of what I think you know already, namely, that I have and always shall have implicit confidence in you, and anything I may write is written from the point of view of a friend and not of an adverse critic. There are two kinds of friends. There is a friend who always tells you everything which he thinks you would like to hear, and there is a friend who tells you things which he thinks you should hear, even if they are not always pleasant. I look upon the latter as being the true friend, and it is from that point of view that I mean to write to you today.

First of all I will deal with the Charteris question. In the note I sent you yesterday I told you that I did not think that you could look upon me as wishing to make Charteris a whipping boy for the Cambrai affair. I have mentioned to you on more than one occasion that he was doing you an infinity of harm by his optimism and by what I consider his inaccurate information, and I have begged you to make a change. You tell me that you invariably make an allowance for the optimism of Charteris. That may be so, but I cannot think that you make sufficient allowance, and the best proof I have of that is your letter of October 8th. That letter is clearly based on wrong information, and for that, although signed by you, I cannot hold you responsible. In view, not only of subsequent events, but of subsequent letters to you, I am sure you would never have put it forward if you had had proper information as to the enemy's reserves and possible reinforcements from the Russian Front.

It appears to me that too often the opinions, not only of the public but even of your subordinates and of the Army as a whole are not put before you. If they had been you would have realised that my view of Charteris as a public danger is shared by practically the whole of the Army, and I feel that if they do not put forward disagreeable facts to you, it is my duty to do so, however unpleasant it may be. I am afraid it is quite impossible for me to allow Charteris to remain as your Intelligence Officer, and much as I dislike giving you any instruction which I know is repugnant to you, I look upon you as a National asset and I cannot allow your loyalty to a subordinate to affect your position. I must, therefore, ask you to make a change within the next month, and shall be glad to hear either of your suggestions as to who should take his place or, failing that, that I should make suggestions to you. So much for Charteris. Now there are other members of your Staff who I think in your interest it would be as well to make a change. The two first are Maxwell and Fowke.

First of all Maxwell. Of him I have nothing to say except that he is undoubtedly a very tired man. He has done you splendid service, but I think that he requires a rest. I do not know at the present that I have any post that I could offer him, but I can assure you that I recognise his good qualities and his excellent work, and it will be my desire as soon as he is rested to find him some further employment. Fowke is a different case. I do not think Fowke is a strong enough man to maintain the discipline of your Army; especially under the present circumstances when everybody is feeling the strain of war. Equally I should be ready, if possible, to find him some other employment if you replace him.

The next case is a still more difficult one to bring to your notice, and that is the question of the retention of Gough in a high command. I believe him to be a most gallant soldier, but that does not affect the question that he has created a feeling of hatred against himself both on the part of officers and men that it is almost impossible to describe to you. Canadians are especially bitter. Sir George Perley has been to see me on the subject and he would have wished to have made a formal protest against his having Canadians under his command in future, but I persuaded him to leave it in my hands, promising to represent his views to you. The feeling in the Canadians is perhaps more intense than in other Units in the Army, but I can assure you that at the present moment there is not a wounded officer or man who comes back, and they naturally talk, who does not express an equally bitter opinion of him. There is nothing I dislike more than to think that the question of an officer in high command should be in any way decided by public opinion; but you must remember this fact, we are going through a very difficult time in this country. Everybody is war weary. The glamour and enthusiasm of the first two years have worn away, and you must take into consideration the views of this country which reflect to a very large extent the views of your own Army. It is not only the letters that come back, but still more the talk of men of all ranks when home on leave which shows that there is a disgruntled feeling in the Army which is impossible to ignore.

Now I come to the Cambrai affair. There is no doubt it has created a great feeling in this country which, personally, I do not share. There must be ups and downs in a war like this, and you cannot always have matters your own way. But there is an unfortunate feeling that somebody is to blame. Who it is naturally nobody knows; but I would ask you to have the most thorough enquiry into the affair, as, indeed, Bonar Law has promised in the House of Commons that you will, and if anybody has been guilty of neglect that that man should be punished. Please don't think that I am asking you to find a scapegoat. Nothing of the kind. I am asking you to find out who let you down—who failed you—and having found him out, send him home because you have no confidence in him. Once you do that the public, and I am one of them, would be absolutely satisfied. But the public will not be satisfied if the whole affair is passed over without a full explanation.

Yet another matter. The public are asking this—

What lines have you got in the rear of our present one to which you can fall back. They have heard of this wonderful Hindenburg line with its extraordinary dugouts, etc. All this information has been used, and rightly used, to show what extraordinary courage it required on the part of our troops to take it. All people are asking if we have got any thing of the same kind behind our line, and if not, why not. We hear of concrete pillboxes—huge dugouts immune from artillery fire, etc., and they feel we ought to have the same, and I should be glad of your assurance that such lines exist.

All these are extremely disagreeable things for me to have to say to you, but I repeat in conclusion what I began with, that they are matters which a true friend must bring to your notice. Your position is unassailable, but only so long as the Country thinks that it is being told the whole truth and that nobody is screened from the punishment he deserves.

I shall back you through thick and thin, and because I am prepared to do so I feel I equally have the right to ask you to take in good part any remarks I may make, to consider them dispassionately, and to as far as possible act on my suggestions. You and I have got to stand or fall together, and that must be my excuse if as a civilian I bring to your notice matters that are continually being brought before me, and ask you to take action which will prevent either of us being the subject of reproach.

10

Derby House,
Stratford Place, W.
18 January 1918

Confidential & Personal.

My dear P.M.,

With reference to the question of a new Ambassador for Paris which you and I discussed at luncheon the other day and whom you wished to appoint with special powers, I think before the man we had in mind would take it his powers would have to be clearly defined.

I do not know what powers have been given to Lord Reading* but I presume that they are largely in excess of those which are given to the ordinary Ambassador. Would they equally apply in the case of Paris? Your answer will probably be No because there is a great difference between Washington and Paris and to that I agree. But the real question is this. Would the Ambassador in Paris be more or less of a colleague of members of the War Cabinet or would he be simply the mouthpiece of that body?

I am sure that what the person in question would first of all consider would be whether or not his acceptance of the post was in the National interest and I am quite sure that he would subordinate all questions of a personal character, which might make him inclined to refuse, if he thought he could be of any real use and assistance: but there is one thing I am convinced of and that is that he would never give up, except to a limited extent, his independence and it is on that question that the difficulty might arise.

A man in office is not only entitled, but it is his duty, to resign if he thinks that the Government to which he belongs is doing something which he disapproves of and which in his opinion is detrimental to the best interests of the Nation. I am naturally only referring to big questions, but would the same liberty be given to him as an Ambassador as would be given to anybody who was in a Government Department at home?

It is always best if possible to take a concrete case. I presume the new Ambassador would be in close touch with Versailles and would be kept fully informed

---

* Lord Reading's appointment as Ambassador to the United States, to replace Sir Cecil Spring-Rice, had been announced at the beginning of January 1918.

of all that was going on there. The man in question* as you know supports the Versailles arrangement and has told both you and me that he thinks great advantage can be gained from it but suppose Versailles put forward a proposal to which the War Cabinet agreed but to which the other Military advisers, Sir Douglas Haig and Sir William Robertson, or anybody who might be in their place, were in strong disagreement. Would he be expected to support the Government view even if he was convinced it was wrong? Personally I do not think that such questions will arise with this particular individual but still he would have the right to have his position made perfectly clear, in order that if he did take an independent line, which if he remained in England he would undoubtedly be entitled to take, he should not be accused of acting disloyally to the Government.

On the other hand I do see that great advantage will be gained by having somebody in Paris who would be in close touch with you and your War Cabinet and who knows what I may call the train of thought there and knowing this would be able to transact business with the French Government which now you have to get done either yourself or by a member of your Government going personally to Paris.

I think also that he probably would be more able to get in personal touch with all political sections in Paris than Bertie has been able to do and by entertaining be able to bring the British Embassy in Paris more, what I may call, 'into the picture' than it is at the present moment.

I only put down these heads because I should like to have another talk with you on the subject because I think the man in question is likely to accept provided he is able to keep his independence—at all events to a limited extent, and is not called upon to be simply

* Lord Derby himself.

a mouthpiece of the Government and gagged on all these questions on which I know he holds a very strong opinion.

Yours v. sincerely,

Derby

The Right Hon.
  D. Lloyd George M.P.

11

29th January, 1918.

Dear Prime Minister,

I have had the article by Colonel Repington in the *Morning Post* of the 24th examined in conjunction with the Man Power Committee's Report—G.185—and some other papers on the subject circulated to the Cabinet, i.e. the Memorandum by the Military Members of the Army Council (G.T.3265), a note by Sir D. Haig dated 8th January, 1918 (W.C.317), a memorandum by myself, dated 14th January (M.P.C.29), another by General Smuts, dated 17th January (M.P.C.30), a note by the Chief of the Imperial General Staff, dated 23rd January, 1918 (M.P.C.31), the Weekly General Staff Summaries, and Sir A. Geddes' speech on Man Power in the House of Commons on 14th January 1918. A schedule showing the results of this comparison is enclosed.

Before I had time to send you this, and answer your letter of the 24th, I received yours of the 28th. Later, I heard from the Cable Censors that Repington had written a reply to the charge that he had been supplied improperly with official information, and that the *Morning Post* was to publish it today. I have now seen this article, and in the face of his statements that many official persons, civil as well as military, have communicated with him from time to time on the subject of man power, and that no Cabinet paper has been given to him by any soldier, I don't see how we can single out the General Staff as the source of his information. With one or two exceptions, Repington's figures and statements are wrong, or are such as his long experience, wide knowledge, and profound study throughout the war would readily furnish him with, or they are such as would naturally come to him in the course of his well-known constant communication with Clemenceau and other French authorities.

I must point out that the Man Power Report was circulated more widely than may be usual with such papers. I enclose the list supplied to me from 2, Whitehall Gardens. I cannot see what other documents than those I have enumerated above Repington could be charged with having been shown, and the principal one is undoubtedly the Man Power Report. It would lead us nowhere to threaten all recipients of the latter with dire pains and penalties, and, as I have said, I can see no ground for singling out the officers of the General Staff for exclusive treatment on these lines.

In reply to your second letter, you should see Lovat Fraser's attack in the *Daily Mail* of yesterday. It is much more "encouraging" to the Enemy than Repington's statements. However, I have sent both to the Director of Public Prosecutions for advice, and I will in due course, when I receive that, submit to the Cabinet whether proceeding shall be taken against either or both. A Prosecution would give really the best opportunity of finding out all that there is to know as to the sources of inspiration of these writers.

Yours sincerely,

Derby.

12

22 Hans Crescent,
S.W.1.

26th April, 1918.

My dear Bonar,

I have been rather worried about the announcement which you made in the House of Commons, to the effect that I had resigned my appointment on the Air Council on the ground that I could not work with the new Chief of the Air Staff. That is not the reason which I gave to Lord Rothermere as you will see by the enclosed copy of my letter to him.

The fact is that my previous relations with Sykes, and my opinion of him, were not secrets, and had I remained in the Air Force, there was grave danger that I might become, however unwillingly, a focus of discontent and opposition.

Further, there was very little question of my "working" with Sykes. I had no executive duties left. The organisation of the Air Force in which I had been engaged since my transfer from the Army Council for the purpose, was complete, and I had clearly told Lord Rothermere, when he asked me to be Vice-President, that I could only hold the position while there was work for me to do.

I am ready to admit that I earnestly desired to escape from the atmosphere of intrigue and falsehood which has enveloped the Air Ministry for the last few months. On the other hand, I quite understand that my action has probably cut me off from any prospect of useful employment, either in the Army or in the Air Force. But I did not allow either of these considerations to influence me. I left, as I said, in the interests of the Service.

I spoke to Baird about this matter and he advised

me to write to you, as there would shortly be an opportunity of correcting the mistake.

Yours very sincerely,

DAVID HENDERSON.

(*Enclosure*)

Dear Lord Rothermere,

After our conversation on Friday last, when I expressed to you and to General Smuts a very unfavourable opinion of Major-General Sykes, and considering my previous relations with that officer, his appointment as Chief of the Air Staff makes it most undesirable, in the interests of the Service, that I should remain in the Air Force.

I am not aware whether the acceptance of a temporary commission in the Royal Air Force, for reasons of administrative convenience, affects my right to refuse attachment to the Royal Air Force given by the Air Force Constitution Act. If this be so, I beg that the point may be waived in my favour, and that this letter may be taken as giving notice that I do not desire to be attached and that my attachment may be annulled.

Yours sincerely,

(Copy initialled) D.H.

13

April 22, 1918.

My dear Prime Minister,

I have recently had an opportunity of seeing the Memorandum which Lord Rothermere addressed to you on the 9th instant in which he reviews the general situation in the Royal Air Force with a view to deciding what reorganisation, if any, is necessary or desirable.

I regret that I am unable to agree with some of the views expressed by Lord Rothermere and, consequently, could not support them in the House of Commons. In view of the Debates which are certain to take place in Parliament on this subject in the near future I thought it advisable to write to you in this sense at the earliest moment, and I most respectfully beg that I may be given an opportunity of laying my views before the War Cabinet. This course is all the more necessary because the opinions which I have formed are largely based on figures and facts which it would be impossible to make public.

Lord Rothermere is unfortunately away in the country ill, and I have to-day sent him the letter of which the enclosed is a copy. There are some other points connected with the Ministry with regard to which I regret that I do not see eye to eye with my Secretary of State and I think it my duty to bring these points before the War Cabinet also.

Yours sincerely,
JOHN BAIRD.

14

Hemsted,
Benenden, Kent.
Tuesday, April 23rd, 1918.

My dear Prime Minister,

I desire to relinquish my office as Secretary of State of the Air Force at the earliest possible moment.

There are three reasons actuating me in reaching this decision. One is that my stock of health is hardly adequate for such an anxious and harassing post.

Another and more decisive reason is that this young Force after all the publicity it has received during the last few weeks requires a rest from comment and criticism. So far no harm has been done. I feel, however, that a continuance during the next few months might impair discipline and prejudice efficiency.

With myself as Secretary of State there is every reason to suppose that comment and criticism will continue. With the office in the hands of someone else there is a fair chance of a moratorium as far as newspaper and parliamentary publicity are concerned.

The danger to discipline through constant publicity is well illustrated in the report of this morning's newspapers of yesterday's proceedings in the House of Commons. Two of the three Members of Parliament pressing Mr. Bonar Law to give an early day for a debate on Air Ministry affairs are officers of the Royal Air Force holding junior Staff appointments under me in the Hotel Cecil. These two officers, viz. Major Rt. Hon. Sir John Simon and Lieut. Rt. Hon. Lord Hugh Cecil, are not privileged persons. Why in the House of Commons should they flout disciplinary codes where elsewhere similar conduct by any other Staff Officer would form the subject of enquiry by his superior officers?

Sequestered in the Hotel Cecil, Major Sir John Simon has acted as an assistant secretary or clerk to Major-General Sir H. Trenchard, late Chief of the Air Staff. Two months ago I mentioned to you the extreme unsuitability of this arrangement with its possible dangers. As events have proved, I was not wrong.

A new Force like the Royal Air Force in which the number of senior officers is extraordinarily small requires iron discipline. Unless this is stamped upon it at its birth it is most improbable it will reach the full measure of its possible achievements in this war.

The third reason for my resignation is that the immediate work I set out to accomplish is finished. The blending of the Royal Naval Air Service and the Royal Flying Corps is complete; their fusion into the Royal Air Force went through on the 1st April without a hitch. So there is no question of "swapping horses". The stream has been crossed.

The recommendations set out in my secret memorandum which received the sanction of the War Cabinet are being carried out. The Strategic Council has been formed and has already held meetings. In a few days Major-General Sykes has impressed his personality on all with whom he has come in contact.

In my opinion this brilliant officer with his singularly luminous mind, great knowledge of Staff work, and grasp of service organisation, is an ideal Chief of Staff of the Royal Air Force. He has the sovereign gifts, particularly necessary now, of elasticity of outlook and receptivity of mind combined with youth and energy.

Aided by the able coadjutors he has found on the Air Council and at the Air Ministry the future of the Air Force can safely be left in his hands.

I cannot close this letter of resignation without an expression of my great respect and regard for yourself.

Yours very faithfully,

ROTHERMERE.

15

Extract of a letter from Winston Churchill to Lord Beaverbrook, 27th November, 1926.

... *The Maurice Debate*. This seems to have made no impression upon me. I may have been in Paris. All I recollect is being horrified to hear Bonar offer Asquith a judicial enquiry. I was with him on the bench and implored that this offer should be withdrawn. I think I was the one who convinced both him and L.G. that same afternoon. It would have been a frightful trap, and no Government ought to put up a set of judges to say whether they are liars or not. Asquith saved the situation by boggling about the enquiry, most foolishly from his point of view; and the Government were able to withdraw their offer in good style. . . .

16

26th February, 1918.

NOTES ON THE RESOLUTION FORWARDED BY THE UNIONIST WAR COMMITTEE TO THE PRIME MINISTER

Dear Prime Minister,

The first half of the Resolution is rather cryptic and may be directed against anyone.

The second half explains itself.

If you intend to act in the spirit of the above Resolution it will be necessary for you to dismiss Rothermere, Beaverbrook and Northcliffe, as none of them will resign. Beaverbrook would continue to support you and your Government up to, and through, the next General Election. I think Rothermere would feel inclined to do the same. Northcliffe may do anything.

My advice is to stand to your guns, for the following reasons:—

1. It is essential that you should stand by your friends and your appointments.

2. That out of the eighty members of the Unionist War Group I do not think more than thirty-five would vote against the Government on this question.

3. The other Conservatives will stand by their leaders.

4. I am almost sure that within two or three months at the latest both Rothermere and Beaverbrook will resign; Rothermere on account of ill-health, and Beaverbrook because he will, by that time, have set up for you a perfectly organised Propaganda Department and will want to regain his liberty.

No pledge is obtainable or reasonable and might even end in deeper difficulty.

I, however, believe that the agitators have very inconvenient proofs of Sutherland's activities, and that, at times, our Press opponents have got the better of him and have given him away. There is also some evidence available to the effect that he has subordinated the interest of your colleagues in his intense loyalty to yourself.

An atmosphere has thereby been created which, I fear, cannot fail to accumulate to your disadvantage.

I do not recommend that so loyal a friend should be thrown to the wolves, but I do recommend that he should be instructed to curtail his activities.

When I first took over, last May, I agreed to leave all connection with the London Press entirely in his hands and have, therefore, no responsibility for any of the so-called "inspirations", but I believe it would be wise that the Whips' Office should resume its traditional function of being the chief repository of information suitable for the Press. Of course I exclude the issue of Government announcements, appointments, etc., which bear the official stamp of No. 10.

I have sounded the following Ministers on the General situation and report as follows:—

Talbot is anxious to find a way out. He thinks the movement serious, but does not think it will be forced to extreme.

Hewart and Illingworth entirely agree with the advice which I submit.

F. E. Smith and W.S.C. think that you should stand by your guns.

Yours sincerely,
Frederick Guest.

The Rt. Hon. David Lloyd George, M.P.

17

1 Carlton House Terrace,
S.W.1.
PRIVATE   November 13, 1918.
My dear Prime Minister,

I received just now your telephone message confirming my departure tomorrow. I have just heard from the King of the Belgians that the Queen and he re-enter Brussels on Saturday. Lady Curzon and I have always promised to be with them on that day and accordingly we are returning to Belgium by motor tomorrow for this ceremony and shall be back in England on Monday.

Meanwhile I should like to report to you the result of my conversation this morning with M. Clemenceau. He treated me as he has done throughout with the greatest confidence and cordiality.

(1) He does not at all want Wilson at the Conference or Conferences. As the Head of a State Wilson ought not to attend the Conference. If he did attend he would probably expect to preside and this Clemenceau thought would be unacceptable to all.

(2) Clemenceau showed me some further messages from Germany appealing to Wilson for compassion. He thinks, and I agree, that this constant communication behind the back of the Allies with Wilson ought to be stopped at once and that all such appeals should be addressed to or communicated, before reply —to the principal Allies.

(3) I do not see how you are to wait till mid-December for Wilson. My own impression is that the Allied representatives should start work at once. I hear that the Italian is coming. Problems are arising every day that call for instant examination, and solution. House's plea that, if the President is coming, he (House) will be without interim authority, is not I

385   2B

think valid. Postpone big decisions if you like. But go ahead with the preparation of all the cases and the settling of all the minor ones.

(4) Clemenceau is very angry with the Italian about their tricks with the Austrian fleet.

(5) I asked him his view about a possible trial of the Kaiser and the Arch-Criminals, and told him we had a Committee investigating the matter and reporting on a possible Tribunal. He said he had not seriously considered the point, but would like my ideas.

Speaking for myself alone, I suggested the possibility of creating—as the first step to a League of Nations—an international tribunal of jurists of the highest eminence (they might or might not include neutrals, probably Yes) for the express purpose of trying the Kaiser, his son and the other offenders. They might be cited before it. I do not know enough of international law to be sure whether Holland having interned them, if she has, could or would give them up for trial. But would that matter in the case of the Kaiser and his son? The charges could be sent to them and their replies invited. Either these would be just and considered, or they would be refused.

In either case the Tribunal could consider the evidence and eventually pronounce its verdict. If the sentence was that of outlawry from the principal countries of the world, it would be a punishment signal, crushing, unheard of in history.

Clemenceau thought that such a proposition had in it immense possibilities. He was greatly taken with the idea. He thought that as an act of international justice, of world retribution, it would be one of the most imposing events in history and that the conception was well worthy of being pursued.

He prayed me to communicate with my Government on the matter and to let him have any papers or reports on the subject that we might prepare.

I pass this on to you at once since you may be talking the matter over with Balfour before you all come here. I pray you to consider it seriously. Public opinion will not willingly consent to let this arch-criminal escape by a final act of cowardice. The supreme and colossal nature of his crime seems to call for some supreme and unprecedented condemnation. Execution, imprisonment, these are not, or may not be, necessary. But continued life, an inglorious and ignoble exile, under the weight of such a sentence as has never before been given in the history of mankind, would be a penance worse than death.

Yours sincerely,

CURZON.

This afternoon in the absence of the Ambassador I was called upon to address a shouting and enthusiastic crowd of English and Dominion soldiers who made their way into the courtyard of this building, and was there and then publicly kissed by Miss Decima Moore!

18

Monday, 7 July 1919

My dear Prime Minister,

I venture, for what they are worth, to put before you some views about the contemplated trial of the Kaiser in England.

I have always been in favour of his trial. Indeed, I was the first to raise the subject in the Imperial War Cabinet last year. On the whole, I adhere to the views which I then expressed, though perhaps less strongly than at the time when the subject was first raised. But I confess that I had never contemplated, and am a good deal staggered at, the idea of the trial taking place in England; and, the more I reflect upon it, the more I am inclined to think that we may be on the verge of committing a great mistake. The considerations which appeal to me are the following:—

In the first place, we cannot get away from the fact that he will have been brought to the country of those whom he regards as his chief enemies, and who have really compassed his downfall. In practice, I fully believe that he would get a fairer trial from us than from any other people; but outside this country it will be said and thought that those whom the German Emperor hated most and did his best to injure have insisted on seizing him and executing the final act of vengeance. There will thus spring up an idea, if he is brought here, that he will not receive fair play; and, if he is condemned and sentenced here, that he has not had it. It will be said that we insisted on getting him, in order to be sure of his fate. Unquestionably there will be this amount of truth in the charge, that, while the feelings towards him in France and Belgium may be even more passionate than they are here, the sentiment of this country as a whole will be one of violent hostility and prejudice, affecting, not, it may be, the minds of the judges, but the temper of the people.

Secondly, does not there seem to be a certain refinement of severity in bringing the Kaiser here, to the country the most famous Sovereign of which was his Grandmother; where his Mother was born; and from which she was married; where he has constantly stayed as a Royal Guest; and where his Cousin is at the present moment on the Throne? I do not suppose that the King was consulted on the matter. I doubt if he knew anything more about it than the rest of us. But surely it is putting him in a very delicate and invidious position if his near relative, however great his crimes, is to be tried almost within sight of the Palace where the King lives and where the culprit has so often stayed? This, it seems to me, is a question of taste rather than of anything else; but a good many people, looking at it from that point of view, will, I

"Hang the Kaiser", was the cry

think, be disposed to hold that such a proceeding ought to be avoided.

Thirdly, if the Kaiser is brought here, we have to choose the place where he and his associates are to be tried. It is really almost inconceivable that he should be placed in a spot where day after day, through a period extending very likely over many months, he will have to be brought backwards and forwards to the Court of Justice amid the jeers and insults of the crowd. Such an arrangement would begin by being disgraceful and, after it had lasted a long time and the public had become indifferent, would end by being ridiculous. The only alternative would be to fix the Court in some place where the Kaiser could be accommodated in close proximity to the building, if not inside it. But such places are not easily available. If he were to be tried in the Royal Gallery of the House of Lords, he might, I suppose, be lodged in the apartments which the Lord Chancellor has been prevented by the Commons from occupying because he insisted on a bath. But surely we do not want him in Westminster, in close proximity to our every day proceedings. Again, it is suggested, I am told, that he might be taken to Hampton Court. But a place of holiday resort, where thousands of people would be hanging about every day is hardly a suitable "mise en scène" for such a trial. Similar objections apply to almost every place that can be suggested. Even if the difficulty can be overcome in the case of the Kaiser, how are we to meet it in the case of his associates? I assume that, if he comes or is brought here, he will make a sustained and prolonged defence. He will summon to his side his sons, his ex-Ministers, his Generals, his friends. He will try to overwhelm the Court with evidence as to his innocence and irresponsibility. He will endeavour to break down the proceedings by every form of delay. We shall run the risk of a trial that may extend over many months, perhaps longer. If Bethmann-Hollweg, Hindenburg,

Ludendorff, and a crowd of other witnesses appear upon the scene, they also will have to be accommodated, and will there not, in their daily procession to the scene of the trial, be an opportunity for the same sort of displays of which I have already spoken?

Fourthly, is it desirable that we should distract the attention of the country from all the difficulties with which we are confronted by providing them with a sensation of this description? They might welcome it, and we might welcome it, to start with. But I cannot help feeling that before long a feeling would grow up that we had made a desperate mistake, and, if it were so, that we should be the sufferers.

Fifthly, let me take the three contingencies which may conceivably occur. The first is that the Dutch Government may decline to surrender the Kaiser, or that he may refuse to come, and the trial will have to take place in his absence. If no one comes to speak on his behalf, would it really do for us to put up some learned British or foreign jurisconsult to plead his case? If, on the other hand, a stream of witnesses comes, unaccompanied by the Kaiser, is it not conceivable that a case may be made which, in the absence of the principal defendant, would result in an inconclusive verdict, if not in an acquittal?

But, however this may be, and whether he comes or not, shall not we be in all probability the main sufferers by any verdict that may be given? If he be pronounced guilty, and sentence be passed upon him, and it is left to us to carry it out, shall not we in the eyes both of Germany and the rest of the world have to bear the entire responsibility, now and in History? Never mind that the Court is international, the verdict will be regarded as having been inspired, just as in all probability it will have to be executed, by ourselves. Would it be possible ever again to make friends with Germany after that? Would not it be a root of bitterness which would last till the end of time?

If, on the other hand, he is acquitted or an inconclusive verdict is reached, upon us will fall the blame and ridicule of the fiasco; and the effects of our military triumph will be largely dissipated by this bathos.

The question therefore arises whether it is possible to extricate ourselves from the position of bringing the Kaiser here, and whether he could be tried anywhere else. I do not, of course, know the arguments which prevailed upon the Council of Four to decide in favour of England. I expect that the other countries represented were only too anxious not to shoulder the responsibility themselves. France and Belgium, I can well imagine, might be considered unsuitable places. Italy is too remote, and the Italians are not to be trusted. But why should Holland be debarred? Is it altogether impossible that the Kaiser should be tried at The Hague? The trial and verdict will surely be independent of the particular locality in which the former will be held, and the judges are as likely to deliver a fair and reasonable finding in one country as they are in another. On the other hand, we would escape all the difficulties, or some at any rate of them, in respect of the contemplated demand of surrender to be addressed to the Dutch Government, and their possible refusal. The Kaiser is already in Holland. It might be easier for them to transfer him from one part of the country to another without raising the question of his leaving Holland. This would also lessen the difficulty as to his witnesses, if he summoned them, reaching the place of trial. It would be much simpler for them to cross a land frontier into Holland than to be brought across the sea to our own shore.

I assume that Holland must have been considered and ruled out for some reason that I do not know, but at least the point seems worthy of consideration.

I have rather hastily dictated this letter, in order to let you know what is in my own mind. I have had a brief talk with both Milner and Winston on the matter, and I find that their views coincide with mine. Insofar as I have spoken to other people, of whatever shade of thought, I find that the same opinions prevail. Indeed I have not come across any one who, whatever he thinks about the wisdom of the trial—and about this there are a good many doubts—, is in favour of the particular suggestion that is made. I did not like to bring the matter before the Cabinet in your absence, and therefore I have written this to you, feeling sure that you will seriously consider the matter and will give the Cabinet the opportunity at an early date of discussing it with fuller knowledge than they now possess.

I believe that the view of the Foreign Office is well-nigh unanimous in the direction which I have described.

I am,

Yours sincerely,
CURZON.

19

Lord Curzon to Lord Lansdowne

(Published by Lord Newton in *Lord Lansdowne: A Biography*, pp. 452–3)

Confidential.   December 3rd, 1916.

I am sorry that you could not be present at the meeting at Bonar Law's which is just over.

It is a long story. For a fortnight *pourparlers* have been going on between Lloyd George and the Prime Minister, in which Bonar Law (without telling us) has taken a prominent part.

The letters were read to us just now. Practically Lloyd George issued an ultimatum to the Prime Minister, putting the latter in the complete background, and constituting a War Committee of three, under himself.

The Prime Minister refused, and stuck to the arrangement (of two Committees) mentioned at the last Cabinet and agreed to at our last meeting in Bonar Law's room, with himself as Chairman. Lloyd George, as the papers of yesterday and today will have shown you, has attempted to force the situation by announcing his own resignation, which is apparently to appear in the Press tomorrow. Derby is to resign with him, and Bonar Law has been so far implicated that his name appears with theirs in the papers, and he told us he meant to resign this afternoon.

We felt three things: (*a*) that this was unfair to the Prime Minister; (*b*) that it placed Lloyd George in a position where he could dictate his terms; (*c*) that Bonar Law ought not to act independently, but that we ought both to think and act unitedly. Accordingly, it was unanimously decided that Bonar Law should see the Prime Minister early this afternoon (he has been summoned back from Walmer, whither, with characteristic nonchalance, he had slipped away yesterday evening); that Bonar Law should tell him that in our opinion the events to which I have referred had rendered internal reconstruction no longer possible; that he (Asquith) should this afternoon place his resignation in the hands of the King (including, of course, ours); and that if he was not able to take that step we placed the whole of our resignations in his hands.

All our colleagues were at the meeting except A.J.B., who is in bed, and yourself.

The object of these tactics, which are, in my opinion, fundamentally sound and essential, is this:

When the Prime Minister resigns, the King will send for Lloyd George. The latter will then, for the first time, be confronted with the difficulties of the situation. He will cease to be a merely destructive and disloyal force. He will have to make terms with the Prime Minister and with all the rest of us. He will soon find out what is the attitude of the Irishmen, the Labour men, and so on. His Government will be dictated to him by others, not shaped exclusively by himself.

For instance, no one of us would accept a dictatorship of Carson and himself. The following, both in the House of Commons and country, of the Prime Minister will become apparent, and Lloyd George will have to make terms with them. In other words, he will for the first time have the responsibilities of his action in breaking up the Government.

In passing, I may say that he does not mean to have Balfour at any cost, and I suppose the majority of the present Government are doomed to disappearance.

Had one felt that reconstitution by and under the present Prime Minister was possible, we should all have preferred to try it. But we know that with him as Chairman, either of the Cabinet or War Committee, it is absolutely impossible to win the War, and it will be for himself and Lloyd George to determine whether he goes out altogether or becomes Lord Chancellor or Chancellor of the Exchequer in a new Government, a nominal Premiership being a protean compromise, which, in our view, could have no endurance.

20

15th March 1919.

My dear Lord Chancellor,

I have received the Report of your Committee on the Land Acquisition Bill with profound disappointment. The Bill was supposed to be one to facilitate acquisition of land for most urgent public purposes, speedily and at a fair price. It has been transformed into a Bill which will be represented as making sure that the landlord gets a good price, that the lawyers get their pickings, and that there should be no undue hurry in the completion of the transaction.

To entrust the valuation of land to a man whose future prosperity and even livelihood depends on the goodwill of owners of land, is to guarantee an interest and bias in favour of the landlord against the State. And as for employing lawyers to argue out the value of the land, would you or any other member of the Committee ever dream of buying an estate assessed by means of a wrangle between rival lawyers on the merits or demerits of the particular fields? Of course you would not. Why then should schemes for housing be condemned to failure by the handicap of such grotesque methods of valuation? This is apart altogether from the piling up of fees and bills of costs, which would be the inevitable result of this unbusinesslike procedure.

It is these methods in the past that have rendered all housing schemes barren. It is owing to these that land producing only a few shillings an acre fetches hundreds of pounds per acre the moment it is requisitioned to build houses for the workmen whose labour has created the adjoining wealth.

I could not accept these alterations and I should be glad if your Committee would reconsider the question before submitting its proposals to the Cabinet.

I trust that the result of the West Leyton election will suffice as a warning to those who have drawn wrong deductions from the overwhelming majority of the last election. Mason's record spread broadcast through the Constituency marked him down as a reactionary. I beg you to assist in making these Bills a reality.

Why was Howard Frank invited to give evidence? He is an out and out landowners man. Surely there ought to have been a witness on the other side brought in to balance his testimony. The country is in no mood to tolerate reactionaries, high or low.

Yours sincerely,
D. LLOYD GEORGE.

21

(*Undated*—8th January 1918)
1 Carlton House Terrace,
S.W.

Private

Dear Prime Minister,

Although I hope I am not quick or resentful of temper, I do not like to let the incident of this morning pass without a word from me.

It was a very trying, and, I think, unmerited experience for a Member of the War Cabinet, who was exercising his legitimate functions, to be pulled up by his Chief, as I was by you this morning, in the presence not merely of his colleagues, but of outsiders. It is quite a new idea that a Cabinet Minister is not to be allowed to express whatever opinions he may choose in Cabinet, until persons other than Cabinet Ministers have spoken. It has certainly not been the rule observed in this Cabinet, where, on scores of occasions Ministers have been asked by yourself to summarise the views which they have placed on paper before their colleagues. This is indeed the ordinary procedure.

It was I, and not Mond or Rothermere or anyone else, who had asked & obtained leave to reopen the question (with what good reasons the result has shown). I had circulated last night a note explaining my reasons, which many of my colleagues, including yourself, had not had time to read. Before you came into the room Bonar Law in the Chair had asked me to open the discussion and in order to shorten the proceedings I had commenced to read my brief memo instead of recapitulating its substance. It was then that you cut me short in a manner which I venture to say left a painful impression on all who heard it.

I certainly felt it acutely myself & that others felt it too was shown by the Archbishop of Canterbury, who came up to me in the H. of Lords this afternoon and said he had been equally astonished at the manner in which a member of the Cabinet could be treated by his Chief and at the good temper with which the latter had borne it.

I do not want to magnify what I am quite content to regard as a trifling incident, & which I should not have noticed had it not occurred before.

I hope that I have always shown in Cabinet courtesy to my colleagues & deference to my chief and I should be sorry if I had done anything this morning to provoke the treatment that I received.

But it is much better to write frankly than to nurse a silent resentment, all the more that our personal relations have always been so pleasant that I, at any rate, could not contemplate a shadow being cast upon them without very sincere regret.

I am,

Yours sincerely,

CURZON.

22

9 Egerton Place,
S.W.3
Jan. 6, 1921.

Confidential

My dear Bonar,

Curzon asked me to dine with him alone two nights ago to talk over what he described as some rather serious matters.

I found him very depressed & very disturbed in mind, uneasy about his position, doubtful of his usefulness & influence—in short very unsettled and wondering whether he could or ought to continue in the Government. I have never before seen him in at all the same mood.

Something of this was due to the impending retirement of Milner with whom he has been on terms of friendship older & more intimate than with any other of his colleagues, but more was due to the course of discussions in Cabinet, to the feeling that the Prime Minister had more than once treated him with scant courtesy—almost with contumely—in the presence of his colleagues & attached little weight to his opinion on matters directly within the sphere of his departmental responsibility. How, he asked, must his colleagues regard him & what use was he under such circumstances? Surely no previous Prime Minister had ever addressed one of his Secretaries of State in such a way or appealed to the votes of minor members of the Cabinet to overrule the advice of two Secretaries of State in the common affairs of their two offices.

I need not tell you that I did all that I could to combat his depression. I assured him of the respect of his colleagues, of his influence & importance in the Government. I told him what I believe is the truth that his resignation would be fatal to the Government & to the Coalition as it now exists & that it must gravely affect my own course of action. Indeed in present conditions I think that the resignation of any one of us three, you, Curzon & myself, would be the end of the combination on whose continuance the Government itself depends, and I put before him as strongly as I could the grounds of public policy on which I hold that it is our duty to maintain that combination if we can.

Lastly—& here I come to the more personal & delicate aspect of the case—I told him that of course I had observed the attacks on himself & his department of which he complained & similar attacks on Winston, that I deeply regretted them, that I, & I was certain all his colleagues, far from misinterpreting his silence as weakness, had admired his self control (which under incomparably less provocation I had myself recently failed to imitate) & been grateful to him for it. I urged that the P.M. did not premeditate these attacks, did not exactly weigh his words or realise the effect of his tone & language, & I suggested that a personal explanation between himself & the P.M. might clear the air & prevent the recurrence of any cause for complaint. Unfortunately, he said, he had already tried this. He had once—or twice—written to the P.M. after one of these scenes & had received a very friendly letter in reply, but then sooner or later the offence was renewed.

It is always dangerous for a third party to meddle in such affairs, but I feel bound to write to you & through you to George. Frankly I have been shocked by the P.M.'s attacks on Curzon on more than one occasion, thinly disguised sometimes as criticisms not of himself but of his department. It has been painful to me to listen to them as I am sure that it has been to you & others. I have wondered at Curzon's reticence under such provocation, & though I do not think that I am generally rash or hot-tempered, I cannot conceive of myself as remaining in the room if I were subject to similar invective.

And I write as one who has no similar cause for complaint. The P.M. has treated me always with great courtesy, & is giving me generous support. It is therefore only as an onlooker, the friend and colleague of both parties, that I write. I am certain that if such attacks are repeated, there will be a smash. I am confident that whatever differences of opinion there may be among us, they are not, at present at any rate, of the insoluble kind. I don't believe that the P.M. wishes to part with Curzon or to quarrel with him or is conscious that on more than one occasion he has spoken to him in a tone & manner which are almost personally insulting. I feel sure that, if the P.M. realised the effect produced not only upon Curzon but upon his other hearers, he has both the good feeling & the good sense to refrain. Finally I suggest—& for this suggestion I appeal to what I believe to be an unbroken Cabinet tradition—that if the Prime Minister & yourself should ever again find yourselves as you did the other day in the question of the administrative arrangements of the Middle East, differing from two important colleagues & those two the ones most immediately concerned, you should not then & there swap them by a poll of the Cabinet but should defer the question for further conference with them.

I address myself directly to you because you & I have been longer & more intimately associated than the Prime Minister & I, & because I know that you have an influence with him to which the rest of us cannot pretend. You will therefore be our best interpreter & you are the man most likely to put things right. But this letter is written for Lloyd George to see, & I hope that you will hand it to him. It is of so personal a character that I do not like to give it even to my very confidential secretary to copy, & I should not like to say so much even to you behind the back, so to speak, of the Prime Minister.

Yrs. ever,
AUSTEN CHAMBERLAIN.

I am leaving early tomorrow so do not trouble to send an answer.

23

Flowerdale House,
Gairloch,
Ross-shire
October 1st, 1921

My dear Winston,

Your memorandum perplexes me. The latter part consists of an incomplete summary of suggestions which were put forward by various members at the Gairloch discussions, and which are the subject of very thorough investigation at the present moment by the

Departments concerned. But the first part consists of an attempt to lay the blame on your colleagues for present unemployment conditions. Although in the first paragraph you attribute the responsibility to the Cabinet as a whole you are careful to point out later on that the Finance Committee of the Cabinet were completely responsible for the policy. This is not in the least accurate inasmuch as all first-class decisions received full Cabinet discussion, and you, amongst others, expressed your views very freely from time to time on all these questions when definite conclusions were being arrived at.

What is it you complain of?—fluctuations. You instance housing. You could not choose a more unfortunate illustration from your point of view. There has been no change in our policy from the start. We assumed a shortage of hundreds of thousands of houses. We urged all those who were concerned in supplying the deficiency—Ministry of Health, Local Authorities, building contractors, landowners etc.—to use the whole of their resources to supply this deficiency without flagging or delay. We have not departed in the least from that policy. The resources of the building industry are necessarily limited. The skilled artizans being the bottle-neck, and by using the whole of our building resources in material and labour we could only turn out so many houses per annum. What did Addison do? He let contracts far in advance of the capacity of the trade to assimilate. The market was glutted with offers. What is the result? Any business man could have told him, in fact every business man did tell him, what the effect would be; prices soared higher and higher. He was urged to halt, but he continued flogging prices up hill in spite of all warnings. You supported him in this very fatuous policy with considerable vehemence and passion, and all those who in future will read your memorandum, are entitled to distil for you such credit as they can out of that fact.

We insisted however, on the advice of the Finance Committee, and compelled Addison to cry a halt. The number of houses being built, so far from being reduced, increased, but contracts were circumscribed. The result was that prices tumbled down. Even then the contracts were still beyond the capacity of the market, and were still being let out. We decided therefore on a further restriction of contracts until those already undertaken had been liquidated. Result, a further fall in prices. But no local authority or builder, who has either the material or the labour for building houses, is prevented from doing so. The Anti-waste campaign was only dangerous where it was justified. It was justified in Mesopotamia, where forces far beyond the need were being kept. That you are putting right. It was justified in the fighting services; it was justified in the excessive staffing of departments; it was certainly justified in the unbusinesslike way in which Addison was forcing up prices over housing. To that extent the Anti-waste campaign has been very useful. It brought the necessary pressure to bear upon Ministers. That is not a change of policy. I had urged all these considerations upon my colleagues for two years. As a matter of fact, I pressed some of these considerations upon you at Deauville two years ago. I consider that Mond is placing our housing programme on a thoroughly businesslike footing, and the only blame I attach to myself is, that out of personal consideration for Addison, I kept him at the Ministry of Health much longer than I ought to have.

You plead for a consistent policy about unemployment. You lay down the principles of that policy in language which I cordially approve. Men who are willing to labour but cannot find it must not be left to starve. I expressed the same sentiments to the Labour Mayors when I said to them that no man who was willing to work ought to be allowed to starve as long as there was a crust in the national cupboard. But you

do less than justice to the Cabinet when you suggest
that this is a new policy which you are inculcating now
for the first time. As you pointed out at Dundee,
no Government has ever taken as great risks in carrying
out this policy as the present Government. £106,000,000
spent on unemployment allowances. That is without
precedent in the history of this or any other country.
Relief work found for something under 100,000. In
the Cabinet of which you and I were members £200,000
was the maximum spent on unemployment in 1908. The
question now is not whether we ought to change our
policy but whether we are not bound to take a step
· forward. All the anticipations of business men as to
trade revival have been falsified. Many expected it last
spring, both here and in America. They were wrong.
Many more expected it in the autumn. It has not yet
arrived. I am afraid therefore that we cannot depend
upon these hopeful anticipations any longer, and that
we must look forward to a further prolonged period of
considerable unemployment. Had it been possible to
trust to a return to what is known in America as
"normalcy", it would have been better in the general
interest to do so rather than resort to artificial stimu-
lants; that is true in every disease; but we cannot do
so, and therefore, as I very emphatically pointed out at
Gairloch, I was of opinion that we must resort to
expedients which can only be justified by the continuance of abnormal conditions.

Hilton Young has done his work uncommonly well.
His investigations have been very thorough and most
helpful. I have not yet had the result of Mond's
enquiries. Those will take another week or fortnight,
but when we meet next week we shall be in a position
at any rate to take big decisions along the lines of the
Gairloch discussions.

As to inflation, there is no question here of a
fluctuating policy. As long as trade was good and
there were plenty of orders and great profits were

being made Chamberlain was perfectly right in pursuing his policy of deflation, but now that trade is depressed and our industries are barely able to keep going we must adapt our financial policy to those conditions. This is a fluctuation not in policy but in conditions, and the fact that we deflated so steadily and courageously in 1919 and 1920 makes it easier for us, without detriment to the national position, to do a little inflation now.

I entreat you to judge more charitably the efforts put forth by your colleagues during the last two years. Abroad this policy has won a good deal of admiration and respect for this country. You will forgive me for writing in this strain, but I know that recrimination will not help in the solution of any problem, and I am anxious to get the full benefit of your resourceful brain without embarking upon discussions which will be not only fruitless but exasperating, and will divert our energies into channels which are neither fertilising nor navigable.

(*Unsigned copy*).

24

8 October 1921

My dear Prime Minister,

I very much appreciate the trouble you have taken to write to me about my recent memorandum on Unemployment and Finance, though I regret to have been the cause of adding to your personal labours at such a busy time.

I am sorry that you think my judgment of the record of the Government in these matters is unduly critical. I do the best I can to defend the Administration in

Parliament & on the platform, but it would be useless for me to pretend that I admire our post-war policy in several important aspects.

The first & greatest mistake in my opinion was leaving the profiteers in possession of their ill-gotten war wealth. Had prompt action been taken at the beginning of 1919, several thousand millions of paper wealth cd have been transferred to the State, & the internal debt reduced accordingly. The question was however deliberately held over & delayed until the moment was lost. Most of this war-made capital has faded as fast as it was created, but the internal debt, wh it might so largely have cancelled, & which was incurred in similar abnormal conditions, towers up over us like a precipice. The assets of taxation to wh the State might have looked have vanished: the war debits of the State are consolidated & will even grow heavier as trade revives & money regains its purchasing power. If I had not pressed this by every means open to me while there was still time to deal with the matter, & more than a year before the House of Commons Committee was appointed wh reported in favour of the principle, I shd not feel entitled to refer to it now. In looking back on this lost opportunity, I feel that it constituted a very great & irreparable disaster to the country.

With regard to the fluctuations in housing policy & in regard to agriculture, it is extraordinary to me that you have not been struck by them. So far as Dundee is concerned, I know from my own personal investigations that up till April the Town Council, in response to the strong pressure of the Ministry of Health, were pressing on with lay-outs & development work for building; that when the new declarations were made on the dismissal of Addison they protested violently against the arrest & curtailment of their work; & I had a bad time with them. Now, almost as soon as this development work has been brought to a standstill, all sorts of new schemes are being considered for increasing employment by starting relief works. I am sure if you make enquiries you will find that many other local bodies have been conscious of similar violent fluctuations—no doubt each explained by a reason very good in itself—in the directions they have received from the Government.

So far as the last part of my memorandum is concerned, it certainly did not originate out of discussions wh we had at Gairloch, altho' these matters were refreshed in my mind by many of yr very illuminating & suggestive comments. But I remember two long discussions wh we had together—the first nearly a year ago in the Hyde Park Hotel after a dinner at wh Max & Rothermere were present, & the second at Lympne at the beginning of this year. In each case I had the feeling that we made great progress in cutting our way into the heart of the post-war monetary & financial mystery, & the contributions of yr own thought, so far as they went, seemed to me of incomparable value & far more searching than I have heard on this subject from anyone else. But it seemed to me that all this process stopped short of reaching any conclusion of a definite character on which a policy or even a provisional policy cd be based; & the fact is undoubtedly as I have stated in my memorandum, that we have not at the present time got a clear view on the fundamental question to wh I have drawn attention. *I* certainly do not pretend to have a clear view upon them, tho' I have a feeling that if we went on hammering away for say a week or two, we shd get to the bottom of it & frame a definite policy wh cd be announced, explained, & defended, & wh wd carry us through the temporary & baffling fluctuations wh are affecting us so violently at the present time. It is quite true that owing to yr vy great skill in navigation we have avoided many dangerous rocks & shoals, & in the Coal Strike have come through one of the greatest industrial hurricanes that have ever blown. But for all that we are drifting about in a fog without a compass.

It was certainly not with any intention of making recriminations about the past, but solely with a view to an amelioration in the future, that I embodied my thoughts in the memorandum wh I have circulated. Still less do I flatter myself with superiority of judgment. But I always try to give the best advice I can sincerely to you & to the Cabinet on the great general questions of our affairs as they come up. If I did not do so, I shd be no use whatever to you or to the Administration.

Let me say in conclusion how glad I am you are reconsidering your decision about going to Washington for the opening of the Conference. I do not think there wd be any necessity for you to exhaust yrself in making speeches to the American multitudes. But I feel you ought to establish friendly personal relations with Harding & Hughes, that you ought to make them conscious of the loyalty & friendliness of our motives, & at the same time of our strong determination not to be ousted from our world-position; & generally to get the Conference started as far as possible on sound lines & to arrive at some informal understandings on its great underlying issues with the Statesmen of America & Japan. This I believe you cd do in a fortnight, with a week at each end for the voyage. Meanwhile I have no doubt that all parties in the country wd respect yr absence & the reasons for it, & that the political position wd be consolidated & not weakened on account of the all-important work on wh you wd be engaged.

Yours sincerely,
WINSTON S. CHURCHILL.

P.S. I was so glad to see you so much restored in health.

W.

STAMFORDHAM MEMORANDA

(Published for the first time)

Buckingham Palace
3.15 p.m., 13 February 1918

I expressed the King's surprise to learn from the Minutes of the Cabinet that Sir William Robertson was no longer Chief of the Imperial General Staff, but that he was to be succeeded by Sir Henry Wilson, and it was suggested that Sir William Robertson should go to Paris as a Member of the Executive Committee of the Supreme War Council.

The Prime Minister when he saw the King on the 4th February never mentioned any idea of this change, indeed he told His Majesty that everything had gone smoothly in Paris the previous week, and that the agreements come to by the Supreme War Council were unanimous, and it was only on the 12th inst. that the King chanced to send for Lord Derby, who then told him of the contemplated new arrangement.

The Prime Minister replied that as Lord Derby told him that he was going to see the King on the 12th he (the Prime Minister) asked him to tell the King everything, and to show him a copy of the conditions which Lord Derby had agreed to and signed, governing the two appointments of C.I.G.S. and Member of the Executive Committee respectively. I said that I had not heard of this document, but the Prime Minister said that he knew Lord Derby had it in his pocket and more than once Mr. Lloyd George said 'Are you sure the King did not see it?' I could only answer that of course I could not be sure as I was not present at the interview, but that His Majesty had not mentioned anything about the document in question. The Prime Minister sent for the original and I brought away a copy. I told him that the King strongly deprecated the idea of Robertson being removed from the office of C.I.G.S., that his loss in that capacity would be an incalculable one to the Army, would be resented in the country, rejoiced in by the enemy, and I thought would damage the Government, and the King considered that Sir William Robertson had enjoyed the absolute confidence of the Army—Officers and Men. The Prime Minister said that he did not share the King's extremely favourable opinion of Sir William Robertson, who had never fought at the Front, had hardly ever visited the trenches, and was not known by the rank and file, and their confidence in him could not be compared to that which they reposed in Sir Herbert Plumer, and Mr. Lloyd George said that the opinions I relied on must be manufactured for the King. The previous week in Paris Robertson never raised any objections to the proposal, but just as on the occasion of Rapallo, he waited until his return to London to make these known far and wide.

The Prime Minister said that Robertson had been offered either Paris or to remain as C.I.G.S., he declined either and wished to dictate to everyone, whereas the Prime Minister repeated what he said on the 22nd January, that Robertson had displayed no capacity as a strategist, and asked where anyone could put their finger on the map and say that this or that is due to Robertson's advice. In fact his forecasts had generally been wrong.

I pointed out that Robertson was only asking to be in a position similar to that of General Foch, who is both C.G.S. and Member of the Executive Committee in France. The Prime Minister replied that there was no analogy. For Foch is on the spot in Paris whereas Sir William Robertson would be in London, while it might be necessary to give orders to the Reserves at a moment's notice in cases of emergency.

Afterwards on returning to Buckingham Palace I rang up Lord Derby and told him of my conversation with the Prime Minister, the former said that Robertson was unreasonable in his demands, swollen headed, and that he (Lord Derby) was so tired of the whole question that he sometimes thought he would be better without Robertson, but himself felt ready to resign.

Later on Lord Derby and Sir William Robertson met in my room, and the whole question was threshed out and examined from all sides. Sir William Robertson gave me a copy of his written opinion as to the suggested plan, which to him had spelt disaster. Lord Derby did not agree, and reminded Sir William Robertson that Sir Douglas Haig had approved of the conditions and thought that they were workable. However, Lord Derby said that he should back up Sir William Robertson. But he knew that if the Prime Minister agreed to Sir W. R.'s terms namely, that he should be both C.I.G.S. in London, and Member of the Executive Committee, with a Deputy to act for him in his absence, Lord Milner and Mr. Barnes would resign: if on the other hand Sir William Robertson were to resign, Lord Curzon, and he (Lord Derby) would leave the Government, and if this resulted in the fall of the Government there was a serious danger of its fate being attributed to the work of the Army and might be a very disagreeable cry with which to go to the country.

I begged Sir William Robertson in the King's name not to relinquish his post as C.I.G.S., but to record his disapproval of the system, his belief that it was unworkable, and might even cost us the War, but for the sake of the King, the Army and the Country, to remain on and do his best to carry out the new arrangement. He undertook to think it over, and said that he had to go with Lord Derby to breakfast with the Prime Minister in the morning. During this discussion Sir W. R. said with considerable warmth that the truth was the Prime Minister hated him.

I reported what had happened to the King at about 8.15 p.m.

14 February 1918

At 8.30 a.m. I sent a note to Sir William Robertson saying that I trusted that after sleeping over the matter he had decided to give effect to the King's wishes. Later on I heard that he had not breakfasted with the Prime Minister, but was to attend the Cabinet and lay before them his views.

Soon after 3.30 p.m. I called at 10 Downing Street, and found that the Cabinet had decided that Sir William Robertson must make up his mind to take either of the two appointments suggested, but he was to see Mr. Balfour about four o'clock.

I went to the War Office and saw Mr. Balfour and Lord Derby, immediately after the former had left Sir William Robertson, upon whom he said he had failed to make any impression, or to divert him from the attitude he had taken up.

I discussed Sir William Robertson's objections to the scheme, which Mr. Balfour thought were exaggerated, and would not hold water. He did not seem to recognize as much as I did the serious view which Sir W. R. took as to the results of the proposed arrangement, and indeed said that Sir William Robertson had not put the case as strongly as I had put it: I replied that I was merely repeating what Sir W. R. had said the previous evening, and I appealed to Lord Derby and asked him to show Mr. Balfour a copy of the paper which Sir William Robertson had given me, but Lord

Derby replied that Sir W. R. had modified his views of the previous evening. I said that Sir William Robertson maintained that one man only could give orders to the Army, and that was the C.I.G.S., whereas by this plan there would be *two* namely, the C.I.G.S. and the member of the Executive Committee.

Later on I saw Lord Derby, who said I was mistaken in thinking that he said Sir William Robertson had changed his views. I told him that Sir William Robertson would not give way or continue to be C.I.G.S. while disapproving of the scheme. Lord Derby said '*He believed it would work* and so did Sir Douglas Haig'. I said I thought there was nothing more to do. Lord Derby asked me to tell Sir William Robertson of the change in the opinion of Lord Curzon and Mr. Balfour, who now no longer supported him, and also to say that Sir H. Plumer would be telegraphed to and offered the appointment of C.I.G.S.

I accordingly wrote to Sir William Robertson, from whom in the meantime I had received a note confirming what he had said in conversation.

16 February 1918

The King saw the Prime Minister. Before doing so Mr. Lloyd George told me that the question of Sir William Robertson had now reached a point that if His Majesty insisted upon his (Sir W. R.) remaining in office on the terms he laid down the Government could not carry on, and the King would have to find other Ministers. The Government *must* govern, whereas this was practically military dictation.

I assured the Prime Minister that His Majesty had no idea of making any such insistence. That since I saw him (Mr. Lloyd George) on the 13th February, I had by the King's instructions done all in my power to induce Sir William Robertson to remain as C.I.G.S.

even though he might consider that the Government's scheme was so dangerous as even risking our loss of the War. But Sir William Robertson said he could not do so, therefore the King regarded the matter as settled, and considered that Sir William Robertson had practically ceased to be C.I.G.S.

The King then saw the Prime Minister, and in discussing the question, stated that in his opinion Sir William Robertson's resignation would be a serious loss to the Army for both Officers and Men had the fullest confidence in him. This however the Prime Minister would not admit. He reminded the King that the scheme was agreed to in Paris when Sir William Robertson never raised a word of objection. Sir Douglas Haig, who after all was the person most concerned, accepted it, and Lord Derby thought it workable; so that the opposition really only came from Sir William Robertson, and Mr. Lloyd George thought that the personal dislike of Sir William Robertson to Sir Henry Wilson was a powerful influence in the case.

The Prime Minister quoted General Smuts as having no opinion of Sir William Robertson as a strategist, and his (Gen. S.'s) last words before leaving for Egypt were to the effect that we should never get on with the War so long as Sir William Robertson remained C.I.G.S.

Mr. Lloyd George asked His Majesty's permission to repeat the offer to Sir William Robertson either to go to Paris as Representative of the Executive, or to remain C.I.G.S. If he refused both, to appoint Sir Henry Wilson C.I.G.S., but without the powers specially granted to Sir William Robertson when he took office. The Prime Minister also asked for permission to consult Sir Douglas Haig, who arrives this evening, as to who should go to Paris.

Later in the day the King saw Lord Derby, who said that he felt there was nothing left for him to do but to resign, though he several times appealed to His

Majesty to advise him as to the proper course he should follow. Lord Derby explained that although he personally thought that the Government's scheme was workable, on the other hand two high authorities— namely Sir William Robertson and Sir Herbert Plumer—both held opposite opinions, and in these circumstances he (Lord Derby) felt that he could not carry out the scheme, especially with Sir Henry Wilson as C.I.G.S.

The King told Lord Derby that after hearing his statement there seemed to be no alternative but his resignation.

Subsequently I saw Lord Derby who told me that he should resign, and that an announcement to that effect would be in Monday's morning newspapers, and that he would make his statement in the House of Lords on Tuesday.

Lord Derby admitted that his case was a weak one, for while supporting the Government's scheme he felt unable to carry it out. Lord Derby added that in his statement he should quote the opinion of Sir William Robertson and Sir Herbert Plumer, although Mr. Bonar Law said that he ought *not* to refer to the latter as the communication made to Sir Herbert Plumer was entirely confidential.

ADDENDUM

Permission to publish the following letter was received after the book had gone into page proof.

Walter Long to Bonar Law, 15th February, 1918

My dear Bonar,

I have seen Robertson. I must say I am horrified at the idea of a change now of all moments & I feel very strongly that every effort should be made to avert it. I do not doubt that the Gov. can ride the storm but I am convinced that it will give the Gov. a very severe shake, what is much worse, may be held, if things go wrong, to have been the cause. Surely so tremendous a step should not be taken without much more deliberation? It is no business of mine as I am not on the War Cabinet, but I confess that having regard to the effect this must have on the Overseas Troops & upon the conduct of the War I think I ought to have been allowed to have a say: however for this it is too late—but not too late to pause before taking a decision which will be irrevocable.

Yours ever,

WALTER H. LONG.

15. ii. 18.

HOUSE OF LORDS DEBATES
28th MARCH, 1945

The Late Earl Lloyd-George of Dwyfor

2 p.m.

The LORD PRIVY SEAL (Lord Beaverbrook): My Lords, in the unavoidable absence of the noble Viscount the Leader of the House, it falls to me to express the sorrow of your Lordships at the death of Earl Lloyd George. There are several members of this House who served under Lloyd George, but of those of his colleagues who knew and felt the full force of his genius, those who served with him in his War Cabinet, nearly all have gone out in front of him. Almost alone the survivor of his war administration is the present Prime Minister. Many will say that Lloyd George's greatest days, his most splendid efforts were in times of peace when he put upon the Statute Book more social legislation than any single statesman in our history; but I do not hold that view. To me his greatest hour came as late as the spring of 1918, when our line of defence had been broken, our troops were in retreat, the Russian Armies were out of the war, and the American Armies had not yet come into it.

The Cabinet at that moment was concerned above all else with the dominant question, "Shall we retreat north and west to protect the Channel ports, or shall we retire south to Paris to sustain contact with the

French Armies?" The history books will tell the truth. A Cabinet of strong men had been diverted for the time by the sheer gravity of the situation from the bigger issue—the issue of defeat or victory. It was at that moment that Lloyd George penetrated the gloom of doubt and indecision. It was in the hour of our peril that he refused to contemplate any plan for retreat. He would talk only of counter-attacks. It was then his leadership showed itself supreme, his courage untarnished. No other moment in Britain's recurring story of escape from disaster can surpass it, save only the decision of the summer nights after the defeat of France in 1940. It was then, I say, that Lloyd George's strength and fortitude, his judgment and courage, led and guided the nation during the weary pilgrimage that was to be so suddenly, so unexpectedly, so completely crowned with victory. If this were a single incident in the life of Lloyd George, it would make for a great name, but the story of Lloyd George as leader of the nation abounds in trials overcome, in temptations resisted, in opportunities for error withstood. On every occasion when men were contained in their conflicting counsels Lloyd George followed his own vision. It seems to me now, as it seemed to me then, he was seldom wrong. It was always the genius of this man that he knew the conditions on the other side of the hill.

It would be wrong of me to attempt any review of Lloyd George's life. This story has been told in part and will no doubt in history be told in full, but I believe it will throw into the shadow every other story, save only the narrative of these present days. In this House we have not seen him, for he was not spared to take his seat. Many present among your Lordships were his supporters. Others marching like Lloyd George himself straight across the political landscape in pursuit of the beliefs which they held, found themselves sometimes his allies and sometimes his opponents. To-day allies and opponents alike are oppressed by a feeling of irreparable personal loss. To his wife and family we will send our deep sympathy. Lloyd George was the idol of the nation, the Premier under whose aegis Germany was overthrown and the Empire saved. He attained an authority greater than that held by any British Prime Minister who had gone before him. He dictated to Europe; he flung out great dynasties with a gesture; he parcelled out the frontiers of races; everything was in his hands, and his hands showed that they had the power to use everything. Now all that is ended. Nothing remains but the picture of him in the days of glory. There on the walls of memory, outstanding in power and vitality, amid the faded pictures of his predecessors, is Lloyd George, Prime Minister of Great Britain.

NOTES

INTRODUCTION

aIntimate Papers of Colonel House, Vol. III, p. 233. *b*Page to Wilson, 7 March, 1918. *Walter Hines Page Papers*, Houghton Library, Harvard University.

Chapter I. THE CLEVEREST MAN IN THE KINGDOM

*a*Robert Blake: *The Unknown Prime Minister*, p. 294. – *bHistory of The Times*, Vol. IV, p. 274. – *c*F. E. Smith: *My American Visit*. – *d*Bonar Law to Borden, 1 May, 1916. *Borden Papers*. – *e*D. Lloyd George: *War Memoirs*, Vol. V, p. 2786. – *fThe Globe*, 18 April, 1918. – *gThe Globe*, 3 May, 1918. – *hThe Morning Post*, 22 April, 1918. – *i*Letter published in *Daily Chronicle, Morning Post* and *Times*, 7 May, 1918. – *j*W. S. Churchill: *The World Crisis, 1916–1918*, Part I, p. 244.

Chapter II. THE FALL OF A GIANT

*a*See Lord Beaverbrook, *Politicians and the War*, Vol. II, pp. 198–9 – *bIbid.*, p. 122. – *c*Lloyd George: *War Memoirs*, Vol. IV, p. 2228. – *d*See *Politicians and the War*, Vol. II, p. 324. – *eIbid.*, p. 342. – *f* See R. S. Baker: *Woodrow Wilson, Life and Letters*, Vol. VII, p. 96. – *g*Tom Clarke: *Northcliffe in History*, p. 120. – *h*Lloyd George: *War Memoirs*, Vol. III, pp. 1688–9. – *i*Baker: *Woodrow Wilson, Life and Letters*, Vol. VII, p. 96. – *j*Robert Cecil to Lloyd George, undated. *Lloyd George Papers*. – *k*Hankey to Lloyd George, 7 June, 1917. *Lloyd George Papers*. – *lHouse of Commons Debates*, Vol. 95, cols. 1105–6. – *mDaily News and Leader*, 21 June, 1917. – *nDaily Chronicle*, 21 June, 1917. – *oDaily News and Leader*, 21 June, 1917. – *pMorning Post*, 30 June, 1917. – *q*David Davies to Lloyd George, dated "Sunday night" (June, 1917). *Lloyd George Papers*. Quoted, Frank Owen: *Tempestuous Journey*, p. 381. – *rIntimate Papers of Colonel House*, Vol. III, p. 89. – *s*Frederick Dixon to Balfour, 22 June, 1917. *Lloyd George Papers*. – *t*Baker: *Woodrow Wilson, Life and Letters*, Vol. VII, p. 96. – *uIbid.*, p. 102, fn. Letter House to Wilson, 7 June, 1917. – *vIbid.*, p. 108. House to Wilson, 12 June, 1917. – *w*Northcliffe to Davies, 20 June, 1917. *Lloyd George Papers*. Quoted, Lloyd George: *War Memoirs*, Vol. III, pp. 1693–5. – *x*Spring-Rice to Balfour, 13 July, 1917. *Lloyd George Papers*. Quoted, *Ibid.*, pp. 1695–6. – *yWalter Hines Page Papers*, Houghton Library, Harvard University. – *z*Spring-Rice to Balfour, 5 July, 1917. *Lloyd George Papers*. Quoted, Lloyd George: *War Memoirs*, Vol. III, p. 1715. – *aaIntimate Papers of Colonel House*, Vol. III, p. 91. – *ab*Diary of E. M. House, Vol. XII, p. 317, 18 October, 1917. – *ac*Quoted, *Intimate Papers of Colonel House*, Vol. III, p. 90. – *adWiseman Papers*, Yale University Library. Quoted, Lloyd George: *War Memoirs*, Vol. III, p. 1697. – *ae*Lloyd George: *War Memoirs*, Vol. IV, p. 1871. – *af*Diary of E. M. House, Vol. XII, p. 359, 16 November, 1917. Quoted, Stanley Morison, "Personality and Diplomacy in Anglo-American relations, 1917": *Essays Presented to Sir Lewis Namier*, ed. R. Pares and A. J. P. Taylor, pp. 465–6, 468. – *agIbid.*, p. 367. 20 November, 1917. *ahIbid.* – *aiThe Times*, 21 November, 1917. – *ajHouse of Commons Debates*, Vol. 104, col. 77.

Chapter III. NABOBS AND TYRANTS

[a]Stephen McKenna: *Reginald McKenna*, p. 236. – [b]Page to Wilson, 16 January, 1918. *Walter Hines Page Papers*, Houghton Library, Harvard University. – [c]McKenna: *Reginald McKenna*, p. 238. – [d]Cunliffe to the Prime Minister, 3 July, 1917. *Lloyd George Papers*. – [e]Letters from Cunliffe to Bonar Law, 3 and 6 July, 1917. *Bonar Law Papers*. – [f]Bonar Law to Lloyd George, 9 July, 1917. *Lloyd George Papers*. – [g]Bonar Law to Lloyd George, 9 July, 1917. *Lloyd George Papers*. – [h]The letter communicating this information to Bonar Law was dated 5 July, but it is not contained in the *Bonar Law* or *Lloyd George Papers*. Bonar Law, however, alludes to it in his letter to Lloyd George of 9 July, 1917. – [i]*Bonar Law Papers*. – [j]*Lloyd George Papers*. – [k]*Lloyd George Papers*. – [l]Cunliffe to Bonar Law, 16 July, 1917. *Bonar Law Papers*. – [m]Cunliffe to Bonar Law, 12 August, 1917. *Bonar Law Papers*. – [n]*The Times*, 9 November, 1917. – [o]*Daily Telegraph*, 26 March, 1918.

Chapter IV. "IF YOU CAN TRUST YOURSELF WHEN ALL MEN DOUBT YOU"

[a]Ian Colvin: *Life of Lord Carson*, Vol. III, p. 150. – [b]*Bonar Law Papers*. – [c]*Daily Telegraph*, 14 May, 1917. – [d]Ed. Robert Blake: *Private Papers of Douglas Haig, 1914–1919*, pp. 208–9. – [e]Churchill to Blumenfeld, 6 September, 1914. From the papers of R. D. Blumenfeld. – [f]Undated. *Bonar Law Papers*. – [g]*Lloyd George Papers*. – [h]Churchill: *The World Crisis, 1916–1918*, Part I, p. 255. – [i]*Lloyd George Papers*. – [j]*Lloyd George Papers*. – [k]Lloyd George: *War Memoirs*, Vol. III, p. 1068. – [l]Bonar Law to Joseph Larmor, 14 October, 1914. *Bonar Law Papers*. – [m]Wilson to Bonar Law, 16 May, 1915. *Bonar Law Papers*. – [n]Churchill to Lloyd George, 9 November, 1921. *Lloyd George Papers*. – [o]*Lloyd George Papers*. – [p]Dr. Addison to Prime Minister, 4 June, 1917. *Lloyd George Papers*. – [q]Guest to Lloyd George, 18 June, 1917. *Lloyd George Papers*. – [r]*Lloyd George Papers*. – [s]*Bonar Law Papers*. – [t]*Bonar Law Papers*. – [u]Derby to Prime Minister, 8 June, 1917. *Lloyd George Papers*. – [v]See *History of The Times, 1912–1921*, Appendix, p. 1006. – [w]Churchill: *The World Crisis, 1916–1918*, Part II, p. 293. – [x]Cable Northcliffe to Churchill, 27 July, 1917. *Wiseman Papers*, Yale University Library. See also Lord Riddell: *War Diary*, p. 259. – [y]*Lloyd George Papers*. – [z]Lloyd George: *War Memoirs*, Vol. III, p. 1072. – [aa]Long to Lloyd George, 18 July, 1917. *Lloyd George Papers*. – [ab]*Morning Post*, 4 August, 1917. – [ac]*Ibid.*, 3 August, 1917. – [ad]*Ibid.*, 18 July, 1917. – [ae]*Ibid.*, 19 July, 1917. – [af]*Ibid.*, 20 July, 1917. – [ag]Long to Bonar Law, 29 July, 1917. *Bonar Law Papers*. – [ah]Churchill: *The World Crisis, 1916–1918*, Part II, p. 335. – [ai]Churchill to Lloyd George, 29 December, 1918. *Lloyd George Papers*.

Chapter V. THE ULSTER PIRATE

[a]Lloyd George: *War Memoirs*, Vol. III, pp. 1175–6. – [b]*Politicians and the War*, Vol. II, p. 335. – [c]Cmd. 2870. *The Record of the Battle of Jutland*. – [d]Letter of 13 December, 1916. Quoted, Colvin: *Life of Lord Carson*, Vol. III, p. 217. – [e]*Daily Express*, 9 March, 1917. – [f]Lloyd George: *War Memoirs*, Vol. III, p. 1150. – [g]*Ibid*. – [h]Figures from *Statistical Review of the War against Merchant Shipping*, Appendix A. – [i]Quoted, Colvin: *Life of Lord Carson*, Vol. III, p. 257. – [j]The

Globe, 7 May, 1917. – *k*30 April, 1917. *Lloyd George Papers*. – *l*Lloyd George:
War Memoirs, Vol. III, p. 1164. – *m*Ibid., p. 1170. – *n*Walter Hines Page Papers,
Houghton Library, Harvard University. – *o*Colvin: *Life of Lord Carson*, Vol.
III, p. 268. – *p*Page to Wilson, 4 May, 1917. *Walter Hines Page Papers*.
Quoted, Hendrick: *The Life and Letters of Walter H. Page*, Vol. II, pp.
259–60. – *q*Quoted, Colvin: *Life of Lord Carson*, Vol. III, p. 266. – *r*Lloyd
George: *War Memoirs*, Vol. III, p. 1176. – *s*Colvin: *Life of Lord Carson*,
Vol. III, p. 269. – *t*See *Private Papers of Douglas Haig, 1914–1919*,
p. 242. – *u*Ibid., p. 255. – *v*Lloyd George Papers. – *w*Lloyd George Papers. –
*x*Lloyd George Papers. – *y*Bonar Law Papers. – *z*Windsor Archives. – *aa*Lloyd
George Papers. Quoted, Owen: *Tempestuous Journey*, p. 417. – *ab*Lloyd George
Papers. Quoted Ibid. – *ac*Lloyd George Papers. Quoted, Owen: *Tempestuous
Journey*, p. 418. – *ad*Lloyd George Papers. – *ae*Christopher Addison: *Four and a
Half Years*, Vol. II, p. 411. – *af*Sir R. H. Bacon: *Life of John Rushworth, Earl
Jellicoe*, p. 377. – *ag*Colvin: *Life of Lord Carson*, Vol. III, p. 287. – *ah*Private
Papers of Douglas Haig, 1914–1919*, p. 255. – *ai*Ibid., pp. 251–2. – *aj*Speech at
the Constitutional Club Luncheon, 20 November, 1917. *The Times*, 21
November, 1917. – *ak*Morning Post*, 17 November, 1917. – *al*Lloyd George
Papers. – *am*House of Commons Debates*, Vol. 103, col. 2024. – *an*Bonar Law
Papers. Quoted, Blake: *The Unknown Prime Minister*, p. 378. – *ao*Bonar Law
to Lloyd George, 19 September, 1918. *Bonar Law Papers*. – *ap*House of
Commons Debates*, Vol. 117, cols. 1233–4.

Chapter VI. ALL THE KING'S MEN

*a*Derby to Lloyd George, 11 December, 1917. *Lloyd George Papers*. – *b*Derby
to Haig, 12 December, 1917. *Lloyd George Papers*. – *c*Lloyd George Papers. –
*d*Derby to Lloyd George, 18 January, 1918. *Lloyd George Papers*. – *e*Derby to
Lloyd George, 29 January, 1918. *Lloyd George Papers*. – *f*Tom Jones: *Lloyd
George*, p. 134. – *g*Balfour Papers. – *h*House of Commons Debates*, Vol.
103, col. 16. – *i*Ibid., col. 30. – *j*Long to Bonar Law, 15 February, 1918.
Bonar Law Papers. – *k*Lord Robert Cecil to Bonar Law, 17 February, 1918.
Bonar Law Papers. – *l*Letter from Curzon to Lloyd George, 18 November,
1917. *Lloyd George Papers*. – *m*See *Private Papers of Douglas Haig, 1914–1919*,
p. 208. – *n*Harold Nicolson: *King George V*, p. 288. – *o*Ibid. – *p*Diary of E. M.
House, Vol. XII, 29 October, 1917. – *q*John Gore: *George V. A Personal Memoir*,
p. 304. – *r*Milner to Lloyd George, 8 February, 1918. *Lloyd George Papers*.
Quoted, Lloyd George: *War Memoirs*, Vol. V, pp. 2790–2. – *s*Bonar Law
Papers. – *t*Nicolson, *King George V*, pp. 321–2. – *u*See *Private Papers of Douglas
Haig, 1914–1919*, p. 286. – *v*Bonar Law Papers. – *w*Bonar Law Papers. – *x*Private
Papers of Douglas Haig, 1914–1919*, p. 288. – *y*Page to Wilson, 7 March, 1918.
Walter Hines Page Papers, Houghton Library, Harvard University.

Chapter VII. THE BIRTH OF THE ROYAL AIR FORCE

*a*The Private Papers of Douglas Haig, 1914–1919*, p. 252. – *b*Ibid., p. 273. –
*c*Ibid., p. 280. – *d*House of Commons Debates*, Vol. 105, col. 43. – *e*Lloyd George
Papers. – *f*Lloyd George Papers. – *g*Daily News*, 16 April, 1918. – *h*Henderson
to Bonar Law, 26 April, 1918. *Bonar Law Papers*. – *i*Baird to Lloyd George, 22
April, 1918. *Lloyd George Papers*. – *j*Rothermere to Lloyd George, 23 April,

1918. *Lloyd George Papers.* – [k]*Lloyd George Papers.* – [l]*Lloyd George Papers.* Quoted Lloyd George: *War Memoirs*, Vol. IV, p. 1877–8. [m]Lloyd George: *War Memoirs*, Vol. IV, p. 1877. – [n]*The Times*, 26 April, 1918. – [o]*Bonar Law Papers.* – [p]*House of Commons Debates*, Vol. 105, col. 1128. – [q]*Ibid.,* col. 1316. – [r]*Ibid.,* col. 1320. – [s]*Ibid.,* col. 1321. – [t]*Ibid.,* cols. 1342–3. – [u]*Ibid.,* col. 1330. – [v]*House of Lords Debates*, Vol. 29, col. 870. – [w]*Lloyd George Papers.* – [x]*Windsor Archives.* – [y]*Windsor Archives.* – [z]*Windsor Archives.* – [aa]*Bonar Law Papers.* [ab]Nicolson: *King George V*, p. 512. – [ac]Diary of E. M. House, Vol. XII, p. 381, 27 November, 1917. – [ad]Stamfordham to Guest, 25 April, 1919. *Lloyd George Papers.* – [ae]Guest to Lloyd George, 17 May, 1920. *Lloyd George Papers.* – [af] See Owen: *Tempestuous Journey,* p. 698.

Chapter VIII. THE LOST BOX

[a]Lloyd George to Bonar Law, 10 April, 1918. *Bonar Law Papers.* – [b]Lloyd George: *War Memoirs*, Vol. V, p. 2973. – [c]Robertson to Milner, 17 May, 1918. *Lloyd George Papers.* – [d]Milner to Lloyd George, 19 May, 1918. *Lloyd George Papers.* – [e]*Westminster Gazette*, 8 May, 1918. – [f]*Manchester Guardian*, 8 May, 1918. – [g]*Morning Post*, 8 May, 1918. – [h]Colvin: *Life of Lord Carson*, Vol. III, p. 351. – [i]L. S. Amery: *My Political Life*, Vol. II, p. 154. – [j]C. Repington: *The First World War, 1914–1918*, Vol. II, p. 298. Quoted, Colvin: *Life of Lord Carson*, Vol. III, pp. 351–2. – [k]*House of Commons Debates*, Vol. 105, col. 2353. – [l]*Ibid.,* col. 2359. [m]*The Private Papers of Douglas Haig, 1914–1919*, p. 309. – [n]Churchill: *The World Crisis, 1916–1918*, Part II, p. 422. – [o]Maurice to Lloyd George, 15 July, 1922. *Lloyd George Papers.*

Chapter IX. "DONT RESIGN: WAIT UNTIL YOU'RE SACKED"

[a]*Lloyd George Papers.* – [b]*House of Commons Debates*, Vol. 104, col. 41. – [c]Cable, 26 August, 1917. *Wiseman Papers*, Yale University Library. – [d]Entry in my diary dated 9 March, 1915. – [e]*Ibid.* – [f]H.R.H. the Duke of Connaught to R. B. Bennett, 14 December, 1916. *Bennett Papers*, University of New Brunswick. – [g]H.R.H. the Duke of Connaught to Sir Robert Borden, 18 April, 1916. *Borden Papers*, University of Toronto. – [h]My files. – [i]*Ibid.* – [j]See Blake: *The Unknown Prime Minister*, p. 346. – [k]Stamfordham to Guest, 8 February, 1918. *Lloyd George Papers.* Quoted, Owen: *Tempestuous Journey*, p. 464. – [l]Lloyd George to Stamfordham, 9 February, 1918. *Lloyd George Papers.* Quoted, Owen: *Tempestuous Journey*, p. 464. – [m]*The Globe*, 8 February, 1918. – [n]*House of Commons Debates*, Vol. 103, cols. 656–7. – [o]Enclosure Salisbury to Bonar Law, 22 February, 1918. *Bonar Law Papers.* – [p]Salisbury to Bonar Law, 22 February, 1918. *Bonar Law Papers.* – [q]My files. – [r]*Lloyd George Papers.* Quoted, *History of The Times*, Vol. IV, pp. 351–2. – [s]See Charles Petrie: *Life and Letters of Austen Chamberlain*, p. 107. – [t]Milner to Lloyd George, 27 February, 1918. *Lloyd George Papers.* – [u]*House of Commons Debates*, Vol. 104, col. 77. – [v]*Ibid.,* col. 130. – [w]*Ibid.,* col. 135. – [x]My files. – [y]*Lloyd George Papers.* – [z]*Lloyd George Papers.* – [aa]*House of Commons Debates*, Vol. 109, col. 958. – [ab]*Ibid.,* col. 1000. – [ac]*Ibid.,* col. 1001. – [ad]*Daily Express*, 29 August, 1918. – [ae]Lloyd George to Bonar Law, 29 August, 1917 (sic). *Bonar Law Papers.* – [af]Churchill to Bonar Law, 8 September, 1918. *Bonar Law Papers.* – [ag]*House of Commons Debates*, Vol. 110, col. 2363. – [ah]*Ibid.,* col. 2380. – [ai]Ludendorff: *My War Memories, 1914–1918.* Vol. I, pp. 361, 365 and 367.

NOTES

Chapter X. HIS ROYAL POMP

[a]Curzon to Lloyd George, 13 November, 1918. *Lloyd George Papers.* –
[b]Quoted: Nicolson, *King George V*, pp. 336–8. – [c]1919, Lloyd George said that
the tribunal would be an Inter-Allied one and it would sit in London. *House of
Commons Debates*, Vol. 117, cols. 1216–17. – [d]Curzon to Lloyd George, 7 July,
1919. *Lloyd George Papers.* – [e]*Lloyd George Papers.* – [f]Quoted, Lord Newton:
Lord Lansdowne: A Biography, pp. 452–3. – [g]Quoted, Stephen Spender and Cyril
Asquith: *Life of Lord Oxford and Asquith*, Vol. II, p. 260. – [h]*Ibid.* – [i]H. H.
Asquith: *Memories and Reflections*, Vol. II, p. 133. – [j]See *Politicians and the War*,
Vol. II, p. 240. – [k]Asquith: *Memories and Reflections*, Vol. II, p. 128 et seq. –
[l]*Lloyd George Papers.* – [m]Curzon to Bonar Law, 25 February, 1918. *Bonar
Law Papers.* Quoted, Ronaldshay: *Life of Lord Curzon*, Vol. III, pp. 195–6. –
[n]Quoted, *Ibid.*, p. 197. – [o]Curzon to Lloyd George, 12 November, 1918.
Lloyd George Papers. – [p]*House of Commons Debates*, Vol. 91, col. 26. – [q]*Bonar
Law Papers.* – [r]Curzon to Lloyd George, 13 November, 1918. *Lloyd George
Papers.* – [s]David Lawrence: *The True Story of Woodrow Wilson*, p. 249. –
[t]Undated. Curzon to Lloyd George. *Lloyd George Papers.* – [u]Lady Curzon:
Reminiscences, p. 180.

Chapter XI. THE HERO

[a]Minute Clive Wigram to Stamfordham, 18 November, 1919. *Windsor Archives.*
– [b]Churchill to Stamfordham, 7 December, 1919. *Windsor Archives.* – [c]*The
Times*, 8 January, 1920. – [d]Milner to Lloyd George, 13 April, 1918. *Lloyd
George Papers.* – [e]Milner to Lloyd George, 7 December, 1918. *Lloyd George
Papers.* – [f]Milner to Lloyd George, 4 January, 1919. *Lloyd George Papers.* –
[g]*Lloyd George Papers.* – [h]Milner to Lloyd George, 3 January, 1921. *Lloyd George
Papers.* – [i]Lloyd George to Birkenhead, 15 March, 1919. *Lloyd George Papers.* –
[j]Undated (8 January, 1918). *Lloyd George Papers.* – [k]Chamberlain to Bonar Law,
6 January, 1921. *Bonar Law Papers.* – [l]Lloyd George to Churchill, 1 October,
1921. *Lloyd George Papers.* – [m]Churchill to Lloyd George, 8 October, 1921.
Lloyd George Papers. – [n]*Lloyd George Papers.* – [o]Lloyd George to Hilton-Young,
26 September, 1921. *Lloyd George Papers.* – [p]Lloyd George to Lloyd Graeme,
26 September, 1921. *Lloyd George Papers.* – [q]Lloyd George to Curzon, 30 April,
1922. *Lloyd George Papers.*

INDEX

ADDISON, Rt. Hon. Christopher,
xxxii, 348
  biographical sketch, ix
  inclusion in War Cabinet objected to by Curzon, 131
  leaves Ministry of Munitions,
175
  halted on house building, 402
  his dismissal, 405
Admiralty against use of convoys,
152–8
Age of Baldwin, The, xli f.
Agriculture declines, 327
Air Board, 131, 219, 220
  independent status, 127
  money squandered, 221
  disloyal complaints, 222
  disaffection at Trenchard's resignation, 225–7
Aisne, battle of, a bitter blow, 115
Aitken, William Maxwell (*see*
Beaverbrook, 1st Baron)
Allenby, General, takes Jerusalem,
Dec. 1917, 187 f.; rejects order,
188 f.
Allied Conference at Rapallo, Nov.
1917, 194–5
  shipping losses, 153–4; an im-
provement, 177
Amery, Leopold Stennett:
  biographical sketch, ix
  records discussion on Maurice's
allegations, 256
Ancre, 229
Anderson, Sir Kenneth, 170
Anglo-French Loan Mission, xxii
Ashton-under-Lyne, xii, 243
Asquith-Brass-Hat Alliance, 117–
18, 121–2, 203
Asquith, Cyril, xxxii
Asquith, Rt. Hon. Herbert Henry,
49, 92, 100, 215, 248, 251, 271,
284, 285
  biographical sketch, x

Asquith, H. H.—contd.
  relinquishes Premiership, xxxv
  attitude to 1916 peace plan,
xxxvii–viii
  desires to take over War Office,
45
  supports military war-time control, 53–4
  efforts for Haldane defeated, 60
  on Balfour's hostility to Northcliffe, 68; disclosure of Balfour's telegram causes a storm,
68–9
  supports Bank of England
Governor's authority, 93–5
  gulf too wide to serve under
Lloyd George, 117
  his Government brought down,
144
  visits G.H.Q. in France, 178–9
  attack on contemplated High
Command changes, 199
  the King's eulogism, 205
  receives little support, 211
  leads conspiracy to oust Lloyd
George, 222
  mild and ineffective in Government crisis, 252
  asks for Select Committee, May
1918, 253
  blunders in not accepting offer
of Court of Honour, 254
  Conservative hate, 257
  charge of "intrigue", 270, 276
  ambiguous part played by
Curzon, 310 12
  asked to resign, 310
  lulled into false sense of security,
312
  receives war medals, 326
  ultimatum by Lloyd George,
392–4
Asquith, Margot (Lady), x
Authorities consulted, 419–23

425

INDEX

INDEX

INDEX

PRINTED IN GREAT BRITAIN BY THE ANCHOR PRESS, LTD., TIPTREE, ESSEX.